NINTH EDITION

CANADIAN OXFORD SCHOOL ATLAS

QUENTIN H. STANFORD
GENERAL EDITOR

OXFORD
UNIVERSITY PRESS

Contents

topographic maps of Canada

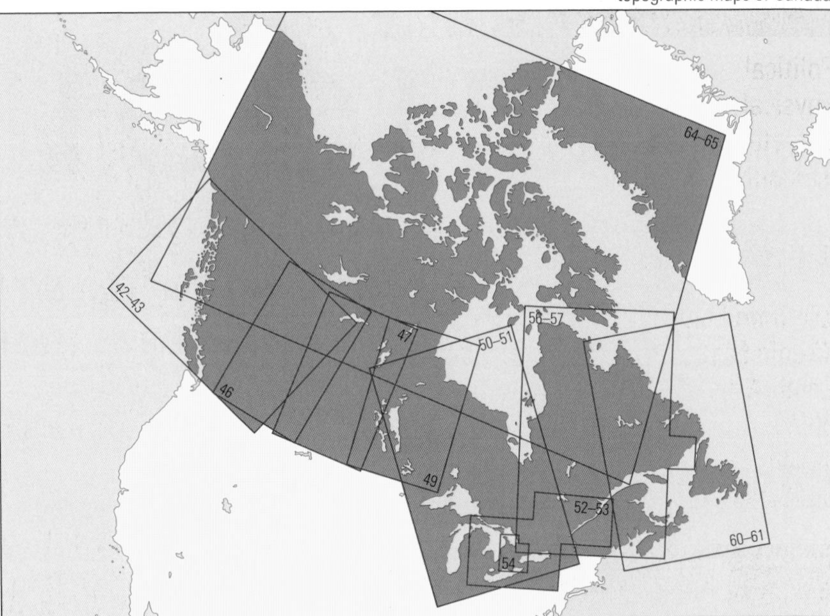

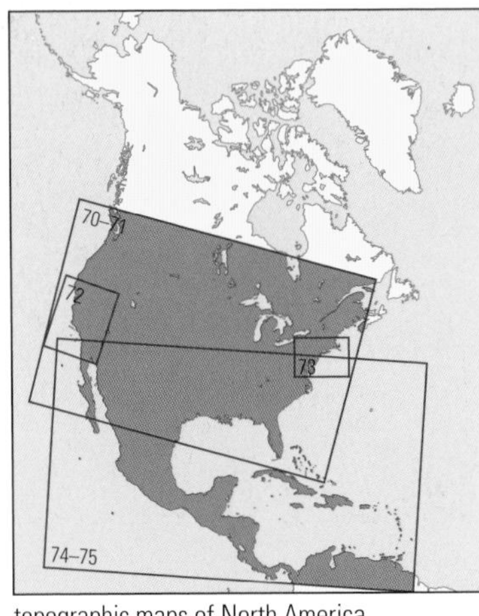

topographic maps of North America

topographic map of South America

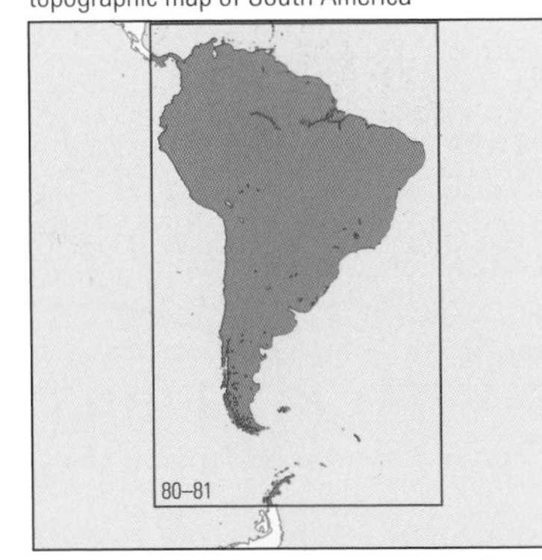

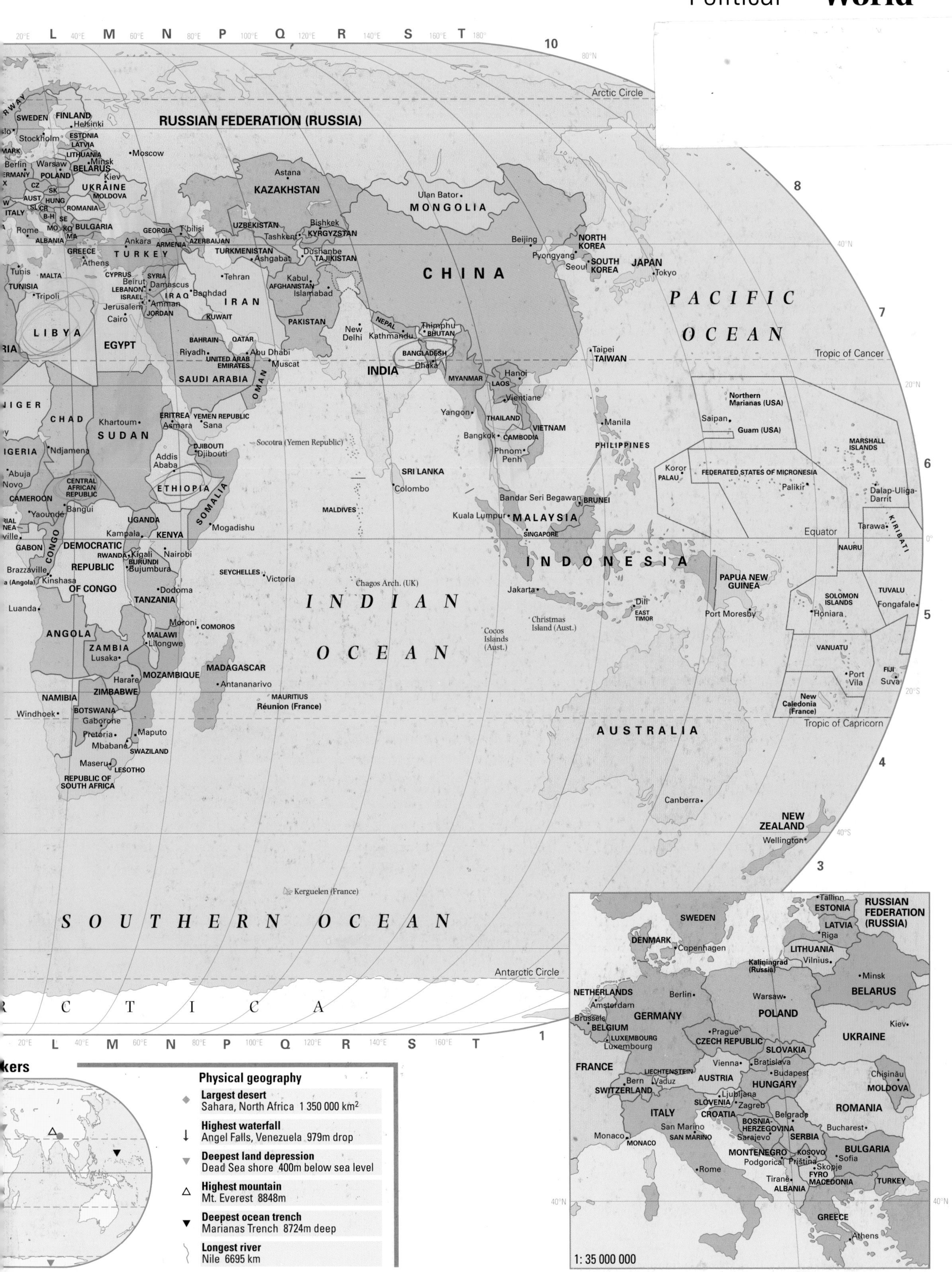

 Eckert IV Projection

In Recognition

In 1957, Oxford University Press Canada published the first *Canadian Oxford School Atlas*. The original idea had been proposed by an editor named Ivon Owen, who spent several years developing it. Although all of the cartographic work and even the printing was done in Britain, the atlas was tailored to the specifications of the Ontario Ministry of Education, and soon became a staple in classrooms across Canada. By 1960, it was being printed and bound in Canada, and today—in its ninth edition—is still Oxford Canada's all-time bestseller.

The first three editions (1957, 1963, and 1972) of the *Canadian Oxford School Atlas* were edited by E.G. Pleva with assistance from Spencer Inch. In 1971, Oxford University Press Canada asked Quentin H. Stanford to fill the role of Geography Consultant on the third edition. He has been an invaluable resource in the adaptation process ever since.

This ninth edition of the *Canadian Oxford School Atlas* is the fifth version for which Quentin H. Stanford has served as General Editor, having previously worked on the fourth (1977), sixth (1992), seventh (1998), and eighth (2003) editions.

Stanford also edited *The Oxford Regional Economic Atlas of the United States and Canada*, 2e (with J. Chapman and J. Sherman) (1975), *Canadian Oxford Intermediate Atlas* (1993), *Canadian Oxford Junior Atlas* (1998), and the *Canadian Oxford World Atlas* 3e (1992), 4e (1998), 5e (2003), and 6e (2008).

His non-atlas titles with Oxford include *Geography: A Study of its Elements* (with W. Moran) (1969); *The World's Population: Problems of Growth* (1972); *Geography: A Study of its Physical Elements* (with W. Moran) (1978); *Geography: A Study of its Physical Elements New Edition* (1988); and *The Global Challenge: A Study of World Issues* (1990).

Oxford University Press Canada would like to thank Quentin H. Stanford for his tremendous contributions throughout the years. We are pleased to present the 50th anniversary edition of the *Canadian Oxford School Atlas*, once again guided by Quentin H. Stanford's expertise and thoughtful assistance.

Acknowledgements

It has been my good fortune to have had an association with OUP Canada since 1963 and especially to have worked on so many editions of the school and world atlas. Atlases are the result of the work of many people both editorial and cartographic, far too many to name. However, I would like to mention a few who have played a prominent role and whose support has made my part in the process an enjoyable one. My thanks go out to Bill Toye, Michael Morrow, Susan Froud, Patti Henderson, and Tracey MacDonald for past editions and David Stover, Linda Masci Linton, Leslie Saffrey, Christine Gordon Manley, and Kingsley Hurlington for this one. On the cartographic side, Carolyn Anderson, Karen Brittin, Tracey Learoyd, and Caleb Gould have had the often difficult task of converting data and vague instructions into maps. I am most grateful to these people and so many others for the opportunity of being a participant in all these editions.

Lastly, I would be remiss if I didn't thank my wife, Joan Stanford. She has been there throughout the whole process with ideas and encouragement and it is to her that I would like to dedicate this 50th anniversary edition.

Quentin H. Stanford

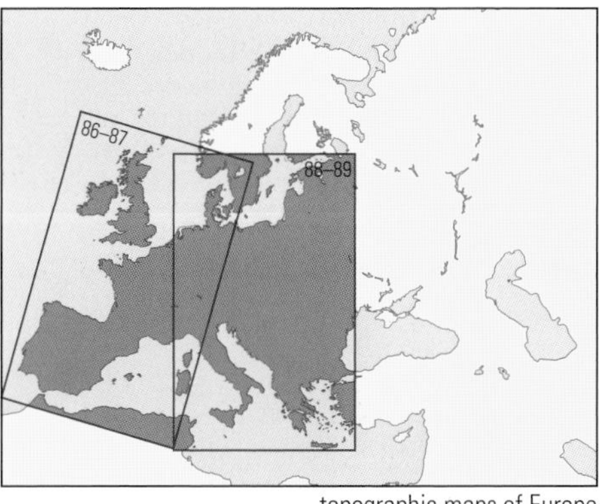

topographic maps of Europe

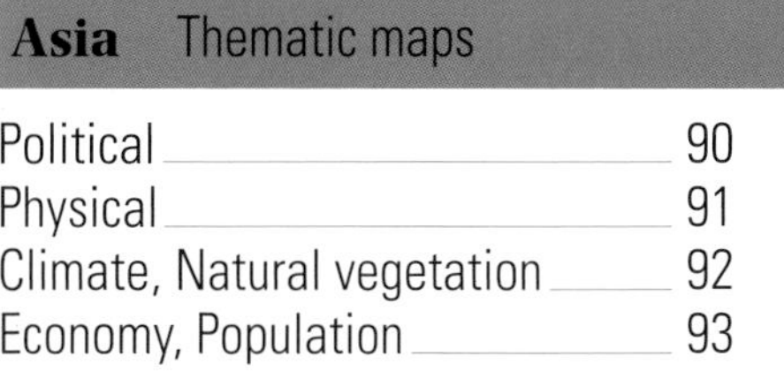

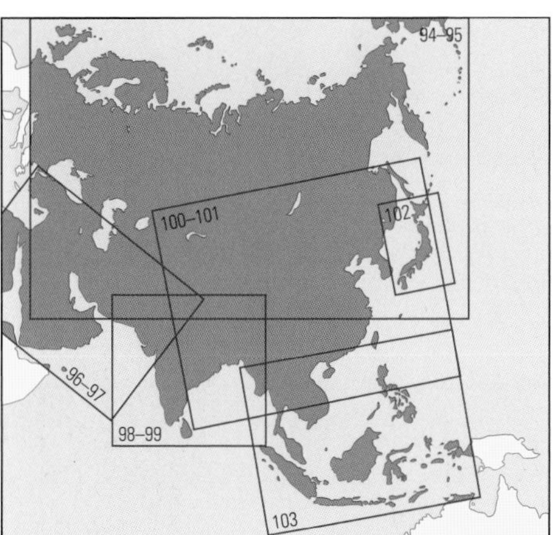

topographic maps of Asia

topographic map of Africa

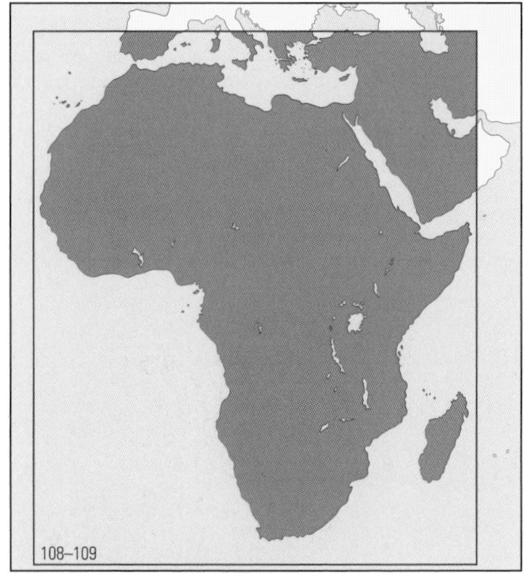

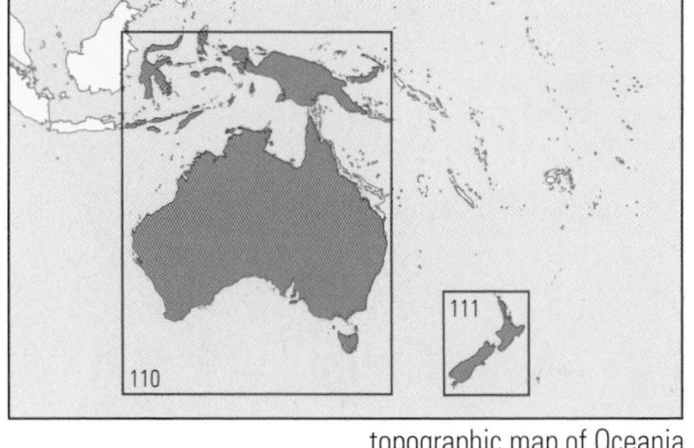

topographic map of Oceania

topographic maps of the Oceans

Types of maps

Maps are representations of the Earth's surface on a flat piece of paper. Maps can include such diverse information as the location of places, the depiction of economic and social data, the type and location of transportation routes, and the portrayal of change through time. Maps are everywhere; we come across them in everyday situations such as malls, schools, road atlases, and increasingly on the Internet. These pictures of the Earth's surface find many ways to attract our attention, orient our inquiries, and ultimately help direct our lives. An effective map is like a narrative — an open-ended and dynamic story that creates a dialogue between it and the user. It is not a straight forward text to be read; rather, it is a series of questions to be asked, ideas to be explored, and preconceptions to be challenged.

The two principal kinds of maps used in this atlas are topographic and thematic maps. Examples of these are shown below. In addition to these types of map, other devices can be used to show information about the Earth. These include globes (a spherical model of the Earth), plans (showing small areas), cross-sections (vertical views), and charts (navigational maps). Satellite imagery has also become an increasingly important means of understanding phenomena on the Earth's surface, and an introduction to the topic can be found on page 9.

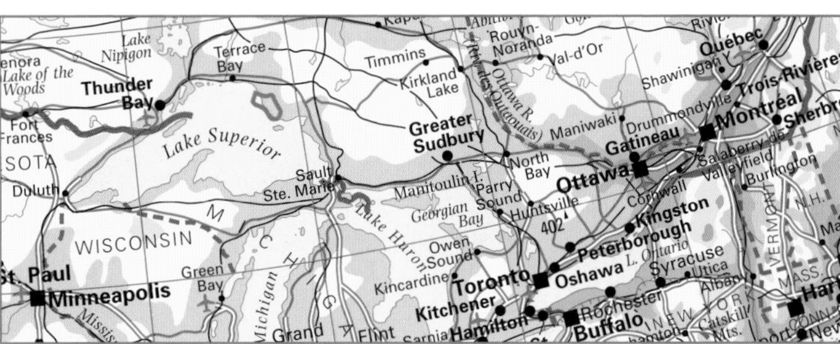

Topographic maps, also known as physical-political maps, are the general purpose maps in most atlases and provide a variety of information such as political boundaries, roads and railways, cities and towns, and the features of the physical landscape. Legends for the topographic maps in this atlas are expained on the opposite page.

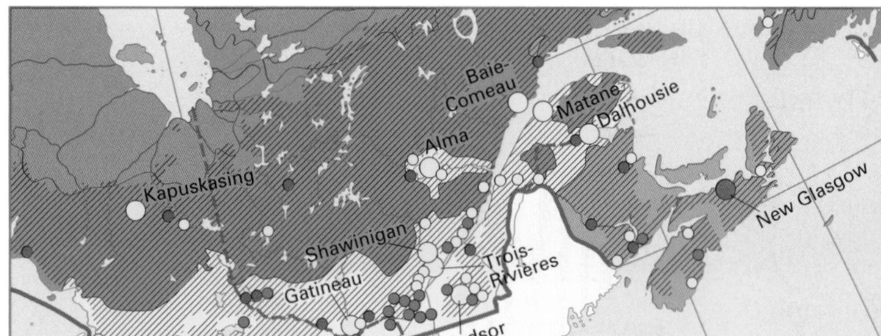

Thematic maps provide information about a variety of specific topics such as agriculture, climate, trade, and quality of life. Many different kinds of symbols are used for this purpose; the main ones are detailed in the section below.

Symbols on thematic maps

Point symbols

Distribution map
Each dot or circle represents a specific quantity.
From p36

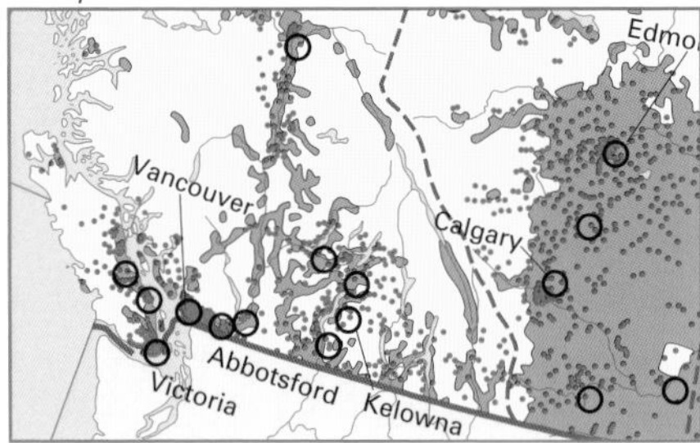

Symbol map
Different shapes, sizes, and colours are used to show, for example, economic or social data.
From p28

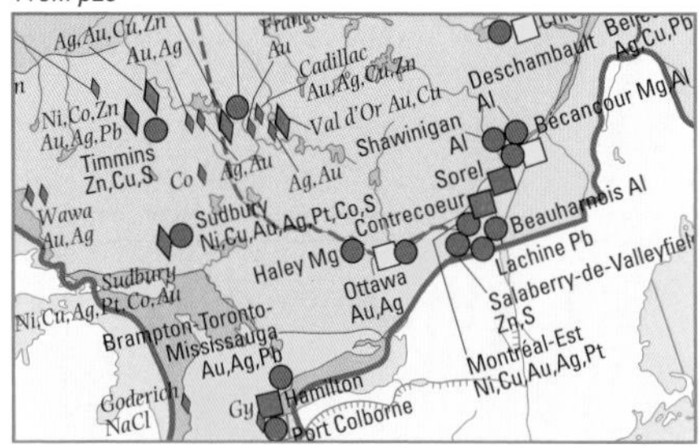

Proportional symbol map
The size or division of the symbol is used to represent quantities.
From p30

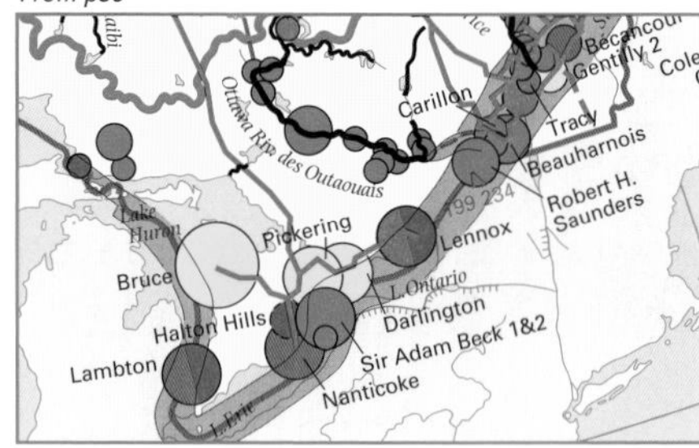

Line symbols

Transfer and transportation map
Lines represent routes or direction of movement.
From p29

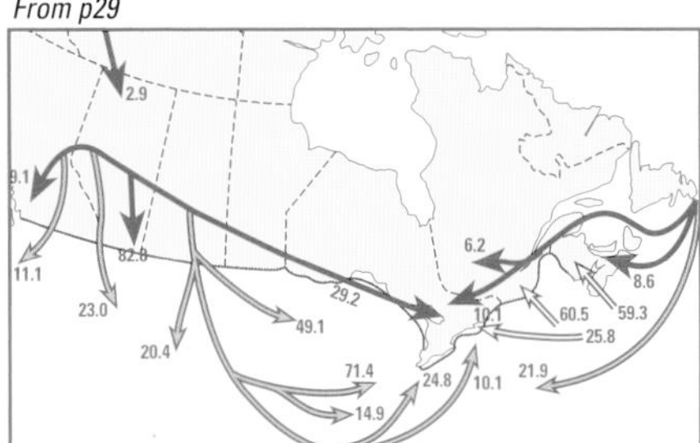

Isoline map
Lines connect places of equal value e.g. temperature (isotherms) or land height (contours).
From p17

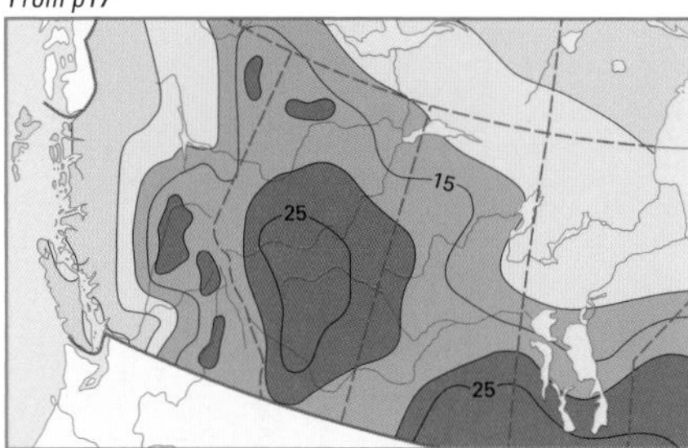

Flowline map
The thickness of the line is proportional to the quantity of what is being transferred.
From p144

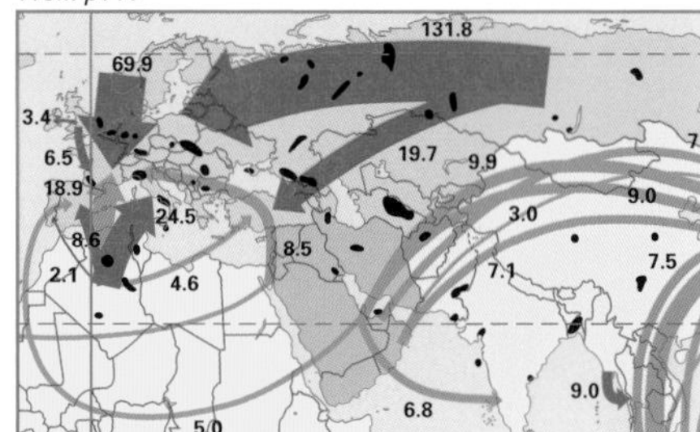

Area symbols

Choropleth map
Graduated colours or shades are used to represent variations in the information being presented.
From p32

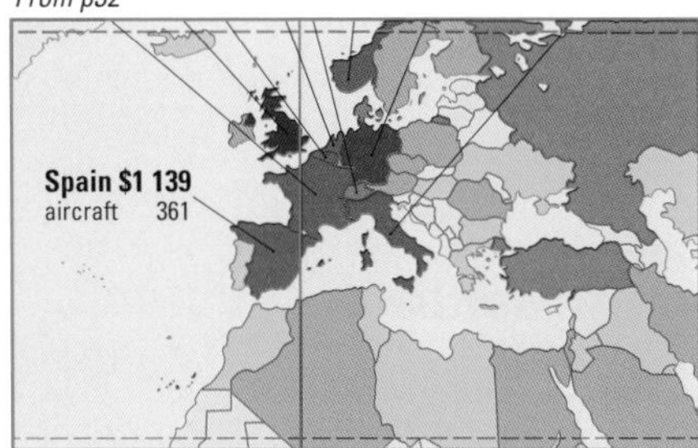

Special purpose map
Colours or shading are used to show different features such as soil types or geology.
From p14

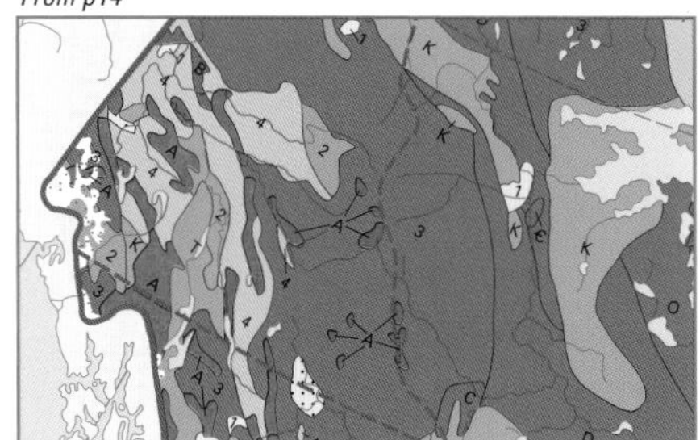

Political map
Colours have no meaning but are simply used to show where one country ends and another begins.
From p118

In the atlas, supplementary information complementing the topics illustrated by maps is provided in the form of tables, graphs, diagrams, satellite images, and text insets. Further information can be found in the two statistical appendixes of Canadian and World data, which begin on page 155.

ographic maps show the main features of the physical landscape well as settlements, communications, and boundaries. Background ours show the height of the land.

ere are small differences in the symbols and colours used for the ps of Canada and those for the rest of the world.

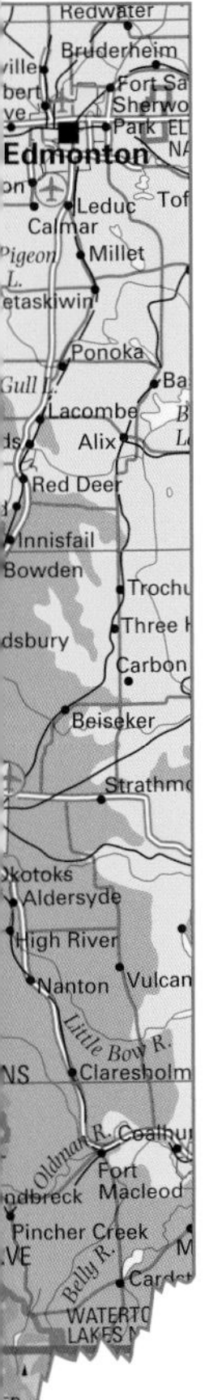

Canadian maps

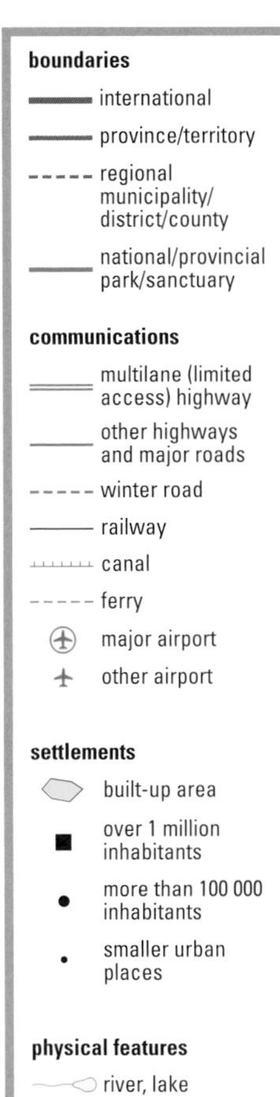

Non-Canadian maps

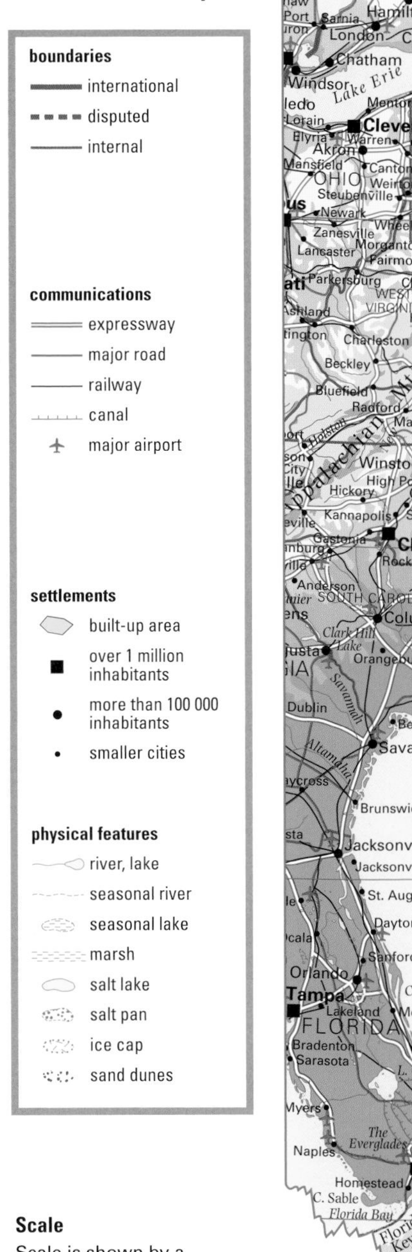

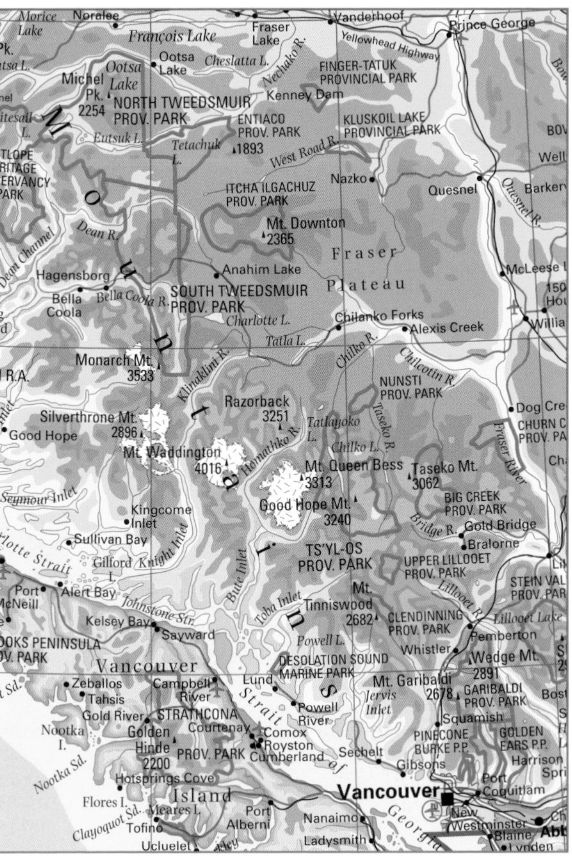

sea ice

unnavigable

pack ice
– fall minimum
– spring maximum

land height and sea depth

metres

3000
2000
1500
1000
500
300
200
100
0 sea level
200
3000
6000

spot height in metres

Scale

Scale is shown by a representative fraction and a scale line.

Scale 1: 5 000 000

0 50 100 150 200 250 km

Sea ice

White stipple patterns over the sea colour show the seasonal extent of sea ice.

Land height and sea depth

Colours on topographic maps refer only to the height of the land or the depth of the sea. They do not give information about land use or other aspects of the environment.

Place names

Anglicized spellings are used. Former names (where places have recently changed their names), and alternative spellings are shown in brackets.

This atlas has been designed for English speaking readers and so all places have been named using the Roman alphabet.

Type style

Contrasting type styles are used to show the difference between physical features, settlements, and administrative areas.

Physical features are separated into two categories, land and water. Land features are shown as roman type:

e.g. Coast Mountains

Water features are shown in italics:

e.g. *Hudson Bay (Baie d'Hudson)*

Peaks are shown in condensed type:

e.g. Mt. Logan 5951

Settlement names are shown in upper and lower case:

e.g. Hamilton

Administrative areas are shown in capital letters:

e.g. ONTARIO

The importance of places is shown by the size of the type and whether the type face is bold or medium:

e.g. **Ottawa** Calgary Louisbourg

On the Canadian maps all Census Metropolitan Areas (CMAs) are shown in bold.

Map projections

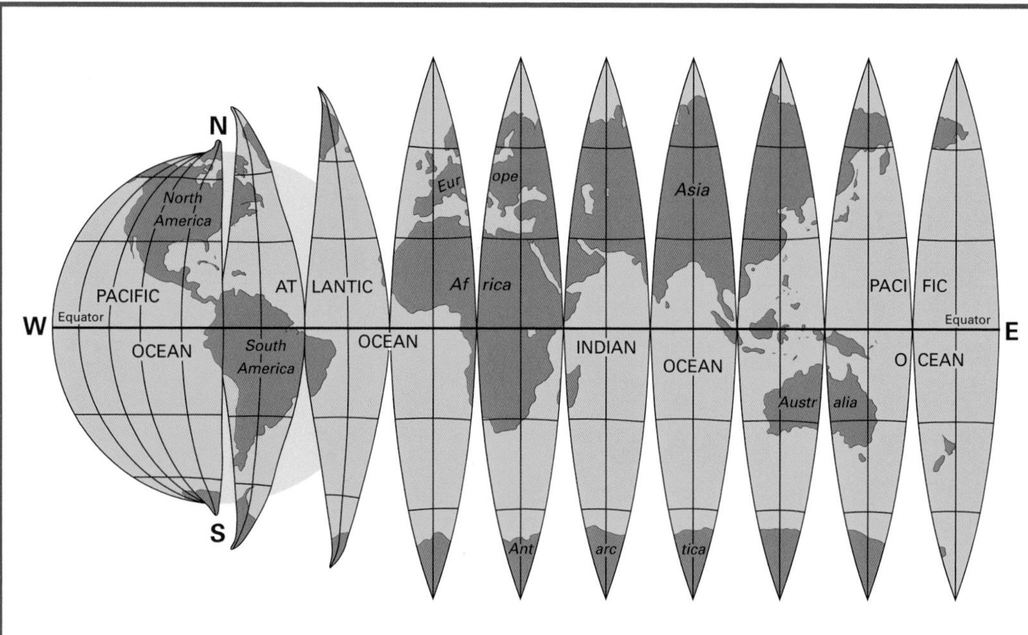

The most accurate way of looking at the Earth's land and sea areas is to use a globe. Globes however, are not always available and are seldom large enough to show much detail. Thus, for most uses, maps are more convenient. To create a map it is necessary to transfer the surface of the globe on to a flat surface. In theory, as the diagram shows, it is necessary to unpeel strips (also known as gores) from the globe's surface, but such a method has obvious drawbacks. Since it is impossible to flatten the curved surface of the Earth without stretching or cutting part of it, it is necessary to employ other methods in order to produce an orderly system of parallels and meridians on which a map can be drawn. Such systems are referred to as **map projections**.

There are two main types of projections: **equal area projections**, where the area of any territory is shown in correct size proportion to other areas, and **conformal projections**, where the emphasis is on showing the shape correctly. No map can be both equal area and conformal, though some projections are designed to minimize distortions in both area and shape.

Polar projections give a good view of the poles. Most other projections do not show Antarctica or the Arctic Ocean accurately.

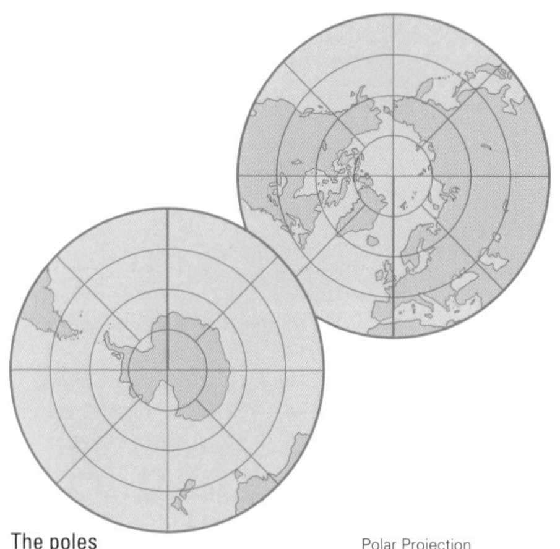

The poles
Polar Projection

The **Oblique Aitoff projection**, created by David Aitoff in 1889, is an equal area projection. The arrangement of the land masses allows a good view of routes in the northern hemisphere. The position of North America and Asia on either side of the Arctic is shown clearly.

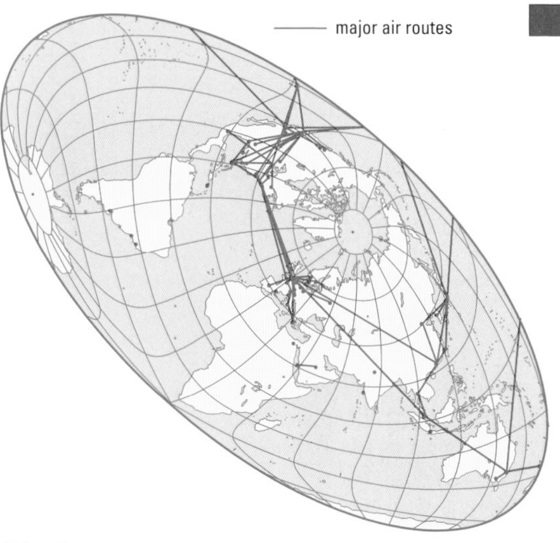

Major air routes
Oblique Aitoff Projection

Mercator's projection is a conformal projection and was initially designed by Gerhardus Mercator in 1569 to be used for navigation. Any straight line on the map is a line of constant compass bearing. Straight lines are not the shortest routes, however. Shape is accurate on a Mercator projection but the size of the land masses is distorted. Land is shown larger the further away it is from the equator. (For example, Alaska is shown four times larger than its actual size).

line of constant compass bearing
shortest route

Navigation chart
Mercator's Proje

Eckert IV projection was designed by the German cartographer Max Eckert (1868–1938). It is an equal area projection, showing the true area of places in relation to each other. This projection is often used in this atlas, the maps permitting fair comparisons to be made between areas of the world.

tropical forest

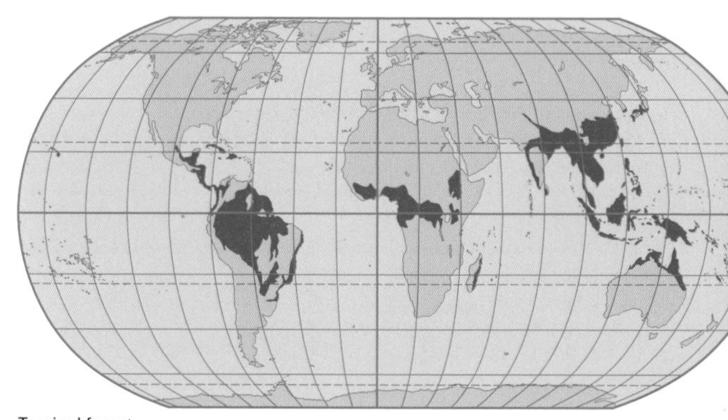

Tropical forest
Eckert IV Proje

Gall's projection represents a compromise between equal area and conformal. A modified version is sometimes used in this atlas as a general world map. This map shows plate boundaries.

plate boundaries

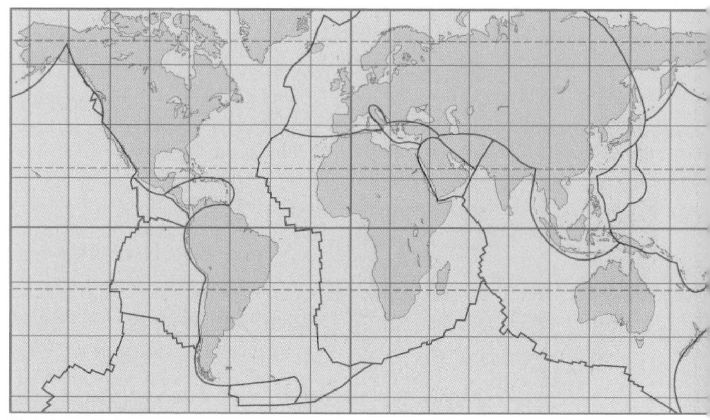

Plate boundaries
Gall's Proje

There are two methods used in the atlas to locate places on maps. Both are shown in the gazetteer (geographical index) on pages 192–231 at the back of the atlas.

The first method is by grid code, where a blue grid (graticule) is superimposed on each topographic map. Each rectangle of the grid is identified vertically by a letter and horizontally by a number. Following each place name in the alphabetical gazetteer is a page number in bold and a letter and number combination (e.g., A2 or D5). This reference gives the page on which the place can be found and the specific rectangle on that page where the place is located. A single rectangle on a map may contain many place names, so it may take some diligence to find a specific place.

More instructions on using the gazetteer are on page 192 of this atlas.

The second method of determining location is by latitude and longitude. Since the Earth is a sphere, a locational grid requires fixed points of reference. The north and south poles, representing the axis of the Earth's rotation, act as these fixed points. A global grid based on these points allows us to pinpoint any place on Earth. The grid consists of two sets of lines. Those running east and west are called "parallels of latitude", and those extending north and south are called "meridians of longitude". Each line is given a value in angular measurement in degrees, minutes, and seconds (see diagram below). For more information on the global grid, see the box below.

This true-colour satellite image shows North and South America as they would appear from space 35 000 km (22 000 miles) above the Earth. The image is a combination of data from two satellites, so that it shows land surface data and a snapshot of the Earth's clouds.

Latitude and longitude
A portion of the Earth is cut away in this drawing to show the angular measurements that are used to locate parallels and meridians.

Parallels of latitude are concentric circles that get smaller in diameter from the equator to the poles. The distance between the parallels remains constant; one degree equals 60 nautical miles (111 km). They are used to determine locations north (N) or south (S) of the equator. The equator is at latitude 0°. The poles are at latitudes 90°N and 90°S.

The Tropics of Cancer (23°26'N) and Capricorn (23°26'S) are parallels of latitude that represent the northern and southern limits of the sun appearing directly overhead. The Arctic (66°33'N) and Antarctic Circles (66°33'S) are also parallels of latitude. During the northern winter solstice (in December) the sun is not visible between the Arctic Circle and the North Pole; during the southern winter solstice (in June) it is not visible between the Antarctic Circle and the South Pole.

Meridians of longitude pass through both poles, intersecting all parallels of latitude at right angles. The distance between meridians gets smaller from a maximum distance at the equator to zero at the poles. Meridians are used to determine locations east (E) and west (W) of the prime meridian, and are numbered from 0° to 180° in both directions from the prime meridian. While the equator serves as a natural starting point for latitude, there is no such natural point for longitude; therefore in 1884, a meridian passing through Greenwich in the United Kingdom was chosen as the prime meridian (0°). On the opposite side of the globe from the prime meridian is the International Date Line, at 180° longitude. Travellers crossing the Date Line from east to west lose a day, while those crossing west to east repeat a day. The designations of 0° and 180° were made to implement the system of Standard Time.

The equator divides the Earth into halves: the northern hemisphere and the southern hemisphere. The prime meridian and the 180° meridian together also divide the Earth into halves: the western hemisphere and the eastern hemisphere.

Lines of latitude and longitude together form a grid. Any position on the surface of the Earth can be located accurately using this grid.

To locate places more precisely, each degree of latitude or longitude can be divided into 60 minutes, and each minute into 60 seconds. A location specified in degrees, minutes, and seconds (for example, 44°25'14"N, 80°45'36"W) describes a location to within a few metres.

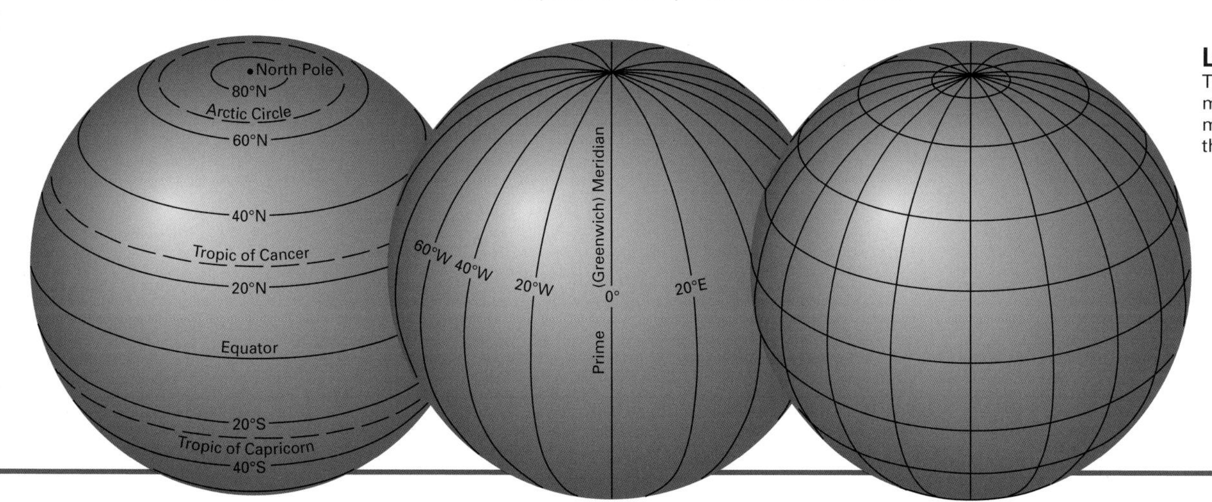

Latitude and longitude
These diagrams show the main parallels of latitude, the meridians of longitude, and the completed grid.

Scale and direction

Scale

Every map and globe has a scale to indicate how much the area on the map has been reduced from its actual size on the Earth's surface. Thus, the map scale indicates the proportion (or ratio) between a distance on a map and the corresponding distance on the Earth's surface.

Scale can be shown in three ways:

The scale statement

1 cm to 5 km — means 1 centimetre on the map represents five kilometres on the Earth's surface.

The representative fraction (RF)

1: 500 000 — means 1 centimetre on the map represents 500 000 centimetres on the Earth's surface, or one of any unit of measurement represents 500 000 of the same units.

The linear scale

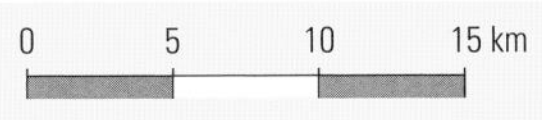

which is a measured line divided into units representing distances on the Earth.

It is important to understand the **relationship between scale and area**. In this atlas, Canada is shown mainly on maps that are at a larger scale than the rest of the world.

For example:
All of northern Africa appears on page 108 at a scale of 1: 26 000 000, while British Columbia, on pages 42–43, has a scale of 1: 5 000 000. We know from the scale that the African map shows a greater area, but how much greater?

The table shows that as the scale doubles, the area it represents increases four times. Thus a square centimetre on the Africa map represents an area more than twenty-seven times larger than a square centimetre on the British Columbia map.

Scale	Scale statement	Area of 1 cm^2
1: 10 000	1 cm to 0.1 km	0.01 km^2
1: 20 000	1 cm to 0.2 km	0.04 km^2
1: 100 000	1 cm to 1 km	1 km^2
1: 200 000	1 cm to 2 km	4 km^2
1: 5 000 000	1 cm to 50 km	2500 km^2
1: 10 000 000	1 cm to 100 km	10 000 km^2
1: 20 000 000	1 cm to 200 km	40 000 km^2

The scale of a map will determine the type and amount of information that can be shown. Larger scale maps (1: 1 000 000 or less) show a smaller area of the Earth than smaller scales (more than 1: 1 000 000). In this atlas, the Canadian urban plans covering the area of a single city have a scale of 1: 300 000, most of the regional Canadian maps covering an entire province have a scale of 1: 5 000 000, and some of those showing the entire Earth's surface have a scale of 1: 95 000 000 or greater. See below for examples of these maps in this atlas.

1: 300 000 scale
Suitable for urban plans.
From p55

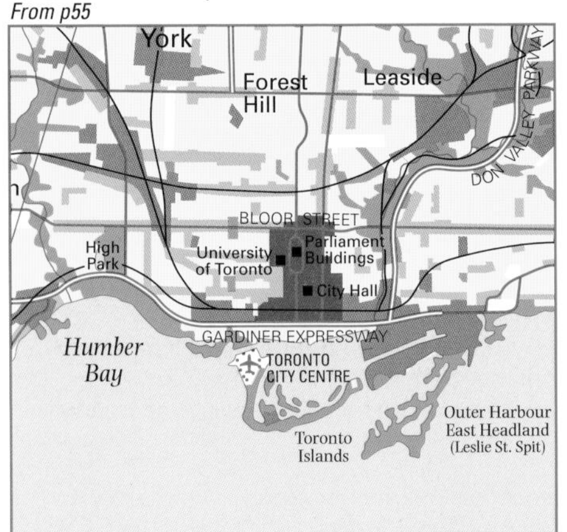

1: 5 000 000 scale
Suitable for maps of the Canadian provinces.
From p51

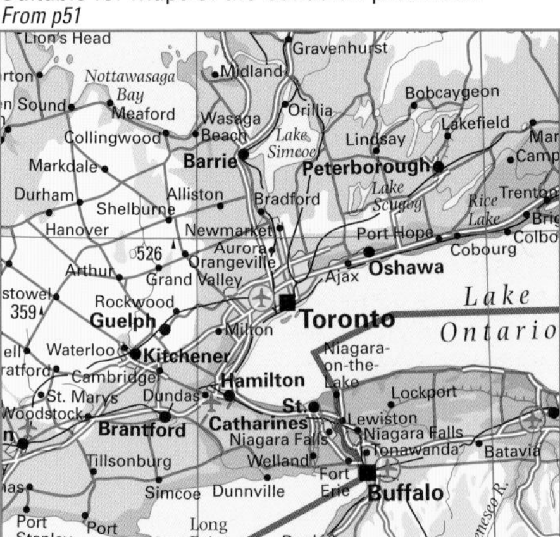

1: 95 000 000 scale
Suitable for maps of the world.
From p120

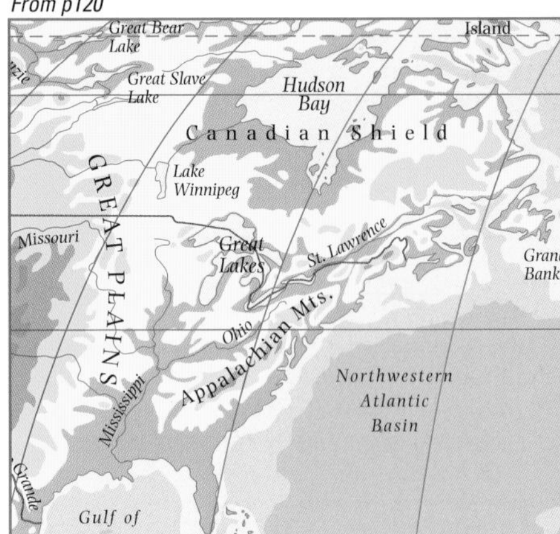

North (N) 0 — North North East — North East — East North East — East 90 — East South East — South East — South South East — South 180 — South South West — South West — West South West — West 270 — West North West — North West — North North West

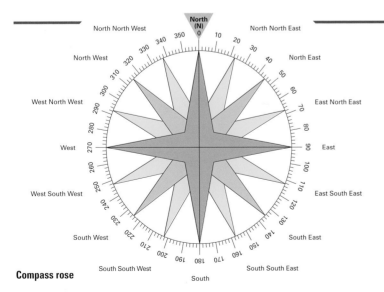

Compass rose

In the atlas, the cardinal points (north, east, south, and west) can be determined from the parallels and meridians. Thus all parallels run north and south, and meridians east and west. Intermediate directions require the application of the compass rose or the use of bearings. Direction using bearings can be determined using a protractor.

Direction

A direction can be expressed in two ways:

1. In terms of north, east, south, and west (the cardinal points of the compass) and various points between, such as east south east or north west (the intermediate points). These are shown on the diagram of the compass rose.

2. In terms of degrees (as a bearing), ranging through the values of the compass from 0° (north), 90° (east), 180° (south) to 359° (one degree west of north). These are also shown on the compass rose diagram.

The North Pole, where all meridians of longitude converge, is referred to as true or geographic north. Likewise, the South Pole is known as the true or geographic south. By convention, most maps are oriented so that true (geographic) north occurs toward the top of the map. Thus, when we refer to north and south on most maps, we are speaking of these poles.

There are also magnetic north and south poles. The magnetic north pole is presently located to the north of Ellesmere Island in the Canadian Arctic *(see pages 40–41)* and is moving about 24 km a year in a north-easterly direction. On a magnetic compass, the north arrow points to this pole.

Maps are devices created to capture phenomena on the Earth's surface in a simplified and accessible form. Depending on the size of the area being captured, the best position for starting to create a map is an elevated vantage point. In the past, views from hills and trees, drawn with paper and pencil, were used to create maps; more recently, photographs from cameras in hot-air balloons and airplanes were used. Today, using digital technology from satellites, we have a constant supply of images covering the entire globe. Technology has always been the close companion of the cartographer in the quest to accurately and effectively capture aspects of the environment.

Since the 1950s, artificial satellites have been in orbit around the Earth. These satellites are positioned at never-before-accessible vantage points high above the Earth. Soaring far above the reconnaissance airplanes used in the first half of the 20th century, the satellites quickly showed their capabilities. From hundreds of kilometres away, humans had their first look at the 'four corners' of the Earth.

As sophisticated as this technology might appear, at its core is one simple element: the camera. A satellite camera contains a series of sensors that are not unlike state-of-the-art digital cameras. These sensors can record information about the environment across a range of both the visible and non-visible parts of the electromagnetic spectrum (see diagram at the top right of this page). Like night-vision goggles, some cameras contain sensors that can detect heat energy (infrared); others contain sensors for energy within the radar portion of the electromagnetic spectrum. Theses sensors are "eyes in the sky", which capture a view of the Earth at a moment in time and allow the user the opportunity to interpret that landscape.

There are many satellites used for Earth observation. Some are privately funded, while others, such as military and environmental satellites, are funded by governments. Some of the satellite images in this atlas were taken by a satellite that orbits the Earth at an altitude of 450 km and has a proven ground resolution of 60 cm, meaning that objects larger than 60 cm on the surface of the Earth can be seen in the images it produces. This orbit allows the satellite to revisit the same location each day. Much of this imagery is shown in natural colours to resemble a digital photograph of the Earth's surface.

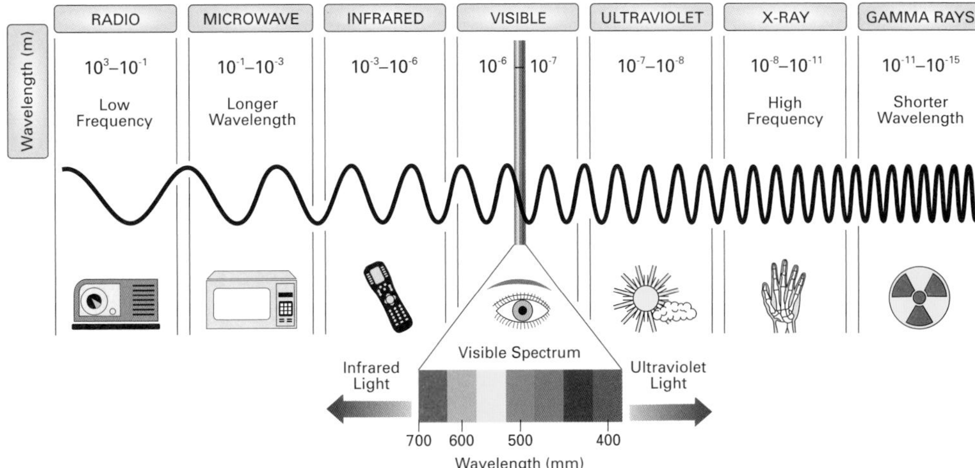

The electromagnetic spectrum
A simple diagram of the electromagnetic spectrum.

To record a scene, the satellite must be positioned over the area of interest. Most satellites are in a sun-synchronous orbit, meaning they are over the same area of the Earth at roughly the same time each day, and always when that area is in daylight. As the sun's energy strikes the surface of the planet, the sensors on the satellite capture the reflected energy. Each sensor on the satellite is responsible for capturing specific wavelengths of energy. The sensors produce a matrix of numbers for each image. This raw data is sent back to ground stations, where it is processed to create usable images such as those in this atlas.

The various objects that make up the Earth's surface such as rocks, soil, vegetation, water, and human artifacts (such as buildings), all absorb and reflect different wavelengths and amounts of energy. The differences in energy absorption and reflection — called a spectral signature — make it possible to distinguish one object from another in an image. For example, a forest may emit some energy at the visible green wavelength, but much more energy in the infrared range. On a satellite image, specific colours are chosen to display these different wavelengths of energy. The result is called a "false-colour composite", where the high levels of infrared energy from a forest could appear red, while urban areas appear blue-green. These images can also be shown in "true colour" to produce realistic landsurface colours. Nearly all of the images used in this atlas are true-colour images.

Satellite imagery has many applications, including environmental monitoring, resource management, disaster preparedness, land-use planning, forest inventories, energy exploration and monitoring, transportation, and security. Most important of all, satellite images are used in the creation of maps.

Vancouver
An oblique satellite view of much of the Lower Mainland of British Columbia from Howe Sound in the north to Point Roberts (part of the USA) in the south.

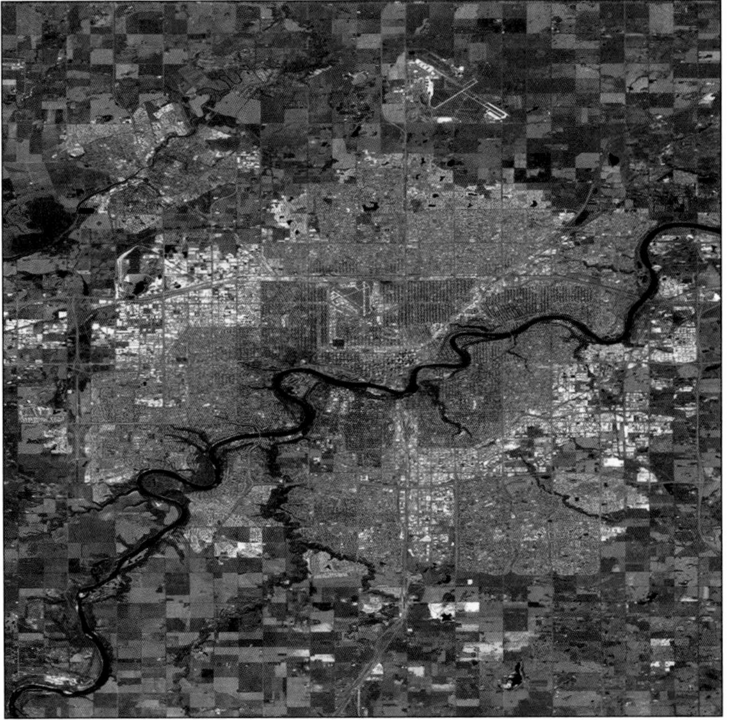

Edmonton
A vertical satellite view of Edmonton, Alberta bisected by the North Saskatchewan River.

The Earth in space

Solar System

Our solar system comprises the sun and eight planets, their 162 moons, three dwarf planets (with four known moons), and thousands of small bodies including asteroids, meteoroids, comets, and interplanetary dust.

The main component of the solar system is the sun, which contains 99.86% of the system's known mass and dominates the system with its gravity. The sun's large mass makes it dense enough to sustain nuclear fusion, releasing enormous amounts of energy. Most of this energy is radiated into space as electromagnetic radiation, including visible light. Jupiter and Saturn together account for more than 90% of the solar system's remaining mass.

Light travels at 299 460 kilometres per second, or 10 trillion kilometres in one year. This distance is known as a light-year. It takes 8 minutes and 17 seconds for light to travel from the sun to the Earth, and about 5.5 hours for light to travel from the sun to the farthest extent of our solar system.

The Milky Way is a spiral galaxy containing at least 200 billion stars, and is approximately 100 000 light-years in diameter. Our sun is a medium-sized star in the Milky Way. Our solar system is located on one of the outer spirals of the galaxy, 28 000 light-years from the galactic centre. The closest star to the Earth outside our solar system, Proxima Centauri, is 4.22 light-years away. Of the known galaxies, one of the farthest from the Earth, called Quasar PKS 2000-330, is more than 13 billion light-years away; the light we see from it comes from a time close to when the universe was born.

All parts of the universe are in constant motion. The entire Milky Way rushes through space at 600 kilometres per second, or 2 160 000 kilometres per hour. It spins around its galactic centre at 800 000 kilometres per hour. The Earth revolves around the sun at 106 300 kilometres per hour, and completes one revolution every 365.26 days. The Earth rotates on its axis once every 23 hours and 56 minutes at 1 600 kilometres per hour at the equator; the rotational speed diminishes toward the poles.

Hubble/GALEX/Spitzer composite image of M81
This image combines data from the Hubble Space Telescope, the Spitzer Space Telescope, and the Galaxy Evolution Explorer (GALEX) missions.

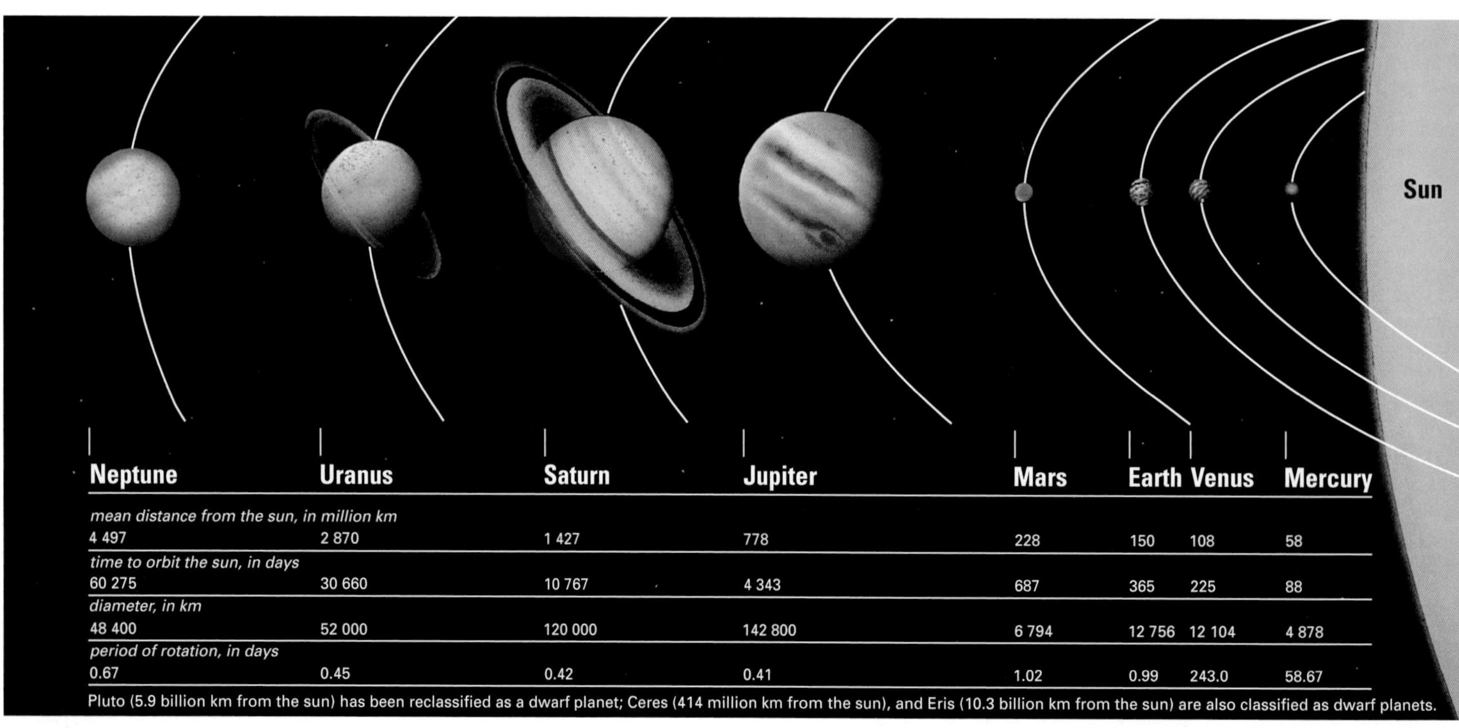

	Neptune	Uranus	Saturn	Jupiter	Mars	Earth	Venus	Mercury
mean distance from the sun, in million km	4 497	2 870	1 427	778	228	150	108	58
time to orbit the sun, in days	60 275	30 660	10 767	4 343	687	365	225	88
diameter, in km	48 400	52 000	120 000	142 800	6 794	12 756	12 104	4 878
period of rotation, in days	0.67	0.45	0.42	0.41	1.02	0.99	243.0	58.67

Pluto (5.9 billion km from the sun) has been reclassified as a dwarf planet; Ceres (414 million km from the sun), and Eris (10.3 billion km from the sun) are also classified as dwarf planets.

Human use of Earth space

Satellites can be placed in different orbits around the Earth. For each satellite purpose there is a preferred orbit.

Low orbits

Satellites in low orbit (300–800 km) must travel rapidly (27 000 km/h) in order to overcome gravity. Satellites that observe the planet, such as those involved in remote sensing, weather, telephone, and data communication, use these orbits, as well as the International Space Station, which orbits the Earth at 354 km.

Polar orbits

These satellites, usually in a low orbit of 700 to 800 km, provide a more global view of the Earth, passing each latitude at approximately the same time through each season.

Elliptical or eccentric orbits

Often used for satellites designed to study particular areas of the Earth and needing to spend long periods over a chosen area.

Geostationary orbits

At 35 880 km above the equator, these are the highest orbits. They enable satellites to view a large area of the Earth. Each orbit takes 24 hours, the same time that it takes the Earth to rotate on its axis; they remain in the same position relative to the Earth. Communications and weather satellites use these orbits.

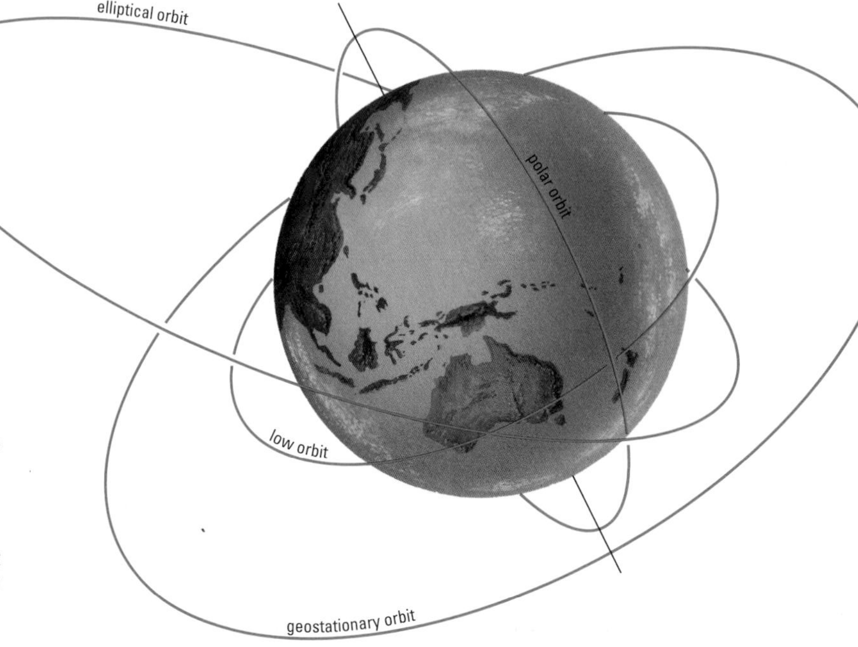

The diagram shows how the Earth revolves around the sun every 365.25 days, while rotating on a tilted axis of 23.5° every 24 hours. The Earth's revolution on its tilted axis causes the four seasons, while its rotation causes day and night.

The Earth revolves around the sun following an elliptical, or slightly egg-shaped, orbit. Thus the distance between the Earth and the sun varies, from a maximum of 152 million kilometres on July 4 to a minimum of 147 million kilometres on January 3. However, this variation has little effect on temperatures on Earth.

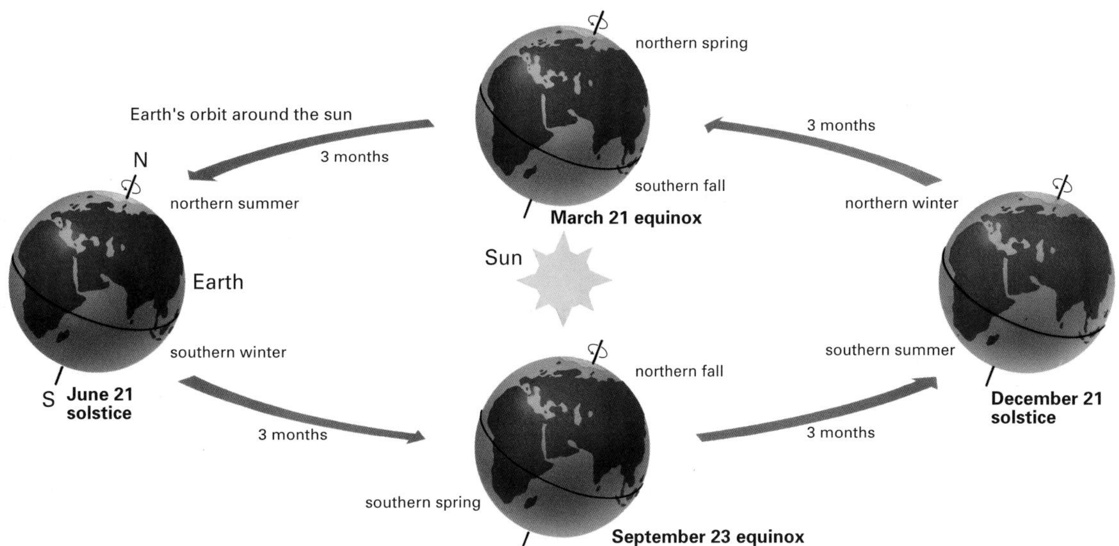

The diagram of the Earth in June and December shows the variations in the length of day and night. In June, the northern hemisphere is tilted at 23.5° towards the sun and as a result it receives more hours of sunshine. The sun's rays strike the Earth's atmosphere over the northern hemisphere more directly than at other times of the year, resulting in summer, with its warm temperatures.

Earth's axis

area of the Earth in sunlight

area of the Earth in darkness

length of day } along each line of latitude

length of night

Six months later, the Earth has revolved halfway around the sun. Now the southern hemisphere is tilted at 23.5° towards the sun. Thus in December it is summer in the southern hemisphere, while it is winter in the northern hemisphere.

June 21

23.5° tilt

North Pole
6 months daylight

Arctic Circle (66.5°N)
24 hours daylight

short night/long day

days and nights of equal length

long night/short day

Tropic of Cancer (23.5°N)
13.5 hours daylight

Equator (0°)
12 hours daylight

Tropic of Capricorn (23.5°S)
10.5 hours daylight

South Pole
6 months darkness

Antarctic Circle (66.5°S)
24 hours darkness

rays of the sun

December 21

23.5° tilt

Arctic Circle (66.5°N)
24 hours darkness

North Pole
6 months darkness

Tropic of Cancer (23.5°N)
10.5 hours daylight

Equator (0°)
12 hours daylight

Tropic of Capricorn (23.5°S)
13.5 hours daylight

short day/long night

days and nights of equal length

long day/short night

Antarctic Circle (66.5°S)
24 hours daylight

South Pole
6 months daylight

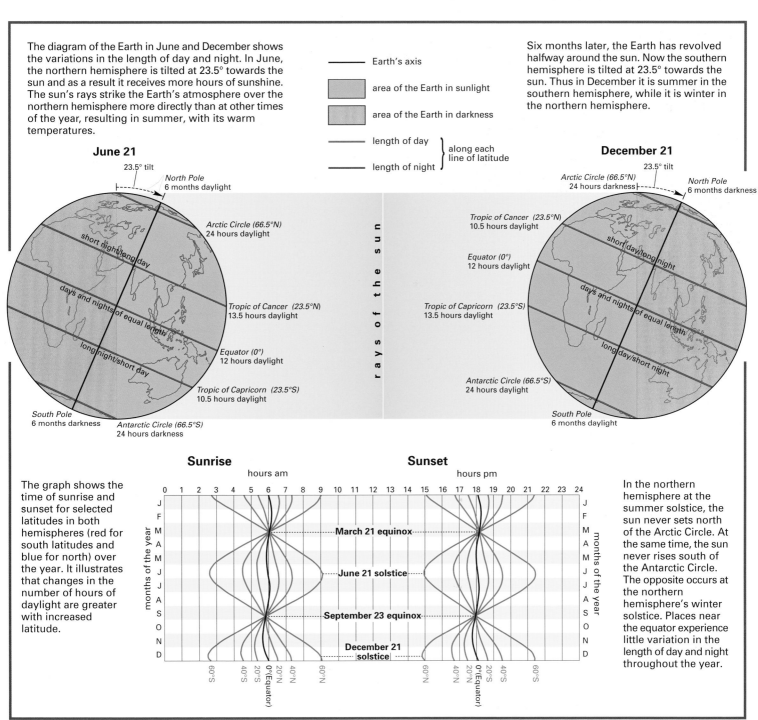

The graph shows the time of sunrise and sunset for selected latitudes in both hemispheres (red for south latitudes and blue for north) over the year. It illustrates that changes in the number of hours of daylight are greater with increased latitude.

Sunrise hours am — **Sunset** hours pm

0 1 2 3 4 5 6 7 8 9 10 11 12 13 14 15 16 17 18 19 20 21 22 23 24

months of the year: J F M A M J J A S O N D

March 21 equinox

June 21 solstice

September 23 equinox

December 21 solstice

60°S 40°S 20°S 0°(Equator) 20°N 40°N 60°N — 60°N 40°N 20°N 0°(Equator) 20°S 40°S 60°S

In the northern hemisphere at the summer solstice, the sun never sets north of the Arctic Circle. At the same time, the sun never rises south of the Antarctic Circle. The opposite occurs at the northern hemisphere's winter solstice. Places near the equator experience little variation in the length of day and night throughout the year.

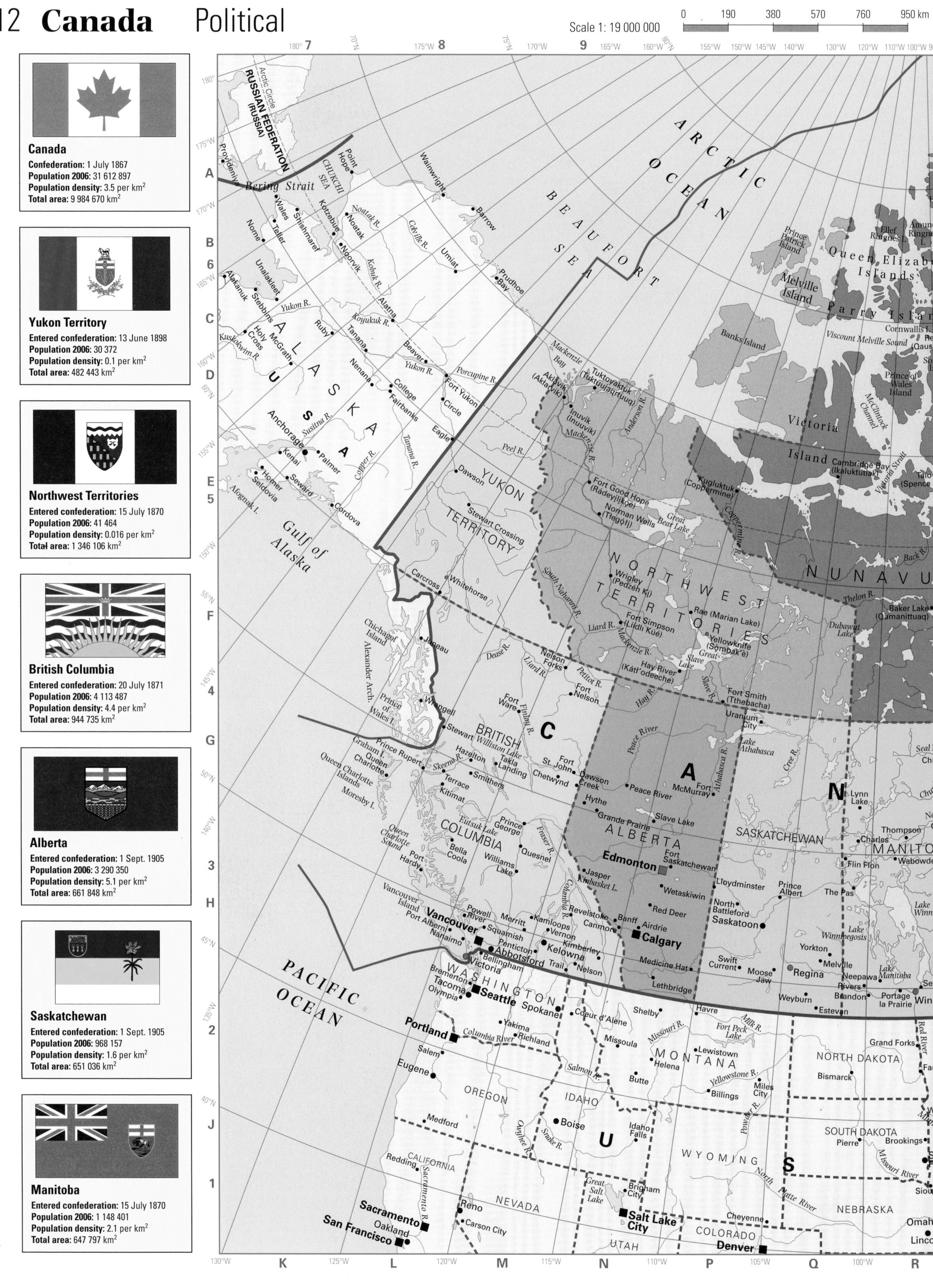
Scale 1: 19 000 000
0 190 380 570 760 950 km
Canada
Confederation: 1 July 1867
Population 2006: 31 612 897
Population density: 3.5 per km²
Total area: 9 984 670 km²
Yukon Territory
Entered confederation: 13 June 1898
Population 2006: 30 372
Population density: 0.1 per km²
Total area: 482 443 km²
Northwest Territories
Entered confederation: 15 July 1870
Population 2006: 41 464
Population density: 0.016 per km²
Total area: 1 346 106 km²
British Columbia
Entered confederation: 20 July 1871
Population 2006: 4 113 487
Population density: 4.4 per km²
Total area: 944 735 km²
Alberta
Entered confederation: 1 Sept. 1905
Population 2006: 3 290 350
Population density: 5.1 per km²
Total area: 661 848 km²
Saskatchewan
Entered confederation: 1 Sept. 1905
Population 2006: 968 157
Population density: 1.6 per km²
Total area: 651 036 km²
Manitoba
Entered confederation: 15 July 1870
Population 2006: 1 148 401
Population density: 2.1 per km²
Total area: 647 797 km²
ARCTIC OCEAN
BEAUFORT SEA
PACIFIC OCEAN
Gulf of Alaska
RUSSIAN FEDERATION (RUSSIA)
ALASKA
YUKON TERRITORY
NORTHWEST TERRITORIES
NUNAVUT
BRITISH COLUMBIA
ALBERTA
SASKATCHEWAN
WASHINGTON
OREGON
IDAHO
MONTANA
WYOMING
NORTH DAKOTA
SOUTH DAKOTA
NEBRASKA
NEVADA
UTAH
COLORADO
CALIFORNIA
Zenithal Equidistant Projection

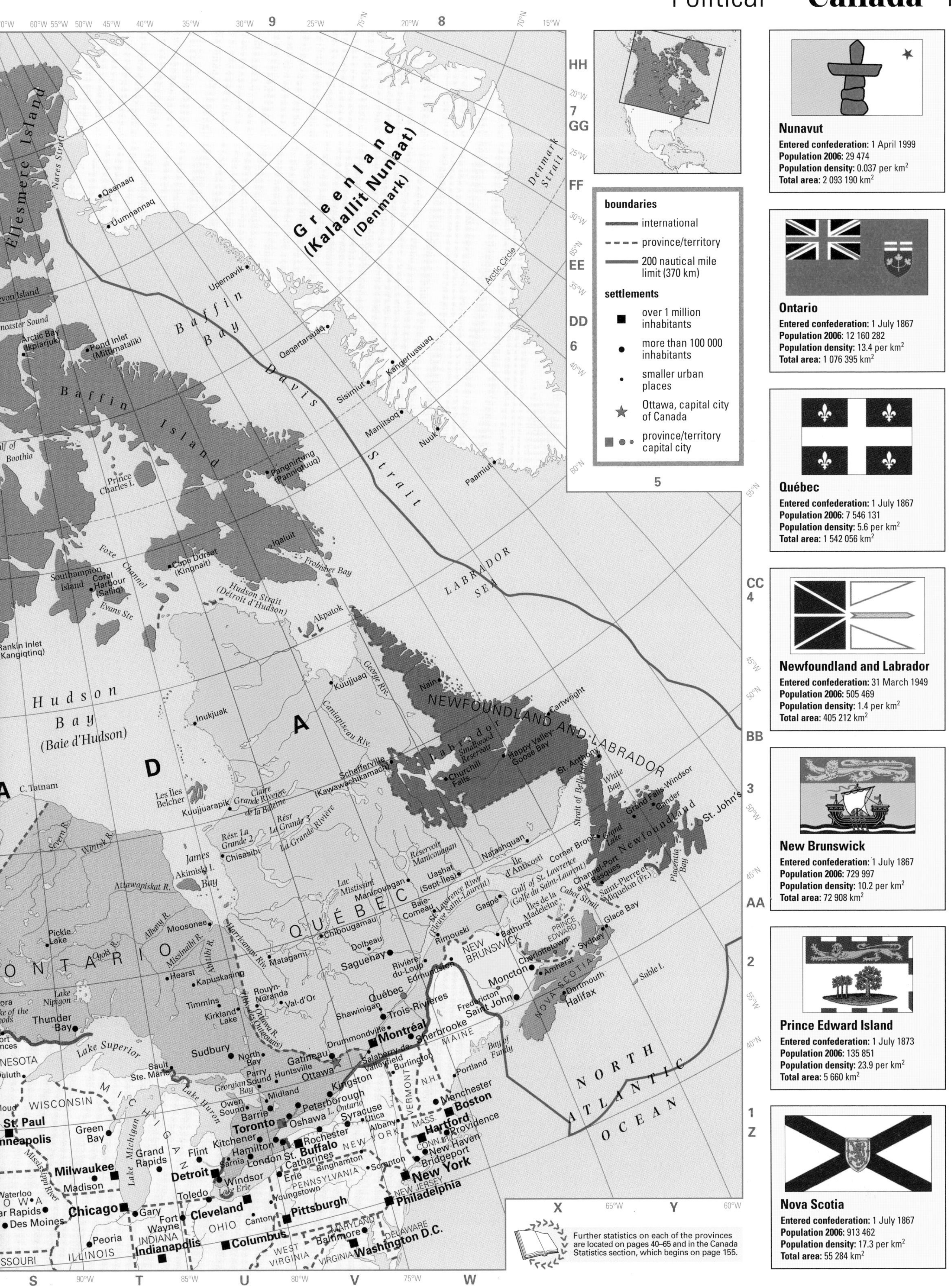
boundaries
international
province/territory
200 nautical mile limit (370 km)
settlements
over 1 million inhabitants
more than 100 000 inhabitants
smaller urban places
Ottawa, capital city of Canada
province/territory capital city
Nunavut
Entered confederation: 1 April 1999
Population 2006: 29 474
Population density: 0.037 per km²
Total area: 2 093 190 km²
Ontario
Entered confederation: 1 July 1867
Population 2006: 12 160 282
Population density: 13.4 per km²
Total area: 1 076 395 km²
Québec
Entered confederation: 1 July 1867
Population 2006: 7 546 131
Population density: 5.6 per km²
Total area: 1 542 056 km²
Newfoundland and Labrador
Entered confederation: 31 March 1949
Population 2006: 505 469
Population density: 1.4 per km²
Total area: 405 212 km²
New Brunswick
Entered confederation: 1 July 1867
Population 2006: 729 997
Population density: 10.2 per km²
Total area: 72 908 km²
Prince Edward Island
Entered confederation: 1 July 1873
Population 2006: 135 851
Population density: 23.9 per km²
Total area: 5 660 km²
Nova Scotia
Entered confederation: 1 July 1867
Population 2006: 913 462
Population density: 17.3 per km²
Total area: 55 284 km²
Further statistics on each of the provinces are located on pages 40–65 and in the Canada Statistics section, which begins on page 155.
Greenland (Kalaallit Nunaat) (Denmark)
Baffin Bay
Baffin Island
Davis Strait
Labrador Sea
Hudson Bay (Baie d'Hudson)
Hudson Strait (Détroit d'Hudson)
James Bay
NEWFOUNDLAND AND LABRADOR
QUÉBEC
ONTARIO
NEW BRUNSWICK
PRINCE EDWARD ISLAND
NOVA SCOTIA
NORTH ATLANTIC OCEAN
Ellesmere Island
Nares Strait
Denmark Strait
Arctic Circle
Foxe Channel
Frobisher Bay
Gulf of St. Lawrence (Golfe du Saint-Laurent)
Bay of Fundy
Lake Superior
Lake Huron
Lake Michigan
Lake Erie
L. Ontario
Iqaluit
Nain
Kuujjuaq
Inukjuak
Schefferville
Happy Valley-Goose Bay
St. John's
Corner Brook
Gander
Québec
Montréal
Ottawa
Toronto
Sudbury
Thunder Bay
Moncton
Fredericton
Saint John
Charlottetown
Halifax
Sydney
Boston
New York
Philadelphia
Washington D.C.
Chicago
Detroit
Cleveland
Pittsburgh
Buffalo
Milwaukee
Minneapolis
St. Paul
Indianapolis
Columbus
Baltimore

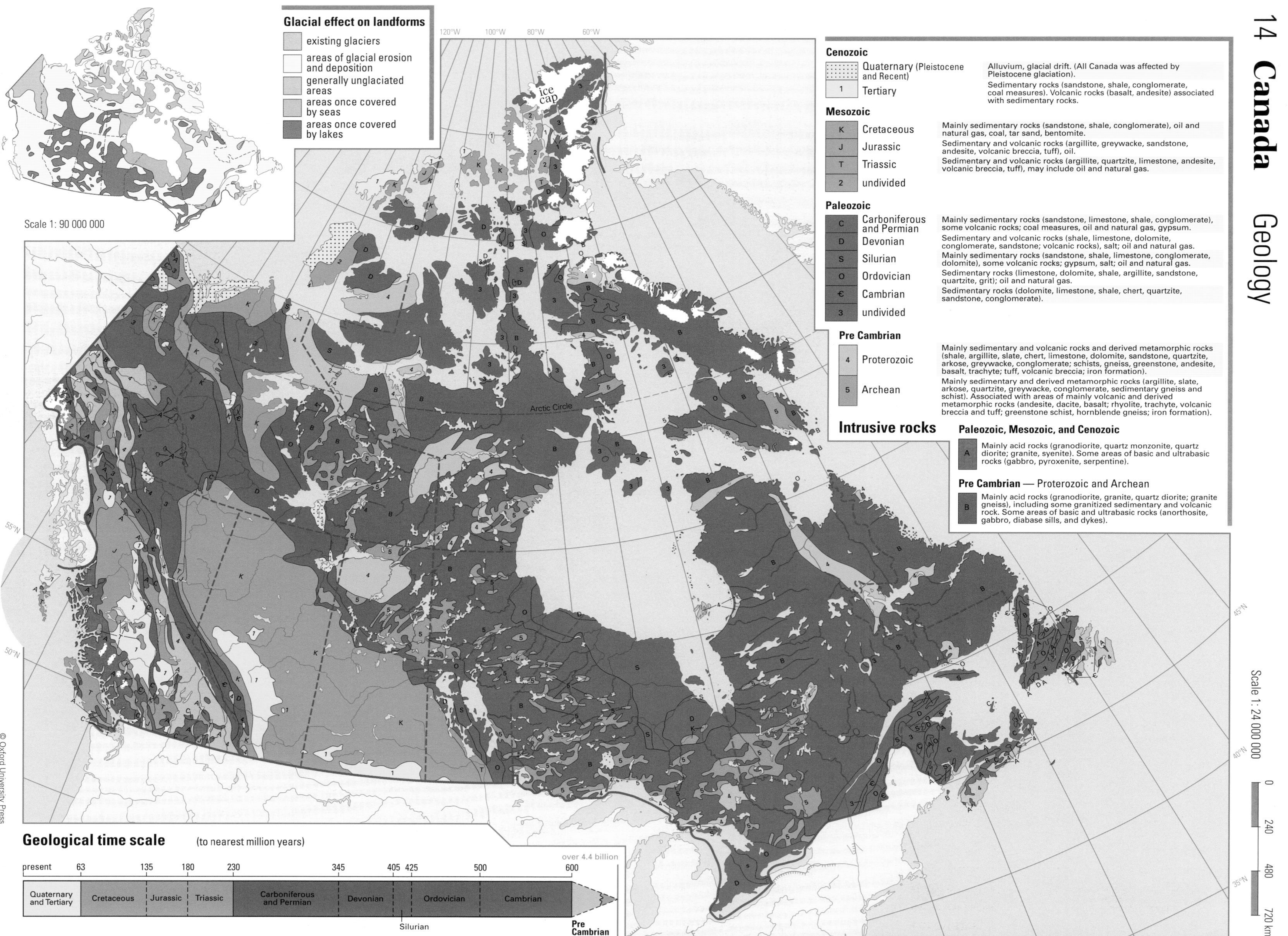
Scale 1: 24 000 000
0
240
480
720 km
Cenozoic
Quaternary (Pleistocene and Recent)
Alluvium, glacial drift. (All Canada was affected by Pleistocene glaciation).
1 Tertiary
Sedimentary rocks (sandstone, shale, conglomerate, coal measures). Volcanic rocks (basalt, andesite) associated with sedimentary rocks.
Mesozoic
K Cretaceous
Mainly sedimentary rocks (sandstone, shale, conglomerate), oil and natural gas, coal, tar sand, bentomite.
J Jurassic
Sedimentary and volcanic rocks (argillite, greywacke, sandstone, andesite, volcanic breccia, tuff), oil.
T Triassic
Sedimentary and volcanic rocks (argillite, quartzite, limestone, andesite, volcanic breccia, tuff), may include oil and natural gas.
2 undivided
Paleozoic
C Carboniferous and Permian
Mainly sedimentary rocks (sandstone, limestone, shale, conglomerate), some volcanic rocks; coal measures, oil and natural gas, gypsum.
D Devonian
Sedimentary and volcanic rocks (shale, limestone, dolomite, conglomerate, sandstone; volcanic rocks), salt; oil and natural gas.
S Silurian
Mainly sedimentary rocks (sandstone, shale, limestone, conglomerate, dolomite), some volcanic rocks; gypsum, salt; oil and natural gas.
O Ordovician
Sedimentary rocks (limestone, dolomite, shale, argillite, sandstone, quartzite, grit); oil and natural gas.
€ Cambrian
Sedimentary rocks (dolomite, limestone, shale, chert, quartzite, sandstone, conglomerate).
3 undivided
Pre Cambrian
4 Proterozoic
Mainly sedimentary and volcanic rocks and derived metamorphic rocks (shale, argillite, slate, chert, limestone, dolomite, sandstone, quartzite, arkose, greywacke, conglomerate; schists, gneiss, greenstone, andesite, basalt, trachyte; tuff, volcanic breccia; iron formation).
5 Archean
Mainly sedimentary and derived metamorphic rocks (argillite, slate, arkose, quartzite, greywacke, conglomerate, sedimentary gneiss and schist). Associated with areas of mainly volcanic and derived metamorphic rocks (andesite, dacite, basalt; rhyolite, trachyte, volcanic breccia and tuff; greenstone schist, hornblende gneiss; iron formation).
Intrusive rocks
Paleozoic, Mesozoic, and Cenozoic
A Mainly acid rocks (granodiorite, quartz monzonite, quartz diorite; granite, syenite). Some areas of basic and ultrabasic rocks (gabbro, pyroxenite, serpentine).
Pre Cambrian — Proterozoic and Archean
B Mainly acid rocks (granodiorite, granite, quartz diorite; granite gneiss), including some granitized sedimentary and volcanic rock. Some areas of basic and ultrabasic rocks (anorthosite, gabbro, diabase sills, and dykes).
Glacial effect on landforms
existing glaciers
areas of glacial erosion and deposition
generally unglaciated areas
areas once covered by seas
areas once covered by lakes
Scale 1: 90 000 000
ice cap
Arctic Circle
120°W
100°W
80°W
60°W
55°N
50°N
45°N
40°N
35°N
Geological time scale
(to nearest million years)
present
63
135
180
230
345
405
425
500
600
over 4.4 billion
Quaternary and Tertiary
Cretaceous
Jurassic
Triassic
Carboniferous and Permian
Devonian
Ordovician
Cambrian
Silurian
Pre Cambrian

Scale 1: 24 000 000

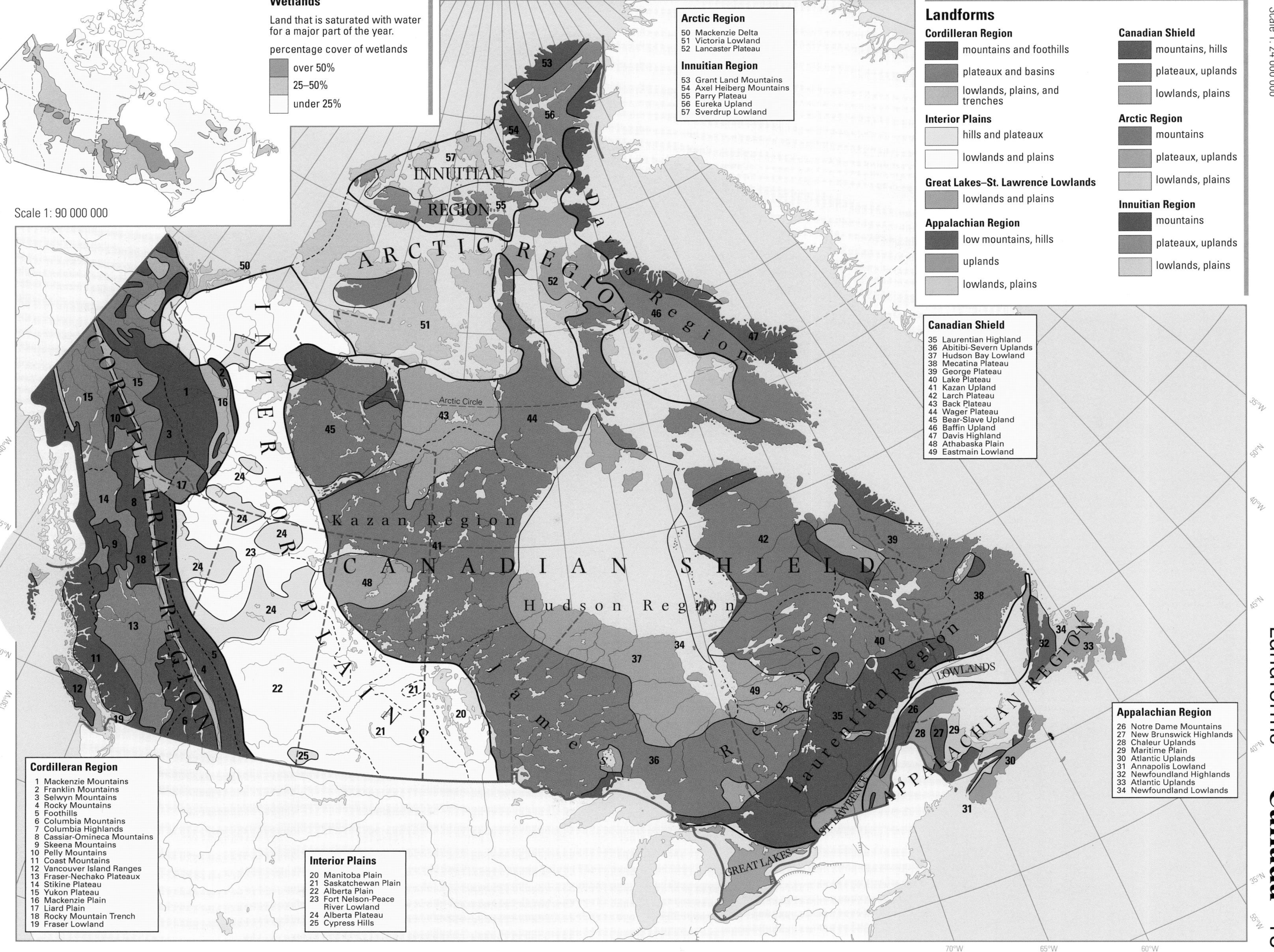
Wetlands
Land that is saturated with water for a major part of the year.
percentage cover of wetlands
over 50%
25–50%
under 25%
Scale 1: 90 000 000
Arctic Region
50 Mackenzie Delta
51 Victoria Lowland
52 Lancaster Plateau
Innuitian Region
53 Grant Land Mountains
54 Axel Heiberg Mountains
55 Parry Plateau
56 Eureka Upland
57 Sverdrup Lowland
Landforms
Cordilleran Region
mountains and foothills
plateaux and basins
lowlands, plains, and trenches
Interior Plains
hills and plateaux
lowlands and plains
Great Lakes–St. Lawrence Lowlands
lowlands and plains
Appalachian Region
low mountains, hills
uplands
lowlands, plains
Canadian Shield
mountains, hills
plateaux, uplands
lowlands, plains
Arctic Region
mountains
plateaux, uplands
lowlands, plains
Innuitian Region
mountains
plateaux, uplands
lowlands, plains
Canadian Shield
35 Laurentian Highland
36 Abitibi-Severn Uplands
37 Hudson Bay Lowland
38 Mecatina Plateau
39 George Plateau
40 Lake Plateau
41 Kazan Upland
42 Larch Plateau
43 Back Plateau
44 Wager Plateau
45 Bear-Slave Upland
46 Baffin Upland
47 Davis Highland
48 Athabaska Plain
49 Eastmain Lowland
INNUITIAN REGION
ARCTIC REGION
Davis Region
Arctic Circle
INTERIOR PLAINS
CORDILLERAN REGION
Kazan Region
CANADIAN SHIELD
Hudson Region
James Region
Laurentian Region
LOWLANDS
APPALACHIAN REGION
ST. LAWRENCE
GREAT LAKES
Appalachian Region
26 Notre Dame Mountains
27 New Brunswick Highlands
28 Chaleur Uplands
29 Maritime Plain
30 Atlantic Uplands
31 Annapolis Lowland
32 Newfoundland Highlands
33 Atlantic Uplands
34 Newfoundland Lowlands
Cordilleran Region
1 Mackenzie Mountains
2 Franklin Mountains
3 Selwyn Mountains
4 Rocky Mountains
5 Foothills
6 Columbia Mountains
7 Columbia Highlands
8 Cassiar-Omineca Mountains
9 Skeena Mountains
10 Pelly Mountains
11 Coast Mountains
12 Vancouver Island Ranges
13 Fraser-Nechako Plateaux
14 Stikine Plateau
15 Yukon Plateau
16 Mackenzie Plain
17 Liard Plain
18 Rocky Mountain Trench
19 Fraser Lowland
Interior Plains
20 Manitoba Plain
21 Saskatchewan Plain
22 Alberta Plain
23 Fort Nelson-Peace River Lowland
24 Alberta Plateau
25 Cypress Hills
140°W
55°N
50°N
130°W
35°W
30°N
40°N
45°N
35°N
55°W
70°W
65°W
60°W

Zenithal Equidistant Projection

Heating the Earth

The Greenhouse Effect

The greenhouse effect is a naturally occurring process that enables the atmosphere to retain heat. Without it, the Earth's average temperature would be -18°C instead of the present +15°C. Climate change is attributed in large measure to increased levels of greenhouse gases largely due to human activity. Information on this subject for Canada occurs on page 25 and for the world on pages 124 and 128.

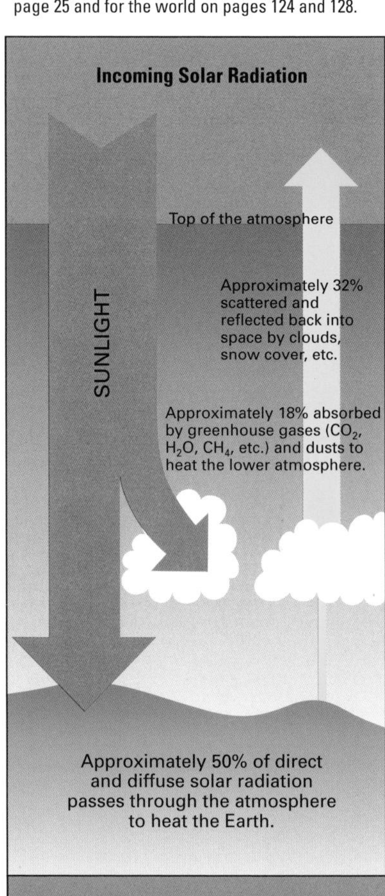
Incoming Solar Radiation
SUNLIGHT
Top of the atmosphere
Approximately 32% scattered and reflected back into space by clouds, snow cover, etc.
Approximately 18% absorbed by greenhouse gases (CO_2, H_2O, CH_4, etc.) and dusts to heat the lower atmosphere.
Approximately 50% of direct and diffuse solar radiation passes through the atmosphere to heat the Earth.

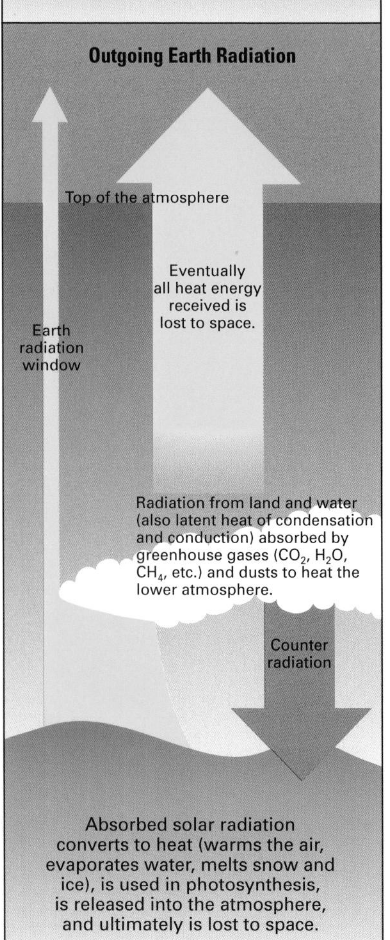
Outgoing Earth Radiation
Top of the atmosphere
Earth radiation window
Eventually all heat energy received is lost to space.
Radiation from land and water (also latent heat of condensation and conduction) absorbed by greenhouse gases (CO_2, H_2O, CH_4, etc.) and dusts to heat the lower atmosphere.
Counter radiation
Absorbed solar radiation converts to heat (warms the air, evaporates water, melts snow and ice), is used in photosynthesis, is released into the atmosphere, and ultimately is lost to space.

Temperature

Isotherms

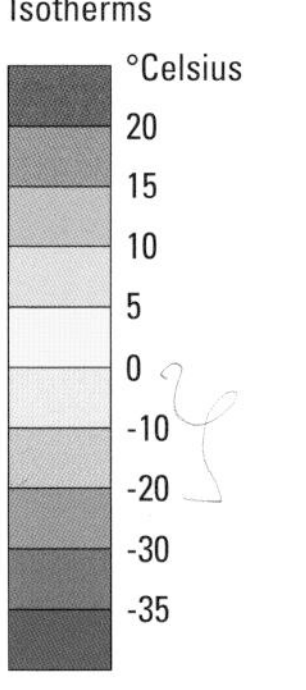
°Celsius
20
15
10
5
0
-10
-20
-30
-35

Isotherms join places having the same average monthly temperature.

Isolines, as seen on the other maps on these pages, join places having the same average temperature range, precipitation, etc.

Permafrost

The state of the ground (soil or rock) that remains below 0°C for more than a year.

approximate southern limit of:

- continuous permafrost (90–100% underlain by permafrost)
- discontinuous permafrost (10–90% underlain by permafrost)

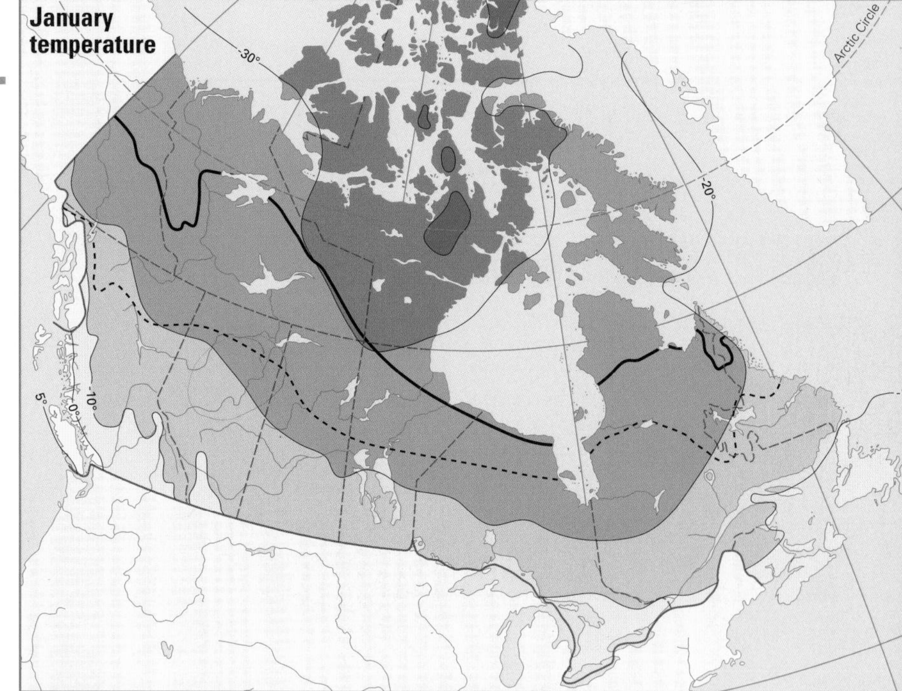
January temperature
Arctic Circle
-30°
-20°
5°
0°
10°

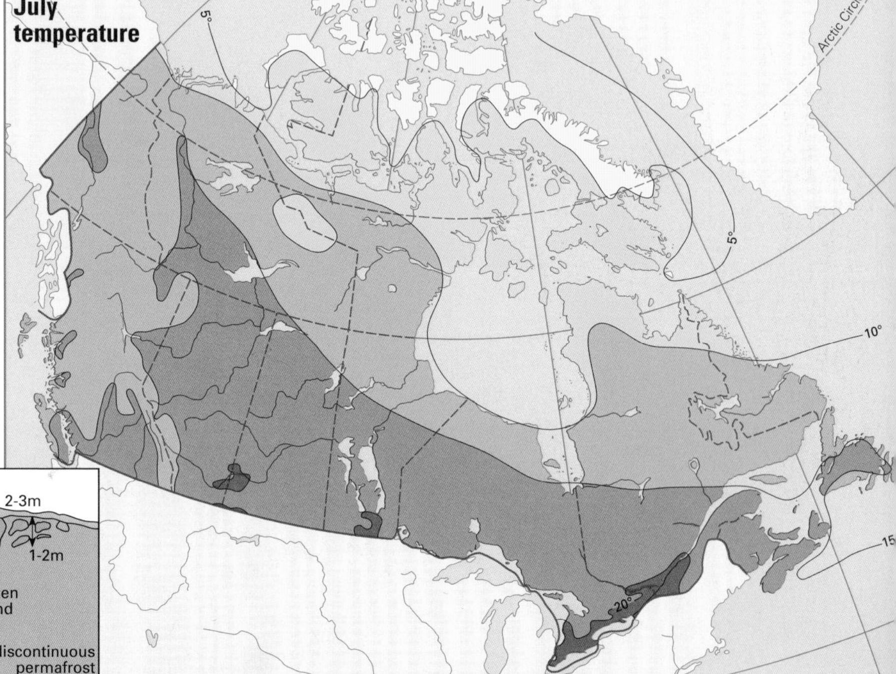
July temperature
Arctic Circle
5°
10°
15
20°

Cross-section showing a typical permafrost distribution in Northern Canada

Limits of continuous and discontinuous permafrost are shown on the map above.

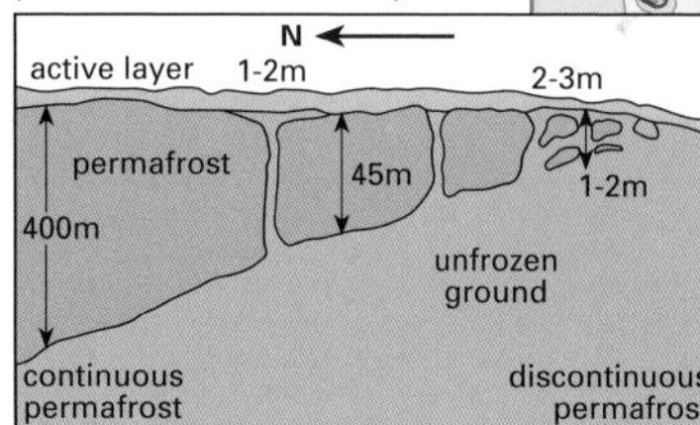
N
active layer 1-2m
2-3m
permafrost
45m
1-2m
400m
unfrozen ground
continuous permafrost
discontinuous permafrost

Temperature range

The difference between the average daily mean temperature in January and July

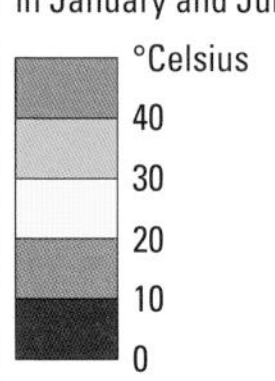
°Celsius
40
30
20
10
0

Monthly average temperatures for selected Canadian locations can be determined from the climate graphs on page 19 and the data in tables 84, 85 and 86 on pages 182–183.

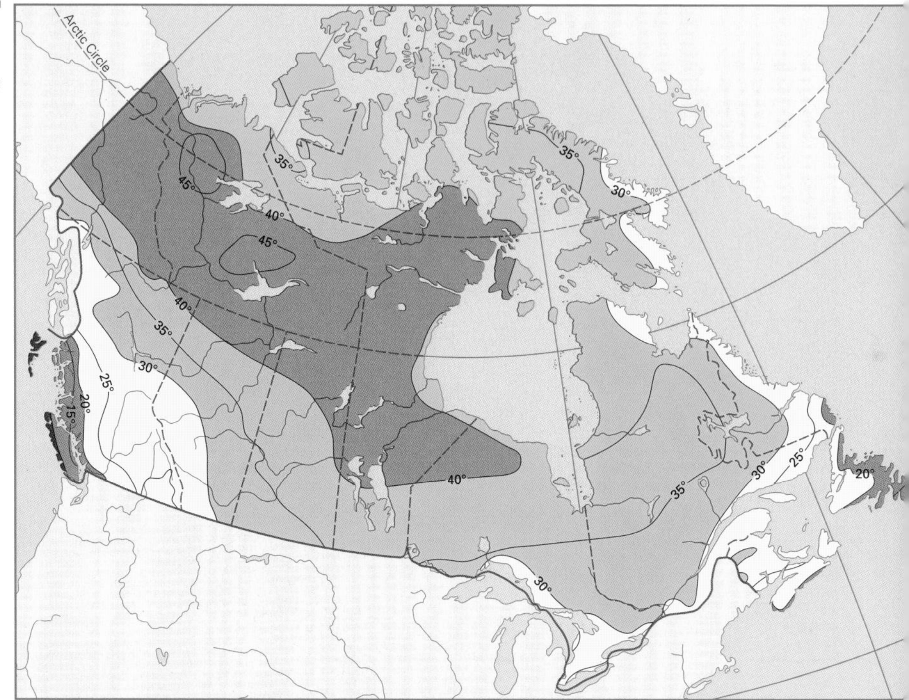
Arctic Circle
35°
30°
45°
40°
45°
40°
35°
30°
25°
20°
15°
40°
35°
30°
30°
25°
20°

Scale 1: 45 000 000

Zenithal Equidistant Projection

Precipitation

mean annual precipitation

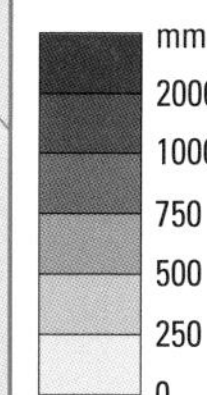

Monthly average precipitation for selected Canadian locations can be determined from the climate graphs on page 19 and the data in tables 84, 85 and 86 on pages 182–183.

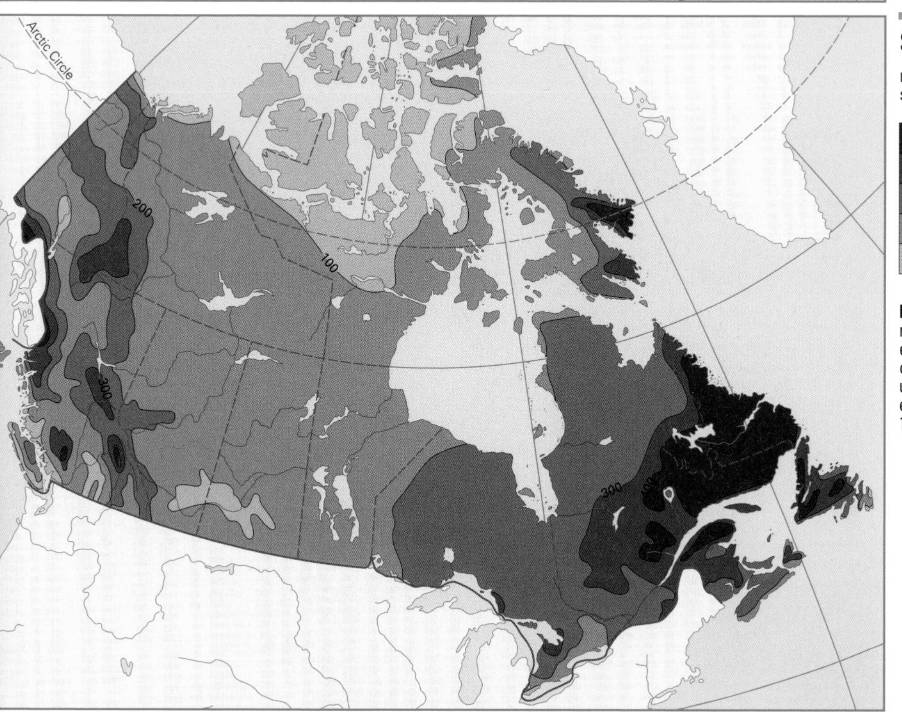

Snow

mean annual snowfall

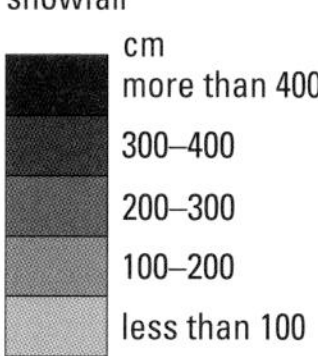

Precipitation includes rain, snow, sleet, hail, etc. Snowfall is converted to water using a 10 to 1 ratio e.g., 10 cm of snow = 1 cm of rain.

Thunderstorms

average annual number of days with thunderstorms

days
20
10
5

Thunderstorms are transient sometimes violent storms caused by strong rising air currents resulting in thunder, lightning, heavy rain, and sometimes hail and high winds.

Scale 1: 45 000 000

Zenithal Equidistant Projection

Air masses and winds

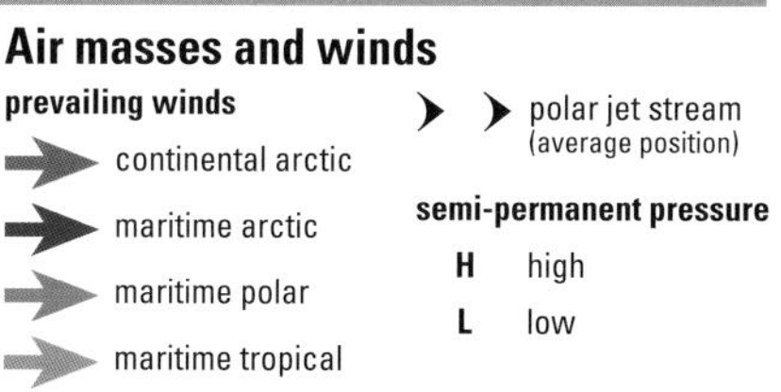

Scale 1: 108 000 000

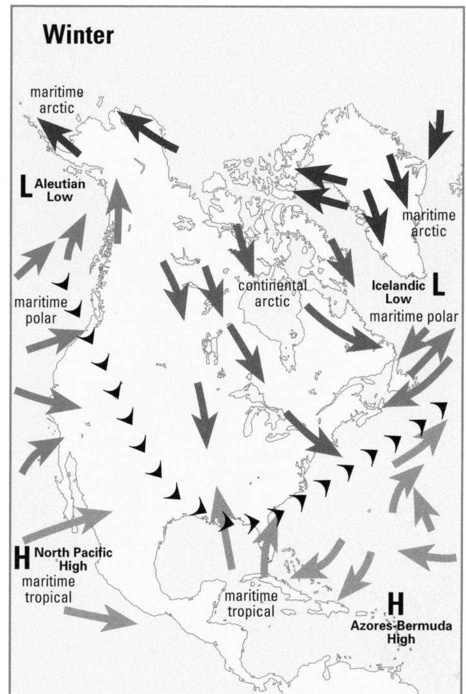

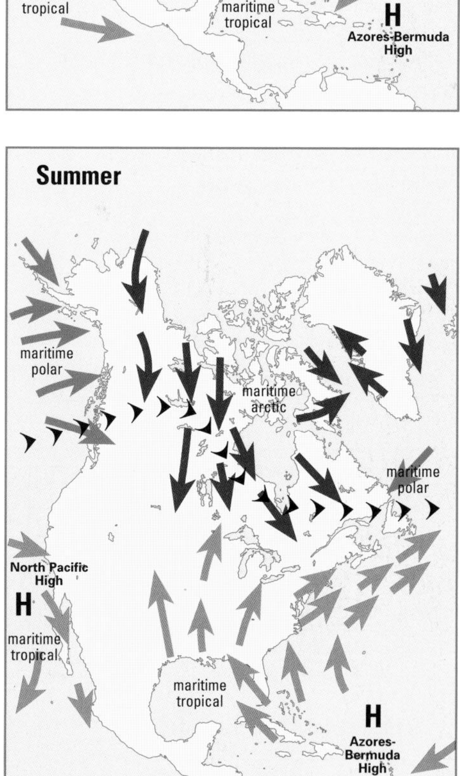

Oblique Mercator Projection

The term **air mass** denotes a mass of air usually several thousands of kilometres in extent, with similar temperature characteristics. Their boundaries are marked by frontal surfaces, along which mid latitude cyclonic storms occur.

Jet streams are high altitude streams of rapidly moving air, characterized by large stationary or slow moving waves. They circle the Earth and change locations with the seasons. They are associated with the fronts between air masses, and thus have a major influence on surface weather.

Humidex

The humidex was developed in Canada in 1965. Its purpose is to combine temperature and humidity into one number to reflect how hot humid weather is perceived by the average person.

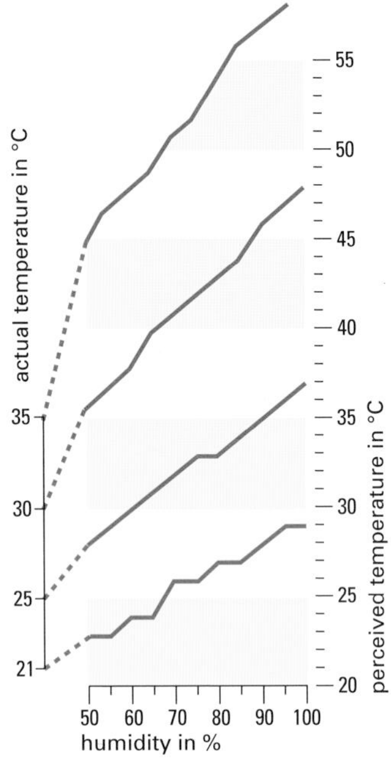

Humidex	Degree of discomfort
over 54	heat stroke imminent
45–54	dangerous
40–45	great discomfort
30–40	some discomfort
under 30	no discomfort

Growing season

average annual length of the growing season in number of days, assuming the growing season is that part of the year when the mean daily temperature is greater than 5.6°C

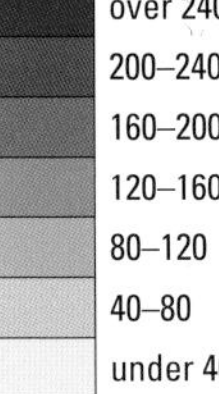

Scale 1: 45 000 000
Zenithal Equidistant Projection

Sunshine

average annual hours

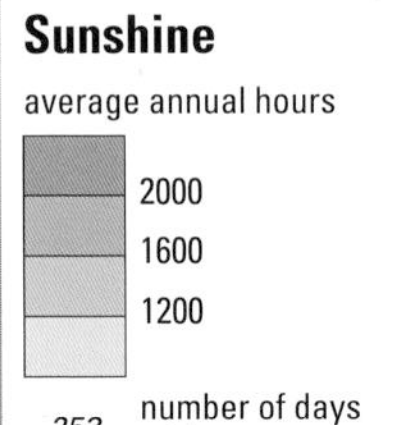

The use of renewable sources such as solar, wind, geothermal, tide, and wave energy to produce electricity will continue to increase in importance to replace non-renewable sources and combat global warming.

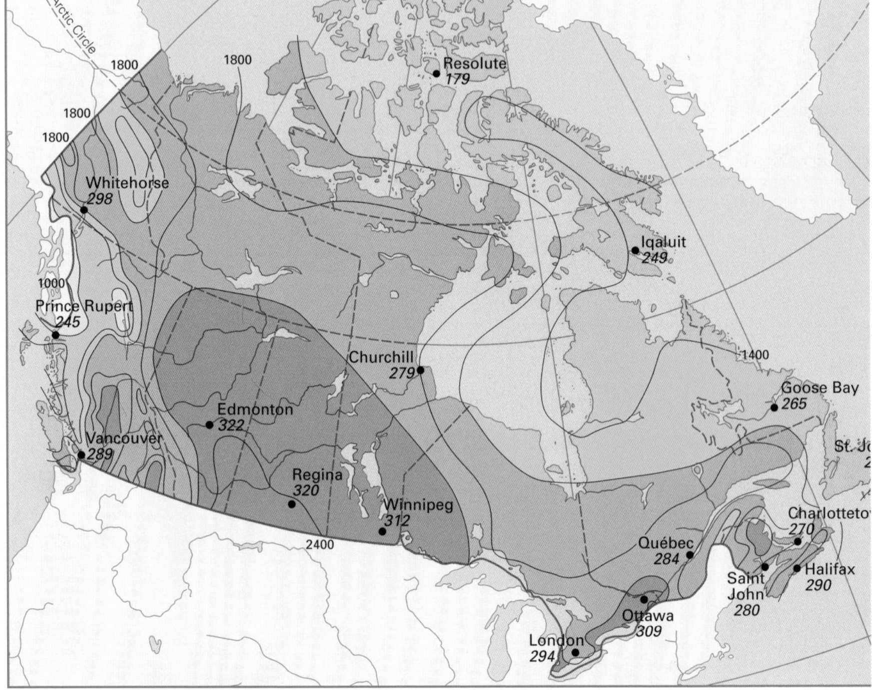

UV Index

The UV Index is a measure of the intensity of the sun's ultraviolet radiation in the sunburning spectrum. As the index increases, the sun's rays do more harm to skin, eyes, and the immune system, and it becomes necessary to take more precautions to protect exposed skin. In Canada, the UV forecast is issued twice daily for 47 locations. The risks from exposure to ultraviolet radiation have increased in recent years due to the thinning of the ozone layer.

UV Index	Description	Sun protection action
over 11	Extreme	take full precautions — unprotected skin will be damaged and can burn in minutes
8–10	Very high	extra precautions required — unprotected skin will be damaged and can burn quickly
6–7	High	protection required — UV damages the skin and can cause sunburn
3–5	Moderate	take precautions — hat, sunglasses and sunscreen
0–2	Low	minimal sun protection required for normal activity

Canadian weather records

highest air temperature	45°C Midale and Yellow Grass, Sask. *5 July 1937*
lowest air temperature	-63°C Snag, Y.T. *3 February 1947*
coldest month	-47.9°C Eureka, N.W.T. *February 1979*
highest sea-level pressure	107.96 kPa Dawson, Y.T. *2 February 1989*
lowest sea-level pressure	94.02 kPa St. Anthony, Nfld. *20 January 1977*
greatest precipitation in 24 hours	489.2 mm Ucluelet Brynnor Mines, B.C. *6 October 1967*
greatest precipitation in one month	2235.5 mm Swanson Bay, B.C. *November 1917*
greatest precipitation in one year	9479 mm Henderson Lake, B.C. *1977*
greatest average annual precipitation	6655 mm Henderson Lake, B.C.
least precipitation in one year	12.7 mm Arctic Bay, N.W.T. *1949*
greatest snowfall in one season	2446.5 cm Revelstoke, B.C. *1971–1972*
highest average annual number of thunderstorm days	34 days London, Ont.

January wind chill

5% chance of having a wind chill value worse than the value shown

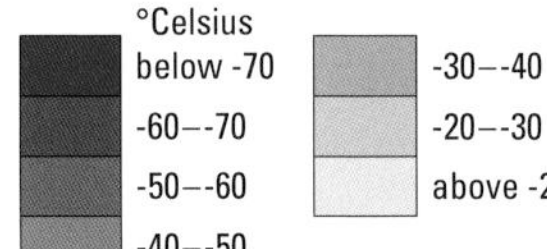

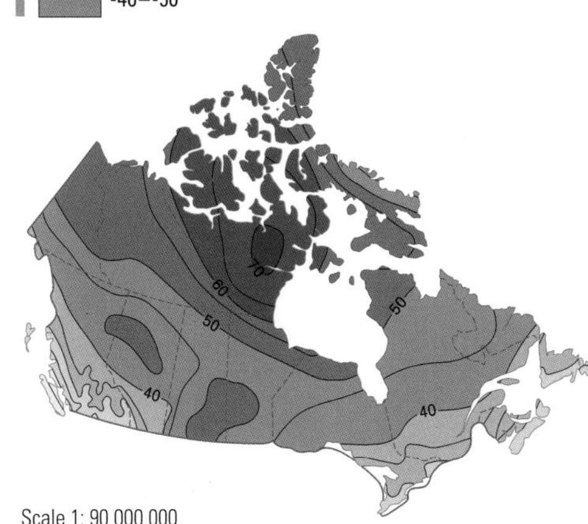

Scale 1: 90 000 000

Wind chill equivalent temperature

Wind chill is a measure of the wind's cooling effect, as on exposed flesh. So as not to confuse it with actual temperature, wind chill is expressed as a temperature index, without the degree symbol.

wind speed at 10 metres in km/h	actual air temperature in °C								
	5	**0**	**-5**	**-10**	**-15**	**-20**	**-25**	**-30**	**-35**
5	4	-2	-7	-13	-19	-24	-30	-36	-41
10	3	-3	-9	-15	-21	-27	-33	-39	-45
15	2	-4	-11	-17	-23	-29	-35	-41	-48
20	1	-5	-12	-18	-24	-31	-37	-43	-49
25	1	-6	-12	-19	-25	-32	-38	-45	-51
30	0	-7	-13	-20	-26	-33	-39	-46	-52
35	0	-7	-14	-20	-27	-33	-40	-47	-53
40	-1	-7	-14	-21	-27	-34	-41	-48	-54
45	-1	-8	-15	-21	-28	-35	-42	-48	-55
50	-1	-8	-15	-22	-29	-35	-42	-49	-56
55	-2	-9	-15	-22	-29	-36	-43	-50	-57
60	-2	-9	-16	-23	-30	-37	-43	-50	-57

Scale 1: 35 000 000 — 0 350 700 1050 km

Climate graphs

for selected stations

- average rainfall in mm
- average snowfall in mm
- average daily temperature in °C
- growing season*
- asl above sea level

10 mm of snowfall is the water equivalent of 1 mm of rainfall

* that part of the year when average daily temperature remains above 5.6°C

Yellowknife 208 m asl

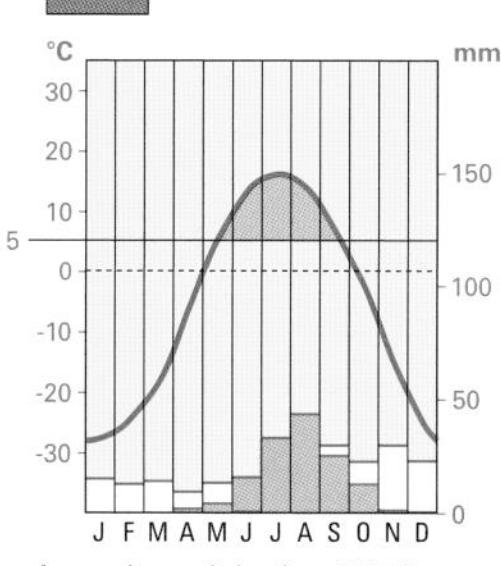

Annual precipitation 267.3 mm

Resolute 67 m asl

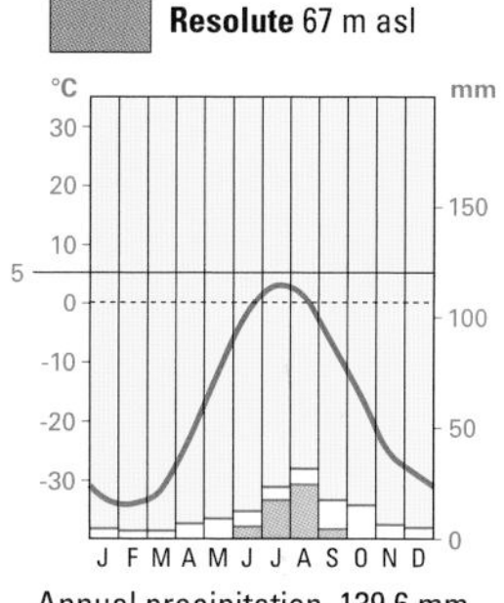

Annual precipitation 139.6 mm

Inukjuak 5 m asl

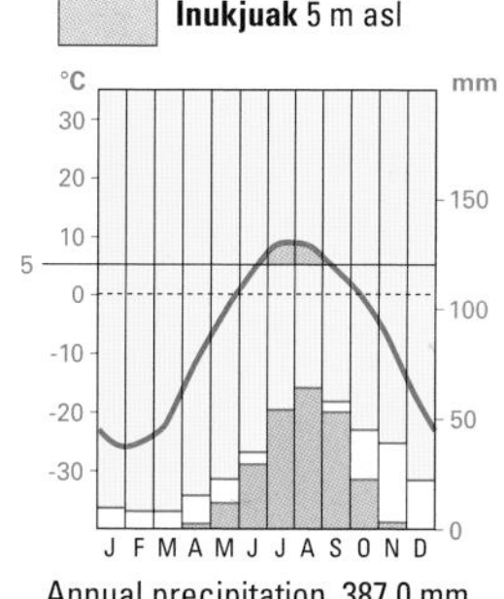

Annual precipitation 387.0 mm

Iqaluit 21 m asl

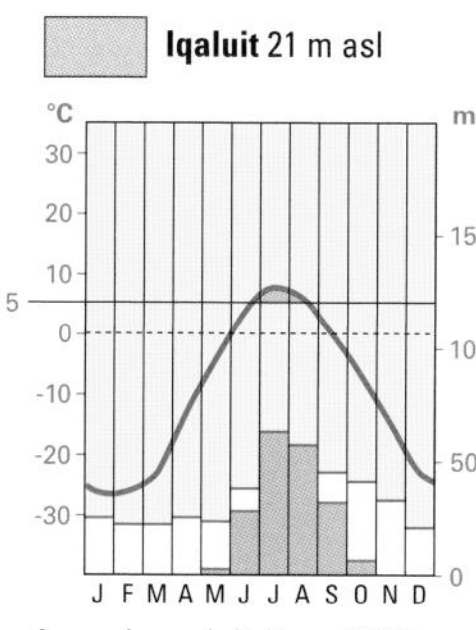

Annual precipitation 433.0 mm

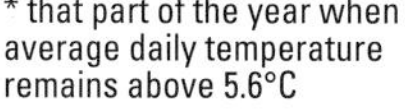

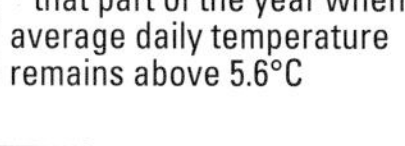

Dawson 320 m asl

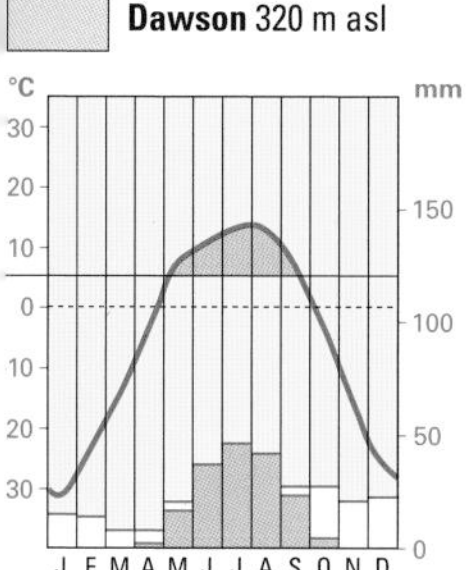

Annual precipitation 306.0 mm

Prince Rupert 34 m asl

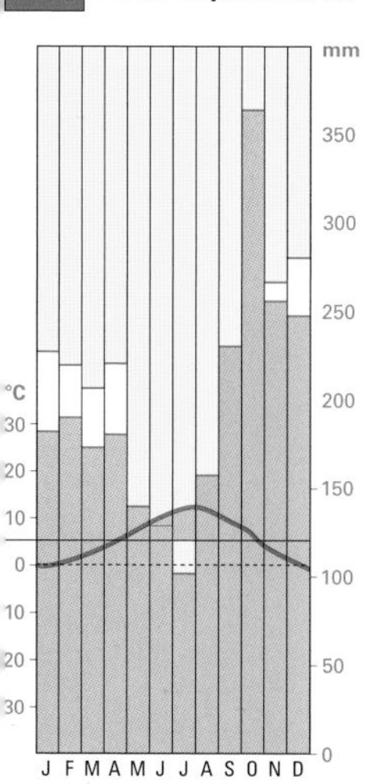

Annual precipitation 2 551.6 mm

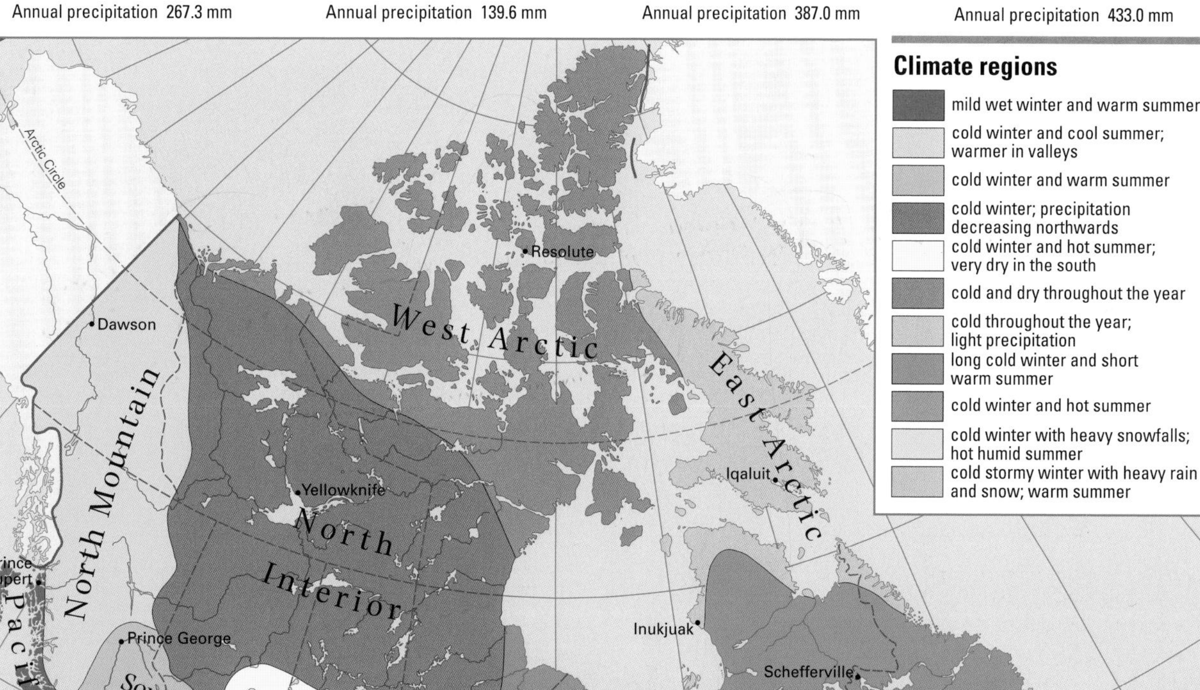

Vancouver 3 m asl

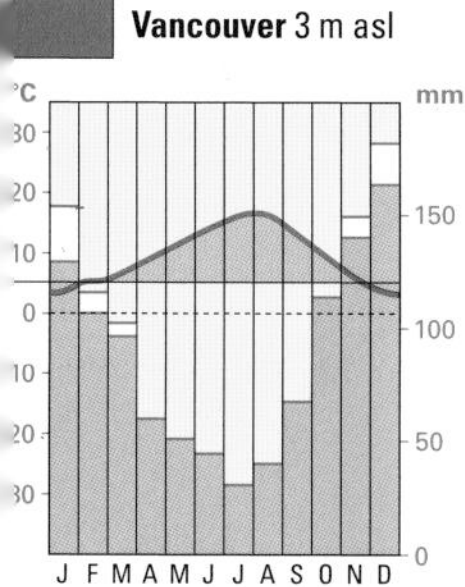

Annual precipitation 1 167.4 mm

Prince George 676 m asl

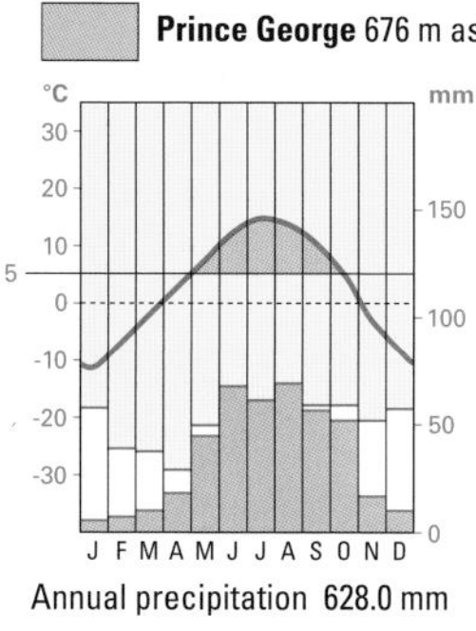

Annual precipitation 628.0 mm

Edmonton 671 m asl

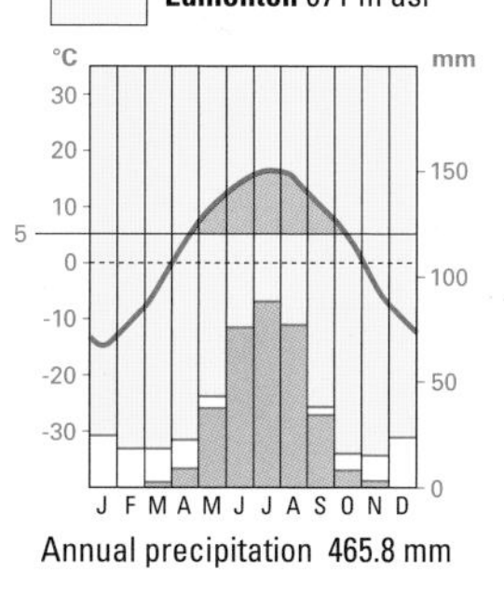

Annual precipitation 465.8 mm

Schefferville 522 m asl

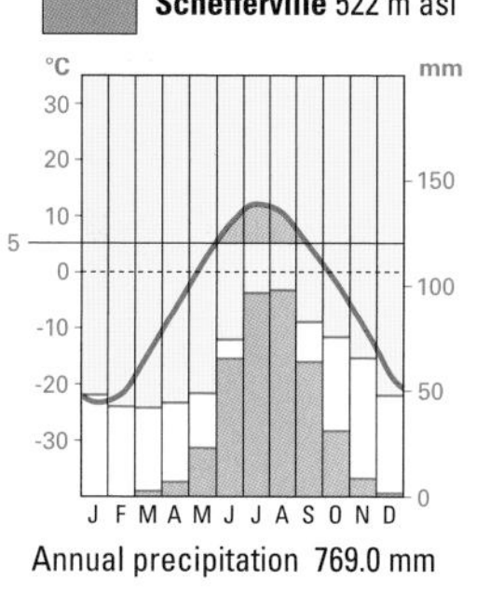

Annual precipitation 769.0 mm

Halifax 32 m asl

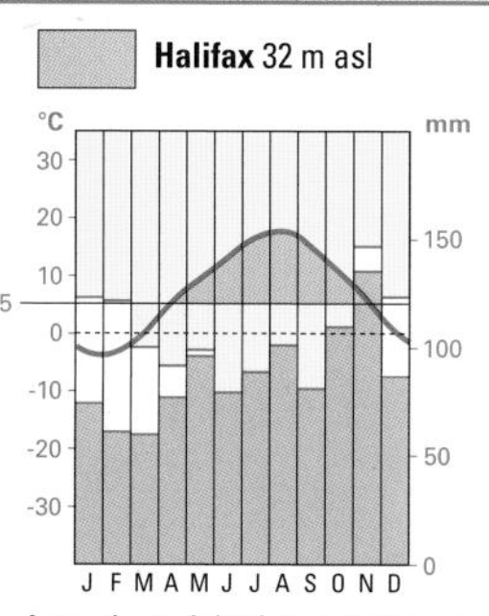

Annual precipitation 1 473.5 mm

Medicine Hat 721 m asl

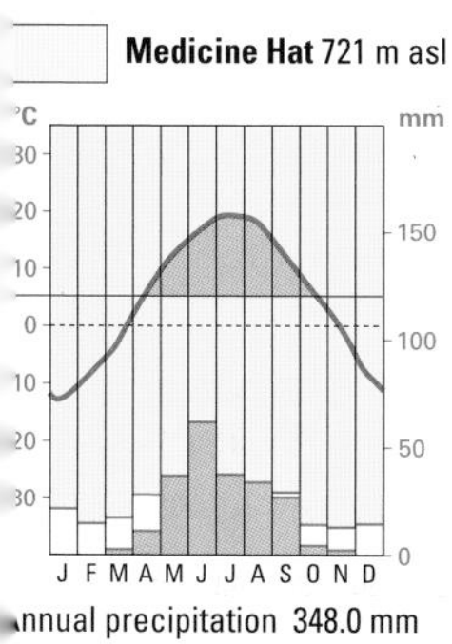

Annual precipitation 348.0 mm

Winnipeg 239 m asl

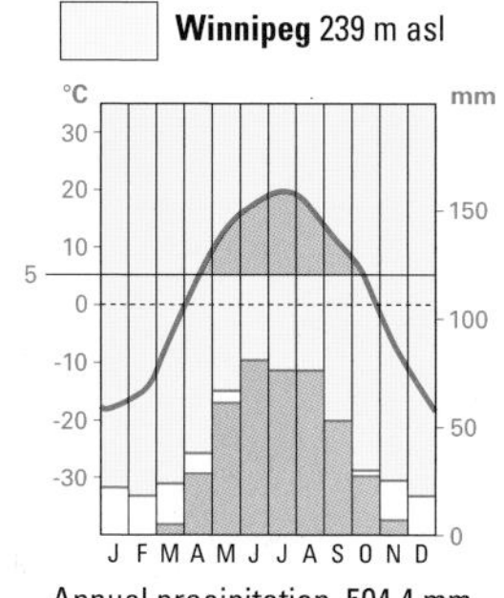

Annual precipitation 504.4 mm

Kapuskasing 229 m asl

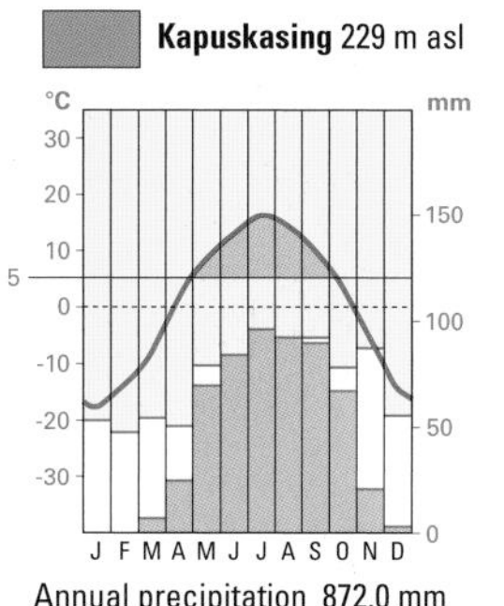

Annual precipitation 872.0 mm

Toronto 173 m asl

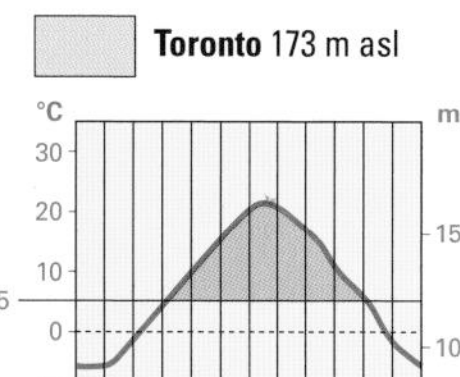

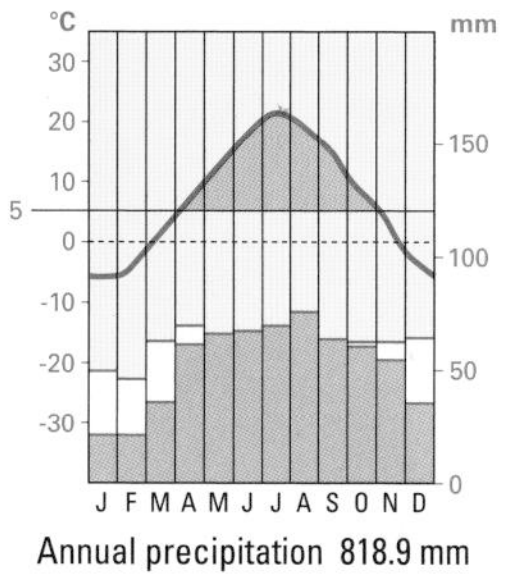

Annual precipitation 818.9 mm

Québec 73 m asl

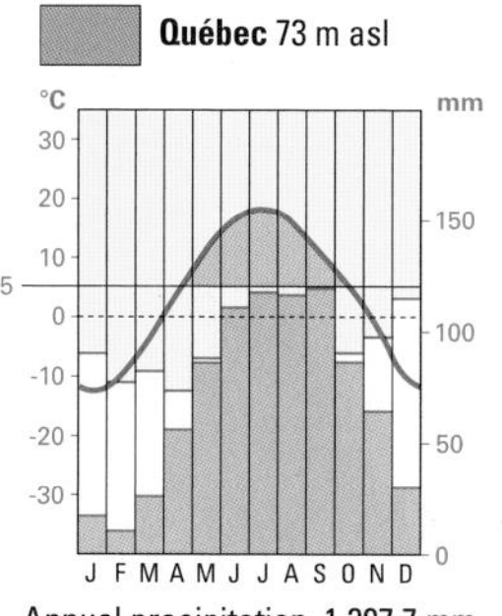

Annual precipitation 1 207.7 mm

Scale 1: 24 000 000

0 240 480 720 km

Natural disturbances such as fire, wind, snow, insects, and fungi are an important and necessary part of forest health. They remove old or otherwise susceptible trees, recycle nutrients, and provide habitat and food for wildlife. They can, however, have serious economic repercussions if they become severe. For example, by 2005, the Mountain Pine Beetle infestation in British Columbia had affected 8.7 million hectares. Beetle outbreaks are also increasingly frequent in Alberta's pine forests. Altogether, on a national scale, the forest area defoliated by insects and beetle-killed trees totalled 13.1 million hectares in 2004. In 2005, some 7 438 fires burned 1.7 million hectares of forest, compared to the 10-year average of 2.4 million hectares.

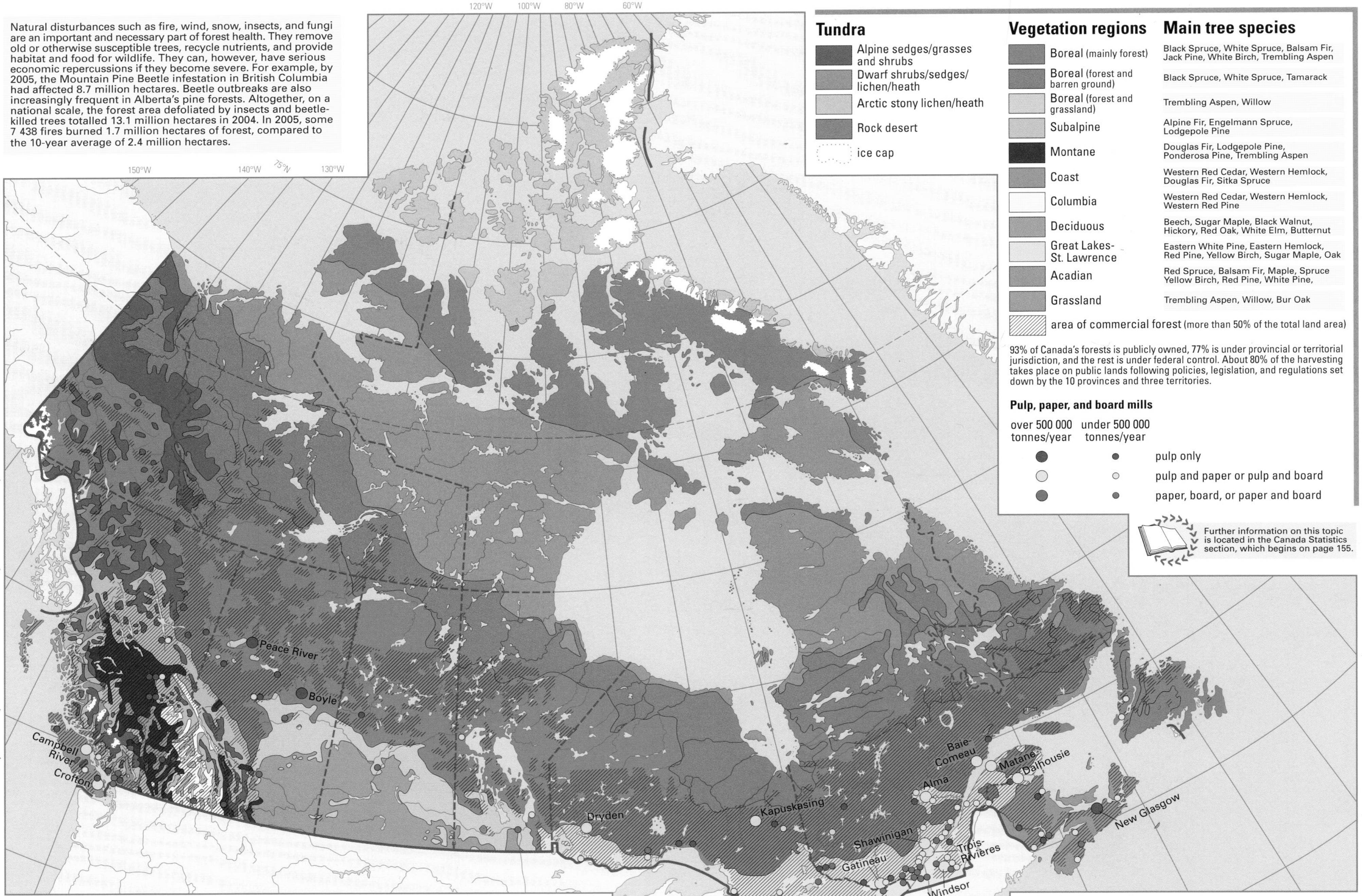

Tundra

- Alpine sedges/grasses and shrubs
- Dwarf shrubs/sedges/lichen/heath
- Arctic stony lichen/heath
- Rock desert
- ice cap

Vegetation regions	Main tree species
Boreal (mainly forest)	Black Spruce, White Spruce, Balsam Fir, Jack Pine, White Birch, Trembling Aspen
Boreal (forest and barren ground)	Black Spruce, White Spruce, Tamarack
Boreal (forest and grassland)	Trembling Aspen, Willow
Subalpine	Alpine Fir, Engelmann Spruce, Lodgepole Pine
Montane	Douglas Fir, Lodgepole Pine, Ponderosa Pine, Trembling Aspen
Coast	Western Red Cedar, Western Hemlock, Douglas Fir, Sitka Spruce
Columbia	Western Red Cedar, Western Hemlock, Western Red Pine
Deciduous	Beech, Sugar Maple, Black Walnut, Hickory, Red Oak, White Elm, Butternut
Great Lakes-St. Lawrence	Eastern White Pine, Eastern Hemlock, Red Pine, Yellow Birch, Sugar Maple, Oak
Acadian	Red Spruce, Balsam Fir, Maple, Spruce Yellow Birch, Red Pine, White Pine,
Grassland	Trembling Aspen, Willow, Bur Oak

area of commercial forest (more than 50% of the total land area)

93% of Canada's forests is publicly owned, 77% is under provincial or territorial jurisdiction, and the rest is under federal control. About 80% of the harvesting takes place on public lands following policies, legislation, and regulations set down by the 10 provinces and three territories.

Pulp, paper, and board mills

over 500 000 tonnes/year — under 500 000 tonnes/year

- pulp only
- pulp and paper or pulp and board
- paper, board, or paper and board

Further information on this topic is located in the Canada Statistics section, which begins on page 155.

120°W 100°W 80°W 60°W 150°W 140°W 75°N 130°W 140°W 55°N 50°N 130°W 45°N 40°N 125°W

Peace River
Boyle
Campbell River
Crofton
Dryden
Kapuskasing
Alma
Baie-Comeau
Matane
Dalhousie
New Glasgow
Shawinigan
Gatineau
Trois-Rivières
Windsor
Brampton
Thorold

White Spruce, Jack Pine, Balsam Fir, Black Spruce, Douglas Fir, Eastern White Pine, Western Red Cedar, White Birch

Trembling Aspen, Sugar Maple, Red Oak, Western Hemlock

Scale 1: 35 000 000

0 350 700 1050 km

Fishing

Atlantic coast fishing

Pacific coast fishing

some major salmon spawning rivers and lakes

sea depth

0–500 m

more than 500 m

Hamilton Bank

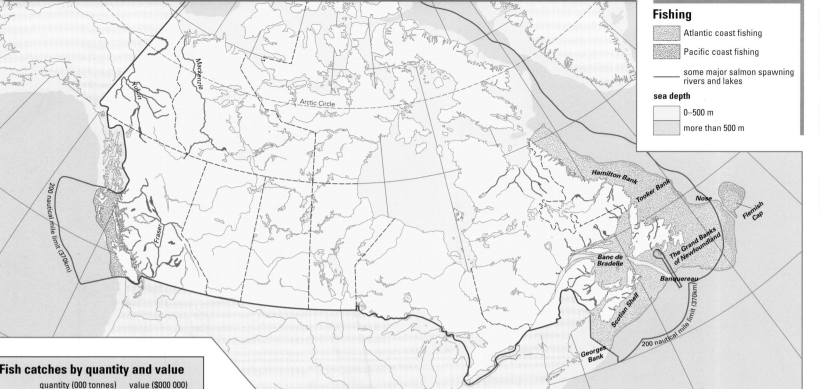

Tooker Bank

Nose

Flemish Cap

The Grand Banks of Newfoundland

Banc de Bradelle

Banquereau

Scotian Shelf

Georges Bank

200 nautical mile limit (370km)

Arctic Circle

Mackenzie

Yukon

Fraser

Pacific Cod

Pacific Halibut

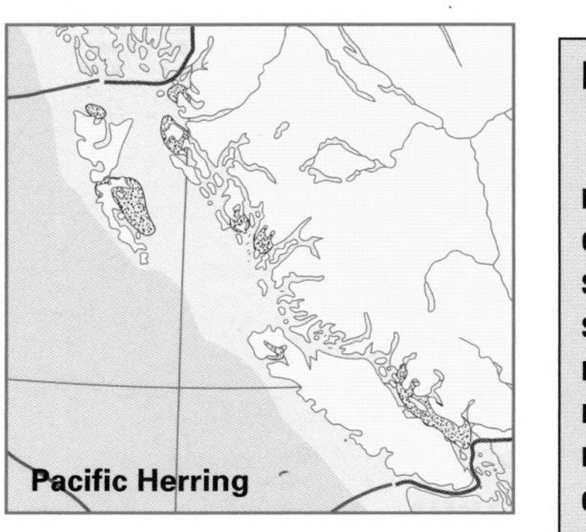

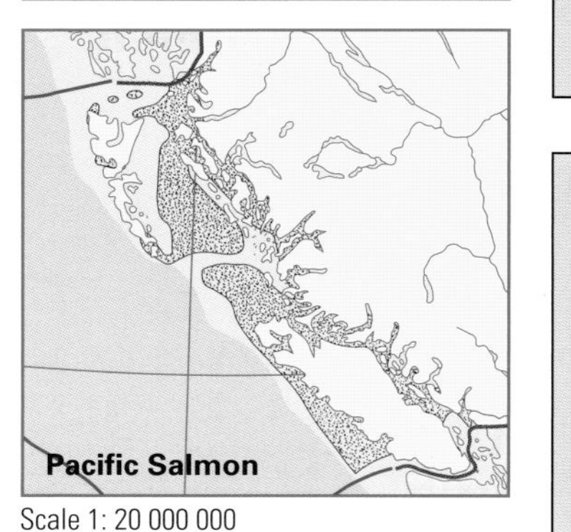

Scale 1: 20 000 000

Further information on this topic is located in the Canada Statistics section, which begins on page 155.

Fish catches by quantity and value

	quantity (000 tonnes) 1990	quantity (000 tonnes) 2006	value ($000 000) 1990	value ($000 000) 2006
Lobster	47.9	52.1	232.2	618.1
Crab	29.2	102.2	59.2	236.7
Shrimp	40.0	179.5	85.4	270.5
Scallop	83.4	63.1	87.4	85.9
Herring	301.3	182.1	110.8	55.6
Halibut	7.5	9.1	31.9	59.1
Hake	94.6	112.6	20.4	38.8
Cod	401.3	28.2	247.2	38.2
Salmon	97.1	23.5	266.6	58.2
All species	1 624.8	1 030.7	1 432.0	1 755.8

Major world fishing countries, 2004

(000 tonnes of catch in live weight)

China	17 271	**Vietnam**	1 879
Peru	9 621	**Iceland**	1 750
Chile	5 326	**Myanmar**	1 587
USA	4 995	**South Korea**	1 584
Indonesia	4 882	**Mexico**	1 478
Japan	4 517	**Malaysia**	1 340
India	3 624	**Canada**	1 191
Russia	3 000	**Bangladesh**	1 187
Thailand	2 845	**Denmark**	1 090
Norway	2 671	**Argentina**	951
Philippines	2 215	**World total**	96 462

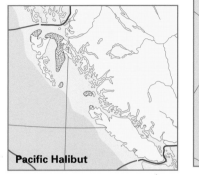

Aquaculture value by species, 2005

% of total value

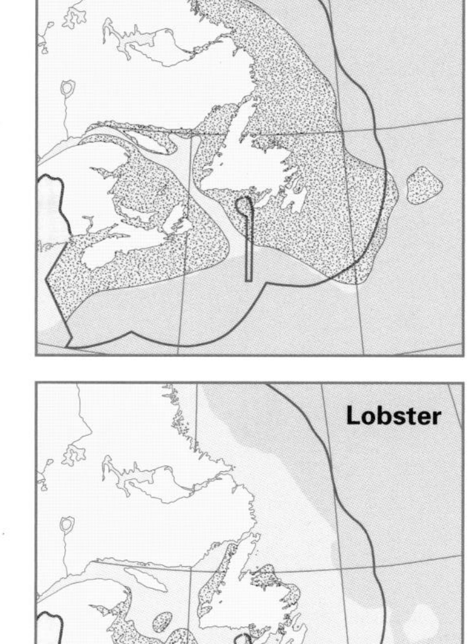

Total production 154 993 tonnes
Total value $715.1 million

In July 1992, the federal government announced a moratorium on the northern cod fishery to rebuild the stock of this species. Moratoria apply to other groundfish, such as haddock, redfish, and plaice, in certain areas, while the government sets out each year a Total Allowable Catch (TAC) for most other groundfish as well as other species.

According to the UN Food and Agriculture Organization, over 70% of the world's fish species are either fully exploited or being depleted. In the last decade in the North Atlantic region, commercial fish populations of cod, hake, haddock, and flounder have fallen by as much as 95%. Overfishing and destructive fishing techniques are the principal causes of the depletion of fish stocks, as well as the endangerment of marine mammals and entire aquatic ecosystems.

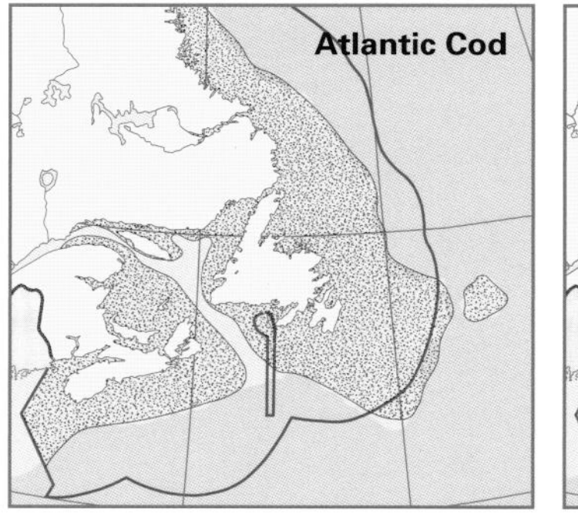

Atlantic Herring

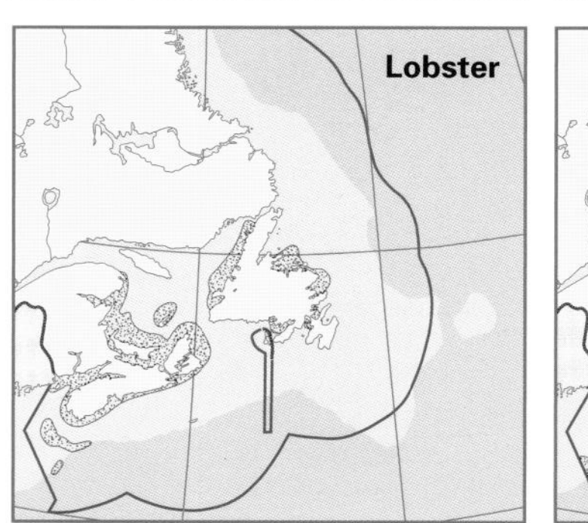

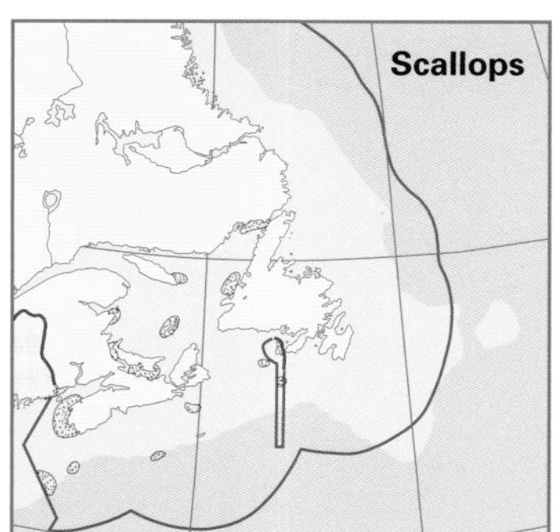

Scale 1: 45 000 000

 Zenithal Equidistant Projection

Scale 1: 35 000 000

0 350 700 1050 km

Soil capability

Soil capability refers to the ability of the land to accommodate agriculture. There are seven classes of soil capability, ranging from Class One (the best soils for agriculture) to Class Seven (no ability to sustain agriculture). The map illustrates classes One to Three while the table shows the distribution of classes One to Six. Class One soils have no limitations for agriculture, Class Two have moderate limitations and Class Three have moderately severe limitations. Class Four soils have marginal capability for the production of field crops. Class Five and Six soils are unsuitable for field crops and are used mainly for pasture and forage production. The factors in determining soil capability include climate, fertility, drainage, stoniness, salinity, and susceptibility to erosion.

Soil capability categories by province

as a percentage for each category

Province	Classes 1, 2 & 3	Class 4	Classes 5 & 6
Newfoundland & Labrador	0.01	0.2	5.9
Prince Edward Island	0.9	0.09	0.2
Nova Scotia	2.5	1.7	0.2
New Brunswick	3.1	7.5	3.2
Québec	4.8	10.5	3.0
Ontario	16.1	10.8	5.6
Manitoba	10.8	9.5	7.9
Saskatchewan	35.8	15.8	21.3
Alberta	22.2	36.9	27.4
British Columbia	1.9	6.3	21.8

Agroclimatic Resource Index

The Agroclimatic Resource Index illustrates agricultural potential in Canada. The index was based on the number of frost-free days divided by sixty days (the minimum growing period for most crops). The index was then adjusted downward to take into account other climatic factors such as the shortage of moisture in the southern Prairies and the lack of sufficient summer heat in coastal areas. The higher the value of the index, the greater the climatic potential for agriculture.

Index value

3

2.5

2

1

Soil capability

land area with Classes One, Two, and Three

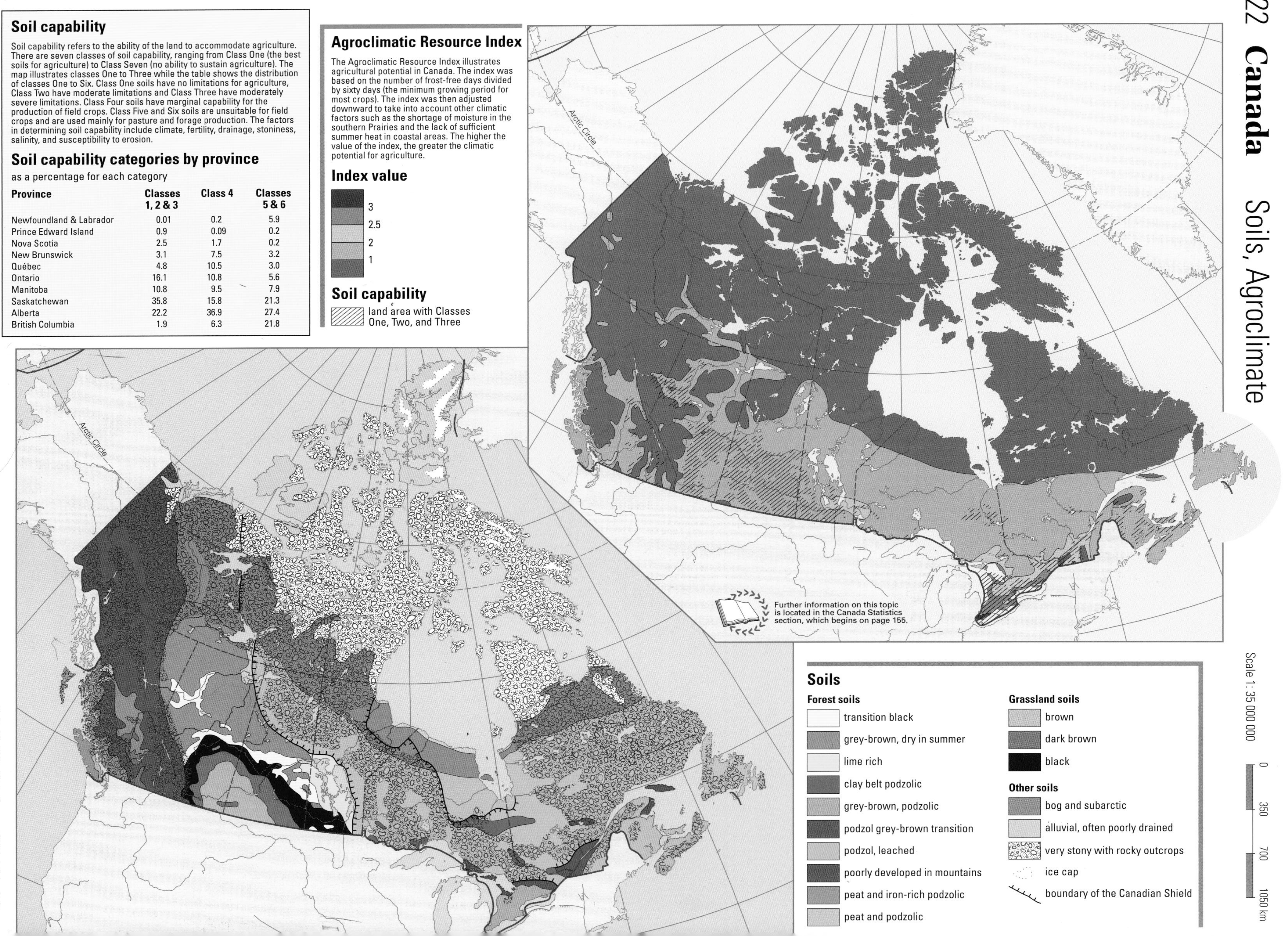

Further information on this topic is located in the Canada Statistics section, which begins on page 155.

Zenithal Equidistant Projection

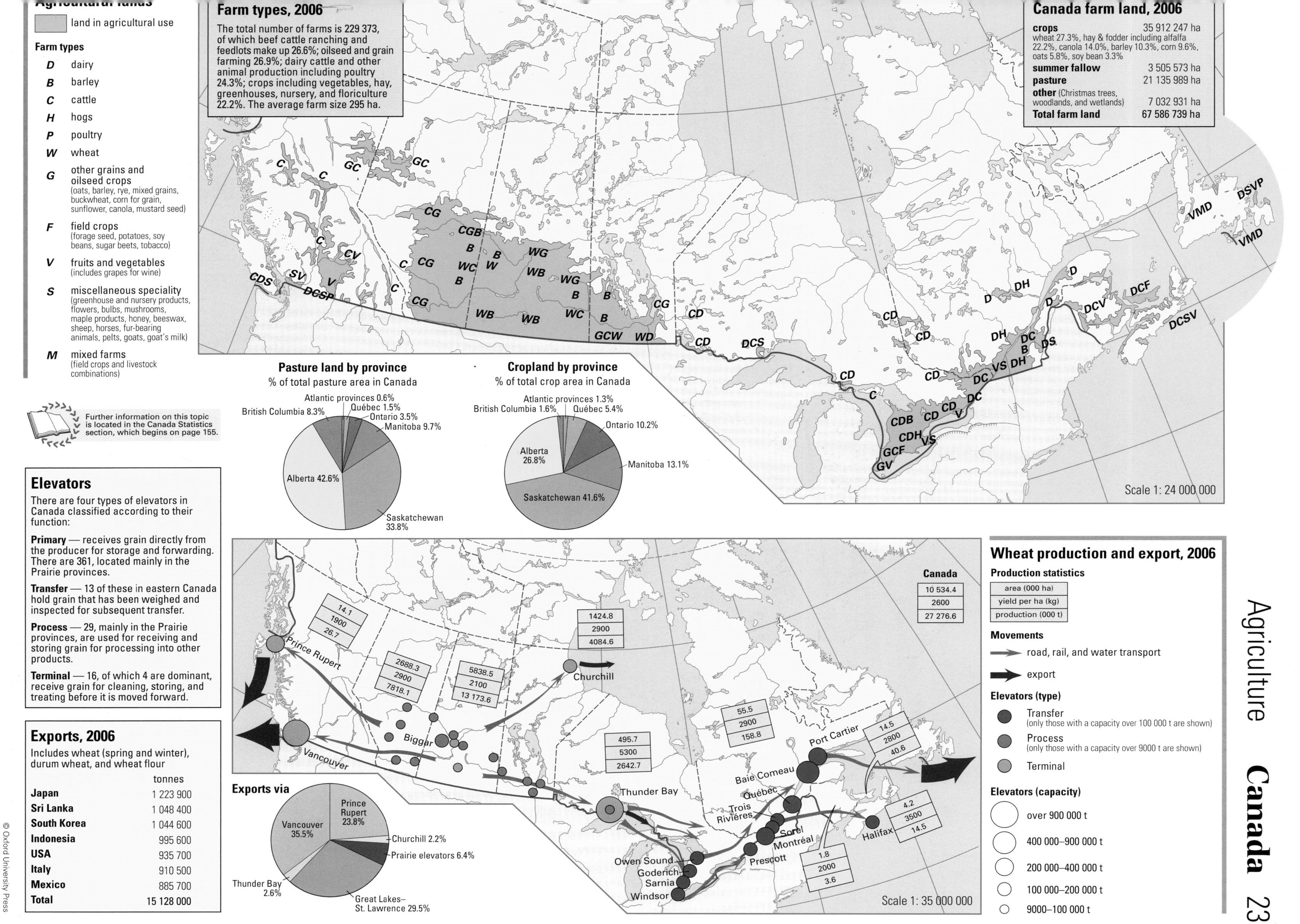

Farm types, 2006

The total number of farms is 229 373, of which beef cattle ranching and feedlots make up 26.6%; oilseed and grain farming 26.9%; dairy cattle and other animal production including poultry 24.3%; crops including vegetables, hay, greenhouses, nursery, and floriculture 22.2%. The average farm size 295 ha.

Canada farm land, 2006

crops wheat 27.3%, hay & fodder including alfalfa 22.2%, canola 14.0%, barley 10.3%, corn 9.6%, oats 5.8%, soy bean 3.3%	35 912 247 ha
summer fallow	3 505 573 ha
pasture	21 135 989 ha
other (Christmas trees, woodlands, and wetlands)	7 032 931 ha
Total farm land	67 586 739 ha

Elevators

There are four types of elevators in Canada classified according to their function:

Primary — receives grain directly from the producer for storage and forwarding. There are 361, located mainly in the Prairie provinces.

Transfer — 13 of these in eastern Canada hold grain that has been weighed and inspected for subsequent transfer.

Process — 29, mainly in the Prairie provinces, are used for receiving and storing grain for processing into other products.

Terminal — 16, of which 4 are dominant, receive grain for cleaning, storing, and treating before it is moved forward.

Exports, 2006

Includes wheat (spring and winter), durum wheat, and wheat flour

	tonnes
Japan	1 223 900
Sri Lanka	1 048 400
South Korea	1 044 600
Indonesia	995 600
USA	935 700
Italy	910 500
Mexico	885 700
Total	15 128 000

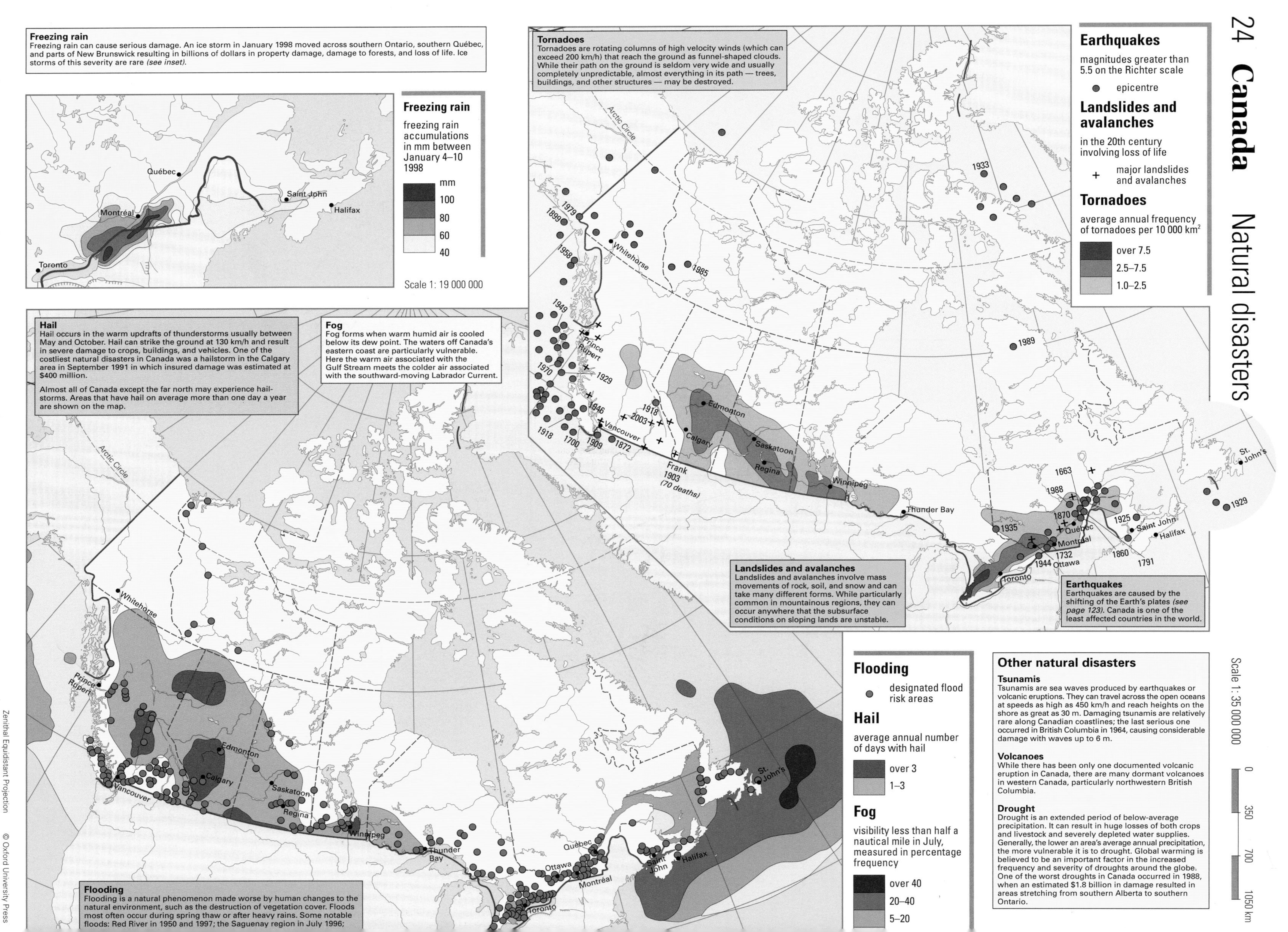
Scale 1: 35 000 000
0 350 700 1050 km
Earthquakes
magnitudes greater than 5.5 on the Richter scale
epicentre
Landslides and avalanches
in the 20th century involving loss of life
major landslides and avalanches
Tornadoes
average annual frequency of tornadoes per 10 000 km²
over 7.5
2.5–7.5
1.0–2.5
Tornadoes
Tornadoes are rotating columns of high velocity winds (which can exceed 200 km/h) that reach the ground as funnel-shaped clouds. While their path on the ground is seldom very wide and usually completely unpredictable, almost everything in its path — trees, buildings, and other structures — may be destroyed.
Landslides and avalanches
Landslides and avalanches involve mass movements of rock, soil, and snow and can take many different forms. While particularly common in mountainous regions, they can occur anywhere that the subsurface conditions on sloping lands are unstable.
Earthquakes
Earthquakes are caused by the shifting of the Earth's plates (see page 123). Canada is one of the least affected countries in the world.
Frank 1903 (70 deaths)
Arctic Circle
Whitehorse
Prince Rupert
Vancouver
Edmonton
Calgary
Saskatoon
Regina
Winnipeg
Thunder Bay
Toronto
Ottawa
Montréal
Québec
Saint John
Halifax
St. John's
Freezing rain
Freezing rain can cause serious damage. An ice storm in January 1998 moved across southern Ontario, southern Québec, and parts of New Brunswick resulting in billions of dollars in property damage, damage to forests, and loss of life. Ice storms of this severity are rare (see inset).
Freezing rain
freezing rain accumulations in mm between January 4–10 1998
mm
100
80
60
40
Scale 1: 19 000 000
Hail
Hail occurs in the warm updrafts of thunderstorms usually between May and October. Hail can strike the ground at 130 km/h and result in severe damage to crops, buildings, and vehicles. One of the costliest natural disasters in Canada was a hailstorm in the Calgary area in September 1991 in which insured damage was estimated at $400 million.
Almost all of Canada except the far north may experience hail-storms. Areas that have hail on average more than one day a year are shown on the map.
Fog
Fog forms when warm humid air is cooled below its dew point. The waters off Canada's eastern coast are particularly vulnerable. Here the warm air associated with the Gulf Stream meets the colder air associated with the southward-moving Labrador Current.
Flooding
Flooding is a natural phenomenon made worse by human changes to the natural environment, such as the destruction of vegetation cover. Floods most often occur during spring thaw or after heavy rains. Some notable floods: Red River in 1950 and 1997; the Saguenay region in July 1996;
Flooding
designated flood risk areas
Hail
average annual number of days with hail
over 3
1–3
Fog
visibility less than half a nautical mile in July, measured in percentage frequency
over 40
20–40
5–20
Other natural disasters
Tsunamis
Tsunamis are sea waves produced by earthquakes or volcanic eruptions. They can travel across the open oceans at speeds as high as 450 km/h and reach heights on the shore as great as 30 m. Damaging tsunamis are relatively rare along Canadian coastlines; the last serious one occurred in British Columbia in 1964, causing considerable damage with waves up to 6 m.
Volcanoes
While there has been only one documented volcanic eruption in Canada, there are many dormant volcanoes in western Canada, particularly northwestern British Columbia.
Drought
Drought is an extended period of below-average precipitation. It can result in huge losses of both crops and livestock and severely depleted water supplies. Generally, the lower an area's average annual precipitation, the more vulnerable it is to drought. Global warming is believed to be an important factor in the increased frequency and severity of droughts around the globe. One of the worst droughts in Canada occurred in 1988, when an estimated $1.8 billion in damage resulted in areas stretching from southern Alberta to southern Ontario.
Zenithal Equidistant Projection

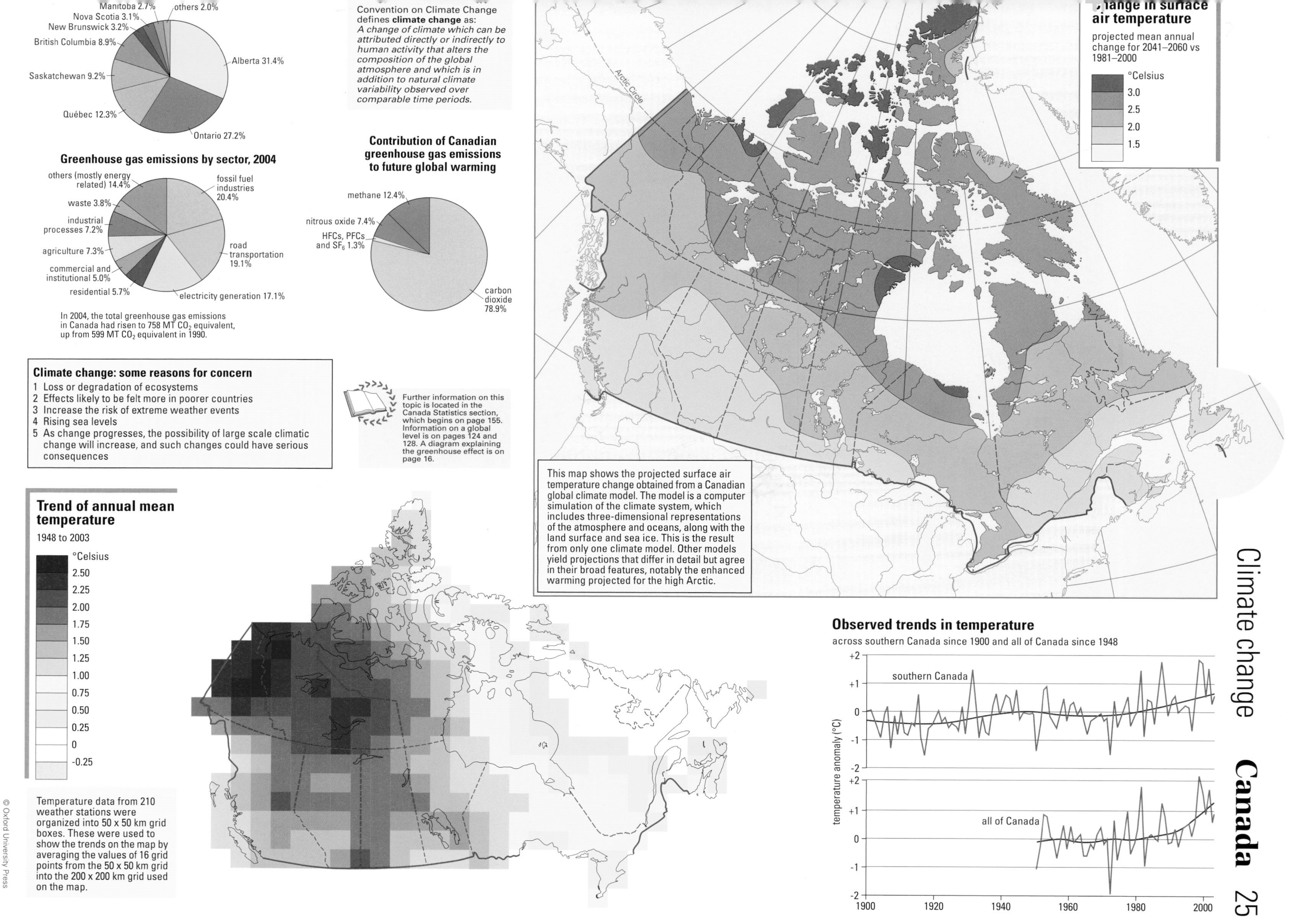
Manitoba 2.7%
others 2.0%
Nova Scotia 3.1%
New Brunswick 3.2%
British Columbia 8.9%
Alberta 31.4%
Saskatchewan 9.2%
Québec 12.3%
Ontario 27.2%
Greenhouse gas emissions by sector, 2004
others (mostly energy related) 14.4%
fossil fuel industries 20.4%
waste 3.8%
industrial processes 7.2%
agriculture 7.3%
road transportation 19.1%
commercial and institutional 5.0%
residential 5.7%
electricity generation 17.1%
In 2004, the total greenhouse gas emissions in Canada had risen to 758 MT CO_2 equivalent, up from 599 MT CO_2 equivalent in 1990.
Convention on Climate Change defines **climate change** as:
A change of climate which can be attributed directly or indirectly to human activity that alters the composition of the global atmosphere and which is in addition to natural climate variability observed over comparable time periods.
Contribution of Canadian greenhouse gas emissions to future global warming
methane 12.4%
nitrous oxide 7.4%
HFCs, PFCs and SF_6 1.3%
carbon dioxide 78.9%
Climate change: some reasons for concern
1 Loss or degradation of ecosystems
2 Effects likely to be felt more in poorer countries
3 Increase the risk of extreme weather events
4 Rising sea levels
5 As change progresses, the possibility of large scale climatic change will increase, and such changes could have serious consequences
Further information on this topic is located in the Canada Statistics section, which begins on page 155. Information on a global level is on pages 124 and 128. A diagram explaining the greenhouse effect is on page 16.
air temperature
projected mean annual change for 2041–2060 vs 1981–2000
°Celsius
3.0
2.5
2.0
1.5
Arctic Circle
This map shows the projected surface air temperature change obtained from a Canadian global climate model. The model is a computer simulation of the climate system, which includes three-dimensional representations of the atmosphere and oceans, along with the land surface and sea ice. This is the result from only one climate model. Other models yield projections that differ in detail but agree in their broad features, notably the enhanced warming projected for the high Arctic.
Trend of annual mean temperature
1948 to 2003
°Celsius
2.50
2.25
2.00
1.75
1.50
1.25
1.00
0.75
0.50
0.25
0
-0.25
Temperature data from 210 weather stations were organized into 50 x 50 km grid boxes. These were used to show the trends on the map by averaging the values of 16 grid points from the 50 x 50 km grid into the 200 x 200 km grid used on the map.
Observed trends in temperature
across southern Canada since 1900 and all of Canada since 1948
southern Canada
all of Canada
temperature anomaly (°C)
+2
+1
0
-1
-2
1900
1920
1940
1960
1980
2000

Scale 1: 23 000 000

Endangered species

There are five classifications of endangered species:

EX	Extinct	species that no longer exist
EXT	Extirpated	species that no longer exist in the wild in Canada, but live elsewhere
E	Endangered	species facing imminent extinction or extirpation
T	Threatened	species that are likely to become endangered in Canada if limiting factors are not reversed
S	Special Concern	species with characteristics that make them particularly sensitive to human activities or natural events

In 2007 in Canada, there were more than 521 species of mammals, birds, reptiles, amphibians, fish, and plants listed in these five categories. Only selected species of birds, mammals, reptiles, and amphibians are shown here.

Terrestrial ecozones

A large or more or less environmentally homogeneous area in terms of landforms, water, soils, vegetation, climate, wildlife, and various human uses that are ecologically related. Considerable variation may occur within an ecozone and boundaries between them are seldom sharply defined.

- Atlantic Maritime
- Mixed-Wood Plain
- Boreal Shield
- Prairie
- Boreal Plain
- Montane Cordillera
- Pacific Maritime
- Boreal Cordillera
- Taiga Cordillera
- Taiga Plain
- Taiga Shield
- Hudson Plain
- Southern Arctic
- Northern Arctic
- Arctic Cordillera

Population by ecozone, 2001

Ecozone	Land area (km^2)	Population	Density (person/km^2)
Atlantic Maritime	192 017	2 537 685	13.216
Mixed-Wood Plain	107 017	15 631 830	146.068
Boreal Shield	1 640 949	2 821 808	1.033
Prairie	443 159	4 222 569	9.528
Boreal Plain	668 664	771 205	1.153
Montane Cordillera	474 753	859 134	1.810
Pacific Maritime	196 200	3 027 206	15.429
Boreal Cordillera	459 864	30 690	0.067
Taiga Cordillera	264 213	370	0.001
Taiga Plain	569 363	20 726	0.036
Taiga Shield	1 122 504	38 116	0.034
Hudson Plain	359 546	9 530	0.027
Southern Arctic	702 542	14 470	0.021
Northern Arctic	1 371 340	20 451	0.015
Arctic Cordillera	234 708	1 304	0.006

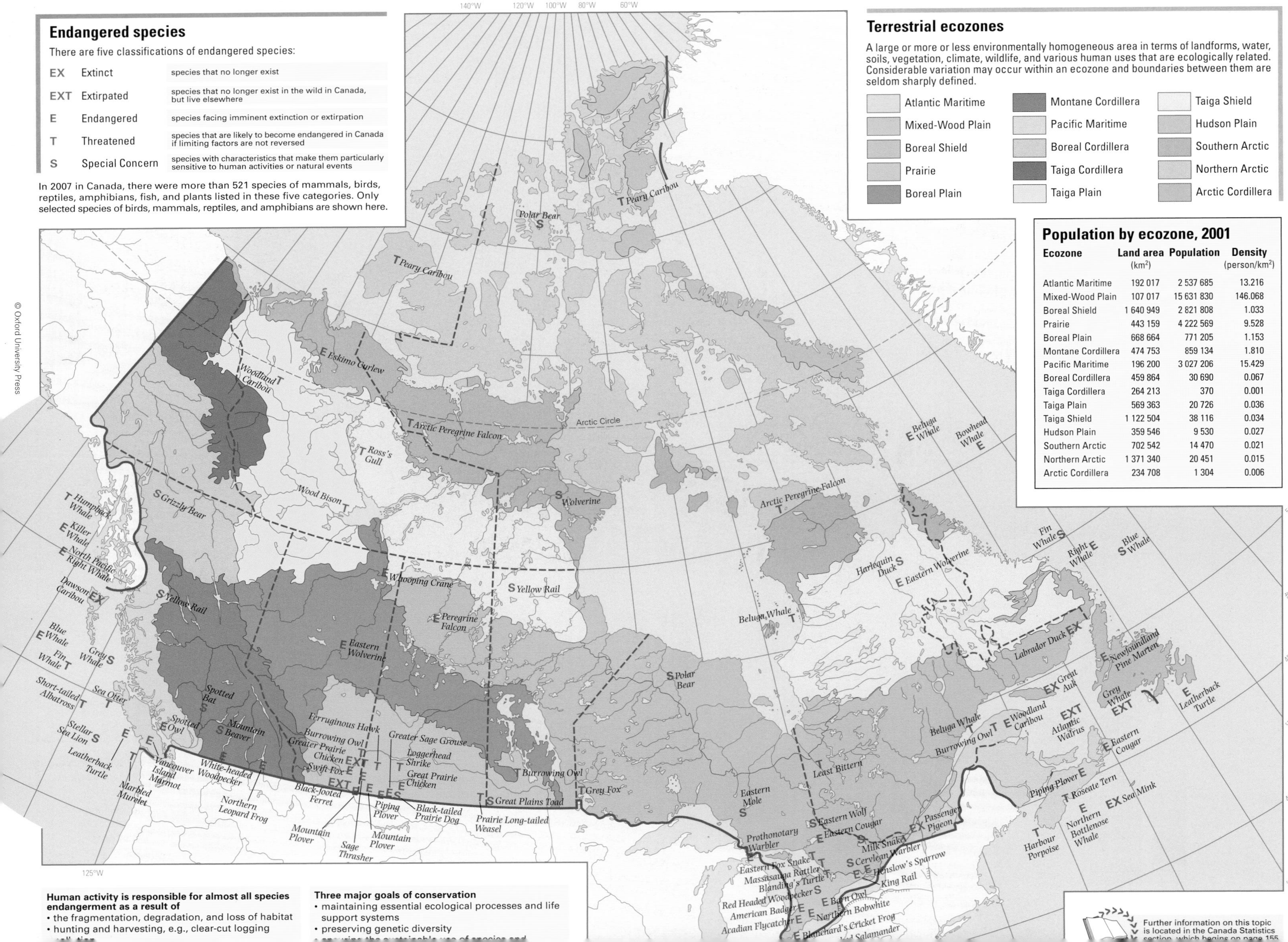

Human activity is responsible for almost all species endangerment as a result of
- the fragmentation, degradation, and loss of habitat
- hunting and harvesting, e.g., clear-cut logging

Three major goals of conservation
- maintaining essential ecological processes and life support systems
- preserving genetic diversity

Further information on this topic is located in the Canada Statistics section, which begins on page 155

Protected lands

- National Parks/National Park Reserves/National Marine Conservation Areas
- selected Provincial/Territorial Parks/Reserves
- Bird/Game Sanctuaries and other Federal designations
- ☆ World Heritage Sites
- ☆ Marine Protected Areas
- ★ selected Ecological Reserves
- Heritage River

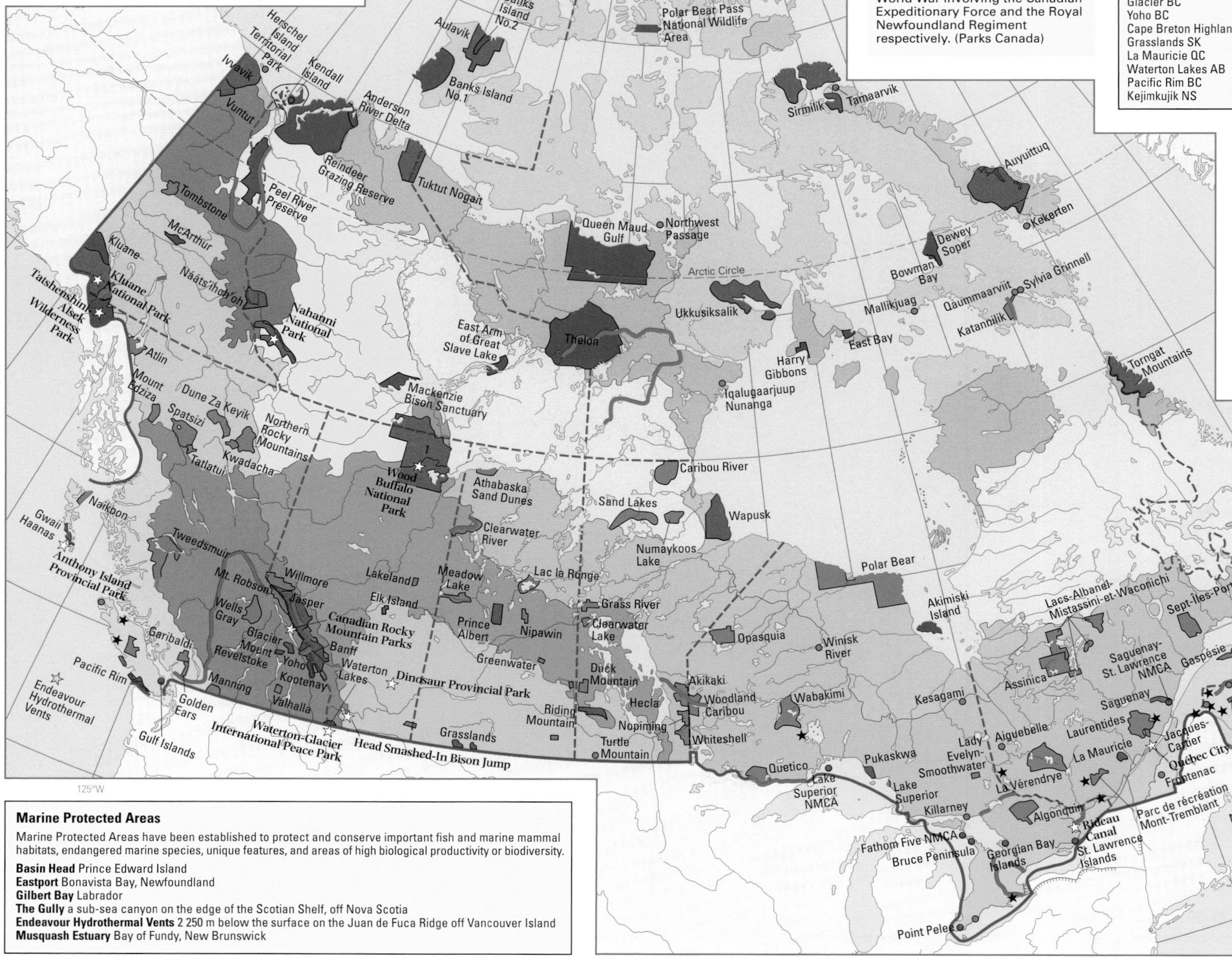

National Parks are a country wide system of representative natural areas of Canadian significance. By law, they are protected to encourage public understanding, appreciation and enjoyment of this natural heritage so as to leave it in an unimpaired state for future generations. (Parks Canada)

There are 925 National Historic Sites of Canada, 157 of which are administered by Parks Canada. Included in the 925 are the sites at Vimy Ridge and Beaumont Hamel in France – battlefields of the First World War involving the Canadian Expeditionary Force and the Royal Newfoundland Regiment respectively. (Parks Canada)

National Parks	Area (km²)
Wood Buffalo AB	44 802
Quttinirpaaq NU	37 775
Sirmilik NU	22 200
Auyuittuq NU	21 469
Ukkusiksalik NU	20 500
Tuktut Nogait NT	16 340
Aulavik NT	12 200
Wapusk MB	11 475
Jasper AB	10 878
Ivvavik YT	10 168
Banff AB	6 641
Vuntut YT	4 345
Prince Albert SK	3 874
Riding Mountain MB	2 973
Pukaskwa ON	1 878
Gros Morne NL	1 805
Kootenay BC	1 406
Glacier BC	1 349
Yoho BC	1 313
Cape Breton Highlands NS	948
Grasslands SK	906
La Mauricie QC	536
Waterton Lakes AB	505
Pacific Rim BC	500
Kejimkujik NS	404
Terra Nova NL	400
Mount Revelstoke BC	260
Forillon QC	240
Kouchibouguac NB	239
Fundy NB	206
Elk Island AB	194
Bruce Peninsula ON	154
Gulf Islands BC	35
Georgian Bay Islands ON	25
Prince Edward Island PE	22
Point Pelee ON	15
St. Lawrence Islands ON	8

National Park Reserves	Area (km²)
Kluane YT	22 013
Torngat Mountains NL	9 700
Nááts'ihch'oh NT	7 600
Nahanni NT	4 765
Gwaii Haanas BC	1 495
Mingan Archipelago QC	151

National Marine Conservation Areas

- Fathom Five ON
- Lake Superior ON
- Saguenay-St. Lawrence QC

Protected lands by province, 2003

as a percentage of the total land area

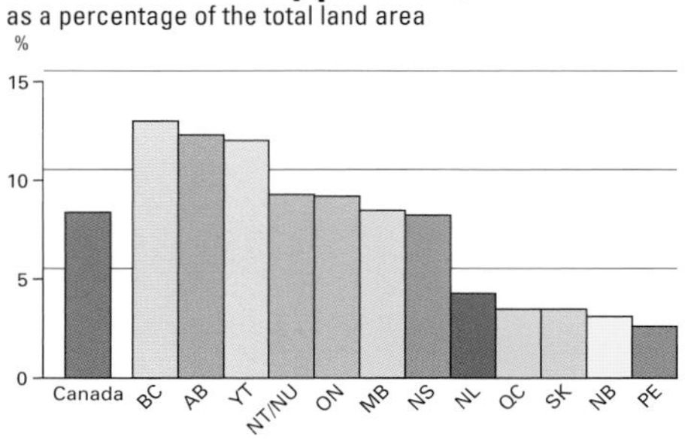

% (0, 5, 10, 15): Canada, BC, AB, YT, NT/NU, ON, MB, NS, NL, QC, SK, NB, PE

Marine Protected Areas

Marine Protected Areas have been established to protect and conserve important fish and marine mammal habitats, endangered marine species, unique features, and areas of high biological productivity or biodiversity.

Basin Head Prince Edward Island
Eastport Bonavista Bay, Newfoundland
Gilbert Bay Labrador
The Gully a sub-sea canyon on the edge of the Scotian Shelf, off Nova Scotia
Endeavour Hydrothermal Vents 2 250 m below the surface on the Juan de Fuca Ridge off Vancouver Island
Musquash Estuary Bay of Fundy, New Brunswick

Further information on this topic is located in the Canada Statistics section, which begins on page 155.

Zenithal Equidistant Projection

Scale 1: 23 000 000

0 230 460 690 km

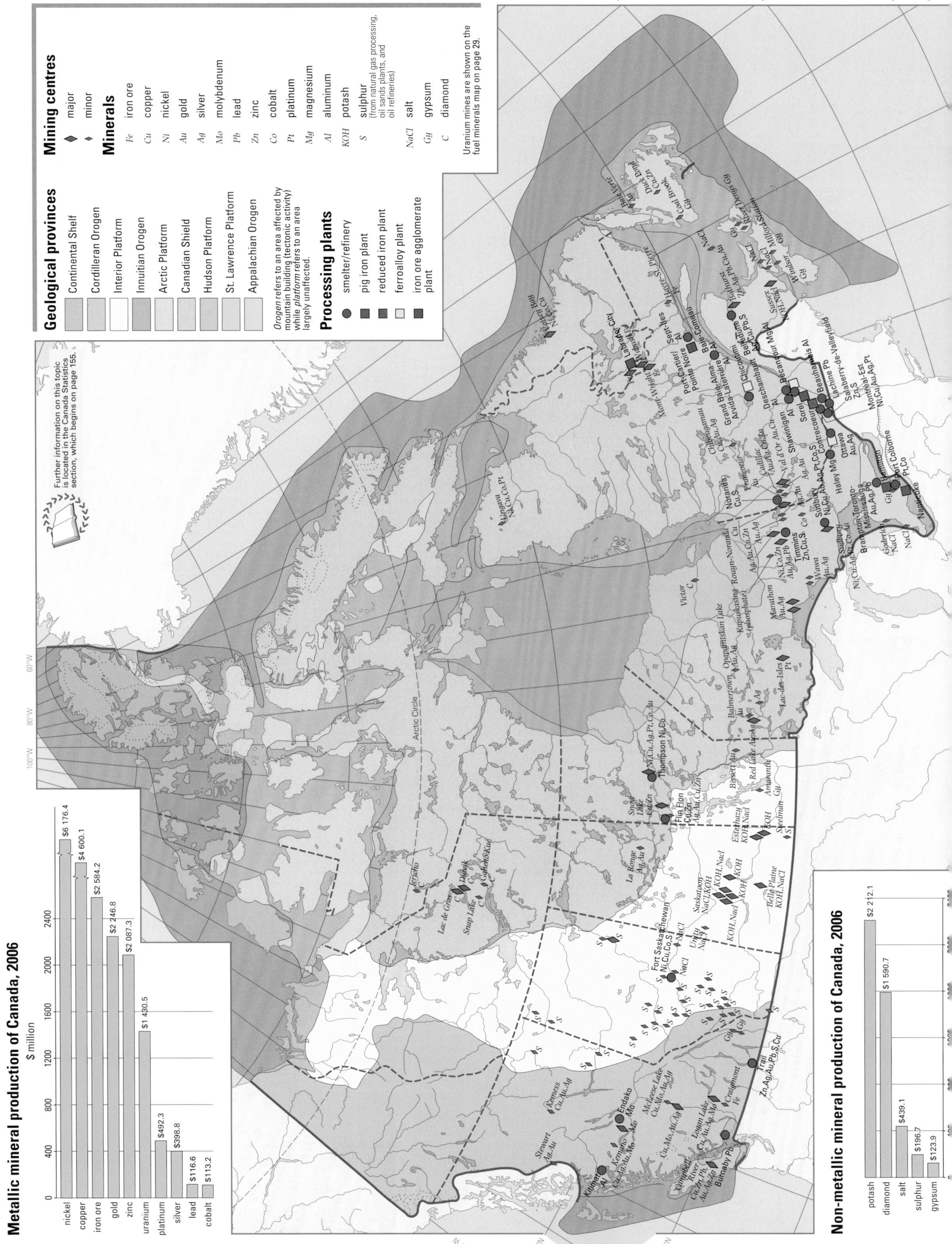

Metallic mineral production of Canada, 2006

$ million

	$ million
nickel	$6 176.4
copper	$4 600.1
iron ore	$2 584.2
gold	$2 246.8
zinc	$2 087.3
uranium	$1 430.5
platinum	$492.3
silver	$398.8
lead	$116.6
cobalt	$113.2

Non-metallic mineral production of Canada, 2006

	$ million
potash	$2 212.1
diamond	$1 590.7
salt	$439.1
sulphur	$196.7
gypsum	$123.9

Further information on this topic is located in the Canada Statistics section, which begins on page 155.

Geological provinces

- Continental Shelf
- Cordilleran Orogen
- Interior Platform
- Innuitian Orogen
- Arctic Platform
- Canadian Shield
- Hudson Platform
- St. Lawrence Platform
- Appalachian Orogen

Orogen refers to an area affected by mountain building (tectonic activity) while *platform* refers to an area largely unaffected.

Processing plants

- smelter/refinery
- pig iron plant
- reduced iron plant
- ferroalloy plant
- iron ore agglomerate plant

Mining centres

- major
- minor

Minerals

Fe	iron ore
Cu	copper
Ni	nickel
Au	gold
Ag	silver
Mo	molybdenum
Pb	lead
Zn	zinc
Co	cobalt
Pt	platinum
Mg	magnesium
Al	aluminum
KOH	potash
S	sulphur (from natural gas processing, oil sands plants, and oil refineries)
NaCl	salt
Gy	gypsum
C	diamond

Uranium mines are shown on the fuel minerals map on page 29.

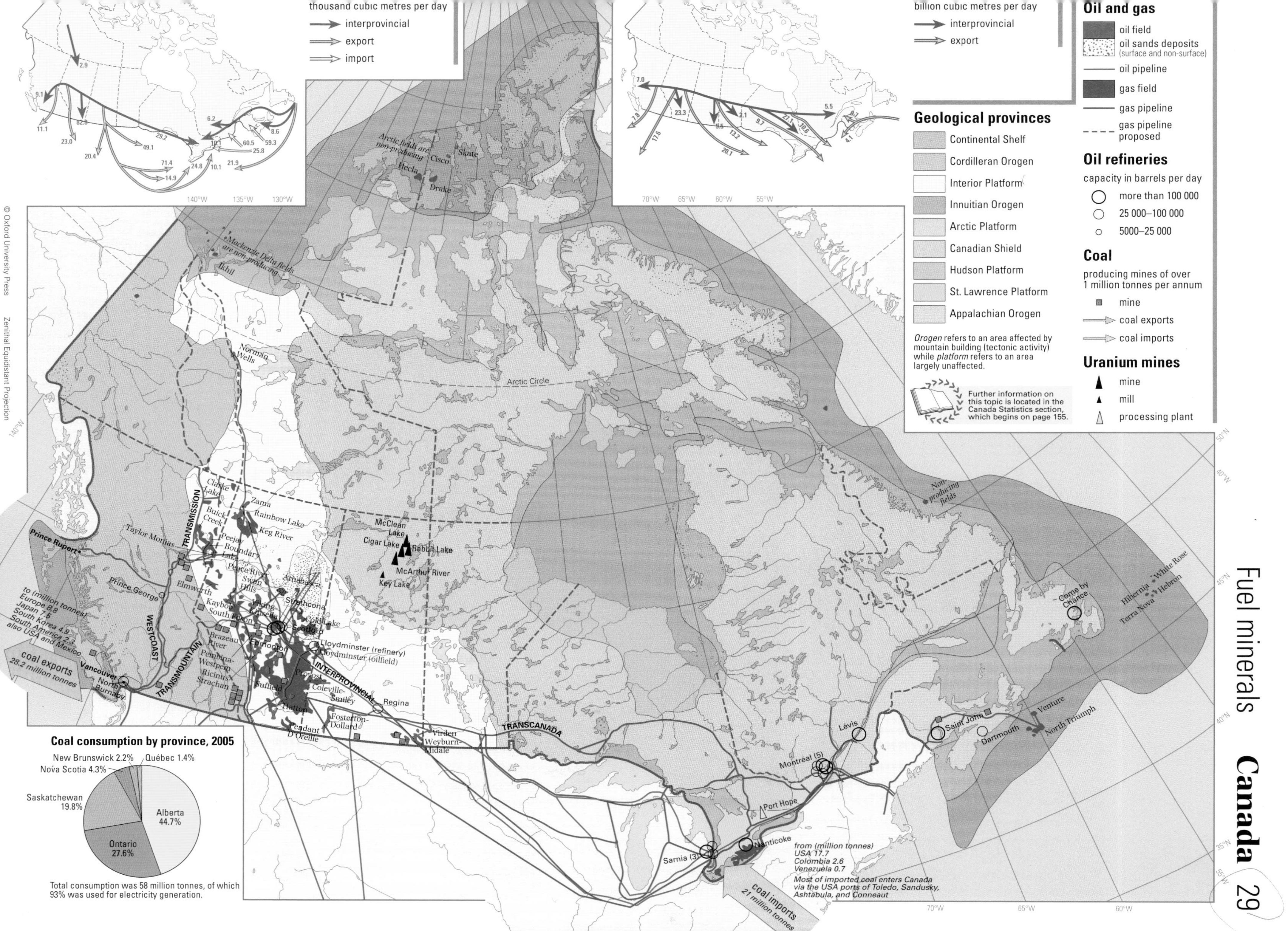
thousand cubic metres per day
interprovincial
export
import
billion cubic metres per day
interprovincial
export
Oil and gas
oil field
oil sands deposits (surface and non-surface)
oil pipeline
gas field
gas pipeline
gas pipeline proposed
Geological provinces
Continental Shelf
Cordilleran Orogen
Interior Platform
Innuitian Orogen
Arctic Platform
Canadian Shield
Hudson Platform
St. Lawrence Platform
Appalachian Orogen
Orogen refers to an area affected by mountain building (tectonic activity) while platform refers to an area largely unaffected.
Further information on this topic is located in the Canada Statistics section, which begins on page 155.
Oil refineries
capacity in barrels per day
more than 100 000
25 000–100 000
5000–25 000
Coal
producing mines of over 1 million tonnes per annum
mine
coal exports
coal imports
Uranium mines
mine
mill
processing plant
Arctic fields are non-producing
Hecla
Cisco
Skate
Drake
Mackenzie Delta fields are non-producing
Ikhil
Norman Wells
Arctic Circle
Non-producing fields
Clarke Lake
Zama
Rainbow Lake
Buick Creek
Keg River
Peejay
Boundary Lake
Taylor Monias
Prince Rupert
TRANSMISSION
Prince George
Elmworth
Peace River
Swan Hills
Athabasca
Kaybob South
Strathcona
Scotford
Cold Lake
McClean Lake
Cigar Lake
Rabbit Lake
McArthur River
Key Lake
Lloydminster (refinery)
Lloydminster (oilfield)
Provost
INTERPROVINCIAL
Coleville-Smiley
Regina
Brazeau River
Pembina-Westpem
Ricinus
Strachan
Suffield
Hatton
Fosterton-Dollard
Pendant D'Oreille
Virden
Weyburn-Midale
TRANSCANADA
WESTCOAST
TRANSMOUNTAIN
Vancouver
North Burnaby
to (million tonnes)
Europe 8.8
Japan 7.5
South Korea 4.9
South America 2.3
also USA and Mexico
coal exports 28.2 million tonnes
Lévis
Montréal (5)
Port Hope
Sarnia (3)
Nanticoke
from (million tonnes)
USA 17.7
Colombia 2.6
Venezuela 0.7
Most of imported coal enters Canada via the USA ports of Toledo, Sandusky, Ashtabula, and Conneaut
coal imports 21 million tonnes
Saint John
Dartmouth
Venture
North Triumph
Come by Chance
Hibernia
Terra Nova
White Rose
Hebron
Coal consumption by province, 2005
New Brunswick 2.2%
Québec 1.4%
Nova Scotia 4.3%
Saskatchewan 19.8%
Alberta 44.7%
Ontario 27.6%
Total consumption was 58 million tonnes, of which 93% was used for electricity generation.
© Oxford University Press
Zenithal Equidistant Projection

Scale 1: 23 000 000

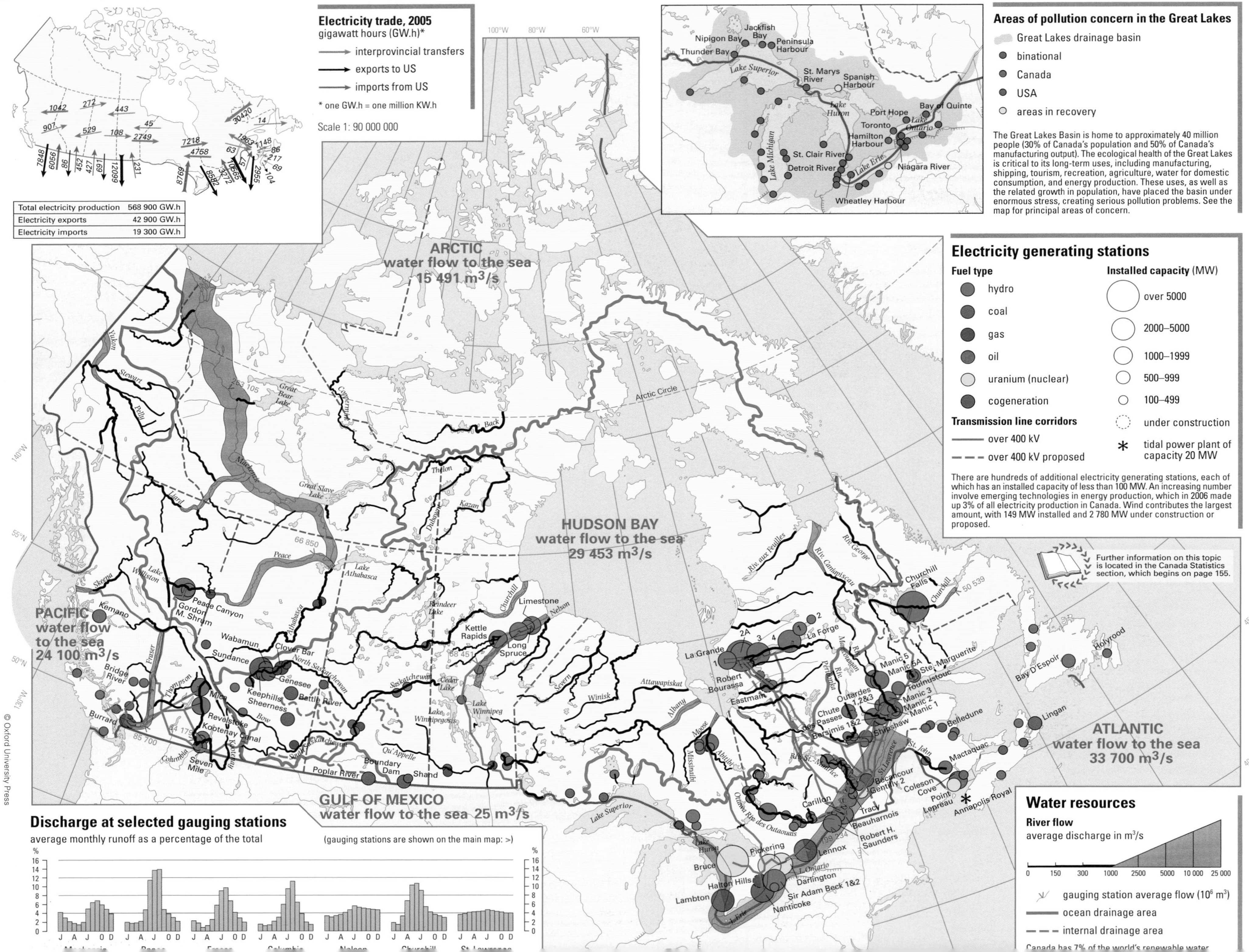

Electricity trade, 2005

gigawatt hours (GW.h)*

- interprovincial transfers
- exports to US
- imports from US

* one GW.h = one million KW.h

Scale 1: 90 000 000

Total electricity production	568 900 GW.h
Electricity exports	42 900 GW.h
Electricity imports	19 300 GW.h

Areas of pollution concern in the Great Lakes

- Great Lakes drainage basin
- binational
- Canada
- USA
- areas in recovery

The Great Lakes Basin is home to approximately 40 million people (30% of Canada's population and 50% of Canada's manufacturing output). The ecological health of the Great Lakes is critical to its long-term uses, including manufacturing, shipping, tourism, recreation, agriculture, water for domestic consumption, and energy production. These uses, as well as the related growth in population, have placed the basin under enormous stress, creating serious pollution problems. See the map for principal areas of concern.

Electricity generating stations

Fuel type

- hydro
- coal
- gas
- oil
- uranium (nuclear)
- cogeneration

Installed capacity (MW)

- over 5000
- 2000–5000
- 1000–1999
- 500–999
- 100–499
- under construction
- * tidal power plant of capacity 20 MW

Transmission line corridors

- over 400 kV
- over 400 kV proposed

There are hundreds of additional electricity generating stations, each of which has an installed capacity of less than 100 MW. An increasing number involve emerging technologies in energy production, which in 2006 made up 3% of all electricity production in Canada. Wind contributes the largest amount, with 149 MW installed and 2 780 MW under construction or proposed.

Further information on this topic is located in the Canada Statistics section, which begins on page 155.

Water resources

River flow

average discharge in m³/s

- gauging station average flow (10^6 m³)
- ocean drainage area
- internal drainage area

Canada has 7% of the world's renewable water

Discharge at selected gauging stations

average monthly runoff as a percentage of the total

(gauging stations are shown on the main map: >)

Scale 1: 21 500 000

0 215 430 645 km

Manufacturing industries, 2006

The colour indicates the major industrial group and the numbers indicate important manufacturing subdivisions in some groups.

- food, beverages, and tobacco
  - 1 food
  - 2 beverages and tobacco
- textiles and clothing
  - 3 textile mills
  - 4 textile mill products
  - 5 clothing
  - 6 leather and allied products
- wood
  - 7 wood products
  - 8 furniture and related products
- paper
  - 9 paper
  - 10 printing and related activities
- chemicals
  - 11 petroleum and coal products
  - 12 chemicals
- plastics and rubber
- non-metallic minerals
- metals
  - 13 primary metals
  - 14 fabricated metal products
- machinery
  - 15 machinery
  - 16 computer and electronic products
  - 17 electrical equipment, appliances, and components
  - 18 transportation equipment
- others
  including the above industrial groups where the value added is less than 5% of the total or where the information is not available for reasons of confidentiality

*$217 279 million value added by manufacturing

The value of manufactured goods shipped, less the cost of materials and supplies used, including fuel and electricity.

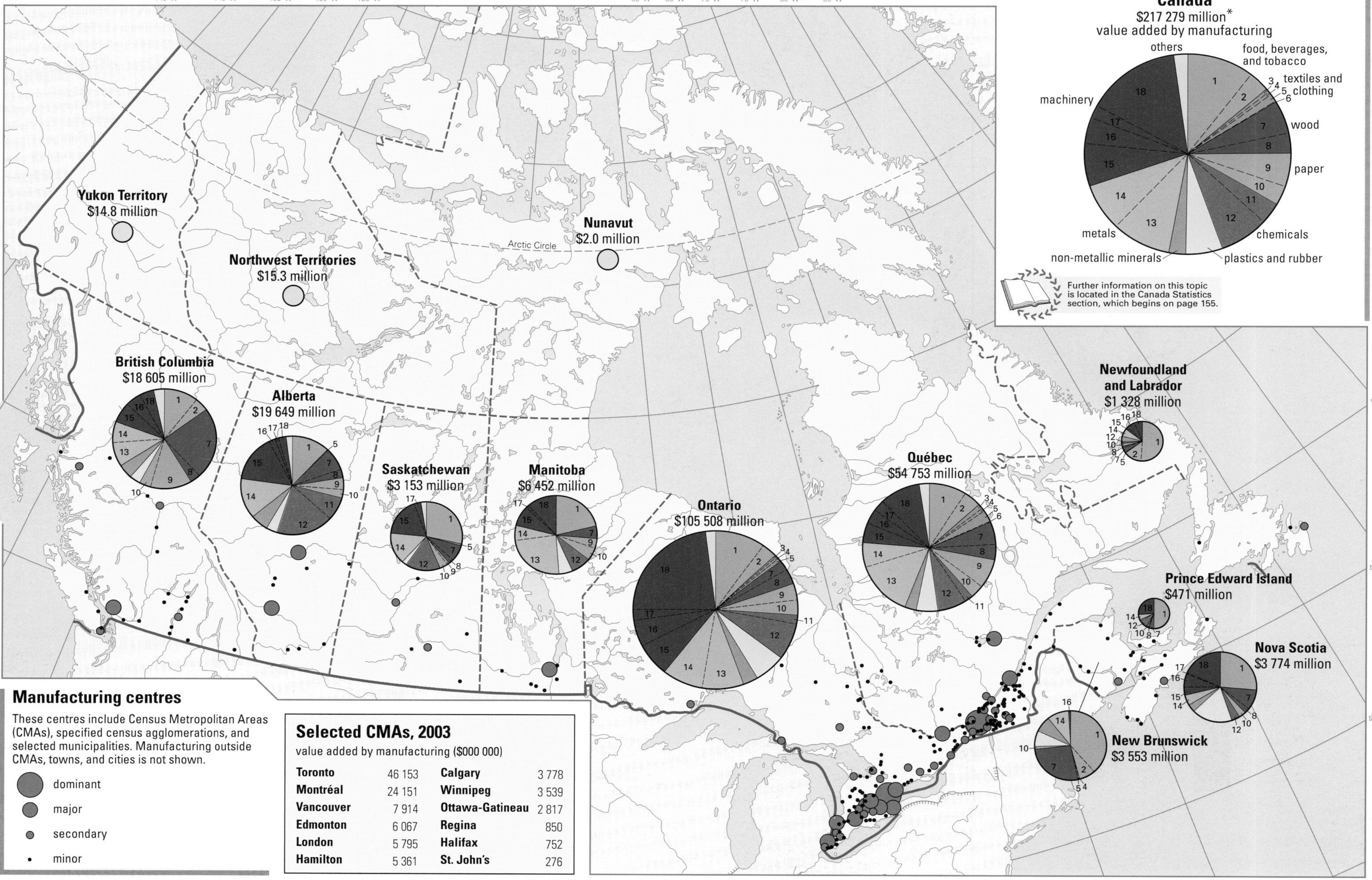

Canada
$217 279 million*
value added by manufacturing
others
food, beverages, and tobacco
textiles and clothing
wood
paper
chemicals
plastics and rubber
non-metallic minerals
metals
machinery
Yukon Territory
$14.8 million
Northwest Territories
$15.3 million
Nunavut
$2.0 million
Arctic Circle
British Columbia
$18 605 million
Alberta
$19 649 million
Saskatchewan
$3 153 million
Manitoba
$6 452 million
Ontario
$105 508 million
Québec
$54 753 million
Newfoundland and Labrador
$1 328 million
Prince Edward Island
$471 million
Nova Scotia
$3 774 million
New Brunswick
$3 553 million
145°W
140°W
135°W
130°W
125°W
85°W
80°W
75°W
70°W
65°W
60°W
55°N
50°N
45°N
40°N

Further information on this topic is located in the Canada Statistics section, which begins on page 155.

Manufacturing centres

These centres include Census Metropolitan Areas (CMAs), specified census agglomerations, and selected municipalities. Manufacturing outside CMAs, towns, and cities is not shown.

- dominant
- major
- secondary
- minor

Selected CMAs, 2003

value added by manufacturing ($000 000)

Toronto	46 153	**Calgary**	3 778
Montréal	24 151	**Winnipeg**	3 539
Vancouver	7 914	**Ottawa-Gatineau**	2 817
Edmonton	6 067	**Regina**	850
London	5 795	**Halifax**	752
Hamilton	5 361	**St. John's**	276

Zenithal Equidistant Projection

Scale 1: 160 000 000

Value of exports, 2006

by country of destination

$ million

- over 5 000
- 3 000–5 000
- 1 000–3 000
- 500–1 000
- 200–500
- 50–200
- under 50

Further information on this topic is located in the Canada Statistics section, which begins on page 155.

All exports exceeding $200 million in value are listed with their value in millions of dollars shown. Because of space limitations it is not possible to show all exports to the USA over $200 million. If a more detailed breakdown is required for the United States or any other country refer to the source for this map: Statistics Canada, Exports by Country Jan-Dec 2006, Cat No. 65-003-XPB.

Trade with the United States Total $336 152

top fifteen exports, 2006

	$ million
fuels	82 468
vehicles	69 894
machinery	34 754
pulp and paper products	15 001
wood products	14 842
plastics	12 880
aluminum products	10 599
iron and steel products	10 368
chemicals	7 723
furniture	6 651
aircraft	5 513
meat and live animals	4 068
copper	3 837
pharmaceutical products	3 772
rubber products	3 422

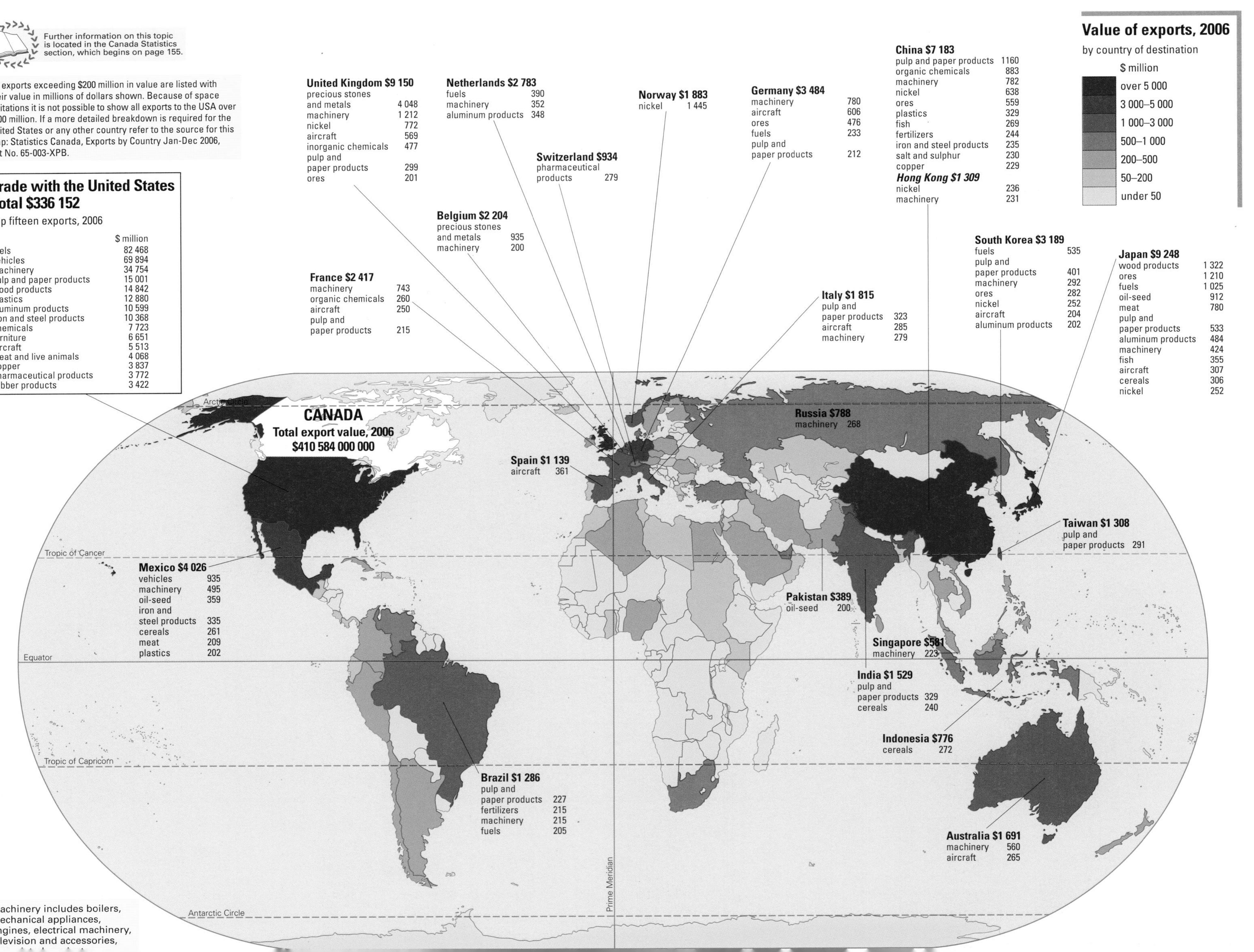

Machinery includes boilers, mechanical appliances, engines, electrical machinery, television and accessories,

Eckert IV Projection

Scale 1: 160 000 000

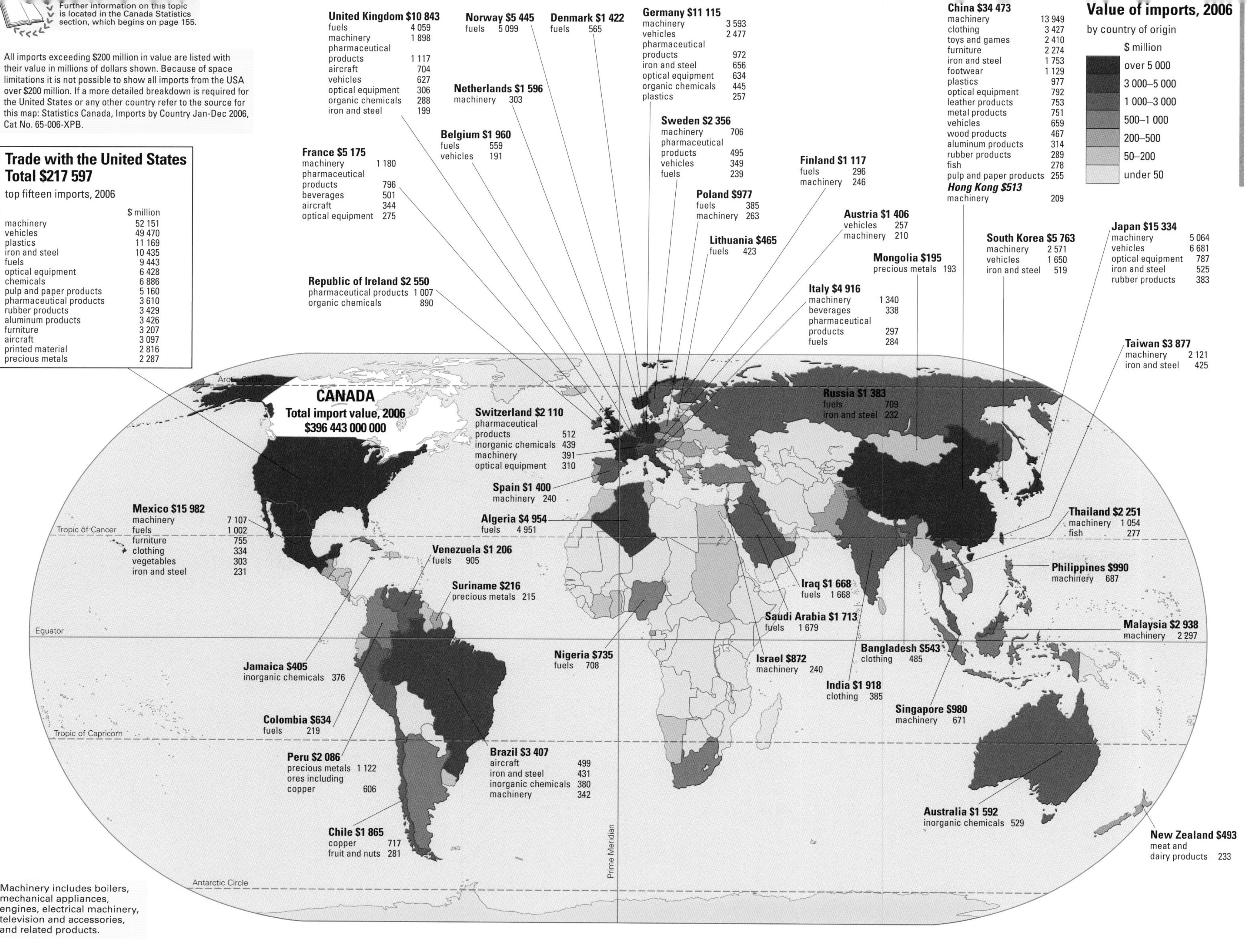

Further information on this topic is located in the Canada Statistics section, which begins on page 155.

All imports exceeding $200 million in value are listed with their value in millions of dollars shown. Because of space limitations it is not possible to show all imports from the USA over $200 million. If a more detailed breakdown is required for the United States or any other country refer to the source for this map: Statistics Canada, Imports by Country Jan-Dec 2006, Cat No. 65-006-XPB.

Trade with the United States Total $217 597

top fifteen imports, 2006

	$ million
machinery	52 151
vehicles	49 470
plastics	11 169
iron and steel	10 435
fuels	9 443
optical equipment	6 428
chemicals	6 886
pulp and paper products	5 160
pharmaceutical products	3 610
rubber products	3 429
aluminum products	3 426
furniture	3 207
aircraft	3 097
printed material	2 816
precious metals	2 287

Machinery includes boilers, mechanical appliances, engines, electrical machinery, television and accessories, and related products.

Eckert IV Projection

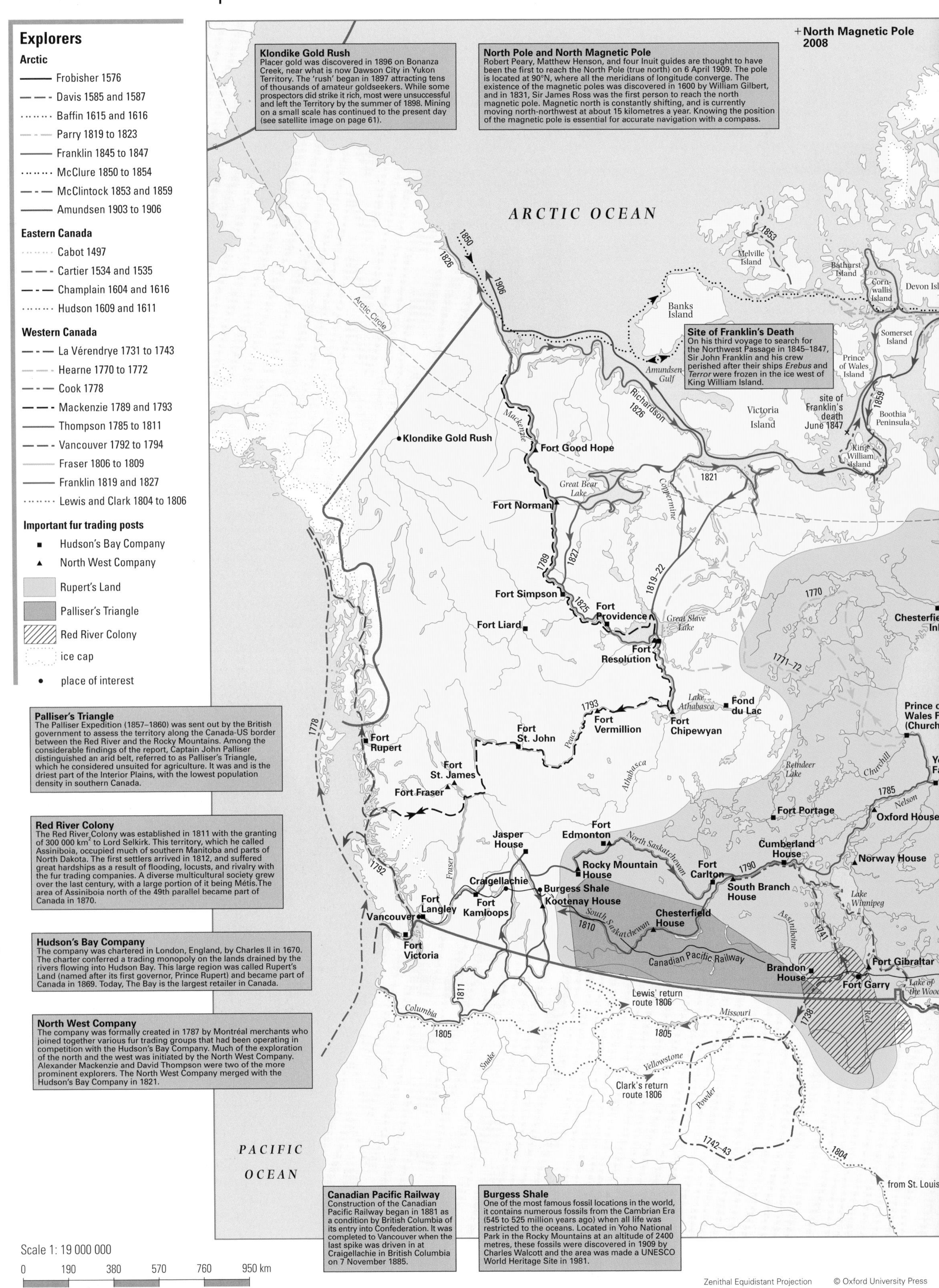
Explorers
Arctic
Frobisher 1576
Davis 1585 and 1587
Baffin 1615 and 1616
Parry 1819 to 1823
Franklin 1845 to 1847
McClure 1850 to 1854
McClintock 1853 and 1859
Amundsen 1903 to 1906
Eastern Canada
Cabot 1497
Cartier 1534 and 1535
Champlain 1604 and 1616
Hudson 1609 and 1611
Western Canada
La Vérendrye 1731 to 1743
Hearne 1770 to 1772
Cook 1778
Mackenzie 1789 and 1793
Thompson 1785 to 1811
Vancouver 1792 to 1794
Fraser 1806 to 1809
Franklin 1819 and 1827
Lewis and Clark 1804 to 1806
Important fur trading posts
Hudson's Bay Company
North West Company
Rupert's Land
Palliser's Triangle
Red River Colony
ice cap
place of interest
Klondike Gold Rush
Placer gold was discovered in 1896 on Bonanza Creek, near what is now Dawson City in Yukon Territory. The 'rush' began in 1897 attracting tens of thousands of amateur goldseekers. While some prospectors did strike it rich, most were unsuccessful and left the Territory by the summer of 1898. Mining on a small scale has continued to the present day (see satellite image on page 61).
North Pole and North Magnetic Pole
Robert Peary, Matthew Henson, and four Inuit guides are thought to have been the first to reach the North Pole (true north) on 6 April 1909. The pole is located at 90°N, where all the meridians of longitude converge. The existence of the magnetic poles was discovered in 1600 by William Gilbert, and in 1831, Sir James Ross was the first person to reach the north magnetic pole. Magnetic north is constantly shifting, and is currently moving north-northwest at about 15 kilometres a year. Knowing the position of the magnetic pole is essential for accurate navigation with a compass.
+North Magnetic Pole 2008
ARCTIC OCEAN
Site of Franklin's Death
On his third voyage to search for the Northwest Passage in 1845–1847, Sir John Franklin and his crew perished after their ships *Erebus* and *Terror* were frozen in the ice west of King William Island.
Palliser's Triangle
The Palliser Expedition (1857–1860) was sent out by the British government to assess the territory along the Canada-US border between the Red River and the Rocky Mountains. Among the considerable findings of the report, Captain John Palliser distinguished an arid belt, referred to as Palliser's Triangle, which he considered unsuited for agriculture. It was and is the driest part of the Interior Plains, with the lowest population density in southern Canada.
Red River Colony
The Red River Colony was established in 1811 with the granting of 300 000 km² to Lord Selkirk. This territory, which he called Assiniboia, occupied much of southern Manitoba and parts of North Dakota. The first settlers arrived in 1812, and suffered great hardships as a result of flooding, locusts, and rivalry with the fur trading companies. A diverse multicultural society grew over the last century, with a large portion of it being Métis. The area of Assiniboia north of the 49th parallel became part of Canada in 1870.
Hudson's Bay Company
The company was chartered in London, England, by Charles II in 1670. The charter conferred a trading monopoly on the lands drained by the rivers flowing into Hudson Bay. This large region was called Rupert's Land (named after its first governor, Prince Rupert) and became part of Canada in 1869. Today, The Bay is the largest retailer in Canada.
North West Company
The company was formally created in 1787 by Montréal merchants who joined together various fur trading groups that had been operating in competition with the Hudson's Bay Company. Much of the exploration of the north and the west was initiated by the North West Company. Alexander Mackenzie and David Thompson were two of the more prominent explorers. The North West Company merged with the Hudson's Bay Company in 1821.
Canadian Pacific Railway
Construction of the Canadian Pacific Railway began in 1881 as a condition by British Columbia of its entry into Confederation. It was completed to Vancouver when the last spike was driven in at Craigellachie in British Columbia on 7 November 1885.
Burgess Shale
One of the most famous fossil locations in the world, it contains numerous fossils from the Cambrian Era (545 to 525 million years ago) when all life was restricted to the oceans. Located in Yoho National Park in the Rocky Mountains at an altitude of 2400 metres, these fossils were discovered in 1909 by Charles Walcott and the area was made a UNESCO World Heritage Site in 1981.
Melville Island
Bathurst Island
Cornwallis Island
Devon Isl
Banks Island
Somerset Island
Prince of Wales Island
Amundsen Gulf
Victoria Island
site of Franklin's death June 1847
Boothia Peninsula
King William Island
Richardson 1826
Klondike Gold Rush
Fort Good Hope
Great Bear Lake
Fort Norman
Coppermine
Fort Simpson
Fort Providence
Great Slave Lake
Fort Liard
Fort Resolution
Lake Athabasca
Fond du Lac
Fort Vermillion
Fort Chipewyan
Fort St. John
Fort Rupert
Fort St. James
Fort Fraser
Reindeer Lake
Churchill
Chesterfield Inlet
Prince of Wales F (Church
Fort Portage
Oxford House
Nelson
Norway House
Cumberland House
Fort Edmonton
North Saskatchewan
Jasper House
Rocky Mountain House
Fort Carlton
South Branch House
Craigellachie
Burgess Shale
Kootenay House
Fort Kamloops
Fort Langley
Vancouver
Fort Victoria
South Saskatchewan
Chesterfield House
Canadian Pacific Railway
Brandon House
Fort Gibraltar
Fort Garry
Lake of the Woods
Lake Winnipeg
Assiniboine
Red
Fraser
Athabasca
Peace
Mackenzie
Arctic Circle
Columbia
Snake
Missouri
Yellowstone
Powder
Lewis' return route 1806
Clark's return route 1806
from St. Louis
PACIFIC OCEAN
1850
1826
1906
1853
1859
1821
1789
1827
1819–22
1825
1770
1771–72
1793
1785
1790
1778
1792
1810
1741
1738
1811
1805
1742–43
1804
Scale 1: 19 000 000
0 190 380 570 760 950 km
Zenithal Equidistant Projection

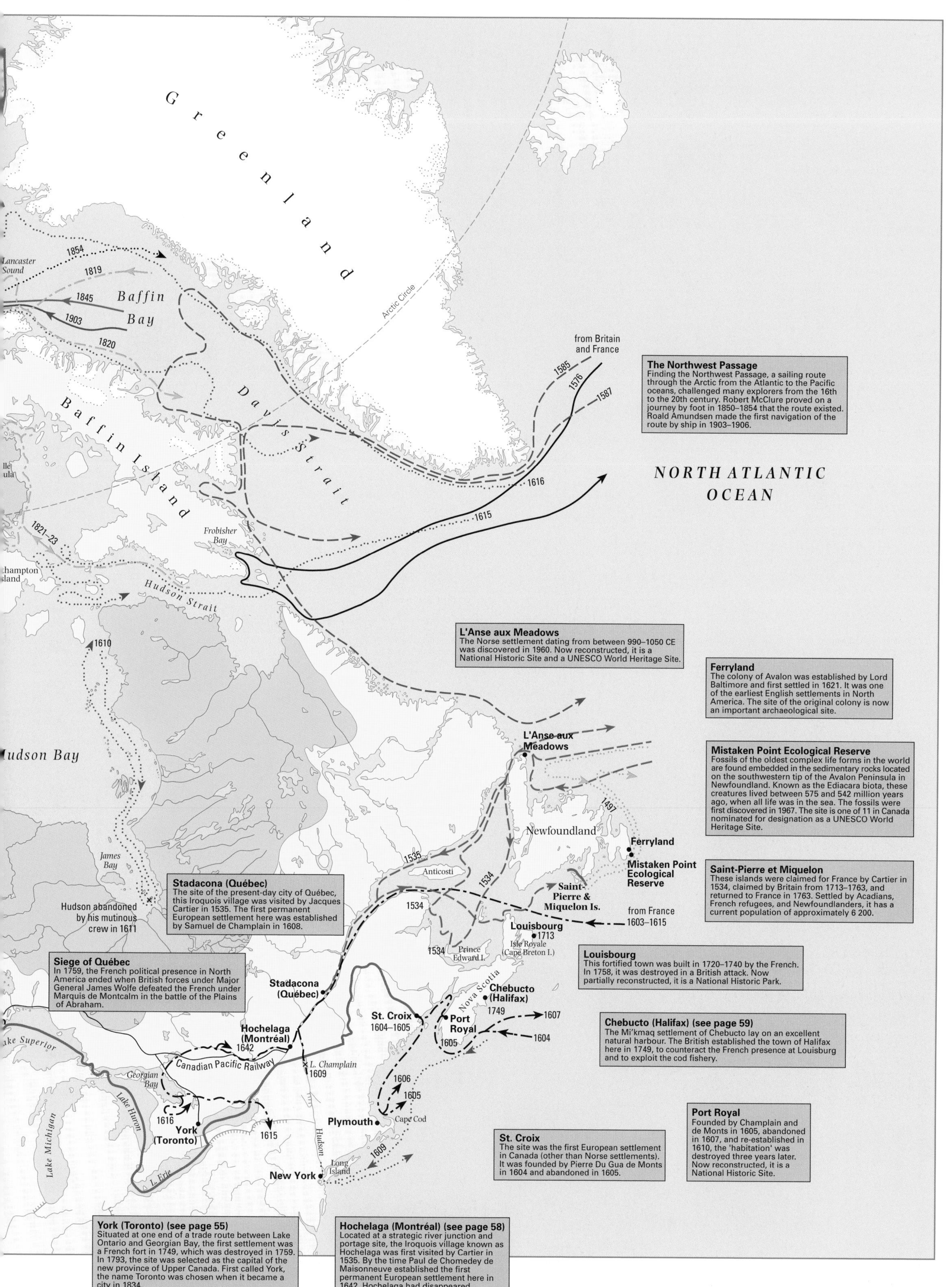
Greenland
Lancaster Sound
1854
1819
1845
Baffin Bay
1903
1820
Arctic Circle
from Britain and France
1585
1576
1587
The Northwest Passage
Finding the Northwest Passage, a sailing route through the Arctic from the Atlantic to the Pacific oceans, challenged many explorers from the 16th to the 20th century. Robert McClure proved on a journey by foot in 1850–1854 that the route existed. Roald Amundsen made the first navigation of the route by ship in 1903–1906.
Baffin Island
Davis Strait
1616
NORTH ATLANTIC OCEAN
1615
Frobisher Bay
1821–23
Hudson Strait
L'Anse aux Meadows
The Norse settlement dating from between 990–1050 CE was discovered in 1960. Now reconstructed, it is a National Historic Site and a UNESCO World Heritage Site.
1610
Ferryland
The colony of Avalon was established by Lord Baltimore and first settled in 1621. It was one of the earliest English settlements in North America. The site of the original colony is now an important archaeological site.
Hudson Bay
L'Anse aux Meadows
Mistaken Point Ecological Reserve
Fossils of the oldest complex life forms in the world are found embedded in the sedimentary rocks located on the southwestern tip of the Avalon Peninsula in Newfoundland. Known as the Ediacara biota, these creatures lived between 575 and 542 million years ago, when all life was in the sea. The fossils were first discovered in 1967. The site is one of 11 in Canada nominated for designation as a UNESCO World Heritage Site.
1497
Newfoundland
Ferryland
Mistaken Point Ecological Reserve
James Bay
1535
Anticosti
1534
Saint-Pierre et Miquelon
These islands were claimed for France by Cartier in 1534, claimed by Britain from 1713–1763, and returned to France in 1763. Settled by Acadians, French refugees, and Newfoundlanders, it has a current population of approximately 6 200.
Stadacona (Québec)
The site of the present-day city of Québec, this Iroquois village was visited by Jacques Cartier in 1535. The first permanent European settlement here was established by Samuel de Champlain in 1608.
Hudson abandoned by his mutinous crew in 1611
1534
Saint-Pierre & Miquelon Is.
from France 1603–1615
Louisbourg 1713
Isle Royale (Cape Breton I.)
1534
Prince Edward I.
Louisbourg
This fortified town was built in 1720–1740 by the French. In 1758, it was destroyed in a British attack. Now partially reconstructed, it is a National Historic Park.
Siege of Québec
In 1759, the French political presence in North America ended when British forces under Major General James Wolfe defeated the French under Marquis de Montcalm in the battle of the Plains of Abraham.
Stadacona (Québec)
Nova Scotia
Chebucto (Halifax)
1749
St. Croix 1604–1605
Port Royal
1607
1604
1605
Chebucto (Halifax) (see page 59)
The Mi'kmaq settlement of Chebucto lay on an excellent natural harbour. The British established the town of Halifax here in 1749, to counteract the French presence at Louisburg and to exploit the cod fishery.
Lake Superior
Hochelaga (Montréal)
1642
Canadian Pacific Railway
L. Champlain 1609
Georgian Bay
Lake Huron
1606
1605
Lake Michigan
1616
York (Toronto)
1615
Plymouth
Cape Cod
Hudson
Port Royal
Founded by Champlain and de Monts in 1605, abandoned in 1607, and re-established in 1610, the 'habitation' was destroyed three years later. Now reconstructed, it is a National Historic Site.
St. Croix
The site was the first European settlement in Canada (other than Norse settlements). It was founded by Pierre Du Gua de Monts in 1604 and abandoned in 1605.
1609
Long Island
New York
L. Erie
York (Toronto) (see page 55)
Situated at one end of a trade route between Lake Ontario and Georgian Bay, the first settlement was a French fort in 1749, which was destroyed in 1759. In 1793, the site was selected as the capital of the new province of Upper Canada. First called York, the name Toronto was chosen when it became a city in 1834.
Hochelaga (Montréal) (see page 58)
Located at a strategic river junction and portage site, the Iroquois village known as Hochelaga was first visited by Cartier in 1535. By the time Paul de Chomedey de Maisonneuve established the first permanent European settlement here in 1642, Hochelaga had disappeared.

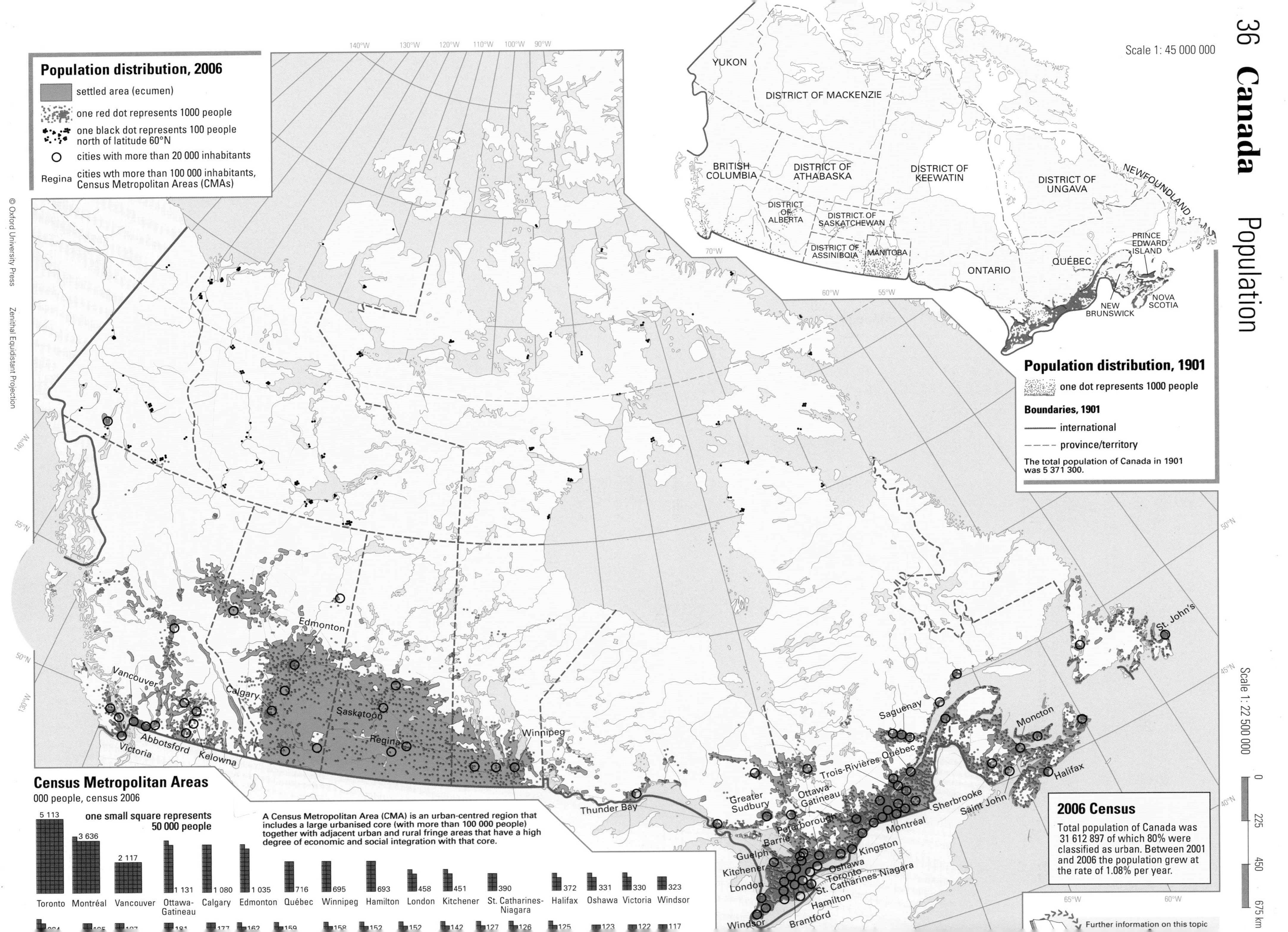
Scale 1: 45 000 000
YUKON
DISTRICT OF MACKENZIE
BRITISH COLUMBIA
DISTRICT OF ATHABASKA
DISTRICT OF KEEWATIN
DISTRICT OF UNGAVA
NEWFOUNDLAND
DISTRICT OF ALBERTA
DISTRICT OF SASKATCHEWAN
DISTRICT OF ASSINIBOIA
MANITOBA
ONTARIO
QUÉBEC
PRINCE EDWARD ISLAND
NEW BRUNSWICK
NOVA SCOTIA
Population distribution, 1901
one dot represents 1000 people
Boundaries, 1901
international
province/territory
The total population of Canada in 1901 was 5 371 300.
Population distribution, 2006
settled area (ecumen)
one red dot represents 1000 people
one black dot represents 100 people north of latitude 60°N
cities with more than 20 000 inhabitants
Regina cities wth more than 100 000 inhabitants, Census Metropolitan Areas (CMAs)
Scale 1: 22 500 000
0 225 450 675 km
Edmonton
Calgary
Saskatoon
Regina
Winnipeg
Vancouver
Abbotsford
Victoria
Kelowna
Thunder Bay
Greater Sudbury
Ottawa-Gatineau
Peterborough
Barrie
Guelph
Kitchener
London
Windsor
Brantford
Hamilton
St. Catharines-Niagara
Toronto
Oshawa
Kingston
Montréal
Trois-Rivières
Québec
Saguenay
Sherbrooke
Saint John
Moncton
Halifax
St. John's
2006 Census
Total population of Canada was 31 612 897 of which 80% were classified as urban. Between 2001 and 2006 the population grew at the rate of 1.08% per year.
Census Metropolitan Areas
000 people, census 2006
one small square represents 50 000 people
A Census Metropolitan Area (CMA) is an urban-centred region that includes a large urbanised core (with more than 100 000 people) together with adjacent urban and rural fringe areas that have a high degree of economic and social integration with that core.
Toronto 5 113
Montréal 3 636
Vancouver 2 117
Ottawa-Gatineau 1 131
Calgary 1 080
Edmonton 1 035
Québec 716
Winnipeg 695
Hamilton 693
London 458
Kitchener 451
St. Catharines-Niagara 390
Halifax 372
Oshawa 331
Victoria 330
Windsor 323
181 177 162 159 158 152 152 142 127 126 125 123 122 117
Further information on this topic
© Oxford University Press
Zenithal Equidistant Projection

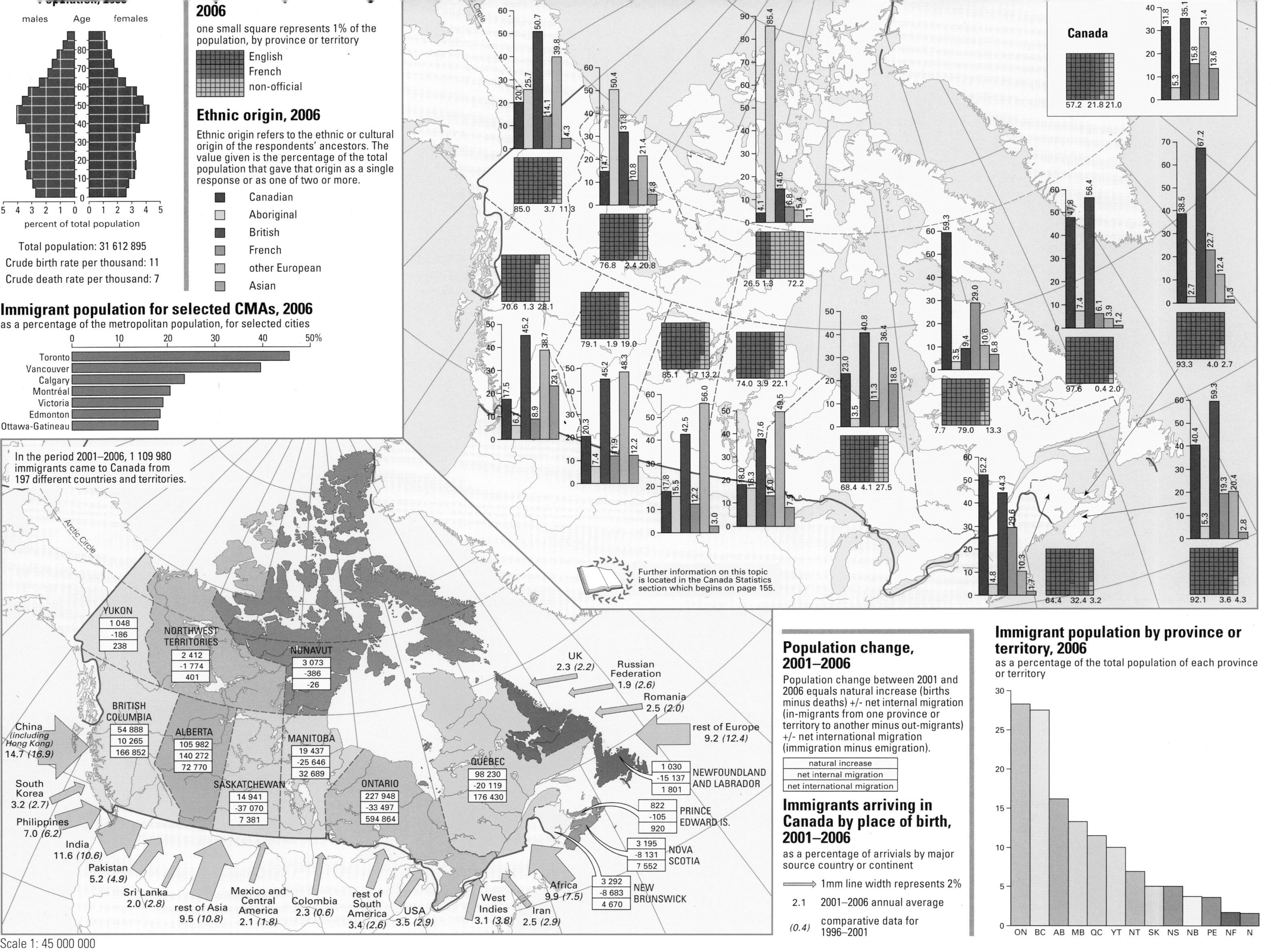
males Age females
percent of total population
Total population: 31 612 895
Crude birth rate per thousand: 11
Crude death rate per thousand: 7
2006
one small square represents 1% of the population, by province or territory
English
French
non-official
Ethnic origin, 2006
Ethnic origin refers to the ethnic or cultural origin of the respondents' ancestors. The value given is the percentage of the total population that gave that origin as a single response or as one of two or more.
Canadian
Aboriginal
British
French
other European
Asian
Immigrant population for selected CMAs, 2006
as a percentage of the metropolitan population, for selected cities
Toronto
Vancouver
Calgary
Montréal
Victoria
Edmonton
Ottawa-Gatineau
Canada
57.2 21.8 21.0
Scale 1: 35 000 000
Further information on this topic is located in the Canada Statistics section which begins on page 155.
In the period 2001–2006, 1 109 980 immigrants came to Canada from 197 different countries and territories.
Arctic Circle
YUKON 1 048 -186 238
NORTHWEST TERRITORIES 2 412 -1 774 401
NUNAVUT 3 073 -386 -26
BRITISH COLUMBIA 54 888 10 265 166 852
ALBERTA 105 982 140 272 72 770
SASKATCHEWAN 14 941 -37 070 7 381
MANITOBA 19 437 -25 646 32 689
ONTARIO 227 948 -33 497 594 864
QUÉBEC 98 230 -20 119 176 430
NEWFOUNDLAND AND LABRADOR 1 030 -15 137 1 801
PRINCE EDWARD IS. 822 -105 920
NOVA SCOTIA 3 195 -8 131 7 552
NEW BRUNSWICK 3 292 -8 683 4 670
China (including Hong Kong) 14.7 (16.9)
South Korea 3.2 (2.7)
Philippines 7.0 (6.2)
India 11.6 (10.6)
Pakistan 5.2 (4.9)
Sri Lanka 2.0 (2.8)
rest of Asia 9.5 (10.8)
Mexico and Central America 2.1 (1.8)
Colombia 2.3 (0.6)
rest of South America 3.4 (2.6)
USA 3.5 (2.9)
West Indies 3.1 (3.8)
Iran 2.5 (2.9)
Africa 9.9 (7.5)
rest of Europe 9.2 (12.4)
Romania 2.5 (2.0)
Russian Federation 1.9 (2.6)
UK 2.3 (2.2)
Scale 1: 45 000 000
Population change, 2001–2006
Population change between 2001 and 2006 equals natural increase (births minus deaths) +/- net internal migration (in-migrants from one province or territory to another minus out-migrants) +/- net international migration (immigration minus emigration).
natural increase
net internal migration
net international migration
Immigrants arriving in Canada by place of birth, 2001–2006
as a percentage of arrivals by major source country or continent
1mm line width represents 2%
2.1 2001–2006 annual average
(0.4) comparative data for 1996–2001
Immigrant population by province or territory, 2006
as a percentage of the total population of each province or territory
ON BC AB MB QC YT NT SK NS NB PE NF N

The 2006 Census recorded over 60 different languages spoken by Aboriginal peoples. Among Canada's First Nations, 29% could speak an Aboriginal language — 51% of those living on reserves and 12% of those living off reserves. The languages with the largest number of speakers were Ojibwa (30 255), Oji-Cree (12 435), and Cree (87 285), (all members of the Algonquin family). Among the 50 485 Inuit, 34 345 were Inuktitut speakers.

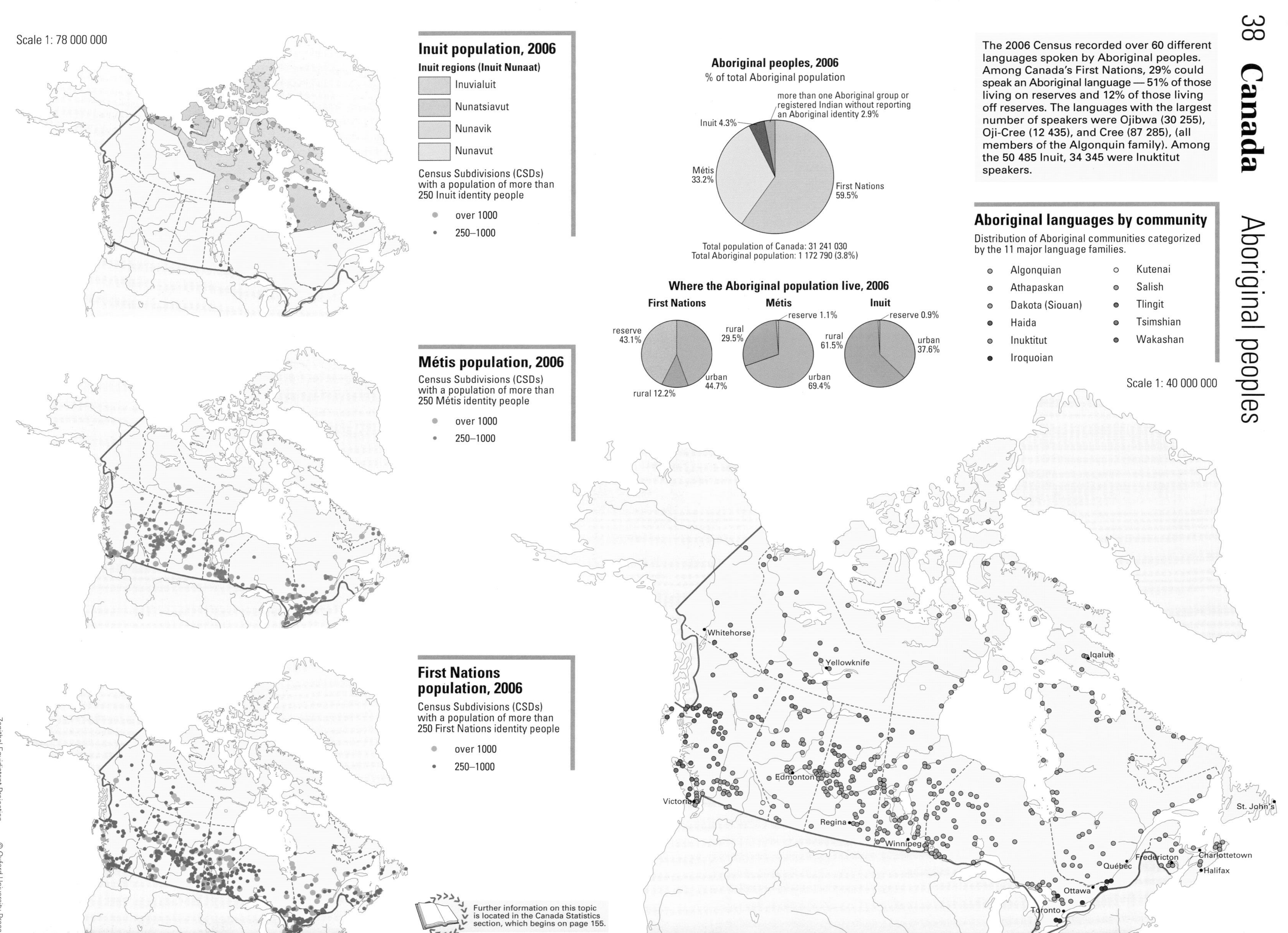

Further information on this topic is located in the Canada Statistics section, which begins on page 155.

Scale 1: 78 000 000

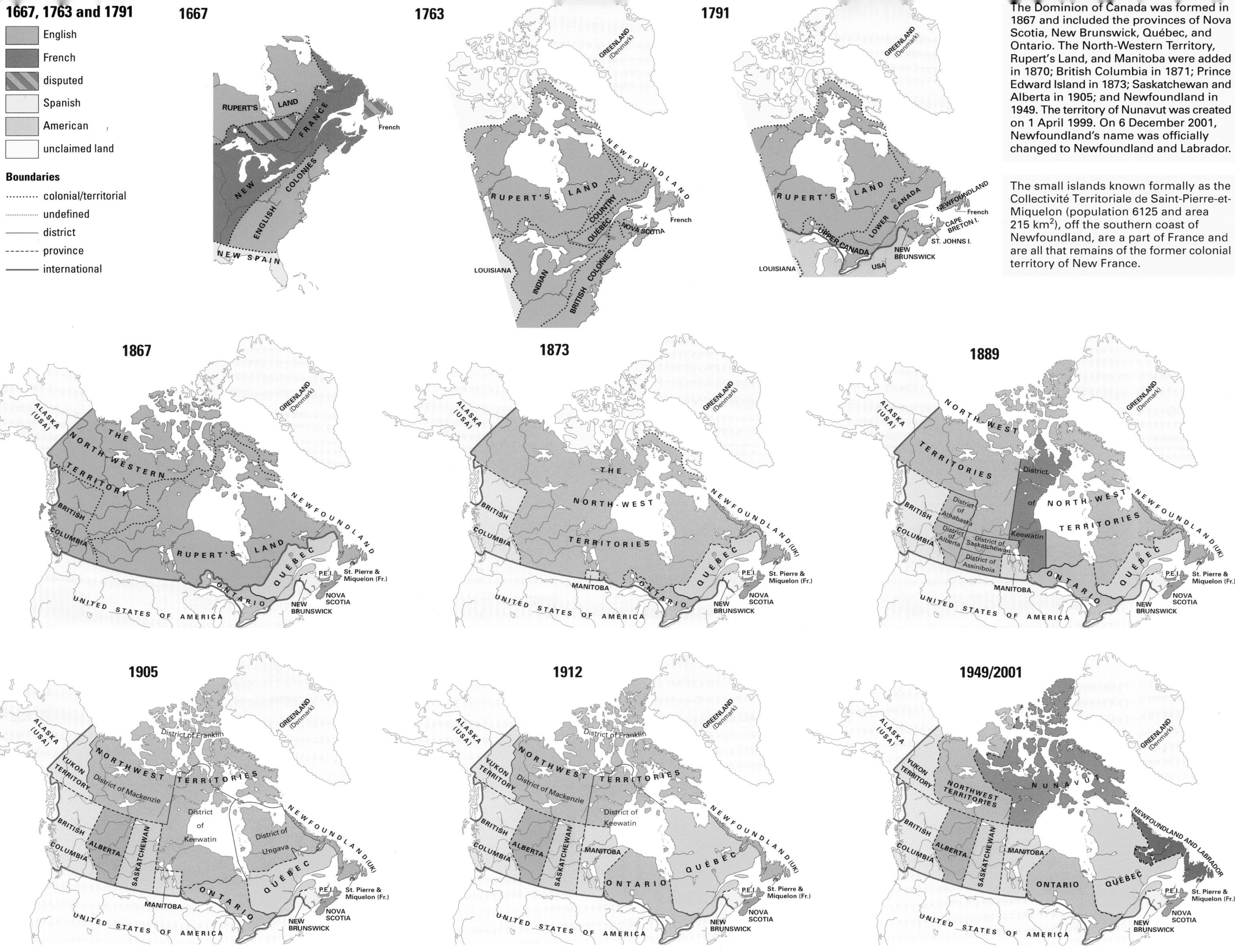

The Dominion of Canada was formed in 1867 and included the provinces of Nova Scotia, New Brunswick, Québec, and Ontario. The North-Western Territory, Rupert's Land, and Manitoba were added in 1870; British Columbia in 1871; Prince Edward Island in 1873; Saskatchewan and Alberta in 1905; and Newfoundland in 1949. The territory of Nunavut was created on 1 April 1999. On 6 December 2001, Newfoundland's name was officially changed to Newfoundland and Labrador.

The small islands known formally as the Collectivité Territoriale de Saint-Pierre-et-Miquelon (population 6125 and area 215 km^2), off the southern coast of Newfoundland, are a part of France and are all that remains of the former colonial territory of New France.

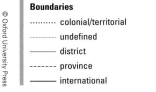

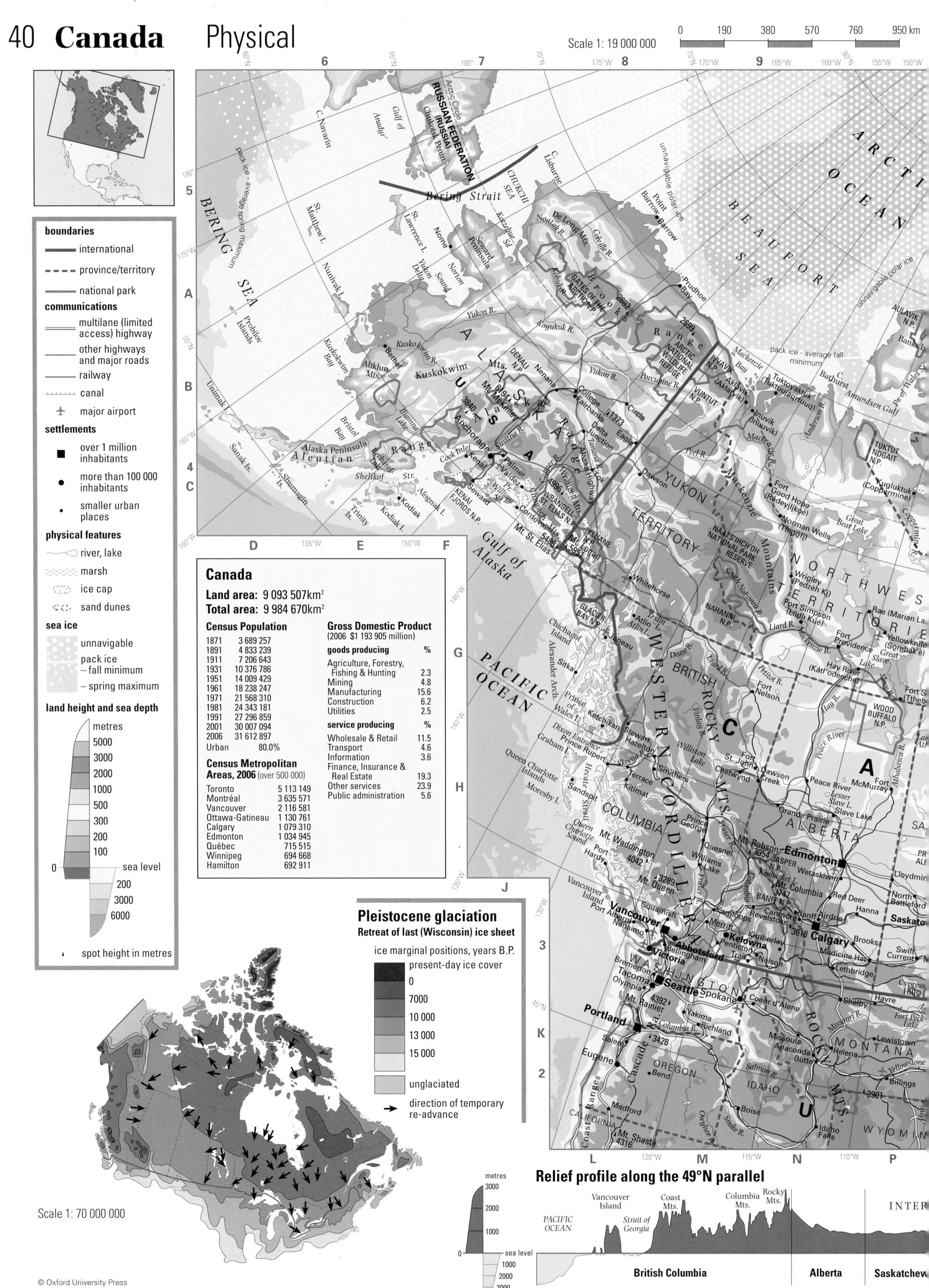

Canada

Land area: 9 093 507km²
Total area: 9 984 670km²

Census Population

1871	3 689 257
1891	4 833 239
1911	7 206 643
1931	10 376 786
1951	14 009 429
1961	18 238 247
1971	21 568 310
1981	24 343 181
1991	27 296 859
2001	30 007 094
2006	31 612 897
Urban	80.0%

Census Metropolitan Areas, 2006 (over 500 000)

Toronto	5 113 149
Montréal	3 635 571
Vancouver	2 116 581
Ottawa-Gatineau	1 130 761
Calgary	1 079 310
Edmonton	1 034 945
Québec	715 515
Winnipeg	694 668
Hamilton	692 911

Gross Domestic Product
(2006 $1 193 905 million)

goods producing	%
Agriculture, Forestry, Fishing & Hunting	2.3
Mining	4.8
Manufacturing	15.6
Construction	6.2
Utilities	2.5
service producing	**%**
Wholesale & Retail	11.5
Transport	4.6
Information	3.6
Finance, Insurance & Real Estate	19.3
Other services	23.9
Public administration	5.6

Distance chart official highway distances, in kilometres

	Calgary	Charlottetown	Edmonton	Fredericton	Halifax	Montréal	Ottawa	Québec	Regina	St. John's	Saskatoon	Thunder Bay	Toronto	Vancouver	Victoria	Whitehorse	Winnipeg	Yellowknife
Calgary	•	4917	299	4558	5042	3743	3553	4014	764	6183	620	2050	3434	1057	1123	2385	1336	1811
Charlottetown		•	4949	359	232	1184	1374	945	4163	1294	4421	2878	1724	5985	6051	7034	3592	6460
Edmonton			•	4598	5082	3764	3574	4035	785	6212	528	2071	3455	1244	1310	2086	1357	1511
Fredericton				•	346	834	1024	586	3813	1622	4070	2527	1373	5634	5700	6684	3241	6109
Halifax					•	1318	1508	912	4297	1349	4554	3011	1857	6119	6185	7168	3726	6593
Montréal						•	190	270	2979	2448	3236	1693	539	4801	4867	5850	2408	5275
Ottawa							•	460	2789	2638	3046	1503	399	4611	4677	5660	2218	5086
Québec								•	3249	2208	3507	1963	810	5071	5137	6120	2678	5546
Regina									•	5427	257	1286	2670	1822	1888	2871	571	2297
St. John's										•	5684	4141	2987	7248	7314	8298	4855	7723
Saskatoon											•	1543	2927	1677	1743	2614	829	2039
Thunder Bay												•	1384	3108	3174	4157	715	3582
Toronto													•	4492	4558	5528	2099	4966
Vancouver														•	66	2697	2232	2411
Victoria															•	2763	2298	2477
Whitehorse																•	3524	2704
Winnipeg																	•	2868
Yellowknife																		•

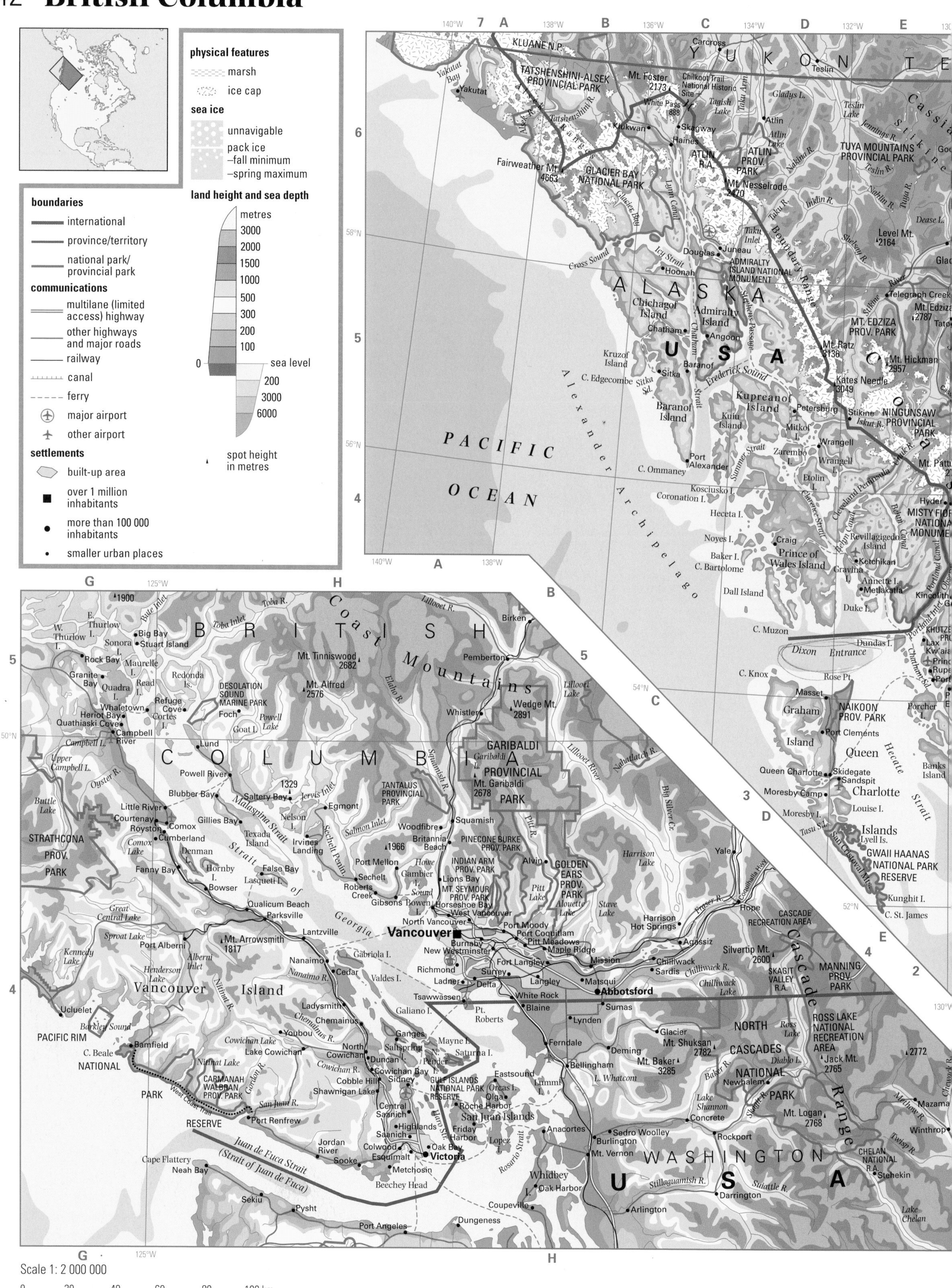
physical features
marsh
ice cap
sea ice
unnavigable
pack ice
–fall minimum
–spring maximum
land height and sea depth
metres
3000
2000
1500
1000
500
300
200
100
0
sea level
200
3000
6000
spot height in metres
boundaries
international
province/territory
national park/ provincial park
communications
multilane (limited access) highway
other highways and major roads
railway
canal
ferry
major airport
other airport
settlements
built-up area
over 1 million inhabitants
more than 100 000 inhabitants
smaller urban places
KLUANE N.P.
Y U K O N T E
TATSHENSHINI-ALSEK PROVINCIAL PARK
Yakutat
Mt. Foster 2173
Chilkoot Trail National Historic Site
White Pass 888
Carcross
Teslin
Atlin
ATLIN PROV. PARK
TUYA MOUNTAINS PROVINCIAL PARK
Skagway
Haines
Klukwan
Fairweather Mt. 4663
GLACIER BAY NATIONAL PARK
Mt. Nesselrode 2470
Juneau
Douglas
Hoonah
ADMIRALTY ISLAND NATIONAL MONUMENT
Boundary Range
Level Mt. 2164
A L A S K A
Chichagof Island
Admiralty Island
Chatham
Angoon
U S A
Kruzof Island
Sitka
Baranof
Baranof Island
C. Edgecombe
Frederick Sound
Kupreanof Island
Petersburg
Mt. Ratz 3136
Kates Needle 3049
Mt. Hickman 2957
Telegraph Creek
Mt. Edziza 2787
MT. EDZIZA PROV. PARK
Stikine
NINGUNSAW PROVINCIAL PARK
Wrangell
PACIFIC OCEAN
Alexander Archipelago
Port Alexander
C. Ommaney
Kosciusko I.
Coronation I.
Heceta I.
Noyes I.
Baker I.
C. Bartolome
Craig
Prince of Wales Island
Dall Island
Ketchikan
Gravina I.
Annette I.
Metlakatla
Duke I.
Kincolith
C. Muzon
Dixon Entrance
Dundas I.
C. Knox
Rose Pt.
Masset
Graham Island
NAIKOON PROV. PARK
Port Clements
Queen Charlotte
Skidegate
Sandspit
Queen Charlotte Islands
Moresby Camp
Moresby I.
Louise I.
Lyell Is.
GWAII HAANAS NATIONAL PARK RESERVE
Kunghit I.
C. St. James
Hecate Strait
Porcher I.
Banks Island
MISTY FIORDS NATIONAL MONUMENT
B R I T I S H C O L U M B I A
Coast Mountains
Mt. Tinniswood 2682
Mt. Alfred 2576
Birken
Pemberton
Whistler
Wedge Mt. 2891
GARIBALDI PROVINCIAL PARK
Mt. Garibaldi 2678
DESOLATION SOUND MARINE PARK
Big Bay
Stuart Island
Sonora I.
Rock Bay
Quadra I.
Campbell River
Quathiaski Cove
Heriot Bay
Whaletown
Refuge Cove
Cortes I.
Lund
Powell River
Saltery Bay
Egmont
TANTALUS PROVINCIAL PARK
Squamish
Woodfibre
Britannia Beach
PINECONE BURKE PROV. PARK
INDIAN ARM PROV. PARK
MT. SEYMOUR PROV. PARK
GOLDEN EARS PROV. PARK
Alvin
Harrison Lake
Yale
Hope
CASCADE RECREATION AREA
Harrison Hot Springs
Agassiz
Chilliwack
Sardis
Silvertip Mt. 2600
SKAGIT VALLEY R.A.
MANNING PROV. PARK
Little River
Courtenay
Comox
Royston
Cumberland
Blubber Bay
Texada Island
Denman I.
Hornby I.
Fanny Bay
Bowser
Lasqueti I.
Sechelt
Roberts Creek
Gibsons
Bowen I.
Port Mellon
Gambier I.
Lions Bay
Horseshoe Bay
West Vancouver
North Vancouver
Vancouver
Burnaby
New Westminster
Port Moody
Port Coquitlam
Pitt Meadows
Maple Ridge
Mission
Fort Langley
Surrey
Langley
Richmond
Ladner
Delta
Tsawwassen
White Rock
Blaine
Pt. Roberts
Matsqui
Abbotsford
Sumas
Lynden
STRATHCONA PROV. PARK
Qualicum Beach
Parksville
Strait of Georgia
Lantzville
Nanaimo
Gabriola I.
Cedar
Valdes I.
Mt. Arrowsmith 1817
Port Alberni
Vancouver Island
Ucluelet
PACIFIC RIM NATIONAL PARK RESERVE
Bamfield
C. Beale
Ladysmith
Chemainus
Youbou
Lake Cowichan
North Cowichan
Duncan
Cowichan Bay
Cobble Hill
Shawnigan Lake
CARMANAH WALBRAN PROV. PARK
Port Renfrew
Galiano I.
Ganges
Saltspring I.
Mayne I.
Saturna I.
GULF ISLANDS NATIONAL PARK RESERVE
Sidney
Central Saanich
Saanich
Highlands
Colwood
Esquimalt
Oak Bay
Victoria
Metchosin
Beechey Head
Sooke
Jordan River
Juan de Fuca Strait (Strait of Juan de Fuca)
Cape Flattery
Neah Bay
Sekiu
Pysht
Port Angeles
Dungeness
San Juan Islands
Friday Harbor
Roche Harbor
Orcas I.
Eastsound
Anacortes
Whidbey I.
Oak Harbor
Coupeville
Ferndale
Bellingham
Deming
Mt. Shuksan 2782
Mt. Baker 3285
Glacier
NORTH CASCADES NATIONAL PARK
ROSS LAKE NATIONAL RECREATION AREA
Jack Mt. 2765
Newhalem
Mt. Logan 2768
Concrete
Rockport
Sedro Woolley
Burlington
Mt. Vernon
W A S H I N G T O N
U S A
Darrington
Arlington
Cascade Range
CHELAN NATIONAL R.A.
Stehekin
Mazama
Winthrop

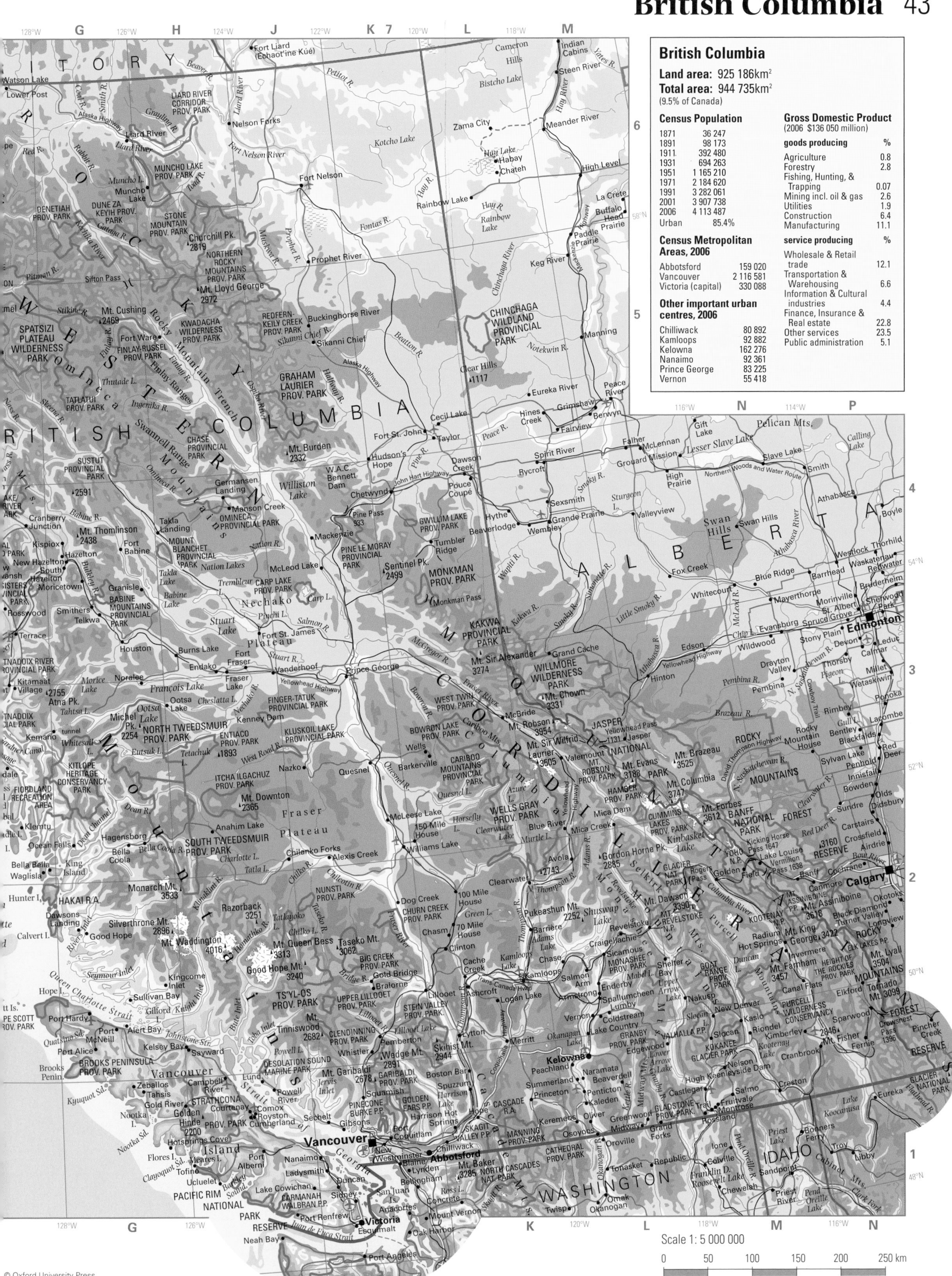

British Columbia

Land area: 925 186km²
Total area: 944 735km²
(9.5% of Canada)

Census Population

Year	Population
1871	36 247
1891	98 173
1911	392 480
1931	694 263
1951	1 165 210
1971	2 184 620
1991	3 282 061
2001	3 907 738
2006	4 113 487
Urban	85.4%

Census Metropolitan Areas, 2006

Abbotsford	159 020
Vancouver	2 116 581
Victoria (capital)	330 088

Other important urban centres, 2006

Chilliwack	80 892
Kamloops	92 882
Kelowna	162 276
Nanaimo	92 361
Prince George	83 225
Vernon	55 418

Gross Domestic Product
(2006 $136 050 million)

goods producing	%
Agriculture	0.8
Forestry	2.8
Fishing, Hunting, & Trapping	0.07
Mining incl. oil & gas	2.6
Utilities	1.9
Construction	6.4
Manufacturing	11.1

service producing	%
Wholesale & Retail trade	12.1
Transportation & Warehousing	6.6
Information & Cultural industries	4.4
Finance, Insurance & Real estate	22.8
Other services	23.5
Public administration	5.1

Vancouver, Calgary

Scale 1: 300 000

0 3 6 9 12 15 km

boundaries
- province
- county/regional municipality/ district

communications
- multilane (limited access) highway
- other highways and major roads
- railway
- canal
- major airport
- other airport

physical features
- river, lake
- marsh
- contours
- spot height in metres

land use
- central business district
- other major commercial areas
- industrial
- residential
- major parks and open spaces
- non-urban

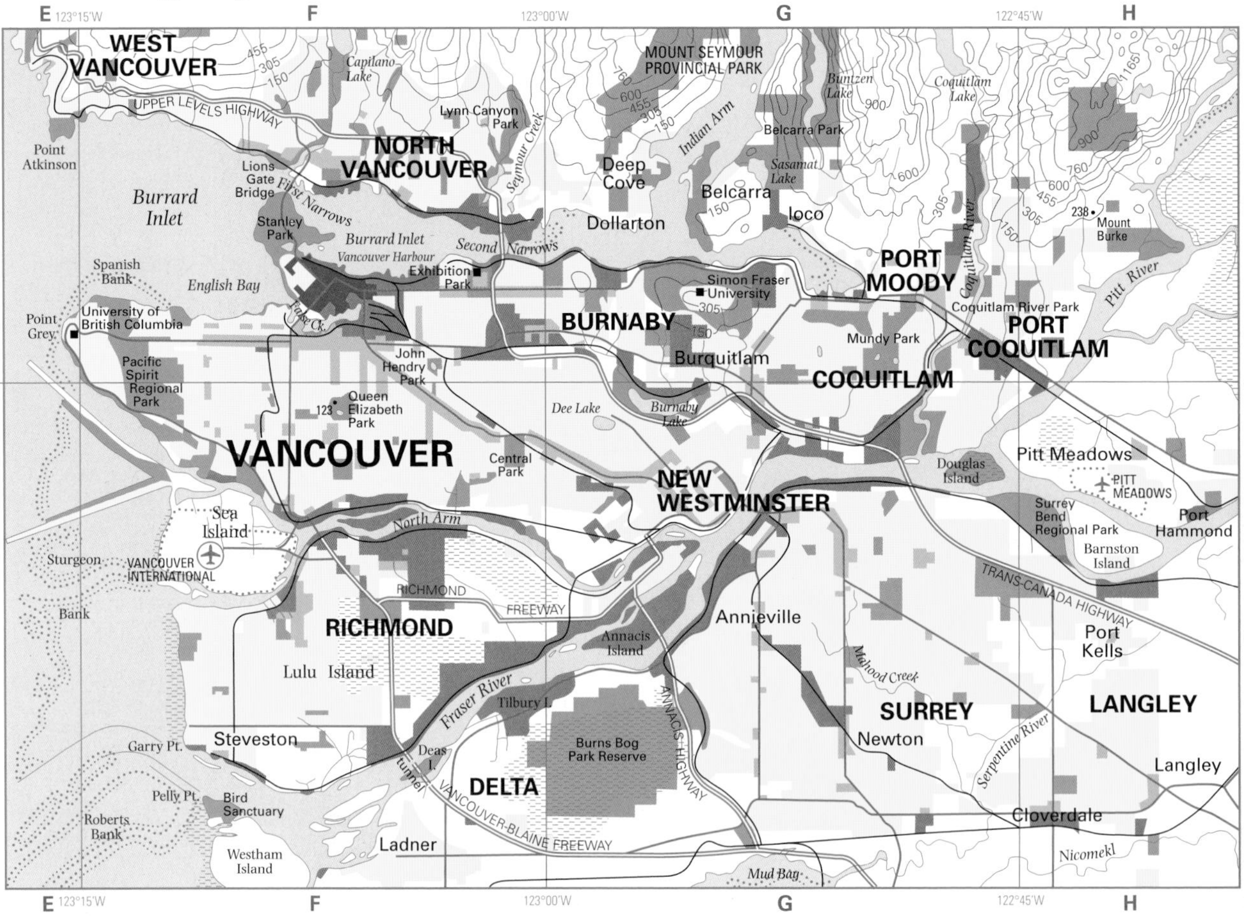

E 123°15'W
F
123°00'W
G
122°45'W
H
4
3
49°15'N
WEST VANCOUVER
Capilano Lake
MOUNT SEYMOUR PROVINCIAL PARK
Buntzen Lake
Coquitlam Lake
UPPER LEVELS HIGHWAY
Lynn Canyon Park
Seymour Creek
Indian Arm
Belcarra Park
NORTH VANCOUVER
Deep Cove
Sasamat Lake
Point Atkinson
Lions Gate Bridge
First Narrows
Burrard Inlet
Belcarra
Ioco
Dollarton
Stanley Park
Burrard Inlet
Vancouver Harbour
Second Narrows
Exhibition Park
PORT MOODY
Coquitlam River
Mount Burke
Pitt River
Spanish Bank
English Bay
Simon Fraser University
Coquitlam River Park
Point Grey
University of British Columbia
False Ck.
BURNABY
PORT COQUITLAM
Mundy Park
Burquitlam
Pacific Spirit Regional Park
John Hendry Park
COQUITLAM
Queen Elizabeth Park
Dee Lake
Burnaby Lake
VANCOUVER
Central Park
Douglas Island
Pitt Meadows
PITT MEADOWS
Sea Island
North Arm
NEW WESTMINSTER
Surrey Bend Regional Park
Port Hammond
Sturgeon
VANCOUVER INTERNATIONAL
RICHMOND
FREEWAY
Barnston Island
Bank
RICHMOND
Annieville
TRANS-CANADA HIGHWAY
Port Kells
Annacis Island
Lulu Island
Fraser River
Mahood Creek
Tilbury I.
SURREY
LANGLEY
Garry Pt.
Steveston
Newton
Serpentine River
Deas I.
Burns Bog Park Reserve
ANNACIS HIGHWAY
Langley
Tunnel
DELTA
Pelly Pt.
Bird Sanctuary
VANCOUVER-BLAINE FREEWAY
Cloverdale
Roberts Bank
Westham Island
Ladner
Nicomekl
Mud Bay

N
B

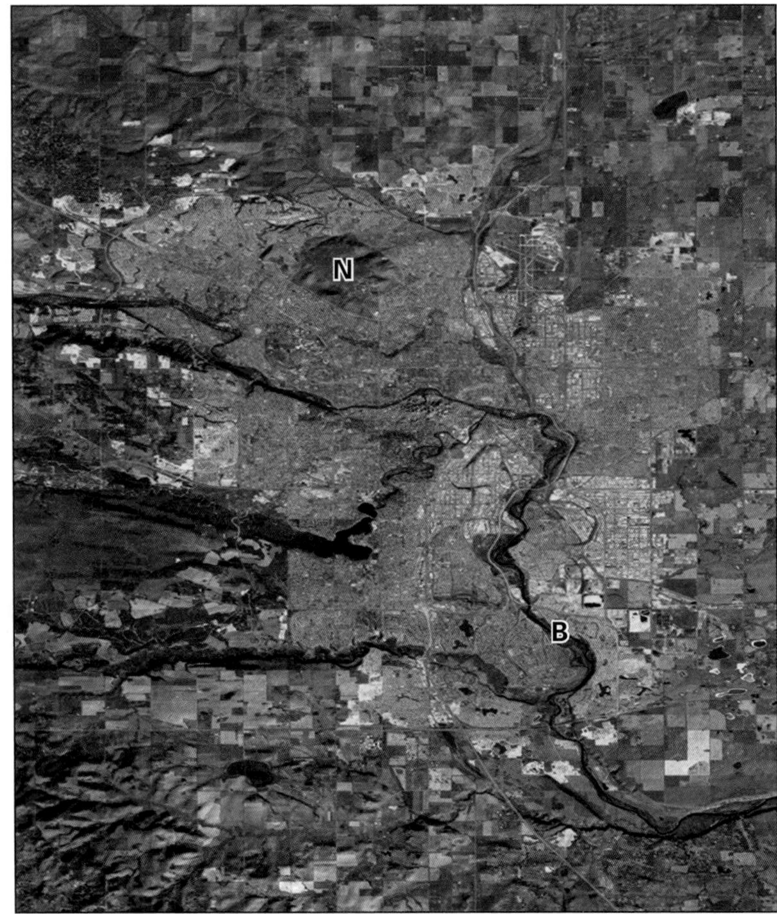

Calgary
In this image of the rapidly expanding city of Calgary, the Bow River (B) and Nose Hill (N) are prominent features.

A
114°00'W
B
2
1
51°00'N
ROCKYVIEW MUNICIPAL DISTRICT
CALGARY CITY
Provincial Correctional Institution
Spyhill Landfill
West Nose Creek
Nose Creek
DEERFOOT TRAIL
STONEY TRAIL
Nose Hill
CALGARY INTERNATIONAL
Bow River
TRANS-CANADA HWY
University of Calgary
TRANS-CANADA HWY
ROCKYVIEW MUNICIPAL DISTRICT
Southern Alberta Institute of Technology
CALGARY
Stampede Park
Elbow River
MACLEOD TRAIL
Sarcee Indian Reserve
Glenmore Reservoir
Canadian Pacific Irrigation Canal
Fish Creek
FISH CREEK PROVINCIAL PARK
FOOTHILLS MUNICIPAL DISTRICT
Lloyd Lake
Bow River

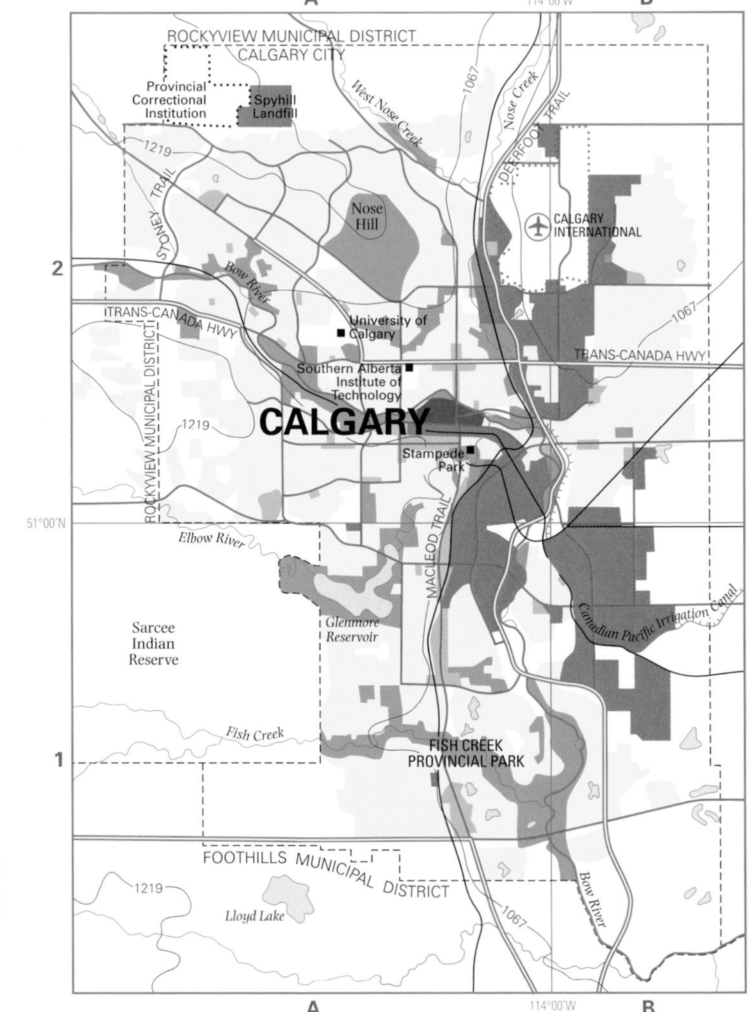

Vancouver

Stanley Park, English Bay, Burrard Inlet, and False Creek (F) surround the central business district of Vancouver.

Victoria

In this image of central Victoria, the Parliament Buildings (P) are visible at the eastern end of Victoria Harbour.

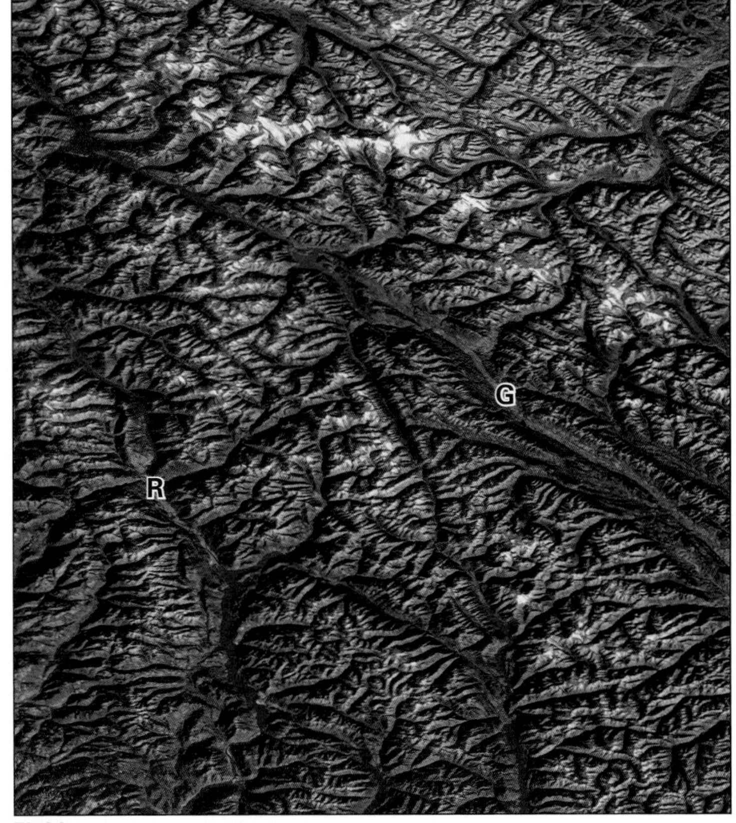

Field

This image shows (from east to west) the Rocky, Purcell, Selkirk, and Monashee Mountains. Golden (G) and Revelstoke (R) are located both on the Columbia River and on the route of the first transcontinental railway.

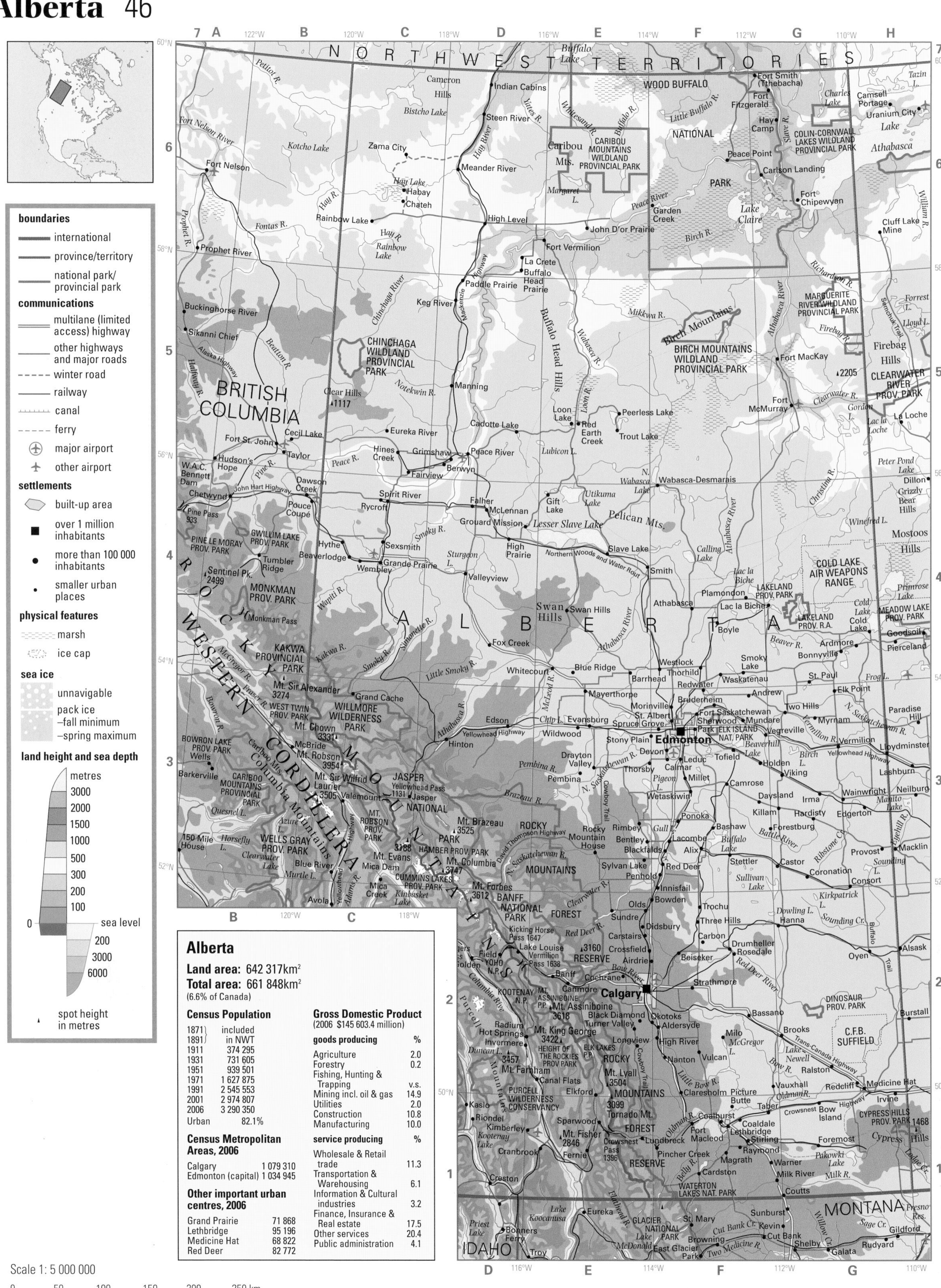

Alberta

Land area: 642 317km²
Total area: 661 848km²
(6.6% of Canada)

Census Population

1871	included in NWT
1891	included in NWT
1911	374 295
1931	731 605
1951	939 501
1971	1 627 875
1991	2 545 553
2001	2 974 807
2006	3 290 350
Urban	82.1%

Census Metropolitan Areas, 2006

Calgary	1 079 310
Edmonton (capital)	1 034 945

Other important urban centres, 2006

Grand Prairie	71 868
Lethbridge	95 196
Medicine Hat	68 822
Red Deer	82 772

Gross Domestic Product
(2006 $145 603.4 million)

goods producing	%
Agriculture	2.0
Forestry	0.2
Fishing, Hunting & Trapping	v.s.
Mining incl. oil & gas	14.9
Utilities	2.0
Construction	10.8
Manufacturing	10.0

service producing	%
Wholesale & Retail trade	11.3
Transportation & Warehousing	6.1
Information & Cultural industries	3.2
Finance, Insurance & Real estate	17.5
Other services	20.4
Public administration	4.1

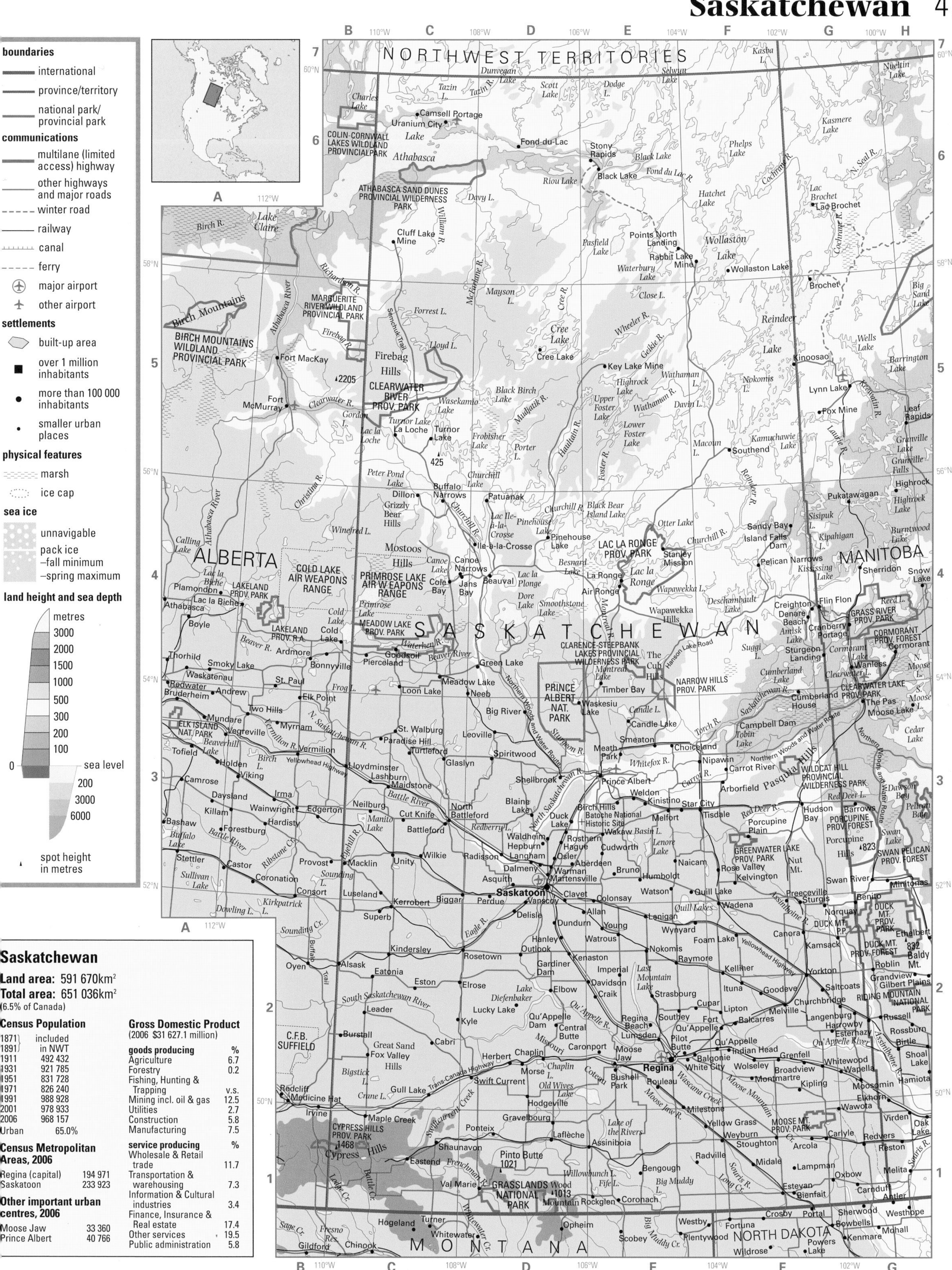

Saskatchewan

Land area: 591 670km²
Total area: 651 036km²
(6.5% of Canada)

Census Population

1871	included
1891	in NWT
1911	492 432
1931	921 785
1951	831 728
1971	926 240
1991	988 928
2001	978 933
2006	968 157
Urban	65.0%

Census Metropolitan Areas, 2006

Regina (capital)	194 971
Saskatoon	233 923

Other important urban centres, 2006

Moose Jaw	33 360
Prince Albert	40 766

Gross Domestic Product
(2006 $31 627.1 million)

goods producing	%
Agriculture	6.7
Forestry	0.2
Fishing, Hunting & Trapping	v.s.
Mining incl. oil & gas	12.5
Utilities	2.7
Construction	5.8
Manufacturing	7.5
service producing	**%**
Wholesale & Retail trade	11.7
Transportation & warehousing	7.3
Information & Cultural industries	3.4
Finance, Insurance & Real estate	17.4
Other services	19.5
Public administration	5.8

ale 1: 5 000 000

0 50 100 150 200 250 km

Central Saskatchewan, Winnipeg

Scale 1: 300 000

0 3 6 9 12 15 km

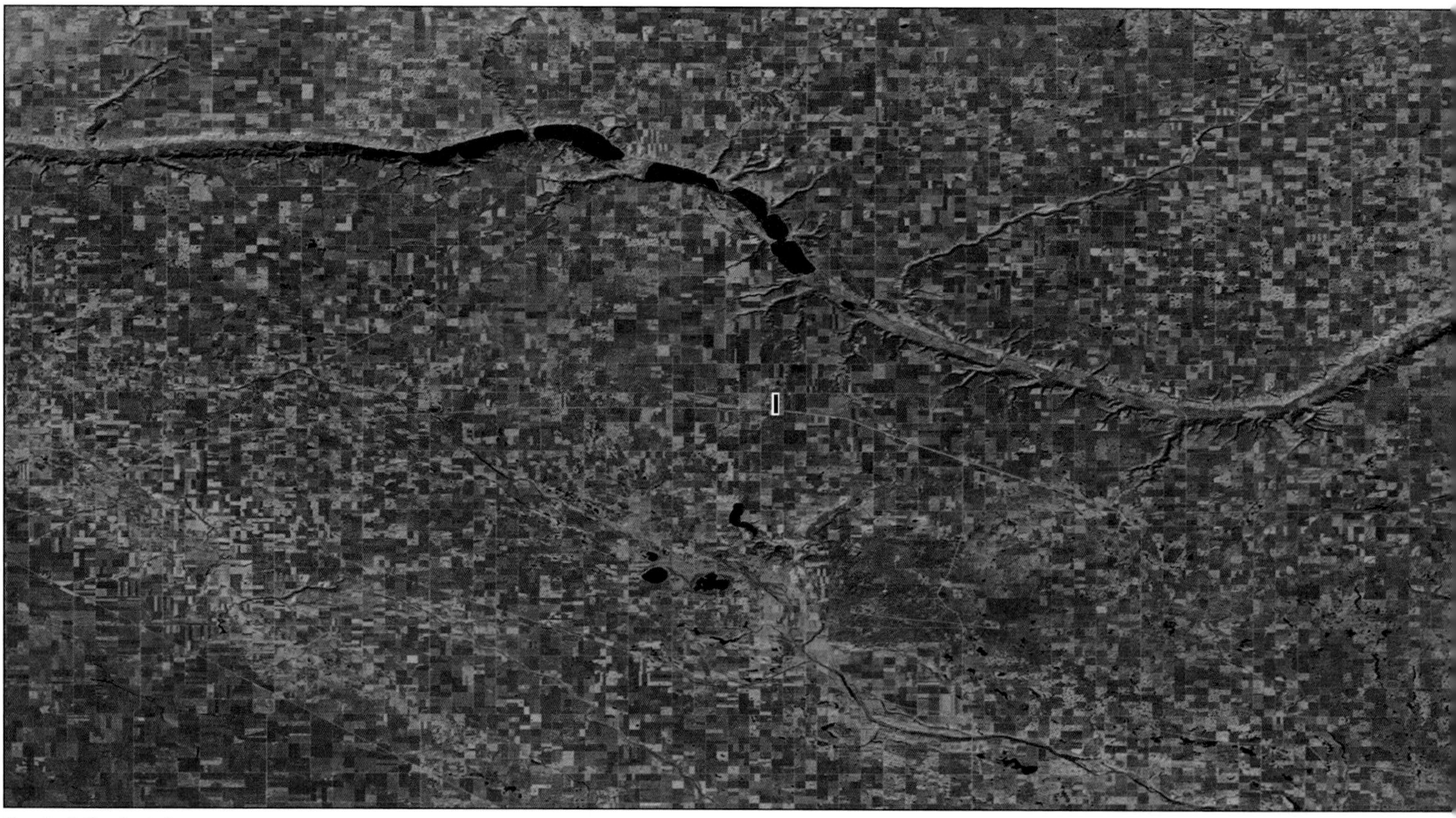

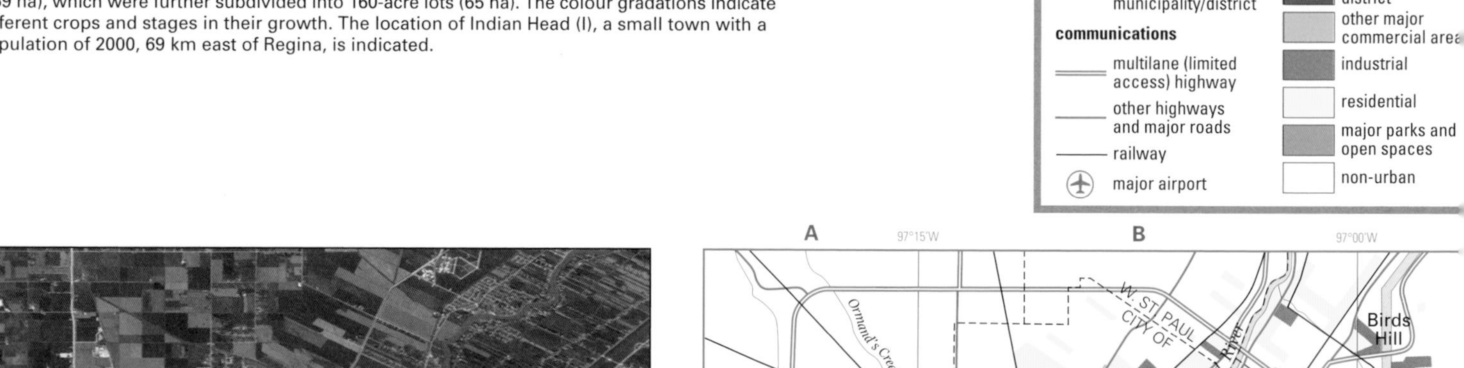

Central Saskatchewan

The image covers a large area of central Saskatchewan east of Regina, with the Qu'Appelle River in the north. The pattern of squares illustrates the division of these lands, beginning in 1872, into square townships of 36 square miles (93.2 km²) consisting of 36 sections of 640 acres each (259 ha), which were further subdivided into 160-acre lots (65 ha). The colour gradations indicate different crops and stages in their growth. The location of Indian Head (I), a small town with a population of 2000, 69 km east of Regina, is indicated.

boundaries

- county/regional municipality/district

communications

- multilane (limited access) highway
- other highways and major roads
- railway
- major airport

land use

- central business district
- other major commercial area
- industrial
- residential
- major parks and open spaces
- non-urban

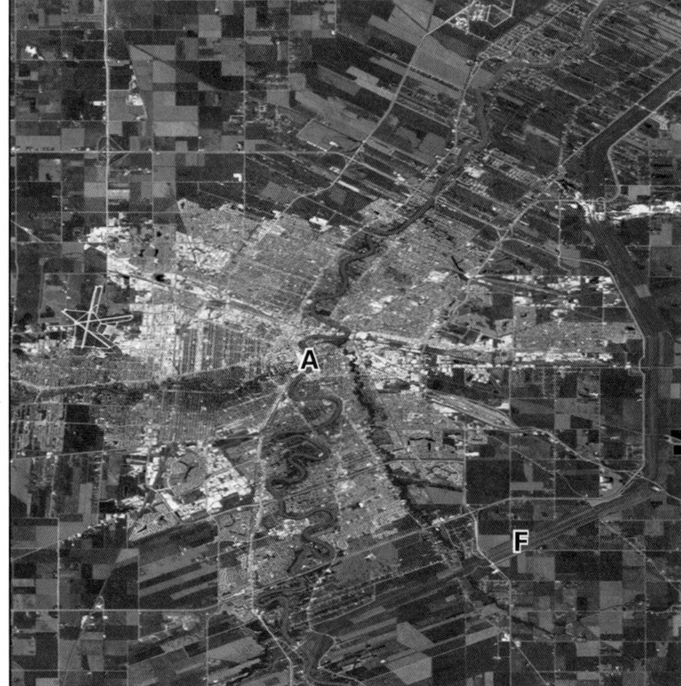

Winnipeg

Winnipeg was first established near the junction of the Red and Assiniboine Rivers (A). This image includes almost the entire built-up area of the city. The airport is shown in the northwest and the Winnipeg Floodway (F) is apparent in the southeast.

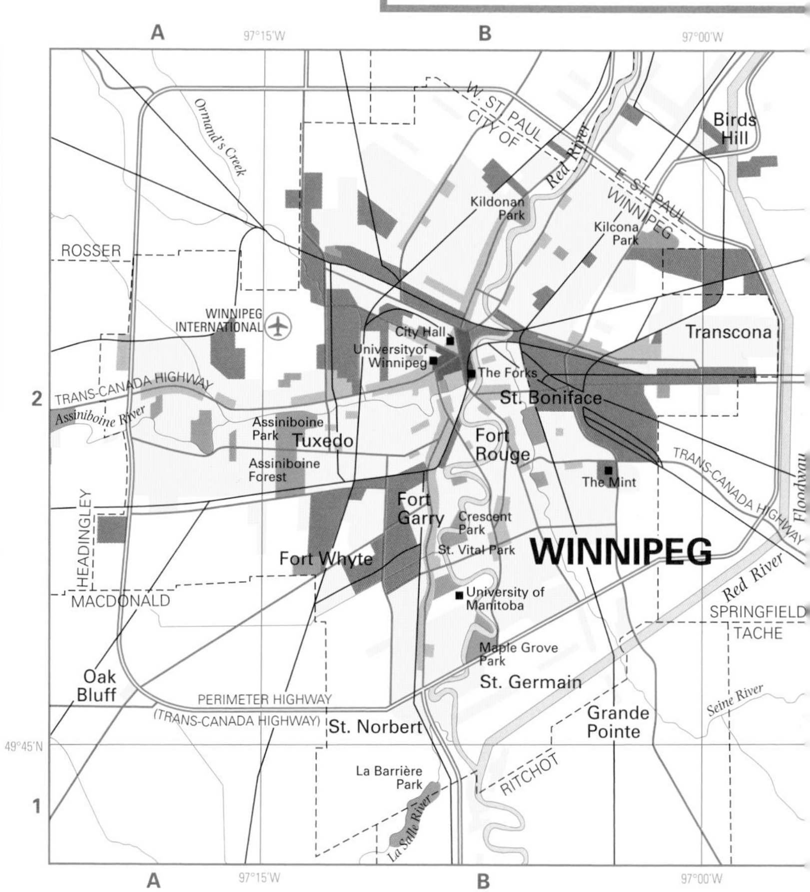

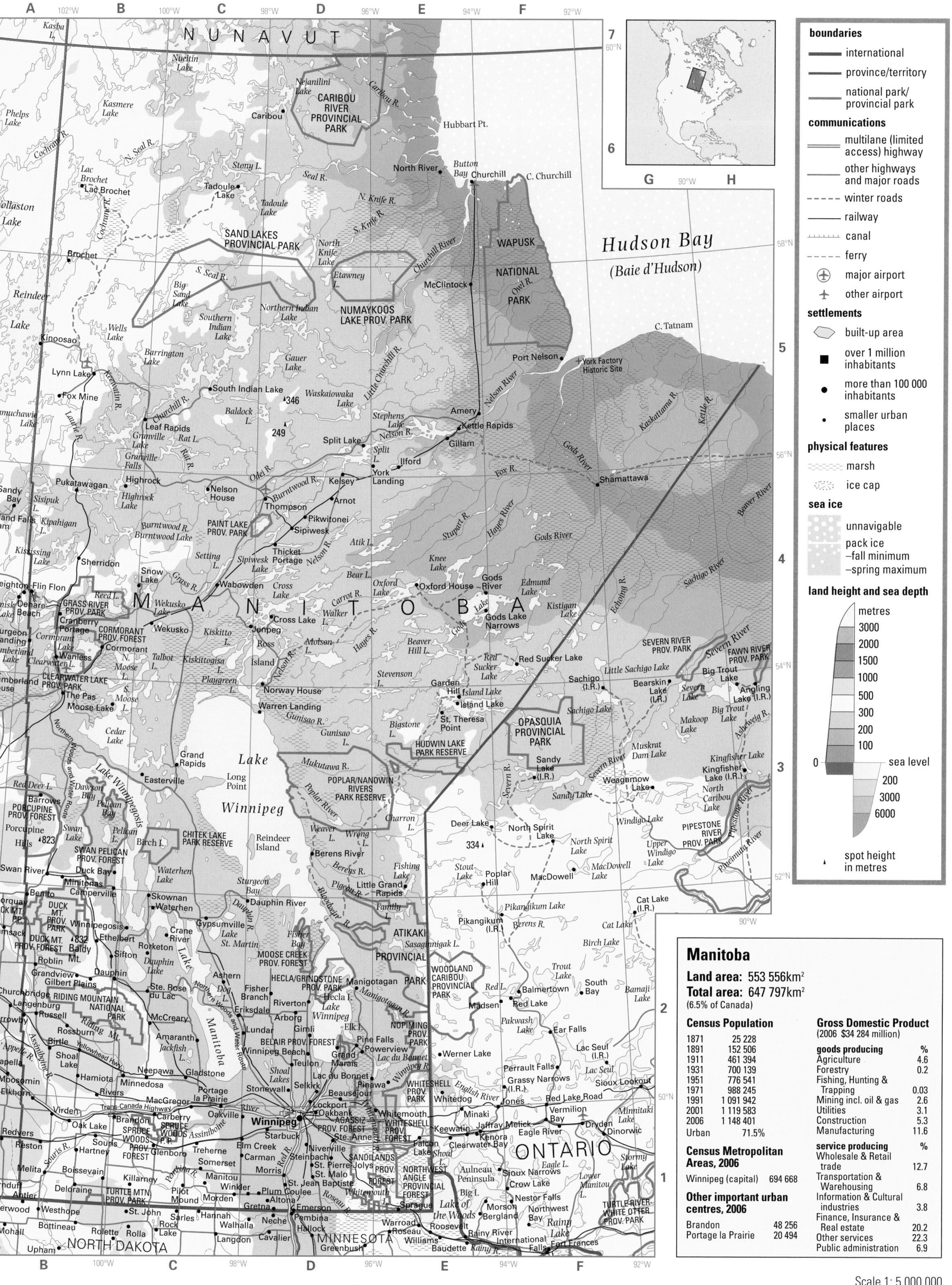

Manitoba

Land area: 553 556km^2

Total area: 647 797km^2

(6.5% of Canada)

Census Population

1871	25 228
1891	152 506
1911	461 394
1931	700 139
1951	776 541
1971	988 245
1991	1 091 942
2001	1 119 583
2006	1 148 401
Urban	71.5%

Census Metropolitan Areas, 2006

Winnipeg (capital)	694 668

Other important urban centres, 2006

Brandon	48 256
Portage la Prairie	20 494

Gross Domestic Product

(2006 $34 284 million)

goods producing	**%**
Agriculture	4.6
Forestry	0.2
Fishing, Hunting & Trapping	0.03
Mining incl. oil & gas	2.6
Utilities	3.1
Construction	5.3
Manufacturing	11.6
service producing	**%**
Wholesale & Retail trade	12.7
Transportation & Warehousing	6.8
Information & Cultural industries	3.8
Finance, Insurance & Real estate	20.2
Other services	22.3
Public administration	6.9

Scale 1: 5 000 000

0 50 100 150 200 250 km

 Conical Orthomorphic Projection

Conical Orthomorphic Projection © Oxford University Press

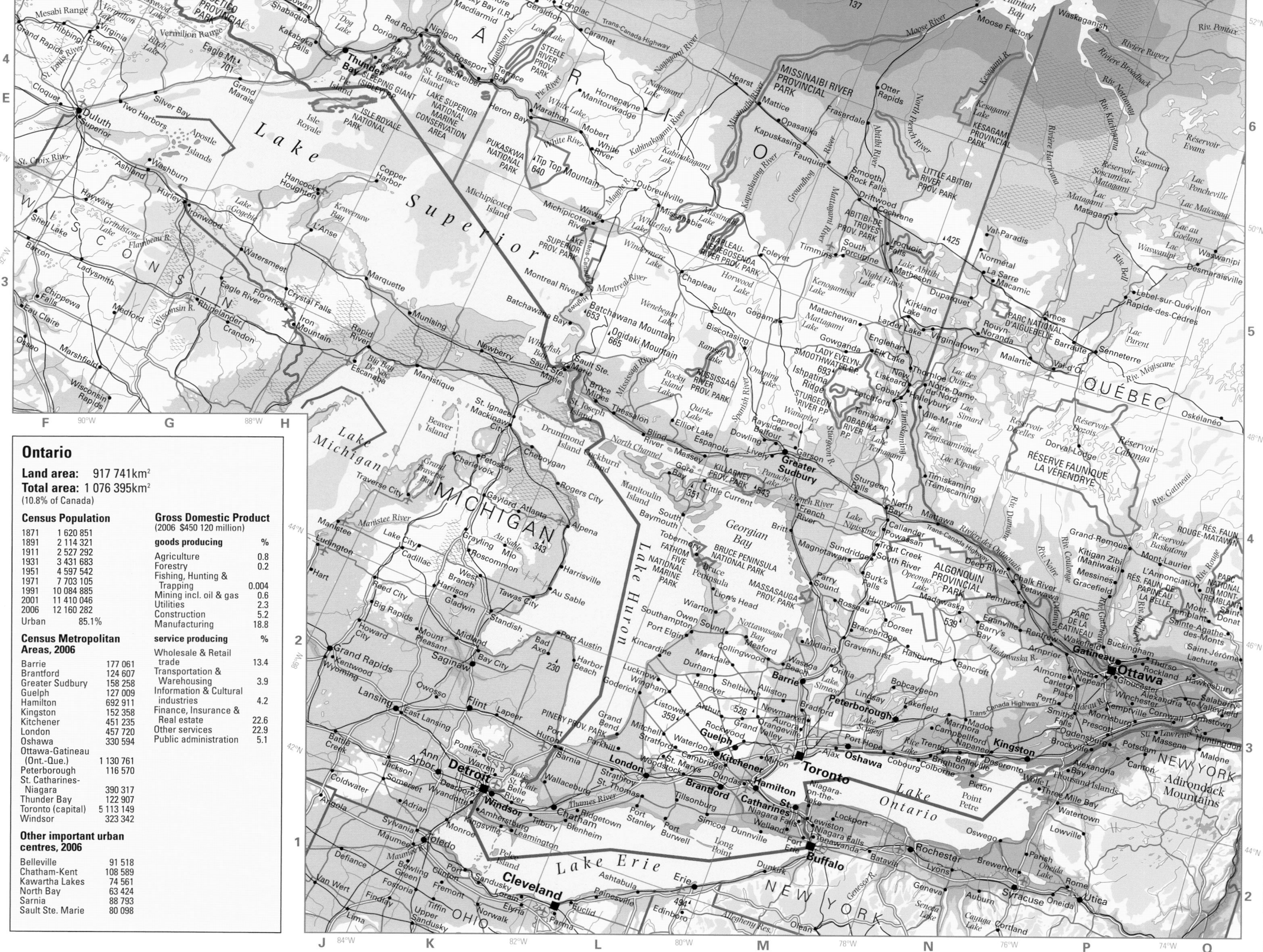

Ontario

Land area: 917 741km²
Total area: 1 076 395km²
(10.8% of Canada)

Census Population

Year	Population
1871	1 620 851
1891	2 114 321
1911	2 527 292
1931	3 431 683
1951	4 597 542
1971	7 703 105
1991	10 084 885
2001	11 410 046
2006	12 160 282
Urban	85.1%

Census Metropolitan Areas, 2006

Barrie	177 061
Brantford	124 607
Greater Sudbury	158 258
Guelph	127 009
Hamilton	692 911
Kingston	152 358
Kitchener	451 235
London	457 720
Oshawa	330 594
Ottawa-Gatineau (Ont.-Que.)	1 130 761
Peterborough	116 570
St. Catharines-Niagara	390 317
Thunder Bay	122 907
Toronto (capital)	5 113 149
Windsor	323 342

Other important urban centres, 2006

Belleville	91 518
Chatham-Kent	108 589
Kawartha Lakes	74 561
North Bay	63 424
Sarnia	88 793
Sault Ste. Marie	80 098

Gross Domestic Product

(2006 $450 120 million)

goods producing	%
Agriculture	0.8
Forestry	0.2
Fishing, Hunting & Trapping	0.004
Mining incl. oil & gas	0.6
Utilities	2.3
Construction	5.2
Manufacturing	18.8
service producing	**%**
Wholesale & Retail trade	13.4
Transportation & Warehousing	3.9
Information & Cultural industries	4.2
Finance, Insurance & Real estate	22.6
Other services	22.9
Public administration	5.1

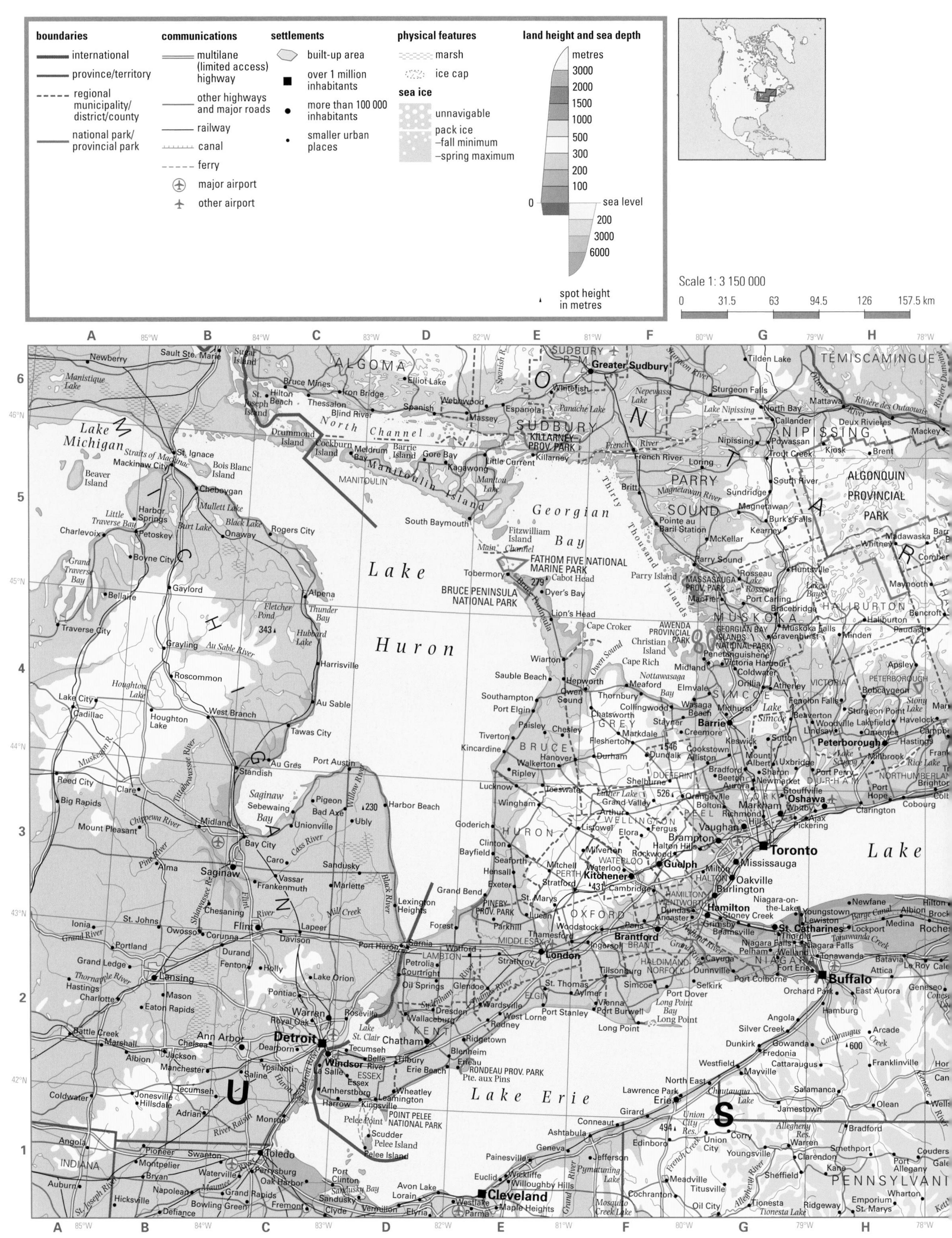
boundaries
international
province/territory
regional municipality/ district/county
national park/ provincial park
communications
multilane (limited access) highway
other highways and major roads
railway
canal
ferry
major airport
other airport
settlements
built-up area
over 1 million inhabitants
more than 100 000 inhabitants
smaller urban places
physical features
marsh
ice cap
sea ice
unnavigable
pack ice
–fall minimum
–spring maximum
land height and sea depth
metres
3000
2000
1500
1000
500
300
200
100
0
sea level
200
3000
6000
spot height in metres
Scale 1: 3 150 000
0
31.5
63
94.5
126
157.5 km
A
B
C
D
E
F
G
H
85°W
84°W
83°W
82°W
81°W
80°W
79°W
78°W
46°N
45°N
44°N
43°N
42°N
6
5
4
3
2
1
Lake Michigan
Lake Huron
Georgian Bay
North Channel
Manitoulin Island
Lake Erie
Lake St. Clair
Saginaw Bay
ALGOMA
SUDBURY
NIPISSING
PARRY SOUND
MUSKOKA
HALIBURTON
SIMCOE
GREY
BRUCE
HURON
PERTH
WELLINGTON
WATERLOO
DUFFERIN
PEEL
YORK
DURHAM
VICTORIA
PETERBOROUGH
NORTHUMBERLAND
OXFORD
MIDDLESEX
ELGIN
LAMBTON
KENT
ESSEX
BRANT
HALDIMAND
NORFOLK
NIAGARA
HAMILTON WENTWORTH
HALTON
MANITOULIN
TEMISCAMINGUE
ONTARIO
MICHIGAN
INDIANA
PENNSYLVANIA
U S
ALGONQUIN PROVINCIAL PARK
FATHOM FIVE NATIONAL MARINE PARK
BRUCE PENINSULA NATIONAL PARK
GEORGIAN BAY ISLANDS NATIONAL PARK
KILLARNEY PROV. PARK
MASSASAUGA PROV. PARK
AWENDA PROVINCIAL PARK
PINERY PROV. PARK
RONDEAU PROV. PARK
POINT PELEE NATIONAL PARK
Greater Sudbury
Sault Ste. Marie
Toronto
Mississauga
Detroit
Windsor
Cleveland
Buffalo
Hamilton
London
Kitchener
Guelph
Oshawa
Barrie
Peterborough
St. Catharines
Brantford
Vaughan
Brampton
Oakville
Burlington
Markham
Saginaw
Flint
Lansing
Toledo
Ann Arbor
Sarnia
Chatham
Erie
Owen Sound
Orillia
North Bay
Huntsville
Conical Orthomorphic Projection
© Oxford University Press

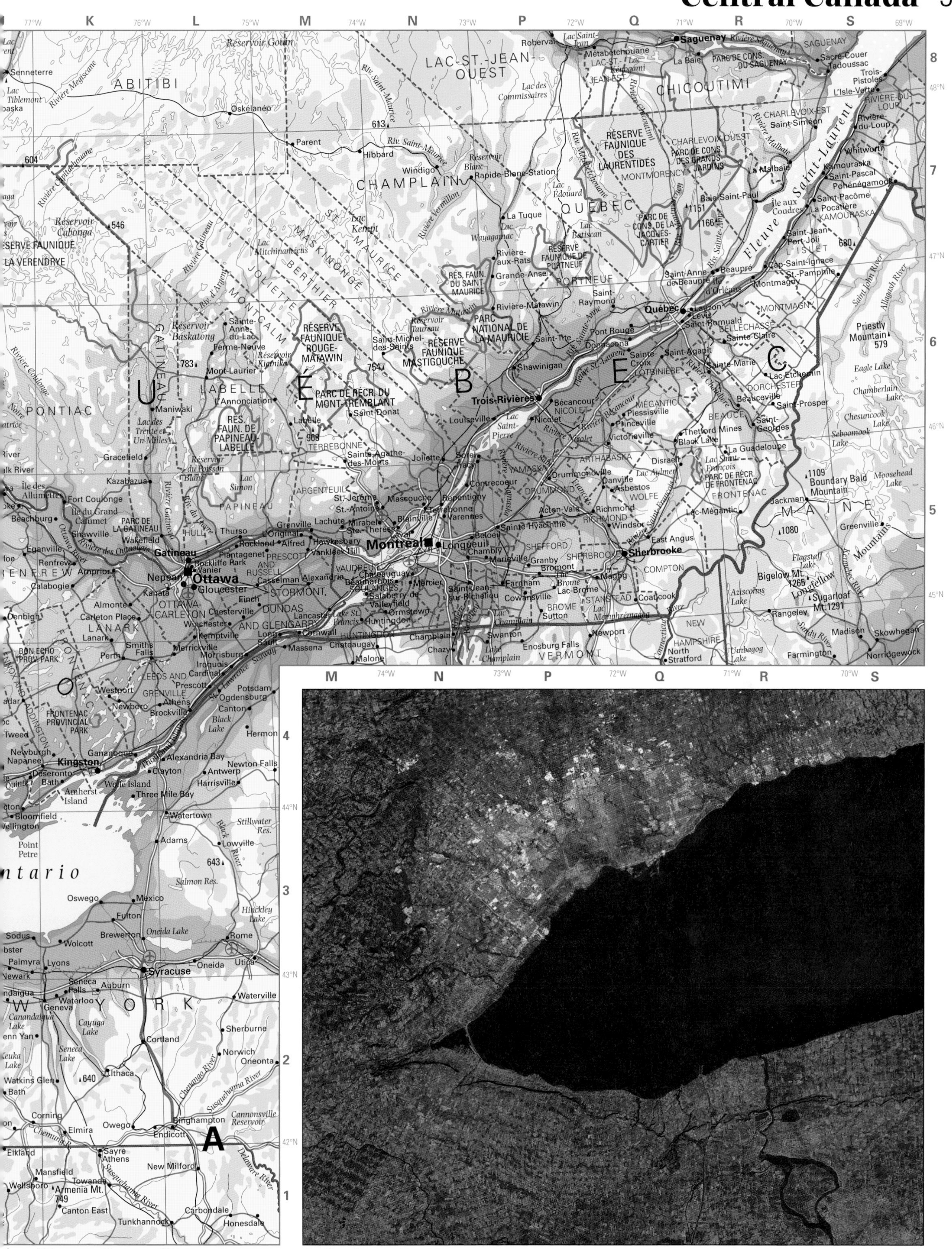

Golden Horseshoe

The Golden Horseshoe extends from Niagara Falls through Hamilton and Toronto, to Oshawa in the east. The Niagara River, separating Canada and the United States, and the Niagara Escarpment are clearly defined south of Lake Ontario.

Central Ontario

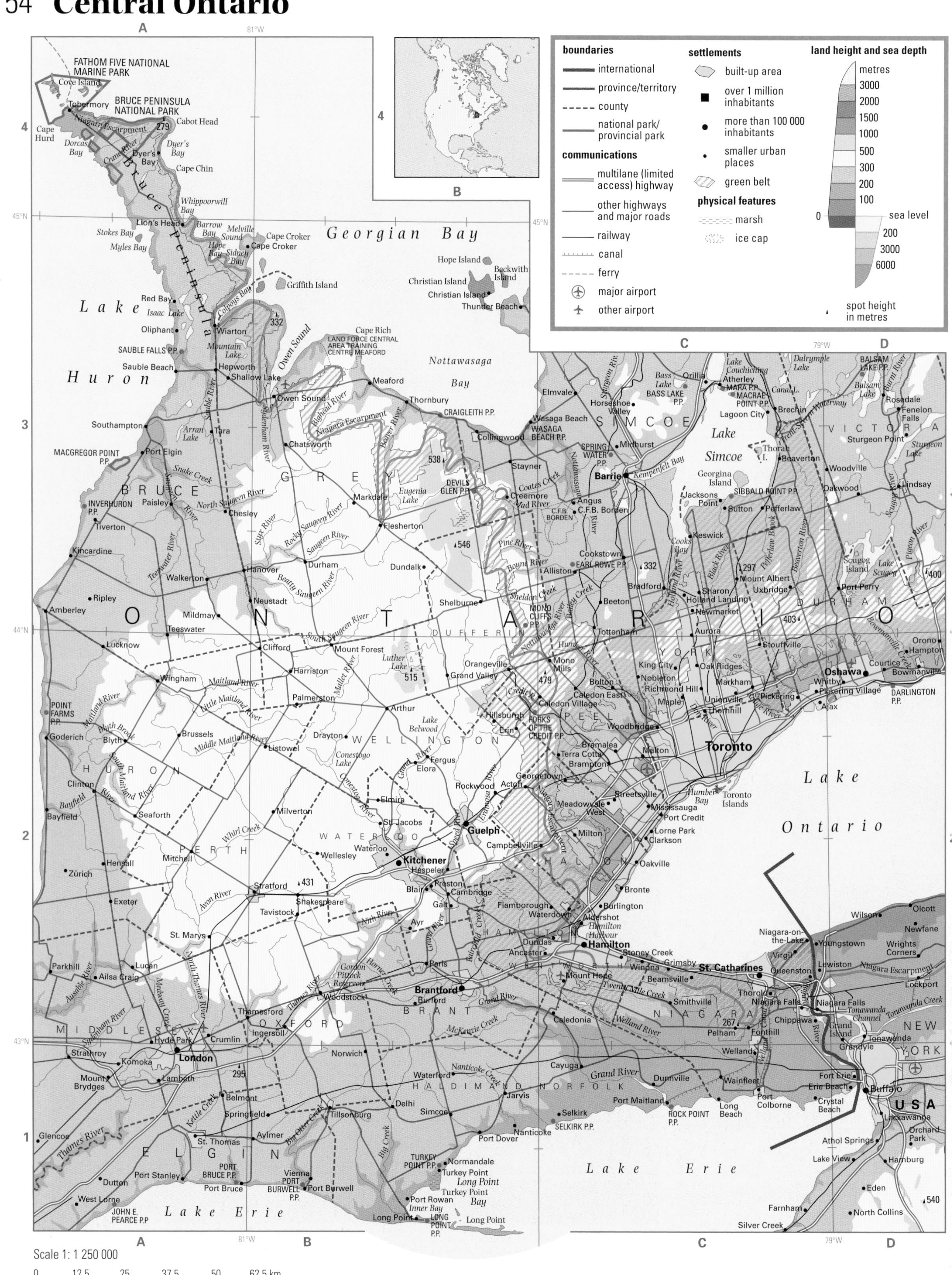

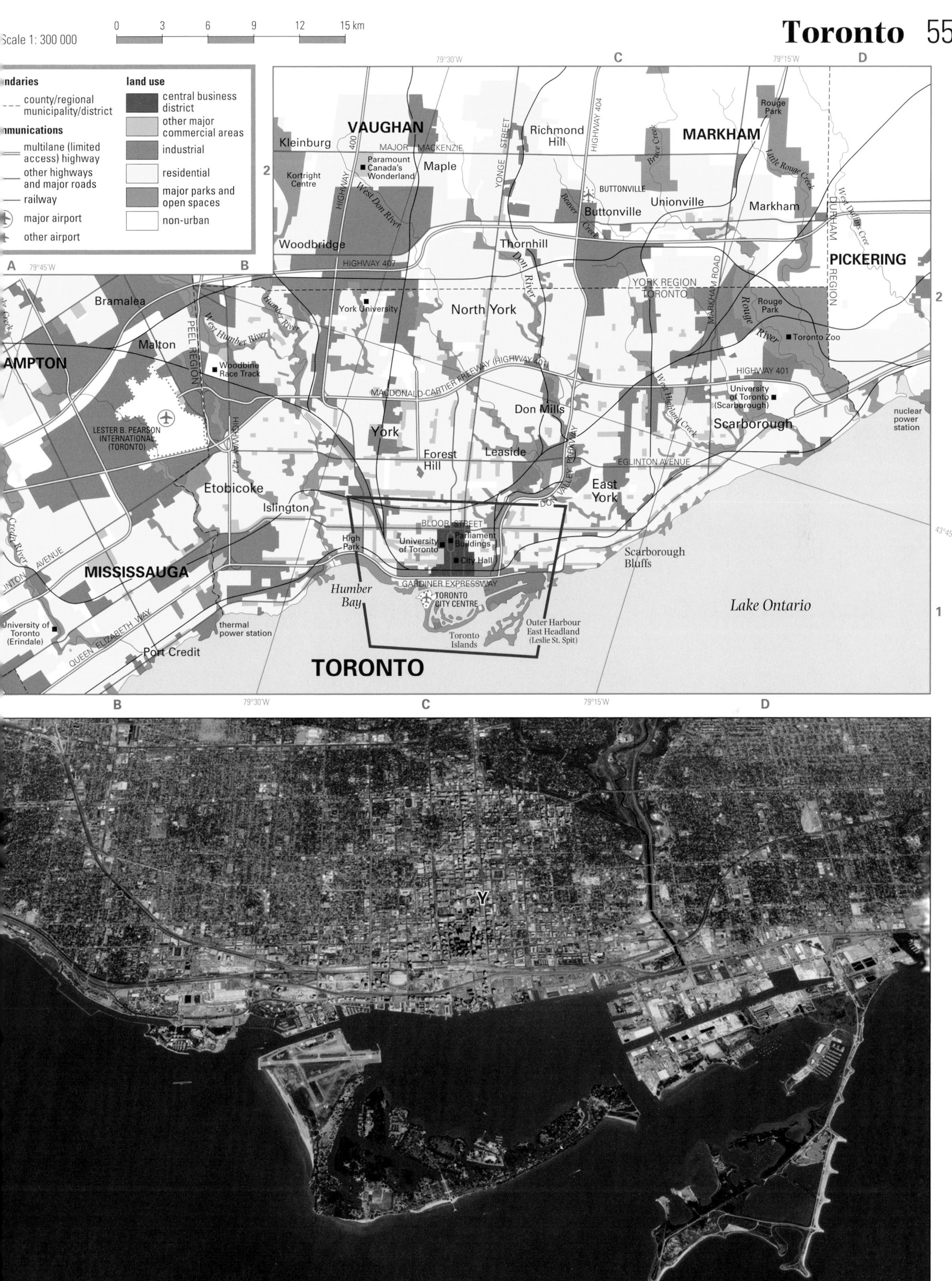
Scale 1: 300 000
0 3 6 9 12 15 km
ndaries
county/regional municipality/district
land use
central business district
other major commercial areas
industrial
residential
major parks and open spaces
non-urban
nmunications
multilane (limited access) highway
other highways and major roads
railway
major airport
other airport
VAUGHAN
Kleinburg
Kortright Centre
Paramount Canada's Wonderland
Maple
Richmond Hill
MARKHAM
Rouge Park
BUTTONVILLE
Buttonville
Unionville
Markham
PICKERING
Woodbridge
Thornhill
HIGHWAY 407
YORK REGION
TORONTO
DURHAM REGION
Bramalea
York University
North York
Rouge Park
Toronto Zoo
Malton
AMPTON
Woodbine Race Track
MACDONALD-CARTIER FREEWAY (HIGHWAY 401)
HIGHWAY 401
University of Toronto (Scarborough)
LESTER B. PEARSON INTERNATIONAL (TORONTO)
York
Don Mills
Scarborough
nuclear power station
Forest Hill
Leaside
EGLINTON AVENUE
Etobicoke
East York
Islington
BLOOR STREET
High Park
University of Toronto
Parliament Buildings
City Hall
Scarborough Bluffs
MISSISSAUGA
GARDINER EXPRESSWAY
Humber Bay
TORONTO CITY CENTRE
Lake Ontario
University of Toronto (Erindale)
thermal power station
Toronto Islands
Outer Harbour East Headland (Leslie St. Spit)
Port Credit
QUEEN ELIZABETH WAY
TORONTO
Y

onto Central Toronto is divided by Yonge Street (Y), which was constructed shortly after the founding of York (Toronto) in 1793.

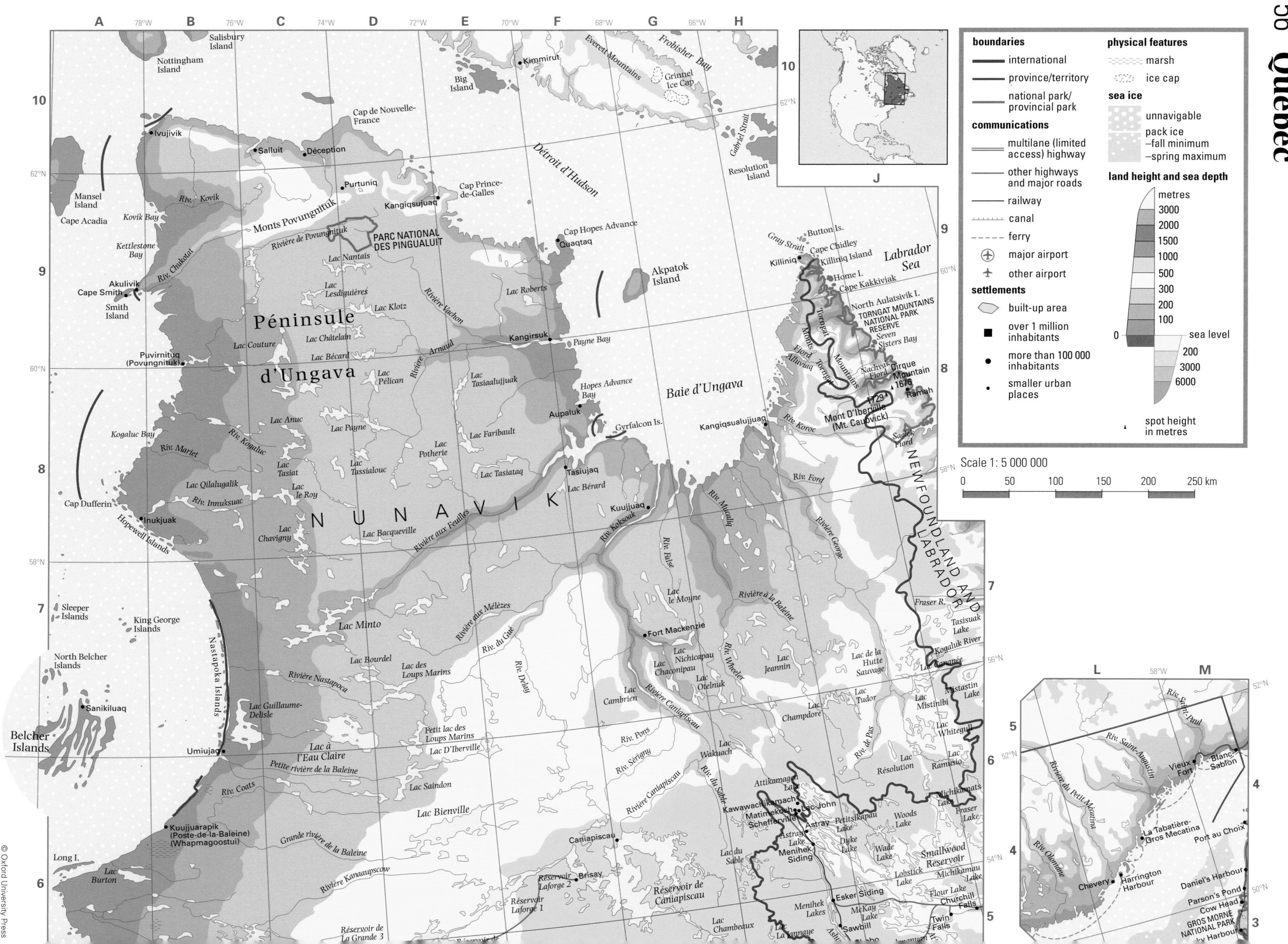

boundaries
international
province/territory
national park/provincial park
communications
multilane (limited access) highway
other highways and major roads
railway
canal
ferry
major airport
other airport
settlements
built-up area
over 1 million inhabitants
more than 100 000 inhabitants
smaller urban places
physical features
marsh
ice cap
sea ice
unnavigable
pack ice –fall minimum –spring maximum
land height and sea depth
metres
3000
2000
1500
1000
500
300
200
100
0
sea level
200
3000
6000
spot height in metres
Scale 1: 5 000 000
0
50
100
150
200
250 km
NUNAVIK
NEWFOUNDLAND AND LABRADOR
Péninsule d'Ungava
Baie d'Ungava
Détroit d'Hudson
Labrador Sea
Frobisher Bay
Gabriel Strait
Resolution Island
Akpatok Island
Grinnell Ice Cap
Everett Mountains
Kimmirut
Big Island
Salisbury Island
Nottingham Island
Mansel Island
Cape Acadia
Ivujivik
Salluit
Déception
Purtuniq
Cap de Nouvelle-France
Kangiqsujuaq
Cap Prince-de-Galles
PARC NATIONAL DES PINGUALUIT
Quaqtaq
Cap Hopes Advance
Kangirsuk
Payne Bay
Aupaluk
Hopes Advance Bay
Tasiujaq
Gyrfalcon Is.
Kuujjuaq
Kangiqsualujjuaq
Killiniq
Killiniq Island
Cape Chidley
Button Is.
Gray Strait
Home I.
Cape Kakkiviak
North Aulatsivik I.
TORNGAT MOUNTAINS NATIONAL PARK RESERVE
Seven Sisters Bay
Nachvak Fiord
Cirque Mountain
1676
Ramah
1729
Mont D'Iberville (Mt. Caubvick)
Saglek Fiord
Monts Torngat
Torngat Mountains
Fjord Alluviaq
Monts Povungnituk
Akulivik
Cape Smith
Smith Island
Kovik Bay
Kettlestone Bay
Puvirnituq (Povungnituk)
Kogaluc Bay
Inukjuak
Hopewell Islands
Cap Dufferin
King George Islands
Sleeper Islands
North Belcher Islands
Belcher Islands
Sanikiluaq
Nastapoka Islands
Umiujaq
Kuujjuarapik (Poste-de-la-Baleine) (Whapmagoostui)
Long I.
Lac Burton
Lac Guillaume-Delisle
Lac à l'Eau Claire
Lac Minto
Lac Bienville
Lac Saindon
Lac D'Iberville
Petit lac des Loups Marins
Lac des Loups Marins
Lac Bourdel
Lac Nantais
Lac Lesdiguières
Lac Klotz
Lac Pélican
Lac Payne
Lac Tasiaalujjuak
Lac Tasiataq
Lac Faribault
Lac Roberts
Lac Bérard
Lac Potherie
Lac Chavigny
Lac Anuc
Lac Couture
Lac Châtelain
Lac Tassialouc
Lac Bacqueville
Lac Qilalugalik
Lac le Roy
Lac Tasiat
Rivière Vachon
Rivière Arnaud
Rivière aux Feuilles
Rivière aux Mélèzes
Riv. Kogaluc
Riv. Kovik
Riv. Chukotat
Riv. Mariet
Riv. Innuksuac
Rivière de Povungnituk
Rivière Nastapoca
Petite rivière de la Baleine
Grande rivière de la Baleine
Riv. Coats
Riv. du Gué
Riv. Delay
Riv. Koksoak
Rivière Caniapiscau
Réservoir de Caniapiscau
Caniapiscau
Brisay
Réservoir Laforge 2
Réservoir Laforge 1
Réservoir de La Grande 3
Rivière Kanaaupscow
Lac Chambeaux
Lac du Sable
Riv. du Sable
Lac Cambrien
Riv. Pons
Riv. Sérigny
Fort Mackenzie
Lac le Moyne
Lac Nichicapau
Lac Chaconipau
Lac Otelnuk
Lac Wakuach
Riv. Wheeler
Riv. False
Riv. Mucalic
Rivière à la Baleine
Lac Jeannin
Lac Champdore
Lac Tudor
Lac de la Hutte Sauvage
Rivière George
Riv. Ford
Riv. Koroc
Riv. de Pas
Lac Résolution
Lac Ramusio
Fraser R.
Tasisuak Lake
Kogaluk River
Mistastin Lake
Lac Mistinibi
Lac Whitegull
Michikamats Lake
Fraser Lake
Woods Lake
Wade Lake
Dyke Lake
Petitsikapau Lake
Smallwood Reservoir
Michikamau Lake
Schefferville
Kawawachikamach
Matimekosh
Lac John
Astray
Astray Lake
Attikamagen Lake
Menihek Lakes
Menihek Siding
Esker Siding
McKay Lake
Sawbill
Churchill Falls
Twin Falls
Lobstick Lake
Flour Lake
Rivière Saint-Paul
Riv. Saint-Augustin
Rivière du Petit Mécatina
Riv. Olomane
Blanc-Sablon
Vieux Fort
La Tabatière-Gros Mecatina
Harrington Harbour
Chevery
Port au Choix
Daniel's Harbour
Parson's Pond
Cow Head
GROS MORNE NATIONAL PARK

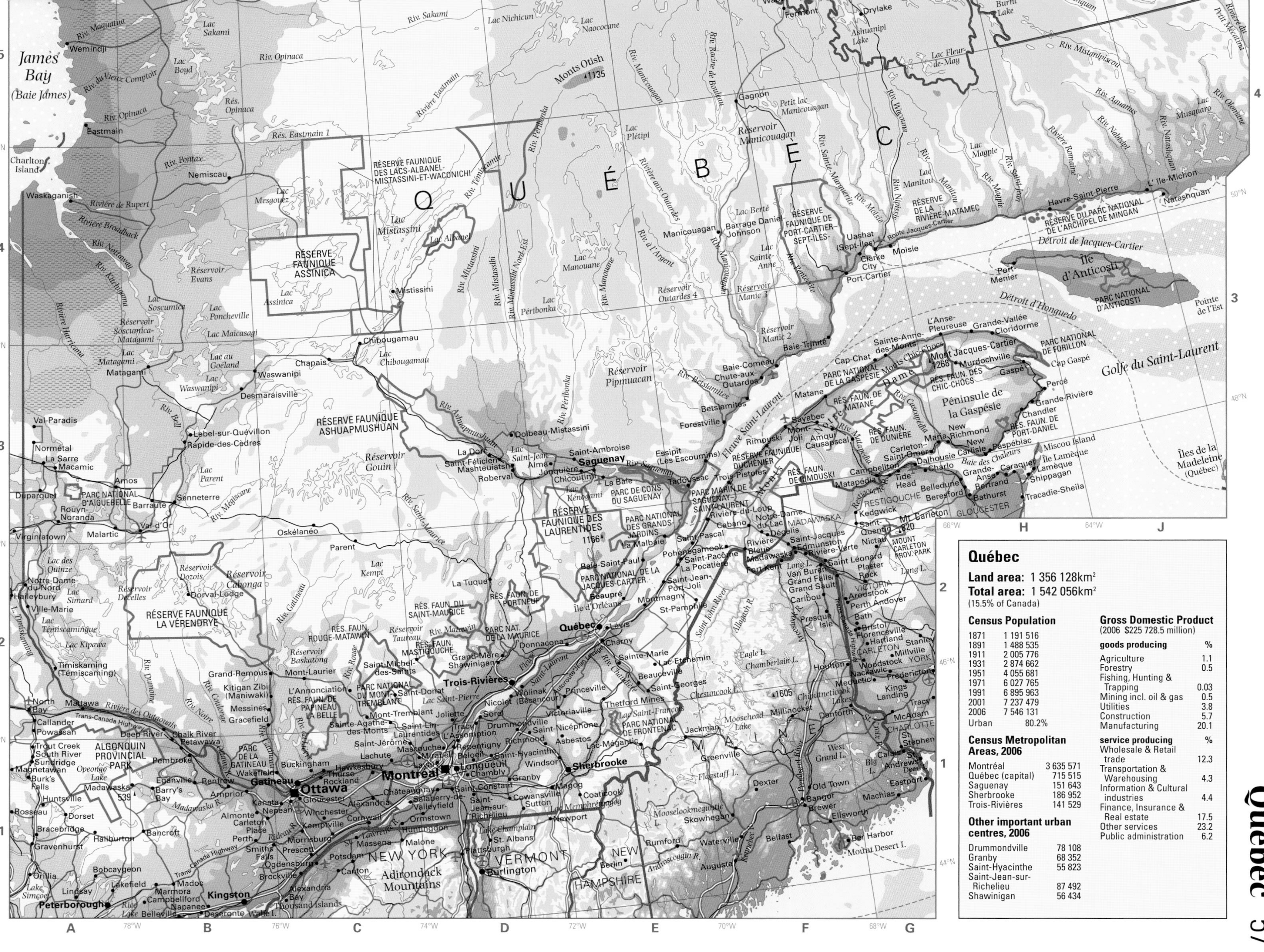

Québec

Land area: 1 356 128km²
Total area: 1 542 056km²
(15.5% of Canada)

Census Population

1871	1 191 516
1891	1 488 535
1911	2 005 776
1931	2 874 662
1951	4 055 681
1971	6 027 765
1991	6 895 963
2001	7 237 479
2006	7 546 131
Urban	80.2%

Census Metropolitan Areas, 2006

Montréal	3 635 571
Québec (capital)	715 515
Saguenay	151 643
Sherbrooke	186 952
Trois-Rivières	141 529

Other important urban centres, 2006

Drummondville	78 108
Granby	68 352
Saint-Hyacinthe	55 823
Saint-Jean-sur-Richelieu	87 492
Shawinigan	56 434

Gross Domestic Product
(2006 $225 728.5 million)

goods producing	%
Agriculture	1.1
Forestry	0.5
Fishing, Hunting & Trapping	0.03
Mining incl. oil & gas	0.5
Utilities	3.8
Construction	5.7
Manufacturing	20.1
service producing	**%**
Wholesale & Retail trade	12.3
Transportation & Warehousing	4.3
Information & Cultural industries	4.4
Finance, Insurance & Real estate	17.5
Other services	23.2
Public administration	6.2

 Conical Orthomorphic Projection

Montréal

Scale 1: 300 000

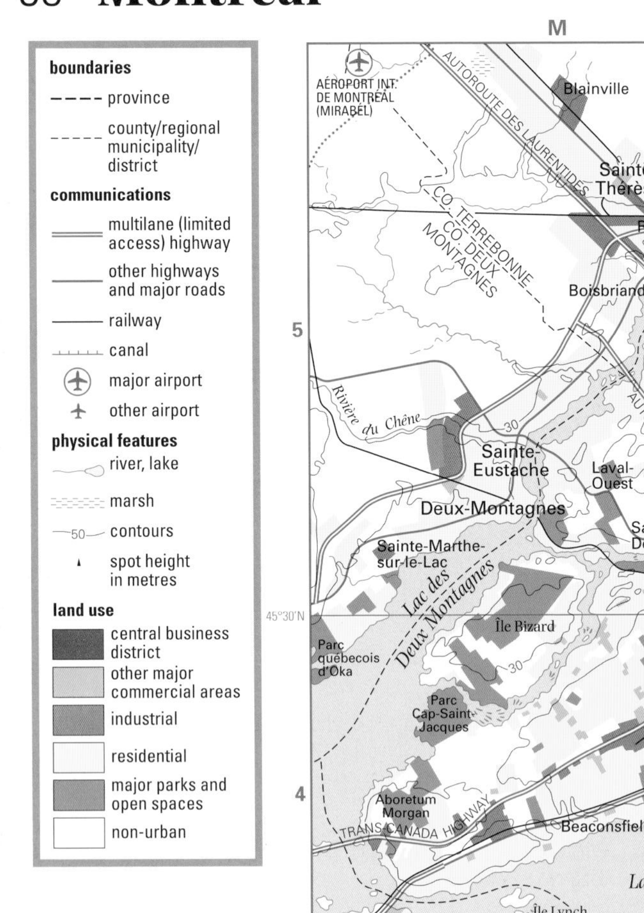

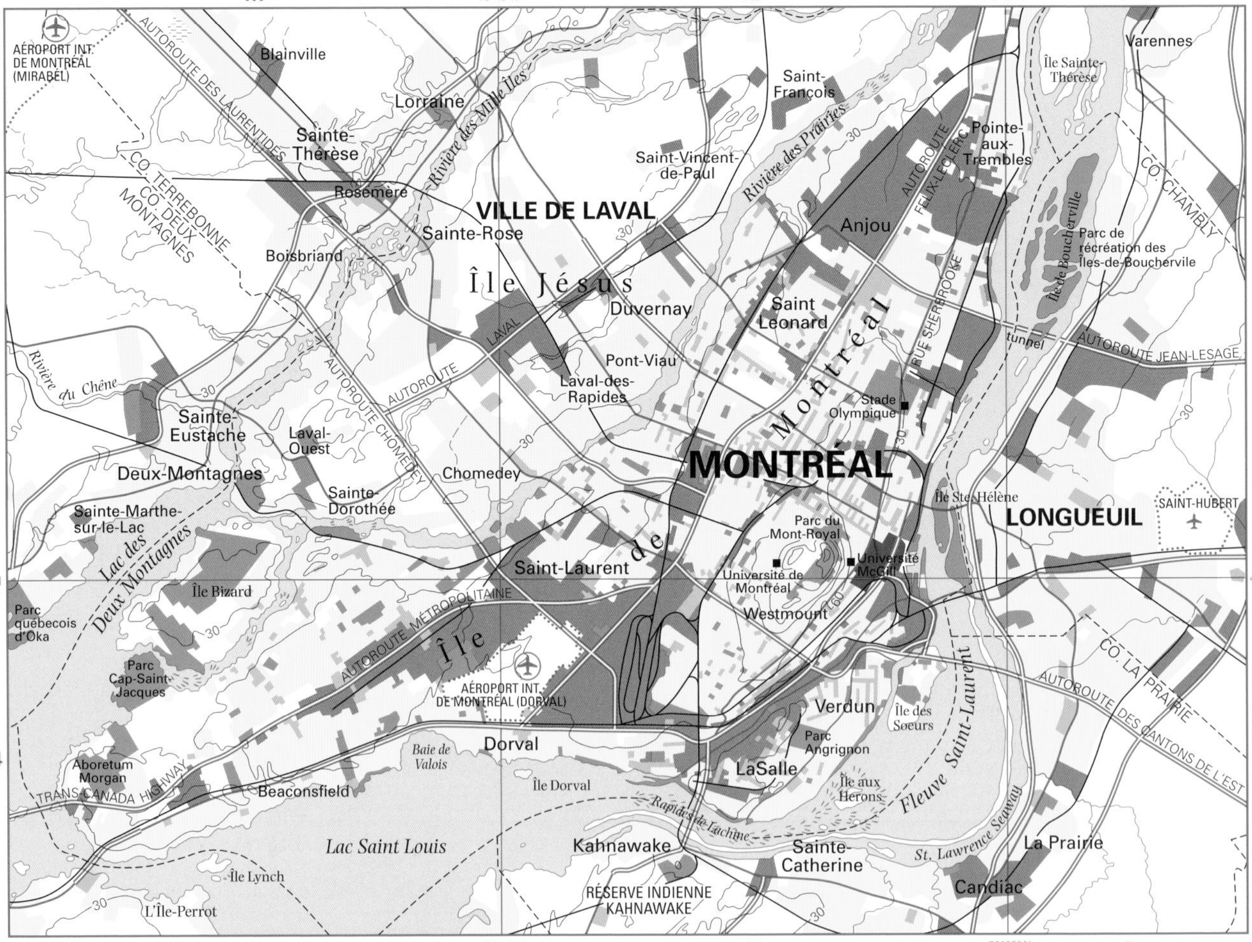

Montréal

The entire urban region of Montréal is visible in the image. Mont-Royal (M) is a prominent feature and the route of the St. Lawrence Seaway (S) can be seen along the south shore of the St. Lawrence.

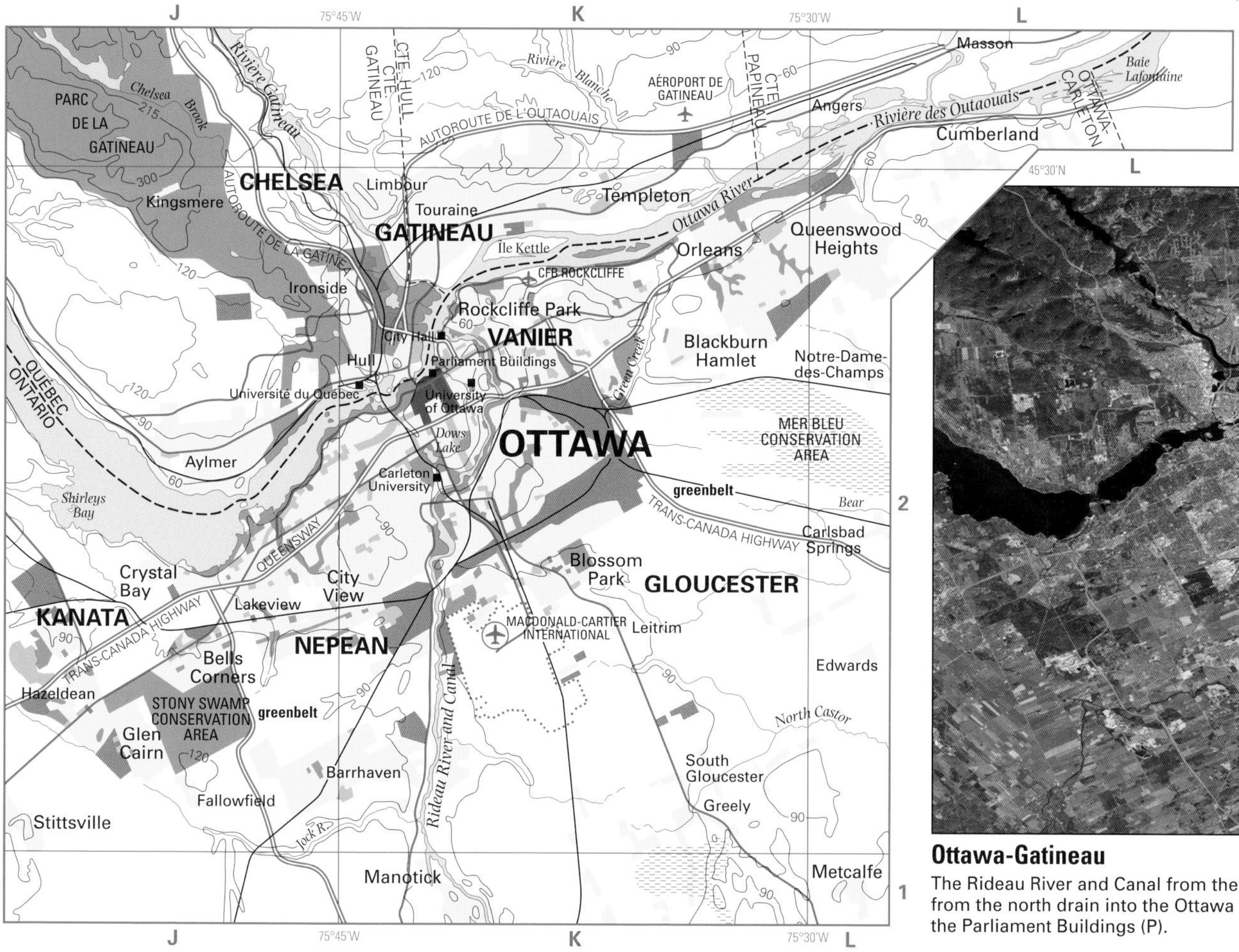

Ottawa-Gatineau

The Rideau River and Canal from the south and the Gatineau River from the north drain into the Ottawa River, just downstream from the Parliament Buildings (P).

Halifax

Halifax Harbour and Bedford Basin separate the cities of Halifax and Dartmouth.

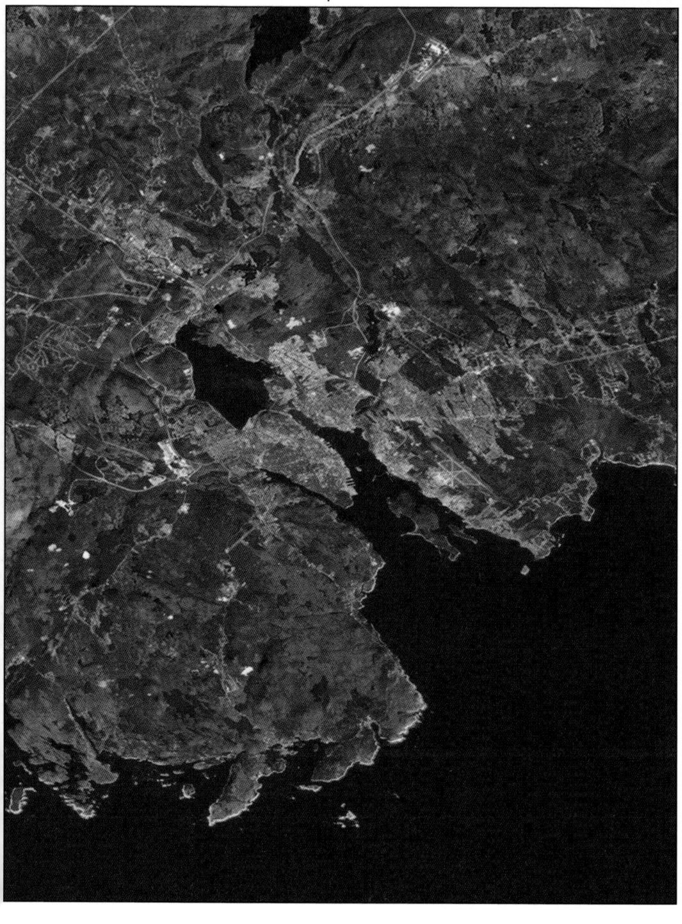

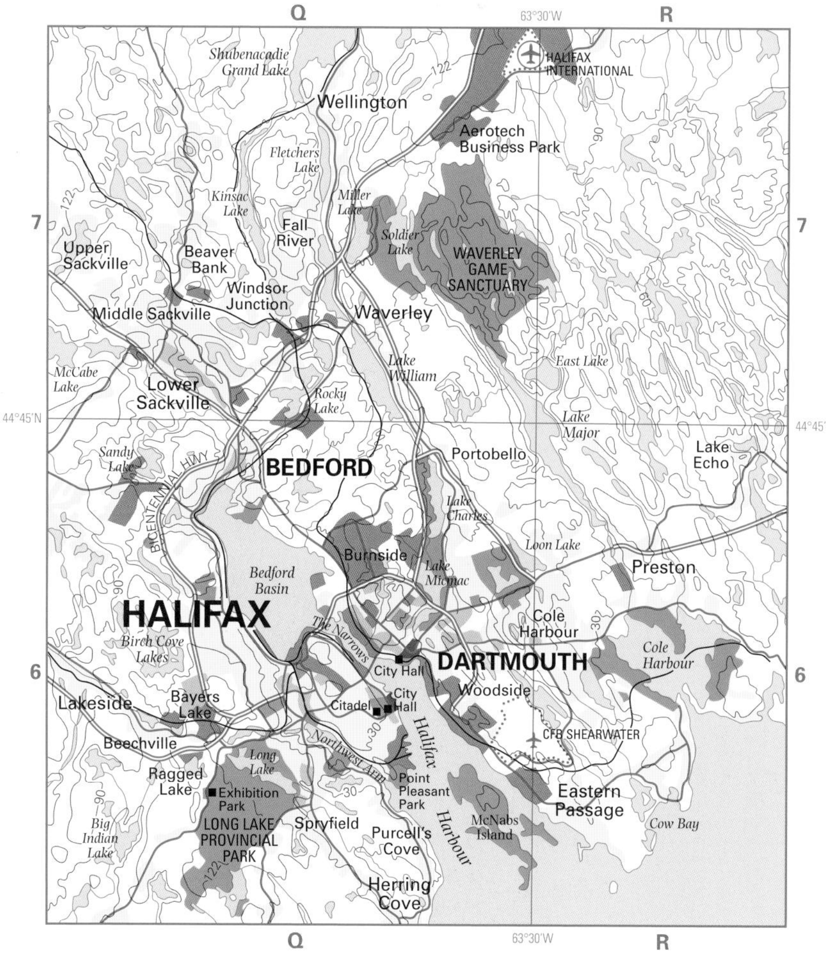

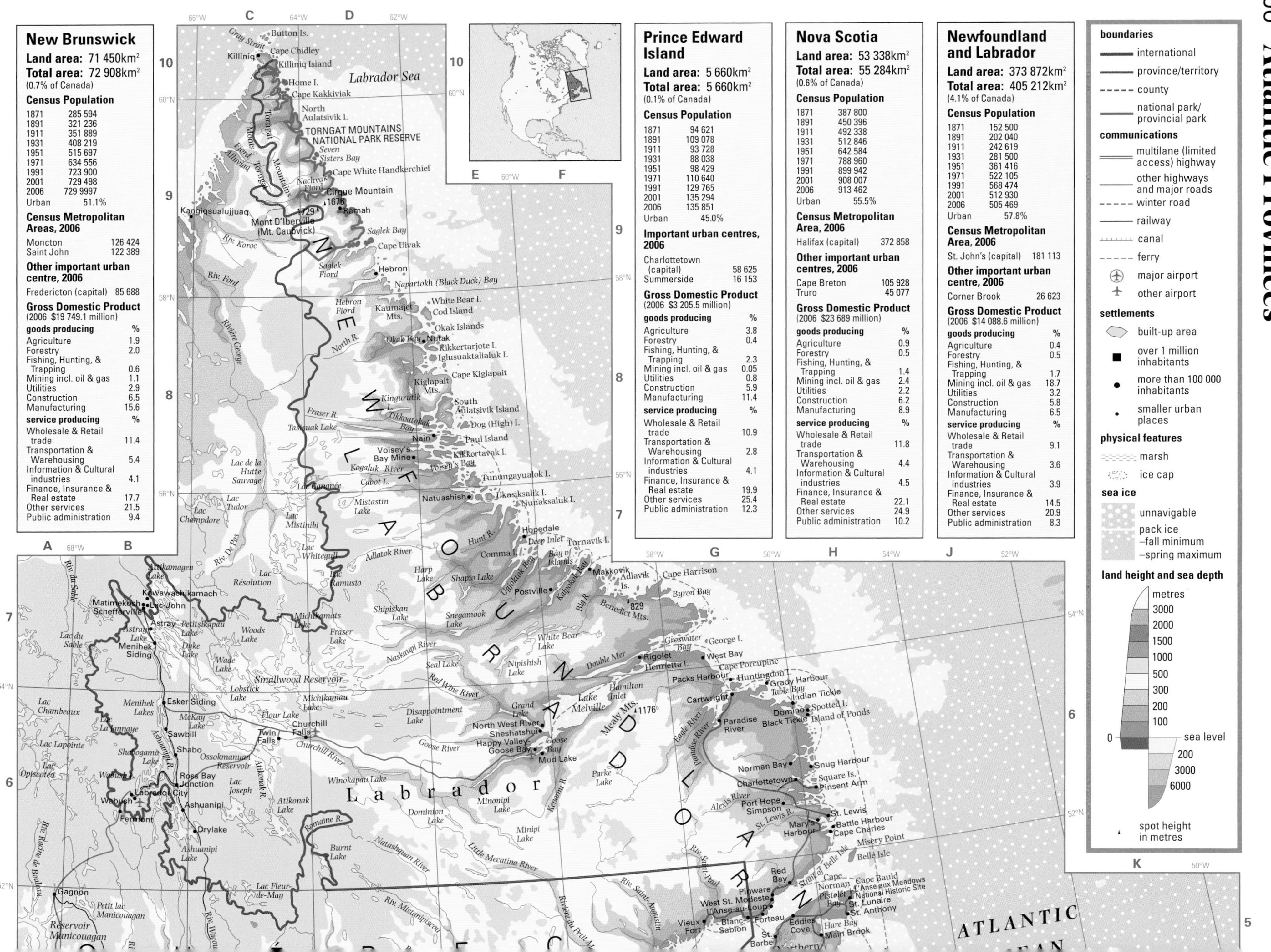

New Brunswick

Land area: 71 450km^2
Total area: 72 908km^2
(0.7% of Canada)

Census Population

1871	285 594
1891	321 236
1911	351 889
1931	408 219
1951	515 697
1971	634 556
1991	723 900
2001	729 498
2006	729 9997
Urban	51.1%

Census Metropolitan Areas, 2006

Moncton	126 424
Saint John	122 389

Other important urban centre, 2006

Fredericton (capital)	85 688

Gross Domestic Product
(2006 $19 749.1 million)

goods producing	%
Agriculture	1.9
Forestry	2.0
Fishing, Hunting, & Trapping	0.6
Mining incl. oil & gas	1.1
Utilities	2.9
Construction	6.5
Manufacturing	15.6
service producing	**%**
Wholesale & Retail trade	11.4
Transportation & Warehousing	5.4
Information & Cultural industries	4.1
Finance, Insurance & Real estate	17.7
Other services	21.5
Public administration	9.4

Prince Edward Island

Land area: 5 660km^2
Total area: 5 660km^2
(0.1% of Canada)

Census Population

1871	94 621
1891	109 078
1911	93 728
1931	88 038
1951	98 429
1971	110 640
1991	129 765
2001	135 294
2006	135 851
Urban	45.0%

Important urban centres, 2006

Charlottetown (capital)	58 625
Summerside	16 153

Gross Domestic Product
(2006 $3 205.5 million)

goods producing	%
Agriculture	3.8
Forestry	0.4
Fishing, Hunting, & Trapping	2.3
Mining incl. oil & gas	0.05
Utilities	0.8
Construction	5.9
Manufacturing	11.4
service producing	**%**
Wholesale & Retail trade	10.9
Transportation & Warehousing	2.8
Information & Cultural industries	4.1
Finance, Insurance & Real estate	19.9
Other services	25.4
Public administration	12.3

Nova Scotia

Land area: 53 338km^2
Total area: 55 284km^2
(0.6% of Canada)

Census Population

1871	387 800
1891	450 396
1911	492 338
1931	512 846
1951	642 584
1971	788 960
1991	899 942
2001	908 007
2006	913 462
Urban	55.5%

Census Metropolitan Area, 2006

Halifax (capital)	372 858

Other important urban centres, 2006

Cape Breton	105 928
Truro	45 077

Gross Domestic Product
(2006 $23 689 million)

goods producing	%
Agriculture	0.9
Forestry	0.5
Fishing, Hunting, & Trapping	1.4
Mining incl. oil & gas	2.4
Utilities	2.2
Construction	6.2
Manufacturing	8.9
service producing	**%**
Wholesale & Retail trade	11.8
Transportation & Warehousing	4.4
Information & Cultural industries	4.5
Finance, Insurance & Real estate	22.1
Other services	24.9
Public administration	10.2

Newfoundland and Labrador

Land area: 373 872km^2
Total area: 405 212km^2
(4.1% of Canada)

Census Population

1871	152 500
1891	202 040
1911	242 619
1931	281 500
1951	361 416
1971	522 105
1991	568 474
2001	512 930
2006	505 469
Urban	57.8%

Census Metropolitan Area, 2006

St. John's (capital)	181 113

Other important urban centre, 2006

Corner Brook	26 623

Gross Domestic Product
(2006 $14 088.6 million)

goods producing	%
Agriculture	0.4
Forestry	0.5
Fishing, Hunting, & Trapping	1.7
Mining incl. oil & gas	18.7
Utilities	3.2
Construction	5.8
Manufacturing	6.5
service producing	**%**
Wholesale & Retail trade	9.1
Transportation & Warehousing	3.6
Information & Cultural industries	3.9
Finance, Insurance & Real estate	14.5
Other services	20.9
Public administration	8.3

boundaries
- international
- province/territory
- county
- national park/provincial park

communications
- multilane (limited access) highway
- other highways and major roads
- winter road
- railway
- canal
- ferry
- major airport
- other airport

settlements
- built-up area
- over 1 million inhabitants
- more than 100 000 inhabitants
- smaller urban places

physical features
- marsh
- ice cap

sea ice
- unnavigable
- pack ice –fall minimum –spring maximum

land height and sea depth
metres: 3000, 2000, 1500, 1000, 500, 300, 200, 100, 0, sea level, 200, 3000, 6000
- spot height in metres

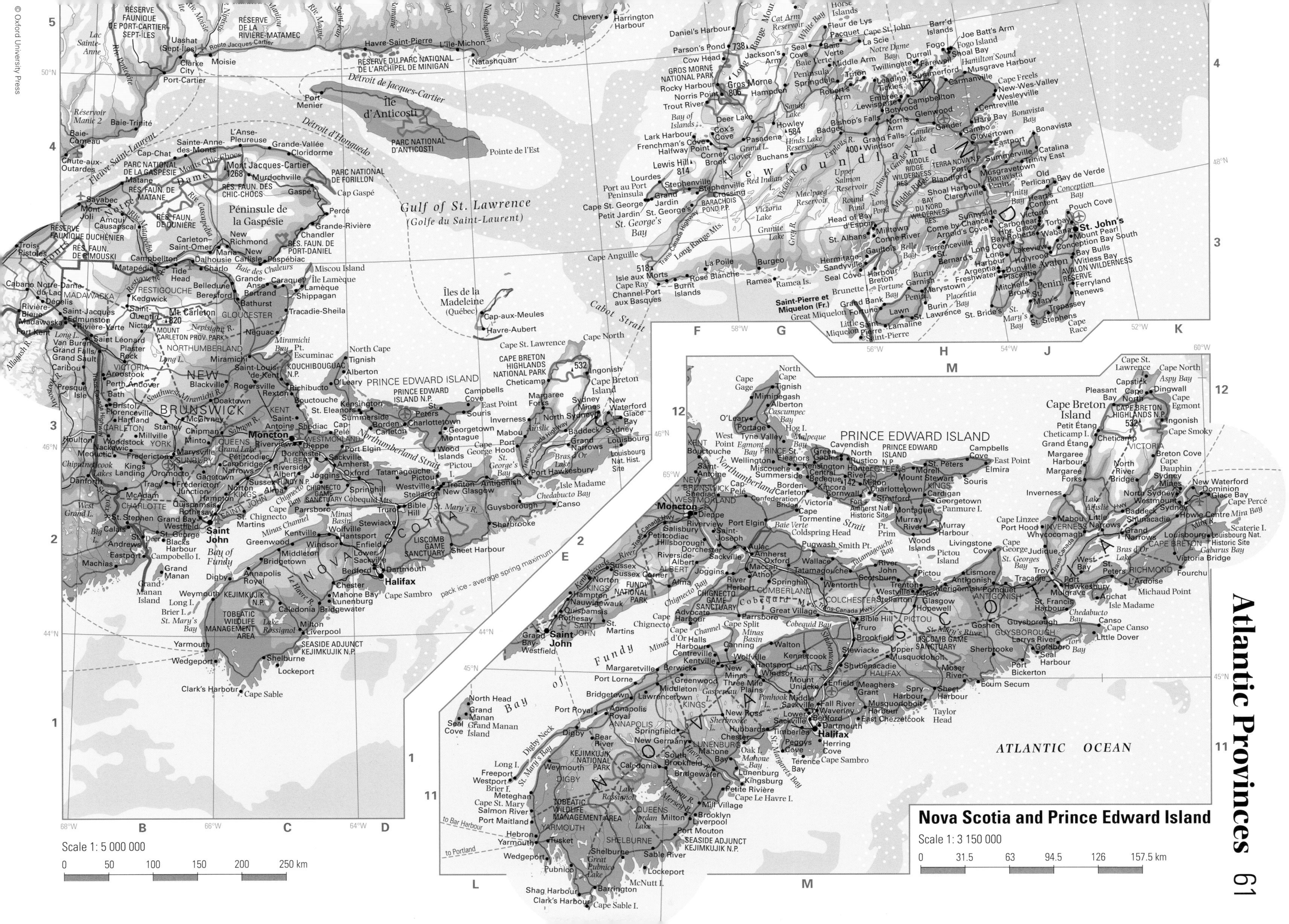
Gulf of St. Lawrence
(Golfe du Saint-Laurent)
Cabot Strait
Île d'Anticosti
Îles de la Madeleine (Québec)
Péninsule de la Gaspésie
NEW BRUNSWICK
PRINCE EDWARD ISLAND
NOVA SCOTIA
Newfoundland
Bay of Fundy
Northumberland Strait
Saint-Pierre et Miquelon (Fr.)
St. John's
Halifax
Moncton
Saint John
Scale 1: 5 000 000
0 50 100 150 200 250 km
Nova Scotia and Prince Edward Island
Scale 1: 3 150 000
0 31.5 63 94.5 126 157.5 km
ATLANTIC OCEAN

Ontario and Québec

The boundary between the sedimentary plains and the Canadian Shield is evident on this image. The lakes, remnants of glaciation, formed along the border between these two geological provinces. Bobcaygeon (B) and Fenelon Falls (F) are identified at either end of Sturgeon Lake.

Beloeil (B) is located on the Richelieu River between Mont St-Bruno and Mont St-Hilaire, two of the eight Monteregian Hills, which rise 200 to 400 m above the surrounding lowland. The long lots associated with the seigneurial system are also evident.

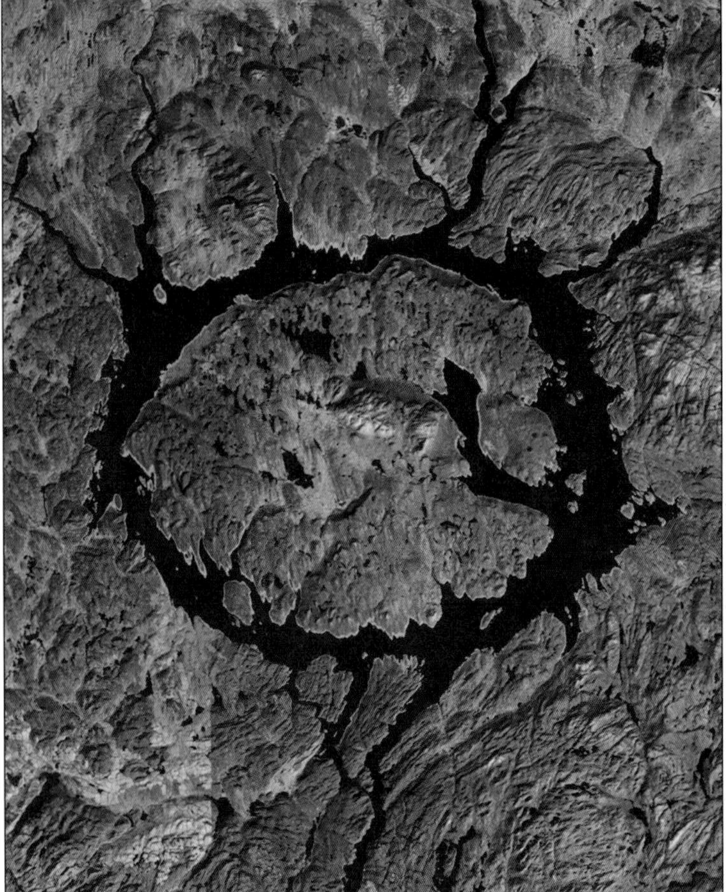

The Manicouagan Crater, one of the largest known impact craters, was created by an asteroid striking the Earth approximately 210 million years ago. Its crater, about 70 km wide, has been preserved in the hard rock of the Canadian Shield.

Québec City, founded in 1608, is the only walled city in North America, which led to its declaration as a UNESCO World Heritage Site. The Plains of Abraham are identified; the old city and its walls are just to the northeast.

t. John's, Canada's oldest city (first permanent settlement 1605), is situated on the ugged coast of the Avalon Peninsula. Cape Spear, the most easterly point in North merica, lies south and east of the city. Signal Hill (S) is a prominent St. John's andmark.

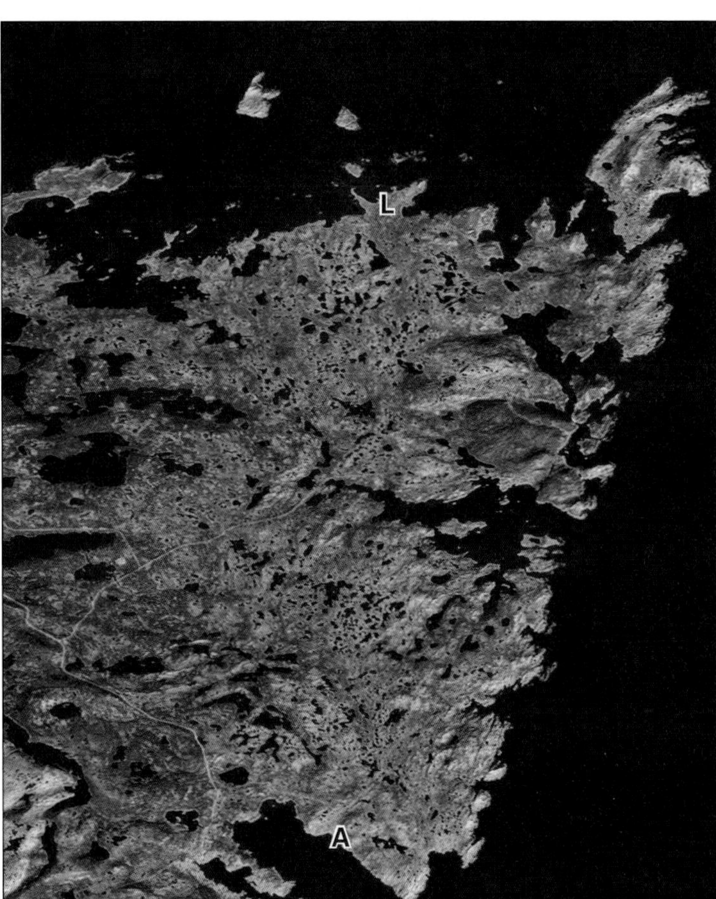

L'Anse aux Meadows (L) is famous as the site of the first European settlement in North America. It is believed that Vikings under Leif Ericsson settled here around 1000 CE. It is recognized as a UNESCO World Heritage Site. The town of St. Anthony (A) is marked for reference.

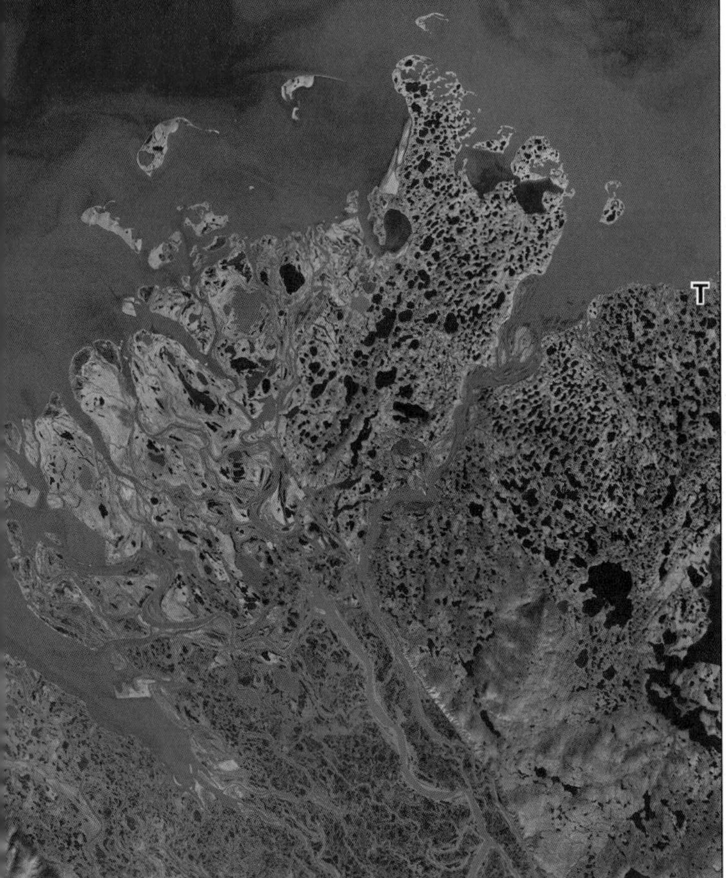

he Mackenzie Delta (13 500 km^2) was formed by deposition from Canada's longest iver. The rivers, lakes, and floodplains of the delta support diverse natural flora and auna. Tuktoyaktuk (T), the largest settlement on the coast, is indicated.

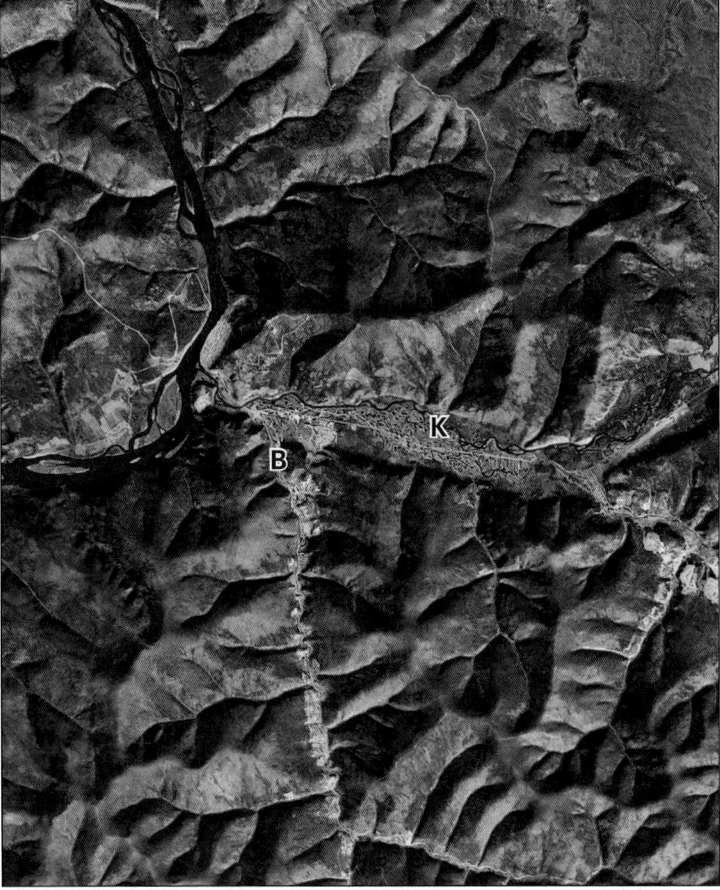

Dawson City on the Yukon River came into existence during the Klondike gold rush in the late 1890s. While the early rush ended quickly, gold has been mined from placer deposits ever since, and the gravel ridges left by this process are evident in the valleys of the Klondike River (K) and Bonanza Creek (B).

Northern Canada

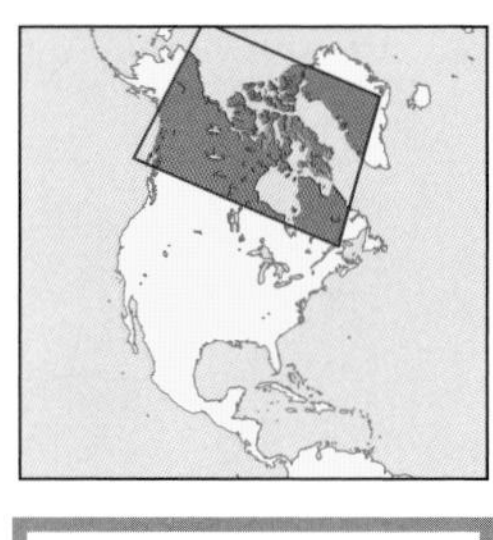

boundaries

- international
- province/territory
- national/provincial park/sanctuary

communications

- multilane (limited access) highway
- other highways and major roads
- winter road
- railway
- major airport
- other airport

settlements

- more than 1000 inhabitants
- less than 1000 inhabitants

physical features

- marsh
- ice cap

sea ice

- unnavigable
- pack ice –fall minimum –spring maximum

land height and sea depth

metres: 3000, 2000, 1000, 500, 300, 200, 100, 0 sea level, 200, 3000, 6000

spot height in metres

Yukon Territory

Land area: 474 391km²
Total area: 482 443km²
(4.8% of Canada)

Census Population

Year	Population
1911	8 512
1931	4 230
1951	9 096
1971	18 390
1991	27 797
2001	28 674
2006	30 372
Urban	59.7%

Important urban centre, 2006

Whitehorse (capital) 22 898

Gross Domestic Product
(2006 $1 199.7 million)

goods producing	%
Agriculture	v.s.
Forestry	0.03
Fishing, Hunting, & Trapping	v.s.
Mining incl. oil & gas	6.3
Utilities	1.4
Construction	9.1
Manufacturing	0.3
service producing	**%**
Wholesale & Retail trade	9.9
Transportation & Warehousing	3.3
Information & Cultural industries	4.6
Finance, Insurance & Real estate	19.3
Other services	24.4
Public administration	23.7

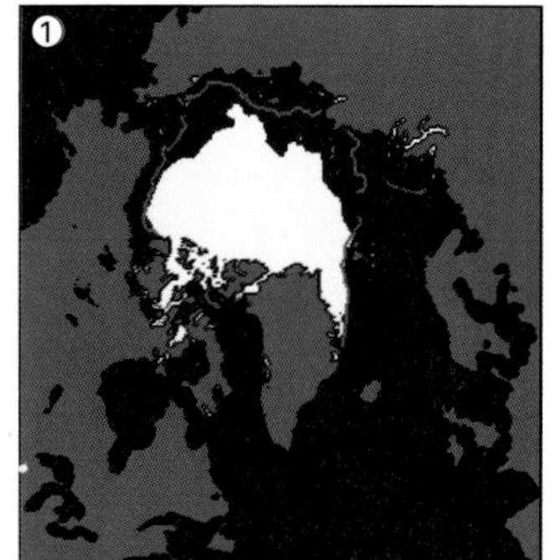

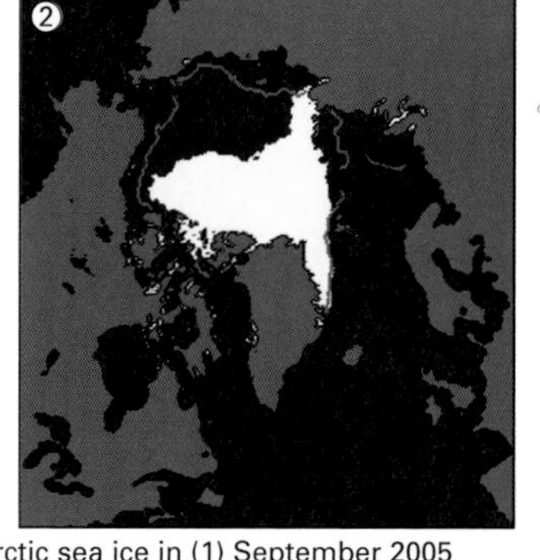

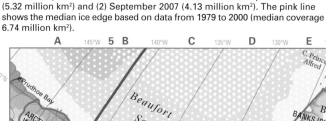

The two maps show the extent of the Arctic sea ice in (1) September 2005 (5.32 million km²) and (2) September 2007 (4.13 million km²). The pink line shows the median ice edge based on data from 1979 to 2000 (median coverage 6.74 million km²).

Scale 1: 12 000 000

0 120 240 360 480 600 km

Conical Orthomorphic Projection

Nunavut

Land area: 1 936 113km²
Total area: 2 093 190km²
(21.0% of Canada)

Census Population

2001	26 745
2006	29 474
Urban	43.4%

Important urban centre, 2006

Iqaluit (capital)	6 184

Gross Domestic Product
(2006 $928.8 million)

goods producing	%
Agriculture	0.0
Forestry	0.0
Fishing, Hunting, & Trapping	0.1
Mining incl. oil & gas	4.2
Utilities	0.7
Construction	17.9
Manufacturing	0.2
service producing	**%**
Wholesale & Retail trade	4.2
Transportation & Warehousing	3.0
Information & Cultural industries	5.3
Finance, Insurance & Real estate	15.1
Other services	22.3
Public administration	25.7

Northwest Territories

Land area: 1 183 085km²
Total area: 1 346 106km²
(13.5% of Canada)

Census Population

1871	56 446*
1891	98 967*
1911	6 507
1931	9 316
1951	16 004
1971	34 805
1991	57 649
2001	37 360
2006	41 464
Urban	58.4%

*includes Saskatchewan and Alberta

Important urban centre, 2006

Yellowknife (capital)	18 700

Gross Domestic Product
(2006 $4 021.8 million)

goods producing	%
Agriculture	v.s.
Forestry	0.02
Fishing, Hunting, & Trapping	v.s.
Mining incl. oil & gas	49.7
Utilities	1.1
Construction	11.3
Manufacturing	0.1
service producing	**%**
Wholesale & Retail trade	3.3
Transportation & Warehousing	4.0
Information & Cultural industries	2.3
Finance, Insurance & Real estate	9.8
Other services	11.6
Public administration	9.1

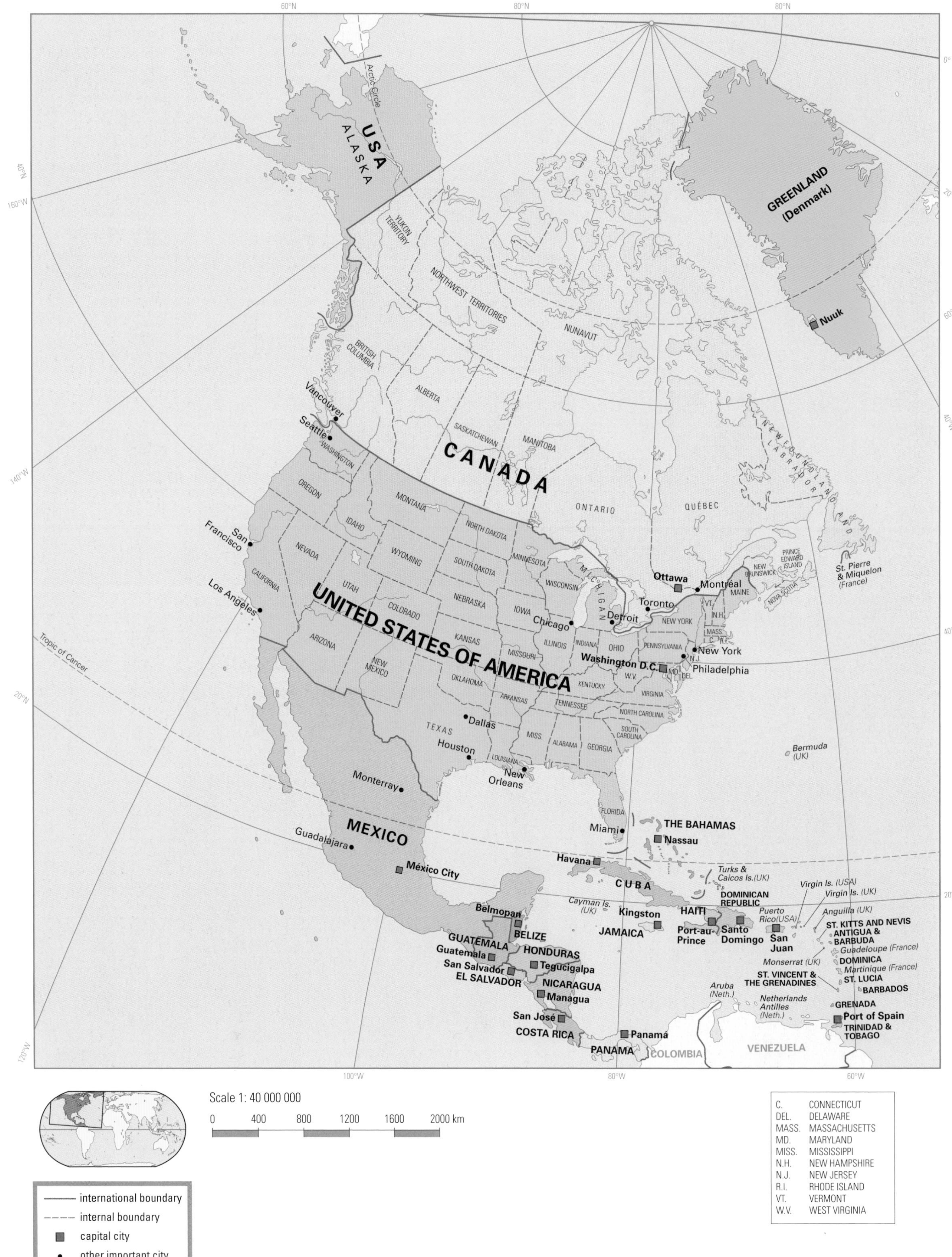
USA
ALASKA
YUKON TERRITORY
NORTHWEST TERRITORIES
NUNAVUT
BRITISH COLUMBIA
ALBERTA
SASKATCHEWAN
MANITOBA
CANADA
ONTARIO
QUÉBEC
NEWFOUNDLAND AND LABRADOR
NEW BRUNSWICK
PRINCE EDWARD ISLAND
NOVA SCOTIA
St. Pierre & Miquelon (France)
GREENLAND (Denmark)
Nuuk
Vancouver
Seattle
Ottawa
Montréal
Toronto
Detroit
Chicago
WASHINGTON
OREGON
IDAHO
MONTANA
NORTH DAKOTA
SOUTH DAKOTA
MINNESOTA
WISCONSIN
MICHIGAN
WYOMING
NEVADA
UTAH
COLORADO
NEBRASKA
IOWA
ILLINOIS
INDIANA
OHIO
PENNSYLVANIA
NEW YORK
MAINE
VT.
N.H.
MASS.
C.
R.I.
N.J.
DEL.
MD.
W.V.
VIRGINIA
KENTUCKY
TENNESSEE
NORTH CAROLINA
SOUTH CAROLINA
GEORGIA
ALABAMA
MISS.
LOUISIANA
ARKANSAS
MISSOURI
KANSAS
OKLAHOMA
TEXAS
NEW MEXICO
ARIZONA
CALIFORNIA
FLORIDA
UNITED STATES OF AMERICA
San Francisco
Los Angeles
Washington D.C.
New York
Philadelphia
Dallas
Houston
New Orleans
Miami
Monterray
Guadalajara
México City
MEXICO
Tropic of Cancer
Arctic Circle
Bermuda (UK)
THE BAHAMAS
Nassau
Havana
CUBA
Turks & Caicos Is.(UK)
Cayman Is. (UK)
Kingston
JAMAICA
HAITI
Port-au-Prince
DOMINICAN REPUBLIC
Santo Domingo
Puerto Rico(USA)
San Juan
Virgin Is. (USA)
Virgin Is. (UK)
Anguilla (UK)
ST. KITTS AND NEVIS
ANTIGUA & BARBUDA
Guadeloupe (France)
Monserrat (UK)
DOMINICA
Martinique (France)
ST. LUCIA
ST. VINCENT & THE GRENADINES
BARBADOS
GRENADA
Port of Spain
TRINIDAD & TOBAGO
Aruba (Neth.)
Netherlands Antilles (Neth.)
Belmopan
BELIZE
GUATEMALA
Guatemala
HONDURAS
Tegucigalpa
San Salvador
EL SALVADOR
NICARAGUA
Managua
San José
COSTA RICA
Panamá
PANAMA
COLOMBIA
VENEZUELA
Scale 1: 40 000 000
0 400 800 1200 1600 2000 km
C. CONNECTICUT
DEL. DELAWARE
MASS. MASSACHUSETTS
MD. MARYLAND
MISS. MISSISSIPPI
N.H. NEW HAMPSHIRE
N.J. NEW JERSEY
R.I. RHODE ISLAND
VT. VERMONT
W.V. WEST VIRGINIA
international boundary
internal boundary
capital city
other important city

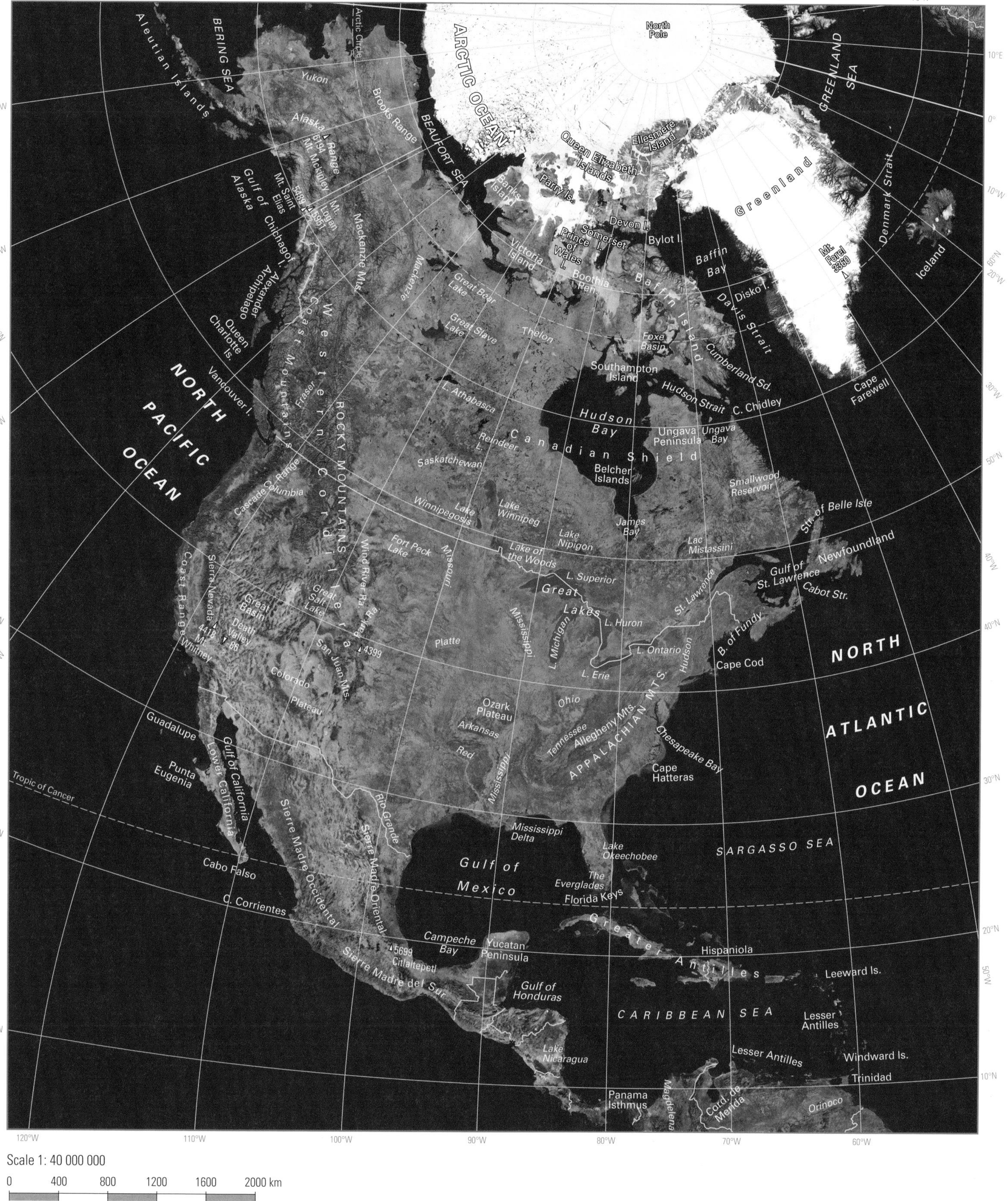

Scale 1: 40 000 000

0 400 800 1200 1600 2000 km

Oblique Mercator Projection

Scale 1: 80 000 000

January temperature

actual surface temperature

°Celsius
25
20
15
10
5
0
-10
-20
-30

• climate station (average January temperature)

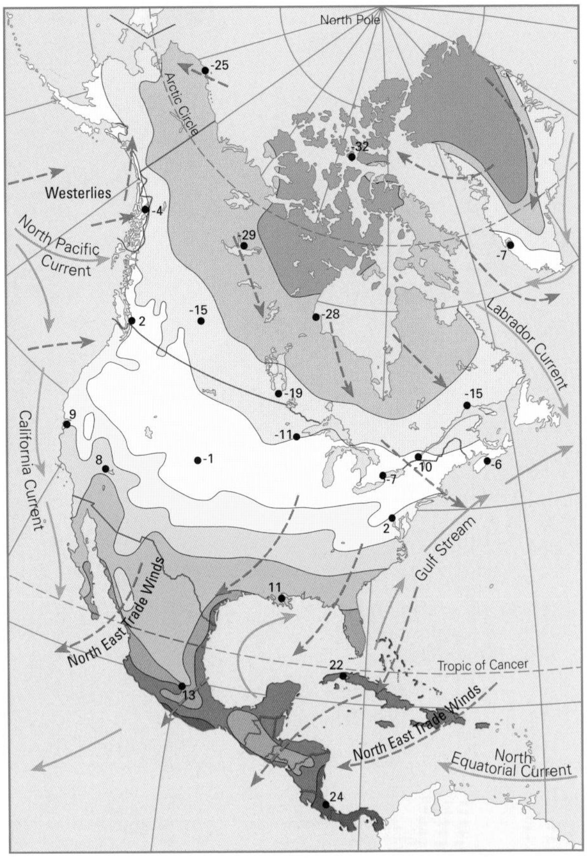

July temperature

actual surface temperature

°Celsius
30
25
20
15
10
5
0
-10

• climate station (average July temperature)

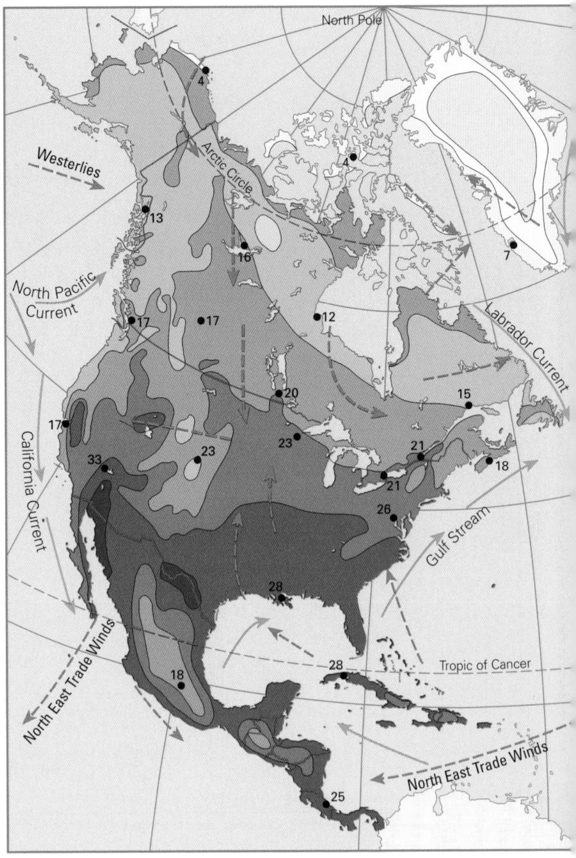

warm sea current
cold sea current
prevailing wind

Precipitation

average annual precipitation

mm
3000
2000
1000
500
250
0

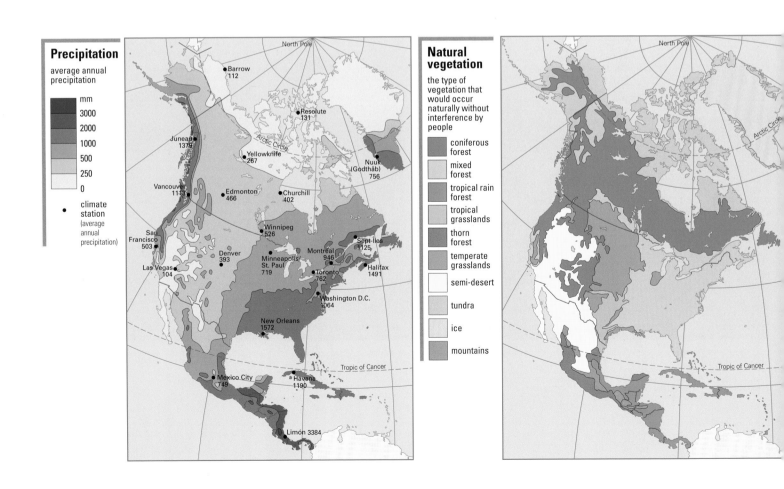

• climate station (average annual precipitation)

Natural vegetation

the type of vegetation that would occur naturally without interference by people

- coniferous forest
- mixed forest
- tropical rain forest
- tropical grasslands
- thorn forest
- temperate grasslands
- semi-desert
- tundra
- ice
- mountains

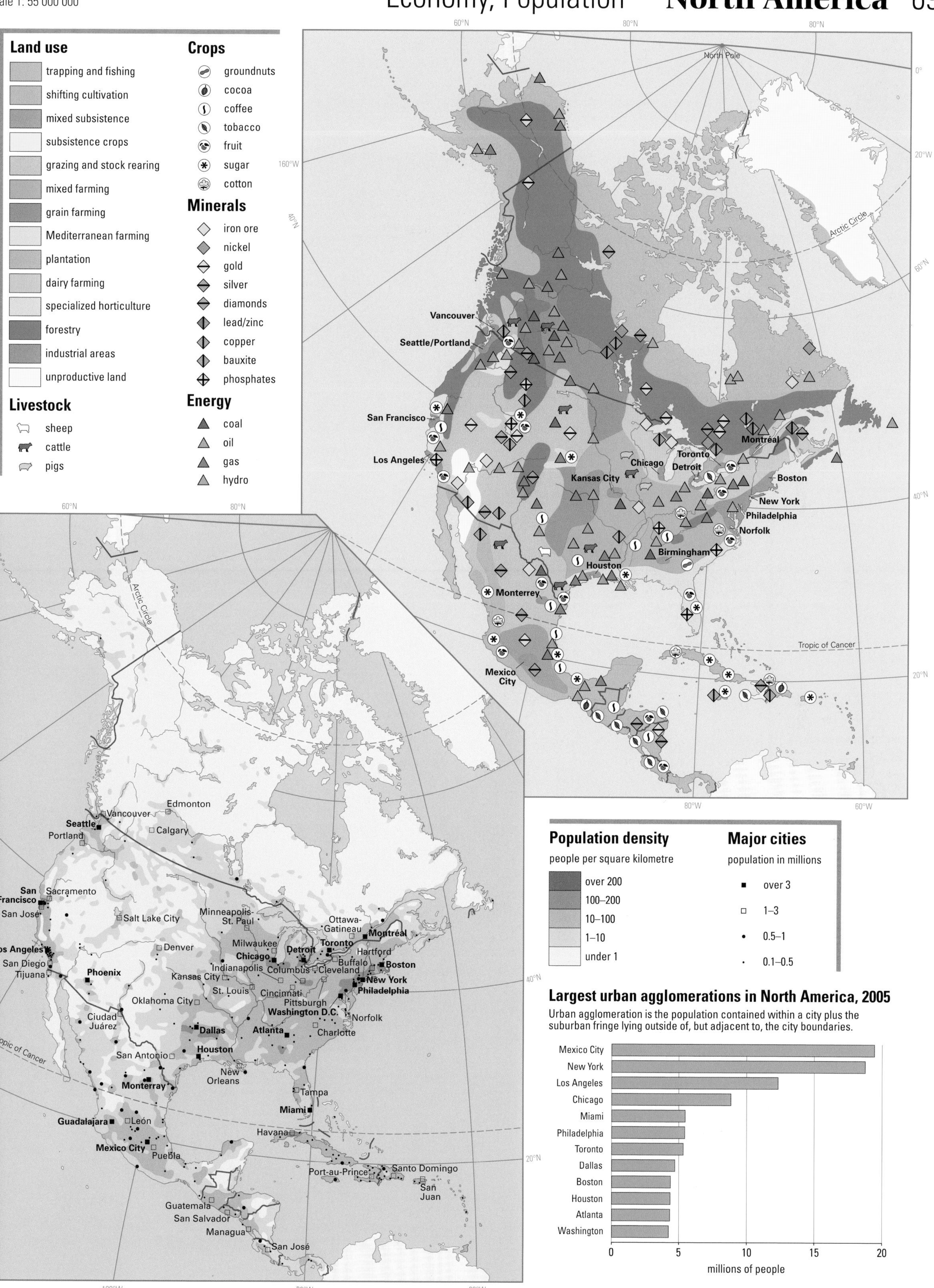
Land use
trapping and fishing
shifting cultivation
mixed subsistence
subsistence crops
grazing and stock rearing
mixed farming
grain farming
Mediterranean farming
plantation
dairy farming
specialized horticulture
forestry
industrial areas
unproductive land
Livestock
sheep
cattle
pigs
Crops
groundnuts
cocoa
coffee
tobacco
fruit
sugar
cotton
Minerals
iron ore
nickel
gold
silver
diamonds
lead/zinc
copper
bauxite
phosphates
Energy
coal
oil
gas
hydro
North Pole
Arctic Circle
Tropic of Cancer
Vancouver
Seattle/Portland
San Francisco
Los Angeles
Chicago
Toronto
Detroit
Montréal
Kansas City
Boston
New York
Philadelphia
Norfolk
Birmingham
Houston
Monterrey
Mexico City
Population density
people per square kilometre
over 200
100–200
10–100
1–10
under 1
Major cities
population in millions
over 3
1–3
0.5–1
0.1–0.5
Edmonton
Vancouver
Seattle
Portland
Calgary
San Francisco
Sacramento
San José
Salt Lake City
Minneapolis-St. Paul
Ottawa-Gatineau
Montréal
Denver
Los Angeles
San Diego
Tijuana
Phoenix
Milwaukee
Detroit
Toronto
Chicago
Hartford
Buffalo
Boston
Indianapolis
Columbus
Cleveland
Kansas City
New York
Philadelphia
St. Louis
Cincinnati
Pittsburgh
Washington D.C.
Norfolk
Oklahoma City
Ciudad Juárez
Dallas
Atlanta
Charlotte
Houston
San Antonio
New Orleans
Monterray
Tampa
Miami
Guadalajara
León
Havana
Mexico City
Puebla
Port-au-Prince
Santo Domingo
San Juan
Guatemala
San Salvador
Managua
San José
Tropic of Cancer
Largest urban agglomerations in North America, 2005
Urban agglomeration is the population contained within a city plus the suburban fringe lying outside of, but adjacent to, the city boundaries.
Mexico City
New York
Los Angeles
Chicago
Miami
Philadelphia
Toronto
Dallas
Boston
Houston
Atlanta
Washington
0
5
10
15
20
millions of people

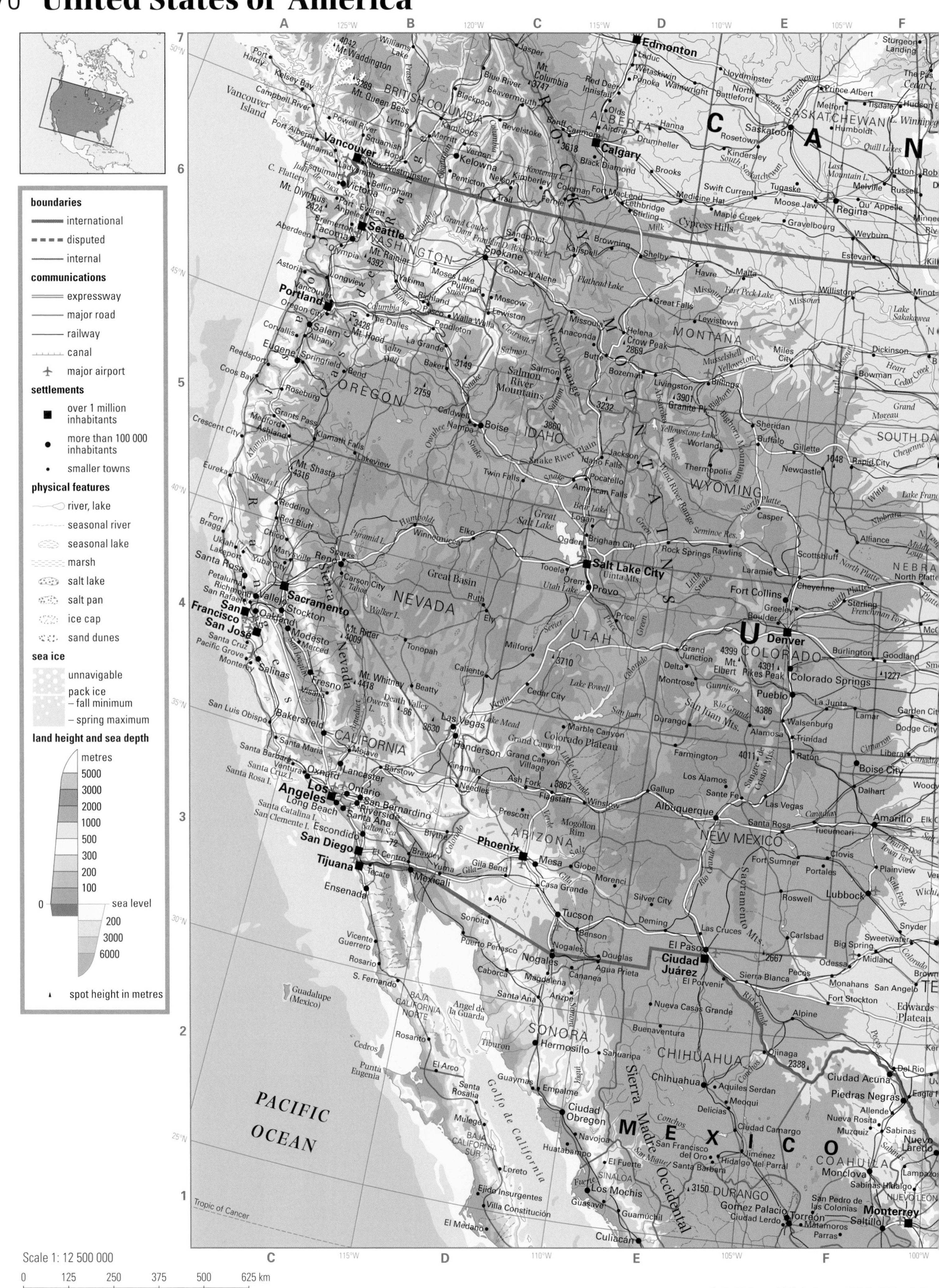

A B C D E F
125°W 120°W 115°W 110°W 105°W 100°W
50°N 45°N 40°N 35°N 30°N 25°N
7 6 5 4 3 2 1
boundaries
international
disputed
internal
communications
expressway
major road
railway
canal
major airport
settlements
over 1 million inhabitants
more than 100 000 inhabitants
smaller towns
physical features
river, lake
seasonal river
seasonal lake
marsh
salt lake
salt pan
ice cap
sand dunes
sea ice
unnavigable
pack ice
– fall minimum
– spring maximum
land height and sea depth
metres
5000
3000
2000
1000
500
300
200
100
0
sea level
200
3000
6000
spot height in metres
BRITISH COLUMBIA
ALBERTA
SASKATCHEWAN
CANADA
WASHINGTON
OREGON
IDAHO
MONTANA
WYOMING
NEVADA
UTAH
COLORADO
CALIFORNIA
ARIZONA
NEW MEXICO
SOUTH DAKOTA
NEBRASKA
ROCKY MOUNTAINS
MEXICO
SONORA
CHIHUAHUA
COAHUILA
DURANGO
SINALOA
BAJA CALIFORNIA NORTE
BAJA CALIFORNIA SUR
NUEVO LEÓN
PACIFIC OCEAN
Golfo de California
Sierra Madre Occidental
Tropic of Cancer
Edmonton
Calgary
Vancouver
Seattle
Portland
Sacramento
San Francisco
San José
Los Angeles
San Diego
Tijuana
Las Vegas
Phoenix
Salt Lake City
Denver
Ciudad Juárez
Monterrey
Great Basin
Great Salt Lake
Colorado Plateau
Scale 1: 12 500 000
0 125 250 375 500 625 km
Conical Orthomorphic Projection
© Oxford University Press

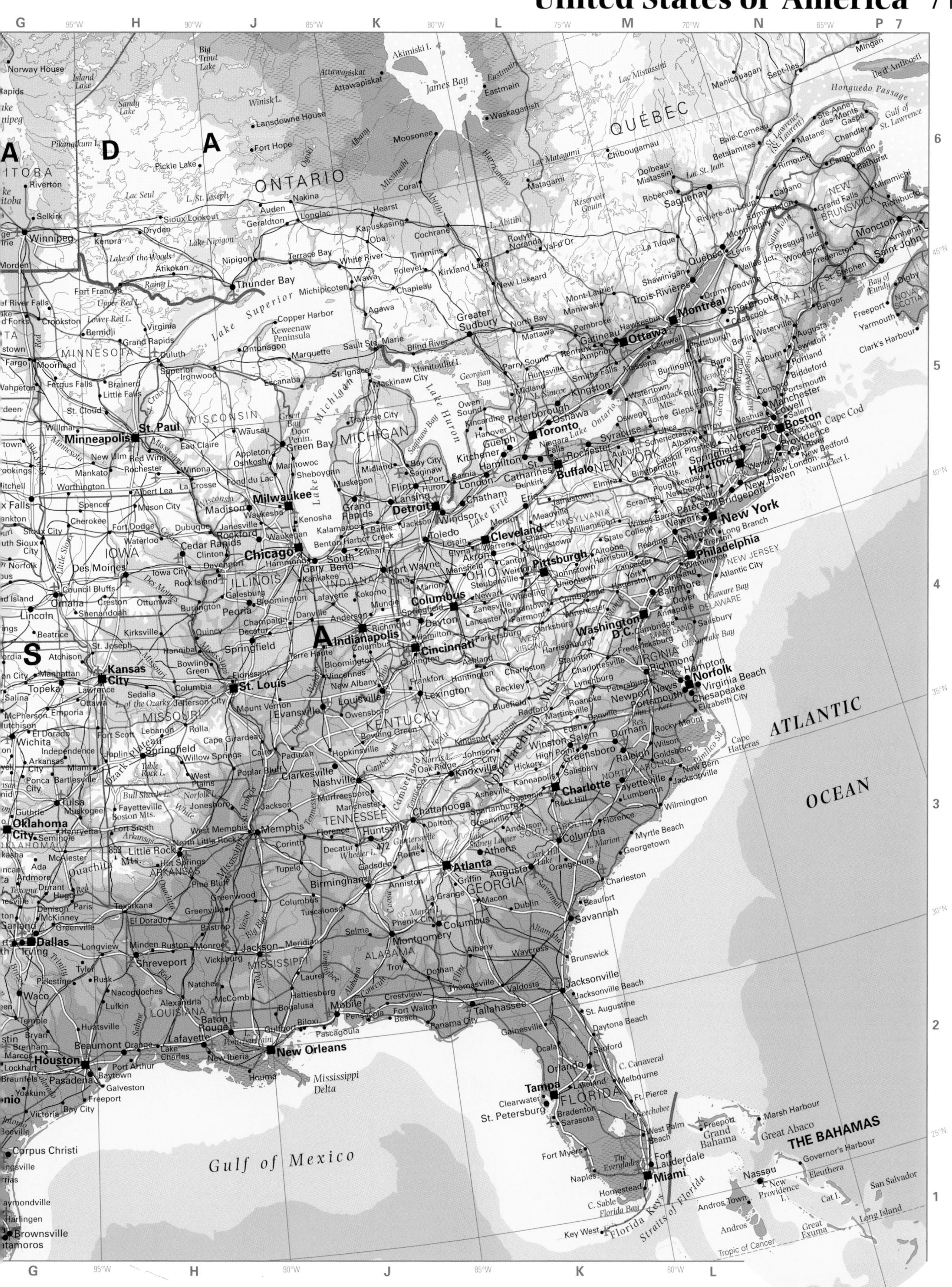

G
H
J
K
L
M
N
P
95°W
90°W
85°W
80°W
75°W
70°W
65°W
45°N
40°N
35°N
30°N
25°N
7
6
5
4
3
2
1
ONTARIO
QUÉBEC
MINNESOTA
WISCONSIN
MICHIGAN
IOWA
ILLINOIS
INDIANA
OHIO
PENNSYLVANIA
NEW YORK
NEW JERSEY
DELAWARE
MARYLAND
WEST VIRGINIA
VIRGINIA
KENTUCKY
MISSOURI
TENNESSEE
NORTH CAROLINA
SOUTH CAROLINA
GEORGIA
ALABAMA
MISSISSIPPI
ARKANSAS
LOUISIANA
FLORIDA
MAINE
VERMONT
NEW HAMPSHIRE
NEW BRUNSWICK
NOVA SCOTIA
THE BAHAMAS
ATLANTIC
OCEAN
Gulf of Mexico
James Bay
Lake Superior
Lake Michigan
Lake Huron
Lake Erie
Lake Ontario
Gulf of St. Lawrence
Bay of Fundy
Mississippi Delta
Straits of Florida
Tropic of Cancer
Winnipeg
Thunder Bay
Minneapolis
St. Paul
Milwaukee
Chicago
Detroit
Toronto
Ottawa
Montréal
Québec
Boston
Hartford
New York
Philadelphia
Baltimore
Washington D.C.
Pittsburgh
Cleveland
Buffalo
Columbus
Cincinnati
Indianapolis
St. Louis
Kansas City
Oklahoma City
Dallas
Houston
New Orleans
Memphis
Nashville
Atlanta
Charlotte
Norfolk
Jacksonville
Tampa
Miami
Nassau
Corpus Christi
Brownsville

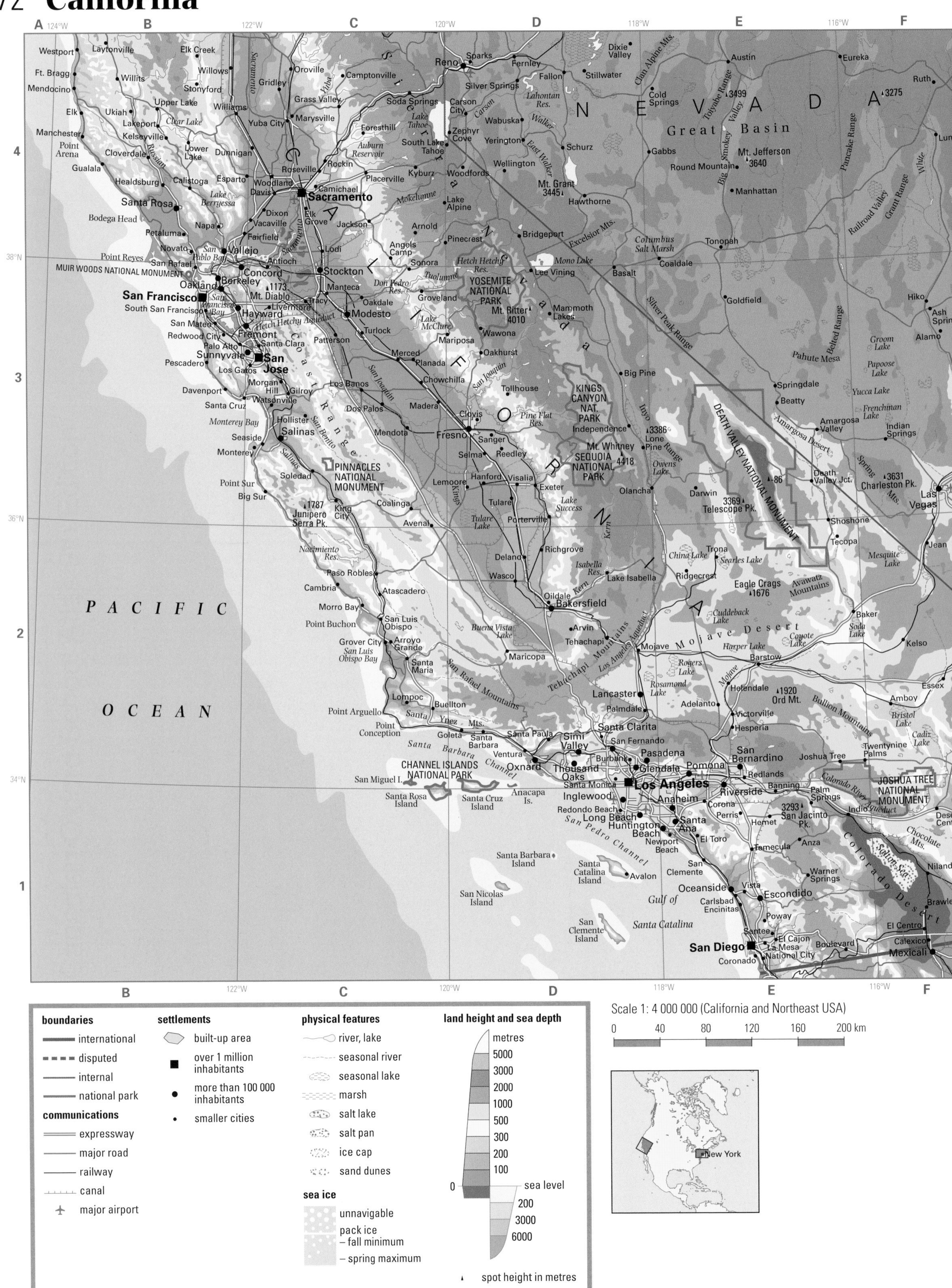

PACIFIC OCEAN
NEVADA
CALIFORNIA
Great Basin
Sierra Nevada
Coast Ranges
Mojave Desert
Colorado Desert
Sacramento
San Francisco
San Jose
Oakland
Berkeley
Stockton
Modesto
Fresno
Bakersfield
Los Angeles
San Diego
Santa Barbara
Reno
Las Vegas
Mexicali
YOSEMITE NATIONAL PARK
KINGS CANYON NAT. PARK
SEQUOIA NATIONAL PARK
DEATH VALLEY NATIONAL MONUMENT
JOSHUA TREE NATIONAL MONUMENT
PINNACLES NATIONAL MONUMENT
CHANNEL ISLANDS NATIONAL PARK
MUIR WOODS NATIONAL MONUMENT
Mt. Whitney 4418
Lake Tahoe
Mono Lake
Salton Sea
Monterey Bay
Santa Barbara Channel
San Pedro Channel
Gulf of Santa Catalina
boundaries
international
disputed
internal
national park
communications
expressway
major road
railway
canal
major airport
settlements
built-up area
over 1 million inhabitants
more than 100 000 inhabitants
smaller cities
physical features
river, lake
seasonal river
seasonal lake
marsh
salt lake
salt pan
ice cap
sand dunes
sea ice
unnavigable
pack ice
– fall minimum
– spring maximum
land height and sea depth
metres
5000
3000
2000
1000
500
300
200
100
0
sea level
200
3000
6000
spot height in metres
Scale 1: 4 000 000 (California and Northeast USA)
0 40 80 120 160 200 km
New York

Lake Ontario
NEW YORK
PENNSYLVANIA
Appalachian Mountains
VERMONT
NEW HAMPSHIRE
MAINE
MASSACHUSETTS
CONNECTICUT
RHODE ISLAND
NEW JERSEY
MARYLAND
DELAWARE
VIRGINIA
WEST VIRGINIA
ATLANTIC OCEAN
Buffalo
Rochester
Syracuse
Albany
Boston
Hartford
Providence
New York
Philadelphia
Baltimore
Washington D.C.
Long Island
Long Island Sound
Massachusetts Bay
Cape Cod
Nantucket Island
Martha's Vineyard
Atlantic City
Cape May
Delaware Bay
Chesapeake Bay
GETTYSBURG NATIONAL MILITARY PARK
SHENANDOAH NATIONAL PARK
boundaries
state
county
communications
expressway/ multilane highway
other highway
railway
canal
major airport
other airport
physical features
river, lake
marsh
contours
spot height in metres
land use
central business district
other major commercial areas
industrial
residential
major parks and open spaces
non-urban
THE BRONX
MANHATTAN
QUEENS
BROOKLYN
RICHMOND
NEWARK
JERSEY CITY
ELIZABETH
NEW YORK
Staten Island
Upper Bay
Lower Bay
Jamaica Bay
JOHN F. KENNEDY INTERNATIONAL AIRPORT
LA GUARDIA AIRPORT
NEWARK INTERNATIONAL AIRPORT
Statue of Liberty
United Nations Headquarters
Central Park
ATLANTIC OCEAN
Scale 1: 300 000
3 6 9 12 15 km
Lambert Conformal Conic Projection

Mexico, Central America, and the Caribbean

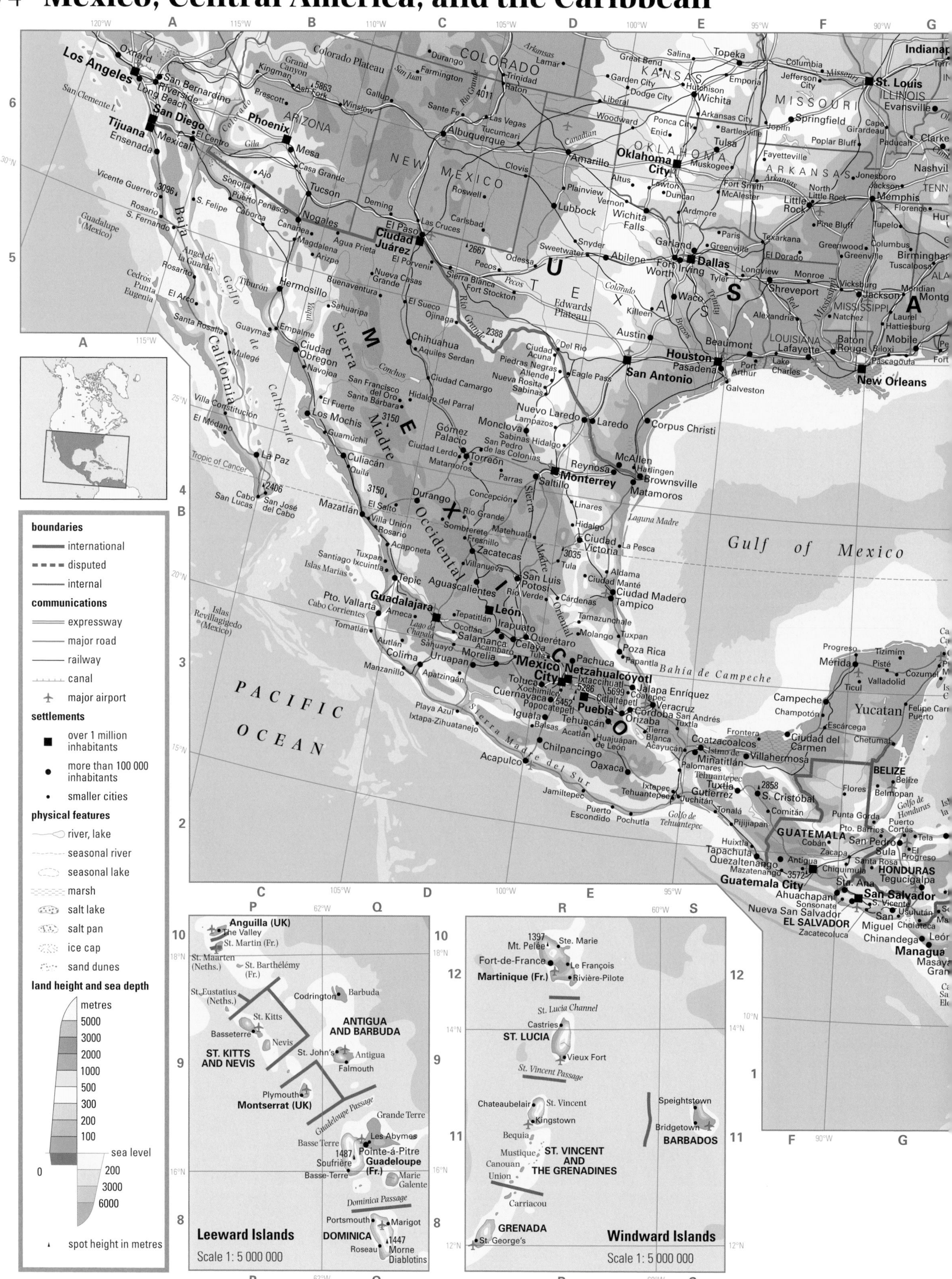

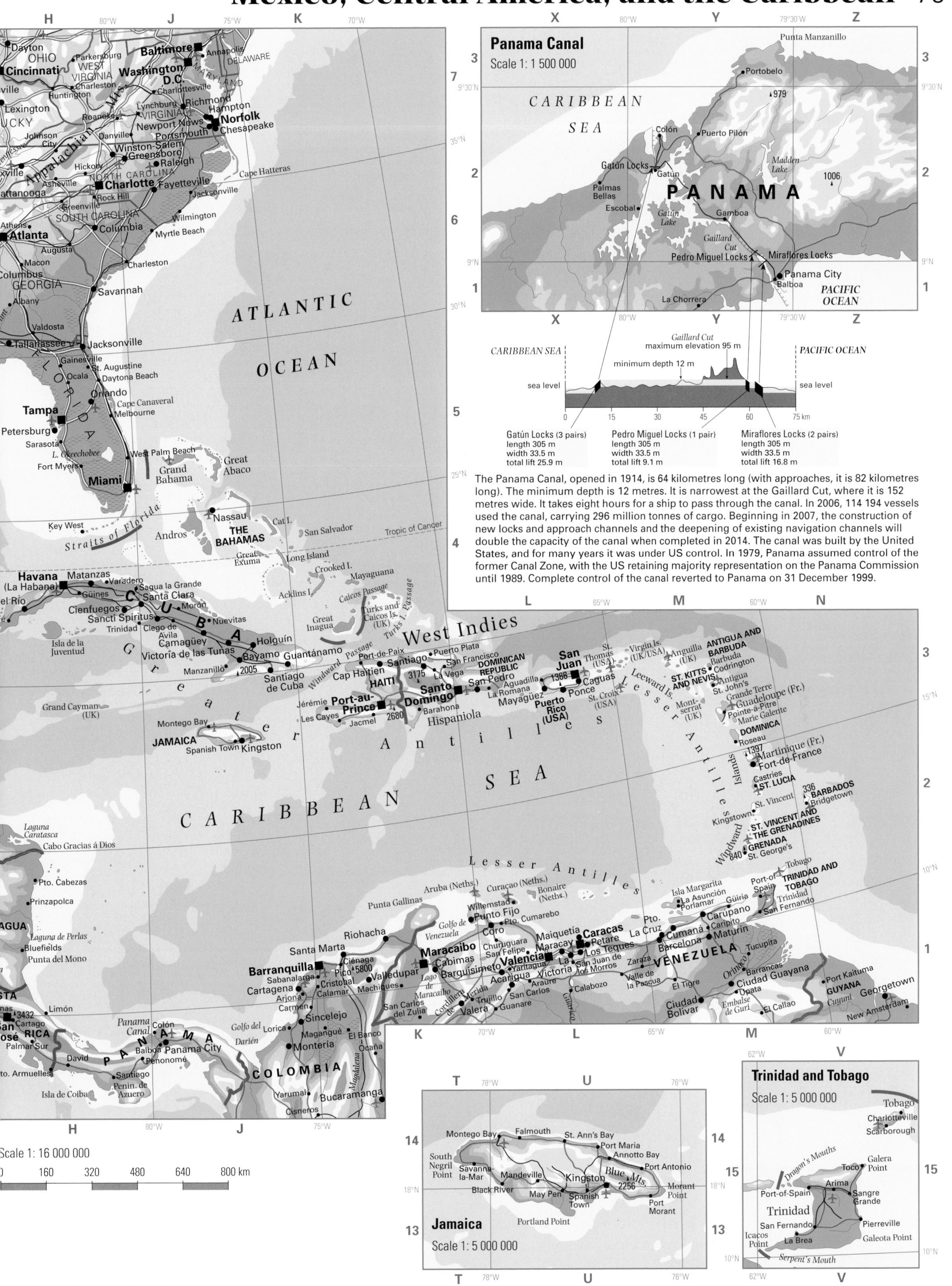

The Panama Canal, opened in 1914, is 64 kilometres long (with approaches, it is 82 kilometres long). The minimum depth is 12 metres. It is narrowest at the Gaillard Cut, where it is 152 metres wide. It takes eight hours for a ship to pass through the canal. In 2006, 114 194 vessels used the canal, carrying 296 million tonnes of cargo. Beginning in 2007, the construction of new locks and approach channels and the deepening of existing navigation channels will double the capacity of the canal when completed in 2014. The canal was built by the United States, and for many years it was under US control. In 1979, Panama assumed control of the former Canal Zone, with the US retaining majority representation on the Panama Commission until 1989. Complete control of the canal reverted to Panama on 31 December 1999.

 Zenithal Equidistant Projection

80°W
60°W
40°W
EL SALVADOR
NICARAGUA
COSTA RICA
PANAMA
Barranquilla
Caracas
Maracaibo
Valencia
VENEZUELA
Georgetown
GUYANA
Paramaribo
SURINAME
Cayenne
French Guiana (France)
Medellín
Bogotá
Cali
COLOMBIA
Equator
0°
Galapagos Islands (Ecuador)
Quito
ECUADOR
Guayaquil
Iquitos
Manaus
Belém
Fortaleza
Rocas Island (Brazil)
Fernando de Noronha (Brazil)
Recife
PERU
B R A Z I L
Lima
Salvador
BOLIVIA
La Paz
Arequipa
Santa Cruz
Brásília
Sucre
PARAGUAY
Rio de Janeiro
20°S
Antofagasta
Asunción
São Paulo
Tropic of Capricorn
C H I L E
Porto Alegre
Córdoba
Rosario
URUGUAY
Santiago
Buenos Aires
Montevideo
Juan Fernandez Is. (Chile)
ARGENTINA
Concepción
Mar del Plata
40°S
Stanley
Falkland Islands (UK)
South Georgia (UK)
Punta Arenas
100°W
80°W
60°W
40°W
20°W
Scale 1: 36 000 000
0 360 720 1080 1440 1800 km
international boundary
internal boundary
capital city
other important city

Oblique Mercator Projection

CARIBBEAN SEA
Punta Gallinas
Margarita
Panama Isthmus
L. Maracaibo
Cord. de Mérida
Llanos
Orinoco
Magdalena
Mt. Roraima 2810
GUIANA HIGHLANDS
Guaviare
Branco
Punta Galera
Cotopaxi 5896
Chimborazo 6310
Equator
Galapagos Islands
Gulf of Guayaquil
Punta Negra
Mouths of the Amazon
Negro
Putumayo
Amazon
Marañon
Juruá
Selvas
Madeira
Tapajós
Xingu
Ucayali
Purus
Parnaíba
6768 Huascarán
ANDES
Serra dos Parecis
Araguaia
Tocantins
São Francisco
Chapada Diamantina
BRAZILIAN HIGHLANDS
Mato Grosso
Serra Geral de Goiás
L. Titicaca
Chiquitos Plateau
Serra do Espinhaço
L. Poopo
Brazil Plateau
Atacama Desert
Paraná
Agulhas Negras 2797
Gran Chaco
6723
Paraná Plateau
Tropic of Capricorn
SOUTH PACIFIC OCEAN
Uruguay
Serra do Mar
Aconcagua 6960
L. Patos
L. Mirim
Río de la Plata
Pampas
SOUTH ATLANTIC OCEAN
Negro
Bahía Blanca
Valdés Peninsula
Chiloé
Patagonia
Gulf of San Jorge
Taitao Peninsula
Strait of Magellan
Falkland Islands
Tierra del Fuego
Cape Horn
South Georgia
SOUTHERN OCEAN

Scale 1: 36 000 000

0 360 720 1080 1440 1800 km

Oblique Mercator Projection

Scale 1: 70 000 000

January temperature

actual surface temperature

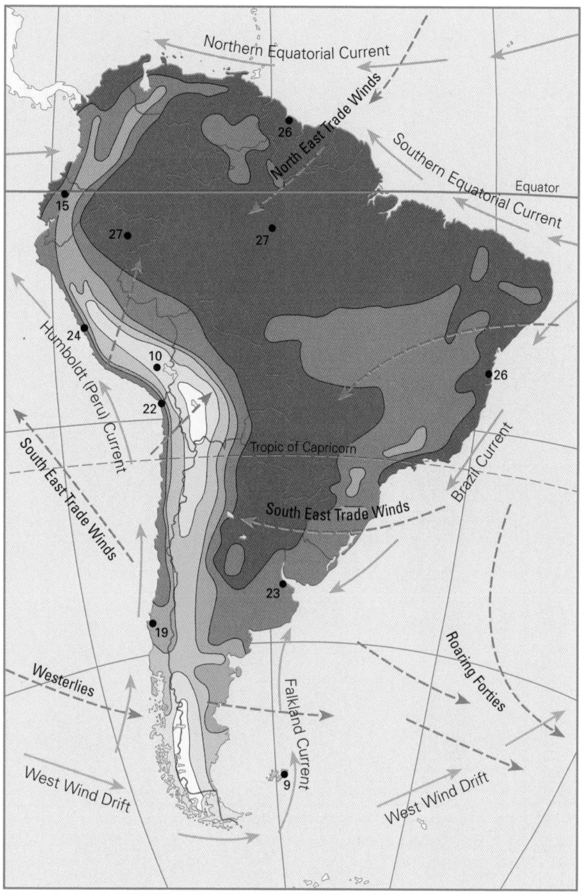

July temperature

actual surface temperature

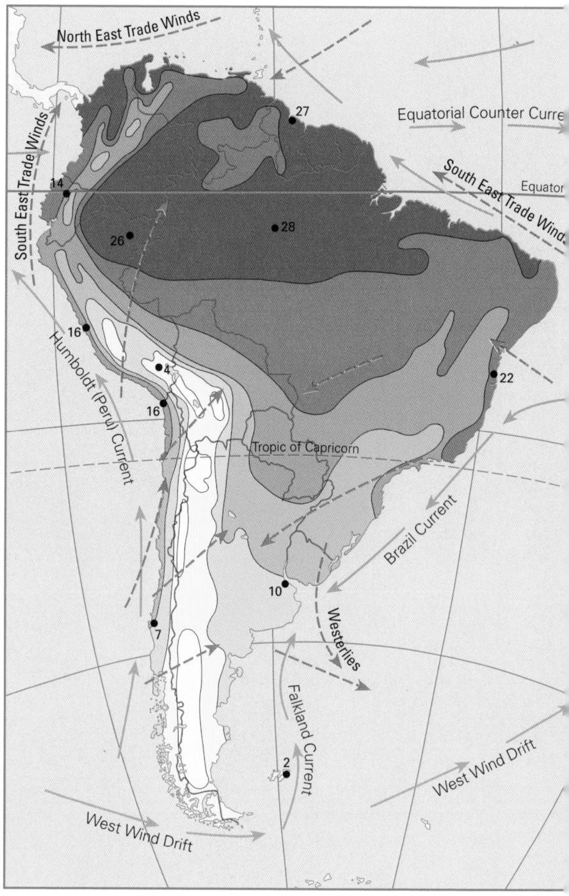

Precipitation

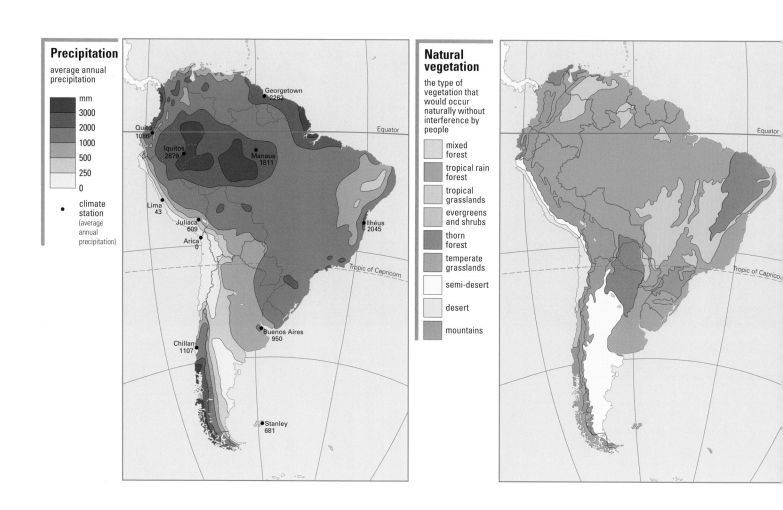

average annual precipitation

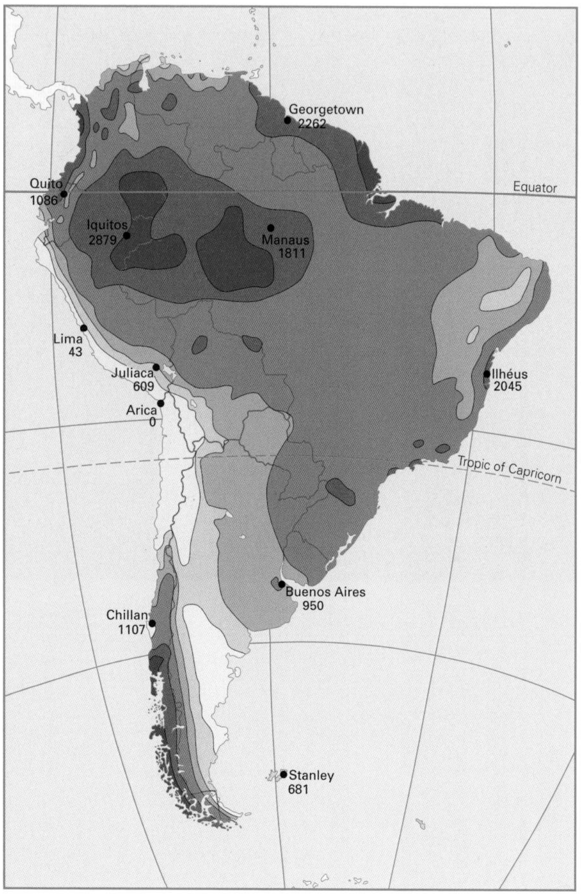

Natural vegetation

the type of vegetation that would occur naturally without interference by people

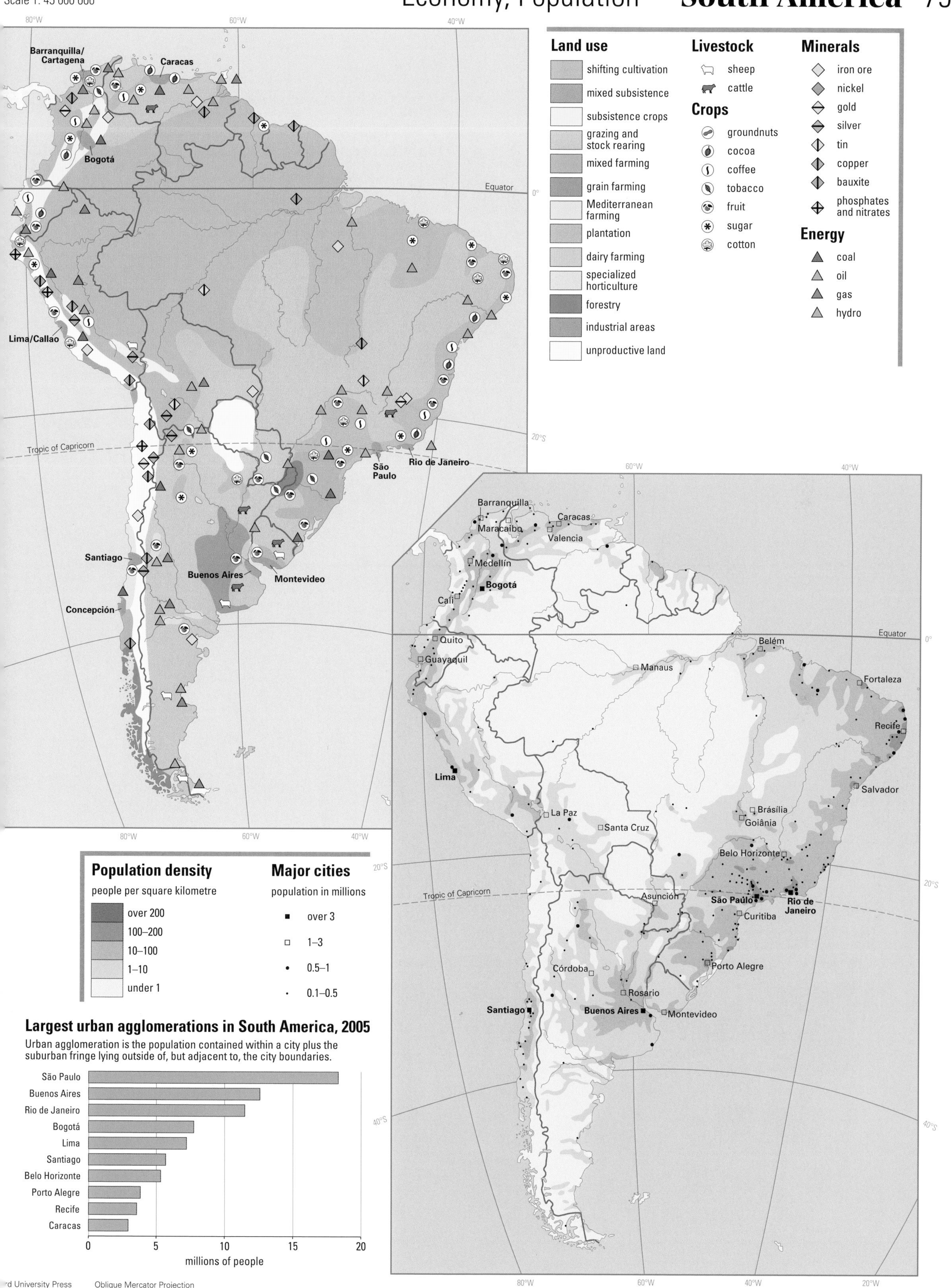
Land use
shifting cultivation
mixed subsistence
subsistence crops
grazing and stock rearing
mixed farming
grain farming
Mediterranean farming
plantation
dairy farming
specialized horticulture
forestry
industrial areas
unproductive land
Livestock
sheep
cattle
Crops
groundnuts
cocoa
coffee
tobacco
fruit
sugar
cotton
Minerals
iron ore
nickel
gold
silver
tin
copper
bauxite
phosphates and nitrates
Energy
coal
oil
gas
hydro
80°W
60°W
40°W
Equator
0°
20°S
Tropic of Capricorn
Barranquilla/ Cartagena
Caracas
Bogotá
Lima/Callao
São Paulo
Rio de Janeiro
Santiago
Buenos Aires
Montevideo
Concepción
Population density
people per square kilometre
over 200
100–200
10–100
1–10
under 1
Major cities
population in millions
over 3
1–3
0.5–1
0.1–0.5
Barranquilla
Maracaibo
Caracas
Valencia
Medellín
Bogotá
Cali
Quito
Guayaquil
Belém
Manaus
Fortaleza
Recife
Lima
Salvador
La Paz
Brasília
Goiânia
Santa Cruz
Belo Horizonte
Asunción
São Paulo
Rio de Janeiro
Curitiba
Porto Alegre
Córdoba
Rosario
Santiago
Buenos Aires
Montevideo
40°S
20°W
Largest urban agglomerations in South America, 2005
Urban agglomeration is the population contained within a city plus the suburban fringe lying outside of, but adjacent to, the city boundaries.
São Paulo
Buenos Aires
Rio de Janeiro
Bogotá
Lima
Santiago
Belo Horizonte
Porto Alegre
Recife
Caracas
0
5
10
15
20
millions of people

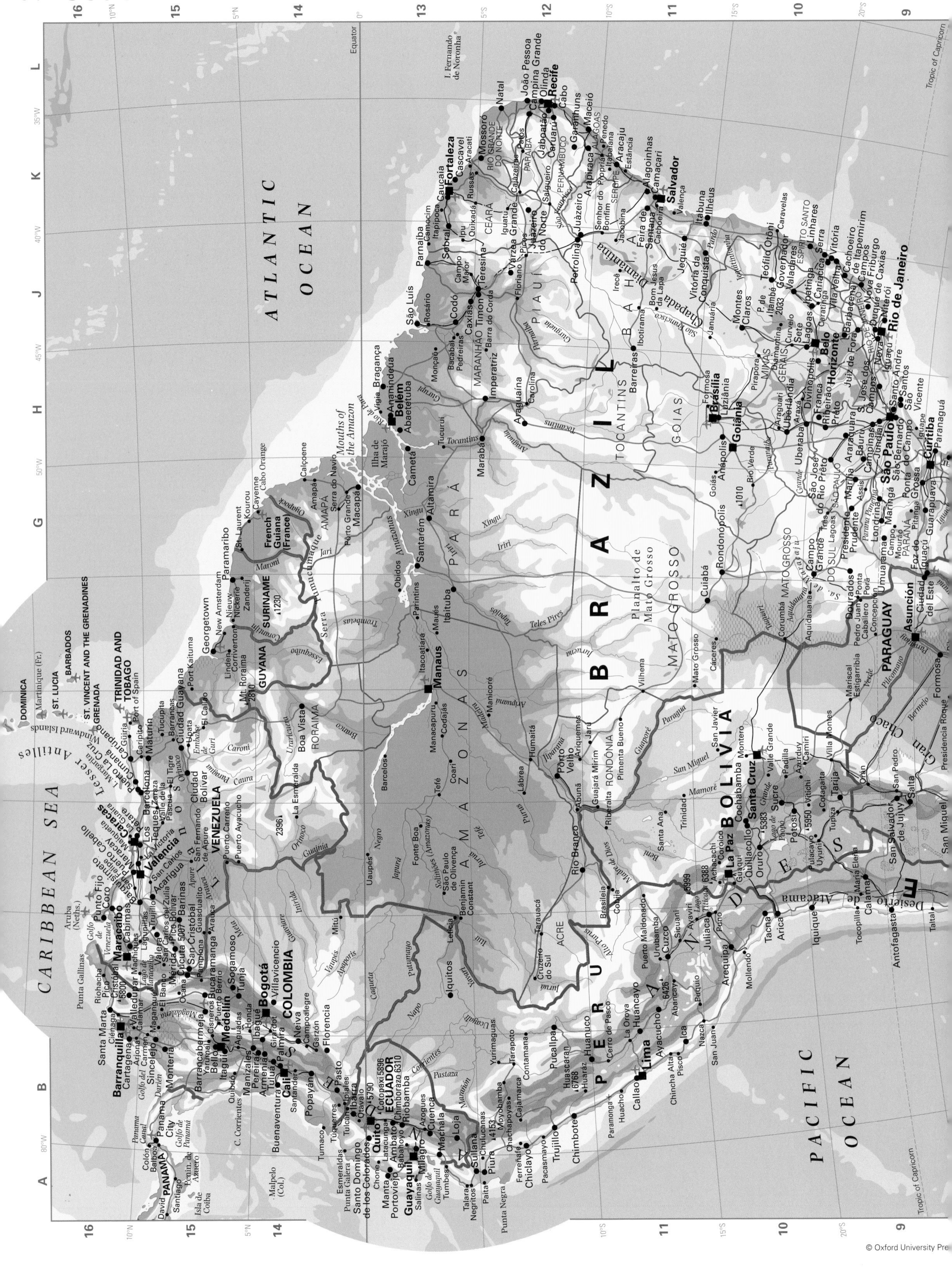
CARIBBEAN SEA
ATLANTIC
OCEAN
PACIFIC
OCEAN
Lesser Antilles
BRAZIL
PERU
BOLIVIA
COLOMBIA
VENEZUELA
ECUADOR
PARAGUAY
GUYANA
SURINAME
French Guiana (France)
PANAMA
TRINIDAD AND TOBAGO
BARBADOS
ST. LUCIA
ST. VINCENT AND THE GRENADINES
GRENADA
DOMINICA
Equator
Tropic of Capricorn

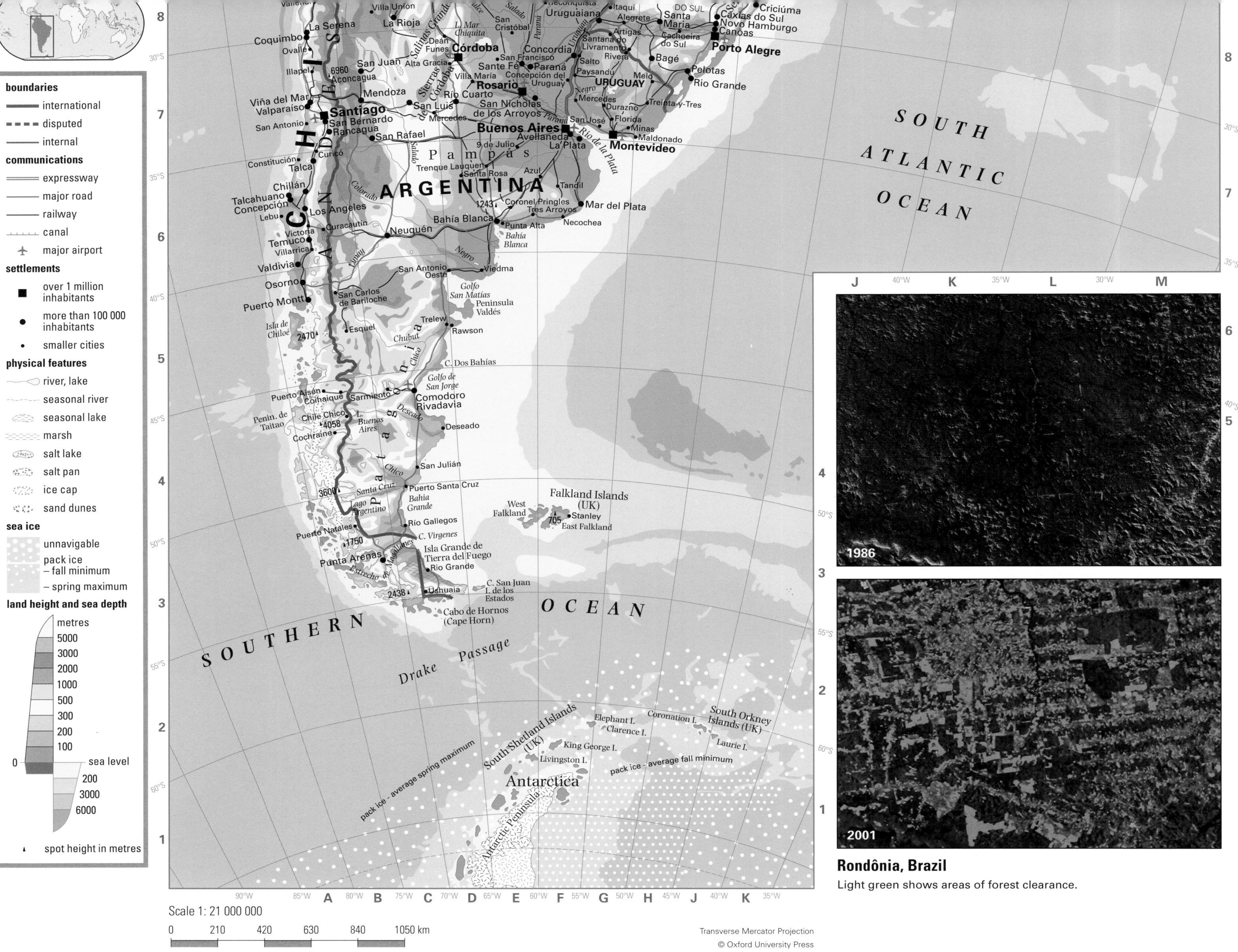

Rondônia, Brazil

Light green shows areas of forest clearance.

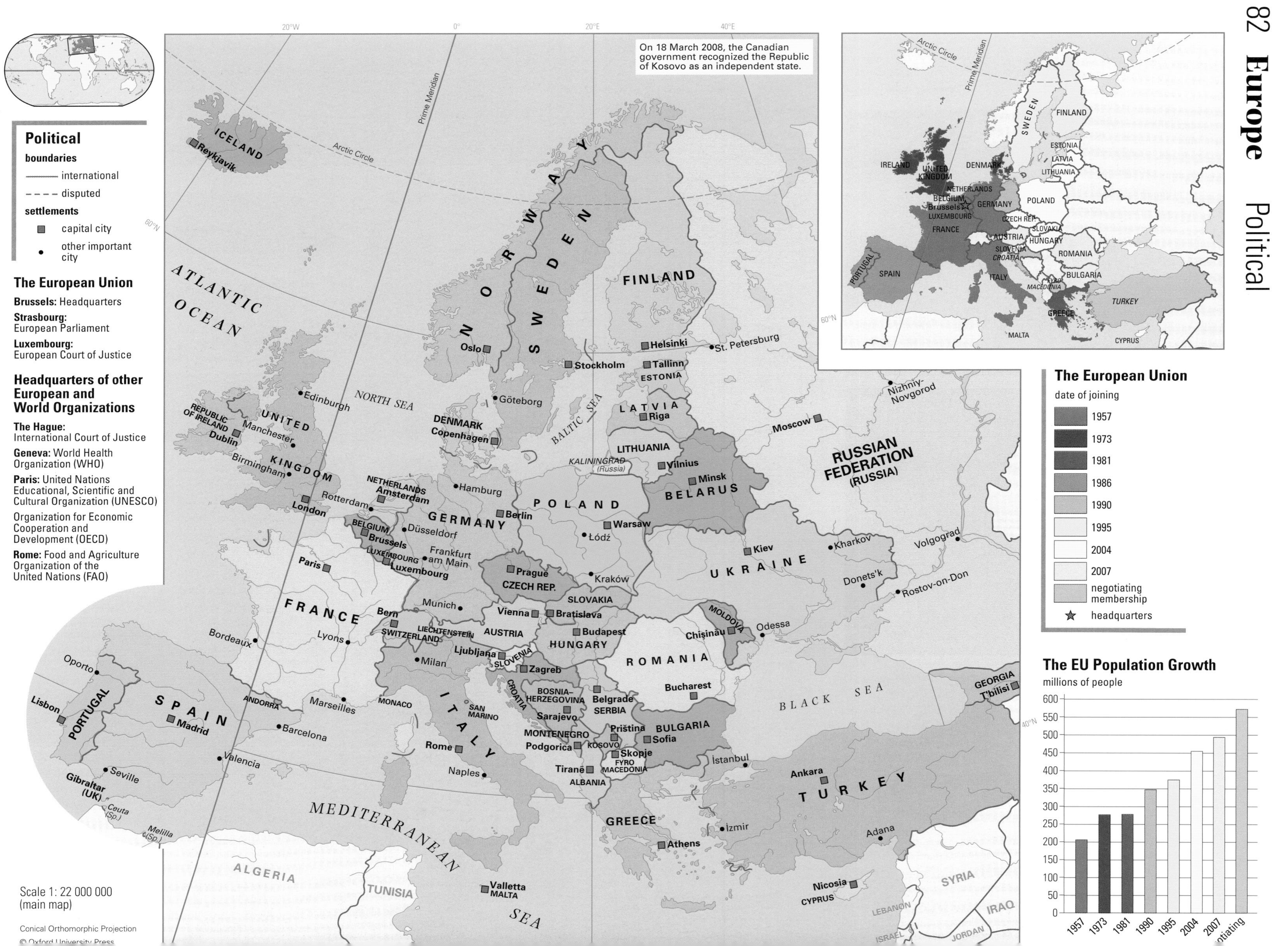

Political
boundaries
international
disputed
settlements
capital city
other important city
The European Union
Brussels: Headquarters
Strasbourg: European Parliament
Luxembourg: European Court of Justice
Headquarters of other European and World Organizations
The Hague: International Court of Justice
Geneva: World Health Organization (WHO)
Paris: United Nations Educational, Scientific and Cultural Organization (UNESCO)
Organization for Economic Cooperation and Development (OECD)
Rome: Food and Agriculture Organization of the United Nations (FAO)
Scale 1: 22 000 000 (main map)
Conical Orthomorphic Projection
© Oxford University Press
On 18 March 2008, the Canadian government recognized the Republic of Kosovo as an independent state.
The European Union
date of joining
1957
1973
1981
1986
1990
1995
2004
2007
negotiating membership
headquarters
The EU Population Growth
millions of people
600
550
500
450
400
350
300
250
200
150
100
50
0
1957
1973
1981
1990
1995
2004
2007
otiating
20°W
0°
20°E
40°E
60°N
40°N
Arctic Circle
Prime Meridian
ATLANTIC OCEAN
NORTH SEA
BALTIC SEA
BLACK SEA
MEDITERRANEAN SEA
ICELAND
Reykjavik
NORWAY
Oslo
SWEDEN
Stockholm
Göteborg
FINLAND
Helsinki
St. Petersburg
ESTONIA
Tallinn
LATVIA
Riga
LITHUANIA
Vilnius
KALININGRAD (Russia)
BELARUS
Minsk
RUSSIAN FEDERATION (RUSSIA)
Moscow
Nizhniy-Novgorod
Volgograd
Rostov-on-Don
UKRAINE
Kiev
Kharkov
Donets'k
Odessa
MOLDOVA
Chişinău
POLAND
Warsaw
Łódź
Kraków
DENMARK
Copenhagen
GERMANY
Berlin
Hamburg
Düsseldorf
Frankfurt am Main
Munich
NETHERLANDS
Amsterdam
Rotterdam
BELGIUM
Brussels
LUXEMBOURG
Luxembourg
UNITED KINGDOM
London
Edinburgh
Manchester
Birmingham
REPUBLIC OF IRELAND
Dublin
FRANCE
Paris
Lyons
Marseilles
Bordeaux
MONACO
SWITZERLAND
Bern
LIECHTENSTEIN
CZECH REP.
Prague
SLOVAKIA
Bratislava
AUSTRIA
Vienna
HUNGARY
Budapest
SLOVENIA
Ljubljana
CROATIA
Zagreb
BOSNIA-HERZEGOVINA
Sarajevo
SERBIA
Belgrade
KOSOVO
Priština
MONTENEGRO
Podgorica
ALBANIA
Tiranë
FYRO MACEDONIA
Skopje
ROMANIA
Bucharest
BULGARIA
Sofia
GREECE
Athens
TURKEY
Ankara
İstanbul
İzmir
Adana
CYPRUS
Nicosia
GEORGIA
T'bilisi
ITALY
Rome
Milan
Naples
SAN MARINO
MALTA
Valletta
SPAIN
Madrid
Barcelona
Valencia
Seville
ANDORRA
PORTUGAL
Lisbon
Oporto
Gibraltar (UK)
Ceuta (Sp.)
Melilla (Sp.)
ALGERIA
TUNISIA
SYRIA
IRAQ
LEBANON
ISRAEL
JORDAN
IRELAND
UNITED KINGDOM
DENMARK
NETHERLANDS
BELGIUM
Brussels
LUXEMBOURG
FRANCE
GERMANY
POLAND
CZECH REP.
SLOVAKIA
AUSTRIA
HUNGARY
SLOVENIA
CROATIA
ROMANIA
BULGARIA
FYRO MACEDONIA
GREECE
TURKEY
CYPRUS
MALTA
ITALY
SPAIN
PORTUGAL
SWEDEN
FINLAND
ESTONIA
LATVIA
LITHUANIA

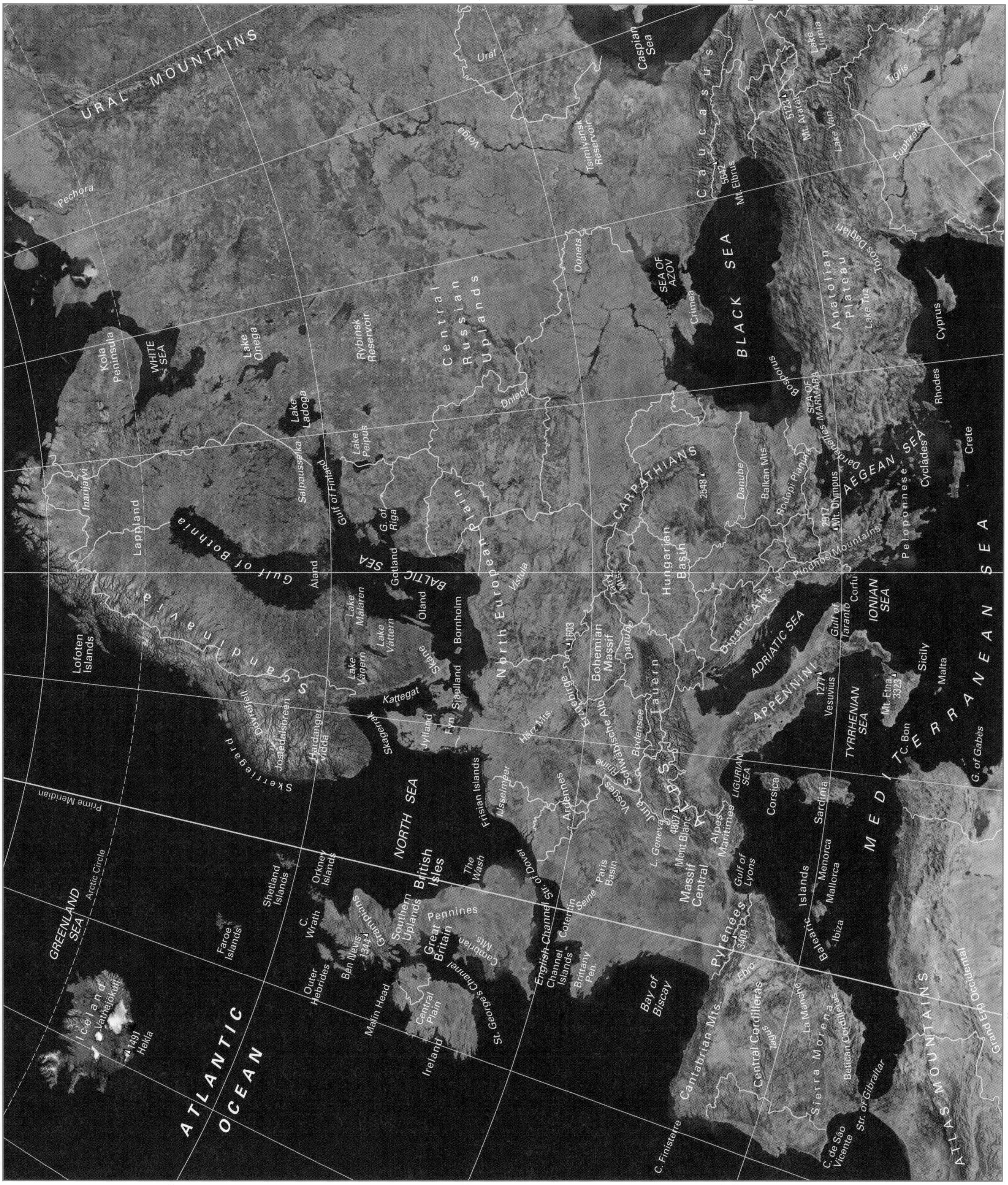

Conical Orthomorphic Projection

Scale 1: 22 000 000

0 220 440 660 880 1100 km

Scale 1: 50 000 000

Conical Orthomorphic Projection

January temperature

actual surface temperature

°Celsius

- 10
- 5
- 0
- -5
- -10
- -15
- -20
- -25

• climate station (average January temperature)

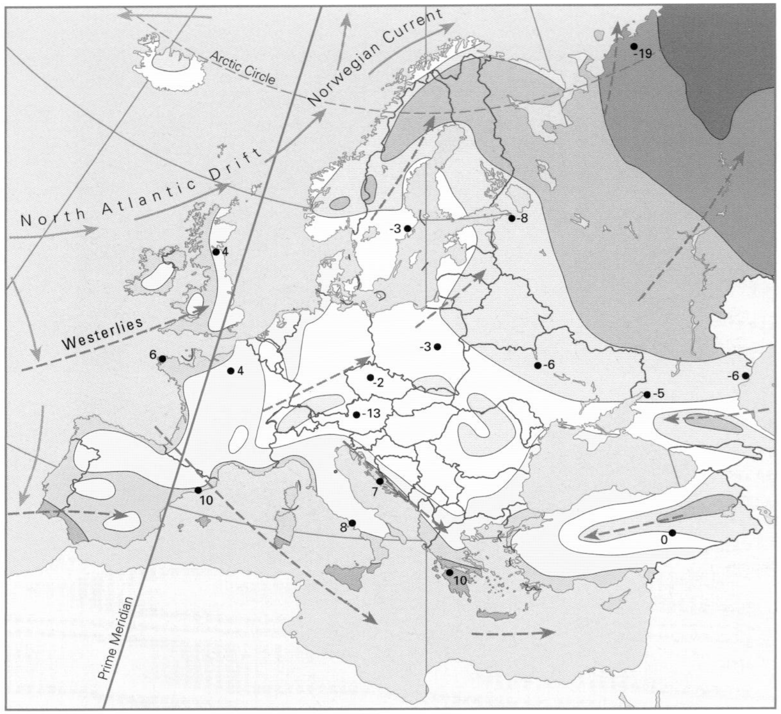

North Atlantic Drift
Norwegian Current
Arctic Circle
Westerlies
Prime Meridian
-19
-3
-8
4
6
4
-3
-2
-6
-13
-5
-6
10
7
8
0
10

warm sea current → cold sea current → prevailing wind

July temperature

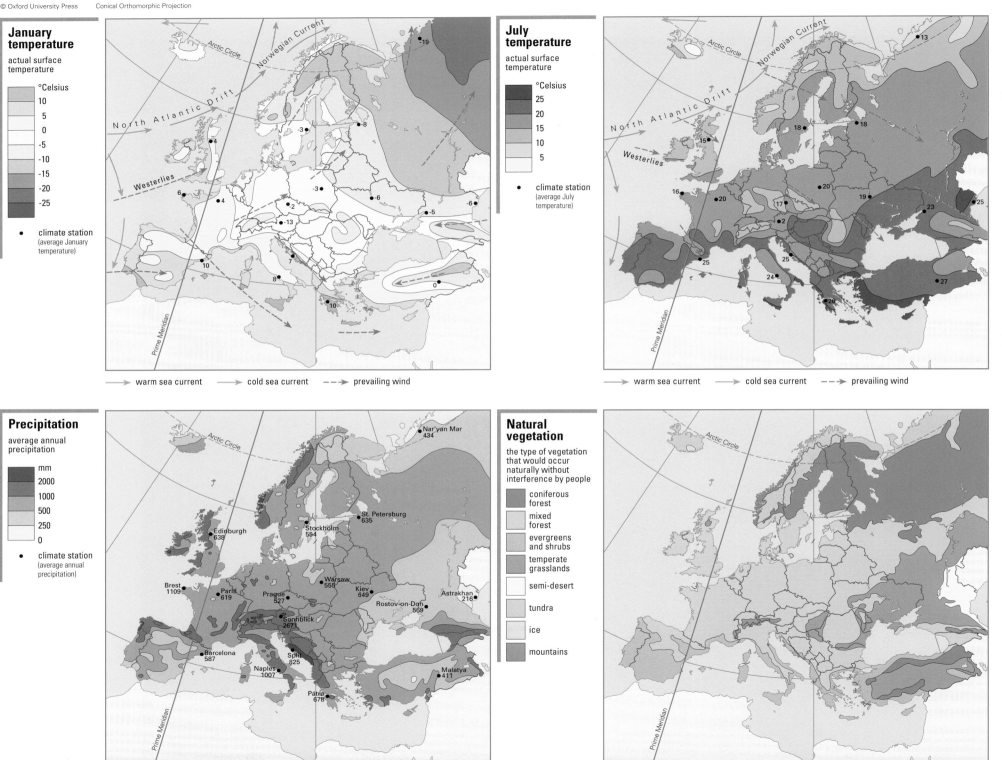

actual surface temperature

°Celsius

- 25
- 20
- 15
- 10
- 5

• climate station (average July temperature)

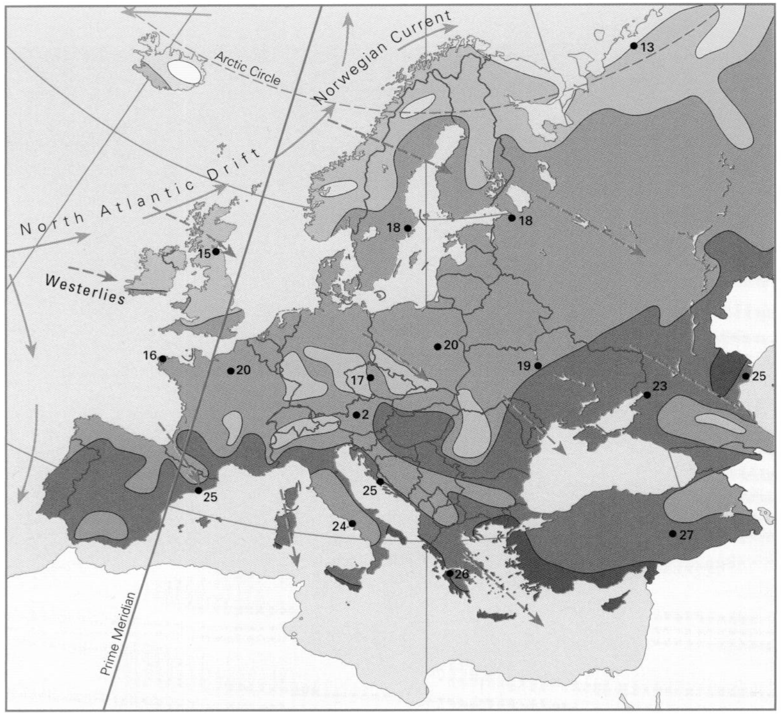

North Atlantic Drift
Norwegian Current
Arctic Circle
Westerlies
Prime Meridian
13
18
18
15
16
20
20
19
17
2
25
23
25
25
24
26
27

warm sea current → cold sea current → prevailing wind

Precipitation

average annual precipitation

mm

- 2000
- 1000
- 500
- 250
- 0

• climate station (average annual precipitation)

Arctic Circle
Prime Meridian
Nar'yan Mar 434
St. Petersburg 635
Stockholm 554
Edinburgh 638
Warsaw 555
Brest 1109
Paris 619
Prague 527
Kiev 649
Astrakhan 216
Rostov-on-Don 569
Sonnblick 2671
Barcelona 587
Split 825
Naples 1007
Malatya 411
Patra 678

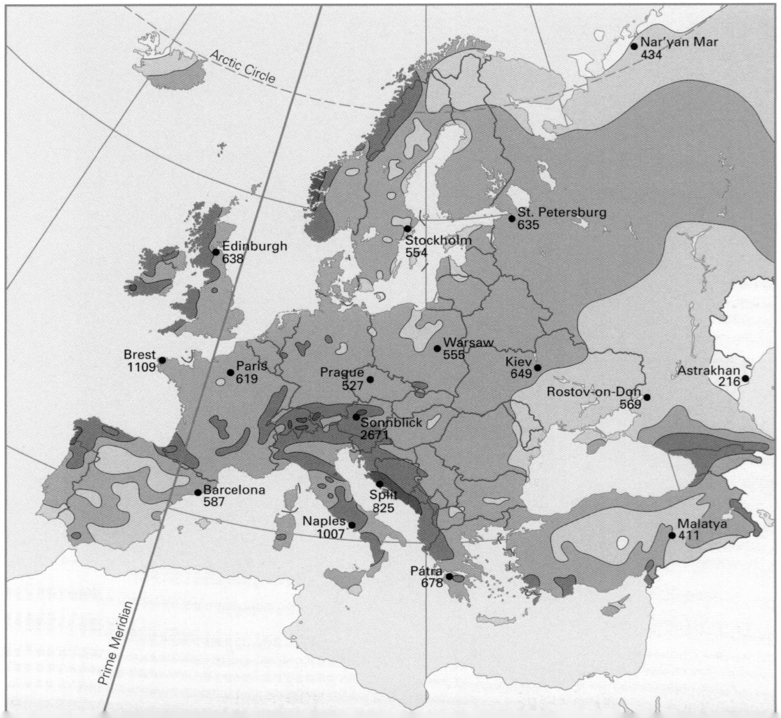

Natural vegetation

the type of vegetation that would occur naturally without interference by people

- coniferous forest
- mixed forest
- evergreens and shrubs
- temperate grasslands
- semi-desert
- tundra
- ice
- mountains

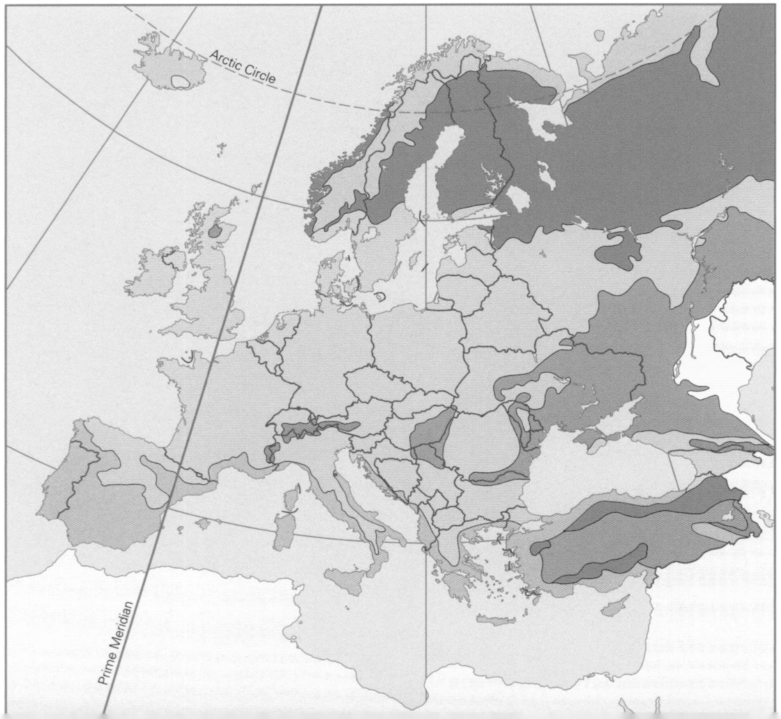

Arctic Circle
Prime Meridian

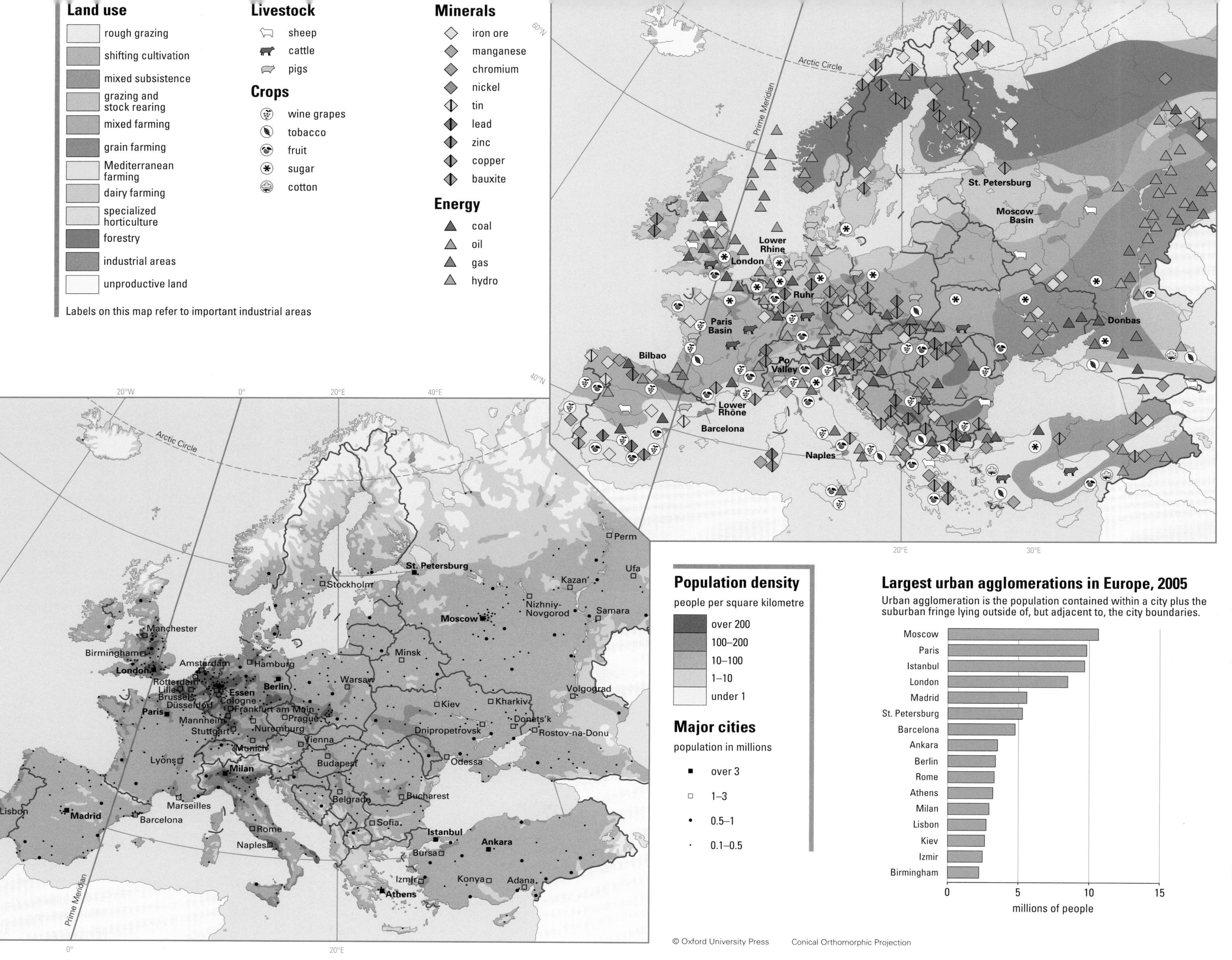
Land use
rough grazing
shifting cultivation
mixed subsistence
grazing and stock rearing
mixed farming
grain farming
Mediterranean farming
dairy farming
specialized horticulture
forestry
industrial areas
unproductive land
Labels on this map refer to important industrial areas
Livestock
sheep
cattle
pigs
Crops
wine grapes
tobacco
fruit
sugar
cotton
Minerals
iron ore
manganese
chromium
nickel
tin
lead
zinc
copper
bauxite
Energy
coal
oil
gas
hydro
Arctic Circle
Prime Meridian
60°N
40°N
20°W
0°
20°E
30°E
40°E
St. Petersburg
Moscow Basin
Lower Rhine
London
Ruhr
Paris Basin
Donbas
Bilbao
Po Valley
Lower Rhône
Barcelona
Naples
Perm
Ufa
St. Petersburg
Stockholm
Kazan'
Nizhniy-Novgorod
Samara
Moscow
Manchester
Birmingham
London
Amsterdam
Hamburg
Minsk
Rotterdam
Lille
Brussels
Düsseldorf
Essen
Cologne
Berlin
Warsaw
Paris
Frankfurt am Main
Prague
Mannheim
Stuttgart
Nuremburg
Munich
Vienna
Volgograd
Kiev
Kharkiv
Donets'k
Dnipropetrovsk
Rostov-na-Donu
Lyons
Milan
Budapest
Odessa
Lisbon
Madrid
Marseilles
Barcelona
Belgrade
Bucharest
Rome
Sofia
Naples
Istanbul
Ankara
Bursa
Izmir
Konya
Adana
Athens
Population density
people per square kilometre
over 200
100–200
10–100
1–10
under 1
Major cities
population in millions
over 3
1–3
0.5–1
0.1–0.5
Largest urban agglomerations in Europe, 2005
Urban agglomeration is the population contained within a city plus the suburban fringe lying outside of, but adjacent to, the city boundaries.
Moscow
Paris
Istanbul
London
Madrid
St. Petersburg
Barcelona
Ankara
Berlin
Rome
Athens
Milan
Lisbon
Kiev
Izmir
Birmingham
0
5
10
15
millions of people
Conical Orthomorphic Projection

Western Europe

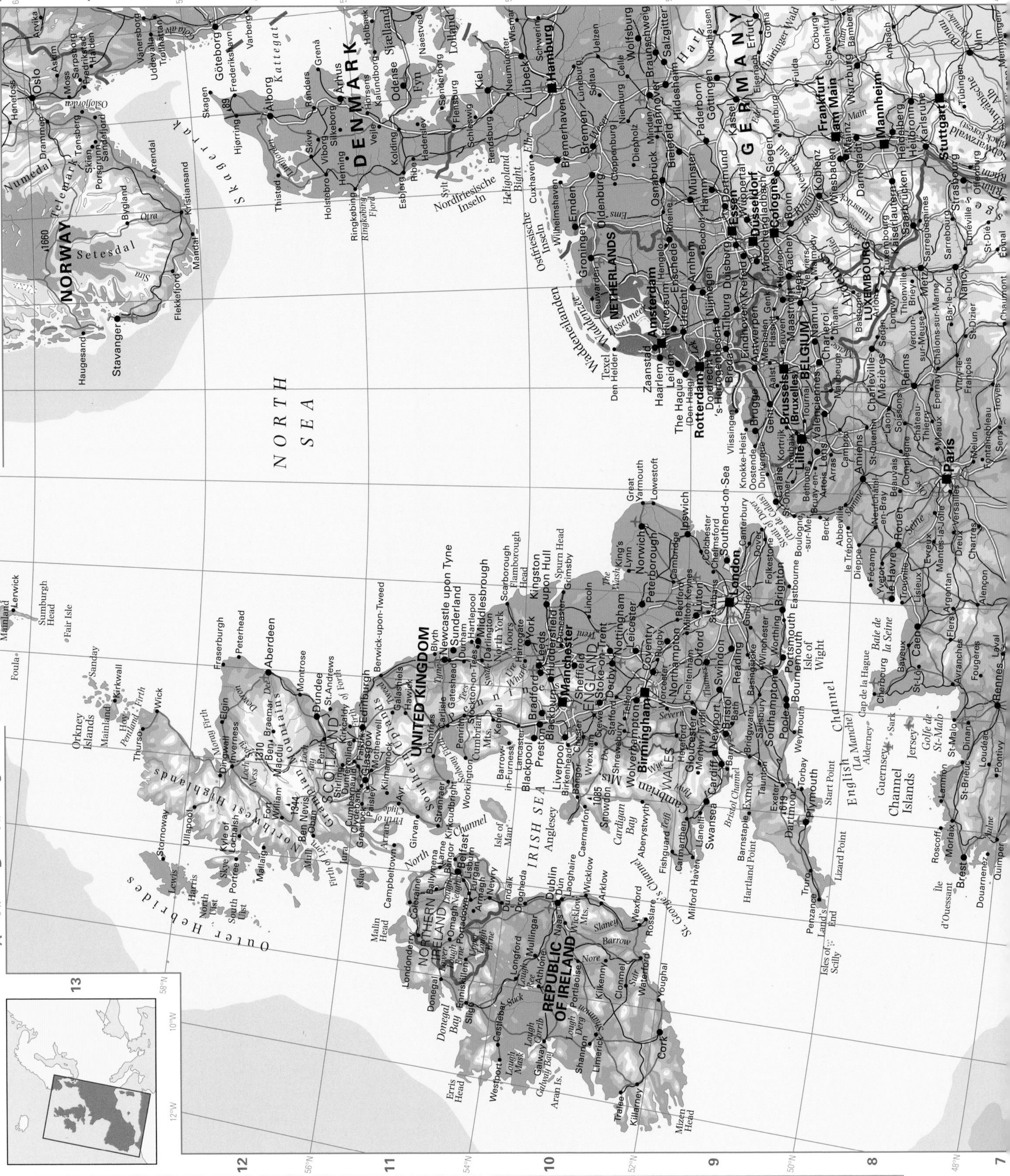

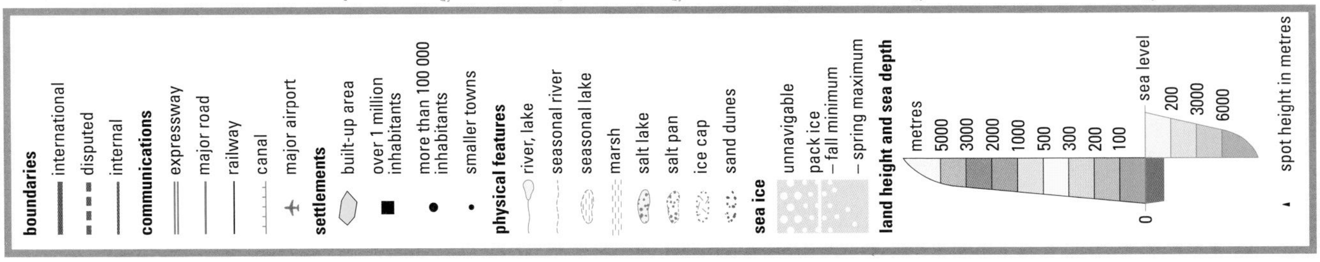

boundaries
- international
- disputed
- internal

communications
- expressway
- major road
- railway
- canal
- major airport

settlements
- built-up area
- over 1 million inhabitants
- more than 100 000 inhabitants
- smaller towns

physical features
- river, lake
- seasonal river
- seasonal lake
- marsh
- salt lake
- salt pan
- ice cap
- sand dunes

sea ice
- unnavigable
- pack ice – fall minimum
- – spring maximum

land height and sea depth

metres 5000 3000 2000 1000 500 300 200 100 0 sea level 200 3000 6000

spot height in metres

FRANCE
SPAIN
PORTUGAL
ALGERIA
MOROCCO
TUNISIA
SWITZERLAND
ANDORRA
MONACO
MEDITERRANEAN SEA
ATLANTIC OCEAN
Bay of Biscay
LIGURIAN SEA
Balearic Islands
Corsica (Corse) (France)
Sardinia (Sardegna) (Italy)
Pyrénées
Pirineos
Massif Central
Cordillera Cantábrica
Sierra Morena
Madrid
Lisbon (Lisboa)
Barcelona
Marseilles
Lyons
Milan
Algiers
Gulf of Valencia
Gulf of Cádiz
Golfe du Lion
Strait of Gibraltar
Scale 1: 6 750 000
0 67.5 135 202.5 270 337.5 km
Conical Orthomorphic Projection
© Oxford University Press

Eastern Europe

ROMANIA
HUNGARY
CROATIA
SLOVENIA
BOSNIA-HERZEGOVINA
SERBIA
MONTENEGRO
KOSOVO
ALBANIA
FYRO MACEDONIA
BULGARIA
GREECE
TURKEY
ITALY
SAN MARINO
SWITZERLAND
UKRAINE
TUNISIA
MALTA
BLACK SEA
SEA OF MARMARA
AEGEAN SEA
MIRTOAN SEA
SEA OF CRETE
IONIAN SEA
ADRIATIC SEA
TYRRHENIAN SEA
LIGURIAN SEA
MEDITERRANEAN SEA
Strait of Otranto
Sicilian Channel
Iónia Nisiá (Ionian Islands)
Dodekánisos (Dodecanese)
Kykládes (Cyclades)
Bucharest
Belgrade
Sofia
Athens
İstanbul
İzmir
Rome (Roma)
Naples
Milan
Tunis
Zagreb
Sarajevo
Skopje
Tiranë
Podgorica
Ljubljana
Sicily
Sardinia (Sardegna) (Italy)
Corsica (Corse) (France)
Kríti (Crete)
Ródos (Rhodes)

Scale 1: 60 000 000

Scale 1: 55 000 000

0 550 1100 1650 2200 2750 km

- international boundary
- disputed boundary
- ceasefire line
- capital city
- other important city

Zenithal Equal Area Projection

cale 1: 55 000 000

550 1100 1650 2200 2750 km

Zenithal equal Area Projection

Scale 1: 120 000 000

January temperature

actual surface temperature

°Celsius: 25, 20, 15, 10, 5, 0, –10, –20, –30, –40, –50

• climate station (average January temperature)

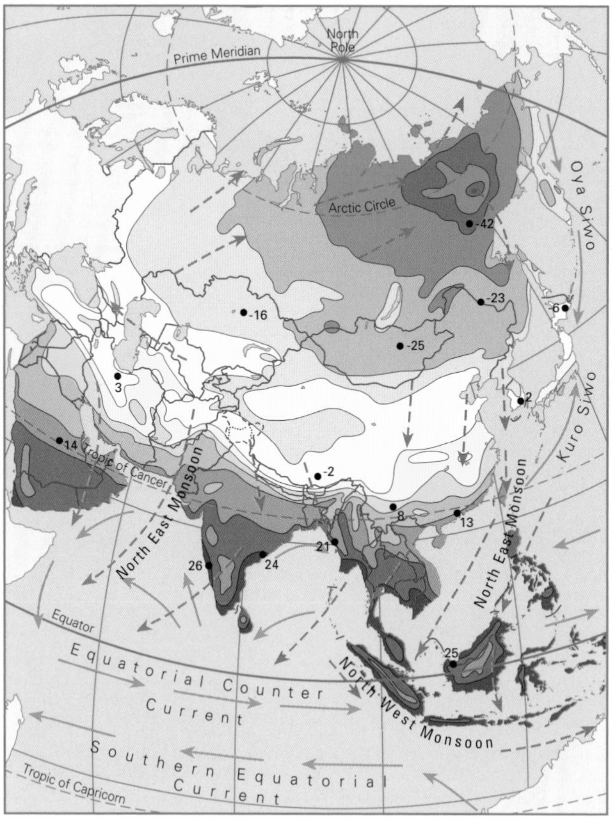

warm sea current — cold sea current — prevailing wind

July temperature

actual surface temperature

°Celsius: 35, 30, 25, 20, 15, 10, 5, 0

• climate station (average July temperature)

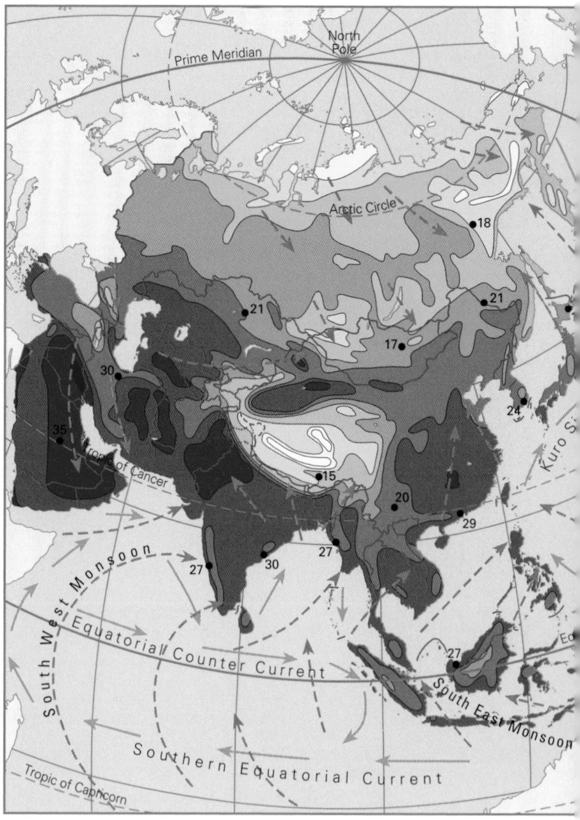

warm sea current — cold sea current — prevailing wind

Precipitation

average annual precipitation

mm: 3000, 2000, 1000, 500, 250, 0

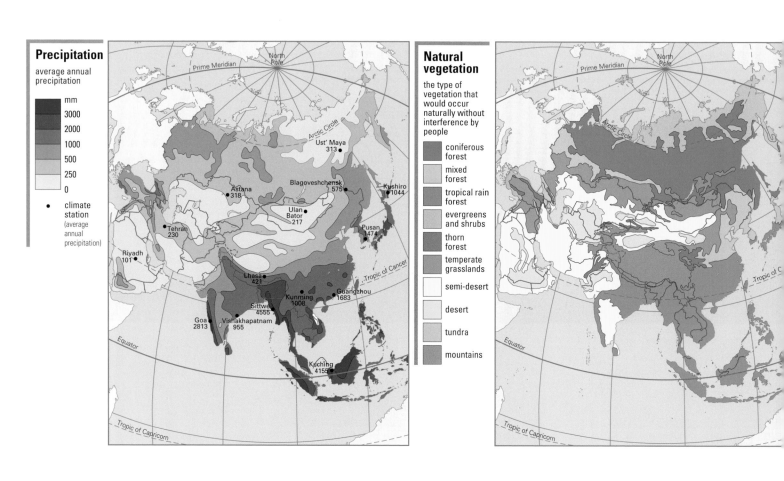

• climate station (average annual precipitation)

Natural vegetation

the type of vegetation that would occur naturally without interference by people

- coniferous forest
- mixed forest
- tropical rain forest
- evergreens and shrubs
- thorn forest
- temperate grasslands
- semi-desert
- desert
- tundra
- mountains

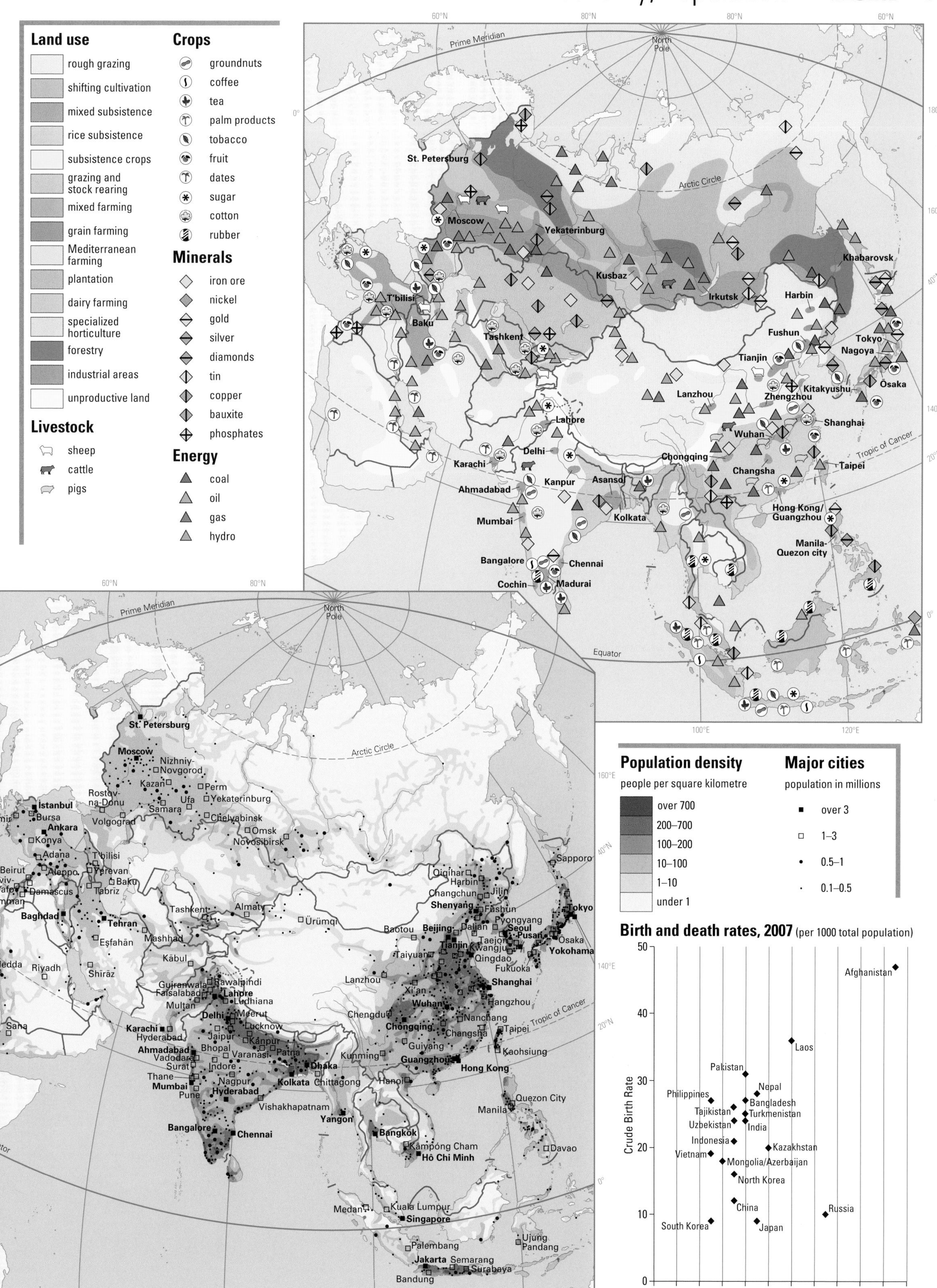

Zenithal Equal Area Projection

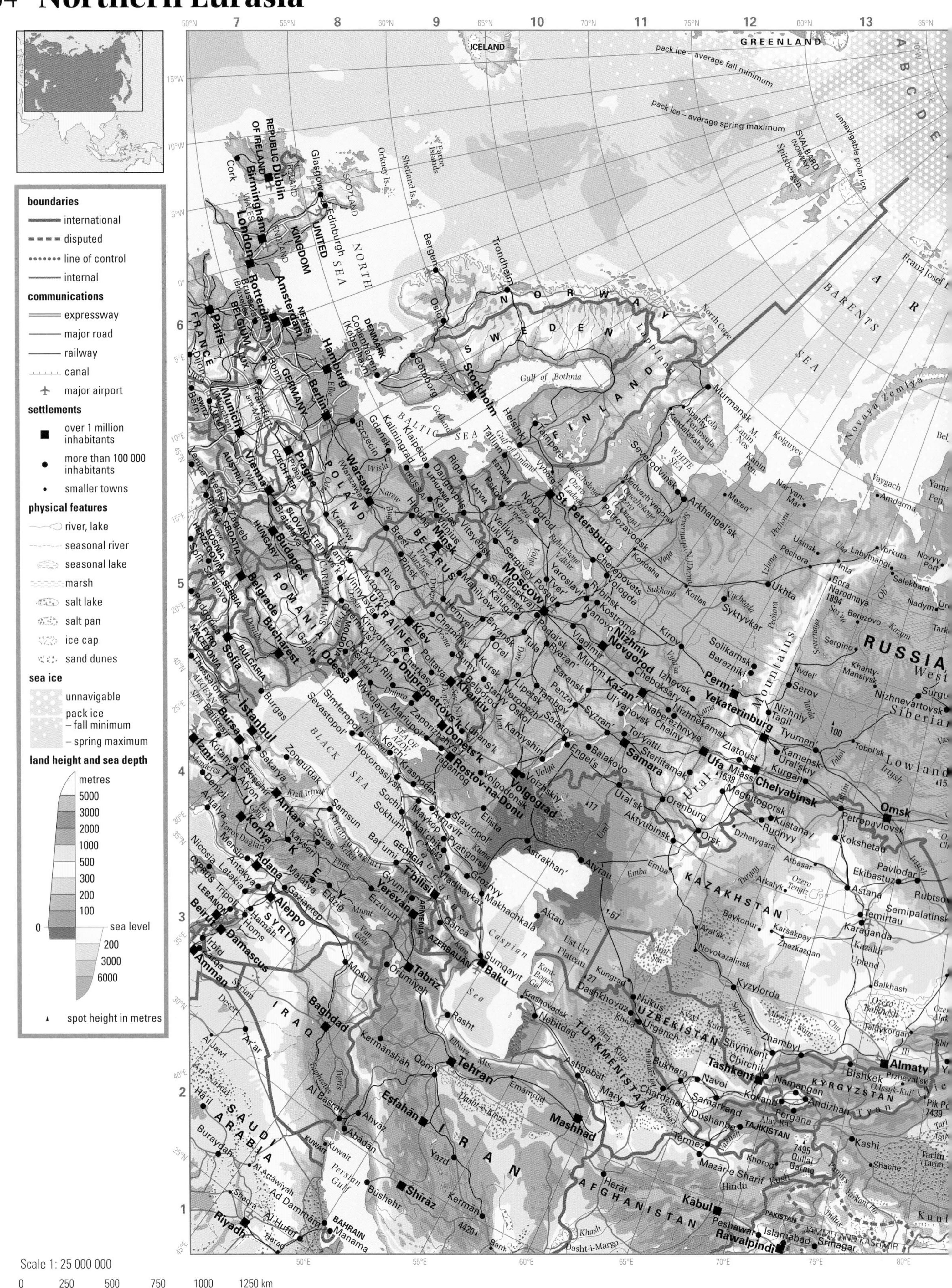
boundaries
international
disputed
line of control
internal
communications
expressway
major road
railway
canal
major airport
settlements
over 1 million inhabitants
more than 100 000 inhabitants
smaller towns
physical features
river, lake
seasonal river
seasonal lake
marsh
salt lake
salt pan
ice cap
sand dunes
sea ice
unnavigable
pack ice
– fall minimum
– spring maximum
land height and sea depth
metres
5000
3000
2000
1000
500
300
200
100
0
sea level
200
3000
6000
spot height in metres
pack ice – average fall minimum
pack ice – average spring maximum
unnavigable polar ice
GREENLAND
ICELAND
NORTH SEA
BALTIC SEA
BARENTS SEA
BLACK SEA
Caspian Sea
Persian Gulf
Gulf of Bothnia
NORWAY
SWEDEN
FINLAND
UNITED KINGDOM
REPUBLIC OF IRELAND
FRANCE
GERMANY
POLAND
BELARUS
UKRAINE
ROMANIA
BULGARIA
TURKEY
SYRIA
IRAQ
IRAN
SAUDI ARABIA
AFGHANISTAN
KAZAKHSTAN
UZBEKISTAN
TURKMENISTAN
KYRGYZSTAN
TAJIKISTAN
PAKISTAN
RUSSIA
Ural Mountains
West Siberian Lowland
Moscow
St Petersburg
London
Paris
Berlin
Stockholm
Kiev
Istanbul
Ankara
Baghdad
Tehran
Tashkent
Almaty
Kābul
Riyadh
Omsk
Yekaterinburg
Volgograd
Scale 1: 25 000 000
0 250 500 750 1000 1250 km
Conical Orthomorphic Projection
© Oxford University Press

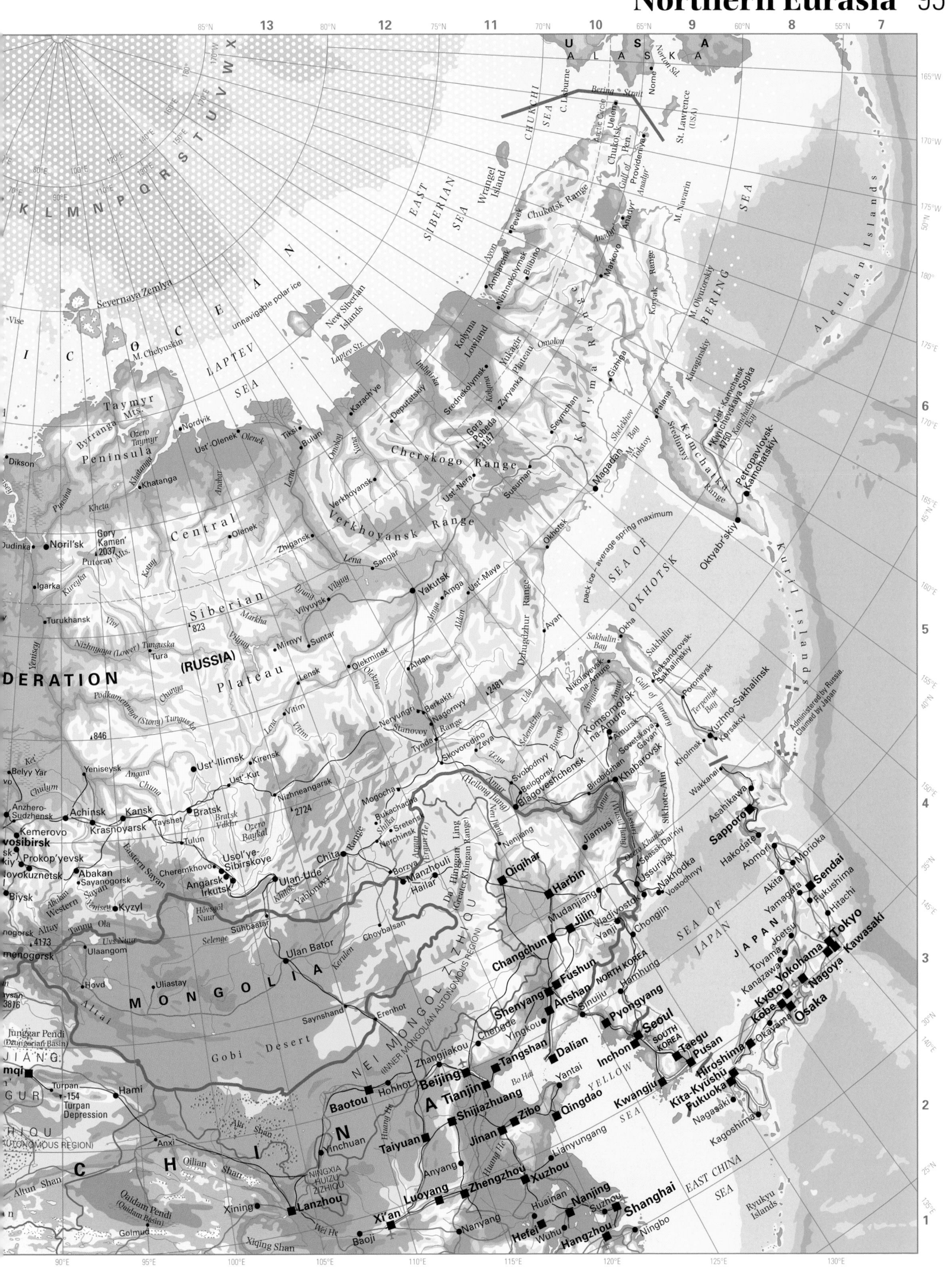
U S A
A L A S K A
Norton Sd.
Nome
Bering Strait
C. Lisburne
CHUKCHI SEA
St. Lawrence (USA)
Arctic Circle
Uelen
Chukotsk Pen.
Gulf of Anadyr'
Provideniya
Wrangel Island
EAST SIBERIAN SEA
Chukotsk Range
Pevek
Anadyr'
Markovo
M. Navarin
BERING SEA
Aleutian Islands
Koryak Range
M. Olyutorskiy
Karaginskiy
Ust'-Kamchatsk
Klyuchevskaya Sopka 4750
Kamchatka Bay
Petropavlovsk-Kamchatskiy
Kamchatka
Sredinnyy Range
Palana
Bilibino
Ambarchik
Nizhnekolymsk
Kolyma Lowland
Yukagir Plateau
Omolon
Kolyma Range
Gizhiga
Shelekhov Bay
M. Tolstoy
Magadan
Seymchan
Srednekolymsk
Zyryanka
Gora Pobeda 3147
Cherskogo Range
Susuman
Ust'-Nera
Verkhoyansk
Verkhoyansk Range
Deputatskiy
Kazach'ye
New Siberian Islands
Laptev Str.
unnavigable polar ice
Severnaya Zemlya
Vise
M. Chelyuskin
LAPTEV SEA
Taymyr Peninsula
Byrranga Mts.
Ozero Taymyr
Nordvik
Ust'-Olenek
Olenek
Tiksi
Bulun
Dikson
Khatanga
Kheta
Anabar
Lena
Omoloy
Yana
Zhigansk
Central Siberian Plateau
Olenek
Gory Kamen' 2037
Putoran Mts.
Dudinka
Noril'sk
Igarka
Kureyka
Turukhansk
Yenisey
Sangar
Yakutsk
Amga
Ust'-Maya
Aldan
Vilyuysk
Vilyuy
Tyung
Markha
823
Nizhnyaya (Lower) Tunguska
Tura
Mirnyy
Suntar
(RUSSIA)
RUSSIAN FEDERATION
Olekminsk
Aldan
Lensk
Podkamennaya (Stony) Tunguska
Chunya
Vitim
Neryungri
Berkakit
Nagornyy
Stanovoy Range
2481
Tynda
Skovorodino
Zeya
846
Okhotsk
pack ice – average spring maximum
SEA OF OKHOTSK
Oktyabr'skiy
Kuril Islands
Administered by Russia. Claimed by Japan.
Dzhugdzhur Range
Ayan
Sakhalin Bay
Okha
Sakhalin
Nikolayevsk-na-Amure
Aleksandrovsk-Sakhalinskiy
Gulf of Tartary
Poronaysk
Terpeniya Bay
Yuzhno-Sakhalinsk
Korsakov
Kholmsk
Komsomol'sk-na-Amure
Amursk
Sovetskaya Gavan'
Khabarovsk
Sikhote-Alin'
Birobidzhan
Blagoveshchensk
Svobodnyy
Belogorsk
Amur (Heilong Jiang)
Ust'-Ilimsk
Kirensk
Yeniseysk
Angara
Ust'-Kut
Nizhneangarsk
Mogocha
2724
Bratsk
Belyy Yar
Anzhero-Sudzhensk
Achinsk
Kansk
Krasnoyarsk
Tayshet
Kemerovo
Novosibirsk
Prokop'yevsk
Novokuznetsk
Abakan
Sayanogorsk
Biysk
Tulun
Ozero Baykal
Usol'ye-Sibirskoye
Cheremkhovo
Angarsk
Irkutsk
Ulan-Ude
Chita
Bukachacha
Sretensk
Nerchinsk
Borzya
Manzhouli
Hailar
Yablonovyy Range
Eastern Sayan
Western Sayan
Kyzyl
Tannu Ola
Altay
4173
Hövsgöl Nuur
Sühbaatar
Selenge
Ulaangom
Uvs Nuur
Leninogorsk
Hovd
Uliastay
MONGOLIA
Ulan Bator
Kerulen
Choybalsan
Saynshand
Erenhot
Gobi Desert
Junggar Pendi (Dzungarian Basin)
Turpan -154
Turpan Depression
Hami
Urumqi
Anxi
Qilian Shan
Altun Shan
Qaidam Pendi (Qaidam Basin)
Golmud
Xining
Lanzhou
NINGXIA HUIZU ZIZHIQU
Yinchuan
Xiqing Shan
Wei He
Baoji
Xi'an
Luoyang
Zhengzhou
Nanyang
Anyang
Taiyuan
Baotou
Hohhot
Huang He
NEI MONGOL ZIZHIQU (INNER MONGOLIAN AUTONOMOUS REGION)
Da Hinggan Ling (Greater Khingan Range)
Nenjiang
Qiqihar
Harbin
Mudanjiang
Jiamusi
Jilin
Changchun
Fushun
Shenyang
Anshan
Yingkou
Chengde
Zhangjiakou
Beijing
Tianjin
Tangshan
Dalian
Bo Hai
Yantai
Shijiazhuang
Zibo
Jinan
Qingdao
Lianyungang
Xuzhou
Huainan
Hefei
Wuhu
Nanjing
Suzhou
Shanghai
Hangzhou
Ningbo
C H I N A
YELLOW SEA
EAST CHINA SEA
Ryukyu Islands
NORTH KOREA
Pyongyang
Sinuiju
Hamhung
Chongjin
Yanji
Vladivostok
Nakhodka
Vostochnyy
Ussuriysk
Spassk-Dal'niy
Ozero Khanka
SOUTH KOREA
Seoul
Inchon
Taegu
Pusan
Kwangju
SEA OF JAPAN
JAPAN
Wakkanai
Asahikawa
Sapporo
Hakodate
Aomori
Morioka
Akita
Sendai
Yamagata
Fukushima
Hitachi
Tokyo
Kawasaki
Yokohama
Joetsu
Toyama
Kanazawa
Nagoya
Kyoto
Kobe
Osaka
Okayama
Hiroshima
Kita-Kyushu
Fukuoka
Nagasaki
Kagoshima

Middle East

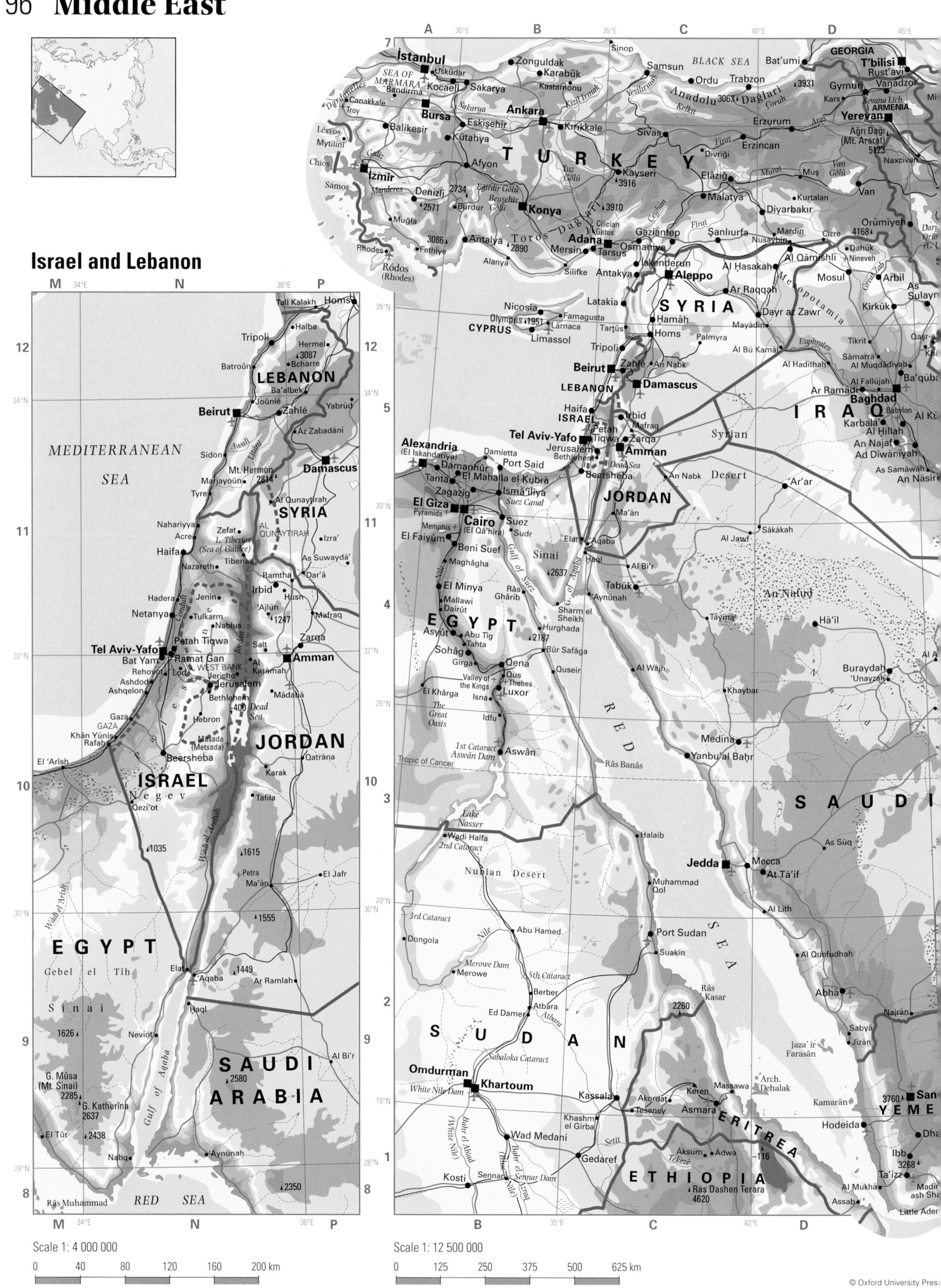
Israel and Lebanon
Scale 1: 4 000 000
0 40 80 120 160 200 km
Scale 1: 12 500 000
0 125 250 375 500 625 km

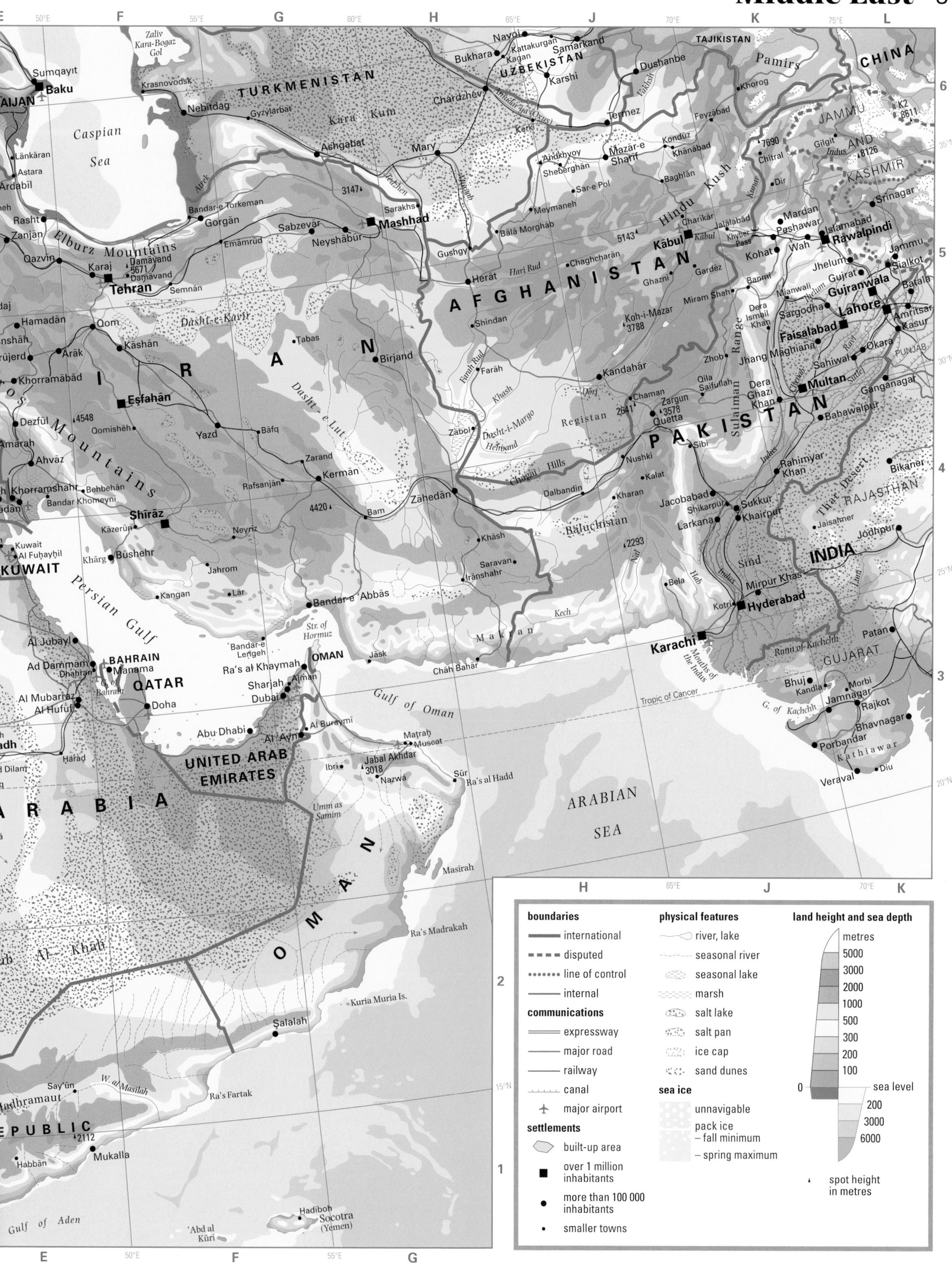
Caspian Sea
TURKMENISTAN
UZBEKISTAN
TAJIKISTAN
CHINA
AFGHANISTAN
PAKISTAN
IRAN
INDIA
KUWAIT
BAHRAIN
QATAR
UNITED ARAB EMIRATES
OMAN
ARABIA
Persian Gulf
Gulf of Oman
ARABIAN SEA
Gulf of Aden
Baku
Tehran
Mashhad
Eşfahān
Shīrāz
Kābul
Karachi
Lahore
Rawalpindi
Faisalabad
Gujranwala
Multan
Hyderabad
Ashgabat
Dushanbe
Samarkand
Muscat
Doha
Dubai
Abu Dhabi
Manama
Elburz Mountains
Zagros Mountains
Dasht-e Kavīr
Dasht-e Lut
Kara Kum
Hindu Kush
Pamirs
Sulaiman Range
Thar Desert
Tropic of Cancer
boundaries
international
disputed
line of control
internal
communications
expressway
major road
railway
canal
major airport
settlements
built-up area
over 1 million inhabitants
more than 100 000 inhabitants
smaller towns
physical features
river, lake
seasonal river
seasonal lake
marsh
salt lake
salt pan
ice cap
sand dunes
sea ice
unnavigable
pack ice – fall minimum
– spring maximum
land height and sea depth
metres
5000
3000
2000
1000
500
300
200
100
0
sea level
200
3000
6000
spot height in metres

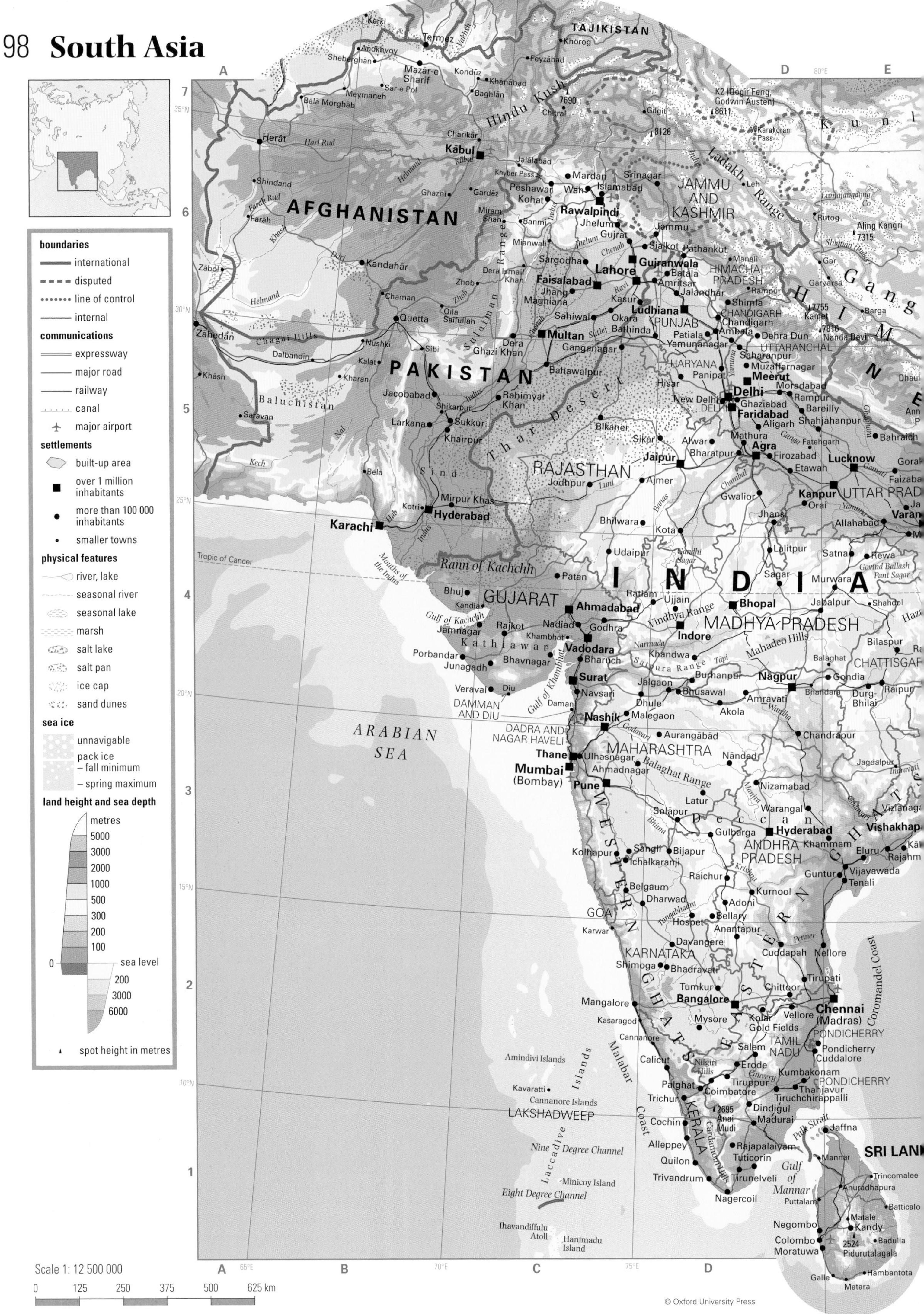
boundaries
international
disputed
line of control
internal
communications
expressway
major road
railway
canal
major airport
settlements
built-up area
over 1 million inhabitants
more than 100 000 inhabitants
smaller towns
physical features
river, lake
seasonal river
seasonal lake
marsh
salt lake
salt pan
ice cap
sand dunes
sea ice
unnavigable
pack ice
– fall minimum
– spring maximum
land height and sea depth
metres
5000
3000
2000
1000
500
300
200
100
0
sea level
200
3000
6000
spot height in metres
Scale 1: 12 500 000
0 125 250 375 500 625 km
A B C D E
1 2 3 4 5 6 7
35°N 30°N 25°N 20°N 15°N 10°N
65°E 70°E 75°E 80°E
AFGHANISTAN
PAKISTAN
INDIA
TAJIKISTAN
SRI LANKA
JAMMU AND KASHMIR
HIMACHAL PRADESH
PUNJAB
CHANDIGARH
HARYANA
UTTARANCHAL
DELHI
RAJASTHAN
UTTAR PRADESH
GUJARAT
MADHYA PRADESH
CHATTISGARH
DAMMAN AND DIU
DADRA AND NAGAR HAVELI
MAHARASHTRA
ANDHRA PRADESH
GOA
KARNATAKA
TAMIL NADU
PONDICHERRY
KERALA
LAKSHADWEEP
ARABIAN SEA
Hindu Kush
Ladakh Range
Sulaiman Range
Thar Desert
Baluchistan
Chagai Hills
Sind
Rann of Kachchh
Kathiawar
Mouths of the Indus
Gulf of Kachchh
Gulf of Khambhat
Vindhya Range
Satpura Range
Mahadeo Hills
Balaghat Range
Deccan
WESTERN GHATS
EASTERN GHATS
Nilgiri Hills
Cardamom Hills
Malabar Coast
Coromandel Coast
Palk Strait
Gulf of Mannar
Amindivi Islands
Laccadive Islands
Cannanore Islands
Nine Degree Channel
Eight Degree Channel
Minicoy Island
Ihavandiffulu Atoll
Hanimadu Island
Tropic of Cancer
Indus
Helmand
Hari Rud
Farah Rud
Khash
Dori
Zhob
Kech
Nal
Hab
Jhelum
Chenab
Ravi
Sutlej
Yamuna
Ganga
Gomati
Chambal
Banas
Luni
Narmada
Tapi
Wardha
Godavari
Manjra
Bhima
Krishna
Tungabhadra
Penner
Cauvery
Indravati
Ghaghara
Kerki
Termez
Andkhvoy
Sheberghan
Mazar-e Sharif
Sar-e Pol
Meymaneh
Bala Morghab
Kondūz
Khānābad
Baghlān
Feyzābād
Khorog
Herāt
Charikār
Kābul
Jalālābād
Shindand
Farāh
Ghazni
Gardēz
Kandahār
Zābol
Zāhedān
Chaman
Quetta
Qila Saifullah
Zhob
Nushki
Dalbandin
Kalat
Khārān
Khāsh
Saravan
Sibi
Jacobabad
Shikarpur
Larkana
Sukkur
Khairpur
Bela
Kotri
Hyderabad
Mirpur Khas
Karachi
Chitral
Gilgit
Mardan
Peshawar
Wah
Islamabad
Rawalpindi
Kohat
Bannu
Miram Shah
Jhelum
Gujrat
Mianwali
Dera Ismail Khan
Sargodha
Faisalabad
Jhang Maghiana
Sahiwal
Okara
Multan
Dera Ghazi Khan
Bahawalpur
Rahimyar Khan
Lahore
Gujranwala
Sialkot
Srinagar
Jammu
Leh
Pathankot
Batala
Amritsar
Jalandhar
Ludhiana
Kasur
Bathinda
Patiala
Ambala
Chandigarh
Shimla
Manali
Rampur
Dehra Dun
Saharanpur
Yamunanagar
Muzaffarnagar
Meerut
Panipat
Hisar
Ganganagar
Moradabad
Rampur
Bareilly
Shahjahanpur
Delhi
New Delhi
Ghaziabad
Faridabad
Aligarh
Mathura
Agra
Firozabad
Etawah
Bikaner
Sikar
Alwar
Bharatpur
Jaipur
Ajmer
Jodhpur
Gwalior
Jhansi
Lucknow
Kanpur
Orai
Allahabad
Varanasi
Faizabad
Bahraich
Fatehgarh
Bhilwara
Kota
Udaipur
Lalitpur
Satna
Rewa
Sagar
Murwara
Jabalpur
Shahdol
Patan
Bhuj
Kandla
Jamnagar
Rajkot
Porbandar
Junagadh
Bhavnagar
Veraval
Diu
Ahmadabad
Nadiad
Khambhat
Godhra
Vadodara
Bharuch
Surat
Navsari
Daman
Ratlam
Ujjain
Indore
Bhopal
Khandwa
Burhanpur
Jalgaon
Bhusawal
Dhule
Malegaon
Nashik
Aurangabad
Akola
Amravati
Nagpur
Gondia
Bhandara
Durg-Bhilai
Raipur
Bilaspur
Balaghat
Chandrapur
Nanded
Thane
Ulhasnagar
Mumbai (Bombay)
Ahmadnagar
Pune
Latur
Solapur
Nizamabad
Warangal
Gulbarga
Hyderabad
Khammam
Kolhapur
Sangli
Ichalkaranji
Bijapur
Raichur
Belgaum
Dharwad
Hospet
Bellary
Adoni
Kurnool
Anantapur
Karwar
Davangere
Shimoga
Bhadravati
Tumkur
Bangalore
Mangalore
Kasaragod
Cannanore
Mysore
Kolar Gold Fields
Vellore
Chennai (Madras)
Tirupati
Chittoor
Cuddapah
Nellore
Guntur
Vijayawada
Tenali
Eluru
Rajahmundry
Vishakhapatnam
Vizianagaram
Jagdalpur
Calicut
Salem
Erode
Pondicherry
Cuddalore
Kumbakonam
Thanjavur
Tiruchchirappalli
Tiruppur
Coimbatore
Palghat
Trichur
Cochin
Alleppey
Quilon
Trivandrum
Nagercoil
Dindigul
Madurai
Rajapalaiyam
Tuticorin
Tirunelveli
Anai Mudi
Kavaratti
Jaffna
Mannar
Trincomalee
Anuradhapura
Puttalam
Batticalo
Matale
Kandy
Negombo
Colombo
Moratuwa
Badulla
Pidurutalagala
Galle
Matara
Hambantota
Barga
Garyarsa
Gar
Rutog
Aling Kangri
Kamet
Nanda Devi
K2 (Gogir Feng, Godwin Austen)
Karakoram Pass
7690
8611
8126
7315
7755
7816
2695
2524
© Oxford University Press

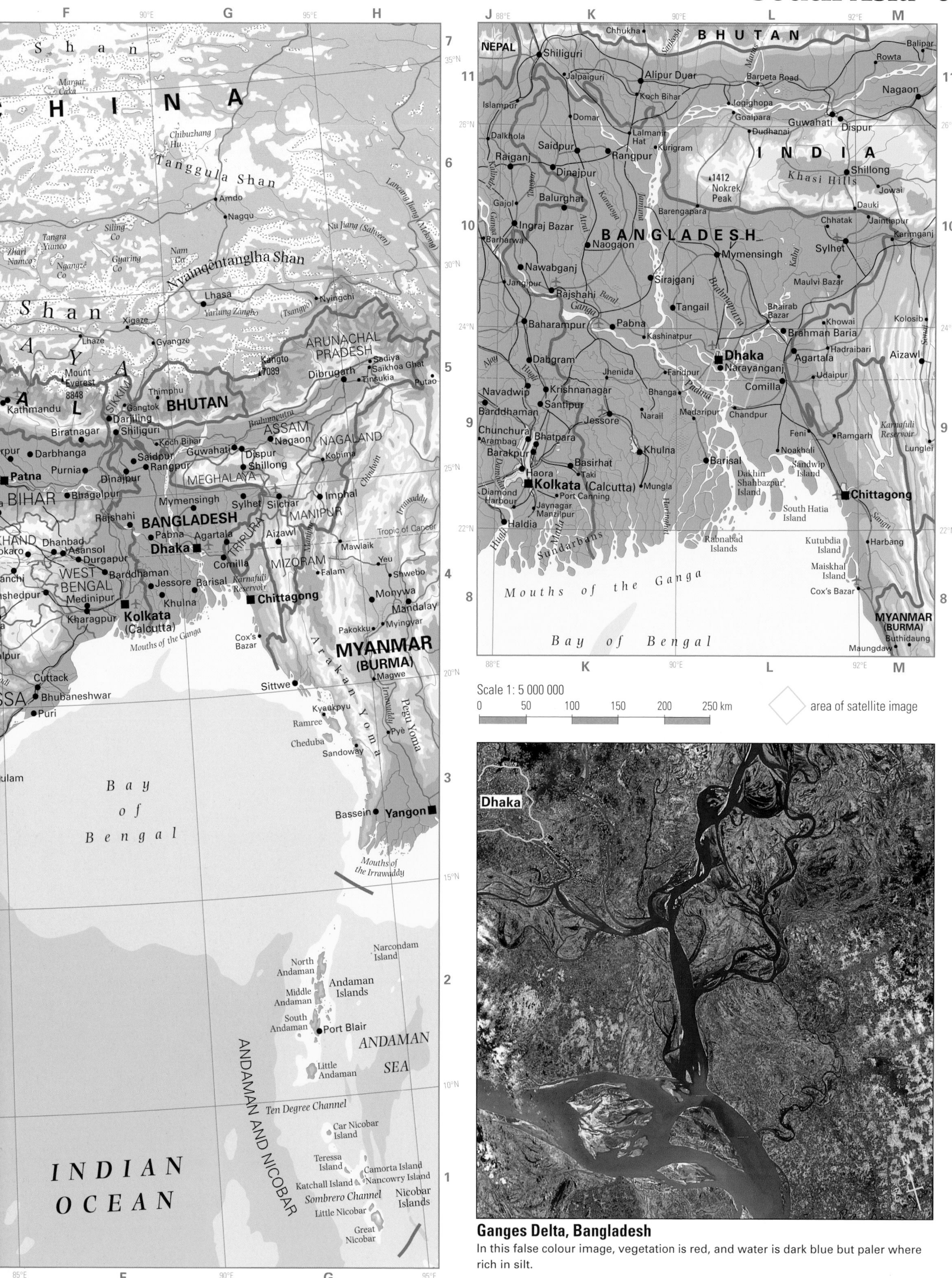

Ganges Delta, Bangladesh

In this false colour image, vegetation is red, and water is dark blue but paler where rich in silt.

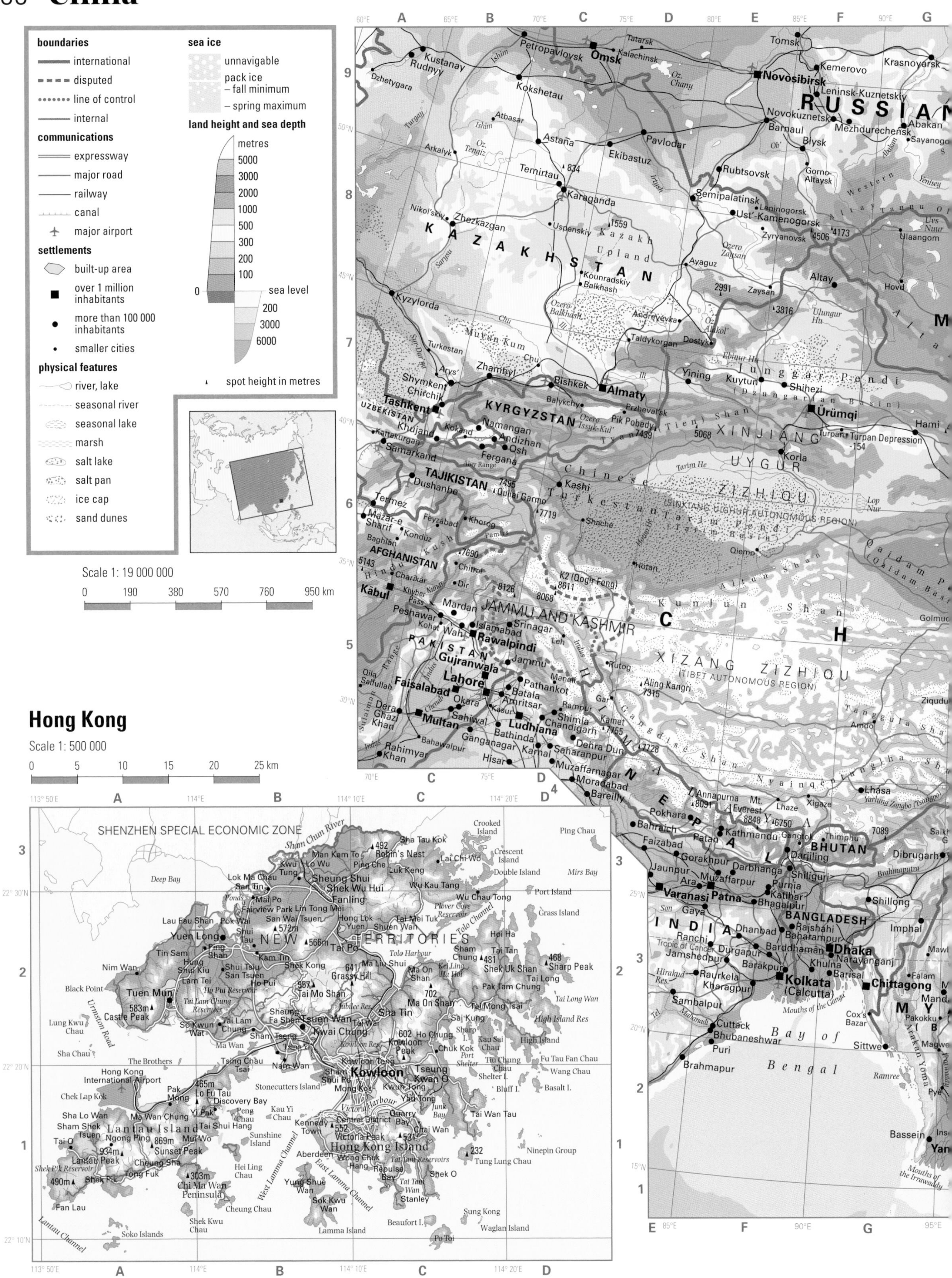
boundaries
international
disputed
line of control
internal
communications
expressway
major road
railway
canal
major airport
settlements
built-up area
over 1 million inhabitants
more than 100 000 inhabitants
smaller cities
physical features
river, lake
seasonal river
seasonal lake
marsh
salt lake
salt pan
ice cap
sand dunes
sea ice
unnavigable
pack ice
– fall minimum
– spring maximum
land height and sea depth
metres
5000
3000
2000
1000
500
300
200
100
0
sea level
200
3000
6000
spot height in metres
Scale 1: 19 000 000
0
190
380
570
760
950 km
Hong Kong
Scale 1: 500 000
0
5
10
15
20
25 km
SHENZHEN SPECIAL ECONOMIC ZONE
Sham Chun River
NEW TERRITORIES
Lantau Island
Hong Kong Island
Kowloon
Victoria Harbour
Hong Kong International Airport
Tuen Mun
Yuen Long
Tai Po
Sha Tin
Tsuen Wan
Kwai Chung
Fanling
Sheung Shui
Deep Bay
Mirs Bay
Lamma Island
Stonecutters Island
Discovery Bay
Lamma Channel
West Lamma Channel
East Lamma Channel
Urmston Road
Lantau Channel
Soko Islands
Po Toi
Waglan Island
Ninepin Group
Tung Lung Chau
Sharp Peak
Castle Peak
Lantau Peak
Victoria Peak
Aberdeen
Stanley
Repulse Bay
Chai Wan
Tseung Kwan O
Sai Kung
Ma On Shan
Tai O
RUSSIA
KAZAKHSTAN
KYRGYZSTAN
UZBEKISTAN
TAJIKISTAN
AFGHANISTAN
PAKISTAN
INDIA
NEPAL
BHUTAN
BANGLADESH
JAMMU AND KASHMIR
XINJIANG UYGUR ZIZHIQU
(SINKIANG UIGHUR AUTONOMOUS REGION)
XIZANG ZIZHIQU
(TIBET AUTONOMOUS REGION)
Kazakh Upland
Dzungarian Basin
Tien Shan
Tarim Basin
Kunlun Shan
Turpan Depression
Bay of Bengal
Omsk
Novosibirsk
Almaty
Bishkek
Tashkent
Dushanbe
Kabul
Islamabad
Rawalpindi
Lahore
Kathmandu
Thimphu
Dhaka
Kolkata (Calcutta)
Ürümqi
Lhasa
K2 (Qogir Feng) 8611
Everest 8848
Annapurna 8091
Gauss Conformal Projection

FEDERATION (RUSSIA)
MONGOLIA
Gobi Desert
NEI MONGOL ZIZHIQU (INNER MONGOLIAN AUTONOMOUS REGION)
CHINA
NORTH KOREA
SOUTH KOREA
JAPAN
TAIWAN
LAOS
THAILAND
VIETNAM
SEA OF OKHOTSK
SEA OF JAPAN
YELLOW SEA
Bo Hai
EAST CHINA SEA
NORTH PACIFIC OCEAN
SOUTH CHINA SEA
Gulf of Tongking
Luzon Strait
Korea Strait
Ryukyu Islands (Nansei-shoto)
Sichuan Pendi (Sichuan Basin)
Great Wall
Tropic of Cancer
Administered by Russia. Claimed by Japan.
Beijing
Tianjin
Shanghai
Nanjing
Wuhan
Chongqing
Chengdu
Xi'an
Lanzhou
Kunming
Guiyang
Guangzhou (Canton)
Hong Kong
Macao
Fuzhou
Hangzhou
Nanchang
Changsha
Zhengzhou
Jinan
Qingdao
Taiyuan
Shijiazhuang
Shenyang
Harbin
Changchun
Jilin
Qiqihar
Dalian
Baotou
Hohhot
Ulan Bator
Irkutsk
Khabarovsk
Vladivostok
Pyongyang
Seoul
Pusan
Taegu
Tokyo
Osaka
Nagoya
Yokohama
Kyoto
Kobe
Sapporo
Hiroshima
Fukuoka
Taibei
Kaohsiung
Hanoi
Vientiane
3 Gorges Project, 1997–2009
boundaries
area affected by project
province
water control
reservoir
dam
gorge
cities and towns
relocated/affected
others
SICHUAN PROVINCE
SHAANXI PROVINCE
HUBEI PROVINCE
HUNAN PROVINCE
Three Gorges Dam
Gezhouba Dam
Sanxia Shuiku (Three Gorges Reservoir)
Qutang Gorge
Wu Gorge
Xiling Gorge
Wanxian
Yichang
Chongqing
Fuling
Wushan
Badong
Zigui
Fengjie
Yungyang
Zhong Xian
Shizhu
Fengdu
Wulong
Baxian
Changshou
Wuxi
Kai Xian
Xingshan
Chang Jiang
Wu Jiang
Daning He

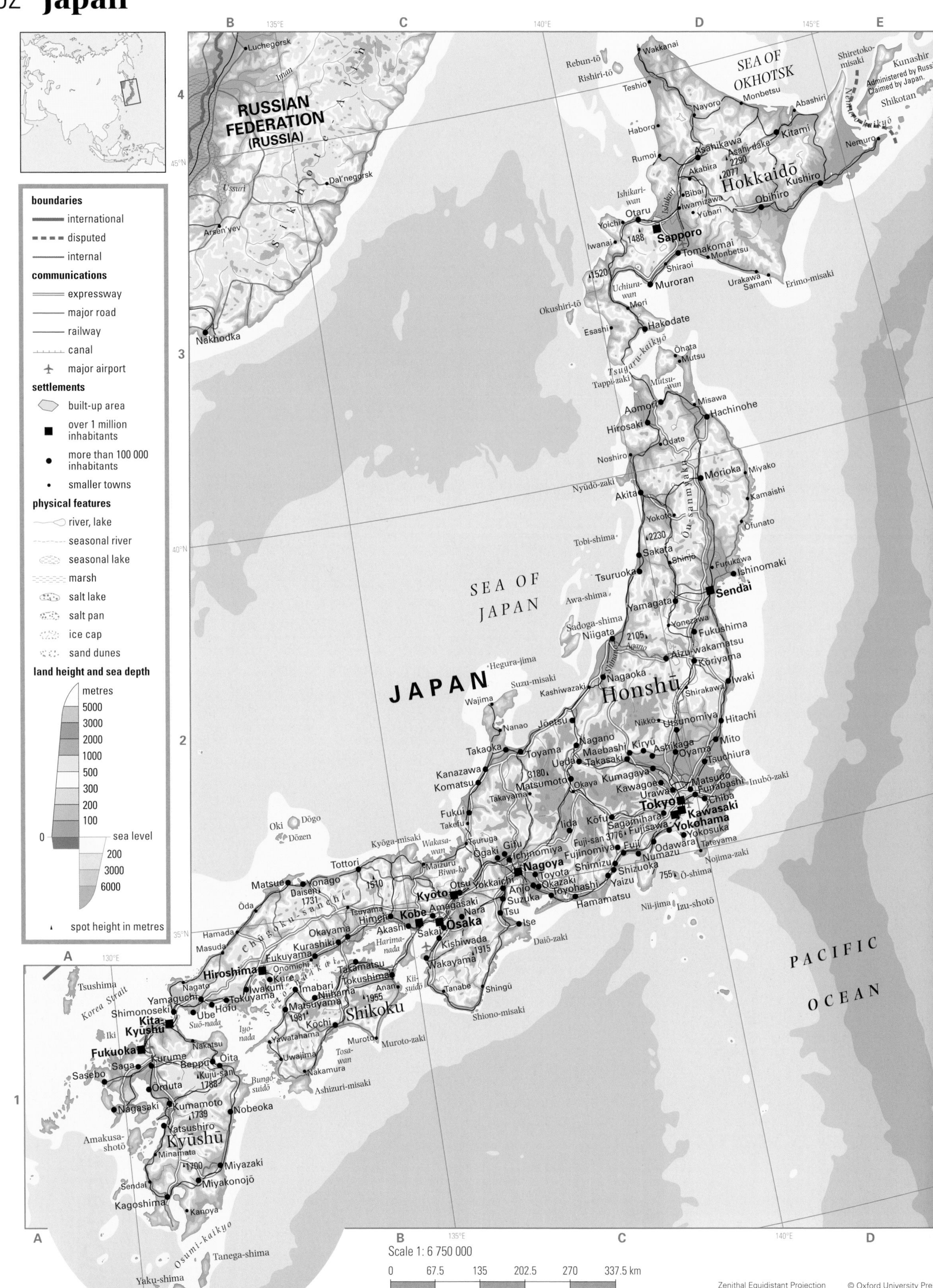
boundaries
international
disputed
internal
communications
expressway
major road
railway
canal
major airport
settlements
built-up area
over 1 million inhabitants
more than 100 000 inhabitants
smaller towns
physical features
river, lake
seasonal river
seasonal lake
marsh
salt lake
salt pan
ice cap
sand dunes
land height and sea depth
metres
5000
3000
2000
1000
500
300
200
100
0
sea level
200
3000
6000
spot height in metres
RUSSIAN FEDERATION (RUSSIA)
SEA OF OKHOTSK
SEA OF JAPAN
JAPAN
PACIFIC OCEAN
Hokkaidō
Honshū
Shikoku
Kyūshū
Sapporo
Sendai
Tokyo
Kawasaki
Yokohama
Nagoya
Kyoto
Kōbe
Ōsaka
Hiroshima
Kita-Kyūshū
Fukuoka
Luchegorsk
Dal'negorsk
Arsen'yev
Nakhodka
Wakkanai
Asahikawa
Kushiro
Hakodate
Aomori
Hachinohe
Morioka
Akita
Niigata
Nagano
Kanazawa
Okayama
Matsuyama
Nagasaki
Kumamoto
Kagoshima
Miyazaki
Kunashir
Administered by Russia. Claimed by Japan.
Scale 1: 6 750 000
0 67.5 135 202.5 270 337.5 km
Zenithal Equidistant Projection

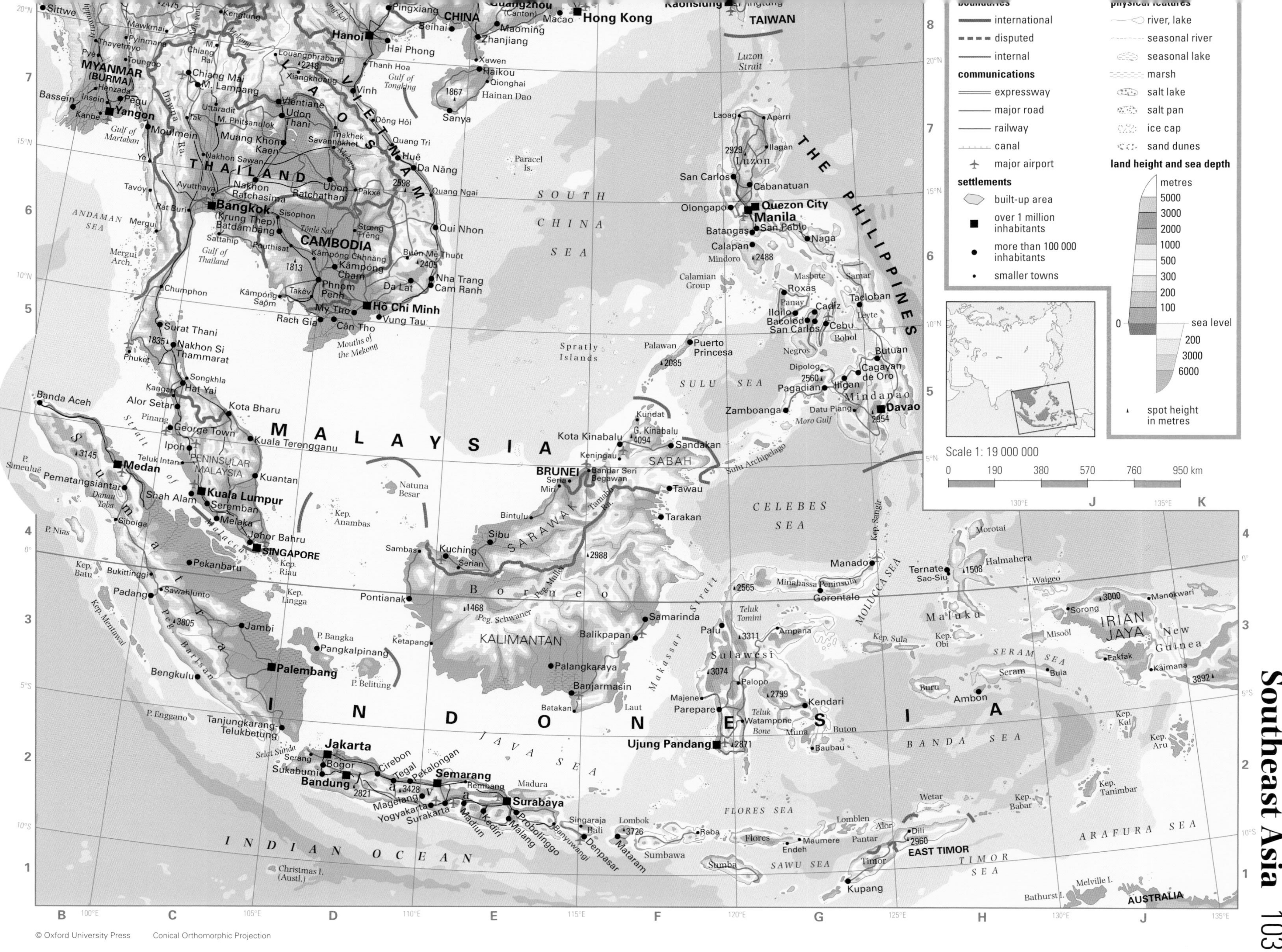

boundaries
international
disputed
internal
communications
expressway
major road
railway
canal
major airport
settlements
built-up area
over 1 million inhabitants
more than 100 000 inhabitants
smaller towns
physical features
river, lake
seasonal river
seasonal lake
marsh
salt lake
salt pan
ice cap
sand dunes
land height and sea depth
metres
5000
3000
2000
1000
500
300
200
100
0
sea level
200
3000
6000
spot height in metres
Scale 1: 19 000 000
0 190 380 570 760 950 km
© Oxford University Press
Conical Orthomorphic Projection
CHINA
TAIWAN
Hong Kong
THE PHILIPPINES
MYANMAR (BURMA)
THAILAND
LAOS
VIETNAM
CAMBODIA
MALAYSIA
SINGAPORE
BRUNEI
INDONESIA
EAST TIMOR
AUSTRALIA
SOUTH CHINA SEA
SULU SEA
CELEBES SEA
JAVA SEA
BANDA SEA
FLORES SEA
SAWU SEA
TIMOR SEA
ARAFURA SEA
SERAM SEA
MOLUCCA SEA
ANDAMAN SEA
INDIAN OCEAN
Gulf of Thailand
Gulf of Tongking
Gulf of Martaban
Strait of Malacca
Makassar Strait
Luzon Strait
Borneo
KALIMANTAN
SARAWAK
SABAH
Sumatra
Sulawesi
Maluku
IRIAN JAYA
New Guinea
Hanoi
Ho Chi Minh
Bangkok (Krung Thep)
Yangon
Kuala Lumpur
Jakarta
Manila
Quezon City
Surabaya
Bandung
Medan
Palembang
Semarang
Ujung Pandang
Davao

Africa Political

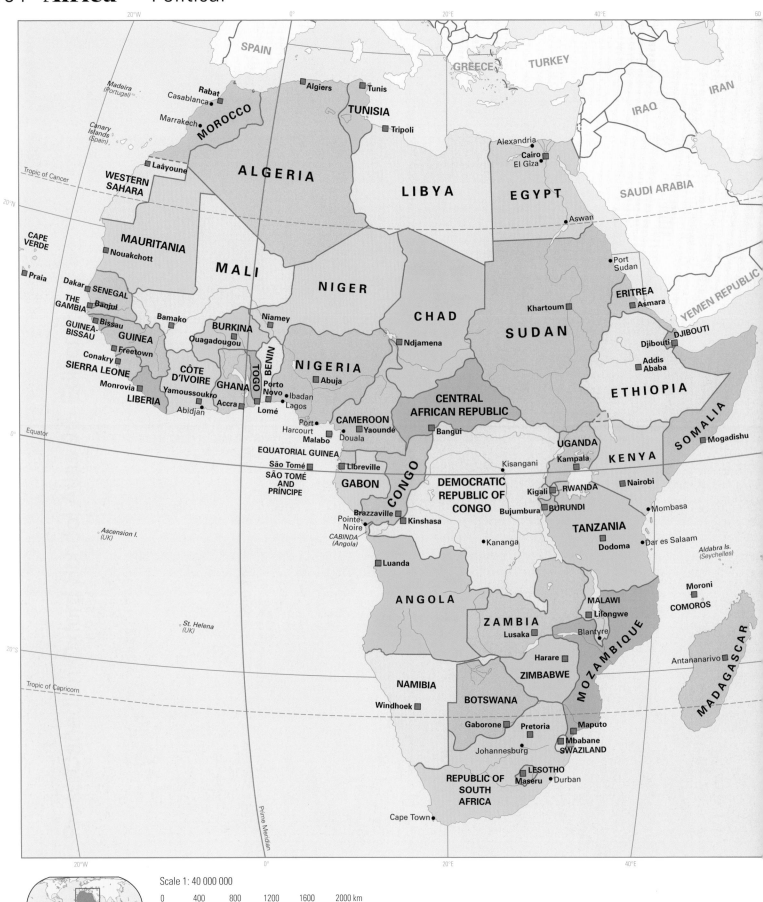

20°W 0° 20°E 40°E 60

SPAIN
GREECE
TURKEY
IRAN
IRAQ
SAUDI ARABIA
YEMEN REPUBLIC

Madeira (Portugal)
Canary Islands (Spain)
Tropic of Cancer
20°N
CAPE VERDE
Praia
Rabat
Casablanca
Marrakech
MOROCCO
Algiers
Tunis
TUNISIA
Tripoli
Laâyoune
WESTERN SAHARA
ALGERIA
LIBYA
Alexandria
Cairo
El Gîza
EGYPT
Aswan
MAURITANIA
Nouakchott
MALI
NIGER
CHAD
SUDAN
Port Sudan
ERITREA
Asmara
Khartoum
Dakar
SENEGAL
THE GAMBIA
Banjul
Bissau
GUINEA-BISSAU
GUINEA
Conakry
Freetown
SIERRA LEONE
Monrovia
LIBERIA
Bamako
BURKINA
Ouagadougou
Niamey
BENIN
TOGO
CÔTE D'IVOIRE
Yamoussoukro
Abidjan
GHANA
Accra
Lomé
Porto Novo
Ibadan
Lagos
NIGERIA
Abuja
Ndjamena
DJIBOUTI
Djibouti
Addis Ababa
ETHIOPIA
CENTRAL AFRICAN REPUBLIC
Bangui
Port Harcourt
Malabo
Douala
CAMEROON
Yaoundé
Equator
0°
EQUATORIAL GUINEA
São Tomé
SÃO TOMÉ AND PRÍNCIPE
Libreville
GABON
CONGO
DEMOCRATIC REPUBLIC OF CONGO
Kisangani
UGANDA
Kampala
KENYA
SOMALIA
Mogadishu
Nairobi
RWANDA
Kigali
Bujumbura
BURUNDI
Mombasa
Brazzaville
Kinshasa
Pointe-Noire
CABINDA (Angola)
Ascension I. (UK)
Kananga
TANZANIA
Dodoma
Dar es Salaam
Aldabra Is. (Seychelles)
Luanda
ANGOLA
Moroni
COMOROS
MALAWI
Lilongwe
Blantyre
ZAMBIA
Lusaka
St. Helena (UK)
20°S
Harare
ZIMBABWE
MOZAMBIQUE
Antananarivo
MADAGASCAR
Tropic of Capricorn
NAMIBIA
Windhoek
BOTSWANA
Gaborone
Pretoria
Maputo
Mbabane
SWAZILAND
Johannesburg
LESOTHO
Maseru
Durban
REPUBLIC OF SOUTH AFRICA
Cape Town
Prime Meridian

20°W 0° 20°E 40°E

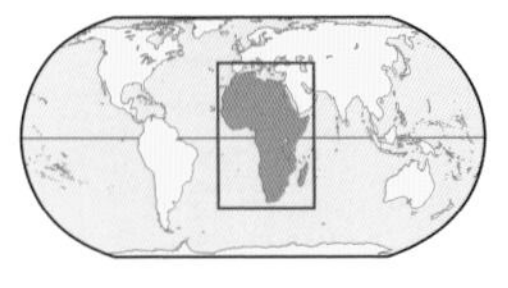

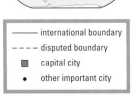

Scale 1: 40 000 000

0 400 800 1200 1600 2000 km

international boundary
disputed boundary
capital city
other important city

Zenithal Equal Area Projection

20°W 10°W 0° 10°E 20°E 30°E 40°E 50°E

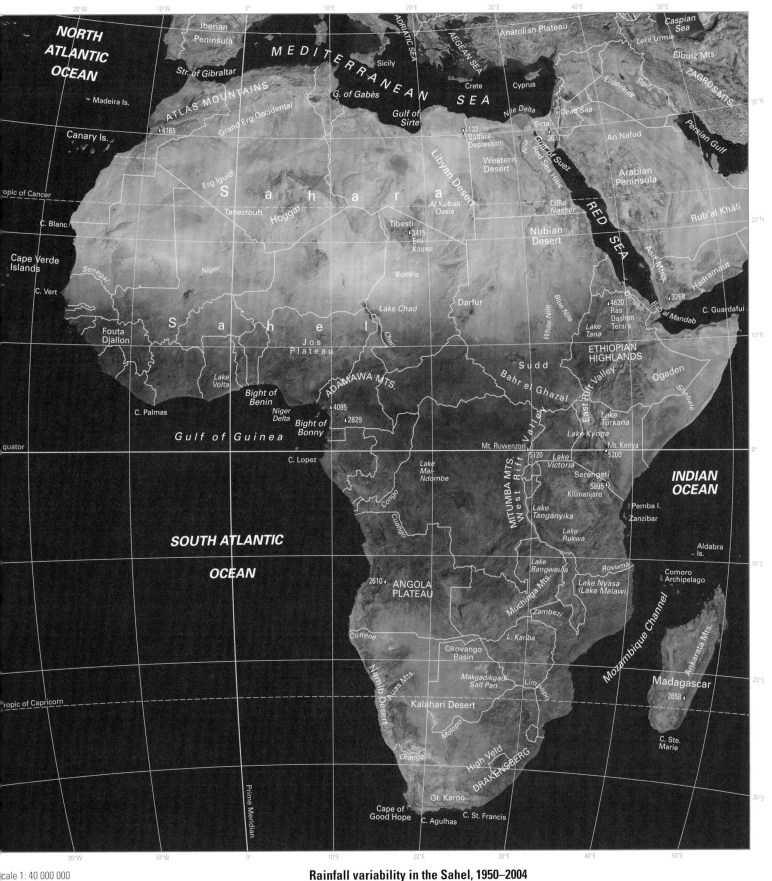

NORTH ATLANTIC OCEAN
Iberian Peninsula
ADRIATIC SEA
AEGEAN SEA
Anatolian Plateau
Caspian Sea
Lake Urmia
Elburz Mts.
ZAGROS MTS.
MEDITERRANEAN SEA
Sicily
Crete
Cyprus
Str. of Gibraltar
ATLAS MOUNTAINS
Madeira Is.
G. of Gabès
Gulf of Sirte
Nile Delta
Dead Sea
Euphrates
Tigris
30°N
Canary Is.
4165
Grand Erg Occidental
-133 Qattara Depression
Sinai
2637
Gulf of Suez
Persian Gulf
An Nafud
Libyan Desert
Western Desert
Nile
Red Sea Hills
Arabian Peninsula
Tropic of Cancer
Erg Iguidi
Sahara
Tanezrouft
Hoggar
Al Kufrah Oasis
Lake Nasser
RED SEA
Rub'al Khālī
C. Blanc
Tibesti
3415 Emi Koussi
Nubian Desert
20°N
Cape Verde Islands
Senegal
Niger
Bodélé
Asir Mts.
Hadramaut
C. Vert
Lake Chad
Darfur
White Nile
Blue Nile
4620 Ras Dashen
Terara
Danakil
3268
Bab al Mandab
C. Guardafui
Sahel
Fouta Djallon
Chari
Jos Plateau
Lake Tana
10°N
ETHIOPIAN HIGHLANDS
Sudd
Bahr el Ghazal
Ogaden
East Rift Valley
Shebele
Lake Volta
Bight of Benin
ADAMAWA MTS.
4095
Niger Delta
2829
Bight of Bonny
C. Palmas
Lake Turkana
Lake Kyoga
Gulf of Guinea
Equator
Mt. Ruwenzori 5120
Mt. Kenya 5200
0°
C. Lopez
Lake Victoria
Lake Mai-Ndombe
West Rift Valley
MITUMBA MTS.
Serengeti
5895 Kilimanjaro
INDIAN OCEAN
Congo
Pemba I.
Zanzibar
Lake Tanganyika
Cuango
SOUTH ATLANTIC OCEAN
Lake Rukwa
Aldabra Is.
Lake Bangweulu
Rovuma
10°S
2610
ANGOLA PLATEAU
Comoro Archipelago
Lake Nyasa (Lake Malawi)
Muchinga Mts.
Zambezi
Mozambique Channel
Ankaratra Mts.
Cunene
L. Kariba
Okovango Basin
Namib Desert
Auas Mts.
Makgadikgadi Salt Pan
Limpopo
Madagascar
20°S
Tropic of Capricorn
2658
Kalahari Desert
Molopo
C. Ste. Marie
Orange
High Veld
DRAKENSBERG
30°S
Prime Meridian
Gt. Karoo
Cape of Good Hope
C. Agulhas
C. St. Francis

20°W 10°W 0° 10°E 20°E 30°E 40°E 50°E

Scale 1: 40 000 000

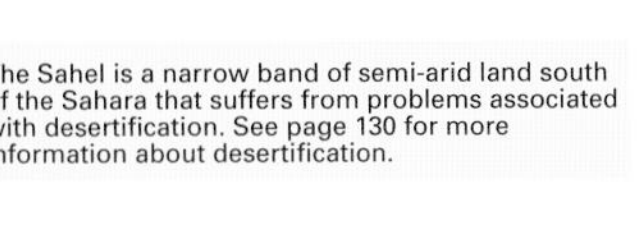

The Sahel is a narrow band of semi-arid land south of the Sahara that suffers from problems associated with desertification. See page 130 for more information about desertification.

Rainfall variability in the Sahel, 1950–2004

0 equals the long term average. Variability is shown as standard deviations above and below this average.

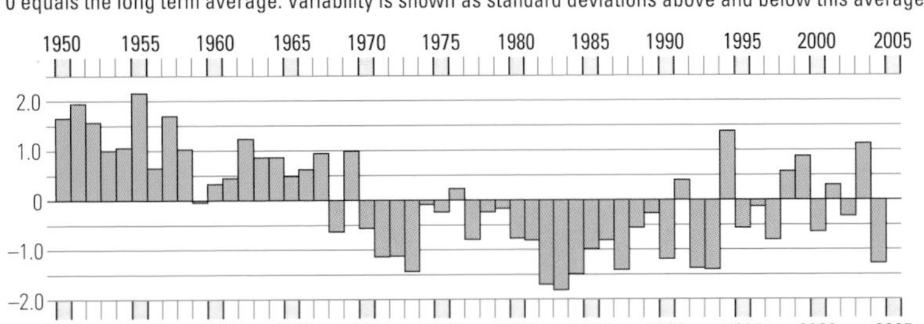

Scale 1: 90 000 000

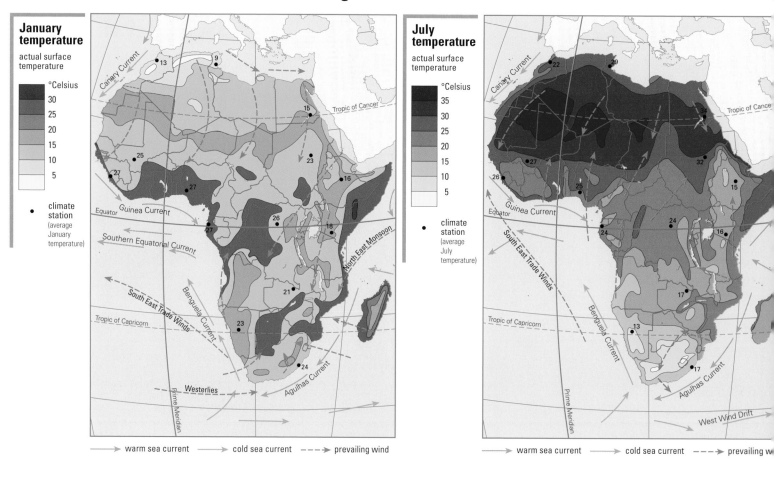

January temperature

actual surface temperature

°Celsius
30
25
20
15
10
5

• climate station (average January temperature)

Canary Current
13
9
Tropic of Cancer
15
25
23
27
16
27
Equator
Guinea Current
27
26
18
Southern Equatorial Current
North East Monsoon
South East Trade Winds
Benguela Current
21
Tropic of Capricorn
23
24
Agulhas Current
Westerlies
Prime Meridian

→ warm sea current → cold sea current - - → prevailing wind

July temperature

actual surface temperature

°Celsius
35
30
25
20
15
10
5

• climate station (average July temperature)

Canary Current
22
29
Tropic of Cancer
34
27
32
26
25
15
Equator
Guinea Current
24
24
16
South East Trade Winds
17
Benguela Current
Tropic of Capricorn
13
17
Agulhas Current
West Wind Drift
Prime Meridian

→ warm sea current → cold sea current - - → prevailing w

Precipitation

average annual precipitation

mm
3000
2000
1000
500
250
0

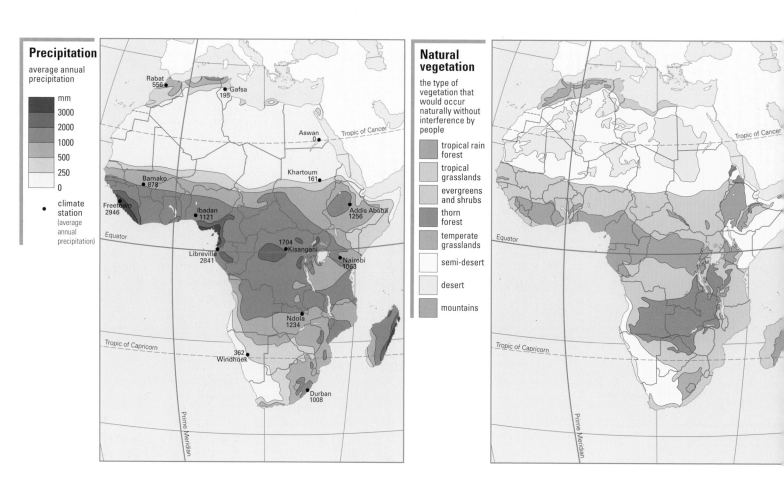

• climate station (average annual precipitation)

Rabat 556
Gafsa 195
Aswan 0
Tropic of Cancer
Khartoum 161
Bamako 878
Freetown 2946
Ibadan 1121
Addis Ababa 1256
Equator
1704 Kisangani
Libreville 2841
Nairobi 1063
Ndola 1234
Tropic of Capricorn
362 Windhoek
Durban 1008
Prime Meridian

Natural vegetation

the type of vegetation that would occur naturally without interference by people

- tropical rain forest
- tropical grasslands
- evergreens and shrubs
- thorn forest
- temperate grasslands
- semi-desert
- desert
- mountains

Tropic of Cancer
Equator
Tropic of Capricorn
Prime Meridian

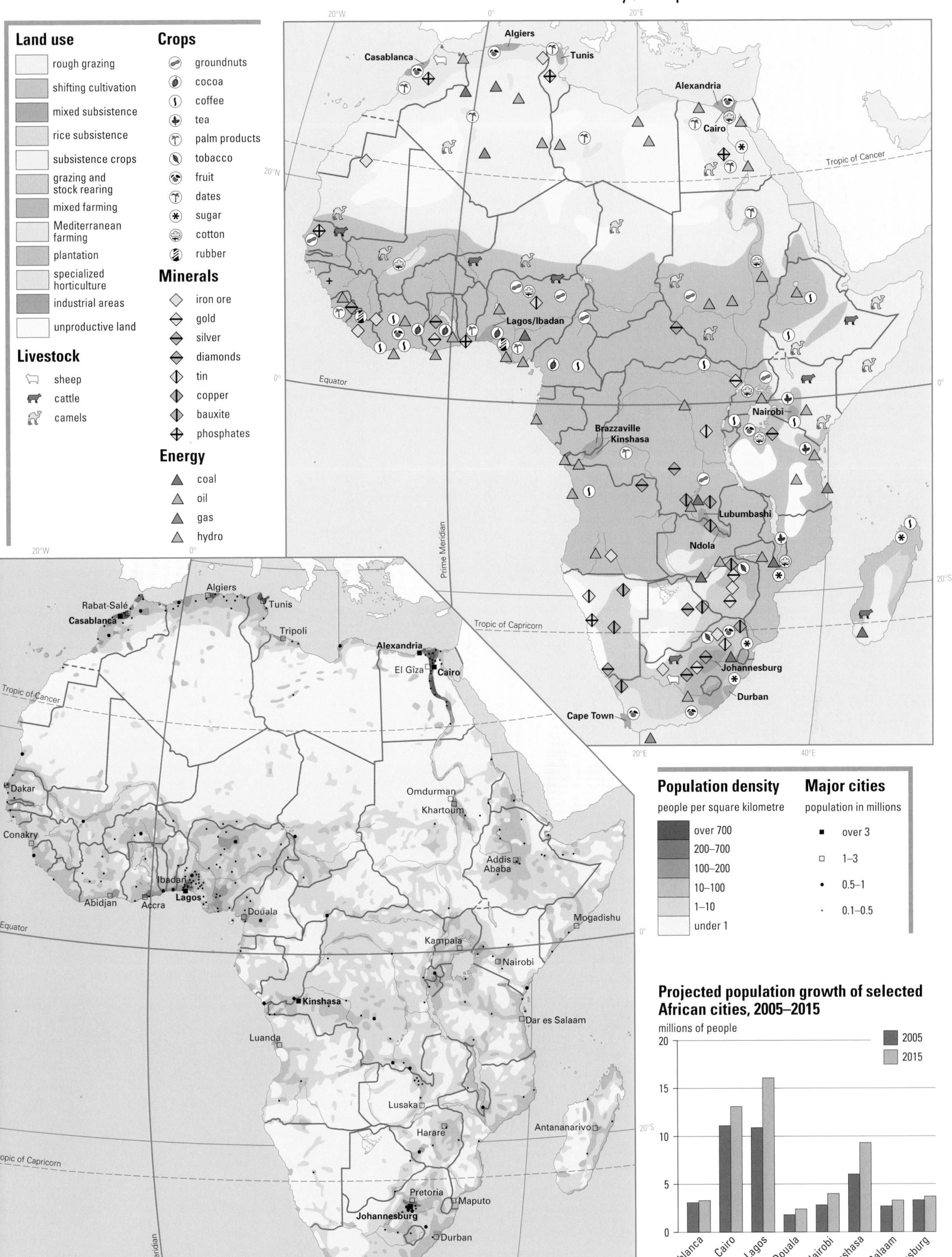
Land use
rough grazing
shifting cultivation
mixed subsistence
rice subsistence
subsistence crops
grazing and stock rearing
mixed farming
Mediterranean farming
plantation
specialized horticulture
industrial areas
unproductive land
Livestock
sheep
cattle
camels
Crops
groundnuts
cocoa
coffee
tea
palm products
tobacco
fruit
dates
sugar
cotton
rubber
Minerals
iron ore
gold
silver
diamonds
tin
copper
bauxite
phosphates
Energy
coal
oil
gas
hydro
Algiers
Casablanca
Tunis
Alexandria
Cairo
Tropic of Cancer
Lagos/Ibadan
Equator
Nairobi
Brazzaville
Kinshasa
Lubumbashi
Ndola
Tropic of Capricorn
Johannesburg
Durban
Cape Town
Prime Meridian
20°W
0°
20°E
40°E
20°N
20°S
Rabat-Salé
Tripoli
El Giza
Dakar
Omdurman
Khartoum
Conakry
Addis Ababa
Ibadan
Lagos
Abidjan
Accra
Douala
Mogadishu
Kampala
Kinshasa
Luanda
Dar es Salaam
Lusaka
Harare
Antananarivo
Pretoria
Maputo
Population density
people per square kilometre
over 700
200–700
100–200
10–100
1–10
under 1
Major cities
population in millions
over 3
1–3
0.5–1
0.1–0.5
Projected population growth of selected African cities, 2005–2015
millions of people
2005
2015
20
15
10
5
0
Casablanca
Cairo
Lagos
Douala
Nairobi
Kinshasa
Dar es Salaam
Johannesburg
Zenithal Equal Area Projection

ATLANTIC OCEAN
INDIAN OCEAN
MEDITERRANEAN SEA
RED SEA
BLACK SEA
Gulf of Aden
Gulf of Guinea
Persian Gulf
MOROCCO
ALGERIA
TUNISIA
LIBYA
EGYPT
WESTERN SAHARA
MAURITANIA
MALI
NIGER
CHAD
SUDAN
ERITREA
DJIBOUTI
ETHIOPIA
SOMALIA
KENYA
UGANDA
RWANDA
BURUNDI
DEMOCRATIC REPUBLIC OF CONGO
CONGO
GABON
EQUATORIAL GUINEA
SÃO TOMÉ AND PRINCIPE
CAMEROON
CENTRAL AFRICAN REPUBLIC
NIGERIA
BENIN
TOGO
GHANA
BURKINA
CÔTE D'IVOIRE
LIBERIA
SIERRA LEONE
GUINEA
GUINEA-BISSAU
THE GAMBIA
SENEGAL
SAUDI ARABIA
YEMEN REPUBLIC
IRAQ
IRAN
SYRIA
JORDAN
ISRAEL
LEBANON
TURKEY
CYPRUS
GREECE
ITALY
SPAIN
PORTUGAL
FRANCE
KUWAIT
BAHRAIN
QATAR
UNITED ARAB EMIRATES
Sahara Desert
Libyan Desert
Nubian Desert
Tropic of Cancer
Equator
Prime Meridian
Cairo
Khartoum
Addis Ababa
Nairobi
Mogadishu
Kampala
Riyadh
Baghdad
Tehran
Damascus
Amman
Beirut
Ankara
Athens
Rome
Madrid
Lisbon
Algiers
Tunis
Tripoli
Rabat-Salé
Dakar
Nouakchott
Bamako
Niamey
Ndjamena
Lagos
Accra
Abidjan
Monrovia
Freetown
Conakry
Bangui
Yaoundé
Douala
Libreville

Suez Canal

The Suez Canal was opened in 1869 and run by the Anglo-French Suez Canal Company until it was nationalized by Egypt in 1956.

The canal is 173 km long (with approaches, it is 184 km long), and connects the Gulf of Suez on the Red Sea with the Mediterranean Sea. It is level throughout and has no locks. It takes 12 hours for a ship to pass through the canal.

From 1967 to 1975, the Suez Canal was closed by war. In 1980, the first part of a two-phase development program was completed when the canal was enlarged to take vessels of up to 150 000 DWT laden, with a draught of up to 16 m. In the second phase, now underway, the canal is being deepened and widened to allow the passage of vessels of up to 180 000 DWT.

On average, 1.7 million tonnes of cargo passed daily through the canal in 2006.

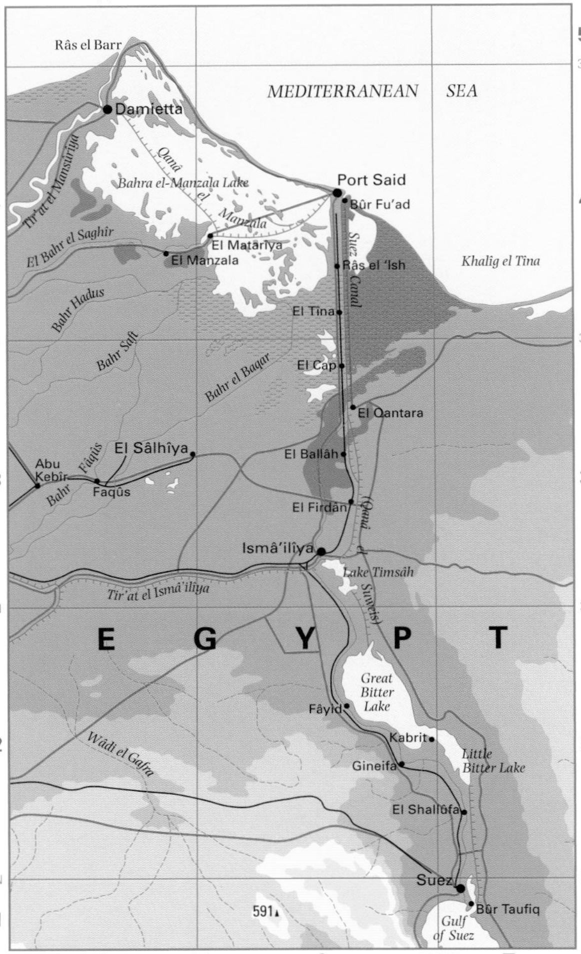

Scale 1: 1 500 000 — 0, 15, 30, 45 km

Scale 1: 26 000 000 — 0, 260, 520, 780, 1040, 1300 km

boundaries
- international
- disputed
- internal

communications
- expressway
- major road
- railway
- canal
- major airport

settlements
- over 1 million inhabitants
- more than 100 000 inhabitants
- smaller cities

physical features
- river, lake
- seasonal river
- seasonal lake
- marsh
- salt lake
- salt pan
- ice cap
- sand dunes

sea ice
- unnavigable
- pack ice – fall minimum
- – spring maximum

land height and sea depth

metres: 5000, 3000, 2000, 1000, 500, 300, 200, 100, 0, sea level, 200, 3000, 6000

spot height in metres

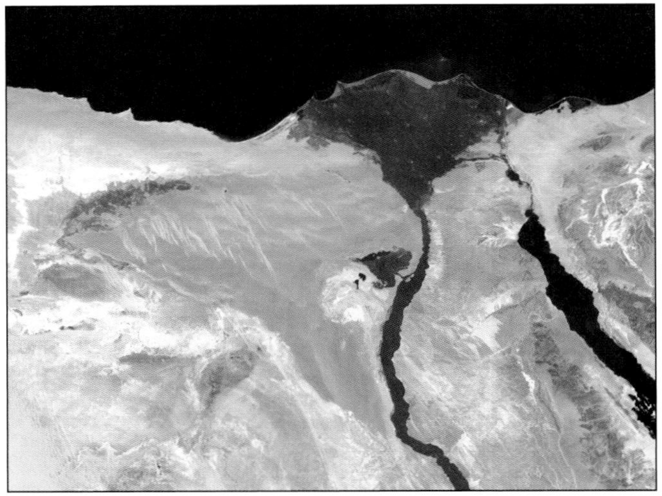

Zenithal Equal Area Projection

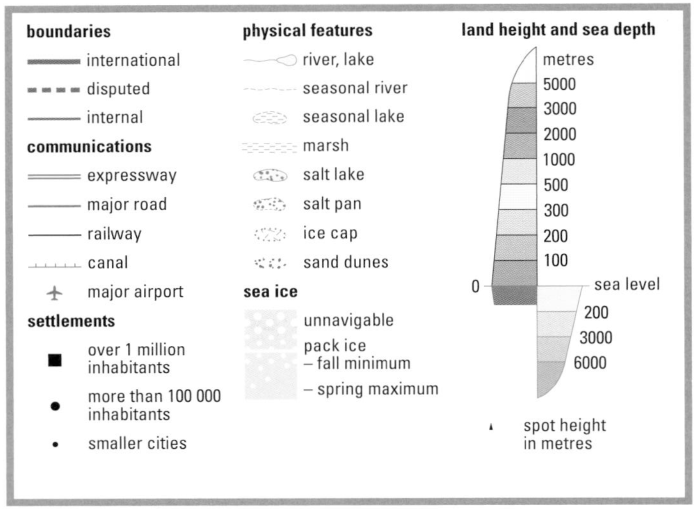

The Nile Delta

This satellite image clearly shows the Nile valley and delta in dark green. The Qattara Depression is also visible to the left of the image.

Australia

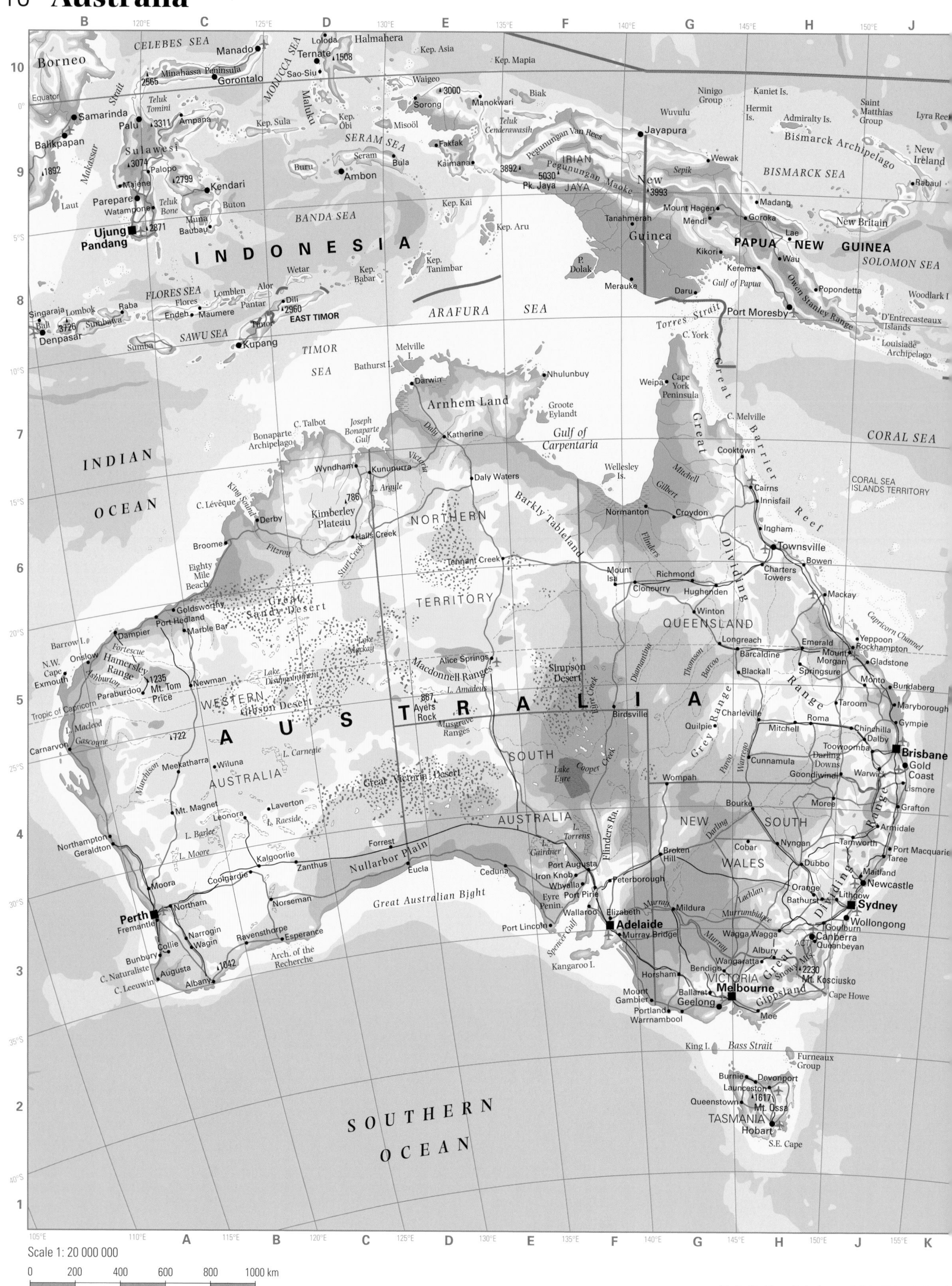

Scale 1: 20 000 000

0 200 400 600 800 1000 km

Zenithal Equidistant Projection

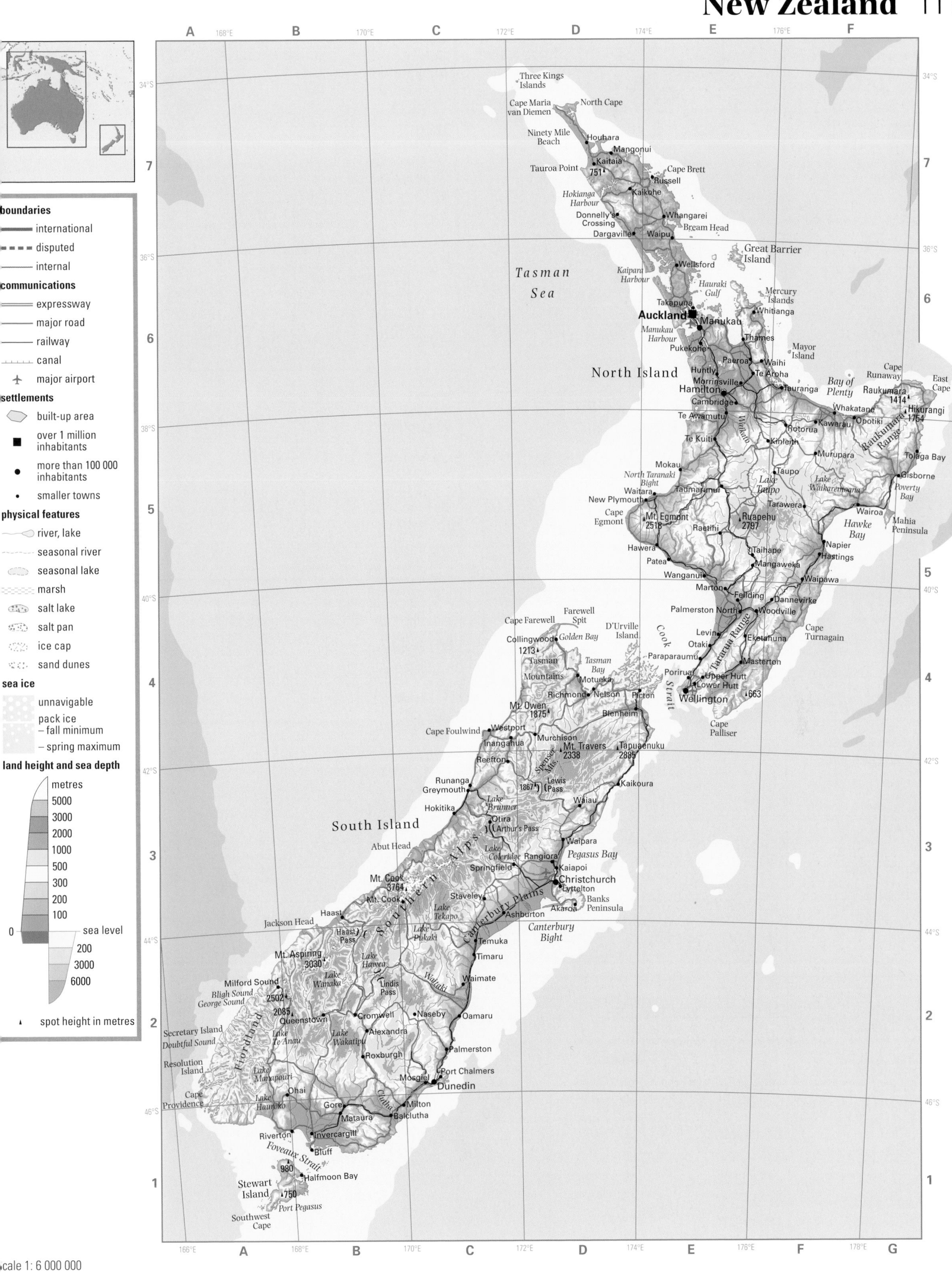

boundaries
international
disputed
internal
communications
expressway
major road
railway
canal
major airport
settlements
built-up area
over 1 million inhabitants
more than 100 000 inhabitants
smaller towns
physical features
river, lake
seasonal river
seasonal lake
marsh
salt lake
salt pan
ice cap
sand dunes
sea ice
unnavigable
pack ice
– fall minimum
– spring maximum
land height and sea depth
metres
5000
3000
2000
1000
500
300
200
100
0
sea level
200
3000
6000
spot height in metres
Tasman Sea
North Island
South Island
Three Kings Islands
Cape Maria van Diemen
North Cape
Ninety Mile Beach
Houhara
Mangonui
Kaitaia
751
Tauroa Point
Cape Brett
Russell
Kaikohe
Hokianga Harbour
Donnelly's Crossing
Whangarei
Bream Head
Dargaville
Waipu
Great Barrier Island
Wellsford
Kaipara Harbour
Hauraki Gulf
Mercury Islands
Takapuna
Auckland
Manukau
Whitianga
Manukau Harbour
Thames
Pukekohe
Mayor Island
Paeroa
Waihi
Huntly
Te Aroha
Morrinsville
Tauranga
Bay of Plenty
Cape Runaway
East Cape
Hamilton
Cambridge
Raukumara
1414
Whakatane
Hikurangi
1754
Te Awamutu
Kawerau
Opotiki
Raukumara Range
Rotorua
Te Kuiti
Kinleith
Waikato
Murupara
Tolaga Bay
Mokau
North Taranaki Bight
Taupo
Gisborne
Waitara
Lake Taupo
Lake Waikaremoana
Poverty Bay
Taumarunui
New Plymouth
Tarawera
Wairoa
Cape Egmont
Mt. Egmont
2518
Ruapehu
2797
Raetihi
Hawke Bay
Mahia Peninsula
Hawera
Napier
Taihape
Hastings
Patea
Mangaweka
Wanganui
Waipawa
Marton
Feilding
Dannevirke
Palmerston North
Woodville
Cape Farewell
Farewell Spit
D'Urville Island
Cook Strait
Cape Turnagain
Collingwood
Golden Bay
Levin
1213
Otaki
Tararua Range
Eketahuna
Tasman Mountains
Paraparaumu
Tasman Bay
Masterton
Motueka
Porirua
Upper Hutt
Lower Hutt
Richmond
Nelson
Picton
Wellington
663
Mt. Owen
1875
Blenheim
Cape Palliser
Cape Foulwind
Westport
Inangahua
Murchison
Mt. Travers
2338
Tapuaenuku
2885
Reefton
Spenser Mts.
Runanga
Greymouth
1867
Lewis Pass
Kaikoura
Hokitika
Lake Brunner
Waiau
Otira
Arthur's Pass
Southern Alps
Abut Head
Waipara
Lake Coleridge
Rangiora
Pegasus Bay
Springfield
Kaiapoi
Mt. Cook
3764
Christchurch
Lyttelton
Staveley
Banks Peninsula
Canterbury Plains
Akaroa
Haast
Lake Tekapo
Ashburton
Jackson Head
Haast Pass
Lake Pukaki
Canterbury Bight
Temuka
Timaru
Mt. Aspiring
3030
Lake Hawea
Lake Wanaka
Lindis Pass
Waitaki
Waimate
Milford Sound
Bligh Sound
George Sound
2502
2085
Queenstown
Cromwell
Naseby
Oamaru
Fiordland
Secretary Island
Doubtful Sound
Lake Te Anau
Lake Wakatipu
Alexandra
Palmerston
Resolution Island
Roxburgh
Lake Manapouri
Port Chalmers
Mosgiel
Dunedin
Cape Providence
Ohai
Lake Hauroko
Gore
Milton
Clutha
Mataura
Balclutha
Riverton
Invercargill
Foveaux Strait
Bluff
980
Halfmoon Bay
Stewart Island
750
Port Pegasus
Southwest Cape
34°S
36°S
38°S
40°S
42°S
44°S
46°S
166°E
168°E
170°E
172°E
174°E
176°E
178°E
A
B
C
D
E
F
G
1
2
3
4
5
6
7

Scale 1: 75 000 000

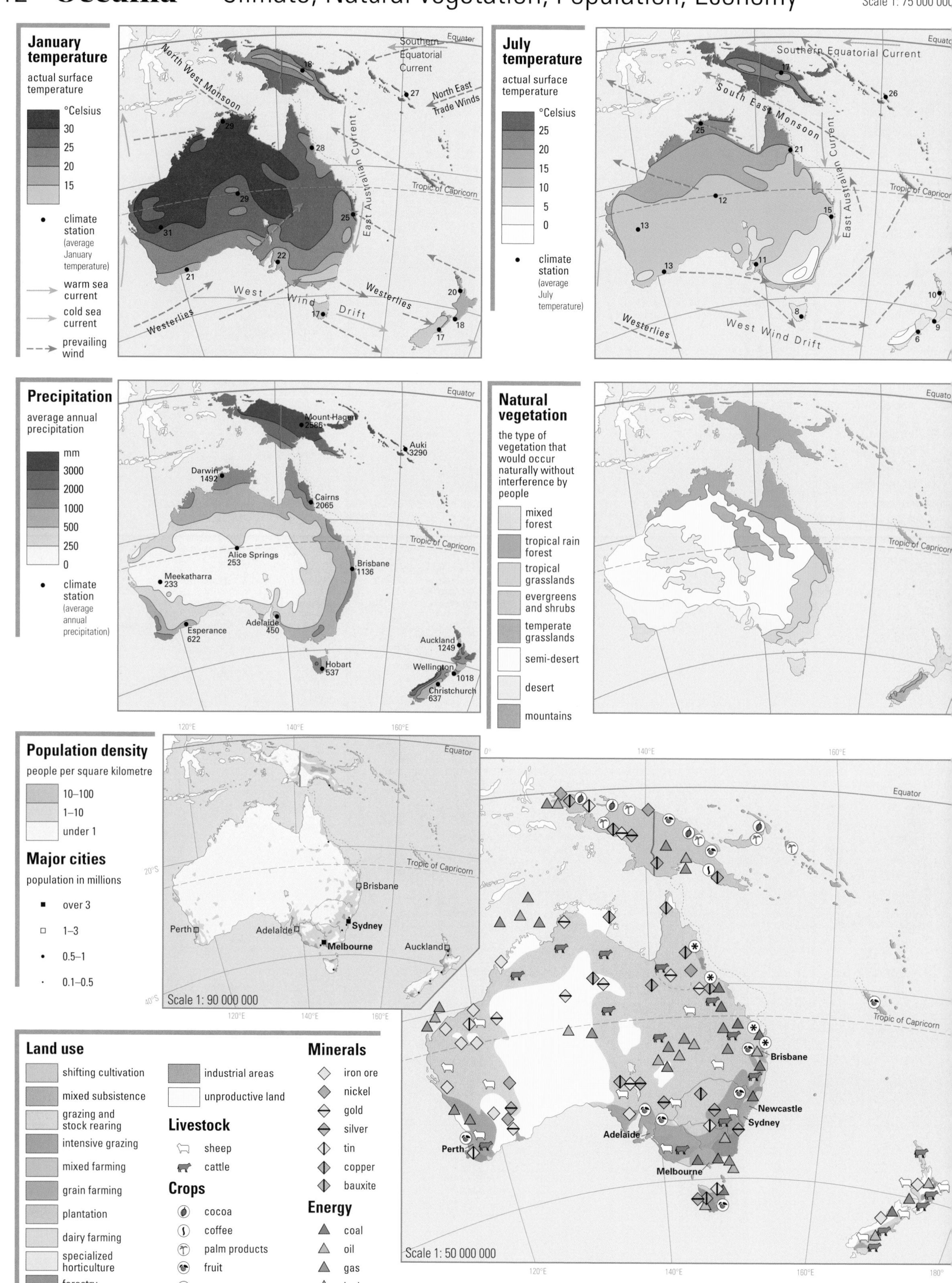
January temperature
actual surface temperature
°Celsius
30
25
20
15
climate station (average January temperature)
warm sea current
cold sea current
prevailing wind
North West Monsoon
Southern Equatorial Current
North East Trade Winds
East Australian Current
Tropic of Capricorn
Equator
West Wind Drift
Westerlies
July temperature
actual surface temperature
°Celsius
25
20
15
10
5
0
climate station (average July temperature)
South East Monsoon
Precipitation
average annual precipitation
mm
3000
2000
1000
500
250
0
climate station (average annual precipitation)
Mount Hagen 2586
Auki 3290
Darwin 1492
Cairns 2065
Alice Springs 253
Brisbane 1136
Meekatharra 233
Adelaide 450
Esperance 622
Auckland 1249
Hobart 537
Wellington 1018
Christchurch 637
Natural vegetation
the type of vegetation that would occur naturally without interference by people
mixed forest
tropical rain forest
tropical grasslands
evergreens and shrubs
temperate grasslands
semi-desert
desert
mountains
Population density
people per square kilometre
10–100
1–10
under 1
Major cities
population in millions
over 3
1–3
0.5–1
0.1–0.5
Perth
Adelaide
Sydney
Melbourne
Auckland
Scale 1: 90 000 000
Land use
shifting cultivation
mixed subsistence
grazing and stock rearing
intensive grazing
mixed farming
grain farming
plantation
dairy farming
specialized horticulture
forestry
industrial areas
unproductive land
Livestock
sheep
cattle
Crops
cocoa
coffee
palm products
fruit
sugar
Minerals
iron ore
nickel
gold
silver
tin
copper
bauxite
Energy
coal
oil
gas
hydro
Newcastle
Scale 1: 50 000 000

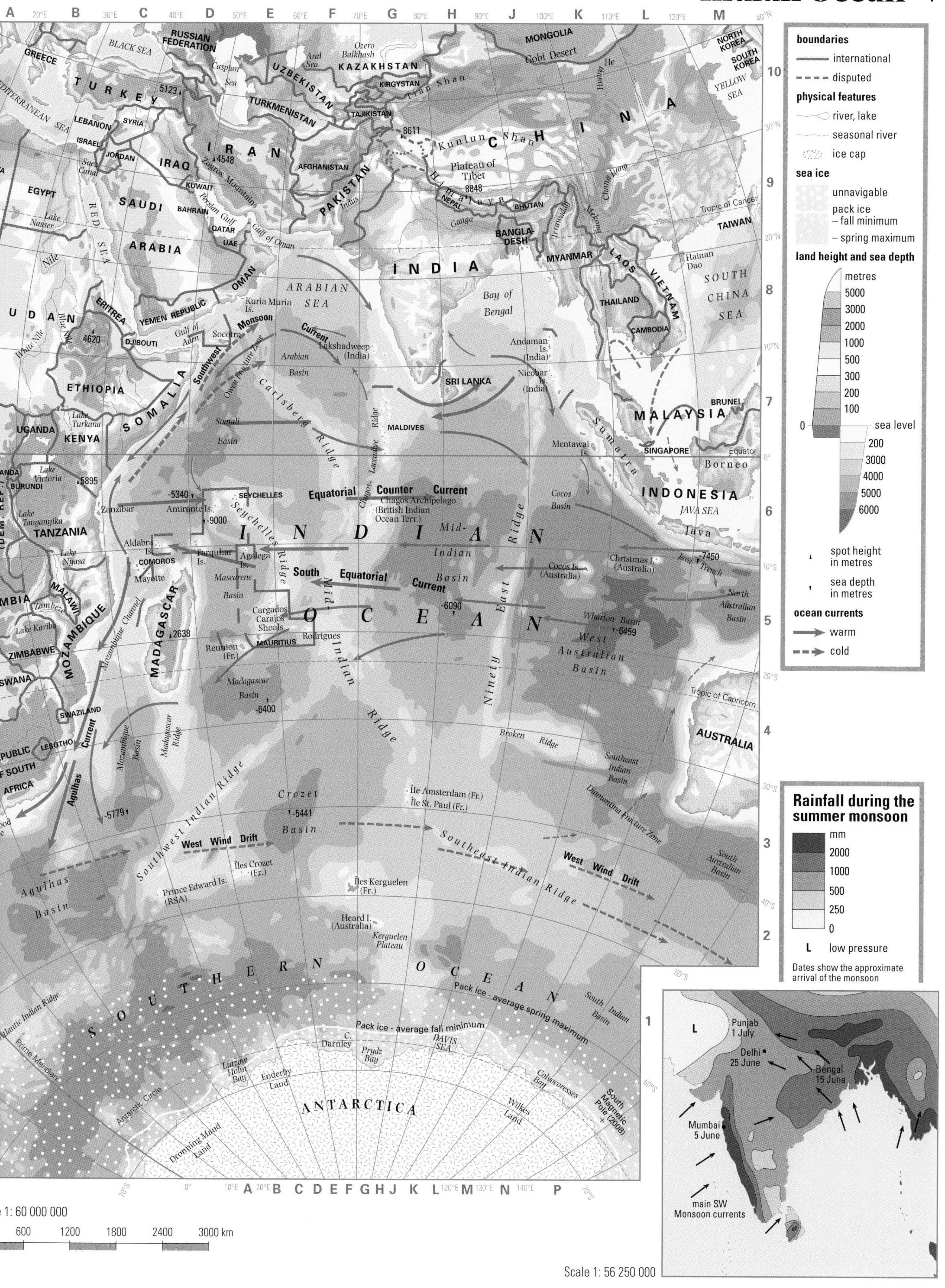
boundaries
international
disputed
physical features
river, lake
seasonal river
ice cap
sea ice
unnavigable
pack ice
– fall minimum
– spring maximum
land height and sea depth
metres
5000
3000
2000
1000
500
300
200
100
0
sea level
200
3000
4000
5000
6000
spot height in metres
sea depth in metres
ocean currents
warm
cold
Rainfall during the summer monsoon
mm
2000
1000
500
250
0
L low pressure
Dates show the approximate arrival of the monsoon
Punjab 1 July
Delhi 25 June
Bengal 15 June
Mumbai 5 June
main SW Monsoon currents
Scale 1: 56 250 000
INDIAN OCEAN
SOUTHERN OCEAN
ANTARCTICA
ARABIAN SEA
Bay of Bengal
INDIA
CHINA
INDONESIA
AUSTRALIA
MADAGASCAR
Equatorial Counter Current
South Equatorial Current
West Wind Drift
Agulhas Current
Southwest Monsoon Current
Mid-Indian Ridge
Ninety East Ridge
Southeast Indian Ridge
Southwest Indian Ridge
Carlsberg Ridge
Pack ice - average spring maximum
Pack ice - average fall minimum
1: 60 000 000
600 1200 1800 2400 3000 km
Modified Zenithal Equidistant Projection

Pacific Ocean

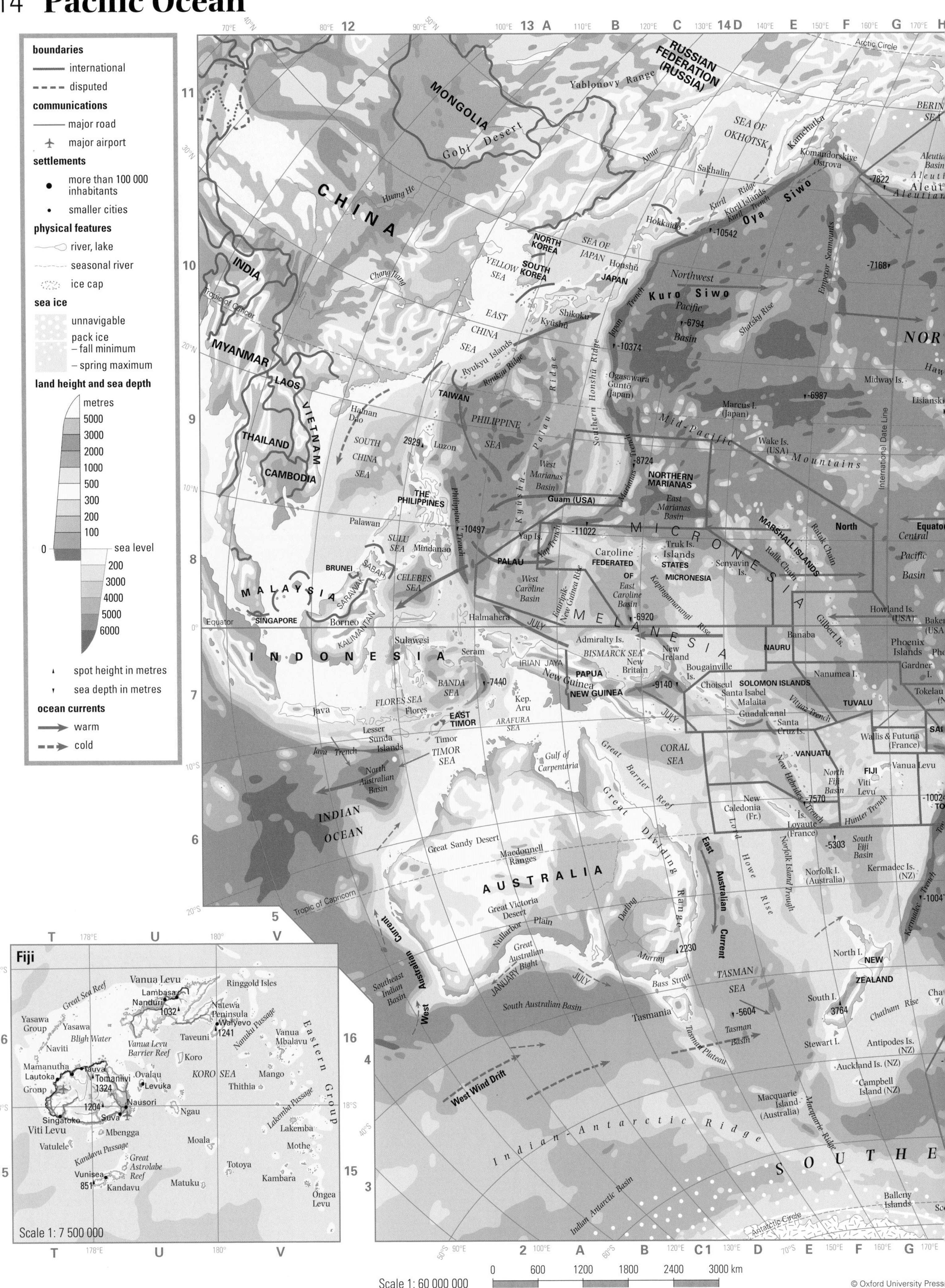

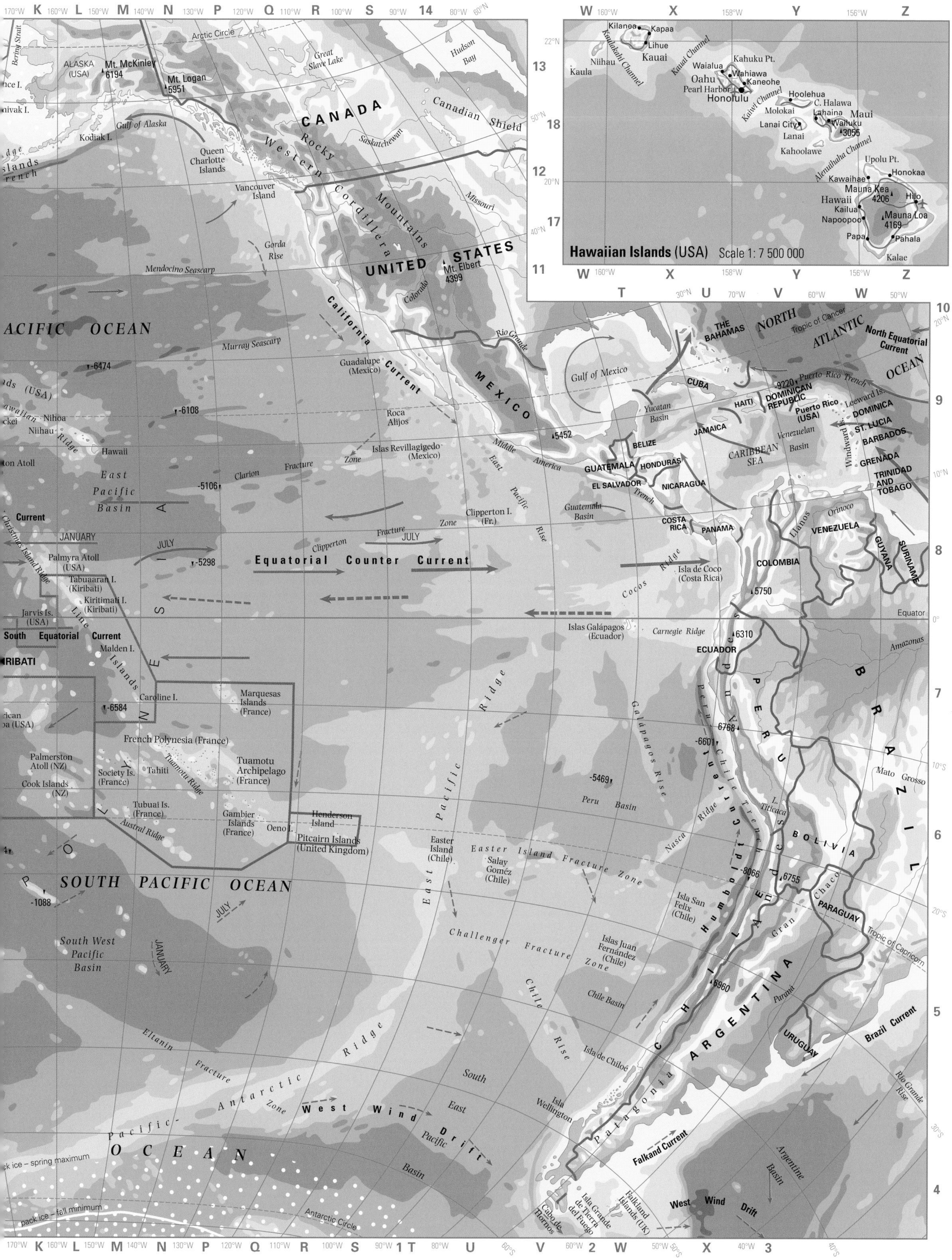

Hawaiian Islands (USA) Scale 1: 7 500 000

Modified Zenithal Equidistant Projection

Atlantic Ocean

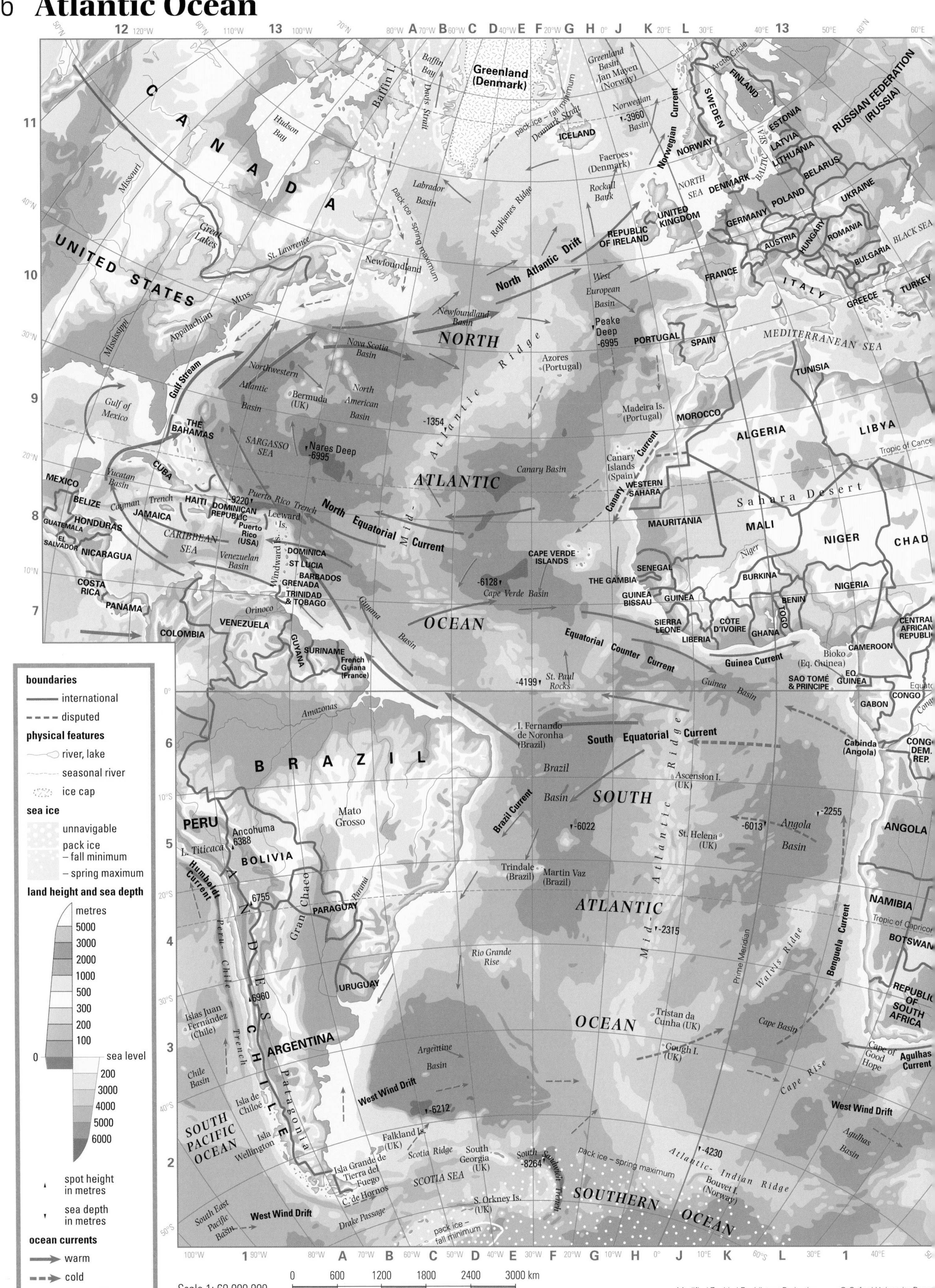

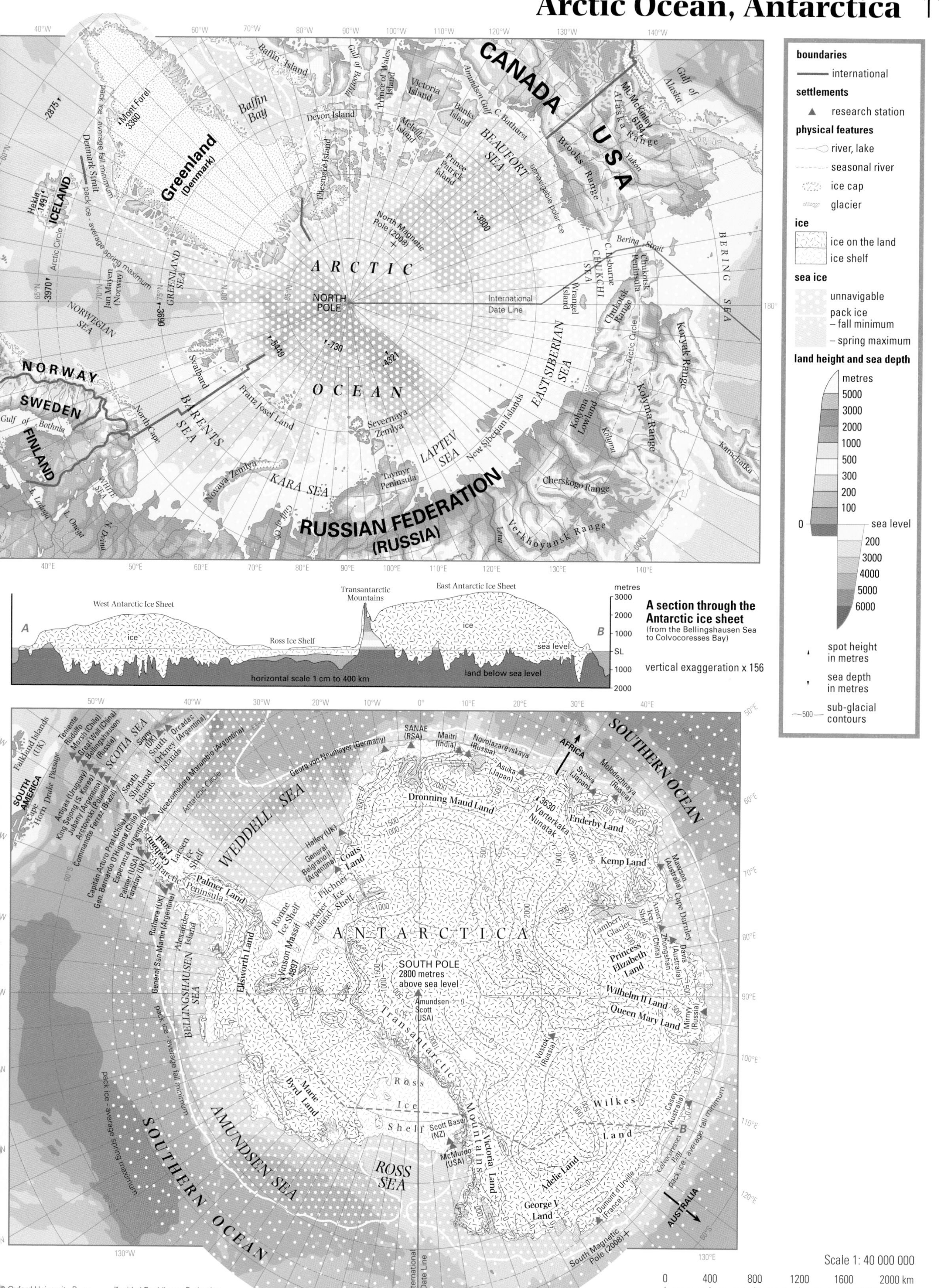
boundaries
international
settlements
research station
physical features
river, lake
seasonal river
ice cap
glacier
ice
ice on the land
ice shelf
sea ice
unnavigable
pack ice
– fall minimum
– spring maximum
land height and sea depth
metres
5000
3000
2000
1000
500
300
200
100
0
sea level
200
3000
4000
5000
6000
spot height in metres
sea depth in metres
sub-glacial contours
A section through the Antarctic ice sheet
(from the Bellingshausen Sea to Colvocoresses Bay)
vertical exaggeration x 156
West Antarctic Ice Sheet
Transantarctic Mountains
East Antarctic Ice Sheet
Ross Ice Shelf
ice
sea level
land below sea level
horizontal scale 1 cm to 400 km
ARCTIC OCEAN
NORTH POLE
Greenland (Denmark)
CANADA
USA
RUSSIAN FEDERATION (RUSSIA)
ICELAND
NORWAY
SWEDEN
FINLAND
ANTARCTICA
SOUTH POLE
2800 metres above sea level
WEDDELL SEA
ROSS SEA
AMUNDSEN SEA
BELLINGSHAUSEN SEA
SCOTIA SEA
SOUTHERN OCEAN
Scale 1: 40 000 000
0 400 800 1200 1600 2000 km

Zenithal Equidistant Projection

Equatorial scale 1: 95 000 000 (main map)

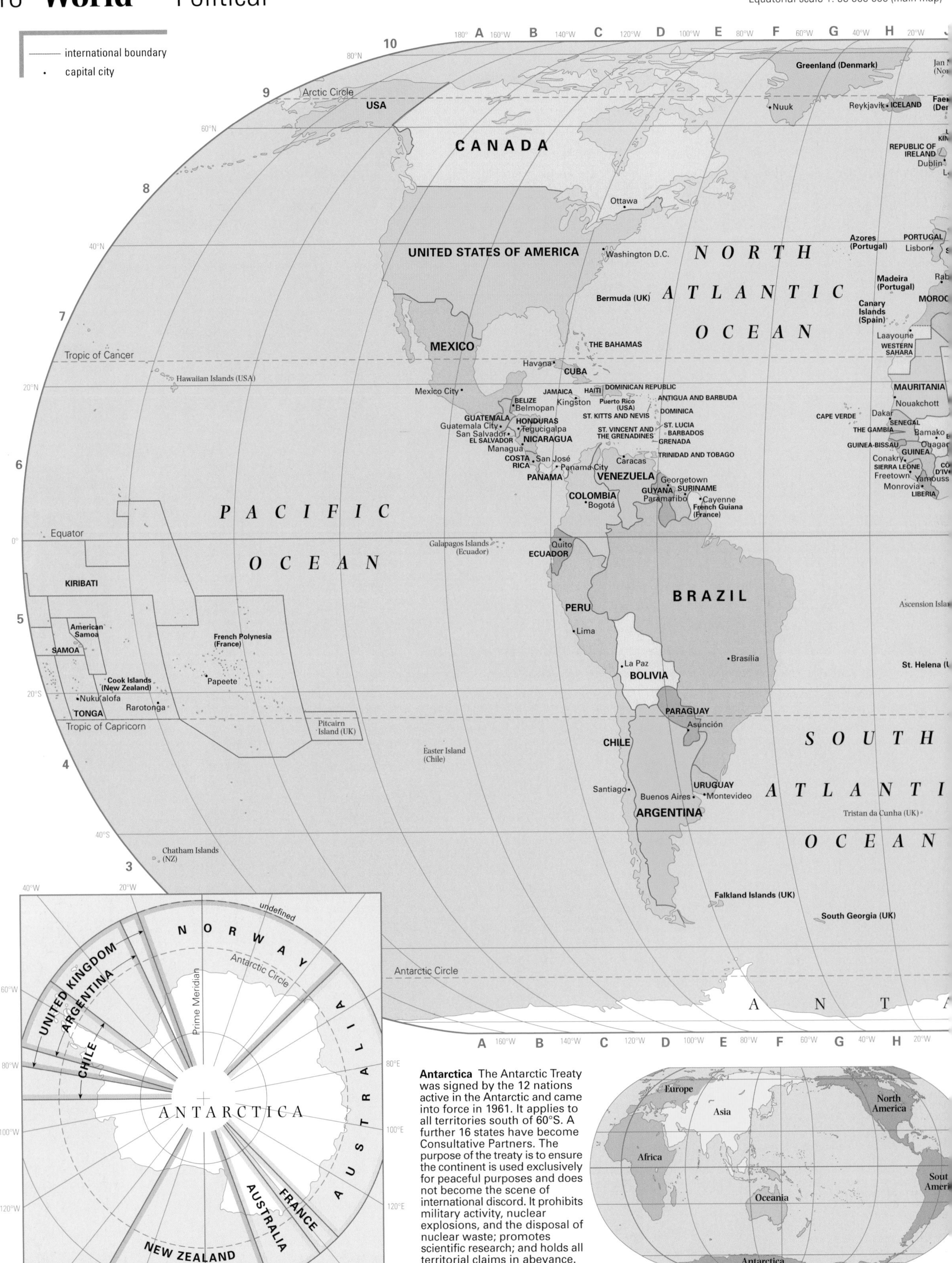

Antarctica The Antarctic Treaty was signed by the 12 nations active in the Antarctic and came into force in 1961. It applies to all territories south of 60°S. A further 16 states have become Consultative Partners. The purpose of the treaty is to ensure the continent is used exclusively for peaceful purposes and does not become the scene of international discord. It prohibits military activity, nuclear explosions, and the disposal of nuclear waste; promotes scientific research; and holds all territorial claims in abeyance.

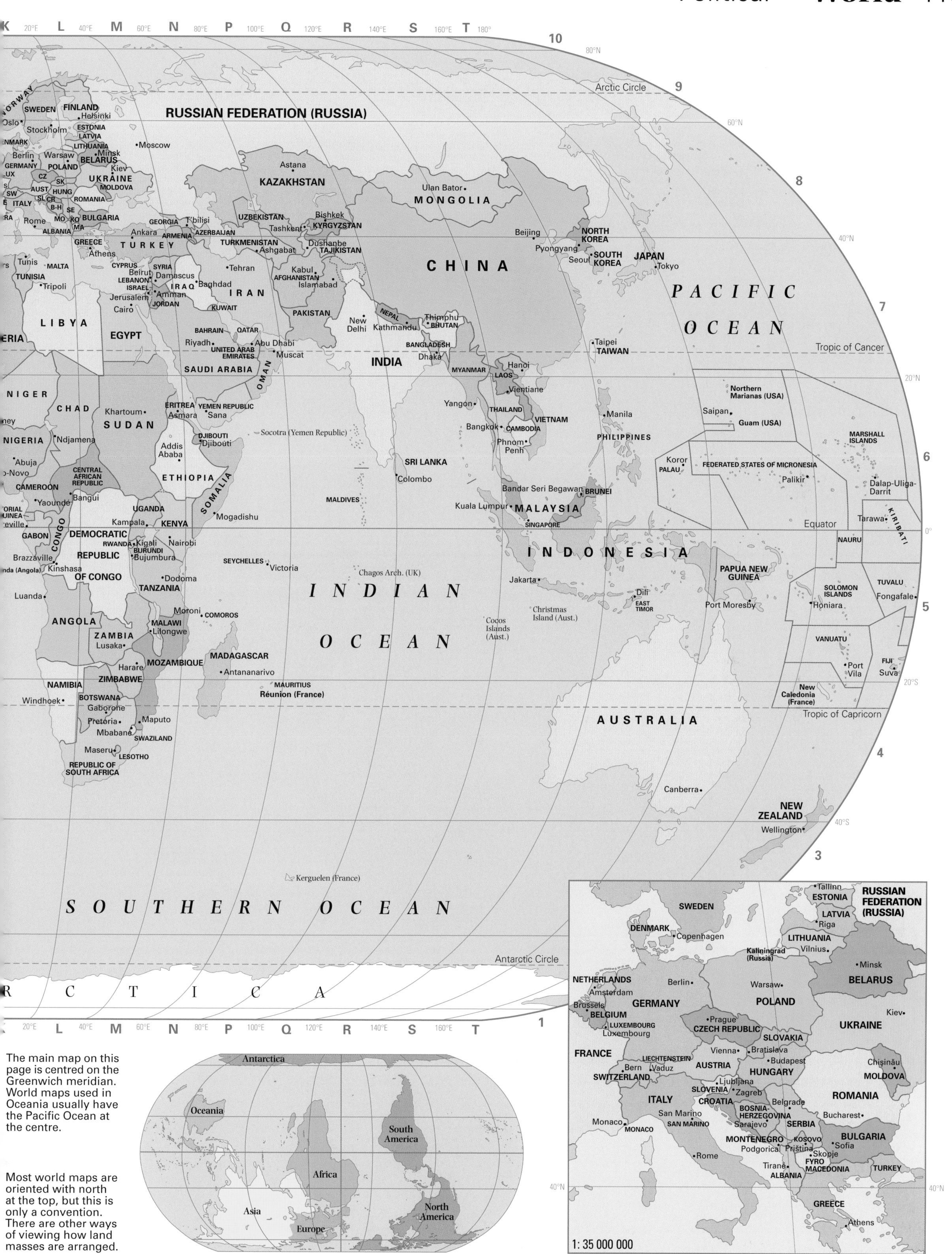
K 20°E L 40°E M 60°E N 80°E P 100°E Q 120°E R 140°E S 160°E T 180°
10
80°N
Arctic Circle
9
60°N
8
40°N
7
Tropic of Cancer
20°N
6
Equator
0°
5
20°S
Tropic of Capricorn
4
40°S
3
Antarctic Circle
1
RUSSIAN FEDERATION (RUSSIA)
NORWAY
SWEDEN
FINLAND
Helsinki
Oslo
Stockholm
ESTONIA
LATVIA
DENMARK
LITHUANIA
Moscow
Minsk
BELARUS
Berlin
Warsaw
GERMANY
POLAND
Kiev
LUX
CZ
SK
UKRAINE
MOLDOVA
AUST
HUNG
ROMANIA
SL
CR
B-H
SE
ITALY
MO
KO
BULGARIA
MA
Rome
ALBANIA
GEORGIA
Tbilisi
ARMENIA
AZERBAIJAN
Ankara
TURKEY
GREECE
Athens
Tunis
MALTA
TUNISIA
Tripoli
CYPRUS
SYRIA
Beirut
Damascus
LEBANON
ISRAEL
IRAQ
Baghdad
Jerusalem
Amman
JORDAN
Cairo
LIBYA
EGYPT
Astana
KAZAKHSTAN
UZBEKISTAN
Bishkek
Tashkent
KYRGYZSTAN
TURKMENISTAN
Ashgabat
Dushanbe
TAJIKISTAN
Tehran
IRAN
Kabul
AFGHANISTAN
Islamabad
KUWAIT
PAKISTAN
BAHRAIN
QATAR
Riyadh
UNITED ARAB EMIRATES
Abu Dhabi
Muscat
SAUDI ARABIA
OMAN
Ulan Bator
MONGOLIA
CHINA
Beijing
NORTH KOREA
Pyongyang
Seoul
SOUTH KOREA
JAPAN
Tokyo
PACIFIC OCEAN
NEPAL
Thimphu
BHUTAN
New Delhi
Kathmandu
BANGLADESH
Dhaka
INDIA
MYANMAR
Hanoi
LAOS
Vientiane
Taipei
TAIWAN
Northern Marianas (USA)
Saipan
Guam (USA)
MARSHALL ISLANDS
ERITREA
YEMEN REPUBLIC
Asmara
Sana
Khartoum
SUDAN
CHAD
NIGER
DJIBOUTI
Djibouti
Socotra (Yemen Republic)
Yangon
THAILAND
Bangkok
CAMBODIA
VIETNAM
Phnom Penh
Manila
PHILIPPINES
NIGERIA
Ndjamena
Addis Ababa
ETHIOPIA
Abuja
CENTRAL AFRICAN REPUBLIC
SOMALIA
SRI LANKA
Colombo
Koror
PALAU
FEDERATED STATES OF MICRONESIA
Palikir
Dalap-Uliga-Darrit
CAMEROON
Bangui
Yaounde
MALDIVES
Bandar Seri Begawan
BRUNEI
Kuala Lumpur
MALAYSIA
SINGAPORE
UGANDA
Kampala
KENYA
Mogadishu
GABON
CONGO
DEMOCRATIC REPUBLIC OF CONGO
RWANDA
Kigali
BURUNDI
Bujumbura
Nairobi
Brazzaville
Kinshasa
SEYCHELLES
Victoria
Chagos Arch. (UK)
INDONESIA
Tarawa
KIRIBATI
NAURU
PAPUA NEW GUINEA
Jakarta
Dodoma
TANZANIA
Luanda
INDIAN OCEAN
Dili
EAST TIMOR
Port Moresby
SOLOMON ISLANDS
Honiara
TUVALU
Fongafale
Moroni
COMOROS
Christmas Island (Aust.)
Cocos Islands (Aust.)
ANGOLA
MALAWI
Lilongwe
ZAMBIA
Lusaka
VANUATU
Port Vila
FIJI
Suva
Harare
MOZAMBIQUE
MADAGASCAR
Antananarivo
NAMIBIA
ZIMBABWE
MAURITIUS
Réunion (France)
Windhoek
BOTSWANA
Gaborone
New Caledonia (France)
Pretoria
Maputo
Mbabane
SWAZILAND
AUSTRALIA
Maseru
LESOTHO
REPUBLIC OF SOUTH AFRICA
Canberra
NEW ZEALAND
Wellington
Kerguelen (France)
SOUTHERN OCEAN
ANTARCTICA
The main map on this page is centred on the Greenwich meridian. World maps used in Oceania usually have the Pacific Ocean at the centre.
Antarctica
Oceania
South America
Africa
Asia
Europe
North America
Most world maps are oriented with north at the top, but this is only a convention. There are other ways of viewing how land masses are arranged.
Tallinn
ESTONIA
RUSSIAN FEDERATION (RUSSIA)
SWEDEN
LATVIA
Riga
DENMARK
Copenhagen
LITHUANIA
Vilnius
Kaliningrad (Russia)
Minsk
BELARUS
NETHERLANDS
Amsterdam
Berlin
Warsaw
Brussels
BELGIUM
GERMANY
POLAND
LUXEMBOURG
Luxembourg
Prague
CZECH REPUBLIC
Kiev
UKRAINE
SLOVAKIA
FRANCE
LIECHTENSTEIN
Vienna
Bratislava
Budapest
Bern
Vaduz
AUSTRIA
HUNGARY
Chişinău
MOLDOVA
SWITZERLAND
Ljubljana
SLOVENIA
Zagreb
ITALY
CROATIA
Belgrade
ROMANIA
BOSNIA-HERZEGOVINA
San Marino
SAN MARINO
Sarajevo
SERBIA
Bucharest
Monaco
MONACO
MONTENEGRO
KOSOVO
BULGARIA
Podgorica
Priština
Sofia
Skopje
FYRO MACEDONIA
Rome
Tirane
ALBANIA
TURKEY
GREECE
Athens
1: 35 000 000
40°N
20°E

Equatorial scale 1: 95 000 000

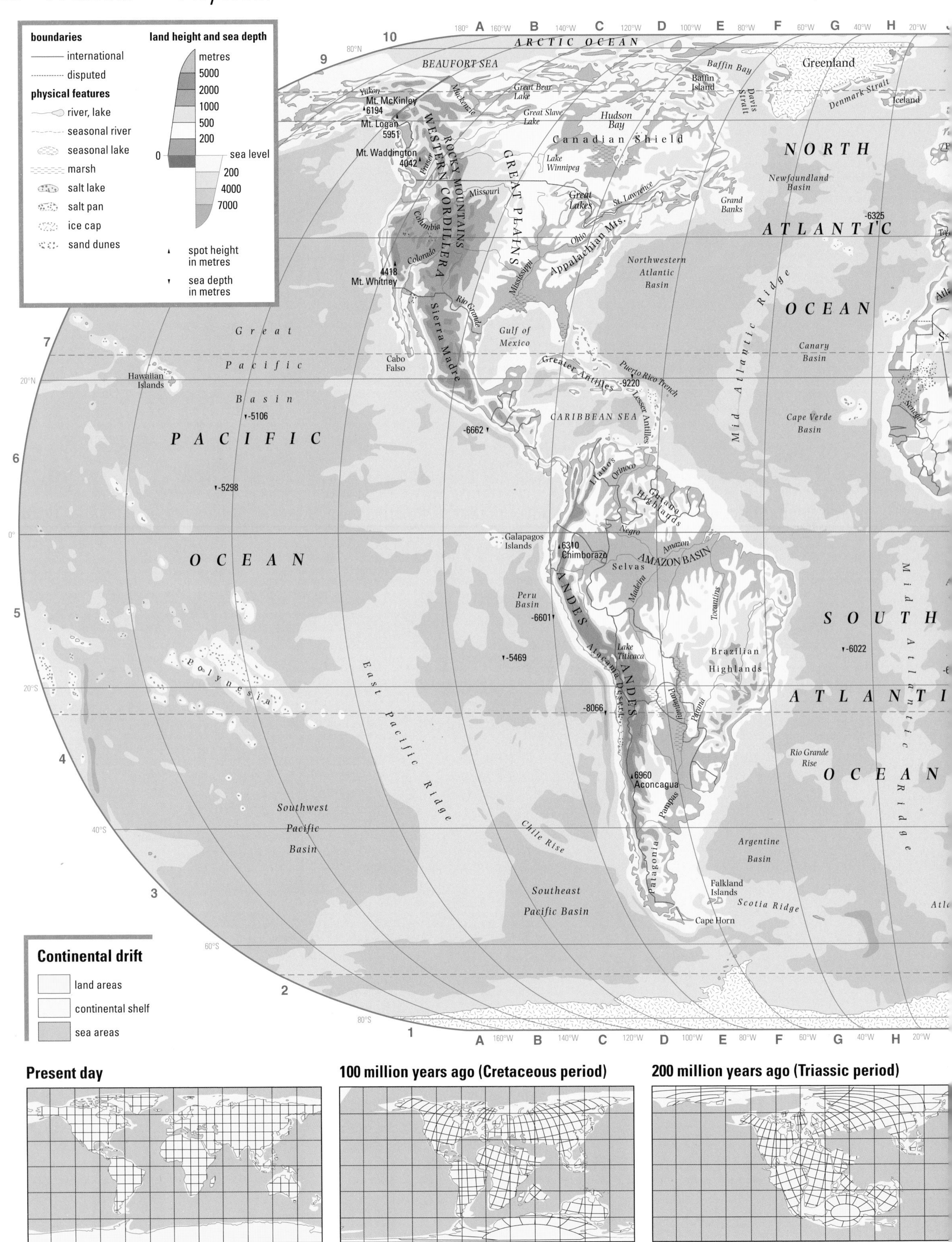
boundaries
international
disputed
physical features
river, lake
seasonal river
seasonal lake
marsh
salt lake
salt pan
ice cap
sand dunes
land height and sea depth
metres
5000
2000
1000
500
200
0
sea level
200
4000
7000
spot height in metres
sea depth in metres
ARCTIC OCEAN
BEAUFORT SEA
Baffin Bay
Baffin Island
Davis Strait
Greenland
Denmark Strait
Iceland
Yukon
Mt. McKinley 6194
Mt. Logan 5951
Mt. Waddington 4042
Mackenzie
Great Bear Lake
Great Slave Lake
Hudson Bay
Canadian Shield
ROCKY MOUNTAINS
WESTERN CORDILLERA
GREAT PLAINS
Lake Winnipeg
Missouri
Great Lakes
St. Lawrence
Columbia
Colorado
Ohio
Appalachian Mts.
Mississippi
4418 Mt. Whitney
Rio Grande
Sierra Madre
Gulf of Mexico
Cabo Falso
NORTH
Newfoundland Basin
Grand Banks
-6325
ATLANTIC
Northwestern Atlantic Basin
Mid Atlantic Ridge
OCEAN
Canary Basin
Great Pacific Basin
Hawaiian Islands
-5106
PACIFIC
-5298
OCEAN
Greater Antilles
Puerto Rico Trench
-9220
Lesser Antilles
CARIBBEAN SEA
-6662
Cape Verde Basin
Senegal
Llanos
Orinoco
Guiana Highlands
Negro
Galapagos Islands
6310 Chimborazo
Amazon
AMAZON BASIN
Selvas
Madeira
Tocantins
ANDES
Peru Basin
-6601
-5469
Lake Titicaca
Atacama Desert
Brazilian Highlands
Paraguay
Paraná
-8066
SOUTH
-6022
ATLANTIC
OCEAN
Polynesia
East Pacific Ridge
Southwest Pacific Basin
Rio Grande Rise
6960 Aconcagua
Pampas
Chile Rise
Argentine Basin
Patagonia
Southeast Pacific Basin
Falkland Islands
Scotia Ridge
Cape Horn
Continental drift
land areas
continental shelf
sea areas
80°N
20°N
0°
20°S
40°S
60°S
80°S
180°
160°W
140°W
120°W
100°W
80°W
60°W
40°W
20°W
A
B
C
D
E
F
G
H
1
2
3
4
5
6
7
9
10

Present day

100 million years ago (Cretaceous period)

200 million years ago (Triassic period)

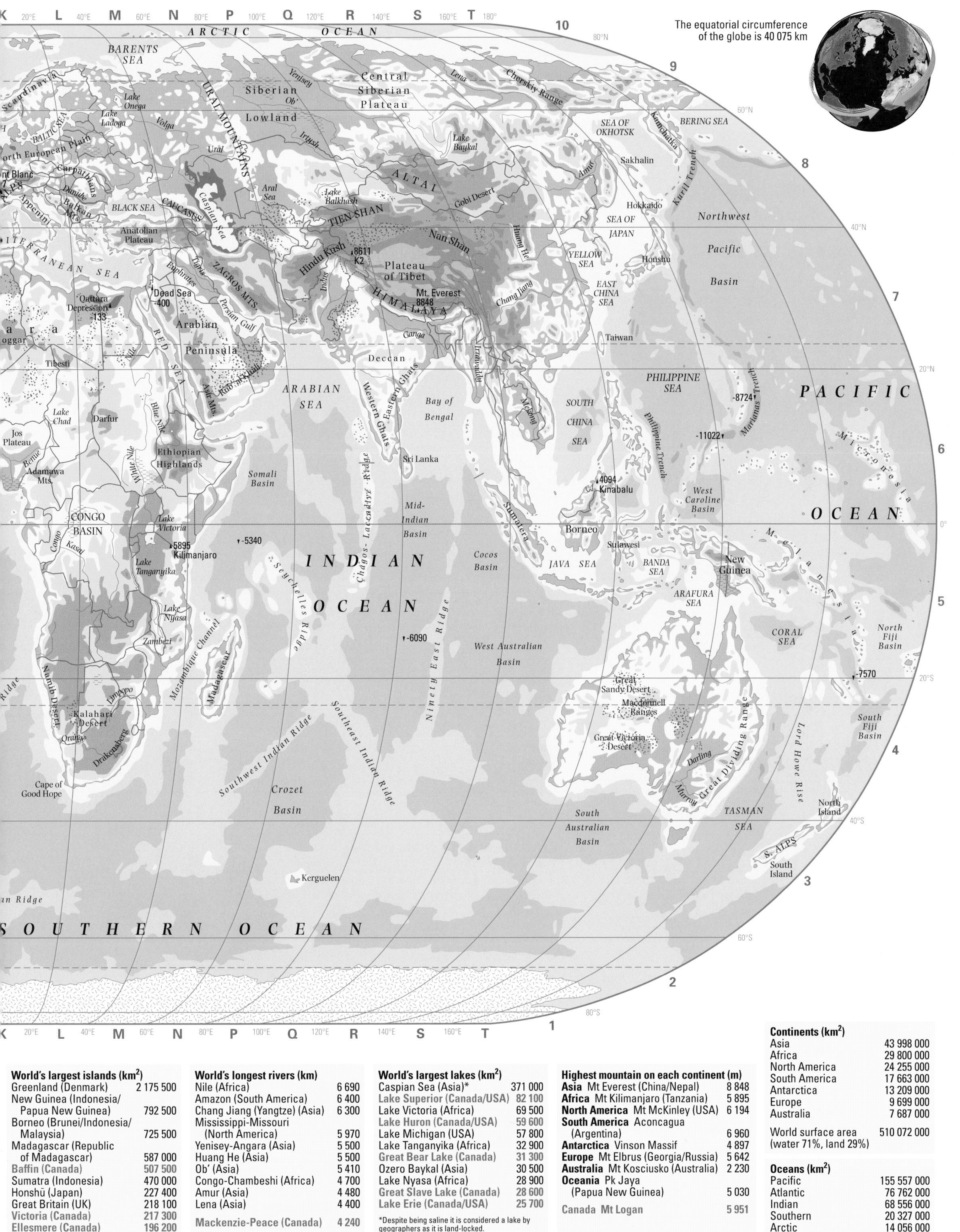

World's largest islands (km²)	
Greenland (Denmark)	2 175 500
New Guinea (Indonesia/ Papua New Guinea)	792 500
Borneo (Brunei/Indonesia/ Malaysia)	725 500
Madagascar (Republic of Madagascar)	587 000
Baffin (Canada)	507 500
Sumatra (Indonesia)	470 000
Honshū (Japan)	227 400
Great Britain (UK)	218 100
Victoria (Canada)	217 300
Ellesmere (Canada)	196 200

World's longest rivers (km)	
Nile (Africa)	6 690
Amazon (South America)	6 400
Chang Jiang (Yangtze) (Asia)	6 300
Mississippi-Missouri (North America)	5 970
Yenisey-Angara (Asia)	5 500
Huang He (Asia)	5 500
Ob' (Asia)	5 410
Congo-Chambeshi (Africa)	4 700
Amur (Asia)	4 480
Lena (Asia)	4 400
Mackenzie-Peace (Canada)	4 240

World's largest lakes (km²)	
Caspian Sea (Asia)*	371 000
Lake Superior (Canada/USA)	82 100
Lake Victoria (Africa)	69 500
Lake Huron (Canada/USA)	59 600
Lake Michigan (USA)	57 800
Lake Tanganyika (Africa)	32 900
Great Bear Lake (Canada)	31 300
Ozero Baykal (Asia)	30 500
Lake Nyasa (Africa)	28 900
Great Slave Lake (Canada)	28 600
Lake Erie (Canada/USA)	25 700

*Despite being saline it is considered a lake by geographers as it is land-locked.

Highest mountain on each continent (m)	
Asia Mt Everest (China/Nepal)	8 848
Africa Mt Kilimanjaro (Tanzania)	5 895
North America Mt McKinley (USA)	6 194
South America Aconcagua (Argentina)	6 960
Antarctica Vinson Massif	4 897
Europe Mt Elbrus (Georgia/Russia)	5 642
Australia Mt Kosciusko (Australia)	2 230
Oceania Pk Jaya (Papua New Guinea)	5 030
Canada **Mt Logan**	**5 951**

Continents (km²)	
Asia	43 998 000
Africa	29 800 000
North America	24 255 000
South America	17 663 000
Antarctica	13 209 000
Europe	9 699 000
Australia	7 687 000
World surface area (water 71%, land 29%)	510 072 000

Oceans (km²)	
Pacific	155 557 000
Atlantic	76 762 000
Indian	68 556 000
Southern	20 327 000
Arctic	14 056 000

 Eckert IV Projection

Equatorial scale 1: 130 000 000

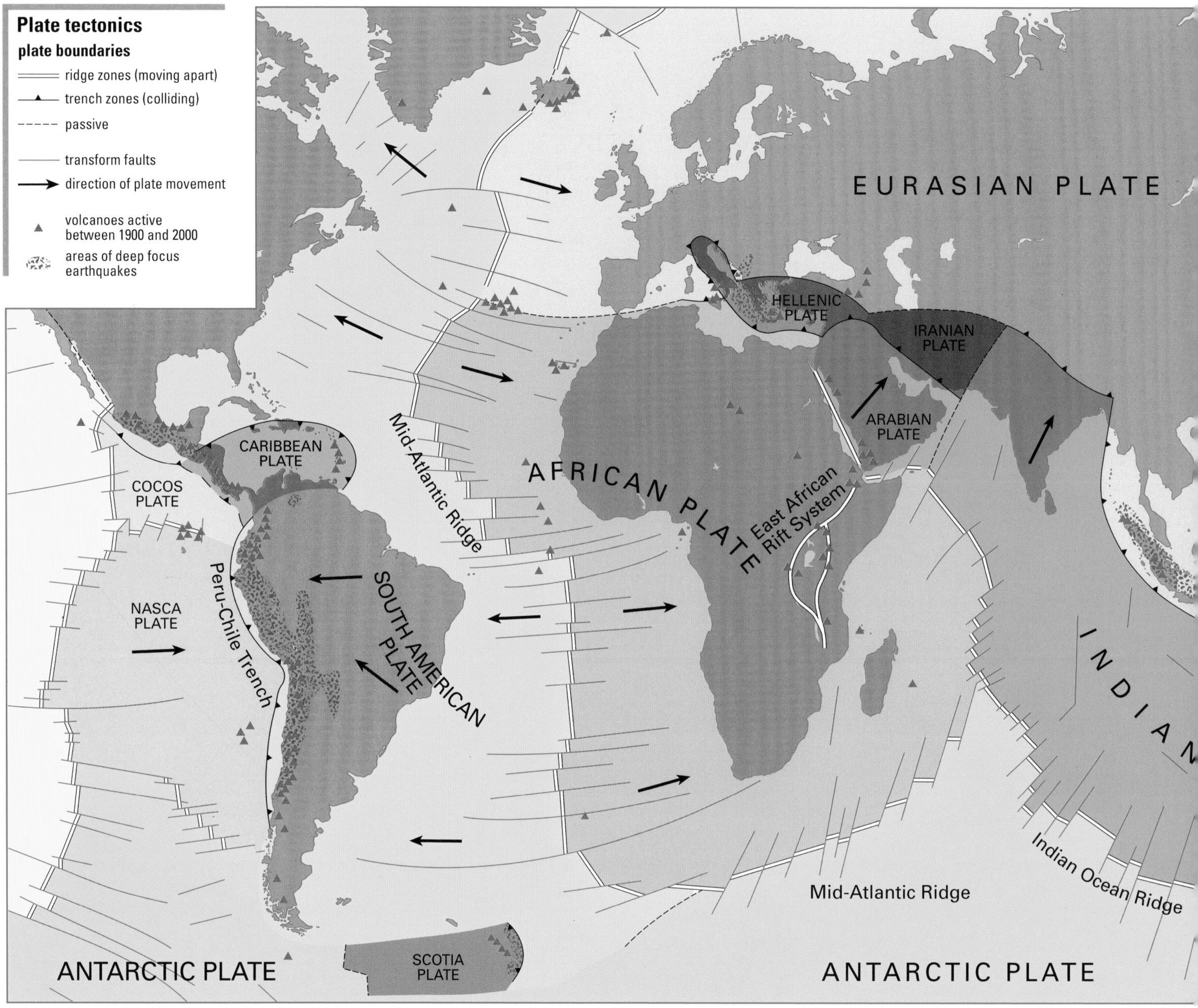

Plate tectonics

plate boundaries

- ridge zones (moving apart)
- trench zones (colliding)
- passive
- transform faults
- direction of plate movement
- volcanoes active between 1900 and 2000
- areas of deep focus earthquakes

EURASIAN PLATE
HELLENIC PLATE
IRANIAN PLATE
ARABIAN PLATE
CARIBBEAN PLATE
COCOS PLATE
Mid-Atlantic Ridge
AFRICAN PLATE
East African Rift System
NASCA PLATE
Peru-Chile Trench
SOUTH AMERICAN PLATE
INDIAN
Indian Ocean Ridge
Mid-Atlantic Ridge
ANTARCTIC PLATE
SCOTIA PLATE
ANTARCTIC PLATE

Structure of the Earth

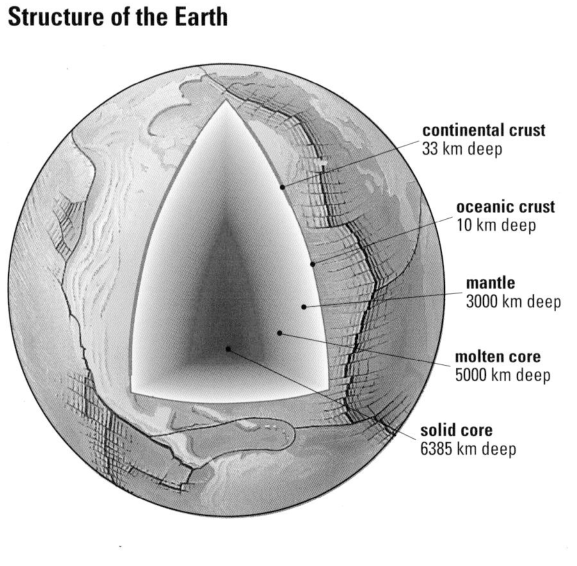

Cross section of a strato volcano

(e.g. Mt. Vesuvius, Italy)

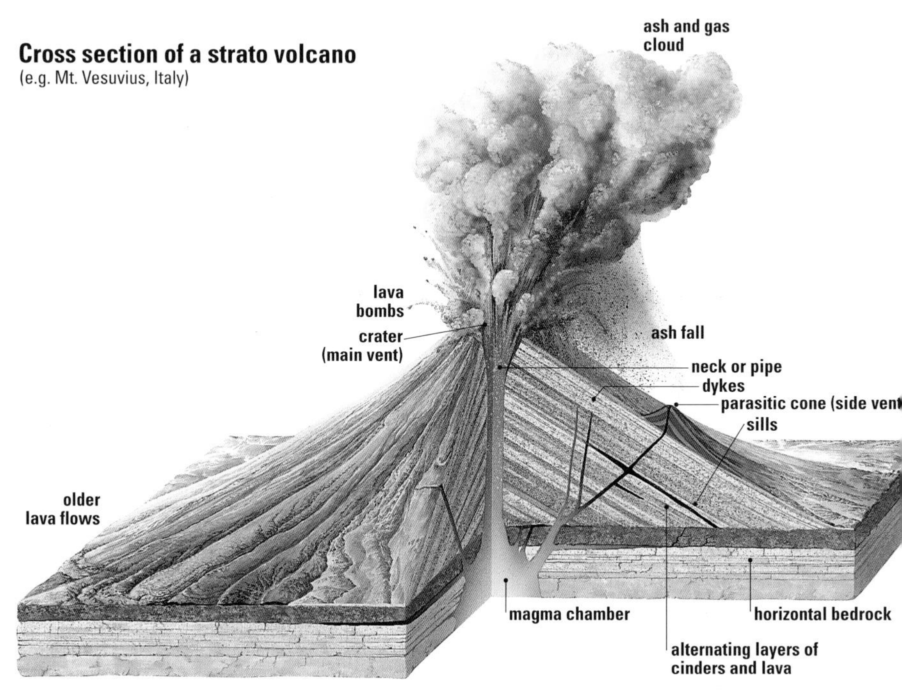

Gall Projection

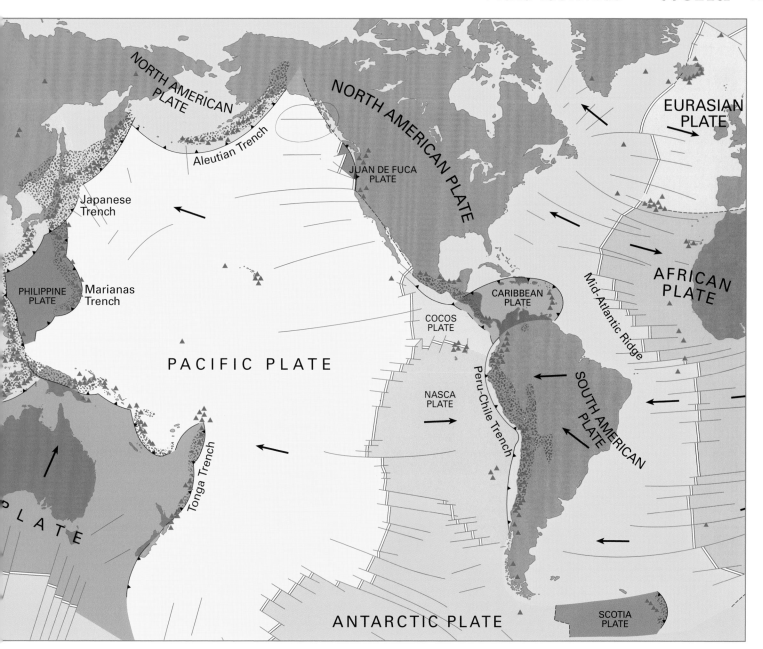

NORTH AMERICAN PLATE
NORTH AMERICAN PLATE
EURASIAN PLATE
Aleutian Trench
JUAN DE FUCA PLATE
Japanese Trench
PHILIPPINE PLATE
Marianas Trench
CARIBBEAN PLATE
AFRICAN PLATE
Mid-Atlantic Ridge
COCOS PLATE
PACIFIC PLATE
NASCA PLATE
Peru-Chile Trench
SOUTH AMERICAN PLATE
Tonga Trench
PLATE
ANTARCTIC PLATE
SCOTIA PLATE

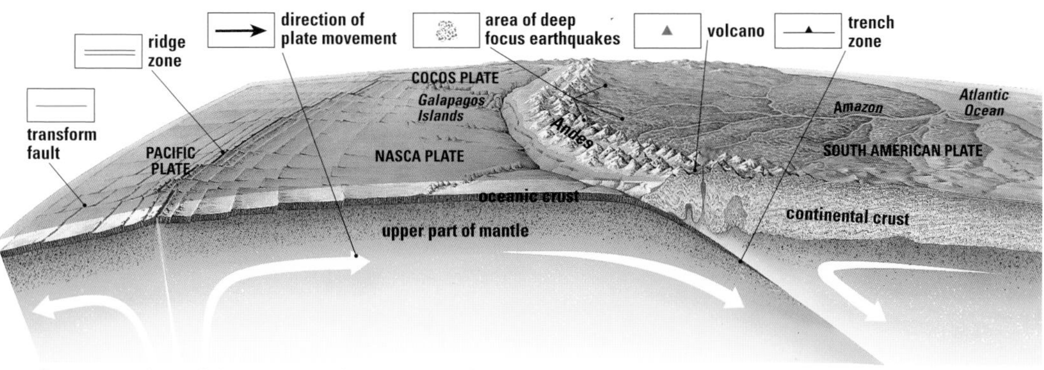

Cross section of the crust and upper mantle

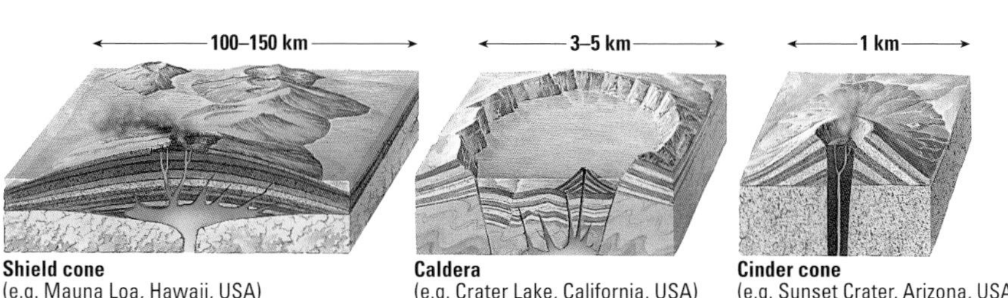

Shield cone
(e.g. Mauna Loa, Hawaii, USA)

Caldera
(e.g. Crater Lake, California, USA)

Cinder cone
(e.g. Sunset Crater, Arizona, USA)

Deadliest earthquakes, 1990–2006

force measured on the Richter scale

Year	Place	Force	Deaths
1990	Northwestern Iran	7.7	37 000
1990	Luzon, Philippines	7.7	1660
1991	Afghanistan/Pakistan	6.8	1000
1991	Uttar Pradesh, India	6.1	1500
1992	Erzincan, Turkey	6.7	2000
1992	Flores Island, Indonesia	7.5	2500
1993	Maharashtra, India	6.3	9800
1994	Cauca, Colombia	6.8	1000
1995	Kobe, Japan	7.2	5500
1995	Sakhalin Island, Russia	7.6	2000
1997	Ardabil, Iran	unknown	>1000
1997	Khorash, Iran	7.1	>1600
1998	Takhar, Afghanistan	6.1	>3800
1998	Northeastern Afghanistan	7.1	>3000
1999	Western Colombia	6.0	1124
1999	Izmit, Turkey	7.4	>17 000
1999	Central Taiwan	7.6	2295
2001	Gujarat, India	6.9	>20 000
2002	Baghlan, Afghanistan	6.0	>2000
2003	Northern Algeria	6.8	>2266
2003	Southeastern Iran	6.6	31 000
2004	Sumatra, Indonesia	9.1	>283 100
2005	Northern Pakistan	6.0	>86 000
2006	Java, Indonesia	6.3	>5 749

 Eckert IV Projection

Scale 1: 240 000 000

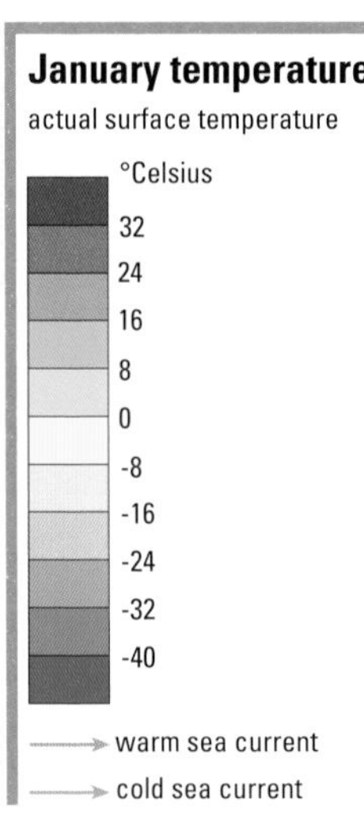

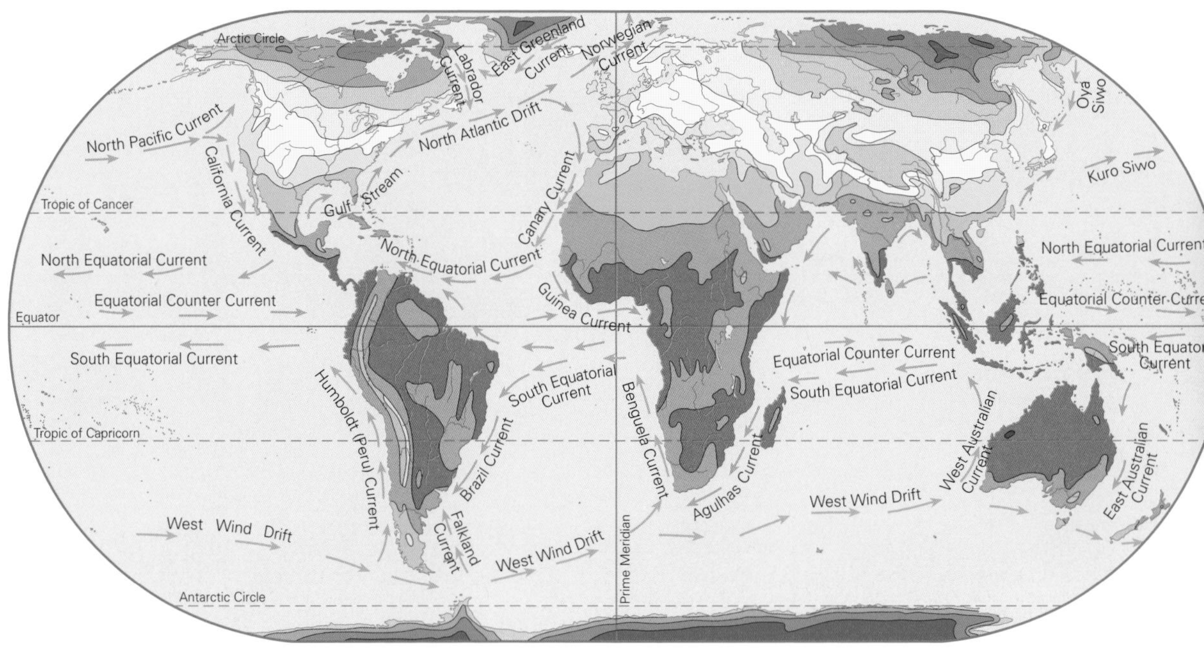

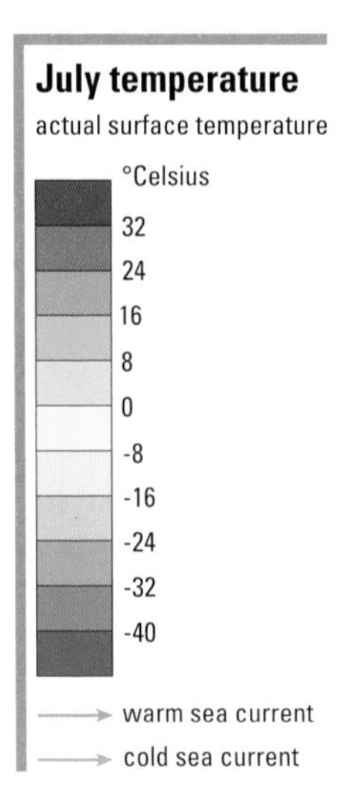

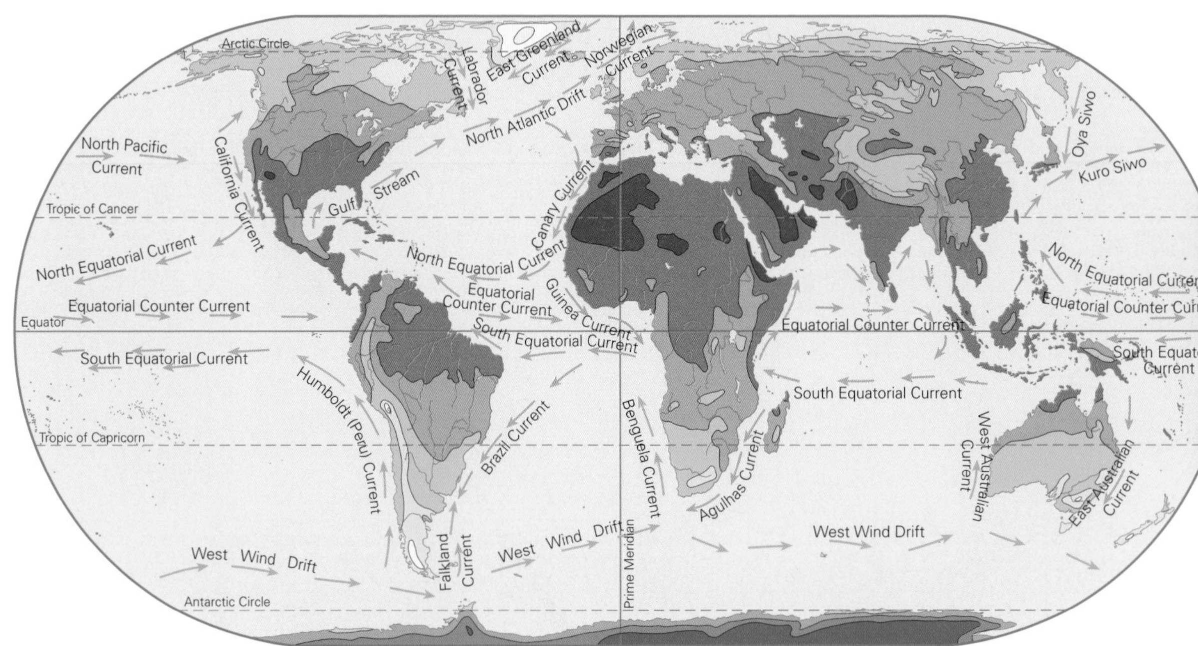

Global warming

predicted annual mean temperature increase by 2050

°Celsius

4.5
4.0
3.5
3.0
2.5
2.0
1.5
1.0

This map shows the projected increase in temperature obtained from a global climate model. This is the result from only one climate model. Other models yield projections that differ in detail but agree in their broad features.

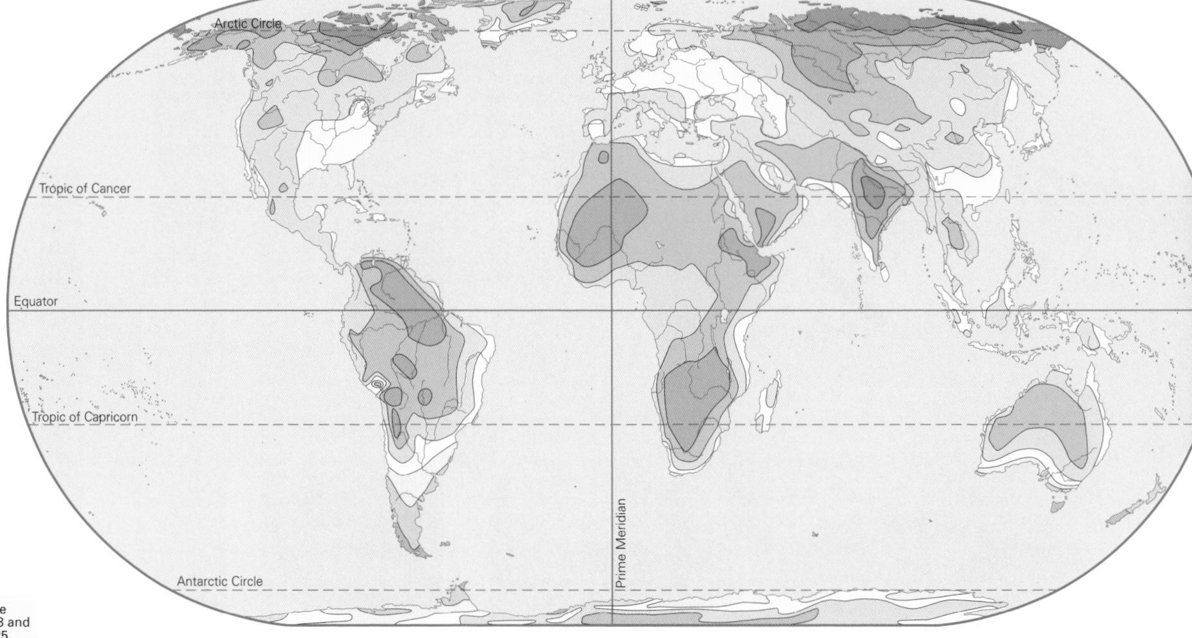

Further information on climate change is located on page 128 and for Canada on pages 16 and 25.

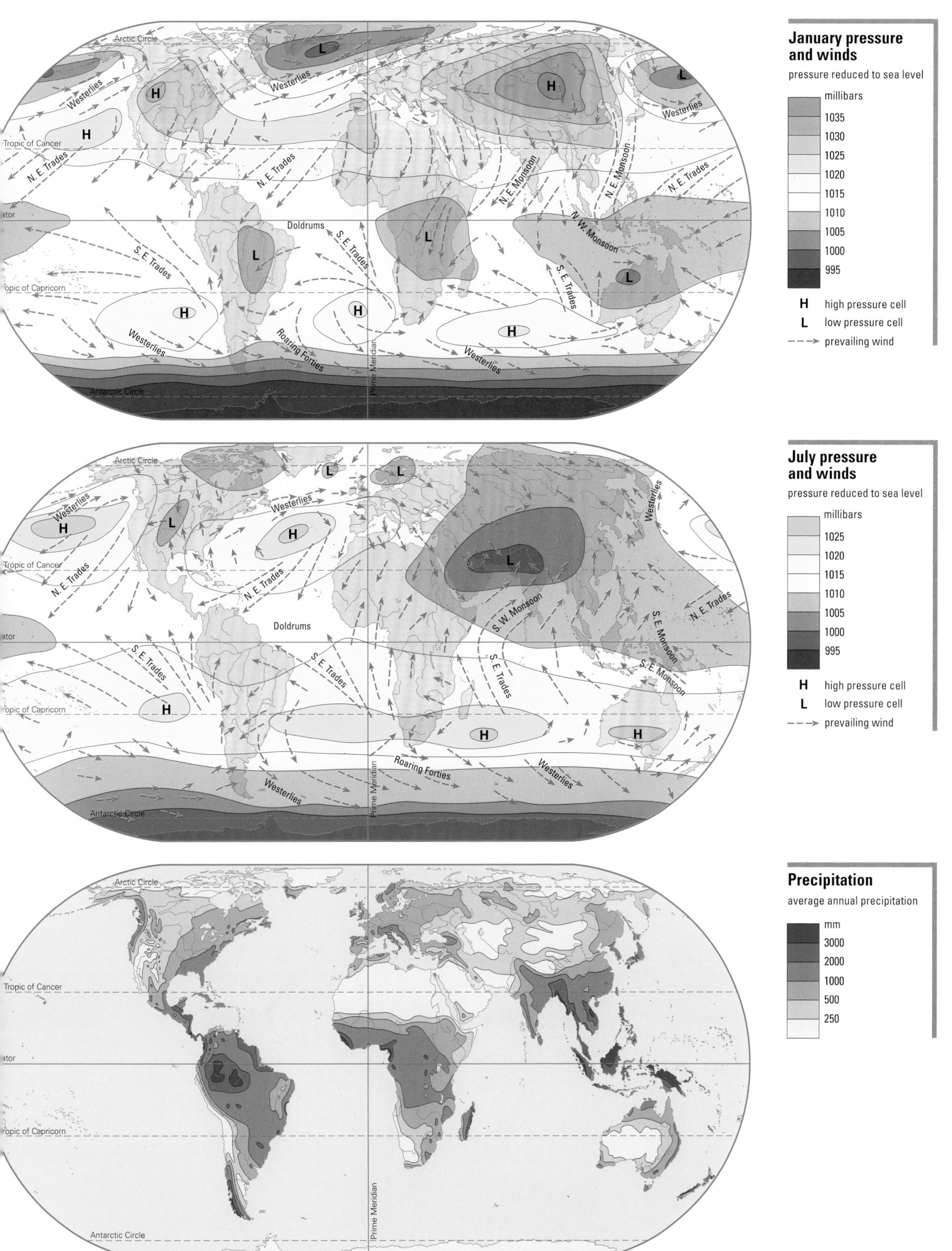
January pressure and winds
pressure reduced to sea level
millibars
1035
1030
1025
1020
1015
1010
1005
1000
995
H high pressure cell
L low pressure cell
prevailing wind
Arctic Circle
Tropic of Cancer
Tropic of Capricorn
Antarctic Circle
Prime Meridian
Westerlies
N. E. Trades
Doldrums
S. E. Trades
Roaring Forties
N. E. Monsoon
N. W. Monsoon
July pressure and winds
pressure reduced to sea level
millibars
1025
1020
1015
1010
1005
1000
995
H high pressure cell
L low pressure cell
prevailing wind
S. W. Monsoon
S. E. Monsoon
Precipitation
average annual precipitation
mm
3000
2000
1000
500
250

 Eckert IV Projection

Climate regions

Equatorial scale 1: 190 000 000

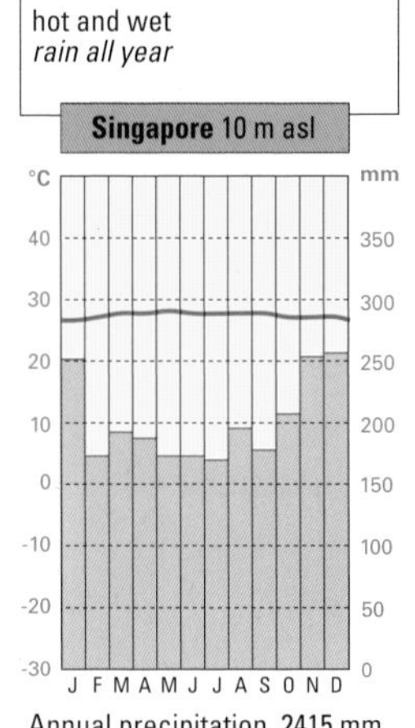

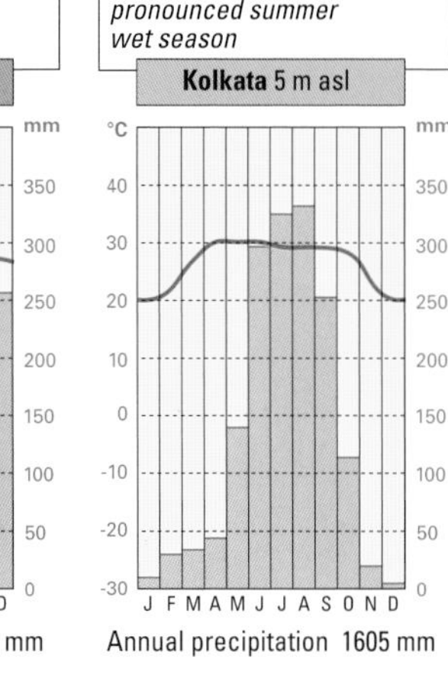

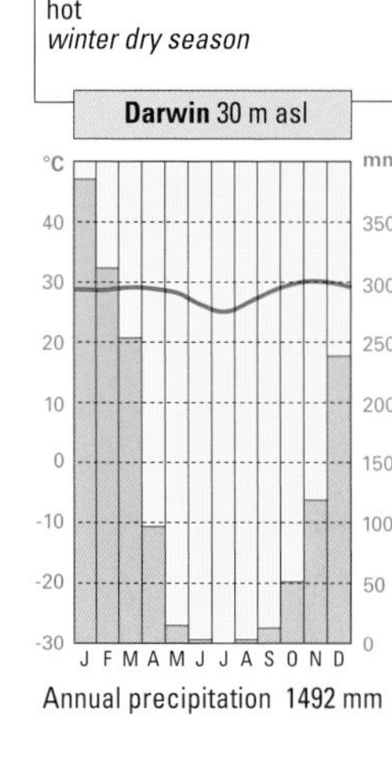

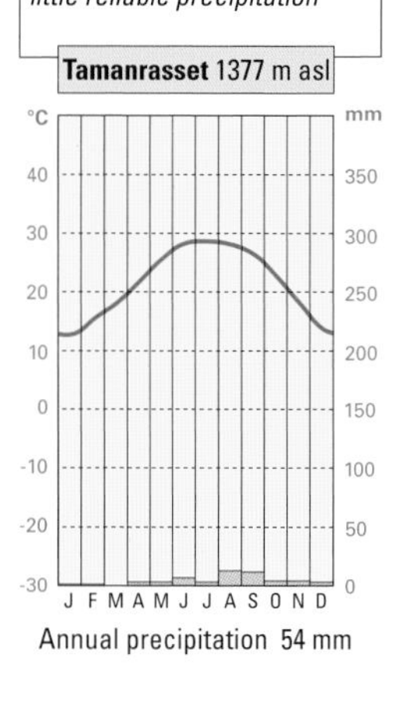

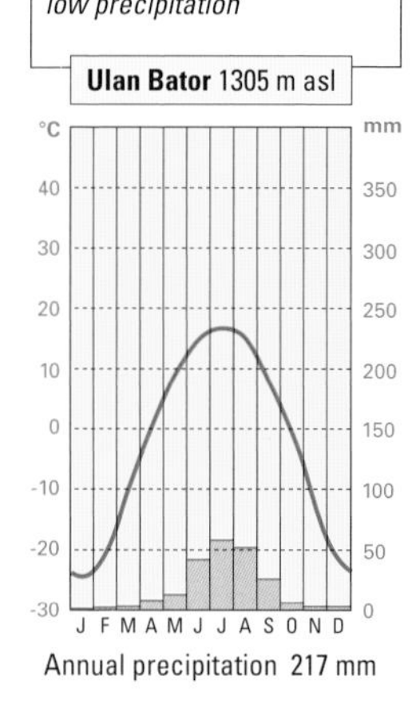

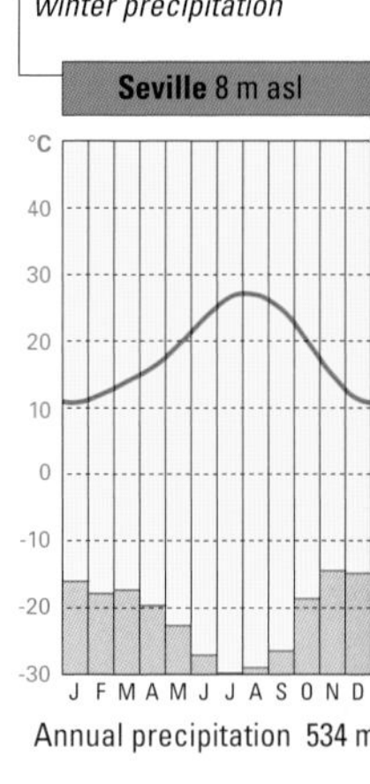

80°N
Arctic Circle
60°N
Iqaluit
Montréal
40°N
Seville
Ulan Bator
Vladivostock
Tokyo
Tropic of Cancer
Tamanrasset
Kolkata
20°N
Equator
0°
Singapore
Darwin
La Paz
20°S
Tropic of Capricorn
Johannesburg
Prime Meridian
40°S
60°S
Antarctic Circle
80°S

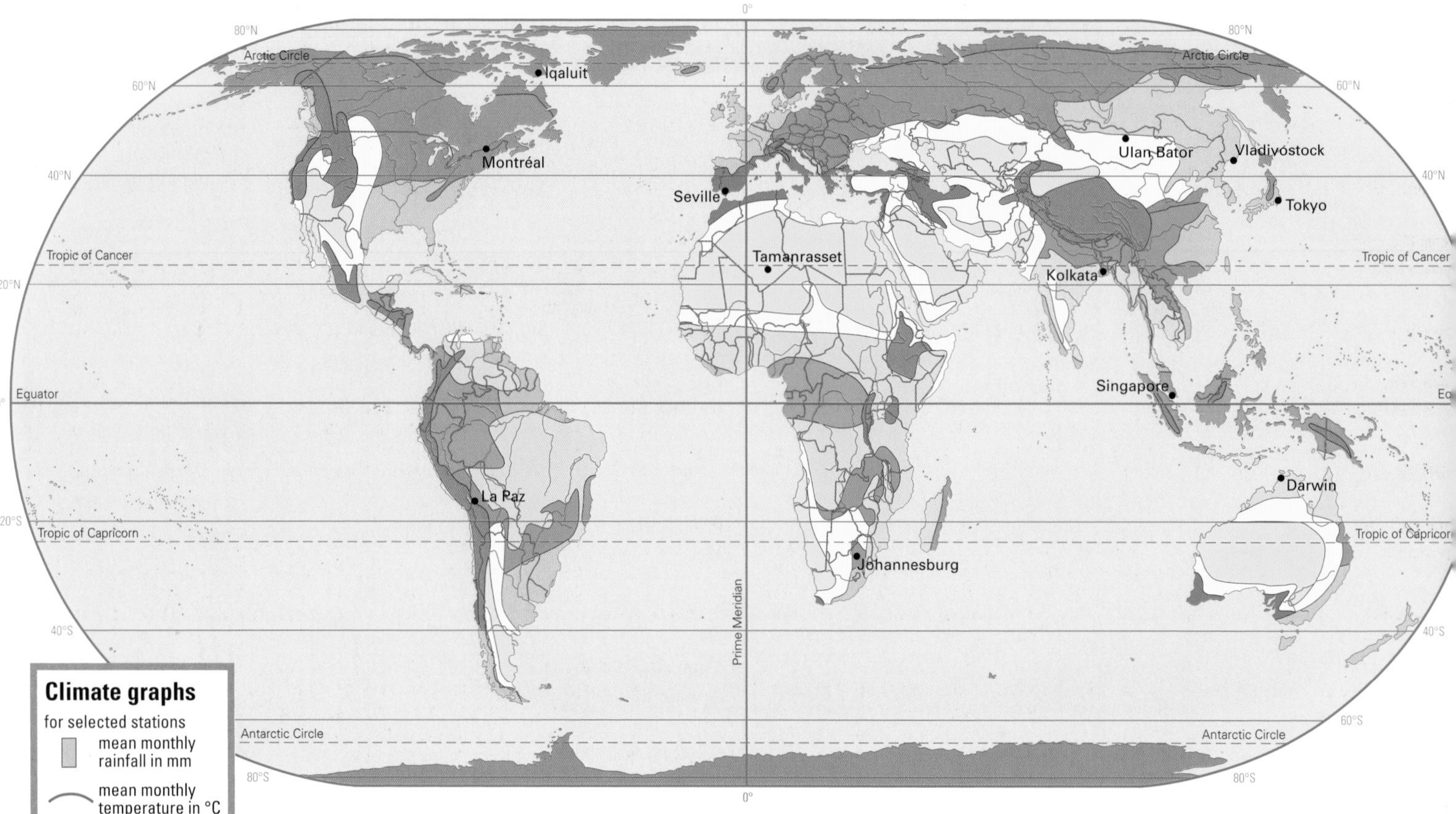

Climate graphs
for selected stations
mean monthly rainfall in mm
mean monthly temperature in °C
asl above sea level

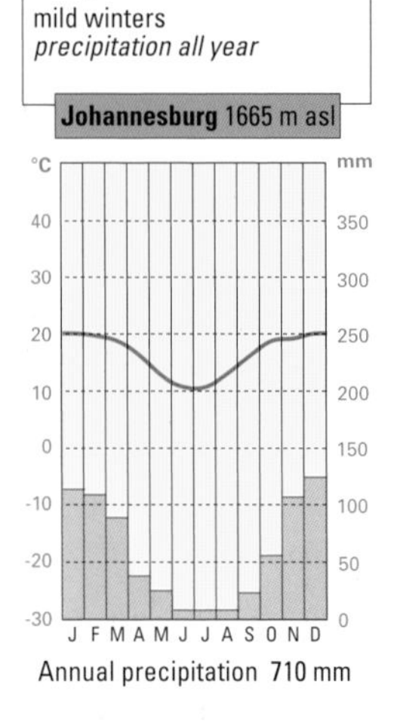

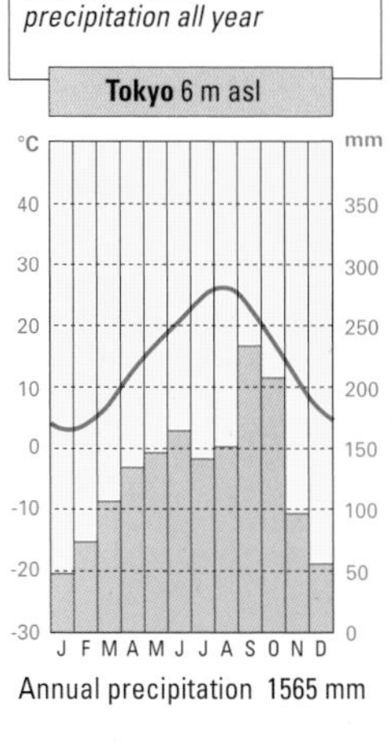

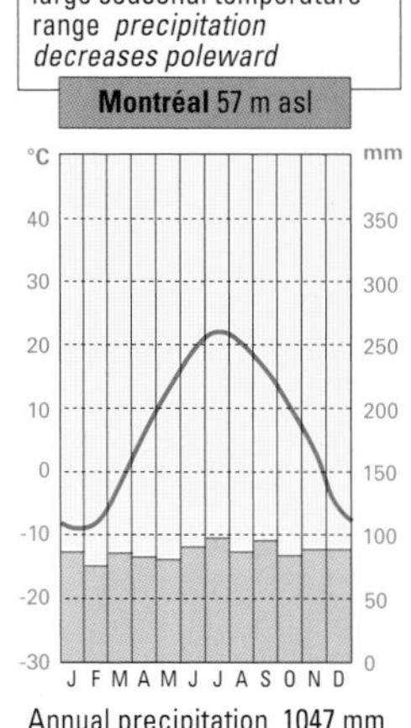

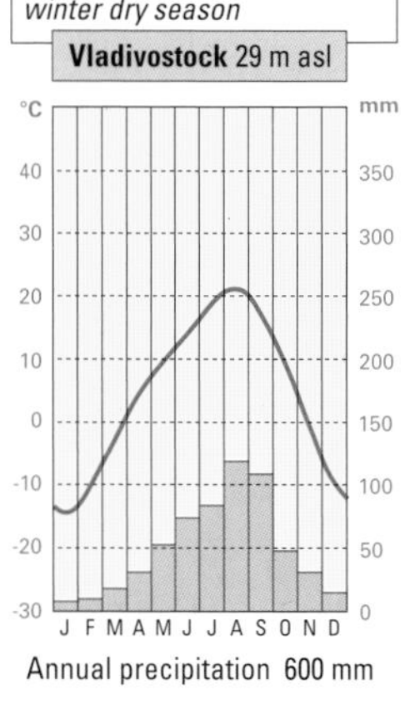

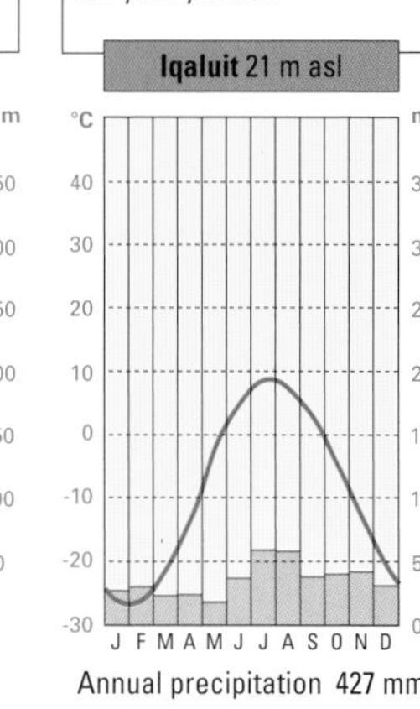

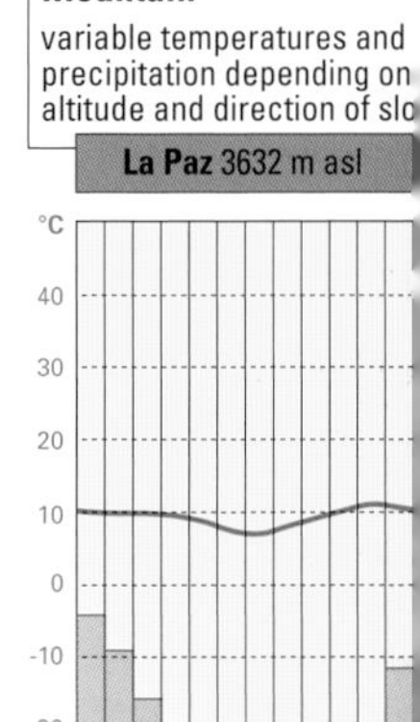

Eckert IV Projection

Climate data

Averages are for 1961–1990

Denver 1626 m		climate station and its height above sea level
Temperature (°C)	high	average daily maximum temperature
	mean	average monthly temperature
	low	average daily minimum temperature
Precipitation (mm)		average monthly precipitation

ver, USA 1626 m

		Jan	Feb	Mar	Apr	May	Jun	Jul	Aug	Sep	Oct	Nov	Dec	YEAR
erature (°C)	high	6.2	8.1	11.2	16.6	21.6	27.4	31.2	29.9	24.9	19.1	11.4	6.9	17.9
	mean	-1.3	0.8	3.9	9.0	14.0	19.4	23.1	21.9	16.8	10.8	3.9	-0.6	10.1
	low	-8.8	-6.6	-3.4	1.4	6.4	11.3	14.8	13.8	8.7	2.4	-3.7	-8.1	2.4
pitation (mm)		13	15	33	43	61	46	49	38	32	25	22	16	393

rgetown, Guyana 2 m

		Jan	Feb	Mar	Apr	May	Jun	Jul	Aug	Sep	Oct	Nov	Dec	YEAR
erature (°C)	high	28.6	28.9	29.2	29.5	29.4	29.2	29.6	30.2	30.8	30.8	30.2	29.1	29.6
	mean	26.1	26.4	26.7	27.0	26.8	26.5	26.6	27.0	27.5	27.6	27.2	26.4	26.8
	low	23.6	23.9	24.2	24.4	24.3	23.8	23.5	23.8	24.2	24.4	24.2	23.8	24.0
pitation (mm)		185	89	111	141	286	328	268	201	98	107	186	262	2262

ngzhou, China 42 m

		Jan	Feb	Mar	Apr	May	Jun	Jul	Aug	Sep	Oct	Nov	Dec	YEAR
erature (°C)	high	18.3	18.4	21.6	25.5	29.4	31.3	32.7	32.6	31.4	28.6	24.4	20.5	26.2
	mean	13.3	14.3	17.7	21.9	25.6	27.3	28.5	28.3	27.1	24.0	19.4	15.0	21.9
	low	5.0	6.6	10.7	16.1	20.7	23.5	25.7	25.2	22.6	17.6	11.9	6.5	16.0
pitation (mm)		43	65	85	182	284	258	228	221	172	79	42	24	1683

ana, Cuba 50 m

		Jan	Feb	Mar	Apr	May	Jun	Jul	Aug	Sep	Oct	Nov	Dec	YEAR
erature (°C)	high	25.8	26.1	27.6	28.6	29.8	30.5	31.3	31.6	31.0	29.2	27.7	26.5	28.8
	mean	22.2	22.4	23.7	24.8	26.1	26.9	27.6	27.8	27.4	26.2	24.5	23.0	25.2
	low	18.6	18.6	19.7	20.9	22.4	23.4	23.8	24.1	23.8	23.0	21.3	19.5	21.6
pitation (mm)		64	69	46	54	98	182	106	100	144	181	88	58	1190

aca, Peru 3827 m

		Jan	Feb	Mar	Apr	May	Jun	Jul	Aug	Sep	Oct	Nov	Dec	YEAR
erature (°C)	high	16.7	16.7	16.5	16.8	16.6	16.0	16.0	17.0	17.6	18.6	18.8	17.7	17.1
	mean	10.2	10.1	9.9	8.7	6.4	4.5	4.3	5.8	8.1	9.5	10.2	10.4	8.2
	low	3.6	3.5	3.2	0.6	-3.8	-7.0	-7.5	-5.4	-1.4	0.3	1.5	3.0	-0.8
ipitation (mm)		133	109	99	43	10	3	2	6	22	41	55	86	609

toum, Sudan 380 m

		Jan	Feb	Mar	Apr	May	Jun	Jul	Aug	Sep	Oct	Nov	Dec	YEAR
erature (°C)	high	30.8	33.0	36.8	40.1	41.9	41.3	38.4	37.3	39.1	39.3	35.2	31.8	37.1
	mean	23.2	25.0	28.7	31.9	34.5	34.3	32.1	31.5	32.5	32.4	28.1	24.5	29.9
	low	15.6	17.0	20.5	23.6	27.1	27.3	25.9	25.3	26.0	25.5	21.0	17.1	22.7
ipitation (mm)		0	0	0	0.5	4	5	46	75	25	5	1	0	161

sa, China 3650 m

		Jan	Feb	Mar	Apr	May	Jun	Jul	Aug	Sep	Oct	Nov	Dec	YEAR
erature (°C)	high	6.9	9.0	12.1	15.6	19.3	22.7	22.1	21.1	19.7	16.3	11.2	7.7	15.3
	mean	-2.1	1.1	4.6	8.1	11.9	15.5	15.3	14.5	12.8	8.1	2.2	-1.7	7.5
	low	-10.1	-6.8	-3.0	0.9	5.0	9.3	10.1	9.4	7.5	1.3	-4.9	-9.0	0.8
ipitation (mm)		1	1	2	5	27	72	119	123	58	10	2	1	421

eville, Gabon 15 m

		Jan	Feb	Mar	Apr	May	Jun	Jul	Aug	Sep	Oct	Nov	Dec	YEAR
erature (°C)	high	29.5	30.0	30.2	30.1	29.4	27.6	26.4	26.8	27.5	28.0	28.4	29.0	28.6
	mean	26.8	27.0	27.1	26.6	26.7	25.4	24.3	24.3	25.4	25.7	25.9	26.2	26.0
	low	24.1	24.0	23.9	23.1	24.0	23.2	22.1	21.8	23.4	23.4	23.4	23.4	23.3
ipitation (mm)		250	243	363	339	247	54	7	14	104	427	490	303	2841

ón, Costa Rica 3 m

		Jan	Feb	Mar	Apr	May	Jun	Jul	Aug	Sep	Oct	Nov	Dec	YEAR
erature (°C)	high	27.9	28.6	29.6	29.6	28.5	27.5	27.7	27.7	27.2	27.0	27.1	27.7	28.0
	mean	24.0	24.3	25.0	25.8	26.1	25.9	25.2	25.6	25.7	25.4	25.1	24.3	25.2
	low	20.3	20.3	20.9	21.6	22.2	22.3	22.1	22.1	22.2	21.9	21.6	20.9	21.5
ipitation (mm)		319	201	193	287	281	276	408	289	163	198	367	402	3384

atya, Turkey 849 m

		Jan	Feb	Mar	Apr	May	Jun	Jul	Aug	Sep	Oct	Nov	Dec	YEAR
erature (°C)	high	2.9	5.3	11.1	18.2	23.5	29.2	33.8	33.4	28.9	20.9	11.8	5.7	18.7
	mean	-0.4	1.5	6.9	13.0	17.8	22.9	27.0	26.5	22.0	14.8	7.6	2.4	13.5
	low	-3.2	-1.7	2.4	7.7	11.8	16.1	19.8	19.4	15.2	9.5	3.7	-0.3	8.4
cipitation (mm)		42	36	60	61	50	22	3	2	6	40	47	42	411

naus, Brazil 84 m

		Jan	Feb	Mar	Apr	May	Jun	Jul	Aug	Sep	Oct	Nov	Dec	YEAR
erature (°C)	high	30.5	30.4	30.6	30.7	30.8	31.0	31.3	32.6	32.9	32.8	32.1	31.3	31.4
	mean	26.1	26.0	26.1	26.3	26.3	26.4	26.5	27.0	27.5	27.6	27.3	26.7	26.7
	low	23.1	23.1	23.2	23.3	23.3	23.0	22.7	23.0	23.5	23.7	23.7	23.5	23.3
cipitation (mm)		260	288	314	300	256	114	88	58	83	126	183	217	2287

Meekatharra, Australia 518 m

		Jan	Feb	Mar	Apr	May	Jun	Jul	Aug	Sep	Oct	Nov	Dec	YEAR
Temperature (°C)	high	38.1	36.5	34.5	29.2	23.6	19.7	18.9	21.0	25.4	29.4	33.1	36.5	28.8
	mean	31.2	30.1	28.0	23.2	17.8	14.3	13.2	14.8	18.4	22.2	25.9	29.3	22.4
	low	24.3	23.7	21.5	17.1	11.9	8.9	7.5	8.5	11.4	15.0	18.6	22.1	15.9
Precipitation (mm)		26	30	22	17	27	36	25	12	6	7	14	11	233

Montréal, Canada 57 m

		Jan	Feb	Mar	Apr	May	Jun	Jul	Aug	Sep	Oct	Nov	Dec	YEAR
Temperature (°C)	high	-5.7	-4.4	1.6	10.6	18.5	23.6	26.1	24.8	19.9	13.3	5.4	-3.0	10.9
	mean	-10.3	-8.8	-2.4	5.7	12.9	18.0	20.8	19.4	14.5	8.3	1.6	-6.9	6.1
	low	-14.6	-13.5	-6.7	0.8	7.4	12.9	15.6	14.3	9.6	4.1	-1.5	-10.8	1.5
Precipitation (mm)		63.3	56.4	67.6	74.8	68.3	82.5	85.6	100.3	86.5	75.4	93.4	85.6	939.7

Ndola, Zambia 1270 m

		Jan	Feb	Mar	Apr	May	Jun	Jul	Aug	Sep	Oct	Nov	Dec	YEAR
Temperature (°C)	high	26.6	26.9	27.4	27.5	26.6	25.1	25.2	27.5	30.5	31.5	29.4	27.0	27.6
	mean	20.8	20.8	21.0	20.5	18.6	16.5	16.7	19.2	22.5	23.7	22.5	21.0	20.3
	low	17.1	17.1	16.5	14.4	10.8	7.9	7.8	10.2	13.6	16.2	17.1	17.2	13.8
Precipitation (mm)		29.3	249	170	46	4	1	0	0	3	32	130	306	1234

Nuukv, Greenland 70 m

		Jan	Feb	Mar	Apr	May	Jun	Jul	Aug	Sep	Oct	Nov	Dec	YEAR
Temperature (°C)	high	-4.4	-4.5	-4.8	-0.8	3.5	7.7	10.6	9.9	6.3	1.7	-1.0	-3.3	1.7
	mean	-7.4	-7.8	-8.0	-3.9	0.6	3.9	6.5	6.1	3.5	-0.6	-3.6	-6.2	-1.4
	low	-10.1	-10.6	-10.6	-6.1	-1.5	1.3	3.8	3.8	1.6	-2.5	-5.8	-8.7	-3.8
Precipitation (mm)		39	47	50	46	55	62	82	89	88	70	74	54	756

Paris, France 65 m

		Jan	Feb	Mar	Apr	May	Jun	Jul	Aug	Sep	Oct	Nov	Dec	YEAR
Temperature (°C)	high	6.0	7.6	10.8	14.4	18.2	21.5	24.0	23.8	20.8	16.0	10.1	6.8	15.0
	mean	3.4	4.2	6.6	9.5	13.2	16.4	18.4	18.0	15.3	11.4	6.7	4.2	10.6
	low	0.9	1.3	2.9	5.0	8.3	11.2	12.9	12.7	10.6	7.7	3.8	1.7	6.6
Precipitation (mm)		54	46	54	47	63	58	84	52	54	56	56	56	650

Qiqihar, China 148 m

		Jan	Feb	Mar	Apr	May	Jun	Jul	Aug	Sep	Oct	Nov	Dec	YEAR
Temperature (°C)	high	-12.7	-7.8	2.3	12.9	21.0	26.2	27.8	26.1	20.1	11.1	-1.3	-10.4	9.6
	mean	-19.2	-14.8	-4.5	6.1	14.4	20.3	22.8	20.9	14.0	4.8	-7.1	-16.2	3.5
	low	-24.5	-20.9	-11.0	-0.9	7.3	14.2	17.9	16.2	8.5	-0.7	-12.0	-21.2	-2.3
Precipitation (mm)		1	2	5	15	31	64	138	94	45	19	4	3	421

Rabat-Salé, Morocco 75 m

		Jan	Feb	Mar	Apr	May	Jun	Jul	Aug	Sep	Oct	Nov	Dec	YEAR
Temperature (°C)	high	17.2	17.7	19.2	20.0	22.1	24.1	26.8	27.1	26.4	24.0	20.6	17.7	21.9
	mean	12.6	13.1	14.2	15.2	17.4	19.8	22.2	22.4	21.5	19.0	15.9	13.2	17.2
	low	8.0	8.6	9.2	10.4	12.7	15.4	17.6	17.7	16.7	14.1	11.1	8.7	12.5
Precipitation (mm)		77	74	61	62	25	7	1	1	6	44	97	101	556

Sittwe, Myanmar 5 m

		Jan	Feb	Mar	Apr	May	Jun	Jul	Aug	Sep	Oct	Nov	Dec	YEAR
Temperature (°C)	high	28.0	29.4	31.4	34.1	31.5	29.5	28.9	28.9	30.1	31.1	30.3	28.5	30.1
	mean	21.4	22.7	24.8	28.9	28.3	27.1	26.8	26.7	27.4	27.6	25.7	22.6	25.8
	low	14.7	15.9	18.2	23.6	25.1	24.6	24.7	24.5	24.6	24.0	21.0	16.6	21.5
Precipitation (mm)		11	8	5	44	268	1091	1155	1025	537	289	105	17	4555

Stockholm, Sweden 52 m

		Jan	Feb	Mar	Apr	May	Jun	Jul	Aug	Sep	Oct	Nov	Dec	YEAR
Temperature (°C)	high	-0.7	-0.6	3.0	8.6	15.7	20.7	21.9	20.4	15.1	9.9	4.5	1.1	10.0
	mean	-2.8	-3.0	0.1	4.6	10.7	15.6	17.2	16.2	11.9	7.5	2.6	-1.0	6.6
	low	-5.0	-5.3	-2.7	1.1	6.3	11.3	13.4	12.7	9.0	5.3	0.7	-3.2	3.6
Precipitation (mm)		39	27	26	30	30	45	72	66	55	50	53	46	539

Tehran, Iran 1191 m

		Jan	Feb	Mar	Apr	May	Jun	Jul	Aug	Sep	Oct	Nov	Dec	YEAR
Temperature (°C)	high	7.2	9.9	15.4	21.9	28.0	34.1	36.8	35.4	31.5	24.0	16.5	9.8	22.5
	mean	3.0	5.3	10.3	16.4	22.1	27.5	30.4	29.2	25.3	18.5	11.6	5.6	17.1
	low	-1.1	0.7	5.2	10.9	16.1	20.9	24.0	23.0	19.2	12.9	6.7	1.3	11.7
Precipitation (mm)		37	34	37	28	15	3	3	1	1	14	21	36	230

Wellington, New Zealand 8 m

		Jan	Feb	Mar	Apr	May	Jun	Jul	Aug	Sep	Oct	Nov	Dec	YEAR
Temperature (°C)	high	21.3	21.1	19.8	17.3	14.8	12.8	12.0	12.7	14.2	15.9	17.8	19.6	16.6
	mean	17.8	17.7	16.6	14.3	11.9	10.1	9.2	9.8	11.2	12.8	14.5	16.4	13.5
	low	14.4	14.3	13.5	11.3	9.1	7.3	6.4	6.9	8.3	9.7	11.3	13.2	10.5
Precipitation (mm)		67	48	76	87	99	113	111	106	82	81	74	74	1018

Scale 1: 240 000 000

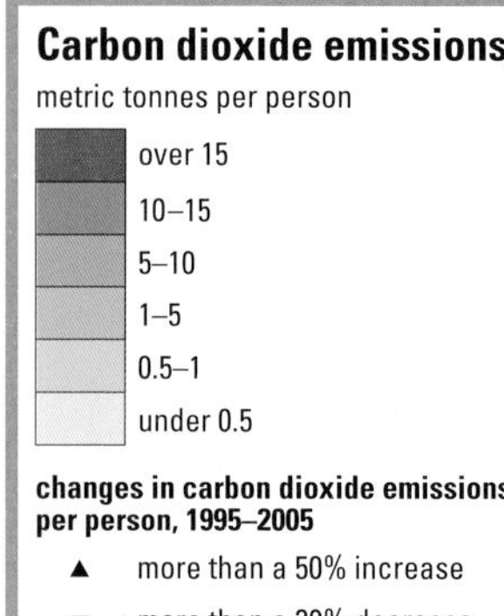

Arctic Circle
Tropic of Cancer
Equator
Tropic of Capricorn
Antarctic Circle
Prime Meridian

Highest carbon dioxide emissions
million metric tonnes

USA	5 957.0
China	5 322.7
Russian Federation	1 696.0
Japan	1 230.4
India	1 165.7
Germany	844.2
Canada	631.3
United Kingdom	577.2
South Korea	499.6
Italy	466.6
World	28 192.7

Summary of atmospheric greenhouse gases

Gas	Anthropogenic sources	Concentrations preindustrial 1860	Concentrations 2004	Annual rate of increase 1994–2004	Lifetime in atmosphere	Contribution to global warming
carbon dioxide (CO_2)	fossil fuels, deforestation, soil destruction	286–288 ppm	377 ppm	1.9 ppm (0.5%)	50-200 years	54%
methane (CH_4)	domesticated livestock, biomass, rice cultivation, oil and gas production, mining	848 ppb	1784 ppb	3.7 ppb (0.2%)	12 +/–3 years	12%
halocarbons e.g., chlorofluorocarbons (CFC 11 & 12) and hydro-fluorocarbons (HFC)	refrigeration, air conditioning, solvents, aerosols	0 0	263 CFC 11 544 CFC 12 ppt	11 ppt (5.0%) CFC 11 19 ppt (5.0%) CFC 12	10s to 100s years	21%
nitrous oxide (N_2O)	fossil fuels, deforestation, fertilizer use	285 ppb	318 ppb	0.8 ppb (0.3%)	114 years	6%
ozone and other trace gases (O_3)	photochemicals, processes, cars, power plants, solvents	25 ppb	29 ppb	unknown	hours to days in upper troposphere	7%

ppm = parts per million; ppb = parts per billion; ppt = parts per trillion
Halocarbons are carbon compounds containing halogens such as chlorine, fluorine, and bromine. They are a product of human activities.
Each greenhouse gas differs in its ability to absorb heat in the atmosphere. CFCs and HFCs are the most heat absorbent. CH_4 traps 27 times and N_2O 270 times more heat than CO_2.

Climate change

The Earth's climate naturally changes over long periods of time. Many scientists now believe that these natural cycles have been interrupted by a rise in the temperature in the lower atmosphere as a consequence of human activity; predictions indicate this trend will continue and may accelerate. The primary cause of rising temperatures is related to the greenhouse effect (see page 16). Increasing amounts of carbon dioxide and other greenhouse gases are being added to the atmosphere as a result of burning fossil fuels, increased road and air transport, and the cutting down of forests makes the problem even worse.

Scientific models that attempt to understand future climate changes predict that rising temperatures will not occur uniformly, while precipitation will increase in some areas and decrease in others. Some of the reasons why we should be concerned about climate change are described on page 27. While it is practically impossible to know the specifics of the changes in climate that will occur in the future, the scientific principles are clear and our knowledge of more detailed implications is rapidly developing. However, uncertainties remain and the possibility of surprises cannot be ruled out.

World temperature forecast 2000–2100

Based on three scenarios from the Intergovernmental Panel on Climate Change which look at population and economic growth, technological change, and associated CO_2 emissions

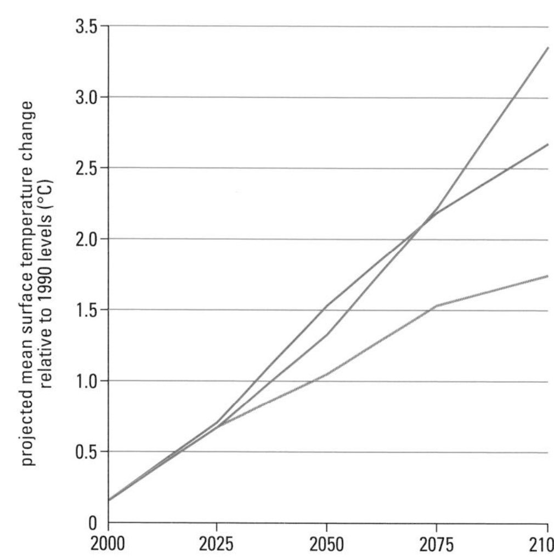

assumes rapid population and economic growth combined with a reliance on fossil and non-fossil ener
assumes high population growth but lower economi growth and less globalization
assumes some reduction in emissions through increas efficiency and improvement in technology

Global CO2 emissions by sector

% of world total

other 4%
other fuel consumption 10%
electricity and heat 32%
land use changes and forestry 24%
manufacturing and construction 13%
transportation 17%

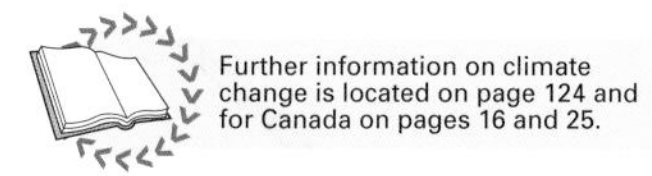

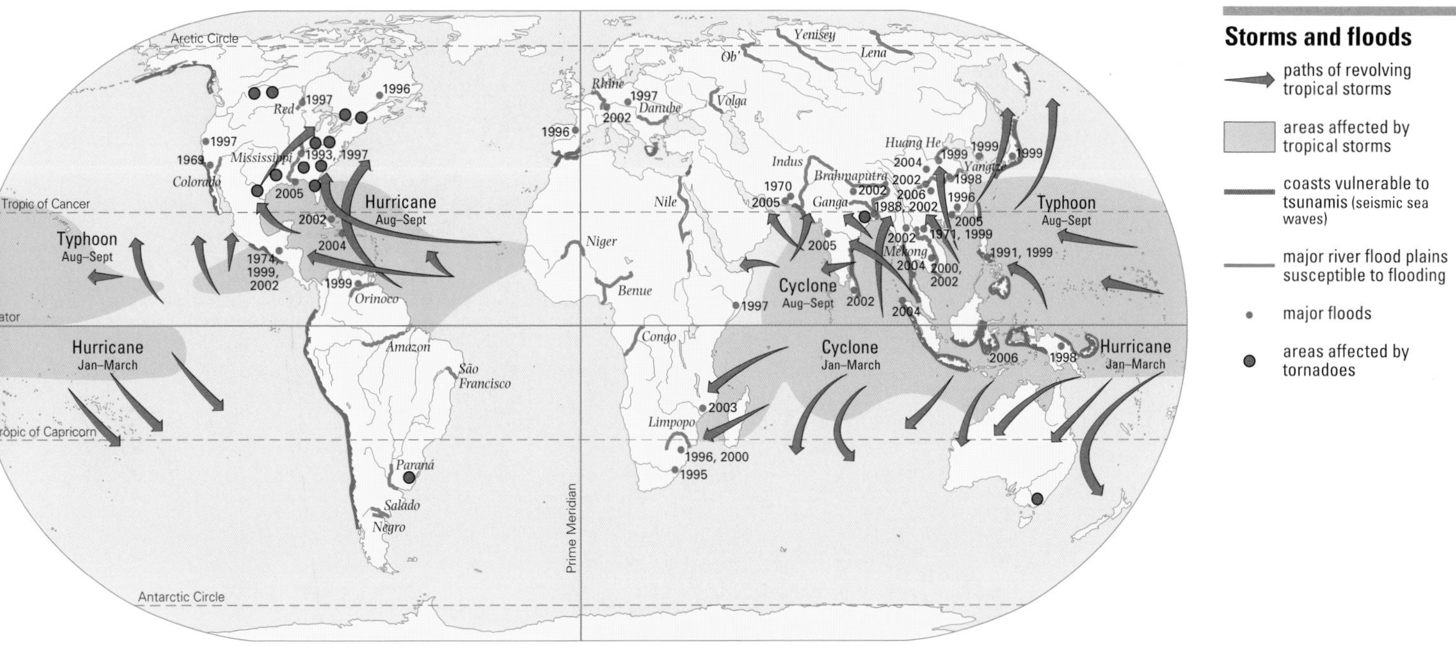

Distribution of the Earth's water

	Volume (km³)	Average residence time
eans and seas	1 370 000 000	4 000+ years
aciers and ice caps	30 000 000	1000s of years
oundwater	4 000 000– 60 000 000	from days to tens of thousands of years
mospheric water	113 000	8 to 10 days
eshwater lakes	125 000	days to years
ine lakes and inland seas	104 000	–
ver channels	1 700	2 weeks
vamps and marshes	3 600	years
ological water plants and animals)	65 000	a few days
oisture in soil	65 000	2 weeks to 1 year

Hurricane Katrina

Winds in this hurricane reached 280 km per hour and caused 1 836 deaths. 29 August 2005.

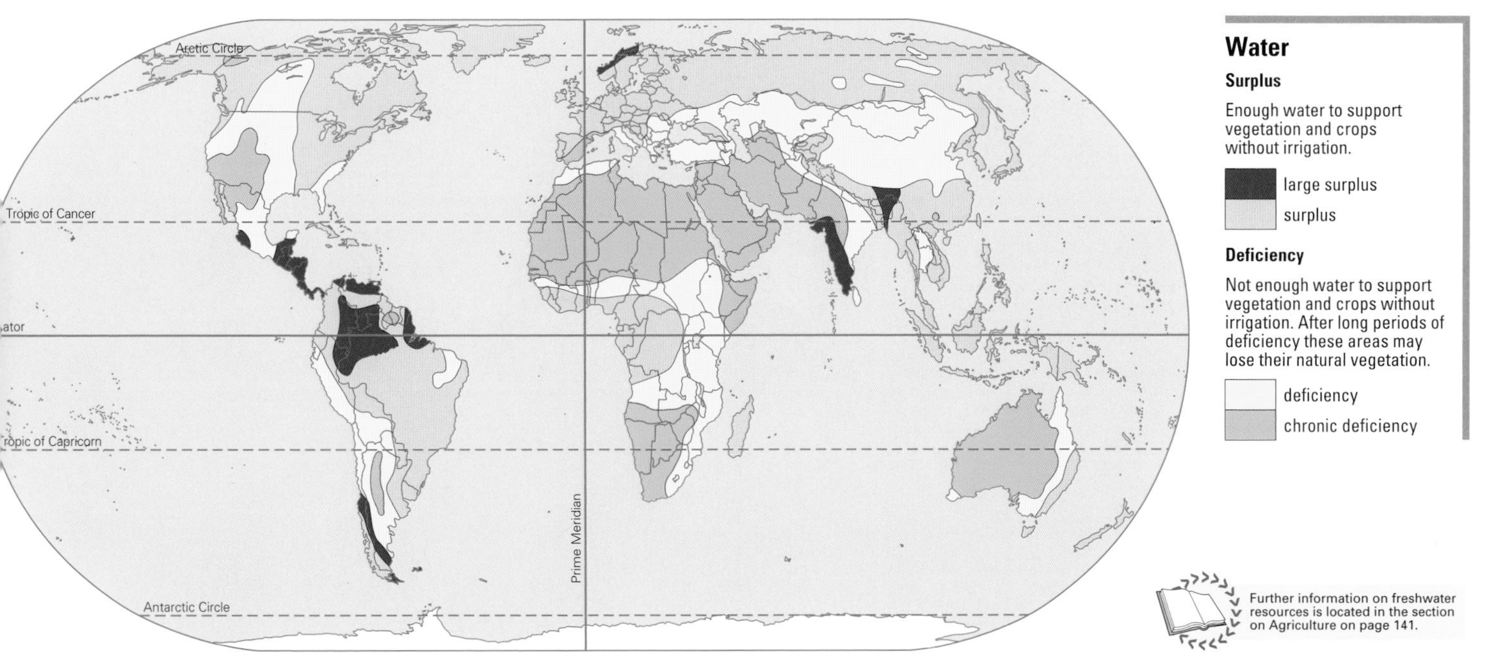

Further information on freshwater resources is located in the section on Agriculture on page 141.

Scale 1: 240 000 000

Global aridity and drought probability

- ● **Extreme arid deserts** 100% drought probability with exceptionally rare rainy spells
- **Arid deserts** shifting dunes and irregular moist years, drought dominating up to 90–95% of the time
- **Extremely arid areas** fine earth lowland areas with droughts dominating up to 60–70% of the time
- **Very frequent droughts** areas of semi-desert with the probability of droughts for 40–50% of the time
- **Frequent droughts** areas of dry steppe and savanna with the probability of droughts 20–25% of the time
- **Rare droughts** areas of steppe, prairie, and savanna with the probability of droughts 10–15% of the time
- □ **Sporadic very rare droughts** areas with the probability of droughts 3–5% of the time

Arctic Circle
Tropic of Cancer
Equator
Tropic of Capricorn
Antarctic Circle
Prime Meridian

Drought and desertification

Drought begins with a deficiency of precipitation over an extended period, relative to a long-term average. It is naturally occurring phenomenon and may occur in any climatic region, though it is rare in the wet topics. Drought may also result from or be intensified by human activity, and is generally believed to be one consequence of global warming.

Desertification is caused by drought, together with human activity in arid, semi-arid, and sub-humid areas. Pressure from growing populations in these fragile ecosystems intensifies the impact of drought, resulting in permanent land degradation and widespread poverty. Though estimates vary, as much as 15% of the world's population and 25% of the world's land areas are affected by desertification.

Aral Sea, Central Asia, 1989–2003

The Aral Sea on the Kazakhstan-Uzbekistan border is a salt lake whose level is maintained by the Amudar'ya and Syrdar'ya rivers. Over the past several decades, the surface area has declined by more than 50 per cent, mainly because of the diversion of water from the two rivers for agricultural purposes. At the same time, its salt content has increased five times, and the lake is now severely polluted.

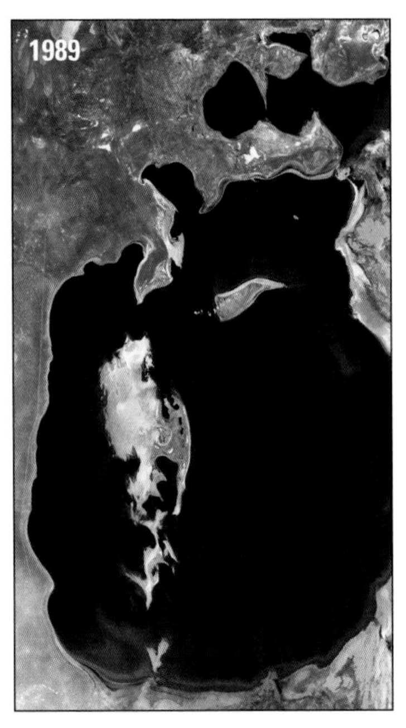

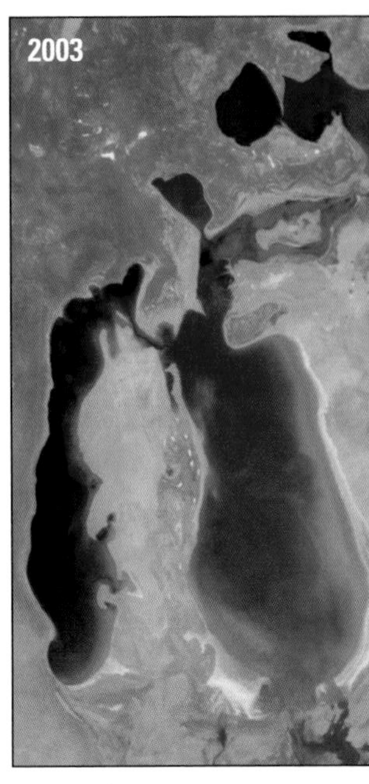

Desertification and tropical deforestation

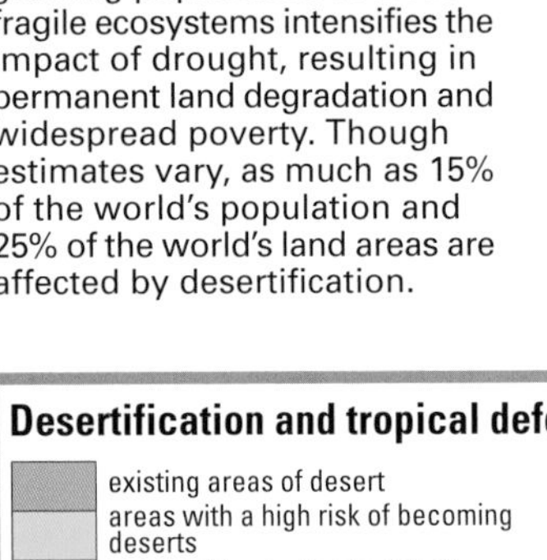

- existing areas of desert
- areas with a high risk of becoming deserts
- areas with a moderate risk of becoming deserts
- existing areas of tropical rain forest
- former areas of tropical rain forest

Countries losing greatest areas of forest, average per year for 2000–2005 (000 hectares)

Brazil	3 103
Indonesia	1 871
Sudan	589
Myanmar	466
Zambia	445
Tanzania	412
Nigeria	410
Congo, Dem. Rep.	319
Zimbabwe	313
Venezuela	288

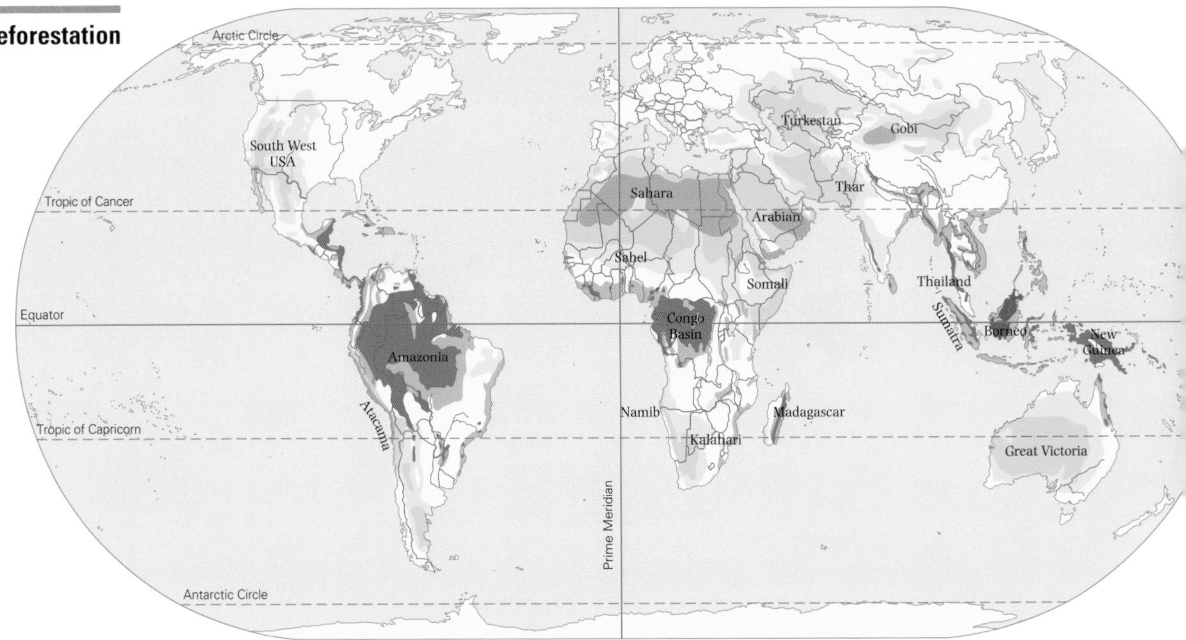

Sea pollution

Major oil spills

- over 100 000 tonnes
- under 100 000 tonnes
- frequent oil slicks from shipping

Other sea pollution

- severe pollution
- moderate pollution
- deep sea dump sites

Major oil spills (000 tonnes)

		000 tonnes
1979	*Ixtoc 1* well blowout, Gulf of Mexico	467
1979	Collision of *Atlantic Empress* and *Aegean Captain*, off Tobago, Caribbean	138
1983	*Nowruz* well blowout, Persian Gulf	267
1989	*Exxon Valdez* spills oil off the coast of Alaska	37
1991	Release of oil by Iraqi troops, *Sea Island* terminal, Persian Gulf	800
2002	*Prestige* oil tanker sinks off the coast of Spain	63
2003	*Tasman Spirit* tanker spills oil in Karachi Port, Pakistan	30

The world's top ten most endangered river basins

As identified by WWF with the primary threat facing each river basin

Over-extraction
Ganges, South Asia
Rio Grande/Rio Bravo del Norte, North America–Central America

Dams and infrastructure
Danube, Europe
Río de la Plata, South America
Salween, Southeast Asia

Invasive species
Murray–Darling, Australia

Climate change
Indus, South Asia
Nile–Lake Victoria, Africa

Over-fishing
Mekong (Lancang), Southeast Asia

Pollution
Yangtze, East Asia

The Antarctic ozone 'hole'

Three dimensional image of ozone depletion over Antarctica in September, 1998. The lowest ozone concentration is shown in blue.

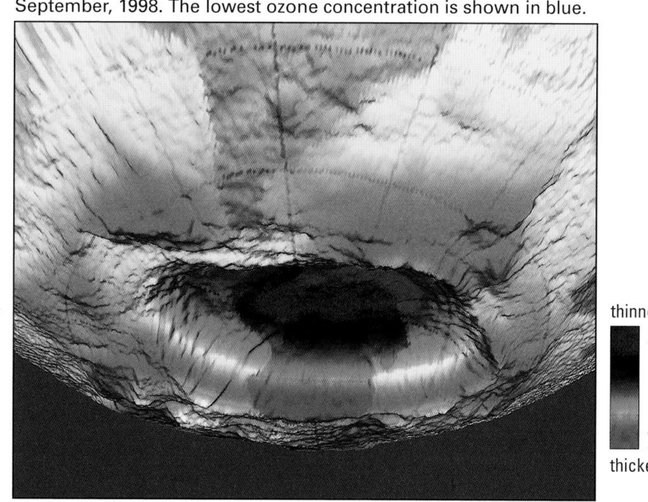

Ozone in the stratosphere absorbs harmful ultraviolet rays. Pollutants in the air destroy ozone, making it thinner. Strong winds and intense cold concentrate the effects of pollutants, so that ozone is thinnest over Antarctica in spring.

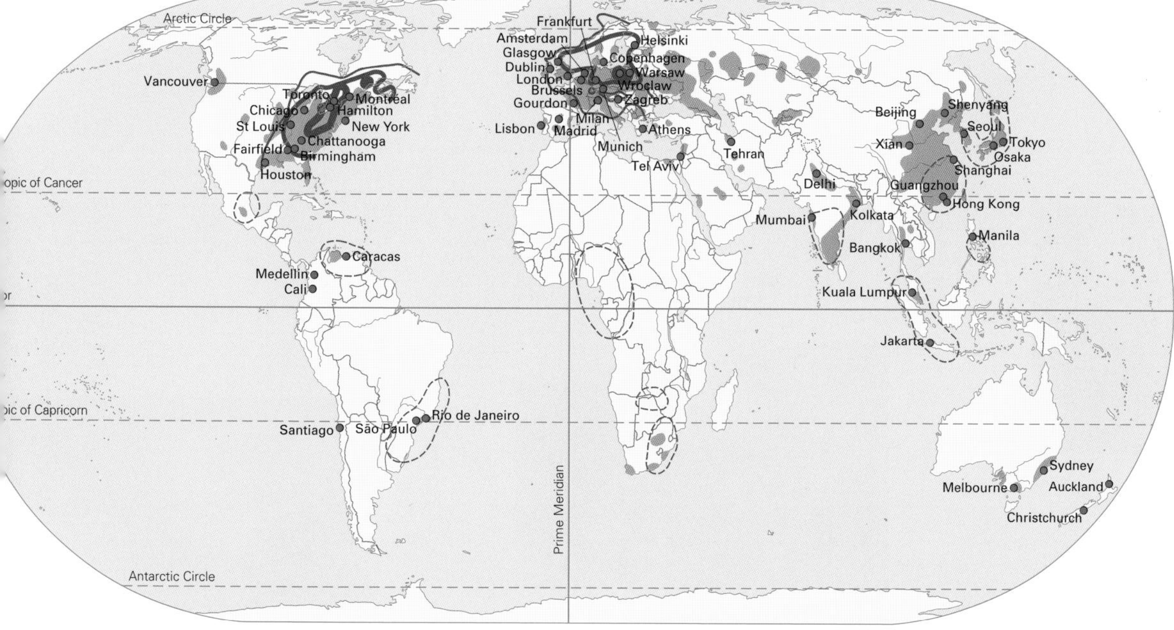

Acid rain

Sulphur and nitrogen emissions
Oxides of sulphur and nitrogen produced by burning fossil fuel react with rain to form dilute sulphuric and nitric acids

- areas with high levels of fossil fuel burning
- cities where sulphur dioxide emissions are recorded and exceed World Health Organization recommended levels

Areas of acid rain deposition
Annual mean values of pH in precipitation

- pH less than 4.2 (most acidic)
- pH 4.2–4.6
- pH 4.6–5.0
- other areas where acid rain is becoming a problem

Lower pH values are more acidic. 'Clean' rain water is slightly acidic with a pH of 5.6. The pH scale is logarithmic, so that a value of 4.6 is ten times as acidic as normal rain.

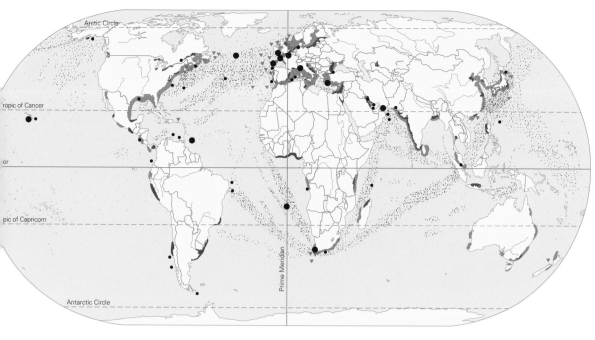

Equatorial scale 1: 105 000 000

Ecosystems

vegetation types are those which would occur naturally without interference by people

- **coniferous forest** cone bearing trees
- **deciduous and mixed forest** leaf shedding and coniferous trees
- **tropical rain forest** many species of lush, tall trees
- **tropical grasslands (savannah)** tall grass parkland with scattered trees
- **evergreen trees and shrubs** plants and small trees with leathery leaves
- **thorn forest** low trees and shrubs with spines or thorns
- **temperate grasslands** prairies, steppes, pampas, and veld
- **semi-desert** short grasses and drought-resistant scrub
- **desert** sand and stones, very little vegetation
- **tundra** moss and lichen, with few trees
- **ice** no vegetation
- **mountains** thin soils, steep slopes, and high altitude affects type of vegetation

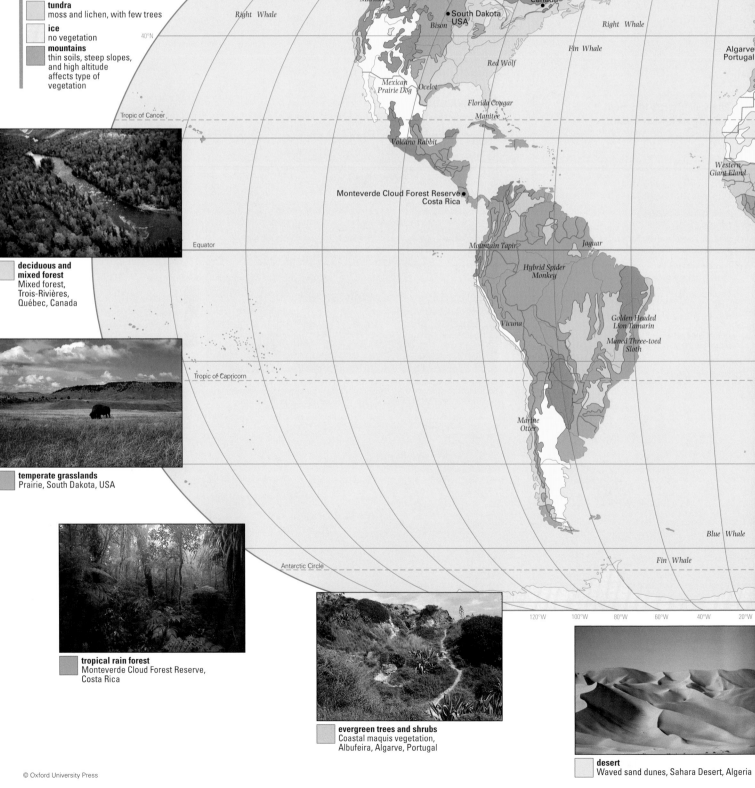

ice
Aerial view of Jameson Land, towards Liverpool Land, Greenland

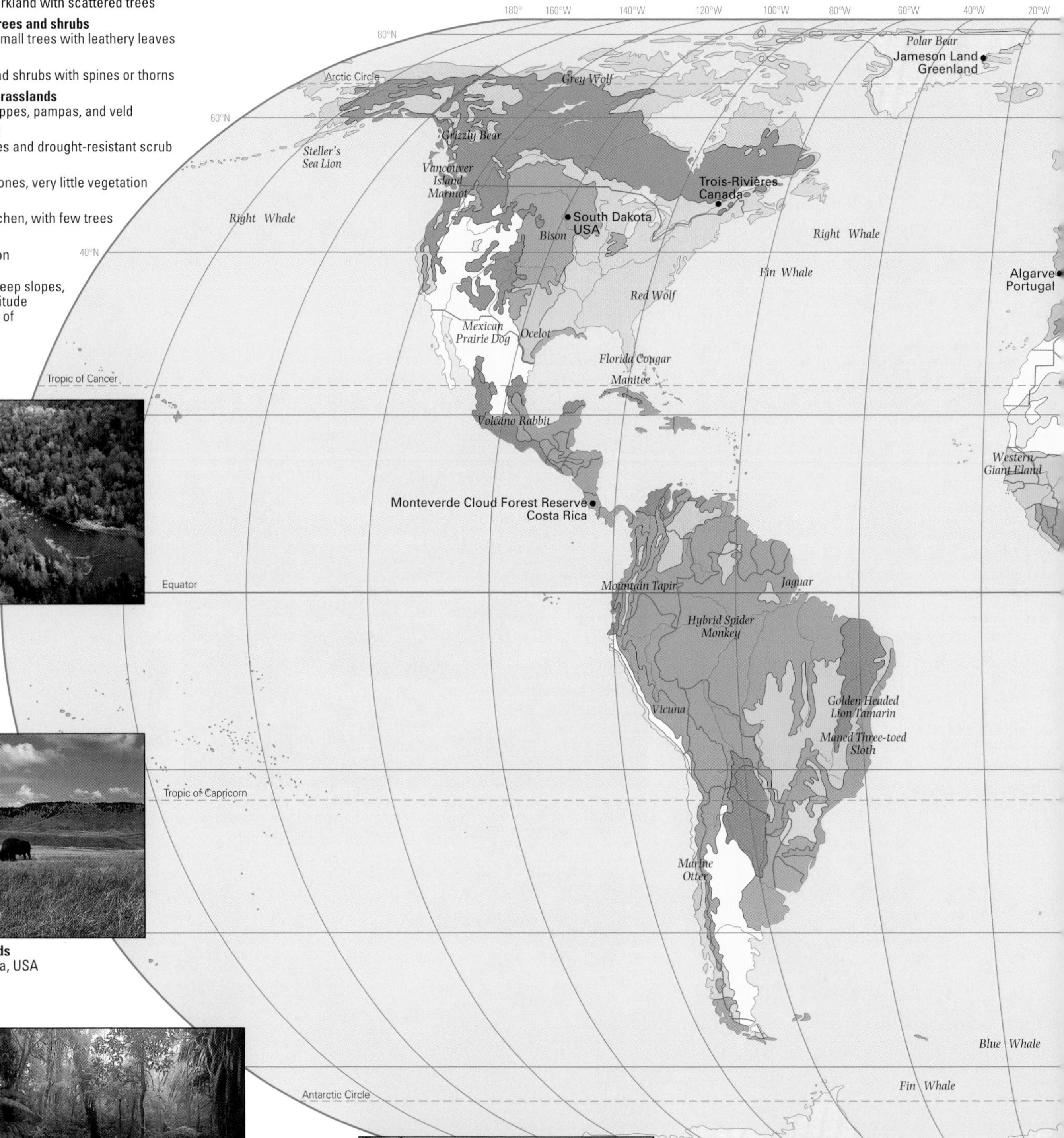

180° 160°W 140°W 120°W 100°W 80°W 60°W 40°W 20°W

80°N
Arctic Circle
60°N
40°N
Tropic of Cancer
Equator
Tropic of Capricorn
Antarctic Circle

Polar Bear
Jameson Land
Greenland
Grey Wolf
Grizzly Bear
Steller's Sea Lion
Vancouver Island Marmot
Trois-Rivières
Canada
South Dakota
USA
Bison
Right Whale
Right Whale
Fin Whale
Algarve
Portugal
Red Wolf
Mexican Prairie Dog
Ocelot
Florida Cougar
Manitee
Volcano Rabbit
Western Giant Eland
Monteverde Cloud Forest Reserve
Costa Rica
Mountain Tapir
Jaguar
Hybrid Spider Monkey
Vicuna
Golden Headed Lion Tamarin
Maned Three-toed Sloth
Marine Otter
Blue Whale
Fin Whale

120°W 100°W 80°W 60°W 40°W 20°W

deciduous and mixed forest
Mixed forest, Trois-Rivières, Québec, Canada

temperate grasslands
Prairie, South Dakota, USA

tropical rain forest
Monteverde Cloud Forest Reserve, Costa Rica

evergreen trees and shrubs
Coastal maquis vegetation, Albufeira, Algarve, Portugal

desert
Waved sand dunes, Sahara Desert, Algeria

coniferous forest
Forest track, Finland

Endangered species

Human activity is primarily responsible for the loss of habitat resulting in the extinction, endangerment, and vulnerability of many species of animals, birds, fish, reptiles, and plants (definitions and Canadian examples are found on page 26). The names on the map represent only a small selection of animals that are classified as endangered.

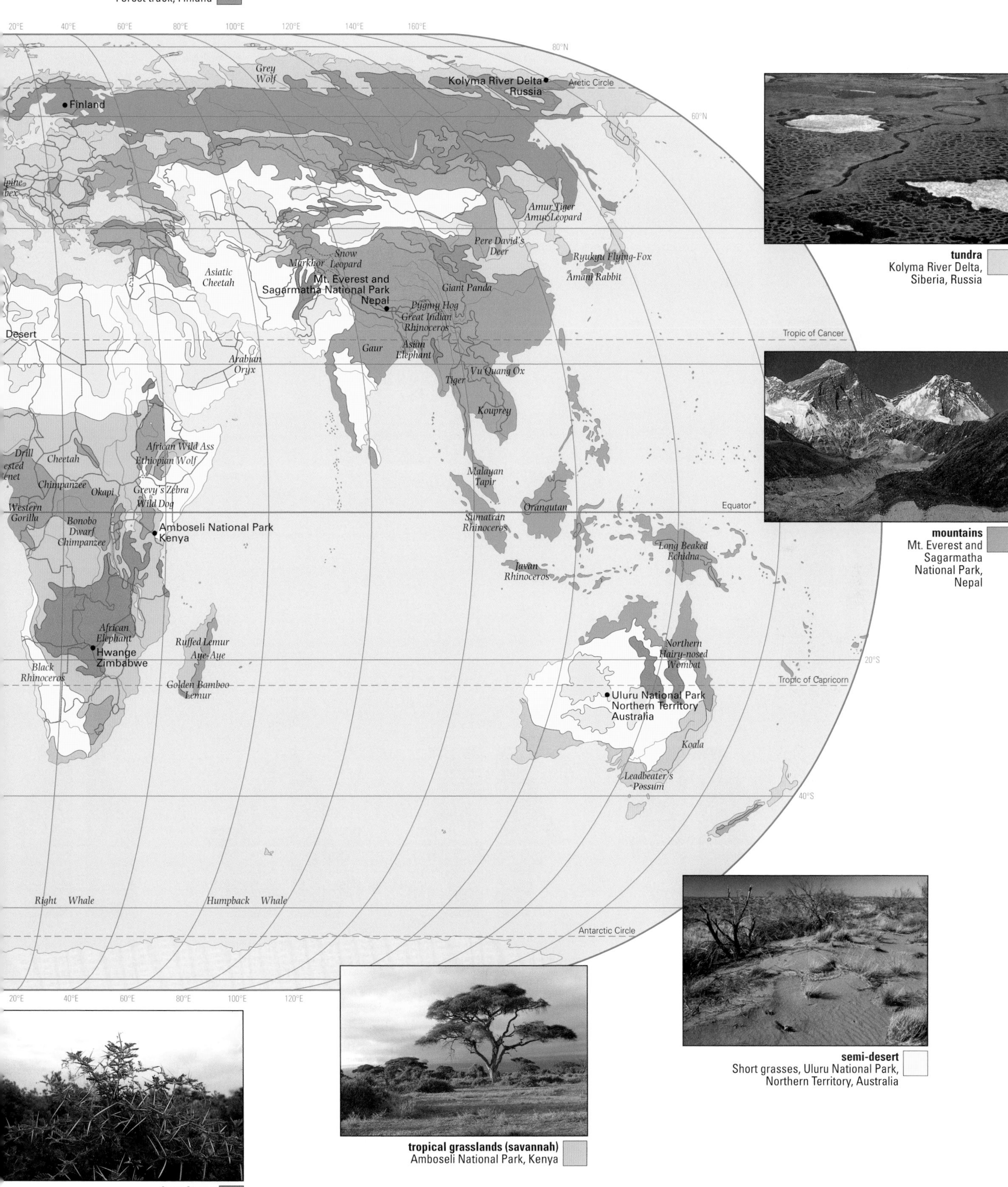

tundra
Kolyma River Delta, Siberia, Russia

mountains
Mt. Everest and Sagarmatha National Park, Nepal

semi-desert
Short grasses, Uluru National Park, Northern Territory, Australia

tropical grasslands (savannah)
Amboseli National Park, Kenya

thorn forest
Acacia thorns, Hwange, Zimbabwe

Eckert IV Projection

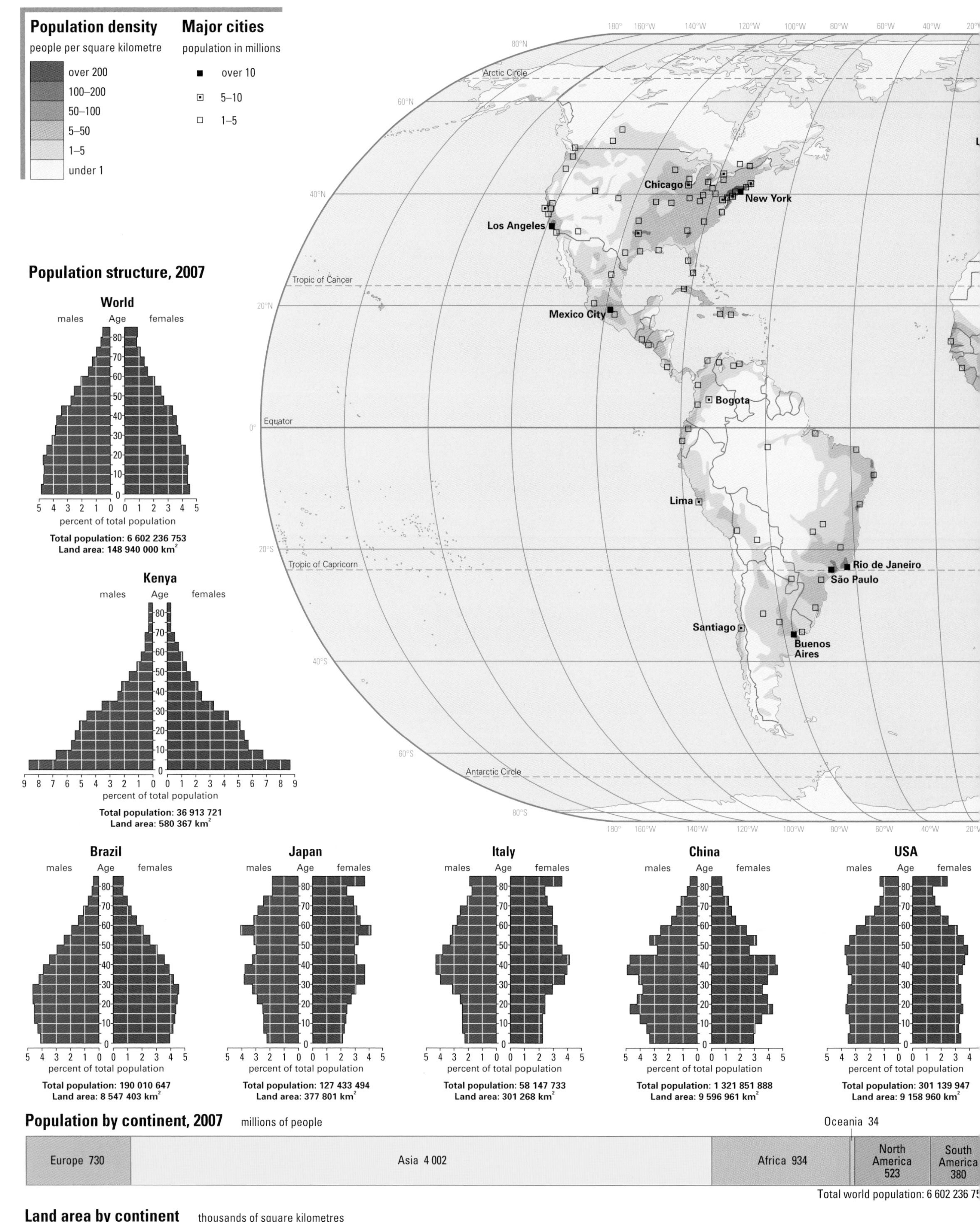
Scale 1: 125 000 00
Population density
people per square kilometre
over 200
100–200
50–100
5–50
1–5
under 1
Major cities
population in millions
over 10
5–10
1–5
Arctic Circle
Tropic of Cancer
Equator
Tropic of Capricorn
Antarctic Circle
80°N
60°N
40°N
20°N
0°
20°S
40°S
60°S
80°S
180°
160°W
140°W
120°W
100°W
80°W
60°W
40°W
Chicago
New York
Los Angeles
Mexico City
Bogota
Lima
Rio de Janeiro
São Paulo
Santiago
Buenos Aires
Population structure, 2007
World
males
Age
females
percent of total population
Total population: 6 602 236 753
Land area: 148 940 000 km²
Kenya
males
Age
females
percent of total population
Total population: 36 913 721
Land area: 580 367 km²
Brazil
Total population: 190 010 647
Land area: 8 547 403 km²
Japan
Total population: 127 433 494
Land area: 377 801 km²
Italy
Total population: 58 147 733
Land area: 301 268 km²
China
Total population: 1 321 851 888
Land area: 9 596 961 km²
USA
Total population: 301 139 947
Land area: 9 158 960 km²
Population by continent, 2007
millions of people
Europe 730
Asia 4 002
Africa 934
Oceania 34
North America 523
South America 380
Total world population: 6 602 236 75
Land area by continent
thousands of square kilometres
Europe 10 498
Asia 44 387
Africa 30 335
Oceania 8 503
North America 24 241
South America 17 832
Antarctica 13 340
Total world land area: 148 940 000 km

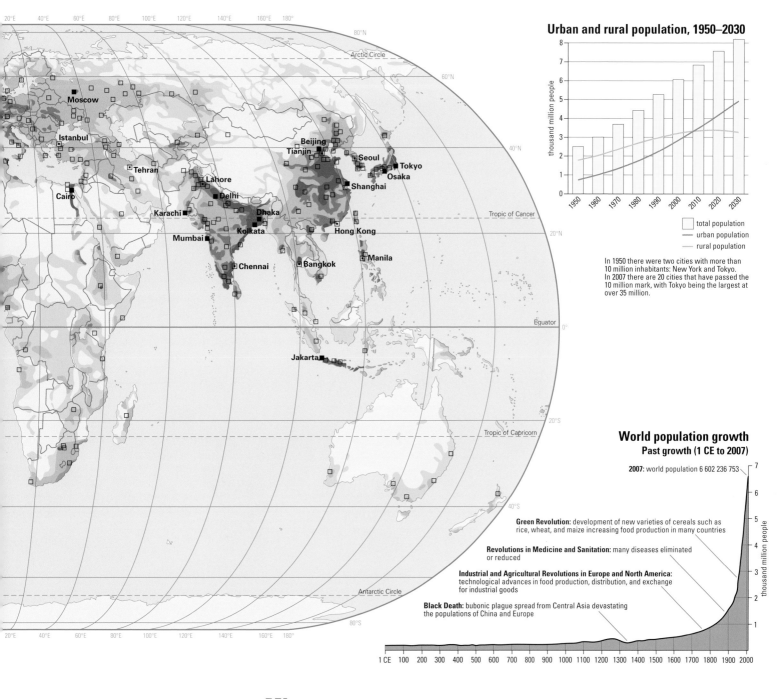

Urban and rural population, 1950–2030

thousand million people

- total population
- urban population
- rural population

In 1950 there were two cities with more than 10 million inhabitants: New York and Tokyo. In 2007 there are 20 cities that have passed the 10 million mark, with Tokyo being the largest at over 35 million.

World population growth

Past growth (1 CE to 2007)

2007: world population 6 602 236 753

Green Revolution: development of new varieties of cereals such as rice, wheat, and maize increasing food production in many countries

Revolutions in Medicine and Sanitation: many diseases eliminated or reduced

Industrial and Agricultural Revolutions in Europe and North America: technological advances in food production, distribution, and exchange for industrial goods

Black Death: bubonic plague spread from Central Asia devastating the populations of China and Europe

thousand million people

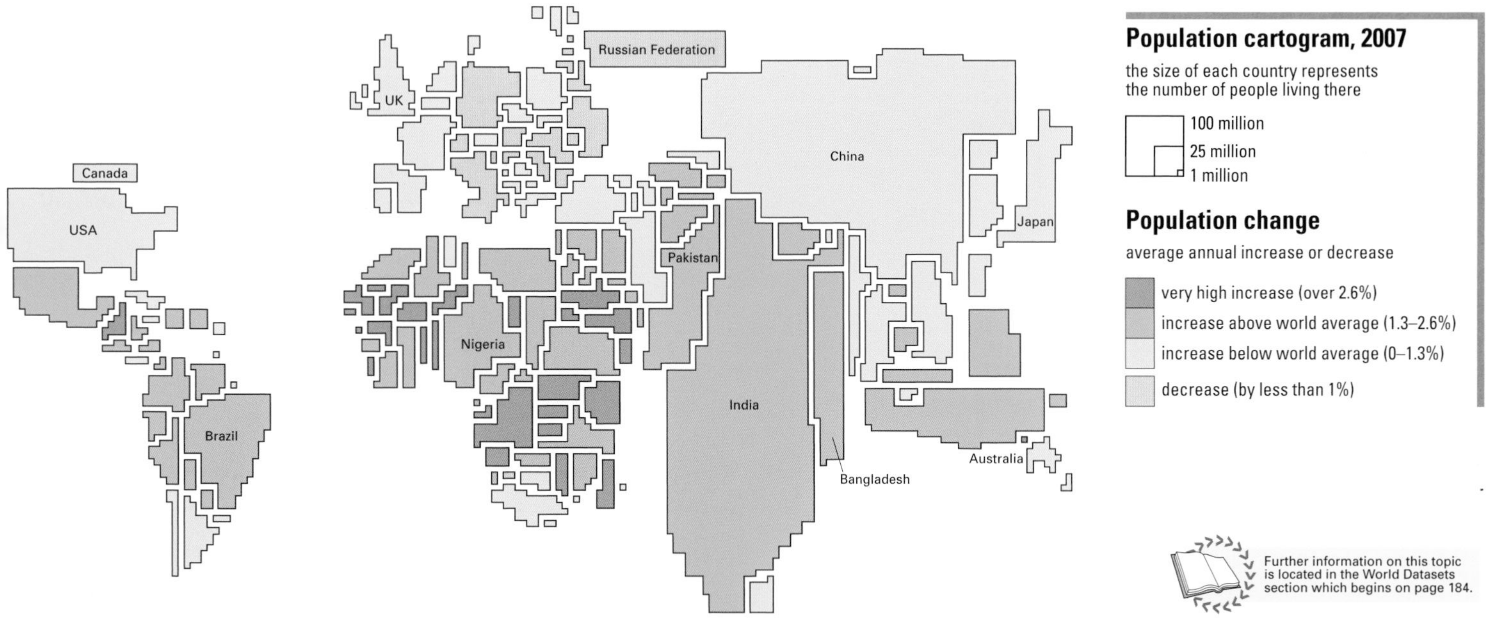

Further information on this topic is located in the World Datasets section which begins on page 184.

Scale 1: 240 000 000

Population change, 1997–2007

percentage population gain or loss

- over 40% gain
- 30–40% gain
- 20–30% gain
- 10–20% gain
- under 10% gain
- 0–20% loss

Highest population gain	
United Arab Emirates	61.8%
Liberia	45.2%
Afghanistan	43.5%
Kuwait	41.9%
Yemen Republic	40.4%
Canada	10.2%
Highest population loss	
Trinidad and Tobago	-7.2%
Latvia	-7.2%
Ukraine	-8.1%
Bulgaria	-9.2%
Montserrat	-14.1%

Population change refers to the growth or decline of a national population over the period 1997 to 2007 resulting from natural increase (births - deaths) and net migration (immigration - emigration).

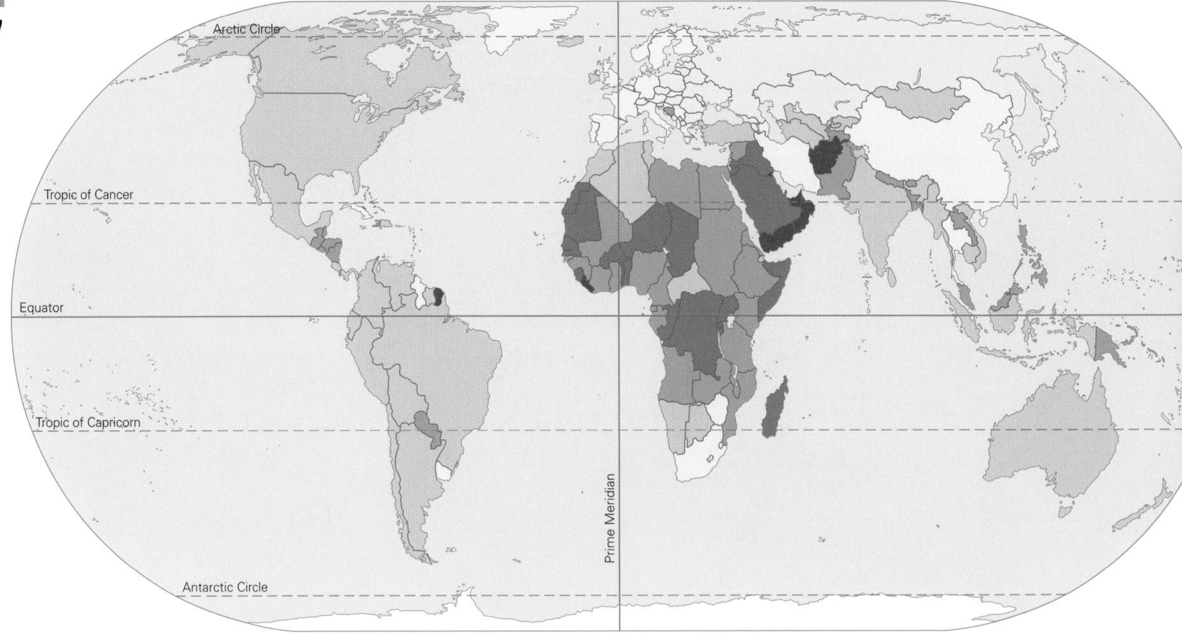

Fertility rate, 2007

average number of children born to women of childbearing age

- over 6 children
- 5–5.9 children
- 4–4.9 children
- 3–3.9 children
- 2–2.9 children
- 1–1.9 children
- o countries with over 40% of the total population under the age of 15 in 2007

Largest families	Number of children
Niger	7.1
Afghanistan	6.8
Angola	6.8
Burundi	6.8
Somalia	6.8
Uganda	6.8
Canada	1.5

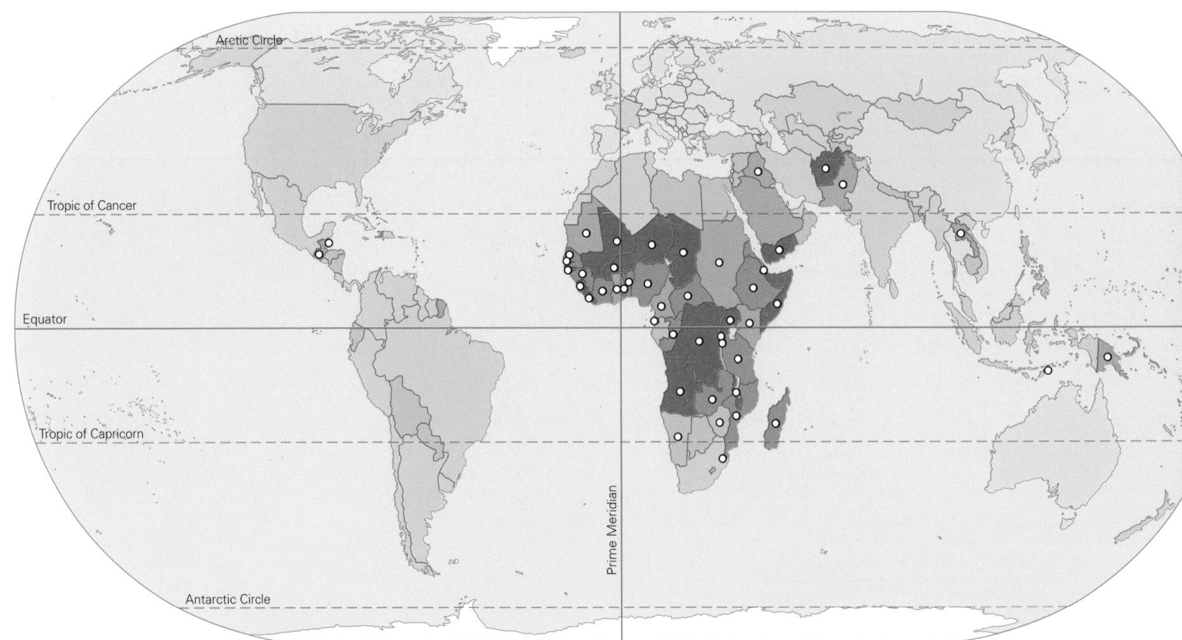

Urban population

percentage of the population living in urban areas

- over 80%
- 60–80%
- 40–60%
- 20–40%
- under 20%
- no data

Most urban in 2005	
Singapore	100.0%
Kuwait	98.3%
Belgium	97.2%
Bahrain	96.5%
Qatar	95.4%
Canada	80.1%
Least urban in 2005	
Sierra Leone	15.1%
Papua New Guinea	13.4%
Uganda	12.6%
Bhutan	11.1%
Burundi	10.0%

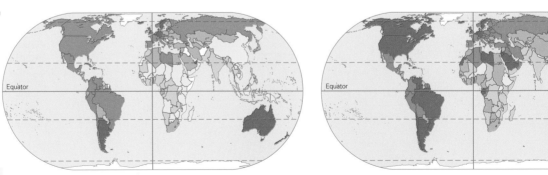

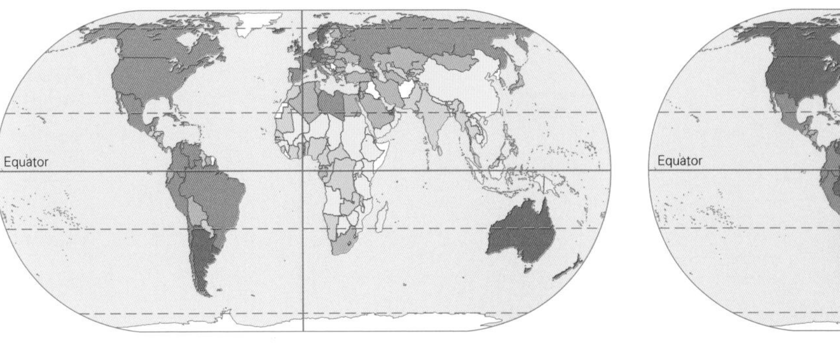

1975

2005

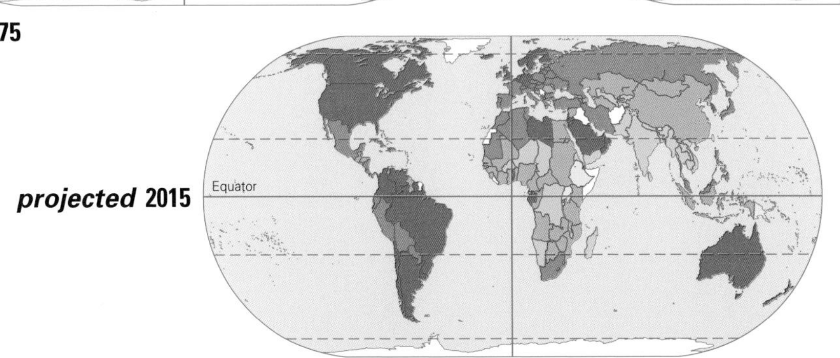

***projected* 2015**

Further information on this topic is located in the World Datasets section, which begins on page 184.

Eckert IV Projection

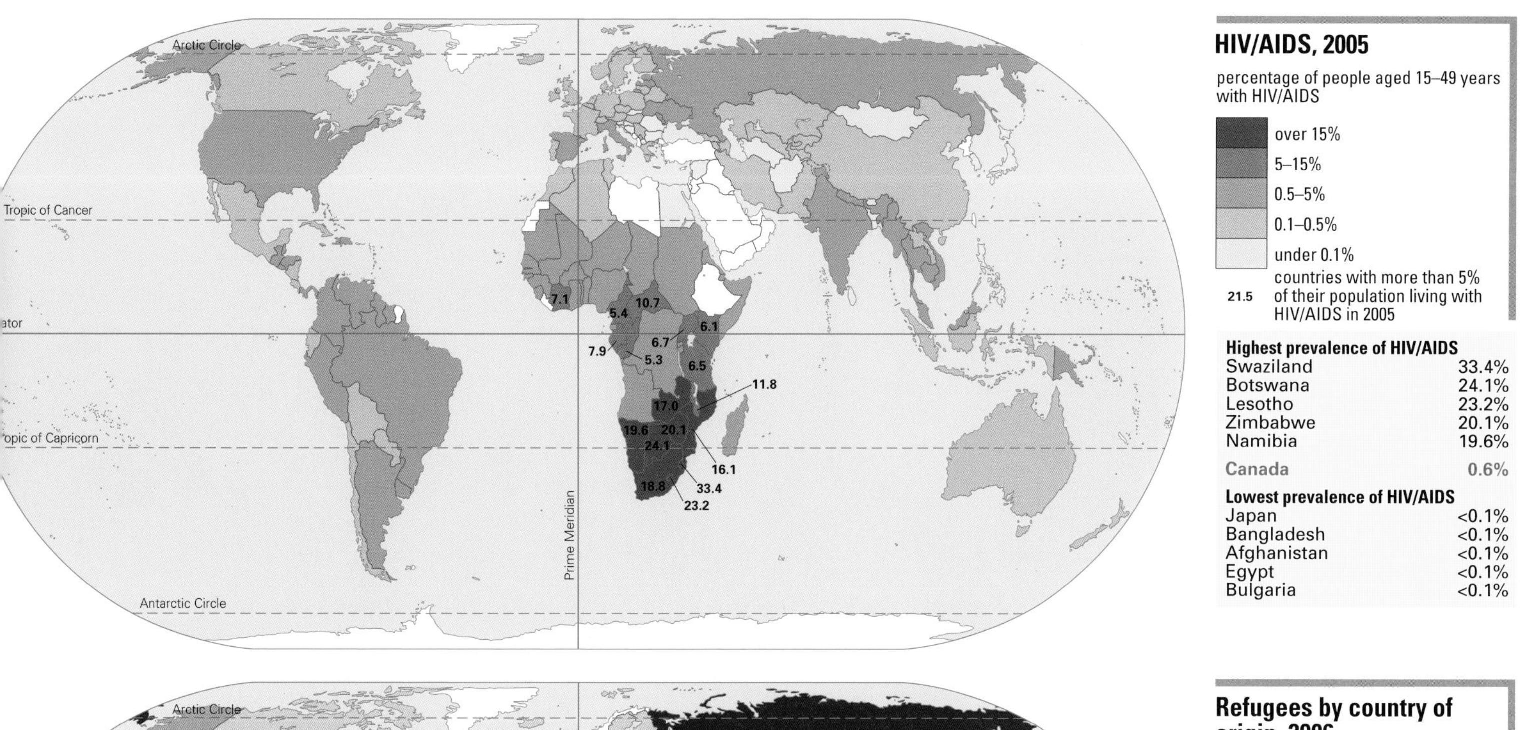

HIV/AIDS, 2005

percentage of people aged 15–49 years with HIV/AIDS

- over 15%
- 5–15%
- 0.5–5%
- 0.1–0.5%
- under 0.1%
- 21.5 countries with more than 5% of their population living with HIV/AIDS in 2005

Highest prevalence of HIV/AIDS	
Swaziland	33.4%
Botswana	24.1%
Lesotho	23.2%
Zimbabwe	20.1%
Namibia	19.6%
Canada	0.6%

Lowest prevalence of HIV/AIDS	
Japan	<0.1%
Bangladesh	<0.1%
Afghanistan	<0.1%
Egypt	<0.1%
Bulgaria	<0.1%

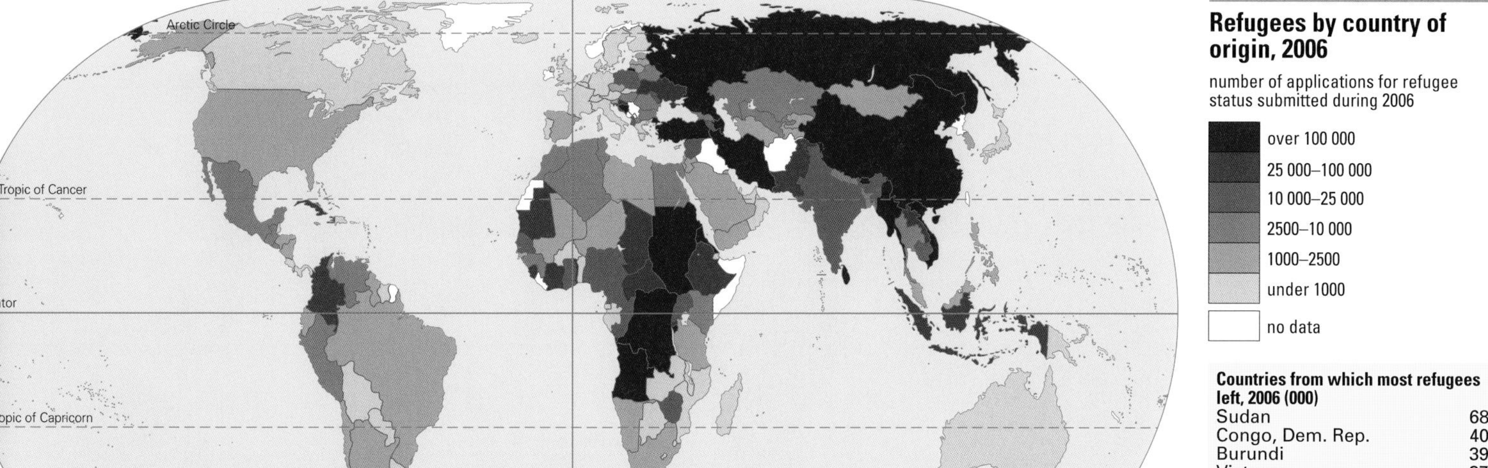

Refugees by country of origin, 2006

number of applications for refugee status submitted during 2006

- over 100 000
- 25 000–100 000
- 10 000–25 000
- 2500–10 000
- 1000–2500
- under 1000
- no data

Countries from which most refugees left, 2006 (000)	
Sudan	686
Congo, Dem. Rep.	402
Burundi	397
Vietnam	374
Turkey	227
Angola	207
Myanmar	203
Bosnia–Herzegovina	200

Civil war in Iraq has resulted in a large number of refugees; estimates in 2007 indicate over 2 million have left the country and an equal number are displaced within the country.

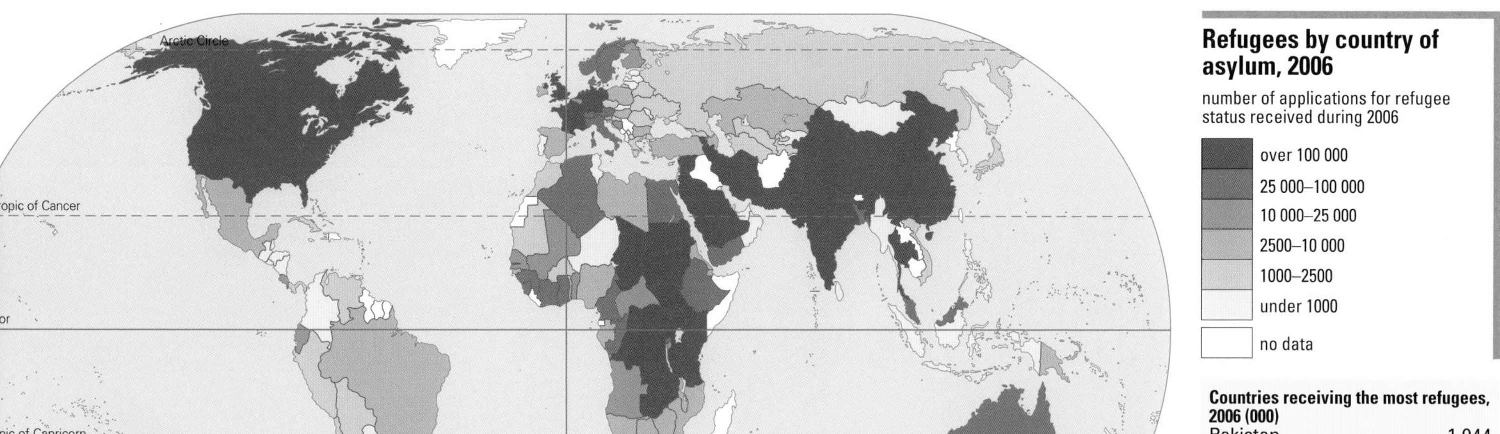

Refugees by country of asylum, 2006

number of applications for refugee status received during 2006

- over 100 000
- 25 000–100 000
- 10 000–25 000
- 2500–10 000
- 1000–2500
- under 1000
- no data

Countries receiving the most refugees, 2006 (000)	
Pakistan	1 044
Iran	968
USA	844
Syria	702
Germany	605
Jordan	500
Tanzania	485
United Kingdom	302
Canada	152

Scale 1: 240 000 000

Purchasing power, 2005

Purchasing Power Parity (PPP) in $US based on Gross Domestic Product (GDP) per person, adjusted for the local cost of living

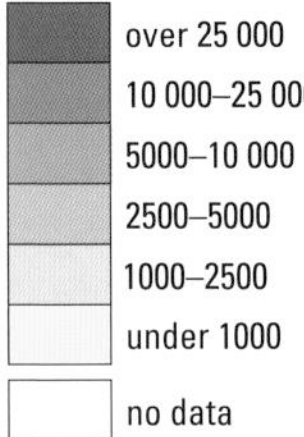

over 25 000
10 000–25 000
5000–10 000
2500–5000
1000–2500
under 1000
no data

Highest purchasing power	
Luxembourg	$60 228
United States	$41 890
Norway	$41 420
Ireland	$38 505
Iceland	$36 510
Canada	$33 375

Lowest purchasing power	
Niger	$781
Tanzania	$744
Congo, Democratic Republic	$714
Burundi	$699
Malawi	$667

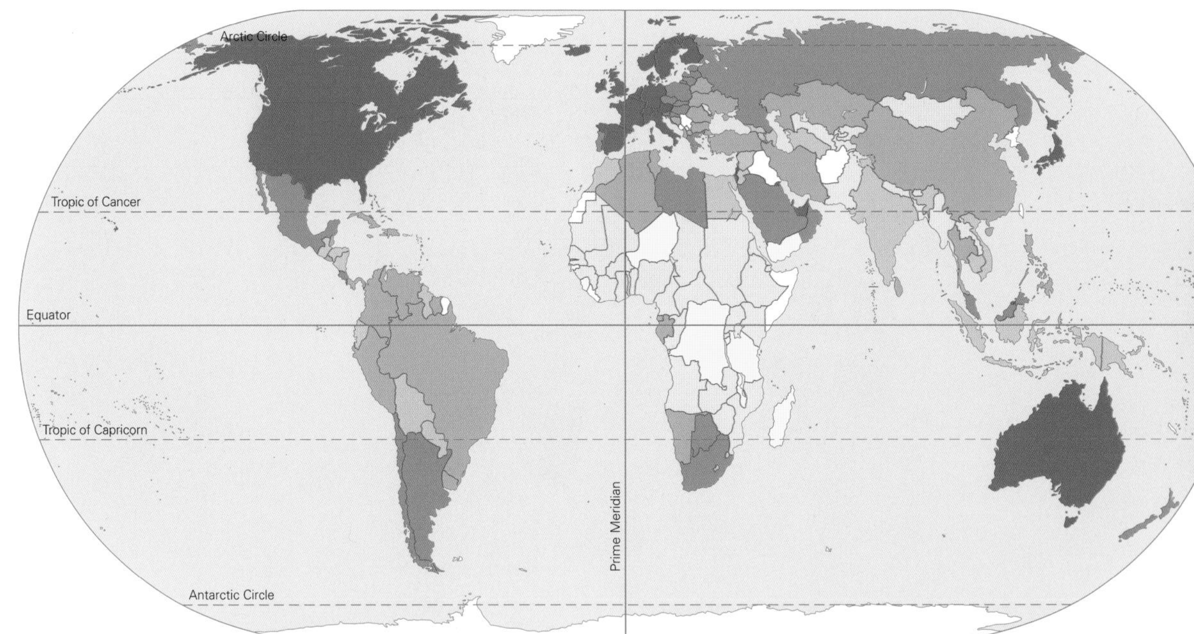

Literacy and schooling, 2005

percentage of people aged 15 and above who can, with understanding, both read and write a short, simple statement on their everyday life

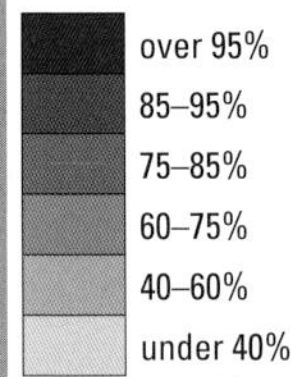

over 95%
85–95%
75–85%
60–75%
40–60%
under 40%
○ countries that spend a greater percentage of their GDP on the military than on education

Highest literacy levels	
Georgia	100.0%
Cuba	99.8%
Estonia	99.8%
Latvia	99.7%
Slovenia	99.7%
Canada	99.0%

Lowest literacy levels	
Niger	28.7%
Afghanistan	28.0%
Chad	25.7%
Mali	24.0%
Burkina	23.8%

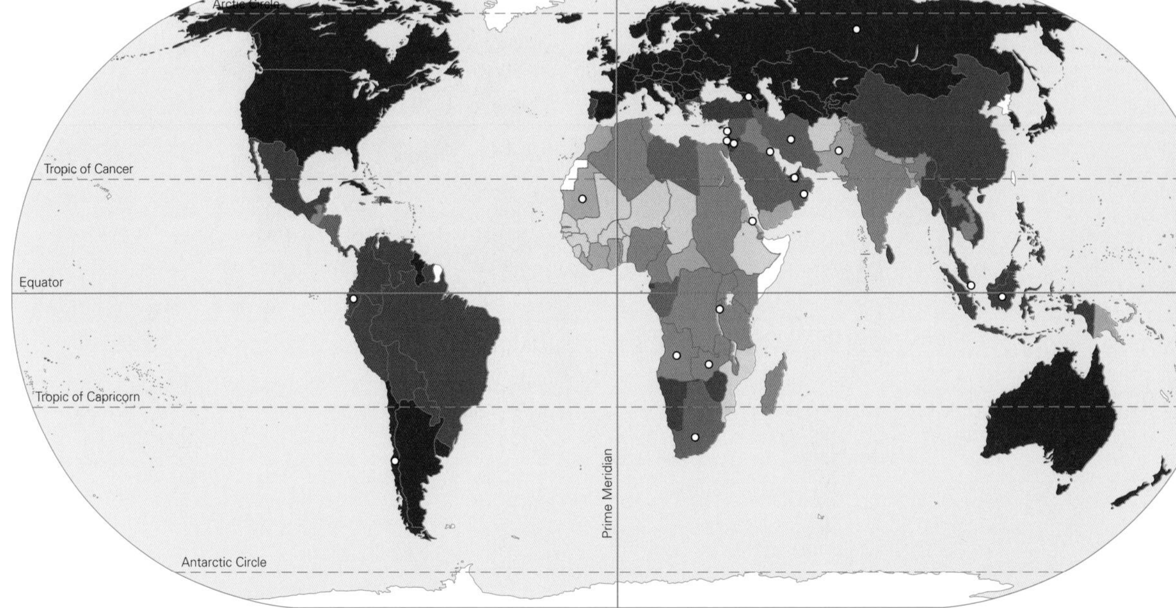

Life expectancy, 2005

average expected lifespan of babies born in 2005

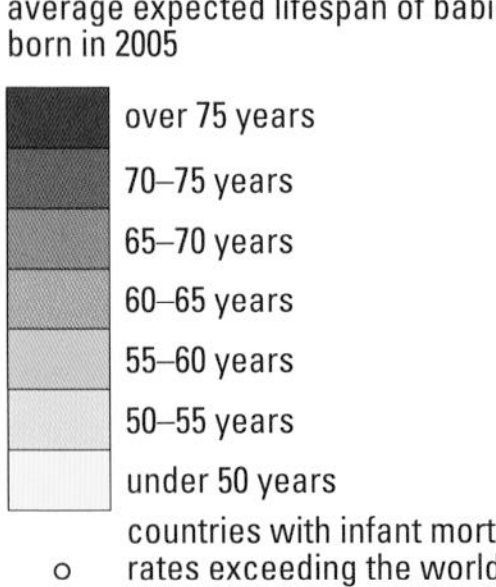

over 75 years
70–75 years
65–70 years
60–65 years
55–60 years
50–55 years
under 50 years
○ countries with infant mortality rates exceeding the world average of 52 per 1000 live births

Highest life expectancy	Years
Japan	82
Iceland	81
Switzerland	81
Australia	80
Spain	80
Canada	80

Lowest life expectancy	
Angola	41
Sierra Leone	41
Swaziland	40
Zambia	40
Zimbabwe	40

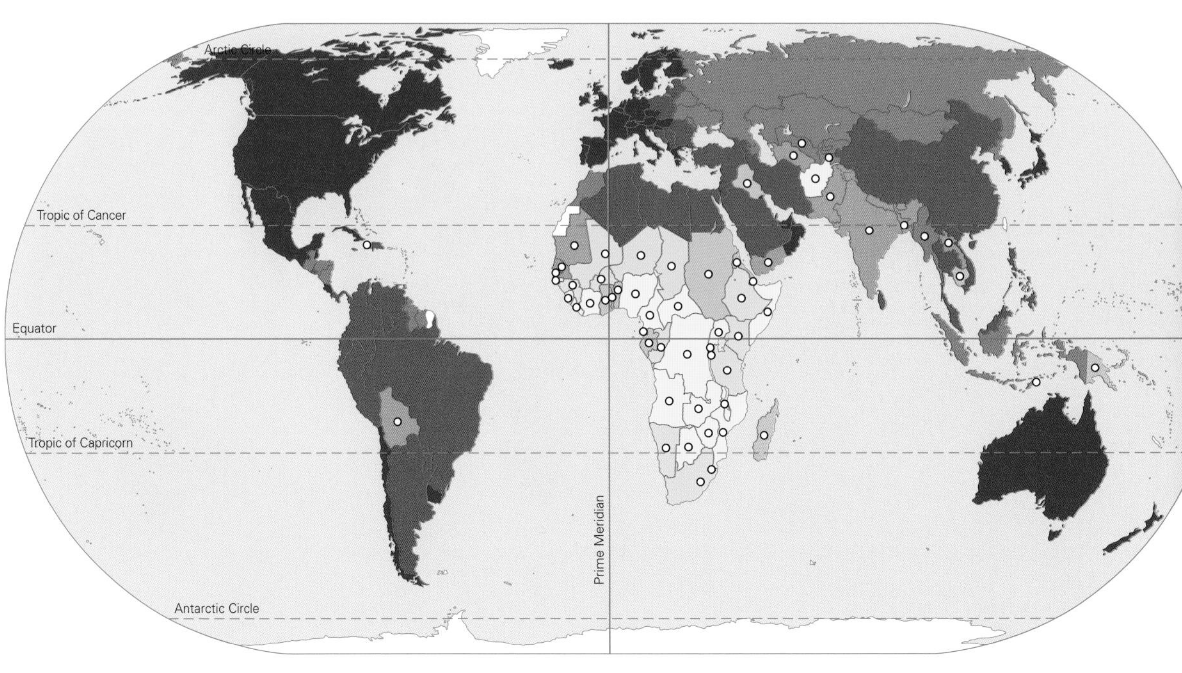

Eckert IV Projection

Further information on this topic is located in the World Datasets section which begins on page 184.

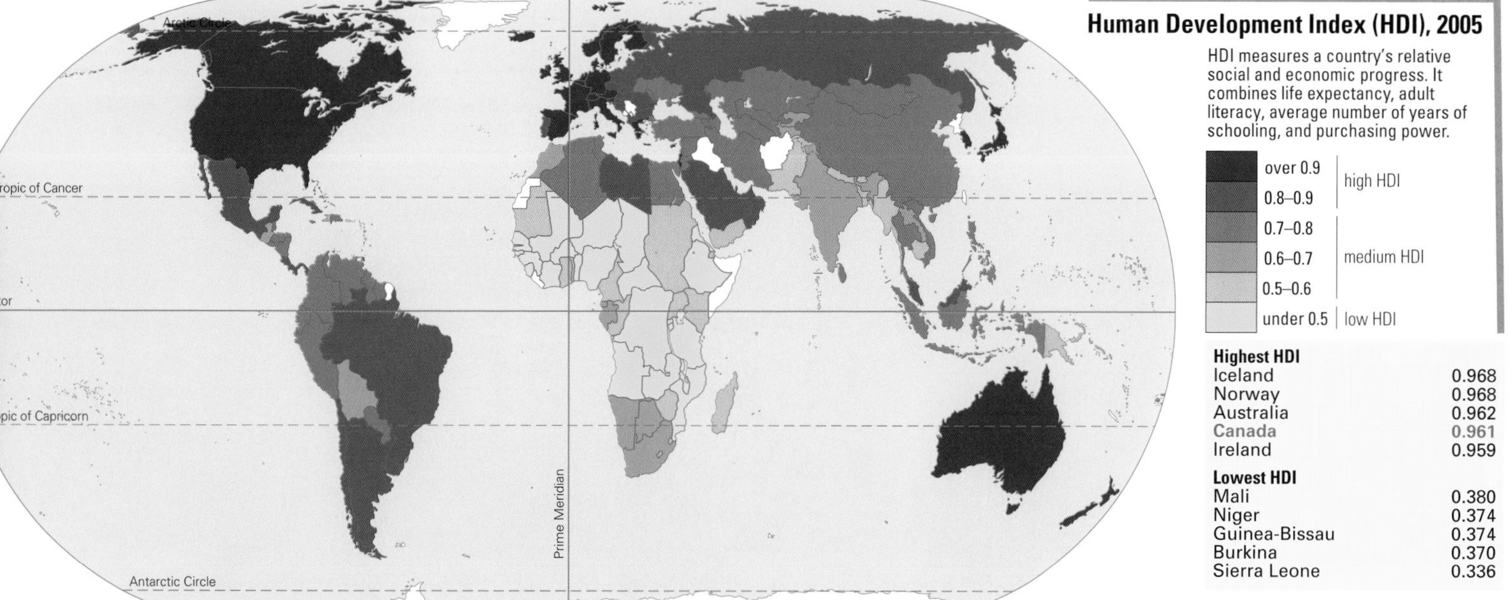

Human Development Index (HDI), 2005

HDI measures a country's relative social and economic progress. It combines life expectancy, adult literacy, average number of years of schooling, and purchasing power.

- over 0.9 — high HDI
- 0.8–0.9 — high HDI
- 0.7–0.8 — medium HDI
- 0.6–0.7 — medium HDI
- 0.5–0.6 — medium HDI
- under 0.5 — low HDI

Highest HDI	
Iceland	0.968
Norway	0.968
Australia	0.962
Canada	0.961
Ireland	0.959
Lowest HDI	
Mali	0.380
Niger	0.374
Guinea-Bissau	0.374
Burkina	0.370
Sierra Leone	0.336

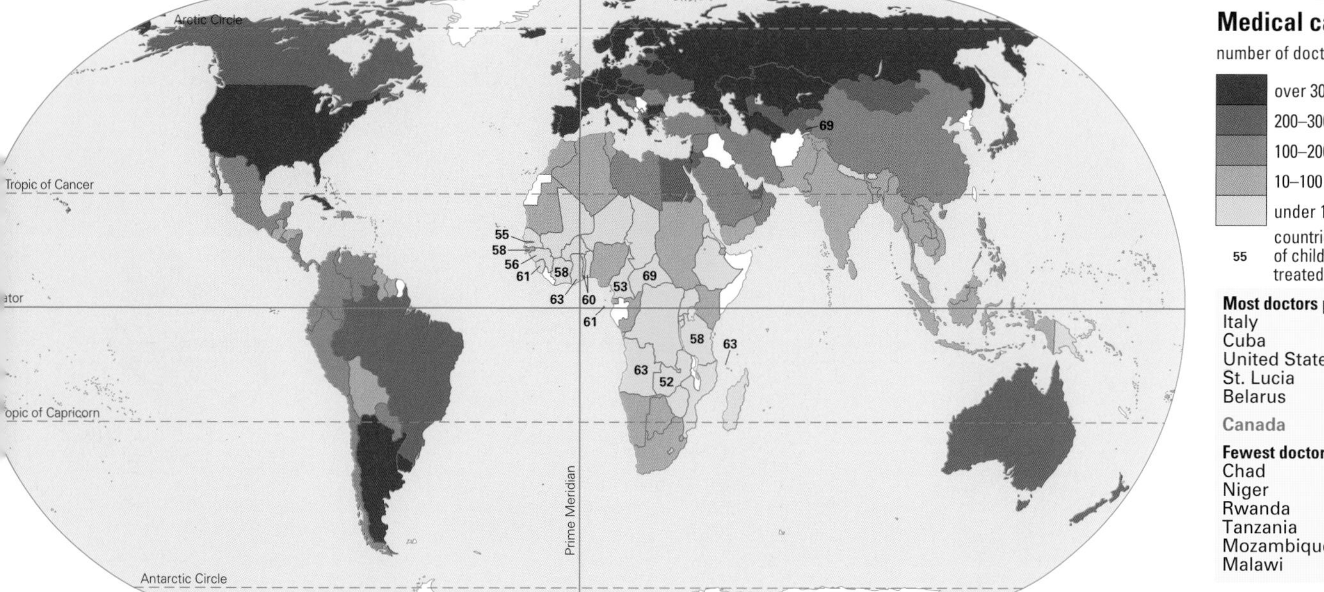

Medical care, 2004

number of doctors per 100 000 people

- over 300
- 200–300
- 100–200
- 10–100
- under 10

55 countries where more than 50% of children under five have been treated for Malaria in 2005

Most doctors per 100 000 people	
Italy	606
Cuba	591
United States	549
St. Lucia	518
Belarus	450
Canada	214
Fewest doctors per 100 000 people	
Chad	3
Niger	3
Rwanda	2
Tanzania	2
Mozambique	2
Malawi	1

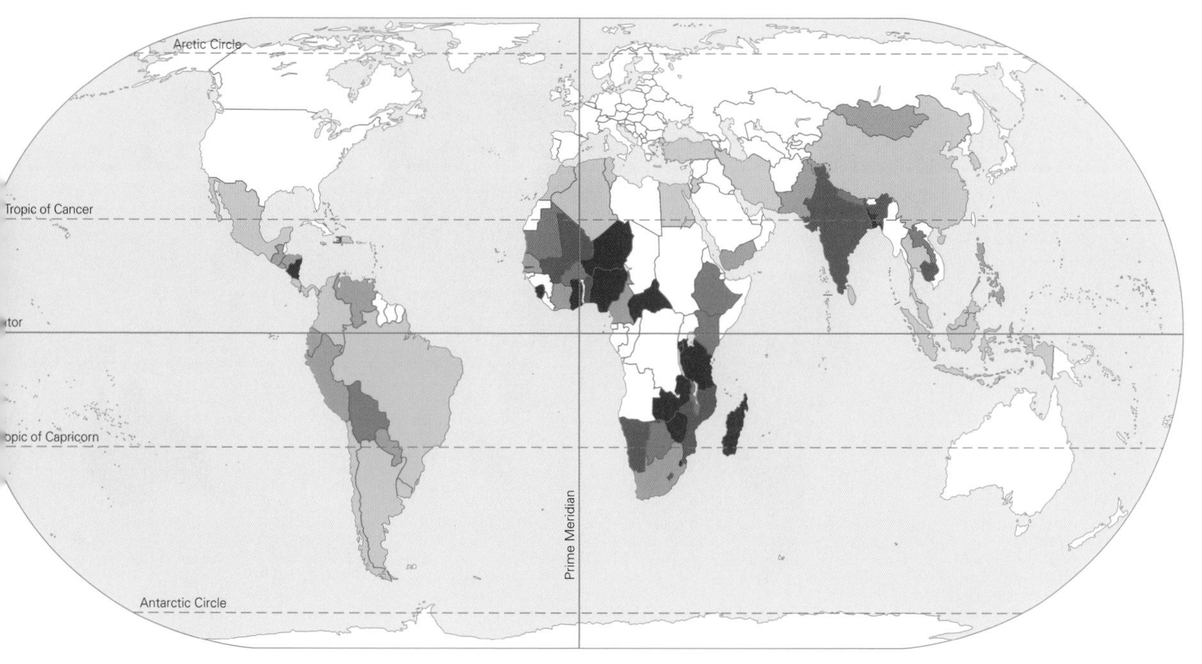

Poverty, 2005

percentage of population living on less than $1 per day

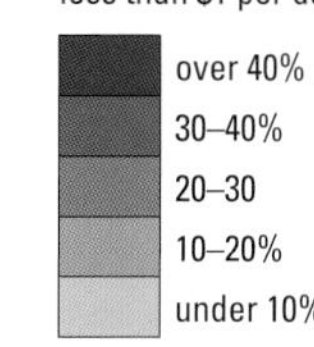

At the beginning of the 21st century, it is estimated that 1.1 billion people were living on less than $1 per day — the majority of them children.

In 2000 the member states of the UN adopted the Millennium Declaration that would provide targets and accountability mechanisms to enable poor people to improve their lives. The eight goals were: eradicate extreme poverty and hunger; achieve universal primary education; promote gender equality; reduce child mortality; improve maternal health; combat HIV/AIDS, malaria, and other diseases; ensure environmental sustainability; and develop a global partnership for development.

Agriculture

Commercial farming
- cereals dominant
- mixed farming and dairy
- mixed farming, fruit and vegetables
- mixed farming, cash crops
- ranching and stock raising

Mainly subsistence farming
- staples: cassava, yam, potatoes
- staples: millet, sorghum, barley, rye
- nomadic herding

Small holding
- rice dominant
- other cereals dominant
- mixed farming and livestock
- mixed farming, fruit and vegetables
- mixed farming, cash crops
- stock raising

Forests
- commercially exploited

Non-agricultural land
- ice, tundra, swamp, desert, montane, and coniferous forest

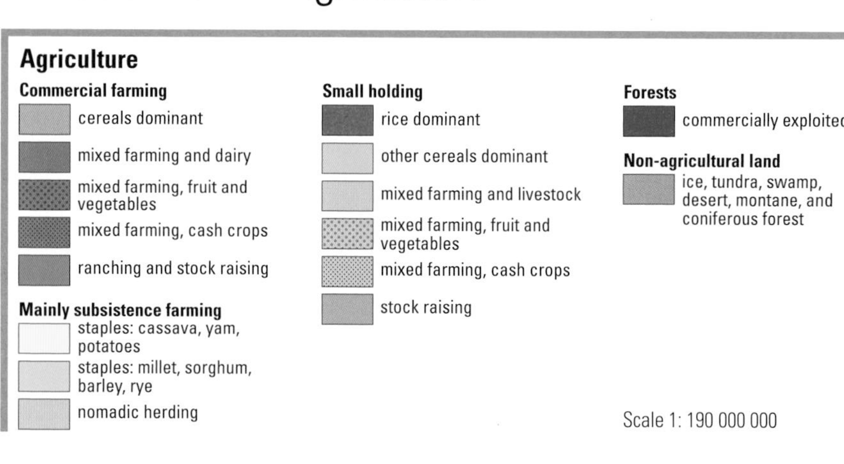

Scale 1: 190 000 000

Agriculture's contribution to Gross Domestic Product (GDP)

percentage of GDP, for selected countries, 2005 (GDP is the annual total value of all goods and services in a country, excluding transactions with other countries)

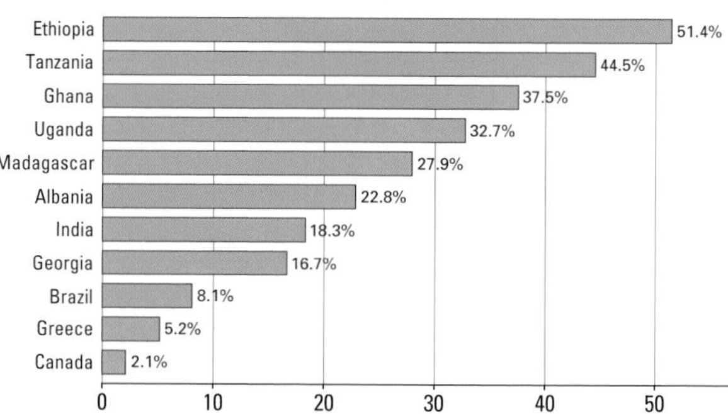

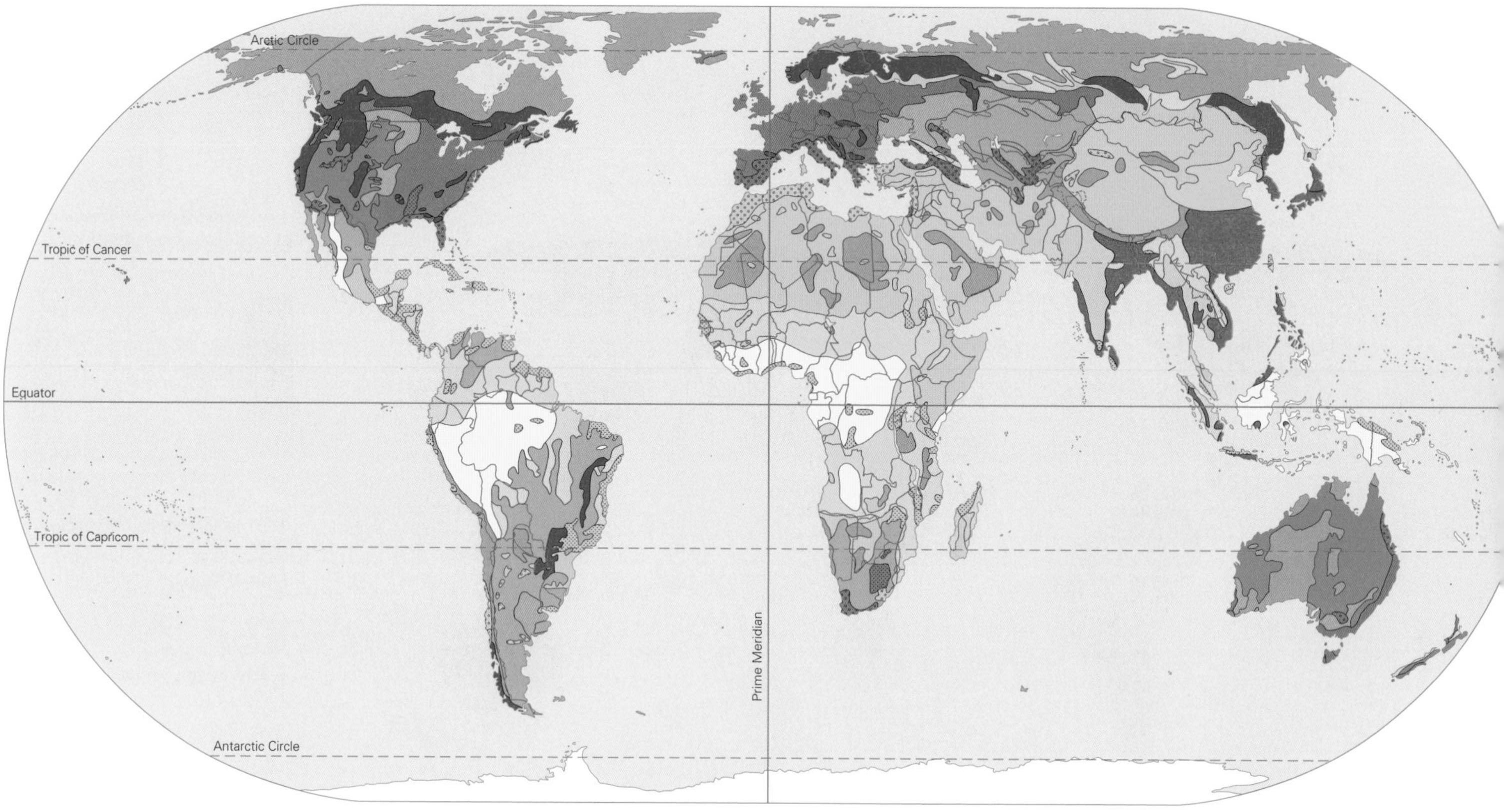

Ethiopia 51.4%
Tanzania 44.5%
Ghana 37.5%
Uganda 32.7%
Madagascar 27.9%
Albania 22.8%
India 18.3%
Georgia 16.7%
Brazil 8.1%
Greece 5.2%
Canada 2.1%
0
10
20
30
40
50

Arctic Circle
Tropic of Cancer
Equator
Tropic of Capricorn
Antarctic Circle
Prime Meridian

Food consumption, 2005

average daily food intake in calories per person

- more than 3500 calories
- 3000–3500 calories
- 2500–3000 calories
- 2000–2500 calories
- less than 2000 calories
- ○ countries with more than 25% of the total population classified by the UN as undernourished (2000–2003)

Highest food consumption	
Romania	4 125
Austria	4 023
Italy	3 730
Israel	3 695
France	3 681
Canada	**3 486**
Lowest food consumption	
Malawi	1 729
Burundi	1 693
Yemen	1 590
Ethiopia	1 582
Congo, Democratic Republic	1 398

Scale 1: 240 000 000

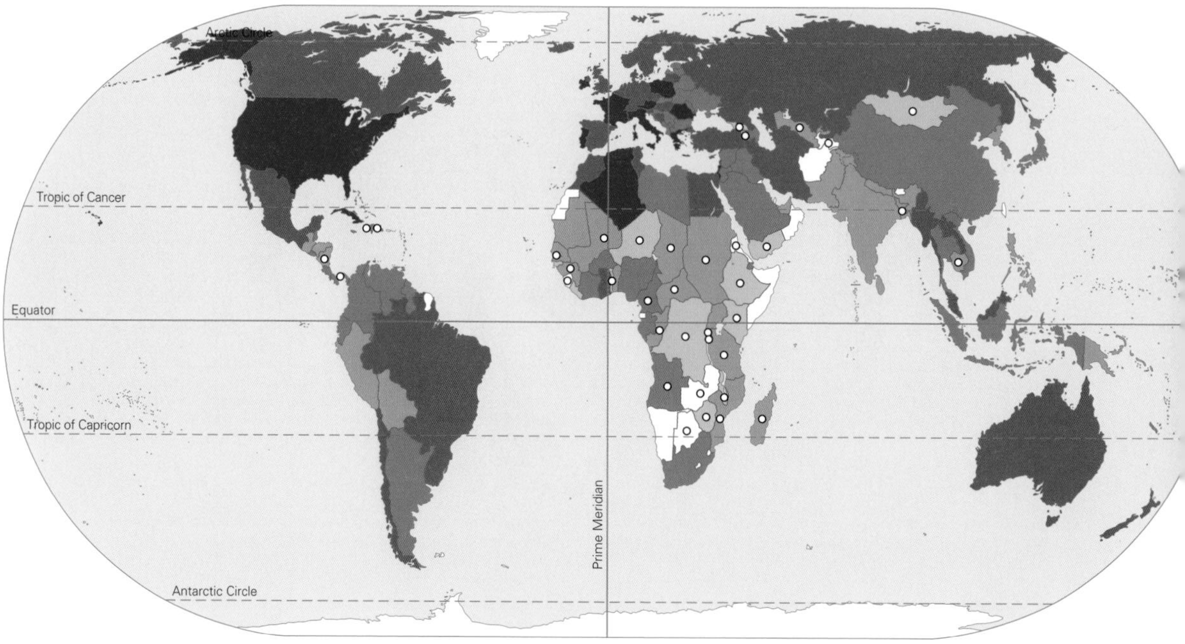

Arctic Circle
Tropic of Cancer
Equator
Tropic of Capricorn
Antarctic Circle
Prime Meridian

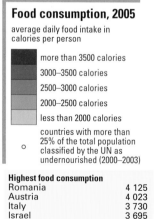

Eckert IV Projection

Scale 1: 240 000 000

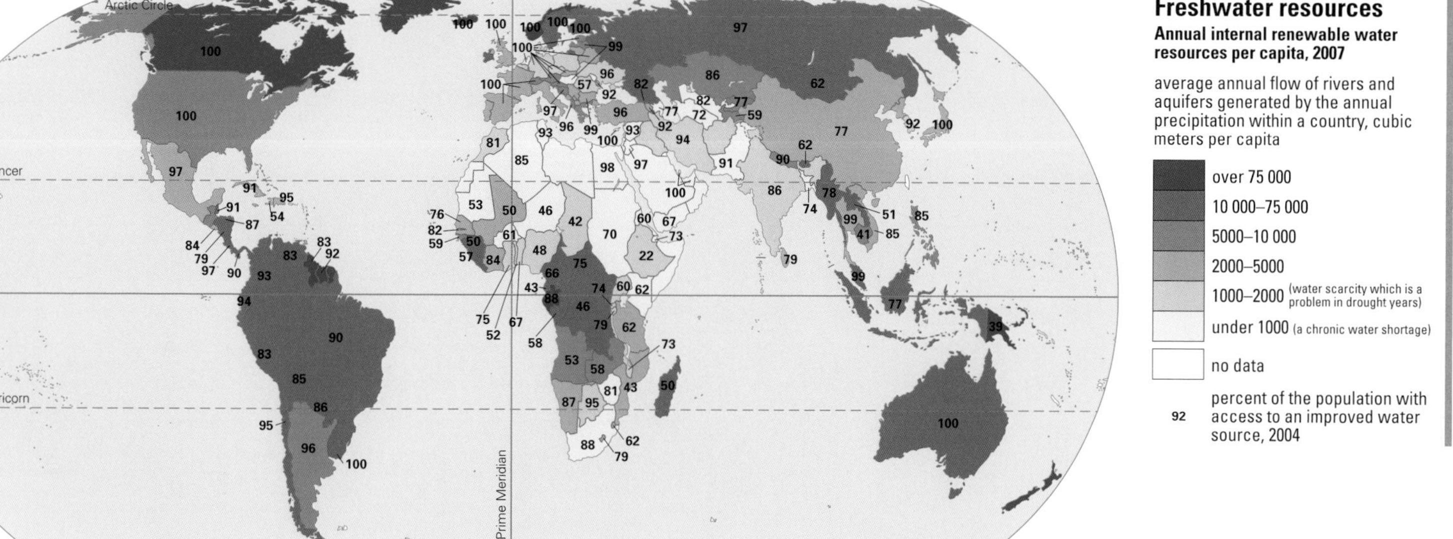

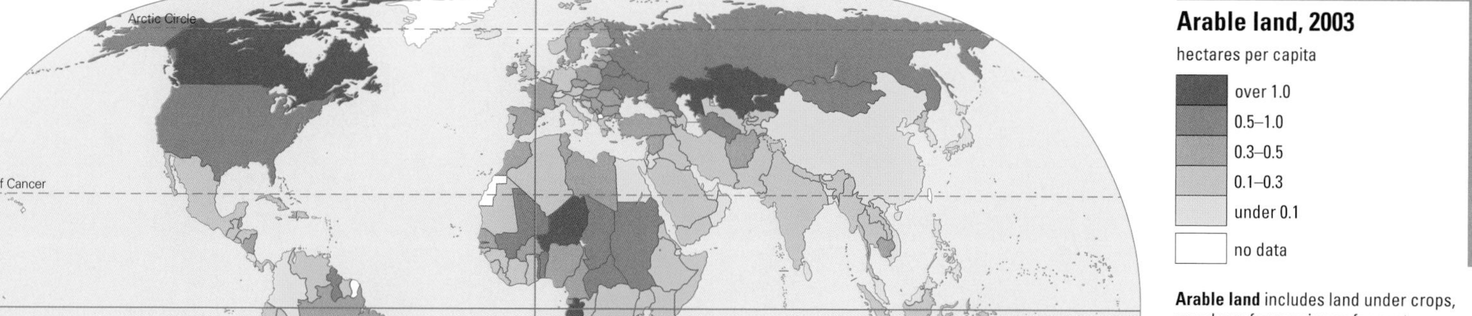

Arable land includes land under crops, meadows for mowing or for pasture, land under market or kitchen gardens, and land temporarily fallow.

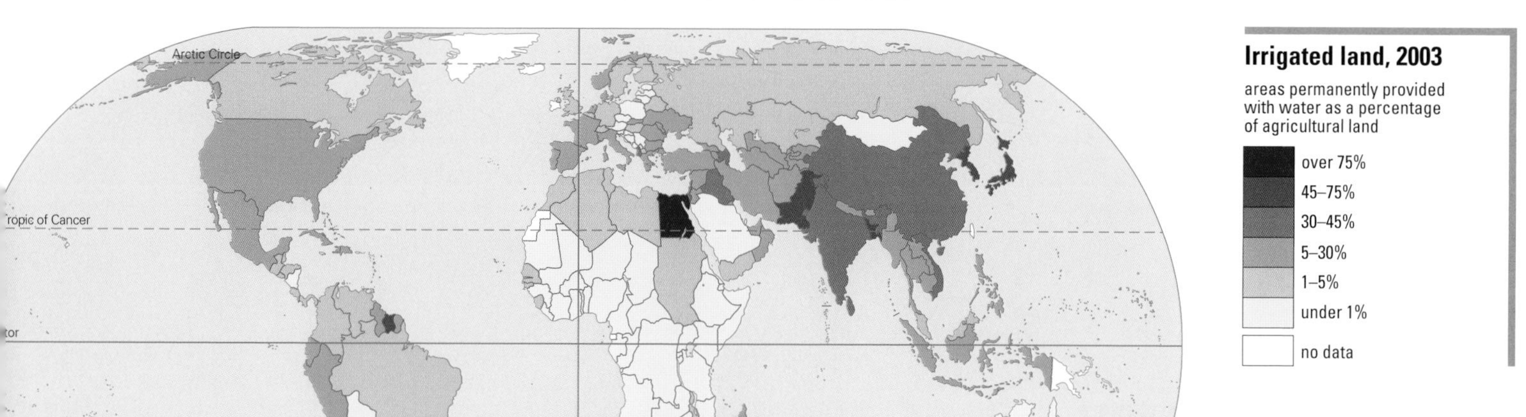

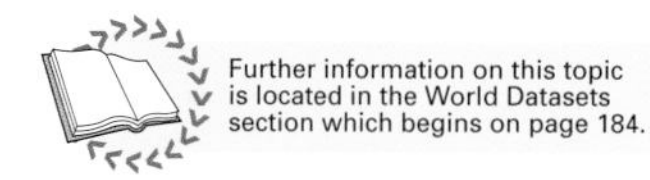
Further information on this topic is located in the World Datasets section which begins on page 184.

Scale 1: 240 000 000

Industrialization, 2006

Industrialized high income economies
Most people live in cities and have high standards of living based on manufacturing and services. High levels of energy consumption

Industrializing upper-middle income economies
Manufacturing and industrial development are growing alongside traditional economies. Most people have rising incomes.

Industrializing lower-middle income economies
Manufacturing and industrial development are growing alongside traditional economies. As a consequence, a middle-income class is emerging, though most people have relatively low incomes.

Agricultural low income economies
Most people live in rural areas and depend on agriculture. Little industrial development. Low incomes.

o more than 40% of the population living below the national poverty line

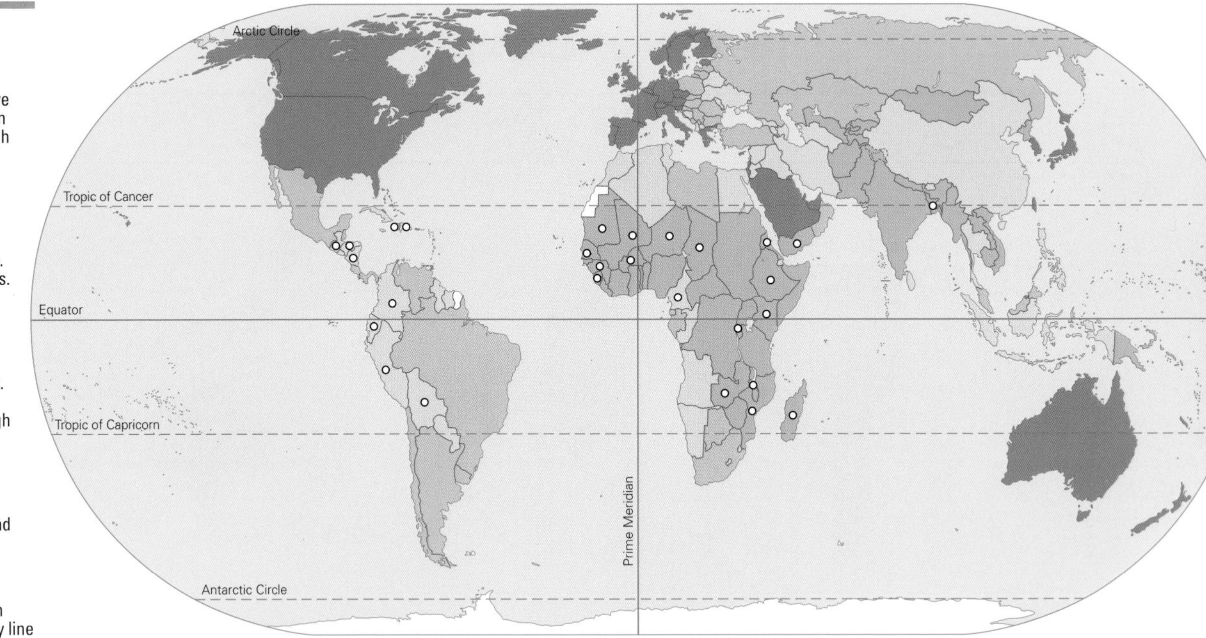

International aid, 2005

Official development assistance (ODA) given or received per person in $US

Countries giving aid

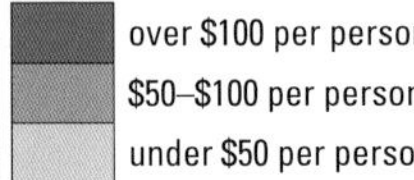

over $100 per person
$50–$100 per person
under $50 per person

Countries receiving aid

under $10 per person
$10–$100 per person
over $100 per person

The economy becomes dependent on financial grants or loans from other, wealthier countries.

Countries giving most aid (total $US)	
USA	$27 622 000 000
Japan	$13 147 000 000
United Kingdom	$10 767 000 000
Germany	$10 082 000 000
Canada	$3 756 000 000

Countries receiving most aid (total $US)	
Nigeria	$6 437 300 000
Indonesia	$2 523 500 000
Ethiopia	$1 937 300 000
Vietnam	$1 904 900 000

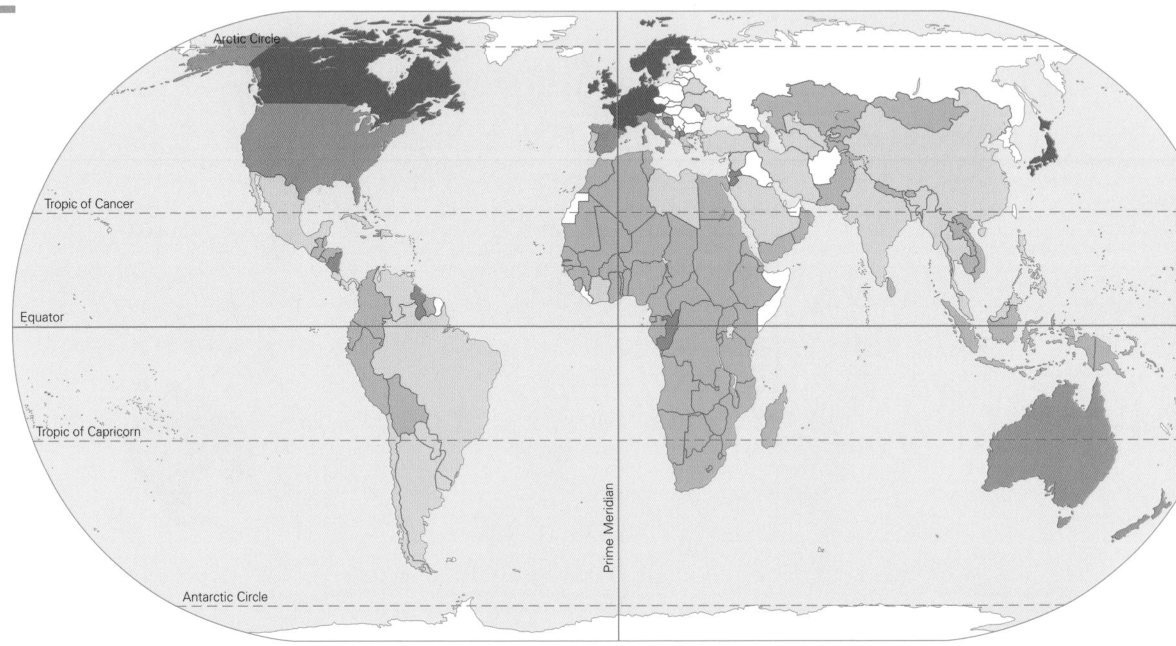

Employment

percentage of the labour force

over 80%
60–80%
30–60%
10–30%
under 10%
no data

Scale 1: 480 000 000

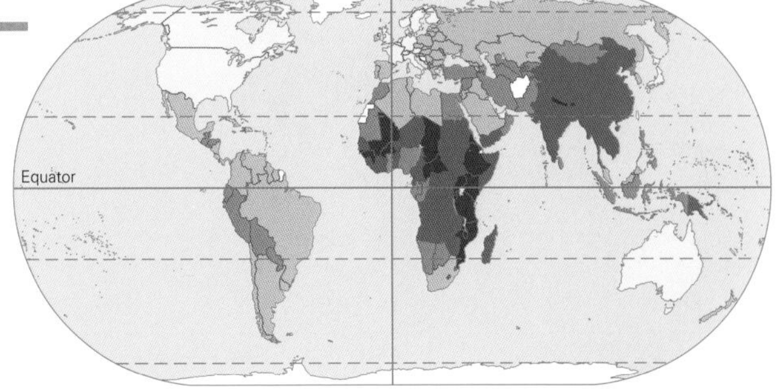

Agriculture

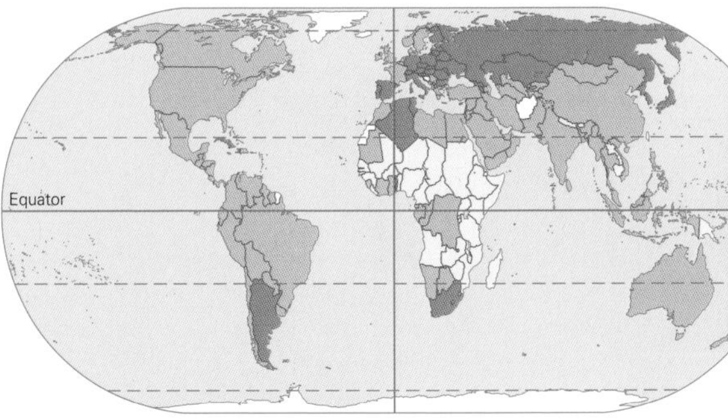

Industry

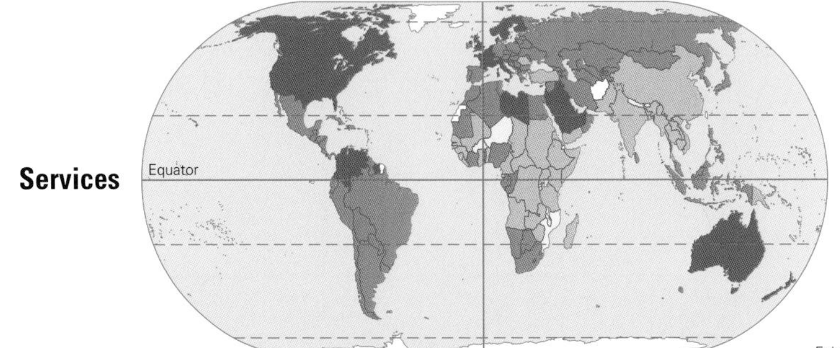

Services

Further information on this topic is located in the World Datasets section which begins on page 184.

Eckert IV Projection

ctor	includes
mary	Farming, fishing, forestry, mining and quarrying
condary	Manufacturing industry, building and construction
tiary	Transport and distribution, wholesale and retail, administration and finance, public services

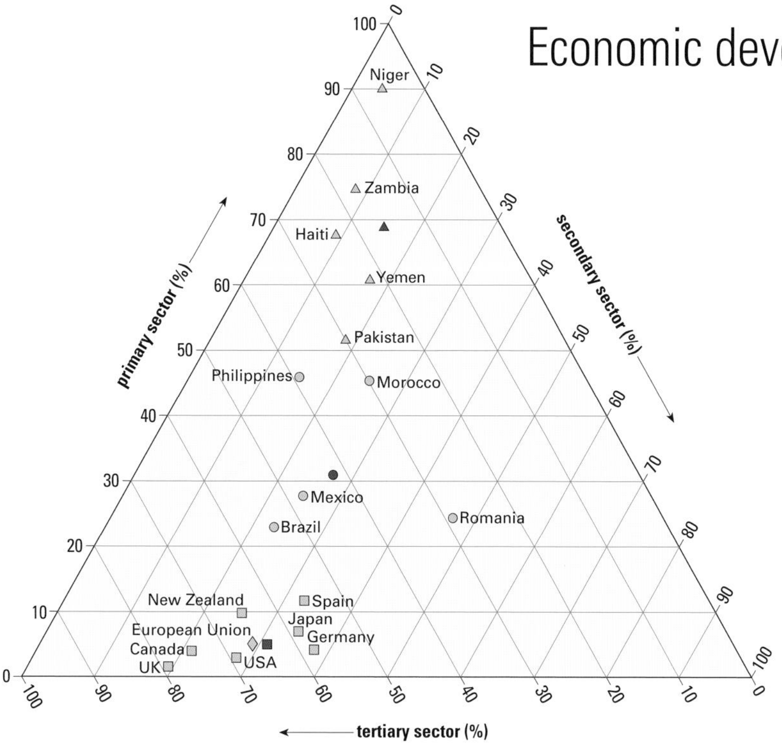

Employment by economic sector

Average for country categories

- ▲ Low income economies
- ● Middle income economies
- ■ High income economies

Selected countries and the European Union

- △ Low income countries
- ○ Middle income countries
- □ High income countries
- ◇ European Union

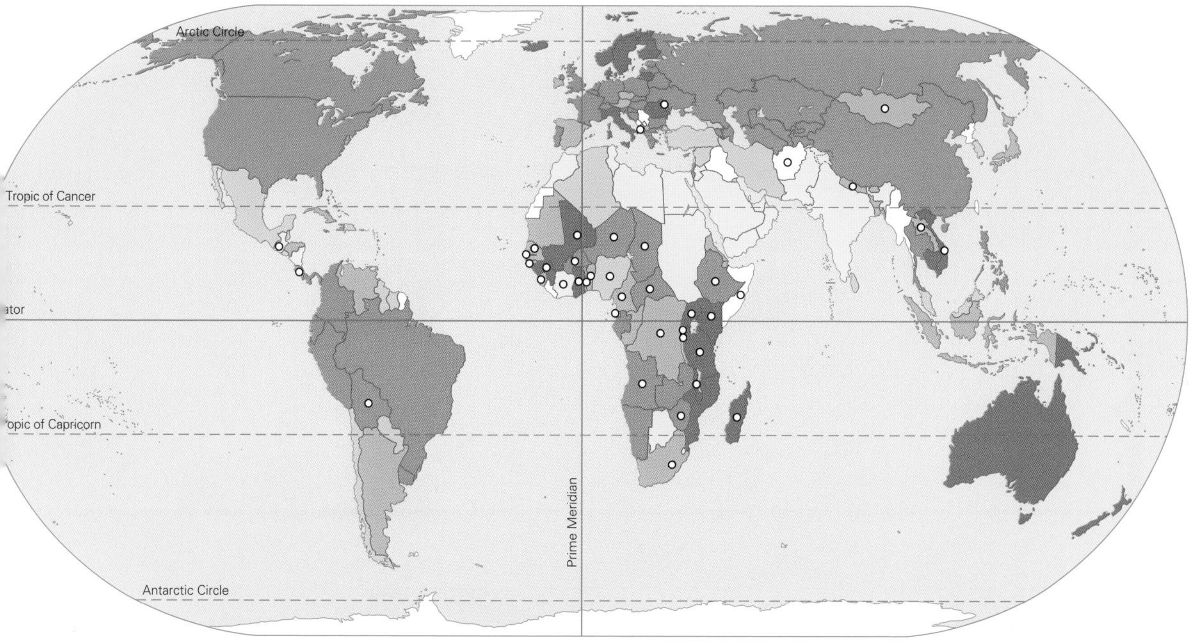

Female income, 2005

percentage of total income earned by females in $US

- over 40%
- 35–40%
- 30–35%
- 25–30%
- under 25%
- ○ countries with more than 20% of children aged 5 to 14 years involved in child labour activities

Highest female earned income ($US)	
Norway	$30 749
Sweden	$29 044
Denmark	$28 766
Iceland	$28 637
Finland	$26 795
Canada	$25 448

Lowest female earned income ($US)	
Niger	$561
Guinea-Bissau	$558
Sierra Leone	$507
Congo, Democratic Republic	$488
Yemen Republic	$424

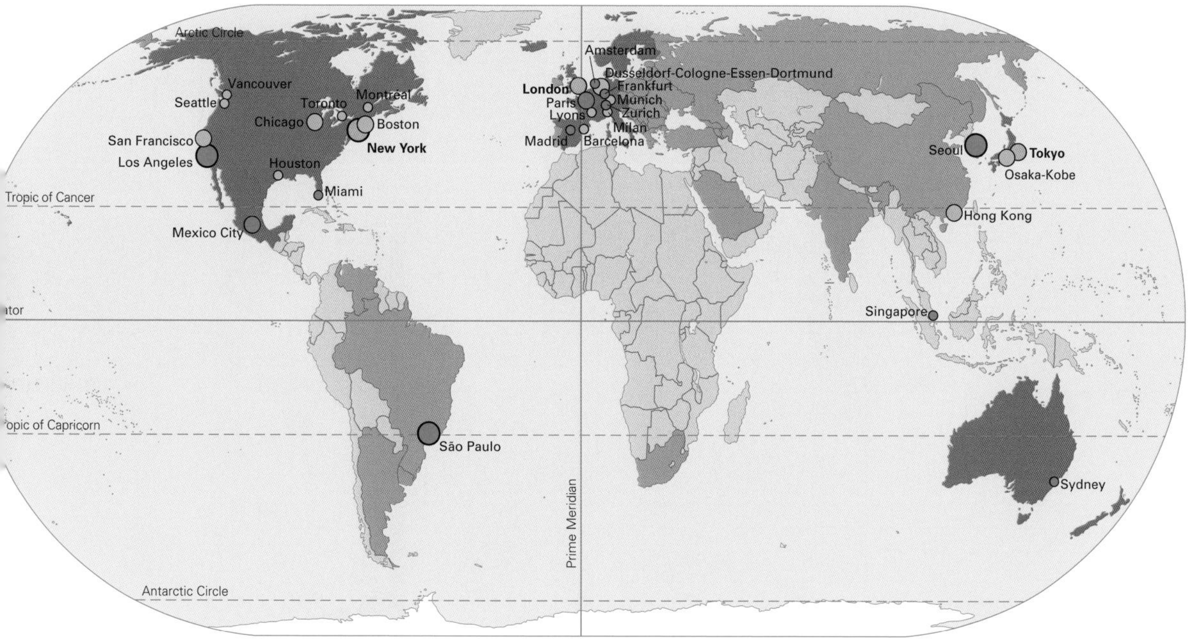

World economy

- economic core (countries dominant in the world economy)
- semi-periphery (countries partially dependent on the core)
- periphery (countries highly dependent on the core)

Global cities

Some geographers have identified a network of global cities arranged in a hierarchy according to the power they exert on the global economy. The map shows one view of this hierarchy. The position of each city in the hierarchy can change rapidly through time.

- cities dominating global financial markets
- cities dominating international and national economies
- cities dominating subnational and regional economies

City population

- 10–25 million
- 5–10 million
- 1–5 million

Source: J. Friedmann, *World Cities in a World-System*. (Cambridge: Cambridge University Press, 1995), p.24.

Scale 1: 240 000 000

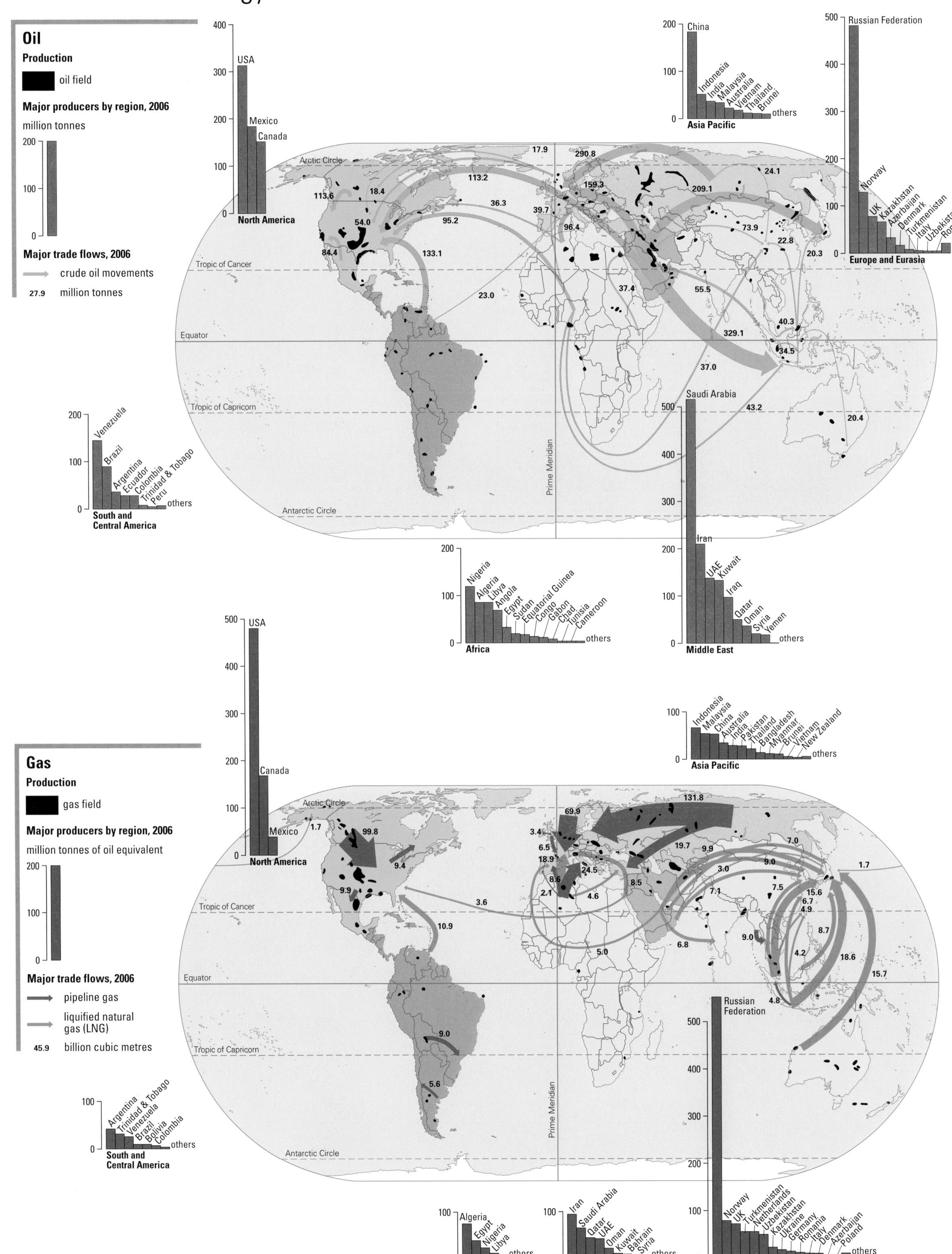
Oil
Production
oil field
Major producers by region, 2006
million tonnes
Major trade flows, 2006
crude oil movements
27.9 million tonnes
USA
Mexico
Canada
North America
China
Indonesia
India
Malaysia
Australia
Vietnam
Thailand
Brunei
others
Asia Pacific
Russian Federation
Norway
UK
Kazakhstan
Azerbaijan
Denmark
Turkmenistan
Italy
Uzbekistan
Europe and Eurasia
Venezuela
Brazil
Argentina
Ecuador
Colombia
Trinidad & Tobago
Peru
South and Central America
Nigeria
Algeria
Libya
Angola
Egypt
Sudan
Equatorial Guinea
Congo
Gabon
Chad
Tunisia
Cameroon
Africa
Saudi Arabia
Iran
UAE
Kuwait
Iraq
Qatar
Oman
Syria
Yemen
Middle East
Arctic Circle
Tropic of Cancer
Equator
Tropic of Capricorn
Antarctic Circle
Prime Meridian
17.9
290.8
113.2
113.6
18.4
159.3
209.1
24.1
36.3
39.7
54.0
95.2
96.4
73.9
22.8
84.4
133.1
20.3
23.0
37.4
55.5
40.3
329.1
34.5
37.0
43.2
20.4
Gas
Production
gas field
Major producers by region, 2006
million tonnes of oil equivalent
Major trade flows, 2006
pipeline gas
liquified natural gas (LNG)
45.9 billion cubic metres
USA
Canada
Mexico
North America
Indonesia
Malaysia
China
Australia
India
Pakistan
Thailand
Bangladesh
Myanmar
Brunei
Vietnam
New Zealand
others
Asia Pacific
Argentina
Trinidad & Tobago
Venezuela
Brazil
Bolivia
Colombia
South and Central America
Algeria
Egypt
Nigeria
Libya
Africa
Iran
Saudi Arabia
Qatar
UAE
Oman
Kuwait
Bahrain
Syria
Middle East
Russian Federation
Norway
UK
Turkmenistan
Netherlands
Uzbekistan
Kazakhstan
Ukraine
Germany
Romania
Italy
Denmark
Azerbaijan
Poland
Europe and Eurasia
131.8
69.9
1.7
99.8
3.4
6.5
18.9
19.7
9.9
7.0
9.4
24.5
3.0
9.0
8.6
8.5
2.1
4.6
7.1
7.5
15.6
6.7
4.9
9.9
3.6
10.9
8.7
6.8
9.0
5.0
4.2
18.6
15.7
4.8
9.0
5.6

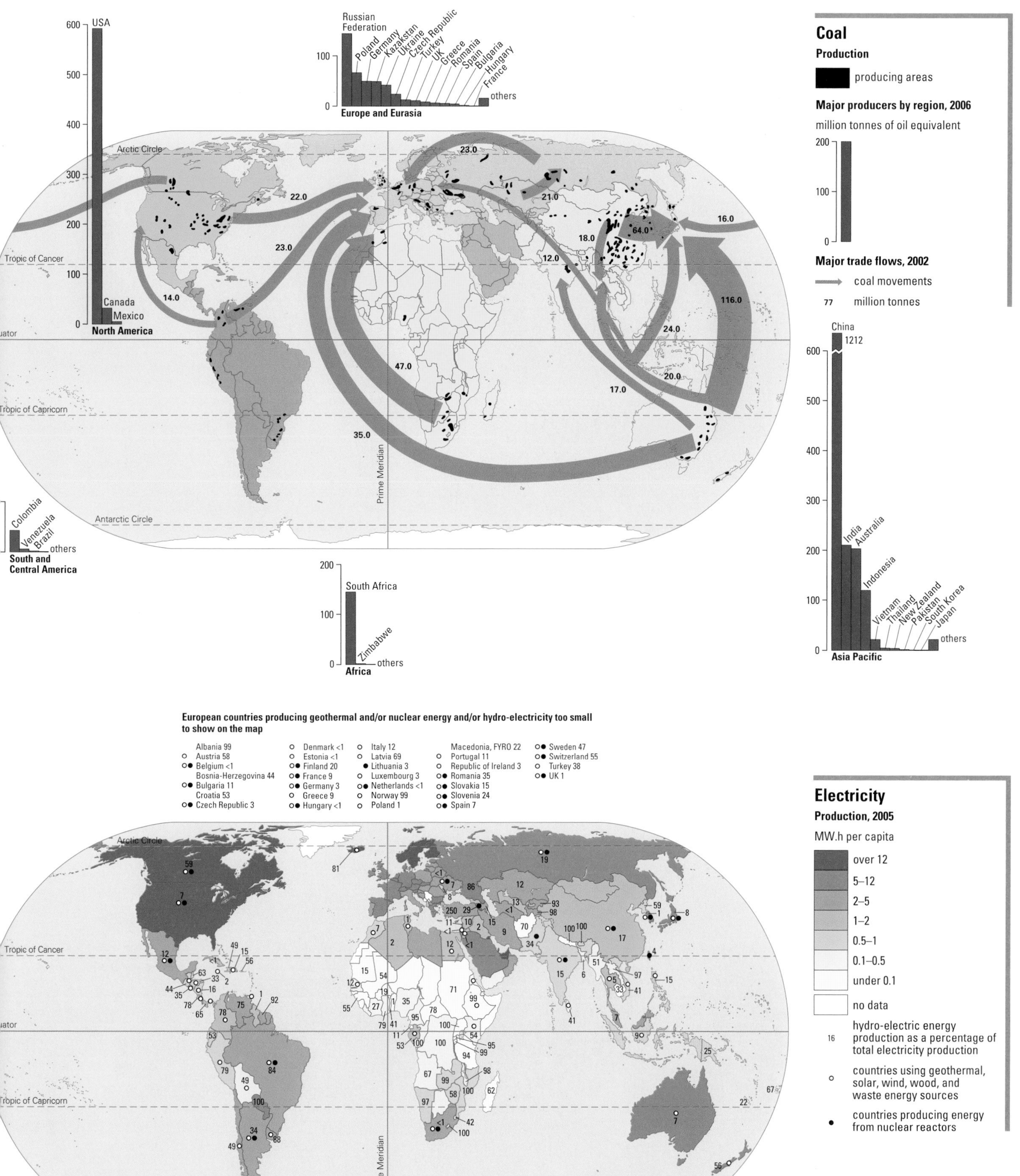
Coal
Production
producing areas
Major producers by region, 2006
million tonnes of oil equivalent
Major trade flows, 2002
coal movements
77 million tonnes
USA
Canada
Mexico
North America
Russian Federation
Poland
Germany
Kazakhstan
Ukraine
Czech Republic
Turkey
UK
Greece
Romania
Spain
Bulgaria
Hungary
France
others
Europe and Eurasia
Colombia
Venezuela
Brazil
others
South and Central America
South Africa
Zimbabwe
others
Africa
China
1212
India
Australia
Indonesia
Vietnam
Thailand
New Zealand
Pakistan
South Korea
Japan
others
Asia Pacific
Arctic Circle
Tropic of Cancer
Equator
Tropic of Capricorn
Antarctic Circle
Prime Meridian
22.0
23.0
14.0
23.0
21.0
16.0
64.0
18.0
12.0
116.0
24.0
20.0
17.0
47.0
35.0
Electricity
Production, 2005
MW.h per capita
over 12
5–12
2–5
1–2
0.5–1
0.1–0.5
under 0.1
no data
16 hydro-electric energy production as a percentage of total electricity production
countries using geothermal, solar, wind, wood, and waste energy sources
countries producing energy from nuclear reactors
European countries producing geothermal and/or nuclear energy and/or hydro-electricity too small to show on the map
Albania 99
Austria 58
Belgium <1
Bosnia-Herzegovina 44
Bulgaria 11
Croatia 53
Czech Republic 3
Denmark <1
Estonia <1
Finland 20
France 9
Germany 3
Greece 9
Hungary <1
Italy 12
Latvia 69
Lithuania 3
Luxembourg 3
Netherlands <1
Norway 99
Poland 1
Macedonia, FYRO 22
Portugal 11
Republic of Ireland 3
Romania 35
Slovakia 15
Slovenia 24
Spain 7
Sweden 47
Switzerland 55
Turkey 38
UK 1

Scale 1: 240 000 000

Energy production, 2005

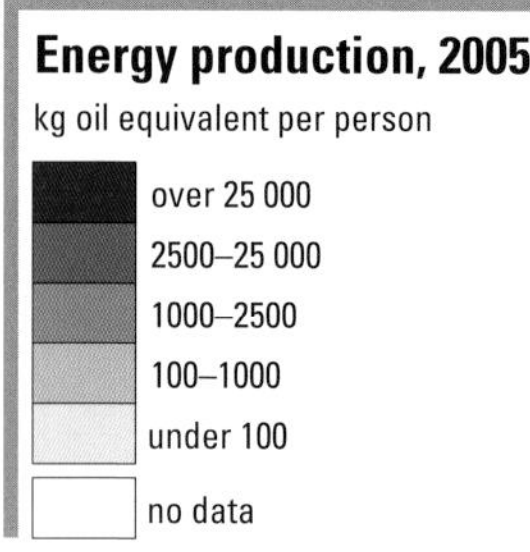

Highest energy producers
kg oil equivalent per person

Qatar	117 511
Kuwait	60 340
Brunei	58 253
Norway	57 630
United Arab Emirates	41 859
Equatorial Guinea	41 283
Trinidad and Tobago	28 628
Saudi Arabia	27 583
Oman	23 411
Libya	17 089
Bahrain	16 747
Canada	14 774
Turkmenistan	14 182
Australia	13 806
Gabon	10 554

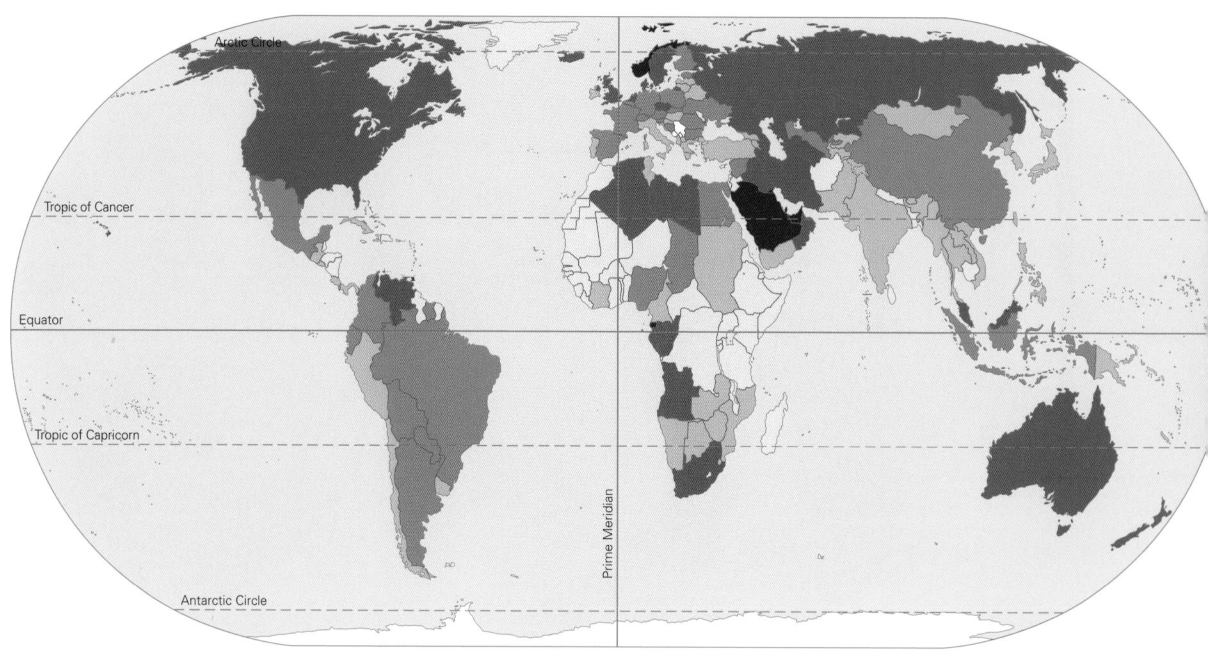

North America
Central and South America
Europe and Eurasia
Middle East
Africa
Asia Pacific

Oil reserves

Proven recoverable reserves
World total: 165 000 000 000 tonnes

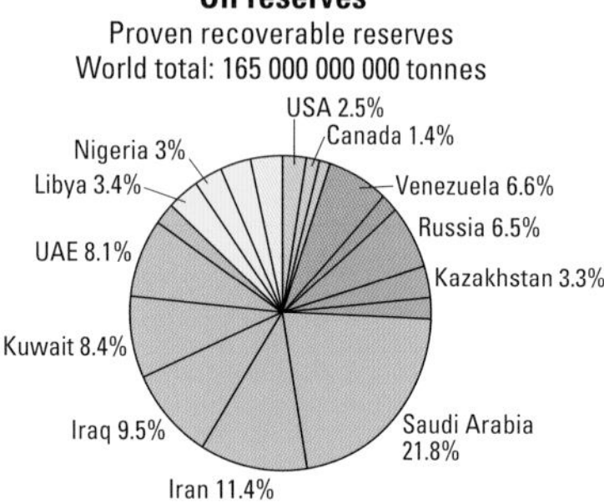

Gas reserves

Proven recoverable reserves
World total: 180 200 000 000 000 m³

USA 3.2%
Canada 0.9%
Venezuela 2.4%
Russia 26.4%
Iran 15.3%
Qatar 14.1%
Nigeria 2.9%
Algeria 2.5%

Coal reserves

Proven recoverable reserves
World total: 909 064 000 000 tonnes

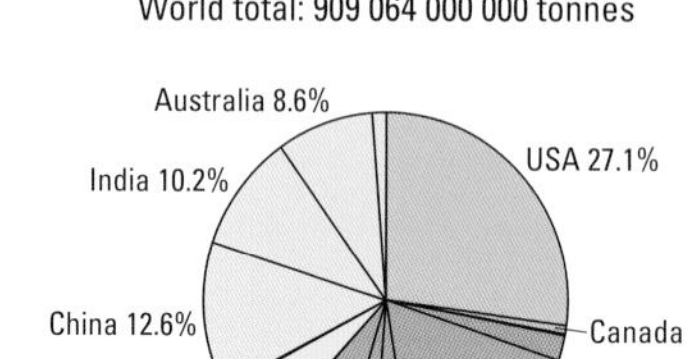

Oil consumption

World total: 3 861 300 000 tonnes

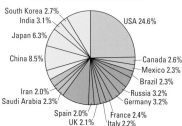

USA 24.6%
Canada 2.6%
Mexico 2.3%
Brazil 2.3%
Russia 3.2%
Germany 3.2%
France 2.4%
Italy 2.2%
UK 2.1%
Spain 2.0%
Saudi Arabia 2.3%
Iran 2.0%
China 8.5%
Japan 6.3%
India 3.1%
South Korea 2.7%

Gas consumption

World total: 2 780 300 000 000 m³

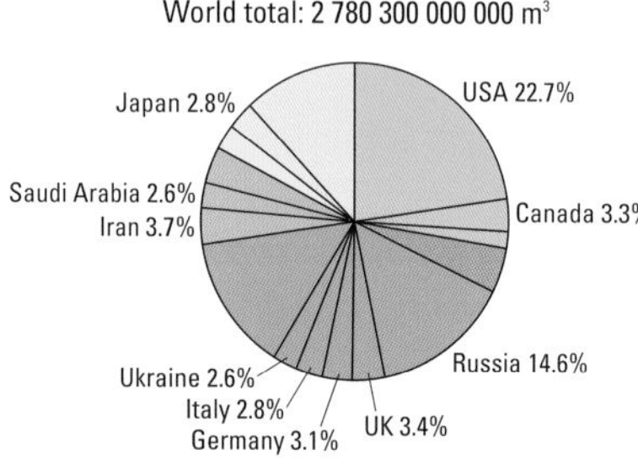

Coal consumption

World total: 2 957 000 000 tonnes oil equivalent

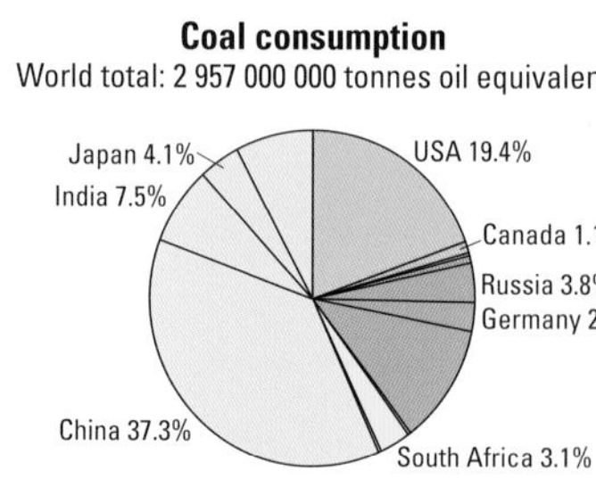

Energy consumption, 2005

kg oil equivalent per person

over 10 000
2500–10 000
1000–2500
250–1000
under 250
no data

Highest energy consumers
kg oil equivalent per person

Qatar	26 555
Bahrain	15 769
United Arab Emirates	12 702
Trinidad and Tobago	12 624
Iceland	12 238
Canada	11 075

Lowest energy consumers
kg oil equivalent per person

Burundi	26
Mali	22
Afghanistan	16
Cambodia	15
Chad	7

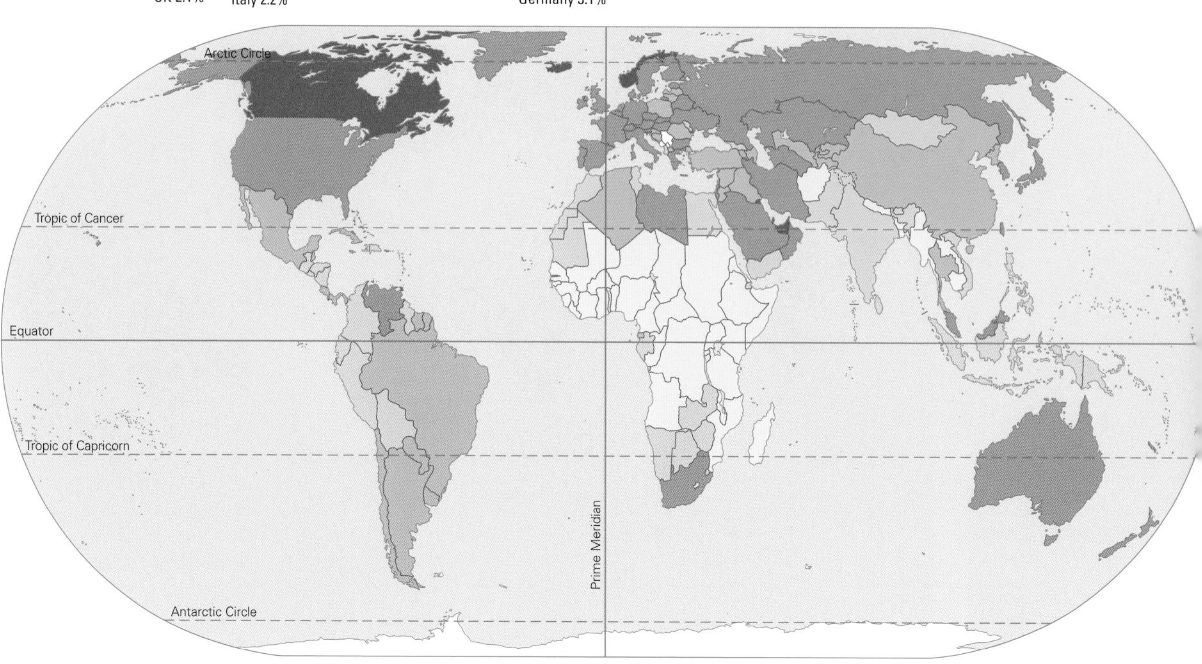

Eckert IV Projection

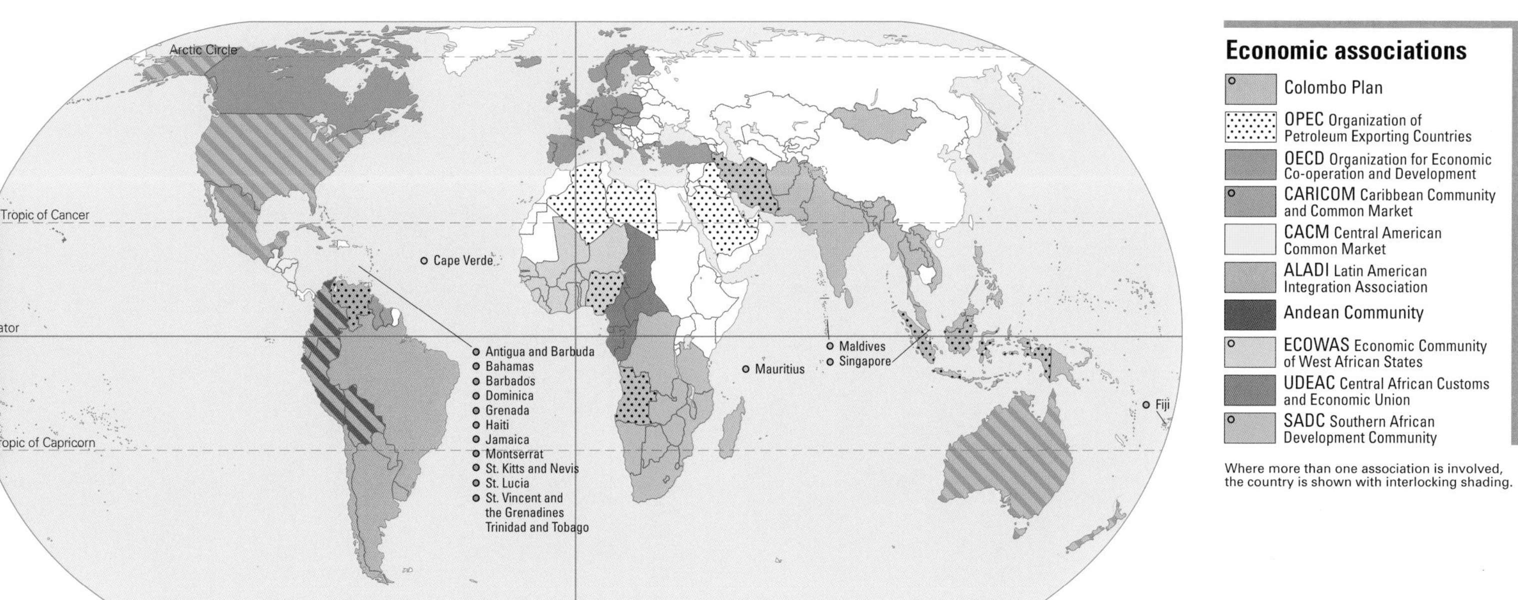

Economic associations

- Colombo Plan
- OPEC Organization of Petroleum Exporting Countries
- OECD Organization for Economic Co-operation and Development
- CARICOM Caribbean Community and Common Market
- CACM Central American Common Market
- ALADI Latin American Integration Association
- Andean Community
- ECOWAS Economic Community of West African States
- UDEAC Central African Customs and Economic Union
- SADC Southern African Development Community

Where more than one association is involved, the country is shown with interlocking shading.

WTO World Trade Organization

• WTO World Trade Organization

● ● Antigua and Barbuda	● ● Maldives
● Bahamas	● ● Malta
● Bahrain	● ● Mauritius
● ● Barbados	● Nauru
● ● Brunei	● Qatar
● Burundi	● ● St. Kitts and Nevis
● ● Cyprus	● ● St. Lucia
● ● Dominica	● ● St. Vincent and the Grenadines
● Fiji	● Samoa
● ● Grenada	● Seychelles
● Haiti	● ● Singapore
● Israel	● ● Solomon Islands
● ● Jamaica	● ● Tonga
● Kiribati	● ● Trinidad and Tobago
● Kuwait	● Tuvalu
● Liechtenstein	● Vanuatu
● Luxembourg	

• Commonwealth of Nations

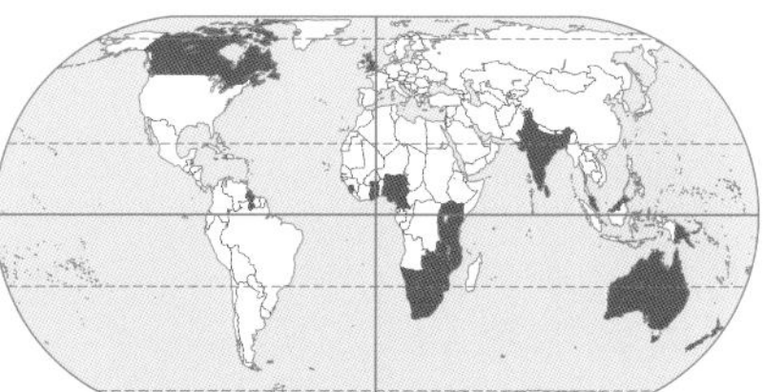

Commonwealth of Nations

UNCTAD

United Nations Conference on Trade and Development

Almost all nations (193) are now members

EU

European Union

For members see page 82.

United Nations

The following countries are **non-members**

Northern Marianas
Taiwan
Vatican City†
Western Sahara

† observer status

Headquarters of selected world organizations

Brussels:
The European Union
North Atlantic Treaty Organization (NATO)

The Hague:
International Court of Justice

New York:
United Nations

Paris:
United Nations Educational, Scientific and Cultural Organization (UNESCO)
Organization for Economic Co-operation and Development (OECD)

Rome:
Food and Agriculture Organization of the United Nations (FAO)

Geneva:
World Health Organization (WHO)
World Trade Organization (WTO)

Washington:
Organization of American States (OAS)

Addis Ababa:
African Union (AU)

Cairo:
Arab League

Singapore:
Asia Pacific Economic Co-operation (APEC)

Strasbourg:
Council of Europe
European Parliament

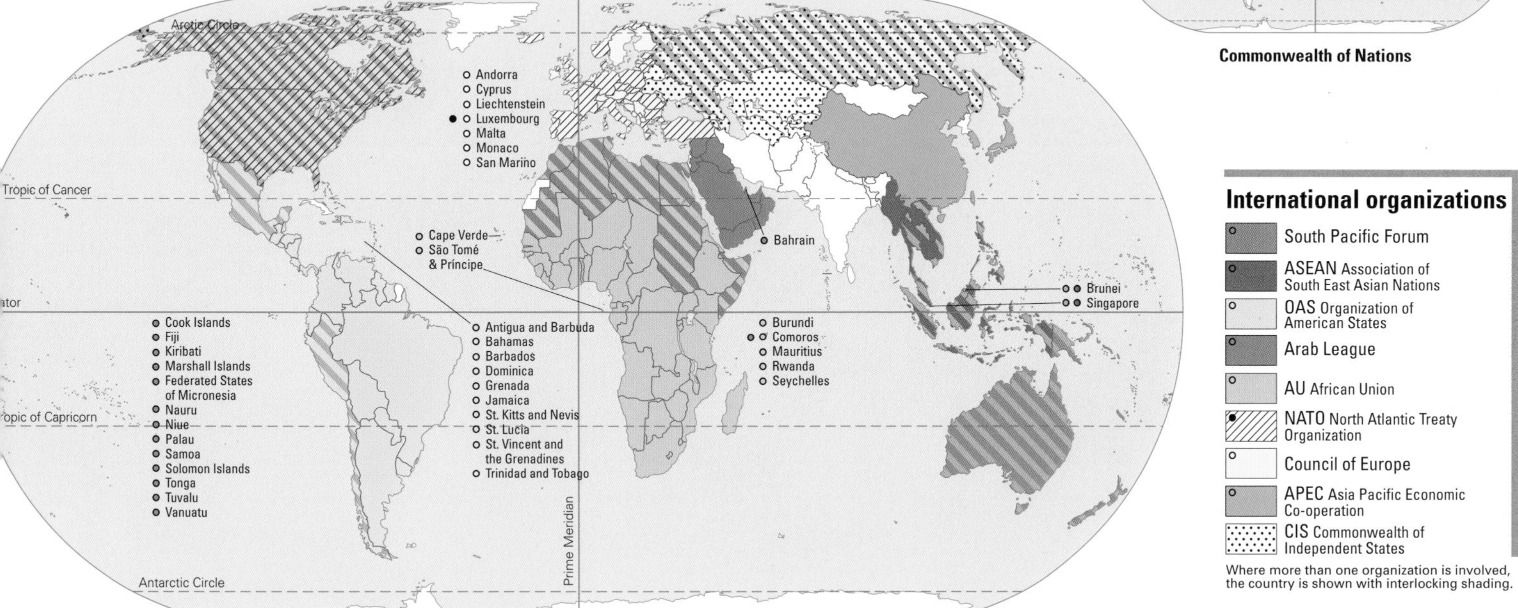

International organizations

- South Pacific Forum
- ASEAN Association of South East Asian Nations
- OAS Organization of American States
- Arab League
- AU African Union
- NATO North Atlantic Treaty Organization
- Council of Europe
- APEC Asia Pacific Economic Co-operation
- CIS Commonwealth of Independent States

Where more than one organization is involved, the country is shown with interlocking shading.

Time zones

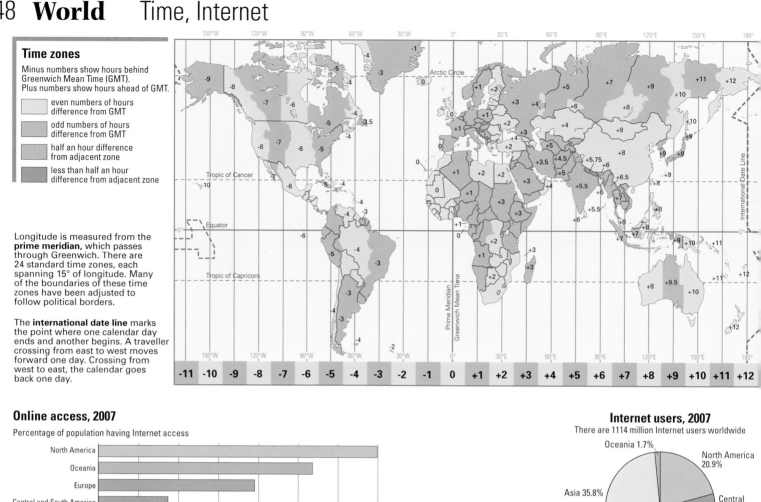

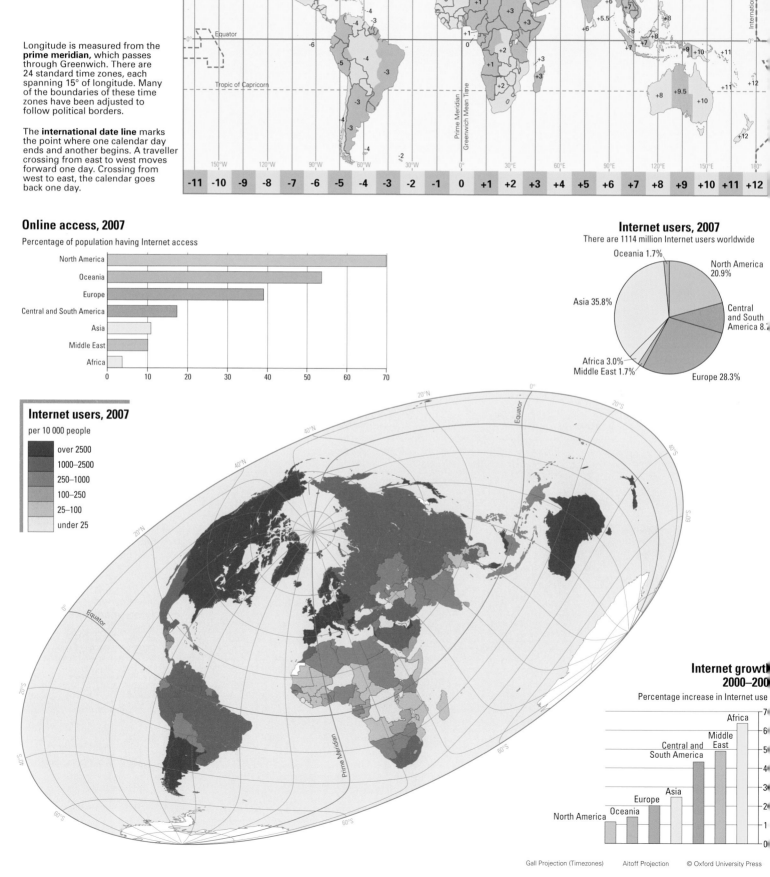

Minus numbers show hours behind Greenwich Mean Time (GMT).
Plus numbers show hours ahead of GMT.

- even numbers of hours difference from GMT
- odd numbers of hours difference from GMT
- half an hour difference from adjacent zone
- less than half an hour difference from adjacent zone

Longitude is measured from the **prime meridian,** which passes through Greenwich. There are 24 standard time zones, each spanning 15° of longitude. Many of the boundaries of these time zones have been adjusted to follow political borders.

The **international date line** marks the point where one calendar day ends and another begins. A traveller crossing from east to west moves forward one day. Crossing from west to east, the calendar goes back one day.

-11 -10 -9 -8 -7 -6 -5 -4 -3 -2 -1 0 +1 +2 +3 +4 +5 +6 +7 +8 +9 +10 +11 +12

Online access, 2007

Percentage of population having Internet access

North America
Oceania
Europe
Central and South America
Asia
Middle East
Africa

0 10 20 30 40 50 60 70

Internet users, 2007

There are 1114 million Internet users worldwide

Oceania 1.7%
North America 20.9%
Central and South America 8.7
Europe 28.3%
Middle East 1.7%
Africa 3.0%
Asia 35.8%

Internet users, 2007

per 10 000 people

- over 2500
- 1000–2500
- 250–1000
- 100–250
- 25–100
- under 25

Internet growth 2000–200

Percentage increase in Internet use

North America
Oceania
Europe
Asia
Central and South America
Middle East
Africa

Gall Projection (Timezones) Aitoff Projection

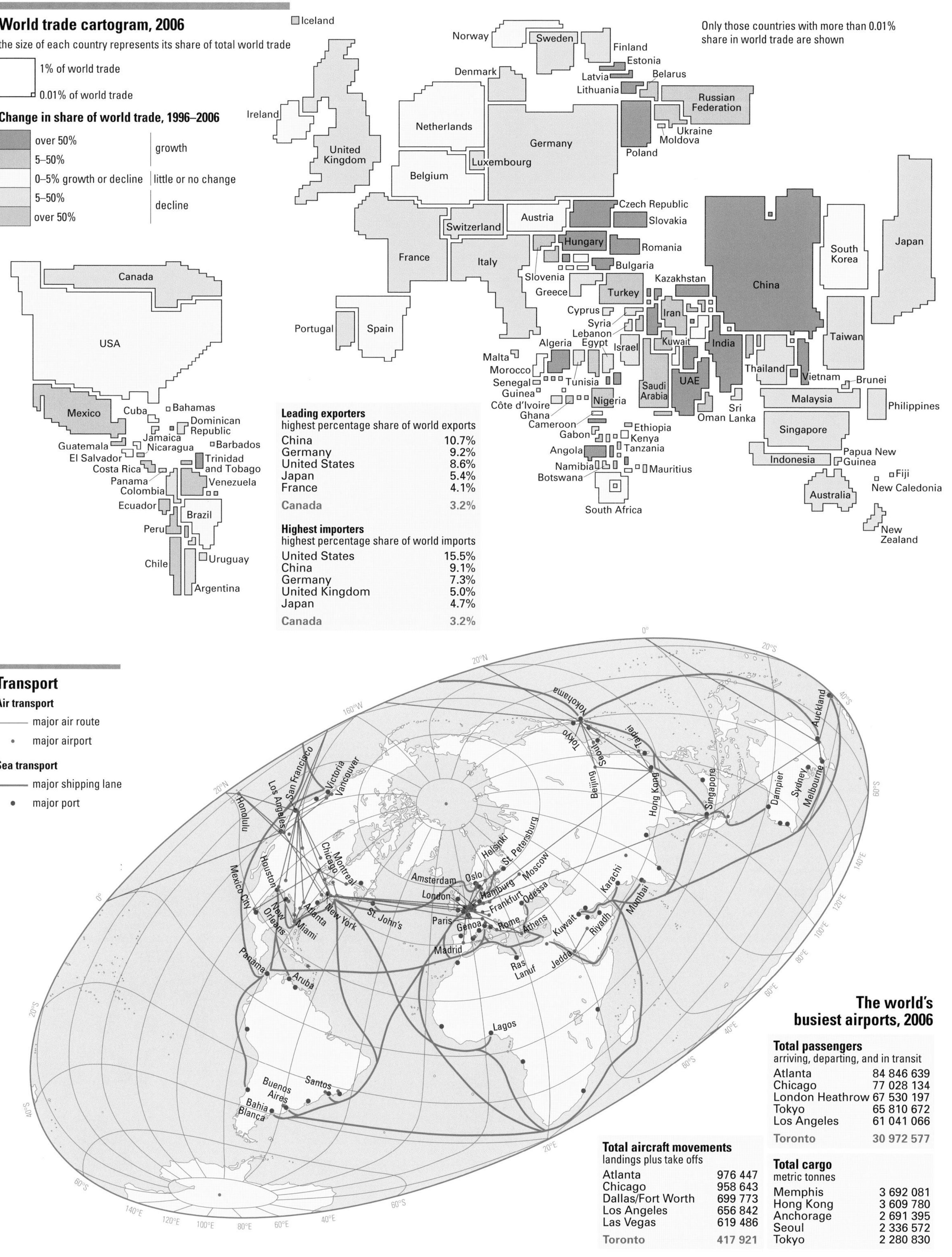

Leading exporters
highest percentage share of world exports

China	10.7%
Germany	9.2%
United States	8.6%
Japan	5.4%
France	4.1%
Canada	3.2%

Highest importers
highest percentage share of world imports

United States	15.5%
China	9.1%
Germany	7.3%
United Kingdom	5.0%
Japan	4.7%
Canada	3.2%

The world's busiest airports, 2006

Total passengers
arriving, departing, and in transit

Atlanta	84 846 639
Chicago	77 028 134
London Heathrow	67 530 197
Tokyo	65 810 672
Los Angeles	61 041 066
Toronto	30 972 577

Total aircraft movements
landings plus take offs

Atlanta	976 447
Chicago	958 643
Dallas/Fort Worth	699 773
Los Angeles	656 842
Las Vegas	619 486
Toronto	417 921

Total cargo
metric tonnes

Memphis	3 692 081
Hong Kong	3 609 780
Anchorage	2 691 395
Seoul	2 336 572
Tokyo	2 280 830

 Oblique Aitoff Projection

Scale 1: 125 000 000 (main map)

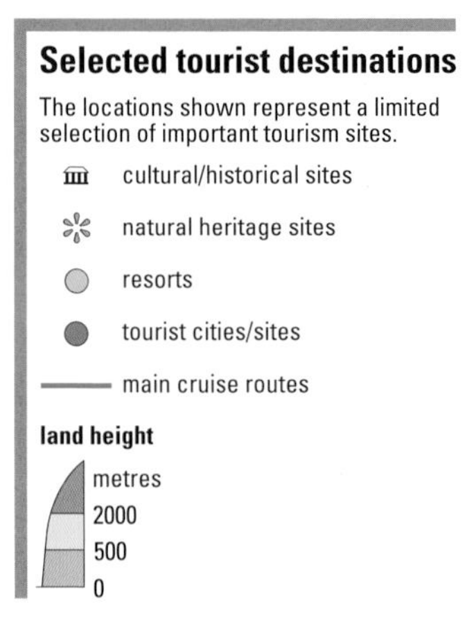

Arctic Circle
Klulane/Wrangell National Parks
Canadian Rocky Mountains Parks
Whistler
Vancouver
Yellowstone
Muskoka-Haliburton
Québec City
Gros Morne National Park
Toronto
Montréal
Boston
Chicago
New York
Washington D.C.
Yosemite
San Francisco
Grand Canyon
California coast
Las Vegas
Myrtle Beach
New Orleans
Bermuda
Disneyland
Miami Beach
Everglades
Miami
Azores
Madeira
Marrakesh
Canary Islands
Tropic of Cancer
Hawaii Volcanoes
Maya sites
Sian Ka'an
Jamaica
Leeward Islands
Acapulco
Barbados
Timbukt
Gambia coast
Cartagena
Panama Canal
Equator
Quito
Galapagos Islands
Amazon
Lima
Machu Picchu
Discovery Coast Atlantic Forest Reserves
Tahiti
Ouro Preto
Rio de Janeiro
Tropic of Capricorn
Iguaçu
Valparaíso
Buenos Aires
Falkland Islands
Cape Horn
Antarctic Circle

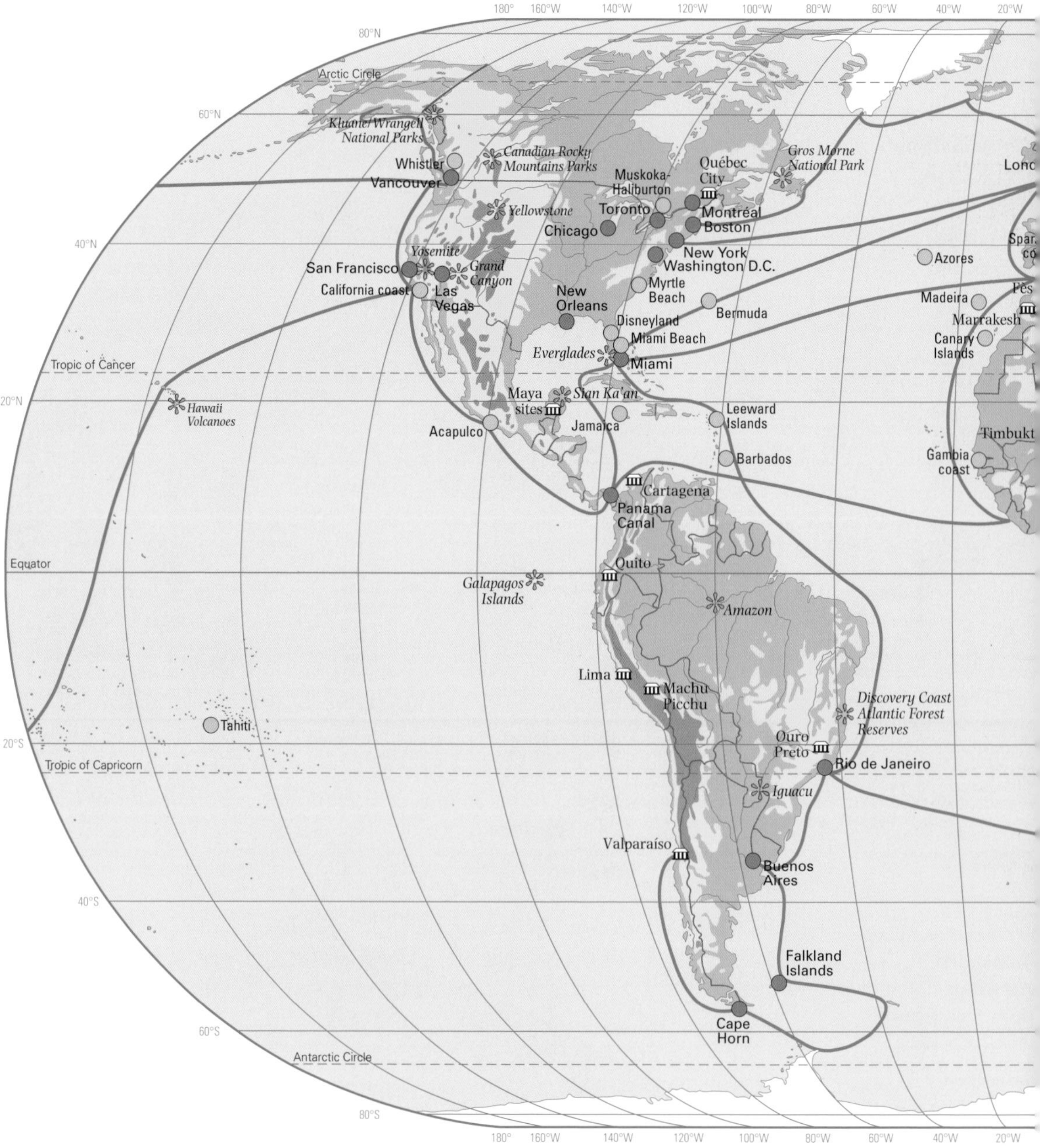

Top tourist destinations, 2006

	arrivals (000)	% change 2005–2006
France	79 100	4.2
Spain	58 500	4.5
USA	51 100	3.8
China	49 600	6.0
Italy	41 100	12.4
United Kingdom	30 700	9.3
Germany	23 600	9.6
Mexico	21 400	-2.6
Austria	20 300	1.5
Russia	20 200	1.3
Canada	**18 300**	**-2.7**

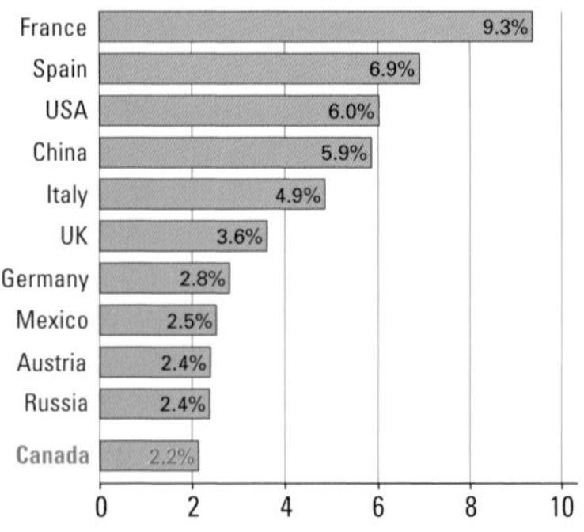

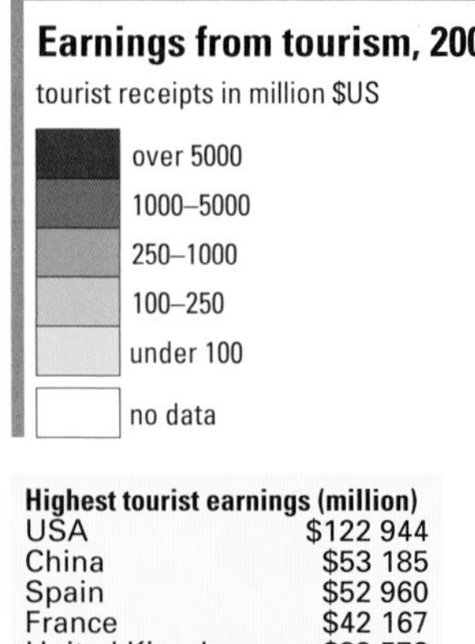

Highest tourist earnings (million)	
USA	$122 944
China	$53 185
Spain	$52 960
France	$42 167
United Kingdom	$39 573
Canada	**$15 830**

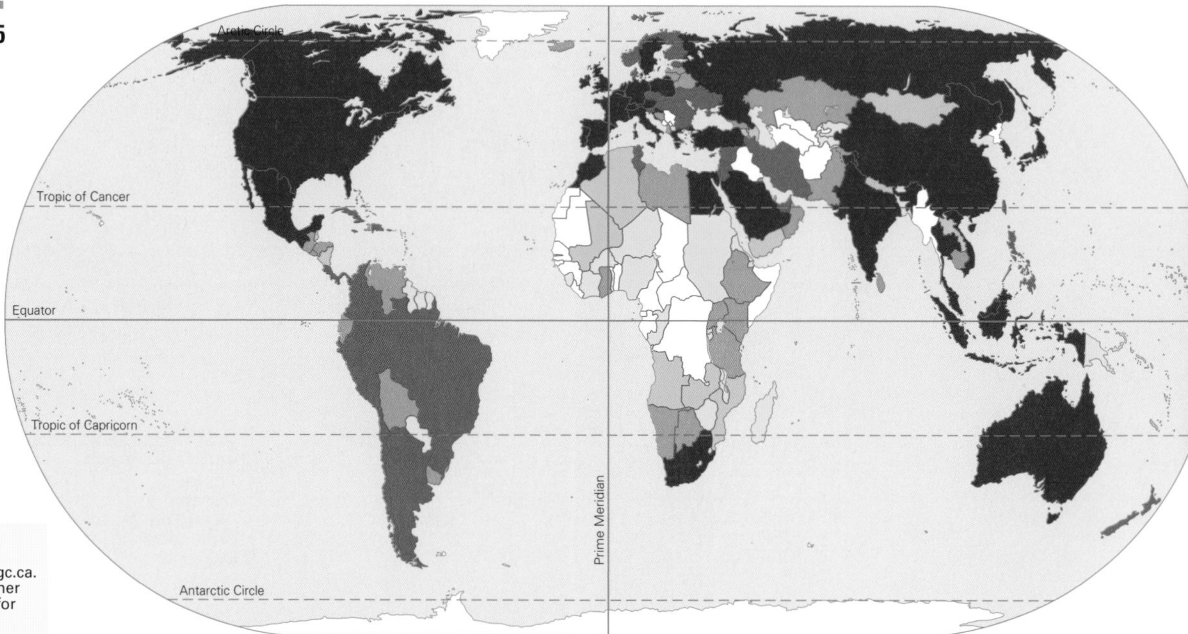

The government of Canada maintains a regularly updated travel advisory for all countries of the world at www.voyage.gc.ca. In February 2008, warnings to avoid either non-essential or all travel were posted for 58 countries.

Eckert IV Projection

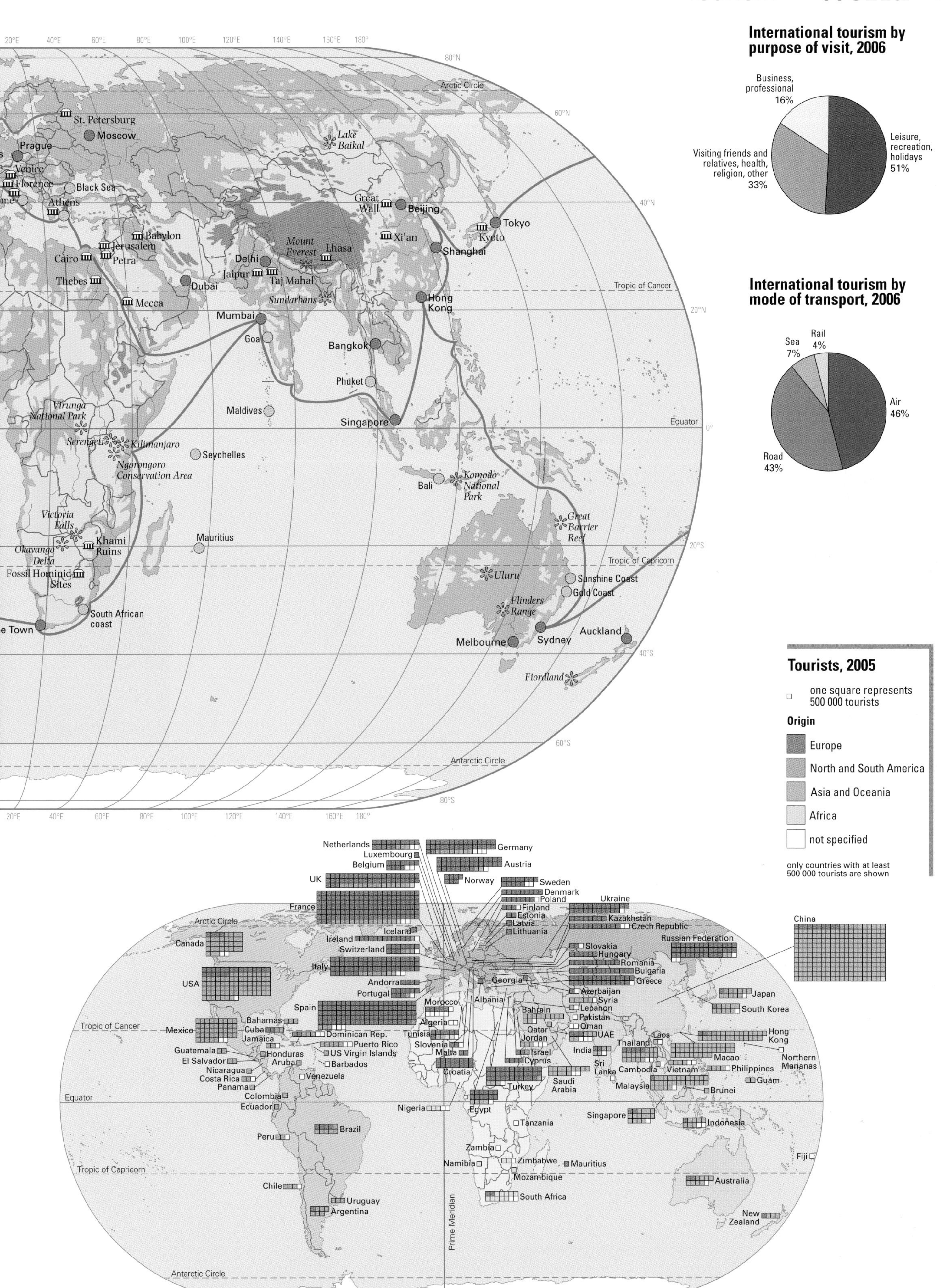
International tourism by purpose of visit, 2006
Business, professional 16%
Leisure, recreation, holidays 51%
Visiting friends and relatives, health, religion, other 33%
International tourism by mode of transport, 2006
Rail 4%
Sea 7%
Air 46%
Road 43%
Tourists, 2005
one square represents 500 000 tourists
Origin
Europe
North and South America
Asia and Oceania
Africa
not specified
only countries with at least 500 000 tourists are shown
St. Petersburg
Moscow
Prague
Venice
Florence
Black Sea
Athens
Lake Baikal
Great Wall
Beijing
Tokyo
Kyoto
Xi'an
Shanghai
Babylon
Jerusalem
Petra
Cairo
Thebes
Mecca
Dubai
Delhi
Jaipur
Taj Mahal
Mount Everest
Lhasa
Sundarbans
Hong Kong
Mumbai
Goa
Bangkok
Phuket
Maldives
Singapore
Virunga National Park
Serengeti
Kilimanjaro
Ngorongoro Conservation Area
Seychelles
Bali
Komodo National Park
Victoria Falls
Okavango Delta
Khami Ruins
Mauritius
Fossil Hominid Sites
South African coast
Great Barrier Reef
Uluru
Sunshine Coast
Gold Coast
Flinders Range
Sydney
Melbourne
Auckland
Fiordland
Arctic Circle
Tropic of Cancer
Equator
Tropic of Capricorn
Antarctic Circle
Netherlands
Luxembourg
Belgium
UK
France
Iceland
Ireland
Switzerland
Italy
Andorra
Portugal
Spain
Germany
Austria
Norway
Sweden
Denmark
Poland
Finland
Estonia
Latvia
Lithuania
Ukraine
Kazakhstan
Czech Republic
Russian Federation
Slovakia
Hungary
Romania
Bulgaria
Greece
Georgia
Azerbaijan
Syria
Lebanon
Pakistan
Oman
UAE
Bahrain
Qatar
Jordan
Israel
Cyprus
Saudi Arabia
Turkey
Egypt
Albania
Morocco
Algeria
Tunisia
Slovenia
Malta
Croatia
Nigeria
Tanzania
Zambia
Namibia
Zimbabwe
Mauritius
Mozambique
South Africa
China
Japan
South Korea
Hong Kong
Northern Marianas
Laos
Thailand
Macao
Philippines
Vietnam
Cambodia
Guam
India
Sri Lanka
Malaysia
Brunei
Singapore
Indonesia
Fiji
Australia
New Zealand
Canada
USA
Mexico
Bahamas
Cuba
Jamaica
Dominican Rep.
Puerto Rico
US Virgin Islands
Barbados
Guatemala
El Salvador
Honduras
Aruba
Nicaragua
Costa Rica
Panama
Venezuela
Colombia
Ecuador
Peru
Brazil
Chile
Uruguay
Argentina
Prime Meridian

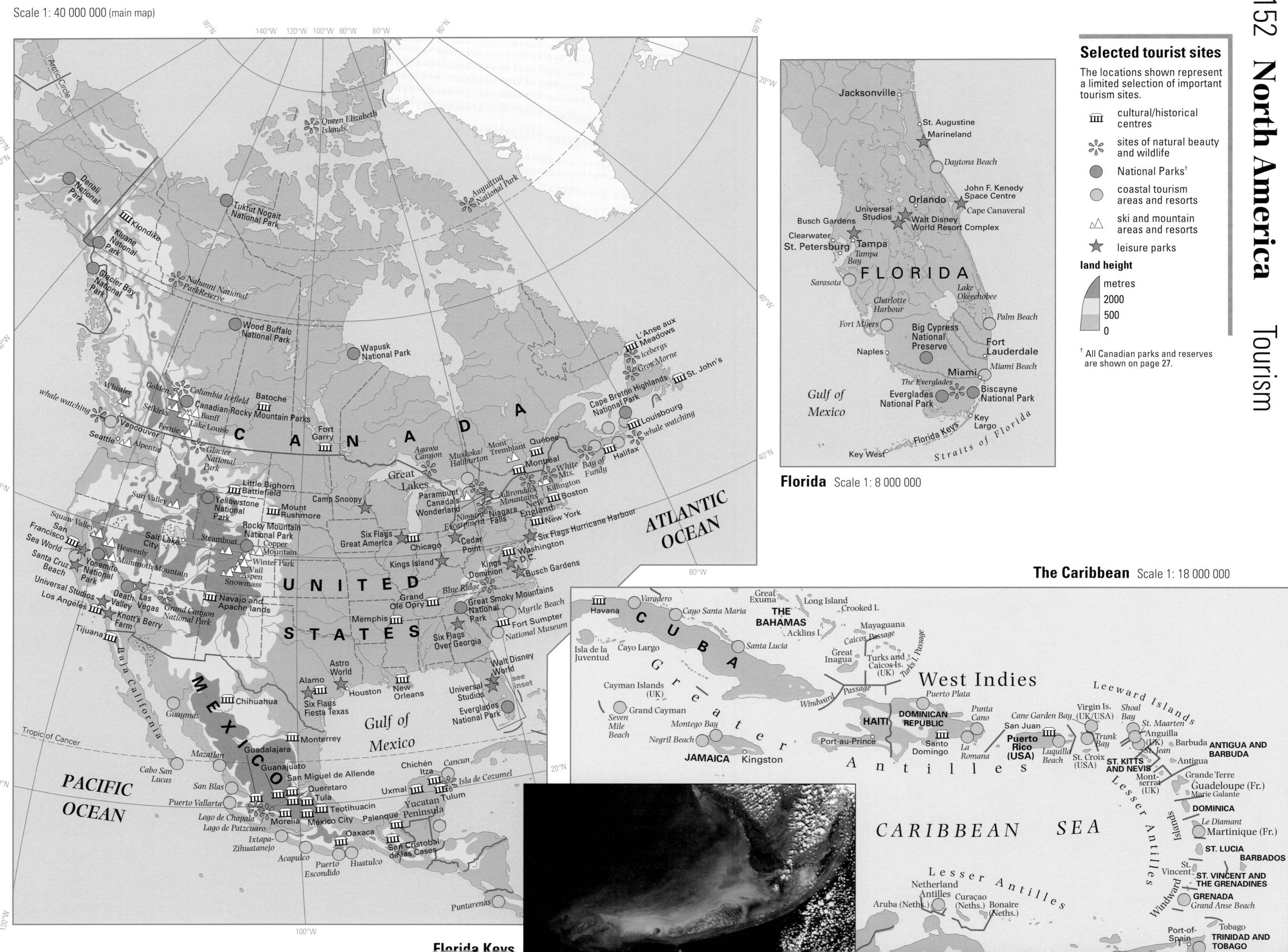
Selected tourist sites
The locations shown represent a limited selection of important tourism sites.
cultural/historical centres
sites of natural beauty and wildlife
National Parks†
coastal tourism areas and resorts
ski and mountain areas and resorts
leisure parks
land height
metres
2000
500
0
† All Canadian parks and reserves are shown on page 27.
Scale 1: 40 000 000 (main map)
Florida Scale 1: 8 000 000
The Caribbean Scale 1: 18 000 000
CANADA
UNITED STATES
MEXICO
ATLANTIC OCEAN
PACIFIC OCEAN
Gulf of Mexico
Great Lakes
Baja California
Yucatan Peninsula
Tropic of Cancer
Arctic Circle
Denali National Park
Klondike
Kluane National Park
Glacier Bay National Park
Tuktut Nogait National Park
Nahanni National Park Reserve
Wood Buffalo National Park
Wapusk National Park
Queen Elizabeth Islands
Auyuittuq National Park
L'Anse aux Meadows
Icebergs
Gros Morne
St. John's
Cape Breton Highlands National Park
Louisbourg
whale watching
Halifax
Bay of Fundy
Québec
Mont Tremblant
Montreal
White Mts.
Killington
Boston
New England
New York
Six Flags Hurricane Harbour
Washington D.C.
Busch Gardens
Kings Dominion
Great Smoky Mountains National Park
Myrtle Beach
Fort Sumpter National Museum
Six Flags Over Georgia
Walt Disney World
Universal Studios
Everglades National Park
see inset
Whistler
Golden
Selkirks
Columbia Icefield
Canadian Rocky Mountain Parks
Banff
Lake Louise
Fernie
Vancouver
Seattle
Alpental
Glacier National Park
Batoche
Fort Garry
Agawa Canyon
Muskoka/ Haliburton
Paramount Canada's Wonderland
Niagara Escarpment
Niagara Falls
Adirondack Mountains
Camp Snoopy
Six Flags Great America
Chicago
Cedar Point
Kings Island
Blue Ridge
Grand Ole Opry
Memphis
New Orleans
Houston
Astro World
Alamo
Six Flags Fiesta Texas
Little Bighorn Battlefield
Mount Rushmore
Yellowstone National Park
Rocky Mountain National Park
Copper Mountain
Winter Park
Vail
Aspen
Snowmass
Steamboat
Sun Valley
Salt Lake City
Squaw Valley
San Francisco
Sea World
Santa Cruz Beach
Heavenly
Yosemite National Park
Mammoth Mountain
Universal Studios
Los Angeles
Death Valley
Las Vegas
Knott's Berry Farm
Grand Canyon National Park
Navajo and Apache lands
Tijuana
Chihuahua
Guaymas
Mazatlán
Cabo San Lucas
Monterrey
Guadalajara
Guanajuato
San Miguel de Allende
Queretaro
Tula
Teotihuacán
México City
Morelia
San Blas
Puerto Vallarta
Lago de Chapala
Lago de Patzcuaro
Ixtapa-Zihuatanejo
Acapulco
Puerto Escondido
Oaxaca
Huatulco
San Cristobal de las Cases
Palenque
Uxmal
Chichén Itza
Cancun
Isla de Cozumel
Tulum
Puntarenas
Jacksonville
St. Augustine
Marineland
Daytona Beach
John F. Kenedy Space Centre
Cape Canaveral
Orlando
Universal Studios
Walt Disney World Resort Complex
Busch Gardens
Clearwater
St. Petersburg
Tampa
Tampa Bay
FLORIDA
Sarasota
Charlotte Harbour
Lake Okeechobee
Palm Beach
Fort Myers
Big Cypress National Preserve
Fort Lauderdale
Naples
Miami Beach
Miami
The Everglades
Everglades National Park
Biscayne National Park
Key Largo
Florida Keys
Key West
Straits of Florida
Havana
Varadero
CUBA
Cayo Santa Maria
Great Exuma
Long Island
Crooked I.
THE BAHAMAS
Acklins I.
Mayaguana
Caicos Passage
Isla de la Juventud
Cayo Largo
Santa Lucia
Great Inagua
Turks and Caicos Is. (UK)
Turks I. Passage
Cayman Islands (UK)
Grand Cayman
Seven Mile Beach
Greater Antilles
Windward Passage
West Indies
Puerto Plata
HAITI
DOMINICAN REPUBLIC
Punta Cano
Montego Bay
Negril Beach
JAMAICA
Kingston
Port-au-Prince
Santo Domingo
La Romana
Cane Garden Bay
San Juan
Puerto Rico (USA)
Luquillo Beach
Virgin Is. (UK/USA)
Trunk Bay
St. Croix (USA)
Shoal Bay
St. Maarten
Anguilla (UK)
St. Jean
Barbuda
ANTIGUA AND BARBUDA
Antigua
ST. KITTS AND NEVIS
Montserrat (UK)
Leeward Islands
Lesser Antilles
Grande Terre
Guadeloupe (Fr.)
Marie Galante
DOMINICA
Le Diamant
Martinique (Fr.)
Windward Islands
ST. LUCIA
BARBADOS
St. Vincent
ST. VINCENT AND THE GRENADINES
GRENADA
Grand Anse Beach
Tobago
TRINIDAD AND TOBAGO
Port-of-Spain
CARIBBEAN SEA
Netherland Antilles
Aruba (Neths.)
Curaçao (Neths.)
Bonaire (Neths.)
Florida Keys

Selected tourist sites
The locations shown represent a limited selection of important tourism sites.
Tuscany sites of natural beauty
cultural/historical centres
archaeological sites
coastal tourism areas and resorts
ski and mountain areas and resorts
leisure parks
land height
metres
2000
500
0
Flight times from London
typical non-stop flight times, 2007
hours
4
Moscow
Istanbul
Athens
3
Helsinki
Lisbon
Rome
Vienna
Madrid
Stockholm
2
Prague
Copenhagen
Berlin
Dublin
Amsterdam
Edinburgh
Paris
Brussels
1
45 minutes
30 minutes
15 minutes
0
London
ATLANTIC OCEAN
NORTH SEA
BALTIC SEA
BLACK SEA
AEGEAN SEA
IONIAN SEA
ADRIATIC SEA
MEDITERRANEAN SEA
FINLAND
RUSSIA
ESTONIA
LATVIA
LITHUANIA
BELARUS
UKRAINE
MOLDOVA
ROMANIA
BULGARIA
TURKEY
GREECE
FYRO MACEDONIA
ALBANIA
KOSOVO
SERBIA
MONTENEGRO
BOSNIA-HERZEGOVINA
CROATIA
SLOVENIA
HUNGARY
SLOVAKIA
POLAND
CZECH REPUBLIC
AUSTRIA
GERMANY
DENMARK
NORWAY
SWEDEN
NETHERLANDS
BELGIUM
LUXEMBOURG
LIECHTENSTEIN
SWITZERLAND
ITALY
SAN MARINO
MONACO
FRANCE
ANDORRA
SPAIN
PORTUGAL
UNITED KINGDOM
REPUBLIC OF IRELAND
Conical Orthomorphic Projection

Scale 1: 55 000 000 (main map)

Selected tourist sites

The locations shown represent a limited selection of important tourism sites.

- cultural/historical centres
- archaeological sites
- sites of natural beauty
- National Parks and wildlife reserves
- coastal tourism areas and resorts

land height

metres
2000
500
0

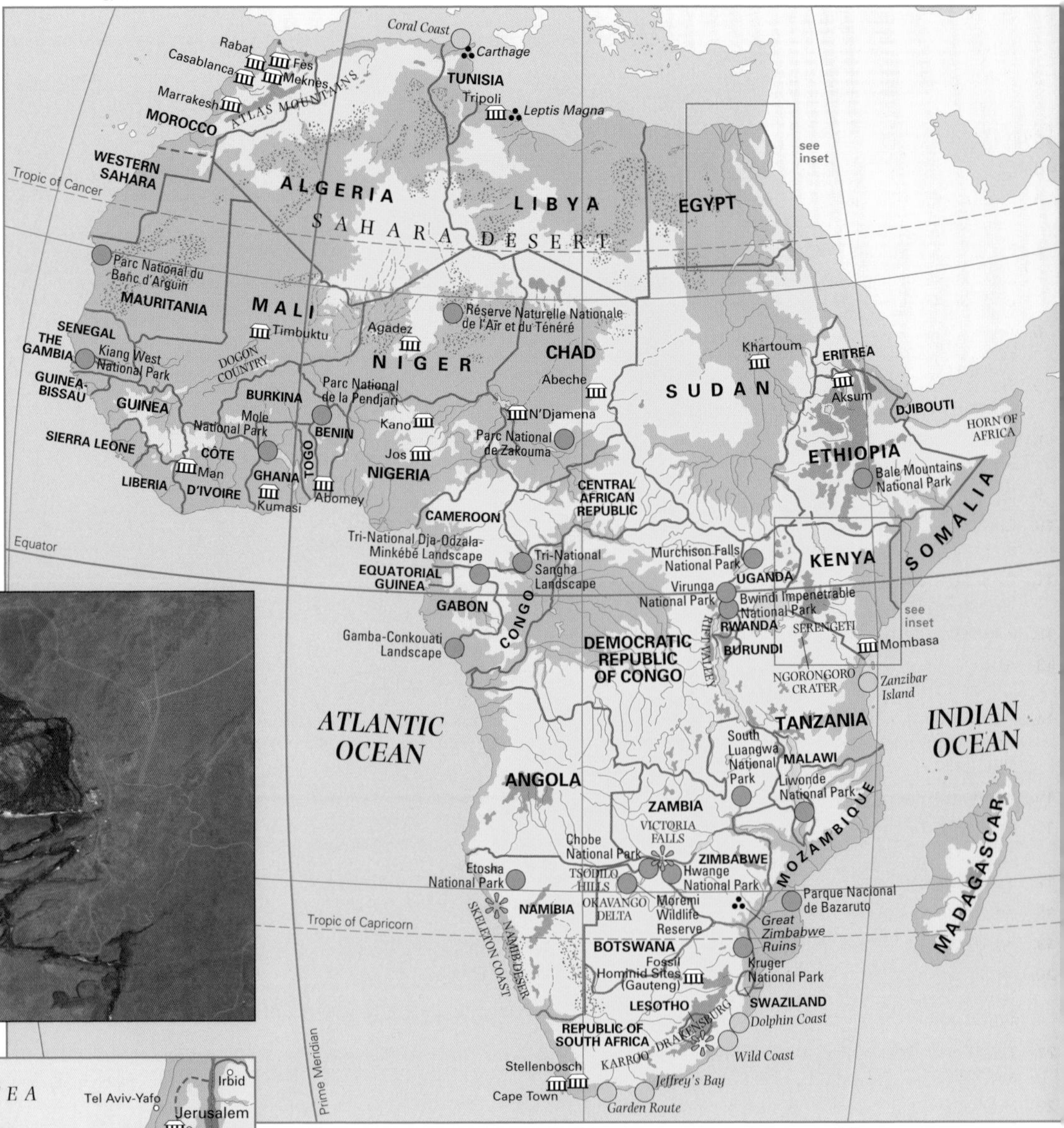

Victoria Falls

The wide Zambezi River, flowing from the top-left of the image, suddenly plunges 130 metres into the narrow gorge below. The tourist town of Victoria Falls (V) can be seen near the gorge.

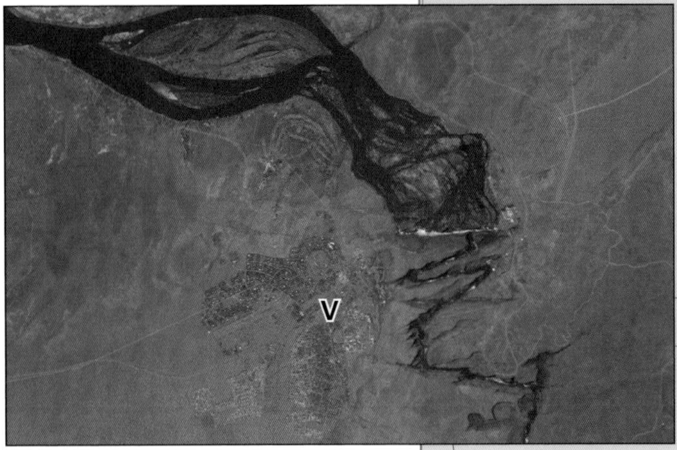

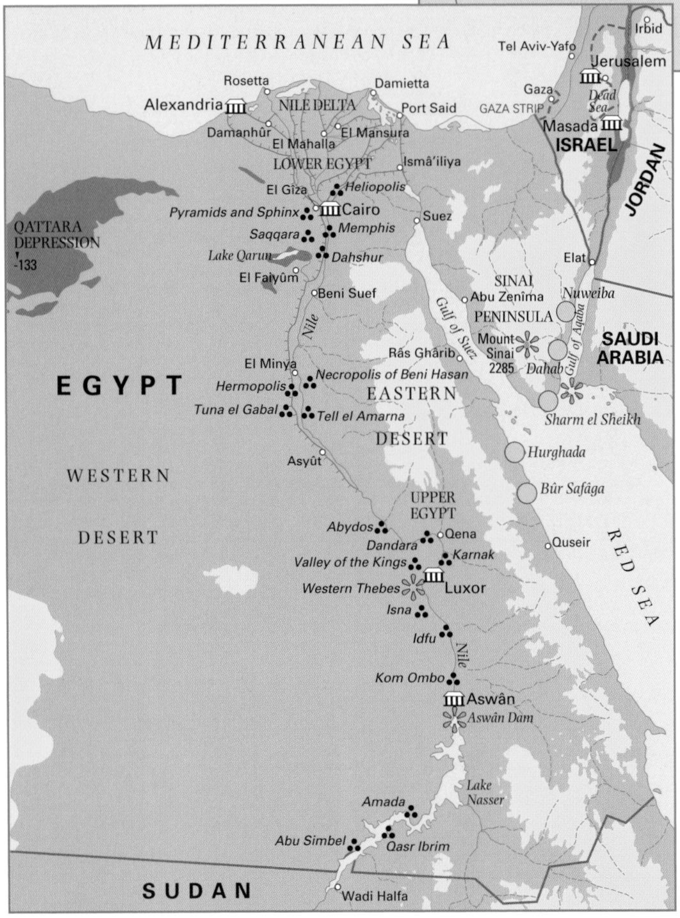

Nile Valley and Eastern Egypt Scale 1: 10 000 000

Kenya Scale 1: 10 000 000

Zenithal Equal Area Projection

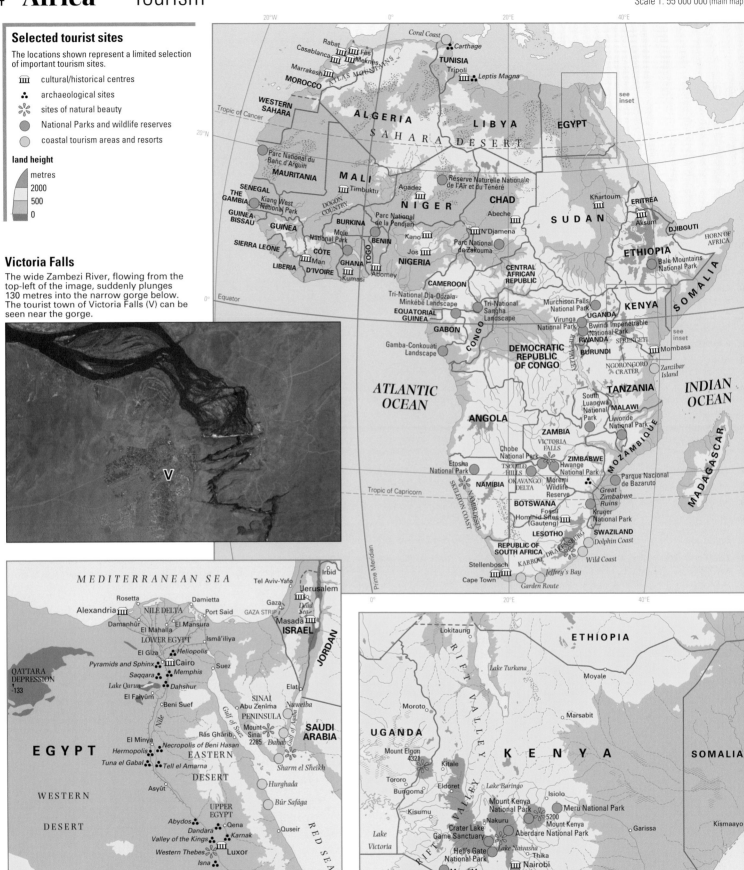

Land

Population

Agriculture

Forestry and Fishing

Mining

Energy

Manufacturing

Trade

The Economy

Transportation and Tourism

Environment

Climate

Land

1. Land and Freshwater Area

Province or Territory	Total Area (km²)	Land (km²)	Fresh Water (km²)	% of Total Area
Newfoundland & Labrador	405 212	373 872	31 340	4.1
Prince Edward Island	5 660	5 660	–	0.1
Nova Scotia	55 284	53 338	1 946	0.6
New Brunswick	72 908	71 450	1 458	0.7
Quebéc	1 542 056	1 365 128	176 928	15.4
Ontario	1 076 395	917 741	158 654	10.8
Manitoba	647 797	553 556	94 241	6.5
Saskatchewan	651 036	591 670	59 366	6.5
Alberta	661 848	642 317	19 531	6.6
British Columbia	944 735	925 186	19 549	9.5
Yukon	482 443	474 391	8 052	4.8
Northwest Territories	1 346 106	1 183 085	163 021	13.5
Nunavut	2 093 190	1 936 113	157 077	21.0
Canada	**9 984 670**	**9 093 507**	**891 163**	**100.0**

SOURCE: Adapted from Natural Resources Canada, "Facts about Canada—Land and Freshwater Areas" http://atlas.nrcan.gc.ca/site/english/learningresources/facts/surfareas.html. 2001 data courtesy of Natural Resouces Canada, Canada Centre for Remote Sensing.

2. Primary Land Cover in Canada

Land Cover Class	Predominant Cover in the Class	Area[1] (000 km²)	% of Canada Total
Forest and taiga	Closed canopy forest and/or open stands of trees with secondary occurrences of wetland, barren land, or others	4 218	42.2
Tundra/sparse vegetation	Well-vegetated to sparsely vegetated or barren land, mostly in arctic or alpine environments	2 303	23.0
Wetland	Treed and non-treed fens, bogs, swamps, marshes, shallow open water, and coastal and shore marshes	1 396	14.0
Fresh water	Lakes, rivers, streams, and reservoirs	891	8.9
Cropland	Cropland, pasture land and orchards	681	6.6
Rangeland	Generally nonfenced pasture land, grazing land; includes natural grassland that is not necessarily used for agriculture	203	2.0
Ice/snow	Permanent ice and snow fields (glaciers, ice caps)	199	2.0
Built-up	Urban and industrial land	94	1.0
Total		**9 985**	**100.0**

NOTE: Data for this table are derived from satellite imagery and may deviate slightly from other sources of data.
[1]Includes the area of all land and fresh water.
SOURCE: Derived from a variety of sources (1991 to 2002), including: Environment Canada, *The State of Canada's Environment*, 1996

Population

3. Total Population Growth, 1851 to 2006

Year	Population (000)	Average Annual Rate of Population Growth (%)
1851	2 436.3	–
1861	3 229.6	2.9
1871	3 689.3	1.3
1881	4 324.8	1.6
1891	4 833.2	1.1
1901	5 371.3	1.1
1911	7 206.6	3.0
1921	8 787.9	2.0
1931	10 376.8	1.7
1941	11 506.7	1.0
1951[1]	14 009.4	1.7
1961	18 238.2	2.5
1971	21 568.3	1.5
1981	24 343.2	1.1
1991	27 296.9	1.5
2001	30 007.1	1.0
2006	31 612.9	1.1

— = nil
NOTE: On 1 January 2008, Statistics Canada estimated Canada's population to be 33 143 610.
[1]Newfoundland included for the first time. [2]Data from Statistics Canada 2001 Census.
SOURCE: Adapted from Statistics Canada, *Canada Year Book*, Catalogue 11-402, 1992; Census of Canada, various years.

4. Components of Population Growth, 1960 to 2006

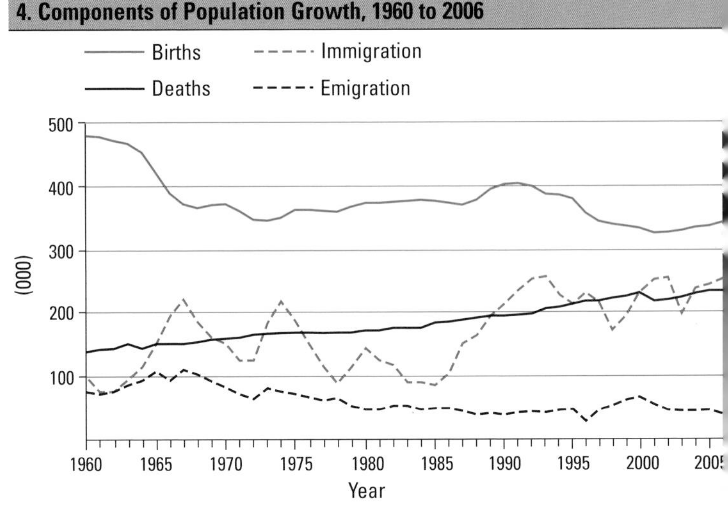

SOURCE: Adapted from Statistics Canada, *Annual Demographic Estimates: Canada Provinces and Territories* 2005-2006, Catalogue 91-215, tables 4.1 -4.4, 27 September 2006, http://www.statcan.ca/english/freepub/91-215-XIE/91-215-XIE2006000.pdf

5. Population Growth, 1961, 1971, 1981, 1991, 2001, 2006, and Population Density, 2006, by Province and Territory

Province or Territory	1961	1971	1981	1991	2001	2006	Population Density (km²) 2006
Newfoundland & Labrador	457 853	522 104	567 181	568 474	512 930	505 469	1.4
Prince Edward Island	104 629	111 641	122 506	129 765	135 294	135 851	23.9
Nova Scotia	737 007	788 960	847 882	899 942	908 007	913 462	17.3
New Brunswick	597 936	634 557	696 403	723 900	729 498	729 997	10.2
Québec	5 259 211	6 027 764	6 438 403	6 895 963	7 237 479	7 546 131	5.6
Ontario	6 236 092	7 703 106	8 625 107	10 084 885	11 410 046	12 160 282	13.4
Manitoba	921 686	988 247	1 026 241	1 091 942	1 119 583	1 148 401	2.1
Saskatchewan	925 181	926 242	968 313	988 928	978 933	968 157	1.6
Alberta	1 331 944	1 627 874	2 237 724	2 545 553	2 974 807	3 290 350	5.1
British Columbia	1 629 082	2 184 021	2 744 467	3 282 061	3 907 738	4 113 487	4.4
Yukon	14 628	18 388	23 153	27 797	28 674	30 372	0.06
Northwest Territories	22 998	34 807	45 741	57 649	37 360	41 464	0.04
Nunavut	n.a.	n.a.	n.a.	n.a.	26 745	29 474	0.02
Canada	**18 238 247**	**21 568 310**	**24 343 181**	**27 296 859**	**30 007 094**	**31 612 897**	**3.5**

n.a. = not available
SOURCE: Adapted from Statistics Canada: *Canada Year Book*, Catalogue 11-402, various years; "A National Overview—Population and Dwelling Counts", 1996 Census of Population, Catalogue 93-357, April 1997; "Population and Dwelling Counts" 2006 Census, Catalogue 97-550-XWE2006002, July 2007, http://www.statcan.ca/bsolc/english/bsolc?catno=97-550-X2006002; Census of Canada, various years.

6. Approximate Geographic Distribution of the Population

Selected Parallels of Latitude	%
South of 49°	70.0
Between 49° and 54°	27.6
Between 54° and 60°	2.1
North of 60°	0.3
Selected Distances North of Canada–US Border	
0–150 km	72.0
151–300 km	13.4
301–600 km	10.4
Over 600 km	4.2

OURCE: Adapted from Statistics Canada, "Census of Population", 1986 Census.

7. Percentage of People Who are Bilingual (English and French), 1971, 1981, 2006

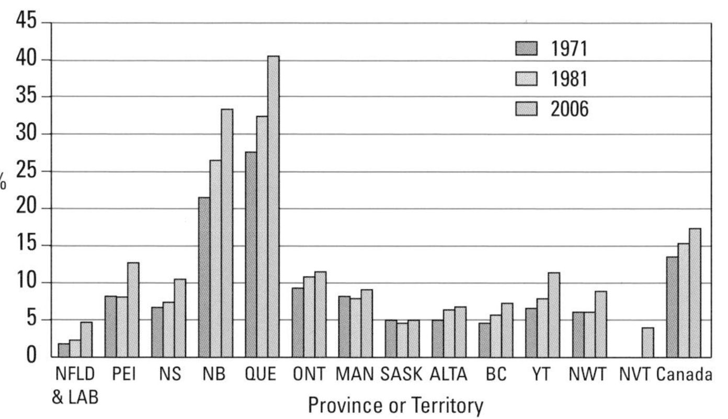

OURCE: Adapted from Statistics Canada, *The Daily*, Catalogue 11-001, 2 December 1997, http://www.statcan. a/Daily/English/971202/d971202.htm; and "Detailed Mother Tongue (186), Knowledge of Official Languages (5), ge Groups (17A) and Sex (3) for the Population of Canada, Provinces, Territories, Census Metropolitan Areas nd Census Agglomerations, 2001 and 2006 Censuses", Catalogue 97-555-XCB2006015, 4 December, 2007, ttp://www.statcan.ca/bsolc/english/bsolc?catno=97-555-X2006015.

8. Population by Mother Tongue,[1] 1991, 2001, 2006

Official Language	1991	2001	2006
English	16 169 875	17 352 315	18 232 200
French	6 502 860	6 703 325	6 970 405
Non-Official Language			
Chinese	498 845	853 745	1 034 085
Indo-European[2]	301 335	627 860	1 018 960
Italian	510 990	469 485	476 905
German	466 245	438 080	466 655
Spanish	177 425	245 500	362 120
Arabic	107 750	199 940	286 790
Tagalog (Filipino)	99 715	174 060	266 445
Portuguese	212 090	213 815	229 280
Aboriginal[3]	172 610	187 675	222 185
Polish	189 815	208 375	217 605
Vietnamese	78 570	122 055	146 410
Ukrainian	187 010	148 090	141 805
Russian	35 300	94 555	136 235
Dutch	149 870	128 670	133 240
Korean	36 185	85 070	128 120
Greek	126 205	120 365	123 575
Romanian	–	–	80 245
Hungarian	79 770	75 555	75 595
Total single response	26 686 850	29 257 885	30 848 270
Total multiple response	307 190	381 145	392 760
Canada	**26 994 045**	**29 639 035**	**31 241 030**

NOTE: Data is listed in order of 2006 population values.

[1]The mother tongue is the language learned at home in childhood and still understood by the individual at the time of the census. Also note that "mother tongue" is the official term used in the census.

[2]Includes the following principal languages: Panjabi (Punjabi) 382 585; Urdu 156 420; Persian (Farsi) 138 075; Tamil 122 020; Gujarati 86 285; Hindi 85 500; Bengali 48 075. [3]Thirty-six Aboriginal languages are listed separately in the 2006 Census, of which Cree with 84 905 speakers, Inuktitut with 32 580, and Ojibway with 25 575 are the largest.

SOURCE: Adapted from Statistics Canada, "1991 and 2001 Census"; and "Detailed Mother Tongue (148), Single and Multiple Language Responses (3) and Sex (3) for the Population of Canada, Provinces, Territories, Census Metropolitan Areas and Census Agglomerations", 2006 Census, Catalogue 97-555-XCB2006007, 4 December 2007, http://www.statcan.ca/bsolc/english/bsolc?catno=97-555-X2006007.

9. Interprovincial Migration[1], 1976 to 2006

Years	NFLD & LAB	PEI	NS	NB	QUE	ONT	MAN	SASK	ALTA	BC	YT	NWT	NVT[2]
1976-1981	-19 860	-15	-8 420	-8 505	-141 725	-78 070	-43 600	5 820	197 645	110 930	-545	-2 015	n.a.
1981-1986	-16 550	1 540	6 275	1 370	-63 295	99 355	-1 555	-2 830	-27 675	9 515	-2 655	-755	n.a.
1986-1991	-13 945	-850	-4 885	-6 060	-25 560	46 965	-35 260	-60 365	-25 005	125 870	790	-1 695	n.a.
1991-1996	-23 240	1 455	-6 450	-1 950	-37 430	-47 025	-19 390	-19 780	3 575	149 935	685	-465	n.a.
1996-2001	-31 055	135	-1 275	-8 425	-57 315	51 905	-18 560	-24 940	119 420	-23 630	-2 760	-3 170	-330
2001-2006	-15 137	-105	-8 131	-8 683	-20 119	-33 497	-25 646	-37 070	140 272	10 265	-186	-1 774	-386

.a. = not available

)ifference between the number of incoming and outgoing migrants.

Vunavut became a territory in 1999.

OURCE: Adapted from Statistics Canada, 2001 Census: analysis series, Profile of the Canadian population by mobility status: Canada, a nation on the move. Table: Net migrants and net migration rates, provinces and territories, 1976 to 2001 age 20). Catalogue: 96F0030XIE2001006. http://www12.statcan.ca/english/census01/products/analytic/companion/mob/pdf/96F0030XIE2001006.pdf.

10. Births, Deaths, Migration, Infant Mortality, and Life Expectancy, 2006

Demographic Category	NFLD & LAB	PEI	NS	NB	QUE	ONT	MAN	SASK	ALTA	BC	YT	NWT	NVT	Canada
Birth rate/1000	8.5	9.7	9.0	9.0	10.9	10.6	12.0	12.1	13.4	9.9	10.0	16.0	24.1	10.9
Death rate/1000	8.9	9.3	9.3	8.8	7.3	7.1	8.7	9.2	6.2	7.2	5.8	3.9	4.3	7.3
Number of immigrants (000)	0.5	0.3	2.2	1.4	42.0	133.1	8.9	2.1	19.9	43.9	0.08	0.07	0.01	251.7
Number of emigrants (000)	0.14	0.14	0.8	0.3	6.1	16.6	1.4	0.5	5.3	7.1	0.02	0.02	0.02	38.6
Interprovincial in-migration (000)	10.5	3.4	16.5	12.1	25.6	64.2	14.2	16.0	109.7	55.8	1.5	2.2	1.1	332.8
Interprovincial out-migration (000)	14.9	3.5	20.4	15.9	33.8	85.6	22.9	25.1	52.6	52.0	1.7	3.6	1.0	332.8
Infant mortality rate/1000[1]	5.1	4.3	4.6	4.3	4.6	5.5	7.0	6.2	5.8	4.3	11.0	0.0	16.1	5.3
Life expectancy at birth (in years)[2] M	75	76	76	76	76	77	76	76	77	78	72[3]	72[3]	72[3]	77
F	81	82	81	82	82	82	81	82	82	83	77[3]	77[3]	77[3]	82

004 data. [2]2000–2002 data. [3]Data combined for all three territories.

OURCE: Adapted from Statistics Canada, *Annual Demographic Estimates: Canada Provinces and Territories*, Catalogue 91-215, 2005–2006, pages 27, 29-30, tables 4-3, 4-4, 4-8, 4-9, 27 September 2006, http://www.statcan.ca/english/ eepub/91-215-XIE/91-215-XIE2006000.pdf; "Life Tables, Canada, Provinces and Territories", Catalogue 84-537, tables 2a-13b, http://www.statcan.ca/english/freepub/84-537-XIE/tables.htm; "Deaths and death rate, by province and territory", tp://www40.statcan.ca/l01/cst01/demo07b.htm; & "Births and birth rate, by province and territory", http://www40.statcan.ca/l01/cst01/demo04b.htm.

11. Canadian Family and Household Structure, 2006

Province or Territory	Total Families	Married Families		Common-law Families		Lone-parent Families		% Couples with Children[1]	% Couples without Children[2]	% One-person Households	% Other[3]
		Number	%	Number	%	Number	%				
NFLD & LAB	155 730	114 630	73.6	16 935	10.9	24 165	15.5	30.4	34.0	20.2	15.4
PEI	39 185	28 700	73.2	4 085	10.4	6 400	16.3	29.6	30.9	24.1	15.5
NS	267 415	187 420	70.1	34 705	13.0	45 290	16.9	25.5	31.9	26.5	16.1
NB	217 795	151 210	69.4	30 995	14.2	35 585	16.3	26.9	32.9	24.3	15.9
QUE	2 121 610	1 156 930	54.5	611 855	28.8	352 825	16.6	25.7	28.7	30.7	14.9
ONT	3 422 315	2 530 560	73.9	351 040	10.3	540 715	15.8	31.2	28.3	24.3	16.3
MAN	312 810	225 875	72.2	33 720	10.8	53 210	17.0	27.6	28.2	28.6	15.5
SASK	267 460	194 165	72.6	28 850	10.8	44 445	16.6	26.4	29.9	28.8	14.9
ALTA	904 845	658 900	72.8	115 685	12.8	130 265	14.4	30.5	28.7	24.6	16.3
BC	1 161 425	844 430	72.7	141 830	12.2	175 165	15.1	26.3	29.6	28.0	16.1
YT	8 335	4 640	55.7	1 965	23.6	1 725	20.7	26.1	24.9	30.9	18.2
NWT	10 880	5 555	51.1	2 990	27.5	2 330	21.4	34.4	22.0	21.7	21.9
NVT	7 035	2 890	41.1	2 205	31.3	1 940	27.6	42.0	10.9	18.3	28.8
Canada	**8 896 840**	**6 105 910**	**68.6**	**1 376 870**	**15.5**	**1 414 060**	**15.9**	**28.5**	**29.0**	**26.8**	**15.8**

[1]Refers to households containing a couple with at least one child aged 24 and under at home. [2]Includes households containing a couple with all children aged 25 and over at home. [3]Includes lone-parent households, multiple-family households, and non-family households other than one-person households.
SOURCE: Adapted from Statistics Canada, "Family portrait: Continuity and change in Canadian families and households in 2006: Findings", Analysis Series, 2006 Census, Catalogue 97-553, 12 September 2007, Table 4 and 5, http://www12.statcan.ca/english/census06/analysis/famhouse/provterr.cfm.

12. Population by Sex and Age Group, 2006

Age Group	Total	Male	Female
0–4	1 690 540	864 600	825 940
5–9	1 809 370	926 860	882 515
10–14	2 079 925	1 065 865	1 014 065
15–24	4 220 875	2 143 235	2 077 645
25–34	4 005 805	1 963 660	2 042 145
35–44	4 818 730	2 369 030	2 449 705
45–54	4 977 905	2 449 095	2 528 805
55–64	3 674 490	1 806 530	1 867 960
65–74	2 288 360	1 087 270	1 201 095
75–84	1 526 280	637 905	888 375
85+	520 605	161 920	358 685
Median age[1]	39.5	38.6	40.4
Total	**31 612 895**	**15 475 970**	**16 136 930**

[1]The median age is an age 'x', such that exactly one half of the population is older than 'x' and the other half is younger than 'x'.
SOURCE: Adapted from Statistics Canada, "Age Groups (13) and Sex (3) for the Population of Canada, Provinces and Territories, 1921 to 2006 Censuses", 2006 Census, Catalogue 97-551-XCB2006005, 17 July 2007, http://www.statcan.ca/bsolc/english/bsolc?catno=97-551-X2006005.

14. Population Totals and Future Projection for Age Categories "Less than 15 Years" and "65 Years and Over"

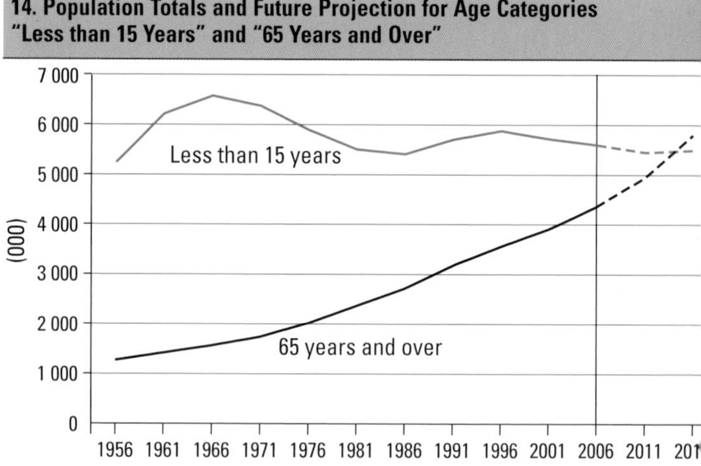

SOURCE: Adapted from Statistics Canada, "Portrait of the Canadian Population in 2006, by Age and Sex: National portrait", Analysis Series, 2006 Census, Catalogue 97-551-XWE2006001, 17 July 2007, Figure 1, http://www12.statcan.ca/english/census06/analysis/agesex/natlportrait1.cfm, accessed 17 July 2007.

13. Aging of the Canadian Population, 1921 to 2006

Year	Age 0–64 %	65 and Over %	Ratio of 65 and Over to 0–64 %	Average Annual Change %
1921	95.2	4.8	5.0	—
1931	94.4	5.6	5.9	0.86
1941	93.3	6.7	7.1	1.27
1951	92.2	7.8	8.4	1.26
1956	92.3	7.7	8.4	-0.04
1961	92.4	7.6	8.3	-0.25
1966	92.3	7.7	8.3	0.15
1971	91.9	8.1	8.8	0.93
1976	91.3	8.7	9.5	1.48
1981	90.3	9.7	10.7	2.40
1986	89.3	10.7	11.9	2.38
1991	88.4	11.6	13.1	2.42
1996	87.8	12.2	13.8	2.60
2001	87.0	13.0	14.9	2.04
2006	86.8	13.2	15.2	2.01

— = nil
SOURCE: Adapted from Statistics Canada: "Age, Sex and Marital Status", 1991 census, Catalogue 93-310, 6 July 1992, http://www.statcan.ca/bsolc/english/bsolc?catno=93-310-X; Report on the Demographic Situation in Canada, Catalogue 91-209, 1991 and 2001, http://www.statcan.ca/bsolc/english/bsolc?catno=91-209-XIE#formatdisp; and the CANSIM database, http://cansim2.statcan.ca, Table 051-0001, accessed 17 October 2007.

15. Aboriginal Population, 2006

Province or Territory	Aboriginal population[1]	First Nation[2]	Métis[2]
Newfoundland and Labrador	23 450	7 765	6 470
Prince Edward Island	1 730	1 230	385
Nova Scotia	24 175	15 240	7 680
New Brunswick	17 655	12 385	4 270
Québec	108 430	65 090	27 980
Ontario	242 495	158 395	73 605
Manitoba	175 395	100 645	71 805
Saskatchewan	141 890	91 400	48 115
Alberta	188 365	97 275	85 500
British Columbia	196 075	129 580	59 445
Yukon	7 580	6 275	805
Northwest Territories	20 635	12 640	3 580
Nunavut	24 920	100	130
Canada	**1 172 790**	**698 025**	**389 785**

[1]This total includes an additional 34 500 persons who reported more than one Aboriginal identity group, and also includes those who reported being a Registered Indian and/or Band member in the census without reporting an Aboriginal identity. The Inuit population of 50 485 is also included in this total (see Table 17).
[2]Includes only persons who reported a First Nation (North American Indian on the census) or Métis identity.
SOURCE: Adapted from Statistics Canada, "Aboriginal Peoples Highlight Tables, 2006 Census", Highlight tables, 2006 Census, Catalogue 97-558-XWE2006002, 15 January 2008, Table 1, http://www.statcan.ca/bsolc/english/bsolc?catno=97-558-X2006002.

16. Population of Census Metropolitan Areas, 1961, 1971, 1981, 1991, 2001, 2006

Census Metropolitan Area	Area (km^2) 2006	1961	1971	1981	1991	2001	2006
Toronto	5 904	1 919 409	2 628 043	3 130 392	3 893 046	4 682 897	5 113 149
Montreal	4 259	2 215 627	2 743 208	2 862 286	3 127 242	3 426 350	3 635 571
Vancouver	2 877	826 798	1 082 352	1 268 183	1 602 502	1 986 965	2 116 581
Ottawa–Gatineau	5 716	457 038	602 510	743 821	920 857	1 063 664	1 130 761
Calgary	5 107	279 062	403 319	625 966	754 033	951 395	1 079 310
Edmonton	9 418	359 821	495 702	740 882	839 924	937 845	1 034 945
Québec	3 277	379 067	480 502	583 820	645 550	682 757	715 515
Winnipeg	5 303	476 543	540 262	592 061	652 354	671 274	694 668
Hamilton	1 372	401 071	498 523	542 095	599 760	662 401	692 911
London	2 665	226 669	286 011	326 817	381 522	432 451	457 720
Kitchener	827	154 864	226 846	287 801	356 421	414 284	451 235
St. Catharines–Niagara	1 398	257 796	303 429	342 645	364 552	377 009	390 317
Halifax	5 496	193 353	222 637	277 727	320 501	359 183	372 858
Oshawa	903	n.a.	120 318	186 446	240 104	296 298	330 594
Victoria	695	155 763	195 800	241 450	287 897	311 902	330 088
Windsor	1 023	217 215	258 643	250 885	262 075	307 877	323 342
Saskatoon	5 207	95 564	126 449	175 058	210 023	225 927	233 923
Regina	3 408	113 749	140 734	173 226	191 692	192 800	194 971
Sherbrooke	1 232	n.a.	n.a.	125 183	139 194	153 811	186 952
St. John's	804	106 666	131 814	154 835	171 859	172 918	181 113
Barrie	897	n.a.	n.a.	n.a.	n.a.	n.a.	177 061
Kelowna	2 904	n.a.	n.a.	n.a.	n.a.	n.a.	162 276
Abbotsford	626	n.a.	n.a.	n.a.	n.a.	n.a.	159 020
Greater Sudbury	3 382	127 446	155 424	156 121	157 613	155 601	158 258
Kingston	1 907	n.a.	n.a.	n.a.	136 401	146 838	152 385
Saguenay	1 754	127 616	133 703	158 229	160 928	154 938	151 643
Trois-Rivières	880	n.a.	n.a.	125 343	136 303	137 507	141 529
Guelph	379	n.a.	n.a.	n.a.	n.a.	n.a.	127 009
Moncton	2 406	n.a.	n.a.	n.a.	n.a.	n.a.	126 424
Brantford	1 073	n.a.	n.a.	n.a.	n.a.	n.a.	124 607
Thunder Bay	2 550	102 085	112 093	121 948	124 427	121 986	122 907
Saint John	3 359	98 083	106 744	121 012	124 981	122 678	122 389
Peterborough	1 506	n.a.	n.a.	n.a.	n.a.	n.a.	116 570

NOTE: Data is listed in order of 2006 population values. n.a. = not available

SOURCE: Adapted from Statistics Canada, "Population and dwelling counts, for census metropolitan areas, 2006 and 2001 censuses", Highlight Tables, 2006 Census, Catalogue 97-550-XWE2006002, 12 July 2007, http://www12.statcan.ca/english/census06/data/popdwell/Table.cfm?T=205&RPP=50.

17. Inuit Population, 2006

Region	Inuit Population
Inuit Nunaat[1]	
Nunatsiavut	2 160
Nunavik	9 565
Nunavut	24 635
Inuvialuit	3 115
Total	**39 475**
Outside Inuit Nunaat	
Rural	2 610
Urban	8 395
Total	**11 005**
Canada	**50 480**

[1]"Inuit Nunaat" is an Inuktitut expression for "Inuit homeland", an area comprising more than one-third of Canada's land mass. The Inuit population map on page 38 shows the regions of Inuit Nunaat.

SOURCE: Adapted from Statistics Canada, http://www12.statcan.ca/english/census06/analysis/aboriginal/inuit.cfm.

18. Aboriginal Languages, 2006

Language	Aboriginal Mother Tongue[1]	Knowledge of an Aboriginal Language[2]
Cree	76 460	87 285
Ojibway	24 410	30 255
Oji-Cree	11 605	12 435
Montagnais-Naskapi	10 470	11 080
Dene	8 495	9 250
Mi'kmaq	7 685	8 540
Siouan languages (Dakota/Sioux)	5 675	6 285
Atikamekw	5 140	5 320
Blackfoot	3 270	4 760
Salish languages n.i.e.	1 990	2 800
Algonquin	2 020	2 560
Dogrib	2 055	2 540
Carrier	1 800	2 320
South Slave	1 575	2 160
Inuktituk	32 380	34 345

n.i.e. = not included elsewhere

[1]"Mother tongue" is the first language learned at home in childhood and still understood. [2]"Knowledge" refers to a language in which the respondent can conduct a conversation.

SOURCE: Adapted from Statistics Canada, "Aboriginal Peoples in Canada in 2006: Inuit, Métis and First Nations, 2006 Census", Analysis Series, 2006 Census, Catalogue 97-551-XWE2006001, 15 January 2008, Table 24, http://www12.statcan.ca/english/census06/analysis/aboriginal/share.cfm.

19. Population by Ethnic Origin, 2001[1] (000)

Ethnic Origin	NFLD & LAB	PEI	NS	NB	QUE	ONT	MAN	SASK	ALTA	BC	YT	NWT	NVT	Canada
Canadian	241.5	52.4	368.9	380.9	4 474.1	2 768.9	206.4	172.4	667.4	720.4	6.1	6.1	1.2	10 066.3
British Isles	285.3	91.3	542.1	332.3	712.0	4 911.3	431.3	411.4	1 488.1	1 860.7	15.4	13.2	4.3	11 098.6
European	19.5	16.8	186.1	75.4	930.1	4 379.6	568.6	541.9	1 588.2	1 591.1	12.1	8.9	1.6	9 919.8
Western European	9.7	11.8	131.5	49.0	219.2	1 685.7	282.7	325.8	862.5	783.1	6.7	4.5	0.7	4 372.8
German	7.4	7.1	101.9	33.8	131.8	1 144.6	216.8	286.1	679.7	561.6	4.8	3.5	0.6	3 179.4
Dutch	2.1	4.6	37.0	15.5	23.0	491.0	55.4	35.4	172.9	196.4	1.5	1.0	0.1	1 036.0
Eastern European	3.1	2.3	25.3	9.0	186.4	1 171.2	265.3	225.7	609.8	493.4	3.5	2.8	0.4	2 998.2
Ukrainian	1.0	0.8	7.5	2.5	32.0	336.4	167.2	129.3	332.2	197.3	1.6	1.4	0.2	1 209.1
Polish	1.0	0.8	11.0	3.1	62.8	465.6	82.4	56.9	170.9	128.4	0.9	0.8	0.1	984.6
Russian	0.6	0.3	3.2	1.3	40.2	167.4	45.6	35.1	92.0	114.1	0.6	0.3	0.07	500.6
Southern European	4.3	2.0	25.3	11.6	505.2	1 642.0	51.2	19.6	168.7	291.3	1.2	1.1	0.2	2 723.7
Greek	0.3	0.2	2.9	1.0	66.0	132.4	3.5	2.5	11.9	21.8	0.07	0.05	0.02	242.7
Italian	1.4	1.0	13.5	5.9	299.7	868.0	21.4	8.0	82.0	143.2	0.6	0.6	0.1	1 445.3
Portuguese	0.9	0.2	3.1	1.7	57.5	282.9	11.1	1.1	17.6	34.7	0.07	0.1	0.05	410.9
Northern European	3.3	1.9	13.8	9.6	20.9	245.6	77.8	112.5	308.4	322.0	2.7	1.9	0.4	1 120.8
Norwegian	1.5	0.4	4.7	2.6	6.4	53.8	18.4	68.7	144.6	129.4	1.3	0.7	0.06	432.5
Jewish	0.5	0.2	3.3	1.4	71.4	177.3	13.2	2.1	14.8	30.8	0.1	0.03	0.03	315.1
French[2]	30.6	30.9	176.4	216.1	2 184.7	2 580.1	148.8	118.5	391.7	364.3	4.3	4.5	1.0	5 000.4
Eastern and Southeastern Asia	2.4	0.5	8.2	4.9	173.3	1 047.1	65.3	19.0	238.8	650.1	1.0	1.5	0.2	2 212.3
Chinese	1.7	0.3	5.1	2.9	91.9	644.5	17.9	11.1	137.6	432.2	0.5	0.5	0.08	1 346.5
Filipino	0.3	0.03	0.8	0.6	25.7	215.8	39.2	4.2	54.3	94.3	0.3	0.8	0.08	436.2
Aboriginal	37.3	3.7	48.2	35.2	264.2	403.8	186.7	149.8	244.6	250.9	7.8	20.9	25.2	1 678.2
South Asian	1.8	0.3	4.8	2.6	77.0	833.3	17.8	5.5	107.7	265.6	0.2	0.2	0.06	1 316.8
East Indian	1.3	0.3	3.9	2.2	41.6	573.3	14.9	4.5	88.2	232.4	0.2	0.1	0.04	962.7
Pakistani	0.3	0.0	0.5	0.3	11.7	91.2	1.1	0.5	11.2	8.0	0.01	0.03	0.0	124.7
Caribbean	0.7	0.3	3.5	1.0	133.6	390.0	8.5	2.1	21.0	17.6	0.08	0.1	0.05	578.7
Jamaican	0.3	0.2	1.0	0.3	11.9	197.6	3.3	0.8	8.7	6.9	0.05	0.07	0.02	231.1
Arab	1.4	0.9	10.6	3.8	202.2	188.0	4.4	2.9	37.9	18.3	0.07	0.2	0.03	470.6
African	1.0	0.5	11.1	3.1	78.0	235.9	11.9	5.0	41.2	32.9	0.1	0.4	0.2	421.2
Latin etc	0.5	0.2	1.5	1.1	101.1	166.3	10.2	3.3	34.5	41.1	0.02	0.1	0.03	360.2
West Asian	0.3	0.05	1.8	0.9	58.3	174.0	3.4	1.8	17.2	44.6	0.03	0.1	0.02	302.6
Oceania	0.1	0.2	0.7	0.2	1.7	16.2	0.9	1.1	9.5	27.7	0.09	0.1	0.02	58.5
Total[3]	**500.6**	**134.2**	**903.1**	**719.7**	**7 435.9**	**12 028.9**	**1 133.5**	**953.9**	**3 256.4**	**4 074.4**	**30.2**	**41.1**	**29.3**	**31 241.0**

[1] "Ethnic origin" refers to the the ethnic or cultural origins of the respondent's ancestors. For example, of the 4 911.3 in Ontario who reported origins in the British Isles, 3 736.6 reported another origin, and many would have reported "Canadian".
[2] Includes both French and Acadian responses.
[3] Represents total population. The sum of specific groups is not equal to the total population due to multiple counts.
SOURCE: Adapted from Statistics Canada, Ethnic origins, 2006 counts, for Canada, provinces and territories - 20% sample data (table). Ethnocultural Portrait of Canada Highlight Tables. 2006 Census. Statistics Canada Catalogue no. 97-562-XWE2006002. Ottawa, 2 April 2008, http://www12.statcan.ca/english/census06/data/highlights/ethnic/index.cfm?Lang=E, accessed 10 April 2008.

20. Immigration of Permanent Residents by Top Ten Source Countries and Source Area, 1997 to 2006

Source Countries	1997	1998	1999	2000	2001	2002	2003	2004	2005	2006
China	18 526	19 790	29 148	36 750	40 365	33 307	36 256	36 429	42 292	33 080
India	19 615	15 375	17 457	26 123	27 904	28 838	24 593	25 575	33 148	30 753
Philippines	10 872	8 184	9 205	10 119	12 928	11 011	11 989	13 303	17 525	17 717
Pakistan	11 239	8 089	9 303	14 201	15 354	14 173	12 351	12 795	13 575	12 332
United States	5 030	4 776	5 533	5 828	5 911	5 294	6 013	7 507	9 262	10 943
Iran	7 486	6 775	5 909	5 617	5 746	7 889	5 651	6 063	5 502	7 073
United Kingdom	4 657	3 899	4 478	4 649	5 360	4 725	5 199	6 062	5 865	6 542
South Korea	4 001	4 917	7 217	7 639	9 608	7 334	7 089	5 337	5 819	6 178
Colombia	571	922	1 296	2 228	2 967	3 226	4 273	4 438	6 031	5 813
France	2 858	3 867	3 923	4 345	4 428	3 963	4 127	5 028	5 430	4 915
Total for top ten only	**118 070**	**87 490**	**98 461**	**121 520**	**134 285**	**123 228**	**119 055**	**123 757**	**144 449**	**135 346**
Total other countries	**97 968**	**86 705**	**91 496**	**105 939**	**116 356**	**105 823**	**102 296**	**112 067**	**117 790**	**116 303**
Total	**216 038**	**174 195**	**189 957**	**227 459**	**250 641**	**229 051**	**221 351**	**235 824**	**262 239**	**251 649**
Source Area										
Asia and Pacific	117 070	84 202	96 581	120 739	132 944	119 059	113 733	114 575	138 057	126 479
Africa and the Middle East	37 795	32 592	33 557	40 909	48 238	46 340	43 678	49 531	49 279	51 863
Europe	38 674	38 538	38 991	42 963	43 295	38 869	37 570	41 902	40 908	37 946
South and Central America	17 422	14 045	15 279	17 007	20 211	19 473	20 349	22 255	24 639	24 306
United States	5 029	4 776	5 532	5 828	5 911	5 294	6 013	7 507	9 262	10 942
not stated	8	17	1	6	34	13	6	52	94	111
Total	**216 038**	**174 195**	**189 957**	**227 459**	**250 641**	**229 051**	**221 351**	**235 824**	**262 239**	**251 649**

NOTE: Data is listed in order of 2006 values.
SOURCE: Adapted from Citizenship and Immigration Canada: "Facts and Figures 2006 Immigration Overview: Permanent Residents: Canada—Permanent Residents by Top Source Countries" http://www.cic.gc.ca/english/resources/statistics/facts2006/permanent/12.asp; "Facts and Figures 2006 Immigration Overview: Permanent Residents: Canada—Permanent Residents by Gender and Source Area" http://www.cic.gc.ca/english/resources/statistics/facts2006/permanent/09.asp. Adapted and reproduced with the permission of the Minister of Public Works and Government Services Canada, 2008.

. Total Population by Visible Minority, 2001 and 2006

	Total Population, 2006	Total Visible Minorities[1,2]		South Asian[3]		Chinese		Black		Filipino	
		2001	2006	2001	2006	2001	2006	2001	2006	2001	2006
FLD & LAB	500 605	3 850	5 720	1 005	1 590	920	1 325	845	905	260	305
EI	134 205	1 180	1 830	110	130	205	250	370	640	35	30
S[4]	903 090	34 525	37 680	2 895	3 810	3 290	4 300	19 670	19 230	655	700
B	719 650	9 425	13 345	1 415	1 960	1 530	2 450	3 845	4 455	355	530
UE[4]	7 435 905	497 975	654 355	59 505	72 845	56 830	79 830	152 195	188 070	18 550	24 200
NT[4]	12 028 895	2 153 045	2 745 205	554 870	794 170	481 505	576 980	411 090	473 765	156 515	203 220
AN[4]	1 133 510	87 115	109 095	12 880	16 560	11 930	13 705	12 820	15 660	30 490	37 790
ASK[4]	953 845	27 580	33 900	4 090	5 130	8 085	9 505	4 165	5 090	3 025	3 770
LTA[4]	3 256 355	329 925	454 200	69 585	103 885	99 100	120 275	31 390	47 075	33 940	51 090
C[4]	4 074 385	836 445	1 008 855	210 290	262 290	365 490	407 225	25 460	28 315	64 005	88 080
T[4]	30 195	1 020	1 220	205	195	225	325	120	125	235	210
WT	41 060	1 545	2 270	190	210	255	320	175	375	465	690
VT[4]	29 325	210	420	25	80	40	80	65	100	35	75
anada[4]	**31 241 030**	**3 983 845**	**5 068 090**	**917 070**	**1 262 865**	**1 029 395**	**1 216 570**	**662 215**	**783 795**	**308 575**	**410 695**

e *Employment Equity Act* defines visible minorities as "persons, other than Aboriginal peoples, who are non-Caucasian in race or non-white in colour." [2]Visible minorities included in the total but not listed separately include people from Latin America and theast Asia.[3]For example, "East Indian", "Pakistani", "Sri Lankan", etc. [4]Excludes census data for one or more incompletely enumerated Indian reserves or Indian settlements.

JRCE: Statistics Canada. "Visible Minority Groups (15) and Sex (3) for Population, for Canada, Provinces, Territories, Census Metropolitan Areas and Census Agglomerations, 2001 Census - 20% Sample Data", Catalogue 97F0010, January 23, 2003; Visible ority groups, 2006 counts, for Canada, provinces and territories - 20% sample data (table). Ethnocultural Portrait of Canada Highlight Tables. 2006 Census. Statistics Canada Catalogue no. 97-562-XWE2006002. Ottawa. Released April 2, 2008. http://www12.can.ca/english/census06/data/highlights/ethnic/index.cfm?Lang=E (accessed April 10, 2008).

2. Numbers of Immigrants and Immigration Rates, Canada, 1944 to 2006

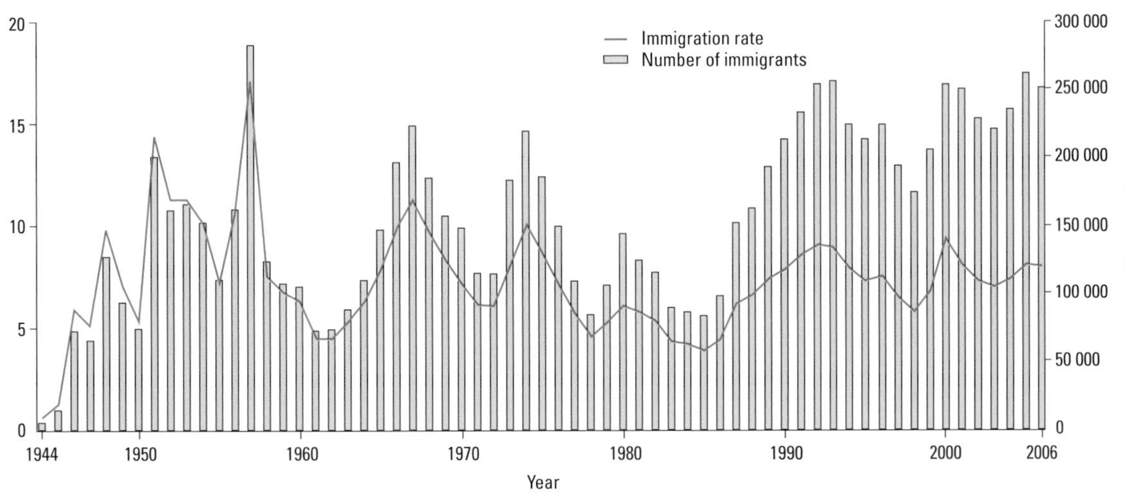

SOURCE: Adapted from Statistics Canada, "Report on the Demographic Situation in Canada", Catalogue 91-209, 2001-2004, http://www.statcan.ca/bsolc/english/bsolc?catno=91-209-X&CHROPG=1; Citizenship and Immigration Canada, "Facts and Figures 2006 Immigration Overview: Permanent and Temporary Residents: Canada --Permanent Residents by Category (No Backlog Reallocation)" http://www.cic.gc.ca/english/resources/statistics/facts2006/overview/01.asp. Adapted and reproduced with the permission of the Minister of Public Works and Government Services Canada, 2008.

3. Immigration of Permanent Residents by Category, 1997 to 2006

ategory	1997	1998	1999	2000	2001	2002	2003	2004	2005	2006
pouses and partners	29 775	28 062	32 790	35 293	37 761	32 742	38 736	43 999	45 406	45 280
arents and grandparents	20 153	14 164	14 481	17 768	21 341	22 234	19 384	12 732	12 474	20 006
thers (including children)	9 610	8 370	7 956	7 550	7 691	7 304	6 993	5 529	5 479	5 222
otal family class	**59 538**	**50 596**	**55 227**	**60 611**	**66 793**	**62 280**	**65 113**	**62 260**	**63 359**	**70 508**
killed workers[1]	104 924	80 811	92 372	118 561	137 200	122 706	105 215	113 445	130 242	105 949
usiness immigrants	19 924	13 777	13 018	13 665	14 587	11 022	8 100	9 759	13 469	12 077
rovincial/territorial nominees	47	0	477	1 252	1 275	2 127	4 418	6 248	8 047	13 336
ive-in caregivers	2 718	2 867	3 260	2 782	2 625	1 985	3 304	4 292	4 552	6 895
otal economic immigrants	**127 613**	**97 455**	**109 127**	**136 260**	**155 687**	**137 840**	**121 037**	**133 744**	**156 310**	**138 257**
overnment-assisted refugees	7 660	7 387	7 443	10 671	8 697	7 505	7 506	7 411	7 416	7 316
rivately sponsored refugees	2 580	2 140	2 330	2 922	3 571	3 039	3 251	3 115	2 976	3 337
efugees landed in Canada	10 429	10 059	11 780	12 993	11 897	10 546	11 265	15 901	19 935	15 892
efugee dependants[2]	3 194	2 919	2 805	3 494	3 749	4 021	3 959	6 259	5 441	5 947
otal refugees	**23 863**	**22 505**	**24 358**	**30 080**	**27 914**	**25 111**	**25 981**	**32 686**	**35 768**	**32 492**
etirees	46	8	9	0	0	n.a.	0	0	0	0
ROC and PDRCC[3]	3 233	2 486	1 020	460	206	125	79	53	20	23
emporary resident permit holders	0	0	0	0	0	n.a.	97	148	123	136
umanitarian and compassionate ases / Public policy	0	0	0	0	0	3 652	9 032	6 932	6 651	10 223
otal other	**3 279**	**2 494**	**1 029**	**460**	**206**	**3 787**	**9 208**	**7 133**	**6 794**	**10 382**
otal immigrants/refugees	**214 293**	**173 050**	**189 741**	**227 411**	**250 600**	**229 018**	**221 339**	**235 823**	**262 231**	**251 639**

cludes independents and assisted relatives. [2]Dependants of refugees landed in Canada including spouses and partners. [3]Deferred removal orders and post-determination refugee claimants.

URCE: Adapted from Citizenship and Immigration Canada, "Facts and Figures 2006 Immigration Overview: Permanent and Temporary Residents: Canada—Permanent Residents by Category (No Backlog Reallocation)" http://www.cic.gc.ca/glish/resources/statistics/facts2006/overview/01.asp. Adapted and reproduced with the permission of the Minister of Public Works and Government Services Canada, 2008.

24. Immigration of Permanent Residents by Category and Source Area, 2006

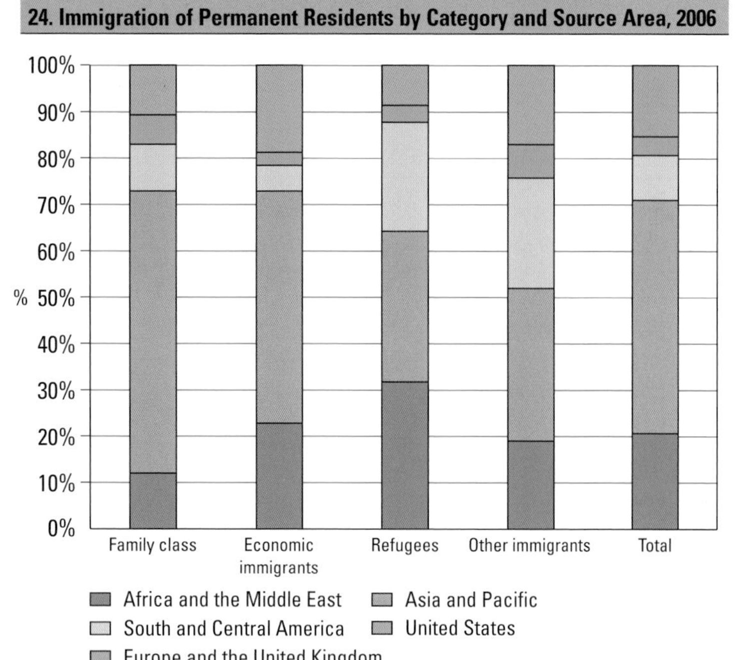

SOURCE: Adapted from Citizenship and Immigration Canada, "Facts and Figures 2006 Immigration Overview: Permanent Residents: Canada—Permanent Residents by Category and Source Area" http://www.cic.gc.ca/english/resources/statistics/facts2006/permanent/10.asp. Adapted and reproduced with the permission of the Minister of Public Works and Government Services Canada, 2008.

26. Employment by Industry and by Sex, 2006

Industry	Number Employed (000)		
	Both Sexes	Men	Women
Agriculture	346.4	239.5	107.0
Forestry, fishing, mining, oil and gas	330.1	269.1	60.9
Utilities	122.0	92.5	29.5
Construction	1 069.7	946.8	122.9
Manufacturing	2 117.7	1 517.8	599.9
Trade	2 633.5	1 340.4	1 293.2
Transportation and warehousing	802.2	616.2	186.0
Finance, insurance, real estate, and leasing	1 040.5	442.7	597.8
Professional, scientific, and technical services	1 089.9	620.1	469.9
Business, building, and other support services	690.0	366.1	323.9
Educational services	1 158.4	410.4	748.0
Health care and social assistance	1 785.5	312.8	1 472.7
Information, culture, and recreation	745.0	394.2	350.8
Accommodation and food services	1 015.0	402.2	612.8
Other services	701.0	327.9	373.1
Public administration	837.4	428.4	409.0
Total all industries	**16 484.3**	**8 727.1**	**7 757.2**

SOURCE: Adapted from Statistics Canada, http://www40.statcan.ca/l01/cst01/labor10a.htm, accessed 23 August 2007.

25. Individuals by Total Income Level, 2001 to 2005

	2001	2002	2003	2004	2005
Under $5 000	2 396 540	2 373 740	2 375 060	2 323 290	2 210 370
$5 000 and over	20 313 370	20 425 240	20 695 140	21 085 590	21 505 290
$10 000 and over	17 629 360	17 807 080	18 119 380	18 572 830	19 129 110
$15 000 and over	14 773 880	14 994 700	15 370 750	15 879 220	16 431 080
$20 000 and over	12 379 840	12 587 440	12 926 300	13 390 830	13 923 310
$25 000 and over	10 475 810	10 698 800	11 041 800	11 493 990	11 999 020
$35 000 and over	7 105 400	7 361 260	7 706 720	8 146 710	8 630 290
$50 000 and over	3 806 950	4 025 790	4 285 870	4 631 570	5 006 340
$75 000 and over	1 335 790	1 450 590	1 589 290	1 788 240	2 020 810
$100 000 and over	611 610	654 580	704 380	791 580	904 600
$150 000 and over	243 760	252 270	267 360	297 810	334 140
$200 000 and over	140 400	143 160	151 740	169 220	188 950
$250 000 and over	92 550	94 020	99 880	112 060	124 890
Total	**22 709 910**	**22 798 980**	**23 070 200**	**23 408 890**	**23 715 660**
Median total income	**22 600**	**23 100**	**23 600**	**24 400**	**25 400**

SOURCE: Adapted from Statistics Canada, http://www40.statcan.ca/l01/cst01/famil105a.htm?sdi=income%20canada, accessed 22 November 2007.

27. Persons in Low Income Before Tax, 1987, 1991, 2001, 2005 (000)

Persons and Age Group	1987	1991	2001	2005
All persons	**4 148**	**4 794**	**4 711**	**4 821**
Under 18 years of age	1 132	1 331	1 191	1 132
18 to 64 years of age	2 342	2 789	2 971	3 112
65 years of age and over	674	675	550	577
Persons in economic families	**2 883**	**3 268**	**3 076**	**3 040**
Under 18 years of age	1 132	1 331	1 191	1 132
18 to 64 years of age	1 542	1 769	1 757	1 770
65 years of age and over	208	168	129	138
Unattached individuals	**1 265**	**1 526**	**1 635**	**1 780**
Under 65 years of age	800	1 019	1 214	1 342
65 years of age and over	465	507	421	438

SOURCE: Adapted from Statistics Canada, http://www40.statcan.ca/l01/cst01/famil41b.htm, accessed 29 January 2008, and http://www40.statcan.ca/l01/cst01/famil41h.htm, accessed 13 May 2008.

28. Employment, Unemployment, and Participation Rates,[1] 2007

Province or Territory	Population Over 15 Years (000)	Labour Force (000)	Employed (000)	Unemployed (000)	Participation Rate (%)	Unemployment Rate (%)
Newfoundland and Labrador	423.1	247.2	213.8	33.5	58.4	13.6
Prince Edward Island	113.4	76.9	68.8	8.1	67.8	10.5
Nova Scotia	764.2	485	442.4	42.6	63.5	8.8
New Brunswick	613.1	390.4	362.2	28.2	63.7	7.2
Québec	6 317.7	4 143.7	3 858.5	285.2	65.6	6.9
Ontario	10 366.6	7 049.9	6 584.7	465.2	68.0	6.6
Manitoba	899.2	621.0	594.9	26.1	69.1	4.2
Saskatchewan	751.1	521.9	496.8	25.1	69.5	4.8
Alberta	2 748.8	2 037.0	1 968.9	68.1	74.1	3.3
British Columbia	3 572.6	2 355.3	2 257.6	97.7	65.9	4.1
Yukon	21.3	16.0	15.3	0.7	75.1	4.4
Northwest Territories	30.8	24.4	22.9	1.6	79.2	6.6
Nunavut	14.2	10.2	9.2	1.0	71.5	9.7
Canada[2]	**26 569.9**	**17 928.3**	**16 848.6**	**1 079.8**	**67.5**	**6.0**

[1]The participation rate is the percentage of the population over 15 years of age in the labour force and includes both employed and unemployed. [2]Values for the provinces and territories may not add up to the totals for Canada, due to rounding and the use of estimated data in some cases.

SOURCE: Adapted from Statistics Canada, *Labour Force Information*, Catalogue 71-001, Issue of July 15 to 21, 2007, pages 23, 25-26, 48, tables 1, 3, 6.2, 10 August 2007, http://www.statcan.ca/bsolc/english/bsolc?catno=71-001-X&CHROPG=1.

9. Distribution of Employed People by Industry and by Province, 2006

Province[1]	Employees (000)													
	All Industries	Agriculture	Forestry, Fishing, Mining, Oil and Gas, Utilities	Construction	Manufacturing	Trade Transportation, and Warehousing	Finance, Insurance, Real Estate, and Leasing	Professional Scientific, and Technical Services	Business, Building, and Other Support Services	Educational Services	Health Care and Social Assistance	Information, Culture, and Recreation	Accommodation, Food, and Other Services	Public Administration
Newfoundland & Labrador	215.7	1.9	18.6	12.9	15.7	49.3	6.5	6.7	8.5	16.6	30.1	8.8	24.7	15.3
Prince Edward Island	68.6	3.9	2.7	5.7	6.6	12.1	2.1	2.8	2.8	4.6	7.9	2.6	8.5	6.3
Nova Scotia	441.8	4.7	14.5	27.3	39.1	96.9	22.3	18.4	28.8	34.7	59.1	16.3	50.5	29.2
New Brunswick	355.4	6.2	13.0	21.1	36.9	76.7	16.4	14.5	21.8	27.2	45.3	160.4	42.7	21.7
Québec	3765.4	65.1	68.5	186.1	581.3	795.7	222.3	241.7	139.8	260.9	454.1	319.6	373.9	215.6
Ontario	6492.7	100.4	87.7	405.2	1007.2	1311.8	476.8	453.8	295.8	444.5	638.2	319.6	637.2	314.5
Manitoba	587.0	29.4	12.1	29.9	66.6	126.4	34.2	23.4	18.3	45.5	79.6	23.7	62.9	35.0
Saskatchewan	491.6	47.8	26.0	29.6	29.3	104.9	25.7	18.9	12.6	38.1	59.5	20.2	51.4	27.5
Alberta	1870.7	52.3	156.4	172.6	137.5	388.6	96.2	142.2	62.7	130.4	179.5	68.3	202.8	81.1
British Columbia	2195.5	34.7	52.4	179.3	197.5	473.2	138.0	167.6	98.8	156.0	232.2	113.2	261.3	91.3
Canada	**16484.3**	**346.4**	**452.1**	**1069.7**	**2117.7**	**3435.7**	**1040.5**	**1089.9**	**690.0**	**1158.4**	**1785.5**	**745.0**	**1716.0**	**837.4**

[1]Data for the three territories is not available.
SOURCE: Adapted from Statistics Canada, "Distribution of employed people, by industry, by province", http://www40.statcan.ca/l01/cst01/labor21a.htm, accessed 15 October 2007.

Agriculture

0. Farm Cash Receipts from Farming Operations, 2006[1] ($000)

	NFLD & LAB	PEI	NS	NB	QUE	ONT	MAN	SASK	ALTA	BC	Canada[2]
Wheat[3]	—	3 671	1 194	324	14 641	279 735	361 157	1 336 020	810 623	5 373	2 812 738
Oats	—	548	96	334	16 410	5 511	98 353	175 367	33 384	1 967	331 970
Barley[3]	—	5 071	493	1 072	14 622	6 625	39 678	214 339	133 028	2 235	417 163
Liquidations	—	—	—	—	—	—	75 214	208 797	121 831	4 924	410 766
Flaxseed	—	—	—	—	—	0	22 198	128 770	3 326	0	154 294
Canola	—	—	—	—	2 777	3 107	384 485	1 114 878	991 041	5 321	2 501 609
Soybeans	—	1 380	—	—	114 650	546 620	17 413	—	—	—	680 063
Corn	—	—	1 586	—	288 047	448 589	14 725	—	550	—	753 497
Potatoes	2 861	201 411	8 160	110 773	118 175	98 054	125 897	28 564	154 147	51 200	899 242
Greenhouse vegetables	216	x	4 533	x	58 709	426 202	x	735	30 459	236 457	758 243
Other vegetables	3 152	13 077	15 363	5 957	251 335	423 859	38 603	1 152	46 582	126 198	925 278
Apples	0	185	10 260	1 682	28 427	56 092	x	x	x	37 420	134 132
Other tree fruits	3	x	366	x	256	45 245	—	x	x	30 787	76 742
Strawberries	480	760	4 400	1 680	22 715	15 300	1 300	500	911	4 280	52 326
Other berries and grapes	137	4 946	25 536	14 724	66 236	75 440	481	926	837	139 994	329 257
Floriculture and nursery	8 377	2 209	37 058	50 406	240 965	987 121	46 031	30 563	146 101	401 656	1 950 488
Tobacco	—	0	0	0	143	178 378	—	—	—	—	178 521
Ginseng	0	0	0	0	0	56 562	0	0	0	7 802	64 364
Lentils	—	—	—	—	—	—	0	206 677	1 543	—	208 220
Dry beans	—	—	—	—	7 424	70 375	41 821	—	23 568	—	143 188
Dry peas	—	—	—	—	0	0	7 483	247 159	71 950	333	326 925
Chick peas	—	—	—	—	—	—	—	44 482	6 763	—	51 245
Forage and grass seed	0	0	0	0	598	2 313	23 750	23 660	21 214	1 375	72 910
Hay and clover	43	510	359	422	13 032	34 186	14 651	24 417	39 072	11 938	138 631
Maple products	—	0	1 159	10 853	152 256	11 007	—	—	—	—	175 275
Forest products	94	x	12 268	x	41 672	19 172	x	x	x	16 534	109 362
Christmas trees	330	242	10 636	6 692	49 261	5 151	121	177	82	562	73 254
Total crops	**15 991**	**237 395**	**134 335**	**215 530**	**1 506 706**	**3 821 883**	**1 275 343**	**3 636 866**	**2 551 378**	**1 086 684**	**14 482 106**
Cattle	1 511	20 175	22 797	20 489	294 950	944 925	450 378	803 450	2 979 307	206 485	5 744 469
Calves	172	354	1 429	2 237	218 910	70 806	82 053	262 447	38 913	73 224	750 546
Hogs	1 167	23 630	22 880	20 454	838 946	851 218	827 838	312 170	495 315	34 391	3 428 012
Lambs	527	388	2 221	1 263	32 604	41 878	5 663	8 729	19 196	9 212	121 681
Dairy	38 778	63 087	107 660	84 365	1 846 187	1 590 920	188 801	133 433	382 095	395 346	4 830 672
Hens and chickens	x	x	53 399	43 238	409 524	495 414	62 980	56 686	137 995	259 767	1 545 233
Turkeys	x	x	6 392	4 669	56 437	127 271	18 047	9 662	23 826	31 932	278 304
Eggs	12 112	3 724	24 735	15 672	98 101	213 511	59 780	20 932	44 320	67 643	560 530
Honey	—	114	1 600	400	6 716	13 972	30 951	44 902	34 699	3 156	136 510
Furs	3 527	1 927	54 280	1 429	3 121	16 797	x	18	2 646	x	96 599
Miscellaneous livestock	540	1 954	6 071	3 486	27 136	44 425	21 334	65 058	108 966	49 011	327 981
Total livestock	**78 973**	**121 106**	**303 621**	**200 379**	**3 849 170**	**4 442 960**	**1 784 444**	**1 728 934**	**4 299 995**	**1 150 406**	**17 959 991**
Stabilization, insurance, income disaster programs, and other payments	**815**	**21 343**	**14 509**	**33 637**	**896 181**	**662 134**	**626 087**	**1 267 192**	**945 115**	**105 146**	**4 572 159**
Total receipts	**95 779**	**379 844**	**452 465**	**449 546**	**6 252 057**	**8 926 977**	**3 685 874**	**6 632 992**	**7 796 488**	**2 342 236**	**37 014 256**

x = confidential to meet secrecy requirements of the Statistics Act; — = nil
[1]Those listed have total production exceeding $60 million. [2]Information about the territories is excluded because of the small number of farms. [3]Includes durum wheat; includes Canadian Wheat Board payments.
SOURCE: Adapted from Statistics Canada, *Farm Cash Receipts: Agriculture Economic Statistics,* Catalogue 21-011, May 2007 issue, vol. 6 no. 1, p. 34. table 1-26, 28 May 2007, http://www.statcan.ca/english/freepub/21-011-XIE/2007001/t027_en.htm.

31. Cash Receipts from Farming by Province, 1983, 1989, 1995, 2000, 2006

Province[1]	Cash Receipts ($000 000)				
	1983	1989	1995	2000	2006
Newfoundland & Labrador	35	58	67	73	96
Prince Edward Island	172	256	311	326	380
Nova Scotia	236	315	329	414	453
New Brunswick	200	272	287	366	450
Québec	2 710	3 649	4 379	5 423	6 252
Ontario	4 990	5 663	6 158	7 579	8 927
Manitoba	1 798	2 102	2 461	3 137	3 686
Saskatchewan	4 026	4 475	5 250	5 781	6 633
Alberta	3 751	4 509	5 846	7 337	7 797
British Columbia	915	1 164	1 527	2 077	2 342
Canada	**18 832**	**22 462**	**26 614**	**32 513**	**37 014**

[1]Information about the territories is excluded because of the small number of farms.
SOURCE: Adapted from Statistics Canada: *Agriculture Economic Statistics,* May 2002, Catalogue 21-603, 28 June 2002, http://www.statcan.ca/bsolc/english/bsolc?catno=21-603-UPE#formatdisp; *Net Farm Income: Agriculture Economic Statistics,* Catalogue 21-011, May 2007 issue, vol. 6, no. 1, page 13, table 1-6, 28 May 2007, http://www.statcan.ca/english/freepub/21-011-XIE/2007001/t027_en.htm.

32. Farm Cash Receipts, 2006 ($000 000)

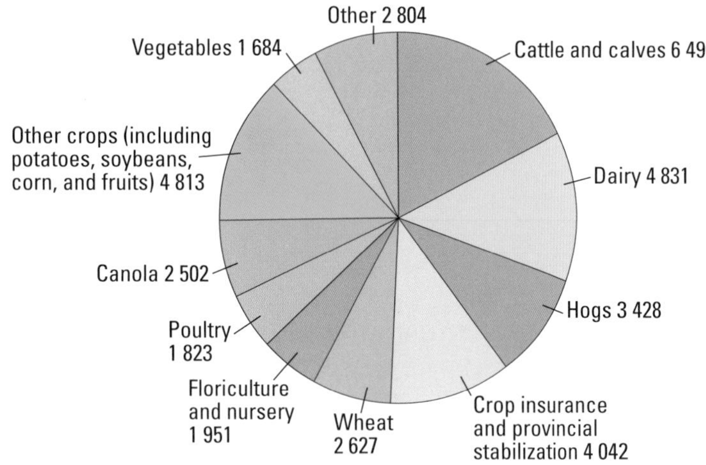

Total cash receipts 2006 = 37 014

SOURCE: Adapted from Statistics Canada, *Farm Cash Receipts: Agriculture Economic Statistics,* Catalogue 21-011, May 2007 issue, vol. 6 no. 1, p. 34. table 1-26, 28 May 2007, http://www.statcan.ca/english/freepub/21-011-XIE/2007001/t027_en.htm.

33. Number of Farms and Average Size, Canada, 1901 to 2006

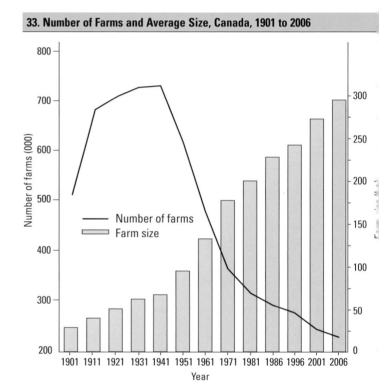

Number of farms (000): 200, 300, 400, 500, 600, 700, 800

Farm size: 0, 50, 100, 150, 200, 250, 300

Number of farms

Farm size

Year: 1901 1911 1921 1931 1941 1951 1961 1971 1981 1986 1996 2001 2006

SOURCE: Adapted from Statistics Canada: 1996, 2001, and 2006 Census of Agriculture; "2006 Census of Agriculture: Farm operations and operators" from *The Daily,* Catalogue 11-001, 16 May 2007, http://www.statcan.ca/Daily/English/070516/d070516a.htm.

34. Agricultural Land Use, 2006

Province[1]	Farmland Area (000 ha)	% Change 1996 to 2006	% Classed as Class 1, 2, or 3 (1996)	Number of Farms	Average Farm Size (ha)	% Change in Farm Size 2001 to 2006	Cropland Area (000 ha)	Summer Fallow Area (000 ha)	Natural & Seeded Pasture (000 ha)
Newfoundland & Labrador	39.2	-10.5	0.005	558	65	+3.2	9.2	0.07	12.6
Prince Edward Island	250.9	-5.4	71.2	1 700	148	+4.2	171.3	0.2	23.2
Nova Scotia	403.0	-5.7	20.7	3 795	106	+1.9	116.6	1.1	55.1
New Brunswick	395.2	nil	17.9	2 776	142	+10.9	152.0	0.9	42.0
Québec	3 462.9	-0.2	1.4	30 675	113	+6.6	1 933.3	4.2	306.0
Ontario	5 386.5	-4.1	6.8	57 211	94	+2.2	1 788.9	11.9	753.7
Manitoba	7 718.6	-0.2	8.0	19 054	405	+12.2	4 701.0	126.6	2 046.5
Saskatchewan	26 002.6	-2.1	25.0	44 329	587	+13.1	14 960.1	2 428.6	7 138.0
Alberta	21 095.4	-0.3	16.2	49 431	427	+8.7	9 621.6	906.3	9 013.6
British Columbia	2 835.5	-12.1	1.0	19 844	143	+11.7	586.2	25.6	1 745.4
Canada[2]	**67 586.7**	**-0.7**	**4.6**	**229 373**	**295**	**+8.1**	**35 912.3**	**3 505.5**	**21 136.1**

[1]Information about the territories is excluded because of the small number of farms. [2]Values for the provinces and territories may not add up to the totals for Canada, due to rounding and the use of estimated data in some cases.
SOURCE: Adapted from Statistics Canada, 1996, 2001, and 2006 Census of Agriculture and "Farm Data and Farm Operator Data", 2006 Census of Agriculture, Catalogue 95-629, released 16 May 2007, Table 4, http://www.statcan.ca/english/freepub/95-629-XIE/2007000/landuse.htm#landuse.

35. Wheat Statistics,[1] 1994–2006

	1994-1995	1995-1996	1996-1997	1997-1998	1998-1999	1999-2000	2000-2001	2001-2002	2002-2003	2003-2004	2004-2005	2005-2006
Carryover from previous crop year	11 118	5 680	6 727	9 046	6 009	7 425	7 699	9 666	6 549	5 725	6 080	7 922
Production	22 920	24 989	29 801	24 280	24 082	26 941	26 519	20 568	16 198	23 552	25 860	25 748
Total supply	34 040	30 689	36 647	33 378	30 171	34 380	34 279	30 331	22 925	29 295	31 955	33 696
Exports	20 771	16 198	19 366	19 366	14 723	18 313	17 108	16 214	9 191	15 726	14 812	15 786
Domestic use	7 589	7 764	8 235	7 373	8 023	8 328	7 512	7 388	8 008	7 488	9 221	8 213
Carryover at the end of the crop year	5 680	6 727	9 046	6 009	7 425	7 739	9 658	6 729	5 725	6 080	7 922	9 698

[1]The crop year begins August 1 and ends July 31.
SOURCE: Adapted from Statistics Canada: *Grain Trade of Canada 1998-1999*, Catalogue 22-201, Table 2 "Supply and Disposition of Principal Grains, Canada, by Crop Year" http://www.statcan.ca/english/freepub/22-201-XIB/0009922-201-XIB.pdf; *Grain Trade of Canada 2000-2001*, Catalogue 22-201, Table 2 "Supply and Disposition of Principal Grains, Canada, by Crop Year" http://www.statcan.ca/english/freepub/22-201-XIB/0000122-201-XIB.pdf; *Cereals and Oilseeds Review*, Vols 24-30, Catalogue 22-007, Table 1, "Supply and disposition of wheat, Canada, by crop year".

36. Canadian Bulk Wheat (including durum) Exports,[1] 1996 to 2006 (000 t)

Country or Region	Average 1996 to 2006	2005/2006
United States	1 597	1 582
Japan	1 390	1 224
Sri Lanka	207	1 048
South Korea	426	1 045
Indonesia	797	996
Italy	625	911
Mexico	785	886
Venezuela	660	581
Iran	1 222	515
Algeria	1 106	358
China	896	160
Total all countries	**15 873**	**15 473**

[1]The crop year begins August 1 and ends July 31.
SOURCES: Canadian Wheat Board, 2005-2006 Statistical Tables, Table 12

37. World Wheat Imports and Exports, 1990, 1998, 2006

Country or Region	Imports (000 000 t)			
	1990	1998	2006	10-Year Average 1996 to 2006
European Union	n.a.	5.1	7.6	7.1
Egypt	6.0	7.1	7.8	7.0
Brazil	2.8	5.7	6.2	6.4
Japan	5.5	6.2	5.5	5.9
Algeria	3.5	5.2	5.5	4.9
Indonesia	2.0	3.7	5.0	4.1
South Korea	4.1	3.9	3.9	3.8
Iran	4.1	3.6	1.1	3.6
Mexico	n.a.	2.2	3.6	2.9
Philippines	n.a.	2.0	3.0	2.7
Iraq	0.2	2.5	4.8	2.6
World total[1]	**90.6**	**104.5**	**113.7**	**108.0**
Country or Region	**Exports (000 000 t)**			
	1990	1998	2006	10-Year Average 1996 to 2006
United States	28.3	28.3	27.4	27.9
European Union	18.5	16.3	15.0	16.4
Canada	21.9	20.0	15.8	16.1
Australia	11.9	15.4	15.2	15.7
Argentina	5.1	9.8	8.3	9.9
Russian Federation	n.a.	1.1	10.7	4.3
Ukraine	n.a.	1.4	6.5	3.2
World total	**90.6**	**104.5**	**113.7**	**108.0**

NOTE: Data is listed in order of 10-year average values.
n.a. = not available
[1]Morocco, United States, Nigeria, Yemen, the Russian Federation, and China imported between 2 and 3 million tonnes a year on average between 1996 and 2006.
SOURCE: (1990 data) Canadian Wheat Board, *CWB Annual Report*, 1990-1991; (1998-2006 data) Canadian Wheat Board, 2005-2006 Statistical Tables, Tables 30 and 31..

38. World Wheat Production, 1990, 1996, 2000, 2005 (000 000 t)

Country or Region	1990	1996	2000	2005
European Union	84.6	118.0	124.2	122.6
China	98.2	110.6	99.6	97.5
India	49.7	62.1	76.4	68.6
USA	74.5	62.0	60.0	57.3
Russian Federation	108.0	34.9	34.5	47.7
Canada	32.7	29.8	26.5	26.8
Australia	15.1	22.9	22.1	24.5
Pakistan	14.4	16.9	21.1	21.5
Ukraine	n.a	13.6	10.2	18.7
Turkey	20.0	16.0	18.0	18.0
Iran	n.a.	11.0	8.0	14.5
Argentina	11.4	15.9	16.2	13.0
World total	**592.4**	**582.6**	**581.5**	**618.9**

NOTE: Data is listed in order of 2005 production values.
SOURCE: Adapted from: (1990 data) CWB Annual Report, 1990-1991; (1996-2005 data) Canadian Wheat Board, 2005-2006 Statistical Tables, Table 29.

39. Natural Resources Summary, 2005[1, 2]

	Forestry	Minerals	Energy	Geomatics[3]	Total Natural Resources	Canada
Gross Domestic Product ($ billion)	$37.6 (3.0%)	$50.7 (4.0%)	$75.2 (5.9%)	$2.4 (0.2%)	$165.9 (13.0%)	$1 276.6 (100%)
Direct employment (thousands of people)	340 (2.1%)	388 (2.4%)	250 (1.5%)	27 (0.01%)	1 005 (6.2%)	16 169 (100%)
New capital investments ($ billion)	$3.5 (1.3%)	$7.4 (2.8%)	$56.4 (21.3%)	n.a.	$67.3 (25.4%)	$265.5 (100%)
Trade ($ billion)						
Domestic exports (excluding re-exports)	$41.9 (10.3%)	$62.1 (15.2%)	$84.8 (20.8%)	$0.5 (0.1%)	$189.3 (46.4%)	$408.1 (100%)
Imports	$10.2 (2.7%)	$56.7 (14.9%)	$34.1 (9.0%)	n.a.	$101 (26.5%)	$380.8 (100%)
Balance of trade[4] (including re-exports)	+$31.9	+$7.5	+$50.7	n.a.	+$90.1	+$55.2

[1]The data reported for each of the natural resource sectors reflect the value of the primary industries and related downstream manufacturing industries as of September 2006. [2]The minerals industry now includes mineral extraction and concentrating, smelting and refining, non-metals and metals-based semi-fabricating industries, and metals fabricating industries. Minerals include uranium mining; energy includes coal mining. [3]Geomatics: The science and technology of gathering, analyzing, interpreting, distributing, and using geographic information. [4]Balance of trade shown in this table is the merchandise balance, which represents the difference between the total exports and imports of goods. Services and capital flows are excluded.
SOURCE: Adapted from *Important Facts on Canada's Natural Resources* (as of October 2005), Catalogue M2-6/2005, ISBN 0-662-69659-X [2006]. Reproduced with the permission of the Minister of Public Works and Government Services Canada, courtesy of Natural Resources Canada, 2007.

Forestry and Fishing

40. Forest Land, Harvests, and Forest Fires, 2005

Province or Territory	Total Land Area (000 000 ha)	Area of Forest and Other Wooded Land (000 000 ha)	Area Defoliated by Insects and Beetles (000 ha)	Total Area Harvested (000 ha)	Total Volume of Roundwood Harvested (000 000 m3)	Area Burned (000 ha)
Newfoundland & Labrador	40.3	20.1	57.9	22.9	2.4	22.8
Prince Edward Island	0.58	0.27	1.1	2.0	0.6	v.s.
Nova Scotia	5.3	4.4	n.a.	54.3	6.3	0.5
New Brunswick	7.3	6.2	nil	111.3 (2004)	11.4 (2004)	0.4
Québec	151.9	84.6	143.2	356.9	38.5	800.1
Ontario	107.5	68.3	1 403.6	225.2	23.4	42.3
Manitoba	63.6	36.4	47.2	13.7	2.1 (2004)	70.0
Saskatchewan	65.2	24.3	196.5	29.9	5.3	213.5
Alberta	65.4	36.4	2 700.0	79.8 (2004)	27.6	60.8
British Columbia	94.6	64.3	11 293.9	197.6	87.0	35.1
Yukon	48.5	22.8	82.6	v.s.	v.s.	170.7
Northwest Territories	128.1	33.4	35.0	0.13	v.s.	218.1
Nunavut	200.6	0.94	nil	nil	nil	nil
Canada	**979.1**	**402.1**	**15 960.9**	**1 108.4**	**191.0**	**1 885.3**

NOTE: Values for the provinces and territories may not add up to the totals for Canada, due to rounding and the use of estimated data in some cases.
— = nil; n.a. = not available; v.s. = very small
[1]Any forested area may be defoliated by more than one insect. Therefore, there can be considerable overlap in the reported figures. The area within which there is moderate to severe defoliation can also include roads, cultivated areas, small lakes, or burned areas. Areas reported as defoliated may include patches of different severity classes. Also, some areas of defoliation may be missed in the overall surveys.
SOURCE: Adapted from Natural Resources Canada, *The State of Canada's Forests 2005-2006* / "Canada's Forests" website, canadaforests.nrcan.gc.ca. Reproduced with the permission of the Minister of Public Works and Government Services, 2008, and the courtesy of the Canadian Forest Service.

41. Wood Pulp Market in Canada, 1995 to 2005

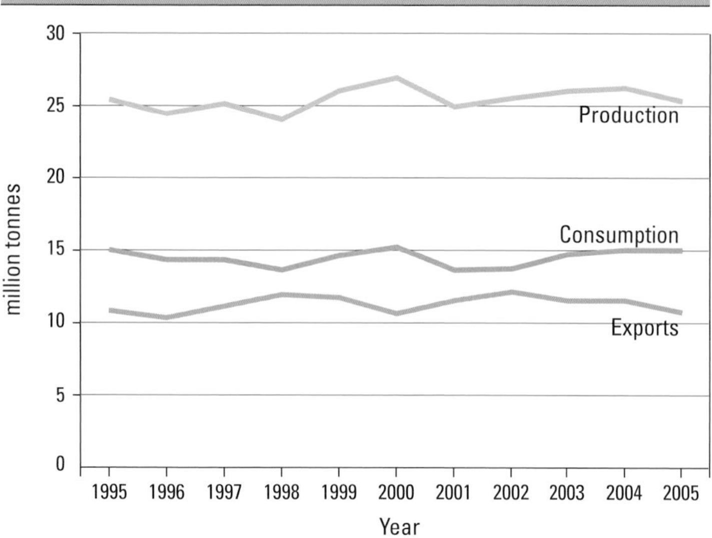

SOURCE: Adapted from Natural Resources Canada, *The State of Canada's Forests 2005–2006* / "Canada's Forests" website, http://canadaforests.nrcan.gc.ca. Reproduced with the permission of the Minister of Public Works and Government Services, 2008, and the courtesy of the Canadian Forest Service.

42. Newsprint Market in Canada, 1995 to 2005

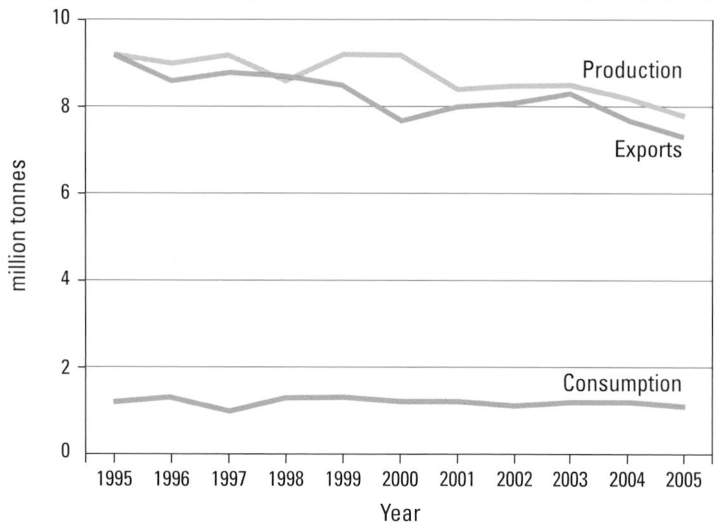

SOURCE: Adapted from Natural Resources Canada, *The State of Canada's Forests 2005–2006* / "Canada's Forests" website, http://canadaforests.nrcan.gc.ca. Reproduced with the permission of the Minister of Public Works and Government Services, 2008, and the courtesy of the Canadian Forest Service.

43. Softwood Lumber Market in Canada, 1995 to 2005

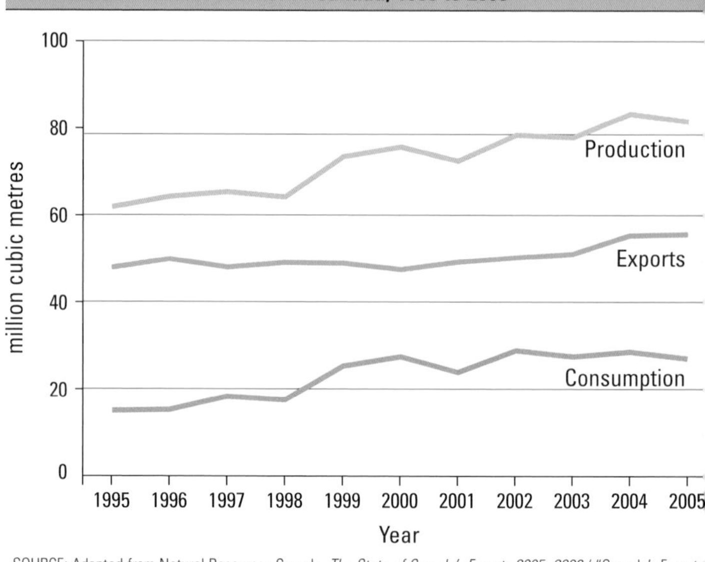

SOURCE: Adapted from Natural Resources Canada, *The State of Canada's Forests 2005–2006* / "Canada's Forests" website, http://canadaforests.nrcan.gc.ca. Reproduced with the permission of the Minister of Public Works and Government Services, 2008, and the courtesy of the Canadian Forest Service.

44. Printing and Writing Paper Market in Canada, 1995 to 2005

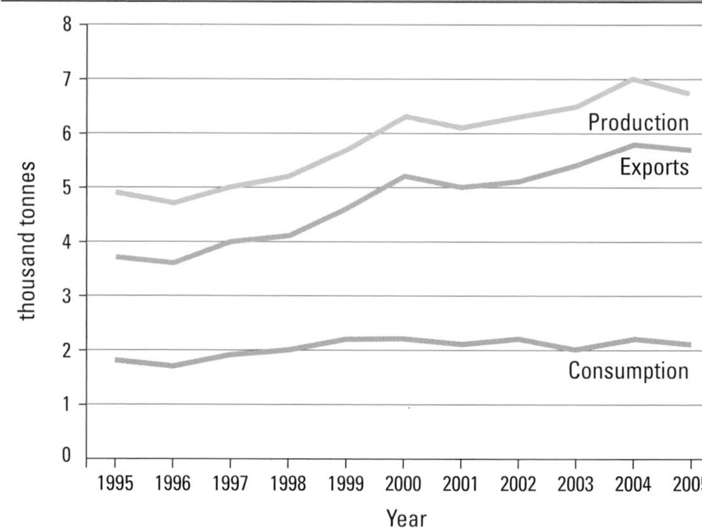

SOURCE: Adapted from Pulp and Paper Products Council (PPPC), *Canadian Pulp and Paper Industry Key Statistics 2006*, p. 3.

45. Commercial Fish Catches, 2000 and 2005[1]

	2000		2005	
	Quantity (tonnes, live weight)	Value ($000)	Quantity (tonnes, live weight)	Value ($000)
Sea fisheries				
Newfoundland and Labrador	278 141	584 319	357 472	517 626
PEI	54 712	129 808	45 873	140 076
Nova Scotia	336 216	704 551	268 211	731 681
New Brunswick	125 570	178 770	119 261	204 951
Québec	60 666	171 548	57 306	152 316
Total Atlantic seafisheries	**855 305**	**1 768 996**	**848 124**	**1 746 650**
Total Pacific seafisheries	**148 195**	**368 797**	**248 520**	**330 121**
Total seafisheries	**1 003 500**	**2 137 793**	**1 096 645**	**2 076 771**
Freshwater fisheries				
New Brunswick	1 611	691	—	—
Québec	1 508	3 960	—	—
Ontario	14 215	40 822	13 384	35 133
Manitoba	15 892	31 954	11 446	22 031
Saskatchewan	4 422	5 305	2 777	2 799
Alberta	1 752	2 508	1 679	2 024
Northwest Territories	1 173	1 580	906	814
Total freshwater fisheries	**40 573**	**86 820**	**30 192**	**62 801**
Total Canada	**1 044 073**	**2 224 613**	**1 126 837**	**2 139 572**

— = nil
Aquaculture in 2004 produced an additional 146 thousand tonnes valued at $527 million.
SOURCE: Adapted from Fisheries and Oceans Canada website: "Summary of Canadian Commercial Catches and Values" 2000-2003, http://www.dfo-mpo.gc.ca/communic/statistics/commercial/landings/sum0003_e.htm; "Summary of Canadian Commercial Catches and Values" 2004-2005, http://www.dfo-mpo.gc.ca/communic/statistics/commercial/landings/sum0407_e.htm. Reproduced with the permission of Her Majesty the Queen in Right of Canada, 2008.

Mining

46. Production of Leading Minerals, 2006[1] ($000 000)

Mineral	NFLD & LAB	PEI	NS	NB	QUE	ONT	MAN	SASK	ALTA	BC	YT	NWT	NVT	Canada
Nickel	1 270.8	—	—	—	628.1	3 269.0	1 008.5	—	—	—	—	—	—	6 176.4
Copper	236.4	—	—	74.0	144.6	1 453.0	423.1	9.6	—	2 259.3	—	—	—	4 600.0
Iron ore	1 543.1	—	—	—	x	—	—	—	—	x	—	—	—	2 584.2
Gold	—	—	—	5.5	508.3	1 246.6	76.1	32.7	1.3	338.8	37.5	—	—	2 246.8
Zinc	—	—	—	902.4	319.0	378.8	369.7	1.9	—	115.4	—	—	—	2 087.3
Uranium	—	—	—	—	—	—	—	1 430.5	—	—	—	—	—	1 430.5
Platinum group	—	—	—	—	x	x	x	—	—	—	—	—	—	492.3
Silver	—	—	—	87.7	74.2	73.5	16.5	0.1	—	146.5	.2	—	—	398.8
Lead	—	—	—	112.9	—	—	—	—	—	3.7	—	—	—	116.6
Cobalt	25.1	—	—	—	13.8	55.3	19.0	—	—	—	—	—	—	113.2
Total metals	**3 075.4**	**—**	**—**	**1 185.3**	**3 213.4**	**6 898.8**	**1 959.0**	**1 475.0**	**1.3**	**3 297.8**	**37.7**	**55.7**	**0**	**21 199.3**
Potash	—	—	—	x	—	—	—	x	—	—	—	—	—	2 212.1
Cement	—	—	x	—	329.0	667.0	—	—	x	310.6	—	—	—	1 702.9
Diamonds	—	—	—	—	—	—	—	—	—	—	—	1 561.5	29.2	1 590.7
Stone	32.9	—	82.9	37.3	366.8	626.5	23.9	—	9.0	81.7	—	6.0	—	1 267.1
Sand and gravel	9.9	x	x	15.6	89.9	431.9	58.8	37.1	306.8	203.7	5.4	5.8	—	1 189.2
Lime	—	—	—	x	x	120.0	x	—	x	x	—	—	—	271.7
Salt	—	—	x	x	x	260.0	x	47.5	21.3	—	—	—	—	439.1
Clay products	—	—	x	—	x	184.9	—	x	x	x	—	—	—	230.9
Peat	x	x	x	74.8	63.1	—	x	x	26.8	x	—	—	—	211.2
Sulphur, elemental	x	—	—	—	—	x	—	2.3	141.3	x	—	—	—	158.4
Gypsum	x	—	105.4	—	—	x	x	—	—	x	—	—	—	123.9
Total non-metals	**46.5**	**3.9**	**x**	**x**	**1 515.1**	**2 492.2**	**127.1**	**x**	**x**	**672.7**	**5.4**	**1 573.3**	**29.2**	**10 199.0**
Total all minerals	**3 121.9**	**3.9**	**309.1**	**1 485.2**	**4 728.5**	**9 390.9**	**2 086.1**	**3 834.1**	**1 321.9**	**5 620.4**	**43.1**	**1 629.0**	**29.2**	**33 603.3**

— = nil; x = confidential to meet secrecy requirements of the Statistics Act.
Preliminary.
OURCE: Adapted from Statistics Canada, *Canada's Mineral Production: Preliminary Estimates 2006*, Catalogue 26-202, Table 1, 6 June 2007, http://www.statcan.ca/bsolc/english/bsolc?catno=26-202-X.

47. Mineral Reserves 1994 to 2005

Mineral	Reserves						Production
	1994	1996	1998	2001	2003	2005	2005
Crude petroleum (000 000 m^3)[1]	1 259.0	1 372.0	1 448.0	644.7	590.0	752.3	146.2[4]
Natural gas (000 000 000 m^3)[1]	2 232.2	1 929.0	1 809.0	1 591.2	1 504.4	1 553.7	170.7
Crude bitumen (000 000 m^3)[1]	158.8	197.5	229.8	1 830.0	1 720.0	1 620.0	n.a.[5]
Coal (megatonnes)[1]	8 623.0	8 623.0	8 623.0	4 555.3	4 423.1	4 291.8	65.3
Copper (000 t)[2]	9 533.0	9 667.0	8 402.0	6 666.0	6 037.0	6 589.0	595.4
Nickel (000 t)[2]	5 334.0	5 632.0	5 683.0	4 335.0	4 303.0	3 960.0	199.9
Lead (000 t)[2]	3 861.0	3 450.0	1 845.0	970.0	749.0	552.0	79.3
Zinc (000 t)[2]	14 514.0	13 660.0	10 159.0	7 808.0	6 251.0	5 063.0	666.7
Molybdenum (000 t)[2]	148.0	144.0	121.0	96.0	78.0	95.0	7.7
Silver (t)[2]	19 146.0	18 911.0	15 738.0	12 593.0	9 245.0	6 990.0	1 123.8
Gold (t)[2]	1 513.0	1 510.0	1 415.0	1 070.0	1 009.0	971.0	119.6
Uranium (000 t)[3]	397.0	369.0	312.0	452.0	429.0	n.a.	12.6

n.a. = not available

[1]Proved reserves recoverable with present technology and prices. [2]Proven and probable reserves. [3]Reserves recoverable from mineable ore. [4]Includes crude bitumen. [5]Included in the production data for crude petroleum.

SOURCE: Adapted from: Statistics Canada, http://www40.statcan.ca/l01/cst01/phys09.htm, accessed in 2002; and Natural Resources Canada, *Canadian Minerals Yearbook 2006*, © Her Majesty the Queen in Right of Canada, 2007. Reproduced with permission.

48. Canada's World Role as a Producer of Certain Important Minerals, 2006

Mineral	Values (% of World Total)	World Total	Rank of Five Leading Countries 1	2	3	4	5
Uranium (U metal content) (mine production)	t (%)	41 827	**Canada** **11 627** **(27.8)**	Australia 9 559 (22.9)	Kazakhstan 4 357 (10.4)	Russia 3 431 (8.2)	Namibia 3 147 (7.5)
Potash (K_2O equivalent) (mine production)	000 t (%)	31 000	**Canada** **10 700** **(34.5)**	Russia 5 000 (16.1)	Belarus 4 500 (14.5)	Germany 3 800 (12.3)	Israel 2 100 (6.8)
Nickel (mine production)	000 t (%)	1449	Russia 300 (20.7)	**Canada** **198** **(13.7)**	Australia 189 (13.0)	Indonesia 148 (10.2)	New Caledonia 112 (7.7)
Cobalt (mine production)	t (%)	54 262	Congo D.R. 22 000 (40.5)	**Canada** **5 533** **(10.2)**	Zambia 5 422 (10.0)	Russia 4 748 (8.8)	Brazil 4 300 (7.9)
Magnesium (metal)	000 t (%)	722	China 468 (64.7)	USA 118 (16.3)	**Canada** **65** **(9.0)**	Russia 38 (5.3)	Israel 28 (3.8)
Titanium concentrate	000 t (%)	4 800	Australia 1 140 (23.8)	South Africa 952 (19.8)	**Canada** **809** **(16.9)**	China 400 (8.3)	Norway 380 (7.9)
Platinum group metals (mine metal content)	kg (%)	495 628	South Africa 299 964 (60.5)	Russia 137 600 (26.3)	**Canada** **21 456** **(5.6)**	USA 18 400 (3.7)	Zimbabwe 8 811 (1.9)
Aluminum (primary metal)	000 t (%)	31 955	China 7 806 (24.4)	Russia 3 647 (11.4)	**Canada** **2 894** **(9.1)**	USA 2 481 (7.8)	Australia 1 903 (6.0)
Gypsum (mine production)	000 t (%)	110 000	USA 17 500 (15.9)	Iran 11 000 (10.0)	**Canada** **9 500** **(8.6)**	Thailand 8 000 (7.3)	Spain/China 7 500 (6.8)
Chrysotile (asbestos) (mine production)	000 t (%)	2 200	Russia 875 (39.8)	China 360 (16.4)	Kazakhstan 350 (15.9)	**Canada** **240** **(10.9)**	Brazil 195 (8.9)
Cadmium (metal)	t (%)	18 440	China 3 000 (16.3)	South Korea 2 582 (14.0)	Japan 2 297 (12.5)	**Canada** **1 703** **(9.2)**	Mexico 1 627 (8.8)
Zinc (mine production)	000 t (%)	10 107	China 2 525 (25.0)	Australia 1 367 (13.5)	Peru 1 202 (11.9)	USA 748 (7.4)	**Canada** **667** **(6.6)**
Molybdenum (Mo content) (mine production)	t (%)	161 570	USA 56 900 (35.2)	Chile 45 500 (28.2)	China 28 500 (17.6)	Peru 9 700 (6.0)	**Canada** **7 910** **(4.9)**
Salt (mine production)	000 t (%)	210 000	USA 45 900 (21.9)	China 38 000 (18.1)	Germany 18 700 (8.9)	India 15 500 (7.4)	**Canada** **13 300** **(6.3)**
Lead (mine production)[1]	000 t (%)	3 333	China 1 023 (30.7)	Australia 767 (23.0)	USA 437 (13.1)	Peru 319 (9.6)	Mexico 134 (4.0)
Gold (mine production)[2]	t (%)	2 441	South Africa 297 (12.2)	Australia 263 (10.8)	USA 261 (10.7)	China 225 (9.2)	Peru 208 (8.5)
Silver[3]	t (%)	20 501	Peru 3 193 (15.6)	Mexico 2 894 (14.1)	China 2 500 (12.2)	Australia 2 407 (11.7)	Chile 1 400 (6.8)
Copper (mine production)[4]	000 t (%)	15 016	Chile 5 321 (35.4)	USA 1 140 (7.6)	Indonesia 1 064 (7.1)	Peru 1 010 (6.7)	Australia 927 (6.2)

[1]Canada ranked 6th. [2]Canada ranked 8th. [3]Canada ranked 8th. [4]Canada ranked 8th. SOURCE: Adapted from Natural Resources Canada, *Canadian Minerals Yearbook 2006*, © Her Majesty the Queen in Right of Canada, 2007. Reproduced with permission.

nergy

49. Coal,[1] Supply and Demand, 1960, 1970, 1980, 1991, 2001, 2005 (10^6 t)

	1960	1970	1980	1991	2000	2005
Production	10.0	15.1	36.7	71.1	70.5	65.3
mports	11.5	18.0	15.6	12.4	25.4	16.3
Total supply	**21.5**	**33.1**	**52.3**	**83.5**	**95.9**	**81.7**
Domestic	20.4	25.7	37.3	49.4	57.3	57.2
Exports	0.9	4.3	15.3	34.1	30.2	25.4
Total demand	**21.3**	**30.0**	**52.6**	**83.5**	**87.5**	**82.6**

ncludes bituminous, sub-bituminous, and lignite.
URCE: Adapted from Statistics Canada, *Canada Year Book*, Catalogue 11-402, 1997, 5 November 1997; *Coal nd Coke Statistics*, Catalogue 45-002, various years, http://www.statcan.ca/bsolc/english/bsolc?catno= 5-002-X&CHROPG=1; and *Energy Statistics Handbook*, Catalogue 57-601, January–March 2007, 17 August 2007, tp://www.statcan.ca/english/freepub/57-601-XIE/57-601-XIE2007001.htm.

50. Marketable Natural Gas, Supply and Demand, 1960, 1970, 1980, 1991, 2001, 2005 (10^9 m^3)

	1960	1970	1980	1991	2000	2005
Production	12.5	52.9	69.8	105.2	171.4	170.7
Imports	0.2	0.3	5.6	0.3	3.9	9.5
Total supply	**12.7**	**53.2**	**75.4**	**105.5**	**175.3**	**180.2**
Domestic	9.4	29.5	43.3	54.8	85.5	73.9
Exports	3.1	22.1	22.6	47.6	108.2	106.3
Total demand	**12.5**	**51.6**	**75.4**	**102.4**	**193.7**	**180.2**

OURCE: Adapted from Statistics Canada, *Canada Year Book*, Catalogue 11-402, 1997, Released November 5, 1997; *upply and Disposition of Crude Oil and Natural Gas*, Catalogue 26-006, various years; and *Energy Statistics andbook*, Catalogue 57-601, January–March 2007, 17 August 2007, http://www.statcan.ca/english/freepub/ 7-601-XIE/57-601-XIE2007001.htm.

51. Electricity, Supply and Demand, 1960, 1970, 1980, 1991, 2000, 2005 (10^9 kWh)

	1960	1970	1980	1991	2000	2005
Production	114.0	204.7	367.3	489.2	585.8	604.2
Imports	1.0	3.2	2.9	6.2	15.3	19.7
Total supply	**115.0**	**207.9**	**370.2**	**495.4**	**601.1**	**623.9**
Domestic	109.0	202.3	239.9	470.8	550.2	580.4
Exports	6.0	5.6	30.3	24.6	50.6	43.5
Total demand	**115.0**	**207.9**	**370.2**	**495.4**	**600.8**	**623.9**

SOURCE: Adapted from Statistics Canada, *Canada Year Book*, Catalogue 11-402, 1997, 5 November 1997; *Electric Power Statistics*, Catalogue 57-001, various years, http://www.statcan.ca/bsolc/english/bsolc?catno= 57-001-X&CHROPG=1; and *Energy Statistics Handbook*, Catalogue 57-601, January–March 2007, 17 August 2007, http://www.statcan.ca/english/freepub/57-601-XIE/57-601-XIE2007001.htm.

52. Crude Oil and Equivalent, Supply and Demand, 1960, 1970, 1980, 1991, 2001, 2005 (10^6 m^3)

	1960	1970	1980	1991	2000	2005
Production	36.5	80.2	89.5	96.7	129.0	146.2
Imports	21.2	33.1	32.2	31.5	53.5	53.8
Total supply	**57.7**	**113.3**	**121.7**	**128.2**	**182.5**	**200.0**
Domestic	46.8	74.3	109.8	84.4	103.1	108.4
Exports	10.7	38.9	11.9	44.2	79.6	91.6
Total demand	**57.5**	**113.2**	**121.7**	**128.6**	**182.7**	**200.0**

SOURCE: Adapted from Statistics Canada, *Canada Year Book*, Catalogue 11-402, 1997, 5 November 1997; *Electric Power Statistics*, Catalogue 57-001, various years, http://www.statcan.ca/bsolc/english/bsolc?catno=57-001-X&CHROPG=1; and *Energy Statistics Handbook*, Catalogue 57-601, January–March 2007, 17 August 2007, http://www.statcan.ca/english/freepub/57-601-XIE/57-601-XIE2007001.htm.

53. Electricity Production and Consumption, 1960, 1970, 1980, 2000, 2005 (GWh)

Province or Territory	1960		1970		1980		2000		2005	
	Production	Consumption	Production	Consumption	Production	Consumption	Production	Consumption	Production	Consumption
Newfoundland & Labrador	1 512	1 427	4 854	4 770	46 374	8 545	43 598	11 817	42 136	11 947
Prince Edward Island	79	79	250	250	127	518	48	1 037	46	1 198
Nova Scotia	1 814	1 733	3 511	3 706	6 868	6 814	11 625	11 505	12 477	12 595
New Brunswick	1 738	1 684	5 142	4 221	9 323	8 838	19 295	16 134	21 063	15 880
Québec	50 433	44 002	75 877	69 730	97 917	118 254	179 757	191 819	180 296	206 909
Ontario	35 815	37 157	63 857	69 488	110 283	106 509	153 221	153 696	158 750	159 161
Manitoba	3 742	4 021	8 449	8 601	19 468	13 927	32 500	21 051	37 049	21 918
Saskatchewan	2 204	2 124	6 011	5 402	9 204	9 827	17 488	18 629	20 020	19 512
Alberta	3 443	3 472	10 035	9 880	23 451	23 172	54 535	59 363	63 636	62 207
British Columbia	13 409	13 413	26 209	25 761	43 416	42 789	68 683	64 052	67 773	65 732
Yukon	89	89	224	220	381	381	298	298	343	343
Northwest Territories	100	100	304	308	494	494	765[1]	765[1]	635	635
Nunavut	—	—	—	—	—	—	—	—	142	142
Canada	**114 378**	**109 304**	**204 723**	**202 337**	**367 306**	**340 068**	**581 813**	**550 166**	**604 500**	**580 649**

OTE: Values for the provinces and territories may not add up to the totals for Canada, due to rounding and the use of estimated data in some cases. [1]Includes Nunavut.
OURCE: Adapted from Statistics Canada, *Electric Power Statistics*, Catalogue 57-001, various years, http://www.statcan.ca/bsolc/english/bsolc?catno=57-001-X&CHROPG=1; and *Electric Power Generation, Transmission and Distribution*, atalogue 57-202, 2005, 26 November 2007, http://www.statcan.ca/bsolc/english/bsolc?catno=57-202-X&CHROPG=1.

54. Primary Energy Production, 1990 to 2005 (petajoules)

Year	Coal	Crude Oil	Natural Gas	Gas Plant Natural Gas Liquids (NGLs)	Primary Electricity, Hydro & Nuclear	Steam & Biomass	Total
1990	1 673.1	3 765.2	4 183.8	390.3	1 305.9	16.0	11 495.4
1991	1 748.0	3 765.4	4 406.0	399.6	1 387.6	20.6	11 887.9
1992	1 553.5	3 931.7	4 864.5	433.5	1 401.8	12.6	12 196.2
1993	1 651.3	4 116.9	5 348.0	484.9	1 472.7	6.8	13 077.8
1994	1 735.3	4 299.9	5 831.3	500.5	1 542.3	4.0	13 913.3
1995	1 800.8	4 457.8	6 129.3	582.3	1 530.0	2.6	14 489.2
1996	1 832.3	4 590.7	6 343.4	589.1	1 583.1	2.5	14 800.3
1997	1 897.3	4 842.6	6 409.5	603.1	1 530.7	1.2	15 284.4
1998	1 651.5	5 021.7	6 664.1	605.2	1 426.2	0	15 368.7
1999	1 589.3	4 788.8	6 857.1	641.4	1 481.7	0	15 358.2
2000	1 509.9	4 999.6	7 062.1	672.2	1 524.6	0	15 768.4
2001	1 533.0	5 056.2	7 202.1	655.8	1 447.9	0	15 894.9
2002	1 429.9	5 359.6	7 249.9	626.2	1 505.3	0	16 171.0
2003	1 326.1	5 679.6	7 065.2	642.9	1 457.1	0	16 170.9
2004	1 415.7	5 869.4	7 095.7	650.7	1 522.2	0	16 553.7
2005	1 400.5	5 632.4	7 249.9	655.8	1 608.7	0	16 547.3

OURCE: Adapted from Statistics Canada, *Energy Statistics Handbook*, Catalogue 57-601, January-March 2007, p. 30, table 2.1-1, 17 August 2007, ttp://www.statcan.ca/english/freepub/57-601-XIE/57-601-XIE2007001.htm.

55. Energy Summary, 1994, 2000 and 2005 (petajoules[1])

	1994	2000	2005
Primary production[2]	13 941	15 768	16 547
Net supply[3]	8 418	9 426	9 990
Producer's own consumption	976	1 257	1 355
Non-energy use	745	789	982
Energy use (final demand)	6 697	7 379	7 654
Industrial	2 086	2 287	2 283
Transportation	2 027	2 280	2 389
Agriculture	195	232	209
Residential	1 277	1 288	1 296
Public administration	145	131	137
Commercial and institutional	967	1 162	1 340

[1]A 30-litre gasoline fill-up contains about one gigajoule of energy. A petajoule is one million gigajoules. [2]Primary energy sources: coal, crude oil, natural gas, natural gas liquids, hydro, and nuclear energy. [3]Net supply of primary and secondary sources. In 2005, Canada exported 8 662 petajoules and imported 3 007.
SOURCE: Adapted from Statistics Canada *Canada Year Book*, Catalogue 11-402, 1997, 5 November 1997; "Energy Summary", http://www.statcan.ca/english/Pgdb/manuf19.htm, accessed 2002; and "Energy supply and demand", http://www40.statcan.ca/l01/cst01/prim71.htm, accessed 21 August 2007.

56. Installed Electrical Generating Capacity by Fuel Type and Region, 1970, 1990, 2000, 2004

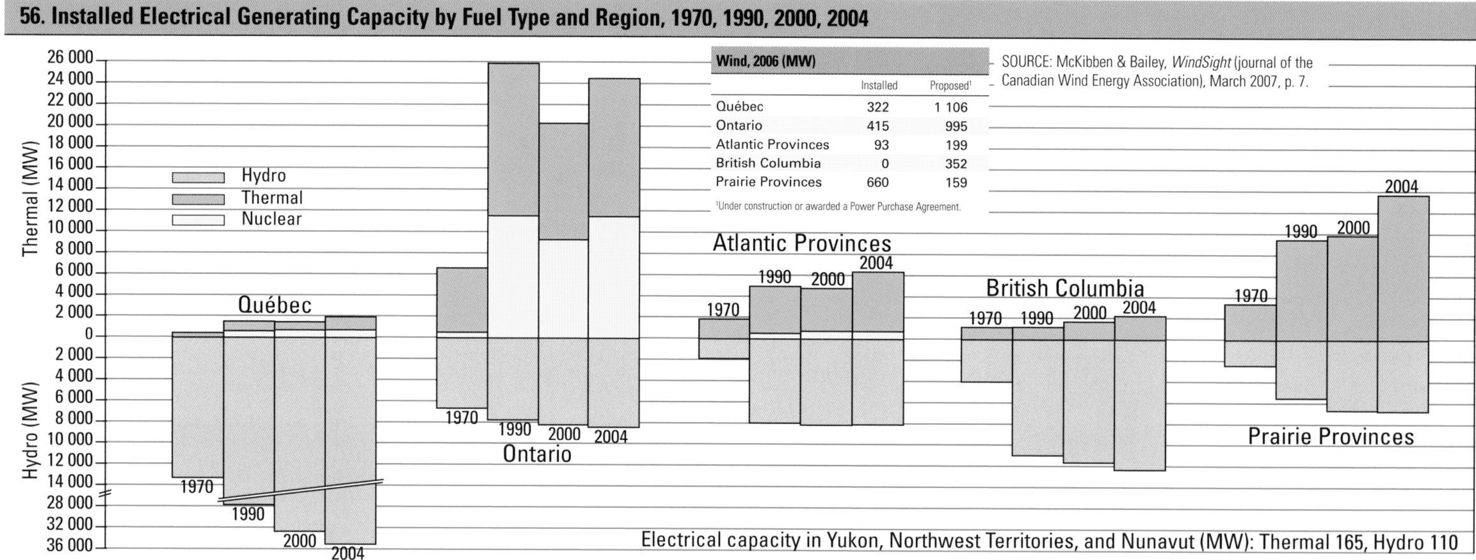

Wind, 2006 (MW)	Installed	Proposed[1]
Québec	322	1 106
Ontario	415	995
Atlantic Provinces	93	199
British Columbia	0	352
Prairie Provinces	660	159

[1]Under construction or awarded a Power Purchase Agreement.

SOURCE: Adapted from Statistics Canada, *Electric Power Generation, Transmission and Distribution*, Catalogue 57-202, 2000, 2 May 2002; and 2004, 29 August 2006, page 8-9, Table 1, http://www.statcan.ca/bsolc/english/bsolc?catno=57-202-X&CHROPG=1.

57. Top World Oil Producers, 2006

Country	Production (thousand barrels per day)
Saudi Arabia	10 719
Russia	9 668
United States	8 367
Iran	4 146
China	3 836
Mexico	3 706
Canada	3 289
United Arab Emirates	2 938
Venezuela	2 802
Norway	2 785
Kuwait	2 674
Nigeria	2 443
Brazil	2 163
Algeria	2 122
Iraq	2 008

SOURCE: Energy Information Administration: Official Energy Statistics from the US Government, "Top World Oil Producers and Consumers" 2006. http://www.eia.doe.gov/emeu/cabs/topworldtables1_2.htm.

58. Top World Oil Consumers, 2006

Country	Consumption (thousand barrels per day)
United States	20 588
China	7 274
Japan	5 222
Russia	3 103
Germany	2 630
India	2 534
Canada	2 218
Brazil	2 183
South Korea	2 157
Saudi Arabia	2 068
Mexico	2 030
France	1 972
United Kingdom	1 816
Italy	1 709
Iran	1 627

SOURCE: Energy Information Administration: Official Energy Statistics from the US Government, "Top World Oil Producers and Consumers" 2006. http://www.eia.doe.gov/emeu/cabs/topworldtables1_2.htm.

59. Conventional Crude Oil and Equivalent, Remaining Established Reserves in Canada, 2005 (000 m³)

	Remaining Reserves at 31 Dec 2004	2005 Gross Additions	2005 Net Production	Remaining Reserves at 31 Dec 2005	Net Change in Reserves during 2005
Crude Oil					
British Columbia	22 162	1 237	1 928	21 471	-691
Alberta	276 632	27 193	33 060	270 765	-5 867
Saskatchewan	187 902	34 264	24 515	197 651	9 749
Manitoba	3 861	893	812	3 942	81
Ontario	1 947	-214	138	1 595	-352
Québec	0	n.a.	n.a.	0	0
New Brunswick	0	n.a.	n.a.	0	0
Mainland territories	6 788	n.a.	1 089	5 699	-1 089
Eastcoast offshore	138 699	151 851	17 685	272 865	134 166
Total crude oil	**637 991**	**215 224**	**79 227**	**773 988**	**135 997**
Mackenzie/Beaufort	53 950	n.a.	n.a.	53 950	0
Arctic islands	0	n.a.	n.a.	0	0
Total frontier areas	**53 950**	**0**	**0**	**53 950**	**0**
Total crude oil	**691 941**	**215 224**	**79 227**	**827 938**	**135 997**
Pentanes plus					
British Columbia	6 477	629	466	6 640	163
Alberta	53 536	9 076	8 830	53 782	246
Saskatchewan	262	61	76	247	-15
Manitoba	0	n.a.	n.a.	0	0
Mainland territories	2 731	n.a.	55	2 676	-55
Eastcoast offshore	7 548	n.a.	185	7 363	-185
Total pentanes plus	**70 554**	**9 766**	**9 612**	**70 708**	**154**
Total crude oil & equivalent	**762 495**	**224 990**	**88 839**	**898 646**	**136 151**

n.a. = not available

SOURCE: Adapted from Canadian Association of Petroleum Producers, *Technical Report, Statistical Handbook for Canada's Upstream Petroleum Industry*, September 2007, 2006-9999, table 2.1a.

60. Marketable Natural Gas, Remaining Established Reserves in Canada, 2005

Area	Remaining Reserves at 31 Dec 2004	2005 Gross Additions	2005 Net Production	Remaining Reserves at 31 Dec 2005	Net Changes in Reserves during 2005
	(000 000 m³ at 101.325 kPa and 15°C)				
British Columbia	289 432	86 354	27 953	347 833	58 401
Alberta	1 175 892	113 301	135 713	1 153 480	-22 412
Saskatchewan	85 007	13 512	6 905	91 614	6 607
Ontario	11 456	1 912	347	13 021	1 565
Québec	105	—	—	105	0
New Brunswick	0	—	—	0	0
Mainland territories	11 872	-125	487	11 260	-612
Eastcoast offshore	19 278	—	4 031	15 247	-4 031
Total	**1 593 042**	**214 954**	**175 436**	**1 632 560**	**39 518**

SOURCE: Adapted from Canadian Association of Petroleum Producers, *Technical Report, Statistical Handbook for Canada's Upstream Petroleum Industry*, September 2007, 2006-9999, table 2.2a.

61. Developed Non-Conventional Oil, Remaining Established Reserves in Canada, 2005 (000 m³)

	Remaining Reserves at 31 Dec 2004	2005 Gross Additions	2005 Net Production	Remaining Reserves at 31 Dec 2005	Net Changes in Reserves during 2005
Mining—upgraded and bitumen[1] (Alberta)	841 235	163 633	31 553	973 315	132 080
In-situ—bitumen[2] (Alberta)	330 868	87 940	25 555	393 253	62 385
Total developed non-conventional oil	**1 172 103**	**251 573**	**57 108**	**1 366 568**	**194 465**
Total conventional & non-conventional oil	**1 934 598**	**476 563**	**145 947**	**2 265 214**	**330 616**

[1]Developed synthetic crude oil reserves are those recoverable from developed commercial projects. [2]Developed bitumen reserves are those recoverable from developed experimental/demonstration and commercial projects.
SOURCE: Adapted from Canadian Association of Petroleum Producers, *Technical Report, Statistical Handbook for Canada's Upstream Petroleum Industry*, September 2007, 2006-9999, table 2.5a.

62. Liquified Petroleum Gases, Remaining Established Reserves in Canada, 2005 (000 m³)

	Ethane, Propane, & Butanes				
	Remaining Reserves at 31 Dec 2004	2005 Gross Additions	2005 Net Production	Remaining Reserves at 31 Dec 2005	Net Change in Reserves during 2005
British Columbia	11 658	3 437	1 667	13 428	1 770
Alberta	113 269	16 064	18 532	110 801	-2 468
Saskatchewan	888	207	244	851	-37
Manitoba	0	0	n.a.	0	0
Total	**125 815**	**19 708**	**20 443**	**125 080**	**-735**

n.a. = not available
SOURCE: Adapted from Canadian Association of Petroleum Producers, *Technical Report, Statistical Handbook for Canada's Upstream Petroleum Industry*, September 2007, 2006-9999, table 2.3a.

63. Energy Supply and Demand, by Fuel Type, 2005 (petajoules)

	Coal	Crude Oil	Natural Gas	Natural Gas[1] Liquids (NGLs)	Primary Electricity, Hydro & Nuclear	Refined Petroleum Products
Production	**1 400.5**	**5 632.4**	**7 249.9**	**655.8**	**1 608.7**	**4 698.8**
Exports	659.6	3 541.3	4 065.9	238.7	156.7	974.5
Imports	486.0	2 072.3	364.4	13.9	70.8	632.4
Energy availability	1 272.3	4 507.1	3 543.1	465.0	1 522.8	4 246.4
Transformed to electricity by utilities	1 077.4	n.a.	280.6	n.a.	n.a.	162.7
Transformed to electricity by industry	0.04	0	67.1	n.a.	n.a.	16.9
Transformed to coke and manufactured gases	125.5	n.a.	n.a.	n.a.	n.a.	n.a.
Transformed to refined petroleum products	n.a.	4 507.1	26.4	60.0	n.a.	n.a.
Transformed to steam generation	0.01	n.a.	24.7	n.a.	0	5.9
Net supply	**70.2**	**0**	**3 144.3**	**405.0**	**1 522.8**	**4 123.0**
Producer consumption	5.8	0	714.5	28.6	152.3	453.7
Non-energy use	10.7	n.a.	162.0	321.3	n.a.	487.3
Energy use, final demand	53.7	0	2 267.8	108.3	1 936.7	3 128.7
Total industrial	52.8	n.a.	896.6	52.2	858.6	265.4
Total transportation	n.a.	n.a.	200.0	10.3	15.3	2 163.2
Agriculture	n.a.	n.a.	19.8	7.0	36.9	144.9
Residential	0.9	n.a.	646.6	12.3	543.6	92.7
Public administration	0.005	n.a.	22.4	0	50.3	63.3
Commercial and other institutional	0	n.a.	482.4	26.5	432.0	399.2

n.a. = not available
[1]Includes propane, butane, and ethane produced by gas plant.
SOURCE: Adapted from Statistics Canada, "Energy supply and demand, by fuel type", http://www40.statcan.ca/l01/cst01/prim72.htm, accessed 21 August 2007.

64. Canadian Imports and Exports of Selected Energy Materials

	1990 ($000 000)		1995 ($000 000)		2000 ($000 000)		2005 ($000 000)	
	Import	Export	Import	Export	Import	Export	Import	Export
Coal	611.4	2 110.3	475.2	2 212.1	946.5	1 659.7	1 265.0	3 182.7
Crude petroleum[1, 2]	5 300.2	5 528.5	5 707.9	8 956.3	13 668.6	19 589.3	21 925.3	29 926.8
Natural gas[2]	0.5	3 276.7	45.4	5 515.6	227.2	20 136.0	3 625.5	35 252.0
Petroleum products	1 583.2	2 651.2	1 167.3	2 562.0	2 351.9	5 598.9	5 790.2	11 454.3
Electricity	557.6	538.3	75.0	1 174.9	621.2	4 059.0	1 233.1	3 121.6
Total	**8 524.0**	**15 180.2**	**8 024.7**	**23 023.2**	**18 482.9**	**53 771.7**	**34 678.5**	**86 977.8**

[1]Main exporting countries 2005: Norway, 25.9%; Algeria, 17.6%; United Kingdom, 15.7%; Saudi Arabia, 8.2%; Iraq, 7.1%. [2]Over 95% of Canada's exports of petroleum and natural gas go to the United States.
SOURCE: Adapted from Statistics Canada, *Imports by Commodity*, 65-007, (Jan-Dec 2006 for 2006 data); *Exports by Commodity*, 65-004 (Jan-Dec 2006 for 2006 data).

Manufacturing

65. Summary Statistics, Annual Census of Manufacturers, 1965, 1970, 1975, 1980, 1984, 1990, 1994, 1999, 2005

Year	Number of Establishments[1]	Production and Related Workers		Cost of Fuel & Electricity ($000 000)	Cost of Materials & Supplies Used ($000 000)	Value of Shipments of Goods of Own Manufacture ($000 000)	Value Added ($000 000)
		Number	Wages ($000 000)				
1965	33 310	1 115 892	5 012	676	18 622	33 889	14 928
1970	31 928	1 167 063	7 232	903	25 700	46 381	20 048
1975	30 100	1 271 786	12 699	1 805	51 178	88 427	36 106
1980	35 495	1 346 187	22 162	4 449	99 898	168 059	65 852
1984	36 464	1 240 816	28 295	7 306	136 134	230 070	88 668
1990	39 864	1 393 324	40 407	7 936	168 664	298 919	122 973
1994	31 974	1 243 026	41 405	9 152	202 655	352 835	142 859
1999	29 822	1 487 098	53 164	11 018	277 803	488 729	202 930
2005	32 582	1 312 484	55 045	16 958	357 040	584 266	211 047

[1]The increase in the number of establishments between 1975 and 1980 was largely a result of the addition of 4 962 small establishments by improved coverage.
SOURCE: Adapted from Statistics Canada, *Manufacturing Industries of Canada, National and Provincial Areas*, Catalogue 31-203, various years; *Canada Year Book*, Catalogue 11-202E, 1976-77; Canada Year Book, Catalogue 11-402, 1992, 21 October 1991; and CANSIM database, http://cansim2.statcan.ca, table number 301-0006, extracted 23 August 2007.

66. Principal Statistics on Manufacturing Industries by Province and Territory, 2005

Province or Territory	Number of Establishments	Number of Production Workers	Production Workers' Wages ($000 000)	Cost of Energy and Water Utility ($000 000)	Cost of Materials, and Supplies ($000 000)	Revenue from Goods Manufactured ($000 000)	Manufacturing Value Added ($000 000)
Newfoundland & Labrador	369	14 136	352.5	140.8	1 290.5	2 407.0	934.4
Prince Edward Island	196	4 973	134.0	33.6	814.8	1 278.9	460.2
Nova Scotia	707	29 867	980.4	335.8	5 390.7	9 598.2	3 874.5
New Brunswick	631	28 028	837.3	438.0	11 225.6	15 542.4	3 981.4
Québec	8 059	342 379	13 047.0	4 212.2	76 924.3	133 791.5	52 742.7
Ontario	13 451	609 718	28 128.6	6 750.4	185 433.9	298 342.8	106 407.1
Manitoba	995	46 432	1 572.1	327.4	7 231.3	13 240.3	5 762.7
Saskatchewan	767	20 071	775.7	371.5	6 343.9	9 728.0	3 019.5
Alberta	3 100	99 697	4 137.6	2 891.5	39 931.9	60 348.5	17 812.5
British Columbia	4 241	116 737	5 064.5	1 454.9	22 377.5	39 875.8	16 015.1
Yukon	35	159	5.0	0.4	9.8	22.5	12.3
Northwest Territories	20	204	9.5	0.4	63.6	83.9	21.3
Nunavut	11	83	1.1	0.6	2.5	5.9	2.8
Canada	**32 582**	**1 312 484**	**55 045.4**	**16 957.5**	**357 040.3**	**584 265.7**	**211 046.6**

SOURCE: Adapted from Statistics Canada, *Manufacturing Industries of Canada, National and Provincial Areas*, 1999, Catalogue 31-203, 18 June 2002; and CANSIM database, http://cansim2.statcan.ca, table number 301-0006, extracted 23 August 2007.

67. Manufacturing Sales, by Subsector, 2002 and 2006 ($000 000)

	2002	2006
Food	64 089.5	72 138.0
Beverage and tobacco products	12 074.4	11 196.7
Textile mills	4 260.6	2 561.6
Textile product mills	2 950.4	2 442.3
Leather and allied products	933.6	459.1
Paper	34 284.4	31 422.4
Printing and related support activities	12 155.3	10 868.4
Petroleum and coal products	33 690.1	61 219.4
Chemicals	40 469.2	53 046.1
Plastics and rubber products	25 286.6	27 808.9
Clothing	8 024.4	5 309.9
Wood products	32 801.6	29 465.4
Non-metallic mineral products	11 630.8	13 945.7
Primary metals	36 074.9	51 273.6
Fabricated metal products	32 210.5	35 411.5
Machinery	27 448.5	31 424.7
Computer and electronic products	22 656.3	19 560.7
Electrical equipment, appliances, and components	10 135.9	10 520.1
Transportation equipment	126 451.6	118 449.0
Furniture and related products	13 916.5	13 358.9
Miscellaneous manufacturing	8 357.6	9 161.9
All manufacturing industries	**559 902.7**	**611 044.4**

SOURCE: Adapted from Statistics Canada, http://www40.statcan.ca/l01/cst01/manuf11.htm, accessed 25 October 2007.

Trade

68. Exports from Canada, Principal Nations, 1991, 1995, 2001, 2006 ($000 000)

Country or Region	1991	1995	2001	2006
United States	103 449	196 161	325 034	336 152
Japan	7 111	11 857	8 067	9 248
United Kingdom	2 920	3 748	4 700	9 150
China	1 849	3 212	3 920	7 183
Mexico	n.a.	1 107	2 353	4 026
Germany	2 125	3 150	2 691	3 484
South Korea	1 861	2 695	1 950	3 189
Netherlands	1 655	1 584	1 541	2 783
France	1 350	1 888	2 035	2 417
Belgium	1 073	1 823	1 837	2 204
Norway	n.a.	n.a.	n.a.	1 883
Italy	1 017	1 768	1 550	1 815
Australia	628	1 139	954	1 691
India	n.a.	n.a.	n.a.	1 529
Hong Kong	817	1 377	1 063	1 309
Taiwan	n.a.	1 683	965	1 308
Total all countries	**138 079**	**247 703**	**373 554**	**410 584**

NOTE: Data is listed in order of 2006 export values.
n.a. = not available
SOURCE: Adapted from Statistics Canada, *Exports by Country*, Catalogue 65-003, various years.

69. Imports to Canada, Principal Nations, 1991, 1995, 2001, 2006 ($000 000)

Country or Region	1991	1995	2001	2006
United States	86 235	150 705	218 408	217 597
China	1 852	4 639	12 712	34 473
Mexico	2 574	5 341	12 110	15 982
Japan	10 249	12 103	14 647	15 334
Germany	3 734	4 801	7 955	11 115
United Kingdom	4 182	5 470	11 631	10 843
South Korea	2 110	3 204	4 601	5 763
Norway	n.a.	2 314	3 500	5 445
France	2 670	3 125	5 510	5 175
Italy	1 792	3 270	4 034	4 916
Taiwan	2 212	2 792	4 410	3 877
Malaysia	n.a.	1 549	1 894	2 938
Ireland	n.a.	189	n.a.	2 550
Sweden	n.a.	1 305	1 708	2 356
Thailand	n.a.	1 014	1 689	2 251
Total all countries	**135 284**	**225 493**	**343 056**	**396 443**

NOTE: Data is listed in order of 2006 export values.
n.a. = not available
SOURCE: Adapted from Statistics Canada, *Imports by Country*, Catalogue 65-006, various years.

70. Principal Commodities Imported and Exported, 2006 ($000 000)

Commodity	Imports	Exports[2]
Mineral fuels	36 273	86 258
Vehicles, rolling stock, parts	67 770	72 202
Wood and articles thereof	3 559	17 313
Machinery[1]	63 520	29 526
Electrical machinery and parts	39 085	16 522
Iron and steel products	18 234	11 759
Plastic products	13 860	14 206
Aircraft and parts	5 965	9 613
Pharmaceutical products	10 148	5 004
Paper and paperboard	6 268	14 218
Precious stones and metals	6 009	8 651
Organic chemicals	7 520	5 141
Aluminum and articles thereof	4 283	12 107
Optical equipment	11 396	4 596
Furniture and related products	7 522	7 172
Pulp wood and cellulose	439	6 649
Clothing and apparel	6 969	2 329
Rubber and articles thereof	5 552	3 639
Total, all commodities	**396 443**	**410 584**

[1]Includes nuclear reactors, boilers, machinery, and mechanical appliances and parts. [2]Nickel and related articles exports $5 820. SOURCE: Adapted from Statistics Canada, *Imports by Country*, Catalogue 65-006, vol. 63 no. 04, Jan to Dec 2006, 19 Feb 2007; and *Exports by Country*, Catalogue 65-003, vol. 63 no. 04, Jan to Dec 2006, 5 March 2007.

The Economy

71. Gross Domestic Product by Industry,[1] Canada, 1980, 1990, 2001, 2006

Industry	1980 (%)	1990 (%)	2001 (%)	2006 (%)
Agricultural, fishing, trapping, and forestry	2.3	3.0	2.3	2.3
Mining	4.1	4.0	3.9	4.8
Manufacturing	17.7	18.1	17.3	15.6
Construction	5.7	6.4	5.3	6.2
Trade (wholesale and retail)	11.4	11.5	11.5	11.5
Finance, insurance, and real estate	13.4	15.7	19.6	19.3
Transportation	4.6	4.7	4.6	4.6
Professional, community, and personal services	22.2	23.1	22.3	23.9
Public administration	7.2	6.7	5.6	5.6
Other (utilities, and information and cultural industries)	11.4	6.8	7.6	6.2

[1]Based on per cent of Canada's GDP.
SOURCE: Adapted from Statistics Canada, *Canadian Economic Observer*, Catalogue 11-010, various years; and "Gross domestic product at basic prices, by industry", http://www40.statcan.ca/l01/cst01/econ41.htm, accessed 21 August 2007.

72. Inflation Rates, 1915 to 2006

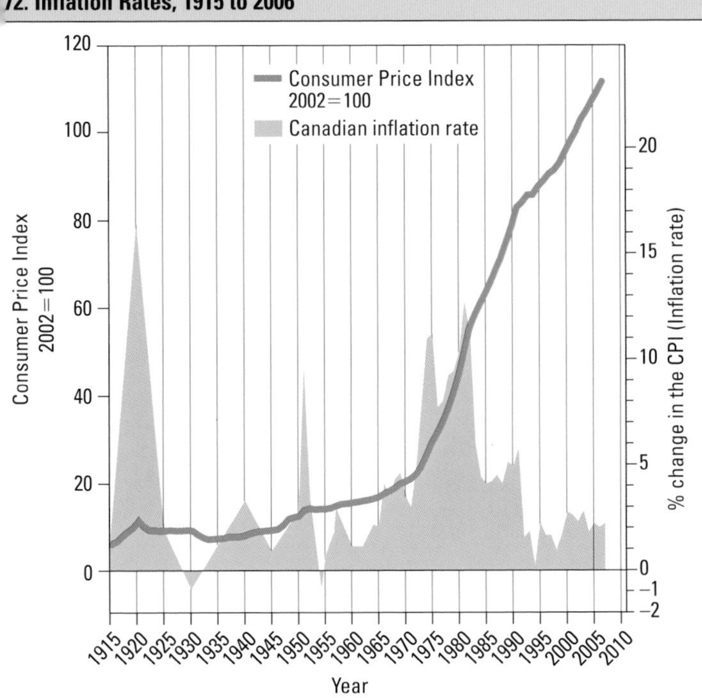

NOTE: Prior to 1950, data was compiled every five years. Since 1950, data has been compiled annually.
SOURCE: Adapted from Statistics Canada, "Consumer Price Index, historical summary", http://www40.statcan.ca/l01/cst01/econ46a.htm

73. Gross Domestic Product by Province and Territory,[1] 1970, 1980, 1990, 2001, 2006

Province or Territory	1970	1980	1990	2001	2006
NFLD & LAB	1.4	1.3	1.3	1.3	1.7
PEI	0.3	0.3	0.3	0.3	0.3
NS	2.5	2.0	2.5	2.3	2.2
NB	1.9	1.6	2.0	1.7	1.8
QUE	25.5	23.3	23.1	21.0	19.7
ONT	42.0	37.1	40.8	40.6	38.7
MAN	4.2	3.6	3.5	3.2	3.1
SASK	3.4	4.0	3.1	3.1	3.1
ALTA	8.0	13.9	10.7	13.9	16.4
BC	10.6	12.4	12.2	12.0	12.5
YT, NWT & NVT	0.3	0.4	0.5	0.6	0.5

[1]Based on per cent of Canada's GDP, expenditure based. SOURCE: Adapted from Statistics Canada, *Canadian Economic Observer*, Catalogue 11-010, various years. "Gross domestic product, expenditure-based, by province and territory", http://www40.statcan.ca/l01/cst01/econ15.htm, accessed 21 August 2007.

74. Foreign Investment in Canada, 1970, 1990, 2000, 2006 ($000 000)

Country or Region	1970	1990	2000	2006
US	22 054	84 311	185 238	273 705
UK	2 641	18 217	19 268	39 012
Other EU	1 617	14 339	58 653	79 353
Japan	103	5 203	8 442	11 309
Other OECD[1]	580	5 871	9 229	19 359
Total	**27 374**	**130 932**	**291 520**	**448 858**

NOTE: Data is listed in order of 2006 investment values.
[1]OECD = Organization for Economic Cooperation and Development. Member countries are shown on the map on page 147.
SOURCE: Adapted from Statistics Canada, Table 376-0053, "International investment position, Canadian direct investment abroad and foreign direct investment in Canada, by industry and country, annual (dollars)", CANSIM (database), Using E-STAT (distributor), http://estat.statcan.ca/cgi-win/cnsmcgi.exe?Lang=E&ESTATFile=EStat\English\CII_1_E.htm&RootDir=ESTAT/, http://estat.statcan.ca/cgi-win/cnsmcgi.exe?Lang=E&ESTATFile=EStat\English\CII_2_E.htm&RootDir=ESTAT/, accessed 16 April 2008.

Transportation and Tourism

75. Principal Seaway Ports,[1] 1995, 2001, and 2006 (000 t)[2]

	Inbound Cargo			Outbound Cargo		
	1995	2001	2006	1995	2001	2006
Canadian ports	**30 289**	**26 022**	**28 230**	**26 622**	**24 471**	**28 664**
Thunder Bay	9	v.s.	—	6 702	6 145	6 203
Port Cartier	4 664	2 733	2 045	2 113	2 068	3 686
Sept-Îles	821	217	292	3 950	2 222	3 029
Québec City	2 247	955	1 837	1 008	883	2 412
Hamilton	11 044	9 947	10 889	702	666	1 725
Goderich	v.s.	v.s.	n.a.	758	1 046	1 599
Pointe-Noire	380	263	—	3 845	3 753	1 588
Toronto[3]	798	3 751	3 361	19	1 623	1 417
Windsor	179	v.s.	382	1 373	773	885
Sarnia	—	—	303	—	—	812
Meldrum Bay	—	—	—	—	—	633
Sault Ste Marie	—	—	—	—	—	504
Picton	239	182	340	567	491	487
Montreal[4]	2 198	1 775	1 785	96	442	451
Nanticoke	n.a.	477	390	n.a.	304	265
Sorel	404	307	537	116	133	187
Baie-Comeau	2 643	1 248	2 136	v.s.	v.s.	—
Trois-Rivieres	803	424	413	78	v.s.	—

	Inbound Cargo			Outbound Cargo		
	1995	2001	2006	1995	2001	2006
US ports	**11 986**	**9 941**	**12 867**	**16 375**	**12 449**	**12 416**
Toledo	264	229	3 458	3 579	2 673	2 487
Duluth	230	270	204	4 510	3 613	1 952
Sandusky	v.s.	v.s.	—	1 660	992	1 597
Chicago	1 168	871	747	1 357	429	840
Ashtabula	710	563	242	660	1 186	604
Milwaukee	228	141	224	769	363	471
Cleveland	2 044	1 692	1 834	400	339	404
Burns Harbor	3 047	1 735	1 968	566	225	376
Detroit	1 935	2 311	1 736	472	130	231
Gary	—	—	541	—	—	188
Essexville	n.a.	400	438	n.a.	v.s.	—

NOTE: Data is listed in order of 2006 cargo totals.
v.s. = very small/unreported; n.a. = not available
[1]Area includes all ports or installations within a 20 km radius of the main harbour. [2]Tonnage figures are limited to cargo volumes moved through seaway lock structures. [3]Includes Port Credit, Lakeview, Bowmanville, Clarkson, Oakville, and Oshawa. [4]Includes Côte Ste. Catherine.
SOURCE: The St. Lawrence Seaway Management Corporation, *St. Lawrence Seaway Traffic Report*, 1995, 2001, and 2006 Navigation Seasons.

76. The St. Lawrence Seaway

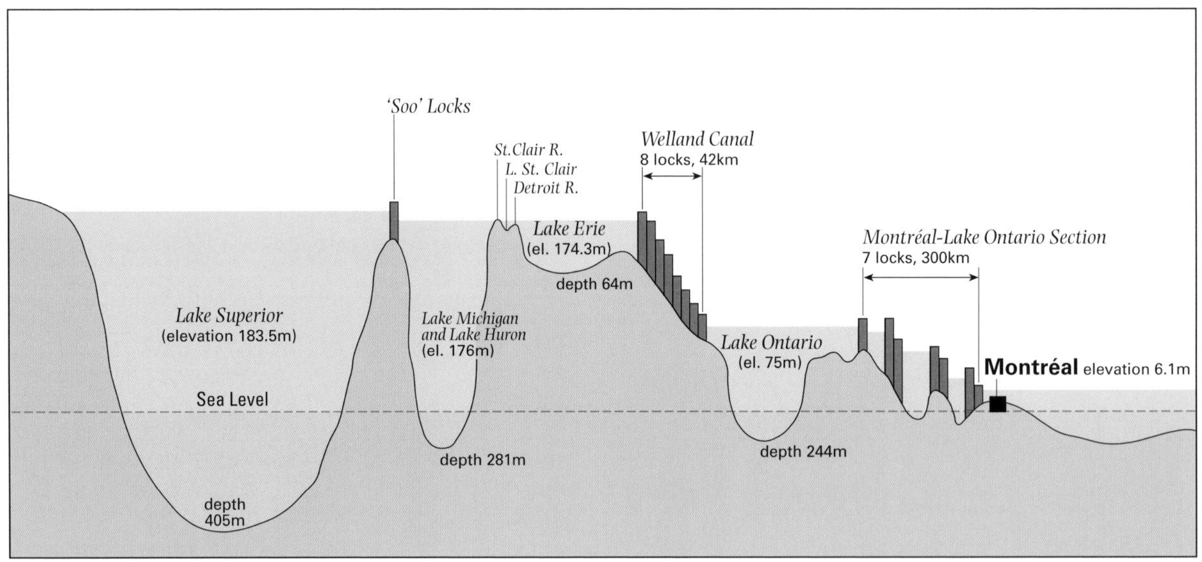

The St. Lawrence Seaway Authority was established in 1951 for the purpose of constructing, operating, and maintaining a deep waterway between the Port of Montréal and Lake Erie, replacing an earlier network of shallow-draught canals. Two of the seven seaway locks along the St. Lawrence River, in the United States, are operated by the US St. Lawrence Seaway Development Corporation.

The St. Lawrence Seaway was officially opened in 1959. It allows navigation by ships not exceeding 222.5 m in length, 23.2 m in width, and loaded to a maximum draught of 7.9 m in a minimum water depth of 8.2 m.

Beginning at Montréal, the Seaway naturally divides into four sections:

1. The Lachine Section required the construction of the 33 km South Shore Canal, to bypass the Lachine Rapids. The St. Lambert and Côte Ste. Catherine locks provide a lift 13.7 m to Lake St. Louis.

2. The Soulanges Section contains the two Beauharnois locks, bypassing the Beauharnois hydroelectric plant to reach Lac Saint-François.

3. The Lac Saint-François Section extends to a point just east of Cornwall, Ontario.

4. The International Rapids Section was developed simultaneously for hydro-electric power generation and navigation. Ontario and the State of New York jointly built the Moses–Saunders Power Dam, the Long Sault and Iroquois control dams, and undertook the flooding of the river above the power dam to form Lake St. Lawrence, the 'head pond' of the generating station. The Wiley–Dondero Canal and the Snell and Eisenhower locks allow ships to bypass the Moses–Saunders power station. The Iroquois lock and adjacent control dam are used to adjust the level of Lake St. Lawrence to that of Lake Ontario.

The Welland Canal joins lakes Ontario and Erie and allows ships to bypass Niagara Falls by means of eight locks. The present Welland Canal, completed in 1932, was later deepened to ensure 7.9 m draught navigation throughout the Seaway.

The final section consists of four parallel locks, the 'Soo' locks, on the St. Mary's River and connects Lake Superior to Lake Huron. This section is not part of the St. Lawrence Seaway Authority.

77. Cargo Loaded and Unloaded at Leading Canadian Ports, Major Commodities, 2004 (000 t)

Port	Domestic Cargo		International Cargo		Total
	Loaded	Unloaded	Loaded	Unloaded	
Vancouver	1 416	281	64 453 (potash, coal, wheat, sulphur)	8 849 (machinery/equipment)	74 998
Come-by-Chance	1 817 (crude petroleum)	15 579 (crude petroleum)	18 708 (crude petroleum)	5 948 (crude petroleum)	42 051
Saint John	1 158 (fuel oil)	1 430	10 772 (fuel oil, gasoline)	12 798 (crude petroleum)	26 158
Port Hawksbury	446	70	13 115 (crude petroleum)	10 343 (crude petroleum)	23 973
Montréal–Contrecoeur	1 209	3 877 (iron ore)	6 659 (wheat, food products)	11 521 (manufactured and miscellaneous goods, fuels)	23 265
Québec-Lévis	2 214 (fuel oil)	1 944 (wheat)	4 599 (wheat, iron ore)	12 891 (crude petroleum)	21 648
Port Cartier	3 684 (iron ore)	1 425 (wheat)	11 322 (iron ore)	1 167 (fodder and feed)	17 597
Sept-Îles–Pointe-Noire	1 730 (iron ore)	568	13 573	1 141 (alumina)	17 011
Newfoundland offshore	15 986 (crude petroleum)	372	0	0	16 359
Fraser River	5 434 (wood chips)	2 914 (limestone)	3 694 (logs, lumber, wood pulp)	2 816 (iron, steel)	14 857
Halifax	1 632	1 283	2 915	5 614	14 208
Nanticoke	671	932 (Manufactured and miscellaneous goods)	654	10 114 (coal)	12 371
Hamilton	625	5 005	643	5 645	11 917

SOURCE: Adapted from Statistics Canada, *Shipping in Canada*, Catalogue 54-205, 2004, p. 62, table 13, 20 July 2007, http://www.statcan.ca/bsolc/english/bsolc?catno=54-205-X.

78. St Lawrence Seaway Traffic by Commodity and by Nationality, 2006[1]

Commodities	Upbound (000 t)	Sources and Destinations of Upbound Commodities (%)	Downbound (000 t)	Sources and Destinations of Downbound Commodities (%)
Corn	—	—	1 729.3	Can to Can 5; US to Can 19; US to For 76
Flaxseed	—	—	467.7	Can to Can 2; Can to For 93; US to For 5
Wheat	11.7	Can to US 100	6 434.9	Can to Can 74; Can to For 6; US to Can 2; US to For 18
Soy beans	—	—	1 583.9	Can to Can 16; Can to For 9; US to Can 39; US to For 36
Canola	—	—	478.9	Can to Can 11; Can to For 89
Beans and peas	—	—	445.4	Can to Can 29; Can to For 49; US to Can 4; US to For 18
Total agricultural	**54.3**		**11 532.3**	
Iron ore	9 150.9	Can to Can 44; Can to US 56	1 859.1	US to Can 89; US to For 11
Bitumenous coal	—	—	3 714.5	Can to Can 12; US to Can 88
Salt	52.9	Can to Can 100	2 891.2	Can to Can 68; Can to US 6; US to Can 26
Coke	785.7	Can to Can 23; Can to US 56; For to Can 8; For to US 13	1 209.9	Can to Can 11; Can to For 4; US to Can 73; US to For 11
Gypsum	927.1	Can to Can 99; Can to US 1	—	—
Stone	443.0	Can to Can 4; Can to US 96	718.3	Can to Can 100
Total mine	**11 819.5**		**11 084.8**	
Iron and steel	3 447.0	Can to Can 1; For to Can 36; For to US 63	18.6	Can to For 98
Fuel oil	525.6	Can to Can 79; Can to US 21	700.9	Can to Can 73; Can to US 6; Can to For 4; US to Can 17
Cement	1 154.7	Can to Can 3; Can to US 97	52.1	Can to Can 100
Furnace slags	632.1	Can to Can 21; Can to US 56; For to US 22	433.3	Can to Can 83; Can to US 17
Cement clinker	1 064.5	Can to US 100	—	—
Steel slab	985.9	Can to Can 9; For to Can 59; For to US 32	—	—
Gasoline	621.0	Can to Can 96; US to Can 3	164.7	Can to Can 15; US to Can 85
Chemicals	391.9	Can to Can 1; US to Can 17; For to Can 74; For to US 9	338.4	Can to Can 7; Can to US 7; Can to For 68; US to Can 18
Total manufactures[2]	**10 463.4**	**Can to Can 16; Can to US 29; For to Can 25; For to US 29**	**2 135.3**	**Can to Can 55; Can to US 7; Can to For 18; US to Can 19**
Grand total	**22 386.7**	**Can to Can 31; Can to US 41; For to Can 13; For to US 15**	**24 777.5**	**Can to Can 40; Can to US 1; Can to For 9; US to Can 34; US to For 16**

— = nil

[1]Includes traffic through both the Montreal–Lake Ontario section and the Welland Canal section. [2]Includes unclassified cargoes.

SOURCE: The St. Lawrence Seaway Management Corporation, *The St. Lawrence Seaway Traffic Report 2006 Navigation Season.*

79. Visits and Expenditures of Canadian Residents in Selected Countries (other than the US), 2005

Country or Region	Visits (000)	Spending ($000 000)	Average Spending per Person per Visit ($)
Austria	152	80	525
Belgium	131	83[1]	629
France	684	834	1 219
Germany	409	279	682
Greece	146	144[1]	992
Ireland (Republic of)	127	146	1 151
Italy	423	618	1 460
Netherlands	266	135	507
Spain	216	225	1 038
Switzerland	164	123	750
United Kingdom	968	1 093	1 129
Other	914	619	1 761
Total Europe	**4 600**	**4 377**	**952**
Total Africa	**253**	**382**	**1 511**
China	170	305	1 795
Hong Kong	171	210	1 231
Japan	151	221	1 464
Other	696	817	2 677
Total Asia	**1 187**	**1 552**	**1 308**
Total Central America	**197**	**115**	**584**
Cuba	518	470	908
Dominican Republic	519	458	881
Other	1 225	522	426
Total Bermuda and Caribbean	**2 262**	**1 450**	**641**
Total South America	**233**	**266**	**1 144**
Mexico	1 007	926	919
Total North America	**1 016**	**928**	**913**
Australia	124	263	2 127
Total Oceania & other ocean islands	**179**	**383**	**2 136**
Total	**9 927**	**9 454**	**952**

[1]Use data with caution.
SOURCE: Adapted from Statistics Canada, *International Travel*, Catalogue 66-201, 2005, p. 49, table 27, 22 December 2006, http://www.statcan.ca/english/freepub/66-201-XIE/2005000/t034_en.htm.

80. Visits and Expenditures of Canadian Residents Returning from the US, by Selected States, 2005

State	Visits (000)	Spending ($000 000)
Arizona	516	437.5
California	1 258	867.6
Florida	2 207	2 353.3
Georgia	903	114.6
Idaho	475	45.5
Illinois	814	174.4
Indiana	534	63.1
Kentucky	498	38.2
Maine	949	186.7
Maryland	620	46.3
Massachusetts	736	208.4
Michigan	2 202	273.1
Minnesota	906	172.1
Montana	564	105.4
Nevada	1 010	777.6
New Hampshire	864	75.2
New York	4 445	696.2
North Carolina	861	107.5
North Dakota	556	86.3
Ohio	879	121.4
Oregon	420	97.7
Pennsylvania	1 439	136.2
South Carolina	784	261.6
Tennessee	517	79.4
Vermont	1 453	119.3
Virginia	897	96.3
Washington	2 057	321.7
West Virginia	462	16.9
Other states	3 671	1 550.0
Total	**33 496**	**9 653.6**

SOURCE: Adapted from Statistics Canada, *International Travel*, Catalogue 66-201, 2005, p. 47, table 25, 22 December 2006, http://www.statcan.ca/english/freepub/66-201-XIE/2005000/t032_en.htm.

81. Trip Characteristics of US Residents Entering Canada, Staying One or More Nights in Provinces Visited, 2005

	Atlantic Provinces[1]	Québec	Ontario	Manitoba	Saskatchewan	Alberta	British Columbia[2]	Canada
Person-visits (000)	989	2 196	7 214	293	181	961	3 793	15 627
Spending in province ($000 000)	461	1 299	2 932	146	125	626	1 875	7 463
Average spending per person-visit ($)	466	591	406	499	691	651	494	478
Person-nights (000)	4 220	7 946	25 320	1 057	692	4 489	13 606	57 331
Average number of nights per visit	4.3	3.6	3.5	3.6	3.8	4.7	3.6	3.7
Average spending per person-night ($)	109	163	116	138	181	139	138	130
Region of Residence (000)								
New England	431	782	348	x	x	39	71	1 682
Middle Atlantic	116	588	1 962	x	x	60	215	2 967
South Atlantic	132	270	708	27[3]	253	130	307	1 598
East North Central	113	205	2 886	35	28	107	237	3 611
West North Central	35[3]	65	526	161	54	105	164	1 111
East South Central	12[3]	34[3]	94	x	x	23[3]	603	231
West South Central	x	64	227	x	93	57	186	604
Mountain	36[3]	51	154	16[1]	23	189	349	818
Pacific	59	135	301	18	12	219	2 042	2 786
Total	**989**	**2 196**	**7 214**	**293**	**181**	**961**	**3 793**	**15 627**
Purpose of Trip (000)								
Business, convention, or employment	57	371	1 027	35	213	171	368	2 050
Visiting friends or relatives	274	378	1 412	63	50	211	594	2 981
Other pleasure, recreation, or holiday	598	1 244	4 029	151	82	448	2 427	8 978
Other	60	203	747	43	293	131	404	1 617
Total	**989**	**2 196**	**7 214**	**293**	**181**	**961**	**3 793**	**15 627**

continued ▶

81. Trip Characteristics of US Residents Entering Canada, Staying One or More Nights in Provinces Visited, 2005 (continued)

	Atlantic Provinces[1]	Québec	Ontario	Manitoba	Saskatchewan	Alberta	British Columbia[2]	Canada
Quarter of Entry (000)								
First	42	399	991	36	10	126	556	2 159
Second	204	552	1 928	85	49	234	982	4 034
Third	623	807	3 054	118	87	462	1 692	6 842
Fourth	121	438	1 241	54	35	139	563	2 591
Total	**989**	**2 196**	**7 214**	**293**	**181**	**961**	**3 793**	**15 627**
Length of Stay (000)								
1 night	164	295	1 789	76	67	126	894	3 412
2 to 6 nights	650	1 700	4 487	175	77	606	2 452	10 148
7 to 13 nights	151	173	788	38	32	202	383	1 768
14 nights and over	23	273	150	x	x	263	65	300
Total	**989**	**2 196**	**7 214**	**293**	**181**	**961**	**3 793**	**15 627**

x = data too small and/or unreliable to be published.
[1]Includes sum of visits to Newfoundland and Labrador, New Brunswick, Nova Scotia, and Prince Edward Island. [2]Includes sum of visits to British Columbia, Yukon Territory, Northwest Territories, and Nunavut. [3]Use data with caution.
SOURCE: Adapted from Statistics Canada, *International Travel*, Catalogue 66-201, 2005, p. 31, table 13, 22 December 2006, http://www.statcan.ca/english/freepub/66-201-XIE/2005000/t014_en.htm.

82. Trip Characteristics of Residents of Countries Other than the US Entering Canada, Staying One or More Nights in Provinces Visited, 2005

	Atlantic Provinces[1]	Québec	Ontario	Manitoba	Saskatchewan	Alberta	British Columbia[2]	Canada
Person-visits (000)	291	1 062	1 989	72	47	821	1 504	5 786
Spending in province ($000 000)	241	1 071	1 792	89	34	829	1 709	5 766
Average spending per person-visit ($)	828	1 009	901	1 235	724	1 010	1 137	997
Person-nights (000)	2 616	12 293	24 247	1 237	540[5]	7 906	19 486	68 325
Average number of nights per visit	9	12	12	17	11[5]	10	13	12
Average spending per person-night ($)	92	87	74	72	63	105	88	84
Area of Residence (000)								
Europe	189	703	1 048	37	30	451	638	3 096
France[3]	x	282	108	x	x	18[5]	21	446
Germany	43	67	123	6[5]	x	87	128	460
Netherlands	9	17	50	x	x	35	50	166
United Kingdom[4]	81	133	430	21	16	226	305	1 211
Other Europe	41	205	337	x	x	84	135	813
Africa	x	35	31	x	x	9	9[5]	91
Asia	39[5]	173	566	17	x	273	634	1 711
China	x	32	64	x	x	18	65	184
Hong Kong	x	11[5]	48	x	x	15	62	139
Japan	x	44	174	10[5]	x	110	213	578
South Korea	x	18[5]	69	x	x	43	107	241
Taiwan	x	x	9[5]	x	x	46	91	150
Other Asia	x	6 4	201	x	x	42	95	418
Central America, Bermuda, and Caribbean	19[5]	27[5]	110	x	x	x	x	173
South America	x	30	84	x	x	7[5]	17[5]	152
North America	16	57	83	x	x	17	59	235
Mexico	x	53	82	x	x	17	59	216
Oceania and other ocean islands	17[5]	37	66	x	x	59	137	327
Australia	15[5]	32	59	x	x	44	114	274
Total	**291**	**1 062**	**1 989**	**72**	**47**	**821**	**1 504**	**5 786**
Purpose of Trip (000)								
Business, convention, or employment	30	206	344	x	6[5]	89	146	826
Visiting friends or relatives	76	303	728	36	18[5]	157	332	1 650
Other pleasure, recreation, or holiday	160	474	733	26	18[5]	515	864	2 790
Other	26	79	184	5[5]	x	60	163	521
Total	**291**	**1 062**	**1 989**	**72**	**47**	**821**	**1 504**	**5 786**
Length of Stay (000)								
1 to 6 nights	164	557	939	30	29	464	783	2 966
7 to 13 nights	75	265	497	13[5]	x	206	359	1 423
14 nights and over	52	240	553	29	11[5]	151	362	1 398
Total	**291**	**1 062**	**1 989**	**72**	**47**	**821**	**1 504**	**5 786**
Quarter of Entry (000)								
First	22	136	224	x	x	106	246	746
Second	85	265	549	19	18	245	400	1 581
Third	161	464	839	30	19[5]	364	626	2 503
Fourth	23	197	376	18	x	105	232	957
Total	**291**	**1 062**	**1 989**	**72**	**47**	**821**	**1 504**	**5 786**

x = data too small and/or unreliable to be published. [1]Includes sum of visits to Newfoundland and Labrador, New Brunswick, Nova Scotia, and Prince Edward Island. [2]Includes sum of visits to British Columbia, Yukon Territory, Northwest Territories, and Nunavut. [3]Includes Andorra and Monaco. [4]Includes Gibraltar. [5]Use data with caution. SOURCE: Adapted from Statistics Canada, *International Travel*, Catalogue 66-201, 2005, p. 36, table 18, 22 December 2006, http://www.statcan.ca/english/freepub/66-201-XIE/2005000/t019_en.htm.

83. Trip Characteristics of Canadian Residents Returning from Countries Other than the US, After a Stay of One or More Nights, by Province of Residence, 2005

	Atlantic Provinces[1]	Québec	Ontario	Manitoba	Saskatchewan	Alberta	British Columbia[2]	Canada
Person-trips (000)	239	1 275	2 975	146	82	569	941	6 229
Spending ($000 000)	342	1 756	4 471	239	127	891	1 602	9 428
Average spending per person-trip ($)	1 430	1 377	1 503	1 630	1 541	1 567	1 702	1 514
Person-nights (000)	3 735	19 954	48 691	2 583	1 420	9 823	20 471	106 676
Average number of nights per trip	15.6	15.6	16.4	17.6	17.2	17.3	21.8	17.1
Average spending per person-night ($)	92	88	92	92	89	91	78	88
Area of Destination (000)								
Europe	83	483	1 249	43[3]	28[3]	155	334	2 375
Africa	x	x	49	x	x	x	14[3]	129
Asia	15[3]	67	357	x	x	85	199	745
Central America	x	x	53[3]	x	x	x	x	83
Bermuda and Caribbean	82	426	671	22[3]	13[3]	99	93	1 406
South America	x	x	70	x	x	x	x	146
Other areas	29[3]	139	305	49	25	151	203	902
Cruises	x	72[3]	219	x	x	44[3]	77	437
Total	**239**	**1 275**	**2 975**	**146**	**82**	**569**	**941**	**6 229**
Purpose of Trip (000)								
Business, convention, or employment	35[3]	141	301	x	x	68	82	647
Visiting friends or relatives	30[3]	124	671	x	x	89	231	1 183
Other pleasure, recreation, or holiday	165	979	1 799	102	54	377	554	4 030
Other	x	x	204	x	x	34[3]	74[3]	369
Total	**239**	**1 275**	**2 975**	**146**	**82**	**569**	**941**	**6 229**
Sex (000								
Male	104	508	1 234	69	33	238	401	2 585
Female	116	633	1 492	66	42	279	470	3 097
Not stated	x	135	250	x	x	52	70	546
Total	**239**	**1 275**	**2 975**	**146**	**82**	**569**	**941**	**6 229**
Age Group (000								
Under 12 years	x	50[3]	114	x	x	25[3]	38[3]	246
12 to 19 years	16[3]	49[3]	115	10[3]	x	30	62	284
20 to 24 years	x	36[3]	98	8[3]	x	29[3]	32[3]	212
25 to 34 years	22[3]	169	315	17[3]	13[3]	70	95	701
35 to 44 years	27	188	371	16[3]	x	75	117	804
45 to 54 years	49	273	545	40	16[3]	128	188	1 238
55 to 64 years	63	259	644	26[3]	19[3]	94	192	1 298
65 years and over	29[3]	116	524	x	10[3]	66	147	901
Not stated	x	135	250	x	x	52	70	546
Total	**239**	**1 275**	**2 975**	**146**	**82**	**569**	**941**	**6 229**
Length of Stay (000)								
1 to 6 nights	x	71	287	x	x	25[3]	33[3]	446
7 to 13 nights	111	581	1 302	72	37	231	319	2 653
14 to 20 nights	56	409	702	33[3]	26[3]	175	285	1 686
21 nights and over	49[3]	214	685	37[3]	x	138	305	1 444
Total	**239**	**1 275**	**2 975**	**146**	**82**	**569**	**941**	**6 229**
Quarter of Re-Entry (000)								
First	76	459	949	71	41	192	281	2 069
Second	80	302	692	32[3]	19[3]	142	218	1 485
Third	54[3]	298	722	x	x	125	229	1 458
Fourth	29[3]	216	613	24[3]	x	110	214	1 217
Total	**239**	**1 275**	**2 975**	**146**	**82**	**569**	**941**	**6 229**

x = data too small and/or unreliable to be published.

[1]Includes Newfoundland and Labrador, New Brunswick, Nova Scotia, and Prince Edward Island. [2]Also includes Yukon Territory, Northwest Territories and Nunavut. [3]Use data with caution.

SOURCE: Adapted from Statistics Canada, *International Travel*, Catalogue 66-201, 2005, p. 46, table 24-3, 22 December 2006, http://www.statcan.ca/english/freepub/66-201-XIE/2005000/t031_en.htm.

84. Trips of One or More Nights between Canada and the US, 1996 to 2005

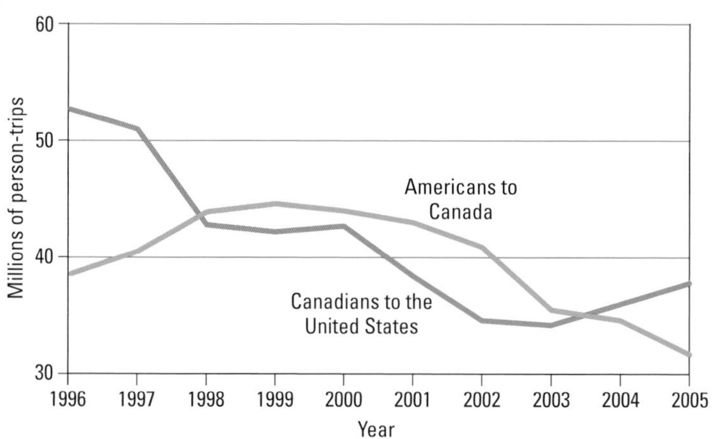

SOURCE: Adapted from Statistics Canada, *International Travel*, Catalogue 66-201, 2005, p. 46, table 6 & p. 26, table 8, 22 December 2006, http://www.statcan.ca/english/freepub/66-201-XIE/2005000/tablesectionlist.htm.

85. Canada's International Travel Deficit, 1996 to 2005

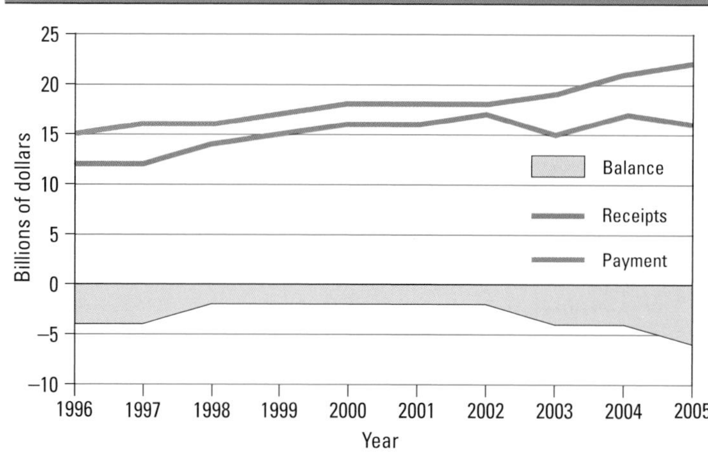

SOURCE: Adapted from Statistics Canada, *International Travel*, Catalogue 66-201, 2005, p. 15, chart 4, 22 December 2006, http://www.statcan.ca/english/freepub/66-201-XIE/2005000/ct004_en.htm.

Environment

86. Biophysical Characteristics of Terrestrial Ecozones

Terrestrial Ecozone	Land Area (km²)	Landforms	Vegetation/Productivity	Surface Materials/Soils	Climate Characteristics
Boreal Shield	1 876 142	Plains; some hills	Evergreen forest; mixed evergreen-deciduous forest	Canadian Shield rock; moraine; lacustrine; podzols;[1] brunisols[2]	Cold; moist
Taiga Shield	1 367 722	Plains; some hills	Open evergreen-deciduous trees; some lichen-shrub tundra	Canadian Shield rock; moraine; cryosols;[3] brunisols[2]	Cold; moist to semi-arid; discontinuous permafrost
Atlantic Maritime	202 619	Hills and coastal plains	Mixed deciduous-evergreen forest stands	Moraine; colluvium; marine; brunisols;[2] podzols;[1] luvisols[4]	Cool; wet
Arctic Cordillera	244 584	Mountains	Mainly unvegetated; some shrub-herb tundra	Ice; snow; colluvium; rock; cryosols[3]	Extremely cold; dry; continuous permafrost
Northern Arctic	1 529 827	Plains; hills	Herb-lichen tundra	Moraine; rock; marine; cryosols[3]	Very cold; dry; continuous permafrost
Southern Arctic	851 673	Plains; hills	Shrub-herb tundra	Moraine; rock; marine; cryosols[3]	Cold; dry; continuous permafrost
Mixedwood Plains	113 971	Plains; some hills	Mixed deciduous-evergreen forest	Moraine; marine; rock; luvisols;[4] brunisols[2]	Cool to mild; moist
Hudson Plains	374 270	Plains	Wetlands; some herb-moss-lichen tundra; evergreen forest	Organic; marine; cryosols[3]	Cold to mild; semi-arid; discontinuous permafrost
Boreal Plains	704 719	Plains; some foothills	Mixed evergreen-deciduous forest	Moraine, lacustrine; organic; luvisols;[4] brunisols[2]	Cold; moist
Prairies	464 070	Plains; some hills	Grass; scattered deciduous forest (aspen parkland)	Moraine; chernozems[5]	Cold; semi-arid
Taiga Plains	610 541	Plains; some foothills	Open to closed mixed evergreen-deciduous forest	Organic; moraine; lacustrine; cryosols;[3] brunisols[2]	Cold; semi-arid to moist; discontinuous permafrost
Montane Cordillera	490 234	Mountains; interior plains	Evergreen forest; alpine tundra; interior grassland	Moraine; colluvium; rock; luvisols;[4] brunisols[2]	Moderately cold; moist to arid
Pacific Maritime	213 000	Mountains; minor coastal plains	Coastal evergreen forest	Colluvium; moraine; rock; podzols;[1] brunisols[2]	Mild; temperate; very wet to cold alpine
Boreal Cordillera	470 476	Mountains; some hills	Largely evergreen forest; some tundra; open woodland	Colluvium; moraine; rock; podzols;[1] cryosols[3]	Moderately cold; moist
Taiga Cordillera	267 283	Mountains	Shrub-herb-moss-lichen tundra	Colluvium; moraine; rock; cryosols;[3] gleysols[6]	Very cold winters; cool summers; minimal precipitation

NOTE: See the maps illustrating Canada's terrestrial ecozones on page 26.

[1]Podzols are acid and well-weathered soils. [2]Brunisols are soils with minimal weathering. [3]Cryosols are frozen soils. [4]Luvisols are temperate-region soils with clay-rich sublayers. [5]Chernozems are organically rich, relatively fertile grassland soils. [6]Gleysols are soils developed under wet conditions and characterized by reduced iron and other elements.

SOURCE: Adapted from: Government of Canada, 1996, *The State of Canada's Environment Part II: Canadian Ecozones*, Minister of Public Works and Government Services Canada, http://www1.ec.gc.ca/~soer/SOE; © Her Majesty The Queen in Right of Canada, Environment Canada, 1996. Reproduced with the permission of the Minister of Public Works and Government Services Canada; Wiken, E.B. et al, 1996, *A Perspective on Canada's Ecosystems: An Overview of the Terrestrial and Marine Ecozones*, Canadian Council on Ecological Areas, Occasional paper No. 14, Ottawa.

87. Greenhouse Gas Emission Trends by Sector, 1990 to 2004

GHG Source/Sink Categories	(megatonnes of CO_2-equivalent emissions)				
	1990	1995	2000	2003	2004
Energy	**475**	**517**	**596**	**622**	**620**
Stationary combustion sources	283	296	347	368	360
Electricity and heat generation	95	101	132	139	130
Fossil fuel industries	53	56	70	77	79
Mining	6	8	10	16	15
Manufacturing industries	55	53	53	50	51
Construction	2	1	1	1	1
Commercial and institutional	26	29	33	38	38
Residential	44	45	45	45	43
Agriculture and forestry	2	3	3	2	2
Transportation[1]	150	160	180	190	190
Domestic aviation	6	6	7	7	8
Road transportation	107	119	131	140	145
Railways	7	6	7	6	6
Domestic marine	5	4	5	6	7
Others	20	30	30	30	30
Fugitive sources	43	57	65	66	67
Coal mining	2	2	0.9	1	1
Oil and natural gas	41	55	64	65	66
Industrial processes	**53**	**56**	**50**	**50**	**54**
Mineral production	8	9	10	9	10
Chemical industry	15	17	7	7	10
Metal production	20	19	19	17	18
Consumption of halocarbons and SF_6	2	2	5	6	6
Other and undifferentiated production	8	9	10	11	12
Solvent and other product use	**0.4**	**0.4**	**0.5**	**0.5**	**0.5**
Agriculture	**45**	**49**	**51**	**53**	**55**
Enteric fermentation	18	21	22	23	24
Manure management	7	7	8	8	8
Agricultural soils	20	21	22	22	22
Waste	**25**	**26**	**28**	**29**	**29**
Solid waste disposal on land	23	25	27	27	27
Wastewater handling	1	1	1	1	1
Waste incineration	0.4	0.3	0.3	0.2	0.3
Land use, land-use change, and forestry	**-82**	**190**	**-130**	**-11**	**81**
Forest land	-110	180	-140	-20	73
Cropland	14	7	3	0.8	0.1
Grassland	-	-	-	-	-
Wetlands	6	3	2	1	1
Settlements	8	7	7	7	7
Total[2]	**599**	**649**	**725**	**754**	**758**

NOTE: Totals may not add due to rounding.
[1]Emissions from fuel ethanol are reported within the gasoline transportation subcategories. [2]National totals exclude all GHGs from the "Land use, land-use change, and forestry" sector.
SOURCE: Adapted from Environment Canada, "National Inventory Report, 1990-2004—Greenhouse Gas Sources and Sinks in Canada", http://www.ec.gc.ca/pdb/ghg/inventory_report/2004_report/ts_3_e.cfm, © Her Majesty The Queen in Right of Canada, Environment Canada, 2006. Reproduced with the permission of the Minister of Public Works and Government Services Canada.

88. Species Extinct, Extirpated, and at Risk in Canada, 2005[1]

Status	Terrestrial Mammals	Marine Mammals	Birds	Fish	Amphibians	Reptiles	Molluscs	Arthropods[2]	Plants	Lichens	Mosses	Total
Extinct	1	1	3	6	0	0	1	0	0	0	1	13
Extirpated	2	2	2	3	1	4	2	3	2	0	1	22
Endangered	9	9	24	26	6	8	12	8	74	2	6	184
Threatened	7	10	10	24	5	13	2	6	48	1	3	129
Special concern	16	12	22	36	7	9	4	2	35	5	4	152
Total	**35**	**34**	**61**	**95**	**19**	**34**	**21**	**19**	**159**	**8**	**15**	**500**

[1]The Status categories are defined on page 25. [2]Formerly described as "lepidopterans".
SOURCE: Adapted from Environment Canada, Canadian Wildlife Service, Committee on the Status of Endangered Wildlife in Canada, 2005, *Canadian Species at Risk*, www.cosewic.gc.ca/eng/sct0/rpt/rpg_csar_e.cfm (accessed March 6, 2006).

89. Selected Environmental Impacts by Type of Transport

	Air	Land	Water	Solid Waste	Noise	Other
Cars and trucks	Air pollution and greenhouse gas emissions	Land taken for highways, roads, parking lots, and other infrastructure; extraction of road building materials; habitat disturbance; corridor creation; release of contaminants (spills, road salt)	Surface and groundwater pollution; modification of water systems through road building	Waste oil, tires and other materials; road vehicles and parts taken out of service	Noise and vibration in cities and along main roads	Animal kills; congestion
Trains	Air pollution and greenhouse gas emissions	Land taken for terminals, track, and rights of way; habitat disturbance; corridor creation	Modification of water systems in railway construction	Rolling stock and related equipment taken out of service	Noise and vibration around terminals and along railway lines	Animal kills
Planes	Air pollution and greenhouse gas emissions	Land taken for terminals and runways; habitat disturbance	Modification of water systems in airport construction	Aircraft and parts taken out of service	Noise and vibration around airports	Bird kills
Water transport	Air pollution and greenhouse gas emissions	Land taken for ports and other infrastructure; habitat disturbance	Release of substances into water (discharge of ballast water, oil spills); modification of water systems in port construction, canal cutting,	Vessels and parts taken out of service	Noise and vibration around terminals and port facilities	Animal kills; introduction of invasive species

SOURCE: United Nations Environment Programme, "Transport and the Environment: Facts and Figures, 1993", *Industry and Environment*, Vol. 16 (January-June), pp. 1-2, as found in Statistics Canada, *Human Activity and the Environment 2000*, Catalogue 11-509.

90. Water Resource Characteristics by Major River Basin

Major River Basin		Mean Annual Streamflow		Mean Annual Precipitation		Dams	
	Total area[1] (km^2)	Rate (m^3/second)	Total (km^3)	Rate (mm)	Volume (km^3)	Number	Generating Capacity[2] (MW)
Pacific Coastal	334 452	16 390	516.9	1 354	451	50	1 648
Fraser–Lower Mainland	233 105	3 972	125.3	670	156	24	848
Okanagan–Similkameen	15 603	74	2.3	466	7	3	594
Columbia	87 321	2 009	63.4	776	68	56	5 153
Yukon	332 906	2 506	79.0	346	115	10	76
Peace–Athabasca	485 146	2 903	91.5	497	241	17	3 427
Lower Mackenzie	1 330 481	7 337	231.4	365	486	18	83
Arctic Coast–Islands	1 764 279	8 744	275.8	189	333	0	0
Missouri	27 097	12	0.4	390	11	2	13
North Saskatchewan	150 151	234	7.4	443	67	6	504
South Saskatchewan	177 623	239	7.5	419	74	21	310
Assiniboine–Red	190 705	50	1.6	450	86	3	168
Winnipeg	107 654	758	23.9	683	74	98	905
Lower Saskatchewan–Nelson	360 883	1 911	60.3	508	183	60	4 941
Churchill	313 572	701	22.1	480	151	12	119
Keewatin–Southern Baffin Island	939 568	5 383	169.8	330	310	0	0
Northern Ontario	691 811	5 995	189.1	674	466	60	1 116
Northern Québec	940 194	16 830	530.8	698	656	66	15 238
Great Lakes–St. Lawrence	582 945	7 197	227.0	957	556	623	12 515
North Shore–Gaspé	369 094	8 159	257.3	994	367	129	10 785
Saint John–St. Croix	41 904	779	24.6	1 147	48	54	1 864
Maritime Coastal	122 056	3 628	114.4	1 251	153	60	411
Newfoundland and Labrador	380 355	9 324	294.0	1 030	392	90	6 693
Canada	**9 978 904**	**105 135**	**3 315.5**	**545**	**5 451**	**1 462**	**67 411**

[1]Area includes the Canadian portion of the Great Lakes. [2]The generating capacity refers to the maximum power capability from hydro plants. The survey coverage for those plants is limited to those utilities and companies which have at least one plant with a total generating capacity of over 500 kilowatts.

SOURCE: Environment Canada, 2003, Canadian Climate Normals, 1971 to 2000, Meteorological Service of Canada, *climate.weatheroffice.ec.gc.ca/climate_normals/index_e.html* (accessed 23 Feb 2005). Pearse, P.H., F. Bertrand and J.W. MacLaren, 1985, Currents of Change: Final Report of the Inquiry on Federal Water Policy, Environment Canada, Ottawa. Fernandes, R., G. Pavlic, W. Chen and R. Fraser, 2001, Canada-wide 1-km2 water fraction, National Topographic Database, Natural Resources Canada, *www.nrcan.gc.ca/ess/_portal_esst.cache/gc_ccrs_e* (accessed 23 Feb 2005). Laycock, A.H., 1987, "The Amount of Canadian Water and its Distribution", in Canadian Aquatic Resources, no. 215 of Canadian Bulletin of Fisheries and Aquatic Sciences, M.C. Healey and R.R. Wallace (eds.), 13–42, Fisheries and Oceans Canada, Ottawa. Natural Resources Canada, GeoAccess Division, 2003, 1:1 Million Digital Drainage Area Framework, version 4.8b. Statistics Canada, 2001 Census of Population. "Electric Power Generating Stations", catalogue no. 57-206-X.; Statistics Canada, *Human Activity and the Environment: Annual Statistics 2006*, Catalogue 16-201, pp. 44–45, 9 November 2006, http://www.statcan.ca/english/freepub/16-201-XIE/16-201-XIE2006000.pdf

91. Total Area Protected, by Province and Territory, 1989 and 2003

Province or Territory	1989		2003		Change in Protected Area as a Share of Total Land, 1989 to 2003
	Total Area Protected[1] (ha)	Protected Area as a Share of Total Land (%)	Total Area Protected[1] (ha)	Protected Area as a Share of Total Land (%)	
Newfoundland and Labrador	367 500	0.9	1 701 412	4.3	3.4
Prince Edward Island	6 000	1.0	14 780	2.6	1.5
Nova Scotia	138 700	2.4	465 363	8.2	5.7
New Brunswick	88 800	1.2	233 443	3.1	1.9
Québec	622 800	0.4	5 217 586	3.5	3.1
Ontario	5 152 900	5.2	9 142 039	9.2	4.0
Manitoba	315 400	0.5	5 402 416	8.5	8.0
Saskatchewan	1 936 000	3.0	2 243 230	3.5	0.5
Alberta	5 642 000	8.7	8 009 229	12.3	3.6
British Columbia	4 958 300	5.4	12 017 617	13.0	7.6
Yukon Territory	3 218 300	6.8	5 678 119	12.0	5.2
Northwest Territories and Nunavut	6 978 550	2.0	31 752 615	9.3	7.2
Canada	**29 425 250**	**3.0**	**81 877 849**	**8.4**	**5.4**

[1] Defined by World Wildlife Fund Canada as those areas that are permanently protected through legislation and that prohibit industrial uses such as logging, mining, hydro-electric development, oil and gas and other large scale developments.
SOURCE: World Wildlife Fund Canada, 2000, *Endangered Spaces: The Wilderness Campaign that Changed the Canadian Landscape 1989-2000*, Toronto; World Wildlife Fund Canada, 2003, *The Nature Audit: Setting Canada's Conservation Agenda for the 21st Century*, Toronto; as found in Statistics Canada, Human Activity and the Environment: Annual Statistics 2006, Catalogue 16-201.

Climate

92. Annual Average "Number of Days with" and Hours of Bright Sunshine

Station	Average[1] Number of Days with:[2]								Bright Sunshine[3] (hours)
	Winds (>63 km/h)	Hail[4]	Thunder[5]	Fog[6]	Freezing Temperatures[7]	Freezing Precipitation[8]	Rain[9]	Snow[10]	
Goose Bay	1	*	9	14	215	13	102	97	1 564.9
St. John's	23	*	3	124	176	38	156	88	1 497.4
Charlottetown	6	*	9	47	169	17	124	68	1 818.4
Halifax	3	*	9	122	163	19	125	64	1 885.0
Saint John	6	*	11	106	173	12	124	59	1 865.3
Kuujjuarapik	3	*	6	45	243	10	83	100	1 497.8
Québec	*	*	24	35	180	15	115	73	1 851.7
Sept-Îles	9	*	7	51	206	8	93	72	1 990.6
Montreal	1	*	25	20	155	13	114	62	2 054.0
Ottawa	*	*	24	35	165	16	107	62	2 008.5
Thunder Bay	*	*	26	38	204	8	88	61	2 202.8
Toronto	*	*	27	35	155	10	99	47	2 045.4
Windsor	2	*	33	37	136	9	105	45	n.a.
The Pas	*	*	23	15	209	12	65	73	2 167.5
Winnipeg	1	3	27	20	195	12	72	57	2 321.4
Churchill	11	*	7	48	258	19	58	100	1 827.9
Regina	9	1	23	29	204	14	59	58	2 331.1
Saskatoon	*	*	19	25	202	9	57	59	2 449.7
Calgary	6	3	25	22	201	5	58	62	2 314.4
Edmonton	*	3	22	17	185	8	70	59	2 263.7
Penticton	*	*	12	1	129	1	78	29	2 032.2
Vancouver	*	*	6	45	55	1	156	15	1 919.6
Prince Rupert	4	8	2	37	107	0	218	35	1 224.1
Alert	10	0	0	46	338	5	10	93	1 767.4
Inuvik	*	*	1	24	267	6	36	99	1 898.8
Yellowknife	*	*	5	21	226	13	46	82	2 276.6
Whitehorse	*	*	6	16	224	1	52	120	1 843.8
Resolute	25	0	*	62	324	13	20	82	1 505.1

* = a value less than 0.5 (but not zero); n.a. = not available
[1]Average, mean, or normal refer to the value of the particular element averaged over the period from 1951-1980. [2]A "day with" is counted once per day regardless of the number of individual occurrences of that phenomenon that day. [3]Bright sunshine is reported in hours and tenths. [4]Hail is a piece of ice with a diameter of 5 mm or more. [5]Thunder is reported when thunder is heard or lightning or hail is seen. [6]Fog is a suspension of small water droplets in air that reduces the horizontal visibility at eye level to less than 1 km. [7]Freezing temperature is a temperature below 0°C. [8]Freezing precipitation is rain or drizzle of any quantity that freezes on impact. [9]Rain is a measurable amount of liquid water (rain, showers, or drizzle) equal to or greater than 0.2 mm. [10]Snow is a measurable amount of solid precipitation (snow, snow grains, ice crystals, or ice and snow pellets) equal to or greater than 0.2 cm.
SOURCE: Adapted from David Phillips, *The Climates of Canada*, Catalogue EN56-1/1990E, Ottawa: Canadian Government Publishing, 1990 and the Environment Canada publications *Canadian Climate Normals 1961-1990* and *Principal Station Data*.

93. Average Monthly Precipitation[1] (mm)

Station	Jan	Feb	Mar	Apr	May	June	July	Aug	Sept	Oct	Nov	Dec	Annual
Goose Bay	64.9	57.0	68.6	57.1	66.4	100.9	119.4	98.3	90.6	78.8	79.9	77.6	959.5
St. John's West	179.4	154.9	146.3	124.5	107.0	93.5	77.8	113.8	117.0	149.0	152.8	163.5	1 579.5
Charlottetown	97.1	82.3	83.1	88.3	94.2	87.5	78.5	90.1	91.9	112.4	115.0	116.7	1 137.1
Halifax	146.9	119.1	122.6	124.4	110.5	98.4	96.8	109.6	94.9	128.9	154.4	167.0	1 473.5
Saint John	128.3	102.6	109.9	109.7	123.1	104.8	103.7	103.0	111.3	122.5	146.2	167.6	1 432.8
Kuujjuarapik	28.1	21.1	21.1	25.1	36.4	57.3	72.7	89.0	93.6	73.3	62.1	35.1	614.9
Québec	90.0	74.4	85.0	75.5	99.9	110.2	118.5	119.6	123.7	96.0	106.1	108.9	1 207.7
Sept-Îles	86.8	68.9	80.9	93.4	96.3	92.4	90.8	99.6	111.5	100.8	99.6	107.0	1 127.9
Montreal	63.3	56.4	67.6	74.8	68.3	82.5	85.6	100.3	86.5	75.4	93.4	85.6	939.7
Ottawa	50.8	49.7	56.6	64.8	76.8	84.3	86.5	87.8	83.6	74.7	81.0	72.9	869.5
Thunder Bay	32.4	25.6	40.9	47.1	69.3	84.0	79.9	88.5	86.4	60.9	49.4	39.3	703.5
Toronto	55.2	52.6	65.2	65.4	68.0	67.0	71.0	82.5	76.2	63.3	76.1	76.5	818.9
Windsor	50.3	53.7	72.0	80.3	75.7	97.0	85.3	85.7	86.7	57.9	75.4	81.6	901.6
The Pas	16.6	15.1	21.0	26.2	33.6	63.1	69.1	65.0	58.3	37.5	26.6	19.8	451.9
Winnipeg	19.3	14.8	23.1	35.9	59.8	83.8	72.0	75.3	51.3	29.5	21.2	18.6	504.4
Churchill	17.3	12.8	18.3	22.6	30.5	44.5	50.7	60.5	52.6	46.5	35.5	19.7	411.6
Regina	14.7	13.0	16.5	20.4	50.8	67.3	58.9	40.0	34.4	20.3	11.7	15.9	364.0
Saskatoon	15.9	12.9	16.0	19.7	44.2	63.4	58.0	36.8	32.1	16.9	14.1	17.2	347.2
Calgary	12.2	9.9	14.7	25.1	52.9	76.9	69.9	48.7	48.1	15.5	11.6	13.2	398.8
Edmonton	22.9	15.5	15.9	21.8	42.8	76.1	101.0	69.5	47.5	17.7	16.0	19.2	465.8
Penticton	27.3	20.6	20.4	25.8	33.0	34.4	23.3	28.4	23.0	15.7	24.3	32.1	308.5
Vancouver	149.8	123.6	108.8	75.4	61.7	45.7	36.1	38.1	64.4	115.3	169.9	178.5	1 167.4
Prince Rupert	250.8	216.5	188.2	181.0	142.0	119.5	112.9	162.8	244.7	378.9	284.4	269.8	2 551.6
Alert	7.8	5.2	6.8	9.4	9.9	12.7	25.0	23.8	24.3	13.2	8.8	7.4	154.2
Inuvik	15.6	11.1	10.8	12.6	19.1	22.2	34.1	43.9	24.2	29.6	17.5	16.8	257.4
Yellowknife	14.9	12.6	10.6	10.3	16.6	23.3	35.2	41.7	28.8	34.8	23.9	14.7	267.3
Whitehorse	16.9	11.9	12.1	8.3	14.4	31.2	38.5	39.3	35.2	23.0	18.9	18.9	268.8
Resolute	3.5	3.2	4.7	6.2	8.3	12.7	23.4	31.5	22.8	13.1	5.7	4.6	139.6

[1]These are statistics for the 1961–1990 period.
SOURCE: Adapted from Environment Canada website http://www.msc-smc.ec.gc.ca/climate/climate_normals/index_e.cfm (accessed 2002). © Her Majesty The Queen in Right of Canada, Environment Canada, 2002. Reproduced with the permission of the Minister of Public Works and Government Services Canada.

94. Average Daily Temperature[1] (°C)

Station	Jan	Feb	Mar	Apr	May	June	July	Aug	Sept	Oct	Nov	Dec	Annual
Goose Bay	-17.3	-15.5	-9.2	-1.8	5.1	10.9	15.5	14.2	9.0	2.5	-4.0	-13.4	-0.3
St. John's West	-4.0	-4.6	-2.0	1.8	6.4	11.3	15.8	15.6	11.8	7.3	3.3	-1.4	5.1
Charlottetown	-7.2	-7.5	-3.0	2.7	9.2	14.8	18.8	18.4	14.0	8.6	3.1	-3.6	5.7
Halifax	-5.8	-6.0	-1.7	3.6	9.4	14.7	18.3	18.1	13.8	8.5	3.2	-3.0	6.1
Saint John	-8.2	-7.7	-2.6	3.2	9.1	13.8	16.9	16.7	12.7	7.5	2.1	-5.0	4.9
Kuujjuarapik	-22.8	-23.1	-17.5	-7.1	1.2	6.3	10.2	10.6	7.2	2.1	-5.0	-16.6	-4.5
Québec	-12.4	-11.0	-4.6	3.3	10.8	16.3	19.1	17.6	12.5	6.5	-0.5	-9.1	4.0
Sept-Îles	-14.6	-13.0	-6.8	0.0	5.9	11.6	15.2	14.2	9.2	3.4	-2.7	-11.0	0.9
Montreal	-10.3	-8.8	-2.4	5.7	12.9	18.0	20.8	19.4	14.5	8.3	1.6	-6.9	6.1
Ottawa	-10.7	-9.2	-2.6	5.9	13.0	18.1	20.8	19.4	14.7	8.3	1.5	-7.2	6.0
Thunder Bay	-15.0	-12.8	-5.6	2.7	9.0	13.9	17.7	16.4	11.2	5.4	-2.6	-11.3	2.4
Toronto	-4.5	-3.8	1.0	7.5	13.8	18.9	22.1	21.1	16.9	10.7	4.9	-1.5	8.9
Windsor	-5.0	-3.9	1.7	8.1	14.4	19.7	22.4	21.3	17.4	10.9	4.7	-1.9	9.1
The Pas	-21.4	-17.5	-10.0	0.5	8.7	14.8	17.7	16.4	9.9	3.5	-7.7	-18.0	-0.3
Winnipeg	-18.3	-15.1	-7.0	3.8	11.6	16.9	19.8	18.3	12.4	5.7	-4.7	-14.6	2.4
Churchill	-26.9	-25.4	-20.2	-10.0	-1.1	6.1	11.8	11.3	5.5	-1.4	-12.5	-22.7	-7.1
Regina	-16.5	-12.9	-6.0	4.1	11.4	16.4	19.1	18.1	11.6	5.1	-5.1	-13.6	2.6
Saskatoon	-17.5	-13.9	-7.0	3.9	11.5	16.2	18.6	17.4	11.2	4.8	-6.0	-14.7	2.0
Calgary	-9.6	-6.3	-2.5	4.1	9.7	14.0	16.4	15.7	10.6	5.7	-3.0	-8.3	3.9
Edmonton	-14.2	-10.8	-5.4	3.7	10.3	14.2	16.0	15.0	9.9	4.6	-5.7	-12.2	2.1
Penticton	-2.0	0.7	4.5	8.7	13.3	17.6	20.3	19.9	14.7	8.7	3.2	-1.1	9.0
Vancouver	3.0	4.7	6.3	8.8	12.1	15.2	17.2	17.4	14.3	10.0	6.0	3.5	9.9
Prince Rupert	0.8	2.5	3.7	5.5	8.4	10.9	12.9	13.3	11.3	8.0	3.8	1.7	6.9
Alert	-31.9	-33.6	-33.1	-25.1	-11.6	-1.0	3.4	1.0	-9.7	-19.5	-27.0	-29.5	-18.1
Inuvik	-28.8	-28.5	-24.1	-14.1	-0.7	10.6	13.8	10.5	3.3	-8.2	-21.5	-26.1	-9.5
Yellowknife	-27.9	-24.5	-18.5	-6.2	5.0	13.1	16.5	14.1	6.7	-1.4	-14.8	-24.1	-5.2
Whitehorse	-18.7	-13.1	-7.2	0.3	6.6	11.6	14.0	12.3	7.3	0.7	-10.0	-15.9	-1.0
Resolute	-32.0	-33.0	-31.2	-23.5	-11.0	-0.6	4.0	1.9	-5.0	-15.2	-24.3	-29.0	-16.6

[1]These are statistics for the 1961–1990 period.
SOURCE: Adapted from Environment Canada website http://www.msc-smc.ec.gc.ca/climate/climate_normals/index_e.cfm (accessed 2002). © Her Majesty The Queen in Right of Canada, Environment Canada, 2002. Reproduced with the permission of the Minister of Public Works and Government Services Canada.

The datasets below are explained on pages 190/

ooo	no data
per capita	for each person

	Land		Population									Employment		
	Area	Arable and permanent crops	Total	Density	Change	Births	Deaths	Fertility	Infant mortality	Life expectancy	Urban	Agriculture	Industry	Services
			2007	2007	1997–2007	2007	2007	2007	2007	2007	2007			
	thousand km²	% of total	millions	persons per km²	%	births per 1000	deaths per 1000	children per mother	per 1000 live births	years	%	%	%	%
Afghanistan	652	12.4	31.9	48.9	43.5	47	21	6.8	166	42	20	ooo	ooo	ooo
Albania	29	24.3	3.6	124.2	5.0	14	6	1.8	8	75	45	55	23	22
Algeria	2382	3.5	33.3	14.0	14.7	21	4	2.4	30	72	58	26	31	43
Andorra	0.5	2.2	0.1	143.6	11.2	11	4	1.3	3	ooo	91	ooo	ooo	ooo
Angola	1247	2.6	12.3	9.8	24.4	49	22	6.8	141	41	40	75	8	17
Antigua and Barbuda	0.4	22.7	0.1	173.7	7.3	21	6	2.3	20	72	39	ooo	ooo	ooo
Argentina	2780	12.6	40.3	14.5	11.3	19	8	2.5	14	75	89	12	32	56
Armenia	30	18.8	3.0	99.1	-2.9	15	9	1.7	26	71	64	18	43	39
Australia	7741	6.3	20.4	2.6	10.1	13	6	1.8	5	81	91	6	26	68
Austria	84	17.4	8.2	97.6	1.6	9	9	1.4	4	80	67	8	38	54
Azerbaijan	87	23.2	8.1	93.3	5.8	18	6	2.1	10	72	52	31	29	40
Bahamas, The	14	0.9	0.3	21.8	8.6	16	7	1.9	13	71	90	5	16	79
Bahrain	0.7	8.5	0.7	1012.2	18.4	21	3	2.6	9	74	100	2	30	68
Bangladesh	144	58.5	150.4	1044.8	22.0	27	8	3.0	65	62	23	65	16	19
Barbados	0.4	39.5	0.3	702.4	4.0	14	8	1.9	14	76	53	14	30	56
Belarus	208	30.4	9.7	46.8	-4.0	9	14	1.2	7	70	73	20	40	40
Belgium	33	25.4	10.4	314.9	1.9	11	10	1.7	4	79	97	3	28	69
Belize	23	4.4	0.3	12.8	28.6	27	5	3.3	25	70	50	33	19	48
Benin	113	25.0	8.1	71.5	33.2	42	12	5.7	98	56	39	63	8	29
Bhutan	47	3.5	2.3	49.5	24.1	20	7	2.9	40	64	31	94	2	4
Bolivia	1099	2.8	9.1	8.3	18.5	29	8	3.7	51	65	63	47	18	35
Bosnia-Herzegovina	51	21.3	4.6	89.3	26.2	9	9	1.2	7	74	46	ooo	ooo	ooo
Botswana	582	0.7	1.8	3.1	17.6	26	27	3.1	56	34	54	46	20	34
Brazil	8547	7.8	190.0	22.2	12.7	21	6	2.3	27	72	81	23	23	54
Brunei	6	1.2	0.4	62.4	23.6	19	3	2.3	7	75	72	2	24	74
Bulgaria	111	32.3	7.3	66.0	-9.2	10	15	1.4	10	73	71	13	48	39
Burkina	274	16.1	14.3	52.3	38.4	45	15	6.2	81	51	16	92	2	6
Burundi	28	48.5	8.4	299.7	37.1	46	16	6.8	107	49	10	92	3	5
Cambodia	181	21.0	14.0	77.3	19.4	26	9	3.4	71	63	15	74	8	18
Cameroon	475	15.1	18.1	38.0	26.4	37	14	4.9	74	50	53	70	9	21
Canada	9971	4.6	33.1	3.5	10.2	11	7	1.5	5	80	81	3	25	72
Cape Verde	4	11.2	0.4	105.9	9.1	30	5	3.5	28	71	56	30	30	40
Central African Republic	623	3.2	4.4	7.0	18.2	38	19	5.0	102	43	38	80	3	17
Chad	1284	2.8	9.9	7.7	36.1	47	16	6.5	102	51	21	83	4	13
Chile	757	3.0	16.3	21.5	11.5	15	5	2.0	8	78	88	19	25	56
China	9598	16.0	1321.9	137.7	6.6	12	7	1.6	27	72	44	72	15	13
Colombia	1139	3.4	44.4	39.0	17.5	20	6	2.4	19	72	72	27	23	50
Comoros	2	59.2	0.7	355.7	34.7	37	7	4.9	59	64	37	78	9	13
Congo	342	0.7	3.8	11.1	35.7	41	14	5.3	75	52	60	49	15	36
Congo, Dem. Rep.	2345	3.3	65.8	28.0	37.0	50	19	6.7	120	45	32	68	13	19
Costa Rica	51	10.3	4.1	81.1	17.5	16	4	1.9	10	79	59	26	27	47
Côte d'Ivoire	322	21.4	18.0	55.9	23.2	38	14	5.0	104	51	47	60	10	30
Croatia	57	28.1	4.5	78.8	1.1	10	12	1.4	6	75	56	16	34	50
Cuba	111	34.2	11.4	102.6	4.0	11	8	1.5	6	77	76	19	30	51
Cyprus	9	12.2	0.8	87.6	6.0	12	6	1.5	6	78	62	14	30	56
Czech Republic	79	41.9	10.2	129.5	-0.7	10	10	1.3	3	76	74	11	45	44
Denmark	43	53.0	5.5	127.2	3.5	12	10	1.9	4	78	72	6	28	66
Djibouti	23	0.04	0.5	21.6	18.8	30	12	4.2	67	54	82	ooo	ooo	ooo
Dominica	0.8	26.7	0.1	90.5	3.0	24	7	3.0	22	74	73	ooo	ooo	ooo
Dominican Republic	49	32.8	9.4	191.1	16.9	24	5	2.9	30	72	65	25	29	46
Ecuador	284	10.5	13.8	48.4	15.5	26	6	3.1	25	75	62	33	19	48
Egypt	1001	3.4	80.3	80.3	21.5	27	6	3.1	33	71	43	40	22	38
El Salvador	21	43.3	6.9	330.9	20.1	25	6	2.9	25	71	59	36	21	43
Equatorial Guinea	28	8.2	0.6	19.7	25.3	40	16	5.6	101	49	39	66	11	23
Eritrea	118	4.3	4.9	41.6	20.9	40	10	5.3	59	57	19	80	5	15

ealth			Energy and trade				Quality of life								
NI	Purchasing power	Growth of PP	Energy consumption	Imports	Exports	Aid received (given)	Human Development Index	Health care	Food consumption	Safe water	Illiteracy male	Illiteracy female	Higher education	Internet users	
05	2005	2005	2005	2006	2006	2005	2005	2004	2005	2004	2005	2005	2005	2007	
ion S$	US$	annual %	kg oil equivalent per capita	US$ per capita	US$ per capita	million US$		doctors per 100 000 people	daily calories per capita	% access	%	%	students per 100 000 people	users per 10 000 people	
7.0	ooo	ooo	16	95	14	ooo	ooo	ooo	ooo	ooo	ooo	ooo	ooo	111	Afghanistan
8.1	5316	5.2	925	850	220	319	0.801	131	2918	96	1	2	1694	609	Albania
9.3	7062	1.1	1084	652	1660	371	0.733	113	3510	85	20	40	2411	573	Algeria
ooo	ooo	ooo	ooo	ooo	ooo	ooo	ooo	ooo	ooo	ooo	ooo	ooo	ooo	3150	Andorra
2.5	2335	1.5	236	967	2917	442	0.446	8	2518	53	17	46	302	64	Angola
0.9	12 500	1.5	2512	8429	929	7	0.815	17	2045	91	ooo	ooo	ooo	4007	Antigua and Barbuda
2.7	14 280	1.1	1892	856	1167	100	0.869	301	2985	96	3	3	ooo	3400	Argentina
4.4	4945	4.4	1597	731	335	193	0.775	359	2380	92	0	1	2872	546	Armenia
3.2	31 794	2.5	6754	6860	6072	(1680)	0.962	247	3330	100	ooo	ooo	5040	7019	Australia
6.2	33 700	1.9	4680	17 105	17 122	(1573)	0.948	338	4023	100	ooo	ooo	2969	5661	Austria
0.6	5016	ooo	1977	650	787	223	0.746	355	2744	77	1	2	1534	803	Azerbaijan
ooo	18 380	0.4	4282	8747	2227	ooo	0.845	105	2521	97	5	5	ooo	6348	Bahamas, The
ooo	21 482	2.3	15 769	12 778	16 518	ooo	0.866	109	ooo	ooo	11	16	2593	2098	Bahrain
6.7	2053	2.9	122	109	80	1321	0.547	26	2309	74	46	59	643	27	Bangladesh
ooo	17 297	1.5	1858	5287	1283	-2	0.892	121	2988	100	0	0	ooo	5985	Barbados
7.0	7918	2.2	2789	2278	2014	54	0.804	455	2885	100	0	1	5406	3507	Belarus
8.7	32 119	1.7	6162	34 012	35 497	(1963)	0.946	449	3109	ooo	ooo	ooo	3718	4850	Belgium
1.0	7109	2.3	1278	2250	887	13	0.778	105	2921	91	ooo	ooo	247	1217	Belize
4.3	1141	1.4	101	125	71	349	0.437	4	2437	67	52	77	ooo	551	Benin
0.8	ooo	5.6	747	139	152	90	0.579	5	ooo	62	ooo	ooo	ooo	308	Bhutan
9.3	2819	1.3	574	313	429	583	0.695	122	2128	85	7	19	3769	506	Bolivia
0.5	7032	12.7	1630	1623	736	546	0.803	134	3068	97	1	6	ooo	1726	Bosnia-Herzegovina
9.8	12 387	4.8	775	1975	2919	71	0.654	40	ooo	95	20	18	620	317	Botswana
5.7	8402	1.1	1252	510	731	192	0.800	115	3244	90	12	11	2293	1720	Brazil
ooo	28 161	-0.8	7593	4325	19 250	ooo	0.894	101	2610	ooo	5	10	1344	3346	Brunei
7.1	9032	1.5	2930	3126	2036	ooo	0.824	356	2839	99	1	2	3074	2867	Bulgaria
5.6	1213	1.3	35	104	32	660	0.370	5	2593	61	69	83	211	52	Burkina
0.7	699	-2.8	25	53	7	365	0.413	3	1693	79	33	48	224	50	Burundi
6.1	2727	5.5	15	353	273	538	0.598	16	2370	41	15	36	404	26	Cambodia
6.4	2299	0.6	135	169	202	414	0.532	19	2634	66	23	40	612	141	Cameroon
2.6	33 375	2.2	11 075	10 805	11 769	(3756)	0.961	214	3486	100	ooo	ooo	4108	6782	Canada
1.0	5803	3.4	203	1355	53	161	0.736	49	2875	80	12	25	771	587	Cape Verde
1.4	1224	-0.6	35	56	28	95	0.384	8	2105	75	35	67	155	33	Central African Republic
4.2	1427	1.7	7	126	379	380	0.388	4	2190	42	59	87	107	45	Chad
8.4	12 027	3.8	1921	2386	3610	152	0.867	109	3079	95	4	4	4073	4235	Chile
3.0	6757	8.8	1279	599	734	1757	0.777	106	2951	77	5	14	1158	1040	China
5.0	7304	0.6	688	597	559	511	0.791	135	2745	93	7	7	2683	1288	Colombia
0.4	1993	-0.4	61	157	16	25	0.561	15	1766	86	36	36	296	293	Comoros
3.8	1262	-1.0	149	459	1730	1449	0.548	20	2026	58	10	21	ooo	132	Congo
6.9	714	-5.2	42	45	37	1828	0.411	11	1398	46	19	46	ooo	23	Congo, Dem. Rep.
0.2	10 180	2.3	1041	2810	2004	30	0.846	132	2618	97	5	5	2559	2048	Costa Rica
5.3	1648	-0.5	156	300	476	119	0.432	12	2268	84	39	61	ooo	99	Côte d'Ivoire
7.1	13 042	2.6	2349	4775	2306	125	0.850	244	2811	100	1	3	2739	3295	Croatia
ooo	6000	3.5	1016	825	235	88	0.838	591	3547	91	0	0	4187	167	Cuba
ooo	22 699	2.3	3990	8660	1666	ooo	0.903	234	3295	100	1	5	2650	3356	Cyprus
4.1	20 538	1.9	4347	9139	9321	ooo	0.891	351	3303	100	ooo	ooo	3286	4995	Czech Republic
1.8	33 973	1.9	3837	15 686	16 864	(2109)	0.949	293	3494	100	ooo	ooo	4288	6918	Denmark
0.8	2178	-2.7	830	692	100	79	0.516	18	2674	73	20	20	214	126	Djibouti
0.3	6393	1.3	678	2357	557	15	0.798	50	3083	97	ooo	ooo	ooo	3462	Dominica
1.8	8217	3.9	774	1216	700	77	0.779	188	2673	95	13	13	3300	1620	Dominican Republic
4.7	4341	0.8	753	892	938	210	0.772	148	2770	94	8	10	ooo	801	Ecuador
2.9	4337	2.4	929	261	174	926	0.708	54	3274	98	17	41	3504	690	Egypt
6.8	5255	1.6	460	1122	517	199	0.735	124	2680	84	18	21	1779	955	El Salvador
2.7	7874	16.6	2492	5000	17 200	39	0.642	30	ooo	43	7	20	ooo	62	Equatorial Guinea
0.8	1109	0.3	61	113	2	355	0.483	5	ooo	60	29	29	105	188	Eritrea

The datasets below are explained on pages 190/1

ooo	no data
per capita	for each person

	Land		Population									Employment		
	Area	Arable and permanent crops	Total	Density	Change	Births	Deaths	Fertility	Infant mortality	Life expectancy	Urban	Agriculture	Industry	Services
			2007	2007	1997–2007	2007	2007	2007	2007	2007	2007			
	thousand km²	% of total	millions	persons per km²	%	births per 1000	deaths per 1000	children per mother	per 1000 live births	years	%	%	%	%
Estonia	45	14.0	1.3	29.2	-6.9	11	13	1.6	4	73	69	14	41	45
Ethiopia	1104	9.7	76.5	69.3	27.8	40	15	5.4	77	49	16	86	2	12
Fiji	18	15.6	0.9	51.0	15.1	21	6	2.5	16	68	51	46	15	39
Finland	338	6.5	5.2	15.5	2.0	11	9	1.8	3	79	62	8	31	61
France	552	35.5	63.7	115.4	5.7	13	9	2.0	4	81	77	5	29	66
French Guiana	91	0.1	0.2	2.2	ooo	31	4	4.0	10	75	76	ooo	ooo	ooo
Gabon	268	1.8	1.5	5.4	29.2	28	12	3.4	62	57	84	51	16	33
Gambia, The	11	22.6	1.7	153.5	36.6	38	11	5.1	75	58	50	82	8	10
Georgia	70	15.3	4.6	66.4	-4.9	11	10	1.3	20	73	52	26	31	43
Germany	357	33.6	82.4	230.8	0.5	8	10	1.3	4	79	75	4	38	58
Ghana	239	26.5	22.9	95.9	24.1	33	10	4.4	59	59	44	59	13	28
Greece	132	29.1	10.7	81.1	1.9	10	9	1.3	4	79	59	23	27	50
Greenland	342	ooo	0.1	0.2	0.5	16	8	2.4	11	70	83	ooo	ooo	ooo
Grenada	0.3	35.3	0.1	299.9	0.0	19	7	2.1	17	65	31	ooo	ooo	ooo
Guatemala	109	17.5	12.7	116.8	21.3	34	6	4.4	34	69	47	52	17	31
Guinea	246	6.3	9.9	40.4	23.6	42	14	5.7	113	54	30	87	2	11
Guinea-Bissau	36	15.2	1.5	40.9	23.3	50	19	7.1	117	46	30	85	2	13
Guyana	215	2.4	0.8	3.6	3.0	21	9	2.7	48	65	28	22	25	53
Haiti	28	39.6	8.7	310.9	24.0	29	11	4.0	57	58	36	68	9	23
Honduras	112	12.7	7.5	66.8	27.5	27	6	3.3	23	71	48	41	20	39
Hungary	93	51.6	10.0	107.1	-2.8	10	13	1.3	6	73	65	15	38	47
Iceland	103	0.07	0.3	2.9	11.3	15	6	2.1	2	81	93	ooo	ooo	ooo
India	3288	51.7	1129.9	343.6	18.7	24	8	2.9	58	64	28	64	16	20
Indonesia	1905	17.7	234.7	123.2	14.8	21	7	2.4	34	69	42	55	14	31
Iran	1633	10.4	65.4	40.0	5.6	18	6	2.0	32	70	67	39	23	38
Iraq	438	13.9	27.5	62.8	32.4	36	11	4.9	94	57	67	16	18	66
Ireland	70	16.0	4.1	58.7	12.0	15	7	1.9	4	78	60	14	29	57
Israel	21	19.2	6.4	306.0	16.2	21	6	2.8	4	80	92	4	29	67
Italy	301	36.7	58.1	193.2	1.2	10	9	1.4	4	81	68	9	31	60
Jamaica	11	25.8	2.8	252.7	9.8	17	6	2.1	24	72	49	25	23	52
Japan	378	12.6	127.4	337.1	1.2	9	9	1.3	3	82	79	7	34	59
Jordan	89	4.5	6.1	68.0	33.7	28	4	3.5	24	72	82	15	23	62
Kazakhstan	2717	8.0	15.3	5.6	-1.3	20	10	2.5	29	66	57	22	32	46
Kenya	580	8.9	36.9	63.6	29.7	40	12	4.9	77	53	19	80	7	13
Kiribati	0.7	50.7	0.1	154.0	25.9	31	8	4.2	43	62	47	ooo	ooo	ooo
Kuwait	18	0.8	2.5	139.2	41.9	21	2	2.6	8	78	98	1	25	74
Kyrgyzstan	199	7.1	5.3	26.6	13.3	23	7	2.8	50	66	35	32	27	41
Laos	237	4.2	6.5	27.5	27.9	36	12	4.8	85	55	21	78	6	16
Latvia	65	28.8	2.3	34.8	-7.2	10	14	1.4	8	72	68	16	40	44
Lebanon	10	30.1	3.9	392.6	14.4	19	5	2.3	17	71	87	7	31	62
Lesotho	30	11.0	2.1	70.8	6.8	28	25	3.5	91	36	13	40	28	32
Liberia	111	5.4	3.2	28.8	45.2	50	19	6.8	138	45	58	ooo	ooo	ooo
Libya	1760	1.2	6.0	3.4	26.8	24	4	3.0	21	73	85	11	23	66
Liechtenstein	0.2	25.0	0.03	171.2	9.4	11	6	1.4	3	80	15	ooo	ooo	ooo
Lithuania	65	45.8	3.6	55.0	-2.4	9	13	1.3	7	71	67	18	41	41
Luxembourg	3	ooo	0.5	160.1	14.1	12	8	1.7	3	78	83	ooo	ooo	ooo
Macedonia, FYRO*	26	23.8	2.1	79.1	3.6	11	9	1.4	13	74	59	21	40	39
Madagascar	587	6.0	19.4	33.1	35.3	40	12	5.2	79	57	26	78	7	15
Malawi	118	20.6	13.6	115.3	26.7	46	18	6.3	96	40	17	87	5	8
Malaysia	330	23.0	24.8	75.2	21.2	23	5	2.9	10	74	62	27	23	50
Maldives	0.3	40.0	0.4	1230.1	34.5	19	3	2.8	15	70	27	32	31	37
Mali	1240	3.8	12.0	9.7	28.0	48	16	6.6	96	53	31	86	2	12
Malta	0.3	31.3	0.4	1339.6	4.9	10	8	1.4	6	80	95	ooo	ooo	ooo
Marshall Islands	0.2	16.7	0.1	309.1	21.6	38	5	4.9	29	70	68	ooo	ooo	ooo
Mauritania	1026	0.5	3.3	3.2	33.8	35	9	4.8	74	62	40	55	10	35

* Former Yugoslav Republic of Macedonia

Wealth			Energy and trade				Quality of life								
ll	Purchasing power	Growth of PP	Energy consumption	Imports	Exports	Aid received (given)	Human Development Index	Health care	Food consumption	Safe water	Illiteracy male	Illiteracy female	Higher education	Internet users	
005	2005	2005	2005	2006	2006	2005	2005	2004	2005	2004	2005	2005	2005	2007	
lion S$	US$	annual %	kg oil equivalent per capita	US$ per capita	US$ per capita	million US$		doctors per 100 000 people	daily calories per capita	% access	%	%	students per 100 000 people	users per 10 000 people	
12.8	15 478	4.2	4337	10 213	7284	ooo	0.860	448	2744	100	0	0	5034	5176	Estonia
11.3	1055	1.5	31	61	14	1937	0.406	3	1582	22	50	77	268	22	Ethiopia
2.7	6049	1.4	767	2002	754	64	0.762	34	3197	47	4	4	1500	807	Fiji
96.9	32 153	2.5	6012	13 245	14 814	(902)	0.952	316	3387	100	ooo	ooo	5833	6229	Finland
59.2	30 386	1.6	4695	8783	8052	(10 026)	0.952	337	3681	100	ooo	ooo	3593	5027	France
ooo	ooo	ooo	1851	ooo	ooo	ooo	ooo	ooo	ooo	ooo	ooo	ooo	ooo	2049	French Guiana
6.1	6954	-0.4	708	1234	4000	54	0.677	29	2705	88	12	20	ooo	458	Gabon
0.4	1921	0.1	68	159	6	58	0.502	11	2537	82	50	50	101	325	Gambia, The
5.8	3365	0.2	829	783	211	310	0.754	409	1797	82	ooo	ooo	3894	400	Georgia
75.6	29 461	1.4	4398	11 027	13 495	(10 082)	0.935	337	3472	100	ooo	ooo	ooo	6117	Germany
10.0	2480	2.0	168	244	165	1120	0.553	15	3098	75	34	50	541	184	Ghana
20.3	23 381	2.5	3196	5905	1953	(384)	0.926	438	3706	ooo	2	6	5823	3351	Greece
ooo	ooo	ooo	3632	ooo	ooo	ooo	ooo	ooo	ooo	ooo	ooo	ooo	ooo	6629	Greenland
0.4	7843	2.5	840	3167	222	45	0.777	50	2310	95	ooo	ooo	ooo	1881	Grenada
30.3	4568	1.3	383	954	482	254	0.689	90	2239	95	25	37	ooo	763	Guatemala
3.9	2316	1.2	60	96	100	182	0.456	11	2428	50	57	82	253	61	Guinea
0.3	827	-2.6	82	79	54	79	0.374	12	1949	59	40	40	ooo	208	Guinea-Bissau
0.8	4508	3.2	734	1106	751	137	0.750	48	2853	83	1	1	969	1806	Guyana
3.9	1663	-2.0	80	201	60	515	0.529	25	1945	54	44	44	ooo	712	Haiti
8.0	3430	0.5	399	742	264	681	0.700	57	2435	87	20	20	1705	381	Honduras
02.9	17 887	3.1	2858	7696	7448	ooo	0.874	333	3272	99	ooo	ooo	4322	3039	Hungary
14.4	36 510	2.2	12 238	20 050	11 527	ooo	0.968	362	3189	100	ooo	ooo	5112	8627	Iceland
04.1	3452	4.2	370	157	108	1724	0.619	60	2417	86	27	52	1076	354	India
77.1	3843	2.1	608	347	446	2524	0.728	13	2893	77	6	13	1660	802	Indonesia
77.3	7968	2.3	2660	786	1134	104	0.759	87	3082	94	12	23	3115	1065	Iran
ooo	ooo	ooo	1192	1042	1104	ooo	ooo	ooo	ooo	ooo	ooo	ooo	1630	13	Iraq
71.1	38 505	6.2	3960	17 758	27 089	(719)	0.959	279	3679	ooo	ooo	ooo	4486	5019	Ireland
28.7	25 864	1.5	3080	7810	7258	ooo	0.932	382	3695	100	2	2	4491	5112	Israel
72.9	28 529	1.3	3445	7528	7067	(5091)	0.941	420	3730	ooo	1	2	3438	5166	Italy
9.1	4291	0.7	1505	2017	707	36	0.736	85	2826	93	26	14	ooo	3937	Jamaica
76.5	31 267	0.8	4416	4546	5097	(13 147)	0.953	198	2679	100	ooo	ooo	3161	6708	Japan
13.5	5530	1.6	1318	1940	877	622	0.773	203	2741	97	5	13	3980	1171	Jordan
44.6	7857	2.0	4686	1642	2663	229	0.794	354	3200	86	0	1	4973	273	Kazakhstan
18.5	1240	-0.1	135	204	96	768	0.521	14	1881	61	22	30	300	317	Kenya
0.1	ooo	ooo	115	634	63	ooo	ooo	ooo	2333	ooo	ooo	ooo	ooo	214	Kiribati
77.7	26 321	0.6	11 476	6663	23 197	ooo	0.891	153	ooo	ooo	6	9	1524	2564	Kuwait
2.3	1927	-1.3	1004	330	153	269	0.696	251	3052	77	1	2	4286	515	Kyrgyzstan
2.6	2039	3.8	120	166	137	296	0.601	ooo	3064	51	23	39	801	43	Laos
15.6	13 646	3.6	1985	5004	2675	ooo	0.855	301	2586	99	0	0	5682	4519	Latvia
22.1	5584	2.8	1655	2474	722	243	0.772	325	3009	100	6	6	4633	1536	Lebanon
1.7	3335	2.3	90	733	347	69	0.549	5	ooo	79	26	10	441	171	Lesotho
0.4	ooo	ooo	57	148	60	ooo	ooo	ooo	1943	ooo	ooo	ooo	ooo	3	Liberia
34.7	10 335	ooo	3332	1178	6695	24	0.818	129	2892	ooo	7	25	6407	326	Libya
ooo	ooo	ooo	ooo	ooo	ooo	ooo	ooo	ooo	ooo	ooo	ooo	ooo	ooo	6176	Liechtenstein
23.6	14 494	1.9	2414	5361	3920	ooo	0.862	397	3196	ooo	0	0	5723	3589	Lithuania
31.4	60 228	3.3	11 060	53 310	45 690	(256)	0.944	266	ooo	100	ooo	ooo	666	6799	Luxembourg
5.7	7200	-0.1	1471	1792	1143	230	0.801	219	2631	ooo	2	6	2427	1909	Macedonia, FYRO*
5.4	923	-0.7	57	79	50	929	0.533	29	2148	50	24	35	242	53	Madagascar
2.1	667	1.0	51	91	41	575	0.437	2	1729	73	25	46	39	45	Malawi
26.1	10 882	3.3	2511	5375	6585	32	0.811	70	3013	99	8	15	2884	4781	Malaysia
0.8	5261	3.8	802	2361	563	67	0.741	92	2791	83	4	4	22	545	Maldives
5.2	1033	2.2	22	159	115	692	0.380	8	2306	50	68	84	241	55	Mali
5.5	19 189	2.7	2522	9940	6663	ooo	0.878	318	3451	100	14	11	2340	3165	Malta
0.2	ooo	ooo	ooo	ooo	ooo	ooo	ooo	ooo	ooo	ooo	ooo	ooo	ooo	397	Marshall Islands
1.8	2234	0.3	341	304	403	190	0.550	11	2371	53	41	57	285	68	Mauritania

The datasets below are explained on pages 190/1

ooo	no data
per capita	for each person

	Land		Population									Employment		
	Area	Arable and permanent crops	Total	Density	Change	Births	Deaths	Fertility	Infant mortality	Life expectancy	Urban	Agriculture	Industry	Services
			2007	2007	1997–2007	2007	2007	2007	2007	2007	2007			
	thousand km²	% of total	millions	persons per km²	%	births per 1000	deaths per 1000	children per mother	per 1000 live births	years	%	%	%	%
Mauritius	2	52.0	1.3	625.4	8.8	14	7	1.7	14	72	42	17	43	40
Mexico	1958	13.9	108.7	55.5	13.4	21	5	2.4	21	75	75	28	24	48
Micronesia, Fed. States	0.7	51.4	0.1	154.1	0.9	26	6	4.1	40	67	22	ooo	ooo	ooo
Moldova	34	64.3	4.3	127.3	-2.0	11	12	1.3	12	69	45	33	30	37
Mongolia	1567	0.8	3.0	1.9	16.2	18	6	2.0	41	66	59	32	22	46
Montenegro	14	ooo	0.7	48.9	-1.1	12	9	1.6	10	73	64	ooo	ooo	ooo
Morocco	447	20.8	33.8	75.5	18.3	21	6	2.4	38	70	55	45	25	30
Mozambique	802	5.5	20.9	26.1	24.7	41	20	5.4	108	43	35	83	8	9
Myanmar	677	15.7	47.4	70.0	10.6	20	10	2.3	75	60	29	73	10	17
Namibia	824	1.0	2.1	2.5	15.8	27	13	3.6	55	52	33	49	15	36
Nauru	0.02	ooo	0.01	676.4	21.7	26	7	3.4	42	62	100	ooo	ooo	ooo
Nepal	147	22.4	28.9	196.6	25.7	28	9	3.1	51	62	14	94	0	6
Netherlands	41	22.9	16.6	404.2	6.2	11	8	1.7	4	80	65	5	26	69
New Zealand	271	12.5	4.1	15.2	12.0	14	7	2.0	5	80	86	10	25	65
Nicaragua	130	16.6	5.7	43.7	23.1	28	5	3.2	26	71	59	28	26	46
Niger	1267	3.6	12.9	10.2	33.4	48	15	7.1	126	56	17	90	4	6
Nigeria	924	35.7	135.0	146.1	27.1	43	18	5.9	100	47	44	43	7	50
Northern Marianas	0.5	17.4	0.1	169.1	35.5	17	2	1.2	7	75	90	ooo	ooo	ooo
North Korea	121	22.4	23.3	192.6	8.0	16	7	2.0	21	71	60	38	32	30
Norway	324	2.7	4.6	14.3	5.0	13	9	1.9	3	80	78	6	25	69
Oman	213	0.3	3.2	15.0	40.3	25	3	3.4	10	74	71	44	24	32
Pakistan	796	27.8	164.7	207.0	23.0	31	8	4.1	78	62	34	52	19	29
Palau	0.5	21.7	0.02	41.7	17.4	14	7	2.1	18	71	77	ooo	ooo	ooo
Panama	76	9.2	3.2	42.7	18.6	20	4	2.4	15	75	64	26	16	58
Papua New Guinea	463	1.9	5.8	12.5	26.8	32	10	4.1	64	57	13	79	7	14
Paraguay	407	7.7	6.7	16.4	29.2	27	6	3.5	36	71	57	39	22	39
Peru	1285	3.4	28.7	22.3	15.9	21	6	2.5	24	70	73	36	18	46
Philippines	300	35.7	91.1	303.6	21.4	27	5	3.4	27	69	48	46	15	39
Poland	323	45.5	38.5	119.3	-0.4	10	10	1.3	6	75	62	27	36	37
Portugal	92	29.4	10.6	115.7	4.8	10	10	1.4	4	78	55	18	34	48
Qatar	11	1.9	0.9	82.5	35.9	17	2	2.8	7	73	100	3	32	65
Romania	238	41.5	22.3	93.6	-1.3	10	12	1.3	14	71	55	24	47	29
Russian Federation	17 075	7.4	141.4	8.3	-4.5	10	15	1.3	10	65	73	14	42	44
Rwanda	26	52.6	9.9	381.1	30.7	43	16	6.1	86	47	17	92	3	5
St. Kitts and Nevis	0.4	22.2	0.04	98.4	0.1	18	9	2.3	15	70	32	ooo	ooo	ooo
St. Lucia	0.6	29.0	0.2	284.4	13.2	15	7	1.7	19	74	28	ooo	ooo	ooo
St. Vincent & the Grenadines	0.4	35.9	0.1	295.4	4.2	18	7	2.0	18	71	45	ooo	ooo	ooo
Samoa	3.0	45.4	0.2	71.4	12.8	29	6	4.4	20	73	22	ooo	ooo	ooo
San Marino	0.06	16.7	0.03	493.6	15.1	10	6	1.2	3	81	84	ooo	ooo	ooo
Sao Tome and Principe	1.0	56.3	0.2	199.6	37.1	35	8	4.1	77	64	58	ooo	ooo	ooo
Saudi Arabia	2150	1.8	27.6	12.8	30.0	30	3	4.1	16	75	81	19	20	61
Senegal	197	12.7	12.5	63.6	31.4	39	10	5.3	61	62	41	77	8	15
Serbia*	88	ooo	10.2	115.3	-1.8	11	12	1.8	13	72	52	ooo	ooo	ooo
Seychelles	0.5	15.6	0.1	163.8	5.0	17	8	2.1	11	72	53	ooo	ooo	ooo
Sierra Leone	72	8.4	6.1	85.3	34.2	46	23	6.1	158	48	36	68	15	17
Singapore	1	1.6	4.6	4553.0	19.7	10	4	1.3	3	80	100	0	36	64
Slovakia	49	31.8	5.4	111.2	1.2	10	10	1.3	7	74	56	12	32	56
Slovenia	20	9.8	2.0	100.5	-0.1	9	9	1.3	3	78	49	6	46	48
Solomon Islands	29	2.6	0.6	19.5	33.6	34	8	4.5	48	62	17	77	7	16
Somalia	638	1.7	9.1	14.3	37.5	46	17	6.8	117	48	34	ooo	ooo	ooo
South Africa	1221	12.9	44.0	36.0	2.7	23	15	2.7	43	51	53	14	32	54
South Korea	99	18.9	49.0	495.4	6.2	9	5	1.1	5	79	82	18	35	47
Spain	506	37.0	40.4	79.9	1.5	11	8	1.4	4	80	77	12	33	55
Sri Lanka	66	29.2	20.9	317.1	10.9	18	7	2.0	11	74	15	48	21	31
Sudan	2506	6.6	39.4	15.7	24.7	33	11	4.5	69	58	41	70	8	22

* includes data for the Republic of Kosovo

…NI	Purchasing power	Growth of PP	Energy consumption	Imports	Exports	Aid received (given)	Human Development Index	Health care	Food consumption	Safe water	Illiteracy male	Illiteracy female	Higher education	Internet users	
…Wealth			Energy and trade				Quality of life								
…05	2005	2005	2005	2006	2006	2005	2005	2004	2005	2004	2005	2005	2005	2007	
…ion US$	US$	annual %	kg oil equivalent per capita	US$ per capita	US$ per capita	million US$		doctors per 100 000 people	daily calories per capita	% access	%	%	students per 100 000 people	users per 10 000 people	
6.5	12 715	3.8	1120	3025	1811	32	0.804	106	3097	100	12	20	1355	2398	Mauritius
2.8	10 751	1.5	1668	2497	2332	189	0.829	198	3117	97	7	10	2313	2132	Mexico
0.3	ooo	ooo	ooo	ooo	ooo	ooo	ooo	ooo	ooo	ooo	ooo	ooo	ooo	1454	Micronesia, Fed. States
3.3	2100	-3.5	823	626	245	192	0.708	264	2953	92	0	1	2818	1476	Moldova
1.9	2107	2.2	885	531	551	212	0.700	263	1995	62	2	3	4848	1031	Mongolia
2.0	ooo	ooo	ooo	2544	921	ooo	ooo	ooo	2679	ooo	ooo	ooo	ooo	1757	Montenegro
2.6	4555	1.5	463	710	383	652	0.646	51	3256	81	34	60	1216	1506	Morocco
6.2	1242	4.3	199	137	117	1286	0.384	3	2392	43	45	75	143	68	Mozambique
ooo	1027	6.6	125	52	90	145	0.583	36	3305	78	6	14	ooo	55	Myanmar
6.0	7586	1.4	727	1460	1324	123	0.650	30	ooo	87	13	17	668	360	Namibia
ooo	ooo	ooo	4448	ooo	ooo	ooo	ooo	ooo	ooo	ooo	ooo	ooo	ooo	263	Nauru
7.4	1550	2.0	60	74	27	428	0.534	21	2341	90	37	65	ooo	87	Nepal
2.0	32 684	1.9	6496	25 239	28 025	(5115)	0.953	315	3427	100	ooo	ooo	3462	7332	Netherlands
6.3	24 996	2.1	5201	6447	5471	(274)	0.943	237	3337	ooo	ooo	ooo	5855	7486	New Zealand
4.9	3674	1.8	342	534	183	740	0.710	37	2402	79	23	23	ooo	246	Nicaragua
3.4	781	-0.5	30	76	43	515	0.374	2	1897	46	57	85	77	23	Niger
3.1	1128	0.8	203	165	394	6437	0.470	28	2848	48	22	40	981	308	Nigeria
ooo	ooo	ooo	ooo	ooo	ooo	ooo	ooo	ooo	ooo	ooo	ooo	ooo	ooo	1187	Northern Marianas
ooo	ooo	ooo	1023	ooo	ooo	ooo	ooo	ooo	2291	ooo	ooo	ooo	ooo	ooo	North Korea
1.5	41 420	2.7	11 318	13 939	26 414	(2786)	0.968	313	3366	100	ooo	ooo	4627	6742	Norway
ooo	15 602	1.8	4650	3521	6963	31	0.814	132	ooo	ooo	13	27	1889	1162	Oman
8.2	2370	1.3	362	180	102	1667	0.551	74	2446	91	36	65	502	715	Pakistan
0.2	ooo	ooo	ooo	ooo	ooo	ooo	ooo	ooo	ooo	ooo	ooo	ooo	ooo	ooo	Palau
5.0	7605	2.2	1791	1520	328	20	0.812	150	2681	90	8	9	3907	946	Panama
4.1	2563	0.2	294	395	723	266	0.530	5	ooo	39	37	49	ooo	276	Papua New Guinea
6.7	4642	-0.6	1748	904	293	51	0.755	111	3101	86	6	7	2528	348	Paraguay
4.0	6039	2.2	570	542	828	398	0.773	117	2411	83	6	18	3251	1591	Peru
7.2	5137	1.6	402	576	526	562	0.771	58	2497	85	8	6	2893	896	Philippines
2.8	13 847	4.3	2398	3273	2865	ooo	0.870	247	3596	ooo	ooo	ooo	5550	2991	Poland
1.3	20 410	2.1	2631	6285	4087	(377)	0.897	342	3547	ooo	4	8	3611	7384	Portugal
ooo	27 664	ooo	26 555	18 266	37 834	ooo	0.875	222	ooo	100	11	11	1201	2657	Qatar
2.8	9060	1.6	2002	2292	1450	ooo	0.813	190	4125	57	2	4	3415	2335	Romania
9.3	10 845	-0.1	5292	1153	2143	ooo	0.802	425	3005	97	0	1	6291	1653	Russian Federation
2.1	1206	0.1	34	52	14	576	0.452	5	1980	74	29	40	292	56	Rwanda
0.4	13 307	2.9	967	7000	782	4	0.821	119	2798	100	ooo	ooo	ooo	2539	St. Kitts and Nevis
0.8	6707	0.9	818	2960	300	11	0.795	517	2159	98	ooo	ooo	1333	3243	St. Lucia
0.4	6568	1.6	699	2750	200	5	0.761	87	ooo	ooo	ooo	ooo	ooo	794	St. Vincent & the Grenadines
0.4	6170	2.5	357	1094	53	44	0.785	70	3093	88	1	2	ooo	433	Samoa
ooo	ooo	ooo	ooo	ooo	ooo	ooo	ooo	ooo	ooo	ooo	ooo	ooo	ooo	5200	San Marino
ooo	2178	0.5	232	354	19	32	0.654	49	ooo	79	8	22	ooo	1453	Sao Tome and Principe
9.2	15 711	0.1	7198	2456	7759	26	0.812	137	2631	ooo	13	24	2611	1055	Saudi Arabia
8.2	1792	1.2	173	281	127	689	0.499	6	2228	76	49	71	507	488	Senegal
6.0	ooo	ooo	ooo	1304	636	ooo	ooo	ooo	2679	ooo	ooo	ooo	ooo	1388	Serbia
0.7	16 106	1.5	3922	7640	4230	19	0.843	151	2992	88	9	8	ooo	3541	Seychelles
1.2	806	-1.4	78	65	36	343	0.336	3	ooo	57	53	76	ooo	19	Sierra Leone
5.6	29 663	3.6	11 649	53 034	60 394	ooo	0.922	140	ooo	100	3	11	ooo	5319	Singapore
3.6	15 871	2.8	3716	8494	7726	ooo	0.863	318	2615	100	ooo	ooo	3368	4647	Slovakia
4.9	22 273	3.2	3953	12 052	11 629	ooo	0.917	225	3087	ooo	0	0	5610	5553	Slovenia
0.3	2031	-2.4	141	333	201	198	0.602	13	2262	70	ooo	ooo	ooo	171	Solomon Islands
ooo	ooo	ooo	32	74	33	ooo	ooo	ooo	ooo	ooo	ooo	ooo	ooo	72	Somalia
5.8	11 110	0.6	2688	1748	1322	700	0.674	77	2874	88	16	19	1568	1027	South Africa
6.9	22 029	4.5	4802	6340	6669	ooo	0.921	157	2969	92	ooo	ooo	6678	6651	South Korea
5.9	27 169	2.5	3795	7833	5086	(3018)	0.949	330	3285	100	ooo	ooo	4169	4392	Spain
2.9	4595	3.7	271	496	333	1189	0.743	55	2200	79	8	11	ooo	141	Sri Lanka
3.4	2083	3.5	113	196	137	1829	0.526	22	2444	70	29	48	ooo	765	Sudan

ooo	no data
per capita	for each person

	Land		**Population**									**Employment**		
	Area	**Arable and permanent crops**	**Total**	**Density**	**Change**	**Births**	**Deaths**	**Fertility**	**Infant mortality**	**Life expectancy**	**Urban**	**Agriculture**	**Industry**	**Service**
			2007	2007	1997–2007	2007	2007	2007	2007	2007	2007			
	thousand km²	% of total	millions	persons per km²	%	births per 1000	deaths per 1000	children per mother	per 1000 live births	years	%	%	%	%
Suriname	163	0.4	0.5	2.9	13.9	21	7	2.5	20	69	74	21	18	61
Swaziland	17	10.9	1.1	66.7	7.5	28	29	3.6	73	33	23	40	22	38
Sweden	450	6.0	9.0	20.1	1.5	12	10	1.9	3	81	84	ooo	ooo	ooo
Switzerland	41	10.5	7.6	184.3	5.0	10	8	1.4	4	81	68	6	35	59
Syria	185	29.3	19.3	104.4	28.1	28	4	3.5	19	73	50	33	24	43
Taiwan	36	ooo	22.9	635.0	5.6	9	6	1.1	5	77	78	ooo	ooo	ooo
Tajikistan	143	7.4	7.1	49.5	20.7	26	7	3.4	65	64	26	41	23	36
Tanzania	945	5.4	39.4	41.7	26.7	40	15	5.4	78	50	23	84	5	11
Thailand	513	37.7	65.1	126.8	8.1	14	7	1.7	20	71	33	64	14	22
Togo	57	46.3	5.7	100.0	32.0	38	10	5.1	91	58	40	66	10	24
Tonga	0.8	64.0	0.1	146.2	20.0	27	6	3.6	12	71	24	ooo	ooo	ooo
Trinidad and Tobago	5	23.8	1.1	211.3	-7.2	14	8	1.6	15	69	12	11	31	58
Tunisia	164	30.0	10.3	62.7	11.3	17	6	2.0	20	74	65	28	33	39
Turkey	775	36.8	71.2	91.8	12.9	19	6	2.2	23	72	66	53	18	29
Turkmenistan	488	3.9	5.1	10.4	19.5	25	8	2.9	74	62	47	37	23	40
Tuvalu	0.02	ooo	0.01	599.6	15.6	27	10	3.7	35	64	47	ooo	ooo	ooo
Uganda	241	29.9	30.3	125.6	38.4	48	16	6.7	83	47	12	85	5	10
Ukraine	604	55.7	46.3	76.7	-8.1	10	16	1.3	10	68	68	20	40	40
United Arab Emirates	84	3.2	4.4	52.9	61.8	17	2	2.7	9	79	74	8	27	65
United Kingdom	245	23.9	60.8	248.1	3.3	12	10	1.8	5	79	90	2	29	69
United States of America	9364	18.5	301.1	32.2	10.3	14	8	2.1	7	78	79	3	28	69
Uruguay	177	7.6	3.5	19.6	5.9	15	9	2.1	15	75	93	14	27	59
Uzbekistan	447	10.8	27.8	62.1	17.7	24	7	2.7	58	67	36	34	25	41
Vanuatu	12	9.8	0.2	17.7	18.1	31	6	4.0	27	67	21	ooo	ooo	ooo
Venezuela	912	3.7	26.0	28.5	16.4	22	5	2.7	18	73	88	12	27	61
Vietnam	332	26.8	85.3	256.8	12.1	19	5	2.1	18	72	27	71	14	15
Western Sahara	252	0.008	0.4	1.5	36.6	28	8	2.9	49	65	92	ooo	ooo	ooo
Yemen	528	3.2	22.2	42.1	40.4	40	9	6.2	75	60	26	61	17	22
Zambia	753	7.0	11.5	15.2	20.4	41	22	5.5	100	38	35	75	8	17
Zimbabwe	391	8.6	12.3	31.5	7.9	31	21	3.8	60	37	36	68	8	24

Explanation of datasets

Land

Area is a country's total area, including areas under inland bodies of water and coastal waterways

Arable and permanent crops percentage of total land area used for arable and permanent crops

Population

Total estimate for mid 2007

Density the total population of a country divided by its land area

Change percentage change in population between 1997 and 2007. Negative numbers indicate a decrease

Births number of births per one thousand people in one year

Deaths number of deaths per one thousand people in one year

Fertility average number of children born to child bearing women

Infant mortality number of deaths of children under one year per 1000 live births

Life expectancy number of years a baby born now can expect to live

Urban percentage of the population living in towns and cities

Employment

Agriculture percentage of the labour force employe in agriculture

Industry percentage of the labour force employe in industry

Services percentage of the labour force employe in services

ealth			Energy and trade				Quality of life								
	Purchasing power	Growth of PP	Energy consumption	Imports	Exports	Aid received (given)	Human Development Index	Health care	Food consumption	Safe water	Illiteracy male	Illiteracy female	Higher education	Internet users	
5	2005	2005	2005	2006	2006	2005	2005	2004	2005	2004	2005	2005	2005	2007	
on $	US$	annual %	kg oil equivalent per capita	US$ per capita	US$ per capita	million US$		doctors per 100 000 people	daily calories per capita	% access	%	%	students per 100 000 people	users per 10 000 people	
1.1	7722	1.1	2204	1640	2400	44	0.774	45	3424	92	8	13	ooo	632	Suriname
2.5	4824	0.2	422	2000	1873	46	0.547	16	ooo	62	19	22	521	307	Swaziland
9.1	32 525	2.1	6481	14 082	16 375	(3362)	0.956	328	3108	100	ooo	ooo	4729	7565	Sweden
1.4	35 633	0.6	4272	18 850	19 661	(1767)	0.955	361	3306	100	ooo	ooo	2685	6776	Switzerland
7.0	3808	1.4	1039	512	463	78	0.724	140	2906	93	12	26	ooo	564	Syria
ooo	ooo	ooo	4912	8827	9729	ooo	ooo	ooo	ooo	ooo	ooo	ooo	ooo	6304	Taiwan
2.2	1356	-4.0	1073	250	203	241	0.673	203	ooo	59	0	1	1834	7	Tajikistan
2.7	744	1.7	47	114	45	1505	0.467	2	2131	62	23	38	133	86	Tanzania
4.6	8677	2.7	1411	1991	2025	-171	0.781	37	2657	99	5	10	3673	1252	Thailand
2.1	1506	ooo	146	200	112	87	0.512	4	1895	52	31	62	ooo	543	Togo
0.2	8177	1.9	439	1194	117	32	0.819	34	ooo	100	1	1	642	298	Tonga
4.2	14 603	4.3	12 624	5895	12 861	-2	0.814	79	2805	91	1	2	1296	1203	Trinidad and Tobago
3.8	8371	3.3	897	1457	1129	377	0.766	134	3484	93	17	35	3107	921	Tunisia
2.2	8407	1.7	1297	1964	1214	464	0.775	135	3212	96	5	20	2923	2109	Turkey
ooo	3838	-6.8	4419	811	1052	28	0.713	418	3112	72	1	2	ooo	52	Turkmenistan
ooo	ooo	ooo	ooo	1900	170	ooo	ooo	ooo	ooo	ooo	ooo	ooo	ooo	1724	Tuvalu
3.0	1454	3.2	36	86	34	1198	0.505	8	2392	60	23	42		175	Uganda
2.6	6848	-2.4	3297	966	823	410	0.788	295	2865	96	0	1	5533	1152	Ukraine
ooo	25 514	-0.9	12 702	37 598	53 597	ooo	0.868	202	2446	100	11	12	1504	3509	United Arab Emirates
3.7	33 238	2.5	4157	10 221	7398	(10 767)	0.946	230	3424	100	ooo	ooo	3798	6229	United Kingdom
2.9	41 890	2.1	8493	6432	3479	(27 622)	0.951	256	3637	100	ooo	ooo	5827	6991	United States of America
5.1	9962	0.8	1118	1399	1163	15	0.852	365	3066	100	4	3	2987	2042	Uruguay
3.8	2063	0.3	2060	146	206	172	0.702	274	2074	82	ooo	ooo	1558	331	Uzbekistan
0.3	3225	ooo	158	700	250	40	0.674	11	2187	60	ooo	ooo	452	337	Vanuatu
1.2	6632	-1.0	2951	1308	2537	49	0.792	194	2509	83	7	7	3950	1284	Venezuela
1.3	3071	5.9	368	526	469	1905	0.733	53	2762	85	6	13	1630	1754	Vietnam
ooo	ooo	ooo	344	ooo	ooo	ooo	ooo	ooo	ooo	ooo	ooo	ooo	ooo	ooo	Western Sahara
3.8	930	1.5	306	230	339	336	0.508	33	1590	67	27	65	959	103	Yemen
5.8	1023	-0.3	261	258	326	945	0.434	12	ooo	58	24	40	ooo	201	Zambia
4.5	2038	-2.1	391	184	160	368	0.513	16	1870	81	7	14	ooo	968	Zimbabwe

Explanation of datasets

ealth

GNI Gross National Income (GNI) is the total value of goods and services produced in a country plus income from abroad.

rchasing power Gross Domestic Product (GDP) is the total value of goods and services produced in a country. Purchasing power parity (PPP) is GDP per person, adjusted for the local cost of living

Growth of PP average annual growth (or decline, shown as a negative value in the table) in purchasing power. This figure shows whether people are becoming better or worse off

Energy and trade

Energy consumption consumption of commercial energy per person shown as the equivalent in kilograms of oil

Imports total value of imports per person shown in US dollars

Exports total value of exports per person shown in US dollars

Aid received (given) amount of economic aid a country has received. Negative values indicate that the repayment of loans exceeds the amount of aid received. Figures in brackets show aid given

Quality of life

HDI Human Development Index (HDI) measures the relative social and economic progress of a country. It combines life expectancy, adult literacy, average number of years of schooling, and purchasing power. Economically more developed countries have an HDI approaching 1.0. Economically less developed countries have an HDI approaching 0.

Health care number of doctors in each country per 100 000 people

Food consumption average number of calories consumed by each person each day

Safe water percentage of the population with access to safe drinking water

Illiteracy percentage of men and women who are unable to read and write

Higher education number of students in higher education per 100 000 people

Internet users the number of internet users per 10 000 people

How to use the gazetteer

To find a place on an atlas map use either the grid code or latitude and longitude.

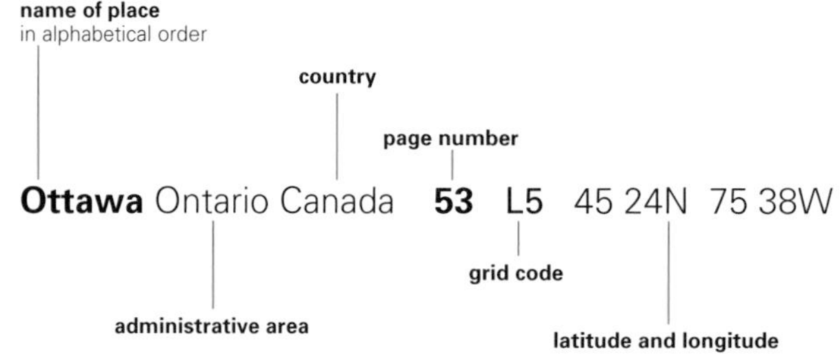

Grid code

Ottawa Ontario Canada **53** L5 45 24N 75 38W

Ottawa is in grid square L5

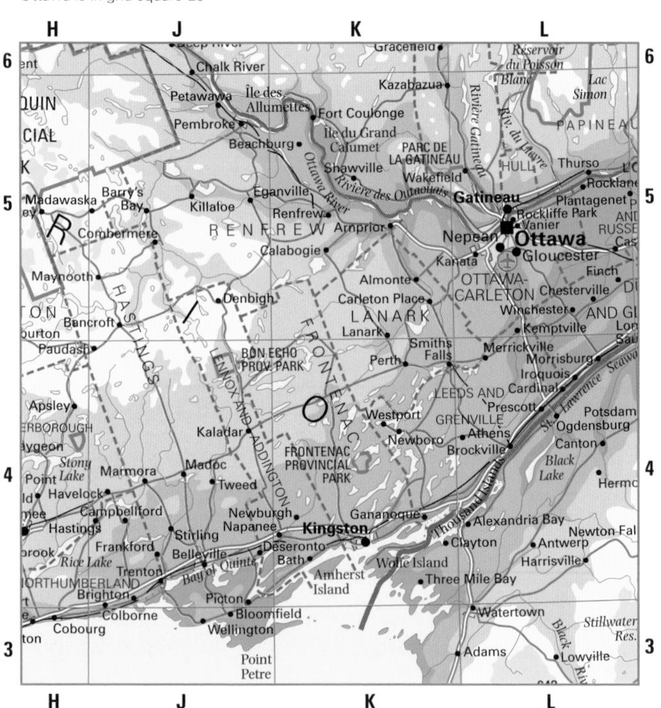

Latitude and longitude

Ottawa Ontario Canada **53** L5 45 24N 75 38W

Ottawa is at latitude 45 degrees, 24 minutes north and 75 degrees, 38 minutes west

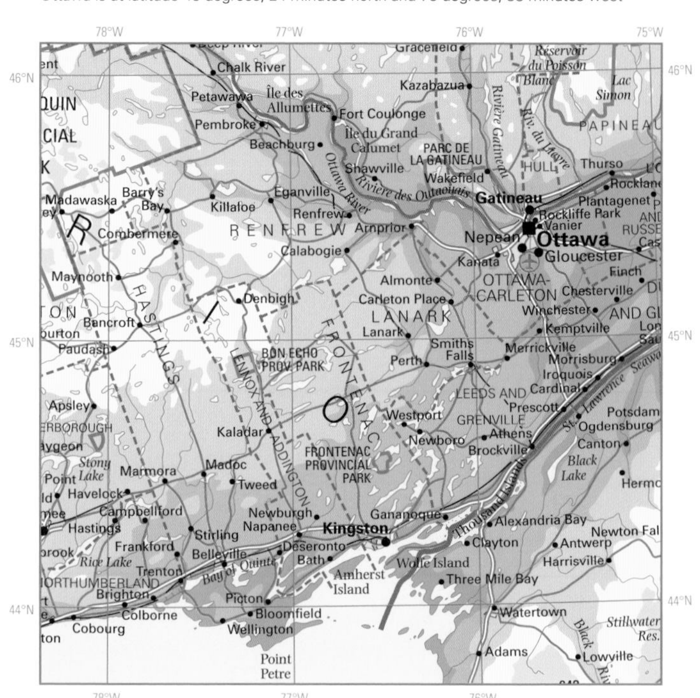

Abbreviations used in the gazetteer

admin.	administrative area
Aust.	Australia
b.	bay or harbour
Bahamas	The Bahamas
bor.	borough
c.	cape, point, or headland
can.	canal
CAR	Central African Republic
CDR	Congo Democratic Republic
Col.	Colombia
Czech Rep.	Czech Republic
d.	desert
dep.	depression
Dom. Rep.	Dominican Republic
Eq. Guinea	Equatorial Guinea
est.	estuary
Fr.	France
g.	gulf
geog. reg.	geographical region
hist. site	historical site
i.	island
in.	inlet
I.R.	Indian Reservation
is.	islands
ist.	isthmus
l.	lake, lakes, lagoon
m.s.	manned meteorological station
mt.	mountain, peak, or spot height
mts.	mountains
Neths.	Netherlands
NZ	New Zealand
p.	peninsula
Philippines	The Philippines
plat.	plateau
PNG	Papua New Guinea
Port.	Portugal
r.	river
res.	reservoir
RoI	Republic of Ireland
RSA	Republic of South Africa
Russia	Russian Federation
salt l.	salt lake
sd.	sound, strait, or channel
Sp.	Spain
St.	Saint
Ste.	Sainte
Switz.	Switzerland
tn.	town
UAE	United Arab Emirates
UK	United Kingdom
USA	United States of America
vol.	volcano
W. Indies	West Indies
Yemen	Yemen Republic

Abbreviations used on the maps

A.C.T.	Australian Capital Territory
Arch.	Archipelago
Arq.	Arquípelago
Aust.	Australia
C.	Cape; Cabo; Cap
Col.	Colombia
Cr.	Creek
Czech Rep.	Czech Republic
D.C.	District of Columbia
E.	East
Eq. Guinea	Equatorial Guinea
Fr.	France
FYROM	Former Yugoslav Republic of Macedonia
G.	Gunung; Gebel; Gulf
Hwy.	Highway
I.	Island; Île; Isla; Ilha
Is.	Islands; Îles; Islas; Ilhas
Kep.	Kepulauan
L.	Lake; Lac; Lago
Mt.	Mount; Mountain; Mont
Mts.	Mountains; Monts
N.	North
NAT. PARK	National Park
Neths	Netherlands
N.P.	National Park
NZ	New Zealand
P.	Pulau
Peg.	Pegunungan
Pen.; Penin.	Peninsula
Pk.	Peak
Port.	Portugal
P.P.	Provincial Park
PROV. PARK	Provincial Park
Pt.	Point
Pte.	Pointe
Pto.	Porto; Puerto
R.	River; Rio
Ra.	Range
R.A.	Recreational Area
Res	Reservoir
RÉS. FAUN.	Réserve Faunique
Riv.	Rivière
RSA	Republic of South Afr
Russia	Russian Federation
S.	South
Sd.	Sound
Sp.	Spain
St.	Saint
Sta.	Santa
Ste.	Sainte
UK	United Kingom
USA	United States of Ame
Yemen	Yemen Republic

A

Abbotsford British Columbia 42 H4 49 02N 122 18W
Abitibi *admin.* Québec 53 K8/L8 48 20N 76 00W
Abitibi-De Troyes Provincial Park Ontario 51 L5 48 50N 80 40W
Abitibi River Ontario 51 L5 49 40N 81 20W
Acton Ontario 54 B2 43 38N 80 04W
Acton Vale Québec 53 P5 45 40N 72 35W
Adams Lake British Columbia 43 L2 51 10N 119 30W
Adams River British Columbia 43 L2 51 40N 119 00W
Adlatok River Newfoundland and Labrador 60 D7 55 28N 62 50W
Adlavik Islands Newfoundland and Labrador 60 F7 54 55N 58 40W
Admiralty Inlet Nunavut 65 N5 72 30N 86 00W
Advocate Harbour *tn.* Nova Scotia 61 M12 45 20N 64 45W
Agassiz Ice Cap Nunavut 65 Q7 80 15N 76 00W
Agassiz Provincial Forest Manitoba 49 D1 49 50N 96 20W
Aguasabon River Ontario 51 H5 48 50N 87 00W
Ailsa Craig *tn.* Ontario 54 A2 43 08N 81 34W
Ainslie, Lake Nova Scotia 61 M12 46 10N 61 10W
Airdrie Alberta 46 E2 51 20N 114 00W
Ajax Ontario 54 C2 43 48N 79 00W
Akimiski Island Nunavut 65 P1 52 30N 81 00W
Akimiski Island Bird Sanctuary Nunavut 65 P1 53 00N 81 00W
Akimiski Strait Nunavut/Ontario 50 L7 52 40N 82 00W
Akłarvik *(Aklavik)* Northwest Territories 64 D4 68 15N 135 02W
Akpatok Island Nunavut 56 F9 60 30N 68 00W
Akulivik Québec 56 A9 60 53N 78 15W
Albany Island Ontario 50 L7 52 15N 81 34W
Albany River Ontario 50 K6 51 40N 83 20W
Albany River Provincial Park Ontario 50 G6 51 30N 88 30W
Alberni Inlet *admin.* British Columbia 42 H4 49 05N 124 52W
Albert *admin.* New Brunswick 61 L12 45 40N 65 10W
Alberta *province* 46
Alberton Prince Edward Island 61 M12 46 50N 64 08W
Aldershot Ontario 54 C2 43 17N 79 51W
Aldersyde Alberta 46 F2 50 44N 113 53W
Alert Bay *tn.* British Columbia 43 G2 50 34N 126 58W
Alexandria Ontario 53 M5 45 19N 74 38W
Alexis Creek *tn.* British Columbia 43 J3 52 05N 123 12W
Alexis River Newfoundland and Labrador 60 G6 52 50N 57 40W
Alfred Ontario 53 M5 45 34N 74 53W
Alfred, Mount British Columbia 42 H5 50 13N 124 07W
Algoma *admin.* Ontario 52 C6/D6 48 00N 84 00W
Algonquin Provincial Park Ontario 52 H5 45 50N 78 30W
Alix Alberta 46 F3 52 25N 113 11W
Allan Saskatchewan 47 D2 51 54N 106 02W
Allan Water *tn.* Ontario 50 F6 50 14N 90 12W
Alliston Ontario 54 C3 44 09N 79 51W
Alma New Brunswick 61 M12 45 36N 64 58W
Alma Québec 57 E3 48 32N 71 41W
Almonte Ontario 53 K5 45 14N 76 12W
Alouette Lake British Columbia 42 H4 49 22N 121 22W
Alsask Saskatchewan 47 C2 51 22N 110 00W
Alsek Ranges *mts.* British Columbia 42 A6/B6 59 30N 137 30W
Altona Manitoba 49 D1 49 06N 97 35W
Alvin British Columbia 42 H4 49 25N 122 34W
Amadjuak Lake Nunavut 65 R3 65 00N 71 08W
Amaranth Manitoba 49 C2 50 36N 98 43W
Amberley Ontario 54 A3 44 02N 81 44W
Amery Manitoba 49 E5 56 45N 94 00W
Amherst Nova Scotia 61 M12 45 50N 64 14W
Amherstburg Ontario 52 C2 42 06N 83 07W
Amherst Island Ontario 53 K4 44 08N 76 43W
Amisk Lake Saskatchewan 47 F4 54 30N 102 15W
Amos Québec 57 A3 48 04N 78 08W
Amqui Québec 57 G3 48 30N 67 30W
Amund Ringnes Islands Nunavut 65 L6 78 00N 96 00W
Amundsen Gulf Northwest Territories 64 E5 70 30N 125 00W
Anahim Lake *tn.* British Columbia 43 H3 52 25N 125 18W
Ancaster Ontario 54 C2 43 13N 79 58W
Anderson River Northwest Territories 64 E4 69 42N 129 01W
Anderson River Delta Bird Sanctuary Northwest Territories 64 E4 69 50N 128 00W
Andrew Alberta 46 F3 53 52N 112 14W
Andrew Gordon Bay Nunavut 65 R3 60 27N 75 30W
Angers Québec 59 L3 45 32N 75 29W
Angikuni Lake Nunavut 65 L3 62 00N 99 45W
Angling Lake *I.R.* Ontario 50 G7 53 50N 89 30W
Anguille, Cape Newfoundland and Labrador 61 F3 47 55N 59 24W
Angus Ontario 54 C3 44 19N 79 53W
Anjou Québec 58 N5 45 36N 73 34W
Annacis Island British Columbia 44 G3 49 09N 122 59W
Annapolis *admin.* Nova Scotia 61 L11 44 40N 65 20W
Annapolis Royal Nova Scotia 61 L11 44 44N 65 32W
Annieville British Columbia 44 G3 49 10N 122 54W
Antigonish Nova Scotia 61 M12 45 39N 62 00W
Antigonish *admin.* Nova Scotia 61 M12 45 30N 62 10W
Anvil Range Yukon Territory 64 D3 62 25N 133 15W
Apsley Ontario 52 H4 44 45N 78 06W
Arborfield Saskatchewan 47 F3 53 06N 103 39W
Arborg Manitoba 49 D2 50 55N 97 12W
Arcola Saskatchewan 47 F1 49 38N 102 26W
Arctic Red River Northwest Territories 64 D4 66 00N 132 00W
Ardmore Alberta 46 G4 54 20N 110 29W
Argenteuil *admin.* Québec 53 M5 45 50N 74 40W
Argentia Newfoundland and Labrador 61 J3 47 17N 53 59W
Arichat Nova Scotia 61 M12 45 31N 61 00W
Aristazabal Island British Columbia 42 F3 52 40N 129 40W
Armstrong British Columbia 43 L2 50 27N 119 14W
Armstrong Ontario 50 G6 50 20N 89 02W
Arnold's Cove *tn.* Newfoundland and Labrador 61 H3 47 45N 54 00W
Arnot Manitoba 49 D4 55 46N 96 42W
Arnprior Ontario 53 K5 45 26N 76 21W
Aroland Ontario 50 H6 50 14N 86 59W
Aroostook New Brunswick 61 B3 46 45N 67 40W
Arran Lake Ontario 54 A3 44 29N 81 16W
Arrowsmith, Mount British Columbia 42 H4 49 00N 124 00W
Arthabaska *admin.* Québec 53 P5 45 58N 72 11W
Arthur Ontario 54 B2 43 50N 80 32W
Artillery Lake Northwest Territories 64 J3 63 09N 107 52W
Arviat *(Eskimo Point)* Nunavut 65 M3 61 10N 94 05W
Asbestos Québec 53 Q5 45 46N 71 56W
Ashcroft British Columbia 43 K2 50 41N 121 17W
Ashern Manitoba 49 C2 51 10N 98 20W
Asheweig River Ontario 50 H7 53 50N 87 50W
Ashihik Lake Yukon Territory 64 C3 61 00N 135 05W
Ashuanipi Newfoundland and Labrador 60 B6 52 46N 66 05W
Ashuanipi Lake Newfoundland and Labrador 60 B6 52 45N 66 15W
Ashuanipi River Newfoundland and Labrador 60 B6 53 50N 66 30W
Aspy Bay Nova Scotia 61 M12 46 50N 60 20W
Asquith Saskatchewan 47 D3 52 08N 107 12W
Assiniboia Saskatchewan 47 E1 49 39N 105 59W
Assiniboine River Manitoba/Saskatchewan 49 C1 49 40N 98 50W
Aston, Cape Nunavut 65 S5 70 00N 67 15W
Astray Newfoundland and Labrador 60 B7 54 36N 66 42W
Astray Lake Newfoundland and Labrador 60 B7 54 36N 66 42W
Athabasca Alberta 46 F4 54 44N 113 15W
Athabasca, Lake Alberta/Saskatchewan 47 C6 59 00N 109 00W
Athabasca River Alberta 46 G5 57 30N 111 40W
Athabasca Sand Dunes Provincial Wilderness Park Saskatchewan 47 C6 59 10N 108 30W
Athens Ontario 53 L4 44 38N 75 57W
Atherley Ontario 54 C3 44 36N 79 21W
Athol Nova Scotia 61 M12 45 40N 64 10W
Atikaki Provincial Park Manitoba 49 E2 51 30N 95 30W
Atik Lake Manitoba 49 D4 55 20N 96 10W
Atikokan Ontario 50 F5 48 45N 91 38W
Atikonak Lake Newfoundland and Labrador 60 C6 52 40N 64 32W
Atikonak River Newfoundland and Labrador 60 C6 53 20N 64 50W
Atkinson, Point British Columbia 44 E4 49 20N 123 16W
Atlin British Columbia 42 D6 59 31N 133 41W
Atlin Lake British Columbia 42 D6 59 31N 133 41W
Atlin Provincial Park British Columbia 42 D6 59 10N 133 50W
Atna Peak British Columbia 43 F3 53 53N 128 07W
Attawapiskat Ontario 50 K7 53 00N 82 30W
Attawapiskat Lake Ontario 50 H7 52 18N 87 54W
Attawapiskat River Ontario 50 K7 53 00N 84 00W
Aubry, Lake Northwest Territories 64 E4 67 23N 126 30W
Auden Ontario 50 H6 50 14N 87 54W
Aujuittuq *(Grise Fiord) tn.* Nunavut 65 P6 76 25N 82 57W
Aulac New Brunswick 61 M12 45 50N 64 20W
Aulavik National Park Northwest Territories 64 G5 73 30N 118 00W
Aulneau Peninsula Ontario 50 D5 49 23N 94 29W
Aupaluk Québec 56 F8 59 12N 69 35W
Aurora Ontario 54 C3 43 00N 79 28W
Ausable River Ontario 54 A2 43 06N 81 36W
Austin Channel Nunavut 65 K6 75 35N 103 25W
Auyuittuq National Park Reserve Nunavut 65 S4 67 00N 67 00W
Avalon Peninsula Newfoundland and Labrador 61 J3 47 30N 53 30W
Avalon Wilderness Reserve Newfoundland and Labrador 61 J3 47 10N 52 40W
Avola British Columbia 43 L2 51 47N 119 19W
Avon River Ontario 54 A2 43 20N 81 10W
Awenda Provincial Park Ontario 54 B3 44 50N 80 00W
Axel Heiberg Island Nunavut 65 M6 80 00N 90 00W
Aylmer Ontario 54 B1 42 47N 80 58W
Aylmer Québec 59 K2 45 23N 75 49W
Aylmer Lake Northwest Territories 64 J3 64 05N 108 30W
Ayr Ontario 54 B2 43 17N 80 26W
Azure Lake British Columbia 43 K3 52 22N 120 07W

B

Babine Lake British Columbia 43 H4 54 45N 125 05W
Babine Mountains Provoncial Park British Columbia 43 G4 54 50N 126 55W
Babine River British Columbia 43 G4 55 44N 127 29W
Bache Peninsula Nunavut 65 Q6 79 08N 76 00W
Backbone Ranges *mts.* Northwest Territories 64 E3 64 30N 130 00W
Back River Nunavut 64 J4 65 00N 105 00W
Baddeck Nova Scotia 61 M12 46 06N 60 45W
Badger Newfoundland and Labrador 61 G4 49 00N 56 04W
Baffin Bay Nunavut 65 S5 72 00N 64 00W
Baffin Island Nunavut 65 Q5 70 00N 75 00W
Baie-Comeau *tn.* Québec 57 F3 49 12N 68 10W
Baie des Chaleurs *b.* Québec/New Brunswick 57 H2 47 59N 65 50W
Baie de Valois *b.* Québec 58 M4 45 27N 73 17W
Baie d'Ungava Québec/Nunavut 56 G8 59 00N 67 30W
Baie James *b.* Québec/Nunavut 57 A5 52 00N 79 00W
Baie Lafontaine *b.* Ontario 59 L3 45 32N 75 18W
Baie-St.-Paul *tn.* Québec 53 R7 47 27N 70 30W
Baie-Trinité *tn.* Québec 57 G3 49 25N 67 20W
Baie Vert *b.* Nova Scotia 61 M12 46 00N 64 00W
Baie Vert *tn.* Newfoundland and Labrador 61 G4 49 55N 56 12W
Baie Verte Peninsula Newfoundland and Labrador 61 G4 49 45N 56 15W
Bailey Creek Ontario 54 C3 44 01N 79 56W
Baillie Island Northwest Territories 64 E5 70 35N 128 10W
Baillie River Northwest Territories/Nunavut 64 J3 64 40N 105 50W
Baird Peninsula Nunavut 65 Q4 68 55N 76 04W
Baker Lake Nunavut 65 L3 64 00N 95 00W
Balcarres Saskatchewan 47 F2 50 49N 103 32W
Baldock Lake Manitoba 49 C5 56 30N 98 25W
Baldy Mountain Manitoba 49 B2 51 27N 100 45W
Balgonie Saskatchewan 47 E2 50 31N 104 15W
Ballantyre Strait Northwest Territories 64 G6 77 25N 114 20W
Balmertown Ontario 50 E6 51 04N 93 41W
Balsam Lake Ontario 54 D3 44 37N 78 51W
Balsam Lake Provincial Park Ontario 54 D3 44 30N 78 50W
Bamaji Lake Ontario 50 F6 51 09N 91 25W
Bancroft Ontario 52 J5 45 03N 77 51W
Banff Alberta 46 E2 51 10N 115 34W
Banff National Park Alberta 46 D2/E2 51 00N 116 00W
Banks Island British Columbia 42 E3 53 30N 130 00W
Banks Island Northwest Territories 64 F4 73 15N 121 30W
Banks Island No 1 Bird Sanctuary Northwest Territories 64 F4 72 30N 124 50W
Banks Island No 2 Bird Sanctuary Northwest Territories 64 F4 73 30N 124 00W
Barachois Pond Provincial Park Newfoundland and Labrador 61 F4 48 28N 58 20W
Baring, Cape Northwest Territories 64 G5 70 02N 117 20W
Barkerville British Columbia 43 K3 53 06N 121 35W
Barkley Sound British Columbia 42 G4 48 58N 125 11W
Barnes Ice Cap Nunavut 65 R5 70 00N 74 00W
Barnfield British Columbia 42 G4 48 50N 125 07W
Barnston Island British Columbia 44 H3 49 11N 122 42W
Barrage Daniel-Johnson Québec 57 F4 50 39N 68 45W
Barraute Québec 57 B3 48 26N 72 15W
Barr'd Islands *tn.* Newfoundland and Labrador 61 H4 49 44N 54 11W
Barrhaven Ontario 59 J2 45 16N 75 47W
Barrhead Alberta 46 E4 54 10N 114 22W
Barrie Ontario 54 C3 44 22N 79 42W
Barrie Island Ontario 52 D5 45 56N 82 39W
Barrière British Columbia 43 K2 51 10N 120 07W
Barrington Nova Scotia 61 L11 43 34N 65 35W
Barrington Lake Manitoba 49 B5 57 00N 100 15W
Barrow Bay Ontario 54 A3 44 58N 81 11W
Barrows Manitoba 49 B2 52 50N 101 26W
Barrow Strait Nunavut 65 M5 74 24N 94 10W
Barry's Bay *tn.* Ontario 52 J5 45 27N 77 41W
Bashaw Alberta 46 F3 52 35N 112 58W
Basin Lake Saskatchewan 47 E3 52 40N 105 10W
Bassano Alberta 46 F2 50 47N 112 28W
Bass Lake Ontario 54 C3 44 36N 79 31W
Bass Lake Provincial Park Ontario 54 C3 44 30N 79 40W
Batchawana Bay *tn.* Ontario 51 J4 46 53N 84 36W
Batchawana Mountain Ontario 51 J4 47 04N 84 24W
Bath New Brunswick 61 B3 46 30N 67 36W
Bath Ontario 53 K4 44 11N 76 47W
Bathurst, Cape Northwest Territories 64 E5 70 31N 127 53W
Bathurst New Brunswick 61 C3 47 37N 65 40W
Bathurst Inlet Nunavut 64 J4 66 49N 108 00W
Bathurst Island Nunavut 65 K6 76 00N 100 00W
Batoche National Historic Site Saskatchewan 47 E3 52 45N 106 00W
Battle Creek Saskatchewan 47 C1 49 20N 109 30W
Battleford Saskatchewan 47 C3 52 45N 108 20W
Battle Harbour *tn.* Newfoundland and Labrador 60 H6 52 16N 55 35W
Battle River Alberta/Saskatchewan 47 C3 52 50N 109 10W
Bauld, Cape Newfoundland and Labrador 60 H5 51 40N 55 25W
Bay Bulls *tn.* Newfoundland and Labrador 61 J3 47 19N 52 50W
Bay de Verde *tn.* Newfoundland and Labrador 61 J4 48 03N 52 54W
Bay du Nord Wilderness Reserve Newfoundland and Labrador 61 H4 48 10N 54 55W
Bayers Lake Nova Scotia 59 Q6 44 38N 63 39W
Bayfield Ontario 54 A2 43 33N 81 41W
Bayfield River Ontario 54 A2 43 34N 81 38W
Bay Roberts *tn.* Newfoundland and Labrador 61 J3 47 36N 53 16W
Beachburg Ontario 53 K5 45 44N 76 51W
Beaconsfield Québec 58 M4 45 26N 73 50W
Beale, Cape British Columbia 42 G4 48 46N 125 10W
Beamsville Ontario 54 C2 43 10N 79 31W
Bear *r.* Ontario 59 L2 45 22N 75 29W
Beardmore Ontario 51 H5 49 36N 87 59W
Bear Island Nunavut 50 L8 64 01N 83 13W
Bear Lake Manitoba 49 D4 55 10N 96 30W
Bear River *tn.* Nova Scotia 61 L11 44 34N 65 40W
Bearskin Lake *I.R.* Ontario 50 F7 53 50N 90 55W
Beatton River British Columbia 43 K5 57 18N 121 15W
Beatty Saugeen River Ontario 54 B3 44 08N 80 54W
Beauce *admin.* Québec 53 R6 46 15N 71 00W
Beauceville Québec 53 R6 46 12N 70 45W
Beaufort Sea 64 C5 72 00N 139 30W
Beauharnois Québec 53 N5 45 18N 73 52W
Beaupré Québec 53 R7 47 03N 70 56W
Beauséjour Manitoba 49 D2 50 04N 96 30W
Beauval Saskatchewan 47 D4 55 09N 107 35W
Beaver Bank Nova Scotia 59 Q7 44 48N 63 39W
Beaver Creek Ontario 55 C2 43 51N 79 23W
Beaver Creek *tn.* Yukon Territory 64 B3 60 20N 140 45W
Beaverdell British Columbia 43 L1 49 25N 119 09W
Beaverhill Lake Alberta 46 F3 53 27N 112 32W
Beaver Hill Lake Manitoba 49 E4 54 20N 95 20W
Beaverlodge Alberta 46 C4 55 13N 119 26W
Beaver River Alberta/Saskatchewan 47 C4 54 20N 108 40W
Beaver River Ontario 54 B3 44 21N 80 33W
Beaverton Ontario 54 C3 44 25N 79 10W
Beaverton River Ontario 54 C3 44 08N 79 06W
Bécancour Québec 53 P6 46 20N 72 30W
Beckwith Island Ontario 54 B3 44 53N 80 06W
Bedford Nova Scotia 61 M11 44 44N 61 41W
Bedford Basin Nova Scotia 59 Q6 44 41N 63 37W
Beechey Head *c.* British Columbia 42 H4 48 19N 123 39W
Beechville Nova Scotia 59 Q6 44 37N 63 42W
Beeton Ontario 54 C3 44 04N 79 46W
Beiseker Alberta 46 F2 51 23N 113 32W
Belair Provincial Forest Manitoba 49 D2 50 38N 96 40W
Belcher Islands Nunavut 65 Q2 56 00N 79 30W
Bella Bella British Columbia 43 F3 52 06N 128 06W
Bella Coola British Columbia 43 G3 52 30N 126 50W
Bella Coola River British Columbia 43 G3 52 22N 126 35W
Bellcarra British Columbia 44 G4 49 19N 122 56W
Belle Bay Newfoundland and Labrador 61 H3 47 37N 55 18W
Bellechasse *admin.* Québec 53 R6 46 40N 70 50W
Belledune New Brunswick 61 C3 47 50N 65 45W
Belle Isle *i.* Newfoundland and Labrador 60 H5 51 57N 55 21W
Belle Isle, Strait of Newfoundland and Labrador 60 G5 51 30N 56 30W
Belle River *tn.* Ontario 52 D2 42 18N 82 43W
Belleville Ontario 53 J4 44 10N 77 23W
Bell-Irving River British Columbia 42 F5 56 42N 129 40W
Bell Island Newfoundland and Labrador 60 H5 50 50N 55 50W
Bell Peninsula Nunavut 65 P3 63 00N 82 00W
Bells Corners Ontario 59 J2 45 19N 75 49W
Belly River Alberta 46 F1 49 10N 113 40W
Belmont Ontario 54 A1 42 52N 81 06W
Beloeil Québec 53 N5 45 34N 73 15W
Belwood, Lake Ontario 54 B2 43 46N 80 20W
Benedict Mountains Newfoundland and Labrador 60 F7 54 45N 58 45W
Bengough Saskatchewan 47 E1 49 25N 105 10W
Benito Manitoba 49 B2 51 55N 101 30W
Bentley Alberta 46 E3 52 28N 114 04W
Berens River Manitoba/Ontario 49 D3 52 10N 96 40W
Berens River *tn.* Manitoba 49 D3 52 22N 97 00W
Beresford New Brunswick 61 C3 47 40N 65 40W
Bergland Ontario 50 D5 48 57N 94 23W
Bernier Bay Nunavut 65 N5 71 05N 88 15W
Berthier *admin.* Québec 53 M7 47 40N 75 20W
Bertrand New Brunswick 61 C3 47 45N 65 05W
Berwick Nova Scotia 61 M12 45 03N 64 44W
Berwyn Alberta 46 D5 56 09N 117 44W
Besnard Lake Saskatchewan 47 D4 55 30N 106 10W
Betsiamites Québec 57 F3 48 56N 68 40W
Bible Hill *tn.* Nova Scotia 61 M12 45 20N 63 10W
Bienfait Saskatchewan 47 F1 49 09N 102 48W
Big Bay *tn.* British Columbia 42 G5 50 24N 125 08W
Big Creek Ontario 54 B1 42 43N 80 33W
Big Creek Provincial Park British Columbia 43 J2 51 10N 123 10W
Biggar Saskatchewan 47 D3 52 03N 107 59W
Bighead River Ontario 54 B3 44 30N 80 47W
Big Indian Lake Nova Scotia 59 Q6 44 35N 63 42W
Big Island Nunavut 65 R3 62 43N 70 43W
Big Island Ontario 50 D5 49 10N 94 30W
Big Muddy Lake Saskatchewan 47 E1 49 10N 104 50W
Big Otter Creek Ontario 54 B1 42 46N 80 51W
Big River Newfoundland and Labrador 60 F7 54 50N 59 40W
Big River *tn.* Saskatchewan 47 D3 53 50N 107 01W

Big Salmon Range *mts.* Yukon Territory 64 D3 62 40N 134 59W
Big Sand Lake Manitoba 49 C5 57 50N 99 30W
Big Silver Creek British Columbia 42 H4 49 50N 121 50W
Bigstick Lake Saskatchewan 47 C2 50 20N 109 50W
Bigstone Lake Manitoba 49 E3 53 30N 95 50W
Big Trout Lake Ontario 50 F7 53 50N 90 00W
Big Trout Lake *tn.* Ontario 50 G7 53 40N 89 50W
Birch Cove Lakes Nova Scotia 59 Q6 44 40N 63 39W
Birch Hills *tn.* Saskatchewan 47 E3 53 00N 105 00W
Birch Island Manitoba 49 C3 52 20N 99 50W
Birch Lake Alberta 46 G3 53 19N 111 35W
Birch Lake Ontario 50 E6 51 20N 92 20W
Birch Mountains Alberta 46 F5 57 20N 113 55W
Birch Mountains Wildland Provincial Park Alberta 46 F5 57 30N 113 00W
Birch River Alberta 46 F6 58 20N 113 20W
Birds Hill *tn.* Manitoba 48 C2 49 58N 96 59W
Birken British Columbia 42 H5 50 29N 112 36W
Birtle Manitoba 49 B2 50 26N 101 04W
Biscotasing Ontario 51 K4 47 17N 82 06W
Bishop's Falls *tn.* Newfoundland and Labrador 61 H4 49 01N 55 30W
Bistcho Lake Alberta 46 C6 59 45N 118 50W
Bjorne Peninsula Nunavut 65 N6 77 37N 87 00W
Black Bear Island Lake Saskatchewan 47 E4 55 45N 105 50W
Black Birch Lake Saskatchewan 47 D5 56 55N 107 25W
Blackburn Hamlet Ontario 59 K2 45 26N 75 33W
Black Diamond Alberta 46 E2 50 45N 114 12W
Blackfalds Alberta 46 F3 52 23N 113 47W
Black Lake Saskatchewan 47 E6 59 10N 104 30W
Black Lake *tn.* Québec 53 Q6 46 03N 71 21W
Black Lake *tn.* Saskatchewan 47 E6 59 05N 105 35W
Black River Ontario 54 C3 44 48N 79 08W
Blacks Harbour New Brunswick 61 B2 45 03N 66 49W
Black Tickle Newfoundland and Labrador 60 D8 53 27N 55 49W
Blackville New Brunswick 61 C3 46 44N 65 51W
Blackwater Lake Northwest Territories 64 F3 64 00N 123 05W
Blaine Lake *tn.* Saskatchewan 47 D3 52 50N 106 54W
Blainville Québec 53 N5 45 39N 73 52W
Blair Ontario 54 B2 43 23N 80 23W
Blanc-Sablon Québec 56 L4 51 26N 57 08W
Blenheim Ontario 52 E2 42 20N 82 00W
Blind River *tn.* Ontario 52 D6 46 10N 82 58W
Bloodvein River Manitoba 49 D2 51 50N 96 40W
Bloomfield Ontario 53 J3 43 59N 77 14W
Blossom Park *tn.* Ontario 59 K2 45 21N 75 37W
Blubber Bay *tn.* British Columbia 42 H4 49 48N 124 37W
Bluenose Lake Nunavut 64 G4 68 30N 119 35W
Blue Ridge *tn.* Alberta 46 E4 54 08N 115 22W
Blue River *tn.* British Columbia 43 L3 52 05N 119 09W
Blyth Ontario 54 A2 43 43N 81 26W
Blyth Brook Ontario 54 A2 43 45N 81 31W
Bobcaygeon Ontario 52 H4 44 32N 78 33W
Boisbriand Québec 58 M5 45 35N 73 51W
Boissevain Manitoba 49 B1 49 14N 100 02W
Bolton Ontario 54 C2 43 53N 79 44W
Bonavista Newfoundland and Labrador 61 J4 48 39N 53 07W
Bonavista Bay Newfoundland and Labrador 61 J4 48 45N 53 30W
Bonavista Peninsula Newfoundland and Labrador 61 J4 48 30N 53 30W
Bon Echo Provincial Park Ontario 53 J4 44 55N 77 15W
Bonnet Plume River Yukon Territory 64 D4 65 25N 135 00W
Bonnyville Alberta 46 G4 54 16N 110 44W
Boothia, Gulf of Nunavut 65 N4 69 00N 88 00W
Boothia Peninsula Nunavut 65 M5 70 30N 94 30W
Borden-Carleton Prince Edward Island 61 M12 46 20N 63 40W
Borden Island Northwest Territories/Nunavut 64 H6 78 30N 111 30W
Borden Peninsula Nunavut 65 P5 73 00N 82 30W
Boston Bar British Columbia 43 K1 49 52N 121 25W
Botwood Newfoundland and Labrador 61 H4 49 09N 55 21W
Bouctouche New Brunswick 61 M12 46 30N 64 40W
Boundary Range *mts.* British Columbia 42 D6 58 00N 133 00W
Bowden Alberta 46 E2 51 55N 114 02W
Bowen Island British Columbia 42 H4 49 23N 123 26W
Bow Island *tn.* Alberta 46 G1 49 52N 111 22W
Bowman Bay Wildlife Sanctuary Nunavut 65 R4 66 00N 74 00W
Bowmanville Ontario 54 D2 43 55N 78 43W
Bowmanville Creek Ontario 54 D3 44 02N 78 47W
Bow River Alberta 46 F2 50 47N 111 55W
Bowron Lake Provincial Park British Columbia 43 K3 53 00N 121 00W
Bowron River British Columbia 43 K3 53 38N 121 40W
Bowser British Columbia 42 H4 49 26N 124 41W
Boyle Alberta 46 F4 54 35N 112 49W
Boyne River Ontario 54 B3 44 07N 80 07W
Bracebridge Ontario 52 G5 45 02N 79 19W
Bradford Ontario 54 C3 44 07N 79 34W
Bralorne British Columbia 43 J2 50 46N 122 51W
Bramalea Ontario 54 C2 43 44N 79 44W
Brampton Ontario 54 C2 43 42N 79 46W
Brandon Manitoba 49 C1 49 50N 99 57W
Brant *admin.* Ontario 54 B2 43 03N 80 29W
Brantford Ontario 54 B2 43 09N 80 17W
Bras d'Or Lake Nova Scotia 61 M12 45 50N 60 50W
Brazeau, Mount Alberta 46 D3 52 33N 117 21W
Brazeau River Alberta 46 D3 52 50N 116 20W
Brechin Ontario 54 C3 44 32N 79 11W
Brent Ontario 52 H6 46 02N 78 29W
Breton Cove *tn.* Nova Scotia 61 M12 46 30N 60 30W
Brevoort Island Nunavut 65 T3 63 19N 64 08W
Bridge River British Columbia 43 J2 50 55N 123 25W
Bridgetown Nova Scotia 61 L11 44 50N 65 20W
Bridgewater Nova Scotia 61 M11 44 23N 64 32W
Brier Island Nova Scotia 61 L11 44 20N 66 20W
Brighton Ontario 52 J4 44 07N 77 45W
Brisay Québec 56 E6 54 25N 70 42W
Bristol New Brunswick 61 B3 46 28N 67 38W
Britannia Beach *tn.* British Columbia 42 H4 49 38N 123 10W
British Columbia *province* 42/43
British Empire Range *mts.* Nunavut 65 P7 82 30N 84 50W
British Mountains 64 B4 69 00N 141 00W
Britt Ontario 52 F5 45 46N 80 33W
Broadview Saskatchewan 47 F2 50 22N 102 31W
Brochet Manitoba 49 B5 57 55N 101 40W
Brockville Ontario 53 L4 44 35N 75 41W
Brodeur Peninsula Nunavut 65 N5 72 00N 87 30W
Brome *admin.* Québec 53 P5 45 10N 72 10W
Bromont Québec 53 P5 45 18N 72 38W
Bronte Ontario 54 C2 43 23N 79 43W
Brookfield Nova Scotia 61 M12 45 15N 63 18W
Brooklyn Nova Scotia 61 M11 44 04N 64 42W
Brooks Alberta 46 G2 50 35N 111 54W
Brooks Peninsula British Columbia 43 G2 50 05N 127 45W
Brooks Peninsula Provincial Park British Columbia 43 G2 50 15N 127 50W
Brown Lake Nunavut 65 M4 65 54N 91 15W
Bruce *admin.* Ontario 54 A3 44 15N 81 24W
Bruce Creek Ontario 55 C2 43 55N 79 20W
Bruce Mines *tn.* Ontario 52 C6 46 18N 83 48W
Bruce Peninsula Ontario 54 A3/A4 45 00N 81 20W
Bruce Peninsula National Park Ontario 54 A4 45 00N 81 20W
Bruderheim Alberta 46 F3 53 47N 112 56W
Brunette Island Newfoundland and Labrador 61 H3 47 16N 55 55W
Bruno Saskatchewan 47 E3 52 17N 105 31W
Brussels Ontario 54 A2 43 44N 81 15W
Buchan Gulf Nunavut 65 R5 71 47N 74 16W
Buchans Newfoundland and Labrador 61 G4 48 49N 56 53W
Buckingham Québec 57 C1 45 35N 75 24W
Buckinghorse River *tn.* British Columbia 43 J5 57 25N 122 50W
Buffalo Head Hills Alberta 46 E5 57 25N 115 55W
Buffalo Head Prairie Alberta 46 D6 58 04N 116 30W
Buffalo Lake Alberta 46 F3 52 27N 112 54W
Buffalo Narrows *tn.* Saskatchewan 47 C4 55 52N 108 28W
Buffalo River Alberta 46 E6 59 25N 114 35W
Buffalo Trail Alberta 46 G2 51 45N 110 35W
Bulkley River British Columbia 43 G4 55 00N 127 10W
Buntzen Lake British Columbia 44 G4 49 20N 124 51W
Burden, Mount British Columbia 43 J5 56 10N 123 09W
Burford Ontario 54 B2 43 46N 80 25W
Burgeo Newfoundland and Labrador 61 G3 47 37N 57 37W
Burin Newfoundland and Labrador 61 H3 47 02N 55 10W
Burin Peninsula Newfoundland and Labrador 61 H3 47 00N 55 40W
Burk's Falls *tn.* Ontario 52 G5 45 37N 79 25W
Burlington Ontario 54 C2 43 19N 79 48W
Burnaby British Columbia 42 H4 49 16N 122 58W
Burnaby Lake British Columbia 44 G3 49 14N 122 57W
Burns Bog Park Reserve British Columbia 44 G3 46 07N 122 58W
Burnside Nova Scotia 59 Q6 44 41N 63 35W
Burnside River Nunavut 64 J4 66 20N 109 30W
Burns Lake *tn.* British Columbia 43 H4 54 14N 125 45
Burnt Islands *tn.* Newfoundland and Labrador 61 F3 47 50N 58 00W
Burnt Lake Québec 57 J5 52 15N 63 50W
Burnt River Ontario 54 D3 44 41N 78 43W
Burntwood Lake Manitoba 49 B4 55 20N 100 10W
Burntwood River Manitoba 49 D4 55 50N 97 40W
Burquitlam British Columbia 44 G4 49 15N 122 56W
Burrard Inlet British Columbia 44 F4 49 19N 123 14W
Burstall Saskatchewan 47 C2 50 40N 109 56W
Bushell Park *tn.* Saskatchewan 47 E2 50 25N 105 30W
Butedale British Columbia 43 F3 53 12N 128 45W
Bute Inlet British Columbia 42 H5 50 31N 124 59W
Buttle Lake British Columbia 42 G4 49 47N 125 30W
Button Bay Manitoba 49 E6 58 50N 94 30W
Button Islands Nunavut 56 H9 60 35N 64 40W
Buttonville Ontario 55 C2 43 51N 79 22W
Byam Channel Nunavut 65 K6 75 10N 105 00W
Byam Martin Island Nunavut 65 K6 75 15N 104 15W
Bylot Island Nunavut 65 Q5 73 30N 79 00W
Byron Bay Newfoundland and Labrador 60 G7 54 40N 57 40W

C

Cabano Québec 57 F2 47 40N 68 56W
Cabot Head Ontario 54 A4 45 15N 81 17W
Cabot Lake Newfoundland and Labrador 60 D8 56 09N 62 37W
Cabot Strait Nova Scotia/Newfoundland and Labrador 61 F3 47 10N 59 30W
Cabri Saskatchewan 47 C2 50 38N 108 28W
Cache Creek *tn.* British Columbia 43 K2 50 46N 121 17W
Cadotte Lake *tn.* Alberta 46 D5 56 25N 116 28W
Calabogie Ontario 53 K5 45 18N 76 43W
Calais New Brunswick 61 B2 45 10N 67 15W
Caledon East Ontario 54 C2 43 52N 79 53W
Caledonia Nova Scotia 61 L11 44 24N 65 02W
Caledonia Ontario 54 C2 43 05N 79 57W
Caledon Village Ontario 54 C2 43 51N 79 59W
Calgary Alberta 46 E2 51 05N 114 05W
Callander Ontario 52 G6 46 13N 79 22W
Calling Lake Alberta 46 F4 55 15N 113 20W
Calmar Alberta 46 F3 53 16N 113 49W
Calvert Island British Columbia 43 F2 51 30N 128 00W
Cambridge Ontario 54 B2 43 22N 80 20W
Cambridge-Narrows New Brunswick 61 C2 45 50N 65 55W
Cameron Hills Alberta 46 C6 59 48N 118 00W
Campbell Dam Saskatchewan 47 F3 53 40N 103 20W
Campbellford Ontario 52 J4 44 18N 77 48W
Campbell Lake British Columbia 42 G4 49 59N 125 30W
Campbell, Mount Yukon Territory 64 C3 64 23N 138 43W
Campbell River *tn.* British Columbia 42 G5 50 00N 125 18W
Campbells Cove *tn.* Prince Edward Island 61 M12 46 30N 62 15W
Campbellton New Brunswick 61 B3 48 00N 66 41W
Campbellton Newfoundland and Labrador 61 H4 49 17N 54 56W
Campbellville Ontario 54 C2 43 29N 79 59W
Camperville Manitoba 49 B2 51 00N 100 08W
Campobello Island New Brunswick 61 B2 44 50N 66 50W
Camrose Alberta 46 F3 53 01N 112 50W
Camsell Portage Saskatchewan 47 C6 59 39N 109 12W
CANADA 12/13
Canal Flats *tn.* British Columbia 43 N2 50 09N 115 50W
Canal Lake Ontario 54 C3 44 34N 79 02W
Candiac Québec 58 N4 45 24N 73 31W
Candle Lake Saskatchewan 47 E3 53 55N 105 10W
Candle Lake *tn.* Saskatchewan 47 E3 53 50N 105 10W
Caniapiscau Québec 56 F6 54 58N 69 47W
Canmore Alberta 46 E2 51 07N 115 18W
Canning Nova Scotia 61 M12 45 10N 64 26W
Canoe Lake Saskatchewan 47 C4 55 10N 108 30W
Canoe Narrows Saskatchewan 47 C4 55 10N 108 09W
Canora Saskatchewan 47 F2 51 38N 102 28W
Canso Nova Scotia 61 M12 45 20N 61 00W
Canso, Cape Nova Scotia 61 M12 45 19N 60 59W
Cap-aux-Meules *tn.* Québec 61 E3 47 25N 62 00W
Cap-Chat *tn.* Québec 57 G3 49 06N 66 42W
Cap de Nouvelle-France *c.* Québec 56 D10 61 30N 73 45W
Cap Dufferin *c.* Québec 56 A8 58 35N 78 32W
Cape Breton *admin.* Nova Scotia 61 M12 45 50N 60 00W
Cape Breton Highlands National Park Nova Scotia 61 M12 46 45N 60 40W
Cape Breton Island Nova Scotia 61 M12 46 45N 60 00W
Cape Charles *tn.* Newfoundland and Labrador 60 H6 52 13N 55 38W
Cape Croker *tn.* Ontario 54 A3 44 56N 81 01W
Cape Dorset Sanctuaries Nunavut 65 Q3 63 50N 77 00W
Cape Le Havre Island Nova Scotia 61 M11 44 10N 64 20W
Cape North *tn.* Nova Scotia 61 M12 46 55N 60 30W
Cape Parry *m.s.* Northwest Territories 64 F5 70 08N 124 34W
Cape Sable Island Nova Scotia 61 L11 43 30N 65 40W
Cape St. George *tn.* Newfoundland and Labrador 61 F4 48 28N 59 15W
Cape Scott Provincial Park British Columbia 43 F2 50 42N 128 20W
Cape Smith *tn.* Nunavut 56 A9 60 44N 78 29W
Cape Tormentine *tn.* New Brunswick 61 M12 46 08N 63 47W
Cap Gaspé *c.* Québec 57 H3 48 46N 64 10W
Cap Hopes Advance *c.* Québec 56 F9 61 00N 69 40W
Capilano Lake British Columbia 44 F4 49 22N 123 06W
Cap Pelé *tn.* New Brunswick 61 M12 46 10N 64 10W
Cap Prince-de-Galles *c.* Québec 56 E9 61 42N 71 30W
Cap-Saint-Ignace *c.* Québec 53 R7 47 00N 70 29W
Capstick Nova Scotia 61 M12 47 00N 60 31W
Caramat Ontario 51 H5 49 37N 86 09W
Caraquet New Brunswick 61 C3 47 48N 64 59W
Carberry Manitoba 49 C1 49 52N 99 20W
Carbon Alberta 46 F2 51 29N 113 11W
Carbonear Newfoundland and Labrador 61 J3 47 44N 53 13W
Carcross Yukon Territory 64 D3 60 11N 134 41W
Cardigan Prince Edward Island 61 M12 46 14N 62 37W
Cardinal Ontario 53 L4 44 47N 75 23W
Cardston Alberta 46 F1 49 12N 113 18W
Cariboo Mountains British Columbia 43 K3 53 20N 120 50W
Cariboo Mountains Provincial Park British Columbia 43 K3 53 00N 120 30W
Caribou Manitoba 49 D6 59 20N 97 50W
Caribou Mountains Alberta 46 E6 59 00N 115 30W
Caribou Mountains Wildland Provincial Park Alberta 46 E6 59 10N 115 00W
Caribou River Manitoba 49 E6 59 30N 95 30W
Caribou River Provincial Park Manitoba 49 D6 59 30N 96 40W
Carleton–St-Omer Québec 57 G3 48 08N 66 10W
Carleton *admin.* New Brunswick 61 B3 46 10N 66 52W
Carleton, Mount New Brunswick 61 B3 47 24N 66 52W
Carleton Place Ontario 53 K5 45 15N 75 45W
Carlsbad Springs Ontario 59 L2 45 22N 75 29W
Carlson Landing Alberta 46 G6 58 59N 111 45W
Carlyle Saskatchewan 47 F1 49 39N 102 18W
Carmacks Yukon Territory 64 C3 62 04N 136 21W
Carman Manitoba 49 D1 49 32N 97 59W
Carmanah Walbran Provincial Park British Columbia 42 H4 48 37N 124 35W
Carmanville Newfoundland and Labrador 61 H4 49 24N 54 18W
Carnduff Saskatchewan 47 G1 49 11N 101 50W
Caronport Saskatchewan 47 E2 50 27N 105 49W
Carp Lake British Columbia 43 J4 54 48N 123 20W
Carp Lake Provincial Park British Columbia 43 J4 54 08N 123 30W
Carrot River Manitoba 49 D4 54 50N 96 40W
Carrot River Saskatchewan 47 E3 53 05N 104 15W
Carrot River *tn.* Saskatchewan 47 F3 53 18N 103 32W
Carstairs Alberta 46 E2 51 34N 114 06W
Cartmel, Mount British Columbia 43 F5 57 45N 129 12W
Cartwright Newfoundland and Labrador 60 G6 53 42N 57 01W
Cascade Range *mts.* British Columbia 42 H4 50 48N 121 15W
Cascade Recreation Area British Columbia 42 H4 49 16N 120 56W
Cascumpec Bay Prince Edward Island 61 M12 46 45N 64 00W
Casselman Ontario 53 L5 45 19N 78 07W
Cassiar Highway British Columbia 42 F5 57 30N 130 10W
Cassier Mountains British Columbia 42/43 E6/F6 59 50N 131 50W
Castlegar British Columbia 43 M1 49 18N 117 41W
Castor Alberta 46 G3 52 13N 111 53W
Catalina Newfoundland and Labrador 61 J4 48 31N 53 05W
Cat Arm Reservoir Newfoundland and Labrador 61 G5 50 10N 56 40W
Cathedral Provincial Park British Columbia 43 K1 49 05N 120 11W
Cat Lake Ontario 50 F6 51 30N 91 50W
Cat Lake *I.R.* Ontario 50 F6 51 40N 91 50W
Caubvick, Mt. Newfoundland and Labrador 60 D9 58 50N 64 40W
Causapscal Québec 57 G3 48 22N 67 14W
Cavendish Prince Edward Island 61 M12 46 30N 63 20W
Cayuga Ontario 54 C1 42 57N 79 50W
Cecil Lake *tn.* British Columbia 43 K5 56 19N 120 40W
Cedar Lake Manitoba 49 B3 53 40N 100 30W
Central Bedeque Prince Edward Island 61 M12 46 20N 63 40W
Central Butte Saskatchewan 47 D2 50 50N 106 30W
Central Patricia Ontario 50 F6 51 30N 90 09W
Central Saanich British Columbia 42 H4 48 32N 123 25W
Centreville Newfoundland and Labrador 61 J4 49 01N 53 53W
Centreville Nova Scotia 61 M12 45 10N 64 30W
C.F.B. Borden Ontario 54 C3 44 18N 79 53W
C.F.B. Suffield Alberta 46 G2 50 35N 110 47W
Chalk River *tn.* Ontario 53 J6 46 01N 77 27W
Chambly Québec 53 N5 45 27N 73 19W
Champlain *admin.* Québec 53 N7 48 20N 74 20W
Chandler Québec 57 H3 48 21N 64 41W
Channel-Port aux Basques Newfoundland and Labrador 61 F3 47 34N 59 09W
Chantrey Inlet Nunavut 65 L4 67 48N 96 20W
Chapais Québec 57 C3 49 47N 74 54W
Chapleau Ontario 51 K4 47 50N 83 24W
Chapleau-Nemegosenda River Provincial Park Ontario 51 K5 48 25N 83 00W
Chaplin Saskatchewan 47 D2 50 29N 106 40W
Chaplin Lake Saskatchewan 47 D2 50 25N 106 30W
Charles Island Nunavut 65 R3 62 39N 74 15W
Charles Lake Alberta 46 G6 59 50N 110 33W
Charles, Lake Nova Scotia 59 Q6 44 43N 63 32W
Charlevoix-Est *admin.* Québec 53 R7 47 50N 70 20W
Charlevoix-Ouest *admin.* Québec 53 R7 47 57N 71 05W
Charlo New Brunswick 61 B3 47 55N 66 20W
Charlotte *admin.* New Brunswick 61 B2 45 20N 67 20W
Charlotte Lake British Columbia 43 H3 52 11N 125 19W
Charlottetown Newfoundland and Labrador 60 G6 52 06N 56 07W
Charlottetown Prince Edward Island 61 M12 46 14N 63 09W
Charlton Island Nunavut 50 M7 52 00N 79 30W
Charny Québec 57 E2 46 43N 71 16W
Charron Lake Manitoba 49 E3 52 40N 95 40W
Chase British Columbia 43 L2 50 49N 119 41W
Chase Provincial Park British Columbia 43 H5 56 30N 125 10W
Chasm British Columbia 43 K2 51 13N 121 28W
Châteauguay Québec 53 N5 45 20N 73 42W
Chateh Alberta 46 C6 58 42N 118 55W

Chatham Ontario 52 D2 42 24N 82 11W
Chatham Sound British Columbia 42 E4 54 30N 130 30W
Chatsworth Ontario 54 B3 44 27N 80 54W
Chedabucto Bay Nova Scotia 61 M12 45 20N 61 10W
Cheepay River Ontario 50 K6 50 50N 83 40W
Chelsea Québec 59 J2 45 29N 75 48W
Chelsea Brook Québec 59 J3 45 31N 75 51W
Chemainus British Columbia 42 H4 48 54N 123 42W
Chemainus River British Columbia 42 H4 48 58N 124 09W
Cheslatta Lake British Columbia 43 H3 53 44N 125 20W
Chesley Ontario 54 A3 44 18N 81 07W
Chester Nova Scotia 61 M11 44 33N 64 16W
Chesterfield Inlet Nunavut 65 M3 63 21N 90 42W
Chesterville Ontario 53 L5 45 06N 75 14W
Cheticamp Nova Scotia 61 M12 46 37N 60 59W
Cheticamp Island Nova Scotia 61 M12 46 40N 61 05W
Chetwynd British Columbia 43 K4 55 38N 121 40W
Chevery Québec 56 L4 50 29N 59 41W
Chibougamau Québec 57 C3 49 56N 72 24W
Chicoutimi Québec 57 E3 48 26N 71 03W
Chicoutimi *admin.* Québec 53 R8 48 10N 71 10W
Chidley, Cape Newfoundland and Labrador 60 C10 60 23N 64 26W
Chignecto Bay Nova Scotia 61 M12 45 40N 64 40W
Chignecto, Cape Nova Scotia 61 M12 45 20N 64 55W
Chignecto Game Sanctuary Nova Scotia 61 M12 45 30N 64 35W
Chilanko Forks British Columbia 43 H3 52 04N 124 00W
Chilcotin River British Columbia 43 J2 51 54N 123 20W
Chilko Lake British Columbia 43 H2 51 15N 124 59W
Chilko River British Columbia 43 J2 51 59N 124 05W
Chilliwack British Columbia 42 H4 49 06N 121 56W
Chilliwack Lake British Columbia 42 H4 49 04N 121 22W
Chilliwack River British Columbia 42 H4 49 04N 121 52W
Chin, Cape Ontario 54 A4 45 05N 81 17W
Chinchaga River Alberta 46 C5 57 30N 119 00W
Chinchaga Wildland Provincial Park Alberta 46 C5 57 10N 119 40W
Chip Lake Alberta 46 E3 53 40N 115 23W
Chipman New Brunswick 61 C3 46 11N 65 54W
Chippawa Ontario 54 C2 43 03N 79 04W
Chisasibi Québec 57 A5 53 50N 79 01W
Chitek Lake Park Reserve Manitoba 49 C3 52 30N 99 30W
Choiceland Saskatchewan 47 E3 53 30N 104 33W
Chomedey Québec 58 M5 45 32N 73 46W
Chorkbak Inlet Nunavut 65 R3 64 30N 74 25W
Chown, Mount Alberta 46 C3 53 24N 119 25W
Christian Island Ontario 54 B3 44 50N 80 14W
Christian Island *tn.* Ontario 54 B3 44 49N 80 10W
Christie Bay Northwest Territories 64 H3 62 32N 111 10W
Christina River Alberta 46 G4 55 50N 111 59W
Churchbridge Saskatchewan 47 G2 50 55N 101 38W
Churchill Manitoba 49 E6 58 45N 94 00W
Churchill, Cape Manitoba 49 F6 59 00N 93 00W
Churchill Falls *tn.* Newfoundland and Labrador 60 D6 53 35N 64 00W
Churchill Lake Saskatchewan 47 C5 56 05N 108 15W
Churchill Peak British Columbia 43 H6 58 20N 125 02W
Churchill River Manitoba/Saskatchewan 49 E6 58 00N 95 00W
Churchill River Newfoundland and Labrador 60 D6 53 20N 63 40W
Churn Creek Provincial Park British Columbia 43 J2 51 25N 122 30W
Chute-aux-Outardes Québec 57 F3 49 17N 68 25W
Cirque Mountain Newfoundland and Labrador 60 D9 58 56N 63 33W
City View Ontario 59 K2 45 21N 75 44W
Claire, Lake Alberta 46 F6/G6 58 30N 112 00W
Clarence Head *c.* Nunavut 65 Q6 76 47N 77 47W
Clarence-Steepbank Lakes Provincial Wilderness Park Saskatchewan 47 E4 54 15N 105 10W
Clarenville Newfoundland and Labrador 61 J4 48 10N 53 58W
Claresholm Alberta 46 F2 50 04N 113 29W
Clarke City Québec 57 G4 50 11N 66 39W
Clark's Harbour *tn.* Nova Scotia 61 L11 43 25N 65 38W
Clarkson Ontario 54 C2 43 30N 79 38W
Clavet Saskatchewan 47 D3 51 59N 106 21W
Clayoquot Sound British Columbia 43 G1 49 12N 126 05W
Clear Hills Alberta 46 C5 56 40N 119 30W
Clearwater British Columbia 43 K2 51 37N 120 03W
Clearwater Bay *tn.* Ontario 50 D5 49 39N 94 48W
Clearwater Lake British Columbia 43 K3 52 13N 120 20W
Clearwater Lake Manitoba 49 B4 53 50N 101 40W
Clearwater Lake Provincial Park Manitoba 49 B4 54 00N 101 00W
Clearwater River Alberta 46 E2 51 59N 115 20W
Clearwater River Alberta 46 G5 56 47N 110 59W
Clearwater River Provincial Park Saskatchewan 47 C5 57 10N 108 10W
Clendinning Provincial Park British Columbia 43 J2 50 25N 123 45W
Clifford Ontario 54 B2 43 58N 80 00W
Clinton British Columbia 43 K2 51 05N 121 38W
Clinton Ontario 54 A2 43 36N 81 33W
Clinton-Colden Lake Northwest Territories 64 J3 64 58N 107 27W
Cloridorme Québec 57 H3 49 10N 64 51W
Close Lake Saskatchewan 47 E5 57 50N 104 40W
Cloverdale British Columbia 44 H3 49 05N 122 46W
Cluff Lake Mine *tn.* Saskatchewan 47 C6 58 20N 109 35W
Coaldale Alberta 46 F1 49 43N 112 37W
Coalhurst Alberta 46 F1 49 45N 112 56W
Coal River British Columbia 43 G6 59 56N 127 11W
Coast Mountains British Columbia 42/43 E5/H2 58 10N 132 40W
Coates Creek Ontario 54 B3 44 22N 80 07W
Coaticook Québec 53 Q5 45 08N 71 40W
Coats Island Nunavut 65 P3 63 30N 83 00W
Cobalt Ontario 51 M4 47 24N 79 41W
Cobble Hill *tn.* British Columbia 42 H4 48 41N 123 39W
Cobequid Bay Nova Scotia 61 M12 45 20N 63 50W
Cobequid Mountains Nova Scotia 61 M12 45 30N 64 50W
Cobourg Ontario 51 M2 43 58N 78 11W
Cochrane Alberta 46 E2 51 11N 114 28W
Cochrane Ontario 51 L5 49 04N 81 02W
Cochrane River Manitoba/Saskatchewan 47 F6 58 50N 102 20W
Cockburn Island Ontario 52 C5 45 55N 83 22W
Cod Island Newfoundland and Labrador 60 E8 57 47N 61 47W
Colborne Ontario 52 J4 44 00N 77 53W
Colchester *admin.* Nova Scotia 61 M12 45 30N 63 30W
Cold Lake Alberta 46 G4 54 00N 110 00W
Cold Lake *tn.* Alberta 46 G4 54 28N 110 15W
Cold Lake Air Weapons Range Alberta 46 G4 55 10N 110 25W
Coldspring Head Nova Scotia 61 M12 45 55N 63 50W
Coldstream British Columbia 43 L2 50 10N 119 12W
Coldwater Ontario 52 G4 44 43N 79 39W
Cole Harbour Nova Scotia 59 R6 44 40N 63 27W
Cole Harbour *tn.* Nova Scotia 59 R6 44 40N 63 30W
Colin-Cornwall Lakes Wildland Provincial Park Alberta 46 G6 59 35N 110 10W
Collingwood Ontario 54 B3 44 30N 80 14W
Collins Ontario 50 G6 50 17N 89 27W
Colonsay Saskatchewan 47 E3 52 00N 105 52W
Colpoys Bay Ontario 54 A3 44 48N 81 04W
Columbia, Mount British Columbia/Alberta 46 D3 52 09N 117 25W
Columbia Mountains British Columbia 43 K3/M2 53 12N 120 49W
Columbia River British Columbia 43 M2 51 15N 116 58W
Colville Lake Northwest Territories 64 E4 67 10N 126 00W
Colwood British Columbia 42 H4 48 27N 123 28W
Combermere Ontario 52 J5 45 22N 77 37W
Comma Island Newfoundland and Labrador 60 E7 55 20N 60 20W
Committee Bay Nunavut 65 N4 68 30N 86 30W
Comox British Columbia 42 H4 49 41N 124 56W
Comox Lake British Columbia 42 G4 49 37N 125 10W
Compton *admin.* Québec 53 Q5 45 20N 71 40W
Conception Bay Newfoundland and Labrador 61 J3 47 45N 53 00W
Conception Bay South *tn.* Newfoundland and Labrador 61 J3 47 30N 53 00W
Conche Newfoundland and Labrador 60 H5 50 53N 55 54W
Conestogo Lake Ontario 54 B2 43 47N 80 44W
Conestogo River Ontario 54 B2 43 41N 80 42W
Conne River *tn.* Newfoundland and Labrador 61 H3 47 50N 55 20W
Consort Alberta 46 G3 52 01N 110 46W
Contrecoeur Québec 53 N5 45 51N 73 15W
Contwoyto Lake Nunavut 64 J4 65 42N 110 50W
Cook's Bay Ontario 54 C3 44 53N 79 31W
Cookstown Ontario 54 C3 44 12N 79 42W
Coppermine River Nunavut 64 H4 67 10N 115 00W
Coquihalla Highway British Columbia 42 H4 49 25N 121 20W
Coquitlam British Columbia 44 G4 49 15N 122 52W
Coquitlam Lake British Columbia 44 G4 49 21N 122 46W
Coquitlam River British Columbia 44 G4 49 17N 122 45W
Cormorant Manitoba 49 B4 54 14N 100 35W
Cormorant Lake Manitoba 49 B4 54 10N 101 30W
Cormorant Provincial Forest Manitoba 49 B4 54 10N 100 50W
Corner Brook *tn.* Newfoundland and Labrador 61 G4 48 58N 57 58W
Cornwall Ontario 53 M5 45 02N 74 45W
Cornwall Prince Edward Island 61 M12 46 10N 63 10W
Cornwallis Island Nunavut 65 L6 75 00N 97 30W
Coronach Saskatchewan 47 E1 49 06N 105 29W
Coronation Alberta 46 G3 52 05N 111 27W
Coronation Gulf Nunavut 64 H4 68 15N 112 30W
Cortes Island British Columbia 42 H5 50 07N 125 01W
Couchiching, Lake Ontario 54 C3 44 39N 79 22W
Courtenay British Columbia 42 H4 49 40N 124 58W
Courtice Ontario 54 D2 43 57N 78 48W
Courtright Ontario 52 D2 42 49N 82 28W
Coutts Alberta 46 G1 49 00N 112 00N
Cove Island Ontario 54 A4 45 19N 81 44W
Cowansville Québec 53 P5 45 13N 72 44W
Cow Bay Nova Scotia 59 R6 44 36N 63 26W
Cow Head *tn.* Newfoundland and Labrador 61 G4 49 55N 57 48W
Cowichan Bay *tn.* British Columbia 42 H4 48 44N 123 40W
Cowichan Lake British Columbia 42 H4 48 50N 124 04W
Cowichan River British Columbia 42 H4 48 48N 123 58W
Cox's Cove *tn.* Newfoundland and Labrador 61 F4 49 07N 58 04W
Craigellachie British Columbia 43 L2 50 59N 118 38W
Craigleith Provinicial Park Ontario 54 B3 44 30N 80 15W
Craik Saskatchewan 47 E2 51 03N 105 50W
Cranberry Junction British Columbia 43 F4 55 35N 128 36W
Cranberry Portage Manitoba 49 B4 54 36N 101 22W
Cranbrook British Columbia 43 N1 49 29N 115 48W
Crane Lake Saskatchewan 47 C2 50 10N 109 20W
Crane River Ontario 54 A4 45 53N 81 31W
Crane River *tn.* Manitoba 49 C2 51 30N 99 18W
Credit River Ontario 54 B2 43 50N 80 02W
Cree Lake Saskatchewan 47 D5 57 30N 106 30W
Creemore Ontario 54 B3 44 20N 80 07W
Cree River Saskatchewan 47 D5 58 00N 106 30W
Creighton Saskatchewan 47 G4 54 46N 101 50W
Cresswell Bay Nunavut 65 M5 72 40N 93 30W
Creston British Columbia 43 M1 49 05N 116 32W
Croker, Cape Ontario 54 B3 44 58N 80 59W
Crossfield Alberta 46 E2 51 26N 114 02W
Cross Lake Manitoba 49 D4 54 50N 97 20W
Cross Lake *tn.* Manitoba 49 D4 54 38N 97 45W
Crow Lake Ontario 50 E5 49 10N 93 56W
Crowsnest Highway Alberta 46 G1 49 50N 111 55W
Crowsnest Pass Alberta/British Columbia 43 N1 49 40N 114 41W
Crumlin Ontario 54 A2 43 01N 81 08W
Crystal Bay Ontario 59 J2 45 21N 75 51W
Crystal Beach *tn.* Ontario 54 C1 42 52N 79 03W
Cub Hills, The Saskatchewan 47 E4 54 20N 104 40W
Cudworth Saskatchewan 47 E3 52 31N 105 44W
Cumberland British Columbia 42 H4 49 37N 124 59W
Cumberland Ontario 59 L3 45 31N 75 23W
Cumberland *admin.* Nova Scotia 61 M12 45 30N 64 10W
Cumberland House *tn.* Saskatchewan 47 F3 53 57N 102 20W
Cumberland Lake Saskatchewan 47 F4 54 10N 102 30W
Cumberland Peninsula Nunavut 65 T4 67 00N 65 00W
Cumberland Sound Nunavut 65 S4 65 30N 66 00W
Cummins Lakes Provincial Park British Columbia 43 L3 52 10N 118 00W
Cupar Saskatchewan 47 E2 50 57N 104 12W
Cushing, Mount British Columbia 43 G5 57 36N 126 51W
Cut Knife Saskatchewan 47 C3 52 45N 109 01W
Cypress Hills Alberta/Saskatchewan 46 G1 49 30N 110 00W
Cypress Hills Provincial Park Alberta/Saskatchewan 46 G1 49 38N 110 00W

D

Dalhousie New Brunswick 61 B4 48 03N 66 22W
Dalhousie, Cape Northwest Territories 64 E5 70 14N 129 42W
Dalmeny Saskatchewan 47 D3 52 22N 106 46W
Dalrymple Lake Ontario 54 C3 44 41N 79 07W
Daniel's Harbour *tn.* Newfoundland and Labrador 61 G5 50 14N 57 35W
Danville Québec 53 P5 45 48N 72 01W
Darlington Provincial Park Ontario 54 D2 44 00N 78 50W
Darnley Bay Northwest Territories 64 F4 69 30N 123 30W
Dartmouth Nova Scotia 61 M11 44 40N 63 35W
Dauphin Manitoba 49 B2 51 09N 100 05W
Dauphin, Cape Nova Scotia 61 M12 46 20N 60 25W
Dauphin Lake Manitoba 49 C2 51 10N 99 30W
Dauphin River Manitoba 49 D2 51 50N 98 20W
Dauphin River *tn.* Manitoba 49 D2 51 50N 98 00W
Davidson Saskatchewan 47 E2 51 15N 105 59W
David Thompson Highway Alberta 46 D3 52 15N 116 35W
Davin Lake Saskatchewan 47 F5 56 45N 103 40W
Davis Strait Greenland/Nunavut 65 T4 65 00N 65 00W
Davy Lake Saskatchewan 47 C6 58 50N 108 10W
Dawson Bay Manitoba 49 B3 52 50N 100 50W
Dawson City Yukon Territory 64 C3 64 04N 139 24W
Dawson Creek *tn.* British Columbia 43 K4 55 44N 120 15W
Dawson, Mount British Columbia 43 M2 51 08N 117 26W
Dawson Range *mts.* Yukon Territory 64 C3 63 00N 139 30W
Dawsons Landing British Columbia 43 G2 51 28N 127 33W
Daysland Alberta 46 F3 52 52N 112 15W
Ddhaw Gro Habitat Protection Area Yukon Territory 64 C3 62 25N 135 50W
Dean Channel British Columbia 43 G3 52 18N 127 35W
Dean River British Columbia 43 G3 52 45N 122 30W
Dease Arm *b.* Northwest Territories 64 F4 66 52N 122 00W
Dease Lake British Columbia 42 E6 58 05N 130 04W
Dease Lake *tn.* British Columbia 42 E6 58 28N 130 00W
Dease River British Columbia 42 F6 59 05N 129 40W
Dease Strait Nunavut 64 J4 68 40N 108 00W
Deas Island British Columbia 44 F3 49 07N 123 04W
Déception Québec 56 C10 62 10N 74 45W
Dee Lake British Columbia 44 G3 49 14N 122 59W
Deep Cove British Columbia 44 G4 49 19N 122 58W
Deep Inlet Newfoundland and Labrador 60 E7 55 22N 60 14W
Deep River *tn.* Ontario 53 J6 46 06N 77 30W
Deer Island New Brunswick 61 B2 45 00N 67 00W
Deer Lake Ontario 50 D7 52 38N 94 25W
Deer Lake *tn.* Newfoundland and Labrador 61 G4 49 11N 57 27W
Delhi Ontario 54 B1 42 51N 80 30W
Déline *(Fort Franklin)* Northwest Territories 64 F4 65 11N 123 26W
Delisle Saskatchewan 47 D2 51 56N 107 10W
Deloraine Manitoba 49 B1 49 11N 100 30W
Delta British Columbia 42 H4 49 06N 123 01W
Dempster Highway Yukon Territory 64 C4 65 30N 138 10W
Denare Beach Saskatchewan 47 F4 54 39N 102 06W
Denbigh Ontario 53 J5 45 08N 77 15W
Denetiah Provincial Park British Columbia 43 G6 58 30N 127 30W
Denínue Kúé *(Fort Resolution)* Northwest Territories 64 H3 61 10N 113 39W
Denman Island British Columbia 42 H4 49 32N 124 49W
Deschambault Lake Saskatchewan 47 F4 54 50N 103 50W
Deseronto Ontario 53 J4 44 12N 77 03W
Desmaraisville Québec 57 B3 49 30N 76 18W
Desolation Sound Marine Park British Columbia 42 H5 50 08N 124 45W
Destruction Bay *tn.* Yukon Territory 64 C3 61 16N 138 50W
Détroit de Jacques-Cartier *sd.* Québec 57 J3 50 10N 64 10W
Détroit d'Honguedo *sd.* Québec 57 H3 49 30N 64 20W
Détroit d'Hudson *sd.* Québec/Nunavut 56 F9 62 00N 70 00W
Deux-Montagnes Québec 58 M5 45 32N 73 56W
Deux Rivières Ontario 52 H6 46 15N 78 17W
Devil's Glen Provincial Park Ontario 54 B3 44 20N 80 30W
Devon Alberta 46 F3 53 22N 113 44W
Devon Island Nunavut 65 N6 75 47N 88 00W
Dewar Lakes Nunavut 65 R4 68 30N 71 20W
Dewey Soper Bird Sanctuary Nunavut 65 R4 66 20N 68 50W
Diamond Jennes Peninsula Northwest Territories 64 G5 71 20N 117 00W
Didsbury Alberta 46 E2 51 40N 114 08W
Diefenbaker, Lake Saskatchewan 47 D2 51 10N 107 30W
Dieppe New Brunswick 61 M12 46 10N 64 40W
Digby Nova Scotia 61 L11 44 37N 65 47W
Digby *admin.* Nova Scotia 61 L11 44 20N 65 40W
Digby Neck *p.* Nova Scotia 61 L11 44 30N 66 00W
Dillon Saskatchewan 47 C6 55 56N 108 54W
Dingwall Nova Scotia 61 M12 46 50N 60 30W
Dinorwic Ontario 50 E5 49 41N 92 30W
Dinosaur Provincial Park Alberta 46 G2 50 47N 111 25W
Disappointment Lake Newfoundland and Labrador 60 D6 53 49N 62 31W
Dismal Lakes Nunavut 64 G4 67 26N 117 07W
Disraeli Québec 53 Q5 45 54N 71 22W
Dixon Entrance *sd.* British Columbia/USA 42 D4/E4 54 28N 132 50W
Doaktown New Brunswick 61 B3 46 34N 66 06W
Dobie River Ontario 50 F6 51 30N 90 05W
Dodge Lake Saskatchewan 47 E6 59 50N 105 25W
Dog Creek *tn.* British Columbia 43 J2 51 35N 122 18W
Dog (High) Island Newfoundland and Labrador 60 E8 56 38N 61 10W
Dog Lake Manitoba 49 C2 51 00N 98 20W
Dog Lake Ontario 51 G5 48 50N 89 30W
Dolbeau-Mistassini Québec 57 D3 48 52N 72 15W
Dollarton British Columbia 44 G4 49 18N 122 58W
Dolphin and Union Strait Nunavut 64 G4 69 05N 114 45W
Dominion Nova Scotia 61 M12 46 14N 60 01W
Dominion Lake Newfoundland and Labrador 60 E6 52 40N 61 43W
Domino Newfoundland and Labrador 60 H6 53 29N 55 48W
Don Mills Ontario 55 C1 43 44N 79 22W
Donnacona Québec 53 Q6 46 41N 71 45W
Don River Ontario 54 C2 43 48N 79 24W
D'Or, Cape Nova Scotia 61 M12 45 20N 64 50W
Dorcas Bay Ontario 54 A4 45 10N 81 38W
Dorchester New Brunswick 61 M12 45 54N 64 32W
Dorchester *admin.* Québec 53 R6 46 20N 70 40W
Dorchester, Cape Nunavut 65 Q4 65 27N 77 27W
Dore Lake Saskatchewan 47 D4 54 50N 107 20W
Dorion Ontario 51 G5 48 49N 88 33W
Dorval Québec 58 N4 44 27N 73 45W
Dorval-Lodge Québec 57 B2 47 27N 77 05W
Double Mer *in.* Newfoundland and Labrador 60 F7 54 04N 59 10W
Douglas Island British Columbia 44 G3 49 13N 122 46W
Dowling Lake British Columbia 46 F2 51 44N 112 00W
Downtown, Mount British Columbia 43 H3 52 45N 124 53W
Dows Lake Ontario 59 K2 45 24N 75 42W
Drayton Ontario 54 B2 43 45N 80 40W
Drayton Valley *tn.* Alberta 46 E3 53 13N 114 59W
Dresden Ontario 52 D2 42 34N 82 11W
Driftwood Ontario 51 L5 49 08N 81 20W
Drowning River Ontario 50 J6 50 30N 86 00W
Drumheller Alberta 46 F2 51 28N 112 40W
Drummond *admin.* Québec 53 P5 45 50N 72 40W

Drummondville Québec 53 P5 45 52N 72 30W
Dryden Ontario 50 E5 49 48N 92 48W
Drylake *tn.* Newfoundland and Labrador 60 C7 52 38N 65 59W
Dubawnt Lake Nunavut 65 K3 63 15N 102 00W
Dubreuilville Ontario 51 J5 48 21N 84 32W
Duck Bay *tn.* Manitoba 49 B3 52 10N 100 10W
Duck Lake *tn.* Saskatchewan 47 D3 52 52N 106 12W
Duck Mountain Provincial Forest Manitoba 49 B2 51 20N 100 50W
Duck Mountain Provincial Park Manitoba 49 B2 51 40N 101 00W
Duck Mountain Provincial Park Saskatchewan 47 G2 51 40N 101 40W
Dufferin *admin.* Ontario 54 B3 44 00N 80 20W
Duncan British Columbia 42 H4 48 46N 123 40W
Duncan, Cape Nunavut 50 L7 52 40N 80 50W
Duncan Lake British Columbia 43 M2 50 23N 116 57W
Dundalk Ontario 54 B3 44 10N 80 24W
Dundas Ontario 54 C2 43 16N 79 57W
Dundas Island British Columbia 42 E4 54 33N 131 20W
Dundas Peninsula Northwest Territories 64 H5 74 50N 111 30W
Dundurn Saskatchewan 47 D2 51 49N 106 30W
Dune Za Keyih Provincial Park British Columbia 43 G6/H6 58 20N 126 00W
Dunnville Ontario 54 C1 42 54N 79 36W
Dunville Newfoundland and Labrador 61 J3 47 16N 53 54W
Duparquet Québec 57 A3 48 32N 79 14W
Durham Ontario 54 B3 44 11N 80 49W
Durham *admin.* Ontario 54 C3/D3 44 04N 79 11W
Durrell Newfoundland and Labrador 61 H4 49 40N 54 44W
Dutton Ontario 54 A1 42 39N 81 30W
Duvernay Québec 58 N5 45 34N 73 41W
Dyer, Cape Nunavut 65 T4 66 37N 61 16W
Dyer's Bay Ontario 54 A4 45 10N 81 18W
Dyer's Bay *tn.* Ontario 54 A4 45 09N 81 20W
Dyke Lake Newfoundland and Labrador 60 B7 54 30N 66 18W

E

Eabamet Lake Ontario 50 H6 51 32N 87 46W
Eagle Lake Ontario 50 E5 49 35N 93 00W
Eagle Plains *tn.* Yukon Territory 64 C4 66 30N 136 50W
Eagle River Newfoundland and Labrador 60 G6 53 10N 58 00W
Eagle River Saskatchewan 47 D2 51 35N 107 40W
Eagle River *tn.* Ontario 50 E5 49 50N 93 12W
Ear Falls *tn.* Ontario 50 E6 50 38N 93 13W
Earl Rowe Provincial Park Ontario 54 C3 44 15N 79 45W
East Angus Québec 53 Q5 45 30N 71 40W
East Bay Bird Sanctuary Nunavut 65 P3 66 20N 74 00W
East Chezzetcook Nova Scotia 61 M11 44 34N 63 14W
Eastend Saskatchewan 47 C1 49 32N 108 50W
Eastern Passage *tn.* Nova Scotia 59 R6 44 36N 63 29W
Easterville Manitoba 49 C3 53 00N 99 40W
East Lake Nova Scotia 59 R7 44 46N 63 29W
Eastmain Québec 57 A5 52 10N 78 30W
East Point Prince Edward Island 61 M12 46 27N 61 59W
Eastport Newfoundland and Labrador 61 J4 48 39N 53 45W
East Thurlow Island British Columbia 42 G5 50 24N 125 26W
East York Ontario 55 C2 43 43N 79 20W
Eatonia Saskatchewan 47 C2 51 13N 109 22W
Echaot'ine Kúé *(Fort Liard)* Northwest Territories 64 F3 60 14N 123 28W
Echoing River Ontario 50 F8 54 30N 92 00W
Eclipse Sound Nunavut 65 Q5 72 38N 79 00W
Ecum Secum Nova Scotia 61 M11 44 58N 62 08W
Eddies Cove *tn.* Newfoundland and Labrador 60 G5 51 25N 56 27W
Edehon Lake Nunavut 65 L3 60 25N 97 15W
Edgerton Alberta 46 G3 52 46N 110 27W
Edgewood British Columbia 43 L1 49 47N 118 08W
Edmonton Alberta 46 F3 53 34N 113 25W
Edmund Lake Manitoba 49 F4 54 50N 93 30W
Edmundston New Brunswick 61 A3 47 22N 68 20W
Edson Alberta 46 D3 53 35N 116 26W
Eduni, Mount Northwest Territories 64 E3 64 13N 128 10W
Edwards Ontario 59 L2 45 19N 75 48W
Edziza, Mount British Columbia 42 E5 57 43N 130 42W
Edzo Northwest Territories 64 G3 63 50N 116 00W
Eganville Ontario 53 J5 45 32N 77 06W
Eglinton Island Northwest Territories 64 G6 75 48N 118 30W
Egmont British Columbia 42 H4 49 45N 123 55W
Egmont Bay Prince Edward Island 61 M12 46 30N 64 20W
Egmont, Cape Nova Scotia 61 M12 46 50N 60 20W
Eileen Lake Northwest Territories 64 J3 62 16N 107 37W
Ekwan Point Ontario 50 K7 53 20N 82 10W
Ekwan River Ontario 50 K7 53 30N 83 40W
Elaho River British Columbia 42 H5 50 14N 123 33W
Elbow Saskatchewan 47 D2 51 08N 106 36W
Elbow River Alberta 44 A1 50 59N 114 13W
Elgin *admin.* Ontario 54 A1 42 38N 81 36W
Elkford British Columbia 43 N2 50 02N 114 55W
Elkhorn Manitoba 49 B1 49 58N 101 14W
Elk Island Manitoba 49 D2 50 50N 96 40W
Elk Island National Park Alberta 46 F3 53 36N 112 53W
Elk Lake *tn.* Ontario 51 L4 47 44N 80 20W
Elk Lakes Provincial Park British Columbia 43 N2 50 00N 115 00W
Elk Point *tn.* Alberta 46 G3 53 54N 110 54W
Ellef Ringnes Island Nunavut 65 K6 78 30N 102 00W
Ellesmere Island Nunavut 65 P6 77 30N 82 30W
Ellice River Nunavut 64 J4 66 20N 105 00W
Elliot Lake *tn.* Ontario 52 D6 46 25N 82 40W
Elm Creek *tn.* Manitoba 49 D1 49 41N 97 59W
Elmira Ontario 54 B2 43 36N 80 34W
Elmira Prince Edward Island 61 M12 46 26N 62 05W
Elmvale Ontario 54 C3 44 35N 79 52W
Elora Ontario 54 B2 43 42N 80 26W
Elrose Saskatchewan 47 C2 51 12N 108 01W
Elsa Yukon Territory 64 C3 63 55N 135 29W
Elvira, Cape Nunavut 64 J5 73 16N 107 10W
Embree Newfoundland and Labrador 61 H4 49 18N 55 02W
Emerald Island Northwest Territories 64 H6 76 48N 114 10W
Emerson Manitoba 49 D1 49 00N 97 11W
Endako British Columbia 43 H4 54 10N 125 21W
Enderby British Columbia 43 L2 50 32N 119 10W
Enfield Nova Scotia 61 M11 44 56N 63 34W
Englee Newfoundland and Labrador 60 G5 50 44N 56 06W
Englehart Ontario 51 M4 47 50N 79 52W
English Bay British Columbia 44 F4 49 17N 123 12W
English River Ontario 50 D6 50 20N 94 50W
Ennadai Lake Nunavut 65 K3 60 58N 101 20W
Enterprise Northwest Territories 64 G3 60 34N 116 15W
Entiaco Provincial Park British Columbia 43 H3 53 15N 125 30W
Eramosa River Ontario 54 B2 43 33N 80 11W
Erieau Ontario 52 E2 42 16N 81 56W
Erie Beach *tn.* Ontario 52 D2 42 16N 82 00W
Erie Beach *tn.* Ontario 54 D1 42 53N 78 56W
Erie, Lake Ontario/USA 52 E2 42 15N 81 00W
Eriksdale Manitoba 49 C2 50 52N 98 07W
Erin Ontario 54 B2 43 48N 80 04W
Escuminac, Point New Brunswick 61 C3 47 04N 64 49W
Esker Siding Newfoundland and Labrador 60 B6 53 53N 66 25W
Eskimo Lakes Northwest Territories 64 D4 68 30N 132 30W
Espanola Ontario 52 E6 46 15N 81 46W
Esquimalt British Columbia 42 H4 48 25N 123 29W
Essex Ontario 52 D2 42 10N 82 49W
Essex *admin.* Ontario 52 D2 42 10N 82 50W
Esterhazy Saskatchewan 47 F2 50 40N 102 02W
Estevan Saskatchewan 47 F1 49 09N 103 00W
Eston Saskatchewan 47 C2 51 09N 108 42W
Etawney Lake Manitoba 49 D5 57 50N 96 40W
Ethelbert Manitoba 49 B2 51 32N 100 25W
Etobicoke Ontario 55 B1 43 38N 79 30W
Etobicoke Creek Ontario 55 A1 43 43N 79 47W
Eugenia Lake Ontario 54 B3 44 20N 80 30W
Eureka *m.s.* Nunavut 65 N6 79 59N 85 57W
Eureka River *tn.* Alberta 46 C5 56 25N 118 48W
Eutsuk Lake British Columbia 43 G3 53 12N 126 32W
Evansburg Alberta 46 E3 53 36N 115 01W
Evans, Mount Alberta 46 C3 52 26N 118 07W
Evans Strait Nunavut 65 P3 63 15N 82 30W
Exeter Ontario 54 A2 43 21N 81 30W
Exploits River Newfoundland and Labrador 61 G4 48 40N 56 30W
Eyehill River Saskatchewan 47 C3 52 25N 109 50W

F

Faber Lake Northwest Territories 64 G3 63 56N 117 15W
Fairchild Creek Ontario 54 B2 43 13N 80 11W
Fairview Alberta 46 C5 56 03N 118 28W
Fairweather Mountain British Columbia/USA 42 B6 58 50N 137 55W
Falcon Lake *tn.* Manitoba 49 E1 49 44N 95 18W
Falher Alberta 46 D4 55 44N 117 12W
Fallowfield Ontario 59 J2 45 17N 75 51W
Fall River *tn.* Nova Scotia 61 M11 44 49N 63 36W
False Creek British Columbia 44 F4 49 16N 123 08W
Family Lake Manitoba 49 E2 51 50N 95 40W
Farewell Newfoundland and Labrador 57 B3 48 26N 72 15W
Farnham Québec 53 P5 45 17N 72 59W
Farnham, Mount British Columbia 43 M2 50 27N 116 37W
Faro Yukon Territory 64 D3 62 30N 133 00W
Fathom Five National Marine Park Ontario 54 A4 54 20N 81 35W
Fauquier Ontario 51 L5 49 19N 81 59W
Fawn River Ontario 50 G8 54 20N 88 40W
Fawn River Provincial Park Ontario 50 G8 54 10N 89 25W
Felix, Cape Nunavut 65 L4 69 54N 97 58W
Fenelon Falls *tn.* Ontario 54 D3 44 32N 78 45W
Fergus Ontario 54 B2 43 43N 80 24W
Ferland Ontario 50 G6 50 18N 88 25W
Ferme-Neuve Québec 53 L6 46 42N 75 28W
Fermont Québec 57 G5 52 00N 68 00W
Fernie British Columbia 43 N1 49 30N 115 00W
Ferryland Newfoundland and Labrador 61 J3 47 01N 54 53W
Field British Columbia 43 M2 51 23N 116 29W
Fife Lake Saskatchewan 47 E1 49 10N 105 55W
Finch Ontario 53 L5 45 08N 75 05W
Finger-Tatuk Provincial Park British Columbia 43 H3 53 30N 124 15W
Finlay Ranges *mts.* British Columbia 43 H5 57 10N 126 00W
Finlay River British Columbia 43 G5 57 20N 125 40W
Finlay-Russel Provincial Park British Columbia 43 G5/H5 57 20N 126 00W
Fiordland Recreation Area British Columbia 43 F3 52 00N 127 00W
Firebag Hills Saskatchewan 47 C5 57 15N 109 50W
Firebag River Alberta 46 G5 57 30N 110 40W
Fish Creek Alberta 44 A1 50 55N 114 10W
Fish Creek Provincial Park Alberta 44 A1 50 55N 114 04W
Fisher Bay Manitoba 49 D2 51 30N 97 30W
Fisher Branch *tn.* Manitoba 49 D2 51 04N 97 38W
Fisher, Mount British Columbia 43 N1 49 35N 115 20W
Fisher Strait Nunavut 65 P3 63 00N 84 00W
Fishing Branch Game Reserve Yukon Territory 64 C4 66 30N 139 30W
Fishing Lake Manitoba 49 E3 52 10N 95 40W
Fitzgerald Alberta 46 G6 59 51N 111 36W
Fitzwilliam Island Ontario 52 E5 45 29N 81 45W
Fjord Alluviaq Québec 56 H8 59 30N 65 30W
Flamborough Ontario 54 C2 43 20N 79 57W
Flathead River British Columbia 43 N1 48 30N 114 10W
Flesherton Ontario 54 B3 44 16N 80 32W
Fletchers Lake Nova Scotia 59 Q7 44 51N 63 35W
Fleur de Lys Newfoundland and Labrador 61 G5 50 07N 56 08W
Fleuve Saint-Laurent *r.* Québec 57 F3 48 20N 69 20W
Flin Flon Manitoba 49 B4 54 50N 102 00W
Florenceville New Brunswick 61 B3 46 20N 67 20W
Flores Island British Columbia 43 G1 49 20N 126 10W
Flour Lake Newfoundland and Labrador 60 C6 53 44N 64 50W
Foam Lake *tn.* Saskatchewan 47 F2 51 38N 103 31W
Foch British Columbia 42 H5 50 07N 124 31W
Foch-Gitnadoix Provincial Park British Columbia 43 F3 54 00N 129 15W
Fogo Newfoundland and Labrador 61 H4 49 43N 54 17W
Fogo Island Newfoundland and Labrador 61 H4 49 40N 54 10W
Foleyet Ontario 51 K5 48 05N 82 26W
Fond du Lac Saskatchewan 47 D6 59 20N 107 09W
Fond du Lac River Saskatchewan 47 E6 59 05N 104 40W
Fontas River British Columbia 43 K6 58 20N 121 25W
Fonthill *tn.* Ontario 54 C2 43 02N 79 17W
Forbes, Mount Alberta 46 D2 51 52N 116 55W
Foremost Alberta 46 G1 49 29N 111 25W
Forest Ontario 52 E3 43 06N 82 00W
Forestburg Alberta 46 G3 52 35N 112 04W
Forest Hill Ontario 55 C1 43 42N 79 25W
Forestville Québec 57 F3 48 45N 69 04W
Forks of the Credit Provincial Park Ontario 54 B2 43 49N 80 02W
Forrest Lake Saskatchewan 47 C5 57 35N 109 10W
Fort Albany Ontario 50 L7 52 12N 81 40W
Fort Babine British Columbia 43 G4 55 20N 126 35W
Fort Chipewyan Alberta 46 G6 58 46N 111 09W
Fort Coulange Québec 53 K5 45 51N 76 46W
Forteau Newfoundland and Labrador 60 G5 51 28N 56 58W
Fort Erie Ontario 54 D1 42 55N 78 56W
Fort Frances Ontario 50 E5 48 37N 93 23W
Fort Fraser British Columbia 43 H4 54 03N 124 30W
Fort Garry Manitoba 48 B2 49 49N 97 10W
Fort Hope *I.R.* Ontario 50 H6 51 37N 87 55W
Fort Langley British Columbia 42 H4 49 11N 122 38W
Fort MacKay Alberta 46 G5 57 11N 111 37W
Fort Mackenzie Québec 56 F7 56 50N 68 56W
Fort Macleod Alberta 46 F1 49 44N 113 24W
Fort McMurray Alberta 46 G5 56 45N 111 27W
Fort Nelson British Columbia 43 J6 58 48N 122 44W
Fort Nelson River British Columbia 43 J6 59 20N 124 05W
Fort Qu'Appelle Saskatchewan 47 F2 50 46N 103 54W
Fort Rouge Manitoba 48 B2 49 52N 97 07W
Fort St. James British Columbia 43 H4 54 26N 124 15W
Fort St. John British Columbia 43 K5 56 14N 120 55W
Fort Saskatchewan Alberta 46 F3 53 42N 113 12W
Fort Severn Ontario 50 H9 56 00N 87 40W
Fortune Newfoundland and Labrador 61 H3 47 04N 55 50W
Fortune Bay Newfoundland and Labrador 61 H3 47 15N 55 30W
Fort Vermilion Alberta 46 E6 58 22N 115 59W
Fort Ware British Columbia 43 H5 57 30N 125 43W
Fort Whyte Manitoba 48 B2 49 49N 97 12W
Fosheim Peninsula Nunavut 65 P6 80 00N 85 00W
Foster, Mount British Columbia 42 C6 59 49N 135 35W
Foster River Saskatchewan 47 E5 56 20N 105 45W
Fourchu Nova Scotia 61 M12 45 43N 60 17W
Fox Creek *tn.* Alberta 46 D4 54 24N 116 48W
Foxe Basin *b.* Nunavut 65 P4 66 20N 79 00W
Foxe Channel Nunavut 65 P3 64 40N 80 00W
Foxe Peninsula Nunavut 65 Q3 65 00N 76 00W
Fox Mine *tn.* Manitoba 49 B5 56 39N 101 38W
Fox River Manitoba 49 F5 56 00N 93 50W
Fox Valley *tn.* Saskatchewan 47 C2 50 29N 109 29W
Frances Lake Yukon Territory 64 E3 61 20N 129 30W
François Lake British Columbia 43 H3 54 00N 125 47W
Frankford Ontario 52 J4 44 12N 77 36W
Franklin Bay Northwest Territories 64 E5 69 45N 126 00W
Franklin Lake Nunavut 65 L4 66 56N 96 03W
Franklin Mountains Northwest Territories 64 F3 61 15N 123 50W
Fraserdale Ontario 51 L5 49 51N 81 37W
Fraser Lake Newfoundland and Labrador 60 D7 54 24N 63 40W
Fraser Lake *tn.* British Columbia 43 H4 54 00N 124 50W
Fraser Plateau British Columbia 43 J3 52 32N 124 10W
Fraser River British Columbia 43 J2 51 36N 122 25W
Fraser River Newfoundland and Labrador 60 D8 56 50N 63 50W
Fredericton New Brunswick 61 B2 45 57N 66 40W
Fredericton Junction New Brunswick 61 B2 45 40N 66 38W
Freels, Cape Newfoundland and Labrador 61 J4 49 15N 53 29W
Freeport Nova Scotia 61 L11 44 17N 66 19W
Frenchman River Saskatchewan 47 D1 49 30N 108 00W
Frenchman's Cove *tn.* Newfoundland and Labrador 61 F4 49 04N 58 10W
French River Ontario 52 F6 46 00N 81 00W
French River *tn.* Ontario 52 F6 46 03N 80 34W
Freshwater Newfoundland and Labrador 61 J3 47 15N 53 59W
Frobisher Bay Nunavut 65 S3 62 15N 65 00W
Frobisher Lake Saskatchewan 47 C5 57 00N 108 00W
Frog Lake Alberta 46 G3 53 55N 110 20W
Frontenac *admin.* Ontario 53 K4 44 40N 76 45W
Frontenac *admin.* Québec 53 R5 45 40N 70 50W
Frontenac Provincial Park Ontario 53 K4 44 32N 76 29W
Frozen Strait Nunavut 65 P4 66 08N 85 00W
Fruitvale British Columbia 43 M1 49 08N 117 28W
Fundy, Bay of New Brunswick/Nova Scotia 61 L11 45 00N 66 00W
Fundy National Park New Brunswick 61 L12 45 40N 65 10W
Fury and Hecla Strait Nunavut 65 P4 69 56N 84 00W

G

Gabarus Bay Nova Scotia 61 M12 45 50N 60 10W
Gabriola Island British Columbia 42 H4 49 10N 123 51W
Gage, Cape Prince Edward Island 61 M12 46 50N 64 20W
Gagetown New Brunswick 61 B2 45 46N 66 29W
Gagnon Québec 57 F4 51 56N 68 16W
Galiano Island British Columbia 42 H4 48 57N 123 25W
Galt Ontario 54 B2 43 21N 80 19W
Gambier Island British Columbia 42 H4 49 30N 123 25W
Gambo Newfoundland and Labrador 61 H4 48 46N 54 14W
Gamet *(Red Lakes)* *tn.* Northwest Territories 64 G3 64 10N 117 20W
Gananoque Ontario 53 K4 44 20N 76 10W
Gander Newfoundland and Labrador 61 H4 48 57N 54 34W
Gander Lake Newfoundland and Labrador 61 H4 48 55N 54 35W
Ganges British Columbia 42 H4 48 51N 123 31W
Garden Creek *tn.* Alberta 46 F6 58 42N 113 53W
Garden Hill *tn.* Manitoba 49 E3 53 52N 94 37W
Gardiner Dam Saskatchewan 47 D2 51 15N 106 40W
Gardner Canal British Columbia 42 F3 53 30N 128 50W
Garibaldi Lake British Columbia 42 H4 49 55N 122 57W
Garibaldi, Mount British Columbia 42 H4 49 53N 123 00W
Garibaldi Provincial Park British Columbia 42 H4 49 58N 122 45W
Garnish Newfoundland and Labrador 61 H3 47 14N 55 22W
Garry Lake Nunavut 65 K4 66 20N 100 00W
Garry Point British Columbia 52 F3 49 07N 123 14W
Gaspé Québec 57 H3 48 50N 64 30W
Gaspereau Lake Nova Scotia 61 M11 44 50N 64 30W
Gataga River British Columbia 43 G6 58 30N 126 40W
Gateshead Island Nunavut 65 K5 70 36N 100 26W
Gatineau Québec 53 L5 45 29N 75 39W
Gatineau *admin.* Québec 53 L6 45 47N 76 05W
Gauer Lake Manitoba 49 D5 57 10N 97 30W
Gaultois Newfoundland and Labrador 61 H3 47 36N 55 54W
Geikie River Saskatchewan 47 E5 57 20N 104 40W
George, Cape Nova Scotia 61 M12 45 50N 61 50W
George Island Newfoundland and Labrador 60 G7 54 16N 57 20W
Georgetown Ontario 54 C2 43 39N 79 56W
Georgetown Prince Edward Island 61 M12 46 12N 62 32W
Georgian Bay Ontario 52 E5 45 00N 81 00W
Georgian Bay Islands National Park Ontario 52 G4 44 53N 79 52W
Georgia, Strait of British Columbia 42 H4 49 39N 124 34W
Georgina Island Ontario 54 C3 44 22N 79 17W
Geraldton Ontario 51 H5 49 44N 86 59W
Germansen Landing British Columbia 43 H4 55 47N 124 42W
Giant's Causeway Northwest Territories 64 F6 75 46N 121 11W
Giants Tomb Island Ontario 54 B3 44 55N 80 00W

Gibsons *tn.* British Columbia 42 H4 49 24N 123 30W
Gifford Island British Columbia 43 G2 50 45N 126 20W
Gift Lake *tn.* Alberta 46 E4 55 50N 115 50W
Gilbert Plains *tn.* Manitoba 49 B2 51 09N 100 28W
Gil Island British Columbia 42 F3 53 10N 129 15W
Gillam Manitoba 49 E5 56 25N 94 45W
Gillies Bay *tn.* British Columbia 42 H4 49 42N 124 28W
Gimli Manitoba 49 D2 50 39N 97 00W
Gitnadoix River Provincial Park British Columbia 43 F4 54 05NN 129 00W
Glace Bay *tn.* Nova Scotia 61 M12 46 11N 59 58W
Glacial Mountain British Columbia 42 F6 58 15N 129 25W
Glacier National Park British Columbia 43 M2 51 00N 117 00W
Gladstone Manitoba 49 C2 50 14N 98 56W
Gladstone Provincial Park British Columbia 43 L1 49 15N 118 10W
Gladys Lake British Columbia 42 D6 59 50N 132 52W
Glaslyn Saskatchewan 47 C3 53 23N 108 22W
Glenboro Manitoba 49 C1 49 35N 99 20W
Glen Cairn Ontario 59 J2 45 15N 75 45W
Glencoe Ontario 54 A1 42 45N 81 44W
Glenmore Reservoir Alberta 44 A1 50 58N 114 08W
Glenwood Newfoundland and Labrador 61 H4 48 59N 54 53W
Gloucester Ontario 53 L5 45 21N 75 39W
Gloucester *admin.* New Brunswick 61 C3 47 30N 65 50W
Glover Island Newfoundland and Labrador 61 G4 48 46N 57 43W
Glovertown Newfoundland and Labrador 61 H4 48 41N 54 02W
Goat Island British Columbia 42 H5 50 03N 124 28W
Goat Range Provincial Park British Columbia 43 M2 50 15N 117 15W
Goderich Ontario 54 A2 43 43N 81 43W
Gods Lake Manitoba 49 E4 54 40N 94 20W
Gods Lake *tn.* Manitoba 49 E4 54 45N 94 00W
Gods Mercy, Bay of Nunavut 65 N3 63 30N 88 10W
Gods River Manitoba 49 F4 56 20N 92 50W
Gogama Ontario 51 L4 47 40N 81 43W
Goldboro Nova Scotia 61 M12 45 12N 61 35W
Gold Bridge British Columbia 43 J2 50 51N 122 51W
Golden British Columbia 43 M2 51 19N 116 55W
Golden Ears Provincial Park British Columbia 42 H4 49 28N 122 25W
Golden Hinde *mt.* British Columbia 43 H1 49 35N 125 40W
Gold River British Columbia 43 G1 49 41N 125 59W
Goldsmith Channel Nunavut 64 J5 73 00N 106 00W
Golfe du Saint-Laurent Québec 57 J3 48 40N 63 20W
Goodeve Saskatchewan 47 F2 51 03N 103 11W
Good Hope British Columbia 43 G2 50 59N 124 01W
Good Hope Lake British Columbia 43 F6 56 15N 129 20W
Good Hope Mountain British Columbia 43 J2 51 08N 124 10W
Goodsoil Saskatchewan 47 C4 54 24N 109 12W
Goose Bay *tn.* Newfoundland and Labrador 60 E6 53 15N 60 20W
Goose River Newfoundland and Labrador 60 E6 53 30N 61 50W
Gordon Horne Peak British Columbia 43 L2 51 47N 118 50W
Gordon Lake Alberta 46 G5 56 30N 110 25W
Gordon Pittock Reservoir Ontario 54 B2 43 11N 80 43W
Gordon River British Columbia 42 H4 48 38N 124 25W
Gore Bay *tn.* Ontario 52 D5 45 55N 82 28W
Goshen Nova Scotia 61 M12 45 20N 62 55W
Gowganda Ontario 51 L4 47 39N 80 46W
Gracefield Québec 53 K6 46 05N 76 05W
Grady Harbour *tn.* Newfoundland and Labrador 60 G6 53 48N 56 25W
Graham Island British Columbia 42 D3 53 50N 132 40W
Graham Island Nunavut 65 M6 77 25N 90 30W
Graham Laurier Provincial Park British Columbia 43 J5 56 30N 123 30W
Granby Québec 53 P5 45 22N 72 43W
Granby Provincial Park British Columbia 43 L1 49 45N 118 30W
Granby River British Columbia 43 L1 49 27N 118 25W
Grand Bank Newfoundland and Labrador 61 H3 47 06N 55 46W
Grand Bay-Westfield *tn.* New Brunswick 61 L12 45 19N 66 14W
Grand Bend Ontario 52 E3 43 21N 81 45W
Grande-Anse New Brunswick 61 C3 47 50N 65 10W
Grande-Anse Québec 53 P7 47 05N 72 55W
Grande Cache Alberta 46 C3 53 50N 119 08W
Grande Pointe Manitoba 48 B2 49 45N 97 03W
Grande Prairie Alberta 43 L4 55 10N 118 40W
Grande-Rivière *tn.* Québec 57 H3 48 23N 64 31W
Grande Rivière de la Baleine *r.* Québec 56 C6 55 15N 77 00W
Grand Étang Nova Scotia 61 M12 46 00N 61 00W
Grande-Vallée *tn.* Québec 57 H3 49 15N 65 10W
Grand Falls/Grand Sault *tn.* New Brunswick 61 B3 47 02N 67 46W
Grand Falls-Windsor *tn.* Newfoundland and Labrador 61 H4 48 56N 55 40W
Grand Forks British Columbia 43 L1 49 02N 118 30W
Grandin, Lake Northwest Territories 64 G3 63 50N 119 50W
Grand Jardin Newfoundland and Labrador 61 F4 48 28N 59 13W
Grand Lake New Brunswick 61 B2 46 00N 66 40W
Grand Lake Newfoundland and Labrador 60 E6 53 40N 60 30W
Grand Lake Newfoundland and Labrador 61 G4 49 00N 57 20W
Grand Manan *tn.* New Brunswick 61 L11 44 41N 66 46W
Grand Manan Island New Brunswick 61 L11 44 45N 66 40W
Grand Marais Manitoba 49 D2 50 30N 96 35W
Grand-Mère Québec 53 P6 46 36N 72 41W
Grand Narrows *tn.* Nova Scotia 61 M12 45 55N 60 50W
Grand Prairie *tn.* Alberta 46 C4 55 10N 118 52W
Grand Rapids *tn.* Manitoba 49 C3 53 12N 99 19W
Grand-Remous Québec 57 C2 46 37N 75 56W
Grand River Ontario 54 C1 42 51N 79 34W
Grand Valley *tn.* Ontario 54 B2 43 54N 80 10W
Grandview Manitoba 49 B2 51 11N 100 51W
Granisle British Columbia 43 G4 54 56N 126 18W
Granite Bay *tn.* British Columbia 42 G5 50 00N 125 00W
Granite Lake Newfoundland and Labrador 61 G4 48 11N 57 01W
Granville Falls Manitoba 49 B5 56 10N 100 20W
Granville Lake Manitoba 49 B5 56 00N 101 00W
Grasslands National Park Saskatchewan 47 D1 49 10N 107 30W
Grass River Manitoba 49 C4 54 50N 99 20W
Grass River Provincial Park Manitoba 49 B4 54 40N 101 40W
Grassy Narrows *I.R.* Ontario 50 E6 50 10N 93 55W
Gravelbourg Saskatchewan 47 D1 49 53N 106 33W
Gravenhurst Ontario 52 G4 44 55N 79 22W
Grayling River British Columbia 43 H6 59 43N 125 55W
Greasy Lake Northwest Territories 64 F3 62 55N 122 15W
Great Bear Lake Northwest Territories 64 F4 66 00N 120 00W
Great Central Lake British Columbia 42 G4 49 22N 125 10W
Greater Sudbury Ontario 52 E6 46 30N 81 01W
Great Plain of the Koukdjuak Nunavut 65 R4 66 25N 72 50W
Great Pubnico Lake Nova Scotia 61 L11 43 50N 65 30W
Great Sand Hills Saskatchewan 47 C2 50 35N 109 20W
Great Slave Lake Northwest Territories 64 H3 62 00N 114 00W
Great Village Nova Scotia 61 M12 45 25N 63 36W
Greely Ontario 59 K2 45 16N 75 33W
Greely Fiord Nunavut 65 P7 80 30N 85 00W
Green Creek Ontario 59 K2 45 25N 75 35W
Green Gables Prince Edward Island 61 M12 46 28N 63 20W
Green Lake British Columbia 43 K2 51 26N 121 12W
Green Lake *tn.* Saskatchewan 47 D4 54 18N 107 49W
Greenville British Columbia 42 F4 55 05N 129 35W
Greenwater Lake Provincial Park Saskatchewan 47 F3 52 35N 103 25W
Greenwood British Columbia 43 L1 49 08N 118 41W
Greenwood Nova Scotia 61 M11 45 00N 64 50W
Grenfell Saskatchewan 47 F2 50 24N 102 56W
Grenville Québec 53 M5 45 40N 74 38W
Gretna Manitoba 49 D1 49 01N 97 34W
Grey *admin.* Ontario 54 B3 44 22N 80 33W
Grey Islands Newfoundland and Labrador 60 H5 50 50N 55 35W
Grey, Point British Columbia 44 E4 49 16N 123 17W
Grey River Newfoundland and Labrador 61 G3 47 50N 56 50W
Griffith Island Ontario 54 B3 44 50N 80 54W
Grimsby Ontario 54 C2 43 12N 79 35W
Grimshaw Alberta 46 D5 56 11N 117 36W
Grinnell Peninsula Nunavut 65 L6 76 40N 95 00W
Grizzly Bear Hills Saskatchewan 47 C4 55 50N 109 30W
Groais Island Newfoundland and Labrador 60 H5 50 57N 55 36W
Gros Morne *mt.* Newfoundland and Labrador 61 G4 49 36N 57 47W
Gros Morne National Park Newfoundland and Labrador 61 G4 49 40N 58 40W
Groswater Bay Newfoundland and Labrador 60 G7 54 20N 57 40W
Grouard Mission Alberta 46 D4 55 30N 116 10W
Groundhog River Ontario 51 K5 49 00N 82 10W
Guelph Ontario 54 B2 43 34N 80 16W
Gull Bay *I.R.* Ontario 50 G5 49 50N 89 00W
Gull Lake Alberta 46 F3 52 34N 114 00W
Gull Lake *tn.* Saskatchewan 47 C2 50 05N 108 30W
Gunisao Lake Manitoba 49 D3 53 30N 96 40W
Gunisao River Manitoba 49 D3 53 30N 96 50W
Guysborough Nova Scotia 61 M12 45 23N 61 30W
Guysborough *admin.* Nova Scotia 61 M12 45 20N 61 40W
Gwaii Haanas National Park Reserve British Columbia 42 E3 52 30N 130 40W
Gwillim Lake Provincial Park British Columbia 43 K4 55 00N 121 00W
Gypsumville Manitoba 49 C2 51 47N 98 38W
Gyrfalcon Islands Nunavut 56 F8 59 05N 69 00W

H

Habay Alberta 46 C6 58 49N 118 44W
Hadley Bay Nunavut 64 J5 72 22N 108 30W
Hagensborg British Columbia 43 G3 52 30N 126 30W
Hague Saskatchewan 47 D3 52 30N 106 25W
Haileybury Ontario 51 M4 47 27N 79 38W
Haines Junction Yukon Territory 64 C3 60 45N 137 21W
Hakai Recreation Area British Columbia 43 G2 50 40N 128 00W
Haldimand-Norfolk *admin.* Ontario 54 B1/C1 42 37N 80 39W
Halfway Point *tn.* Newfoundland and Labrador 61 F4 48 59N 58 06W
Halfway River British Columbia 43 J5 56 42N 122 30W
Haliburton Ontario 52 H5 45 03N 78 31W
Haliburton *admin.* Ontario 52 H5 45 05N 78 50W
Halifax Nova Scotia 61 M11 44 40N 63 41W
Halifax *admin.* Nova Scotia 61 M12 45 00N 63 00W
Halifax Harbour Nova Scotia 59 Q6 44 39N 63 33W
Hall Peninsula Nunavut 65 S3 68 40N 66 00W
Halls Harbour Nova Scotia 61 M12 45 12N 64 37W
Halton *admin.* Ontario 54 C2 43 26N 79 57W
Hamber Provincial Park British Columbia 43 M3 53 20N 117 55W
Hamilton Ontario 54 C2 43 15N 79 50W
Hamilton Harbour Ontario 54 C2 43 16N 80 50W
Hamilton Inlet Newfoundland and Labrador 60 F6 54 18N 57 30W
Hamilton Sound Newfoundland and Labrador 61 H4 49 30N 54 15W
Hamilton-Wentworth *admin.* Ontario 54 B2/C2 43 14N 80 09W
Hamiota Manitoba 49 B2 50 11N 100 38W
Hampden Newfoundland and Labrador 61 G4 49 33N 56 51W
Hampton New Brunswick 61 L12 45 30N 65 50W
Hampton Ontario 54 D2 43 52N 78 43W
Hanley Saskatchewan 47 D2 51 37N 106 26W
Hanna Alberta 46 G2 51 38N 111 56W
Hannah Bay Ontario 51 L6/M6 51 20N 80 00W
Hanover Ontario 54 A3 44 10N 81 03W
Hanson Lake Road Saskatchewan 47 E4 54 20N 104 35W
Hants *admin.* Nova Scotia 61 M12 45 10N 63 40W
Hantsport Nova Scotia 61 M12 45 04N 64 12W
Happy Valley-Goose Bay Newfoundland and Labrador 60 E6 53 18N 60 16W
Harbour Breton *tn.* Newfoundland and Labrador 61 H3 47 29N 55 50W
Harbour Deep *tn.* Newfoundland and Labrador 61 G5 50 22N 56 31W
Harbour Grace *tn.* Newfoundland and Labrador 61 J3 47 42N 53 13W
Hardisty Alberta 46 G3 52 40N 111 18W
Hardisty Lake Northwest Territories 64 G3 64 30N 117 45W
Hare Bay Newfoundland and Labrador 60 H5 51 15N 55 45W
Hare Bay *tn.* Newfoundland and Labrador 61 J4 48 51N 54 00W
Hare Indian River Northwest Territories 64 E4 66 40N 128 00W
Haro Strait British Columbia 42 H4 48 36N 123 17W
Harp Lake Newfoundland and Labrador 60 E7 55 05N 61 50W
Harrington Harbour *tn.* Québec 56 L4 50 31N 59 30W
Harrison, Cape Newfoundland and Labrador 60 G7 54 57N 57 57W
Harrison Hot Springs *tn.* British Columbia 42 H4 49 17N 121 47W
Harrison Lake British Columbia 42 H4 49 30N 122 10W
Harriston Ontario 54 B2 43 54N 80 52W
Harrow Ontario 52 D2 42 02N 82 55W
Harrowby Manitoba 49 B2 50 45N 101 28W
Harry Gibbons Bird Sanctuary Nunavut 65 N3 63 50N 86 00W
Hartland New Brunswick 61 B3 46 18N 67 31W
Hartney Manitoba 49 B1 49 29N 100 31W
Hart River Yukon Territory 64 C4 65 40N 137 10W
Hastings Ontario 52 J4 44 18N 77 57W
Hastings *admin.* Ontario 52 J4/J5 44 45N 77 40W
Hatchet Lake Saskatchewan 47 F6 58 50N 103 30W
Haultain River Saskatchewan 47 D5 56 20N 106 20W
Havelock Ontario 52 J4 44 26N 77 53W
Havre-Aubert Québec 61 E3 47 15N 61 51W
Havre Saint-Pierre Québec 57 J4 50 20N 63 38W
Hawkes Bay *tn.* Newfoundland and Labrador 61 G5 50 36N 57 10W
Hawkesbury Ontario 53 M5 45 36N 74 37W
Hay Camp Alberta 46 G6 59 31N 111 23W
Hay, Cape Northwest Territories 64 H5 74 25N 113 00W
Hayes River Manitoba 49 F4 55 20N 93 50W
Hay Lake Alberta 46 C6 58 52N 119 20W
Hay River Alberta/Northwest Territories 46 C6 58 20N 119 00W
Hazeldean Ontario 59 J2 45 18N 75 55W
Hazelton British Columbia 43 G4 55 17N 127 42W
Hazen Strait Northwest Territories/Nunavut 64 J6 77 00N 110 00W
Head of Bay d'Espoir Newfoundland and Labrador 61 H3 47 56N 55 45W
Hearst Ontario 51 K5 49 42N 83 40W
Heart's Content Newfoundland and Labrador 61 J3 47 53N 53 22W
Hebron Newfoundland and Labrador 60 D9 58 12N 62 38W
Hebron Nova Scotia 61 L11 43 57N 66 03W
Hebron Fiord *in.* Newfoundland and Labrador 60 D9 58 09N 62 45W
Hecate Strait British Columbia 42 E3 53 40N 131 10W
Hecla and Griper Bay Northwest Territories/Nunavut 64 H6 76 25N 113 00W
Hecla/Grindstone Provincial Park Manitoba 49 D2 51 10N 96 30W
Hecla Island Manitoba 49 D2 51 00N 96 30W
Height of the Rockies Provincial Park British Columbia 43 N2 50 15N 115 00W
Henrietta Island Newfoundland and Labrador 60 F7 54 05N 58 28W
Henrietta Maria, Cape Ontario 50 K8 55 00N 82 30W
Henry Kater Peninsula Nunavut 65 S4 69 20N 67 20W
Hensall Ontario 54 A2 43 26N 81 31W
Hepburn Saskatchewan 47 D3 52 30N 106 45W
Hepworth Ontario 54 A3 44 37N 81 09W
Herbert Saskatchewan 47 D2 50 26N 107 12W
Heriot Bay *tn.* British Columbia 42 G5 50 06N 125 12W
Hermitage Sandyville Newfoundland and Labrador 61 H3 47 33N 55 56W
Heron Bay *I.R.* Ontario 51 H5 48 40N 86 17W
Herring Cove Nova Scotia 61 M11 44 35N 63 35W
Herschel Yukon Territory 64 C4 69 34N 139 00W
Herschel Island Yukon Territory 64 C4 69 34N 139 00W
Hespeler Ontario 54 B2 43 26N 80 20W
Hess River Yukon Territory 64 D3 63 25N 133 50W
Hibbard Québec 53 M7 47 53N 74 03W
Hickman, Mount British Columbia 42 E5 57 15N 131 07W
Highlands British Columbia 42 H4 48 30N 123 30W
High Level *tn.* Alberta 46 D6 58 10N 117 20W
High Prairie *tn.* Alberta 46 D4 55 26N 116 29W
High River *tn.* Alberta 46 F2 50 35N 113 52W
Highrock Manitoba 49 B4 55 50N 100 22W
Highrock Lake Manitoba 49 B4 55 45N 100 20W
Highrock Lake Saskatchewan 47 E5 57 00N 105 20W
Hillsborough New Brunswick 61 M12 45 56N 64 40W
Hillsburgh Ontario 54 B2 43 46N 80 10W
Hilton Beach *tn.* Ontario 52 C6 46 16N 83 56W
Hinds Lake Reservoir Newfoundland and Labrador 61 G4 49 10N 56 50W
Hines Creek *tn.* Alberta 46 C5 56 15N 118 36W
Hinton Alberta 46 D3 53 25N 117 34W
Hoare Bay Nunavut 65 T4 65 17N 62 55W
Hodgeville Saskatchewan 47 D2 50 07N 106 58W
Hog Island Prince Edward Island 61 M12 46 53N 63 50W
Holden Alberta 46 F3 53 14N 112 14W
Holland Landing Ontario 54 C3 44 05N 79 29W
Holland River Ontario 54 C3 44 01N 79 39W
Holyrood Newfoundland and Labrador 61 J3 47 23N 53 08W
Homathko River British Columbia 43 H2 51 00N 125 05W
Home Bay Nunavut 65 S4 69 00N 87 00W
Home Island Newfoundland and Labrador 60 C10 60 10N 64 14W
Hope British Columbia 42 H4 49 21N 121 28W
Hope Bay Ontario 54 A3 44 55N 81 14W
Hopedale Newfoundland and Labrador 60 E7 55 28N 60 13W
Hope Island British Columbia 43 G2 50 55N 127 55W
Hope Island Ontario 54 B3 44 54N 80 11W
Hopes Advance Bay Québec 56 F8 59 20N 69 40W
Hopewell Nova Scotia 61 M12 45 29N 62 41W
Hopewell Islands Nunavut 56 A8 58 20N 78 10W
Hornaday River Northwest Territories 64 F4 69 00N 123 00W
Hornby Island British Columbia 42 H4 49 31N 124 40W
Hornepayne Ontario 51 J5 49 13N 84 47W
Horner Creek Ontario 54 B2 43 12N 80 35W
Horn Mountains Northwest Territories 64 G3 62 15N 119 15W
Horsefly Lake British Columbia 43 K3 52 25N 121 00W
Horse Islands Newfoundland and Labrador 61 H5 50 13N 55 48W
Horseshoe Bay *tn.* British Columbia 42 H4 49 22N 123 17W
Horseshoe Valley Ontario 54 C3 44 34N 79 41W
Horton River Northwest Territories 64 F4 68 50N 123 50W
Horwood Lake Ontario 51 K5 48 00N 82 20W
Hottah Lake Northwest Territories 64 G4 65 04N 118 30W
Houston British Columbia 43 G4 54 24N 126 39W
Houston Point Nunavut 50 L7 58 20N 81 00W
Howe Sound British Columbia 42 H4 49 30N 123 25W
Howie Centre Nova Scotia 61 M12 46 05N 60 15W
Howley Newfoundland and Labrador 61 G4 49 10N 57 07W
Hubbards Nova Scotia 61 M11 44 38N 64 03W
Hubbart Point Manitoba 49 E6 59 21N 94 41W
Hudson Bay *(Baie d'Hudson)* Canada 65 N3/P2 60 00N 85 00W
Hudson Bay *tn.* Saskatchewan 47 F3 52 45N 102 45W
Hudson's Hope British Columbia 43 K5 56 00N 121 59W
Hudson Strait *(Detroit d'Hudson)* Nunavut 65 R3 62 00N 70 00W
Hudwin Lake Park Reserve Manitoba 49 E3 53 15N 95 00W
Hugh Keenleyside Dam British Columbia 43 M1 49 33N 118 00W
Hull Québec 59 K2 45 25N 75 44W
Hull *admin.* Québec 53 L5 45 40N 75 40W
Humber Bay Ontario 54 C2 43 36N 79 27W
Humber River Ontario 54 C2 43 58N 79 37W
Humboldt Saskatchewan 47 E3 52 12N 105 07W
150 Mile House British Columbia 43 K3 52 05N 121 56W

100 Mile House British Columbia 43 K2 51 36N 121 18W
Hunter Island British Columbia 43 F2 51 57N 128 05W
Hunter River *tn.* Prince Edward Island 61 M12 46 20N 63 20W
Huntingdon Québec 53 M5 45 05N 74 11W
Huntingdon *admin.* Québec 53 M5 45 00N 74 20W
Huntingdon Island Newfoundland and Labrador 60 G6 53 47N 56 55W
Hunt River Newfoundland and Labrador 60 E7 55 20N 61 10W
Huntsville Ontario 52 G5 45 20N 79 13W
Hurd, Cape Ontario 54 A4 45 14N 81 44W
Huron *admin.* Ontario 54 A2 43 27N 81 35W
Huron, Lake Ontario/USA 52 D4/D5 45 00N 83 00W
Hyde Park Ontario 54 A2 43 00N 81 20W
Hythe Alberta 46 C4 55 18N 119 33W

I

Igluligaarjuk *(Chesterfield Inlet) tn.* Nunavut 65 M3 63 21N 90 42W
Iglulik *(Igloolike)* Nunavut 65 P4 69 23N 81 46W
Iglusuaktalialuk Island Newfoundland and Labrador 60 E8 57 20N 61 30W
Ignace Ontario 50 F5 49 26N 91 40W
Ikaahuk *(Sachs Harbour) tn.* Northwest Territories 64 E5 71 59N 125 13W
Ikpiarjuk *(Arctic Bay) tn.* Nunavut 65 N5 73 05N 85 20W
Île-à-la-Crosse *tn.* Saskatchewan 47 D4 55 28N 107 53W
Île aux Coudres *i.* Québec 53 R7 47 23N 70 20W
Île aux Herons Québec 58 N4 45 26N 73 35W
Île Bizard *i.* Québec 58 M4 45 29N 73 54W
Île d'Anticosti *i.* Québec 57 J3 49 20N 62 30W
Île de Montréal *i.* Québec 58 M4 45 30N 73 43W
Île des Allumettes *i.* Québec 53 J5 45 55N 77 08W
Île des Soeurs *i.* Québec 58 N4 45 28N 73 33W
Île d'Orléans *i.* Québec 53 R6 46 55N 71 00W
Île Dorval *i.* Québec 58 N4 45 26N 73 44W
Île Jésus *i.* Québec 58 N5 45 35N 73 45W
Île Kettle *i.* Québec 59 K2 45 28N 75 39W
Île Lamèque *i.* New Brunswick 61 C3 47 50N 64 40W
Île Lynch *i.* Québec 58 M4 45 25N 73 54W
Île Ste. Hélène *i.* Québec 58 N5 45 31N 73 32W
Île Sainte-Thérèse *i.* Québec 58 P5 45 39N 73 28W
Îles-de-Boucherville *is.* Québec 58 P5 45 36N 73 28W
Îles de la Madeleine *is.* Québec 61 E3 47 40N 61 50W
Îles du Grand Calumet *is.* Québec 53 K5 45 30N 76 35W
Ilford Manitoba 49 E5 56 04N 95 40W
Indian Arm *b.* British Columbia 44 G4 49 19N 122 55W
Indian Arm Provincial Park British Columbia 42 H4 49 22N 122 45W
Indian Cabins Alberta 46 D6 59 52N 117 02W
Indian Head *tn.* Saskatchewan 47 F2 50 35N 103 37W
Indian Tickle Newfoundland and Labrador 60 H6 53 34N 56 00W
Ingenika River British Columbia 43 G5 56 48N 126 11W
Ingersoll Ontario 54 B2 43 03N 80 53W
Ingonish Nova Scotia 61 M12 46 42N 60 22W
Inklin River British Columbia 42 D6 58 54N 132 50W
Inner Bay Ontario 54 B1 42 35N 80 26W
Innisfail Alberta 46 F3 52 01N 113 59W
Inside Passage British Columbia 42/43 F3 53 38N 129 40W
Inukjuak Québec 56 A8 58 40N 78 15W
Inuvik Northwest Territories 64 D4 68 16N 133 40W
Inverhuron Provincial Park Ontario 54 A3 44 20N 81 30W
Invermere British Columbia 43 M2 50 30N 116 00W
Inverness Nova Scotia 61 M12 46 14N 61 19W
Inverness *admin.* Nova Scotia 61 M12 46 00N 61 30W
Ioco *tn.* British Columbia 44 G4 49 18N 122 51W
Iqaluit Nunavut 65 S3 60 00N 65 00W
Iqaluktuutiaq *(Cambridge Bay) tn.* Nunavut 64 K4 69 09N 105 00W
Irma Alberta 46 G3 52 55N 111 14W
Iron Bridge *tn.* Ontario 52 C6 46 17N 83 14W
Ironside Québec 59 J2 45 27N 75 46W
Iroquois Ontario 53 L4 44 51N 75 19W
Iroquois Falls *tn.* Ontario 51 L5 48 47N 80 41W
Irvine Alberta 46 G1 49 57N 110 17W
Irvines Landing British Columbia 42 H4 49 37N 124 02W
Isaac Lake Ontario 54 A3 44 46N 81 13W
Isachsen Nunavut 65 K6 78 47N 103 30W
Ishpatina Ridge Ontario 51 L4 47 19N 80 44W
Iskut River British Columbia 42 E5 56 45N 131 10W
Island Falls Dam Saskatchewan 47 F4 55 30N 102 20W
Island Lake Manitoba 49 E3 53 50N 94 00W
Island Lake *tn.* Manitoba 49 E3 53 50N 94 00W
Island of Ponds *tn.* Newfoundland and Labrador 60 H6 53 20N 55 50W
Islands, Bay of Newfoundland and Labrador 60 F7 55 09N 59 49W
Islands, Bay of Newfoundland and Labrador 61 F4 49 10N 58 14W
Isle aux Morts *tn.* Newfoundland and Labrador 61 F3 47 35N 58 59W
Isle Madame *i.* Nova Scotia 61 M12 45 30N 60 50W
Isle Royale *i.* Ontario 51 G4 48 10N 88 30W
Isle Royale National Park Ontario 51 G4 48 10N 88 30W
Islington Ontario 55 B1 43 38N 79 32W
Itcha Ilgachuz Provincial Park British Columbia 43 H3 52 50N 125 00W
Itchen Lake Northwest Territories 64 H4 65 33N 112 50W
Ituna Saskatchewan 47 F2 51 09N 103 24W
Ivujivik Québec 56 B10 62 25N 77 54W
Ivvavik National Park Yukon Territory 64 C4 69 20N 139 30W

J

Jackfish Lake Manitoba 49 C2 50 30N 99 20W
Jackson's Arm *tn.* Newfoundland and Labrador 61 G4 49 53N 56 47W
Jacksons Point *tn.* Ontario 54 C3 44 18N 79 22W
Jaffray Melick Ontario 50 D5 49 49N 94 25W
Jakes Corner *tn.* Yukon Territory 64 D3 60 20N 133 58W
James Bay Ontario/Québec 50 L7/M7 53 45N 81 00W
James Ross, Cape Northwest Territories 64 H4 74 40N 114 25W
James Ross Strait Nunavut 65 L4 69 40N 96 00W
Jans Bay *tn.* Saskatchewan 47 C4 55 09N 108 08W
Jarvis Ontario 54 B1 42 52N 80 08W
Jasper Alberta 46 C3 52 55N 118 05W
Jasper National Park Alberta 46 C3/D3 53 00N 118 00W
Jellicoe Ontario 51 H5 49 41N 87 31W
Jennings River British Columbia 42 E6 59 33N 131 40W
Jenpeg Manitoba 49 C4 54 30N 98 00W
Jervis Inlet British Columbia 42 H4 49 47N 124 04W
Jock River Ontario 59 J2 45 15N 75 46W
Joe Batt's Arm *tn.* Newfoundland and Labrador 61 H4 49 44N 54 10W
Joggins Nova Scotia 61 M12 45 42N 64 27W
John D'or Prairie Alberta 46 E6 58 30N 115 08W
John E. Pearce Provincial Park Ontario 54 A1 42 37N 81 27W
John Hart Highway British Columbia 43 K4 55 40N 121 38W
Johnsons Crossing *tn.* Yukon Territory 64 D3 60 29N 133 17W
Johnstone Strait British Columbia 43 G2/H2 50 23N 126 30W
Joliette Québec 53 N6 46 02N 73 27W
Joliette *admin.* Québec 53 L7 47 40N 75 40W
Jones Ontario 50 D5 49 59N 94 05W
Jones Sound Nunavut 65 N6 76 00N 88 00W
Jonquière Québec 57 E3 48 25N 71 14W
Jordan Lake Nova Scotia 61 L11 44 05N 65 20W
Jordan River *tn.* British Columbia 42 H4 48 26N 123 59W
Juan de Fuca Strait British Columbia 42 H4 48 30N 124 31W
Judique Nova Scotia 61 M12 45 55N 61 30W

K

Kabania Lake Ontario 50 G7 52 12N 88 20W
Kabinakagami, Lake Ontario 51 J5 48 54N 84 25W
Kabinakagami River Ontario 51 J5 49 10N 84 10W
Kagawong Ontario 52 D5 45 54N 82 15W
K'ágee *(Kakisa)* Northwest Territories 64 G3 60 58N 117 30W
K'áhbamítúe *(Colville Lake) tn.* Northwest Territories 64 E4 67 02N 126 07W
Kahnawake Québec 58 N4 45 25N 73 42W
Kaipokok Bay Newfoundland and Labrador 60 F7 54 00N 59 35W
Kakabeta Falls *tn.* Ontario 51 G5 48 24N 89 40W
Kakkiviak, Cape Newfoundland and Labrador 60 C10 60 05N 64 15W
Kakwa Provincial Park British Columbia 43 K4 54 05N 120 20W
Kakwa River Alberta 46 C4 54 15N 119 45W
Kaladar Ontario 53 J4 44 39N 77 07W
Kaleden British Columbia 43 L1 49 20N 119 38W
Kamilukuak Lake Nunavut 65 K3 62 22N 101 40W
Kaminak Lake Nunavut 65 M3 62 10N 95 00W
Kamloops British Columbia 43 K2 50 39N 120 24W
Kamloops Lake British Columbia 43 K2 50 45N 120 40W
Kamouraska Québec 53 S7 47 34N 69 51W
Kamouraska *admin.* Québec 53 S7 47 10N 69 50W
Kamsack Saskatchewan 47 G2 51 34N 101 51W
Kamuchawie Lake Saskatchewan 47 F5/G5 56 20N 102 20W
Kanata Ontario 53 L5 45 20N 75 53W
Kangiqsualujjuaq Québec 56 G8 58 48N 66 08W
Kangiqsujuaq Québec 56 E9 61 40N 71 59W
Kangiqtinq *(Rankin Inlet)* Nunavut 65 M3 62 49N 92 05W
Kangiqtugaapik *(Clyde River)* Nunavut 65 S5 70 30N 68 30W
Kangirsuk Québec 56 E9 60 00N 70 00W
Kapiskau River Ontario 50 K7 52 30N 82 50W
Kapuskasing Ontario 51 K5 49 25N 82 26W
Kapuskasing River Ontario 51 K5 48 40N 82 50W
Kasabonika *I.R.* Ontario 50 G7 53 32N 88 37W
Kasabonika Lake Ontario 50 G7 53 35N 88 35W
Kasba Lake Northwest Territories/Nunavut 65 K3 60 18N 102 07W
Kashechewan *I.R.* Ontario 50 L7 52 18N 81 37W
Kaskattama River Manitoba 49 G5 56 25N 91 10W
Kaslo British Columbia 43 M1 49 54N 116 57W
Kasmere Lake Manitoba 49 B6 59 30N 101 10W
Katannilik Territorial Park Nunavut 65 S3 63 00N 69 55W
Kates Needle *mt.* British Columbia 42 D5 57 02N 132 05W
Kátł'odeeche *(Hay River)* Northwest Territories 64 G3 60 51N 115 42W
Kaumajet Mountains Newfoundland and Labrador 60 D8 57 48N 61 51W
Kawawachikamach Québec 56 G6 54 50N 67 00W
Kazabazua Québec 53 K5 45 56N 76 01W
Kearney Ontario 52 G5 45 35N 79 17W
Kechika River British Columbia 43 G6 58 44N 127 25W
Kedgwick New Brunswick 61 B3 47 38N 67 21W
Keele Peak Yukon Territory 64 D3 63 25N 130 17W
Keele River Northwest Territories 64 E3 64 15N 126 00W
Keewatin Ontario 50 D5 49 47N 94 30W
Keewatin River Manitoba 49 B5 56 59N 100 59W
Keg River *tn.* Alberta 46 D5 57 46N 117 39W
Keith Arm *b.* Northwest Territories 64 F4 65 20N 122 15W
Kejimkujik National Park Nova Scotia 61 L11 44 20N 65 20W
Kekerton Territorial Park Nunavut 65 S4 65 40N 65 15W
Keller Lake Northwest Territories 64 F3 64 00N 121 30W
Kellett, Cape Northwest Territories 64 E5 71 59N 126 00W
Kellett Strait Northwest Territories 64 G6 75 45N 117 30W
Kelliher Saskatchewan 47 F2 51 15N 103 41W
Kelowna British Columbia 43 L1 49 50N 119 29W
Kelsey Manitoba 49 D5 56 04N 96 30W
Kelsey Bay *tn.* British Columbia 43 H2 50 22N 125 29W
Kelvington Saskatchewan 47 F3 52 10N 103 30W
Kemano British Columbia 43 G3 53 39N 127 58W
Kempenfelt Bay Ontario 54 C3 44 22N 79 39W
Kemptville Ontario 53 L5 45 01N 75 38W
Kenamu River Newfoundland and Labrador 60 E6 52 50N 60 20W
Kenaston Saskatchewan 47 D2 51 30N 106 15W
Kendall Island Bird Sanctuary Northwest Territories 64 C4 69 30N 135 00W
Kennebecasis River New Brunswick 61 L12 45 30N 65 55W
Kennedy Lake British Columbia 42 G4 49 12N 125 32W
Kennetcook Nova Scotia 61 M12 45 10N 63 43W
Kenney Dam British Columbia 43 H3 53 38N 124 59W
Kenogami River Ontario 51 J6 50 50N 84 30W
Kenogamissi Lake Ontario 51 L5 48 15N 81 33W
Kenora Ontario 50 D5 49 47N 94 26W
Kensington Prince Edward Island 61 M12 46 26N 63 39W
Kent *admin.* New Brunswick 61 C3 46 30N 65 20W
Kent *admin.* Ontario 52 D2 42 25N 82 10W
Kent Peninsula Nunavut 64 J4 68 30N 106 00W
Kentville Nova Scotia 61 M12 45 04N 64 30W
Keremeos British Columbia 43 L1 49 12N 119 50W
Kerrobert Saskatchewan 47 C2 51 56N 109 09W
Kesagami Lake Ontario 51 L6 50 00N 80 00W
Kesagami Provincial Park Ontario 51 L6 50 30N 80 10W
Kesagami River Ontario 51 L6 50 30N 80 10W
Keswick Ontario 54 C3 44 15N 79 28W
Kettle Creek Ontario 54 A1 42 47N 81 13W
Kettle Rapids *tn.* Manitoba 49 E5 56 25N 94 30W
Kettle River British Columbia 43 L1 49 10N 119 02W
Kettle River Manitoba 49 H5 56 40N 89 50W
Kettlestone Bay Québec 56 B9 61 20N 77 54W
Keyano Québec 56 D5 53 52N 73 30W
Key Lake Mine *tn.* Saskatchewan 47 E5 57 10N 105 30W
Khutzeymafeen Provincial Park British Columbia 42 F4 54 45N 129 50W
Kicking Horse Pass Alberta/British Columbia 43 M2 51 28N 116 23W
Kiglapait, Cape Newfoundland and Labrador 60 E9 57 06N 61 22W
Kiglapait Mountains Newfoundland and Labrador 60 E8 57 06N 61 35W
Kikerk Lake Nunavut 64 H4 66 55N 113 20W
Kikkertarjote Island Newfoundland and Labrador 60 E8 57 30N 61 28W
Kikkertavak Island Newfoundland and Labrador 60 E8 56 22N 61 35W
Killaloe Ontario 53 J5 45 33N 77 26W
Killam Alberta 46 G3 52 47N 111 51W
Killarney Manitoba 49 C1 49 12N 99 40W
Killarney Ontario 52 E5 45 59N 81 30W
Killarney Provincial Park Ontario 52 E6 46 00N 81 00W
Killiniq Nunavut 56 H9 60 30N 64 50W
Killiniq Island Newfoundland and Labrador/Nunavut 60 C10 60 24N 64 31W
Kimberley British Columbia 43 N1 49 40N 115 58W
Kimmirut *(Lake Harbour)* Nunavut 65 S3 62 50N 69 50W
Kinbasket Lake British Columbia 43 M2 51 57N 118 02W
Kincardine Ontario 54 A3 44 11N 81 38W
Kincolith British Columbia 42 F4 55 00N 129 57W
Kincora Prince Edward Island 61 M12 46 20N 63 40W
Kindersley Saskatchewan 47 C2 51 27N 109 08W
King Christian Island Nunavut 65 K6 77 45N 102 00W
King City Ontario 54 C2 43 54N 79 31W
Kingcome Inlet British Columbia 43 G2 50 58N 125 15W
Kingfisher Lake Ontario 50 G7 53 05N 89 49W
Kingfisher Lake *I.R.* Ontario 50 G7 53 02N 89 50W
Kinggauk *(Bathurst Inlet) tn.* Nunavut 64 J4 66 50N 108 01W
King George, Mount British Columbia 43 N2 50 36N 115 26W
King Island British Columbia 43 G3 52 10N 127 35W
Kingnait *(Cape Dorset) tn.* Nunavut 65 Q3 64 10N 76 40W
Kings *admin.* New Brunswick 61 L12 45 30N 65 40W
Kings *admin.* Nova Scotia 61 M11 44 50N 64 50W
Kings *admin.* Prince Edward Island 61 M12 46 20N 62 40W
Kingsburg Nova Scotia 61 M11 44 20N 64 10W
Kings Landing New Brunswick 61 B2 45 50N 67 00W
Kingsmere Québec 59 J2 45 29N 75 50W
Kingston Ontario 53 K4 44 14N 76 30W
Kingsville Ontario 52 D2 42 02N 82 45W
Kingurutik Lake Newfoundland and Labrador 60 D8 56 49N 62 20W
King William Island Nunavut 65 L4 69 00N 97 30W
Kinistino Saskatchewan 47 E3 52 28N 105 01W
Kinoje River Ontario 50 L6 51 40N 81 50W
Kinoosao Saskatchewan 47 F5 57 07N 102 02W
Kinsac Lake Nova Scotia 59 Q7 44 50N 63 38W
Kinusheseo River Ontario 50 K8 54 30N 83 50W
Kiosk Ontario 52 H6 46 05N 78 53W
Kipahigan Lake Manitoba 49 B4 55 20N 101 50W
Kipling Saskatchewan 47 F2 50 08N 102 40W
Kirkland Lake Ontario 51 L5 48 10N 80 02W
Kirkpatrick Lake Alberta 46 G2 51 52N 111 18W
Kiskittogisa Lake Manitoba 49 C4 54 10N 98 50W
Kiskitto Lake Manitoba 49 C4 54 20N 98 50W
Kispiox British Columbia 43 G4 55 21N 127 41W
Kississing Lake Manitoba 49 B4 55 10N 101 30W
Kistigan Lake Manitoba 49 F4 54 50N 92 40W
Kitamaat Village British Columbia 43 F3 53 58N 128 38W
Kitchener Ontario 54 B2 43 27N 80 03W
Kitimat British Columbia 42 F4 54 05N 128 38W
Kitlope Heritage Conservancy Park British Columbia 43 G3 53 00N 127 30W
Klappan River British Columbia 42 F6 57 50N 129 40W
Kleinburg Ontario 55 B2 43 50N 79 36W
Klemtu British Columbia 43 F3 52 32N 128 24W
Klinaklini River British Columbia 43 H2 51 18N 125 45W
Klondike Highway Yukon Territory 64 C3 62 55N 136 10W
Klondike River Yukon Territory 64 C3 64 20N 138 50W
Kluane Lake Yukon Territory 64 C3 62 20N 139 00W
Kluane National Park Yukon Territory 64 C3 60 30N 139 00W
Kluane Wildlife Sanctuary Yukon Territory 64 B3 61 30N 139 50W
Kluskoil Lake Provincial Park British Columbia 43 J3 53 15N 124 00W
Knee Lake Manitoba 49 E4 55 10N 94 40W
Knight Inlet British Columbia 43 H2 50 45N 125 36W
Knox, Cape British Columbia 42 D4 54 09N 133 05W
Koch Island Nunavut 65 Q4 69 38N 78 15W
Kogaluc Bay Québec 56 B8 56 10N 63 30W
Kogaluk River Newfoundland and Labrador 60 D8 56 10N 63 30W
Kokanee Glacier Park British Columbia 43 M1 49 45N 117 10W
Komoka Ontario 54 A1 42 56N 81 26W
Kootenay Lake British Columbia 43 M1 49 35N 116 30W
Kootenay National Park British Columbia 43 M2 51 15N 116 25W
Kopka River Ontario 50 G6 50 00N 90 00W
Kotcho Lake British Columbia 43 K6 59 05N 121 10W
Kouchibouguac National Park New Brunswick 61 C3 46 45N 64 50W
Koukdjuuak River Nunavut 65 R4 66 50N 72 50W
Kovik Bay Québec 56 B9 61 35N 77 54W
Kugaaruk *(Pelly Bay)* Nunavut 65 N4 68 32N 89 48W
Kugluktuk *(Coppermine)* Nunavut 64 H4 65 00N 110 00W
Kunghit Island British Columbia 42 E3 52 02N 131 02W
Kuujjuaq Québec 56 F8 58 25N 68 55W
Kuujjuarapik Québec 56 B6 55 15N 77 41W
Kwadacha Wilderness Provincial Park British Columbia 43 H5 57 35N 125 30W
Kwataboahegan River Ontario 51 K6 51 10N 82 30W
Kyle Saskatchewan 47 C2 50 50N 108 02W
Kyuquot Sound British Columbia 43 G1 50 02N 127 22W

L

La Baie Québec 57 E3 48 20N 70 52W
Labelle Québec 53 M6 46 17N 74 45W
Labelle *admin.* Québec 53 L6 46 30N 75 40W
Laberge, Lake Yukon Territory 64 D3 61 10N 134 59W
Labrador *geog. reg.* Newfoundland and Labrador 60 D6/E6 54 00N 64 00W
Labrador City Newfoundland and Labrador 60 B6 52 57N 66 55W
Labrador Sea 65 T2/U2 59 30N 60 00W
Lac Abitibi *l.* Ontario/Québec 51 M5 48 40N 79 40W
Lac Albanel *l.* Québec 57 D4 51 N 73 20W
Lac à l'Eau Claire *l.* Québec 56 C7 56 20N 74 30W
Lac Anuc *l.* Québec 56 C8 59 15N 75 10W
Lac Assinica *l.* Québec 57 C4 50 20N 75 12W
Lac au Goéland *l.* Québec 57 B3 49 45N 76 55W

Lac Aylmer *l.* Québec **53** Q5 45 50N 71 20W
Lac Bacqueville *l.* Québec **56** D8 58 05N 74 00W
Lac Batiscan *l.* Québec **53** Q7 47 23N 71 53W
Lac Bécard *l.* Québec **56** D9 60 05N 73 45W
Lac Belot *l.* Northwest Territories **64** E4 66 53N 126 16W
Lac Bérard *l.* Québec **56** E8 58 25N 70 05W
Lac Bermen *l.* Québec **56** F5 53 40N 69 00W
Lac Berté *l.* Québec **57** F4 50 52N 68 35W
Lac Bienville *l.* Québec **56** D6 55 30N 73 00W
Lac Bourdel *l.* Québec **56** C7 56 42N 74 15W
Lac Boyd *l.* Québec **57** B5 52 45N 76 45W
Lac Brochet *l.* Manitoba **49** B6 58 40N 101 20W
Lac Brochet *tn.* Manitoba **49** B6 58 45N 101 30W
Lac Brome *l.* Québec **53** P5 45 15N 72 30W
Lac Brome *tn.* Québec **53** P5 45 13N 72 30W
Lac Burton *l.* Québec **56** A6 54 45N 79 25W
Lac Cambrien *l.* Québec **56** F7 56 30N 69 22W
Lac Cananée *l.* Québec **56** H7 56 05N 64 05W
Lac Chaconipau *l.* Québec **56** F7 56 20N 68 45W
Lac Champdoré *l.* Québec **56** H5 55 50N 65 50W
Lac Champlain *l.* Québec/USA **53** N4 45 08N 73 08W
Lac Châtelain *l.* Québec **56** C9 60 20N 74 20W
Lac Chavigny *l.* Québec **56** C8 58 10N 75 10W
Lac Chibougamau *l.* Québec **57** C3 49 55N 74 20W
Lac Couture *l.* Québec **56** C9 60 00N 75 20W
Lac de Gras *l.* Northwest Territories **64** J3 64 10N 109 00W
Lac de la Hutte Sauvage *l.* Québec **56** H7 56 18N 65 00W
Lac des Bois *l.* Northwest Territories **64** E4 65 00N 127 00W
Lac des Commissaires *l.* Québec **53** P8 48 09N 72 13W
Lac des Deux Montagnes *l.* Québec **58** M4 45 30N 73 58W
Lac des Loups Marins *l.* Québec **56** D7 56 30N 73 30W
Lac des Mille Lacs *l.* Ontario **50** F5 48 53N 90 22W
Lac des Quinze *l.* Québec **57** A2 47 45N 79 15W
Lac des Trente et Un Milles *l.* Québec **53** L6 46 18N 75 43W
Lac d'Iberville *l.* Québec **56** D6 55 55N 73 25W
Lac du Bonnet *l.* Manitoba **49** E2 50 30N 95 50W
Lac du Bonnet *tn.* Manitoba **49** D2 50 16N 96 03W
Lac Duncan *l.* Québec **57** A5 53 25N 78 00W
Lac du Sable *l.* Québec **56** G6 54 25N 67 59W
Lac Édouard *l.* Québec **53** P7 47 40N 72 16W
Lac-Etchemin *tn.* Québec **53** R6 46 23N 70 32W
Lac Faribault *l.* Québec **56** E8 59 10N 72 00W
Lac Fleur-de-May *l.* Newfoundland and Labrador **60** C6 52 00N 65 02W
Lac Goatanaga *l.* Québec **53** J7 47 42N 77 28W
Lac Guillaume-Delisle *l.* Québec **56** B7 56 15N 77 20W
Lachute Québec **53** M5 51 00N 71 00W
Lac Île-à-la Crosse *l.* Saskatchewan **47** D4 55 40N 107 30W
Lac Jeannin *l.* Québec **56** G7 56 25N 66 30W
Lac-John Québec **56** G6 54 49N 66 47W
Lac Joseph *l.* Newfoundland and Labrador **60** C6 52 45N 65 18W
Lac Kempt *l.* Québec **53** M7 47 28N 74 08W
Lac Kénogami *l.* Québec **57** E3 48 22N 71 25W
Lac Kipawa *l.* Québec **51** M4 46 55N 79 06W
Lac Klotz *l.* Québec **56** D9 60 30N 73 30W
Lac la Biche *l.* Alberta **46** F4 54 55N 112 58W
Lac la Biche *tn.* Alberta **46** G4 54 46N 111 58W
Lac la Croix *l.* Ontario **51** F5 48 21N 92 09W
Lac la Loche *l.* Saskatchewan **47** C5 56 30N 109 40W
Lac la Martre *l.* Northwest Territories **64** G3 63 20N 118 30W
Lac la Plonge *l.* Saskatchewan **47** D4 55 05N 107 00W
Lac la Ronge *l.* Saskatchewan **47** E4 55 10N 105 00W
Lac la Ronge Provincial Park Saskatchewan **47** E4 55 20N 104 45W
Lac le Moyne *l.* Québec **56** F7 57 10N 68 33W
Lac Le Roy *l.* Québec **56** C8 58 35N 75 25W
Lac Lesdiguière *l.* Québec **56** C9 60 00N 74 20W
Lac Magpie *l.* Québec **57** H4 51 00N 64 40W
Lac Maicasagi *l.* Québec **57** B4 50 00N 76 45W
Lac Manitou *l.* Québec **57** H4 50 50N 65 20W
Lac Manouane *l.* Québec **57** E4 50 45N 70 45W
Lac Matagami *l.* Québec **57** B3 49 55N 77 50W
Lac Maunoir *l.* Northwest Territories **64** E4 67 30N 125 55W
Lac-Mégantic *tn.* Québec **53** R5 45 34N 70 53W
Lac Memphrémagog *l.* Québec **53** P5 45 05N 72 13W
Lac Mesgouez *l.* Québec **57** C4 51 25N 75 00W
Lac Minto *l.* Québec **56** C7 57 5N 75 00W
Lac Mistassini *l.* Québec **57** D4 51 00N 73 20W
Lac Mistinibi *l.* Québec **56** H6 55 50N 64 20W
Lac Mitchinamécus *l.* Québec **53** M7 47 20N 75 00W
Lac Musquaro *l.* Québec **57** K4 50 50N 60 50W
Lac Nantais *l.* Québec **56** C9 61 10N 74 20W
Lac Naococane *l.* Québec **57** E5 52 53N 70 40W
Lac Nichicapau *l.* Québec **56** F7 56 42N 68 28W
Lac Nichicun *l.* Québec **57** E5 53 05N 71 05W
Lacombe Alberta **46** F3 52 28N 113 44W
Lac Opiscotéo *l.* Québec **57** F5 53 15N 68 20W
Lac Otelnuk *l.* Québec **56** F7 56 10N 68 20W
Lac Parent *l.* Québec **53** J8 48 30N 77 08W
Lac Payne *l.* Québec **56** C8 59 25N 74 25W
Lac Pélican *l.* Québec **56** D8 59 57N 73 40W
Lac Péribonka *l.* Québec **57** E4 50 10N 71 23W
Lac Plétipi *l.* Québec **57** E4 51 0N 70 10W
Lac Poncheville *l.* Québec **57** B4 50 12N 77 00W
Lac Potherie *l.* Québec **56** D8 58 50N 72 25W
Lac Qilalugalik *l.* Québec **56** B8 58 35N 76 00W
Lac Ramusio *l.* Québec **56** J6 55 10N 63 59W
Lac Résolution *l.* Québec **56** H6 55 15N 64 40W
La Crete Alberta **46** D6 58 11N 116 30W
Lac Roberts *l.* Québec **56** E9 60 25N 70 25W
Lac Saindon *l.* Québec **56** D6 55 35N 73 30W
Lac Sainte-Anne *l.* Québec **57** G4 50 5N 68 00W
Lac Saint-François *l.* Québec **53** Q5 45 56N 71 08W
Lac Saint-Jean *l.* Québec **57** D3/E3 48 35N 72 00W
Lac-St.-Jean-Est *admin.* Québec **53** Q8 48 20N 71 40W
Lac-St.-Jean-Ouest *admin.* Québec **53** N8/P8 48 20N 72 20W
Lac Saint-Louis *l.* Québec **58** M4 45 25N 73 49W
Lac Saint-Patrice *l.* Québec **53** J6 46 20N 77 30W
Lac Saint-Pierre *l.* Québec **53** P6 46 12N 72 49W
Lac Sakami *l.* Québec **57** B5 53 20N 76 50W
Lac Seul *l.R.* Ontario **50** E6 50 15N 92 15W
Lac Seul *l.* Ontario **50** E6 50 20N 92 00W
Lac Simard *l.* Québec **57** A2 47 40N 78 50W
Lac Simon *l.* Québec **53** L5 45 55N 75 05W
Lac Soscumica *l.* Québec **57** B4 50 15N 77 35W
Lac Tasiaalujjuak *l.* Québec **56** E8 59 35N 71 59W
Lac Tasiat *l.* Québec **56** C8 59 05N 75 25W
Lac Tasiataq *l.* Québec **56** E8 58 40N 71 40W
Lac Tassialouc *l.* Québec **56** D8 58 59N 74 00W
Lac Témiscamingue *l.* Québec **57** A2 47 28N 79 30W
Lac Tiblemont *l.* Québec **53** J8 48 17N 77 20W
Lac Tudor *l.* Québec **56** H6 55 58N 65 30W
Lac Wakuach *l.* Québec **56** G6 55 35N 67 40W
Lac Waswanipi *l.* Québec **57** B3 49 35N 76 36W
Lac Wayagamac *l.* Québec **53** P7 47 23N 72 35W
Lac Whitegull *l.* Québec **56** H6 55 25N 64 30W
Ladner British Columbia **42** H4 49 06N 123 05W
Lady Evelyn-Smoothwater Provincial Park Ontario **51** L4 47 20N 80 30W
Ladysmith British Columbia **42** H4 48 57N 123 50W
Laflèche Saskatchewan **47** D1 49 44N 106 32W
Lagoon City Ontario **54** C3 44 31N 79 11W
La Grande 2 *dam* Québec **57** B5 53 45N 77 38W
La Grande 3 *dam* Québec **57** B5 53 40N 76 09W
La Grande 4 *dam* Québec **56** D5 53 59N 72 50W
La Grande Rivière *r.* Québec **57** C5 53 34N 74 36W
La Guadeloupe Québec **53** R5 45 58N 70 57W
Lake Country *tn.* British Columbia **43** L2 50 02N 119 25W
Lake Cowichan *tn.* British Columbia **42** H4 48 50N 124 04W
Lake Echo *tn.* Nova Scotia **59** R6 44 44N 63 24W
Lakefield Ontario **52** H4 44 26N 78 16W
Lakeland Provincial Park Alberta **46** G4 54 45N 112 25W
Lakeland Provincial Recreation Area Alberta **46** G4 54 45N 111 15W
Lake Louise *tn.* Alberta **46** D2 51 25N 116 14W
Lake of Bays *tn.* Ontario **52** G5 45 00N 79 00W
Lake of the Rivers Saskatchewan **47** E1 49 50N 105 30W
Lakeside Nova Scotia **59** Q6 44 38N 63 42W
Lake Superior National Marine Conservation Area Ontario **51** G5/H5 48 30N 87 30W
Lake Superior Provincial Park Ontario **51** J4 47 35N 85 45W
Lakeview Newfoundland and Labrador **61** J3 47 20N 54 10W
Lakeview Ontario **59** J2 45 20N 75 48W
La Loche Saskatchewan **47** C5 56 31N 109 27W
La Malbaie Québec **53** R7 47 39N 70 11W
Lamaline Newfoundland and Labrador **61** H3 46 52N 55 49W
Lambeth Ontario **54** A1 42 54N 81 20W
Lambton *admin.* Ontario **52** D2 42 45N 82 05W
Lambton, Cape Northwest Territories **64** F4 71 05N 123 09W
Lamèque New Brunswick **61** C3 47 45N 64 40W
Lampman Saskatchewan **47** F1 49 23N 102 48W
Lanark Ontario **53** K5 45 01N 74 30W
Lanark *admin.* Ontario **53** K5 45 05N 76 20W
Lancaster Ontario **53** M5 45 08N 74 30W
Lancaster Sound Nunavut **65** N5 74 00N 87 30W
Land's End Northwest Territories **64** F6 76 22N 122 33W
Langenburg Saskatchewan **47** G2 50 50N 101 42W
Langham Saskatchewan **47** D3 52 22N 106 55W
Langley British Columbia **42** H4 49 06N 122 38W
Lanigan Saskatchewan **47** E2 51 50N 105 01W
L'Annonciation Québec **53** M6 46 24N 74 52W
Lansdowne House *tn.* Ontario **50** H7 52 05N 88 00W
L'Anse-au-Loup Newfoundland and Labrador **60** G5 51 31N 56 45W
L'Anse aux Meadows National Historic Site Newfoundland and Labrador **60** H5 51 36N 55 32W
L'Anse Pleureuse Québec **57** H3 49 15N 65 40W
Lantzville British Columbia **42** H4 49 15N 124 05W
La Pocatière Québec **53** R7 47 22N 70 03W
La Poile Newfoundland and Labrador **61** F3 47 41N 58 42W
La Prairie Québec **58** P4 45 25N 73 29W
Larder Lake *tn.* Ontario **51** M5 48 05N 79 38W
L'Ardoise Nova Scotia **61** M12 45 37N 60 46W
Lark Harbour *tn.* Newfoundland and Labrador **61** F4 49 06N 58 23W
La Ronge Saskatchewan **47** E4 55 07N 105 18W
Larrys River *tn.* Nova Scotia **61** M12 45 15N 61 25W
Larsen Sound Nunavut **65** L5 70 35N 98 00W
La Salle Ontario **52** C2 42 15N 83 05W
LaSalle Québec **58** N4 44 26N 73 37W
La Salle River Manitoba **48** B1 49 42N 97 16W
La Sarre Québec **57** A3 48 50N 79 20W
La Scie Newfoundland and Labrador **61** H4 49 57N 55 36W
Lashburn Saskatchewan **47** C3 53 08N 109 36W
Lasqueti Island British Columbia **42** H4 49 28N 124 20W
Last Mountain Lake Saskatchewan **47** E2 51 40N 106 55W
La Tabatière–Gros Mecatina Québec **56** L4 50 50N 58 57W
Latchford Ontario **51** M4 47 20N 79 49W
La Tuque Québec **53** P7 47 26N 72 47W
Laurie River Manitoba **49** B5 56 30N 101 30W
Lauzon Québec **53** Q6 46 49N 71 10W
Laval Québec **53** N5 45 38N 73 45W
Laval-des-Rapides Québec **58** N5 45 33N 73 42W
Laval-Ouest Québec **58** M5 45 33N 73 50W
Lawn Newfoundland and Labrador **61** H3 46 57N 55 32W
Lawrencetown Nova Scotia **61** L11 44 54N 65 10W
Lax Kw'aiaams British Columbia **42** E4 54 32N 130 25W
Leader Saskatchewan **47** C2 50 55N 109 31W
Leading Tickles Newfoundland and Labrador **61** H4 49 30N 55 28W
Leaf Rapids *tn.* Manitoba **49** B5 56 30N 100 00W
Leamington Ontario **52** D2 42 03N 83 36W
Leaside Ontario **55** C1 43 44N 79 15W
Lebel-sur-Quévillon Québec **57** B3 49 05N 77 08W
Leduc Alberta **46** F3 53 17N 113 30W
Leeds and Grenville *admin.* Ontario **53** K4/L4 44 35N 76 00W
Le Havre River Nova Scotia **61** M11 44 30N 64 30W
Leitrim Ontario **59** K2 45 20N 75 35W
Lemieux Islands Nunavut **65** T3 63 40N 64 20W
Lennox and Addington *admin.* Ontario **53** J4 44 30N 77 00W
Lenore Lake Saskatchewan **47** E3 52 50N 104 40W
Leoville Saskatchewan **47** D3 53 39N 107 33W
Lesser Slave Lake Alberta **46** E4 55 25N 115 25W
Lethbridge Alberta **46** F1 49 43N 112 48W
Level Mountain British Columbia **42** E6 58 33N 131 25W
Lévis Québec **53** Q6 46 47N 71 12W
Lewis Hill *mt.* Newfoundland and Labrador **61** F4 49 48N 58 30W
Lewisporte Newfoundland and Labrador **61** H4 49 15N 55 03W
Liard River Northwest Territories **64** F3 60 00N 120 00W
Liard River *tn.* British Columbia **43** G6 59 28N 126 18W
Liard River Corridor Provincial Park British Columbia **43** H6 59 20N 125 30W
Liddon Gulf Northwest Territories **64** H6 75 03N 113 00W
Líídlı Kúé *(Fort Simpson)* Northwest Territories **64** F3 61 46N 121 15W
L'île-Michon *tn.* Québec **57** J4 50 13N 62 02W
L'Île-Perrot *i.* Québec **58** M4 45 24N 73 55W
Lillooet British Columbia **43** K2 50 41N 121 59W
Lillooet Lake British Columbia **42** H5 50 15N 122 38W
Lillooet River British Columbia **42** H4 49 59N 122 25W
Limbour Québec **59** K2 45 29N 75 44W
Lindsay Ontario **54** D3 44 21N 78 44W
Linzee, Cape Nova Scotia **61** M12 46 00N 61 30W
Lions Bay *tn.* British Columbia **42** H4 49 28N 123 13W
Lions Head *tn.* Ontario **54** A3 44 59N 81 16W
Lipton Saskatchewan **47** F2 50 55N 103 49W
Liscomb Game Sanctuary Nova Scotia **61** M12 45 10N 62 40W
L'Islet *admin.* Québec **53** R7 47 00N 70 20W
L'Isle-Verte Québec **53** S8 48 00N 69 21W
Lismore Nova Scotia **61** M12 45 42N 62 16W
Listowel Ontario **54** B2 43 44N 80 57W
Little Abitibi River Provincial Park Ontario **51** L5 49 45N 81 00W
Little Bow River Alberta **46** F2 50 20N 113 40W
Little Buffalo River Alberta **46** F6 59 45N 113 30W
Little Churchill River Manitoba **49** E5 56 40N 96 00W
Little Current *tn.* Ontario **52** E5 45 58N 81 56W
Little Current River Provincial Park Ontario **50** H6 50 45N 86 15W
Little Dover Nova Scotia **61** M12 45 20N 61 05W
Little Grand Rapids *tn.* Manitoba **49** E3 52 10N 95 30W
Little Maitland River Ontario **54** A2 43 48N 81 10W
Little Mecatina River Newfoundland and Labrador **60** E6 52 40N 61 30W
Little Narrows *tn.* Nova Scotia **61** M12 45 59N 61 00W
Little River *tn.* British Columbia **42** H4 49 45N 124 56W
Little Rouge Creek Ontario **55** D2 43 54N 79 14W
Little Sachigo Lake Ontario **50** E8 54 09N 92 11W
Little Smoky River Alberta **46** D4 54 05N 117 45W
Liverpool Nova Scotia **61** M11 44 03N 64 43W
Liverpool Bay Northwest Territories **64** D4 69 45N 130 00W
Livingstone Cove *tn.* Nova Scotia **61** M12 45 52N 61 58W
Lloyd George, Mount British Columbia **43** H5 57 50N 124 58W
Lloyd Lake Alberta **44** A1 50 52N 114 10W
Lloyd Lake Saskatchewan **47** C5 57 20N 108 40W
Lloydminster Saskatchewan **47** C3 53 18N 110 00W
Lobstick Lake Newfoundland and Labrador **60** C7 54 00N 65 00W
Lockeport Nova Scotia **61** E6 43 40N 65 10W
Lockport Manitoba **49** D2 50 04N 97 00W
Lodge Creek Alberta/Saskatchewan **46** G1 49 15N 110 05W
Logan Lake *tn.* British Columbia **43** K2 50 28N 120 50W
Logan, Mount Yukon Territory **64** B3 60 34N 140 25W
Logan Mountains Yukon Territory **64** E3 60 30N 128 30W
London Ontario **54** A1 42 58N 81 15W
Long Beach *tn.* Ontario **54** C1 42 51N 79 23W
Long Cove *tn.* Newfoundland and Labrador **61** J3 47 34N 53 40W
Long Creek Saskatchewan **47** F1 49 20N 103 55W
Long Harbour *tn.* Newfoundland and Labrador **61** J3 47 26N 53 48W
Long Island Nova Scotia **61** L11 44 20N 66 15W
Longlac Ontario **51** H5 49 47N 86 34W
Long Lake New Brunswick **61** B3 47 00N 66 50W
Long Lake Nova Scotia **59** Q6 44 37N 63 37W
Long Lake Ontario **51** H5 49 00N 87 00W
Long Lake *l.R.* Ontario **51** H5 49 45N 86 32W
Long Lake Provincial Park Nova Scotia **59** Q6 44 36N 63 38W
Long Point Manitoba **49** C3 52 50N 98 20W
Long Point Ontario **54** B1 42 33N 80 04W
Long Point *tn.* Ontario **54** B1 42 34N 80 15W
Long Point Bay Ontario **54** B1 42 40N 80 14W
Long Point Provincial Park Ontario **54** B1 42 40N 80 15W
Long Pond Newfoundland and Labrador **61** H4 48 00N 55 52W
Long Range Mountains Newfoundland and Labrador **61** F3 50 00N 57 00W
Long Sault Ontario **53** M5 45 02N 74 53W
Longueuil Québec **53** N5 45 32N 73 31W
Longview Alberta **46** E2 50 32N 114 14W
Lookout, Cape Ontario **50** K8 55 18N 83 56W
Loon Lake Nova Scotia **59** Q6 44 42N 63 30W
Loon Lake *tn.* Alberta **46** E5 56 32N 115 24W
Loon Lake *tn.* Saskatchewan **47** C4 54 00N 109 10W
Loon River Alberta **46** E5 56 40N 115 20W
L'Original Ontario **53** M5 45 37N 74 42W
Loring Ontario **52** F5 45 56N 80 00W
Lorne Park *tn.* Ontario **54** C2 43 31N 79 36W
Lorraine Québec **58** M5 45 38N 73 47W
Lotbinière *admin.* Québec **53** Q6 46 20N 71 65W
Lougheed Island Nunavut **65** J6 77 26N 105 06W
Louisbourg Nova Scotia **61** N12 45 56N 59 58W
Louisbourg National Historic Site Nova Scotia **61** N12 45 55N 60 00W
Louise Island British Columbia **42** E3 52 59N 131 50W
Louiseville Québec **53** P6 46 16N 72 56W
Lourdes Newfoundland and Labrador **61** F4 48 39N 59 00W
Low, Cape Nunavut **65** N3 63 07N 85 18W
Lower Arrow Lake British Columbia **43** L1 49 40N 118 09W
Lower Foster Lake Saskatchewan **47** E5 56 30N 105 10W
Lower Manitou Lake Ontario **50** E5 49 15N 93 00W
Lower Post British Columbia **43** F6 59 56N 128 09W
Lower Sackville Nova Scotia **61** M11 44 40N 63 40W
Lubicon Lake Alberta **46** E5 56 23N 115 56W
Lucan Ontario **54** A2 43 11N 81 24W
Lucknow Ontario **54** A2 43 58N 81 31W
Lucky Lake *tn.* Saskatchewan **47** D2 50 59N 107 10W
Lulu Island British Columbia **44** F3 49 09N 123 09W
Lumby British Columbia **43** L2 50 15N 118 58W
Lumsden Saskatchewan **47** E2 50 39N 104 52W
Lund British Columbia **42** H4 49 59N 124 46W
Lundar Manitoba **49** C2 50 41N 98 01W
Lundbreck Alberta **46** E1 49 36N 114 10W
Lunenburg Nova Scotia **61** M11 44 23N 64 21W
Lunenburg *admin.* Nova Scotia **61** M11 44 35N 64 30W
Luseland Saskatchewan **47** C3 52 06N 109 24W
Luther Lake Ontario **54** B2 43 52N 80 26W
Łutselk'e *(Snowdrift)* Northwest Territories **64** H3 62 24N 110 44W
Lyall, Mount Alberta/British Columbia **46** E2 50 05N 114 42W
Lyell Islands British Columbia **42** E3 52 00N 131 00W
Lynn Lake *tn.* Manitoba **49** B5 56 51N 101 01W
Lynx Lake Northwest Territories **64** J3 62 25N 106 15W
Lytton British Columbia **43** K2 50 12N 121 34W

M

Maaset British Columbia **42** D4 54 00N 132 01W
Mabel Lake British Columbia **43** L2 50 35N 118 40W
Mabou Nova Scotia **61** M12 46 04N 61 22W
McAdam New Brunswick **61** B2 45 34N 67 20W
MacAlpine Lake Nunavut **65** K4 66 45N 130 00W
Macamic Québec **57** A3 48 46N 79 02W
McBride British Columbia **43** K3 53 21N 120 19W
McCabe Lake Nova Scotia **59** Q7 44 47N 63 43W
Maccan Nova Scotia **61** M12 45 43N 64 16W
McClintock Manitoba **49** E5 57 50N 94 10W
McConnell River Bird Sanctuary Nunavut **65** M3 60 30N 94 00W
McCreary Manitoba **49** C2 50 45N 99 30W
Macdiarmid Ontario **51** G5 49 23N 88 08W
MacDowell Ontario **50** E7 52 10N 92 40W
MacDowell Lake Ontario **50** E7 52 15N 92 42W
McFarlane River Saskatchewan **47** D5 57 50N 107 55W
McGivney New Brunswick **61** B3 46 22N 66 34W
MacGregor Manitoba **49** C1 49 57N 98 48W
McGregor Lake Alberta **46** F2 50 25N 112 52W
Macgregor Point Provincial Park Ontario **54** A3 44 25N 81 27W
McGregor River British Columbia **43** K4 54 10N 121 20W
McKay Lake Newfoundland and Labrador **60** C6 53 44N 65 37W
Mackay Lake Northwest Territories **64** H3 63 55N 110 25W

McKeller Ontario 52 G5 45 30N 79 00W
Mackenzie British Columbia 43 J4 55 18N 123 10W
Mackenzie Bay Yukon Territory 64 C4 69 00N 137 30W
Mackenzie Bison Sanctuary Northwest Territories 64 G3 61 30N 116 30W
McKenzie Creek Ontario 54 B2 43 02N 80 17W
Mackenzie Highway Alberta 46 D5 57 55N 117 40W
Mackenzie King Island Northwest Territories/Nunavut 64 H6 77 45N 111 00W
Mackenzie Mountains Yukon Territory/Northwest Territories 64 E3 66 00N 132 00W
Mackenzie River Northwest Territories 64 E4 66 20N 125 55W
Mackey Ontario 52 J6 46 10N 77 49W
Macklin Saskatchewan 47 C3 52 20N 109 58W
Maclean Strait Nunavut 65 K6 77 30N 102 30W
McLeese Lake *tn.* British Columbia 43 J3 52 25N 122 20W
McLennan Alberta 46 D4 55 42N 116 54W
McLeod Lake *tn.* British Columbia 43 J4 55 00N 123 00W
McLeod River Alberta 46 E3 53 40N 116 20W
M'Clintock Channel Nunavut 65 K5 72 00N 102 00W
M'Clure, Cape Northwest Territories 64 F4 74 32N 121 19W
M'Clure Strait Northwest Territories 64 G5 74 59N 120 10W
Macmillan Pass Yukon Territory 64 D3 63 25N 130 00W
Macmillan River Yukon Territory 64 D3 63 00N 134 00W
McNabs Island Nova Scotia 59 Q6 44 37N 63 31W
McNutt Island Nova Scotia 61 L11 43 40N 65 20W
Macoun Lake Saskatchewan 47 F5 56 30N 103 40W
Macrae Point Provincial Park Ontario 54 C3 44 30N 79 10W
McTavish Arm *b.* Northwest Territories 64 G4 66 06N 118 04W
MacTier Ontario 52 G4 45 08N 79 47W
McVicar Arm *b.* Northwest Territories 64 F3 65 20N 120 10W
Madawaska Ontario 52 J5 45 30N 77 59W
Madawaska *admin.* New Brunswick 61 A3/B3 47 30N 68 00W
Madawaska River Ontario 51 N3 45 10N 77 30W
Madoc Ontario 53 J4 44 30N 77 29W
Mad River Ontario 54 B3 44 18N 80 02W
Madsen Ontario 50 E6 50 58N 93 55W
Maelpaeg Réservoir Newfoundland and Labrador 61 G4 48 20N 56 40W
Magnetawan Ontario 52 G5 45 40N 79 39W
Magnetawan River Ontario 52 F5 45 46N 80 37W
Magog Québec 53 P5 45 16N 72 09W
Magpie River Ontario 51 J5 48 00N 84 50W
Magrath Alberta 46 F1 49 27N 112 52W
Maguse Lake Nunavut 65 M3 61 40N 95 10W
Mahone Bay Nova Scotia 61 M11 44 25N 64 15W
Mahone Bay *tn.* Nova Scotia 61 M11 44 27N 64 24W
Mahood Creek British Columbia 44 G3 49 09N 122 50W
Maidstone Saskatchewan 47 C3 53 06N 109 18W
Main Brook *tn.* Newfoundland and Labrador 60 G5 51 11N 56 01W
Main Channel Ontario 52 E5 45 00N 82 00W
Maitland River Ontario 54 A2 43 50N 81 28W
Major, Lake Nova Scotia 59 R6 44 45N 63 30W
Makkovik Newfoundland and Labrador 60 F7 55 05N 59 11W
Makoop Lake Ontario 50 F7 53 24N 90 50W
Malartic Québec 57 A3 48 09N 78 09W
Malaspina Strait British Columbia 42 H4 49 47N 124 30W
Mallet River Ontario 54 B2 43 51N 80 42W
Mallikjuaq Territorial Park Nunavut 65 Q3 64 14N 76 34W
Malpeque Bay Prince Edward Island 61 M12 46 35N 63 50W
Malton Ontario 54 C2 43 42N 79 38W
Manicouagan Québec 57 F4 50 40N 68 46W
Manigotagan Manitoba 49 D2 51 00N 96 10W
Manigotagan River Manitoba 49 E2 51 00N 96 10W
Manitoba *province* 49
Manitoba, Lake Manitoba 49 C2 50 30N 98 15W
Manito Lake Saskatchewan 47 C3 52 40N 109 20W
Manitou Manitoba 49 C1 49 15N 98 32W
Manitou Lake Ontario 52 E5 45 48N 82 00W
Manitoulin *admin.* Ontario 52 C5/D5 45 45N 82 30W
Manitoulin Island Ontario 52 D5 45 50N 82 20W
Manitouwadge Ontario 51 J5 49 10N 85 55W
Maniwaki Québec 53 L6 46 22N 75 58W
Manning Alberta 46 D5 56 55N 117 37W
Manning Provincial Park British Columbia 42 H4 49 09N 120 50W
Manotick Ontario 59 K1 45 14N 75 43W
Mansel Island Nunavut 65 Q3 62 00N 80 00W
Manson Creek *tn.* British Columbia 43 H4 55 40N 124 32W
Maple Ontario 54 C2 43 50N 79 30W
Maple Creek *tn.* Saskatchewan 47 B1 49 55N 109 28W
Maple Ridge British Columbia 42 H4 49 13N 122 36W
Mara Provincial Park Ontario 54 C3 44 30N 79 15W
Marathon Ontario 51 H5 48 44N 86 23W
Margaree Forks Nova Scotia 61 M12 46 20N 61 10W
Margaree Harbour *tn.* Nova Scotia 61 M12 46 26N 61 08W
Margaret Lake Alberta 46 E6 58 56N 115 25W
Margaretville Nova Scotia 61 L12 45 05N 65 05W
Marguerite River Wildland Provincial Park Alberta 46 G5 57 35N 110 10W
Maria Québec 57 H3 48 10N 65 59W
Marieville Québec 53 N5 45 27N 73 08W
Markdale Ontario 54 B3 44 19N 80 39W
Markham Ontario 54 C2 43 53N 79 14W
Markham Bay Nunavut 65 R3 63 02N 72 00W
Marmora Ontario 52 J4 44 29N 77 41W
Marten Falls *I.R.* Ontario 50 J6 51 40N 85 55W
Martensville Saskatchewan 47 D3 52 10N 106 30W
Mary's Harbour *tn.* Newfoundland and Labrador 60 H6 52 19N 55 50W
Marystown Newfoundland and Labrador 61 H3 47 10N 55 09W
Marysville New Brunswick 61 B2 45 58N 66 35W
Mascouche Québec 53 N5 45 47N 73 49W
Mashteuiatsh Québec 57 D3 48 34N 72 15W
Maskinongé *admin.* Québec 53 M7 47 40N 74 50W
Massasauga Provincial Park Ontario 52 F5 45 12N 80 02W
Massey Ontario 52 D6 46 12N 82 05W
Massey Sound Nunavut 65 L6 78 00N 95 00W
Matachewan Ontario 51 L4 47 56N 80 39W
Matagami Québec 57 B3 49 40N 77 40W
Matane Québec 57 G3 48 50N 67 31W
Matapédia Québec 57 G2 47 59N 66 58W
Matheson Ontario 51 L5 48 32N 80 28W
Matimekosh Québec 56 G6 54 49N 66 48W
Matsqui British Columbia 42 H4 49 05N 122 22W
Mattagami Lake Ontario 51 L4 47 54N 81 35W
Mattagami River Ontario 51 L5 49 00N 81 50W
Mattawa Ontario 52 H6 46 19N 78 42W
Mattice Ontario 51 K5 49 36N 83 16W
Maurelle Island British Columbia 42 G5 50 16N 125 11W
Mayerthorpe Alberta 46 E3 53 57N 115 08W
Mayne Island British Columbia 42 H4 48 50N 123 18W
Maynooth Ontario 52 J5 45 14N 77 57W
Mayo Yukon Territory 64 C3 63 34N 135 52W
Mayo Lake Yukon Territory 64 C3 135 00N 63 50W
Mayson Lake Saskatchewan 47 D5 57 50N 107 30W
Meadow Lake *tn.* Saskatchewan 47 C4 54 09N 108 26W
Meadow Lake Provincial Park Saskatchewan 47 C4 54 30N 108 00W
Meadowvale West Ontario 54 C2 43 35N 79 45W
Meaford Ontario 54 B3 44 36N 80 35W
Meaghers Grant Nova Scotia 61 M11 44 57N 63 15W
Mealy Mountains Newfoundland and Labrador 60 F6 53 10N 60 00W
Meander River *tn.* Alberta 46 D6 59 02N 117 42W
Meath Park *tn.* Saskatchewan 47 E3 53 27N 105 22W
Medicine Hat Alberta 46 G2 50 03N 110 41W
Meductic New Brunswick 61 B2 45 55N 67 30W
Medway Creek Ontario 54 A2 43 07N 81 18W
Medway River Nova Scotia 61 M11 44 15N 64 50W
Mégantic *admin.* Québec 53 Q6 46 10N 71 40W
Meighen Island Nunavut 65 L7 80 00N 99 30W
Melbourne Island Nunavut 64 J4 68 30N 104 45W
Meldrum Bay *tn.* Ontario 52 C5 45 56N 83 06W
Melfort Saskatchewan 47 E3 52 52N 104 38W
Melita Manitoba 49 B1 49 16N 101 00W
Melville Saskatchewan 47 F2 50 57N 102 49W
Melville Hills Northwest Territories/Nunavut 64 F4 69 00N 121 00W
Melville Island Northwest Territories/Nunavut 64 H6 75 30N 112 00W
Melville, Lake Newfoundland and Labrador 60 F6 53 45N 59 00W
Melville Peninsula Nunavut 65 P4 68 00N 84 00W
Melville Sound Nunavut 64 J4 68 05N 107 30W
Melville Sound Ontario 54 A3 43 00N 81 04W
Menihek Lakes Newfoundland and Labrador 60 B6 53 50N 66 50W
Menihek Siding Newfoundland and Labrador 60 B7 54 28N 66 36W
Mercier Québec 53 N5 45 20N 73 45W
Mercy Bay Northwest Territories 64 G5 74 05N 119 00W
Merigomish Nova Scotia 61 M12 45 37N 62 25W
Merrickville Ontario 53 L4 44 55N 75 50W
Merritt British Columbia 43 K2 50 09N 120 49W
Mersey River Nova Scotia 61 M11 44 10N 65 00W
Messines Québec 57 B2 46 15N 76 01W
Metabetchouane Québec 53 Q8 48 26N 71 52W
Meta Incognita Peninsula Nunavut 65 S3 63 30N 70 00W
Metcalfe Ontario 59 L1 45 14N 75 29W
Metchosin British Columbia 42 H4 48 22N 123 32W
Meteghan Nova Scotia 61 L11 44 12N 66 10W
Meziadin Junction British Columbia 43 F5 56 10N 129 15W
Mica Creek *tn.* British Columbia 43 L3 52 00N 118 28W
Mica Dam British Columbia 43 L3 52 04N 118 28W
Michaud Point Nova Scotia 61 M12 45 35N 60 40W
Michel Peak British Columbia 43 G3 53 30N 126 25W
Michikamats Lake Newfoundland and Labrador 60 C7 54 38N 64 19W
Michikamau Lake Newfoundland and Labrador 60 D6 54 00N 64 00W
Michipicoten Island Ontario 51 J4 47 45N 85 45W
Michipicoten River *tn.* Ontario 51 J4 47 56N 84 52W
Micmac, Lake Nova Scotia 59 Q6 44 41N 63 32W
Midale Saskatchewan 47 F1 49 23N 103 21W
Middle Arm Newfoundland and Labrador 61 G4 49 42N 56 06W
Middle Maitland River Ontario 54 A2 43 43N 81 11W
Middle Ridge Newfoundland and Labrador 61 H4 48 20N 55 15W
Middle Ridge Wilderness Reserve Newfoundland and Labrador 61 H4 48 30N 55 15W
Middle Sackville Nova Scotia 61 M11 44 47N 63 41W
Middlesex *admin.* Ontario 54 A2 42 46N 81 46W
Middleton Nova Scotia 61 L11 44 56N 65 04W
Midhurst Ontario 54 C3 44 26N 79 45W
Midland Ontario 52 G4 44 45N 79 53W
Midway British Columbia 43 L1 49 02N 118 45W
Midway Mountains British Columbia 43 L1 49 25N 118 45W
Mikkwa River Alberta 46 E5 57 40N 114 08W
Mildmay Ontario 54 A3 44 03N 81 08W
Milestone Saskatchewan 47 E1 49 59N 104 31W
Milk River Alberta 46 G1 49 10N 110 05W
Milk River *tn.* Alberta 46 F1 49 09N 112 05W
Millbrook Ontario 52 H4 44 09N 78 28W
Miller Lake Nova Scotia 59 Q7 44 49N 63 35W
Millet Alberta 46 F3 53 06N 113 28W
Mill Island Nunavut 65 Q3 64 00N 78 00W
Milltown Newfoundland and Labrador 61 H3 47 54N 55 46W
Mill Village Nova Scotia 61 M11 44 10N 64 40W
Millville New Brunswick 61 B3 46 08N 67 12W
Milo Alberta 46 F2 50 34N 112 53W
Milton Nova Scotia 61 M11 44 04N 64 44W
Milton Ontario 54 C2 43 31N 79 53W
Milton Prince Edward Island 61 M12 46 20N 63 10W
Milverton Ontario 54 B2 43 34N 80 55W
Miminegash Prince Edward Island 61 M12 46 54N 64 15W
Minaki Ontario 50 D5 50 00N 94 40W
Minas Basin Nova Scotia 61 M12 45 15N 64 15W
Minas Channel Nova Scotia 61 M12 45 10N 64 50W
Minden Ontario 52 H4 44 56N 78 44W
Minipi Lake Newfoundland and Labrador 60 E6 52 25N 60 45W
Miniss Lake Ontario 50 F6 50 48N 90 50W
Minitonas Manitoba 49 B3 52 04N 101 02W
Minnedosa Manitoba 49 C2 50 14N 99 50W
Minnitaki Lake Ontario 50 F5 49 58N 92 00W
Minonipi Lake Newfoundland and Labrador 60 E6 52 50N 60 50W
Minto New Brunswick 61 B3 46 05N 66 05W
Minto Yukon Territory 64 C3 62 34N 136 50W
Minto Inlet Northwest Territories 64 G5 71 20N 117 00W
Mira Bay Nova Scotia 61 N12 46 05N 59 50W
Mirabel Québec 53 M5 45 41N 74 20W
Miramichi New Brunswick 61 C3 46 55N 65 35W
Miramichi Bay New Brunswick 61 C3 47 05N 65 00W
Mira River Nova Scotia 61 M12 46 00N 60 10W
Miscouche Prince Edward Island 61 M12 46 26N 63 52W
Miscou Island New Brunswick 61 C3 47 50N 64 30W
Misery Point Newfoundland and Labrador 60 H6 52 01N 55 18W
Mishkeegogamang Ontario 50 F6 50 52N 90 13W
Missanabie Ontario 51 J5 48 19N 84 05W
Missinaibi Lake Ontario 51 K5 48 23N 83 40W
Missinaibi River Ontario 51 K5 49 30N 83 20W
Missinaibi River Provincial Park Ontario 51 K6 50 00N 83 15W
Mission British Columbia 42 H4 49 08N 122 20W
Missisa Lake Ontario 50 J7 52 18N 85 12W
Mississagi River Ontario 51 K4 46 10N 83 01W
Mississagi River Provincial Park Ontario 51 K4 47 10N 82 35W
Mississauga Ontario 54 C2 43 38N 79 36W
Missouri Coteau *hills* Saskatchewan 47 D2 50 40N 106 30W
Mistastin Lake Newfoundland and Labrador 60 D7 55 50N 63 00W
Mistissini Québec 57 D4 50 25N 73 50W
Mitchell Ontario 54 A2 43 27N 81 13W
Mitchells Brook *tn.* Newfoundland and Labrador 61 J3 47 08N 53 31W
Mittimatalik *(Pond Inlet) tn.* Nunavut 65 Q5 72 40N 77 59W
Mobert *I.R.* Ontario 51 J5 48 40N 85 40W
Moisie Québec 57 G4 50 12N 66 06W
Molson Lake Manitoba 49 D4 54 20N 96 50W
Monarch Mountain British Columbia 43 H2 51 55N 125 57W
Monashee Mountains British Columbia 43 L2 51 30N 118 50W
Monashee Provincial Park British Columbia 43 L2 50 30N 118 15W
Moncton New Brunswick 61 M12 46 04N 64 50W
Monkman Pass British Columbia 43 K4 54 30N 121 10W
Monkman Provincial Park British Columbia 43 K4 54 00N 121 10W
Mono Cliffs Provincial Park Ontario 54 B3 44 02N 80 03W
Mono Mills Ontario 54 C2 43 55N 79 57W
Montague Prince Edward Island 61 M12 46 10N 62 39W
Montcalm *admin.* Québec 53 L7 47 40N 76 15W
Mont D'Iberville *mt.* Québec/Newfoundland 60 D9 58 50N 64 40W
Mont Jacques-Cartier *mt.* Québec 57 H3 49 00N 66 00W
Mont-Joli *tn.* Québec 57 F3 48 36N 68 14W
Mont-Laurier *tn.* Québec 53 L6 46 33N 75 31W
Montmagny Québec 53 R6 46 58N 70 34W
Montmagny *admin.* Québec 53 R6 46 50N 70 20W
Montmartre Saskatchewan 47 F2 50 13N 103 26W
Montmorency *admin.* Québec 53 Q7 47 34N 71 20W
Montréal Québec 53 N5 45 32N 73 36W
Montreal Lake Saskatchewan 47 E4 54 15N 105 30W
Montreal River Ontario 51 J4 47 20N 84 20W
Montreal River Saskatchewan 47 E4 54 50N 105 30W
Montreal River *tn.* Ontario 51 J4 47 14N 84 39W
Montrose British Columbia 43 M1 49 06N 117 30W
Monts Chic-Chocs *mts.* Québec 57 G3 49 00N 66 40W
Monts Notre Dame *mts.* Québec 57 F3 48 00N 69 00W
Monts Otish *mts.* Québec 57 E5 52 30N 70 20W
Monts Povungnituk *mts.* Québec 56 C9 61 30N 75 59W
Monts Torngat *mts.* Québec/Newfoundland 56 H8 59 00N 64 15W
Mont Tremblant Québec 57 C2 46 07N 74 35W
Moose Creek Provincial Forest Manitoba 49 D2 51 30N 96 45W
Moose Factory Ontario 51 L6 51 16N 80 37W
Moose Jaw Saskatchewan 47 E2 50 23N 105 35W
Moosejaw River Saskatchewan 47 E2 50 15N 105 10W
Moose Lake *tn.* Manitoba 49 B3 53 43N 100 20W
Moose Mountain Creek Saskatchewan 47 F2 50 15N 103 25W
Moose Mountain Provincial Park Saskatchewan 47 F1 49 50N 102 20W
Moose River *tn.* Ontario 51 L6 50 48N 81 18W
Moosomin Saskatchewan 47 G2 50 09N 101 41W
Moosonee Ontario 51 L6 51 18N 80 39W
Morden Manitoba 49 C1 49 12N 98 05W
Morell Prince Edward Island 61 M12 46 25N 62 42W
Moresby Camp British Columbia 42 D3 53 05N 132 04W
Moresby Island British Columbia 42 D3 53 00N 132 00W
Morice Lake British Columbia 43 G3/G4 53 55N 127 30W
Moricetown British Columbia 43 G4 55 02N 127 20W
Morinville Alberta 46 F3 53 48N 113 39W
Morris Manitoba 49 D1 49 22N 97 21W
Morrisburg Ontario 53 L4 44 54N 75 11W
Morse Saskatchewan 47 D2 50 24N 107 00W
Morson Ontario 50 D5 49 03N 94 19W
Moser River *tn.* Nova Scotia 61 M11 44 58N 62 18W
Mostoos Hills Saskatchewan 47 C4 55 20N 109 30W
Mould Bay *m.s.* Northwest Territories 64 G6 76 14N 119 20W
Mountain Lake Ontario 54 A3 44 42N 81 02W
Mount Albert *tn.* Ontario 54 C3 44 07N 79 18W
Mount Blanchet Provincial Park British Columbia 43 H4 55 15N 125 55W
Mount Burke British Columbia 44 H4 49 18N 122 42W
Mount Carleton Provincial Park New Brunswick 61 B3 47 20N 66 30W
Mount Edziza Provincial Park British Columbia 42 E5 57 40N 131 40W
Mount Forest *tn.* Ontario 54 B2 43 58N 80 44W
Mount Hope *tn.* Ontario 54 C2 43 09N 79 54W
Mount Pearl *tn.* Newfoundland and Labrador 61 J3 47 31N 52 47W
Mount Revelstoke National Park British Columbia 43 L2/M2 50 40N 118 00W
Mount Robson Provincial Park British Columbia 43 L3 52 50N 118 40W
Mount Brydges *tn.* Ontario 54 A1 42 54N 81 30W
Mount Seymour Provincial Park British Columbia 42 G4 49 22N 122 56W
Mount Stewart *tn.* Prince Edward Island 61 M12 46 22N 62 52W
Mount Uniacke *tn.* Nova Scotia 61 M11 44 54N 63 50W
Mud Bay British Columbia 44 G3 49 04N 122 53W
Mudjatik River Saskatchewan 47 D5 56 40N 107 10W
Mud Lake *tn.* Newfoundland and Labrador 60 E6 53 19N 60 10W
Mukutawa River Manitoba 49 D3 53 10N 97 10W
Mulgrave Nova Scotia 61 M12 45 36N 61 25W
Muncho Lake British Columbia 43 H6 59 05N 125 47W
Muncho Lake *tn.* British Columbia 43 H6 59 00N 125 46W
Muncho Lake Provincial Park British Columbia 43 H6 58 50N 125 40W
Mundare Alberta 46 F3 53 36N 112 20W
Murdochville Québec 57 H3 48 57N 65 30W
Murray Harbour *tn.* Prince Edward Island 61 M12 46 00N 62 32W
Murray River *tn.* Prince Edward Island 61 M12 46 00N 62 38W
Murtle Lake British Columbia 43 L3 52 09N 119 40W
Musgrave Harbour Newfoundland and Labrador 61 J4 49 27N 53 58W
Musgravetown Newfoundland and Labrador 61 J4 48 24N 53 53W
Muskoka Falls *tn.* Ontario 52 G4 44 59N 79 16W
Muskrat Dam Lake Ontario 50 F7 53 25N 91 40W
Muskwa River British Columbia 43 J6 58 30N 123 20W
Musquodoboit Harbour Nova Scotia 61 M11 44 48N 63 10W
Muzon, Cape British Columbia 42 D4 54 41N 132 40W
Myles Bay Ontario 54 A3 44 56N 81 23W
Myrnam Alberta 46 G3 53 40N 111 14W

N

Nachvak Fiord *in.* Newfoundland and Labrador 60 D9 59 03N 63 45W
Nackawic New Brunswick 61 B2 46 00N 67 15W
Nagagami Lake Ontario 51 J5 49 25N 85 01W
Nagagami River Ontario 51 J5 49 30N 84 50W

Nahanni National Park Reserve Northwest Territories 64 E3 61 30N 126 00W
Nahatlatch River British Columbia 42 H4 49 55N 121 59W
Nahlin River British Columbia 42 E6 58 58N 131 30W
Naicam Saskatchewan 47 E3 52 26N 104 31W
Naikoon Provincial Park British Columbia 42 E3 53 59N 131 35W
Nain Newfoundland and Labrador 60 E8 56 32N 61 41W
Nakina Ontario 50 H6 50 11N 86 43W
Nakina River British Columbia 42 D6 59 07N 132 59W
Nakusp British Columbia 43 M2 50 15N 117 45W
Nanaimo British Columbia 42 H4 49 08N 123 58W
Nanaimo River British Columbia 42 H4 49 08N 123 54W
Nanisivik Nunavut 65 P5 73 00N 79 58W
Nansen Sound Nunavut 65 M7 81 00N 90 35W
Nanticoke Ontario 54 B1 42 48N 80 04W
Nanticoke Creek Ontario 54 B1 42 56N 80 16W
Nanton Alberta 46 F2 50 21N 113 46W
Napaktokh (Black Duck) Bay Newfoundland and Labrador 60 D9 58 01N 62 19W
Napaktulik Lake Nunavut 64 H4 66 30N 112 50W
Napanee Ontario 53 K4 44 15N 76 57W
Naramata British Columbia 43 L1 49 36N 119 36W
Nares Strait 65 R6 78 30N 72 30W
Narrow Hills Provincial Park Saskatchewan 47 E4 54 10N 103 30W
Narrows, The *sd.* Nova Scotia 59 Q6 44 40N 63 35W
Naskaupi River Newfoundland and Labrador 60 D7 54 20N 62 40W
Nass River British Columbia 42 F4 55 10N 129 20W
Nastapoka Islands Nunavut 56 B7 56 50N 76 50W
Natashquan Québec 57 K4 50 10N 61 50W
Natashquan River Newfoundland and Labrador 60 D6 52 30N 62 50W
Nation Lakes British Columbia 43 H4 55 08N 125 15W
Nation River British Columbia 43 H4 55 11N 124 25W
Natuashish Newfoundland and Labrador 60 E7 55 51N 62 04W
Naujat *(Repulse Bay)* Nunavut 65 N4 66 32N 86 15W
Nauwigewauk New Brunswick 61 L12 45 28W 65 53W
Nazko British Columbia 43 J3 53 00N 123 37W
Nechako Plateau British Columbia 43 H4/J4 54 40N 124 40W
Nechako River British Columbia 43 H3 53 35N 124 50W
Neeb Saskatchewan 47 D4 54 00N 107 50W
Neepawa Manitoba 49 C2 50 14N 99 29W
Neguac New Brunswick 61 C3 47 14N 65 03W
Neilburg Saskatchewan 47 C3 52 50N 109 38W
Nejanilini Lake Manitoba 49 D6 59 50N 97 20W
Nelson British Columbia 43 M1 49 29N 117 17W
Nelson Forks *tn.* British Columbia 43 H6 59 30N 124 00W
Nelson House *tn.* Manitoba 49 C4 55 49N 98 51W
Nelson Island British Columbia 42 H4 49 43N 124 03W
Nelson River Manitoba 49 F5 56 50N 93 40W
Némiscau Québec 57 B4 51 20N 77 01W
Nepean Ontario 53 L5 45 16N 75 48W
Nepewassi Lake Ontario 52 F6 46 22N 80 38W
Nepisiguit River New Brunswick 61 B3 47 20N 66 30W
Nesselrode, Mount British Columbia 42 C6 58 55N 134 20W
Nestor Falls *tn.* Ontario 50 E5 49 05N 93 55W
Nettilling Lake Nunavut 65 R4 66 30N 71 10W
Neustadt Ontario 54 A3 44 04N 81 00W
New Aiyansh British Columbia 43 F4 55 15N 129 02W
Newboro Ontario 53 K4 44 39N 76 19W
New Brunswick *province* 61 B3/C3
Newburgh Ontario 53 K4 44 19N 76 52W
New Carlisle Québec 57 H3 48 00N 65 22W
New Denver British Columbia 43 M1 49 59N 117 22W
Newell, Lake Alberta 46 G2 50 26N 111 55W
Newfoundland *i.* Newfoundland and Labrador 61 G4 53 51N 56 56W
Newfoundland and Labrador *province* 60/61
New Germany Nova Scotia 61 M11 44 34N 64 44W
New Glasgow Nova Scotia 61 M12 45 36N 62 38W
New Hazelton British Columbia 43 G4 55 15N 127 30W
New Liskeard Ontario 51 M4 47 31N 79 41W
Newmarket Ontario 54 C3 44 03N 79 27W
New Minas Nova Scotia 61 M12 45 00N 64 30W
New Richmond Québec 57 H3 48 12N 65 52W
New Ross Nova Scotia 61 M11 44 44N 64 27W
Newton British Columbia 44 G3 49 07N 122 50W
New Waterford Nova Scotia 61 M12 46 17N 60 05W
New Westminster British Columbia 42 H4 49 10N 122 58W
New-Wes-Valley Newfoundland and Labrador 61 J4 49 12N 53 31W
Niagara *admin.* Ontario 54 C2 43 02N 79 34W
Niagara Escarpment Ontario 54 B3 44 30N 80 45W
Niagara Falls *tn.* Ontario 54 C2 43 05N 79 06W
Niagara-on-the-Lake Ontario 54 C2 43 14N 79 16W
Nicolet Québec 53 P6 46 14N 72 36W
Nicolet *admin.* Québec 53 P6 46 00N 72 30W
Nicomekl *r.* British Columbia 44 H3 49 05N 122 43W
Nictau New Brunswick 61 B3 47 16N 67 11W
Night Hawk Lake Ontario 51 L5 48 28N 80 58W
Ningunsaw Provincial Park British Columbia 42 E5 56 50N 130 00W
Nipawin Saskatchewan 47 E3 53 23N 104 01W
Nipigon Ontario 51 G5 49 02N 88 26W
Nipigon Bay Ontario 51 G5 48 50N 88 10W
Nipigon, Lake Ontario 50 G5 49 50N 88 30W
Nipishish Lake Newfoundland and Labrador 60 E7 54 10N 60 30W
Nipissing Ontario 52 G6 46 05N 79 31W
Nipissing *admin.* Ontario 52 G6/H6 46 00N 79 00W
Nipissing, Lake Ontario 52 G6 46 17N 80 00W
Nirjutiqavvik National Wildlife Area Nunavut 65 Q6 76 00N 79 55W
Nisgara Memorial Lava Bed Park British Columbia 43 F4 55 15N 128 55W
Nisling Range *mts.* Yukon Territory 64 C3 62 00N 138 40W
Nitchequon Québec 57 E5 53 10N 70 58W
Nith River Ontario 54 B2 43 12N 80 22W
Nitinat Lake British Columbia 42 H4 48 45N 124 42W
Nitinat River British Columbia 42 H4 49 06N 124 35W
Niverville Manitoba 49 D1 49 39N 97 03W
Nobleton Ontario 54 C2 43 53N 79 39W
Nokomis Saskatchewan 47 E2 51 30N 105 00W
Nokomis Lake Saskatchewan 47 F5 56 55N 103 00W
Nootka Island British Columbia 43 G1 49 45N 126 50W
Nootka Sound British Columbia 43 G1 49 34N 126 39W
Nopiming Provincial Park Manitoba 49 E2 50 40N 95 10W
Noralee British Columbia 43 G3 53 59N 126 26W
Norman Bay *tn.* Newfoundland and Labrador 60 G6 52 55N 56 10W
Norman, Cape Newfoundland and Labrador 60 H5 51 38N 55 54W
Normandale Ontario 54 B1 42 41N 80 19W
Normansland Point Ontario 50 L7 52 00N 81 00W
Normétal Québec 57 A3 48 59N 79 53W
Norquay Saskatchewan 47 F2 51 52N 102 00W
Norris Arm *tn.* Newfoundland and Labrador 61 H4 49 05N 55 15W
Norris Point *tn.* Newfoundland and Labrador 61 G4 49 31N 57 53W
North Arm *b.* Northwest Territories 64 G3 62 05N 114 40W
North Arm *r.* British Columbia 44 F3 49 12N 123 05W
North Aulatsivik Island Newfoundland and Labrador 60 C9 59 46N 64 05W
North Battleford Saskatchewan 47 C3 52 47N 108 19W
North Bay *tn.* Ontario 52 G6 46 20N 79 28W
North, Cape Nova Scotia 61 M12 47 10N 60 00W
North Cape Prince Edward Island 61 M12 47 10N 64 00W
North Caribou Lake Ontario 50 F7 52 50N 90 40W
North Castor *r.* Ontario 59 K2 45 18N 75 31W
North Channel Ontario 52 C6/D6 46 00N 83 00W
North Cowichan British Columbia 42 H4 48 51N 123 41W
Northern Indian Lake Manitoba 49 D5 57 30N 97 30W
Northern Peninsula Newfoundland and Labrador 60 G5 50 30N 57 00W
Northern Rocky Mountains Provincial Park British Columbia 43 H6 58 00N 124 00W
Northern Woods and Water Route Canada 47 D4 54 10N 107 20W
North French River Ontario 51 L6 50 20N 81 00W
North Head *tn.* New Brunswick 61 L11 44 46N 66 45W
North Kent Island Nunavut 65 M6 76 40N 90 14W
North Knife Lake Manitoba 49 D6 58 10N 96 40W
North Knife River Manitoba 49 E6 58 40N 95 50W
North Moose Lake Manitoba 49 B4 54 00N 100 10W
North Pender Island British Columbia 42 H4 48 49N 123 17W
North River *tn.* Manitoba 49 E6 58 55N 94 30W
North River *tn.* Newfoundland and Labrador 60 F7 53 49N 57 05W
North River Bridge *tn.* Nova Scotia 61 M12 46 19N 60 40W
North Rustico Prince Edward Island 61 M12 46 26N 63 20W
North Saskatchewan River Alberta/Saskatchewan 47 D3 52 40N 106 40W
North Saugeen River Ontario 54 A3 44 18N 81 10W
North Seal River Manitoba 49 B6 59 00N 100 30W
North Spirit Lake Ontario 50 E7 52 31N 92 55W
North Spirit Lake *tn.* Ontario 50 E7 52 31N 93 01W
North Sydney Nova Scotia 61 M12 46 13N 60 15W
North Thames River Ontario 54 A2 43 02N 81 14W
North Thompson River British Columbia 43 L2 51 32N 120 00W
North Tweedsmuir Provincial Park British Columbia 43 G3 53 30N 126 30W
North Twin Island Nunavut 50 M7 53 20N 80 00W
Northumberland *admin.* New Brunswick 61 B3 47 10N 66 30W
Northumberland Strait Atlantic Provinces 61 M12 46 30N 64 30W
North Vancouver British Columbia 42 H4 49 21N 123 05W
North Wabasca Lake Alberta 46 F5 56 10N 113 55W
Northwest Angle Provincial Park Manitoba 49 E1 49 20N 95 30W
Northwest Bay *tn.* Ontario 50 E5 48 50N 93 38W
Northwest Gander River Newfoundland and Labrador 61 H4 48 30N 55 40W
Northwest Passage Territorial Park Nunavut 65 L4 68 35N 50 29W
North West River *tn.* Newfoundland and Labrador 60 E6 53 32N 60 08W
Northwest Territories *territory* 64
North York Ontario 55 C2 43 46N 79 26W
Norton New Brunswick 61 L12 45 38N 65 43W
Norway House *tn.* Manitoba 49 D3 53 59N 97 50W
Norwich Ontario 54 B1 42 59N 80 36W
Nose Creek Alberta 44 A2 51 08N 114 02W
Nose Hill Alberta 44 A2 51 06N 114 07W
Notekwin River Alberta 46 C5 56 55N 118 20W
Notre Dame Bay Newfoundland and Labrador 61 H4 49 45N 55 00W
Notre-Dame-des-Champs Ontario 59 L2 45 25N 75 28W
Nottawasaga Bay Ontario 54 B3 44 40N 80 30W
Nottawasaga River Ontario 54 C3 43 27N 79 53W
Nottingham Island Nunavut 65 Q3 63 05N 78 00W
Nova Scotia *province* 61 C1/E3
Nueltin Lake Manitoba/Nunavut 49 C6 60 00N 99 55W
Numaykoos Lake Provincial Park Manitoba 49 D5 57 55N 96 00W
Nunaksaluk Island Newfoundland and Labrador 60 E7 55 49N 60 20W
Nunavut *territory* 64/65
Nunsti Provincial Park British Columbia 43 J2 51 40N 123 50W
Nutak Newfoundland and Labrador 60 E8 57 28N 61 52W
Nut Mountain Saskatchewan 47 F3 52 20N 102 50W

O

Oakbank Manitoba 49 D1 49 57N 96 54W
Oak Bay British Columbia 42 H4 48 27N 123 18W
Oak Bluff Manitoba 48 A1 49 46N 97 18W
Oak Island Nova Scotia 61 M11 44 30N 63 55W
Oak Lake *tn.* Manitoba 49 B1 49 40N 100 45W
Oak Ridges Ontario 54 C2 44 55N 79 27W
Oakville Manitoba 49 C1 49 56N 98 00W
Oakville Ontario 54 C2 43 27N 79 41W
Oakwood Ontario 54 D3 44 20N 78 52W
Obabika River Provincial Park Ontario 51 L4 47 00N 80 30W
Obaska Québec 53 J8 48 12N 77 20W
O'Briens Landing Ontario 50 F5 49 50N 91 10W
Observatory Inlet British Columbia 42 F4 55 05N 129 59W
Ocean Falls *tn.* British Columbia 43 G3 52 24N 127 42W
Odei River Manitoba 49 C4 55 50N 98 00W
Ogidaki Mountain Ontario 51 K4 46 57N 83 59W
Ogilvie Mountains Yukon Territory 64 C4 65 05N 139 00W
Ogoki Ontario 50 J6 51 38N 85 57W
Ogoki Lake Ontario 50 H6 50 50N 87 10W
Ogoki Reservoir Ontario 50 G6 50 48N 88 18W
Ogoki River Ontario 50 H6 51 10N 86 30W
Oil Springs *tn.* Ontario 52 D2 42 47N 82 07W
Okak Bay Newfoundland and Labrador 60 D8 57 28N 62 20W
Okak Islands Newfoundland and Labrador 60 E8 57 30N 61 50W
Okanagan Lake British Columbia 43 L2 49 45N 119 32W
Okotoks Alberta 46 F2 50 44N 113 59W
Old Crow Yukon Territory 64 C4 67 34N 139 43W
Old Crow River Yukon Territory 64 C4 68 00N 140 00W
Oldman River Alberta 46 G1 49 50N 112 00W
Old Perlican Newfoundland and Labrador 61 J4 48 05N 53 01W
Olds Alberta 46 E2 51 50N 114 06W
Old Wives Lake Saskatchewan 47 D2 50 15N 106 40W
O'Leary Prince Edward Island 61 M12 46 43N 64 15W
Oliphant Ontario 54 A3 44 44N 81 16W
Oliver British Columbia 43 L1 49 10N 119 37W
Omemee Ontario 52 H4 44 19N 78 33W
Omineca Mountains British Columbia 43 G5/H4 57 15N 127 50W
Omineca Provincial Park British Columbia 43 H4 55 50N 124 45W
Omineca River British Columbia 43 H4 56 02N 126 00W
Onaman Lake Ontario 50 H6 50 00N 87 26W
Onaping Lake Ontario 51 L4 46 57N 81 30W
Ontario *province* 50
Ontario, Lake Ontario/USA 52/53 H3/K3
Ootsa Lake British Columbia 43 G3 53 40N 126 30W
Ootsa Lake *tn.* British Columbia 43 H3 53 42N 125 56W
Opasatika Ontario 51 K5 49 32N 82 52W
Opasquia Provincial Park Ontario 50 E7 53 30N 93 10W
Opeongo Lake Ontario 51 M3 45 42N 78 23W
Opinnagau River Ontario 50 K8 54 20N 83 50W
Orangeville Ontario 54 B2 43 55N 80 06W
Orillia Ontario 54 C3 44 36N 79 26W
Orleans Ontario 59 K2 45 28N 75 34W
Ormand's Creek *tn.* Manitoba 48 A2 49 58N 97 16W
Ormatown Québec 53 M5 45 08N 74 02W
Oromocto New Brunswick 61 B2 45 50N 66 28W
Orono Ontario 54 D2 43 59N 78 36W
Oshawa Ontario 54 D2 43 53N 78 51W
Oskélanéo Québec 53 L8 48 07N 75 14W
Osler Saskatchewan 47 D3 52 22N 106 32W
Osoyoos British Columbia 43 L1 49 00N 119 29W
Ospika River British Columbia 43 J5 56 55N 124 10W
Ossokmanuan Reservoir Newfoundland and Labrador 60 C6 53 25N 65 00W
Otoskwin-Attawapiskat Provincial Park Ontario 50 G6 52 15N 88 00W
Otoskwin River Ontario 50 G6 51 50N 89 40W
Ottawa Ontario 53 L5 45 24N 75 38W
Ottawa-Carleton *admin.* Ontario 53 L5 45 31N 75 22W
Ottawa Islands Nunavut 65 P2 59 10N 80 25W
Ottawa River Ontario/Québec 53 K5 45 34N 76 30W
Otter Lake Saskatchewan 47 E4 55 35N 104 30W
Otter Rapids *tn.* Ontario 51 L6 50 12N 81 40W
Outer Harbour East Headland Ontario 55 C1 43 38N 79 19W
Outlook Saskatchewan 47 D2 51 30N 107 03W
Owen Sound Ontario 54 B3 44 38N 80 56W
Owen Sound *tn.* Ontario 54 B3 44 34N 80 56W
Owl River Manitoba 49 F5 57 50N 93 20W
Oxbow Saskatchewan 47 F1 49 16N 102 12W
Oxford Nova Scotia 61 M12 45 43N 63 52W
Oxford *admin.* Ontario 54 B2 43 06N 80 59W
Oxford House *tn.* Manitoba 49 E4 54 58N 95 17W
Oxford Lake Manitoba 49 E4 54 40N 95 50W
Oyen Alberta 46 G2 51 22N 110 28W
Oyster River British Columbia 42 G4 49 50N 125 42W
Ozhiski Lake Ontario 50 G7 52 01N 88 30W

P

Pacific Rim National Park Reserve British Columbia 42 G4 48 52N 125 35W
Packs Harbour *tn.* Newfoundland and Labrador 60 G6 53 51N 56 59W
Pacquet Newfoundland and Labrador 61 H4 49 59N 55 53W
Paddle Prairie *tn.* Alberta 46 D5 57 57N 117 29W
Paint Lake Provincial Park Manitoba 49 D4 55 30N 97 40W
Paisley Ontario 54 A3 44 17N 81 16W
Pakashkan Lake Ontario 50 F5 49 21N 90 15W
Pakowki Lake Alberta 46 G1 49 20N 111 55W
Pakwash Lake Ontario 50 E6 50 45N 93 30W
Palmerston Ontario 54 B2 43 50N 80 50W
Panache Lake Ontario 52 E6 46 15N 81 20W
Panmure Island Prince Edward Island 61 M12 46 10N 62 30W
Panniqtuuq *(Pangnirtung)* Nunavut 65 S4 66 05N 65 45W
Papineau *admin.* Québec 53 L5 45 40N 75 30W
Paradise Hill *tn.* Saskatchewan 47 C3 53 32N 109 26W
Paradise River Newfoundland and Labrador 60 G6 52 50N 57 50W
Paradise River *tn.* Newfoundland and Labrador 60 G6 53 27N 57 17W
Parc de Conservation du Saguenay Québec 53 R8 48 15N 70 45W
Parc de la Gatineau Québec 53 K5 45 31N 75 53W
Parc de Récréation des Îles-de-Boucherville Québec 58 P5 45 36N 73 27W
Parc Marin du Saguenay–Saint-Laurent Québec 57 F3 48 00N 69 38W
Parc National d'Aiguebelle Québec 57 A3 48 30N 78 50W
Parc National d'Anticosti Québec 57 H3/J3 49 25N 62 58W
Parc National de Forillon Québec 57 H3 49 00N 64 00W
Parc National de Frontenac Québec 53 Q5 45 52N 71 17W
Parc National de la Gaspésie Québec 57 G3 48 52N 65 57W
Parc National de la Jacques-Cartier Québec 53 Q7 47 23N 71 30W
Parc National de la Mauricie Québec 53 N6/P6 46 50N 73 05W
Parc National des Grands-Jardins Québec 53 R7 47 47N 70 59W
Parc National des Pingualuit Québec 56 D9 61 25N 73 30W
Parc National du Mont-Tremblant Québec 53 M6 46 20N 74 43W
Parc québecois d'Oka Québec 58 M4 45 24N 73 58W
Parent Québec 53 M7 47 55N 74 36W
Paris Ontario 54 B2 43 12N 80 25W
Parke Lake Newfoundland and Labrador 60 F6 53 10N 58 50W
Parkhill Ontario 54 A2 43 10N 81 41W
Parksville British Columbia 42 H4 49 20N 124 19W
Parrsboro Nova Scotia 61 M12 45 25N 64 21W
Parry Island Ontario 52 F5 45 17N 80 11W
Parry Islands Northwest Territories/Nunavut 64 H6 75 30N 110 00W
Parry Sound *admin.* Ontario 52 F5/G5 45 22N 80 08W
Parry Sound *tn.* Ontario 52 F5 45 21N 80 03W
Parson's Pond *tn.* Newfoundland and Labrador 61 G5 50 02N 57 43W
Pasadena Newfoundland and Labrador 61 G4 49 01N 57 36W
Pasfield Lake Saskatchewan 47 E6 58 20N 105 45W
Pasqui Hills Saskatchewan 47 F3 53 10N 103 00W
Pass Lake Ontario 51 G5 48 34N 88 44W
Pattullo, Mount British Columbia 42 F5 56 15N 129 43W
Patuanak Saskatchewan 47 D4 55 53N 107 38W
Paudash Ontario 52 J4 44 56N 78 04W
Paulatuuq *(Paulatuk)* Northwest Territories 64 F4 69 49N 123 59W
Paul Island Newfoundland and Labrador 60 E8 56 30N 61 25W
Payne Bay Québec 56 F8 60 00N 70 01W

Peace Point *tn.* Alberta 46 F6 59 07N 112 27W
Peace River Alberta 46 E6 58 40N 114 30W
Peace River *tn.* Alberta 46 D5 56 15N 117 18W
Peachland British Columbia 43 L1 49 49N 119 48W
Peary Channel Nunavut 65 K6 79 40N 101 30W
Peawanuk Ontario 50 J8 55 00N 85 30W
Pedzéh Kį *(Wrigley)* Northwest Territories 64 F3 63 16N 123 39W
Peel *admin.* Ontario 54 C2 43 49N 79 57W
Peel River Yukon Territory 64 C4 66 05N 136 00W
Peel River Game Reserve Northwest Territories 64 D4 66 30N 134 00W
Peel Sound Nunavut 65 L5 73 15N 96 30W
Peerless Lake Alberta 46 E5 56 40N 114 35W
Pefferlaw Ontario 54 C3 44 18N 79 14W
Pefferlaw Brook Ontario 54 C3 44 10N 79 15W
Peggys Cove *tn.* Nova Scotia 61 M11 44 30N 63 50W
Pelee Island Ontario 52 D1 41 47N 82 40W
Pelee Island *tn.* Ontario 52 D1 41 45N 82 40W
Pelee Point Ontario 52 D1 41 45N 82 39W
Pelham Ontario 54 C2 43 02N 79 19W
Pelican Bay Manitoba 49 B3 52 40N 100 30W
Pelican Lake Manitoba 49 B3 52 30N 100 30W
Pelican Mountains Alberta 46 E4 55 35N 114 00W
Pelican Narrows *tn.* Saskatchewan 47 F4 55 12N 102 55W
Pelly Bay Nunavut 65 N4 68 53N 89 51W
Pelly Crossing Yukon Territory 64 C3 62 48N 136 30W
Pelly Mountains Yukon Territory 64 D3 62 10N 134 10W
Pelly Point British Columbia 44 F3 49 06N 123 13W
Pelly River Yukon Territory 64 D3 62 30N 134 50W
Pemberton British Columbia 42 H5 50 19N 122 49W
Pembina Alberta 46 E3 53 08N 115 09W
Pembina River Alberta 46 E3 53 15N 116 05W
Pembina River Manitoba 49 C1 49 10N 99 10W
Pembroke Ontario 53 J5 45 49N 77 08W
Penetanguishene Ontario 52 G4 44 47N 79 56W
Penhold Alberta 46 F3 52 08N 113 52W
Péninsule de la Gaspésie *p.* Québec 57 H3 48 30N 65 30W
Péninsule d'Ungava *p.* Québec 56 C8/C9 60 50N 76 00W
Penticton British Columbia 43 L1 49 30N 119 38W
Percé Québec 57 H3 48 32N 64 14W
Percé, Cape Nova Scotia 61 N12 46 10N 59 40W
Perdue Saskatchewan 47 D3 52 05N 107 33W
Perrault Falls *tn.* Ontario 50 E6 50 20N 93 08W
Perry Island *tn.* Nunavut 65 K4 67 48N 102 33W
Perth Ontario 53 K4 44 54N 76 15W
Perth *admin.* Ontario 54 A2 43 22N 81 10W
Perth Andover New Brunswick 61 B3 46 45N 67 42W
Petawawa Ontario 53 J5 45 54N 77 17W
Peterborough Ontario 52 H4 44 19N 78 20W
Peterborough *admin.* Ontario 52 H4 44 40N 78 30W
Peter Pond Lake Saskatchewan 47 C5 56 00N 108 50W
Petitcodiac New Brunswick 61 L12 45 57N 65 11W
Petite Rivière *tn.* Nova Scotia 61 M11 44 15N 64 25W
Petite Rivière de la Baleine *r.* Québec 56 C6 55 55N 75 58W
Petit Étang Nova Scotia 61 M12 46 39N 61 00W
Petit Jardin Nova Scotia 61 F4 48 28N 59 14W
Petit Lac de Loups Marins *l.* Québec 56 D7 56 30N 73 30W
Petit Lac Manicouagan *l.* Québec 57 G4 52 10N 67 40W
Petitot River British Columbia 43 K6 59 55N 122 15W
Petitsikapau Lake Newfoundland and Labrador 60 B7 54 37N 66 25W
Petre, Point Ontario 53 J3 43 50N 77 09W
Petrolia Ontario 52 D2 42 52N 82 09W
Phelps Lake Saskatchewan 47 F6 59 20N 102 55W
Philpots Island Nunavut 65 Q5 74 57N 79 58W
Pickerel Lake Ontario 51 F5 48 37N 91 19W
Pickering Ontario 54 C2 43 48N 79 11W
Pickering Village Ontario 54 C2 43 51N 79 02W
Pickle Lake *tn.* Ontario 50 F6 51 28N 90 12W
Pic River Ontario 51 H5 48 50N 86 20W
Picton Ontario 53 J4 44 00N 77 07W
Pictou Nova Scotia 61 M12 45 41N 62 42W
Pictou *admin.* Nova Scotia 61 M12 45 30N 62 40W
Pictou Island Nova Scotia 61 M12 45 41N 62 42W
Picture Butte *tn.* Alberta 46 F1 49 53N 112 47W
Pie Island Ontario 51 G5 48 15N 89 06W
Pierceland Saskatchewan 47 C4 54 20N 109 40W
Pigeon Lake Alberta 46 E3 53 01N 114 02W
Pigeon River Manitoba 49 D3 52 10N 96 50W
Pigeon River Ontario 54 D3 44 13N 78 42W
Pikangikum *I.R.* Ontario 50 E6 51 48N 93 59W
Pikangikum Lake Ontario 50 E6 51 48N 94 00W
Pikwitonei Manitoba 49 D4 55 35N 97 11W
Pilot Butte *tn.* Saskatchewan 47 E2 50 29N 104 29W
Pilot Mound *tn.* Manitoba 49 C1 49 13N 98 52W
Pinawa Manitoba 49 E2 50 13N 95 56W
Pincher Creek *tn.* Alberta 46 F1 49 29N 113 57W
Pinchi Lake British Columbia 43 H4 54 36N 124 25W
Pinecone Burke Provincial Park British Columbia 42 H4 49 30N 122 40W
Pine Falls *tn.* Manitoba 49 D2 50 33N 96 14W
Pinehouse Lake Saskatchewan 47 D4 55 35N 106 50W
Pinehouse Lake *tn.* Saskatchewan 47 D4 55 31N 106 36W
Pineimuta River Ontario 50 F7 52 10N 90 40W
Pine Le Moray Provincial Park British Columbia 43 J4 55 20N 122 30W
Pine Pass British Columbia 43 J4 55 30N 122 25W
Pine River British Columbia 43 K4 55 50N 121 50W
Pine River Ontario 54 B3 44 18N 80 06W
Pinery Provincial Park Ontario 52 E3 43 16N 81 50W
Pinsent Arm Newfoundland and Labrador 60 H6 52 41N 55 53W
Pinto Butte *mt.* Saskatchewan 47 B1 49 21N 107 25W
Pinware Newfoundland and Labrador 60 G5 51 37N 56 42W
Pipestone River Ontario 50 F7 52 20N 90 10W
Pipestone River Provincial Park Ontario 50 G7 52 55N 90 00W
Pistolet Bay Newfoundland and Labrador 60 H5 51 35N 55 45W
Pitman River British Columbia 43 G6 58 00N 128 15W
Pitt Island British Columbia 42 F3 53 38N 129 59W
Pitt Lake British Columbia 42 H4 49 25N 122 33W
Pitt Meadows *tn.* British Columbia 42 H4 49 13N 122 42W
Pitt River British Columbia 42 H4 49 42N 122 40W
Placentia Newfoundland and Labrador 61 J3 47 14N 53 58W
Placentia Bay Newfoundland and Labrador 61 H3 47 00N 54 30W
Plamondon Alberta 46 F4 54 51N 112 20W
Plantagenet Ontario 53 L5 45 32N 75 00W
Plaster Rock *tn.* New Brunswick 61 B3 46 55N 67 24W
Playgreen Lake Manitoba 49 C3 53 50N 98 10W
Pleasant Bay *tn.* Nova Scotia 61 M12 46 50N 60 48W
Pledger Lake Ontario 51 K6 50 53N 83 42W
Plum Coulee Manitoba 49 D1 49 12N 97 45W
Plum Point *tn.* Newfoundland and Labrador 60 G5 51 04N 56 53W
Pohénégamook Québec 53 S7 47 28N 69 17W
Pointe au Baril Station *tn.* Ontario 52 F5 45 36N 80 22W
Pointe aux Pins Ontario 52 E2 42 29N 84 28W
Pointe-aux-Trembles Québec 58 N5 45 38N 73 30W
Pointe de l'Est *c.* Québec 57 K3 49 00N 64 00W
Pointe Louis-XIV *c.* Québec 65 P1 54 38N 79 45W
Point Farms Provincial Park Ontario 54 A2 43 48N 81 42W
Point Lake Northwest Territories 64 H4 65 15N 113 04W
Point Pelee National Park Ontario 52 D1 41 57N 82 31W
Points North Landing Saskatchewan 47 E6 58 20N 104 10W
Polar Bear Provincial Park Ontario 50 J8 54 50N 84 30W
Pomquet Nova Scotia 61 M12 45 34N 61 50W
Pond Inlet Nunavut 65 Q5 72 41N 78 00W
Ponhook Lake Nova Scotia 61 M11 44 50N 64 10W
Ponoka Alberta 46 F3 52 42N 113 33W
Ponteix Saskatchewan 47 D1 49 45N 107 20W
Pontiac *admin.* Québec 52 K6 46 28N 77 40W
Pont Rouge Québec 53 Q5 46 45N 71 43W
Pont-Viau Québec 58 N5 45 33N 73 41W
Poplar Hill *tn.* Ontario 50 D7 52 05N 94 18W
Poplar/Nanowin Rivers Park Reserve Manitoba 49 D3 53 00N 96 50W
Poplar River Manitoba 49 D3 52 50N 97 00W
Porcher Island British Columbia 42 E3 54 00N 130 30W
Porcupine, Cape Newfoundland and Labrador 60 G6 53 56N 57 08W
Porcupine Hills Manitoba/Saskatchewan 47 G3 52 30N 101 40W
Porcupine Plain *tn.* Saskatchewan 47 F3 52 36N 103 15W
Porcupine Provincial Forest Manitoba 49 B3 52 30N 101 20W
Portabello Nova Scotia 59 Q6 44 44N 63 32W
Portage Prince Edward Island 61 M12 46 42N 64 08W
Portage la Prairie Manitoba 49 C1 49 58N 98 20W
Port Alberni British Columbia 42 H4 49 11N 124 49W
Port Alice British Columbia 43 G2 50 23N 127 24W
Port au Choix Newfoundland and Labrador 61 G5 50 43N 57 22W
Port au Port Peninsula Newfoundland and Labrador 61 F4 48 35N 59 00W
Port Bickerton *tn.* Nova Scotia 61 M12 45 10N 61 40W
Port Blandford *tn.* Newfoundland and Labrador 61 H4 48 21N 54 10W
Port Bruce Ontario 54 A1 42 40N 81 00W
Port Bruce Provincial Park Ontario 54 A1 42 40N 81 00W
Port Burwell Ontario 54 B1 42 39N 80 47W
Port Burwell Provincial Park Ontario 54 B1 42 40N 80 45W
Port Carling Ontario 52 G5 45 07N 79 35W
Port Cartier Québec 57 G4 50 02N 66 58W
Port Clements British Columbia 42 D3 53 41N 132 11W
Port Colborne Ontario 54 C1 42 53N 79 16W
Port Coquitlam British Columbia 42 H4 49 16N 122 45W
Port Credit Ontario 54 C2 43 33N 79 36W
Port Dover Ontario 54 B1 42 47N 80 12W
Port Edward British Columbia 42 E4 54 11N 130 16W
Port Elgin New Brunswick 61 M12 46 03N 64 08W
Port Elgin Ontario 54 A3 44 25N 81 23W
Porter Lake Saskatchewan 47 D5 56 20N 107 10W
Port Essington British Columbia 42 F4 54 08N 129 58W
Port Hammond British Columbia 44 H3 49 12N 122 40W
Port Hardy British Columbia 43 G2 50 37N 127 15W
Port Hawkesbury Nova Scotia 61 M12 45 36N 61 22W
Port Hood Nova Scotia 61 M12 46 00N 61 32W
Port Hope Ontario 51 M2 43 58N 78 18W
Port Hope Simpson Newfoundland and Labrador 60 G6 52 33N 56 18W
Port Kells British Columbia 44 H3 49 09N 122 43W
Portland Inlet British Columbia 42 E4 54 40N 130 30W
Port Lorne Nova Scotia 61 L11 44 50N 65 20W
Port McNeill British Columbia 43 G2 50 30N 127 01W
Port Maitland Nova Scotia 61 L11 43 59N 66 04W
Port Maitland Ontario 54 C1 42 51N 79 33W
Port Mellon British Columbia 42 H4 49 31N 123 30W
Port Menier Québec 57 H3 49 50N 64 20W
Port Moody British Columbia 42 H4 49 13N 122 57W
Port Mouton Nova Scotia 61 M11 43 58N 64 50W
Port Nelson Manitoba 49 F5 57 10N 92 35W
Portneuf *admin.* Québec 53 P7 46 50N 72 20W
Port Perry Ontario 54 D3 44 06N 78 58W
Port Renfrew British Columbia 42 H4 48 00N 124 00W
Port Rowan Ontario 54 B1 42 38N 80 27W
Port Royal Nova Scotia 61 L11 44 45N 65 40W
Port Saunders Newfoundland and Labrador 61 G5 50 39N 57 18W
Port Stanley Ontario 54 A1 42 40N 81 14W
Postville Newfoundland and Labrador 60 F7 54 54N 59 47W
Pouce Coupé British Columbia 43 K4 55 40N 120 08W
Pouch Cove *tn.* Newfoundland and Labrador 61 J3 47 46N 52 46W
Powassan Ontario 52 G6 46 05N 79 22W
Powell Lake British Columbia 42 H5 50 08N 124 26W
Powell River *tn.* British Columbia 42 H4 49 54N 124 34W
Powerview Manitoba 49 D2 50 30N 96 10W
Preeceville Saskatchewan 47 F2 51 58N 102 40W
Prescott Ontario 53 L4 44 43N 75 33W
Prescott and Russell *admin.* Ontario 53 M5 45 30N 74 45W
Preston Nova Scotia 59 R6 44 41N 63 26W
Preston Ontario 54 B2 43 23N 80 21W
Price Island British Columbia 43 F3 52 25N 128 40W
Prim, Point Prince Edward Island 61 M12 46 10N 63 00W
Primrose Lake Saskatchewan 47 C4 54 50N 109 30W
Primrose Lake Air Weapons Range Saskatchewan 47 C4 55 00N 109 00W
Prince *admin.* Prince Edward Island 61 M12 46 30N 64 00W
Prince Albert Saskatchewan 47 E3 53 13N 105 45W
Prince Albert National Park Saskatchewan 47 D3/D4 54 00N 106 00W
Prince Albert Peninsula Northwest Territories 64 H5 72 30N 117 00W
Prince Albert Sound Northwest Territories 64 G5 70 15N 117 30W
Prince Alfred, Cape Northwest Territories 64 F5 74 20N 124 46W
Prince Charles Island Nunavut 65 Q4 67 40N 77 00W
Prince Edward Island *province* 61 M12
Prince Edward Island National Park Prince Edward Island 61 M12 46 10N 63 10W
Prince George British Columbia 43 J3 53 55N 122 49W
Prince Gustaf Adolf Sea Nunavut 65 J6 78 30N 107 00W
Prince of Wales Icefield Nunavut 65 Q6 78 00N 80 00W
Prince of Wales Island Nunavut 65 L5 73 00N 98 00W
Prince of Wales Strait Northwest Territories 64 G5 71 00N 119 50W
Prince Patrick Island Northwest Territories 64 G6 77 00N 120 00W
Prince Regent Inlet Nunavut 65 M5 72 40N 91 00W
Prince Rupert British Columbia 42 E4 54 09N 130 20W
Princess Margaret Range *mts.* Nunavut 65 M6 81 00N 92 30W
Princess Royal Island British Columbia 43 F3 53 04N 129 00W
Princeton British Columbia 43 K1 49 25N 120 35W
Princeville Québec 53 Q6 46 10N 71 52W
Prophet River British Columbia 43 J6 58 20N 123 00W
Prophet River *tn.* British Columbia 43 J6 58 20N 122 50W
Provost Alberta 46 G3 52 21N 110 16W
Pubnico Nova Scotia 61 L11 43 42N 65 48W
Pugwash Nova Scotia 61 M12 45 52N 63 40W
Pukaskwa National Park Ontario 51 J5 48 20N 85 40W
Pukatawagan Manitoba 49 B4 55 46N 101 14W
Pukeashun Mountain British Columbia 43 L2 51 12N 119 14W
Purcell Mountains British Columbia 43 M2 50 58N 116 59W
Purcell's Cove *tn.* Nova Scotia 59 Q6 44 35N 63 33W
Purcell Wilderness Conservancy British Columbia 43 M2 50 00N 116 00W
Purtuniq Québec 56 D9 61 52N 74 00W
Puvirnituq Québec 56 B9 59 45N 77 20W

Q

Qamanittuaq *(Baker Lake)* *tn.* Nunavut 65 L3 64 20N 96 10W
Qaummaarviit Territorial Park Nunavut 65 S3 63 45N 69 00W
Qausuittuq *(Resolute)* Nunavut 65 M5 74 40N 95 00W
Qikiqtarjuaq *(Broughton Island)* Nunavut 65 T4 67 40N 63 50W
Quadra Island British Columbia 42 G5 50 11N 125 20W
Qualicum Beach *tn.* British Columbia 42 H4 49 21N 124 27W
Qu'Appelle Saskatchewan 47 F2 50 33N 103 54W
Qu'Appelle Dam Saskatchewan 47 D2 50 55N 106 20W
Qu'Appelle River Saskatchewan 47 F2 50 30N 102 20W
Quaqtaq Québec 56 F9 61 00N 69 40W
Quathiaski Cove *tn.* British Columbia 42 G5 50 03N 125 11W
Quatsino Sound British Columbia 43 G2 50 25N 128 55W
Québec Québec 53 Q6 46 49N 71 13W
Québec *admin.* Québec 53 P7/Q7 47 50N 72 30W
Québec *province* 56/57
Queen Bess, Mount British Columbia 43 H2 51 13N 124 35W
Queen Charlotte British Columbia 42 D3 53 18N 132 04W
Queen Charlotte Islands British Columbia 42 D3/E3 53 30N 131 50W
Queen Charlotte Sound British Columbia 43 F2 51 48N 129 25W
Queen Charlotte Strait British Columbia 43 G2 51 00N 127 55W
Queen Elizabeth Foreland Nunavut 65 T3 62 23N 64 28W
Queen Elizabeth Islands Northwest Territories 64 G6 77 30N 120 00W
Queen Maud Gulf Nunavut 65 K4 68 00N 101 00W
Queen Maud Gulf Migratory Bird Sanctuary Nunavut 65 K4 67 30N 103 20W
Queens *admin.* New Brunswick 61 C3 45 50N 65 50W
Queens *admin.* Nova Scotia 61 L11 44 10N 65 10W
Queens *admin.* Prince Edward Island 61 M12 46 20N 63 10W
Queenston Ontario 54 C2 43 09N 79 03W
Queenswood Heights Ontario 59 L2 45 28N 75 29W
Quesnel British Columbia 43 J3 53 03N 122 31W
Quesnel Lake British Columbia 43 K3 52 30N 121 20W
Quesnel River British Columbia 43 J3 52 58N 122 29W
Quetico Provincial Park Ontario 51 F5 48 30N 91 30W
Quill Lake *tn.* Saskatchewan 47 E3 52 03N 104 12W
Quill Lakes Saskatchewan 47 E2 52 03N 104 12W
Quince, Bay of Ontario 53 J4 44 07N 77 32W
Quirke Lake Ontario 51 K4 46 28N 82 33W
Quispamsis New Brunswick 61 L12 45 25N 65 55W
Quoich River Nunavut 65 M3 64 50N 94 40W
Quttinirpaaq National Park Nunavut 65 R7 82 00N 72 30W

R

Raanes Peninsula Nunavut 65 N6 78 30N 85 45W
Rabbit Lake Mine Saskatchewan 47 F2 58 10N 103 42W
Rabbit River British Columbia 43 G6 59 20N 127 20W
Race, Cape Nova Scotia 61 J3 46 39N 53 04W
Rádeyįlįkóé *(Fort Good Hope)* Northwest Territories 64 E4 66 16N 128 37W
Radisson Québec 57 B5 53 43N 77 46W
Radisson Saskatchewan 47 D3 52 27N 107 24W
Radium Hot Springs British Columbia 43 L2 50 39N 116 09W
Radville Saskatchewan 47 E1 49 28N 104 19W
Rae Northwest Territories 64 G3 62 50N 116 03W
Rae River Nunavut 64 G4 68 10N 116 50W
Rae Strait Nunavut 65 L4 68 50N 95 00W
Ragged Lake Nova Scotia 59 Q6 44 37N 63 39W
Rainbow Lake Alberta 46 C6 58 17N 119 16W
Rainbow Lake *tn.* Alberta 46 C6 58 30N 119 23W
Rainy Lake Ontario 50 E5 48 00N 93 00W
Rainy River Ontario 50 D5 48 40N 94 10W
Rainy River *tn.* Ontario 50 D5 48 44N 94 33W
Ralston Alberta 46 G2 50 15N 111 10W
Ralz, Mount British Columbia 42 D5 57 24N 132 19W
Ramah Newfoundland and Labrador 60 D9 58 50N 63 12W
Ramea Newfoundland and Labrador 61 G3 47 31N 57 23W
Ramea Islands Newfoundland and Labrador 61 G3 47 31N 57 22W
Ramsey Lake Ontario 51 K4 47 13N 82 15W
Rankin Inlet Nunavut 65 M3 62 45N 92 05W
Rapide-Blanc-Station Québec 53 N7 47 00N 73 00W
Rapide-des-Cèdres Québec 57 B3 49 00N 77 09W
Rapides de Lachine Québec 58 N4 45 26N 73 39W
Rat Lake Manitoba 49 C5 56 10N 99 40W
Rat River Manitoba 49 C5 56 10N 99 20W
Ray, Cape Newfoundland and Labrador 61 F3 47 37N 59 19W
Raymond Alberta 46 F1 49 27N 112 39W
Raymore Saskatchewan 47 E2 51 24N 104 32W
Razorback *mt.* British Columbia 43 H2 51 28N 124 35W
Read Island British Columbia 42 G5 50 11N 125 05W
Red Bay *tn.* Newfoundland and Labrador 60 G5 51 44N 56 25W
Red Bay *tn.* Ontario 54 A3 44 47N 81 19W
Redberry Lake Saskatchewan 47 D3 52 45N 107 20W
Redcliff Alberta 46 G2 50 05N 110 47W
Red Deer Alberta 46 F3 52 15N 113 48W
Red Deer Lake Manitoba 49 B3 52 50N 101 30W
Red Deer River Alberta 46 F2 51 20N 112 35W

Red Deer River Saskatchewan 47 F3 52 50N 103 05W
Red Earth Creek *tn.* Alberta 46 E5 56 33N 115 15W
Redfern-Keily Creek Provincial Park British Columbia 43 J5 57 25N 124 00W
Red Indian Lake Newfoundland and Labrador 61 G4 48 40N 57 10W
Red Lake Ontario 50 E6 51 10N 93 50W
Red Lake *tn.* Ontario 50 E6 51 01N 93 50W
Red Lake Road *tn.* Ontario 50 E5 49 59N 93 22W
Redonda Island British Columbia 42 H5 50 15N 124 50W
Red River British Columbia 43 F6 59 23N 128 14W
Red River Manitoba 49 D1 49 30N 97 20W
Red Rock Ontario 51 G5 48 55N 88 15W
Redstone River Northwest Territories 64 E3 63 47N 128 00W
Red Sucker Lake Manitoba 49 F4 54 10N 94 10W
Red Sucker Lake *tn.* Manitoba 49 F4 54 11N 93 34W
Redvers Saskatchewan 47 G1 49 34N 101 42W
Redwater Alberta 46 F3 53 57N 113 06W
Red Wine River Newfoundland and Labrador 60 E7 54 10N 62 00W
Reed Lake Manitoba 49 B4 54 30N 100 10W
Refuge Cove *tn.* British Columbia 42 H5 50 07N 124 51W
Regina Saskatchewan 47 E2 50 30N 104 38W
Regina Beach *tn.* Saskatchewan 47 E2 50 49N 105 00W
Reindeer Grazing Reserve Northwest Territories 64 D4 69 00N 132 00W
Reindeer Island Manitoba 49 D3 52 30N 97 20W
Reindeer Lake Saskatchewan/Manitoba 47 F5 57 30N 102 30W
Reindeer River Saskatchewan 47 F5 56 10N 103 10W
Reliance Northwest Territories 64 J3 62 42N 109 08W
Renews Newfoundland and Labrador 61 J3 46 56N 52 56W
Renfrew Ontario 53 K5 45 28N 76 44W
Renfrew *admin.* Ontario 53 J5/K5 45 28N 76 41W
Rennie Lake Northwest Territories 64 J3 61 32N 105 35W
Repentigny Québec 53 N5 45 44N 73 27W
Réserve de la Rivière Matamec Québec 57 H4 50 30N 65 30W
Réserve du Parc National de l'Archipelago de Mingan Québec 57 J4 50 10N 62 30W
Réserve Faunique Ashuapmushuan Québec 57 D3 49 00N 73 30W
Réserve Faunique Assinica Québec 57 C4 50 48N 75 40W
Réserve Faunique Duchénier Québec 57 F3 48 08N 68 40W
Réserve Faunique de Dunière Québec 57 G3 48 30N 66 40W
Réserve Faunique de Matane Québec 57 G3 48 45N 67 00W
Réserve Faunique de Papineau-Labelle Québec 53 L6 46 20N 75 21W
Réserve Faunique de Port-Cartier–Sept-Îles Québec 57 G4 50 30N 67 30W
Réserve Faunique de Portneuf Québec 53 P7 47 10N 72 20W
Réserve Faunique de Port-Daniel Québec 57 H3 48 13N 65 00W
Réserve Faunique de Rimouski Québec 57 F3 48 00N 68 20W
Réserve Faunique des Chic-Chocs Québec 57 H3 49 10N 65 10W
Réserve Faunique des Laurentides Québec 53 Q7 47 50N 71 47W
Réserve Faunique des Lacs-Albanel-Mistassini-et-Waconichi Québec 57 C4 50 10N 74 20W
Réserve Faunique du Saint-Maurice Québec 53 N7 47 08N 73 18W
Réserve Faunique la Vérendrye Québec 53 J7/K7 47 08N 73 18W
Réserve Faunique Mastigouche Québec 53 N6 46 35N 73 47W
Réserve Faunique Rouge-Matawin Québec 53 M6 46 52N 74 35W
Réservoir Baskatong *res.* Québec 53 L6 47 00N 76 00W
Réservoir Blanc *res.* Québec 53 N7 47 49N 73 06W
Réservoir Cabonga *res.* Québec 53 K7 47 31N 76 45W
Réservoir Caniapiscau *res.* Québec 56 F6 54 10N 69 10W
Réservoir de La Grande 2 *res.* Québec 57 B5 53 38N 78 40W
Réservoir de La Grande 3 *res.* Québec 56 C5 54 10N 72 30W
Réservoir de La Grande 4 *res.* Québec 56 D5 53 59N 72 50W
Réservoir Dozois *res.* Québec 53 J7 47 30N 77 26W
Réservoir du Poisson Blanc *res.* Québec 53 L6 46 05N 75 50W
Réservoir Eastmain 1 *res.* Québec 57 C5 52 10N 75 45W
Réservoir Evans *res.* Québec 57 B4 50 45N 76 50W
Réservoir Gouin *res.* Québec 57 C3 48 30N 74 00W
Réservoir Kiamika *res.* Québec 53 L6 46 40N 75 05W
Réservoir Laforge 1 *res.* Québec 56 E6 54 20N 71 50W
Réservoir Laforge 2 *res.* Québec 56 E6 54 30N 71 20W
Réservoir Manic 2 *res.* Québec 57 F3 49 30N 68 25W
Réservoir Manic 3 *res.* Québec 57 F4 50 00N 68 40W
Réservoir Manicouagan *res.* Québec 57 F4 51 00N 58 00W
Réservoir Opinaca *res.* Québec 57 B5 52 30N 75 30W
Réservoir Outardes 4 *res.* Québec 57 F4 50 20N 69 20W
Réservoir Pipmuacan *res.* Québec 57 E3 49 30N 70 10W
Réservoir Soscumica-Matagami *res.* Québec 57 B4 50 10N 77 32W
Réservoir Taureau *res.* Québec 53 N6 46 47N 73 47W
Resolution Island Nunavut 65 T3 61 18N 64 53W
Restigouche *admin.* New Brunswick 61 B3 47 40N 67 10W
Restigouche River New Brunswick 61 B3 47 35N 67 30W
Reston Manitoba 49 B1 49 33N 101 05W
Revelstoke British Columbia 43 L2 51 02N 118 12W
Revelstoke, Lake British Columbia 43 L2 51 32N 118 40W
Rexton New Brunswick 61 C3 46 41N 64 56W
Ribstone Creek Alberta 46 G3 52 10N 111 55W
Rice Lake Ontario 52 H4 44 12N 78 10W
Richard Collinson Inlet Northwest Territories 64 H5 72 45N 113 55W
Richards Island Northwest Territories 64 C4 69 20N 134 30W
Richardson Mountains Yukon Territory/Northwest Territories 64 C4 67 50N 137 00W
Richardson River Alberta 46 G6 58 15N 110 55W
Rich, Cape Ontario 54 B3 44 43N 80 39W
Richibucto New Brunswick 61 C3 46 42N 64 54W
Richmond British Columbia 42 H4 49 09N 123 09W
Richmond Québec 53 P5 45 40N 72 10W
Richmond *admin.* Nova Scotia 61 M12 45 40N 60 40W
Richmond *admin.* Québec 53 P5 45 30N 72 10W
Richmond Hill *tn.* Ontario 54 C2 43 53N 79 26W
Rideau River Ontario 51 P3 44 50N 76 00W
Rideau River and Canal Ontario 59 K2 45 16N 75 43W
Ridgetown Ontario 52 E2 42 26N 81 54W
Riding Mountain Manitoba 49 B2 50 40N 100 40W
Riding Mountain National Park Manitoba 49 B2 50 50N 100 30W
Rigolet Newfoundland and Labrador 60 F7 54 11N 58 26W
Rimbey Alberta 46 E3 52 38N 114 41W
Rimouski Québec 57 F3 48 27N 68 32W
Riondel British Columbia 43 M1 49 46N 116 51W
Riou Lake Saskatchewan 47 D6 59 00N 106 30W
Ripley Ontario 54 A3 44 04N 81 34W
River Herbert *tn.* Nova Scotia 61 M12 45 42N 64 25W
River John *tn.* Nova Scotia 61 M12 45 44N 63 03W
Rivers *tn.* Manitoba 49 B2 50 02N 100 14W
Riverside-Albert New Brunswick 61 M12 45 40N 64 40W
Rivers Inlet British Columbia 43 G2 51 30N 127 30W
Riverton Manitoba 49 D2 51 00N 97 00W
Riverview New Brunswick 61 M12 46 06N 64 51W
Rivière Aguanus *r.* Québec 57 J4 51 15N 62 05W
Rivière à la Baleine *r.* Québec 56 G7 57 00N 67 40W
Rivière à l'Argent *r.* Québec 57 F4 50 30N 69 40W
Rivière Arnaud *r.* Québec 56 D8 59 37N 72 55W
Rivière Ashuapmushuan *r.* Québec 57 D3 49 22N 73 25W
Rivière aux Feuilles *r.* Québec 56 D8 57 45N 73 00W
Rivière aux Mélèzes *r.* Québec 56 D7 56 50N 72 15W
Rivière aux Outardes *r.* Québec 57 F4 51 38N 69 55W
Rivière-aux-Rats *tn.* Québec 53 P7 47 11N 72 52W
Rivière Bécancour *r.* Québec 53 P6/Q6 46 15N 72 20W
Rivière Bell *r.* Québec 57 B3 49 30N 77 30W
Rivière Betsiamites *r.* Québec 57 F3 49 27N 69 30W
Rivière Blanche *r.* Québec 59 K3 45 32N 75 38W
Rivière Broadback *r.* Québec 57 A4 51 15N 78 42W
Rivière Caniapiscau *r.* Québec 56 F7 56 38N 69 15W
Rivière Capitachouane *r.* Québec 53 K7 47 42N 76 49W
Rivière Casapédia *r.* Québec 57 G3 48 45N 66 20W
Rivière Chaudière *r.* Québec 53 Q6 46 30N 71 10W
Rivière Chicoutimi *r.* Québec 53 Q8 48 11N 71 29W
Rivière Chukotat *r.* Québec 56 B9 61 02N 77 15W
Rivière Coats *r.* Québec 56 B6 55 30N 76 50W
Rivière Coulonge *r.* Québec 53 J6 46 44N 77 10W
Rivière d'Argent *r.* Québec 53 L7 46 59N 75 00W
Rivière Delay *r.* Québec 56 E7 56 50N 71 10W
Rivière de Pas *r.* Québec 56 H6 55 12N 65 35W
Rivière de Rupert *r.* Québec 57 A4 51 22N 78 10W
Rivière des Mille Îles *r.* Québec 58 M5 45 37N 73 47W
Rivière des Outaouais *r.* Ontario/Québec 52 H6 45 35N 76 30W
Rivière des Prairies *r.* Québec 58 N5 45 36N 73 37W
Rivière du Chêne *r.* Québec 58 M5 45 34N 73 59W
Rivière du Gué *r.* Québec 56 E7 56 48N 72 00W
Rivière du Lièvre *r.* Québec 53 L5 45 50N 75 39W
Rivière-du-Loup *admin.* Québec 53 S7 47 50N 69 20W
Rivière-du-Loup *tn.* Québec 53 S7 47 49N 69 32W
Rivière Dumoine *r.* Québec 52 J6 46 20N 77 52W
Rivière du Petit Mécatina *r.* Québec 57 K4 51 50N 60 10W
Rivière du Sable *r.* Québec 56 F6 55 28N 68 20W
Rivière du Vieux Comptoir *r.* Québec 57 A5 52 33N 78 40W
Rivière Eastmain *r.* Québec 57 D5 52 20N 73 00W
Rivière False *r.* Québec 56 F7 57 40N 68 30W
Rivière Ford *r.* Québec 56 H8 58 20N 65 30W
Rivière Gatineau *r.* Québec 53 L5 45 58N 75 52W
Rivière George *r.* Québec 56 H7 57 50N 65 30W
Rivière Harricana *r.* Québec 57 A4 50 40N 79 20W
Rivière Innuksuac *r.* Québec 56 B8 58 40N 77 30W
Rivière Kanaaupscow *r.* Québec 56 C6 54 40N 75 00W
Rivière Kitchigama *r.* Québec 57 A4 50 50N 78 10W
Rivière Kogaluc *r.* Québec 56 B8 59 33N 76 18W
Rivière Koksoak *r.* Québec 56 F7 57 50N 69 10W
Rivière Koroc *r.* Québec 56 H8 58 40N 65 20W
Rivière Kovik *r.* Québec 56 B9 61 50N 77 20W
Rivière Magpie *r.* Québec 57 H4 50 42N 64 25W
Rivière Malbaie *r.* Québec 53 R7 48 01N 70 40W
Rivière Manicouagan *r.* Québec 57 F4 50 51N 68 55W
Rivière Manitou *r.* Québec 57 H4 51 08N 65 20W
Rivière Manouane *r.* Québec 57 E4 50 05N 70 59W
Rivière Maquatua *r.* Québec 57 A5 53 05N 78 40W
Rivière Mariet *r.* Québec 56 B8 59 05N 77 30W
Rivière Matapédia *r.* Québec 57 G3 48 30N 67 30W
Rivière Matawin *r.* Québec 53 N6 46 55N 73 39W
Rivière-Matawin *tn.* Québec 53 P6 46 54N 72 55W
Rivière Mégiscane *r.* Québec 57 B3 48 17N 76 50W
Rivière Métabetchouane *r.* Québec 53 P7 47 59N 72 05W
Rivière Mistanipiscou *r.* Québec 57 J4 51 50N 62 25W
Rivière Mistassibi *r.* Québec 57 D4 50 20N 72 15W
Rivière Mistassibi Nord-Est *r.* Québec 57 E4 50 01N 71 59W
Rivière Mistassini *r.* Québec 57 D4 50 20N 72 40W
Rivière Moisie *r.* Québec 57 G4 50 52N 66 33W
Rivière Montmorency *r.* Québec 53 Q7 47 19N 71 12W
Rivière Mucaliq *r.* Québec 56 G8 58 15N 67 30W
Rivière Nabisipi *r.* Québec 57 J4 50 59N 62 32W
Rivière Nastapoca *r.* Québec 56 C7 56 52N 75 30W
Rivière Natashquan *r.* Québec 57 K4 51 00N 61 35W
Rivière Nicolet *r.* Québec 53 P6 46 14N 72 35W
Rivière Nipissis *r.* Québec 57 H4 50 30N 66 00W
Rivière Noire *r.* Québec 53 J6 46 40N 77 23W
Rivière Nottaway *r.* Québec 57 A4 51 05N 78 20W
Rivière Olomane *r.* Québec 57 K4 50 58N 60 35W
Rivière Opinaca *r.* Québec 57 A5 52 20N 78 00W
Rivière Pentecôte *r.* Québec 57 G4 50 18N 67 35W
Rivière Peribonka *r.* Québec 57 E3 48 58N 71 30W
Rivière Pons *r.* Québec 56 F6 55 50N 69 50W
Rivière Pontax *r.* Québec 57 B4 51 50N 77 05W
Rivière Racine de Bouleau *r.* Québec 57 F5 52 00N 68 40W
Rivière Richelieu *r.* Québec 53 N5 45 03N 73 25W
Rivière Romaine *r.* Québec 57 J4 51 10N 63 40W
Rivière Saguenay *r.* Québec 57 E3 48 20N 70 43W
Rivière Saint-Augustin *r.* Québec 56 L4 51 58N 60 10W
Rivière Sainte-Anne *r.* Québec 53 P6 46 40N 72 11W
Rivière Sainte-Marguerite *r.* Québec 57 G4 51 20N 66 59W
Rivière Saint-François *r.* Québec 53 Q5 45 40N 71 30W
Rivière Saint-Jean *r.* Québec 57 H4 50 50N 64 03W
Rivière Saint-Maurice *r.* Québec 53 N7 47 55N 73 46W
Rivière Saint-Paul *r.* Québec 56 M4 51 55N 57 59W
Rivière Sakami *r.* Québec 57 D5 53 05N 73 15W
Rivière Sérigny *r.* Québec 56 F6 55 30N 69 59W
Rivière Témiscamie *r.* Québec 57 D4 51 15N 72 40W
Rivière Vachon *r.* Québec 56 D9 60 40N 72 25W
Rivière Vermillion *r.* Québec 53 N7 47 19N 73 22W
Rivière-Verte *tn.* New Brunswick 61 A3 47 19N 68 09W
Rivière Wacouna *r.* Québec 57 H4 50 57N 65 40W
Rivière Wheeler *r.* Québec 56 G7 56 25N 67 35W
Rivière Yamaska *r.* Québec 53 P5 45 40N 73 00W
Robert's Arm *tn.* Newfoundland and Labrador 61 H4 49 29N 55 49W
Roberts Creek *tn.* British Columbia 42 H4 49 25N 123 37W
Roberval Québec 57 D3 48 31N 72 16W
Roblin Manitoba 49 B2 51 15N 101 20W
Robson, Mount British Columbia 43 L3 53 08N 118 18W
Rock Bay *tn.* British Columbia 42 G5 50 18N 125 31W
Rockcliffe Park Ontario 53 L5 45 27N 75 39W
Rockglen Saskatchewan 47 E1 49 11N 105 57W
Rockland Ontario 53 L5 45 33N 75 18W
Rock Point Provincial Park Ontario 54 C1 42 50N 79 30W
Rockwood Ontario 54 B2 43 37N 80 10W
Rocky Bay *I.R.* Ontario 51 G5 49 26N 88 08W
Rocky Harbour *tn.* Newfoundland and Labrador 61 G4 49 39N 57 55W
Rocky Island Lake Ontario 51 K4 46 55N 83 04W
Rocky Lake Nova Scotia 59 Q7 44 45N 63 36W
Rocky Mountain House Alberta 46 E3 52 22N 114 55W
Rocky Mountains Forest Reserve Alberta 46 D3/E2 52 30N 116 30W
Rocky Mountain Trench British Columbia 43 H5 57 50N 126 00W
Rocky Saugeen River Ontario 54 B3 44 13N 80 52W
Roddickton Newfoundland and Labrador 60 G5 50 52N 56 08W
Rodney Ontario 52 E2 42 34N 81 41W
Roes Welcome Sound Nunavut 65 N3 63 30N 87 30W
Rogers Pass British Columbia 43 M2 51 23N 117 23W
Rogersville New Brunswick 61 C3 46 44N 65 28W
Romaine River Newfoundland and Labrador 60 D6 52 30N 64 00W
Rondeau Provincial Park Ontario 52 E2 42 17N 81 51W
Root River Ontario 50 F6 50 50N 91 40W
Rorketon Manitoba 49 C2 51 24N 99 35W
Roseau River Manitoba 49 D1 49 10N 96 50W
Rose Blanche Newfoundland and Labrador 61 F3 47 37N 58 41W
Rosedale Alberta 46 F2 51 26N 112 38W
Rosedale Ontario 54 D3 44 34N 78 47W
Rosemère Québec 58 M5 45 38N 73 49W
Rose Point British Columbia 42 E4 54 11N 131 39W
Rosetown Saskatchewan 47 D2 51 34N 107 59W
Rose Valley *tn.* Saskatchewan 47 F3 52 19N 103 49W
Ross Bay Junction *tn.* Newfoundland and Labrador 60 B6 53 03N 66 12W
Rossburn Manitoba 49 B2 50 40N 100 49W
Rosseau Ontario 52 G5 45 16N 79 39W
Rosseau, Lake Ontario 52 G5 45 10N 79 35W
Rossignol, Lake Nova Scotia 61 L11 44 10N 65 20W
Ross Island Manitoba 49 D4 54 20N 97 50W
Rossland British Columbia 43 M1 49 05N 117 48W
Rossport Ontario 51 H5 48 50N 87 31W
Ross River *tn.* Yukon Territory 64 D3 62 02N 132 28W
Rosswood British Columbia 43 F4 54 49N 128 42W
Rosthern Saskatchewan 47 D3 52 40N 106 20W
Rothesay New Brunswick 61 L12 45 23N 66 00W
Rouge River Ontario 54 C2 43 52N 79 15W
Rouleau Saskatchewan 47 E2 50 12N 104 56W
Round Pond Newfoundland and Labrador 61 H4 48 10N 55 50W
Route Jacques-Cartier Québec 57 H4 50 20N 66 00W
Rouyn-Noranda Québec 57 A3 48 15N 79 00W
Rowley Island Nunavut 65 Q4 69 06N 77 52W
Royston British Columbia 42 H4 49 39N 124 57W
Russell Manitoba 49 B2 50 47N 101 17W
Russell, Cape Northwest Territories 64 G6 75 15N 117 35W
Russell Point *c.* Northwest Territories 64 H5 73 30N 115 00W
Rycroft Alberta 46 C4 55 45N 118 43W

S

Saamba Tu *(Trout Lake) tn.* Northwest Territories 64 F3 61 00N 121 30W
Saanich British Columbia 42 H4 48 28N 123 22W
Sabine Peninsula Nunavut 64 J6 76 20N 109 30W
Sable, Cape Nova Scotia 61 C1 43 23N 65 37W
Sable Island Nova Scotia 41 Z2 43 57N 60 00W
Sable River *tn.* Nova Scotia 61 L11 43 50N 65 05W
Sachigo *I.R.* Ontario 50 E7 53 50N 92 10W
Sachigo Lake Ontario 50 E7 53 49N 92 08W
Sachigo River Ontario 50 F8 54 50N 90 50W
Sackville New Brunswick 61 M12 45 54N 64 23W
Sacré-Coeur Québec 53 S8 48 26N 68 35WE
Saglek Bay Newfoundland and Labrador 60 D9 58 30N 63 00W
Saglek Fiord Newfoundland and Labrador 60 D9 58 29N 63 15W
Saguenay Québec 53 R8 48 25N 71 04W
Saguenay *admin.* Québec 53 S8 48 20N 70 00W
Saint-Agapit Québec 53 Q6 46 34N 71 26W
St. Albans Newfoundland and Labrador 61 H3 47 52N 55 51W
St. Albert Alberta 46 F3 53 38N 113 38W
Saint-Ambroise Québec 57 E3 48 33N 71 20W
St. Andrews New Brunswick 61 B2 45 05N 67 04W
St. Anthony Newfoundland and Labrador 60 H5 51 22N 55 35W
Saint-Antoine New Brunswick 61 M12 46 22N 64 50W
St. Antoine Québec 53 M5 45 47N 74 01W
St. Barbe Newfoundland and Labrador 60 G5 51 13N 56 45W
St. Bernard's Newfoundland and Labrador 61 H3 47 32N 54 47W
St. Boniface Manitoba 48 B2 49 53N 97 06W
St. Bride's Newfoundland and Labrador 61 H3 46 55N 54 10W
St. Catharines Ontario 54 C2 43 10N 79 15W
St. Clair, Lake Ontario/USA 52 D2 42 28N 82 40W
Saint-Constant Québec 57 D1 45 22N 73 33W
St. Croix River New Brunswick 61 B2 45 30N 67 40W
Saint-Donat Québec 53 M6 46 19N 74 15W
Sainte-Agathe-des-Monts Québec 53 M6 46 03N 74 19W
Ste. Anne Manitoba 49 D1 49 40N 96 40W
Ste. Anne de Beaupré Québec 53 R7 47 02N 70 58W
Sainte-Anne-des-Monts Québec 57 G3 49 07N 66 29W
Sainte-Anne-du-Lac Québec 53 L6 46 54N 75 20W
Sainte-Catherine Québec 58 N4 45 25N 73 35W
Sainte-Claire Québec 53 R6 46 37N 70 51W
Sainte-Croix Québec 53 Q6 46 38N 71 43W
Sainte-Dorothée Québec 58 M5 45 32N 73 49W
Sainte-Eustache Québec 58 M5 45 33N 73 54W
Sainte-Hyacinthe Québec 53 P5 45 38N 72 57W
St. Eleanors Prince Edward Island 61 M12 46 30N 63 50W
Saint Elias Mountains Yukon Territory 64 C3 60 12N 140 57W
Sainte-Marie Québec 53 Q6 46 26N 71 00W
Sainte-Marthe-sur-le-Lac Québec 58 M5 45 31N 73 55W

Sainte-Rose Québec 58 M5 45 36N 73 47W
Ste. Rose du Lac Manitoba 49 C2 51 04N 99 31W
Sainte-Thérèse Québec 53 N5 45 38N 73 50W
Saint-Félicien Québec 57 D3 48 38N 72 29W
St. Francis Harbour *tn.* Nova Scotia 61 M12 45 30N 61 20W
St. Francis, Lake Québec 53 M5 45 05N 74 30W
Saint-François Québec 58 N5 45 38N 73 35W
St. George New Brunswick 61 B2 45 08N 66 50W
St. George's Newfoundland and Labrador 61 F4 48 26N 58 29W
Saint-Georges Québec 53 P6 46 38N 72 35W
Saint-Georges Québec 53 R6 46 08N 70 40W
St. George's Bay Newfoundland and Labrador 61 F4 48 28N 59 16W
St. Georges Bay Nova Scotia 61 M12 45 40N 61 40W
St. Germain Manitoba 48 B2 49 46N 97 07W
St. Ignace Island Ontario 51 H5 48 45N 87 55W
St. Jacobs Ontario 54 B2 43 32N 80 33W
Saint-Jacques New Brunswick 61 A3 47 20N 68 28W
St. James, Cape British Columbia 42 E2 51 58N 131 00W
St. Jean Baptiste Manitoba 49 D1 49 15N 97 20W
Saint-Jean-Port-Joli Québec 53 R7 47 13N 70 16W
Saint-Jean-sur-Richelieu Québec 53 N5 45 18N 73 18W
St.-Jerôme Québec 53 M5 45 47N 74 01W
Saint John New Brunswick 61 L12 45 16N 66 03W
Saint John *admin.* New Brunswick 61 L12 45 20N 65 50W
St. John Bay Newfoundland and Labrador 60 G5 50 55N 57 09W
St. John, Cape Newfoundland and Labrador 61 H4 50 00N 55 32W
St. John, Lake Ontario 54 C3 44 38N 79 19W
St. John's Newfoundland and Labrador 61 J3 47 34N 52 43W
St. Joseph New Brunswick 61 M12 45 59N 64 30W
St. Joseph Island Ontario 52 C6 46 13N 83 57W
St. Joseph, Lake Ontario 50 F6 51 05N 90 35W
Saint-Laurent Québec 58 N5 45 31N 73 42W
St. Lawrence Newfoundland and Labrador 61 H3 46 55N 55 24W
St. Lawrence, Cape Nova Scotia 61 M12 47 10N 60 40W
St. Lawrence, Gulf of Québec 57 J3 48 40N 63 20W
St. Lawrence River Québec 57 C1 45 00N 75 00W
St. Lawrence Seaway Ontario/Québec/USA 53 L4 44 38N 78 34W
Saint Léonard New Brunswick 61 B3 47 10N 67 55W
Saint Leonard Québec 58 N5 45 34N 73 35W
St. Lewis Newfoundland and Labrador 60 H6 52 22N 55 41W
St. Lewis River Newfoundland and Labrador 60 G6 52 20N 56 50W
Saint-Lin-Laurentides Québec 57 D1 45 51N 73 45W
Saint-Louis de-Kent New Brunswick 61 C3 46 50N 65 00W
St. Lunaire Newfoundland and Labrador 60 H5 51 30N 55 29W
St. Malo Manitoba 49 D1 49 20N 96 55W
St. Margarets Bay Nova Scotia 61 M11 44 30N 64 50W
St. Martin, Lake Manitoba 49 C2 51 40N 98 20W
St. Martins New Brunswick 61 L12 45 20N 65 30W
St. Mary, Cape Nova Scotia 61 L11 44 10N 66 10W
St. Mary's Newfoundland and Labrador 61 J3 46 55N 53 34W
St. Marys Ontario 54 A2 43 15N 81 09W
St. Mary's Bay Newfoundland and Labrador 61 J3 46 50N 53 45W
St. Mary's Bay Nova Scotia 61 L11 44 20N 66 10W
St. Mary's River Nova Scotia 61 M12 45 20N 62 30W
St.-Maurice *admin.* Québec 53 M7 47 40N 74 30W
Saint-Michel-des-Saints Québec 53 N6 46 40N 73 55W
Saint-Nicéphore Québec 57 D1 45 51N 72 27W
St. Norbert Manitoba 48 B2 49 46N 97 12W
Saint-Pacôme Québec 53 S7 47 24N 69 58W
St.-Pamphile Québec 53 S6 46 58N 69 48W
Saint-Pascal Québec 53 S7 47 32N 69 48W
St. Paul Alberta 46 G4 53 59N 111 17W
St. Peters Nova Scotia 61 M12 45 40N 60 53W
St. Peters Prince Edward Island 61 M12 46 26N 62 35W
St. Pierre-Jolys Manitoba 49 D1 49 28N 96 58W
Saint-Prosper Québec 53 R6 46 12N 70 29W
Saint-Quentin New Brunswick 61 B3 47 30N 67 20W
Saint-Raymond Québec 53 Q6 46 54N 71 50W
St. Romauld Québec 53 Q6 46 52N 71 49W
Saint-Siméon Québec 53 S7 47 50N 69 55W
St. Stephen New Brunswick 61 B2 45 12N 67 18W
St. Stephens Newfoundland and Labrador 61 J3 46 47N 53 37W
St. Theresa Point *tn.* Manitoba 49 E3 53 45N 94 50W
St. Thomas Ontario 54 A1 42 46N 81 12W
Saint-Tite Québec 53 P6 46 44N 72 34W
Saint-Vincent-de-Paul Québec 58 N5 45 38N 73 39W
St. Walburg Saskatchewan 47 C3 53 38N 109 12W
Sakami Québec 57 B5 53 50N 76 10W
Salaberry-de-Valleyfield Québec 53 M5 45 16N 74 11W
Salisbury New Brunswick 61 L12 46 02N 65 03W
Salisbury Island Nunavut 65 Q3 63 10N 77 20W
Salliq *(Coral Harbour) tn.* Nunavut 65 P3 64 10N 83 15W
Salluit Québec 56 C10 62 20N 75 40W
Salmo British Columbia 43 M1 49 11N 117 16W
Salmon Arm *tn.* British Columbia 43 L2 50 41N 119 18W
Salmon Inlet British Columbia 42 H4 49 39N 123 47W
Salmon River New Brunswick 61 C3 46 10N 65 50W
Salmon River *tn.* Nova Scotia 61 L11 44 10N 66 10W
Saltcoats Saskatchewan 47 F2 51 03N 102 12W
Saltery Bay *tn.* British Columbia 42 H4 49 47N 124 10W
Saltspring Island British Columbia 42 H4 48 50N 123 30W
Sambro, Cape Nova Scotia 61 M11 44 30N 63 30W
San Cristoval Mountains British Columbia 42 E3 52 30N 131 30W
Sandilands Provincial Forest Manitoba 49 D1/E1 49 30N 96 00W
Sand Lakes Provincial Park Manitoba 49 C5 58 00N 98 30W
Sandspit British Columbia 42 E3 53 14N 131 50W
Sandy Bay *tn.* Saskatchewan 47 F4 55 30N 102 10W
Sandy Lake Newfoundland and Labrador 61 G4 49 20N 56 50W
Sandy Lake Nova Scotia 59 Q6 44 44N 63 40W
Sandy Lake Ontario 50 E7 53 02N 93 00W
Sandy Lake *I.R.* Ontario 50 E7 53 04N 93 20W
Sanikiluaq *(Sanikilluaq)* Nunavut 65 Q2 56 32N 79 14W
Sanirajak *(Hall Beach) tn.* Nunavut 65 P4 68 46N 81 12W
San Juan River British Columbia 42 H4 48 37N 124 20W
Sardis British Columbia 42 H4 49 07N 121 57W
Sarnia Ontario 52 D2 42 58N 82 23W
Sasaginnigak Lake Manitoba 49 E2 51 30N 95 30W
Sasamat Lake British Columbia 44 G4 49 19N 122 52W
Saskatchewan *province* 47
Saskatchewan River Manitoba/Saskatchewan 47 F3 53 50N 103 10W
Saskatoon Saskatchewan 47 D3 52 10N 106 40W
Saturna Island British Columbia 42 H4 48 47N 123 07W
Sauble Beach *tn.* Ontario 54 A3 44 38N 81 17W
Sauble Falls Provincial Park Ontario 54 A3 44 40N 81 15W
Sauble River Ontario 54 A3 44 36N 81 09W
Saugeen River Ontario 54 A3 44 23N 81 18W
Sault Ste. Marie Ontario 51 J4 46 31N 84 20W
Savant Lake Ontario 50 F6 50 30N 90 25W
Savant Lake *tn.* Ontario 50 F6 50 14N 90 43W
Sawbill Newfoundland and Labrador 60 B6 53 37N 66 21W
Sayabec Québec 57 G3 48 35N 67 41W
Sayward British Columbia 43 H2 50 19N 125 58W
Scarborough Ontario 55 D2 43 46N 79 14W
Scarborough Bluffs Ontario 55 D1 43 42N 79 15W
Scaterie Island Nova Scotia 61 N12 46 00N 59 40W
Schefferville Québec 56 G6 54 47N 66 48W
Schreiber Ontario 51 H5 48 48N 87 17W
Schultz Lake Nunavut 65 L3 64 45N 97 30W
Scotsburn Nova Scotia 61 M12 45 40N 62 51W
Scott Islands British Columbia 43 F2 50 48N 128 38W
Scott Lake Saskatchewan 47 D6 59 50N 106 30W
Scudder Ontario 52 D1 41 47N 82 39W
Scugog Island Ontario 54 D3 44 10N 78 52W
Scugog, Lake Ontario 54 D3 44 10N 78 51W
Scugog River Ontario 54 D3 44 16N 78 46W
Seaforth Ontario 54 A2 43 03N 81 24W
Sea Island British Columbia 44 F3 49 11N 123 11W
Seal Cove *tn.* Newfoundland and Labrador 61 G3 47 30N 56 00W
Seal Cove *tn.* Newfoundland and Labrador 61 G4 49 56N 56 23W
Seal Cove *tn.* Nova Scotia 61 L11 44 38N 66 52W
Seal Harbour *tn.* New Brunswick 61 M12 45 10N 61 30W
Seal Lake Newfoundland and Labrador 60 E7 54 20N 61 40W
Seal River Manitoba 49 D6 58 50N 97 00W
Sechelt British Columbia 42 H4 49 28N 123 46W
Sechelt Peninsula British Columbia 42 H4 49 45N 123 58W
Seine River Manitoba 48 C2 49 46N 97 02W
Selkirk Manitoba 49 D2 50 10N 96 52W
Selkirk Ontario 54 C1 42 50N 79 55W
Selkirk Mountains British Columbia 43 M2 51 40N 118 20W
Selkirk Provincial Park Ontario 54 C1 42 50N 80 00W
Selwyn Lake Northwest Territories 64 K3 60 05N 104 25W
Selwyn Mountains Yukon Territory 64 D3 64 30N 134 50W
Semchuck Trail Saskatchewan 47 C5 57 35N 109 20W
Senneterre Québec 53 J8 48 24N 77 16W
Sentinel Peak British Columbia 43 K4 54 56N 121 59W
Serpentine River British Columbia 44 G3 49 06N 122 46W
Seseganaga Lake Ontario 50 F6 50 00N 90 28W
Setting Lake Manitoba 49 C4 55 10N 98 50W
Seven Sisters Bay Newfoundland and Labrador 60 D9 59 25N 63 45W
Seven Sisters Provincial Park British Columbia 43 F4 55 00N 128 10W
70 Mile House British Columbia 43 K2 51 21N 121 25W
Severn Lake Ontario 50 F7 53 54N 90 48W
Severn River Ontario 50 H8 55 30N 88 30W
Severn River Provincial Park Ontario 50 F8 54 15N 90 30W
Sexsmith Alberta 46 C4 55 21N 118 47W
Seymour Creek British Columbia 44 F4 49 18N 123 01W
Seymour Inlet British Columbia 43 G2 51 03N 127 05W
Shabaqua Ontario 51 G5 48 35N 89 54W
Shabo Newfoundland and Labrador 60 B6 53 19N 66 12W
Shabogamo Lake Newfoundland and Labrador 60 B6 53 15N 66 30W
Shag Harbour *tn.* Nova Scotia 61 L11 43 30N 65 40W
Shakespeare Ontario 54 B2 43 22N 80 50W
Shaler Mountains Northwest Territories 64 H5 72 10N 111 00W
Shallow Lake *tn.* Ontario 54 A3 44 38N 81 06W
Shamattawa Manitoba 49 F4 55 51N 92 05W
Shamattawa River Ontario 50 J8 54 05N 85 50W
Shapio Lake Newfoundland and Labrador 60 E7 55 00N 61 18W
Sharon Ontario 54 C3 44 06N 79 26W
Shaunavon Saskatchewan 47 C1 49 40N 108 25W
Shawinigan Québec 53 P6 46 34N 72 45W
Shawinigan Lake *tn.* British Columbia 42 H4 48 38N 123 39W
Shawville Québec 53 K5 45 36N 76 30W
Shebandowan Ontario 51 F5 48 38N 90 04W
Shediac New Brunswick 61 M12 46 13N 64 35W
Sheet Harbour *tn.* Nova Scotia 61 M11 44 56N 62 31W
Shefford *admin.* Québec 53 P5 45 30N 72 45W
Shelburne Nova Scotia 61 M11 43 37N 65 20W
Shelburne Ontario 54 B3 44 05N 80 13W
Shelburne *admin.* Nova Scotia 61 L11 43 50N 65 30W
Sheldon Creek Ontario 54 B3 44 05N 80 06W
Shellbrook Saskatchewan 47 D3 53 14N 106 24W
Shelsey River British Columbia 42 E6 58 33N 132 02W
Shelter Bay *tn.* British Columbia 43 M2 50 38N 117 59W
Shepherd Bay Nunavut 65 M4 65 00N 90 00W
Sherbrooke Nova Scotia 61 M12 45 10N 61 58W
Sherbrooke Québec 53 Q5 45 24N 71 54W
Sherbrooke *admin.* Québec 53 P5 45 20N 72 10W
Sherbrooke Lake Nova Scotia 61 M11 44 40N 64 40W
Sherridon Manitoba 49 B4 55 07N 101 05W
Sherwood Park *tn.* Alberta 46 F3 53 31N 113 19W
Sheshatshui Newfoundland and Labrador 60 E6 53 30N 60 10W
Shibogama Lake Ontario 50 G7 53 35N 88 15W
Shipiskan Lake Newfoundland and Labrador 60 D7 54 39N 62 19W
Shippagan New Brunswick 61 C3 47 45N 64 44W
Shirleys Bay Ontario 59 J2 45 22N 75 54W
Shoal Bay *tn.* Newfoundland and Labrador 61 H4 49 41N 54 12W
Shoal Harbour *tn.* Newfoundland and Labrador 61 J4 48 11N 53 59W
Shoal Lake Ontario/Manitoba 50 D5 49 33N 95 01W
Shoal Lake *tn.* Manitoba 49 B2 50 28N 100 35W
Shoal Lakes Manitoba 49 D2 50 25N 97 35W
Shubenacadie Nova Scotia 61 M12 45 05N 63 25W
Shubenacadie Grand Lake Nova Scotia 59 Q7 44 53N 63 37W
Shubenacadie River Nova Scotia 61 M12 45 20N 63 30W
Shunacadie Nova Scotia 61 M12 46 00N 60 40W
Shuswap Lake British Columbia 43 L2 51 00N 119 00W
Sibbald Point Provincial Park Ontario 54 C3 44 15N 79 20W
Sicamous British Columbia 43 L2 50 50N 119 00W
Sidney British Columbia 42 H4 48 39N 123 25W
Sidney Bay Ontario 54 A3 44 55N 81 04W
Sifton Manitoba 49 B2 51 21N 100 09W
Sifton Pass British Columbia 43 G5 57 51N 126 17W
Sikanni Chief British Columbia 43 J5 57 11N 122 43W
Sikanni Chief River British Columbia 43 J5 57 16N 125 25W
Silver Dollar Ontario 50 F5 49 50N 91 15W
Silverthrone Mountain British Columbia 43 G2 51 30N 126 03W
Silvertip Mountain British Columbia 42 H4 49 09N 121 12W
Simcoe Ontario 54 B1 42 50N 80 19W
Simcoe *admin.* Ontario 54 C3 44 32N 79 54W
Simcoe, Lake Ontario 54 C3 44 23N 79 18W
Simonette River Alberta 46 C4 54 25N 118 20W
Simpson Bay Nunavut 64 H4 69 00N 113 40W
Simpson Peninsula Nunavut 65 N4 68 34N 88 45W
Simpson Strait Nunavut 65 L4 68 27N 97 45W
Sioux Lookout Ontario 50 F6 50 07N 91 54W
Sioux Narrows Ontario 50 D5 49 23N 94 08W
Sipiwesk Manitoba 49 D4 55 27N 97 24W
Sipiwesk Lake Manitoba 49 D4 55 10N 97 50W
Sir Alexander, Mount British Columbia 43 K3 53 52N 120 25W
Sir James McBrien, Mount Yukon Territory 64 E3 62 15N 128 01W
Sirmilik National Park Nunavut 65 P5/Q5 73 00N 80 00W
Sir Wilfred Laurier, Mount British Columbia 43 L3 52 45N 119 40W
Sisipuk Lake Manitoba 49 B4 55 30N 101 40W
Skagit Valley Recreation Area British Columbia 42 H4 49 06N 121 09W
Skeena Mountains British Columbia 42/43 F5 57 30N 129 59W
Skeena River British Columbia 43 F4 54 15N 129 15W
Skidegate British Columbia 42 E3 53 13N 132 02W
Skihist Mountain British Columbia 43 K2 50 12N 122 53W
Skownan Manitoba 49 C2 51 58N 99 35W
Slave Lake *tn.* Alberta 46 E4 55 17N 114 43W
Slave River Alberta/Northwest Territories 64 H3 60 30N 112 50W
Sleeping Giant (Sibley) Provincial Park Ontario 51 G5 48 10N 88 50W
Slocan British Columbia 43 M1 49 46N 117 28W
Slocan Lake British Columbia 43 M1 49 50N 117 20W
Smallwood Reservoir Newfoundland and Labrador 60 C7 54 10N 64 00W
Smeaton Saskatchewan 47 E3 53 30N 104 50W
Smith Alberta 46 E4 55 10N 114 02W
Smith Arm *b.* Northwest Territories 64 F4 66 15N 124 00W
Smith Bay Nunavut 65 Q6 77 12N 78 50W
Smithers British Columbia 43 G4 54 45N 127 10W
Smith Island Nunavut 56 A9 60 44N 78 30W
Smith Point Nova Scotia 61 M12 45 52N 63 25W
Smith River British Columbia 43 G6 59 56N 126 28W
Smiths Falls *tn.* Ontario 53 K4 44 45N 76 01W
Smithville Ontario 54 C2 43 06N 79 32W
Smoky, Cape Nova Scotia 61 M12 46 40N 60 20W
Smoky Lake *tn.* Alberta 46 F4 54 07N 112 28W
Smoky River Alberta 46 C4 55 30N 118 00W
Smooth Rock Falls *tn.* Ontario 51 L5 49 17N 81 38W
Smoothrock Lake Ontario 50 G6 50 30N 89 30W
Smoothstone Lake Saskatchewan 47 D4 54 40N 106 30W
Snake Creek Ontario 54 A3 44 23N 81 16W
Snake River Yukon Territory 64 D4 65 20N 133 30W
Snegamook Lake Newfoundland and Labrador 60 E7 54 33N 61 27W
Snowbird Lake Northwest Territories 65 K3 60 41N 102 56W
Snow Lake *tn.* Manitoba 49 B4 54 56N 100 00W
Snug Harbour *tn.* Newfoundland and Labrador 60 H6 52 53N 55 52W
Soldier Lake Nova Scotia 59 Q7 44 49N 63 33W
Sǫmbak'è *(Yellowknife)* Northwest Territories 64 H3 62 30N 114 29W
Somerset Manitoba 49 C1 49 26N 98 39W
Somerset Island Nunavut 65 M5 73 15N 93 30W
Sonora Island British Columbia 42 G5 50 21N 125 13W
Sooke British Columbia 42 H4 48 20N 123 42W
Sorel Québec 53 N6 46 03N 73 06W
Soulanges *admin.* Québec 53 M5 45 15N 74 20W
Sounding Creek Alberta 46 G2 51 40N 111 05W
Sounding Lake Alberta 46 G3 52 08N 110 29W
Souris Manitoba 49 B1 49 38N 100 17W
Souris Prince Edward Island 61 M12 46 22N 62 16W
Souris River Manitoba/USA 49 B1 49 30N 100 50W
Southampton Ontario 54 A3 44 29N 81 22W
Southampton Island Nunavut 65 P3 64 50N 85 00W
South Aulatsivik Island Newfoundland and Labrador 60 E8 56 46N 61 30W
South Bay *tn.* Ontario 50 E6 51 03N 92 45W
South Brookfield Nova Scotia 61 M11 44 23N 64 58W
Southend Saskatchewan 47 F5 56 20N 103 14W
Southern Indian Lake Manitoba 49 C5 57 00N 98 00W
Southey Saskatchewan 47 E2 50 57N 104 33W
South Gloucester Ontario 59 K2 45 17N 75 34W
South Hazelton British Columbia 43 G4 55 12N 127 42W
South Henik Lake Nunavut 65 L3 61 30N 97 30W
South Indian Lake *tn.* Manitoba 49 C5 56 48N 98 55W
South Knife River Manitoba 49 D6 58 20N 96 10W
South Maitland River Ontario 54 A2 43 39N 81 27W
South Moose Lake Manitoba 49 B3 53 40N 100 10W
South Nahanni River Northwest Territories 64 E3 61 30N 123 22W
South Porcupine Ontario 51 L5 48 28N 81 13W
South River *tn.* Ontario 52 G5 45 50N 79 23W
South Saskatchewan River Saskatchewan 47 C2 50 50N 110 00W
South Saugeen River Ontario 54 B3 44 00N 80 45W
South Seal River Manitoba 49 C5 58 00N 99 10W
South Tweedsmuir Provincial Park British Columbia 43 H3 52 30N 126 00W
South Twin Island Nunavut 50 M7 53 10N 79 50W
Southwest Miramichi River New Brunswick 61 B3 46 30N 66 50W
Spallumcheen British Columbia 43 L2 50 24N 119 14W
Spanish Ontario 52 D6 46 12N 82 12W
Spanish River Ontario 52 E6 46 32N 81 57W
Sparwood British Columbia 43 N1 49 55N 114 53W
Spatsizi Plateau Wilderness Park British Columbia 43 F5/G5 57 30N 128 30W
Speed River Ontario 54 B2 43 29N 80 17W
Spicer Islands Nunavut 65 Q4 63 19N 71 52W
Spirit River *tn.* Alberta 46 C4 55 46N 118 51W
Spiritwood Saskatchewan 47 D3 53 24N 107 33W
Split, Cape Nova Scotia 61 M12 45 20N 64 30W
Split Lake Manitoba 49 E5 56 10N 95 50W
Split Lake *tn.* Manitoba 49 D5 56 16N 96 08W
Spotted Island Newfoundland and Labrador 60 H6 53 31N 55 47W
Sprague Manitoba 49 E1 49 02N 95 36W
Springdale Newfoundland and Labrador 61 G4 49 30N 56 04W
Springfield Nova Scotia 61 M11 44 37N 64 52W
Springfield Ontario 54 B1 42 49N 80 57W
Springhill Nova Scotia 61 M12 45 40N 64 04W
Spring Water Provincial Park Ontario 54 C3 44 30N 79 45W
Sproat Lake British Columbia 42 G4 49 16N 125 05W
Spruce Grove Alberta 46 F3 53 32N 113 55W

Spruce Woods Provincial Forest Manitoba 49 C1 49 40N 99 40W
Spruce Woods Provincial Park Manitoba 49 C1 49 40N 99 10W
Spryfield Nova Scotia 59 L3 44 36N 63 40W
Spry Harbour *tn.* Nova Scotia 61 M11 44 50N 62 45W
Spuzzum British Columbia 43 K1 49 40N 121 25W
Squamish British Columbia 42 H4 49 41N 123 11W
Squamish River British Columbia 42 H5 49 42N 123 11W
Square Islands Newfoundland and Labrador 60 H6 52 45N 55 52W
Stanley New Brunswick 61 B3 46 17N 66 45W
Stanley Mission Saskatchewan 47 E4 55 24N 104 34W
Stanstead *admin.* Québec 53 P5 45 10N 72 10W
Starbuck Manitoba 49 D1 49 47N 97 38W
Star City Saskatchewan 47 E3 52 52N 104 20W
Stave Lake British Columbia 42 H4 49 21N 122 19W
Stayner Ontario 54 B3 44 25N 80 06W
Steele River Provincial Park Ontario 51 H5 49 25N 86 40W
Steen River *tn.* Alberta 46 D6 59 38N 117 10W
Stefansson Island Nunavut 65 K5 73 20N 105 00W
Steinbach Manitoba 49 D1 49 32N 96 40W
Stein Valley Provincial Park British Columbia 43 J2 50 10N 122 10W
Stellarton Nova Scotia 61 M12 45 34N 62 40W
Stephens Lake Manitoba 49 E5 56 30N 95 00W
Stephenville Newfoundland and Labrador 61 F4 48 33N 57 32W
Stephenville Crossing Newfoundland and Labrador 61 F4 48 30N 58 26W
Stettler Alberta 46 F3 52 19N 112 43W
Stevenson Lake Manitoba 49 E3 53 50N 95 50W
Steveston British Columbia 44 F3 49 07N 123 10W
Stewart British Columbia 42 F4 55 07N 129 58W
Stewart Yukon Territory 64 C3 63 15N 139 15W
Stewart Crossing Yukon Territory 64 C3 60 37N 128 37W
Stewart River Yukon Territory 64 C3 63 40N 138 20W
Stewiacke Nova Scotia 61 M12 45 09N 63 22W
Stikine British Columbia 42 E5 56 42N 131 45W
Stikine Range *mts.* British Columbia 42 E6/F6 57 00N 127 20W
Stikine River British Columbia 42 E5 58 00N 131 20W
Stikine River Recreation Area British Columbia 43 F5 58 07N 129 35W
Stirling Alberta 46 F1 49 34N 112 30W
Stirling Ontario 53 J4 44 18N 77 33W
Stittsville Ontario 59 J2 45 16N 75 54W
Stokes Bay Ontario 54 A3 45 00N 81 23W
Stone Mountain Provincial Park British Columbia 43 H6 58 35N 124 40W
Stonewall Manitoba 49 D2 50 08N 97 20W
Stoney Creek *tn.* Ontario 54 C2 43 13N 79 46W
Stony Lake Manitoba 49 C6 58 50N 98 30W
Stony Lake Ontario 52 H4 44 33N 78 06W
Stony Plain *tn.* Alberta 46 E3 53 32N 114 00W
Stony Rapids *tn.* Saskatchewan 47 E6 59 14N 105 48W
Stony Swamp Conservation Area Ontario 59 J2 45 15N 75 49W
Storkerson Peninsula Nunavut 64 J5 72 30N 106 30W
Stormont, Dundas and Glengarry *admin.* Ontario 53 M5 45 10N 75 00W
Stormy Lake Ontario 50 E5 49 23N 92 18W
Stouffville Ontario 54 C2 43 59N 79 15W
Stoughton Saskatchewan 47 F1 49 40N 103 00W
Stout Lake Ontario 50 D7 52 08N 94 35W
Strasbourg Saskatchewan 47 E2 51 05N 104 58W
Stratford Ontario 54 B2 43 07N 81 00W
Strathcona Provincial Park British Columbia 42 G4 49 40N 125 30W
Strathmore Alberta 46 F2 51 03N 113 23W
Strathroy Ontario 54 A1 42 57N 81 40W
Streetsville Ontario 54 C2 43 25N 79 44W
Stuart Island *tn.* British Columbia 42 G5 50 22N 125 09W
Stuart Lake British Columbia 43 H4 54 35N 124 40W
Stuart River British Columbia 43 J4 54 10N 124 05W
Stupart River Manitoba 49 E4 55 30N 94 30W
Sturgeon Bay Manitoba 49 D3 51 50N 98 00W
Sturgeon Falls *tn.* Ontario 52 G6 46 22N 79 57W
Sturgeon Lake Alberta 46 D4 55 06N 117 32W
Sturgeon Lake Ontario 50 F5 50 00N 91 00W
Sturgeon Lake Ontario 54 D3 44 30N 78 43W
Sturgeon Landing Saskatchewan 47 G4 54 18N 101 49W
Sturgeon Point *tn.* Ontario 54 D3 44 28N 78 42W
Sturgeon River Ontario 51 L4 47 00N 80 30W
Sturgeon River Saskatchewan 47 D3 53 30N 106 20W
Sturgeon River Provincial Park Ontario 51 L4 47 00N 80 50W
Sturgis Saskatchewan 47 F2 51 58N 102 32W
Styx River Ontario 54 B3 44 15N 80 58W
Sudbury *admin.* Ontario 52 E6 47 10N 82 00W
Sudbury, Regional Municipality of Ontario 52 E6 46 32N 81 00W
Suggi Lake Saskatchewan 47 F4 54 20N 103 10W
Sullivan Bay *tn.* British Columbia 43 G2 50 55N 126 52W
Sullivan Lake Alberta 46 F3 52 00N 112 00W
Sultan Ontario 51 K4 47 36N 82 45W
Summer Beaver Ontario 50 G7 52 50N 88 30W
Summerford Newfoundland and Labrador 61 H4 49 29N 54 47W
Summerland British Columbia 43 L1 49 35N 119 41W
Summerside Prince Edward Island 61 M12 46 24N 63 46W
Summerville Newfoundland and Labrador 61 J4 48 27N 53 33W
Sunbury *admin.* New Brunswick 61 B2 45 50N 66 40W
Sundre Alberta 46 E2 51 48N 114 38W
Sundridge Ontario 52 G5 45 46N 79 24W
Sunnyside Newfoundland and Labrador 61 J3 47 51N 53 55W
Superb Saskatchewan 47 C2 51 56N 109 25W
Superior, Lake Ontario/USA 51 G4/H4 48 00N 88 00W
Surrey British Columbia 42 H4 49 08N 122 50W
Sussex New Brunswick 61 L12 45 43N 65 32W
Sussex Corner New Brunswick 61 L12 45 40N 65 30W
Sustut Provincial Park British Columbia 43 G5 56 20N 126 50W
Sutton Ontario 54 C3 44 18N 79 22W
Sutton Québec 53 P5 45 05N 72 36W
Sutton Lake Ontario 50 J8 54 15N 84 44W
Sutton River Ontario 50 J8 54 50N 84 30W
Svendsen Peninsula Nunavut 65 P6 77 45N 84 00W
Sverdrup Islands Nunavut 65 L6 79 00N 96 00W
Swan Hills Alberta 46 E4 54 45N 115 45W
Swan Hills *tn.* Alberta 46 E4 54 43N 115 24W
Swan Lake Manitoba 49 B3 52 20N 100 50W
Swan Lake/Kispoix River Provincial Park British Columbia 43 F4 55 55N 128 25W
Swannell Range British Columbia 43 H5 56 38N 126 10W
Swan Pelican Provincial Forest Manitoba 49 B3 52 30N 100 30W
Swan River *tn.* Manitoba 49 B3 52 06N 101 17W
Swift Current *tn.* Saskatchewan 47 D2 50 17N 107 49W
Swift Current Creek Saskatchewan 47 C1 49 40N 108 30W
Swinburne, Cape Nunavut 65 L5 71 13N 98 33W
Swindle Island British Columbia 43 F3 52 33N 128 25W
Sydenham River Ontario 52 D2 42 40N 82 20W
Sydenham River Ontario 54 B3 44 32N 80 57W
Sydney Nova Scotia 61 M12 46 10N 60 10W
Sydney Mines *tn.* Nova Scotia 61 M12 46 16N 60 15W
Sylvan Lake *tn.* Alberta 46 E3 52 19N 114 05W
Sylvia Grinnell Territorial Park Nunavut 65 S3 63 45N 68 38W

T

Taber Alberta 46 F1 49 48N 112 09W
Table Bay Newfoundland and Labrador 60 G6 53 40N 56 25W
Tadoule Lake Manitoba 49 C6 58 30N 98 50W
Tadoussac Québec 53 S8 48 09N 69 43W
Tagish Yukon Territory 64 D3 60 18N 134 16W
Tagish Lake British Columbia 42 C6 59 50N 134 33W
Tahiryauk Lake Northwest Territories 64 H5 70 56N 112 15W
Tahoe Lake Nunavut 64 J4 70 15N 108 45W
Tahsis British Columbia 43 G1 49 50N 126 39W
Tahtsa Lake British Columbia 43 G3 53 41N 127 30W
Takla Lake British Columbia 43 H4 55 12N 125 45W
Takla Landing British Columbia 43 H4 55 27N 125 59W
Taku Arm *l.* British Columbia 42 C6 60 10N 134 05W
Taku River British Columbia 42 D6 58 43N 133 20W
Talbot Lake Manitoba 49 C4 54 00N 99 40W
Taloyoak *(Spence Bay)* Nunavut 65 M4 69 30N 93 20W
Taltson River Northwest Territories 64 H3 60 40N 111 30W
Tamaarvik Territorial Park Nunavut 65 Q5 72 35N 77 28W
Tantalus Provincial Park British Columbia 42 H4 49 50N 123 16W
Tara Ontario 54 A3 44 29N 81 09W
Taseko Mountain British Columbia 43 J2 51 12N 123 07W
Taseko River British Columbia 43 J2 51 35N 123 40W
Tasisuak Lake Newfoundland and Labrador 60 D8 56 45N 62 46W
Tasiujaq Québec 56 F8 58 40N 70 00W
Tasu Sound British Columbia 42 D3 52 40N 132 03W
Tatamagouche Nova Scotia 61 M12 45 43N 63 19W
Tatamagouche Bay Nova Scotia 61 M12 45 45N 63 15W
Tathlina Lake Northwest Territories 64 G3 60 33N 117 39W
Tatla Lake British Columbia 43 H3 51 59N 124 25W
Tatlatui Provincial Park British Columbia 43 G5 57 00N 127 20W
Tatlayoko Lake British Columbia 43 H2 51 39N 124 23W
Tatnam, Cape Manitoba 49 G5 57 25N 91 00W
Tatogga British Columbia 42 F5 57 45N 129 58W
Tatshenshini River British Columbia 42 B6 59 30N 137 30W
Tavistock Ontario 54 B2 43 19N 80 50W
Taylor British Columbia 43 K5 56 09N 120 40W
Taylor Head *p.* Nova Scotia 61 M11 44 40N 62 30W
Tazin Lake Saskatchewan 47 C6 59 50N 109 10W
Tazin River Saskatchewan 47 D6 59 50N 108 00W
Tecumseh Ontario 52 D2 42 18N 82 49W
Teeswater Ontario 54 A2 43 59N 81 18W
Teeswater River Ontario 54 A3 44 07N 81 22W
Teetl'it Zheh *(Fort McPherson)* Northwest Territories 64 D4 67 29N 134 50W
Tehek Lake Nunavut 65 L3 64 55N 95 38W
Telegraph Creek *tn.* British Columbia 42 E5 57 56N 131 11W
Telkwa British Columbia 43 G4 54 44N 127 05W
Temagami Ontario 51 M4 47 04N 79 47W
Temagami, Lake Ontario 51 L4 47 00N 80 05W
Témiscamingue *admin.* Québec 52 H6 46 44N 79 06W
Templeton Québec 59 K2 45 29N 75 36W
Terence Bay Nova Scotia 61 M11 44 20N 63 40W
Terrace British Columbia 43 F4 54 31N 128 32W
Terrace Bay *tn.* Ontario 51 H5 48 47N 87 06W
Terra Cotta Ontario 54 C2 43 42N 79 55W
Terra Nova National Park Newfoundland and Labrador 61 H4 48 40N 54 20W
Terrebonne Québec 53 N5 45 42N 73 37W
Terrebonne *admin.* Québec 53 M6 46 00N 74 30W
Terrenceville Newfoundland and Labrador 61 H3 47 40N 54 44W
Teslin Yukon Territory 64 D3 60 10N 132 42W
Teslin Lake British Columbia/Yukon Territory 64 D3 59 50N 132 25W
Teslin River British Columbia 42 E6 59 20N 131 50W
Tetachuk Lake British Columbia 43 H3 53 38N 127 40W
Teulon Manitoba 49 D2 50 26N 97 18W
Texada Island British Columbia 42 H4 49 30N 124 30W
Thamesford Ontario 54 A2 43 03N 81 00W
Thames River Ontario 52 E2 42 19N 82 27W
Thelon River Northwest Territories 64 K3 64 40N 102 30W
Thelon Wildlife Sanctuary Northwest Territories/Nunavut 65 K3 64 30N 103 00W
The Pas Manitoba 49 B3 53 49N 101 14W
Thesiger Bay Northwest Territories 64 E5 71 30N 124 05W
Thessalon Ontario 52 C6 46 15N 83 34W
Thetford Mines *tn.* Québec 53 Q6 46 06N 71 18W
Thicket Portage Manitoba 49 D4 55 20N 97 42W
Thirty Thousand Islands Ontario 52 F5 45 56N 80 57W
Thlewiaza River Nunavut 65 L3 60 50N 98 00W
Thomas Hubbard, Cape Nunavut 65 M6 81 45N 90 10W
Thomlinson, Mount British Columbia 43 G4 55 30N 127 30W
Thompson Manitoba 49 D4 55 45N 97 54W
Thompson River British Columbia 43 K2 50 12N 121 30W
Thomsen River Northwest Territories 64 G5 73 00N 119 50W
Thorah Island Ontario 54 C3 44 27N 79 13W
Thorhild Alberta 46 F4 54 10N 113 07W
Thornbury Ontario 54 B3 44 34N 80 27W
Thornhill *tn.* Ontario 54 C2 43 49N 79 26W
Thornloe Ontario 51 M4 47 42N 79 41W
Thorold Ontario 54 C2 43 08N 79 14W
Thorsby Alberta 46 E3 53 14N 114 03W
Thousand Islands Ontario 53 K4/L4 44 22N 75 55W
Three Hills *tn.* Alberta 46 F2 51 42N 113 16W
Three Mile Plains *tn.* Nova Scotia 61 M11 44 55N 64 10W
Thunder Bay *tn.* Ontario 51 G5 48 27N 89 12W
Thurso Québec 53 L5 45 38N 75 19W
Thutade Lake British Columbia 43 G5 56 59N 126 40W
Tide Head *tn.* New Brunswick 61 B3 47 58N 66 49W
Tignish Prince Edward Island 61 M12 46 58N 64 03W
Tikkoatokak Bay Newfoundland and Labrador 60 D8 56 42N 62 12W
Tilbury Ontario 52 D2 42 16N 82 26W
Tilbury Island British Columbia 44 F3 49 08N 123 02W
Tilden Lake *tn.* Ontario 52 G6 46 37N 79 39W
Tillsonburg Ontario 54 B1 42 53N 80 44W
Timber Bay Saskatchewan 47 E4 54 09N 105 40W
Timberlea Nova Scotia 61 M11 44 40N 63 45W
Timiskaming Québec 51 M4 46 44N 79 05W
Timiskaming, Lake Ontario 51 M4 46 52N 79 15W
Timmins Ontario 51 L5 48 30N 81 20W
Tinniswood, Mount British Columbia 42 H5 50 19N 123 47W
Tip Top Mountain Ontario 51 J5 48 16N 85 59W
Tirya River British Columbia 42 E6 58 46N 130 50W
Tisdale Saskatchewan 47 E3 52 51N 104 01W
Tiverton Ontario 54 A3 44 15N 81 33W
Tłegǫ́hłį *(Norman Wells) tn.* Northwest Territories 64 E4 65 19N 126 46W
Toad River *tn.* British Columbia 43 H6 58 50N 125 12W
Toba Inlet British Columbia 42 H5 50 25N 124 30W
Toba River British Columbia 42 H5 50 31N 124 18W
Tobeatic Wildlife Management Area Nova Scotia 61 L11 44 12N 65 25W
Tobermory Ontario 54 A4 45 15N 81 39W
Tobin Lake Saskatchewan 47 F3 53 30N 103 30W
Tofield Saskatchewan 46 F3 53 22N 112 40W
Tofino British Columbia 43 H1 49 05N 125 51W
Tombstone Territorial Park Yukon Territory 64 C3 64 30N 138 15W
Torbay Newfoundland and Labrador 61 J3 47 40N 52 44W
Tor Bay Nova Scotia 61 M12 45 15N 61 15W
Torch River Saskatchewan 47 F3 53 40N 103 50W
Tornado Mountain Alberta/British Columbia 43 N1 49 57N 114 35W
Torngat Mountains Newfoundland and Labrador 60 C9 59 00N 63 40W
Torngat Mountains National Park Reserve Newfoundland and Labrador 60 C9/D9 59 00N 63 30W
Toronto Ontario 54 C2 43 42N 79 46W
Toronto Islands Ontario 54 C2 43 42N 79 25W
Tottenham Ontario 54 C3 44 02N 79 48W
Touraine Québec 59 K2 45 29N 75 42W
Tracadie Nova Scotia 61 M12 45 38N 61 40W
Tracadie-Sheila New Brunswick 61 C3 47 32N 64 57W
Tracy New Brunswick 61 B2 45 41N 66 42W
Tracy Québec 53 N5 45 59N 73 04W
Trail British Columbia 43 M1 49 04N 117 39W
Trans-Canada Highway Canada 47 C2 50 10N 108 30W
Transcona Manitoba 48 C2 49 54N 97 01W
Treherne Manitoba 49 C1 49 39N 98 41W
Trembleur Lake British Columbia 43 H4 54 50N 124 55W
Trenton Nova Scotia 61 M12 45 37N 62 38W
Trenton Ontario 52 J4 44 07N 77 34W
Trent-Severn Waterway Ontario 54 C3 44 20N 79 23W
Trepassey Newfoundland and Labrador 61 J3 46 45N 53 20W
Trinity Bay Newfoundland and Labrador 61 J3 47 50N 53 40W
Trinity East Newfoundland and Labrador 61 J4 48 23N 53 20W
Triton Newfoundland and Labrador 61 H4 49 30N 55 30W
Trochu Alberta 46 F2 51 50N 113 13W
Trois-Pistoles Québec 53 S8 48 08N 69 10W
Trois-Rivières *tn.* Québec 53 P6 46 21N 72 34W
Trout Creek *tn.* Ontario 52 G5 45 59N 79 22W
Trout Lake Ontario 50 E6 51 20N 93 20W
Trout Lake *tn.* Alberta 46 E5 56 30N 114 32W
Trout River *tn.* Newfoundland and Labrador 61 H4 49 29N 58 08W
Troy Nova Scotia 61 M12 45 40N 61 30W
Truro Nova Scotia 61 M12 45 24N 63 18W
Tsawwassen British Columbia 42 H4 49 03N 123 06W
Tsiigehtchic *(Arctic Red River)* Northwest Territories 64 D4 67 27N 133 46W
Ts'yl-os Provincial Park British Columbia 43 H2 51 10N 123 50W
Tthebacha *(Fort Smith)* Northwest Territories 64 H3 60 01N 111 55W
Tthenáágóo *(Nahanni Butte) tn.* Northwest Territories 64 F3 61 30N 123 20W
Tthets'éhk'édéli *(Jean Marie River) tn.* Northwest Territories 64 F3 61 32N 120 38W
Tuchitua Yukon Territory 64 E3 61 20N 129 00W
Tuktut Nogait National Park Northwest Territories 64 F4 69 00N 121 50W
Tuktuujaqrtuuq *(Tuktoyaktuk)* Northwest Territories 64 D4 69 24N 133 01W
Tulemalu Lake Nunavut 65 L3 62 58N 99 25W
Tulit'a *(Fort Norman)* Northwest Territories 64 E3 64 55N 125 29W
Tumbler Ridge *tn.* British Columbia 43 K4 55 10N 121 01W
Tungsten Northwest Territories 64 E3 61 59N 128 09W
Tunungayualok Island Newfoundland and Labrador 60 E8 56 05N 61 05W
Turkey Point Ontario 54 B1 42 37N 80 20W
Turkey Point *tn.* Ontario 54 B1 43 41N 80 20W
Turkey Point Provincial Park Ontario 54 B1 42 45N 80 20W
Turnagain River British Columbia 43 F6 58 25N 129 08W
Turnavik Island Newfoundland and Labrador 60 F7 55 18N 59 21W
Turner Valley *tn.* Alberta 46 E2 50 40N 114 17W
Turnor Lake Saskatchewan 47 C5 56 35N 109 10W
Turnor Lake *tn.* Saskatchewan 47 C5 56 25N 108 40W
Turtleford Saskatchewan 47 C3 53 25N 108 588W
Turtle Mountain Provincial Park Manitoba 49 B1 49 00N 100 10W
Turtle River-White Otter Provincial Park Ontario 50 E5 49 15N 92 10W
Tusket Nova Scotia 61 L11 43 53N 65 58W
Tuxedo Manitoba 48 B2 49 51N 97 13W
Tuya Mountains Provincial Park British Columbia 42 E6 59 18N 130 35W
Tweed Ontario 53 J4 44 29N 77 19W
Twenty Mile Creek Ontario 54 C2 43 09N 79 48W
Twillingate Newfoundland and Labrador 61 H4 49 39N 54 46W
Twin Falls *tn.* Newfoundland and Labrador 60 C6 53 30N 64 32W
Twin Islands Nunavut 50 M7 53 20N 80 10W
Two Hills *tn.* Alberta 46 G3 53 43N 11 45W
Tyne Valley *tn.* Prince Edward Island 61 M12 46 36N 63 57W

U

Uashat Québec 57 G4 50 10N 66 00W
Ucluelet British Columbia 42 G4 48 55N 125 34W
Ugjoktok Bay Newfoundland and Labrador 60 E7 55 08N 60 30W
Uivak, Cape Newfoundland and Labrador 60 D9 58 29N 62 34W
Ukasiksalik Island Newfoundland and Labrador 60 E7 55 55N 60 47W
Ukkusiksalik National Park Nunavut 65 M4/N4 65 48N 90 00W
Uluqsaquuq *(Holman)* Northwest Territories 64 G5 70 44N 117 44W
Umingmaktok Nunavut 64 J4 65 00N 105 00W
Umiujaq Québec 56 B7 56 00N 76 44W
Ungava Bay *(Baie d'Ungava)* Québec 65 S2 58 00N 72 30W
Unionville Ontario 54 C2 43 51N 79 19W
United States Range *mts.* Nunavut 65 R7 82 25N 68 00W

Unity Saskatchewan 47 C3 52 27N 109 10W
Upper Arrow Lake British Columbia 43 M2 50 25N 117 56W
Upper Campbell Lake British Columbia 42 G4 49 57N 125 36W
Upper Foster Lake Saskatchewan 47 E5 56 40N 105 35W
Upper Liard Yukon Territory 64 E3 60 00N 129 20W
Upper Lillooet Provincial Park British Columbia 43 J2 51 35N 123 40W
Upper Musquodoboit Nova Scotia 61 M12 45 10N 62 58W
Upper Sackville Nova Scotia 59 Q7 44 48N 63 42W
Upper Salmon Reservoir Newfoundland and Labrador 61 G4 48 20N 55 30W
Upper Windigo Lake Ontario 50 F7 52 30N 91 35W
Uqsuqtuq *(Gjoa Haven)* Nunavut 65 L4 68 39N 96 09W
Uranium City Saskatchewan 47 C6 59 32N 108 43W
Utikuma Lake Alberta 46 E4 55 50N 115 25W
Uxbridge Ontario 54 C3 44 07N 79 09W

V

Valdes Island British Columbia 42 H4 49 05N 123 40W
Val-d'Or Québec 57 B3 48 07N 77 47W
Valemount British Columbia 43 L3 52 50N 119 15W
Valhalla Provincial Park British Columbia 43 L1 49 00N 118 00W
Valleyview Alberta 46 D4 55 04N 117 17W
Val Marie Saskatchewan 47 D1 49 15N 107 44W
Val-Paradis Québec 57 A3 49 10N 79 17W
Vancouver British Columbia 42 H4 49 13N 123 06W
Vancouver Island British Columbia 42 G4/H4 48 55N 124 33W
Vanderhoof British Columbia 43 H3 54 00N 124 00W
Vanier Ontario 53 L5 45 27N 75 40W
Vankleek Hill Ontario 53 M5 45 31N 74 39W
Vanscoy Saskatchewan 47 D3 52 01N 106 59W
Vansittart Island Nunavut 65 P4 65 50N 84 00W
Varennes Québec 53 N6 45 39N 73 26W
Vaudreil *admin.* Québec 53 M5 45 20N 74 20W
Vaughan Ontario 55 B2 43 39N 79 25W
Vauxhall Alberta 46 F2 50 04N 112 07W
Vegreville Alberta 46 F3 53 30N 112 03W
Verdun Québec 58 N4 44 28N 73 35W
Vermilion Alberta 46 G3 53 22N 110 51W
Vermilion Bay Ontario 50 E5 49 51N 93 21W
Vermilion Pass Alberta/British Columbia 46 D2 51 14N 116 03W
Vermilion River Alberta 46 G3 53 40N 111 25W
Vernon British Columbia 43 L2 50 17N 119 19W
Victoria British Columbia 42 H4 48 26N 123 20W
Victoria Newfoundland and Labrador 61 J3 47 46N 53 14W
Victoria Prince Edward Island 61 M12 46 10N 63 30W
Victoria *admin.* New Brunswick 61 B3 47 10N 67 30W
Victoria *admin.* Nova Scotia 61 M12 46 30N 60 30W
Victoria *admin.* Ontario 54 D3 44 45N 79 03W
Victoria Bridge Nova Scotia 61 M12 45 50N 60 20W
Victoria Harbour Ontario 52 G4 44 45N 79 45W
Victoria Island Northwest Territories/Nunavut 64 H5 70 45N 115 00W
Victoria Lake Newfoundland and Labrador 61 G4 48 18N 57 20W
Victoria River Newfoundland and Labrador 61 G4 48 30N 57 50W
Victoriaville Québec 53 Q6 46 04N 71 57W
Vienna Ontario 54 B1 42 39N 80 47W
Vieux Fort Québec 57 M4 51 59N 57 59W
Viking Alberta 46 G3 53 06N 111 488W
Virden Manitoba 49 B1 49 50N 100 57W
Virgil Ontario 54 C2 43 13N 79 07W
Virginiatown Ontario 51 M5 48 08N 79 35W
Viscount Melville Sound Northwest Territories/Nunavut 64 H5 74 10N 105 00W
Voisey's Bay Newfoundland and Labrador 60 E8 56 15N 61 50W
Voisey's Bay Mine Newfoundland and Labrador 60 D8 54 41N 62 12W
Vulcan Alberta 46 F2 50 24N 113 15W
Vuntut National Park Yukon Territory 64 C4 69 30N 139 30W

W

Wabakimi Lake Ontario 50 G6 50 38N 89 45W
Wabakimi Provincial Park Ontario 50 G6 50 30N 90 00W
Wabana Newfoundland and Labrador 61 J3 47 38N 52 57W
Wabasca-Desmarais Alberta 46 F4 55 59N 113 50W
Wabasca River Alberta 46 E5 57 30N 115 15W
Wabowden Manitoba 49 C4 54 57N 98 38W
Wabuk Point Ontario 50 J8 55 20N 85 05W
Wabush Newfoundland and Labrador 60 B6 52 55N 66 52W
Wabush Lake Newfoundland and Labrador 60 B6 53 05N 66 52W
Wabuskasing Ontario 50 E6 50 20N 93 10W
W.A.C. Bennet Dam British Columbia 43 J4 55 00N 122 11W
Waddington, Mount British Columbia 43 H2 51 22N 125 14W
Wade Lake Newfoundland and Labrador 60 C7 54 20N 65 38W
Wadena Saskatchewan 47 F2 51 57N 103 58W
Wager Bay Nunavut 65 N4 66 00N 89 00W
Waglisla British Columbia 43 F3 52 05N 128 10W
Wainfleet Ontario 54 C1 42 52N 79 22W
Wainwright Alberta 46 G3 52 49N 110 52W
Wakaw Saskatchewan 47 E3 52 40N 105 45W
Wakefield Québec 53 K5 45 39N 75 56W
Waldheim Saskatchewan 47 D3 52 39N 106 40W
Wales Island Nunavut 65 N4 68 01N 86 40W
Walker Lake Manitoba 49 D4 54 40N 96 40W
Walkerton Ontario 54 A3 44 08N 81 10W
Wallace Nova Scotia 61 M12 45 48N 63 26W
Wallaceburg Ontario 52 D2 42 34N 82 22W
Walton Nova Scotia 61 M12 45 14N 64 00W
Wanapitei Lake Ontario 51 L4 46 45N 80 45W
Wanless Manitoba 49 B4 54 11N 101 21W
Wapawekka Hills Saskatchewan 47 E4 54 50N 104 30W
Wapawekka Lake Saskatchewan 47 E4 55 00N 104 30W
Wapella Saskatchewan 47 G2 50 16N 101 59W
Wapikopa Lake Ontario 50 G7 52 54N 87 50W
Wapiti River Alberta 46 C4 54 40N 119 50W
Wapusk National Park Manitoba 49 F5 57 45N 93 20W
Wardsville Ontario 52 E2 42 39N 81 45W
Warman Saskatchewan 47 D3 52 19N 104 34W
Warner Alberta 46 F1 49 17N 112 12W
Warrender, Cape Nunavut 65 P5 74 28N 81 46W
Warren Landing *tn.* Manitoba 49 D3 53 42N 97 54W
Wasaga Beach *tn.* Ontario 54 B3 44 31N 80 02W
Wasaga Beach Provincial Park Ontario 54 B3 44 30N 80 05W
Wascana Creek Saskatchewan 47 E2 50 20N 104 20W
Wasekiu Lake *tn.* Saskatchewan 47 D3 53 55N 106 00W
Waskaganish Québec 57 A4 51 30N 79 45W
Waskaiowaka Lake Manitoba 49 D5 56 40N 96 40W
Waskamio Lake Saskatchewan 47 C5 56 50N 108 30W
Waskatenau Alberta 46 F4 54 06N 112 48W
Waswanipi Québec 57 C3 49 41N 75 57W
Waterbury Lake Saskatchewan 47 E6 58 10N 104 55W
Waterdown Ontario 54 C2 43 20N 79 54W
Waterford Ontario 54 B1 42 55N 80 19W
Waterhen Manitoba 49 C2 51 50N 99 30W
Waterhen Lake Manitoba 49 C3 52 00N 99 20W
Waterhen River Saskatchewan 47 C4 54 25N 108 50W
Waterloo Ontario 54 B2 43 28N 80 32W
Waterloo *admin.* Ontario 54 B2 43 30N 80 46W
Waterton Lakes National Park Alberta 46 F1 49 00N 114 45W
Watford Ontario 52 E2 42 57N 81 53W
Wathaman Lake Saskatchewan 47 F5 57 00N 104 10W
Wathaman River Saskatchewan 47 E5 56 50N 104 50W
Watrous Saskatchewan 47 E2 51 40N 105 29W
Watson Saskatchewan 47 E3 52 09N 104 31W
Watson Lake *tn.* Yukon Territory 64 E3 60 07N 128 49W
Waverley Nova Scotia 61 M11 44 48N 63 38W
Waverley Game Sanctuary Nova Scotia 59 Q7 44 49N 63 31W
Wawa Ontario 51 J4 48 00N 84 49W
Wawota Saskatchewan 47 G1 49 56N 102 00W
Weagamow Lake *tn.* Ontario 50 F7 52 53N 91 22W
Weaver Lake Manitoba 49 D3 52 40N 96 40W
Webbwood Ontario 52 E6 46 16N 81 53W
Webequie Ontario 50 H7 52 59N 87 21W
Wedge Mountain British Columbia 42 H5 50 07N 122 49W
Wedgeport Nova Scotia 61 L11 43 44N 66 00W
Wekusko Manitoba 49 C4 54 31N 99 45W
Wekusko Lake Manitoba 49 C4 54 30N 99 40W
Wekweti *(Snare Lakes)* Northwest Territories 64 H3 64 10N 114 20W
Weldon Saskatchewan 47 E3 53 00N 105 08W
Welland Ontario 54 C1 42 59N 79 14W
Welland Canal Ontario 54 C2 43 14N 79 13W
Welland River Ontario 54 C2 43 05N 79 46W
Wellesley Ontario 54 B2 43 27N 80 46W
Wellington Nova Scotia 59 Q7 44 50N 63 38W
Wellington Ontario 53 J3 43 57N 77 21W
Wellington *admin.* Ontario 54 B2 43 46N 80 41W
Wellington Channel Nunavut 65 L6 75 00N 93 00W
Wells British Columbia 43 K3 53 00N 121 30W
Wells Gray Provincial Park British Columbia 43 K3 52 00N 120 00W
Wells Lake Manitoba 49 B5 57 10N 100 30W
Wembley Alberta 46 C4 55 09N 119 08W
Wemindji Québec 57 A5 52 59N 78 50W
Wenebegon Lake Ontario 51 K4 47 23N 83 06W
Wentworth Nova Scotia 61 M12 45 39N 63 35W
Werner Lake Ontario 50 D6 50 27N 94 54W
Wesleyville Newfoundland and Labrador 61 J4 49 09N 53 34W
West Bay *tn.* Newfoundland and Labrador 60 G7 54 08N 57 26W
West Bay *tn.* Nova Scotia 61 M12 45 40N 61 10W
West Don River Ontario 55 B2 43 49N 79 31W
West Duffins Creek Ontario 55 D2 43 53N 79 10W
Western River Nunavut 64 J4 66 40N 107 00W
Westham Island British Columbia 44 F3 49 05N 123 10W
West Highland Creek Ontario 55 C2 43 46N 79 15W
West Humber River Ontario 55 B1 43 48N 79 43W
Westlock Alberta 46 F4 54 09N 113 52W
West Lorne Ontario 54 A1 42 36N 81 35W
Westmorland *admin.* New Brunswick 61 M12 46 10N 64 50W
Westmount Nova Scotia 61 M12 46 10N 60 10W
Westmount Québec 58 N4 44 29N 73 36W
West Nose Creek Alberta 44 A2 51 15N 114 11W
West Point Prince Edward Island 61 M12 46 38N 64 26W
Westport Nova Scotia 61 L11 44 20N 66 20W
Westport Ontario 53 K4 44 41N 76 24W
West Road River British Columbia 43 H3 53 12N 123 50W
West St. Modeste Newfoundland and Labrador 60 G5 51 36N 56 42W
West Thurlow Island British Columbia 42 G5 50 27N 125 35W
West Twin Provincial Park British Columbia 43 K3 53 20N 120 30W
West Vancouver British Columbia 42 H4 49 22N 123 11W
Westville Nova Scotia 61 M12 45 34N 62 44W
Wetaskiwin Alberta 46 F3 52 57N 113 20W
Weyburn Saskatchewan 47 F1 49 39N 103 51W
Weymouth Nova Scotia 61 L11 44 26N 66 00W
Whale Cove *(Tikirarjuaq) tn.* Nunavut 65 M3 62 10N 92 36W
Whaletown British Columbia 42 G5 50 06N 125 02W
What *(Lac la Martre)* Northwest Territories 64 G3 63 00N 117 30W
Wheatley Ontario 52 D2 42 06N 82 27W
Wheeler River Saskatchewan 47 E5 57 30N 105 10W
Whippoorwill Bay Ontario 54 A4 45 01N 81 15W
Whirl Creek Ontario 54 A2 43 29N 81 07W
Whistler British Columbia 42 H5 50 08N 122 58W
Whitby Ontario 54 D2 43 52N 78 56W
White Bay Newfoundland and Labrador 61 G5 50 00N 56 32W
White Bear Island Newfoundland and Labrador 60 E8 57 54N 61 42W
White Bear Lake Newfoundland and Labrador 60 F7 54 32N 59 30W
White City Saskatchewan 47 E2 50 35N 104 20W
Whitecourt Alberta 46 E4 54 10N 115 41W
Whitedog Ontario 49 D6 50 09N 94 55W
Whitefish Ontario 52 E6 46 23N 81 22W
Whitefish Bay Ontario 51 J4 46 38N 84 33W
Whitefish Lake Northwest Territories 64 J3 62 30N 106 40W
Whitefish Lake Ontario 51 J5 48 05N 84 10W
Whitefox River Saskatchewan 47 E3 53 25N 104 55W
White Handkerchief, Cape Newfoundland and Labrador 60 D9 59 17N 63 23W
Whitehorse Yukon Territory 64 C3 60 41N 135 08W
White Lake Ontario 51 J5 48 50N 85 30W
Whitemouth Manitoba 49 E1 49 58N 95 59W
Whitemouth Lake Manitoba 49 E1 49 10N 96 00W
Whitemouth River Manitoba 49 E1 49 50N 97 10W
White Otter Lake Ontario 50 F5 49 07N 91 52W
White Pass British Columbia 42 C6 59 37N 135 07W
White River Ontario 51 J5 48 30N 86 20W
White River Yukon Territory 64 B3 62 25N 140 05W
White River *tn.* Ontario 51 J5 48 35N 85 16W
White Rock British Columbia 42 H4 49 02N 122 50W
Whitesail Lake British Columbia 43 G3 53 25N 127 10W
Whitesand River Alberta 46 E6 59 00N 115 00W
Whiteshell Provincial Forest Manitoba 49 E1 49 50N 95 40W
Whiteshell Provincial Park Manitoba 49 E2 50 00N 95 20W
Whitewater Creek Saskatchewan/USA 47 D1 48 50N 107 40W
Whitewater Lake Ontario 50 G6 50 40N 89 30W
Whitewood Saskatchewan 47 F2 50 19N 102 16W
Whitney Ontario 52 H5 45 29N 78 15W
Whitworth Québec 53 S7 47 42N 69 17W
Wholdaia Lake Northwest Territories 64 K3 60 43N 104 10W
Whycocomagh Nova Scotia 61 M12 45 58N 61 08W
Wiarton Ontario 54 A3 44 44N 81 19W
Wildcat Hill Provincial Wilderness Area Saskatchewan 47 F3 53 20N 102 20W
Wildwood Alberta 46 E3 53 37N 115 14W
Wilkie Saskatchewan 47 C3 52 27N 108 42W
William, Lake Nova Scotia 59 Q7 44 46N 63 34W
William River Saskatchewan 47 C6 58 50N 108 55W
Williams Lake *tn.* British Columbia 43 J3 52 08N 122 07W
Williston Lake British Columbia 43 J4 56 00N 124 00W
Willmore Wilderness Park Alberta 46 C3 53 40N 119 30W
Will, Mount British Columbia 43 F5 57 30N 128 44W
Willowbunch Lake Saskatchewan 47 D1 49 20N 105 50W
Willow Lake Northwest Territories 64 G3 60 00N 115 00W
Winchester Ontario 53 L5 45 06N 75 21W
Windermere Lake Ontario 51 K4 47 58N 83 47W
Windigo Québec 53 N7 47 45N 73 22W
Windigo Lake Ontario 50 F7 52 35N 91 32W
Windsor Nova Scotia 61 M11 45 00N 64 09W
Windsor Ontario 52 C2 42 18N 83 00W
Windsor Québec 53 P5 45 35N 72 01W
Windsor Junction Nova Scotia 59 Q7 44 48N 63 38W
Winefred Lake Alberta 46 G4 55 30N 110 31W
Wingham Ontario 54 A2 43 54N 81 19W
Winisk Lake Ontario 50 H7 52 55N 87 22W
Winisk River Ontario 50 H7 54 50N 86 10W
Winisk River Provincial Park Ontario 50 H7 52 50N 87 30W
Winkler Manitoba 49 C1 49 12N 97 55W
Winnipeg Manitoba 49 D1 49 53N 97 10W
Winnipeg Beach *tn.* Manitoba 49 D2 50 30N 97 00W
Winnipeg, Lake Manitoba 49 C3/D3 53 00N 97 00W
Winnipegosis Manitoba 49 C2 51 40N 99 59W
Winnipegosis, Lake Manitoba 49 B3 52 10N 100 00W
Winnipeg River Manitoba 49 E2 50 20N 95 30W
Winokapau Lake Newfoundland and Labrador 60 D6 53 10N 62 52W
Winona Ontario 54 C2 43 12N 79 38W
Witless Bay *tn.* Newfoundland and Labrador 61 J3 47 16N 52 50W
Wolfe *admin.* Québec 53 Q5 45 40N 71 40W
Wolfe Island Ontario 53 K4 44 31N 75 59W
Wolfville Nova Scotia 61 M12 45 06N 64 22W
Wollaston, Cape Northwest Territories 64 G5 71 06N 118 04W
Wollaston Lake Saskatchewan 47 F6 58 20N 103 00W
Wollaston Lake *tn.* Saskatchewan 47 F6 58 05N 103 38W
Wollaston Peninsula Northwest Territories/Nunavut 64 H4 70 00N 115 00W
Wolseley Saskatchewan 47 F2 50 25N 103 15W
Woodbridge Ontario 54 C2 43 47N 79 36W
Wood Buffalo National Park Alberta/Northwest Territories 46 F6 59 00N 112 30W
Woodfibre British Columbia 42 H4 49 36N 123 00W
Wood Islands Prince Edward Island 61 M12 45 50N 62 40W
Woodland Caribou Provincial Park Ontario 50 D6 51 10N 94 20W
Wood Mountain Saskatchewan 47 D1 49 15N 106 20W
Woodside Nova Scotia 59 Q6 44 39N 63 31W
Woods Lake Newfoundland and Labrador 60 C7 54 30N 65 13W
Woods, Lake of the Ontario 50 D5 49 15N 94 45W
Woodstock New Brunswick 61 B3 46 10N 67 36W
Woodstock Ontario 54 B2 43 07N 80 46W
Woodville Ontario 54 D3 44 24N 78 44W
Wrong Lake Manitoba 49 E3 52 40N 96 10W
Wunnummin Lake Ontario 50 G7 52 55N 89 10W
Wynniatt Bay Northwest Territories 64 H5 72 45N 110 30W
Wynyard Saskatchewan 47 E2 51 50N 104 10W

Y

Yale British Columbia 42 H4 49 31N 121 29W
Yamaska *admin.* Québec 53 P5 46 00N 72 50W
Yarmouth Nova Scotia 61 L11 43 50N 66 08W
Yarmouth *admin.* Nova Scotia 61 L11 44 50N 65 40W
Yates River Alberta 46 D6 59 40N 116 25W
Yathkyed Lake Nunavut 65 L3 62 40N 98 00W
Yellow Grass Saskatchewan 47 E1 49 49N 104 11W
Yellowhead Highway Alberta 46 G3 53 20N 110 45W
Yellowhead Pass Alberta/British Columbia 46 C3 52 53N 118 28W
Yellowknife River Northwest Territories 64 H3 62 35N 114 10W
Yoho National Park British Columbia 43 M2 51 00N 116 00W
York New Brunswick 61 B3 46 10N 66 50W
York *admin.* Ontario 54 C2 43 57N 79 39W
York Ontario 55 C2 43 41N 79 28W
York, Cape Nunavut 65 N5 73 48N 87 00W
York Factory Manitoba 49 F5 57 08N 92 25W
York Landing Manitoba 49 E5 56 05N 95 59W
Yorkton Saskatchewan 47 F2 51 12N 102 29W
Youbou British Columbia 42 H4 48 52N 124 12W
Young Saskatchewan 47 E2 51 45N 105 45W
Yukon River Yukon Territory/USA 64 C3 63 00N 138 50W
Yukon Territory *territory* 64

Z

Zama City Alberta 46 C6 59 08N 118 43W
Zeballos British Columbia 43 G1 49 57N 126 10W
Zhahti Koé *(Fort Providence)* Northwest Territories 64 G3 61 03N 117 40W
Zürich Ontario 54 A2 43 25N 81 37W

A

Aachen Germany 86 J9 50 46N 6 06E
Aalst Belgium 86 H9 50 57N 4 03E
Aba Nigeria 108 F9 5 06N 7 21E
Abādān Irān 97 E5 30 20N 48 15E
Abadla Algeria 108 D14 31 01N 2 45W
Abaetetuba Brazil 80 H13 1 45S 48 54W
Abakan Russia 95 M7 53 43N 91 25E
Abakan *r.* Russia 95 L7 52 00N 90 00E
Abancay Peru 80 C11 13 37S 72 52W
Abashiri Japan 102 D3 44 02N 114 17E
Abbe, Lake Ethiopia 108 N10 11 00N 44 00E
Abbeville Fr. 86 F9 50 06N 1 51E
'Abd al Kūrī *i.* Yemen 97 F1 11 55N 52 20E
Abéché Chad 108 J10 13 49N 20 49E
Abeokuta Nigeria 108 E9 7 10N 3 26E
Aberdeen UK 86 D12 57 10N 2 04W
Aberdeen HK China 100 B1 22 14N 114 09E
Aberdeen Maryland USA 73 B1 39 31N 76 10N
Aberdeen South Dakota USA 71 G6 45 28N 98 30W
Aberdeen Washington USA 70 B6 46 58N 123 49W
Aberystwyth UK 86 C10 52 25N 4 05W
Abhā Saudi Arabia 96 D2 18 14N 42 31E
Abidjan Côte d'Ivoire 108 D9 5 19N 4 01W
Abilene Texas USA 70 G3 32 27N 99 49W
Absaroka Range *mts.* USA 70 D6/E5 45 00N 110 00W
Abu Dhabi UAE 97 F3 24 28N 54 25E
Abu Hamed Sudan 108 L11 19 32N 33 20E
Abuja Nigeria 108 F9 9 10N 7 11E
Āl Bū Kamāl Syria 96 D5 34 29N 40 56E
Abu Kebir Egypt 109 R3 30 44N 31 48E
Abunã Brazil 80 D12 9 41S 65 20W
Acambaro Mexico 74 D3 20 00N 100 42W
Acaponeta Mexico 74 C4 22 30N 102 25W
Acapulco Mexico 74 E3 16 51N 99 56W
Acarigua Venezuela 80 D15 9 35N 69 12W
Acatlán Mexico 74 E3 18 12N 98 02W
Acayucán Mexico 74 E3 17 59N 94 58W
Accra Ghana 108 D9 5 33N 0 15W
Achacachi Bolivia 80 D10 16 01S 68 44W
Achinsk Russia 95 M8 56 20N 90 33E
Acklins Island Bahamas 75 K4 22 30N 74 30W
Aconcagua *mt.* Argentina 81 C7 32 40S 70 02W
Acre Israel 96 N11 32 55N 35 04E
Acre *admin.* Brazil 80 C12 8 30S 71 30W
Ada Oklahoma USA 71 G3 34 47N 96 41W
Adaga *r.* Sp. 87 C4 40 45N 4 45W
Adams New York USA 53 K3 43 49N 76 01W
Adana Turkey 96 C6 37 00N 35 19E
Ad Dakhla Western Sahara 108 A12 23 50N 15 58W
Ad Dammām Saudi Arabia 97 F4 26 25N 50 06E
Ad Dilam Saudi Arabia 97 E3 23 59N 47 06E
Ad Dir'īyah Saudi Arabia 97 E3 24 45N 46 32E
Addis Ababa Ethiopia 108 M9 9 03N 38 42E
Addison New York USA 53 J2 42 06N 77 14W
Ad Dīwānīyah Iraq 96 D5 32 00N 44 57E
Adelaide Aust. 110 F3 34 56S 138 36E
Adelanto California USA 72 E2 34 35N 117 24W
Adelie Land *geog. reg.* Antarctica 117 70 00S 135 00E
Aden Yemen 96 E1 12 50N 45 03E
Aden, Gulf of Indian Ocean 97 E1 12 30N 47 30E
Adirondack Mountains New York USA 71 M5 43 15N 74 40W
Admiralty Island Alaska USA 42 C5 57 45N 134 30W
Admiralty Island National Monument Alaska USA 42 C6 58 05N 134 00W
Admiralty Islands PNG 110 H9 2 30S 147 00E
Adoni India 98 D3 15 38N 77 16E
Adra Sp. 87 D2 36 45N 3 01W
Adrar Algeria 108 D13 27 51N 0 19W
Adrian Michigan USA 51 J1 41 54N 84 02W
Adriatic Sea Mediterranean Sea 89 E5 43 00N 15 00E
Ādwa Ethiopia 108 M10 14 12N 38 56E
Aegean Sea Mediterranean Sea 89 K3 39 00N 24 00E
AFGHANISTAN 97 H5/K6
Afyon Turkey 96 B6 38 46N 30 32E
Agadez Niger 108 F11 17 00N 7 56E
Agadir Morocco 108 C14 30 30N 9 40W
Agano *r.* Japan 102 C2 37 50N 139 30E
Agartala India 99 G4 23 49N 91 15E
Agen Fr. 87 F6 44 12N 0 38E
Ágios Nikólaos Greece 89 K1 35 11N 25 43E
Agout *r.* Fr. 87 G5 43 50N 1 50E
Agra India 98 D5 27 09N 78 00E
Agri *r.* Italy 89 F4 40 00N 16 00E
Ağri Daği *mt.* Turkey 96 D6 39 44N 44 15E
Agrigento Italy 89 D2 37 19N 13 35E
Agrínio Greece 89 H3 38 38N 21 25E
Aguadas Col. 80 B15 5 36N 75 30W
Aguadilla Puerto Rico 75 L3 18 27N 67 08W
Agua Prieta Mexico 74 C6 31 20N 109 32W
Aguascalientes Mexico 74 D4 21 51N 102 18W
Agueda *r.* Sp. 87 B4 40 50N 6 50W
Aguilas Sp. 87 E2 37 25N 1 35W
Aguiles Serdan Mexico 74 C5 28 40N 105 57W
Agulhas Basin Indian Ocean 113 A2 45 00S 20 00E
Agulhas, Cape RSA 109 J1 34 50S 20 00E
Ahmadabad India 98 C4 23 03N 72 40E
Ahmadnagar India 98 C3 19 08N 74 48E
Ahuachapán El Salvador 74 G2 13 57N 89 49W
Ahvāz Iran 97 E5 31 17N 48 43E
Ain *r.* Fr. 87 H7 46 30N 5 30E
Aïn Sefra Algeria 108 D14 32 45N 0 35W
Aïr *mts.* Niger 108 F11 19 10N 8 20E
Aire-sur-l'Adour Fr. 87 E5 43 42N 0 15W
Aix-en-Provence Fr. 87 H5 43 31N 5 27E
Aizawl India 99 M9 23 43N 92 47E
Aizu-wakamatsu Japan 102 C2 37 30N 139 58E
Ajaccio France 87 K4 41 55N 8 43E
Ajay *r.* India 99 J9 23 50N 88 00E
Ajdabiya Libya 108 J14 30 46N 20 14E
'Ajlūn Jordan 96 N11 32 20N 35 35E
Ajman UAE 97 G4 25 23N 55 26E
Ajmer India 98 C5 26 29N 74 40E
Ajo Arizona USA 70 D3 32 24N 112 51W
Akabira Japan 102 D3 43 40N 141 55E
Akaroa NZ 111 D3 43 49S 172 58E
Akashi Japan 102 B1 34 39N 135 00E
Aketi CDR 108 J8 2 42N 23 51E
Akita Japan 102 D2 39 44N 140 05E
Akobo Sudan 108 L9 7 50N 33 05E
Akola India 98 D4 20 49N 77 05E
Ákra Akrítas *c.* Greece 89 H2 36 43N 21 52E
Ákra Kafiréas *c.* Greece 89 K3 38 10N 24 35E
Ákra Maléas *c.* Greece 89 J2 36 27N 23 12E
Ákra Taínaro *c.* Greece 89 J2 36 23N 22 29E
Akron Ohio USA 71 K5 41 04N 81 31W
Aktau Kazakhstan 94 H5 43 37N 51 11E
Aktyubinsk Kazakhstan 94 H7 50 16N 57 13E
Alabama *r.* Alabama USA 71 J3 31 00N 88 00W
Alabama *state* USA 71 J3 32 00N 87 00W
Alagoas *admin.* Brazil 80 K12 9 30S 37 00W
Alagoinhas Brazil 80 K11 12 09S 38 21W
Alagón *r.* Sp. 87 B3 40 00N 6 30W
Alajuela Costa Rica 75 H2 10 00N 84 12W
Al 'Amārah Iraq 97 E5 31 51N 47 10E
Alamo Nevada USA 72 F3 37 23N 115 10W
Alamosa Colorado USA 70 E4 37 28N 105 54W
Åland *is.* Finland 88 G14 60 15N 20 00E
Alanya Turkey 96 B6 36 32N 32 02E
Al Artāwīyah Saudi Arabia 96 E4 26 31N 45 21E
Ala Shan *mts.* China 101 J6/J7 40 00N 102 30E
Alaska *state* USA 42 C5 58 00N 135 00W
Alaska, Gulf of Alaska USA 115 M13 58 00N 147 00W
Alaska Range *mts.* Alaska USA 64 A3/B3 62 30N 145 00W
Al 'Ayn UAE 97 G3 24 10N 55 43E
Alay Range *mts.* Asia 94 K4 39 00N 70 00E
Albacete Sp. 87 E3 39 00N 1 52W
Alba Iulia Romania 89 J7 46 04N 23 33E
ALBANIA 89 G4/H4
Albany Aust. 110 B3 34 57S 117 54E
Albany Georgia USA 71 K3 31 37N 84 10W
Albany New York USA 71 M5 42 40N 73 49W
Albany Oregon USA 70 B5 44 38N 123 07W
Al Başrah Iraq 97 E5 30 30N 47 50E
Al Bayda Libya 108 J14 32 00N 21 30E
Albert, Lake Uganda/CDR 108 L8 2 00N 31 00E
Albert Lea Minnesota USA 71 H5 43 38N 93 16W
Albi Fr. 87 G5 43 56N 2 08E
Albion Michigan USA 52 B2 42 14N 84 45W
Albion New York USA 52 H3 43 14N 78 11W
Al Bi'r Saudi Arabia 96 C4 28 50N 36 16E
Ålborg Denmark 88 B12 57 05N 9 50E
Albuquerque New Mexico USA 70 E4 35 05N 106 38W
Al Buraymī Oman 97 G3 24 16N 55 48E
Alcalá de Henares Sp. 87 D4 40 28N 3 22W
Alcamo Italy 89 D2 37 58N 12 58E
Alcañiz Sp. 87 E4 41 03N 0 09W
Alcázar de San Juan Sp. 87 D3 39 24N 3 12W
Alcira Sp. 87 E3 39 10N 0 27W
Alcoy Sp. 87 E3 38 42N 0 29W
Aldabra Islands Indian Ocean 113 D6 9 00S 46 00E
Aldama Mexico 74 E4 22 54N 98 05W
Aldan Russia 95 Q8 58 44N 124 22E
Aldan *r.* Russia 95 R8 59 00N 132 30E
Alderney *i.* British Isles 86 D8 49 43N 2 12W
Alegrete Brazil 81 F8 29 45S 55 40W
Aleksandrovsk-Sakhalinskiy Russia 95 S7 50 55N 142 12E
Alençon Fr. 86 F8 48 25N 0 05E
Alenuihaha Channel *sd.* Hawaiian Islands 115 Y18 20 20N 156 20W
Aleppo Syria 96 C6 36 14N 37 10E
Alès Fr. 87 H6 44 08N 4 05E
Alessándria Italy 89 B6 44 55N 8 37E
Aleutian Basin Pacific Ocean 114 J13 54 00N 178 00W
Aleutian Islands Pacific Ocean 114 H13 52 00N 178 00W
Aleutian Ridge Pacific Ocean 114 H13 53 55N 178 00W
Aleutian Trench Pacific Ocean 114 H13 50 55N 178 00W
Alexander Archipelago *is.* Alaska USA 42 B5/D4 57 00N 137 30W
Alexander Bay *tn.* RSA 109 H2 28 40S 16 30E
Alexander Island Antarctica 117 71 00S 70 00W
Alexandra NZ 111 B2 45 15S 169 23E
Alexandria Egypt 108 K14 31 13N 29 55E
Alexandria Romania 89 K5 43 59N 25 19E
Alexandria Louisiana USA 71 H3 31 19N 92 29W
Alexandria Bay *tn.* New York USA 51 P3 44 20N 75 55W
Alexandroúpoli Greece 89 K4 40 51N 25 53E
Alfambra *r.* Sp. 87 E4 40 40N 1 00W
Alfeiós *r.* Greece 89 H2 37 30N 21 45E
Al Fuḩayḩil Kuwait 97 E4 29 07N 47 02E
Algeciras Sp. 87 C2 36 08N 5 27W
ALGERIA 108 C13
Alghero Italy 89 B4 40 34N 8 19E
Algiers Algeria 108 E15 36 50N 3 00E
Al Hadīthah Iraq 96 D5 34 06N 42 25E
Al Hariq Saudi Arabia 97 E3 23 34N 46 35E
Al Ḩasakah Syria 96 D6 36 32N 40 44E
Al Ḩillah Iraq 96 D5 32 28N 44 29E
Al Hufūf Saudi Arabia 97 E4 25 20N 49 34E
Aliákmanas *r.* Greece 89 J4 40 00N 22 00E
Alicante Sp. 87 E3 38 21N 0 29W
Alice Texas USA 71 G2 27 45N 98 06W
Alice Springs *tn.* Aust. 110 E5 23 42S 133 52E
Aligarh India 98 D5 27 54N 78 04E
Aling Kangri *mt.* China 100 E5 32 51N 81 03E
Alipur Duar India 99 K11 26 27N 89 38E
Al Jahrah Kuwait 97 E4 29 22N 47 40E
Al Jawf Libya 108 J12 24 12N 23 18E
Al Jawf Saudi Arabia 96 C4 29 49N 39 52E
Al Jubayl Saudi Arabia 97 E4 26 59N 49 40E
Aljustrel Port. 87 A2 37 52N 8 10W
Al Karāmah Jordan 96 N10 31 58N 35 34E
Al Khums Libya 108 G14 32 39N 14 16E
Al Kufrah Oasis Libya 108 J12 24 10N 23 15E
Al Kūt Iraq 96 E5 32 30N 45 51E
Allagash River Maine USA 53 S6 46 45N 69 20W
Allahabad India 98 E5 25 27N 81 50E
Allegheny River Pennsylvania USA 52 G1 41 40N 79 30W
Allegheny Mountains Pennsylvania USA 73 A2 40 30N 78 25W
Allegheny Reservoir Pennsylvania/New York USA 51 M1 41 52N 79 00W
Allende Mexico 74 D5 28 22N 100 50W
Allentown Pennsylvania USA 71 L5 40 37N 75 30W
Alleppey India 98 D1 9 30N 76 22E
Alliance Nebraska USA 70 F5 42 08N 102 54W
Allier *r.* Fr. 87 G7 46 40N 3 00E
Al Līth Saudi Arabia 96 D3 20 10N 40 20E
Alma Michigan USA 52 B3 43 23N 84 40W
Almada Port. 87 A3 38 40N 9 09W
Almadén Sp. 87 C3 38 47N 4 50W
Almansa Sp. 87 E3 38 52N 1 06W
Almanzora *r.* Sp. 87 D2 37 15N 2 10W
Almaty Kazakhstan 94 K5 43 19N 76 55E
Almería Sp. 87 D2 36 50N 2 26W
Älmhult Sweden 88 E12 56 32N 14 10E
Almodôvar Port. 87 A2 37 31N 8 03W
Al Mubarraz Saudi Arabia 97 E4 25 26N 49 37E
Al Mukhā Yemen 96 D1 13 20N 43 16E
Al Muqdādīyah Iraq 96 D5 33 58N 44 58E
Alor *i.* Indonesia 103 G2 8 15S 124 30E
Alor Setar Malaysia 103 C5 6 07N 100 21E
Alpena Michigan USA 51 K3 45 03N 83 27W
Alpes Maritimes *mts.* Fr./Italy 87 J5/J6 44 15N 6 45E
Alpi Carniche *mts.* Europe 89 D7 46 00N 13 00E
Alpi Cozie *mts.* Europe 87 J6 45 00N 8 00E
Alpi Dolomitiche *mts.* Italy 89 C7 46 00N 12 00E
Alpi Graie *mts.* Europe 89 A6 45 00N 7 00E
Alpi Lepontine *mts.* Switz. 87 K7 46 26N 8 30E
Alpine Texas USA 70 F3 30 22N 103 40W
Alpi Pennine *mts.* Italy/Switz. 87 J7 45 55N 7 30E
Alpi Retiche *mts.* Switz. 87 K7/L7 46 25N 9 45E
Alps *mts.* Europe 87 J6/L7 46 00N 7 30E
Al Qāmishlī Syria 96 D6 37 03N 41 15E
Al Qunayţirah Syria 96 N11 33 08N 35 49E
Al Qunfudhah Saudi Arabia 96 D2 19 09N 41 07E
Alsek River Alaska USA 42 A6 59 15N 138 40W
Alta Gracia Argentina 81 E7 31 42S 64 25W
Altai *mts.* Mongolia 100 G8 47 00N 92 30E
Altamaha *r.* Georgia USA 71 K3 32 00N 82 00W
Altamira Brazil 80 G13 3 13S 52 15W
Altamura Italy 89 F4 40 49N 16 34E
Altay China 100 F8 47 48N 88 07E
Altay *mts.* Russia 95 L7 51 00N 89 00E
Alto Molocue Mozambique 109 M4 15 38S 37 42E
Altoona Pennsylvania USA 71 L5 40 32N 78 32W
Alto Purus *r.* Peru 80 C11 10 30S 72 00W
Altun Shan *mts.* China 100 E6/F6 37 30N 86 00E
Altus Oklahoma USA 70 G3 34 39N 99 21W
Alva Oklahoma USA 71 G4 36 48N 98 40W
Al Wajh Saudi Arabia 96 C4 26 16N 32 28E
Alwar India 98 D5 27 32N 76 35E
Amadeus, Lake Aust. 110 E5 24 00S 132 30E
Amadi Sudan 108 L9 5 32N 30 20E
Amagasaki Japan 102 C1 34 42N 135 23E
Amakusa-shotō *is.* Japan 102 B1 32 50N 130 05E
Amapá Brazil 80 G14 2 00N 50 50W
Amapá *admin.* Brazil 80 G14 2 00N 52 30W
Amargosa Desert Nevada USA 72 E3 36 45N 116 37W
Amargosa Valley *tn.* Nevada USA 72 E3 36 40N 116 22W
Amarillo Texas USA 70 F4 35 14N 101 50W
Amazonas *admin.* Brazil 80 D13 4 30S 65 00W
Amazonas *r.* Brazil 80 G13 2 00S 53 00W
Amazon, Mouths of the *est.* Brazil 80 G14 1 00N 51 00W
Ambala India 98 D6 30 19N 76 49E
Ambarchik Russia 95 U10 69 39N 162 37E
Ambato Ecuador 80 B13 1 18S 78 39W
Ambon Indonesia 103 H3 3 41S 128 10E
Ambovombe Madagascar 109 P2 25 10S 46 06E
Amboy California USA 72 F2 34 33N 115 44W
Amderma Russia 94 J10 66 44N 61 35E
Amdo China 100 G5 32 22N 91 07E
Ameca Mexico 74 D4 20 34N 104 03W
American Falls *tn.* Idaho USA 70 D5 42 47N 112 50W
American Samoa Pacific Ocean 115 K6 15 00S 170 00W
Amery Ice Shelf Antarctica 117 70 00S 70 00E
Amfípoli Greece 89 J4 40 48N 23 52E
Amga Russia 95 R9 61 51N 131 59E
Amga *r.* Russia 95 R9 60 30N 130 00E
Amgun' *r.* Russia 95 R7 52 00N 137 00E
Amiens Fr. 86 G8 49 54N 2 18E
Amindivi Islands India 98 C2 11 23N 72 23E
Amirante Islands Seychelles 113 E6 5 00S 55 00E
Amman Jordan 96 C5 31 04N 46 17E
Amorgós *i.* Greece 89 K2 36 50N 25 55E
Ampana Indonesia 103 G3 0 54S 121 35E
Amravati India 98 D4 20 58N 77 50E
Amritsar India 98 C6 31 35N 74 56E
Amsterdam Neths. 86 H10 52 22N 4 54E
Amsterdam New York USA 73 C3 42 57N 74 11W
Amstetten Austria 88 E8 48 08N 14 52E
Am Timan Chad 108 J10 10 59N 20 18E
Amudar'ya *r.* Asia 94 J4/J5 40 00N 64 00E
Amundsen Sea Southern Ocean 117 72 00S 130 00W
Amur *r.* Asia 101 P9 52 30N 126 30E
Amursk Russia 95 R7 50 16N 136 55E
Anabar *r.* Russia 95 P11 71 30N 113 00E
Anacapa Islands California USA 72 D2 34 01N 119 23W
Anaconda Montana USA 70 D6 46 09N 112 56W
Anacortes Washington USA 42 H4 48 29N 122 35W
Anadolu Dağlari *mts.* Turkey 96 C7/D7 40 30N 38 30E
Anadyr' Russia 95 V9 64 50N 178 00E
Anadyr' *r.* Russia 95 V10 65 00N 175 00E
Anadyr', Gulf of Russia 95 W9 65 00N 178 00W
Anáfi *i.* Greece 89 K2 36 20N 25 45E
Anaheim California USA 72 E1 33 50N 117 54W
Anai Mudi *mt.* India 98 D2 10 20N 77 15E
Anan Japan 102 B1 33 54N 134 40E
Ananindeua Brazil 80 H13 1 22S 48 20W
Anantapur India 98 D2 14 42N 77 05E
Anápolis Brazil 80 H10 16 19S 48 58W
Ancona Italy 89 D5 43 37N 13 31E
Andaman and Nicobar *admin.* India 99 G1 12 30N 92 45E
Andaman Islands India 99 G2 12 00N 94 00E
Anderson South Carolina USA 71 K3 34 30N 82 39W
Anderson Indiana USA 71 J5 40 05N 85 41W
Andes *mts.* South America 80/81 B14 10 00S 77 00W
Andhra Pradesh *admin.* India 98 D3 16 00N 79 00E
Andizhan Uzbekistan 94 K5 40 40N 72 12E
Andkhvoy Afghanistan 97 J6 36 59N 65 08E
ANDORRA 87 F5
Andorra la Vella Andorra 87 F5 42 30N 1 30E
Andros *i.* Bahamas 75 J4 24 00N 78 00W
Ándros *i.* Greece 89 K2 37 49N 24 54E
Androscoggin River Maine USA 57 E1 44 27N 70 50W
Andújar Sp. 87 C3 38 02N 4 03W
Andulo Angola 109 H5 11 29S 16 43E
Angara *r.* Russia 95 M8 58 00N 97 30E
Angarsk Russia 95 N7 52 31N 103 55E
Angel de la Guarda *i.* Mexico 74 B5 29 00N 113 30W
Angelholm Sweden 88 D12 56 15N 12 50E
Angels Camp California USA 72 C4 38 04N 120 34W
Angers Fr. 87 E7 47 29N 0 32W
Anglesey *i.* UK 86 C10 53 18N 4 25W
ANGOLA 109 H5
Angola Indiana USA 51 J1 41 38N 84 59W
Angola New York USA 52 G2 42 39N 79 02W
Angola Basin Atlantic Ocean 116 J5 15 00S 3 00E
Angoon Alaska USA 42 C5 57 30N 133 35W
Angoulême Fr. 87 F6 45 40N 0 10E
Anguilla *i.* Leeward Islands 74 P10 18 14N 63 05W
Anjō Japan 102 C1 34 56N 137 05E
Ankara Turkey 96 B6 39 55N 32 50E
Ankaratra *mt.* Madagascar 109 P4 19 25S 47 12E
'Annaba Algeria 108 F15 36 55N 7 47E
An Nabk Saudi Arabia 96 C5 31 21N 37 20E
An Nabk Syria 96 C5 34 02N 36 43E
An Nafud *d.* Saudi Arabia 96 D4 28 20N 40 30E
An Najaf Iraq 96 D5 31 59N 44 19E
Annapolis Maryland USA 71 L4 38 59N 76 30W
Annapurna *mt.* Nepal 98 E5 28 34N 83 50E
Ann Arbor Michigan USA 51 K2 42 17N 83 45W
An Nāsirīyah Iraq 96 E5 31 04N 46 17E
Annecy Fr. 87 J6 45 54N 6 07E
Annette Island Alaska USA 42 E4 55 10N 131 30W
Anniston Alabama USA 71 J3 33 38N 85 50W
Annotto Bay *tn.* Jamaica 75 U14 18 16N 76 47W
Anqing China 101 M5 30 46N 119 40E
Ansbach Germany 88 C8 49 18N 10 36E
Anshan China 101 N7 41 05N 122 58E
Anshun China 101 K4 26 15N 105 51E
Antakya Turkey 96 C6 36 12N 36 10E
Antalya Turkey 96 B6 36 53N 30 42E
Antananarivo Madagascar 109 P4 18 52S 47 30E
Antarctica 117
Antarctic Peninsula Antarctica 117 68 00S 65 00W
Antequera Sp. 87 C2 37 01N 4 34W
Antibes Fr. 87 J5 43 35N 7 07E
Antigua Guatemala 74 F2 14 33N 90 42W
Antigua *i.* Antigua & Barbuda 74 Q9 17 09N 61 49W
ANTIGUA AND BARBUDA 74 Q9
Antioch California USA 72 C4 38 00N 121 49W
Antipodes Islands Southern Ocean 114 H3 49 42S 178 50E
Antofagasta Chile 80 C9 23 40S 70 23W
Antsiranana Madagascar 109 P5 12 19S 49 17E

Name	Page	Grid	Lat	Long
Antwerp New York USA	53	L4	44 13N	75 38W
Antwerpen Belgium	86	H9	51 13N	4 25W
Anuradhapura Sri Lanka	98	E1	8 20N	80 25E
Anxi China	100	H7	40 32N	95 57E
Anyang China	101	L6	36 04N	114 20E
Anza California USA	72	E1	33 33N	116 41W
Anzhero-Sudzhensk Russia	95	L8	56 10N	86 01E
Aomori Japan	102	D3	40 50N	140 43E
Aosta Italy	89	A6	45 43N	7 19E
Aozou Strip Chad	108	H12	23 00N	17 00E
Apaporis *r.* Col.	80	C14	1 00N	72 30W
Aparri Philippines	103	G7	18 22N	121 40E
Apatity Russia	94	F10	67 32N	33 21E
Apatzingán Mexico	74	D3	19 05N	102 20W
Apostle Islands Wisconsin USA	51	F4	47 02N	90 30W
Appalachian Mountains USA	71	K4	37 00N	82 00W
Appennini *mts.* Italy	89	B6/E4	43 00N	12 30E
Appennino Abruzzese *mts.* Italy	89	D5/E4	42 00N	14 00E
Appennino Ligure *mts.* Italy	89	B6	44 00N	9 00E
Appennino Lucano *mts.* Italy	89	E4	40 30N	15 30E
Appennino Tosco-Emiliano *mts.* Italy	89	C6/D5	44 00N	12 00E
Appleton Wisconsin USA	71	J5	44 17N	88 24W
Apure *r.* Venezuela	80	D15	7 40N	68 00W
'Aqaba Jordan	96	C5	29 32N	35 00E
Aqaba, Gulf of Middle East	96	N9	28 40N	34 40E
Aquidauana Brazil	80	F9	20 27S	55 45W
Aquidauana *r.* Brazil	80	F10	20 00S	56 00W
Arabian Basin Indian Ocean	113	F7/F8	10 00N	65 00E
Arabian Sea Indian Ocean	113	F8	17 00N	60 00E
Aracaju Brazil	80	K11	10 54S	37 07W
Aracati Brazil	80	K13	4 32S	37 45W
Arad Romania	89	H7	46 10N	21 19E
Arafura Sea Indonesia	103	J2	8 00S	132 00E
Aragón *r.* Sp.	87	E5	42 15N	1 40W
Araguaia *r.* Brazil	80	H12	7 20S	49 00W
Araguaína Brazil	80	H12	7 16S	48 18W
Araguari Brazil	80	H10	18 38S	48 13W
Arāk Iran	97	E5	34 05N	49 42E
Aral Sea *l.* Asia	94	H5/J6	45 00N	60 00E
Aral'sk Kazakhstan	94	J6	46 56N	61 43E
Arambag India	99	K9	22 50N	87 59E
Aranda de Duero Sp.	87	D4	41 40N	3 41W
Aran Islands RoI	86	A10	53 10N	9 50W
Aranjuez Sp.	87	D4	40 02N	3 37W
Arapiraca Brazil	80	K12	9 45S	36 40W
Ar'ar Saudi Arabia	96	D5	30 58N	41 03E
Araraquara Brazil	80	H9	21 46S	48 08W
Ararat, Mount Turkey	96	D6	39 44N	44 15E
Aras *r.* Turkey	96	D7	40 00N	43 30E
Arauca Col.	80	C15	7 04N	70 41W
Arauca *r.* Venezuela	80	D15	7 10N	68 30W
Araxá Brazil	80	H10	19 37S	46 50W
Araz *r.* Iran	96	E6	38 40N	46 30E
Arbil Iraq	96	D6	36 12N	44 01E
Arcachon Fr.	87	E6	44 40N	1 11W
Arcade New York USA	52	H2	42 32N	78 25W
Arctic National Wildlife Refuge Alaska USA	40	F7/G7	68 30N	144 30W
Arctic Ocean	117			
Arda *r.* Bulgaria	89	K4	41 30N	26 00E
Ardabil Iran	97	E6	38 15N	48 18E
Ardennes *mts.* Belgium	86	H9/J9	50 10N	5 45E
Ardila *r.* Sp.	87	B3	38 15N	6 50W
Ardmore Oklahoma USA	71	G3	34 11N	97 08W
Arendal Norway	86	K13	58 27N	8 56E
Arequipa Peru	80	C10	16 25S	71 32W
Arezzo Italy	89	C5	43 28N	11 53E
Argentan Fr.	86	E8	48 45N	0 01W
ARGENTINA	81	D6		
Argentine Basin Atlantic Ocean	116	J3	42 00S	45 00W
Argeș *r.* Romania	89	K6	44 00N	26 00E
Argun *r.* Asia	101	M9	51 30N	120 00E
Argyle, Lake Aust.	110	D6	17 00S	128 30E
Århus Denmark	88	C12	56 15N	10 10E
Arica Chile	80	C10	18 30S	70 20W
Arima Trinidad and Tobago	75	V15	10 38N	61 17W
Aripuanã *r.* Brazil	80	E12	7 00S	60 30W
Ariquemes Brazil	80	E12	9 55S	63 06W
Arizona *state* USA	70	D3	34 00N	112 00W
Arizpe Mexico	74	B6	30 20N	110 11W
Arjona Col.	80	B16	10 14N	75 22W
Arkalyk Kazakhstan	94	J7	50 17N	66 51E
Arkansas *r.* USA	70	G4	36 00N	99 00W
Arkansas *state* USA	71	H3	34 00N	93 00W
Arkansas City Kansas USA	71	G4	37 03N	97 02W
Arkhangel'sk Russia	94	G9	64 32N	40 40E
Arklow RoI	86	B10	52 48N	6 09W
Arlanza *r.* Sp.	87	D5	42 00N	3 30W
Arlanzón *r.* Sp.	87	D5	42 00N	4 00W
Arles Fr.	87	H5	43 41N	4 38E
Arlington Washington USA	42	H4	48 08N	122 15W
Arlit Niger	108	F11	18 50N	7 00E
Arlon Belgium	86	H8	49 41N	5 49E
Armagh UK	86	B11	54 21N	6 39W
Armavir Russia	94	G5	44 59N	41 40E
ARMENIA	94	G5		
Armenia Col.	80	B14	4 32N	75 40W
Armenia Mountain Pennsylvania USA	53	K1	41 45N	76 55W
Armidale Aust.	110	J3	30 32S	151 40E
Arnhem Neths.	86	H9	52 00N	5 53E
Arnhem Land *geog. reg.* Aust.	110	E7	13 00S	133 00E
Arno *r.* Italy	89	C5	43 00N	10 00E
Arnold California USA	72	C4	38 15N	120 20W
Aroostook River Maine USA	57	F2	46 48N	68 30W
Arquipélago dos Bijagós *is.* Guinea-Bissau	108	A10	11 20N	16 40W
Ar Ramādī Iraq	96	D5	33 27N	43 19E
Ar Ramlah Jordan	96	N9	29 28N	25 58E
Arran *i.* UK	86	C11	55 35N	5 15W
Ar Raqqah Syria	96	C6	35 57N	39 03E
Arras Fr.	86	G9	50 17N	2 46E
Arroyo Grande California USA	72	C2	35 08N	120 34W
Árta Greece	89	H3	39 10N	20 59E
Artigas Uruguay	81	F7	30 25S	56 28W
Arua Uganda	108	L8	3 02N	30 56E
Aruba *i.* Neths.	80	C16	12 30N	70 00W
Arunachal Pradesh *admin.* India	99	G5/H5	28 00N	95 00E
Arusha Tanzania	108	M7	3 23S	36 40E
Aruwimi *r.* CDR	108	K8	2 00N	25 00E
Arvika Sweden	88	D13	59 41N	12 38E
Arvin California USA	72	D2	35 11N	118 50W
Asahi-dake *mt.* Japan	102	D3	43 42N	142 54E
Asahikawa Japan	102	D3	43 46N	142 23E
Asamankese Ghana	108	D9	5 45N	0 45W
Asansol India	99	F4	23 40N	86 59E
Asbury Park *tn.* New Jersey USA	73	C2	40 14N	74 00W
Ascension Island Atlantic Ocean	116	G6	7 57S	14 22W
Ascoli Piceno Italy	89	D5	42 52N	13 35E
Assab Eritrea	108	N10	13 01N	42 47E
Asenovgrad Bulgaria	89	K4	42 00N	24 53E
Ashburton NZ	111	C3	43 54S	171 45E
Ashburton *r.* Aust.	110	B5	22 30S	116 00E
Ashdod Israel	96	N10	31 48N	34 48E
Asheville North Carolina USA	71	K4	35 35N	82 35W
Ash Fork Arizona USA	70	D4	35 13N	112 29W
Ashgabat Turkmenistan	94	H4	37 58N	58 24E
Ashikaga Japan	102	C2	36 21N	139 26E
Ashizuri-misaki *c.* Japan	102	B1	32 42N	133 00E
Ashland Kentucky USA	71	K4	38 28N	82 40W
Ashland Oregon USA	70	B5	42 14N	122 44W
Ashland Wisconsin USA	51	F4	46 35N	90 53W
Ashqelon Israel	96	N10	31 40N	34 35E
Ash Springs *tn.* Nevada USA	72	F3	37 32N	115 12W
Ashtabula Ohio USA	51	L1	41 52N	80 48W
Askim Norway	86	L13	59 15N	11 10E
Asmara Eritrea	108	M11	15 20N	38 58E
Assam *admin.* India	99	G5	26 20N	92 00E
As Samāwah Iraq	96	E5	31 18N	45 18E
Assis Brazil	80	G9	22 37S	50 25W
Assisi Italy	89	D5	43 04N	12 37E
As Sulaymaniyah Iraq	96	E6	35 32N	45 27E
As Sūq Saudi Arabia	96	D3	21 55N	42 02E
As Suwaydā' Syria	96	P11	32 43N	36 33E
Astana Kazakhstan	94	K7	51 10N	71 28E
Asti Italy	89	B6	44 54N	8 13E
Astoria Oregon USA	70	B6	46 12N	123 50W
Astrakhan' Russia	94	G6	46 22N	48 04E
Astypálaia *i.* Greece	89	L2	36 30N	26 20E
Asunción Paraguay	80	F8	25 15S	57 40W
Aswa *r.* Uganda	108	L8	3 30N	32 30E
Aswân Egypt	108	L12	24 05N	32 56E
Aswân Dam Egypt	108	L12	23 40N	31 50E
Asyût Egypt	108	L13	27 14N	31 07E
Atar Mauritania	108	B12	20 32N	13 08W
Atascadero California USA	72	C2	35 30N	120 40W
Atbara Sudan	108	L11	17 42N	34 00E
Atbara *r.* Sudan	108	M11	17 28N	34 30E
Atbasar Kazakhstan	94	J7	51 49N	68 18E
Atchison Kansas USA	71	G4	39 33N	95 09W
Athens Greece	89	J2	38 00N	23 44E
Athens Georgia USA	71	K3	33 57N	83 24W
Athens Pennsylvania USA	53	K1	41 57N	76 31W
Athlone RoI	86	B10	53 25N	7 56W
Athol Springs *tn.* New York USA	54	D1	42 45N	78 49W
Áthos *mt.* Greece	89	K4	40 10N	24 19E
Ati Chad	108	H10	13 11N	18 20E
Atlanta Georgia USA	71	K3	33 45N	84 23W
Atlanta Michigan USA	51	J3	45 00N	84 08W
Atlantic City New Jersey USA	71	M4	39 23N	74 27W
Atlantic-Indian Ridge Atlantic Ocean	116	H1/K1	53 00S	3 00E
Atlantic Ocean	116			
Atlas Saharien *mts.* Algeria	108	D14	33 30N	1 00E
Atrai *r.* India/Bangladesh	99	K10	25 10N	88 50E
At Tā'if Saudi Arabia	96	D3	21 15N	40 21E
Attica New York USA	52	H2	42 52N	78 17W
Atyrau Kazakhstan	94	H6	47 08N	51 59E
Aubagne Fr.	87	H5	43 17N	5 35E
Aubenas Fr.	87	H6	44 37N	4 24E
Auburn Indiana USA	52	A1	41 22N	85 02W
Auburn Maine USA	71	M5	44 04N	70 27W
Auburn Massachusetts USA	73	E3	42 11N	71 51W
Auburn New York USA	71	L5	42 57N	76 34W
Auburn Reservoir California USA	72	C4	39 05N	120 55W
Auch Fr.	87	F5	43 40N	0 36E
Auckland NZ	111	E6	36 51S	174 46E
Auckland Islands Southern Ocean	114	G2	50 35S	116 00E
Aude *r.* Fr.	87	G5	43 00N	2 00E
Au Gres Michigan USA	52	C3	44 03N	83 40W
Augsburg Germany	88	C8	48 21N	10 54E
Augusta Aust.	110	B3	34 19S	115 09E
Augusta Georgia USA	71	K3	33 29N	82 00W
Augusta Maine USA	71	N5	44 17N	69 50W
Aulne *r.* Fr.	86	D8	48 10N	4 00W
Aurangābād India	98	D3	19 52N	75 22E
Aurillac Fr.	87	G6	44 56N	2 26E
Au Sable Michigan USA	51	K3	44 23N	83 20W
Au Sable *r.* Michigan USA	51	J3	44 39N	84 08W
Austin Nevada USA	72	E4	39 30N	117 05W
Austin Texas USA	71	G3	30 18N	97 47W
AUSTRALIA	110			
Australian Capital Territory *admin.* Aust.	110	H2	35 00S	144 00E
AUSTRIA	88/89	D7/E7		
Autlán Mexico	74	D3	19 48N	104 20W
Autun Fr.	87	H7	46 58N	4 18E
Auxerre Fr.	86	G7	47 48N	3 35E
Avallon Fr.	87	G7	47 30N	3 54E
Avalon California USA	72	D1	33 21N	118 19W
Avawatz Mountains California USA	72	E2	35 32N	116 30W
Aveiro Port.	87	A4	40 38N	8 40W
Avellaneda Argentina	81	F7	34 40S	58 20W
Avenal California USA	72	C3	36 00N	120 10W
Avesta Sweden	88	F14	60 09N	16 10E
Aveyron *r.* Fr.	87	G6	44 30N	2 05E
Avezzano Italy	89	D5	42 02N	13 26E
Avila Sp.	87	C4	40 39N	4 42W
Avilés Sp.	87	C5	43 33N	5 55W
Avon Lake *tn.* Ohio USA	52	D1	41 31N	82 01W
Avranches Fr.	86	E8	48 42N	1 21W
Awali *r.* Lebanon	96	N11	33 35N	35 32E
Awash Ethiopia	108	N9	9 01N	41 10E
Awash *r.* Ethiopia	108	N9	10 00N	40 00E
Awa-shima *i.* Japan	102	C2	38 40N	139 15E
Awbārī Libya	108	G13	26 35N	12 46E
Ayacucho Peru	80	C11	13 10S	74 15W
Ayaguz Kazakhstan	94	L6	47 59N	80 27E
Ayamonte Sp.	87	B2	37 13N	7 24W
Ayan Russia	95	R8	56 29N	138 07E
Ayaviri Peru	80	C11	14 53S	70 35W
Ayers Rock *mt.* Aust.	110	E4	25 18S	131 18E
'Aynūnah Saudi Arabia	96	C4	28 06N	35 08E
Ayod Sudan	108	L9	8 08N	31 24E
Ayon *i.* Russia	95	U10	69 55N	169 10E
Ayr UK	86	C11	55 28N	4 38W
Ayutthaya Thailand	103	C6	14 20N	100 35E
AZERBAIJAN	94	G4		
Aziscohos Lake Maine USA	53	R5	45 08N	70 59W
Azogues Ecuador	80	B13	2 46S	78 56W
Azores *is.* Atlantic Ocean	116	F10	38 30N	28 00W
Azoum *r.* Chad	108	J10	12 00N	21 00E
Azuero, Peninsula de Panama	75	H1	7 40N	81 00W
Azul Argentina	81	F6	36 46S	59 50W
Azurduy Bolivia	80	E10	20 00S	64 29W
Az Zabadānī Syria	96	P11	33 42N	36 03E
B				
Ba'albek Lebanon	96	P12	34 00N	36 12E
Babahoyo Ecuador	80	B13	1 53S	79 31W
Bab el Mandab *sd.* Red Sea	108	N10	12 30N	47 00E
Babylon *hist. site* Iraq	96	D5	32 33N	44 25E
Bacabal Brazil	80	J13	4 15S	44 45W
Bacău Romania	89	L7	46 33N	26 58E
Bacolod Philippines	103	G6	10 38N	122 58E
Badajoz Sp.	87	B3	38 53N	6 58W
Badalona Sp.	87	G4	41 27N	2 15E
Bad Axe Michigan USA	51	K2	43 48N	82 59W
Baden Austria	88	F7	48 01N	16 14E
Badulla Sri Lanka	98	E1	6 59N	81 03E
Bafoussam Cameroon	108	G9	5 31N	10 25E
Bāfq Iran	97	G5	31 35N	55 21E
Bagé Brazil	81	G7	31 22S	54 06W
Baghdad Iraq	96	D5	33 20N	44 26E
Baghlān Afghanistan	97	J6	36 11N	68 44E
BAHAMAS, THE	75	J4		
Baharampur India	99	K10	24 06N	88 15E
Bahawalpur Pakistan	98	C5	29 24N	71 47E
Bahia *admin.* Brazil	80	J11	12 00S	42 30W
Bahía Blanca Argentina	81	E6	38 45S	62 15W
Bahía Blanca *b.* Argentina	81	E6	39 00S	61 00W
Bahia de Campeche *b.* Mexico	74	E4/F4	20 00N	95 00W
Bahía Grande *b.* Argentina	81	D3	51 30S	68 00W
Bahra el Manzala Lake Egypt	109	R4	31 18N	31 54E
Bahraich India	98	E5	27 35N	81 36E
BAHRAIN	97	F4		
Bahrain, Gulf of The Gulf	97	F4	25 55N	50 30E
Bahr el Abiad *r.* Sudan	108	L10	14 00N	32 20E
Bahr el Arab *r.* Sudan	108	K9	10 00N	27 30E
Bahr el Azraq *r.* Sudan	108	L10	13 30N	33 45E
Bahr el Baqar *r.* Egypt	109	S3	30 54N	32 02E
Bahr el Ghazal *r.* Chad	108	H10	14 00N	16 00E
Bahr Faqus *r.* Egypt	109	R3	30 42N	31 42E
Bahr Hadus *r.* Egypt	109	R4	31 01N	31 43E
Bahr Saft *r.* Egypt	109	R3	30 57N	31 48E
Baia Mare Romania	88	J7	47 39N	23 36E
Baicheng China	101	N8	45 37N	122 48E
Baie de la Seine *b.* Fr.	86	E8	49 40N	0 30W
Baja Hungary	89	G7	46 11N	18 58E
Baja California *p.* Mexico	74	A6/C4	27 30N	113 00W
Baker California USA	72	E2	35 16N	116 06W
Baker Oregon USA	70	C5	44 46N	117 50W
Baker Island Alaska USA	42	D4	55 30N	133 30W
Baker Islands Pacific Ocean	114	J8	0 30N	173 00W
Baker, Mount Washington USA	42	H4	48 48N	121 50W
Baker River Washington USA	42	H4	48 40N	121 30W
Bakersfield California USA	70	C4	35 25N	119 00W
Balaghat India	98	E4	21 48N	80 16E
Balaghat Range *mts.* India	98	D3	18 45N	77 00E
Balakovo Russia	94	G7	52 04N	47 46E
Balama Mozambique	109	M5	13 19S	38 35E
Bala Morghab Afghanistan	97	H6	35 35N	63 21E
Balassagyarmat Hungary	88	G7	48 06N	19 17E
Balaton *l.* Hungary	89	F7	47 00N	17 30E
Balboa Panama	75	J1	8 57N	79 33W
Balclutha NZ	111	B1	46 14S	169 44E
Balearic Islands Mediterranean Sea	87	F3/H3	40 00N	2 00E
Bali *i.* Indonesia	103	E2/F2	8 30S	115 00E
Balikesir Turkey	96	A6	39 37N	27 51E
Balikpapan Indonesia	103	F3	1 15S	116 50E
Balipar India	99	M11	27 00N	92 30E
Balkhash Kazakhstan	94	K6	46 50N	74 57E
Ballarat Aust.	110	G2	37 36S	143 58E
Balleny Islands Southern Ocean	114	G1	66 30S	164 00E
Ballymena UK	86	B11	54 52N	6 17W
Balsas Mexico	74	E3	18 00N	99 44W
Balta Ukraine	88	M7	47 58N	29 39E
Bălți Moldova	88	L7	47 44N	28 41E
Baltic Sea Europe	88	G12	55 15N	17 00E
Baltimore Maryland USA	71	L4	39 18N	76 38W
Baluchistan *geog. reg.* Pakistan	98	A5	27 30N	65 00E
Balurghat India	99	K10	25 12N	88 50E
Bam Iran	97	G4	29 07N	58 20E
Bamako Mali	108	C10	12 40N	7 59W
Bambari CAR	108	J9	5 40N	20 37E
Bamberg Germany	88	C8	49 54N	10 54E
Bamenda Cameroon	108	G9	5 55N	10 09E
Banas *r.* India	98	D5	26 00N	75 00E
Banda Aceh Indonesia	103	B5	5 30N	95 20E
Bandama Blanc *r.* Côte d'Ivoire	108	C9	8 00N	5 45W
Bandar-e 'Abbās Iran	97	G4	27 12N	56 15E
Bandar-e Lengeh Iran	97	F4	26 34N	54 52E
Bandar-e Torkeman Iran	97	F6	36 55N	54 01E
Bandar Khomeyni Iran	97	E5	30 40N	49 08E
Bandar Seri Begawan Brunei	103	F4	4 53N	115 00E
Banda Sea Indonesia	103	H2	5 50S	126 00E
Bandirma Turkey	96	A7	40 21N	27 58E
Bandundu CDR	108	H7	3 20S	17 24E
Bandung Indonesia	103	D2	6 57S	107 34E
Banfora Burkina	108	D10	10 36N	4 45W
Bangalore India	98	D2	12 58N	77 35E
Bangassou CAR	108	J8	4 41N	22 48E
Bangkok Thailand	103	C6	13 44N	100 30E
BANGLADESH	99	F4/G4		
Bangor Wales UK	86	C10	53 13N	4 08W
Bangor Northern Ireland UK	86	C11	54 40N	5 40W
Bangor Maine USA	71	N5	44 49N	68 47W
Bangui CAR	108	H8	4 23N	18 37E
Bangweulu, Lake Zambia	109	K5	11 15S	29 45E
Banja Luka Bosnia-Herzegovina	89	F6	44 47N	17 11E
Banjarmasin Indonesia	103	E3	3 22S	114 33E
Banjul The Gambia	108	A10	13 28N	16 39W
Banmi Pakistan	98	C6	33 00N	70 30E
Banning California USA	72	E1	33 55N	116 52W
Banská Bystrica Slovakia	88	G8	48 44N	19 10E
Banyuwangi Indonesia	103	E2	8 12S	114 22E
Baoding China	101	M6	38 54N	115 26E
Baoji China	101	K5	34 23N	107 16E
Baotou China	101	K7	40 38N	109 59E
Ba'qūbah Iraq	96	D5	33 45N	44 40E
Baracaldo Sp.	87	D5	43 17N	2 59W
Barahona Dom. Rep.	75	K3	18 13N	71 07W
Barakpur India	99	K9	22 45N	88 23E
Baral *r.* Bangladesh	99	K10	24 20N	89 05E
Baranof Alaska USA	42	C5	57 05N	134 50W
Baranof Island Alaska USA	42	C5	57 30N	135 00W
Barbacena Brazil	80	J9	21 13S	43 47W
BARBADOS	74	S11		
Barbastro Sp.	87	F5	42 02N	0 07E
Barbuda *i.* Antigua & Barbuda	74	Q9	17 41N	61 48W
Barcaldine Aust.	110	H5	23 31S	145 15E
Barcellona Italy	89	E3	38 10N	15 15E
Barcelona Sp.	87	G4	41 25N	2 10E
Barcelona Venezuela	80	E16	10 08N	64 43W
Barcelonnette Fr.	87	J6	44 24N	6 40E
Barcelos Brazil	80	E13	0 59S	62 58W
Barcoo *r.* Aust.	110	G5	24 00S	144 00E
Barcs Hungary	89	F6	45 58N	17 30E
Barddhaman India	99	F4	23 20N	88 00E
Bareilly India	98	D5	28 20N	79 24E
Barents Sea Arctic Ocean	117		75 00N	40 00E
Barge Canal New York USA	52	H3	43 14N	78 23W
Barharwa India	99	J10	24 51N	87 49E
Bari Italy	89	F4	41 07N	16 52E
Barinas Venezuela	80	C15	8 36N	70 15W
Barisal Bangladesh	99	L9	22 41N	90 20E
Barkly Tableland *geog. reg.* Aust.	110	F6	17 30S	137 00E
Bârlad Romania	89	L7	46 14N	27 40E
Bar-le-Duc Fr.	86	H8	48 46N	5 10E
Barlee, Lake Aust.	110	B4	28 30S	120 00E
Barletta Italy	89	F4	41 20N	16 17E
Barnaul Russia	95	L7	53 21N	83 45E
Barnstaple UK	86	C9	51 05N	4 04W
Barpeta Road *tn.* India	99	L11	26 27N	90 56E
Barquisimeto Venezuela	80	D16	10 03N	69 18W
Barra do Corba Brazil	80	H12	5 30S	45 12W
Barrancabermeja Col.	80	C15	7 06N	73 54W
Barrancas Venezuela	80	E15	8 45N	62 13W
Barranquilla Col.	80	C16	11 10N	74 50W
Barre Vermont USA	71	M5	44 13N	72 31W
Barreiras Brazil	80	J11	12 09S	44 58W
Barreiro Port.	87	A3	38 40N	9 05W
Barron Wisconsin USA	51	F3	45 24N	91 50W
Barrow Alaska USA	40	D8	71 18N	156 43W

Barrow *r.* RoI 86 B10 52 38N 6 58W
Barrow-in-Furness UK 86 D11 54 07N 3 14W
Barrow Island Aust. 110 B5 21 00S 115 00E
Barry UK 86 D9 51 24N 3 18W
Barstow California USA 70 C3 34 55N 117 01W
Bartlesville Oklahoma USA 71 G4 36 44N 95 59W
Bartolome, Cape Alaska USA 42 D4 55 15N 133 39W
Basalt Nevada USA 72 D3 38 02N 118 18W
Basalt Island HK China 100 D1 22 18N 114 21E
Basel Switz. 87 J7 47 33N 7 36E
Basingstoke UK 86 E9 51 16N 1 05W
Basirhat India 99 K9 22 39N 88 52E
Bassas da India *i.* Mozambique Channel 109 M3 22 00S 40 00E
Bassein Myanmar 103 A7 16 46N 94 45E
Basse Terre Lesser Antilles 74 Q9 16 00N 61 20W
Basseterre St. Kitts and Nevis 74 P9 17 18N 62 43W
Basse Terre *i.* Lesser Antilles 74 Q9 16 10N 61 40W
Bass Strait Aust. 110 H2 40 00S 145 00E
Basswood Lake Minnesota USA 51 F5 48 00N 91 50W
Bastia Fr. 87 K5 42 14N 9 26E
Bastogne Belgium 86 H8 50 00N 5 43E
Bastrop Louisiana USA 71 H3 32 49N 91 54W
Bata Eq. Guinea 108 F8 1 51N 9 49E
Batakan Indonesia 103 E3 4 03S 114 39E
Batala India 98 D6 31 48N 75 17E
Batang China 101 H5 30 02N 99 01E
Batangafo CAR 108 H9 7 27N 18 11E
Batangas Philippines 103 G6 13 46N 121 01E
Batavia New York USA 51 M2 42 59N 78 10W
Batdâmbâng Cambodia 103 C6 13 06N 103 13E
Bath UK 86 D9 51 23N 2 22W
Bath New York USA 53 J2 42 20N 77 18W
Batha *r.* Chad 108 H10 13 00N 19 00E
Bathinda India 98 C6 30 10N 74 58E
Bathurst Aust. 110 H3 33 27S 149 35E
Bathurst Island Aust. 110 E7 12 00S 130 00E
Batna Algeria 108 F15 35 34N 6 10E
Baton Rouge Louisiana USA 71 H3 30 30N 91 10W
Batroûn Lebanon 96 N12 36 16N 35 40E
Batticaloa Sri Lanka 98 E1 7 43N 81 42E
Battle Creek *tn.* Michigan USA 71 J5 42 20N 85 21W
Bat Yam Israel 96 N10 31 59N 34 45E
Baubau Indonesia 103 G2 5 30S 122 37E
Bauchi Nigeria 108 F10 10 16N 9 50E
Baudette Minnesota USA 49 E1 48 42N 94 34W
Bauru Brazil 80 H9 22 19S 49 07W
Bautzen Germany 88 E9 51 11N 14 29E
Bayamo Cuba 75 J4 20 23N 76 39W
Bay City Michigan USA 71 K5 43 35N 83 52W
Bay City Texas USA 71 G2 28 59N 96 00W
Baydhabo Somalia 108 N8 3 08N 43 34E
Bayerische Alpen *mts.* Germany 89 C7 47 00N 11 00E
Bayeux Fr. 86 E8 49 16N 0 42W
Baykonur Kazakhstan 94 J6 47 50N 66 03E
Bayonne Fr. 87 E5 43 30N 1 28W
Bayonne New Jersey USA 73 H1 40 39N 74 07W
Bayreuth Germany 88 C8 49 27N 11 35E
Bay Ridge *tn.* New York USA 73 H1 40 37N 74 02W
Baytown Texas USA 71 H2 29 43N 94 59W
Baza Sp. 87 D2 37 30N 2 45W
Bcharre Lebanon 96 P12 34 15N 36 00E
Bear Lake USA 70 D5 42 00N 111 20W
Beatrice Nebraska USA 71 G5 40 17N 96 45W
Beatty Nevada USA 70 C4 36 54N 116 45W
Beaufort South Carolina USA 71 K3 32 26N 80 40W
Beaufort Island HK China 100 C1 22 11N 114 15E
Beaumont Texas USA 71 H3 30 04N 94 06W
Beaune Fr. 87 H7 47 02N 4 50E
Beauvais Fr. 86 G8 49 26N 2 05E
Beaver Island Michigan USA 51 J3 45 39N 85 30W
Béchar Algeria 108 D14 31 35N 2 17W
Beckley West Virginia USA 71 K4 37 46N 81 12W
Bedford UK 86 E10 52 08N 0 29W
Bedford Pennsylvania USA 73 A2 40 01N 78 31W
Beersheba Israel 96 N10 31 15N 34 47E
Beeville Texas USA 71 G2 28 25N 97 47W
Behbehān Iran 97 F5 30 34N 50 18E
Behm Canal *sd.* Alaska USA 42 D4/E5 56 00N 131 00W
Bei'an China 101 P8 48 16N 126 36E
Beihai China 101 K3 21 29N 109 10E
Beijing China 101 M6 39 55N 116 26E
Beira Mozambique 109 L4 19 49S 34 52E
Beirut Lebanon 96 N11 33 52N 35 30E
Beja Port. 87 B3 38 01N 7 52W
Bejaïa Algeria 108 F15 36 49N 5 03E
Béjar Sp. 87 C4 40 24N 5 45W
Békéscsaba Hungary 89 H7 46 45N 21 09E
Bela Pakistan 98 B5 26 12N 66 20E
BELARUS 94 E7
Belém Brazil 80 H13 1 27S 48 29W
Belfast UK 86 C11 54 35N 5 55W
Belfast Maine USA 57 F1 44 26N 69 01W
Belfort Fr. 87 J7 47 38N 6 52E
Belgaum India 98 C3 15 54N 74 36E
BELGIUM 86 G9/H9
Belgorod Russia 94 F7 50 38N 36 36E
Belgrade Serbia 89 H6 44 50N 20 30E
BELIZE 74 G3
Belize Belize 74 G3 17 29N 88 10W
Bellac Fr. 87 F7 46 07N 1 04E
Bellaire Michigan USA 52 A4 44 59N 85 12W
Bellary India 98 D3 15 11N 76 54E
Bella Vista Argentina 81 F8 28 31S 59 00W
Belle-Île *i.* Fr. 87 D7 47 20N 3 10W
Bellingham Washington USA 70 B6 48 45N 122 29W
Bellingshausen Sea Southern Ocean 117 71 00S 85 00W
Bello Col. 80 B15 6 20N 75 41W
Belluno Italy 89 D7 46 08N 12 13E
Belmopan Belize 74 G3 17 13N 88 48W
Belogorsk Russia 95 Q7 50 55N 128 26E
Belo Horizonte Brazil 80 J10 19 54S 43 54W
Belted Range *mts.* Nevada USA 72 E3 37 28N 116 05W
Belyy *i.* Russia 94 K11 73 00N 70 00E
Belyy Yar Russia 95 L8 58 28N 85 03E
Bembézar *r.* Sp. 87 C2/C3 38 00N 5 15W
Bemidji Minnesota USA 71 H6 47 29N 94 52W
Benavente Sp. 87 C4 42 00N 5 40W
Bend Oregon USA 70 B5 44 04N 121 20W
Bender-Bayla Somalia 108 Q9 9 30N 50 50E
Bendigo Aust. 110 G2 36 48S 144 21E
Benevento Italy 89 E4 41 08N 14 46E
Bengal, Bay of Indian Ocean 99 F3 17 00N 88 00E
Bengbu China 101 M5 32 56N 117 27E
Benghazi Libya 108 J14 32 07N 20 04E
Bengkulu Indonesia 103 C3 3 46S 102 16E
Benguela Angola 109 G5 12 34S 13 24E
Beni *r.* Bolivia 80 D11 13 00S 67 30W
Beni Abbès Algeria 108 D14 30 11N 2 14W
Benicarló Sp. 87 F4 40 25N 0 25E
Beni Mellal Morocco 108 C14 32 22N 6 29W
BENIN 108 E10
Benin, Bight of *b.* West Africa 108 E9 5 50N 2 30E
Benin City Nigeria 108 F9 6 19N 5 41E
Beni Suef Egypt 108 L13 29 05N 31 05E
Benjamin Constant Brazil 80 C13 4 23S 69 59W
Ben Macdui *mt.* UK 86 D12 57 04N 3 40W
Ben Nevis *mt.* UK 86 C12 56 40N 5 00W
Bennington Vermont USA 73 D3 42 53N 73 12W
Benson Arizona USA 70 D3 31 58N 110 19W
Benton Harbor *tn.* Michigan USA 71 J5 42 07N 86 27W
Benue *r.* Nigeria/Cameroon 108 F9 8 00N 7 40E
Benxi China 101 N7 41 21N 123 45E
Beppu Japan 102 B1 33 18N 131 30E
Bequia *i.* Lesser Antilles 74 R11 13 01 61 13W
Berat Albania 89 H4 40 43N 19 46E
Berber Sudan 108 L11 18 01N 34 00E
Berbera Somalia 108 P10 10 28N 45 02E
Berbérati CAR 108 H8 4 19N 15 51E
Berck Fr. 86 F9 50 24N 1 35E
Berdychiv Ukraine 88 M8 49 54N 28 39E
Beregovo Ukraine 88 J8 48 13N 22 39E
Berezniki Russia 94 H8 59 26N 56 49E
Berezovo Russia 94 J9 63 58N 65 00E
Bérgamo Italy 89 B6 45 42N 9 40E
Bergerac Fr. 87 F6 44 50N 0 29E
Ber Harbor *tn.* Maine USA 57 F1 44 24N 68 10W
Bering Sea Pacific Ocean 114/115 H13 60 00N 175 00W
Berkakit Russia 95 Q8 56 36N 124 49E
Berkeley California USA 72 B3 37 53N 122 17W
Berkner Island Antarctica 117 80 00S 45 00W
Berlin Germany 88 D10 52 32N 13 25E
Berlin New Hampshire USA 71 M5 44 27N 71 13W
Bermejo *r.* Argentina 80 E8 25 00S 61 00W
Bermuda *i.* Atlantic Ocean 116 B10 32 50N 64 20W
Bern Switz. 87 J7 46 57N 7 26E
Berner Alpen *mts.* Switz. 87 J7/K7 46 25N 7 30E
Berryessa, Lake California USA 72 B4 38 37N 122 15W
Bertoua Cameroon 108 G8 4 34N 13 42E
Berwick Pennsylvania USA 73 B2 41 04N 76 15W
Berwick-upon-Tweed UK 86 E11 55 46N 2 00W
Besançon Fr. 87 H7 47 14N 6 02E
Beskidy Zachodnie *mts.* Poland 88 H8 50 00N 20 00E
Bethel Alaska USA 40 C6 60 48N 161 50W
Bethesda Maryland USA 73 B1 38 58N 77 06W
Bethlehem Middle East 96 N10 31 42N 35 12E
Bethlehem Pennsylvania USA 73 C2 40 37N 75 23W
Béthune Fr. 86 G9 50 32N 2 38E
Betsiboka *r.* Madagascar 109 P4 17 00S 46 30E
Beyla Guinea 108 C9 8 42N 8 39W
Beyşehir Gölü *l.* Turkey 96 B6 37 40N 31 43E
Béziers Fr. 87 G5 43 21N 3 13E
Bhadravati India 98 D2 13 54N 75 38E
Bhagalpur India 99 F5 25 14N 86 59E
Bhairab Bazar Bangladesh 99 L10 24 04N 91 00E
Bhandara India 98 D4 21 10N 79 41E
Bhanga Bangladesh 99 L9 23 24N 89 58E
Bharatpur India 98 D5 27 14N 77 29E
Bharuch India 98 C4 21 40N 73 02E
Bhatpara India 99 K9 22 51N 88 24E
Bhavnagar India 98 C4 21 46N 72 14E
Bhilwara India 98 C5 25 23N 74 39E
Bhima *r.* India 98 D3 17 00N 76 00E
Bhopal India 98 D4 23 17N 77 28E
Bhubaneshwar India 99 F4 20 13N 85 50E
Bhuj India 98 B4 23 12N 69 54E
Bhusawal India 98 D4 21 01N 75 50E
BHUTAN 99 G5
Biała Podlaska Poland 88 J9 52 03N 23 05E
Białystok Poland 88 J10 53 09N 23 10E
Biarritz Fr. 87 E5 43 29N 1 33W
Bibai Japan 102 D3 43 21N 141 53E
Bida Nigeria 108 F9 9 06N 5 59E
Biddeford Maine USA 71 M5 43 29N 70 27W
Biebrza *r.* Poland 88 J10 53 00N 22 00E
Biel Switz. 87 J7 46 27N 8 13E
Bielefeld Germany 88 B10 52 02N 8 32E
Biella Italy 89 B6 45 34N 8 04E
Bielsko-Biała Poland 88 G8 49 50N 19 00E
Bielsk Podlaski Poland 88 J10 52 47N 23 11E
Biferno *r.* Italy 89 E4 41 00N 14 00E
Big Bay De Noc *b.* Michigan USA 51 H3 45 55N 86 50W
Big Black *r.* Mississippi USA 71 H3 33 00N 90 00W
Bigelow Mountain Maine USA 53 R5 45 10N 70 18W
Bighorn *r.* USA 70 E6 45 00N 108 00W
Bighorn Mountains USA 70 E5 44 00N 108 00W
Big Lake Maine USA 57 G1 44 10N 67 45W
Big Muddy Creek *r.* Montana USA 47 E1 48 50N 105 20W
Big Pine California USA 72 D3 37 10N 118 18W
Big Rapids *tn.* Michigan USA 51 J2 43 42N 85 29W
Big Sioux *r.* Minnesota/South Dakota USA 71 G5 44 00N 96 00W
Big Smokey Valley Nevada USA 72 E4 38 52N 117 08W
Big Spring *tn.* Texas USA 70 F3 32 15N 101 30W
Big Sur California USA 72 C3 36 15N 121 47W
Bihać Bosnia-Herzegovina 89 E6 44 49N 15 53E
Bihar *admin.* India 99 F5 24 40N 86 00E
Biharamulo Tanzania 108 L7 2 37S 31 20E
Bijapur India 98 D3 16 47N 75 48E
Bījār Iran 97 E6 35 52N 47 39E
Bikaner India 98 C5 28 01N 73 22E
Bilaspur India 98 E4 27 51N 82 00E
Bila Tserkva Ukraine 88 N8 49 49N 30 10E
Bilbao Sp. 87 D5 43 15N 2 56W
Bilibino Russia 95 U10 68 00N 166 15E
Billings Montana USA 70 E6 45 47N 108 30W
Biloxi Mississippi USA 71 J3 30 24N 88 55W
Binghampton New York USA 71 L5 42 06N 75 55W
Bintulu Malaysia 103 E4 3 10N 113 02E
Bioko *i.* Eq. Guinea 108 F8 3 00N 8 20E
Birao CAR 108 J10 10 11N 22 49E
Biratnagar Nepal 99 F5 26 27N 87 17E
Birch Lake Minnesota USA 51 F4 47 35N 91 55W
Birdsville Aust. 110 F4 25 50S 139 20E
Birjand Iran 97 G5 32 55N 59 10E
Birkenhead UK 86 D10 53 24N 3 02W
Birmingham UK 86 E10 52 30N 1 50W
Birmingham Alabama USA 71 J3 33 30N 86 55W
Birnin Kebbi Nigeria 108 E10 12 30N 4 11E
Birobidzhan Russia 95 R6 48 49N 132 54E
Birzai Lithuania 88 K12 56 12N 24 48E
Biscay, Bay of Atlantic Ocean 87 D6 45 30N 2 50W
Bishkek Kyrgyzstan 94 K5 42 53N 74 46E
Bismarck North Dakota USA 70 F6 46 50N 100 48W
Bismarck Archipelago *is.* PNG 110 H9/J9 2 00S 146 00E
Bismarck Sea PNG 110 H9 3 30S 148 00E
Bissau Guinea-Bissau 108 A10 11 52N 15 39W
Bistrița Romania 89 K7 47 08N 24 30E
Bistrița *r.* Romania 89 K7 47 00N 25 00E
Bitola FYROM 89 H4 41 01N 21 21E
Bitterroot Range *mts.* USA 70 D6 46 00N 114 00W
Biwa-ko *l.* Japan 102 C2 35 20N 135 20E
Biysk Russia 95 L7 52 35N 85 16E
Bizerte Tunisia 108 F15 37 18N 9 52E
Blackall Aust. 110 H5 24 23S 145 27E
Blackburn UK 86 D10 53 45N 2 29W
Black Lake Michigan USA 52 B5 45 30N 84 20W
Black Lake New York USA 53 L4 44 30N 75 30W
Black Point *c.* HK China 100 A2 22 25N 113 54E
Blackpool UK 86 D10 53 50N 3 03W
Black River Michigan USA 52 D3 43 25N 82 35W
Black River New York USA 53 L3 43 47N 75 30W
Black River *tn.* Jamaica 75 U14 18 02N 77 52W
Black Volta *r.* Africa 108 D9 9 00N 2 40W
Blackwell Oklahoma USA 71 G4 36 47N 97 18W
Blagoevgrad Bulgaria 89 J5 42 01N 23 05E
Blagoveshchensk Russia 95 Q7 50 19N 127 30E
Blaine Washington USA 42 H4 49 00N 122 44W
Blantyre Malawi 109 L4 15 46S 35 00E
Blenheim NZ 111 D4 41 31S 173 57E
Blida Algeria 108 E15 36 30N 2 50E
Bligh Water *sd.* Fiji 114 T16 17 00S 178 00E
Bloemfontein RSA 109 K2 29 07S 26 14E
Bloomfield New Jersey USA 73 H2 40 37N 74 10W
Bloomington Illinois USA 71 J5 40 29N 89 00W
Bloomington Indiana USA 71 J4 39 10N 86 31W
Bloomsburg Pennsylvania USA 73 B2 41 00N 76 27W
Bluefield West Virginia USA 71 K4 37 14N 81 17W
Bluefields Nicaragua 75 H2 12 00N 83 49W
Blue Mountains Jamaica 75 U14 18 00N 76 30W
Bluff NZ 111 B1 46 36S 168 20E
Bluff Island HK China 100 D1 22 19N 114 21E
Blumenau Brazil 80 H8 26 55S 49 07W
Blyth UK 86 E11 55 07N 1 30W
Blythe California USA 70 D3 33 38N 114 35W
Bo Sierra Leone 108 B9 7 58N 11 45W
Boa Vista Brazil 80 E14 2 49N 60 40W
Bobo Dioulasso Burkina 108 D10 11 11N 4 18W
Bocholt Germany 88 A9 51 49N 6 37E
Bodega Head *c.* California USA 72 B4 38 18N 123 06W
Bodélé *dep.* Chad 108 H11 17 00N 17 50E
Bodensee *l.* Switz. 87 K7 47 40N 9 30E
Bogalusa Louisiana USA 71 J3 30 56N 89 53W
Bogor Indonesia 103 D2 6 34S 106 45E
Bogotá Col. 80 C14 4 38N 74 05W
Bo Hai *b.* China 101 M6 38 30N 118 30E
Böhmer Wald *mts.* Germany 88 D8 49 00N 13 00E
Bohol *i.* Philippines 103 G5 10 00N 124 00E
Bois Blanc Island Michigan USA 52 B5 45 45N 84 30W
Boise Idaho USA 70 C5 43 38N 116 12W
Boise City Oklahoma USA 70 F4 36 44N 102 31W
Bokaro India 99 F4 23 46N 85 55E
Boké Guinea 108 B10 10 57N 14 13W
Bolesławiec Poland 88 E9 51 16N 15 34E
Bolgatanga Ghana 108 D10 10 44N 0 53W
Bolhrad Ukraine 89 M6 45 42N 28 35E
BOLIVIA 80 D10
Bolmen *l.* Sweden 88 D12 57 00N 13 30E
Bologna Italy 89 C6 44 30N 11 20E
Bolzano Italy 89 C7 46 30N 11 22E
Boma CDR 109 G6 5 50S 13 03E
Bom Jesus da Lapa Brazil 80 J11 13 16S 43 23W
Bomu *r.* Central Africa 108 J8 4 50N 24 00E
Bonaire *i.* Lesser Antilles 75 L2 12 15N 68 27W
Bonaparte Archipelago *is.* Aust. 110 D7 19 00S 126 00E
Bondo CDR 108 J8 1 22N 23 54E
Bongor Chad 108 H10 10 18N 15 20E
Bonifacio Fr. 87 K4 41 23N 9 10E
Bonifacio, Strait of Fr./Sp. 87 K4 41 20N 8 45E
Bonn Germany 88 A9 50 44N 7 06E
Bonners Ferry *tn.* Idaho USA 43 M1 48 41N 116 20W
Bonny, Bight of *b.* West Africa 108 F8 2 10N 7 30E
Bonthe Sierra Leone 108 B9 7 32N 12 30W
Boosaaso Somalia 108 P10 11 18N 49 10E
Bor Sudan 108 L9 6 18N 31 34E
Borås Sweden 88 D12 57 44N 12 55E
Bordeaux Fr. 87 E6 44 50N 0 34W
Borgholm Sweden 88 F12 56 51N 16 40E
Borislav Ukraine 88 J8 49 18N 23 28E
Borneo *i.* Indonesia/Malaysia 103 D3/F5 1 00N 113 00E
Bornholm *i.* Denmark 88 E11 55 02N 15 00E
Borūjerd Iran 97 E5 33 55N 48 48E
Borzya Russia 95 P7 50 24N 116 35E
Bosna *r.* Bosnia-Herzegovina 89 G6 45 00N 18 00E
BOSNIA-HERZEGOVINA 89 F6/H6
Bossangoa CAR 108 H9 6 27N 17 21E
Bosso Niger 108 G10 13 43N 13 19E
Boston Massachusetts USA 71 M5 42 20N 71 05W
Boston Mountains Arkansas USA 71 H4 36 00N 94 00W
Botoşani Romania 88 L7 47 44N 26 41E
BOTSWANA 109 J3/K3
Bottineau North Dakota USA 49 B1 48 48N 100 28W
Bouaké Côte d'Ivoire 108 D9 7 42N 5 00W
Bouar CAR 108 H9 5 58N 15 35E
Bouârfa Morocco 108 D14 32 30N 1 59W
Bougainville Island PNG 114 F7 5 58N 15 35E
Bougouni Mali 108 C10 11 25N 7 28W
Boulder Colorado USA 70 E5 40 02N 105 16W
Boulevard California USA 72 E1 32 39N 116 15W
Boulogne-sur-Mer Fr. 86 F9 50 43N 1 37E
Boundary Bald Mountain Maine USA 53 R5 45 45N 70 14W
Bourem Mali 108 D11 16 59N 0 20W
Bourges Fr. 87 G7 47 05N 2 23E
Bourke Aust. 110 H3 30 09S 145 59E
Bournemouth UK 86 E9 50 43N 1 54W
Bou Saâda Algeria 108 F15 35 10N 4 09E
Bousso Chad 108 H10 10 32N 16 45E
Bouvet Island Atlantic Ocean 116 J1 54 26S 3 24E
Bowbells North Dakota USA 47 F1 48 53N 102 15W
Bowen Aust. 110 H5 20 00S 148 10E
Bowling Green Kentucky USA 71 J4 37 00N 86 29W
Bowling Green Missouri USA 71 H4 39 21N 91 11W
Bowling Green Ohio USA 51 K1 41 22N 83 39W
Bowman North Dakota USA 70 F6 46 11N 103 26W
Boyne City Michigan USA 52 B5 45 13N 85 00W
Boyoma Falls CDR 108 J8 0 18N 25 30E
Bozeman Montana USA 70 D6 45 40N 111 00W
Bozoum CAR 108 H9 6 16N 16 22E
Brač *i.* Croatia 89 F5 43 00N 16 00E
Bradenton Florida USA 71 K2 27 29N 82 33W
Bradford UK 86 D10 53 48N 1 45W
Bradford Pennsylvania USA 52 H1 41 57N 78 38W
Brady Texas USA 70 G3 31 08N 99 22W
Braemar UK 86 D12 57 01N 3 23W
Braga Port. 87 A4 41 32N 8 26W
Bragança Brazil 80 H13 1 02S 46 46W
Bragança Port. 87 B4 41 47N 6 46W
Brahman Baria Bangladesh 99 L9 23 58N 91 04E
Brahmaputra *r.* India/Bangladesh 99 G5 26 40N 93 00E
Brăila Romania 89 L6 45 17N 27 58E
Brainerd Minnesota USA 71 H6 46 20N 94 10W
Branco *r.* Brazil 80 E14 0 00 62 00W
Brandenburg Germany 88 D10 52 25N 12 34E
Brasileia Brazil 80 D11 10 59S 68 45W
Brásilia Brazil 80 H10 15 45S 47 57W
Braşov Romania 89 K6 45 39N 25 35E
Bratislava Slovakia 88 F8 48 10N 17 10E
Bratsk Russia 95 N8 56 20N 101 50E
Bratsk Vodokhrahnilishche *res.* Russia 95 N8 56 00N 102 00E
Brattleboro Vermont USA 73 D3 42 51N 72 34W

Name	Page	Grid	Latitude	Longitude
Braunschweig Germany	**88**	C10	52 15N	10 30E
Brawley California USA	**70**	C3	32 59N	115 30W
BRAZIL	**80**	F11		
Brazil Basin Atlantic Ocean	**116**	F5/F6	10 00S	26 00W
Brazos *r.* Texas USA	**71**	G3	32 00N	97 00W
Brazzaville Congo	**108**	H7	4 14S	15 14E
Breda Neths.	**86**	H9	51 35N	4 46E
Bremen Germany	**88**	B10	53 05N	8 48E
Bremerhaven Germany	**88**	B10	53 33N	8 35E
Bremerton Washington USA	**70**	B6	47 34N	122 40W
Brenham Texas USA	**71**	G3	30 09N	96 24W
Brenner Pass Austria/Italy	**89**	C7	47 02N	11 32E
Brescia Italy	**89**	C6	45 33N	10 13E
Brest Belarus	**88**	J10	52 08N	23 40E
Brest Fr.	**86**	C8	48 23N	4 30W
Brewer Maine USA	**57**	F1	44 52N	68 01W
Brewerton New York USA	**51**	N2	43 14N	76 08W
Bria CAR	**108**	J9	67 32N	22 00E
Briançon Fr.	**87**	J6	44 53N	6 39E
Bridgeport California USA	**72**	D4	38 14N	119 15W
Bridgeport Connecticut USA	**71**	M5	41 12N	73 12W
Bridgeton New Jersey USA	**73**	C1	39 26N	75 14W
Bridgetown Barbados	**74**	S11	13 06N	59 37W
Bridgwater UK	**86**	D9	51 08N	3 00W
Briey Fr.	**86**	H8	49 15N	5 57E
Brigham City Utah USA	**70**	D5	41 30N	112 02W
Brighton UK	**86**	E9	50 50N	0 10W
Brighton Beach *tn.* New York USA	**73**	J1	40 34N	73 58W
Brindisi Italy	**89**	F4	40 37N	17 57E
Brisbane Aust.	**110**	J4	27 30S	153 00E
Bristol UK	**86**	D9	51 27N	2 35W
Bristol Channel UK	**86**	C9/D9	51 20N	3 50W
Bristol Lake California USA	**72**	F2	34 30N	115 40W
Brive-la-Gaillarde Fr.	**87**	F6	45 09N	1 32E
Brno Czech Rep.	**88**	F8	49 13N	16 40E
Brockport New York USA	**52**	J3	43 13N	77 56W
Brockton Massachusetts USA	**71**	M5	42 06N	71 01W
Brody Ukraine	**88**	K9	50 05N	25 08E
Broken Hill *tn.* Aust.	**110**	G3	31 57S	141 30E
Broken Ridge Indian Ocean	**113**	J3	30 00S	93 00E
Bronx *admin.* New York USA	**73**	D2	40 48N	73 50W
Brookings South Dakota USA	**71**	G5	44 19N	96 47W
Brooklyn *admin.* New York USA	**73**	D2	40 41N	73 57W
Broome Aust.	**110**	C6	17 58S	122 15E
Browning Montana USA	**70**	D6	48 33N	113 00W
Brownsville Texas USA	**71**	G2	25 54N	97 30W
Brownwood Texas USA	**70**	G3	31 42N	98 59W
Bruay-en-Artois Fr.	**86**	G9	50 29N	2 33E
Brugge Belgium	**86**	G9	51 13N	3 14E
BRUNEI	**103**	E4/F4		
Brunswick Georgia USA	**71**	K3	31 09N	81 30W
Brussels Belgium	**86**	H9	50 50N	4 21E
Bryan Ohio USA	**52**	B1	41 30N	84 34W
Bryan Texas USA	**71**	G3	30 41N	96 24W
Bryansk Russia	**94**	F7	53 15N	34 09E
Brzeg Poland	**88**	F9	50 52N	17 27E
Bucaramanga Col.	**80**	C15	7 08N	73 10W
Bucharest Romania	**89**	L6	44 25N	26 07E
Buchanan Liberia	**108**	B9	5 57N	10 02W
Budapest Hungary	**89**	G7	47 30N	19 03E
Budjala CAR	**108**	H8	2 38N	19 48E
Buellton California USA	**72**	C2	34 37N	120 11W
Buenaventura Col.	**80**	B14	3 54N	77 02W
Buenaventura Mexico	**74**	C5	29 50N	107 30W
Buena Vista Lake California USA	**72**	D2	35 13N	119 18W
Buenos Aires Argentina	**81**	F7	34 40S	58 30W
Buenos Aires, Lake Argentina/Chile	**81**	C4	47 00S	72 00W
Buffalo New York USA	**71**	L5	42 52N	78 55W
Buffalo Wyoming USA	**70**	E5	44 21N	106 40W
Buhusi Romania	**89**	L7	46 44N	26 41E
Bujumbura Burundi	**108**	K7	3 22S	29 19E
Bukachacha Russia	**95**	P7	53 00N	116 58E
Bukama CDR	**109**	K6	9 13S	25 52E
Bukavu CDR	**108**	K7	2 30S	28 50E
Bukhara Uzbekistan	**94**	J4	39 47N	64 26E
Bukittinggi Indonesia	**103**	C3	0 18S	100 20E
Bukoba Tanzania	**108**	L7	1 19S	31 49E
Bula Indonesia	**103**	J3	3 07S	130 27E
Bulawayo Zimbabwe	**109**	K3	20 10S	28 43E
BULGARIA	**89**	J5/K5		
Bullion Mountains California USA	**72**	E2	34 30N	116 15W
Bull Shoals Lake USA	**71**	H4	36 00N	93 00W
Bulun Russia	**95**	Q11	70 45N	127 20E
Bumba CDR	**108**	J8	2 10N	22 30E
Bunbury Aust.	**110**	B3	33 20S	115 34E
Bundaberg Aust.	**110**	J5	24 50S	152 21E
Bungo-suidō *sd.* Japan	**102**	B1	33 00N	132 30E
Bunia CDR	**108**	L8	1 33N	30 13E
Buôn Mê Thuôt Vietnam	**103**	D6	12 41N	108 02E
Bura Kenya	**108**	M7	1 06S	39 58E
Buraydah Saudi Arabia	**96**	D4	26 20N	43 59E
Burbank California USA	**72**	D2	34 10N	118 17W
Burdur Turkey	**96**	B6	37 44N	30 17E
Bureya *r.* Russia	**95**	R7	52 00N	133 00E
Bûr Fu'ad Egypt	**109**	S4	31 50N	32 19E
Burgas Bulgaria	**89**	L5	42 30N	27 29E
Burgos Sp.	**87**	D5	42 21N	3 41W
Burgsvik Sweden	**88**	G12	57 03N	18 19E
Burhanpur India	**98**	D4	21 18N	76 08E
BURKINA	**108**	D10		
Burlington Colorado USA	**70**	F4	39 17N	102 17W
Burlington Iowa USA	**71**	H5	40 50N	91 07W
Burlington Vermont USA	**71**	M5	44 28N	73 14W
Burlington Washington USA	**42**	H4	48 26N	122 20W
Burnie Aust.	**110**	H1	41 03S	145 55E
Bursa Turkey	**96**	A7	40 12N	29 04E
Bûr Safâga Egypt	**108**	L13	25 43N	33 55E
Bûr Taufiq Egypt	**109**	T1	29 57N	32 34E
Burt Lake Michigan USA	**52**	B5	45 30N	84 40W
Buru *i.* Indonesia	**103**	H3	3 30S	126 30E
BURUNDI	**108**	K7/L7		
Burwell Nebraska USA	**70**	G5	41 48N	99 09W
Būshehr Iran	**97**	F4	28 57N	50 52E
Busira *r.* CDR	**108**	H7/J7	1 00S	20 00E
Busto Arsizio Italy	**89**	B6	45 37N	8 51E
Buta CDR	**108**	J8	2 49N	24 50E
Butare Rwanda	**108**	K7	2 35S	29 44E
Buthidaung Myanmar	**99**	M8	20 49N	92 34E
Buton *i.* Indonesia	**103**	G2/G3	5 00S	122 45E
Butte Montana USA	**70**	D6	46 00N	112 31W
Butuan Philippines	**103**	H5	8 56N	125 31E
Buulobarde Somalia	**108**	P8	3 50N	45 33E
Buzău Romania	**89**	L6	45 09N	26 49E
Bydgoszcz Poland	**88**	F10	53 16N	18 00E
Bygland Norway	**86**	J13	58 50N	7 49E
Byrranga Mountains Russia	**95**	M11	75 00N	100 00E
Bytom Poland	**88**	G9	50 21N	18 51E

C

Name	Page	Grid	Latitude	Longitude
Cabanatuan Philippines	**103**	G7	15 30N	120 58E
Cabimas Venezuela	**80**	C16	10 26N	71 27W
Cabinda *admin.* Angola	**108**	G6	5 30S	12 20E
Cabinet Mountains Montana USA	**43**	N1	48 15N	115 45W
Cabo Brazil	**80**	K12	8 16S	35 00W
Cabo Blanco *c.* Costa Rica	**75**	G1	9 36N	85 06W
Cabo Catoche *c.* Mexico	**74**	G4	21 38N	87 08W
Cabo Corrientes *c.* Col.	**80**	B15	5 29N	77 36W
Cabo Corrientes *c.* Mexico	**74**	C4	20 25N	105 42W
Cabo de Gata *c.* Sp.	**87**	D2	36 44N	2 10W
Cabo de Hornos *c.* Chile	**81**	D2	56 00S	67 15W
Cabo de la Nao *c.* Sp.	**87**	F3	38 44N	0 14E
Cabo Delgado *c.* Mozambique	**109**	N5	10 45S	40 45E
Cabo de Palos *c.* Sp.	**87**	E2	37 38N	0 40W
Cabo de Peñas *c.* Sp.	**87**	C5	43 39N	5 50W
Cabo de São Vicente *c.* Port.	**87**	A2	37 01N	8 59W
Cabo de Tortosa *c.* Sp.	**87**	F4	40 44N	0 54E
Cabo Dos Bahías *c.* Argentina	**81**	D5	45 00S	65 30W
Cabo Espichel *c.* Port.	**87**	A3	38 24N	9 13W
Cabo Finisterre *c.* Sp.	**87**	A5	42 52N	9 16W
Cabo Gracias á Dios *c.* Nicaragua	**75**	H3	15 00N	83 10W
Cabo Orange *c.* Brazil	**80**	G14	4 25N	51 32W
Cabo Ortegal *c.* Sp.	**87**	B5	43 46N	7 54W
Cabora Bassa Dam Mozambique	**109**	L4	16 00S	33 00E
Caborca Mexico	**74**	B6	30 42N	112 10W
Cabo San Juan *c.* Argentina	**81**	E3	54 45S	63 46W
Cabo San Lucas Mexico	**74**	C4	22 50N	109 52W
Cabo Santa Elena *c.* Costa Rica	**74**	G2	10 54N	85 56W
Cabo Vírgenes *c.* Argentina	**81**	D3	52 20S	68 00W
Cabrera *i.* Sp.	**87**	G3	39 00N	2 59E
Cabriel *r.* Sp.	**87**	E3	39 20N	1 15W
Čačak Serbia	**89**	H5	43 54N	20 22E
Cáceres Brazil	**80**	F10	16 05S	57 40W
Cáceres Sp.	**87**	B3	39 29N	6 23W
Cachoeira Brazil	**80**	K11	12 35S	38 59W
Cachoeira do Sol Brazil	**81**	G7	30 03S	52 52W
Cachoeiro de Itapemirim Brazil	**80**	J9	20 51S	41 07W
Cadillac Michigan USA	**51**	J3	44 14N	85 23W
Cadiz Philippines	**103**	G6	10 57N	123 18E
Cádiz Sp.	**87**	B2	36 32N	6 18W
Cádiz, Gulf of Sp.	**87**	B2	36 30N	7 15W
Cadiz Lake California USA	**72**	F2	34 17N	115 23W
Caen Fr.	**86**	E8	49 11N	0 22W
Caernarfon UK	**86**	C10	53 08N	4 16W
Cagayan de Oro Philippines	**103**	G5	8 29N	124 40E
Cágliari Italy	**89**	B3	39 13N	9 08E
Caguas Puerto Rico	**75**	L3	18 41N	66 04W
Cahors Fr.	**87**	F6	44 28N	0 26E
Caicos Passage *sd.* W. Indies	**75**	K4	22 20N	72 30W
Cairns Aust.	**110**	H6	16 51S	145 43E
Cairo Egypt	**108**	L13	30 00N	31 15E
Cairo Illinois USA	**71**	J4	37 01N	89 09W
Cajamarca Peru	**80**	B12	7 09S	78 32W
Cajàzeiras Brazil	**80**	K12	6 52S	38 31W
Cakovec Croatia	**89**	F7	46 24N	16 26E
Calabar Nigeria	**108**	F8	4 56N	8 22E
Calahorra Sp.	**87**	E5	46 19N	1 58W
Calais Fr.	**86**	F9	50 57N	1 52E
Calais Maine USA	**57**	G1	44 11N	67 16W
Calama Chile	**80**	D9	22 30S	68 55W
Calamar Col.	**80**	C16	10 16N	74 55W
Calamian Group *is.* Philippines	**103**	F6/G6	12 00N	120 00E
Calamocha Sp.	**87**	E4	40 54N	1 18W
Calapan Philippines	**103**	G6	13 23N	121 10E
Calatayud Sp.	**87**	E4	41 21N	1 39W
Calçoene Brazil	**80**	G14	2 30N	50 55W
Caldas da Rainha Port.	**87**	A3	39 24N	9 08W
Caldwell Idaho USA	**70**	C5	43 39N	116 40W
Caledonia New York USA	**52**	J2	42 58N	77 51W
Calexico California USA	**72**	F1	32 40N	115 30W
Cali Col.	**80**	B14	3 24N	76 30W
Calicut India	**98**	D2	11 15N	75 45E
Caliente Nevada USA	**70**	D4	37 36N	114 31W
California *state* USA	**70**	C4	35 00N	119 00W
Calistoga California USA	**72**	B4	38 36N	122 35W
Callao Peru	**80**	B11	12 05S	77 08W
Caltanissetta Italy	**89**	E2	37 29N	14 04E
Calvi Fr.	**87**	K5	42 34N	8 44E
Calvinia RSA	**109**	H1	31 25S	19 47E
Camaçari Brazil	**80**	K11	12 44S	38 16W
Camacupa Angola	**109**	H5	12 03S	17 50E
Camagüey Cuba	**75**	J4	21 25N	77 55W
CAMBODIA	**103**	C6/D6		
Cambrai Fr.	**86**	G9	50 10N	3 14E
Cambria California USA	**72**	C2	35 34N	121 05W
Cambrian Mountains UK	**86**	D10	52 15N	3 45W
Cambridge NZ	**111**	E6	37 53S	175 28E
Cambridge UK	**86**	F10	52 12N	0 07E
Cambridge Maryland USA	**71**	L4	38 34N	76 04W
Camden New Jersey USA	**73**	C1	39 57N	75 07W
CAMEROON	**108**	G9		
Cametá Brazil	**80**	H13	2 12S	49 30W
Camiri Bolivia	**80**	E9	20 08S	63 33W
Camocim Brazil	**80**	J13	2 55S	40 50W
Camorta Island Nicobar Islands	**99**	G1	7 30N	93 30E
Campbell Island Southern Ocean	**114**	G2	52 30S	169 10E
Campbeltown UK	**86**	C11	55 26N	5 36W
Campeche Mexico	**74**	F3	19 50N	90 30W
Câmpina Romania	**89**	K6	45 08N	25 44E
Campina Grande Brazil	**80**	K12	7 15S	35 50W
Campinas Brazil	**80**	H9	22 54S	47 06W
Campoalegre Col.	**80**	B14	2 49N	75 19W
Campobasso Italy	**89**	E4	41 33N	14 39E
Campo Grande Brazil	**80**	G9	20 24S	54 35W
Campo Maior Brazil	**80**	J13	4 50S	42 12W
Campo Mourão Brazil	**80**	G9	24 01S	52 24W
Campos Brazil	**80**	J9	21 46S	41 21W
Camptonville California USA	**72**	C4	39 28N	121 01W
Cam Rahn Vietnam	**103**	D6	11 54N	109 14E
Canadian *r.* USA	**70**	F4	35 00N	104 00W
Canajoharie New York USA	**73**	C3	42 55N	74 46W
Canakkale Turkey	**96**	A7	40 09N	26 25E
Canal du Midi Fr.	**87**	G5	43 20N	2 00E
Canandaigua New York USA	**53**	J2	42 53N	77 17W
Canandaigua Lake New York USA	**53**	J2	42 50N	77 17W
Cananea Mexico	**74**	B6	30 59N	110 20W
Canary Basin Atlantic Ocean	**116**	E9/F9	26 20N	30 00W
Canary Islands Sp.	**108**	A13	28 30N	15 10W
Canaveral, Cape Florida USA	**71**	K2	28 28N	80 28W
Canberra Aust.	**110**	H2	35 18S	149 08E
Cancún Mexico	**74**	G4	21 09N	86 45W
Cangamba Angola	**109**	H5	13 40S	19 47E
Cangzhou China	**101**	M6	38 19N	116 54E
Canisteo New York USA	**52**	J2	42 16N	77 37W
Cannanore India	**98**	D2	11 53N	75 23E
Cannanore Islands India	**98**	C2	10 05N	72 10E
Cannes Fr.	**87**	J5	43 33N	7 00E
Cannonsville Reservoir New York USA	**53**	L2	42 05N	75 20W
Canõas Brazil	**81**	G8	28 55S	51 10W
Canouan *i.* Lesser Antilles	**74**	R11	12 43N	61 20W
Canterbury UK	**86**	F9	51 17N	1 05E
Canterbury Plains NZ	**111**	C2/D3	43 45S	171 56E
Can Tho Vietnam	**103**	D6	10 03N	105 46E
Canton New York USA	**51**	P3	44 36N	75 10W
Canton Ohio USA	**71**	K5	40 48N	81 23W
Canton East Pennsylvania USA	**53**	K1	41 38N	76 50W
Cap Corse *c.* Fr.	**87**	K5	43 00N	9 21E
Cap d'Ambre *c.* Madagascar	**109**	P5	12 00S	49 15E
Cap de Creus *c.* Sp.	**87**	G5	42 19N	3 19E
Cap de la Hague *c.* Fr.	**86**	E8	49 44N	1 56W
Cape Basin Atlantic Ocean	**116**	J3	36 00S	6 00E
Cape Coast *tn.* Ghana	**108**	D9	5 10N	1 13W
Cape Cod Bay Massachusetts USA	**73**	E2	41 00N	70 00W
Cape Girardeau *tn.* Missouri USA	**71**	J4	37 19N	89 31W
Cape May *tn.* New Jersey USA	**73**	C1	38 56N	74 54W
Cape Rise Atlantic Ocean	**116**	K2	42 00S	11 00E
Cape Town RSA	**109**	H1	33 56S	18 28E
CAPE VERDE	**116**	E8		
Cape Verde Basin Atlantic Ocean	**116**	E8	11 00N	35 00W
Cape York Peninsula Aust.	**110**	G7	12 30S	142 30E
Cap-Haïtien Haiti	**75**	K3	19 47N	72 17W
Capo Carbonara *c.* Italy	**89**	B3	39 07N	9 33E
Capo Passero *c.* Italy	**89**	E2	36 42N	15 09E
Capo Santa Maria di Leuca *c.* Italy	**89**	G3	39 47N	18 22E
Capo San Vito *c.* Italy	**89**	D3	38 12N	12 43E
Capri *i.* Italy	**89**	E4	40 33N	14 15E
Capricorn Channel Aust.	**110**	J5	23 00S	152 30E
Caprivi Strip *geog. reg.* Namibia	**109**	J4	17 30S	27 50E
Cap Ste. Marie *c.* Madagascar	**109**	P2	25 34S	45 10E
Cap Vert *c.* Senegal	**108**	A10	14 43N	17 33W
Caqueta *r.* Col.	**80**	C13	0 05S	72 30W
Caracal Romania	**89**	K6	44 07N	24 18E
Caracas Venezuela	**80**	D16	10 35N	66 56W
Caratinga Brazil	**80**	J10	19 50S	42 06W
Caravelas Brazil	**80**	K10	17 45S	39 15W
Carbondale Pennsylvania USA	**53**	L1	41 35N	75 31W
Carcassonne Fr.	**87**	G5	43 13N	2 21E
Cardamom Hills India	**98**	D1	9 50N	77 00E
Cárdenas Mexico	**74**	E4	22 00N	99 41W
Cardiff UK	**86**	D9	51 30N	3 13W
Cardigan Bay UK	**86**	C10	52 30N	4 30W
Carei Romania	**88**	J7	47 40N	22 28E
Cargados Carajos Shoals Indian Ocean	**113**	E5	16 00S	60 00E
Cariacica Brazil	**80**	J10	20 15S	40 23W
Caribbean Sea Central America	**75**	J3/L3	15 00N	75 00W
Caribou Maine USA	**57**	F2	46 52N	68 01W
Caripito Venezuela	**80**	E16	10 07N	63 07W
Carlisle UK	**86**	D11	54 54N	2 55W
Carlsbad California USA	**72**	E1	33 09N	117 20W
Carlsbad New Mexico USA	**70**	F3	32 25N	104 14W
Carlsberg Ridge Indian Ocean	**113**	F7	5 00N	65 00E
Carmarthen UK	**86**	C9	51 51N	4 20W
Carmen Col.	**80**	B15	9 46N	75 06W
Carmichael California USA	**72**	C4	38 36N	121 20W
Carnarvon Aust.	**110**	A5	24 51S	113 45E
Carnegie, Lake Aust.	**110**	C4	27 00S	124 00E
Carnegie Ridge Pacific Ocean	**115**	T7	1 30S	95 00W
Car Nicobar Island Nicobar Islands	**99**	G1	9 00N	93 00E
Carnot CAR	**108**	H8	4 59N	15 56E
Caro *r.* Michigan USA	**52**	C3	43 29N	83 24W
Carolina Brazil	**80**	H12	7 20S	47 25W
Caroline Island Kiribati	**115**	M7	10 00S	150 00W
Caroline Islands Pacific Ocean	**114**	E8	8 00N	148 00E
Caroni *r.* Venezuela	**80**	E15	7 00N	62 30W
Carpathians *mts.* Europe	**88/89**	G8/K7	49 00N	22 00E
Carpatii Meridionali *mts.* Romania	**89**	J6/K6	45 00N	24 00E
Carpentaria, Gulf of Aust.	**110**	F6/F7	13 30S	138 00E
Carpentras Fr.	**87**	H6	44 03N	5 03E
Carriacou *i.* Lesser Antilles	**74**	R11	12 30N	61 27W
Carrion *r.* Sp.	**87**	C5	42 30N	4 45W
Carson *r.* Nevada USA	**72**	D4	39 15N	119 36W
Carson City Nevada USA	**70**	C4	39 10N	119 46W
Cartagena Col.	**80**	B16	10 24N	75 33W
Cartagena Sp.	**87**	E2	37 36N	0 59W
Cartago Costa Rica	**75**	H1	9 50N	83 52W
Carteret New Jersey USA	**73**	H1	40 34N	74 13W
Caruarú Brazil	**80**	K12	8 15S	35 55W
Carúpano Venezuela	**80**	E16	10 39N	63 14W
Casablanca Morocco	**108**	C14	33 39N	7 35W
Casa Grande Arizona USA	**70**	D3	32 52N	111 46W
Cascade Range *mts.* North America	**70**	B5/B6	48 00N	121 00W
Cascais Port.	**87**	A3	38 41N	9 25W
Cascavel Brazil	**80**	K13	4 10S	38 15W
Caserta Italy	**89**	E4	41 04N	14 20E
Casper Wyoming USA	**70**	E5	42 50N	106 20W
Cassino Italy	**89**	D4	41 29N	13 50E
Cass River Michigan USA	**52**	C3	43 30N	83 30W
Castellane Fr.	**87**	J5	43 50N	6 30E
Castellón de la Plana Sp.	**87**	E3	39 59N	0 03W
Castelo Branco Port.	**87**	B3	39 50N	7 30W
Castlebar Rol	**86**	A10	53 52N	9 17W
Castle Peak HK China	**100**	A2	22 23N	113 57E
Castres Fr.	**87**	G5	43 36N	2 14E
Castries St. Lucia	**74**	R12	14 02N	60 59W
Castrovillari Italy	**89**	F3	39 48N	16 12E
Catamarca Argentina	**81**	D8	28 28S	65 46W
Catánia Italy	**89**	E2	37 31N	15 06E
Catanzaro Italy	**89**	F3	38 54N	16 36E
Cataract, 1st Egypt	**108**	L12	24 00N	32 45E
Cataract, 2nd Sudan	**108**	L12	21 40N	31 12E
Cataract, 3rd Sudan	**108**	L11	19 45N	30 25E
Cataract, 5th Sudan	**108**	L11	18 25N	33 52E
Cathedral Provincial Park Washington USA	**43**	K1/L1	48 55N	120 00W
Cat Island Bahamas	**75**	J4	24 30N	75 30W
Catskill Mountains New York USA	**71**	L5	42 10N	74 20W
Cattaraugus New York USA	**52**	H2	42 20N	78 50W
Cattaraugus Creek New York USA	**52**	H2	42 28N	78 30W
Caucaia Brazil	**80**	K13	3 44S	38 45W
Caura *r.* Venezuela	**80**	E15	6 00N	64 00W
Cauvery *r.* India	**98**	D2	11 05N	78 15E
Cavalier North Dakota USA	**49**	D1	48 47N	97 38W
Caxias Brazil	**80**	J13	4 53S	43 20W
Caxias do Sul Brazil	**81**	G8	29 14S	51 10W
Cayenne French Guiana	**80**	G14	4 55N	52 18W
Cayman Trench Caribbean Sea	**116**	A8	15 00N	80 00W
Cayuga Lake New York USA	**51**	N2	42 40N	76 50W
Ceará *admin.* Brazil	**80**	J12	5 30S	40 00W
Cebu Philippines	**103**	G6	10 17N	123 56E
Cedar *r.* Iowa USA	**71**	H5	42 00N	92 00W
Cedar City Utah USA	**70**	D4	37 40N	113 04W
Cedar Creek *r.* North Dakota USA	**70**	F6	46 00N	102 00W
Cedar Grove New Jersey USA	**73**	H2	40 51N	74 14W
Cedar Rapids *tn.* Iowa USA	**71**	H5	41 59N	91 39W
Cedros *i.* Mexico	**74**	A5	28 00N	115 00W
Ceduna Aust.	**110**	E3	32 07S	133 42E
Ceerigaabo Somalia	**108**	P10	10 40N	47 20E
Cegléd Hungary	**89**	G7	47 10N	19 47E
Celaya Mexico	**74**	D4	20 32N	100 48W
Celebes Sea Indonesia	**103**	G4	3 00N	122 00E
Celje Slovenia	**89**	E7	46 15N	15 16E
Celle Germany	**88**	C10	52 37N	10 05E

CENTRAL AFRICAN REPUBLIC **108** H9/J9
Central District HK China **100** C1 22 17N 114 10E
Central Pacific Basin Pacific Ocean **114** J8 10 00N 177 00W
Central Siberian Plateau Russia **95** N10 65 00N 110 00E
Cerro de Pasco Peru **80** B11 10 43S 76 15W
Cesis Latvia **88** K12 57 18N 25 18E
České Budějovice Czech Rep. **88** E8 48 58N 14 29E
Ceuta *territory* Sp. **87** C1 35 53N 5 19W
Cévennes *mts.* Fr. **87** G6 44 20N 3 30E
Ceyhan *r.* Turkey **96** C6 37 45N 36 45E
Cèze *r.* Fr. **87** H6 44 30N 4 00E
Chachapoyas Peru **80** B12 6 13S 77 54W
CHAD **108** H10
Chad, Lake West Africa **108** G10 13 50N 14 00E
Chagai Hills Afghanistan/Pakistan **98** A5 29 30N 63 00E
Chaghcharan Afghanistan **97** J5 34 28N 65 03E
Chagos Archipelago Indian Ocean **113** G6 6 00S 73 00E
Chagos-Laccadive Ridge Indian Ocean **113** G6 0 00 75 00E
Chāh Bahār Iran **97** H4 25 16N 60 41E
Chaine des Mitumba *mts.* CDR **109** K6 7 30S 27 30E
Chai Wan HK China **100** C1 22 16N 114 14E
Chalkída Greece **89** J3 38 28N 23 36E
Chalkidikí *p.* Greece **89** J4 40 30N 23 00E
Chalkyitsik Alaska USA **64** B4 66 38N 143 49W
Challenger Fracture Zone Pacific Ocean **115** R4/T4 33 30S 100 00W
Châlons-sur-Marne Fr. **86** H8 48 58N 4 22E
Chalon-sur-Saône Fr. **87** H7 46 47N 4 51E
Chaman Pakistan **98** B6 30 55N 66 27E
Chambal *r.* India **98** D5 26 00N 77 00E
Chamberlain Lake Maine USA **53** S6 46 15N 69 20W
Chambersburg Pennsylvania USA **73** B1 39 56N 77 39W
Chambéry Fr. **87** H6 45 34N 5 55E
Chamo, Lake Ethiopia **108** M9 5 55N 37 35E
Champaign Illinois USA **71** J5 40 07N 88 14W
Champlain New York USA **53** N4 44 59N 73 29W
Champlain, Lake Vermont USA **53** N4 44 53N 73 10W
Champotón Mexico **74** F3 19 20N 90 43W
Chañaral Chile **80** C8 26 23S 70 40W
Chandigarh India **98** D6 30 44N 76 54E
Chandigarh *admin.* India **98** D6 30 44N 76 54E
Chandpur Bangladesh **99** L9 23 15N 90 40E
Chandrapur India **98** D3 19 58N 79 21E
Changara Mozambique **109** L4 16 50S 33 17E
Changchun China **101** P7 43 53N 125 20E
Changde China **101** L4 29 03N 111 35E
Chang Jiang *r.* China **101** K5 31 00N 110 00E
Changsha China **101** L4 28 10N 113 00E
Changzhi China **101** L6 36 05N 113 12E
Changzhou China **101** N5 31 39N 120 45E
Chaniá Greece **89** K1 35 31N 24 01E
Channel Island National Park California USA **72** C2 34 04N 120 00W
Channel Islands British Isles **86** D8 49 30N 2 30W
Chaoyang China **101** N7 41 36N 120 25E
Chaozhou China **101** M3 23 42N 116 36E
Chapada Diamantina *mts.* Brazil **80** J11 12 30S 42 30W
Chapecó Brazil **80** G8 27 14S 52 41W
Chardzhev Turkmenistan **94** J4 39 09N 63 34E
Chari *r.* Chad/Sudan **108** H10 11 00N 16 00E
Charikar Afghanistan **97** J5 35 01N 69 11E
Charleroi Belgium **86** H9 50 25N 4 27E
Charleston South Carolina USA **71** L3 32 48N 79 58W
Charleston West Virginia USA **71** K4 38 23N 81 40W
Charleston Peak *mt.* Nevada USA **72** F3 36 16N 115 41W
Charlestown Rhode Island USA **73** E2 41 23N 71 39W
Charleville-Mézières Fr. **86** H8 49 46N 4 43E
Charlevoix Michigan USA **51** J3 45 18N 85 15W
Charlotte North Carolina USA **71** K4 35 03N 80 50W
Charlottesville Virginia USA **71** L4 38 02N 78 29W
Charlotteville Trinidad and Tobago **75** V15 11 16N 60 36W
Charters Towers Aust. **110** H5 20 02S 146 20E
Chartres Fr. **86** F8 48 27N 1 30E
Chateaubelair St. Vincent and the Grenadines **74** R11 13 17N 61 15W
Châteaubriant Fr. **86** E7 47 43N 1 22W
Chateaugay New York USA **53** M4 44 55N 74 06W
Châteauroux Fr. **87** F7 46 49N 1 41E
Château-Thierry Fr. **86** G8 49 03N 3 24E
Châtellerault Fr. **87** F7 46 49N 0 33E
Chatham Alaska USA **42** C5 57 30N 135 00W
Chatham Massachusetts USA **73** F2 41 41N 69 58W
Chatham Rise Pacific Ocean **114** H3 45 00S 175 00E
Chatham Strait *sd.* Alaska USA **42** C5 57 45N 134 50W
Châtillon-sur-Seine Fr. **86** H7 47 52N 4 35E
Chattanooga Tennessee USA **71** J4 35 02N 85 18W
Chattisgarh *admin.* India **98** E4 22 30N 82 30E
Chaumont Fr. **86** H8 48 07N 5 08E
Chautauqua Lake New York USA **52** G2 42 12N 79 30W
Chazy New York USA **53** N4 44 53N 73 29W
Cheb Czech Rep. **88** D9 50 08N 12 28E
Cheboksary Russia **94** G8 56 08N 47 12E
Cheboygan Michigan USA **51** J3 45 39N 84 28W
Cheju do *i.* South Korea **101** P5 33 00N 126 30E
Chek Lap Kok *i.* HK China **100** A1 22 18N 113 56E
Chelan, Lake Washington USA **42** H4 48 06N 120 20W
Chelan National Recreation Area Washington USA **42** H4 48 25N 120 30W
Chełm Poland **88** J9 51 08N 23 29E
Chelmsford UK **86** F9 51 44N 0 28E
Chelsea Michigan USA **52** B2 42 19N 84 01W
Cheltenham UK **86** D9 51 54N 2 04W
Chelyabinsk Russia **94** J8 55 12N 61 25E
Chemnitz Germany **88** D9 50 50N 12 55E
Chemung River New York USA **53** K2 42 02N 76 50W
Chenab *r.* Pakistan **98** C6 32 30N 74 00E
Chenango River New York USA **53** L2 42 28N 75 40W
Chengde China **101** M7 40 59N 117 52E
Chengdu China **101** J5 30 37N 104 06E
Chennai India **98** E2 13 05N 80 18E
Cher *r.* Fr. **87** F7 47 17N 0 50E
Cherbourg Fr. **86** E8 49 38N 1 37W
Cheremkhovo Russia **95** N7 53 08N 103 01E
Cherepovets Russia **94** F8 59 09N 37 50E
Chernihiv Ukraine **88** N9 51 30N 31 18E
Chernivtsi Ukraine **88** K8 48 19N 25 52E
Chernyakhovsk Russia **88** H11 54 36N 21 48E
Cherokee Iowa USA **71** G5 42 45N 95 32W
Cherskogo Range *mts.* Russia **95** R10/S9 66 30N 140 00E
Chervonograd Ukraine **88** K9 50 25N 24 10E
Chesaning Michigan USA **52** B3 43 12N 84 08W
Chesapeake Virginia USA **71** L4 36 45N 76 15W
Chesapeake Bay Maryland USA **71** L4 39 00N 76 20W
Chester UK **86** D10 53 12N 2 54W
Chester Maryland USA **73** B1 38 59N 76 17W
Chesuncook Lake Maine USA **53** S6 46 00N 69 22W
Chetumal Mexico **74** G3 18 30N 88 17W
Cheung Chau *i.* HK China **100** B1 22 10N 114 02E
Cheung Sha HK China **100** A1 22 14N 113 57E
Chewack River Washington USA **42** H4 48 45N 120 10W
Chewelah Washington USA **43** M1 48 17N 117 44W
Cheyenne Wyoming USA **70** F5 41 08N 104 50W
Cheyenne *r.* USA **70** F5 44 00N 102 00W
Chhatak Bangladesh **99** L10 25 02N 91 38E
Chhukha Bhutan **99** K11 27 01N 89 35E
Chiai Taiwan **101** N3 23 09N 120 11E
Chiang Mai Thailand **103** B7 18 48N 98 59E
Chiba Japan **102** D2 35 38N 140 07E
Chicago Illinois USA **71** J5 41 50N 87 45W
Chicapa *r.* Angola/CDR **109** J6 8 00S 20 30E
Chichagof Island Alaska USA **42** C5 57 40N 136 00W
Chickasha Oklahoma USA **71** G4 35 03N 97 57W
Chicken Alaska USA **64** B3 64 04N 142 00W
Chiclayo Peru **80** B12 6 47S 79 47W
Chico California USA **70** B4 39 46N 121 50W
Chico *r.* Argentina **81** D4 49 00S 70 00W
Chico *r.* Argentina **81** D5 45 00S 67 30W
Chienti *r.* Italy **89** D5 43 00N 14 00E
Chieti Italy **89** E5 42 21N 14 10E
Chihuahua Mexico **74** C5 28 40N 106 06W
CHILE **80/81** C5/C8
Chile Basin Pacific Ocean **115** T4 36 00S 84 00W
Chile Chico Chile **81** C4 46 34S 71 44W
Chile Rise Pacific Ocean **115** S4 40 00S 92 00W
Chillán Chile **81** C6 36 37S 72 10W
Chilpancingo Mexico **74** E3 17 33N 99 30W
Chilumba Malawi **109** L5 10 25S 34 18E
Chilung Taiwan **101** N4 25 10N 121 43E
Chi Ma Wan Peninsula HK China **100** A1 22 14N 113 58E
Chimborazo *mt.* Ecuador **80** B13 1 29S 78 52W
Chimbote Peru **80** B12 9 04S 78 34W
CHINA **100/101**
China Lake California USA **72** E2 35 45N 117 36W
Chinandega Nicaragua **74** G2 12 35N 87 10W
Chincha Alta Peru **80** B11 13 25S 76 07W
Chinchilla Aust. **110** J4 26 42S 150 35E
Chinde Mozambique **109** M4 18 35S 36 28E
Chinese Turkestan *geog. reg.* China **100** D6 40 00N 80 00E
Chingola Zambia **109** K5 12 31S 27 53E
Chinju South Korea **101** P6 35 10N 128 06E
Chinko *r.* CAR **108** J9 5 00N 24 00E
Chinook Montana USA **47** C1 48 36N 109 14W
Chíos Greece **89** L3 38 23N 26 07E
Chíos *i.* Greece **89** K3/L3 38 00N 26 00E
Chippewa Falls *tn.* Wisconsin USA **51** F3 44 56N 91 23W
Chippewa River Michigan USA **52** B3 43 36N 84 45W
Chiquimula Guatemala **74** G2 14 48N 89 32W
Chirchik Uzbekistan **94** J5 41 28N 69 31E
Chişinău Moldova **89** M7 47 00N 28 50E
Chita Russia **95** P7 52 03N 113 35E
Chitembo Angola **109** H5 13 33S 16 47E
Chitral Pakistan **98** C7 35 52N 71 58E
Chittagong Bangladesh **99** L9 22 20N 91 48E
Chittoor India **98** D2 13 13N 79 06E
Chocolate Mountains California USA **72** F1 33 30N 115 30W
Choiseul *i.* Solomon Islands **114** F7 5 58N 15 35E
Chojnice Poland **88** F10 53 42N 17 32E
Cholet Fr. **87** E7 47 04N 0 53W
Choluteca Honduras **74** G2 13 15N 87 10W
Chone Ecuador **80** A13 0 44S 80 04W
Chongjin North Korea **101** P7 41 50N 129 55E
Chongju South Korea **101** P6 36 39N 127 27E
Chongqing China **101** K4 29 30N 106 35E
Chonju South Korea **101** P6 35 50N 127 50E
Chornobyl Ukraine **88** N9 51 17N 30 15E
Chott El Jerid *salt l.* Tunisia **108** F14 30 00N 9 00E
Chott Melrhir *salt l.* Algeria **108** F14 33 30N 6 10E
Chowchilla California USA **72** C3 37 07N 120 14W
Choybalsan Mongolia **101** L8 48 02N 114 32E
Christchurch NZ **111** D3 43 32S 172 38E
Christmas Island Aust. **103** D1 10 15S 106 00E
Chu *r.* Asia **94** K5 45 00N 72 30E
Chubut *r.* Argentina **81** D5 43 30S 67 30W
Chūgoku-sanchi *mts.* Japan **102** B1 35 00N 133 00E
Chukchi Sea Arctic Ocean **117** 70 00N 170 00W
Chuk Kok HK China **100** C2 22 21N 114 15E
Chukotsk Peninsula Russia **95** W10 66 00N 175 00W
Chukotsk Range *mts.* Russia **95** V10 68 00N 175 00E
Chulucanas Peru **80** A12 5 08S 80 10W
Chulym *r.* Russia **95** L8 57 30N 87 30E
Chumphon Thailand **103** B6 10 30N 99 11E
Chuna *r.* Russia **95** M8 57 30N 98 00E
Chunchon South Korea **101** P6 37 56N 127 40E
Chunchura India **99** K9 22 55N 88 15E
Ch'ungju South Korea **101** P6 36 59N 127 53E
Chunya *r.* Russia **95** N9 62 00N 101 00E
Chur Switz. **87** K7 46 52N 9 32E
Ciego de Avila Cuba **75** J4 21 51N 78 47W
Ciénaga Col. **80** C16 11 01N 74 15W
Cienfuegos Cuba **75** H4 22 10N 80 27W
Cimarron *r.* USA **70** F4 37 00N 103 00W
Cimislia Moldova **89** M7 46 30N 28 50E
Cinca *r.* Sp. **87** F4 41 45N 0 15E
Cincinnati Ohio USA **71** K4 39 10N 83 30W
Circle Alaska USA **64** B4 65 50N 144 11W
Cirebon Indonesia **103** D2 6 46S 108 33E
Cisco Texas USA **70** G3 32 23N 98 59W
Cisneros Col. **80** B15 6 32N 75 04W
Citlaltépetl *mt.* Mexico **74** E3 19 00N 97 18W
City Island New York USA **73** J2 40 51N 73 48W
Ciucea Romania **89** J7 46 58N 22 50E
Ciudad Acuna Mexico **74** D5 29 20N 100 58W
Ciudad Bolívar Venezuela **80** E15 8 06N 63 36W
Ciudad Camargo Mexico **74** C5 27 41N 105 10W
Ciudad del Carmen Mexico **74** F3 18 38N 91 50W
Ciudad del Este Paraguay **80** G8 25 32S 54 34W
Ciudadela Sp. **87** G3 40 00N 3 50E
Ciudad Guayana Venezuela **80** E15 8 22N 62 37W
Ciudad Juárez Mexico **74** C6 31 42N 106 29W
Ciudad Lerdo Mexico **74** D5 25 34N 103 30W
Ciudad Madero Mexico **74** E4 22 19N 97 50W
Ciudad Manté Mexico **74** E4 22 44N 98 59W
Ciudad Obregón Mexico **74** C5 27 28N 109 59W
Ciudad Real Sp. **87** D3 38 59N 3 55W
Ciudad Rodrigo Sp. **87** B4 40 36N 6 33W
Ciudad Victoria Mexico **74** E4 23 43N 99 10W
Civitavecchia Italy **89** C5 42 05N 11 47E
Cizre Turkey **96** D6 37 21N 42 11E
Clan Alpine Mountains Nevada USA **72** E4 39 34N 117 53W
Clare Michigan USA **52** B3 43 49N 84 47W
Claremont New Hampshire USA **73** D3 43 22N 72 20W
Clarence Island South Shetland Islands **81** G1 61 10S 54 00W
Clarence Strait *sd.* Alaska USA **42** D4 56 00N 133 30W
Clarendon Pennsylvania USA **52** G1 41 46N 79 06W
Clarion Fracture Zone Pacific Ocean **115** N9 18 00N 130 00W
Clark Fork *r.* Montana USA **43** N1 48 00N 115 55W
Clark Hill Lake South Carolina USA **71** K3 33 00N 82 00W
Clarksburg West Virginia USA **71** K4 39 16N 80 22W
Clarks Ferry *tn.* Pennsylvania USA **73** B2 40 25N 77 56W
Clarksville Tennessee USA **71** J4 36 31N 87 21W
Clayton New York USA **53** K4 44 15N 76 06W
Clearfield Pennsylvania USA **73** A2 41 01N 78 26W
Clear Lake California USA **72** B4 39 04N 122 48W
Clearwater Florida USA **71** K2 27 57N 82 48W
Clearwater *r.* Idaho USA **70** C6 46 00N 116 00W
Clermont-Ferrand Fr. **87** G6 45 47N 3 05E
Cleveland Ohio USA **71** K5 41 30N 81 41W
Cleveland Peninsula Alaska USA **42** D4 55 30N 132 00W
Clinton Iowa USA **71** H5 41 51N 90 12W
Clinton Oklahoma USA **70** G4 35 32N 98 59W
Clipperton Fracture Zone Pacific Ocean **115** P8/Q9 10 00N 120 00W
Clipperton Island Pacific Ocean **115** R9 10 20N 109 13W
Cloncurry Aust. **110** G5 20 41S 140 30E
Clonmel RoI **86** B10 52 21N 7 42W
Cloppenburg Germany **88** B10 52 52N 8 02E
Cloquet Minnesota USA **51** E4 46 43N 92 27W
Cloverdale California USA **72** B4 38 47N 123 01W
Clovis California USA **72** D3 36 47N 119 43W
Clovis New Mexico USA **70** F3 34 14N 103 13W
Cluj-Napoca Romania **89** J7 46 47N 23 37E
Clyde Ohio USA **52** D1 41 17N 82 58W
Clydebank UK **86** C11 55 54N 4 24W
Coaldale Nevada USA **72** E4 38 02N 117 52W
Coalinga California USA **72** C3 36 08N 120 22W
Coari Brazil **80** E13 4 08S 63 07W
Coast Ranges *mts.* California USA **70** B4/B6 41 00N 123 00W
Coatepec Mexico **74** E3 19 29N 96 59W
Coats Land *geog. reg.* Antarctica **117** 77 00S 25 00W
Coatzacoalcos Mexico **74** F3 18 10N 94 25W
Cobán Guatemala **74** F3 15 28N 90 20W
Cobar Aust. **110** H3 31 32S 145 51E
Cobija Bolivia **80** D11 11 01S 68 45W
Coburg Germany **88** C9 50 15N 10 58E
Cochabamba Bolivia **80** D10 17 26S 66 10W
Cochin India **98** D1 9 56N 76 15E
Cochraine Chile **81** C4 47 16S 72 33W
Cochranton Pennsylvania USA **52** F1 41 32N 80 03W
Cocos Basin Indian Ocean **113** J6 5 00S 96 00E
Cocos Islands Indian Ocean **113** J5 12 30S 97 00E
Cocos Ridge Pacific Ocean **115** S8 4 00N 90 00W
Codajás Brazil **80** E13 3 55S 62 00W
Cod, Cape Massachusetts USA **71** N5 42 05N 70 12W
Codó Brazil **80** J13 4 28S 43 51W
Codrington Antigua and Barbuda **74** Q9 17 43N 61 49W
Coeur d'Alene Idaho USA **70** C6 47 40N 116 46W
Cognac Fr. **87** E6 45 42N 0 19W
Coihaique Chile **81** C4 45 35S 72 08W
Coimbatore India **98** D2 11 00N 76 57E
Coimbra Port. **87** A4 40 12N 8 25W
Colchester UK **86** F9 51 54N 0 54E
Cold Springs *tn.* Nevada USA **72** E4 39 22N 117 53W
Coldwater Michigan USA **51** J1 41 56N 84 59W
Coleen River Alaska USA **64** B4 67 30N 142 30W
Coleraine UK **86** B11 55 08N 6 40W
Colima Mexico **74** D3 19 14N 103 41W
College Alaska USA **64** A3 64 54N 147 55W
Collie Aust. **110** B3 33 20S 116 06E
Collingwood NZ **111** D4 40 41S 172 41E
Colmar Fr. **86** J8 48 05N 7 21E
Cologne Germany **88** A9 50 56N 6 57E
COLOMBIA **80** C14
Colombo Sri Lanka **98** D1 6 55N 79 52E
Colón Panama **75** J1 9 21N 79 54W
Colorado *r.* Argentina **81** D6 37 30S 69 00W
Colorado *r.* North America **70** D3 33 00N 114 00W
Colorado *r.* Texas USA **71** G2 29 00N 96 00W
Colorado *state* USA **70** E4/F4 39 00N 106 00W
Colorado Desert California USA **72** E1/F1 33 18N 116 00W
Colorado Plateau Arizona USA **70** D4 36 00N 111 00W
Colorado River Aqueduct California USA **72** E1 34 00N 116 30W
Colorado Springs *tn.* Colorado USA **70** F4 38 50N 104 50W
Columbia Missouri USA **71** H4 38 58N 92 20W
Columbia South Carolina USA **71** K3 34 00N 81 00W
Columbia *r.* North America **70** B6 46 00N 120 00W
Columbus Georgia USA **71** K3 32 28N 84 59W
Columbus Indiana USA **71** J4 39 12N 85 57W
Columbus Mississippi USA **71** J3 33 30N 88 27W
Columbus Nebraska USA **71** G5 41 27N 97 21W
Columbus Ohio USA **71** K5 39 59N 83 03W
Columbus Salt Marsh Nevada USA **72** E4 38 06N 117 57W
Colville Washington USA **43** M1 48 33N 117 55W
Colvocoresses Bay Antarctica **117** 66 00S 120 00E
Comilla Bangladesh **99** L9 23 28N 91 10E
Comitán Mexico **74** F3 16 18N 92 09W
Como Italy **89** B6 45 48N 9 05E
Comodoro Rivadavia Argentina **81** D4 45 50S 67 30W
COMOROS **109** N5
Compiègne Fr. **86** G8 49 25N 2 50E
Comrat Moldova **89** M7 46 18N 28 40E
Conakry Guinea **108** B9 9 30N 13 43W
Concepción Chile **81** C5 36 50S 73 03W
Concepción Mexico **74** D4 24 38N 101 25W
Concepción Paraguay **80** F9 23 22S 57 26W
Concepción del Uruguay Argentina **81** F7 32 30S 58 15W
Conchos *r.* Mexico **74** C5 27 30N 107 00W
Concord California USA **72** B3 37 59N 122 03W
Concord New Hampshire USA **71** M5 43 13N 71 34W
Concordia Argentina **81** F7 31 25S 58 00W
Concordia Kansas USA **71** G4 39 35N 97 39W
Concrete Washington USA **42** H4 48 30N 121 45W
Condom Fr. **87** F5 43 58N 0 23E
Conduit *r.* Israel **96** N11 32 25N 35 00E
Conecuh *r.* Alabama USA **71** J3 31 00N 87 00W
Conesus Lake New York USA **52** J2 42 48N 77 44W
Coney Island New York USA **73** J1 40 34N 74 00W
CONGO **108** H7
Congo *r.* Congo/CDR **108** H7 2 00S 17 00E
CONGO DEMOCRATIC REPUBLIC **108** H7
Conneaut Ohio USA **52** F1 41 58N 80 34W
Connecticut *r.* North America **71** M5 43 00N 72 00W
Connecticut *state* USA **71** M5 41 00N 73 00W
Constanța Romania **89** M6 44 12N 28 40E
Constantine Algeria **108** F15 36 22N 6 40E
Constitución Chile **81** C6 31 05S 57 51W
Contamana Peru **80** B12 7 19S 75 04W

Cook Islands Pacific Ocean 115 L6 19 30S 159 50W
Cook, Mount NZ 111 C3 43 36S 170 09E
Cook Strait NZ 111 E4 41 24S 174 36E
Cooktown Aust. 110 H6 15 29S 145 15E
Coolgardie Aust. 110 C3 31 01S 121 12E
Cooper Creek Aust. 111 F4 28 00S 138 00E
Coosa *r.* Alabama USA 71 J3 33 00N 86 00W
Coos Bay *tn.* Oregon USA 70 B5 43 23N 124 12W
Copenhagen Denmark 88 D11 55 43N 12 34E
Copiapó Chile 80 C8 27 20S 70 23W
Copper Harbor Michigan USA 71 J6 47 28N 87 54W
Coquimbo Chile 81 C8 29 57S 71 25W
Coral Sea Pacific Ocean 110 J7 15 00S 154 00E
Coral Sea Islands Territory *admin.* Aust. 110 J6 17 00S 150 00E
Corantijn *r.* Suriname 80 F14 4 30N 57 30W
Cordillera Cantabrica *mts.* Sp. 87 B5/C5 43 00N 5 30W
Córdoba Argentina 81 E7 31 25S 64 11W
Córdoba Mexico 74 E3 18 55N 96 55W
Córdoba Sp. 87 C2 37 53N 4 46W
Corfu Greece 89 G3 39 38N 19 55E
Corinth Mississippi USA 71 J3 34 58N 88 30W
Cork RoI 86 A9 51 54N 8 28W
Corning New York USA 53 J2 42 09N 77 05W
Cornwall Bridge *tn.* Connecticut USA 73 D2 41 49N 73 22W
Coro Venezuela 80 D16 11 20N 70 00W
Coroico Bolivia 80 D10 16 19S 67 45W
Coromandel Coast India 98 E2 12 30N 81 30E
Corona California USA 72 E1 33 52N 117 34W
Coronado California USA 72 E1 32 40N 117 07W
Coronation Island South Orkney Islands 81 H1 61 00S 46 00W
Coronation Island Alaska USA 42 C4 55 50N 134 15N
Coronel Pringles Argentina 81 E6 37 56S 61 25W
Corpus Christi Texas USA 71 G2 27 47N 97 26W
Corrientes Argentina 80 F8 27 30S 58 48W
Corrientes *r.* Peru 80 B13 2 30S 76 30W
Corriverton Guyana 80 F15 5 53N 57 10W
Corry Pennsylvania USA 52 G1 41 56N 79 39W
Corsica *i.* Fr. 87 K4/K5 42 00N 9 00E
Corte Fr. 87 K5 41 18N 9 08E
Cortland New York USA 51 N2 42 36N 76 11W
Çoruh *r.* Turkey 96 D7 40 45N 40 45E
Corumbá Brazil 80 F10 19 00S 57 35W
Corunna Michigan USA 52 B2 42 58N 84 05W
Corvallis Oregon USA 70 B5 44 34N 123 16W
Cosenza Italy 89 F3 39 17N 16 16E
Costa Blanca *geog. reg.* Sp. 87 E3 38 15N 0 20W
Costa Brava *geog. reg.* Sp. 87 G4 41 40N 3 50E
Costa del Sol *geog. reg.* Sp. 87 C2 36 40N 4 40W
COSTA RICA 75 H1
Cotagaita Bolivia 80 D9 20 47S 65 40W
Côte D'Azur *geog. reg.* Fr. 87 J5 43 00N 7 00E
CÔTE D'IVOIRE 108 C9
Cotonou Benin 108 E9 6 24N 2 31E
Cotopaxi *mt.* Ecuador 80 B13 0 40S 78 28W
Cottbus Germany 88 E9 51 43N 14 21E
Coudersport Pennsylvania USA 52 H1 41 47N 78 00W
Council Bluffs Iowa USA 71 G5 41 14N 95 54W
Coupeville Washington USA 42 H4 48 08N 122 38W
Coventry UK 86 E10 52 25N 1 30W
Covilhã Port. 87 B4 40 17N 7 30W
Covington Kentucky USA 71 K4 39 04N 84 30W
Cox's Bazar Bangladesh 99 L8 21 25N 91 59E
Coyote Lake California USA 72 E2 35 05N 116 45W
Cozumel Mexico 74 G4 20 33N 86 55W
Craig Alaska USA 42 D4 55 29N 133 06W
Craiova Romania 89 J6 44 18N 23 47E
Crandon Wisconsin USA 51 G3 45 34N 88 54W
Cremona Italy 89 C6 45 08N 10 01E
Cres *i.* Croatia 89 E6 45 00N 14 00E
Crescent City California USA 70 B5 41 46N 124 13W
Crescent Island HK China 100 C3 22 32N 114 19E
Creston Iowa USA 71 H5 41 04N 94 20W
Crestview Florida USA 71 J3 30 44N 86 34W
Crete, Sea of Mediterranean Sea 89 K2/L2 36 00N 25 00E
Crewe UK 86 D10 53 05N 2 27W
Criciúma Brazil 81 H8 28 45S 49 25W
CROATIA 89 F6
Cromwell NZ 111 E6 36 51S 169 12E
Crooked Island Bahamas 75 B2 45 03N 74 10W
Crooked Island HK China 100 C3 22 33N 114 18E
Crookston Minnesota USA 71 G6 47 47N 96 36W
Crosby North Dakota USA 47 F1 48 59N 103 20W
Cross Sound Alaska USA 42 B6 58 00N 137 00W
Crotone Italy 89 F3 39 05N 17 08E
Crow Peak *mt.* Montana USA 70 D6 46 19N 111 56W
Croydon Aust. 110 G6 18 10S 142 15E
Crozet Basin Indian Ocean 113 E3/F2 40 00S 55 00E
Cruzeiro do Sul Brazil 80 C12 7 40S 72 39W
Crystal Falls *tn.* Michigan USA 51 G4 46 06N 89 20W
Cuando *r.* Southern Africa 109 J4 16 00S 21 30E
Cuango *r.* Angola 109 H6 9 00S 18 30E
Cuanza *r.* Angola 109 H6 9 40S 15 00E
CUBA 75 H4
Cubango *r.* Southern Africa 109 H4 17 00S 18 00E
Cúcuta Col. 80 C15 7 55N 73 31W
Cuddalore India 98 D2 11 43N 79 46E
Cuddapah India 98 D2 14 30N 78 50E
Cuddeback Lake California USA 72 E2 35 17N 117 29W
Cuenca Ecuador 80 B13 2 54S 79 00W
Cuenca Sp. 87 D4 40 04N 2 07W
Cuernavaca Mexico 74 E3 18 57N 99 15W
Cuiabá Brazil 80 F10 15 32S 56 05W
Cuito *r.* Angola 109 H4 17 30S 19 30E
Culiacán Mexico 74 C4 24 50N 107 23W
Cumaná Venezuela 80 E16 10 29N 64 12W
Cumberland Maryland USA 71 L4 39 40N 78 47W
Cumberland *r.* North America 71 J4 37 00N 86 00W
Cumberland Plateau USA 71 J4/K4 36 00N 85 00W
Cumbernauld UK 86 D11 55 57N 4 00W
Cumbrian Mountains UK 86 D11 54 30N 3 00W
Cunene *r.* Angola/Namibia 109 G4 17 00S 13 30E
Cuneo Italy 89 A6 44 24N 7 33E
Cunnamula Aust. 110 H4 28 04S 145 40E
Curaçao *i.* Lesser Antilles 75 L2 12 20N 68 20W
Curacautin Chile 81 C6 38 28S 71 52W
Curicó Chile 81 C6 35 00S 71 15W
Curitiba Brazil 80 H8 25 25S 49 25W
Curvelo Brazil 80 J10 18 45S 44 27W
Cut Bank Montana USA 46 F1 48 37N 112 18W
Cut Bank Creek *r.* Montana USA 46 F1 48 40N 112 50W
Cuttack India 99 F4 20 26N 85 56E
Cuxhaven Germany 88 B10 53 52N 8 42E
Cuzco Peru 80 C11 13 32S 71 59W
CYPRUS 96 B5
CZECH REPUBLIC 88 D8
Częstochowa Poland 88 G9 50 49N 19 07E

D

Dabgram India 99 K9 23 50N 88 17E
Dabola Guinea 108 B10 10 48N 11 02W
Dadra and Nagar Haveli *admin.* India 98 C4 20 00N 73 00E
Da Hinggan Ling *mts.* China 101 M8 50 00N 122 00E
Dahūk Iraq 96 D6 36 52N 43 00E
Daiō-zaki *c.* Japan 102 C1 34 16N 136 55E
Daisen *mt.* Japan 102 B2 35 23N 133 34E
Dakar Senegal 108 A10 14 38N 17 27W
Dakhin Shahbazpur Island Bangladesh 99 L9 22 30N 90 45E
Dakhla Oasis Egypt 108 K13 26 00N 28 00E
Dalälven *r.* Sweden 88 F14 60 30N 17 00E
Da Lat Vietnam 103 D6 11 56N 108 25E
Dalbandin Pakistan 98 A5 28 56N 64 30E
Dalby Aust. 110 J4 27 11S 151 12E
Dalhart Texas USA 70 F4 36 05N 102 32W
Dali China 101 J4 25 33N 100 09E
Dalian China 101 N6 38 53N 121 37E
Dalkhola India 99 J10 25 57N 87 51E
Dallas Texas USA 71 G3 32 47N 96 48W
Dall Island Alaska USA 42 D4 55 00N 133 00W
Daloa Côte d'Ivoire 108 C9 6 56N 6 28W
Dalton Georgia USA 71 K3 34 46N 84 59W
Daly *r.* Aust. 110 E7 14 00S 132 00E
Daly Waters *tn.* Aust. 110 E6 16 13S 133 20E
Daman India 98 C4 20 15N 72 58E
Damascus Syria 96 C5 33 30N 36 19E
Damāvand Iran 97 F6 35 47N 52 04E
Damāvand *mt.* Iran 97 F6 35 56N 52 08E
Damba Angola 109 H6 6 44S 15 20E
Damietta Egypt 109 R4 31 26N 31 48E
Damman and Diu *admin.* India 98 C4 15 00N 74 00E
Damodar *r.* India 99 K9 22 30N 88 00E
Dampier Aust. 110 B5 20 45S 116 48E
Da Năng Vietnam 103 D7 16 04N 108 14E
Danau Toba *l.* Indonesia 103 B4 2 30N 98 30E
Danbury Connecticut USA 71 M5 41 24N 73 26W
Dandong China 101 N7 40 08N 124 24E
Danforth Maine USA 57 G1 45 42N 67 50W
Danielson Connecticut USA 73 E2 41 48N 71 53W
Danli Honduras 74 G2 14 02N 86 30W
Dannevirke NZ 111 F4 40 12S 176 06E
Danville Illinois USA 71 J5 40 09N 87 37W
Danville Pennsylvania USA 73 B2 40 58N 76 37W
Danville Virginia USA 71 L4 36 34N 79 25W
Daqing China 101 P8 46 28N 125 01E
Dar'ā Syria 96 P11 32 37N 36 06E
Darbhanga India 99 F5 26 10N 85 54E
Dardanelles *sd.* Turkey 96 A7 40 08N 26 10E
Dar es Salaam Tanzania 109 M6 6 51S 39 18E
Darfur *geog. reg.* Sudan 108 J10 14 30N 24 30E
Dargaville NZ 111 D7 35 56S 173 52E
Darjiling India 99 F5 27 02N 88 20E
Darling *r.* Aust. 110 G3 30 30S 144 00E
Darling Downs *mts.* Aust. 110 H4 28 00S 148 30E
Darlington UK 86 E11 54 31N 1 34W
Darmstadt Germany 88 B8 49 52N 8 39E
Darnah Libya 108 J14 32 46N 22 39E
Daroca Sp. 87 E4 41 07N 1 25W
Darrington Washington USA 42 H4 48 15N 121 37W
Dartmoor *hills* UK 86 C9 50 35N 3 50W
Daru PNG 110 G8 9 05S 143 10E
Darwin Aust. 110 E7 12 23S 130 44E
Darwin California USA 72 E3 36 17N 117 36W
Daryācheh-ye Orūmīyeh *l.* Iran 96 E6 37 20N 45 55E
Dashkhovuz Turkmenistan 94 H5 41 49N 59 58E
Dasht-e-Kavir *geog. reg.* Iran 97 F5/G5 34 30N 54 30E
Dasht-e-Lut *geog. reg.* Iran 97 G5 32 00N 57 00E
Dasht-i-Margo *d.* Afghanistan 97 H5 30 30N 62 30E
Datong China 101 L7 40 02N 113 33E
Datong Shan *mts.* China 101 H6/J6 38 00N 99 00E
Datong He *r.* China 101 J6 37 30N 102 00E
Datu Piang Philippines 103 G5 7 02N 124 30E
Dauki India 99 L10 25 10N 92 00E
Davangere India 98 D2 14 30N 75 52E
Davao Philippines 103 H5 7 05N 125 38E
Davenport California USA 72 B3 37 02N 122 14W
Davenport Iowa USA 71 H5 41 32N 90 36W
David Panama 75 H1 8 26N 82 26W
Davidson Mountains Alaska USA 64 B4 68 30N 143 30W
Davis California USA 72 C4 38 33N 121 46W
Davison Michigan USA 52 C3 43 02N 83 30W
Davos Switz. 87 K7 46 47N 9 50E
Dawna Range *mts.* Myanmar/Thailand 103 B7 17 10N 98 00E
Dax Fr. 87 E5 43 43N 1 03W
Dayr az Zawr Syria 96 D6 35 20N 40 02E
Dayton Ohio USA 71 K4 39 45N 84 10W
Daytona Beach *tn.* Florida USA 71 K2 29 11N 81 01W
De Aar RSA 109 J1 30 40S 24 01E
Dead Sea Israel/Jordan 96 N10 31 35N 35 30E
Deán Funes Argentina 81 E7 30 25S 64 22W
Dearborn Michigan USA 51 K2 42 18N 83 16W
Death Valley California USA 70 C4 36 00N 117 00W
Death Valley Junction *tn.* California USA 72 E3 36 18N 116 25W
Death Valley National Monument California USA 72 E3 36 30N 117 00W
Debrecen Hungary 89 H7 47 30N 21 37E
Debre Mark'os Ethiopia 108 M10 10 19N 37 41E
Debre Tabor Ethiopia 108 M10 11 50N 38 06E
Decatur Alabama USA 71 J3 34 36N 87 00W
Decatur Illinois USA 71 J4 39 51N 88 57W
Deccan *plat.* India 98 D3 18 00N 78 00E
Dee *r.* UK 86 D10 53 15N 3 10W
Deep Bay HK China 100 A3 22 30N 113 58E
Defiance Ohio USA 51 J1 41 17N 84 22W
Degeh Bur Ethiopia 108 N9 8 11N 43 31E
Dehra Dun India 98 D6 30 19N 78 03E
Dej Romania 89 J7 47 08N 23 55E
Dekese CDR 108 J7 3 28S 21 24E
Delano California USA 72 D2 35 46N 119 15W
Delaware *state* USA 71 L4 39 00N 75 00W
Delaware Bay Delaware/New Jersey USA 71 L4 39 10N 75 10W
Delaware River Delaware USA 73 C1 39 40N 75 30W
Delhi India 98 D5 28 40N 77 14E
Delhi *admin.* India 98 D5 28 40N 77 14E
Del Rio Texas USA 70 F2 29 23N 100 56W
Delta Colorado USA 70 E4 38 42N 108 04W
Delta Junction Alaska USA 64 A3 63 30N 146 00W
Dembi Dolo Ethiopia 108 L9 8 34N 34 50E
Deming New Mexico USA 70 E3 32 17N 107 46W
Deming Washington USA 42 H4 48 50N 122 17W
Denali National Park Alaska USA 40 E6 63 00N 151 00W
Den Helder Neths. 86 H10 52 58N 4 46E
Denison Texas USA 71 G3 33 47N 96 34W
Denizli Turkey 96 A6 37 46N 29 05E
DENMARK 88 B11
Denmark Strait Atlantic Ocean 116 F13 66 30N 25 00W
Denpasar Indonesia 103 F2 8 40S 115 14E
Denton Texas USA 71 G3 33 14N 97 18W
D'Entrecasteaux Islands PNG 110 J7/J8 9 15S 150 45E
Denver Colorado USA 70 E4 39 45N 105 00W
Dépression du Mourdi *dep.* Chad 108 J11 17 00N 22 41E
Deputatskiy Russia 95 R10 69 15N 139 59E
Dera Ghazi Khan Pakistan 98 C6 30 05N 70 44E
Dera Ismail Khan Pakistan 98 C6 31 51N 70 56E
Derby Aust. 110 C6 17 19S 123 38E
Derby UK 86 E10 52 55N 1 30W
Derby Connecticut USA 73 D2 41 20N 73 06W
Dese Ethiopia 108 M10 11 05N 39 40E
Deseado Argentina 81 D4 47 44S 65 56W
Deseado *r.* Argentina 81 D4 47 00S 68 00W
Desert Center California USA 72 F1 33 44N 115 23W
Desierto de Atacama *d.* Chile 80 C9 22 30S 70 00W
Des Moines Iowa USA 71 H5 41 35N 93 35W
Des Moines *r.* Iowa USA 71 H5 41 00N 92 00W
Desna *r.* Russia/Ukraine 88 N9 52 00N 32 30E
Dessau Germany 88 D9 51 51N 12 15E
Detroit Michigan USA 71 K5 42 23N 83 05W
Deva Romania 89 J6 45 53N 22 55E
Deveron *r.* UK 86 D12 57 35N 2 35W
Devil's Lake *tn.* North Dakota USA 71 G6 48 03N 98 57W
Devonport Aust. 110 H1 41 09S 146 16E
Dexter Maine USA 57 F1 45 01N 69 19W
Dezfūl Iran 97 E5 32 23N 48 28E
Dezhou China 101 M6 37 29N 116 11E
Dhahran Saudi Arabia 97 F4 26 13N 50 02E
Dhaka Bangladesh 99 L9 23 42N 90 22E
Dhamār Yemen 96 D1 14 33N 44 30E
Dhanbad India 99 F4 23 47N 86 32E
Dharoor *r.* Somalia 108 P10 10 00N 54 00E
Dharwad India 98 D3 15 30N 75 04E
Dhaulagiri *mt.* Nepal 98 E5 28 40N 83 28E
Dhule India 98 C4 20 52N 74 50E
Diablo Lake Washington USA 42 H4 48 45N 121 05W
Diablo, Mount California USA 72 C3 37 50N 121 47W
Diamantina Brazil 80 J10 18 17S 43 37W
Diamantina *r.* Aust. 110 G5 24 00S 143 00E
Diamantina Fracture Zone Indian Ocean 113 K3 38 00S 110 00E
Diamond Harbour *tn.* India 99 K9 22 10N 88 13E
Dibrugarh India 99 G5 27 29N 95 00E
Dickinson North Dakota USA 70 F6 46 54N 102 48W
Diepholz Germany 88 B10 52 37N 8 22E
Dieppe Fr. 86 F8 49 55N 1 05E
Digne-les-Bains Fr. 87 J6 44 05N 6 14E
Dijon Fr. 87 H7 47 20N 5 02E
Dikson Russia 95 L11 73 32N 80 39E
Dikwa Nigeria 108 G10 12 01N 13 55E
Dili East Timor 103 H2 8 33S 125 34E
Dimitrovgrad Bulgaria 89 K5 42 03N 25 34E
Dinajpur Bangladesh 99 K10 25 38N 88 44E
Dinan Fr. 86 D8 48 27N 2 02W
Dinant Belgium 86 H9 50 16N 4 55E
Dinara Planina *mts.* Europe 89 F5 44 00N 17 00E
Dindigul India 98 D2 10 23N 78 00E
Dingwall UK 86 C12 57 35N 4 29W
Dipolog Philippines 103 G5 8 34N 123 23E
Dire Dawa Ethiopia 108 N9 9 35N 41 50E
Disappointment, Lake Aust. 110 C5 23 00S 123 00E
Discovery Bay *tn.* HK China 100 B1 22 18N 114 01E
Dispur India 99 G5 26 07N 91 48E
Diu India 98 C4 20 41N 71 03E
Divinópolis Brazil 80 J9 20 08S 44 55W
Divriği Turkey 96 C6 39 23N 38 06E
Dixie Valley *tn.* Nevada USA 72 D4 39 41N 118 04W
Dixon California USA 72 C4 38 26N 121 53W
Diyarbakir Turkey 96 D6 37 55N 40 14E
Djambala Congo 108 G7 2 32S 14 43E
Djanet Algeria 108 F12 24 27N 9 32E
Djelfa Algeria 108 E14 34 43N 3 14E
DJIBOUTI 108 N10
Djibouti Djibouti 108 N10 11 35N 43 11E
Djougou Benin 108 E9 9 40N 1 47E
Dnestr *r.* Ukraine 88 K8 48 00N 27 30E
Doboj Bosnia-Herzegovina 89 G6 44 44N 18 05E
Dobrich Bulgaria 89 L5 43 34N 27 51E
Dobrogea *geog. reg.* Romania 89 M6 44 00N 29 00E
Dodekánisos *is.* Greece 89 L2 37 00N 26 00E
Dodge City Kansas USA 70 F4 37 45N 100 02W
Dōgo *i.* Japan 102 B2 36 20N 133 15E
Doha Qatar 97 F4 25 15N 51 36E
Dolina Ukraine 88 J8 49 00N 23 59E
Dolo Odo Ethiopia 108 N8 4 11N 42 03E
Domar Bangladesh 99 K11 26 08N 88 57E
DOMINICA 74 Q8
DOMINICAN REPUBLIC 75 L3
Dominica Passage *sd.* Caribbean Sea 74 Q8 15 10N 61 15W
Don *r.* Russia 94 G7 50 00N 41 00E
Donau *r.* Germany/Austria 88 C8 48 00N 16 00E
Don Benito Sp. 87 C3 38 57N 5 52W
Doncaster UK 86 E10 53 32N 1 07W
Donegal RoI 86 A11 54 39N 8 07W
Donegal Bay RoI 86 A11 54 30N 8 30W
Dongchuan China 101 J4 26 07N 103 05E
Đông Hới Vietnam 103 D7 17 32N 106 35E
Dongola Sudan 108 L11 19 10N 30 27E
Dongou Congo 108 H8 2 02N 18 02E
Donnelly's Crossing NZ 111 D7 35 42S 173 36E
Don Pedro Reservoir California USA 72 C3 37 45N 120 23W
Donting Hu *l.* China 101 L4 29 00N 112 30E
Door Peninsula Wisconsin USA 71 J5 45 00N 87 00W
Dora Bāltea *r.* Italy 89 A6 45 45N 8 00E
Dordogne *r.* Fr. 87 F6 44 55N 0 30E
Dordrecht Neths. 86 H9 51 48N 4 40E
Dori *r.* Afghanistan 97 H5/J5 31 20N 65 00E
Dornbirn Austria 87 K7 47 25N 9 46E
Dortmund Germany 88 A9 51 32N 7 27E
Dos Palos California USA 72 C3 36 59N 120 39W
Dosso Niger 108 E10 13 03N 3 10E
Dothan Alabama USA 71 J3 31 12N 85 25W
Douala Cameroon 108 F8 4 04N 9 43E
Douarnenez Fr. 86 C8 48 05N 4 20W
Double Island HK China 100 C3 22 31N 114 19E
Doubtful Sound NZ 111 A2 44 16S 166 51E
Doubs *r.* Fr. 87 J7 47 20N 6 25E
Douglas Alaska USA 42 C6 58 15N 134 24W
Douglas Arizona USA 70 E3 31 21N 109 34W
Dourados Brazil 80 G9 22 09S 54 52W
Douro *r.* Port./Sp. 87 B4 41 00N 8 30W
Dover UK 86 F9 51 08N 1 19E
Dover Delaware USA 71 L4 39 10N 75 32W
Dover New Hampshire USA 73 E3 43 12N 70 53W
Dover, Strait of *sd.* English Channel 86 F9 51 00N 1 20W
Dōzen *is.* Japan 102 B2 36 05N 133 00E
Dragon's Mouths Trinidad and Tobago 75 V15 10 37N 61 50W
Draguignan Fr. 87 J5 43 32N 6 28E
Drakensberg *mts.* RSA 109 K1/L2 30 00S 28 00E
Drake Passage *sd.* Southern Ocean 81 C2/E2 58 00S 66 00W
Dráma Greece 89 K4 41 10N 24 11E
Drammen Norway 88 L13 59 45N 10 15E
Drau *r.* Austria 89 E7 46 00N 14 00E
Drava *r.* Europe 89 F7 46 00N 18 00E
Dresden Germany 88 D9 51 03N 13 45E
Dreux Fr. 86 F8 48 44N 1 23E
Drin *r.* Albania 89 G5 42 00N 20 00E
Drina *r.* Europe 89 G6 44 00N 19 30E
Drobeta-Turnu-Severin Romania 89 J6 44 36N 22 39E
Drohobyč Ukraine 88 J8 49 22N 23 33E

Drôme *r.* Fr. 87 H6 44 50N 5 00E
Dronning Maud Land *geog. reg.* Antarctica 117 73 00S 10 00E
Drummond Island Michigan USA 51 K3 46 00N 83 50W
Dubai UAE 97 G4 25 14N 55 17E
Dubbo Aust. 110 H3 32 16S 148 41E
Dublin RoI 86 B10 53 20N 6 15W
Dublin Georgia USA 71 K3 32 31N 82 54W
Dubno Ukraine 88 K9 50 28N 25 40E
Du Bois Pennsylvania USA 73 A2 41 07N 78 48W
Dubrovnik Croatia 89 G5 42 40N 18 07E
Dubuque Iowa USA 71 H5 42 31N 90 41W
Dudhanai India 99 L10 25 57N 90 47E
Dudinka Russia 95 L10 69 27N 86 13E
Duero *r.* Sp./Port. 87 B4 41 25N 6 30W
Dugi Otok *i.* Croatia 89 E5/E6 44 00N 15 00E
Duisburg Germany 88 A9 51 26N 6 45E
Duke Island Alaska USA 42 E4 54 50N 131 30W
Dulce *r.* Argentina 81 E8 29 00S 63 00W
Duluth Minnesota USA 71 H6 46 45N 92 10W
Dumfries UK 86 D11 55 04N 3 37W
Duna *r.* Hungary 89 G6/G7 46 00N 19 00E
Dunaújváros Hungary 89 G7 47 00N 18 55E
Dunav *r.* Serbia/Bulgaria 89 J5 45 00N 20 00E
Duncan Oklahoma USA 71 G3 34 30N 97 57W
Dundalk RoI 86 B11 54 01N 6 25W
Dundee UK 86 D12 56 28N 3 00W
Dunedin NZ 111 C2 45 53S 170 30E
Dunfermline UK 86 D12 56 04N 3 29W
Dungeness Washington USA 42 H4 48 07N 123 06W
Dunkerque Fr. 86 G9 51 02N 2 23E
Dunkirk New York USA 71 L5 42 29N 79 21W
Dún Laoghaire RoI 86 B10 53 17N 6 08W
Dunnigan California USA 72 C4 38 53N 121 57W
Duque de Caxias Brazil 80 J9 22 46S 43 18W
Durand Michigan USA 52 C2 42 55N 83 58W
Durango Mexico 74 D4 24 01N 104 40W
Durango Colorado USA 70 E4 37 16N 107 53W
Durant Oklahoma USA 71 G3 33 59N 96 24W
Durazno Uruguay 81 F7 33 22S 56 31W
Durban RSA 109 L2 29 53S 31 00E
Durgapur India 99 F4 24 47N 87 44E
Durg-Bhilai India 98 E4 21 12N 81 20E
Durham UK 86 E11 54 47N 1 34W
Durham North Carolina USA 71 L4 36 00N 78 54W
Durrës Albania 89 G4 41 18N 19 28E
Dushanbe Tajikistan 94 J4 38 38N 68 51E
Düsseldorf Germany 88 A9 51 13N 6 47E
Duyun China 101 K4 26 16N 107 29E
Dzhetygara Kazakhstan 94 J7 52 14N 61 10E
Dzhugdzhur Range *mts.* Russia 95 R8 57 00N 137 00E

E

Eagle Alaska USA 64 B3 64 46N 141 20W
Eagle Crags *mt.* California USA 72 E2 35 25N 117 04W
Eagle Lake Maine USA 53 S6 46 25N 69 20W
Eagle Mountain Minnesota USA 51 F4 47 54N 90 31W
Eagle Pass *tn.* Texas USA 70 F2 28 44N 100 31W
Eagle River *tn.* Wisconsin USA 51 G3 45 55N 89 14W
East Aurora New York USA 52 H2 42 46N 78 37W
Eastbourne UK 86 F9 50 46N 0 17E
East Cape NZ 111 G6 37 41S 178 33E
East Caroline Basin Pacific Ocean 114 E8 4 00N 148 00E
East China Sea China/Japan 101 N5/N6 32 00N 126 00E
Easter Island Pacific Ocean 115 R5 27 05S 109 20W
Easter Island Fracture Zone Pacific Ocean 115 R5 24 00S 100 00W
Eastern Ghats *mts.* India 98 D2/E3 15 00N 80 00E
Eastern Group *is.* Fiji 114 V16 17 40S 178 30W
Eastern Sayan *mts.* Russia 95 M7 53 00N 97 30E
East Falkland *i.* Falkland Islands 81 F3 52 00S 58 50W
East Glacier Park *tn.* Montana USA 46 F1 48 27N 113 13W
East Lamma Channel HK China 100 B1 22 14N 114 09E
East Lansing Michigan USA 51 J2 42 44N 84 29W
East London RSA 109 K1 33 00S 27 54E
East Marianas Basin Pacific Ocean 114 F9 13 00N 153 00E
East Pacific Basin Pacific Ocean 115 L9 16 00N 153 00E
East Pacific Ridge Pacific Ocean 115 Q4/R7 20 00S 113 00W
East Pacific Rise Pacific Ocean 115 R9 13 00N 103 00W
Eastport Maine USA 57 G1 44 55N 67 01W
East Rift Valley East Africa 108 M8 6 00N 37 00E
East River New York USA 73 J2 40 48N 73 55W
East Siberian Sea Arctic Ocean 117 72 00N 165 00E
Eastsound Washington USA 42 H4 48 43N 123 05W
EAST TIMOR 103 H2
East Walker *r.* Nevada USA 72 D4 38 48N 119 03W
Eaton Rapids *tn.* Michigan USA 52 B2 42 30N 84 40W
Eau Claire *tn.* Wisconsin USA 71 H5 44 50N 91 30W
Eauripik-New Guinea Rise Pacific Ocean 114 E8 2 00N 142 00E
Ebensburg Pennsylvania USA 73 A2 40 29N 78 44W
Eberswalde-Finow Germany 88 D10 52 50N 13 53E
Ebinur Hu *l.* China 100 E7 45 00N 83 00E
Ebolowa Cameroon 108 G8 2 56N 11 11E
Ebro *r.* Sp. 87 F4 43 00N 4 30W
Ech Cheliff Algeria 108 E15 36 05N 1 15E
Ecija Sp. 87 C2 37 33N 5 04W
ECUADOR 80 B13
Ed Damer Sudan 108 L11 17 37N 33 59E
Ed Debba Sudan 108 L11 18 02N 30 56E
Edéa Cameroon 108 G8 3 47N 10 13E
Eden New York USA 54 D1 42 39N 78 55W
Eden North Carolina USA 71 L4 36 30N 79 46W
Eder *r.* Germany 88 B9 51 00N 9 00E
Edessa Greece 89 J4 40 48N 22 03E
Edgecombe, Cape Alaska USA 42 C5 57 00N 135 45W
Edgewood Maryland USA 73 B1 39 25N 76 18W
Edinboro Pennsylvania USA 51 L1 41 52N 80 08W
Edinburgh UK 86 D11 55 57N 3 13W
Edward, Lake CDR/Uganda 108 K7 0 30S 29 00E
Edwards Plateau Texas USA 70 F3 31 00N 100 00W
Eger Hungary 88 H7 47 53N 20 28E
Eğirdir Gölü *l.* Turkey 96 B6 37 52N 30 51E
Egmont, Mount NZ 111 E5 39 18S 174 04E
EGYPT 108 K13
Eifel *plat.* Germany 88 A9 50 00N 7 00E
Eight Degree Channel Indian Ocean 98 C1 8 00N 73 30E
Eighty Mile Beach Aust. 110 C6 19 00S 121 00E
Eindhoven Neths. 86 H9 51 26N 5 30E
Eisenach Germany 88 C9 50 59N 10 19E
Eketahuna NZ 111 E4 40 39S 175 42E
Ekibastuz Kazakhstan 94 K7 51 50N 75 10E
Eksjö Sweden 88 E12 57 40N 15 00E
El Arco Mexico 74 B5 28 00N 113 25W
Elat Israel 96 B4 29 33N 34 57E
Elâzığ Turkey 96 C6 38 41N 39 14E
El Bahr el Saghir Egypt 109 R4 31 38N 31 39E
El Ballâh Egypt 109 S3 30 47N 32 19E
El Banco Col. 80 C15 9 04N 73 59W
Elbasan Albania 89 H4 41 07N 20 05E
El Bayadh Algeria 108 E14 33 40N 1 00E
Elbe *est.* Europe 88 B10 54 00N 9 00E
Elbert, Mount Colorado USA 70 E4 39 05N 106 27W
Elbląg Poland 88 G11 54 10N 19 25E
Elburz Mountains Iran 97 F6 36 15N 51 00E
El Cajon California USA 72 E1 32 48N 116 58W
El Callao Venezuela 80 E15 7 18N 61 50W
El Cap Egypt 109 S3 30 55N 32 23E
El Centro California USA 70 C3 32 47N 115 33W
Elche Sp. 87 E3 38 16N 0 41W
Elda Sp. 87 E3 38 29N 0 47W
El Dorado Arkansas USA 71 H3 33 12N 92 40W
El Dorado Kansas USA 71 G4 37 51N 96 52W
Eldoret Kenya 108 M8 0 31N 35 17E
Elephant Island South Shetland Islands 81 F1 62 00S 55 00W
El Faiyûm Egypt 108 L13 29 19N 30 50E
El Fasher Sudan 108 K10 13 37N 25 22E
El Ferrol del Caudillo Sp. 87 A5 43 29N 8 14W
El Firdân Egypt 109 S3 30 42N 32 20E
El Fuerte Mexico 74 C5 26 28N 108 35W
Elgin UK 86 D12 57 39N 3 20W
El Gîza Egypt 108 L13 30 01N 31 12E
El Golea Algeria 108 E14 30 35N 2 51E
Elgon, Mount Uganda/Kenya 108 L8 1 07N 34 35E
Elista Russia 94 G6 46 18N 44 14E
Elizabeth Aust. 110 F3 34 45S 138 39E
Elizabeth New Jersey USA 73 H1 40 39N 74 13W
Elizabeth City North Carolina USA 71 L4 36 18N 76 16W
El Jadida Morocco 108 C14 33 19N 8 35W
El Jafr Jordan 96 P10 30 16N 36 11E
Elk Poland 88 J10 53 51N 22 20E
Elk California USA 72 B4 39 08N 123 43W
Elk City Oklahoma USA 70 G4 34 25N 99 26W
Elk Creek *tn.* California USA 72 B4 39 36N 122 34W
Elk Grove California USA 72 C4 38 26N 121 26W
El Khârga Egypt 108 L13 25 27N 30 32E
Elkhart Indiana USA 71 J5 41 52N 85 56W
Elkhorn *r.* Nebraska USA 71 G5 42 00N 98 00W
Elkland Pennsylvania USA 53 J1 42 00N 77 20W
Elko Nevada USA 70 C5 40 50N 115 46W
Ellis Island New Jersey USA 73 H1 40 42N 74 02W
Ellsworth Maine USA 57 F1 44 34N 68 24W
Ellsworth Land *geog. reg.* Antarctica 117 75 00S 80 00W
El Mahalla El Kubra Egypt 108 L14 30 59N 31 10E
El Manzala Egypt 109 R4 31 09N 31 57E
El Matarîya Egypt 109 S4 31 10N 32 02E
El Médano Mexico 74 B4 24 35N 111 29W
Elmhurst Pennsylvania USA 73 C2 41 20N 75 32W
el Milk *r.* Sudan 108 K11 17 00N 29 00E
El Minya Egypt 108 L13 28 06N 30 45E
Elmira New York USA 71 L5 42 06N 76 50W
El Muglad Sudan 108 K10 11 01N 27 50E
El Obeid Sudan 108 L10 13 11N 30 10E
El Paso Texas USA 70 E3 31 45N 106 30W
El Porvenir Mexico 74 C6 31 15N 105 48W
El Progreso Honduras 74 G3 15 20N 87 50W
El Puerto de Santa Maria Sp. 87 B2 36 36N 6 14W
El Qantara Egypt 109 S3 30 53N 32 20E
El Reno Oklahoma USA 71 G4 35 32N 97 57W
El Sâlhîya Egypt 109 R3 30 47N 31 59E
El Salto Mexico 74 C4 23 47N 105 22W
EL SALVADOR 74 G2
El Shallûfa Egypt 109 T2 30 06N 32 33E
El Sueco Mexico 74 C5 29 54N 106 22W
Eltanin Fracture Zone Pacific Ocean 115 M3 52 00S 135 00W
El Tigre Venezuela 80 E15 8 44N 64 18W
El Tîna Egypt 109 S4 31 03N 32 19E
El Toro California USA 72 E1 33 36N 117 40W
Eluru India 98 E3 16 45N 81 10E
Elvas Port. 87 B3 38 53N 7 10W
Ely Nevada USA 70 D4 39 15N 114 53W
Elyria Ohio USA 71 K5 41 22N 82 06W
Emāmrūd Iran 97 F6 36 15N 54 59E
Emba Kazakhstan 94 H6 48 47N 58 05E
Emba *r.* Kazakhstan 94 H6 47 30N 56 00E
Embalse de Guri *l.* Venezuela 80 E15 7 30N 62 30W
Emden Germany 88 A10 53 23N 7 13E
Emerald Aust. 110 H5 23 30S 148 08E
Emi Koussi *mt.* Chad 108 H11 19 52N 18 31E
Empalme Mexico 74 B5 28 00N 110 49W
Emperor Seamounts Pacific Ocean 114 G12 42 00N 169 00E
Emporia Kansas USA 71 G4 38 24N 96 10W
Emporium Pennsylvania USA 52 H1 41 30N 78 14W
Ems *r.* Germany 88 A10 53 00N 7 00E
Encarnación Paraguay 80 F8 27 20S 55 50W
Encinitas California USA 72 E1 33 04N 117 17W
Endeh Indonesia 103 G2 8 51S 121 40E
Enderby Land *geog. reg.* Antarctica 117 65 00S 45 00E
Endicott New York USA 53 K2 42 06N 76 00W
Engel's Russia 94 G7 51 30N 46 07E
England *admin.* UK 86 D11 53 00N 2 00W
Enid Oklahoma USA 71 G4 36 24N 97 54W
Enna Italy 89 E2 37 34N 14 16E
En Nahud Sudan 108 K10 12 41N 28 28E
Enniskillen UK 86 B11 54 21N 7 38W
Enns *r.* Austria 88 E7 48 00N 14 40E
Enosburg Falls *tn.* Vermont USA 53 P4 44 55N 72 49W
Enschede Neths. 86 J10 52 13N 6 55E
Ensenada Mexico 74 A6 31 53N 116 38W
Entebbe Uganda 108 L8 0 04N 32 27E
Enugu Nigeria 108 F9 6 20N 7 29E
Épernay Fr. 86 G8 49 02N 3 58E
Épinal Fr. 86 J8 48 10N 6 28E
EQUATORIAL GUINEA 108 F8
Erechim Brazil 80 G8 27 35S 52 15W
Erenhot China 101 L7 43 50N 112 00E
Erfurt Germany 88 C9 50 58N 11 02E
Erg Chech *geog. reg.* Algeria 108 D12 24 30N 3 00W
Erg Iguidi *geog. reg.* Algeria 108 C13 26 00N 6 00W
Erie Pennsylvania USA 71 K5 42 07N 80 05W
Erimo-misaki *c.* Japan 102 D3 41 55N 143 13E
ERITREA 108 N10
Erode India 98 D2 11 21N 77 43E
Erris Head *c.* RoI 86 A11 54 20N 10 00W
Er Roseires Sudan 108 L10 11 52N 34 23E
Erzgebirge *mts.* Europe 88 D9 50 00N 13 00E
Erzincan Turkey 96 C6 39 44N 39 30E
Erzurum Turkey 96 D6 39 57N 41 17E
Esashi Japan 102 D3 41 54N 140 09E
Esbjerg Denmark 88 B11 55 20N 8 20E
Escanaba Michigan USA 71 J6 45 47N 87 04W
Escárcega Mexico 74 F3 18 39N 90 43W
Escobal Panama 75 Y2 9 11N 79 59W
Escondido California USA 70 C3 33 07N 117 05W
Eşfahān Iran 97 F5 32 41N 51 41E
Eskilstuna Sweden 88 F13 59 22N 16 31E
Eskişehir Turkey 96 B6 39 46N 30 30E
Esmeraldas Ecuador 80 B14 0 56N 79 40W
Esparto California USA 72 B4 38 42N 122 00W
Esperance Aust. 110 C3 33 49S 121 52E
Espírito Santo *admin.* Brazil 80 J10 18 40S 40 00W
Espoo Finland 88 K14 60 10N 24 40E
Esquel Argentina 81 C5 42 55S 71 20W
Es Semara Western Sahara 108 B13 26 25N 11 30W
Essen Germany 88 A9 51 27N 6 57E
Essequibo *r.* Guyana 80 F14 2 30N 58 00W
Essex California USA 72 F2 34 45N 115 15W
Estância Brazil 80 K11 11 15S 37 28W
ESTONIA 88 J13
Estrecho de Magallanes *sd.* Chile 81 C3 53 00S 71 00W
Etawah India 98 D5 26 46N 79 01E
ETHIOPIA 108 M9
Etna, Mount Italy 89 E2 37 45N 15 00E
Etolin Island Alaska USA 42 D5 56 10N 132 30W
Etosha Pan *salt l.* Namibia 109 H4 18 30S 16 30E
Eucla Aust. 110 D3 31 40S 128 51E
Euclid Ohio USA 51 L1 41 34N 81 32W
Eugene Oregon USA 70 B5 44 03N 123 04W
Euphrates *r.* Iraq/Syria/Turkey 96 D5 34 40N 42 00E
Eureka California USA 70 B5 40 49N 124 10W
Eureka Montana USA 43 N1 48 56N 115 05W
Eureka Nevada USA 72 F4 39 49N 115 58W
Evansville Indiana USA 71 J4 38 00N 87 33W
Eveleth Minnesota USA 51 E4 47 28N 92 32W
Everest, Mount China/Nepal 99 F5 27 59N 86 56E
Everett Washington USA 70 B6 47 59N 122 14W
Evora Port. 87 B3 38 46N 7 41W
Evreux Fr. 86 F8 49 03N 1 11E
Evvoia *i.* Greece 89 K3 38 00N 24 00E
Excelsior Mountains Nevada USA 72 D4 38 15N 118 30W
Exeter UK 86 D9 50 43N 3 31W
Exeter California USA 72 D3 36 18N 119 08W
Exmoor *hills* UK 86 D9 51 08N 3 40W
Exmouth Aust. 110 A5 21 54S 114 10E
Eyasi, Lake Tanzania 108 M7 4 00S 35 00E
Eyre Creek Aust. 110 F4 26 00S 138 00E
Eyre, Lake Aust. 110 F4 28 00S 136 00E
Eyre Peninsula Aust. 110 F3 34 00S 136 00E

F

Fada Chad 108 J11 17 14N 21 32E
Faeroes *i.* Atlantic Ocean 116 H13 62 00N 7 00W
Fafan *r.* Ethiopia 108 N9 7 30N 44 00E
Fagersta Sweden 88 E13 59 59N 15 49E
Fairbanks Alaska USA 64 A3 64 50N 147 50W
Fairfield California USA 72 B4 38 14N 122 03W
Fair Isle *i.* UK 86 E13 59 32N 1 38W
Fairmont West Virginia USA 71 K4 39 28N 80 08W
Fairview Park HK China 100 B2 22 29N 114 03E
Faisalabad Pakistan 98 C6 31 25N 73 09E
Faizabad India 98 E5 26 46N 82 08E
Fakfak Indonesia 103 J3 2 55S 132 17E
Falam Myanmar 100 G3 22 58N 93 45E
Falfurrias Texas USA 71 G2 27 17N 98 10W
Falkenburg Sweden 88 D12 56 55N 12 30E
Falkirk UK 86 D11 55 59N 3 48W
Falkland Islands South Atlantic Ocean 81 E3/F3 52 30S 60 00W
Falköping Sweden 88 D13 58 10N 13 32E
Fallon Nevada USA 72 D4 39 29N 118 46W
Fall River *tn.* Massachusetts USA 71 M5 41 41N 71 08W
Falmouth Antigua and Barbuda 74 Q9 17 01N 61 46W
Falmouth Jamaica 75 U14 18 29N 77 39W
Falmouth Massachusetts USA 73 E2 41 34N 70 37W
Famagusta Cyprus 96 B6 35 07N 33 57E
Fan Lau HK China 100 A1 22 12N 113 51E
Fanling HK China 100 B2 22 29N 114 07E
Fâqûs Egypt 109 R3 30 44N 31 48E
Farafangana Madagascar 109 P3 22 50S 47 50E
Farāh Afghanistan 97 H5 32 22N 62 07E
Farah Rud *r.* Afghanistan 97 H5 32 00N 62 00E
Fargo North Dakota USA 71 G6 46 52N 96 49W
Faridabad India 98 D5 28 24N 77 18E
Faridpur Bangladesh 99 K9 23 29N 89 31E
Farmington Maine USA 53 R4 44 41N 70 11W
Farmington New Mexico USA 70 E4 36 43N 108 12W
Farnham New York USA 54 C1 42 36N 79 05W
Faro Port. 87 B2 37 01N 7 56W
Farquhar Islands Seychelles 109 Q6 9 00N 50 00E
Fastov Ukraine 88 M9 50 08N 29 59E
Fatehgarh India 98 D5 27 22N 79 38E
Faya-Largeau Chad 108 H11 17 58N 19 06E
Fayetteville Arkansas USA 71 H4 36 03N 94 10W
Fayetteville North Carolina USA 71 L4 35 03N 78 53W
Fâyid Egypt 109 S2 30 18N 31 19E
Fderik Mauritania 108 B12 22 30N 12 30W
Fécamp Fr. 86 F8 49 45N 0 23E
FEDERATED STATES OF MICRONESIA 114 E8/F8
Feilding NZ 111 E4 40 14S 175 34E
Feira de Santana Brazil 80 K11 12 17S 38 53W
Felipe Carrillo Puerto Mexico 74 G3 19 51N 88 02W
Feni Bangladesh 99 L9 23 00N 91 24E
Fenton Michigan USA 52 C2 42 48N 83 42W
Fergana Uzbekistan 94 K5 40 23N 71 19E
Fergus Falls *tn.* Minnesota USA 71 G6 46 18N 96 07W
Ferndale Washington USA 42 H4 48 50N 122 35W
Fernley Nevada USA 72 D4 39 36N 119 17W
Ferrara Italy 89 C6 44 50N 11 38E
Ferreñafe Peru 80 B12 6 42S 79 45W
Fès Morocco 108 C14 34 05N 5 00W
Fethiye Turkey 96 A6 36 37N 29 06E
Feyzābād Afghanistan 97 K6 37 06N 70 34E
Fianarantsoa Madagascar 109 P3 21 27S 47 05E
Fier Albania 89 G4 40 44N 19 33E
Figeac Fr. 87 G6 44 32N 2 01E
Figueira da Foz Port. 87 A4 40 09N 8 51W
Figueres Sp. 87 G5 42 16N 2 57E
FIJI 114
Filchner Ice Shelf Antarctica 117 80 00S 37 00W
Findlay Ohio USA 51 K1 41 01N 83 39W
FINLAND 94 E9
Finland, Gulf of Finland/Russia 88 J13 59 40N 23 30E
Fiordland NZ 111 A2 45 09S 167 18E
Firat *r.* Turkey/Syria/Iraq 96 C6 37 30N 38 00E
Firozabad India 98 D5 27 09N 78 24E
Firth of Clyde *est.* UK 86 C11 55 30N 5 00W
Firth of Forth *est.* UK 86 D12 56 05N 3 00W
Firth of Lorn *est.* UK 86 B12 56 15N 6 00W
Fish *r.* Namibia 109 H2 26 30S 17 30E
Fishguard UK 86 C9 51 59N 4 59W
Fitchburg Massachusetts USA 73 E3 42 35N 71 48W
Fitzroy *r.* Aust. 110 C6 18 00S 124 00E
Flagstaff Arizona USA 70 D4 35 12N 111 38W
Flagstaff Lake Maine USA 53 R5 45 14N 70 20W
Flambeau River Wisconsin USA 51 F3 45 59N 90 30W
Flamborough Head *c.* UK 86 E11 54 06N 0 04W

Place	Page	Grid	Lat	Long
Flatbush New York USA	73	J1	40 38N	73 56W
Flathead Lake Montana USA	70	D6	47 55N	114 05W
Flathead River Montana USA	46	E1	48 55N	114 30W
Flatlands New York USA	73	J1	40 37N	73 54W
Flattery, Cape Washington USA	70	B6	48 24N	124 43W
Flekkefjord Norway	86	J13	58 17N	6 40E
Flensburg Germany	88	B11	54 47N	9 27E
Flers Fr.	86	E8	48 45N	0 34W
Fletcher Pond *l.* Michigan USA	52	C4	44 59N	83 53W
Flinders *r.* Aust.	110	G6	19 00S	141 30E
Flinders Range *mts.* Aust.	110	F3	32 00S	138 00E
Flint Michigan USA	71	K5	43 03N	83 40W
Flint *r.* Georgia USA	71	K3	31 00N	84 00W
Flint River Michigan USA	52	C3	43 12N	83 50W
Florence Italy	89	C5	43 47N	11 15E
Florence Alabama USA	71	J3	34 48N	87 40W
Florence South Carolina USA	71	L3	34 12N	79 44W
Florence Wisconsin USA	51	G3	45 55N	88 15W
Florencia Col.	80	B14	1 37N	75 37W
Flores Guatemala	74	G3	16 58N	89 50W
Flores *i.* Indonesia	103	G2	8 30S	121 00E
Flores Sea Indonesia	103	F2/G2	7 00S	119 00E
Floresti Moldova	88	M7	47 52N	28 12E
Floriano Brazil	80	J12	6 45S	43 00W
Florianópolis Brazil	81	H8	27 35S	48 31W
Florida Uruguay	81	F7	34 04S	56 14W
Florida *state* USA	71	K2	28 00N	82 00W
Florida Bay Florida USA	71	K2	25 00N	81 00W
Florida Keys *is.* Florida USA	71	K1	25 00N	80 00W
Flórina Greece	89	H4	40 48N	21 26E
Florissant Missouri USA	71	H4	38 49N	90 24W
Flushing New York USA	73	J2	40 45N	73 49W
Focşani Romania	89	L6	45 41N	27 12E
Fóggia Italy	89	H4	41 28N	15 33E
Fohnsdorf Austria	89	E7	47 13N	14 40E
Foix Fr.	87	F5	42 57N	1 35E
Folkestone UK	86	F9	51 05N	1 11E
Fond du Lac Wisconsin USA	71	J5	43 48N	88 27W
Fontainebleau Fr.	86	G8	48 24N	2 42E
Fonte Boa Brazil	80	D13	2 33S	65 59W
Foresthill *tn.* California USA	72	C4	39 02N	120 49W
Forest Hills *tn.* New York USA	73	J1	40 43N	73 51W
Forlì Italy	89	D6	44 13N	12 02E
Formentera *i.* Sp.	87	F3	38 41N	1 30E
FORMER YUGOSLAV REPUBLIC OF MACEDONIA (FYROM)	89	H4/J4		
Formosa Argentina	80	F8	26 07S	58 14W
Formosa Brazil	80	H10	15 30S	47 22W
Forrest Aust.	110	D3	30 49S	128 03E
Fortaleza Brazil	80	K13	3 45S	38 35W
Fort Bragg California USA	70	B4	39 29N	123 46W
Fort Collins Colorado USA	70	E5	40 35N	105 05W
Fort-de-Fr. Lesser Antilles	74	R12	14 36N	61 05W
Fort Dodge Iowa USA	71	H5	42 31N	94 10W
Fortescue *r.* Aust.	110	B5	21 30S	117 30E
Fort Kent Maine USA	57	F2	47 15N	68 35W
Fort Lauderdale Florida USA	71	K2	26 08N	80 08W
Fort Myers Florida USA	71	K2	26 39N	81 51W
Fort Peck Lake Montana USA	70	E6	48 01N	106 28W
Fort Pierce Florida USA	71	K2	27 28N	80 20W
Fort Portal Uganda	108	L8	0 40N	30 17E
Fort Scott Kansas USA	71	H4	37 52N	94 43W
Fort Smith Arkansas USA	71	H4	35 22N	94 27W
Fort Stockton Texas USA	70	F3	30 54N	102 54W
Fort Sumner New Mexico USA	70	F3	34 27N	104 16W
Fortuna North Dakota USA	47	F1	48 58N	103 49W
Fort Walton Beach *tn.* Florida USA	71	J3	30 25N	86 38W
Fort Wayne Indiana USA	71	J5	41 05N	85 08W
Fort Worth Texas USA	71	G3	32 45N	97 20W
Fort Yukon Alaska USA	64	A4	66 35N	145 20W
Foshan China	101	L3	23 03N	113 08E
Fostoria Ohio USA	51	K1	41 09N	83 24W
Fougères Fr.	86	E8	48 21N	1 12W
Foula *i.* UK	86	D14	60 08N	2 05W
Foumban Cameroon	108	G9	5 43N	10 50E
Fouta Djallon *geog. reg.* Guinea	108	B10	12 00N	13 10W
Foz do Iguaçú Argentina	80	G8	25 33S	54 31W
Framingham Massachusetts USA	73	E3	42 17N	71 25W
Franca Brazil	80	H9	20 33S	47 27W
FRANCE	86/87			
Francis Case, Lake South Dakota USA	70	G5	43 00N	99 00W
Francistown Botswana	109	K3	21 11S	27 32E
Frankenmuth Michigan USA	52	C3	43 19N	83 44W
Frankfort Kentucky USA	71	K4	38 11N	84 53W
Frankfurt am Main Germany	88	B9	50 06N	8 41E
Frankfurt an der Oder Germany	88	E10	52 20N	14 32E
Fränkische Alb *mts.* Germany	88	C8	49 00N	11 00E
Franklin D. Roosevelt Lake Washington USA	70	C6	48 05N	118 15W
Franklinville New York USA	52	H2	42 20N	78 27W
Franz Josef Land *is.* Russia	94	G13	80 00N	50 00E
Fraserburgh UK	86	E12	57 42N	2 00W
Frederick Maryland USA	73	B1	39 25N	77 25W
Fredericksburg Virginia USA	71	L4	38 18N	77 30W
Frederick Sound Alaska USA	42	C5/D5	57 00N	134 00W
Frederikshavn Denmark	88	C12	57 28N	10 33E
Fredonia New York USA	52	G2	42 27N	79 22W
Fredrikstad Norway	86	L13	59 20N	10 50E
Freeport Texas USA	71	G2	28 56N	95 20W
Freetown Sierra Leone	108	B9	8 30N	13 17W
Freewood Acres New Jersey USA	73	C2	40 10N	74 14W
Freiburg im Breisgau Germany	88	A7	48 00N	7 52E
Fréjus Fr.	87	J5	43 26N	6 44E
Fremantle Aust.	110	B3	32 07S	115 44E
Fremont California USA	72	C3	37 32N	121 59W
Fremont Ohio USA	51	K1	41 21N	83 07W
French Creek *r.* Pennsylvania USA	52	F1	41 40N	80 10W
French Guiana *territory* Fr.	80	G14	5 00N	53 00W
Frenchman Fork *r.* USA	70	F5	40 00N	103 00W
Frenchman Lake Nevada USA	72	F3	36 50N	115 58W
French Polynesia Pacific Ocean	115	M6	21 00S	150 00W
Fresnillo Mexico	74	D4	23 10N	102 54W
Fresno California USA	70	C4	36 41N	119 47W
Fresno Reservoir Montana USA	47	B1/C1	48 42N	110 00W
Friday Harbor *tn.* Washington USA	42	H4	48 36N	123 05W
Frontera Mexico	74	F3	18 32N	92 39W
Frosinone Italy	89	D4	41 38N	13 22E
Frýdek-Místek Czech Rep.	88	G8	49 42N	18 20E
Fuerteventura *i.* Canary Islands	108	B13	28 25N	14 00W
Fuji Japan	102	C2	35 10N	138 37E
Fujinomiya Japan	102	C2	35 16N	138 33E
Fuji-san *mt.* Japan	102	C2	35 23N	138 42E
Fujisawa Japan	102	C2	35 20N	139 29E
Fukui Japan	102	C2	36 04N	136 12E
Fukuoka Japan	102	B1	33 39N	130 21E
Fukushima Japan	102	D2	37 44N	140 28E
Fukuyama Japan	102	B1	34 29N	133 21E
Fulda Germany	88	B9	50 33N	9 41E
Fulton New York USA	73	B3	43 19N	76 25W
Funabashi Japan	102	C2	35 42N	139 59E
Funchal Madeira	108	A14	32 40N	16 55W
Furneaux Group *is.* Aust.	110	H1	45 00S	148 00E
Furukawa Japan	102	D2	38 34N	140 56E
Fushun China	101	N7	41 50N	123 54E
Fu Tau Fan Chau *i.* HK China	100	D2	22 20N	114 22E
Fuxin China	101	N7	42 04N	121 39E
Fuzhou China	101	M4	26 09N	119 17E
Fyn *i.* Denmark	88	C11	55 30N	10 00E

G

Place	Page	Grid	Lat	Long
Gaalkacyo Somalia	108	P9	6 47N	47 12E
Gabbs Nevada USA	72	E4	38 53N	117 57W
Gabès Tunisia	108	G14	33 52N	10 06E
GABON	108	G7		
Gaborone Botswana	109	K3	24 45S	25 55E
Gabrovo Bulgaria	89	K5	42 52N	25 19E
Gadsden Alabama USA	71	J3	34 00N	86 00W
Gaeta Italy	89	D4	41 13N	13 36E
Gafsa Tunisia	108	F14	34 28N	8 43E
Gagnoa Côte d'Ivoire	108	C9	6 04N	5 55W
Gaillard Cut Panama	75	Y2	9 05N	79 40W
Gainesville Florida USA	71	K2	29 37N	82 21W
Gainesville Texas USA	71	G3	33 09N	97 38W
Gairdner, Lake Aust.	110	F3	32 50S	136 00E
Gajol India	99	K10	25 10N	88 14E
Galápagos Rise Pacific Ocean	115	T6	12 00S	87 00W
Galashiels UK	86	D11	55 37N	2 49W
Galata Montana USA	46	G1	48 27N	111 20W
Galaţi Romania	89	M6	45 27N	28 02E
Galeota Point Trinidad and Tobago	75	V15	10 09N	60 00W
Galera Point Trinidad and Tobago	75	V15	10 49N	60 54W
Galesburg Illinois USA	71	H5	40 58N	90 22W
Galeton Pennsylvania USA	52	J1	41 44N	77 40W
Galle Sri Lanka	98	E1	6 01N	80 13E
Gallego *r.* Sp.	87	E4/E5	41 55N	0 56W
Gallipoli Italy	89	G4	40 03N	17 59E
Gallup New Mexico USA	70	E4	32 32N	108 46W
Galveston Texas USA	71	H2	29 17N	94 48W
Galway RoI	86	A10	53 16N	9 03W
Galway Bay RoI	86	A10	53 15N	9 15W
Gambia *r.* Senegal/The Gambia	108	B10	13 45N	13 15W
GAMBIA, THE	108	A10		
Gambier Islands Pacific Ocean	115	N5	23 10S	135 00W
Gamboa Panama	75	Y2	9 08N	79 42W
Gandak *r.* India	99	E5	26 30N	85 00E
Gandhi Sagar *l.* India	98	D4	24 30N	75 30E
Ganga *r.* India	98	E5	25 00N	83 30E
Ganga, Mouths of the *est.* Bangladesh/India	99	F4	21 30N	89 00E
Ganganagar India	98	C5	29 54N	73 56E
Gangdisê Shan *mts.* China	100	E5	31 00N	82 30E
Gangtok India	99	F5	27 20N	88 39E
Ganzhou China	101	L4	25 45N	114 51E
Gao Mali	108	D11	16 19N	0 09W
Gap Fr.	87	J6	44 33N	6 05E
Garanhuns Brazil	80	K12	8 53S	36 28W
Gard *r.* Fr.	87	H5	44 05N	4 20E
Garden City Kansas USA	70	F4	37 57N	100 54W
Gardēz Afghanistan	97	J5	33 37N	69 07E
Gardner Island Kiribati	114	J7	4 40S	174 32W
Garissa Kenya	108	M7	0 27S	39 39E
Garland Texas USA	71	G3	32 55N	96 37W
Garonne *r.* Fr.	87	E6	44 45N	0 15E
Garoua Cameroon	108	G9	9 17N	13 22E
Gary Indiana USA	71	J5	41 34N	87 20W
Garzón Col.	80	B14	2 14N	75 37W
Gascoyne *r.* Aust.	110	A5	25 00S	114 00E
Gastonia North Carolina USA	71	K4	35 14N	81 12W
Gateshead UK	86	E11	54 58N	1 35W
Gates of the Arctic National Park Alaska USA	40	E7	67 30N	155 00W
Gatún Panama	75	Y2	9 16N	79 55W
Gatún Lake Panama	75	Y2	9 15N	79 50W
Gávdos *i.* Greece	89	K1	34 00N	24 00E
Gaya India	99	F4	24 48N	85 00E
Gaylord Michigan USA	51	J3	45 01N	84 41W
Gaza Middle East	96	N10	31 30N	34 28E
Gaza *territory* Middle East	96	N10	31 28N	34 05E
Gaziantep Turkey	96	C6	37 04N	37 21E
Gbarnga Liberia	108	C9	7 02N	9 26W
Gdańsk Poland	88	G11	54 22N	18 41E
Gdańsk, Gulf of Baltic Sea	88	G11	54 00N	19 00E
Gdynia Poland	88	G11	54 31N	18 30E
Gedaref Sudan	108	M10	14 01N	35 24E
Gediz *r.* Turkey	96	A6	38 40N	27 30E
Geelong Aust.	110	G2	38 10S	144 26E
Gejiu China	101	J3	23 25N	103 05E
Gela Italy	89	E2	37 04N	14 15E
Genale *r.* Ethiopia	108	N9	6 00N	40 00E
Geneina Sudan	108	J10	13 27N	22 30E
Geneseo New York USA	52	J2	42 48N	77 49W
Geneseo River New York USA	51	M2	42 40N	78 00W
Geneva Switz.	87	J7	46 13N	6 09E
Geneva New York USA	51	N2	42 51N	77 01W
Geneva Ohio USA	52	F1	41 48N	80 57W
Genil *r.* Sp.	87	C2	37 20N	4 45W
Genk Belgium	86	H9	50 58N	5 30E
Genoa Italy	89	B6	44 24N	8 56E
Gent Belgium	86	G9	51 02N	3 42E
Georgetown Guyana	80	F15	6 46N	58 10W
George Town Malaysia	103	C5	5 25N	100 20E
Georgetown South Carolina USA	71	L3	33 23N	79 18W
George V Land *geog. reg.* Antarctica	117		70 00S	150 00E
GEORGIA	94	G5		
Georgia *state* USA	71	K3	33 00N	83 00W
Gera Germany	88	D9	50 51N	12 11E
Geraldton Aust.	110	A4	28 49S	144 36E
GERMANY	88	A9		
Gerona Sp.	87	G4	41 59N	2 49E
Getafe Sp.	87	D4	40 18N	3 44W
Gettysburg Pennsylvania USA	73	B1	39 49N	77 14W
Gettysburg National Military Park Pennsylvania USA	73	B1	39 57N	77 15W
Ghadamis Libya	108	F14	30 08N	9 30E
Ghaghara *r.* India/Nepal	98	E5	27 20N	81 30E
GHANA	108	D9		
Ghanzi Botswana	109	J3	21 42S	21 39E
Ghardaïa Algeria	108	E14	32 20N	3 40E
Gharyan Libya	108	G14	32 10N	13 01E
Ghat Libya	108	G12	24 58N	10 11E
Ghaziabad India	98	D5	28 39N	77 26E
Ghazni Afghanistan	97	J5	33 33N	68 26E
Ghisonaccia Fr.	87	K5	42 01N	9 24E
Gibraltar *territory* U.K.	87	C2	36 09N	5 21W
Gibraltar, Strait of Sp./Morocco	87	C1	35 58N	5 30W
Gibson Desert Aust.	110	C5	25 00S	123 00E
Gidole Ethiopia	108	M9	5 38N	37 28E
Gifu Japan	102	C2	35 27N	136 46E
Gigüela *r.* Sp.	87	D3	39 40N	3 15W
Gijón Sp.	87	C5	43 32N	5 40W
Gila *r.* USA	70	D3	33 00N	114 00W
Gila Bend Arizona USA	70	D3	32 56N	112 42W
Gilbert *r.* Aust.	110	G6	17 00S	142 30E
Gilbert Islands Pacific Ocean	114	H7/H8	0 00	173 00E
Gildford Montana USA	46	G1	48 39N	110 35W
Gilgit Kashmir	98	C7	35 54N	74 20E
Gillette Wyoming USA	70	E5	44 18N	105 30W
Gilroy California USA	72	C3	37 01N	121 38W
Gineifa Egypt	109	S2	30 12N	32 26E
Ginir Ethiopia	108	N9	7 06N	40 40E
Gippsland *geog. reg.* Aust.	110	H2	37 30S	147 00E
Girard Pennsylvania USA	52	F2	42 01N	80 20W
Girardot Col.	80	C14	4 19N	74 47W
Girga Egypt	108	L13	26 17N	31 58E
Gironde *r.* Fr.	87	E6	45 30N	0 45W
Girvan UK	86	C11	55 15N	4 51W
Gisborne NZ	111	G5	38 40S	178 01E
Giurgiu Romania	89	K5	43 53N	25 58E
Gizhiga Russia	95	U9	62 00N	160 34E
Gjirokastër Albania	89	H4	40 05N	20 10E
Glacier Washington USA	42	H4	48 53N	121 57W
Glacier Bay *r.* Alaska USA	42	B6	58 45N	136 15W
Glacier Bay National Park Alaska USA	42	B6	58 45N	136 30W
Glacier National Park Montana USA	46	E1/F1	48 50N	114 00W
Gladstone Aust.	110	J5	23 52S	151 16E
Gladwin Michigan USA	51	J2	43 59N	84 30W
Glasgow UK	86	C11	55 53N	4 15W
Glendale California USA	72	D2	34 09N	118 16W
Glen Ridge New Jersey USA	73	H2	40 47N	74 13W
Glens Falls *tn.* New York USA	71	M5	43 17N	73 41W
Gliwice Poland	88	G9	50 20N	18 40E
Globe Arizona USA	70	D3	33 23N	110 48W
Głogów Poland	88	F9	51 40N	16 06E
Gloucester UK	86	D9	51 53N	2 14W
Gloucester Massachusetts USA	73	E3	42 37N	70 40W
Gloversville New York USA	73	C3	43 03N	74 20W
Gniezno Poland	88	F10	52 32N	17 32E
Goa *admin.* India	98	C3	15 00N	74 00E
Goalpara India	99	L11	26 08N	90 36E
Gobabis Namibia	109	H3	22 30S	18 58E
Gobi Desert Mongolia	101	H7	48 30N	100 00E
Godavari *r.* India	98	C3	20 00N	75 00E
Godhra India	98	C4	22 49N	73 40E
Goiânia Brazil	80	H10	16 43S	49 18W
Goiás Brazil	80	G10	15 57S	50 07W
Goiás *admin.* Brazil	80	H11	14 00S	48 00W
Golan Heights *territory* Middle East	96	N11	33 00N	35 55E
Gold Coast *tn.* Aust.	110	J4	27 59S	153 22E
Goldfield *tn.* Nevada USA	72	E3	37 42N	117 15W
Goldsboro North Carolina USA	71	L4	35 23N	78 00W
Goldsworthy Aust.	110	B5	20 20S	119 31E
Goleta California USA	72	D2	34 26N	119 50W
Golfe de Gabès *g.* Tunisia	108	G14	34 20N	10 30E
Golfe de St-Malo *g.* Fr.	86	D8	48 55N	2 30W
Golfe du Lion *g.* Fr.	87	G5/H5	43 10N	4 00E
Golfo de California *g.* Mexico	74	B5/C4	27 00N	111 00W
Golfo de Guayaquil *g.* Ecuador	80	A13	3 00S	81 30W
Golfo de Honduras *g.* Caribbean Sea	74	G3	17 00N	87 30W
Golfo del Darién *g.* Col./Panama	75	J1	9 00N	77 00W
Golfo de San Jorge *g.* Argentina	81	D4	47 00S	66 00W
Golfo de Tehuantepec *g.* Mexico	74	E3/F3	15 30N	95 00W
Golfo de Venezuela *g.* Venezuela	80	C16	12 00N	71 30W
Golfo di Cágliari *g.* Italy	89	B3	39 00N	9 00E
Golfo di Catania *g.* Italy	89	E2	37 30N	15 20E
Golfo di Gaeta *g.* Italy	89	D4	41 00N	13 00E
Golfo di Genova *g.* Italy	89	B6	44 00N	9 00E
Golfo di Squillace *g.* Italy	89	F3	38 30N	17 00E
Golfo di Táranto *g.* Italy	89	F4	40 00N	17 00E
Golfo di Venézia *g.* Adriatic Sea	89	D6	45 00N	13 00E
Golfo San Matías *g.* Argentina	81	E5	42 00S	64 00W
Golmud China	100	G6	36 22N	94 55E
Gomati *r.* India	98	E5	26 50N	81 00E
Gomera *i.* Canary Islands	108	A13	28 08N	17 14W
Gómez Palacio Mexico	74	D5	25 39N	103 30W
Gonder Ethiopia	108	M10	12 39N	37 29E
Gondia India	98	E4	21 23N	80 14E
Good Hope, Cape of RSA	109	H1	34 30S	19 00E
Goodland Kansas USA	70	F4	39 20N	101 43W
Goondiwindi Aust.	110	J4	28 30S	150 17E
Gorakhpur India	98	E5	26 45N	83 23E
Gora Narodnaya *mt.* Russia	94	J10	65 02N	60 01E
Gora Pobeda *mt.* Russia	95	S10	65 10N	146 00E
Gorda Rise Pacific Ocean	115	N12	43 00N	130 00W
Gore Ethiopia	108	M9	8 10N	35 29E
Gore NZ	111	B1	46 06S	168 56E
Gorgān Iran	97	F6	36 50N	54 29E
Gorizia Italy	89	D6	45 57N	13 37E
Görlitz Germany	88	E9	51 09N	15 00E
Goroka PNG	110	H8	6 02S	145 22E
Gorontalo Indonesia	103	G4	0 33N	123 05E
Gory Kamen' *mt.* Russia	95	M10	69 06N	94 59E
Goryn' *r.* Ukraine	88	L9	51 00N	26 00E
Gorzów Wielkopolski Poland	88	E10	52 42N	15 12E
Gostivar FYROM	89	H4	41 47N	20 55E
Göta älv *r.* Sweden	88	C12	58 00N	12 00E
Göteborg Sweden	86	C12	57 45N	12 00E
Gotha Germany	88	C9	50 57N	10 43E
Gotland *i.* Sweden	88	G12	57 30N	18 40E
Göttingen Germany	88	B9	51 32N	9 57E
Gough Island Atlantic Ocean	116	H2	40 20S	10 00W
Goulburn Aust.	110	H3	34 47S	149 43E
Gouré Niger	108	G10	13 59N	10 15E
Governador Valadares Brazil	80	J10	18 51S	41 57W
Govind Ballash Pant Sagar *l.* India	98	E4	24 30N	82 30E
Gowanda New York USA	52	H2	42 27N	78 56W
Grafton Aust.	110	J4	29 40S	152 56E
Graham Texas USA	71	G3	33 07N	98 36W
Graham Land *geog. reg.* Antarctica	117		67 00S	64 00W
Grahamstown RSA	109	K1	33 18S	26 32E
Grampian Pennsylvania USA	73	A2	40 58N	78 37W
Grampian Mountains UK	86	C12	56 45N	4 00W
Granada Nicaragua	74	G2	11 58N	85 59W
Granada Sp.	87	D2	37 10N	3 35W
Gran Canaria *i.* Canary Islands	108	A13	28 00N	15 35W
Gran Chaco *geog. reg.* Argentina	80	E8/E9	25 00S	62 30W
Grand *r.* South Dakota USA	70	F6	46 00N	102 00W
Grand Bahama *i.* Bahamas	75	J5	27 00N	78 00W
Grand Canyon USA	70	D4	36 04N	112 07W
Grand Canyon Village Arizona USA	70	D4	36 02N	112 09W
Grand Cayman *i.* Caribbean Sea	75	H3	19 20N	81 15W
Grand Coulee Dam Washington USA	70	C6	47 59N	118 58W
Grande *r.* Bolivia	80	E10	18 00S	65 00W
Grande *r.* Brazil	80	G10	20 00S	50 00W

Grand Erg Occidental *geog. reg.* Algeria 108 E14 30 35N 0 30E
Grand Erg Oriental *geog. reg.* Algeria 108 F14 30 15N 6 45E
Grande Terre *i.* Lesser Antilles 74 Q9 17 00N 61 40W
Grand Forks North Dakota USA 71 G6 47 57N 97 05W
Grand Island *tn.* Nebraska USA 71 G5 40 56N 98 21W
Grand Junction *tn.* Colorado USA 70 E4 39 04N 108 33W
Grand Ledge Michigan USA 52 B2 42 45N 84 44W
Grand Marais Minnesota USA 51 F4 47 45N 90 20W
Grand Rapids *tn.* Michigan USA 71 J5 42 57N 86 40W
Grand Rapids *tn.* Minnesota USA 71 H6 47 13N 93 31W
Grand Rapids *tn.* Ohio USA 52 C1 41 23N 83 52W
Grand River Michigan USA 52 A2 42 55N 85 15W
Grand River Ohio USA 52 F1 41 25N 80 57W
Grand Traverse Bay Michigan USA 51 J3 45 00N 85 30W
Grandyle New York USA 54 D2 43 01N 78 57W
Granite Peak Montana USA 70 E6 45 10N 109 50W
Grant, Mount Nevada USA 72 D4 38 34N 118 48W
Grant Range *mts.* Nevada USA 72 F4 38 24N 115 27W
Grants Pass *tn.* Oregon USA 70 B5 42 26N 123 20W
Grasse Fr. 87 J5 43 40N 5 56E
Grass Island HK China 100 D2 22 29N 114 22E
Grass Valley *tn.* California USA 72 C4 39 13N 121 04W
Grassy Hill *mt.* HK China 100 B2 22 25N 114 10E
Gravesend New York USA 73 J1 40 36N 73 58W
Gravina Island Alaska USA 42 E4 55 25N 131 45W
Grayling Michigan USA 51 J3 44 39N 84 43W
Graz Austria 89 E7 47 05N 15 22E
Great Abaco *i.* Bahamas 75 J5 26 40N 77 00W
Great Astrolabe Reef Fiji 114 U15 18 45S 178 50E
Great Australian Bight *b.* Aust. 110 D3/E3 33 00S 130 00E
Great Barrier Island NZ 111 E6 36 13S 175 24E
Great Barrier Reef Aust. 110 G7/H6 15 00S 146 00E
Great Basin *dep.* Nevada USA 70 C4 40 00N 117 00W
Great Bend Kansas USA 71 G4 38 22N 98 47W
Great Bitter Lake Egypt 109 S2 30 22N 32 22E
Great Dividing Range *mts.* Aust. 110 G7/H2 35 00S 148 00E
Greater Antilles *is.* W. Indies 75 H4/L3 19 00N 78 00W
Great Exuma *i.* Bahamas 75 J4 23 30N 76 00W
Great Falls *tn.* Montana USA 70 D6 47 30N 111 16W
Great Inagua *i.* Bahamas 75 K4 21 40N 73 00W
Great Karoo *mts.* RSA 109 J1 32 30S 22 30E
Great Neck New York USA 73 K2 40 48N 72 44W
Great Nicobar *i.* Nicobar Islands 99 G1 6 30N 94 00E
Great Salt Lake Utah USA 70 D5 41 10N 112 40W
Great Sand Sea *d.* Sahara Desert 108 J13 27 00N 25 00E
Great Sandy Desert Aust. 110 C5/D5 21 00S 124 00E
Great Sea Reef Fiji 114 T16 16 30S 178 00E
Great Victoria Desert Aust. 110 D4/E4 28 00S 130 00E
Great Wall China 101 L6 40 00N 111 00E
Great Yarmouth UK 86 F10 52 37N 1 44E
Great Zab *r.* Iraq 96 D6 36 00N 44 00E
GREECE 89 H3/K3
Greeley Colorado USA 70 F5 40 26N 104 43W
Green *r.* USA 70 D5 42 00N 110 00W
Green *r.* USA 70 E4 39 00N 110 00W
Green Bay Wisconsin USA 71 J6 45 00N 87 00W
Green Bay *tn.* Wisconsin USA 71 J5 44 32N 88 00W
Greenbush Minnesota USA 49 D1 48 42N 96 11W
Greenfield Massachusetts USA 73 D3 42 36N 72 36W
GREENLAND 65 U6
Greenland Basin Atlantic Ocean 116 H14 72 00N 0 00
Greenland Sea Arctic Ocean 117 76 00N 5 00W
Green Mountains Vermont USA 71 M5 43 00N 73 00W
Greenock UK 86 C11 55 57N 4 45W
Greensboro North Carolina USA 71 L4 36 03N 79 50W
Greenville Liberia 108 C9 5 01N 9 03W
Greenville Maine USA 53 S5 45 28N 69 36W
Greenville Mississippi USA 71 H3 33 23N 91 03W
Greenville South Carolina USA 71 K3 34 52N 82 25W
Greenville Texas USA 71 G3 33 09N 97 06W
Greenwood Mississippi USA 71 H3 33 31N 90 10W
Grenå Denmark 88 C12 56 25N 10 53E
GRENADA 74 R11
Grenoble Fr. 87 H6 45 11N 5 43E
Greymouth NZ 111 C3 42 27S 171 12E
Grey Range *mts.* Aust. 110 G4 27 00S 144 00E
Gridley California USA 72 C4 39 24N 121 42W
Griffin Georgia USA 71 K3 33 15N 84 17W
Grimsby UK 86 E10 53 35N 0 05W
Grindstone Lake Wisconsin USA 51 F3 45 59N 91 20W
Groningen Neths. 86 J10 53 13N 6 35E
Groom Lake Nevada USA 72 F3 37 18N 115 49W
Groote Eylandt *i.* Aust. 110 F7 14 00S 137 00E
Grootfontein Namibia 109 H4 19 32S 18 05E
Grosseto Italy 89 C5 42 46N 11 07E
Gross Glockner *mt.* Austria 89 D7 47 05N 12 44E
Groveland California USA 72 C3 37 43N 120 56W
Grover City California USA 72 C2 35 08N 120 35W
Groznyy Russia 94 G5 43 21N 45 42E
Grudziądz Poland 88 G10 53 29N 18 45E
Guadalajara Mexico 74 D4 20 40N 103 20W
Guadalajara Sp. 87 D4 40 37N 3 10W
Guadalcanal *i.* Solomon Islands 114 G7 9 30S 160 00E
Guadalope *r.* Sp. 87 E4 40 50N 0 30W
Guadalquivir *r.* Sp. 87 C2 37 45N 5 30W
Guadalupe *i.* Mexico 74 A5 29 00N 118 24W
Guadeloupe *i.* Lesser Antilles 74 Q9 16 30N 61 30W
Guadeloupe Passage *sd.* Caribbean Sea 74 Q9 16 40N 61 50W
Guadiana *r.* Sp./Port. 87 B3 38 30N 7 30W
Guadix Sp. 87 D2 37 19N 3 08W
Guainía *r.* Col./Venezuela 80 D14 2 30N 67 30W
Guajará Mirim Brazil 80 D11 10 50S 65 21W
Gualala California USA 72 B4 38 45N 123 31W
GUAM 114 E9
Guamúchil Mexico 74 C5 25 28N 108 10W
Guangzhou China 101 L3 23 08N 113 20E
Guantánamo Cuba 75 J4 20 09N 75 14W
Guaporé *r.* Brazil/Bolivia 80 E11 13 00S 62 00W
Guaqui Bolivia 80 D10 16 38S 68 50W
Guarapuava Brazil 80 G8 25 22S 51 28W
Guarda Port. 87 B4 40 32N 7 17W
Guardiana *r.* Sp. 87 C3 39 00N 4 00W
Guasdualito Venezuela 80 C15 7 15N 70 40W
GUATEMALA 74 F3
Guatemala Basin Pacific Ocean 115 S9 12 00N 95 00W
Guatemala City Guatemala 74 F2 14 38N 90 22W
Guaviare *r.* Col. 80 C14 3 00N 70 00W
Guayaquil Ecuador 80 A13 2 13S 79 54W
Guaymas Mexico 74 B5 27 59W 110 54W
Guéret Fr. 87 F7 46 10N 1 52E
Guernsey *i.* British Isles 86 D8 46 27N 2 35W
Guildford UK 86 E9 51 14N 0 35W
Guilin China 101 L4 25 21N 110 11E
Guimarães Port. 87 A4 41 26N 8 19W
GUINEA 108 B10
Guinea Basin Atlantic Ocean 116 H7 1 00N 8 00W
GUINEA-BISSAU 108 A10
Güines Cuba 75 H4 22 50N 82 02W
Güiria Venezuela 80 E16 10 37N 62 21W
Guiyang China 101 K4 26 35N 106 40E
Gujarat *admin.* India 98 C4 23 20N 72 00E
Gujranwala Pakistan 98 C6 32 06N 74 11E
Gujrat Pakistan 98 C6 32 35N 74 06E
Gulbarga India 98 D3 17 22N 76 47E
Gulfport Mississippi USA 71 J3 30 21N 89 08W
Gulu Uganda 108 L8 2 46N 32 21E
Gunnison *r.* Colorado USA 70 E4 38 00N 107 00W
Guntersville Lake Alabama USA 71 J3 34 00N 86 00W
Guntur India 98 E3 16 20N 80 27E
Gunung Kinabalu *mt.* Malaysia 103 F5 6 03N 116 32E
Gurgueia *r.* Brazil 80 J12 9 00S 44 00W
Gurupi *r.* Brazil 80 H13 4 00S 47 00W
Gusev Russia 88 J11 54 32N 22 12E
Gushgy Turkmenistan 97 H6 36 03N 62 43E
Güstrow Germany 88 D10 53 48N 12 11E
Guthrie Oklahoma USA 71 G4 35 53N 97 26W
Guwahati India 99 G5 26 10N 91 45E
GUYANA 80 F14
Guyana Basin Atlantic Ocean 116 D7 8 00N 50 00W
Gwalior India 98 D5 26 12N 78 09E
Gweru Zimbabwe 109 K4 19 27S 29 49E
Gyda Peninsula Russia 95 K11 70 00N 77 30E
Gympie Aust. 110 J4 26 10S 152 35E
Gyöngyös Hungary 88 G7 47 46N 20 00E
Györ Hungary 89 F7 47 41N 17 40E

H

Haapsalu Estonia 88 J13 58 58N 23 32E
Haarlem Neths. 86 H10 52 23N 4 39E
Haast NZ 111 B3 43 53S 169 03E
Hab *r.* Pakistan 98 B5 25 20N 67 00E
Habbān Yemen 97 E1 14 21N 47 04E
Haboro Japan 102 D3 44 23N 141 43E
Hachinohe Japan 102 D3 40 30N 141 30E
Hackensack River New Jersey USA 73 H2 40 47N 74 06W
Hadejia Nigeria 108 G10 12 30N 10 03E
Hadejia *r.* Nigeria 108 F10 4 10N 9 30E
Hadera Israel 96 N11 32 26N 34 55E
Haderslev Denmark 88 B11 55 15N 9 30E
Hadhramaut *geog. reg.* Yemen 97 E2 15 40N 47 30E
Hadīboh Yemen 97 F1 12 36N 53 59E
Hadraibari India 99 L9 23 55N 91 50E
Haeju North Korea 101 P6 38 04N 125 40E
Hagerstown Maryland USA 71 L4 39 39N 77 44W
Ha Giang Vietnam 101 J3 22 50N 105 00E
Haifa Israel 96 N11 32 49N 34 59E
Haikou China 101 L3 20 00N 110 25E
Hā'il Saudi Arabia 96 D4 27 31N 41 45E
Hailar China 101 M8 49 15N 119 41E
Hainan Dao *i.* China 101 K2/L2 18 50N 109 50E
Haines Alaska USA 42 C6 59 11N 135 23W
Hai Phong Vietnam 101 K3 20 50N 106 41E
HAITI 75 K3
Hakodate Japan 102 D3 41 46N 140 44E
Halaib Sudan 108 M12 22 12N 36 35E
Halawa, Cape Hawaiian Islands 115 Y18 21 09N 157 15W
Halba Lebanon 96 P12 34 33N 36 04E
Halden Norway 86 L13 59 08N 11 13E
Haldia India 99 K9 22 02N 88 05E
Halle Germany 88 C9 51 28N 11 58E
Hallock Minnesota USA 49 D1 48 50N 96 59W
Halls Creek *tn.* Aust. 110 D6 18 17S 127 38E
Halmahera *i.* Indonesia 103 H4 0 30S 127 00E
Halmstad Sweden 88 D12 56 41N 12 55E
Hamada Japan 102 B1 34 56N 132 04E
Hamadān Iran 97 E5 34 46N 48 35E
Ḥamāh Syria 96 C6 35 10N 36 45E
Hamamatsu Japan 102 C1 34 42N 137 42E
Hambantota Sri Lanka 98 E1 6 07N 81 07E
Hamburg Germany 88 C10 53 33N 10 00E
Hamburg New York USA 52 H2 42 43N 78 50W
Hamden Connecticut USA 73 D2 41 20N 72 55W
Hamersley Range *mts.* Aust. 110 B5 22 00S 117 00E
Hamhung North Korea 101 P6 39 54N 127 35E
Hami China 100 G7 42 37N 93 32E
Hamilton NZ 111 E6 37 47S 175 17E
Hamilton Ohio USA 71 K4 39 23N 84 33W
Hamm Germany 88 A9 51 40N 7 49E
Hammond Indiana USA 71 J5 41 36N 87 30W
Hampton Virginia USA 71 L4 37 02N 76 23W
Hancock Maryland USA 73 B1 39 41N 78 10W
Hancock Michigan USA 51 G4 47 08N 88 36W
Hancock New York USA 73 C2 41 58N 75 17W
Handan China 101 L6 36 35N 114 31E
Hanford California USA 72 D3 36 20N 119 38W
Hangzhou China 101 N5 30 18N 120 07E
Hanimadu Island Maldives 98 C1 6 30N 73 00E
Hanko Finland 88 J13 50 50N 23 00E
Hannah North Dakota USA 49 C1 48 58N 98 42W
Hannibal Missouri USA 71 H4 39 41N 91 20W
Hannover Germany 88 B10 52 23N 9 44E
Hanöbukten *b.* Sweden 88 E11 55 50N 14 30E
Hanoi Vietnam 101 K3 21 01N 105 52E
Hanover Pennsylvania USA 73 B1 39 48N 76 59W
Haora India 99 K9 22 35N 88 19E
Ḥaql Saudi Arabia 96 B4 29 14N 34 56E
Ḥaraḍ Saudi Arabia 97 E3 24 12N 49 12E
Harare Zimbabwe 109 L4 17 50S 31 03E
Harbang Bangladesh 99 M8 21 56N 92 05E
Harbin China 101 P8 45 45N 126 41E
Harbor Beach *tn.* Michigan USA 51 K2 43 51N 82 39W
Harbor Springs *tn.* Michigan USA 52 B5 45 25N 84 59W
Harer Ethiopia 108 N9 9 20N 42 10E
Hargeysa Somalia 108 N9 9 31N 44 02E
Harima-nada *sea* Japan 102 B1 34 30N 134 30E
Haringhat *r.* Bangladesh 99 K9 22 10N 89 55E
Hari Rud *r.* Afghanistan 97 H5 34 00N 64 00E
Harlem New York USA 73 J2 40 48N 73 56W
Harlingen Texas USA 71 G2 26 12N 97 43W
Harper Liberia 108 C8 4 25N 7 43W
Harper Lake California USA 72 E2 35 03N 117 15W
Harris *i.* UK 86 B12 57 50N 6 55W
Harrisburg Pennsylvania USA 71 L5 40 17N 76 54W
Harrison Michigan USA 51 J3 44 01N 84 48W
Harrisonburg Virginia USA 71 L4 38 27N 78 54W
Harrisville Michigan USA 51 K3 44 39N 83 19W
Harrisville New York USA 53 L4 44 09N 75 20W
Harrogate UK 86 E11 54 00N 1 33W
Hart Michigan USA 51 H2 43 42N 86 21W
Hartford Connecticut USA 71 M5 41 46N 72 42W
Hartland Point *c.* UK 86 C9 51 02N 4 31W
Hartlepool UK 86 E11 54 41N 1 13W
Haryana *admin.* India 98 D5 29 20N 75 30E
Harz *mts.* Europe 88 C9 52 00N 10 00E
Hasselt Belgium 86 H9 50 56N 5 20E
Hassi Messaoud Algeria 108 F14 31 52N 5 43E
Hastings NZ 111 F5 39 39S 176 51E
Hastings Michigan USA 52 A2 42 38N 85 17W
Hastings Nebraska USA 71 G5 40 37N 98 22W
Hatteras, Cape North Carolina USA 71 L4 35 14N 75 31W
Hattiesburg Mississippi USA 71 J3 31 20N 89 19W
Hat Yai Thailand 103 C5 7 00N 100 25E
Haud *geog. reg.* Africa 108 N9/P9 8 00N 50 00E
Haugesund Norway 86 H13 59 25N 5 16E
Hauraki Gulf NZ 111 E6 36 38S 175 04E
Haut Atlas *mts.* Morocco 108 C14 30 45N 6 50W
Havana Cuba 75 H4 23 07N 82 25W
Haverhill New Hampshire USA 73 E3 42 47N 71 05W
Havre Montana USA 70 E6 48 34N 109 40W
Hawaii *i.* Hawaiian Islands 115 Z17 19 50N 157 50W
Hawaiian Islands Pacific Ocean 108 J10 25 00N 166 00W
Hawaiian Ridge Pacific Ocean 115 K10 23 00N 166 00W
Hawera NZ 111 E5 39 35S 174 17E
Hawick UK 86 D11 55 25N 2 47W
Hawthorne Nevada USA 72 D4 38 33N 118 37W
Hayward California USA 72 B3 37 40N 122 07W
Hayward Wisconsin USA 51 F4 46 01N 91 29W
Hazaribagh Range *mts.* India 98/99 E4 22 30N 84 00E
Hazleton Pennsylvania USA 73 C2 40 58N 75 59W
Healdsburg California USA 72 B4 38 36N 122 53W
Heard Island Indian Ocean 113 G1 53 07S 73 20E
Heart *r.* North Dakota USA 70 F6 47 00N 102 00W
Hebi China 101 L6 35 57N 114 08E
Hebron Middle East 96 N10 31 32N 35 06E
Heceta Island Alaska USA 42 D4 55 45N 134 40W
Hechuan China 101 K5 30 02N 106 5E
Heerlen Neths. 86 H9 50 53N 5 59E
Hefei China 101 M5 31 55N 117 18E
Hegang China 101 Q8 47 36N 130 30E
Hegura-jima *i.* Japan 102 C2 37 52N 136 56E
Heidelberg Germany 88 B8 49 25N 8 42E
Heilbronn Germany 88 B8 49 08N 9 14E
Hei Ling Chau *i.* HK China 100 B1 22 15N 114 02E
Hekou China 101 J3 22 30N 104 00E
Helan Shan *mts.* China 101 K6 38 00N 106 00E
Helena Montana USA 70 D6 46 35N 112 00W
Helendale California USA 72 E2 34 45N 117 19W
Heligoland Bight *b.* Germany 88 B11 54 00N 8 00E
Hellín Sp. 87 E3 38 31N 1 43W
Helmand *r.* Afghanistan 97 H5 30 00N 62 30E
Helsingborg Sweden 88 D12 56 03N 12 43E
Helsingør Denmark 88 D12 56 03N 12 38E
Helsinki Finland 88 K14 60 08N 25 00E
Hemet California USA 72 E1 33 45N 116 58W
Henares *r.* Sp. 87 D4 40 45N 3 10W
Henderson Nevada USA 70 D4 36 01N 115 00W
Henderson Island Pacific Ocean 115 N5 23 00S 127 00W
Hengelo Neths. 86 J10 52 16N 6 46E
Hengyang China 101 L4 26 58N 112 31E
Henryetta Oklahoma USA 71 G4 35 27N 96 00W
Henzada Myanmar 103 B7 17 36N 95 26E
Herāt Afghanistan 97 H5 34 20N 62 12E
Hérault *r.* Fr. 87 G5 43 50N 3 30E
Hereford UK 86 D10 52 04N 2 43W
Hermel Lebanon 96 P12 34 25N 36 23E
Hermon New York USA 53 L4 44 28N 75 12W
Hermon, Mount Lebanon/Syria 96 N11 33 24N 35 50E
Hermosillo Mexico 74 B5 29 15N 110 59W
Herning Denmark 88 B12 56 08N 8 59E
Hesperia California USA 72 E2 34 25N 117 19W
Hetch Hetchy Aqueduct California USA 72 C3 37 35N 121 45W
Hetch Hetchy Reservoir California USA 72 D3 37 57N 119 45W
Hibbing Minnesota USA 51 E4 47 25N 92 56W
Hickory North Carolina USA 71 K4 35 44N 81 23W
Hicksville Ohio USA 52 B1 41 18N 84 45W
Hidalgo Mexico 74 E4 24 16N 99 28W
Hidalgo del Parral Mexico 74 C5 26 58N 105 40W
High Island HK China 100 D2 22 21N 114 21E
High Island Reservoir HK China 100 D2 22 22N 114 20E
High Point *tn.* North Carolina USA 71 L4 35 58N 80 00W
High Veld *mts.* RSA 109 K2 28 00S 28 00E
Hiiumaa *i.* Estonia 88 J13 58 55N 22 30E
Hiko Nevada USA 72 F3 37 36N 115 14W
Hildesheim Germany 88 B10 52 09N 9 58E
Hillsdale Michigan USA 52 B1 41 56N 84 37W
Hilo Hawaiian Islands 115 Z17 19 42N 155 04W
Hilton New York USA 52 J3 43 17N 77 47W
Hilversum Neths. 86 H10 52 14N 5 10E
Himachal Pradesh *admin.* India 98 D6 32 00N 77 30E
Himalaya *mts.* Asia 98/99 D6 28 00N 85 00E
Himeji Japan 102 B1 34 50N 134 40E
Hinckley Lake New York USA 53 L3 43 20N 75 10W
Hindu Kush *mts.* Afghanistan 97 J5/K6 35 00N 70 00E
Hirakud Reservoir India 98 E4 21 40N 83 40E
Hirosaki Japan 102 D3 40 34N 140 28E
Hiroshima Japan 102 B1 34 23N 132 27E
Hisar India 98 D5 29 10N 75 45E
Hispaniola *i.* W. Indies 75 K3/L3 18 00N 70 00W
Hitachi Japan 102 D2 36 35N 140 40E
Hjørring Denmark 88 B12 57 28N 9 59E
Ho Ghana 108 E9 6 38N 0 38E
Hobart Aust. 110 H1 42 54S 147 18E
Hoboken New Jersey USA 73 H1 40 44N 74 02W
Hobyo Somalia 108 P9 5 20N 48 30E
Hô Chi Minh Vietnam 103 D6 10 46N 106 43E
Ho Chung HK China 100 C2 22 22N 114 14E
Hodeida Yemen 96 D1 14 50N 42 58E
Hódmezovásárhely Hungary 89 H7 46 26N 20 21E
Hof Germany 88 C9 50 19N 11 56E
Hofu Japan 102 B1 34 02N 131 34E
Hogeland Montana USA 47 C1 48 51N 108 39W
Hoggar *mts.* Algeria 108 F12 23 45N 6 00E
Hohhot China 101 L7 40 49N 111 37E
Hoi Ha HK China 100 C2 22 28N 114 20E
Hokitika NZ 111 C3 42 43S 170 58E
Hokkaidō *i.* Japan 102 D3 43 30N 143 00E
Holbaek Denmark 88 C11 56 33N 10 19E
Holguín Cuba 75 J4 20 54N 76 15W
Hollister California USA 72 C3 36 47N 121 25W
Holly Michigan USA 52 C2 42 48N 83 37W
Holstebro Denmark 88 B12 56 22N 8 38E
Holston *r.* USA 71 K4 37 00N 82 00W
Holyoke Massachusetts USA 73 D3 42 13N 72 38N
Homestead Florida USA 71 K2 25 29N 80 29W
Homs Syria 96 C5 34 42N 36 40E
Honda Col. 80 C15 5 15N 74 50W
HONDURAS 74 G2
Hønefoss Norway 86 L14 60 10N 10 16E
Honesdale Pennsylvania USA 53 L1 41 34N 75 15W
Hong Kong *admin.* China 101 L3 23 00N 114 00E
Hong Kong Island HK China 100 B1/C1 22 15N 114 12E
Hong Lok Yuen HK China 100 B2 22 27N 114 09E
Honokaa Hawaiian Islands 115 Z18 20 04N 155 27W
Honolulu Hawaiian Islands 115 Y18 21 19N 157 50W
Honshū *i.* Japan 102 C2 37 15N 139 00E
Hood, Mount Oregon USA 70 B6 45 24N 121 41W
Hoolehua Hawaiian Islands 115 Y18 21 11N 157 06W

Hoonah Alaska USA 42 C6 58 06N 135 25W
Hopkinsville Kentucky USA 71 J4 36 50N 87 30W
Ho Pui HK China 100 B2 22 24N 114 04E
Ho Pui Reservoir HK China 100 B2 22 25N 114 05E
Hormuz, Strait of The Gulf 97 G4 26 35N 56 30E
Hornell New York USA 52 J2 42 20N 77 40W
Horsens Denmark 88 B11 55 53N 9 53E
Horsham Aust. 110 G2 36 45S 142 15E
Hospet India 98 D3 15 16N 76 20E
Hospitalet Sp. 87 G4 41 21N 2 06E
Hotan China 100 D6 37 07N 79 57E
Hotan He *r.* China 100 E6 39 00N 80 30E
Hot Springs *tn.* Arkansas USA 71 H3 34 30N 93 02W
Houghton Michigan USA 51 G4 47 07N 88 35W
Houghton Lake Michigan USA 52 B4 44 20N 84 45W
Houghton Lake *tn.* Michigan USA 52 B4 44 17N 84 45W
Houhara NZ 111 D7 34 48S 173 06E
Houlton Maine USA 57 G2 46 09N 67 50W
Houma China 101 L6 35 36N 111 15E
Houma Louisiana USA 71 H2 29 35N 90 44W
Houston Texas USA 71 G2 29 45N 95 25W
Hovd Mongolia 100 G8 48 00N 91 43E
Hövsgöl Nuur *l.* Mongolia 101 J9 51 00N 100 30E
Howar *r.* Sudan 108 K11 17 00N 25 00E
Howard City Michigan USA 51 J2 43 23N 85 28W
Howe, Cape Aust. 110 H2 37 20S 149 59E
Howland Islands Pacific Ocean 114 J8 2 00N 177 00W
Hoy *i.* UK 86 D13 58 48N 3 20W
Hradec Králové Czech Rep. 88 E9 50 13N 15 50E
Hrodna Belarus 88 J10 53 40N 23 50E
Hron *r.* Slovakia 88 G8 48 00N 18 00E
Hsinchu Taiwan 101 N3 24 48N 120 59E
Huacho Peru 80 B11 11 05S 77 36W
Huaide China 101 N7 43 30N 124 48E
Huainan China 101 M5 32 41N 117 06E
Huajuápan de León Mexico 74 E3 17 50N 97 48W
Huambo Angola 109 H5 12 44S 15 47E
Huancayo Peru 80 B11 12 05S 75 12W
Huang He *r.* China 101 L6 38 00N 111 00E
Huangshi China 101 M5 30 13N 115 05E
Huanuco Peru 80 B12 9 55S 76 11W
Huaráz Peru 80 B12 9 33S 77 31W
Huascaran *mt.* Peru 80 B12 9 08S 77 36W
Huashixia China 101 H6 35 13N 99 12E
Hubbard Lake Michigan USA 52 C4 44 50N 83 30W
Huddersfield UK 86 E10 53 39N 1 47W
Hudson River New York USA 73 D2/D3 42 00N 73 55W
Huê Vietnam 103 D7 16 28N 107 35E
Huelva Sp. 87 B2 37 15N 6 56W
Huelva *r.* Sp. 87 B2 37 50N 6 30W
Huesca Sp. 87 E5 42 08N 0 25W
Hughenden Aust. 110 G5 20 50S 144 10E
Hugli *r.* India 99 K8 22 00N 88 00E
Hugo Oklahoma USA 71 G3 34 01N 95 31W
Huixtla Mexico 74 F3 15 09N 92 30W
Huizhou China 101 L3 23 08N 114 28E
Humaitá Brazil 80 E12 7 33S 63 01W
Humboldt *r.* Nevada USA 70 C5 41 00N 118 00W
HUNGARY 88/89 F7
Hungnam North Korea 101 P6 39 49N 127 40E
Hung Shui Kiu HK China 100 A2 22 25N 113 59E
Hunjiang China 101 P7 41 54N 126 23E
Hunsrück *mts.* Germany 88 J8/J9 50 00N 7 00E
Hunter Trench Pacific Ocean 114 H5 23 00S 175 00E
Huntington West Virginia USA 71 K4 38 24N 82 26W
Huntington Beach *tn.* California USA 72 D1 33 40N 118 00W
Huntly NZ 111 E6 37 34S 175 10E
Huntsville Alabama USA 71 J3 34 44N 86 35W
Huntsville Texas USA 71 G3 30 43N 95 34W
Hurghada Egypt 108 L13 27 17N 33 47E
Hurley Wisconsin USA 51 F4 46 26N 90 10W
Huron River Michigan USA 52 C2 42 10N 83 15W
Huskvarna Sweden 88 E12 57 47N 14 15E
Husn Jordan 96 N11 32 29N 35 53E
Hutchinson Kansas USA 71 G4 38 03N 97 56W
Huzhou China 101 N5 30 56N 120 04E
Hvar *i.* Croatia 89 F5 43 00N 17 00E
Hwange Zimbabwe 109 K4 18 22S 26 29E
Hyder Alaska USA 42 E4 55 45N 130 10W
Hyderabad India 98 D3 17 22N 78 26E
Hyderabad Pakistan 98 B5 25 23N 68 24E

I

Ialomiţa *r.* Romania 89 L6 44 00N 27 00E
Iaşi Romania 89 L7 47 09N 27 38E
Ibadan Nigeria 108 E9 7 23N 3 56E
Ibagué Col. 80 B14 4 25N 75 20W
Ibarra Ecuador 80 B14 0 23N 78 05W
Ibb Yemen 96 D1 14 03N 44 10E
Ibi Nigeria 108 F9 8 11N 9 44E
Ibiza Sp. 87 F3 38 54N 1 26E
Ibiza *i.* Sp. 87 F3 39 00N 1 20E
Ibotirama Brazil 80 J11 12 13S 43 12W
Ibrī Oman 97 G3 23 15N 56 35E
Ica Peru 80 B11 14 02S 75 48W
Icacos Point Trinidad and Tobago 75 V15 10 41N 61 42W
ICELAND 116 F13
Ichalkaranji India 98 C3 16 40N 74 33E
Ichinomiya Japan 102 C2 35 18N 136 48E
Icy Strait *sd.* Alaska USA 42 C6 58 20N 135 45W
Idaho *state* USA 70 D5 44 00N 115 00W
Idaho Falls *tn.* Idaho USA 70 D5 43 30N 112 01W

Idfu Egypt 108 L12 24 58N 32 50E
Igarka Russia 95 L10 67 31N 86 33E
Iglesias Italy 89 B3 39 19N 8 32E
Iguaçu *r.* Brazil 80 G8 26 00S 51 00W
Iguala Mexico 74 E3 18 21N 99 31W
Iguape Brazil 80 H9 24 37S 47 30W
Iguatu Brazil 80 K12 6 22S 39 20W
Ihavandiffulu Atoll *i.* Maldives 98 C1 7 00N 72 55E
Ihosy Madagascar 109 P3 22 23S 46 09E
Iida Japan 102 C2 35 32N 137 48E
IJsselmeer *l.* Neths. 86 H10 52 50N 5 15E
Ikaría *i.* Greece 89 L2 37 35N 26 10E
Ikela CDR 108 J7 1 06S 23 06E
Iki *i.* Japan 102 A1 33 50N 129 40E
Ilagan Philippines 103 G7 17 07N 121 53E
Île Amsterdam *i.* Indian Ocean 113 G3 37 56S 77 40E
Ilebo CDR 108 J7 4 20S 20 35E
Ile de Jerba *i.* Tunisia 108 G14 33 40N 11 00E
Île de l'Europe *i.* Mozambique Channel 109 N3 22 20S 40 20E
Île de Ré *i.* Fr. 87 E7 46 10N 1 26W
Île d'Oléron *i.* Fr. 87 E6 45 55N 1 16W
Île d'Ouessant *i.* Fr. 86 C8 48 28N 5 05W
Île d'Yeu *i.* Fr. 87 D7 46 43N 2 20W
Ilesa Nigeria 108 E9 7 39N 4 38E
Île St. Paul *i.* Indian Ocean 113 G3 38 44S 77 30E
Îles Crozet *is.* Indian Ocean 113 E2 46 27S 52 00E
Îles d'Hyères *is.* Fr. 87 J5 43 10N 6 25E
Îles Kerguelen *is.* Indian Ocean 113 F2 49 30S 69 30E
Îles Loyauté *is.* Pacific Ocean 114 G5 21 00S 167 00E
Ilha Bazaruto *i.* Mozambique 109 M3 21 40S 35 30E
Ilha de Marajó *i.* Brazil 80 G13 1 30S 50 00W
Ilha Fernando de Noronha *i.* Brazil 80 L13 3 50S 32 25W
Ilhéus Brazil 80 K11 14 50S 39 06W
Ili *r.* Asia 94 K5 44 00N 78 00E
Iligan Philippines 103 G5 8 12N 124 13W
Illapel Chile 81 C7 31 40S 71 13W
Illinois *state* USA 71 J5 40 00N 89 00W
Illizi Algeria 108 F13 26 45N 8 30E
Iloilo Philippines 103 G6 10 41N 122 33E
Ilorin Nigeria 108 E9 8 32N 4 34E
Imabari Japan 102 B1 34 04N 132 59E
Imi Ethiopia 108 N9 6 28N 42 10E
Imperatriz Brazil 80 H12 5 32S 47 28W
Imperia Italy 89 B5 43 53N 8 03E
Impfondo Congo 108 H8 1 36N 18 00E
Imphal India 99 G4 24 47N 93 55E
Inangahua NZ 111 C4 41 52S 171 57E
Inca Sp. 87 G3 39 43N 2 54E
Inchon South Korea 101 P6 37 30N 126 38E
Independence California USA 72 D3 36 48N 118 14W
Independence Kansas USA 71 G4 37 13N 95 43W
INDIA 98/99 B4/F4
Indiana *state* USA 71 J5 40 00N 86 00W
Indian Antarctic Basin Southern Ocean 114 A2 57 00S 113 00E
Indian-Antarctic Ridge Southern Ocean 114 A3 51 00S 124 00E
Indianapolis Indiana USA 71 J4 39 45N 86 10W
Indian Ocean 113
Indian Springs *tn.* Nevada USA 72 F3 36 33N 115 40W
Indigirka *r.* Russia 95 S10 70 00N 147 30E
Indio California USA 72 E1 33 44N 116 14W
INDONESIA 103 C3/H3
Indravati *r.* India 98 E3 19 00N 81 30E
Indre *r.* Fr. 87 F7 46 50N 1 25E
Indus *r.* Pakistan 98 B5 28 00N 69 00E
Indus, Mouths of the *est.* Pakistan 98 B4 24 00N 67 00E
Ingham Aust. 110 H6 18 35S 146 12E
Inglewood California USA 72 D1 33 58N 118 22W
Ingolstadt Germany 88 C8 48 46N 11 27E
Ingraj Bazar India 99 K10 24 59N 88 10E
Inhambane Mozambique 109 M3 23 51S 35 29E
Inirida *r.* Col. 80 D14 2 30N 70 00W
Inn *r.* Europe 89 C7 48 00N 12 00E
Innisfail Aust. 110 H6 17 30S 146 00E
Innsbruck Austria 89 C7 47 17N 11 25E
Inongo CDR 108 H7 1 55S 18 20E
Inowrocław Poland 88 G10 52 49N 18 12E
In Salah Algeria 108 E13 27 20N 2 03E
Insein Myanmar 103 B7 16 54N 96 08E
Inta Russia 94 J10 66 04N 60 01E
Inubō-zaki *c.* Japan 102 D2 35 41N 140 52E
Invercargill NZ 111 B1 46 25S 168 22E
Inverness UK 86 C12 57 27N 4 15W
Inyo Range *mts.* California USA 72 D3 36 37N 117 52W
Ioánnina Greece 89 H3 39 40N 20 51E
Ione Washington USA 43 M1 48 45N 117 25W
Ionia Michigan USA 52 A2 42 58N 85 06W
Iónia Nisiá Greece 89 G3 39 00N 20 00E
Ionian Sea Mediterranean Sea 89 F2/G2 38 00N 27 00E
Íos *i.* Greece 89 K2 36 00N 25 00E
Iowa *state* USA 71 H5 42 00N 94 00W
Iowa City Iowa USA 71 H5 41 39N 91 31W
Ipatinga Brazil 80 J10 19 32S 42 30W
Ipiales Col. 80 B14 0 52N 77 38W
Ipoh Malaysia 103 C4 4 36N 101 05E
Ipswich UK 86 F10 52 04N 1 10E
Ipu Brazil 80 J13 4 32S 40 44W
Iquique Chile 80 C9 20 15S 70 08W
Iquitos Peru 80 C13 3 51S 73 13W
Irákleio Greece 89 K1 35 20N 25 08E

IRAN 97 F5/G5
Irānshahr Iran 97 H4 27 15N 60 41E
Irapuato Mexico 74 D4 20 40N 101 30W
IRAQ 96 D5
Irbid Jordan 96 C5 32 33N 35 51E
Irecê Brazil 80 J11 11 22S 41 51W
Irian Jaya *admin.* Indonesia 103 J3 3 00S 133 00E
Iriri *r.* Brazil 80 G13 5 00S 54 50W
Irkutsk Russia 95 N7 52 18N 104 15E
Iron Knob *tn.* Aust. 110 F3 32 44S 137 08E
Iron Mountain *tn.* Michigan USA 51 G3 45 49N 88 04W
Ironwood Michigan USA 71 H6 46 25N 90 08W
Irrawaddy *r.* Myanmar 103 A8 20 00N 95 00E
Irtysh *r.* Asia 94 K8 57 30N 72 30E
Irún Sp. 87 E5 43 20N 1 48W
Irving Texas USA 71 G3 32 49N 96 57W
Irvington New Jersey USA 73 H1 40 44N 74 15W
Isabella Reservoir California USA 72 D2 35 41N 118 28W
Ise Japan 102 C1 34 29N 136 41E
Isère *r.* Fr. 87 H6 45 17N 5 47E
Ishikari *r.* Japan 102 D3 43 20N 141 45E
Ishikari-wan *b.* Japan 102 D3 43 30N 141 00E
Ishim *r.* Russia 94 J8 56 00N 69 00E
Ishinomaki Japan 102 D2 38 25N 141 18E
Isiro CDR 108 K8 2 50N 27 40E
Iskenderun Turkey 96 C6 36 37N 36 08E
Iskŭr *r.* Bulgaria 89 K5 43 30N 24 00E
Isla Asinara *i.* Italy 89 B4 41 00N 8 00E
Isla de Chiloé *i.* Chile 81 C5 42 30S 74 00W
Isla de Coco *i.* Costa Rica 115 S8 4 00N 85 00W
Isla de Coiba *i.* Panama 75 H1 7 40N 82 00W
Isla de Cozumel *i.* Mexico 74 G4 20 30N 87 00W
Isla de la Juventud *i.* Cuba 75 H4 22 00N 82 30W
Isla d'Elba *i.* Italy 89 C5 42 00N 10 00E
Isla de los Estados *i.* Argentina 81 E3 55 00S 64 00W
Isla Grande de Tierra del Fuego *i.* Chile/Argentina 81 D3 54 00S 67 30W
Islamabad Pakistan 98 C6 33 40N 73 08E
Isla Margarita *i.* Venezuela 80 E16 11 30N 64 00W
Islampur India 99 K11 26 16N 88 11E
Island Beach New Jersey USA 73 C1 39 55N 74 05W
Isla San Felix *i.* Chile 115 U5 26 23S 80 05W
Islas de la Bahia *is.* Honduras 74 G3 16 40N 86 00W
Islas Galápagos *i.* Ecuador 115 S7 0 05S 90 00W
Islas Juan Fernández *is.* Chile 115 T4 33 30S 80 00W
Islas Marias *is.* Mexico 74 C4 22 00N 107 00W
Islas Revillagigedo *is.* Pacific Ocean 74 B3 19 00N 112 30W
Isla Wellington *i.* Chile 115 U3 48 50S 79 00W
Islay *i.* UK 86 B11 55 48N 6 12W
Isle of Man British Isles 86 C11 54 15N 4 15W
Isle of Wight *i.* UK 86 E9 50 40N 1 20W
Isle Royale *i.* Michigan USA 51 G4 48 00N 89 0W
Isle Royale National Park Michigan USA 51 G4 48 00N 89 0W
Ismâ'ilîya Egypt 109 S3 30 36N 32 16E
Isoka Zambia 109 L5 10 09S 32 39E
Isola Lipari *is.* Italy 89 E3 38 00N 14 00E
ISRAEL 96 N9
Istanbul Turkey 96 A7 41 02N 28 57E
Istmo de Tehuantepec *ist.* Mexico 74 F3 17 20N 93 10W
Istres Fr. 87 H5 43 30N 4 59E
Itabaiana Brazil 80 K11 10 42S 37 37W
Itabuna Brazil 80 K11 14 48S 39 18W
Itacoatiara Brazil 80 F13 3 06S 58 22W
Itagüi Col. 80 B15 6 13N 75 40W
Itaituba Brazil 80 F13 4 15S 55 56W
Itajaí Brazil 80 H8 26 50S 48 39W
ITALY 89 C5/D5
Itapipoca Brazil 80 K13 3 29S 39 35W
Itaqui Brazil 81 F8 29 10S 56 30W
Ithaca New York USA 53 K2 42 27N 76 30W
Itui *r.* Brazil 80 C12 5 30S 71 00W
Ivano-Frankivs'k Ukraine 88 K8 48 40N 24 40E
Ivanovo Russia 94 G8 57 00N 41 00E
Ivdel' Russia 94 J9 60 45N 60 30E
Iwaki Japan 102 D2 37 03N 140 58E
Iwakuni Japan 102 B1 34 10N 132 09E
Iwamizawa Japan 102 D3 43 12N 141 47E
Iwanai Japan 102 D3 43 01N 140 32E
Iwo Nigeria 108 E9 7 38N 4 11E
Ixtaccihuati *mt.* Mexico 74 E3 19 11N 98 38W
Ixtapa-Zihuatanejo Mexico 74 D3 17 39N 101 35W
Ixtepec Mexico 74 E3 16 32N 95 10W
Iyo-nada *b.* Japan 102 B1 33 50N 132 00E
Izhevsk Russia 94 H8 56 49N 53 11E
Izhma *r.* Russia 94 H9 64 00N 54 00E
Izmayil Ukraine 89 M6 45 20N 28 48E
Izmir Turkey 96 A6 38 25N 27 10E
Izra' Syria 96 P11 32 52N 36 15E
Izu-shotō *is.* Japan 102 C1 34 20N 139 20E

J

Jabal Akhdar *mt.* Oman 97 G3 24 00N 56 30E
Jabal al Akhdar *mts.* Libya 108 J14 33 00N 22 00E
Jabal as Sawdā' *mts.* Libya 108 G13 29 00N 15 00E
Jabalpur India 98 D4 23 10N 79 59E
Jablonec Czech Rep. 88 E9 50 44N 15 10E
Jaboatão Brazil 80 K12 8 05S 35 00W
Jackman Maine USA 53 R5 45 37N 70 16W
Jack Mountain Washington USA 42 H4 48 45N 120 55W
Jackson California USA 72 C4 38 19N 120 47W
Jackson Michigan USA 71 K5 42 15N 84 24W

Jackson Mississippi USA 71 H3 32 20N 90 11W
Jackson Tennessee USA 71 J4 35 37N 88 50W
Jackson Wyoming USA 70 D5 43 28N 110 45W
Jackson Heights New York USA 73 J2 40 45N 73 52W
Jacksonville Florida USA 71 K3 30 20N 81 40W
Jacksonville North Carolina USA 71 L3 34 45N 77 26W
Jacksonville Beach *tn.* Florida USA 71 K3 30 18N 81 24W
Jack Wade Alaska USA 64 B3 64 05N 141 35W
Jacmel Haiti 75 K3 18 18N 72 32W
Jacobabad Pakistan 98 B5 28 16N 68 30E
Jacobina Brazil 80 J11 11 13S 40 30W
Jaén Sp. 87 D2 37 46N 3 48W
Jaffna Sri Lanka 98 E1 9 40N 80 01E
Jagdalpur India 98 E3 19 04N 82 05E
Jahrom Iran 97 F4 28 29N 53 32E
Jaintiapur Bangladesh 99 M10 25 06N 92 08E
Jaipur India 98 D5 26 53N 75 50E
Jakarta Indonesia 103 D2 6 08S 106 45E
Jalālābād Afghanistan 97 C6 34 26N 70 25E
Jalandhar India 98 D6 31 18N 75 40E
Jalapa Enriquez Mexico 74 E3 19 32N 96 56W
Jalgaon India 98 D4 21 01N 75 39E
Jalón *r.* Sp. 87 E4 41 30N 1 35W
Jalpaiguri India 99 K11 26 29N 88 47E
Jālū Libya 108 J13 29 02N 21 33E
JAMAICA 75 J3
Jamaica New York USA 73 J1 40 42N 73 48W
Jamaica Bay New York USA 73 J1 40 37N 73 50W
Jambi Indonesia 103 C3 1 34S 103 37E
James *r.* South Dakota USA 71 G5 44 00N 98 00W
James *r.* Virginia USA 71 L4 37 00N 77 00W
Jamestown New York USA 71 L5 42 05N 79 15W
Jamestown North Dakota USA 71 G6 46 54N 98 42W
Jamiltepec Mexico 74 E3 16 18N 97 51W
Jammu India 98 C6 32 43N 74 54E
Jammu and Kashmir *state* Southern Asia 98 D6 29 40N 76 30E
Jamnagar India 98 C4 22 28N 70 06E
Jamshedpur India 99 F4 22 47N 86 12E
Jamuna *r.* Bangladesh 99 K10 25 00N 89 40E
Janesville Wisconsin USA 71 J5 42 42N 89 02W
Jangipur India 99 K10 24 27N 88 04E
Jan Mayen *i.* Arctic Ocean 117 71 00N 9 00W
Januária Brazil 80 J10 15 28S 44 23W
JAPAN 102
Japan, Sea of Pacific Ocean 102 C2 39 00N 137 00E
Japan Trench Pacific Ocean 114 E11 35 00N 143 00E
Japurá *r.* Brazil 80 D13 2 00S 67 30W
Jari *r.* Brazil 80 G14 2 00N 54 00W
Jarú Brazil 80 E11 10 24S 62 45W
Jarvis Islands Pacific Ocean 115 K8 0 00 163 00W
Jāsk Iran 97 G4 25 40N 57 46E
Jasło Poland 88 H8 49 45N 21 28E
Jastrowie Poland 88 F10 53 25N 16 50E
Jaunpur India 98 E5 25 44N 82 41E
Java *i.* Indonesia 103 D2/E2 7 00S 110 00E
Java Sea Indonesia 103 E2 5 00S 112 00E
Java Trench Indian Ocean 113 L5 10 00S 110 00E
Jayapura Indonesia 110 G9 2 37S 140 39E
Jaynagar Manzilpur India 99 K9 22 10N 88 24E
Jaza'ir Farasān *is.* Saudi Arabia 96 D2 16 45N 42 10E
Jean Nevada USA 72 F2 35 46N 115 20W
Jebel Abyad Plateau Sudan 108 K11 18 00N 28 00E
Jebel Marra *mts.* Sudan 108 J10 13 00N 24 00E
Jedda Saudi Arabia 96 C3 21 30N 39 10E
Jefferson Ohio USA 52 F1 41 44N 80 46W
Jefferson City Missouri USA 71 H4 38 33N 92 10W
Jefferson, Mount Nevada USA 72 E4 38 47N 116 58W
Jelenia Góra Poland 88 E9 50 55N 15 45E
Jelgava Latvia 88 J12 56 39N 23 40E
Jena Germany 88 C9 50 56N 11 35E
Jenin Jordan 96 N11 32 28N 35 18E
Jequié Brazil 80 J11 13 52S 40 06W
Jequitinhonha *r.* Brazil 80 J10 16 00S 41 00W
Jérémie Haiti 75 K3 18 40N 74 09W
Jerez de la Frontera Sp. 87 B2 36 41N 6 08W
Jerez de los Caballeros Sp. 87 B3 38 20N 6 45W
Jericho Middle East 96 N10 31 51N 35 27E
Jersey *i.* British Isles 86 D8 49 13N 2 07W
Jersey City New Jersey USA 73 C2 40 43N 74 06W
Jerusalem Israel/Jordan 96 N10 31 47N 35 13E
Jessore Bangladesh 99 K9 23 10N 89 12E
Jezioro Sniardwy *i.* Poland 88 H10 53 00N 21 00E
Jhang Maghiana Pakistan 98 C6 31 19N 72 22E
Jhansi India 98 D5 25 27N 78 34E
Jharkhand *admin.* India 99 E4/F4 23 50N 85 00E
Jhelum *r.* Pakistan 98 C6 32 30N 72 30E
Jhenida Bangladesh 99 K9 23 32N 89 09E
Jiamusi China 101 Q8 46 59N 130 29E
Ji'an China 101 M4 27 08N 115 00E
Jiangmen China 101 L3 22 40N 113 05E
Jiaxing China 101 N5 30 15N 120 52E
Jiayuguan China 101 H6 39 47N 98 14E
Jihlavá Czech Rep. 88 E8 49 24N 15 34E
Jilin China 101 P7 43 53N 126 35E
Jiloca *r.* Sp. 87 E4 41 08N 1 45W
Jima Ethiopia 108 M9 7 39N 36 47E
Jinan China 101 M6 36 41N 117 00E
Jingdezhen China 101 M4 29 17N 117 12E
Jinhua China 101 M4 29 06N 119 40E

Place	Page	Grid	Latitude	Longitude
Jining China	101	L7	40 58N	113 01E
Jining China	101	M6	35 25N	116 40E
Jinja Uganda	108	L8	0 27N	33 14E
Jinsha Jiang *r.* China	101	J4	27 30N	103 00E
Jinxi China	101	N7	40 46N	120 47E
Jinzhou China	101	N7	41 07N	121 06E
Jiparaná *r.* Brazil	80	E12	8 00S	62 30W
Jiu *r.* Romania	89	J6	44 00N	24 00E
Jiujiang China	101	M4	29 41N	116 03E
Jixi China	101	Q8	45 17N	131 00E
Jīzān Saudi Arabia	96	D2	16 56N	42 33E
João Pessoa Brazil	80	K12	7 06S	34 53W
Jodhpur India	98	C5	26 18N	73 08E
Jōetsu Japan	102	C2	37 06N	138 15E
Jogighopa India	99	L11	26 12N	90 34E
Johannesburg RSA	109	K2	26 10S	28 02E
John Day *r.* Oregon USA	70	B5/C5	45 00N	120 00W
John H. Kerr Reservoir USA	71	L4	37 00N	78 00W
Johnson City Tennessee USA	71	K4	36 20N	82 23W
Johnston Atoll *is.* Pacific Ocean	115	K9	17 00N	168 00W
Johnstown Pennsylvania USA	71	L5	40 20N	78 56W
Johor Bahru Malaysia	103	C4	1 27N	103 45E
Joinville Brazil	80	H8	26 20S	48 55W
Jonesboro Arkansas USA	71	H4	35 50N	90 41W
Jonesville Michigan USA	52	B1	41 59N	84 39W
Jönköping Sweden	88	E12	57 45N	14 10E
Joplin Missouri USA	71	H4	37 04N	94 31W
JORDAN	96	C5		
Jordan *r.* Middle East	96	N11	32 15N	32 10E
Jos Nigeria	108	F9	9 54N	8 53E
Joseph Bonaparte Gulf Aust.	110	D7	14 00S	128 30E
Joshua Tree *tn.* California USA	72	E2	34 09N	116 20W
Joshua Tree National Monument California USA	72	F1	33 54N	116 00W
Jos Plateau Nigeria	108	F9	9 30N	8 55E
Joûnié Lebanon	96	N11	33 58N	35 38E
Jowai India	99	M10	25 26N	92 16E
Juan de Fuca Strait North America	70	B6	48 00N	124 00W
Juàzeiro Brazil	80	J12	9 25S	40 30W
Juàzeiro do Norte Brazil	80	K12	7 10S	39 18W
Juba Sudan	108	L8	4 50N	31 35E
Jubba *r.* Somalia	108	N8	3 00N	42 30E
Jubilee Reservoir HK China	100	B2	22 23N	114 09E
Júcar *r.* Sp.	87	E3	39 08N	1 50W
Juchitán Mexico	74	E3	16 27N	95 05W
Juiz de Fora Brazil	80	J9	21 47S	43 23W
Juliaca Peru	80	C10	15 29S	70 09W
Julijske Alpe *mts.* Europe	89	D7	46 00N	13 00E
Junagadh India	98	C4	21 32N	70 32E
Junction City Kansas USA	71	G4	39 02N	96 51W
Jundiaí Brazil	80	H9	23 10S	46 54W
Juneau Alaska USA	42	C6	58 20N	134 20W
Jungfrau *mt.* Switz.	87	J7	46 33N	7 58E
Junggar Pendi China	100	E7/G7	44 00N	87 30E
Junipero Serra Peak *mt.* California USA	72	C3	36 09N	121 26W
Junk Bay HK China	100	C1	22 18N	114 15E
Jur *r.* Sudan	108	K9	8 00N	28 00E
Jura *i.* UK	86	C11/C12	55 55N	6 00W
Jura *mts.* Fr./Switz.	87	H7/J7	46 30N	6 00E
Jura Krakowska *mts.* Poland	88	G9/H9	50 00N	20 00E
Jurmala Latvia	88	J12	56 59N	23 35E
Juruá *r.* Brazil	80	C12	9 30S	73 00W
Juruá *r.* Brazil	80	D13	4 30S	67 00W
Juruena *r.* Brazil	80	F11	10 00S	57 40W

K

Place	Page	Grid	Latitude	Longitude
K2 *mt.* China/India	100	D6	35 47N	76 30E
Kabrit Egypt	109	S2	30 16N	32 29E
Kābul Afghanistan	97	J5	34 30N	69 10E
Kabwe Zambia	109	K5	14 29S	28 25E
Kachchh, Gulf of India	98	B4	22 40N	69 30E
Kadoma Zimbabwe	109	K4	18 21N	29 55E
Kaduna Nigeria	108	F10	10 28N	7 25E
Kaduna *r.* Nigeria	108	F10	10 00N	6 30E
Kaédi Mauritania	108	B11	16 12N	13 32W
Kaesong South Korea	101	P6	37 59N	126 30E
Kafue Zambia	109	K4	15 44S	28 10E
Kafue *r.* Zambia	109	K5	16 00S	27 00E
Kagoshima Japan	102	B1	31 37N	130 32E
Kahoolawe *i.* Hawaiian Islands	115	Y18	20 30N	156 40W
Kahuku Point *c.* Hawaiian Islands	115	Y18	21 42N	158 00W
Kaiapoi NZ	111	D3	43 23S	172 39E
Kaifeng China	101	L5	34 47N	114 20E
Kaikohe NZ	111	D7	35 25S	173 48E
Kaikoura NZ	111	D3	42 24S	173 41E
Kailua Hawaiian Islands	115	Z17	19 43N	155 59W
Kaimana Indonesia	103	J3	3 39S	133 44E
Kainji Reservoir Nigeria	108	E10	10 25N	4 56E
Kaipara Harbour NZ	111	E6	36 12S	174 06E
Kairouan Tunisia	108	G14	35 42N	10 01E
Kaiserslautern Germany	88	A8	49 27N	7 47E
Kaitaia NZ	111	D7	35 07S	173 16E
Kaiwi Channel *sd.* Hawaiian Islands	115	Y18	21 20N	157 30W
Kākināda India	98	E3	16 59N	82 20E
Kalae *c.* Hawaiian Islands	115	Z17	18 58N	155 24W
Kalahari Desert Southern Africa	109	J3	23 30S	23 00E
Kalamáta Greece	89	J2	37 02N	22 07E
Kalamazoo Michigan USA	71	J5	42 17N	85 36W
Kalambo Falls Tanzania/Zambia	109	L6	8 35S	31 13E
Kalat Pakistan	98	B5	29 01N	66 38E
Kalémié CDR	109	K6	5 57S	29 10E
Kalgoorlie Aust.	110	C3	30 49S	121 29E
Kalimantan *admin.* Indonesia	103	E3	0 00	115 00E
Kalindri *r.* India	99	J10	25 30N	88 00E
Kaliningrad Russia	88	H11	54 40N	20 30E
Kaliningrad *admin.* Russia	88	H11	54 40N	21 00E
Kalispell Montana USA	70	D6	48 12N	114 19W
Kalisz Poland	88	G9	51 46N	18 02E
Kalmar Sweden	88	F12	56 39N	16 20E
Kalni *r.* Bangladesh	99	L10	24 45N	91 15E
Kalomo Zambia	109	K4	17 02S	26 29E
Kaluga Russia	94	F7	54 31N	36 16E
Kalundborg Denmark	88	C11	55 42N	11 06E
Kama *r.* Russia	94	H8	57 00N	55 00E
Kamaishi Japan	102	D2	39 18N	141 52E
Kamarān *i.* Yemen	96	D2	15 21N	42 40E
Kambara *i.* Fiji	114	V15	18 57S	178 58W
Kamchatka *p.* Russia	95	T7	57 30N	160 00E
Kamchatka Bay Russia	95	U7	55 00N	164 00E
Kamchiya *r.* Bulgaria	89	L5	43 00N	27 00E
Kamensk-Ural'skiy Russia	94	J8	56 29N	61 49E
Kamet *mt.* India	98	D6	30 55N	79 36E
Kamina CDR	109	K6	8 46S	25 00E
Kampala Uganda	108	L8	0 19N	32 35E
Kâmpóng Cham Cambodia	103	D6	11 59N	105 26E
Kâmpóng Chhnăng Cambodia	103	C6	12 16N	104 39E
Kam Tin HK China	100	B2	22 26N	114 04E
Kam'yanets'-Podil's'kyy Ukraine	88	L8	48 40N	26 36E
Kamyshin Russia	94	G7	50 05N	45 24E
Kananga CDR	109	J6	5 53S	22 26E
Kanazawa Japan	102	C2	36 35N	136 38E
Kanbe Myanmar	103	B7	16 45N	96 04E
Kandahār Afghanistan	97	J5	31 35N	65 45E
Kandalaksha Russia	94	F10	67 09N	32 31E
Kandavu *i.* Fiji	114	U15	19 10S	178 30E
Kandavu Passage *sd.* Fiji	114	T15	18 50S	178 00E
Kandi Benin	108	E10	11 05N	2 59E
Kandla India	98	C4	23 03N	70 11E
Kandy Sri Lanka	98	E1	7 17N	80 40E
Kane Pennsylvania USA	52	H1	41 41N	78 49W
Kaneohe Hawaiian Islands	115	Y18	21 25N	157 48W
Kangan Iran	97	F4	27 51N	52 07E
Kangar Malaysia	103	C5	6 27N	100 11E
Kangaroo Island Aust.	110	F2	35 50S	137 50E
Kangnung South Korea	101	P6	37 48N	127 52E
Kaniet Islands PNG	110	H9	0 53S	145 30E
Kanin Peninsula Russia	94	G10	68 00N	45 00E
Kankakee Illinois USA	71	J5	41 08N	87 52W
Kankan Guinea	108	C10	10 22N	9 11W
Kannapolis North Carolina USA	71	K4	35 30N	80 36W
Kano Nigeria	108	F10	12 00N	8 31E
Kanoya Japan	102	B1	31 22N	130 50E
Kanpur India	98	E5	26 27N	80 14E
Kansas *state* USA	70/71	G4	38 00N	98 00W
Kansas City Missouri USA	71	H4	39 02N	94 33W
Kansk Russia	95	M8	56 11N	95 48E
Kanye Botswana	109	J3	24 59S	25 19E
Kaohsiung Taiwan	101	N3	22 36N	120 17E
Kaolack Senegal	108	A10	14 09N	16 08W
Kapaa Hawaiian Islands	115	X19	22 04N	159 20W
Kapfenberg Austria	89	E7	47 27N	15 18E
Kapingamarangi Rise Pacific Ocean	114	F8	3 00N	154 00E
Kaposvár Hungary	89	F7	46 21N	17 49E
Kara Bogaz Gol *b.* Turkmenistan	94	H5	42 00N	53 00E
Karabük Turkey	96	B7	41 12N	32 36E
Karachi Pakistan	98	B4	24 51N	67 02E
Karaganda Kazakhstan	94	K6	49 53N	73 07E
Karaginskiy *i.* Russia	95	U8	58 00N	164 00E
Karaj Iran	97	F6	35 48N	50 58E
Karak Jordan	96	N10	31 11N	35 42E
Karakoram Pass China/Kashmir	98	D7	35 33N	77 51E
Kara Kum *geog. reg.* Turkmenistan	94	H4/J4	40 00N	60 00E
Karasburg Namibia	109	H2	28 00S	18 43E
Kara Sea Russia	95	K11	75 00N	70 00E
Karatoya *r.* Bangladesh	99	K10	25 15N	89 15E
Karbalā' Iraq	96	D5	32 37N	44 03E
Karcag Hungary	89	H7	47 19N	20 53E
Kariba Dam Zambia/Zimbabwe	109	K4	16 31S	28 50E
Kariba, Lake Zambia/Zimbabwe	109	K4	17 00S	28 00E
Karibib Namibia	109	H3	21 59S	15 51E
Karimganj India	99	M10	24 50N	92 21E
Karisimbi, Mount Rwanda/CDR	108	K7	1 32S	29 27E
Karlino Poland	88	E11	54 02N	15 52E
Karlovac Croatia	89	E6	45 30N	15 34E
Karlovy Vary Czech Rep.	88	D9	50 13N	12 52E
Karlshamn Sweden	88	E12	56 10N	14 50E
Karlskoga Sweden	88	E13	59 19N	14 33E
Karlskrona Sweden	88	E12	56 10N	15 35E
Karlsruhe Germany	88	B8	49 00N	8 24E
Karlstad Sweden	88	D13	59 24N	13 32E
Karnafuli Reservoir Bangladesh	99	M9	22 30N	92 20E
Karnataka *admin.* India	98	D2	14 40N	75 30E
Kárpathos *i.* Greece	89	L1	35 30N	27 12E
Karpenísi Greece	89	H3	38 55N	21 47E
Kars Turkey	96	D7	40 35N	43 05E
Karsakpay Kazakhstan	94	J6	47 47N	66 43E
Karwar India	98	C2	14 50N	74 09E
Kasai *r.* Angola/CDR	108	H7	4 00S	19 00E
Kasama Zambia	109	L5	10 10S	31 11E
Kasaragod India	98	C2	12 30N	74 59E
Kasempa Zambia	109	K5	13 28S	25 48E
Kasese Uganda	108	L8	0 10N	30 06E
Kāshān Iran	97	F5	33 59N	51 35E
Kashi China	100	D6	39 29N	76 02E
Kashinatpur Bangladesh	99	K9	23 58N	89 37E
Kashiwazaki Japan	102	C2	37 22N	138 33E
Kásos *i.* Greece	89	L1	35 20N	26 55E
Kassala Sudan	108	M11	15 24N	36 30E
Kassel Germany	88	B9	51 18N	9 30E
Kastamonu Turkey	96	B7	41 22N	33 47E
Kastoriá Greece	89	H4	40 33N	21 15E
Kasur Pakistan	98	C6	31 07N	74 30E
Kataba Zambia	109	K4	16 02S	25 03E
Katchall Island India	99	G1	7 57N	93 22E
Kateríni Greece	89	J4	40 15N	22 30E
Katha Myanmar	100	H3	24 11N	96 20E
Katherine Aust.	110	E7	14 29S	132 20E
Kathiawar *p.* India	98	C4	21 10N	71 00E
Kathmandu Nepal	99	F5	27 42N	85 19E
Katmai National Park Alaska USA	40	D5/E5	58 15N	155 00W
Katowice Poland	88	G9	50 15N	18 59E
Katrineholm Sweden	88	F13	58 59N	16 15E
Katsina Nigeria	108	F10	13 00N	7 32E
Katsina Ala Nigeria	108	F9	7 10N	9 30E
Kattegat *sd.* Denmark/Sweden	88	C12	57 00N	11 00E
Kauai *i.* Hawaiian Islands	115	X18	22 00N	159 30W
Kauai Channel *sd.* Hawaiian Islands	115	X18	21 45N	158 50W
Kaula *i.* Hawaiian Islands	115	W18	21 35N	160 40W
Kaulakahi Channel *sd.* Hawaiian Islands	115	X18	21 58N	159 50W
Kaunas Lithuania	88	J11	54 52N	23 55E
Kaura Namoda Nigeria	108	F10	12 39N	6 38E
Kau Sai Chau *i.* HK China	100	C2	22 22N	114 19E
Kau Yi Chau *i.* HK China	100	B1	22 17N	114 04E
Kavajë Albania	89	G4	41 11N	19 33E
Kavála Greece	89	K4	40 56N	24 25E
Kavaratti India	98	C2	10 33N	72 39E
Kawagoe Japan	102	C2	35 55N	139 30E
Kawaihae Hawaiian Islands	115	Z18	20 02N	155 05W
Kawasaki Japan	102	C2	35 30N	139 45E
Kawerau NZ	111	F5	38 05S	176 42E
Kaya Burkina	108	D10	13 04N	1 09W
Kayes Mali	108	B10	14 26N	11 28W
Kayseri Turkey	96	C6	38 42N	35 28E
Kazach'ye Russia	95	R11	70 46N	136 15E
KAZAKHSTAN	94	H6/J6		
Kazakh Upland Kazakhstan	94	K6	47 00N	75 00E
Kazan' Russia	94	G8	55 45N	49 10E
Kazanlŭk Bulgaria	89	K5	42 37N	25 23E
Kazatin Ukraine	88	M8	49 41N	28 49E
Kāzerūn Iran	97	F4	29 35N	51 40E
Kazym *r.* Russia	94	J9	63 00N	67 30E
Kéa *i.* Greece	89	K2	37 00N	24 00E
Kearney Nebraska USA	70	G5	40 42N	99 04W
Kearny New Jersey USA	73	H2	40 45N	74 07W
Kecskemét Hungary	89	G7	46 56N	19 43E
Kediri Indonesia	103	E2	7 45S	112 01E
Keene New Hampshire USA	73	D3	42 56N	72 17W
Keetmanshoop Namibia	109	H2	26 36S	18 08E
Kefallonia *i.* Greece	89	H3	38 00N	20 00E
Kei Ling Ha Hoi *b.* HK China	100	C2	22 26N	114 17E
K'elafo Ethiopia	108	N9	5 37N	44 10E
Kelkit *r.* Turkey	96	C7	40 20N	37 40E
Kelseyville California USA	72	B4	38 58N	122 50W
Kelso California USA	72	F2	35 01N	115 39W
Kemerovo Russia	95	L8	55 25N	86 05E
Kemp Land *geog. reg.* Antarctica	117		65 00S	60 00E
Kempten Germany	88	C7	47 44N	10 19E
Kenai Fjords National Park Alaska USA	40	E5/F5	60 00N	150 00W
Kendal UK	86	D11	54 20N	2 45W
Kendari Indonesia	103	G3	3 57S	122 36E
Kenema Sierra Leone	108	B9	7 57N	11 11W
Kengtung Myanmar	101	H3	21 15N	99 40E
Keningau Malaysia	103	F5	5 21N	116 11E
Kénitra Morocco	108	C14	34 20N	6 34W
Kenmare North Dakota USA	47	F1	48 40N	101 59W
Kennebec River Maine USA	53	S5	45 10N	69 42W
Kennebunk Maine USA	73	E3	43 24N	70 31W
Kennedy Town HK China	100	B1	22 17N	114 07E
Kenosha Wisconsin USA	71	J5	42 34N	87 50W
Kentucky *state* USA	71	J4	37 00N	85 00W
Kentwood Michigan USA	51	J2	42 54N	85 35W
KENYA	108	M7		
Kenya, Mount Kenya	108	L13	0 10S	37 19E
Kepulauan Anambas *is.* Indonesia	103	D4	3 00N	106 20E
Kepulauan Aru *is.* Indonesia	103	J2	6 00S	134 30E
Kepulauan Babar *is.* Indonesia	103	H2	7 50S	129 30E
Kepulauan Batu *is.* Indonesia	103	B3	0 18S	98 29E
Kepulauan Kai *is.* Indonesia	103	J2	5 30S	132 30E
Kepulauan Lingga *is.* Indonesia	103	C3	0 10S	104 30E
Kepulauan Mentawai *is.* Indonesia	103	B3	2 00S	99 00E
Kepulauan Obi *is.* Indonesia	103	H3	1 30S	127 30E
Kepulauan Riau *is.* Indonesia	103	C4	0 30N	104 30E
Kepulauan Sangir *is.* Indonesia	103	H4	3 00N	125 30E
Kepulauan Sula *is.* Indonesia	103	G3	1 50S	124 50E
Kepulauan Tanimbar *is.* Indonesia	103	J2	7 30S	131 30E
Kerala *admin.* India	98	D1/D2	10 10N	76 30E
Kerema PNG	110	H8	7 59S	145 46E
Keren Eritrea	108	M11	15 46N	38 30E
Kerguelen Plateau Indian Ocean	113	G1	55 00S	80 00E
Kérkyra *i.* Greece	89	G3	39 00N	19 00E
Kermadec Islands Pacific Ocean	114	J5	30 00S	178 30W
Kermadec Trench Pacific Ocean	114	J4	33 00S	177 00W
Kermān Iran	97	G5	30 18N	57 05E
Kermānshāh Iran	97	E5	34 19N	47 04E
Kern *r.* California USA	72	D2	36 00N	118 28W
Kerrville Texas USA	70	G3	30 03N	99 09W
Kerulen *r.* Mongolia	101	L8	47 30N	112 30E
Ket' *r.* Russia	95	L8	58 30N	87 00E
Ketapang Indonesia	103	E3	1 50S	110 00E
Ketchikan Alaska USA	42	E4	55 25N	131 40W
Kętrzyn Poland	88	H10	54 05N	21 24E
Kettle Creek *r.* Pennsylvania USA	52	J1	41 30N	77 40W
Keuka Lake New York USA	53	J2	42 30N	77 10W
Kevin Montana USA	46	G1	48 45N	111 57W
Keweenaw Bay Michigan USA	51	G4	47 05N	88 15W
Keweenaw Peninsula Michigan USA	71	J6	47 00N	88 00W
Key West Florida USA	71	K1	24 34N	81 48W
Khabarovsk Russia	95	R6	48 32N	135 08E
Khalig el Tîna Egypt	109	T4	31 08N	32 36E
Khambhat India	98	C4	22 19N	72 39E
Khambhat, Gulf of India	98	C4	20 30N	72 00E
Khammam India	98	E3	17 15N	80 11E
Khānābād Afghanistan	97	J6	36 42N	69 08E
Khānaqīn Iraq	96	E5	34 22N	45 22E
Khandwa India	98	D4	21 49N	76 23E
Khanty-Mansiysk Russia	94	J9	61 01N	69 00E
Khān Yūnis Middle East	96	N10	31 21N	34 18E
Kharagpur India	99	F4	22 23N	87 22E
Kharan Pakistan	98	B5	28 32N	65 26E
Khārg *i.* Iran	97	F4	29 14N	50 20E
Khartoum Sudan	108	L11	15 33N	32 35E
Khāsh Iran	97	H4	28 14N	61 15E
Khash *r.* Afghanistan	97	H5	31 30N	62 30E
Khasi Hills *mts.* India	99	L10	25 34N	91 30E
Khaskovo Bulgaria	89	K4	41 57N	25 32E
Khatanga Russia	95	N11	71 59N	102 31E
Khatanga *r.* Russia	95	N11	72 30N	102 30E
Khaybar Saudi Arabia	96	C4	25 50N	39 00E
Khemisset Morocco	108	C14	33 50N	6 03W
Kheta *r.* Russia	95	M11	71 30N	95 00E
Khilok *r.* Russia	95	N7	51 00N	107 30E
Khiva Uzbekistan	94	J5	41 25N	60 49E
Khmel'nyts'kyy Ukraine	88	L8	49 25N	26 59E
Kholmsk Russia	95	S6	47 02N	142 03E
Khorog Tajikistan	94	K4	37 22N	71 32E
Khorramābād Iran	97	E5	33 29N	48 21E
Khorramshahr Iran	97	E5	30 25N	48 09E
Khotin Ukraine	88	L8	48 30N	26 31E
Khouribga Morocco	108	C14	32 54N	6 57W
Khowai India	99	L10	24 05N	91 36E
Khulna Bangladesh	99	K9	22 49N	89 34E
Khyber Pass Afghanistan/Pakistan	98	C6	34 06N	71 05E
Kibombo CDR	108	K7	3 58S	25 54E
Kiel Germany	88	C11	54 20N	10 08E
Kielce Poland	88	H9	50 51N	20 39E
Kiev Ukraine	88	N9	50 25N	30 30E
Kigali Rwanda	108	L7	1 56S	30 04E
Kigoma Tanzania	108	K7	4 52S	29 36E
Kii-suidō *sd.* Japan	102	B1	34 00N	134 45E
Kikinda Serbia	89	H6	45 50N	20 30E
Kikori PNG	110	G8	7 25S	144 13E
Kikwit CDR	108	H6	5 02S	18 51E
Kilanea Hawaiian Islands	115	X19	22 05N	159 35W
Kilimanjaro *mt.* Tanzania	108	M7	3 04S	37 22E
Kilkenny RoI	86	B10	52 39N	7 15W
Kilkís Greece	89	J4	40 59N	22 52E
Killarney RoI	86	A10	52 03N	9 30W
Killeen Texas USA	71	G3	31 08N	97 44W
Kilmarnock UK	86	C11	55 36N	4 30W
Kilwa Masoko Tanzania	109	M6	8 55S	39 31E
Kimberley RSA	109	J2	28 45S	24 46E
Kimberley Plateau Aust.	110	D6	17 30S	126 00E
Kimchaek North Korea	101	P7	40 41N	129 12E
Kindia Guinea	108	B10	10 03N	12 49W
Kindu CDR	108	K7	3 00S	25 56E
King City California USA	72	C3	36 13N	121 09W
King George Island South Shetland Islands	81	F1	62 00S	58 00W
King Island Aust.	110	G2	40 00S	144 00E
Kingman Arizona USA	70	D4	35 12N	114 02W
Kings *r.* California USA	72	D3	36 32N	119 30W
Kings Canyon National Park California USA	72	D3	36 45N	118 30W
King's Lynn UK	86	F10	52 45N	0 24E
King Sound Aust.	110	C6	16 00S	123 00E
Kings Point *tn.* New York USA	73	J2	40 49N	73 45W
Kingsport Tennessee USA	71	K4	36 33N	82 34W
Kingston Jamaica	75	U13	17 58N	76 48W
Kingston New York USA	73	C2	41 56N	74 00W
Kingston upon Hull UK	86	E10	53 45N	0 20W
Kingstown St. Vincent and The Grenadines	74	R11	13 12N	61 14W
Kingsville Texas USA	71	G2	27 32N	97 53W
Kinkala Congo	108	G7	4 18S	14 49E
Kinleith NZ	111	E5	38 15S	175 56E

Place	Page	Grid	Lat	Long
Kinshasa CDR	108	H7	4 18S	15 18E
Kipili Tanzania	109	L6	7 30S	30 39E
Kirensk Russia	95	N8	57 45N	108 02E
KIRIBATI	114/115	H8/L7		
Kirikkale Turkey	96	B6	39 51N	33 32E
Kiritimati Island Kiribati	115	L8	2 10N	157 00W
Kirkcaldy UK	86	D12	56 07N	3 10W
Kirkcudbright UK	86	C11	54 50N	4 03W
Kirksville Missouri USA	71	H5	40 12N	92 35W
Kirkūk Iraq	96	D6	35 28N	44 26E
Kirkwall UK	86	D13	58 59N	2 58W
Kirov Russia	94	G8	58 00N	49 38E
Kiryū Japan	102	C2	36 26N	139 18E
Kisangani CDR	108	K8	0 33N	25 14E
Kishiwada Japan	102	C1	34 28N	135 22E
Kiskunfélegyháza Hungary	89	G7	46 42N	19 52E
Kiskunhalas Hungary	89	G7	46 26N	19 29E
Kismaayo Somalia	108	N7	0 25S	42 31E
Kisumu Kenya	108	L7	0 08S	34 47E
Kita-Kyūshu Japan	102	B1	33 52N	130 49E
Kitami Japan	102	D3	43 51N	143 54E
Kittery Maine USA	73	E3	43 06N	70 46W
Kitwe Zambia	109	K5	0 08S	30 30E
Kivu, Lake CDR/Rwanda	108	K7	2 00S	29 00E
Kızıl Irmak *r.* Turkey	96	B7	40 30N	34 00E
Kykládes *is.* Greece	89	K2	37 00N	25 00E
Kladno Czech Rep.	88	E9	50 10N	14 07E
Klagenfurt Austria	89	E7	46 38N	14 20E
Klaipėda Lithuania	88	H11	55 43N	21 07E
Klamath *r.* USA	70	B5	42 00N	123 00W
Klamath Falls *tn.* Oregon USA	70	B5	42 14N	121 47W
Klatovy Czech Rep.	88	D8	49 24N	13 17E
Klerksdorp RSA	109	K2	26 52S	26 39E
Klintehamn Sweden	88	G12	57 24N	18 14E
Kłodzko Poland	88	F9	50 28N	16 40E
Klukwan Alaska USA	42	C6	59 25N	135 55W
Klyuchevskaya Sopka *mt.* Russia	95	U8	56 03N	160 38E
Knokke-Heist Belgium	86	G9	51 21N	3 19E
Knoxville Tennessee USA	71	K4	36 00N	83 57W
Kōbe Japan	102	C1	34 40N	135 12E
Koblenz Germany	88	A9	50 21N	7 36E
Kobryn Belarus	88	K10	52 16N	24 22E
Kocaeli Turkey	96	A7	40 47N	29 55E
Koch Bihar India	99	F5	26 18N	89 32E
Kōchi Japan	102	B1	33 33N	133 32E
Kodiak Alaska USA	40	E5	57 46N	152 30W
Kodiak Island Alaska USA	115	L13	57 20N	153 40W
Kodok Sudan	108	L9	9 51N	32 07E
Koforidua Ghana	108	D9	6 01N	0 12W
Kōfu Japan	102	C2	35 42N	138 34E
Kohat Pakistan	98	C6	33 37N	71 30E
Kohima India	99	G5	25 40N	94 08E
Koh-i-Mazar *mt.* Afghanistan	97	J5	32 30N	66 23E
Kokand Uzbekistan	94	K5	40 33N	70 55E
Kokomo Indiana USA	71	J5	40 30N	86 09W
Kokshetau Kazakhstan	94	J7	53 18N	69 25E
Kola Peninsula Russia	94	F10	67 30N	37 30E
Kolar Gold Fields *tn.* India	98	D2	12 54N	78 16E
Kolding Denmark	88	B11	55 29N	9 30E
Kolguyev *i.* Russia	94	G10	69 00N	49 30E
Kolhapur India	98	C3	16 40N	74 20E
Kolin Czech Rep.	88	E9	50 02N	15 11E
Kolka Latvia	88	J12	57 44N	22 27E
Kolkata India	99	F4	22 30N	88 20E
Kolobrzeg Poland	88	E11	54 10N	15 35E
Kolomyya Ukraine	88	K8	48 31N	25 00E
Kolosib India	99	M10	24 05N	92 50E
Kolpashevo Russia	95	L8	58 21N	82 59E
Kolwezi CDR	109	K5	10 45S	25 25E
Kolyma *r.* Russia	95	T10	66 30N	152 00E
Kolyma Lowland Russia	95	T10	69 00N	155 00E
Kolyma Range *mts.* Russia	95	T9	63 00N	160 00E
Komandorskiye Ostrova *is.* Russia	114	G13	60 00N	175 00W
Komárno Slovakia	88	G7	47 46N	18 05E
Komatsu Japan	102	C2	36 25N	136 27E
Komotiní Greece	89	K4	41 06N	25 25E
Kömpóng Saôm Cambodia	103	C6	10 38N	103 28E
Komsomol'sk-na-Amure Russia	95	R7	50 32N	136 59E
Kondūz Afghanistan	97	J6	36 45N	68 51E
Kongolo CDR	108	K6	5 20S	27 00E
Kongsvinger Norway	88	C14	60 12N	12 01E
Konin Poland	88	G10	52 12N	18 12E
Konosha Russia	94	G9	60 58N	40 08E
Konstanz Germany	88	B7	47 40N	9 10E
Konya Turkey	96	B6	37 51N	32 30E
Koocanusa, Lake Montana USA	43	N1	48 55N	115 10W
Koper Slovenia	89	D6	45 31N	13 44E
Kopychintsy Ukraine	88	K8	49 10N	25 58E
Korçë Albania	89	H4	40 38N	20 44E
Korčula *i.* Croatia	89	F5	43 00N	17 00E
Korea Bay China/North Korea	101	N6	39 00N	124 00E
Korea Strait Japan/South Korea	101	P5/Q6	33 00N	129 00E
Korhogo Côte d'Ivoire	108	C9	9 22N	5 31W
Korinthiakós Kólpos *g.* Greece	89	J3	38 00N	22 00E
Kórinthos Greece	89	J2	37 56N	22 55E
Kōriyama Japan	102	D2	37 23N	140 22E
Korla China	100	F7	41 48N	86 10E
Koro *i.* Fiji	114	U16	17 20S	179 25E
Koro Sea Fiji	114	U16	17 35S	180 00
Korosten' Ukraine	88	M9	51 00N	28 30E
Korsakov Russia	95	S6	46 36N	142 50E
Kortrijk Belgium	86	G9	50 50N	3 17E
Koryak Range *mts.* Russia	95	V9	62 00N	170 00E
Kós *i.* Greece	89	L2	36 45N	27 10E
Kosciusko Island Alaska USA	42	D4	56 00N	133 45W
Kosciusko, Mount Aust.	110	H2	36 28S	148 17E
Košice Slovakia	88	H8	48 44N	21 15E
KOSOVO	89	H5		
Kosovska Mitrovica Kosovo	89	H5	42 54N	20 52E
Kosti Sudan	108	L10	13 11N	32 28E
Kostroma Russia	94	G8	57 46N	40 59E
Koszalin Poland	88	F11	54 10N	16 10E
Kota India	98	D5	25 11N	75 58E
Kota Bharu Malaysia	103	C5	6 08N	102 14E
Kota Kinabalu Malaysia	103	F5	5 59N	116 04E
Kotlas Russia	94	G9	61 15N	46 35E
Kotri Pakistan	98	B5	25 22N	68 18E
Kotto *r.* CAR	108	J9	7 00N	22 30E
Kotuy *r.* Russia	95	N10	67 30N	102 00E
Koudougou Burkina	108	D10	12 15N	2 23W
Koulamoutou Gabon	108	G7	1 12S	12 29E
Koulikoro Mali	108	C10	12 55N	7 31W
Koumra Chad	108	H9	8 56N	17 32E
Kourou French Guiana	80	G15	5 08N	52 37W
Kovel' Ukraine	88	K9	51 12N	24 48E
Kowloon HK China	100	C1	22 19N	114 11E
Kowloon Peak *mt.* HK China	100	C2	22 20N	114 14E
Kowloon Reservoirs HK China	100	B2	22 21N	114 09E
Kowloon Tong HK China	100	C2	22 20N	114 11E
Kozáni Greece	89	H4	40 18N	21 48E
Kpalimé Togo	108	E9	6 55N	0 44E
Kragujevac Serbia	89	H5	44 01N	20 55E
Kraków Poland	88	G9	50 03N	19 55E
Kraljevo Serbia	89	H5	43 44N	20 41E
Kranj Slovenia	89	E7	46 15N	14 20E
Krasnodar Russia	94	F6	45 02N	39 00E
Krasnovodsk Turkmenistan	94	H5	40 01N	53 00E
Krasnoyarsk Russia	95	M8	56 05N	92 46E
Krefeld Germany	88	A9	51 20N	6 32E
Kremenets Ukraine	88	K9	50 05N	25 48E
Krems Austria	88	E8	48 25N	15 36E
Kribi Cameroon	108	F8	2 56N	9 56E
Krishna *r.* India	98	D3	16 00N	77 30E
Krishnanagar India	99	K9	23 25N	88 30E
Kristiansand Norway	86	J13	58 08N	8 01E
Kristianstad Sweden	88	E12	56 02N	14 10E
Kristinehamn Sweden	88	E13	59 17N	14 09E
Kríti *i.* Greece	89	K1	35 00N	25 00E
Krk *i.* Croatia	89	E6	45 00N	14 00E
Krosno Poland	88	J8	49 40N	21 46E
Kruševac Serbia	89	H5	43 34N	21 20E
Kruzof Island Alaska USA	42	C5	57 15N	135 40W
Kuala Lumpur Malaysia	103	C4	3 09N	101 42E
Kuala Terengganu Malaysia	103	C5	5 20N	103 09E
Kuantan Malaysia	103	C4	3 48N	103 19E
Kuching Malaysia	103	E4	1 35N	110 21E
Kuito Angola	109	H5	12 25S	16 56E
Kuiu Island Alaska USA	42	C5/D5	56 45N	134 00W
Kujū-san *mt.* Japan	102	B1	33 07N	131 14E
Kukës Albania	89	H5	42 05N	20 24E
Kuldiga Latvia	88	H12	56 58N	21 58E
Kuma *r.* Russia	94	G5	45 00N	45 00E
Kumagaya Japan	102	C2	36 09N	139 22E
Kumamoto Japan	102	B1	32 50N	130 42E
Kumanovo FYROM	89	H5	42 07N	21 40E
Kumasi Ghana	108	D9	6 45N	1 35W
Kumba Cameroon	108	F8	4 39N	9 26E
Kumbakonam India	98	D2	10 59N	79 24E
Kunar *r.* Afghanistan/Pakistan	97	K6	34 50N	71 05E
Kunashir *i.* Russia	102	E3	44 30N	146 20E
Kundat Malaysia	103	F5	6 54N	116 50E
Kungrad Uzbekistan	94	H5	43 06N	58 54E
Kunlun Shan *mts.* China	100	E6/F6	36 30N	85 00E
Kunming China	101	J4	25 04N	102 41E
Kunsan South Korea	101	P6	35 57N	126 42E
Kununurra Aust.	110	D6	15 42S	128 50E
Kupa *r.* Croatia	89	E6	45 30N	15 00E
Kupang Indonesia	103	G1	10 13S	123 38E
Kupreanof Island Alaska USA	42	D5	56 50N	133 30W
Kurashiki Japan	102	B1	34 36N	133 43E
Kure Japan	102	B1	34 14N	132 32E
Kuressaare Estonia	88	J13	59 22N	28 40E
Kureyka *r.* Russia	95	M10	67 30N	91 00E
Kurgan Russia	94	J8	55 30N	65 20E
Kuria Muria Islands Oman	97	G2	17 30N	56 00E
Kurigram Bangladesh	99	K10	25 49N	89 39E
Kuril Islands Russia	95	T6	50 00N	155 00E
Kuril Ridge Pacific Ocean	114	F12	47 50N	152 00E
Kuril Trench Pacific Ocean	114	F12	45 40N	154 00E
Kurnool India	98	D3	15 51N	78 01E
Kursk Russia	94	F7	51 45N	36 14E
Kurskiy Zaliv *g.* Russia	88	H11	55 00N	21 00E
Kurtalan Turkey	96	D6	37 55N	41 44E
Kurume Japan	102	B1	33 20N	130 29E
Kushiro Japan	102	D3	42 58N	144 24E
Kustanay Kazakhstan	94	J7	53 15N	63 40E
Kütahya Turkey	96	A6	39 25N	29 56E
Kutno Poland	88	G10	52 13N	19 20E
Kutubdia Island Bangladesh	99	L8	21 50N	91 52E
Kuvango Angola	109	H5	14 27S	16 20E
KUWAIT	97	E4		
Kuwait Kuwait	97	E4	29 20N	48 00E
Kuytun China	100	E7	44 30N	85 00E
Kwai Chung HK China	100	B2	22 22N	114 07E
Kwangju South Korea	101	P6	35 07N	126 52E
Kwango *r.* CDR	109	H6	6 00S	17 00E
Kwekwe Zimbabwe	109	K4	18 55S	29 49E
Kwilu *r.* CDR	109	H6	6 00S	19 00E
Kwun Tong HK China	100	C1	22 18N	114 13E
Kwu Tung HK China	100	B3	22 31N	114 06E
Kyburz California USA	72	C4	38 47N	120 19W
Kyle of Lochalsh UK	86	C12	57 17N	5 43W
Kyoga, Lake Uganda	108	L8	2 00N	34 00E
Kyōga-misaki *c.* Japan	102	C2	35 48N	135 12E
Kyōto Japan	102	C2	35 02N	135 45E
Kyparissiakós Kólpos *g.* Greece	89	H2	37 00N	21 00E
KYRGYZSTAN	94	K5		
Kythira *i.* Greece	89	J2	36 00N	23 00E
Kýthnos *i.* Greece	89	K2	37 25N	24 25E
Kyūshū *i.* Japan	102	B1	32 20N	131 00E
Kyushu-Palau Ridge Pacific Ocean	114	D9	15 00N	135 00E
Kyustendil Bulgaria	89	J5	42 26N	22 40E
Kyzyl Russia	95	M7	51 45N	94 28E
Kyzyl Kum *d.* Asia	94	J5	43 00N	65 00E
Kzylorda Kazakhstan	94	J5	44 25N	65 28E

L

Place	Page	Grid	Lat	Long
Laascaanood Somalia	108	P9	8 35N	46 55E
Laâyoune Western Sahara	108	B13	27 10N	13 11W
la Baule-Escoublac Fr.	87	D7	47 18N	2 22W
Labé Guinea	108	B10	11 17N	12 11W
Labrador Basin Atlantic Ocean	116	C12	58 00N	50 00W
Lábrea Brazil	80	E12	7 20S	64 46W
La Brea Trinidad and Tobago	75	V15	10 14N	61 37W
Labytnangi Russia	94	J10	66 43N	66 28E
Lac Alaotra *l.* Madagascar	109	P4	17 30S	54 00E
Laccadive Islands India	98	C1/C2	11 00N	72 00E
La Ceiba Honduras	74	G3	15 45N	86 45W
Lac Fitri *l.* Chad	108	H10	13 00N	17 30E
Lachlan *r.* Aust.	110	H3	34 00S	145 00E
La Chorrera Panama	75	Y1	8 51N	79 46W
Lackawanna New York USA	54	D1	42 49N	78 49W
Lac Léman *l.* Switz.	87	J7	46 20N	6 20E
Lac Mai-Ndombe *l.* CDR	108	H7	2 00S	18 20E
La Coruña Sp.	87	A5	43 22N	8 24W
La Crosse Wisconsin USA	71	H5	43 48N	91 04W
Lacul Razim *l.* Romania	89	M6	45 00N	29 00E
Ladakh Range *mts.* Kashmir	98	D6	34 30N	78 30E
Ladozhskoye Ozero *l.* Russia	94	F9	61 00N	30 00E
Ladysmith RSA	109	K2	28 34S	29 47E
Ladysmith Wisconsin USA	51	F3	45 28N	91 06W
Lae PNG	110	H8	6 43S	147 01E
La Esmeralda Venezuela	80	D14	3 11N	65 33W
Lafayette Indiana USA	71	J5	40 25N	86 54W
Lafayette Louisiana USA	71	H3	30 12N	92 18W
La Fé Cuba	75	H4	22 02N	84 15W
Laghouat Algeria	108	E14	33 49N	2 55E
Lago Argentino *l.* Argentina	81	C3	50 10S	72 30W
Lago de Chapala *l.* Mexico	74	D4	20 05N	103 00W
Lago de Maracaibo *l.* Venezuela	80	C15	9 50N	71 30W
Lago de Nicaragua *l.* Nicaragua	75	G2	11 50N	86 00W
Lago de Poopó *l.* Bolivia	80	D10	18 30S	67 20W
Lago di Bolsena *l.* Italy	89	C5	42 00N	12 00E
Lago di Como *l.* Italy	89	B6	46 00N	9 00E
Lago di Garda *l.* Italy	89	C6	45 00N	10 00E
Lago Maggiore *l.* Italy	89	B6	46 00N	8 00E
Lagos Nigeria	108	E9	6 27N	3 28E
Lagos Port.	87	A2	37 05N	8 40W
Lago Titicaca *l.* Peru/Bolivia	80	C10	16 00S	69 30W
La Grande Oregon USA	70	C6	45 21N	118 05W
La Grange Georgia USA	71	J3	33 02N	85 02W
La Guaira Venezuela	80	D16	10 38N	66 55W
Laguna Caratasca *l.* Honduras	75	H3	15 05N	84 00W
Laguna de Perlas *l.* Nicaragua	75	H2	12 30N	83 30W
Laguna Madre *l.* Mexico	74	E4	25 00N	98 00W
Laguna Mar Chiquita *l.* Argentina	81	E7	30 30S	62 30W
Lagunillas Venezuela	80	C16	10 07N	71 16W
Lahaina Hawaiian Islands	115	Y18	20 23N	156 40W
Lahontan Reservoir Nevada USA	72	D4	39 20N	119 08W
Lahore Pakistan	98	C6	31 34N	74 22E
Lai Chi Wo HK China	100	C3	22 32N	114 15E
Lajes Brazil	81	G8	27 48S	50 20W
La Junta Colorado USA	70	F4	37 59N	103 34W
Lake Alpine *tn.* California USA	72	D4	38 30N	120 00W
Lake Charles *tn.* Louisiana USA	71	H3	30 13N	93 13W
Lake City *tn.* Michigan USA	51	J3	44 19N	85 13W
Lake Gogebic Michigan USA	51	G4	46 30N	89 30W
Lake Isabella *tn.* California USA	72	D2	35 37N	118 28W
Lakeland Florida USA	71	K2	28 02N	81 59W
Lakemba Passage *sd.* Fiji	114	V16	18 10S	179 00W
Lake Orion *tn.* Michigan USA	52	C2	42 47N	83 13W
Lakeport California USA	70	B4	39 04N	122 56W
Lake Success California USA	72	D3	36 07N	118 55W
Lake Timsâh Egypt	109	S3	30 34N	32 18E
Lakeview Oregon USA	70	B5	42 13N	120 21W
Lake View *tn.* New York USA	54	D1	42 43N	78 56W
Lakshadweep *admin.* India	98	C1/C2	9 30N	73 00E
La Línea de la Concepción Sp.	87	C2	36 10N	5 21W
Lalitpur India	98	D4	24 42N	78 24E
Lalmanir Hat Bangladesh	99	K10	25 51N	89 34E
La Maddalena Italy	89	B4	41 13N	9 25E
La Mancha *admin.* Sp.	87	D3	39 10N	2 45W
Lamar Colorado USA	70	F4	38 04N	102 37W
Lambaréné Gabon	108	G7	0 41S	10 13E
Lambasa Fiji	114	U16	16 25S	179 24E
Lambert Glacier Antarctica	117		73 00S	70 00E
Lambertville New Jersey USA	73	C2	40 22N	74 57W
Lamego Port.	87	B4	41 05N	7 49W
La Mesa California USA	72	E1	32 45N	117 00W
Lamía Greece	89	J3	38 55N	22 26E
Lamma Island HK China	100	B1	22 12N	114 08E
Lampazos Mexico	74	D5	27 00N	100 30W
Lam Tei Hong Kong China	100	A2	22 25N	113 59E
Lamu Kenya	108	N7	2 17S	40 54E
Lanai *i.* Hawaiian Islands	115	Y18	20 50N	156 55W
Lanai City Hawaiian Islands	115	Y18	20 50N	156 56W
Lancang Jiang *r.* China	101	H4/H5	30 00N	98 00E
Lancaster UK	86	D11	54 03N	2 48W
Lancaster California USA	70	C3	34 42N	118 09W
Lancaster Ohio USA	71	K4	39 43N	82 37W
Lancaster Pennsylvania USA	71	L5	40 01N	76 19W
Land's End *c.* UK	86	C9	50 03N	5 44W
Landshut Germany	88	D8	48 31N	12 10E
Landskrona Sweden	88	D12	55 53N	12 50E
Langdon North Dakota USA	49	C1	48 50N	98 25W
Langon Fr.	87	E6	44 33N	0 14W
Langres Fr.	86	H7	47 53N	5 20E
Lannion Fr.	86	D8	48 44N	3 27W
L'Anse Michigan USA	51	G4	46 45N	88 26W
Lansing Michigan USA	71	K5	42 44N	85 34W
Lantau Channel HK China	100	A1	22 11N	113 52E
Lantau Island HK China	100	A1	22 15N	113 56E
Lantau Peak *mt.* HK China	100	A1	22 15N	113 55E
Lanzarote *i.* Canary Islands	108	B13	29 00N	13 38W
Lanzhou China	101	J6	36 01N	103 45E
Laoag Philippines	103	G7	18 14N	120 36E
Lao Cai Vietnam	101	J3	22 30N	103 57E
Laon Fr.	86	G8	49 34N	3 37E
La Oroya Peru	80	B11	11 36S	75 54W
LAOS	103	C7/D7		
La Paz Bolivia	80	D10	16 30S	68 10W
La Paz Mexico	74	B4	24 10N	110 17W
Lapeer Michigan USA	51	K2	43 03N	83 19W
La Pesca Mexico	74	E4	23 46N	97 47W
La Plata Argentina	81	F6	34 52S	57 55W
Laptev Sea Arctic Ocean	117		76 00N	125 00E
Laptev Strait Russia	95	S11	73 00N	141 00E
L'Aquila Italy	89	D5	42 22N	13 24E
Lār Iran	97	F4	27 42N	54 19E
Larache Morocco	108	C15	35 12N	6 10W
Laramie Wyoming USA	70	E5	41 20N	105 38W
Lärbro Sweden	88	G12	57 47N	18 50E
Laredo Texas USA	70	G2	27 32N	99 22W
La Rioja Argentina	81	D8	29 26S	66 50W
Lárisa Greece	89	J3	39 38N	22 25E
Larkana Pakistan	98	B5	27 32N	68 18E
Larnaca Cyprus	96	B5	34 54N	33 29E
Larne UK	86	C11	54 51N	5 49W
la Rochelle Fr.	87	E7	46 10N	1 10W
la Roche-sur-Yon Fr.	87	E7	46 40N	1 25W
La Romana Dom. Rep.	75	L3	18 27N	68 57W
Larsen Ice Shelf Antarctica	117		67 00S	62 00W
Las Cruces New Mexico USA	70	E3	32 18N	106 47W
La Serena Chile	81	C8	29 54S	71 18W
la Seyne-sur-Mer Fr.	87	H5	43 06N	5 53E
Lashio Myanmar	101	H3	22 58N	97 48E
Las Marismas *geog. reg.* Sp.	87	B2/C2	36 55N	6 00W
Las Palmas Canary Islands	108	A13	28 08N	15 27W
La Spézia Italy	89	B6	44 07N	9 48E
Las Vegas Nevada USA	70	C4	36 10N	115 10W
Las Vegas New Mexico USA	70	E4	35 36N	105 15W
Latacunga Ecuador	80	B13	0 58S	78 36W
Latakia Syria	96	C6	35 31N	35 47E
Latina Italy	89	D4	41 28N	12 53E
Latur India	98	D3	18 24N	76 34E
LATVIA	88	J12		
Lau Fau Shan HK China	100	A2	22 28N	113 59E
Launceston Aust.	110	H1	41 25S	147 07E
Laurel Mississippi USA	71	J3	31 41N	89 09W
Laurie Island South Orkney Islands	81	J1	61 30S	46 00W
Lausanne Switz.	87	J7	46 32N	6 39E
Laut *i.* Indonesia	103	F3	4 40S	116 00E
Lautoka Fiji	114	T16	17 36S	177 28E
Laval Fr.	86	E8	48 04N	0 45W
La Vega Dom. Rep.	75	K3	19 15N	70 33W
Laverton Aust.	110	C4	28 49S	122 25E
La Victoria Venezuela	80	D16	10 16N	67 21W
Lawrence Kansas USA	71	G4	38 58N	95 15W
Lawrence Massachusetts USA	73	E3	42 41N	71 11W
Lawrence Park *tn.* Pennsylvania USA	52	F2	42 08N	80 02W
Lawton Oklahoma USA	71	G3	34 36N	98 25W
Laylá Saudi Arabia	97	E3	22 16N	46 45E
Laysan *i.* Hawaiian Islands	114	J10	25 46N	171 44W
Laytonville California USA	72	B4	39 41N	123 29W
LEBANON	96	N11/P12		
Lebanon Missouri USA	71	H4	37 40N	92 40W
Lebanon Pennsylvania USA	73	B2	40 23N	76 20W
Lebu Chile	81	C6	37 38S	73 43W
Lecce Italy	89	G4	40 21N	18 11E
Leeds UK	86	E10	53 50N	1 35W
Leeuwarden Neths.	86	H10	53 12N	5 48E
Leeuwin, Cape Aust.	110	B3	34 24S	115 09E
Lee Vining California USA	72	D3	37 58N	119 09W
Leeward Islands Lesser Antilles	75	M3	17 30N	64 00W

Lefkáda *i.* Greece 89 H3 38 45N 20 40E
Le François Martinique 74 R12 14 37N 60 54W
Leganés Sp. 87 D4 40 20N 3 46WE
Legnica Poland 88 F9 51 12N 16 10E
le Havre Fr. 86 F8 49 30N 0 06E
Leicester UK 86 E10 52 38N 1 05W
Leiden Neths. 86 H10 52 10N 4 30E
Leipzig Germany 88 D9 51 20N 12 25E
Leiria Port. 87 A3 39 45N 8 49W
Leivadiá Greece 89 J3 38 26N 22 53E
Leizhou Bandao *p.* China 101 L3 21 00N 110 00E
Lek *r.* Neths. 86 H9 51 48N 4 47E
le Mans Fr. 86 F7 48 00N 0 12E
Lemoore California USA 72 D3 36 18N 119 47W
Lena *r.* Russia 95 Q10 70 00N 125 00E
Leninogorsk Kazakhstan 95 L7 50 23N 83 32E
Leninsk-Kuznetskiy Russia 95 L7 54 44N 86 13E
Lens Fr. 86 G9 50 26N 2 50E
Lensk Russia 95 P9 60 48N 114 55E
Leoben Austria 89 E7 47 23N 15 06E
León Mexico 74 D4 21 10N 101 42W
León Nicaragua 74 G2 12 24N 86 52W
León Sp. 87 C5 42 35N 5 34W
Leon *r.* Texas USA 71 G3 32 00N 98 00W
Leonora Aust. 110 C4 28 54S 121 20E
le Puy Fr. 87 G6 45 03N 3 53E
Léré Chad 108 G9 9 41N 14 17E
Le Roy New York USA 52 J2 42 59N 77 59W
Lerwick UK 86 E14 60 09N 1 09W
Les Abymes Guadeloupe 74 Q9 16 15N 61 31W
Les Cayes Haiti 75 K3 18 15N 73 46W
Leskovac Serbia 89 J5 43 00N 21 57E
LESOTHO 109 K2
les Sables-d'Olonne Fr. 87 E7 46 30N 1 47W
Lesser Antilles *is.* W. Indies 75 L2 18 00N 65 00W
Lésvos *i.* Greece 89 L3 39 00N 26 00E
Leszno Poland 88 F9 51 51N 16 35E
Leticia Col. 80 C13 4 09S 69 57W
le Tréport Fr. 86 F9 50 04N 1 22E
Leuven Belgium 86 H9 50 53N 4 42E
Lévêque, Cape Aust. 110 C6 16 25S 122 55E
Levice Slovakia 88 G8 48 14N 18 35E
Levin NZ 111 E4 40 37S 175 17E
Levuka Fiji 114 U16 17 42N 178 50E
Lewis *i.* UK 86 B12 58 15N 6 30W
Lewiston Idaho USA 70 C6 46 25N 117 00W
Lewiston Maine USA 71 M5 44 08N 70 14W
Lewiston New York USA 51 M2 43 10N 79 02W
Lewistown Montana USA 70 E6 47 04N 109 26W
Lewistown Pennsylvania USA 73 B2 40 36N 77 34W
Lexington Kentucky USA 71 K4 38 03N 84 30W
Lexington Heights *tn.* Michigan USA 52 D3 43 15N 82 32W
Leyte *i.* Philippines 103 G6/H6 11 00N 125 00E
Lezhë Albania 89 G4 41 47N 19 39E
Lhasa China 100 G4 29 41N 91 10E
Lhaze China 100 F4 29 08N 87 43E
Lianyungang China 101 M5 34 37N 119 10E
Liaoyang China 101 N7 41 16N 123 12E
Liaoyuan China 101 P7 42 53N 125 10E
Libby Montana USA 43 N1 48 25N 115 33W
Libenge CDR 108 H8 3 39N 18 39E
Liberal Kansas USA 70 F4 37 03N 100 56W
Liberec Czech Rep. 88 E9 50 48N 15 05E
LIBERIA 108 B9/C9
Liberty New York USA 73 C2 41 48N 74 44W
Libourne Fr. 87 E6 44 55N 0 14W
Libreville Gabon 108 F8 0 30N 9 25E
LIBYA 108 G13
Libyan Desert North Africa 108 J13 25 00N 25 00E
Libyan Plateau Egypt 108 K14 31 00N 26 00E
Licata Italy 89 D2 37 07N 13 57E
Lichinga Mozambique 109 M5 13 19S 35 13E
Lidköping Sweden 88 D13 58 30N 13 10E
LIECHTENSTEIN 87 K7
Liège Belgium 86 H9 50 38N 5 35E
Lienz Austria 89 D7 46 51N 12 50E
Liepaja Latvia 88 H12 56 30N 21 00E
Ligurian Sea Mediterranean Sea 89 B5 44 00N 9 00E
Lihue Hawaiian Islands 115 X18 21 59N 159 23W
Likasi CDR 109 K5 10 58S 26 47E
Lille Fr. 86 G9 50 39N 3 05E
Lilongwe Malawi 109 L5 13 58S 33 49E
Lim *r.* Europe 89 G5 43 00N 19 00E
Lima Peru 80 B11 12 04S 77 03W
Lima Ohio USA 71 K5 40 43N 84 06W
Lima *r.* Port. 87 A4 42 00N 8 30W
Limassol Cyprus 96 B5 34 04N 33 03E
Limay *r.* Argentina 81 D6 39 30S 69 30W
Limbe Cameroon 108 F8 3 58N 9 10E
Limerick RoI 86 A10 52 04N 8 38W
Limfjorden *sd.* Denmark 88 B12 57 00N 8 50E
Límnos *i.* Greece 89 K3 39 00N 25 00E
Limoges Fr. 87 F6 45 50N 1 15E
Limón Costa Rica 75 H2 10 00N 83 01W
Limoux Fr. 87 G5 43 03N 2 13E
Limpopo *r.* Southern Africa 109 L3 22 30S 32 00E
Linares Mexico 74 E4 24 54N 99 38W
Linares Sp. 87 D3 38 05N 3 38W
Lincoln UK 86 E10 53 14N 0 33W
Lincoln Nebraska USA 71 G5 40 49N 96 41W
Linden Guyana 80 F15 5 59N 58 19W
Linden New Jersey USA 73 H1 40 37N 74 13W
Line Islands Kiribati 115 L7 0 00 155 00W
Linhares Brazil 80 K10 19 22S 40 04W
Linköping Sweden 88 E13 58 25N 15 35E
Linton North Dakota USA 70 F6 46 17N 100 14W
Lin Tong Mei HK China 100 B2 22 29N 114 06E
Linxia China 101 J6 35 31N 103 08E
Linz Austria 88 E8 48 19N 14 18E
Lipetsk Russia 94 F7 52 37N 39 36E
Lisbon Port. 87 A3 38 44N 9 08W
Lisburn UK 86 B11 54 31N 6 03W
Lisianski *i.* Hawaiian Islands 114 J10 26 04N 173 58W
Lisieux Fr. 86 F8 49 09N 0 14E
Lismore Aust. 110 J4 28 48S 153 17E
Lităni *r.* Lebanon 96 N11 33 35N 35 40E
Lithgow Aust. 110 J3 33 30S 150 09E
LITHUANIA 88 J11
Little Aden Yemen 96 D1 12 47N 44 55E
Little Andaman *i.* Andaman Islands 99 G2 10 30N 92 40E
Little Bitter Lake Egypt 109 T2 30 14N 32 33E
Little Colorado *r.* Arizona USA 70 D4 36 00N 111 00W
Little Falls *tn.* Minnesota USA 71 H6 45 58N 94 20W
Little Missouri *r.* USA 70 F6 46 00N 104 00W
Little Nicobar *i.* Nicobar Islands 99 G1 7 00N 94 00E
Little Rock Kansas USA 71 H3 34 42N 92 17W
Little Sioux *r.* USA 71 G5 42 00N 96 00W
Little Snake *r.* USA 70 E5 41 00N 108 00W
Little Traverse Bay Michigan USA 52 A5 45 25N 85 00W
Liuzhou China 101 K3 24 17N 109 15E
Livermore California USA 72 C3 37 40N 121 46W
Liverpool UK 86 D10 53 25N 2 55W
Livingston Montana USA 70 D6 45 40N 110 33W
Livingstone Zambia 109 K4 17 50S 25 53E
Livingston Island South Shetland Islands 81 E1 62 38S 60 30W
Livorno Italy 89 C5 43 33N 10 18E
Liwale Tanzania 109 M6 9 47S 38 00E
Lizard Point UK 86 C8 49 56N 5 13W
Ljubljana Slovenia 89 E7 46 04N 14 30E
Ljungby Sweden 88 D12 56 49N 13 55E
Llanelli UK 86 C9 51 42N 4 10W
Llanos *geog. reg.* Venezuela 80 D15 7 30N 67 30W
Lleida Sp. 87 F4 41 37N 0 38E
Lobatse Botswana 109 K2 25 11S 25 40E
Lobito Angola 109 G5 12 20S 13 34E
Loch Ness *l.* UK 86 C12 57 02N 4 30W
Loch Tay *l.* UK 86 D12 56 31N 4 10W
Lockhart Texas USA 71 G2 29 54N 97 14W
Lock Haven *tn.* Pennsylvania USA 73 B2 41 09N 77 28W
Lockport New York USA 51 M2 43 10N 78 42W
Lod Israel 96 N10 31 57N 34 54E
Lodi California USA 72 C4 38 07N 121 18W
Łodz Poland 88 G9 51 49N 19 28E
Lo Fu Tau *mt.* HK China 100 A1 22 18N 114 00E
Logan Utah USA 70 D5 41 45N 111 50W
Logan, Mount Washington USA 42 H4 48 30N 121 00W
Logone *r.* Chad 108 G10 11 00N 15 00E
Logroño Sp. 87 D5 42 28N 2 26W
Loir *r.* Fr. 87 F7 47 30N 0 35E
Loire *r.* Fr. 87 E7 47 20N 1 20W
Loja Ecuador 80 B13 3 59S 79 16W
Loja Sp. 87 C2 37 10N 4 09W
Lok Ma Chau HK China 100 B3 22 31N 114 05E
Lokoja Nigeria 108 F9 7 49N 6 44E
Lol *r.* Sudan 108 K9 9 00N 28 00E
Lolland *i.* Denmark 88 C11 54 45N 12 20E
Lomami *r.* CDR 108 K6 5 30S 25 30E
Lomblen *i.* Indonesia 103 G2 8 30S 123 30E
Lombok *i.* Indonesia 103 F2 8 30S 116 30E
Lomé Togo 108 E9 6 10N 1 21E
Lomela CDR 108 J7 2 19S 23 15E
Lomela *r.* CDR 108 J7 3 00S 23 00E
Lompoc California USA 72 C2 34 39N 120 27W
Łomza Poland 88 J10 53 11N 22 04E
London UK 86 E9 51 30N 0 10W
Londonderry UK 86 B11 54 59N 7 19W
Londrina Brazil 80 G9 23 18S 51 13W
Lone Pine California USA 72 D3 36 35N 118 04W
Long Beach *tn.* California USA 70 C3 33 47N 118 15W
Long Beach Island New Jersey USA 73 C1 39 40N 74 15W
Long Branch New Jersey USA 71 M5 40 17N 73 59W
Longfellow Mountains Maine USA 53 R5/S5 45 10N 70 00W
Longford RoI 86 B10 53 44N 7 47W
Long Island Bahamas 75 J4/K4 23 20N 75 00W
Long Island New York USA 73 D2 40 43N 73 05W
Long Island City New York USA 73 J2 40 46N 73 55W
Long Island Sound New York USA 73 D2 40 50N 73 05W
Long Lake Maine USA 57 F2 47 14N 68 18W
Longreach Aust. 110 G5 23 30S 144 15E
Longview Texas USA 71 H3 32 20N 94 45W
Longview Washington USA 70 B6 46 08N 122 56W
Longwy Fr. 86 H8 49 32N 5 46E
Lopez, Cape Gabon 108 F7 0 36S 8 45E
Lopez Island Washington USA 42 H4 48 25N 123 05W
Lop Nur *l.* China 100 G7 40 15N 90 20E
Lorain Ohio USA 71 K5 41 28N 82 11W
Lorca Sp. 87 E2 37 40N 1 41W
Lord Howe Rise Pacific Ocean 114 F5 27 30S 162 00E
Lorient Fr. 86 D7 47 45N 3 21W
Los Alamos Mexico USA 70 E4 35 52N 106 19W
Los Angeles Chile 81 C6 37 28S 72 23W
Los Angeles California USA 70 C3 34 00N 118 15W
Los Angeles Aqueduct California USA 72 D2 35 12N 118 08W
Los Banos California USA 72 C3 37 03N 120 53W
Los Gatos California USA 72 C3 37 13N 121 57W
Los Mochis Mexico 74 C5 25 48N 109 00W
Los Teques Venezuela 80 D16 10 25N 67 01W
Lot *r.* Fr. 87 F6 44 35N 1 10E
Louangphrabang Laos 103 C7 19 53N 102 10E
Loubomo Congo 108 G7 4 09S 12 47E
Loudéac Fr. 86 D8 48 11N 2 45W
Lough Corrib *l.* RoI 86 A10 53 10N 9 10W
Lough Derg *l.* RoI 86 A10 52 55N 8 15W
Lough Mask *l.* RoI 86 A10 53 40N 9 30W
Lough Neagh *l.* UK 86 B11 54 35N 6 30W
Lough Ree *l.* RoI 86 B10 53 35N 8 00W
Louisade Archipelago *is.* PNG 110 J7 12 00S 153 00E
Louisiana *state* USA 71 H3 32 00N 92 00W
Louis Trichardt RSA 109 K3 23 01S 29 43E
Louisville Kentucky USA 71 J4 38 13N 85 48W
Lourdes Fr. 87 E5 43 06N 0 02W
Lowell Massachusetts USA 71 M5 42 38N 71 19W
Lower Bay New York USA 73 H1 40 32N 74 04W
Lower Hutt NZ 111 E4 41 13S 174 55E
Lower Lake *tn.* California USA 72 B4 38 55N 122 37W
Lower Lough Erne *l.* UK 86 B11 54 30N 7 45W
Lower Red Lake Minnesota USA 71 H6 48 00N 95 00W
Lowestoft UK 86 F10 52 29N 1 45E
Łowicz Poland 88 G10 52 06N 19 55E
Lo Wu HK China 100 B3 22 32N 114 07E
Lowville New York USA 51 P2 43 47N 75 29W
Loznica Serbia 89 G6 44 31N 19 14E
Lualaba *r.* CDR 108 K7 4 00S 26 30E
Luanda Angola 109 G6 8 50S 13 15E
Luangwa *r.* Zambia 109 L5 12 00S 32 30E
Luanshya Zambia 109 K5 13 09S 28 24E
Luarca Sp. 87 B5 43 33N 6 31W
Luau Angola 109 J5 10 42S 22 12E
Lubango Angola 109 G5 14 55S 13 30E
Lubbock Texas USA 70 F3 33 35N 101 53W
Lübeck Germany 88 C10 53 52N 10 40E
Lubilash *r.* CDR 109 J6 4 00S 24 00E
Lublin Poland 88 J9 51 18N 22 31E
Lubumbashi CDR 109 K5 11 41S 27 29E
Lucena Sp. 87 C2 37 25N 4 29W
Luckenwalde Germany 88 D10 52 05N 13 11E
Lucknow India 98 E5 26 50N 80 54E
Lucusse Angola 109 J5 12 38S 20 52E
Lüderitz Namibia 109 H2 26 38S 15 10E
Ludhiana India 98 D6 30 56N 75 52E
Ludington Michigan USA 51 H2 43 57N 86 26W
Luena Angola 109 H5 11 47S 19 52E
Lufkin Texas USA 71 H3 31 21N 94 47W
Lugo Sp. 87 B5 43 00N 7 33W
Lugoj Romania 89 H6 45 41N 21 57E
Luiana *r.* Angola 109 J4 17 00S 21 00E
Luk Keng HK China 100 C3 22 32N 114 13E
Łuków Poland 88 J9 51 57N 22 21E
Lulua *r.* CDR 109 J6 9 00S 22 00E
Lumberton North Carolina USA 71 L3 34 37N 79 03W
Lummi Island Washington USA 42 H4 48 40N 122 36W
Lund Sweden 88 D12 55 42N 13 10E
Lund Nevada USA 72 F4 38 53N 115 01W
Lüneburg Germany 88 C10 53 15N 10 24E
Lunéville Fr. 86 J8 48 35N 6 30E
Lung Kwu Chau *i.* HK China 100 A2 22 23N 113 53E
Lunglei India 99 M9 22 54N 92 49E
Lungue Bungo *r.* Angola/Zambia 109 J5 13 00S 22 00E
Luni *r.* India 98 C5 26 00N 73 00E
Luoshan China 101 L5 31 12N 114 30E
Luoyang China 101 L5 34 47N 112 26E
Lurgan UK 86 B11 54 28N 6 20W
Lurio *r.* Mozambique 109 M5 14 00S 39 00E
Lusaka Zambia 109 K4 15 26S 28 20E
Lusambo CDR 108 J7 4 59S 23 26E
Lüshun China 101 N6 38 46N 121 15E
Luton UK 86 E9 51 53N 0 25W
Luts'k Ukraine 88 K9 50 42N 25 15E
Luuq Somalia 108 N8 2 52N 42 34E
LUXEMBOURG 86 H8
Luxembourg Luxembourg 86 J8 49 37N 6 08E
Luxor Egypt 108 L13 25 41N 32 24E
Luzern Switz. 87 K7 47 03N 8 17E
Luzhou China 101 K4 28 55N 105 25E
Luziânia Brazil 80 H10 16 16S 47 57W
Luzon *i.* Philippines 103 G7 15 00N 122 00E
Luzon Strait China/Philippines 103 G8 20 00N 121 30E
L'viv Ukraine 88 K8 49 50N 24 00E
Lyna *r.* Poland 88 H11 54 00N 20 00E
Lynchburg Virginia USA 71 L4 37 24N 79 09W
Lynden Washington USA 42 H4 48 56N 122 28W
Lynn Massachusetts USA 73 E3 42 28N 70 58W
Lynn Canal *sd.* Alaska USA 42 C6 58 50N 135 05W
Lyons Fr. 87 H6 45 46N 4 50E
Lyons New York USA 51 N2 43 04N 76 59W
Lyttelton NZ 111 D3 43 36S 172 42E

M

Ma'ān Jordan 96 C5 30 11N 35 43E
Ma'anshan China 101 M5 31 49N 118 32E
Maastricht Neths. 86 H9 50 51N 5 42E
Mabalane Mozambique 109 L3 23 51S 32 38E
McAlester Oklahoma USA 71 G3 34 56N 95 46W
McAllen Texas USA 71 G2 26 13N 98 15W
Macao China 101 L3 22 10N 113 40E
Macapá Brazil 80 G14 0 04N 51 04W
Macarata Italy 89 D5 43 18N 13 27E
McClure, Lake California USA 72 C3 37 38N 120 16W
McComb Mississippi USA 71 H3 31 13N 90 29W
McCook Nebraska USA 70 F5 40 13N 100 35W
McDonald, Lake Montana USA 46 E1/F1 48 50N 114 00W
Macdonnell Ranges *mts.* Aust. 110 E5 24 00S 132 30E
Maceió Brazil 80 K12 9 40S 35 44W
Machala Ecuador 80 B13 3 20S 79 57W
Machanga Mozambique 109 L3 20 58N 35 01E
Machias Maine USA 57 G1 44 50N 67 20W
Machiques Venezuela 80 C16 10 04N 72 37W
Mackay Aust. 110 H5 21 10S 149 10E
Mackay, Lake Aust. 110 D5 22 30S 128 00E
Mackinac, Straits of *sd.* Michigan USA 52 B5 45 48N 84 43W
Mackinaw City Michigan USA 71 K6 45 47N 84 43W
McKinney Texas USA 71 G3 33 14N 96 37W
Macleod, Lake Aust. 110 A5 24 00S 113 30E
Mâcon Fr. 87 H7 46 18N 4 50E
Macon Georgia USA 71 K3 32 49N 83 37W
McPherson Kansas USA 71 G4 38 22N 97 41W
Macquarie Island Southern Ocean 114 F2 54 29S 158 58E
Macquarie Ridge Southern Ocean 114 F2 55 00S 160 00E
Mādabā Jordan 96 N10 31 44N 35 48E
MADAGASCAR 109 P2/P5
Madagascar Basin Indian Ocean 113 E4 25 00S 55 00E
Madagascar Ridge Indian Ocean 113 D3 30 00S 45 00E
Madang PNG 110 H8 5 14S 145 45E
Madaripur Bangladesh 99 L9 23 09N 90 11E
Madden Lake Panama 75 Y2 9 15N 79 35W
Madeira *r.* Brazil 80 E12 6 00S 61 30W
Madeira Islands Atlantic Ocean 108 A14 32 45N 17 00W
Madera California USA 72 C3 36 59N 120 12W
Madhya Pradesh *admin.* India 98 D4/E4 23 00N 78 30E
Madīnat ash Sha'b Yemen 96 D1 12 50N 44 56E
Madison Maine USA 53 S4 44 48N 69 53W
Madison Wisconsin USA 71 J5 43 04N 89 22W
Madiun Indonesia 103 E2 7 37S 111 33E
Mado Gashi Kenya 108 M8 0 45N 39 11E
Madre de Dios *r.* Bolivia 80 D11 12 00S 68 00W
Madrid Sp. 87 D4 40 25N 3 43W
Madura *i.* Indonesia 103 E2 7 00S 113 00E
Madurai India 98 D1 9 55N 78 07E
Maebashi Japan 102 C2 36 24N 139 04E
Maevantanana Madagascar 109 P4 16 57S 46 50E
Mafia Island Tanzania 109 M6 7 00S 39 00E
Mafikeng RSA 109 K2 25 53S 25 39E
Mafraq Jordan 96 C5 32 20N 36 12E
Magadan Russia 95 T8 59 38N 150 50E
Magangué Col. 80 C15 9 14N 74 47W
Magdalena Mexico 74 B6 30 38N 110 59W
Magdalena *r.* Col. 80 C15 8 00N 73 30W
Magdeburg Germany 88 C10 52 08N 11 37E
Magelang Indonesia 103 E2 7 28S 110 11E
Magnitogorsk Russia 94 H7 53 28N 59 06E
Mahadeo Hills India 98 D4 22 30N 78 30E
Mahajanga Madagascar 109 P4 15 40S 46 20E
Mahanadi *r.* India 99 E4 21 00N 85 00E
Maharashtra *admin.* India 98 C3 19 30N 75 00E
Mahón Sp. 87 H3 39 54N 4 15E
Maiduguri Nigeria 108 G10 11 53N 13 16E
Main *r.* Germany 88 B8 50 00N 8 00E
Maine *state* USA 71 N6 45 00N 70 00W
Mainland *i.* Orkney Islands UK 86 D13 59 00N 3 15W
Mainland *i.* Shetland Islands UK 86 E14 60 15N 1 20W
Maintirano Madagascar 109 N4 18 01S 44 03E
Mainz Germany 88 B8 50 00N 8 16E
Mai Po Hong Kong China 100 B2 22 29N 114 03E
Maiquetía Venezuela 80 D16 10 38N 66 59W
Maiskhal Island Bangladesh 99 L8 21 36N 91 53E
Maitland Aust. 110 J3 32 33S 151 33E
Maizuru Japan 102 C2 35 30N 135 20E
Majene Indonesia 103 F3 3 33S 118 59E
Maji Ethiopia 108 M9 6 12N 35 32E
Makassar Strait *sd.* Indonesia 103 F3/F4 0 00 119 00E
Makeni Sierra Leone 108 B9 8 57N 12 02W
Makgadikgadi Salt Pan Botswana 109 K3 21 00S 26 00E
Makhachkala Russia 94 G5 42 59N 47 30E
Makó Hungary 89 H7 46 11N 20 30E
Makokou Gabon 108 G8 0 38N 12 47E
Makurdi Nigeria 108 F9 7 44N 8 35E
Malabar Coast India 98 C2/D1 12 00N 74 00E
Malabo Eq. Guinea 108 F8 3 45N 8 48E
Malacca, Strait of Indonesia 103 B5/C4 4 00N 100 00E
Málaga Sp. 87 C2 36 43N 4 25W
Malaga New Jersey USA 73 C1 39 34N 75 03W
Malaita *i.* Solomon Islands 114 G7 9 00S 161 00E
Malakal Sudan 108 L9 9 31N 31 40E
Malang Indonesia 103 E2 7 59S 112 45E
Malanje Angola 109 H6 9 32S 16 20E
Mälaren *l.* Sweden 88 F13 59 30N 17 00E
Malaspina Glacier Alaska USA 64 B2 59 50N 140 40W
Malatya Turkey 96 C6 38 22N 38 18E
MALAWI 109 L5
MALAYSIA 103 C5/E5
Malbork Poland 88 G11 54 02N 19 01E
MALDIVES 113 G7
Maldonado Uruquay 81 G7 34 57S 54 59W
Malegaon India 98 C4 20 32N 74 38E
Malema Mozambique 109 M5 14 57S 37 25E

Name	Page	Grid	Lat	Long
MALI	108	C10		
Malin Head *c.* RoI	86	B11	55 30N	7 20W
Ma Liu Shui HK China	100	C2	22 25N	114 12E
Mallaig UK	86	C12	57 00N	5 50W
Mallorca *i.* Sp.	87	G3	39 50N	2 30E
Malmédy Belgium	86	J9	50 26N	6 02E
Malmesbury RSA	109	H1	33 28S	18 43E
Malmö Sweden	88	D12	55 35N	13 00E
Malone New York USA	51	P3	44 51N	74 18W
Malonga CDR	109	J5	10 26S	23 10E
Malpelo *i.* Col.	80	A14	4 00N	81 35W
MALTA	89	E1		
Malta Montana USA	70	E6	48 22N	107 51W
Malta *i.* Mediterranean Sea	89	E1	35 00N	14 00E
Maluku *is.* Indonesia	103	H3	4 00S	127 00E
Mamanutha Group *is.* Fiji	114	T16	17 40S	177 00E
Mambasa CDR	108	K8	1 20N	29 05E
Mammoth Lakes *tn.* California USA	72	D3	37 38N	118 58W
Mamoré *r.* Bolivia	80	E10	15 00S	65 00W
Man Côte d'Ivoire	108	C9	7 31N	7 37W
Manacapuru Brazil	80	E13	3 16S	60 37W
Manacor Sp.	87	G3	39 35N	3 12E
Manado Indonesia	103	G4	1 32N	124 55E
Managua Nicaragua	74	G2	12 06N	86 18W
Manali India	98	D6	32 12N	77 06E
Manama Bahrain	97	F4	26 12N	50 38E
Manas *r.* India/Bhutan	99	L11	27 00N	91 00E
Manaus Brazil	80	F13	3 06S	60 00W
Manchester UK	86	D10	53 30N	2 15W
Manchester California USA	72	B4	38 58N	123 42W
Manchester Connecticut USA	73	D2	41 47N	72 32W
Manchester Michigan USA	52	B2	42 10N	84 01W
Manchester New Hampshire USA	71	M5	42 59N	71 28W
Manchester Tennessee USA	71	J4	35 29N	86 04W
Mandal Norway	86	J13	58 02N	7 30E
Mandalay Myanmar	100	H3	21 57N	96 04E
Mandeville Jamaica	75	U14	18 02N	77 31W
Manfredonia Italy	89	E4	41 37N	15 55E
Mangalore India	98	C2	12 54N	74 51E
Mango *i.* Fiji	114	V16	17 20S	179 20W
Mangoky *r.* Madagascar	109	N3	22 00S	45 00E
Mangonui NZ	111	D7	34 59S	173 32E
Mangui China	101	N9	52 05N	122 17E
Manhattan Kansas USA	71	G4	39 11N	96 35W
Manhattan Nevada USA	72	E4	38 31N	117 05W
Manhattan New York USA	73	J2	40 48N	73 58W
Mania *r.* Madagascar	109	P4	19 30S	50 30E
Manica Mozambique	109	L4	18 56S	32 52E
Manicoré Brazil	80	E12	5 48S	61 16W
Manila Philippines	103	G6	14 37N	120 58E
Manipur *admin.* India	99	G4	24 30N	94 00E
Manipur *r.* India/Myanmar	99	G4	24 00N	93 00E
Manistee Michigan USA	51	H3	44 14N	86 19W
Manistee River Michigan USA	51	J3	44 20N	85 30W
Manistique Michigan USA	51	H3	45 57N	86 14W
Manistique Lake Michigan USA	52	A6	46 25N	85 45W
Manitowoc Wisconsin USA	71	J5	44 04N	87 40W
Manizales Col.	80	B15	5 03N	75 32W
Manjra *r.* India	98	D3	18 30N	77 30E
Man Kam To HK China	100	B3	22 32N	114 08E
Mankato Minnesota USA	71	H5	44 10N	94 00W
Mannar Sri Lanka	98	D1	8 58N	79 54E
Mannar, Gulf of India/Sri Lanka	98	D1	8 30N	79 00E
Mannheim Germany	88	B8	49 30N	8 28E
Manokwari Indonesia	103	J3	0 53S	134 05E
Manresa Sp.	87	F4	41 43N	1 50E
Mansa Zambia	109	K5	11 10S	28 52E
Mansfield Ohio USA	71	K5	40 46N	82 31W
Mansfield Pennsylvania USA	53	J1	41 47N	77 05W
Manta Ecuador	80	A13	0 59S	80 44W
Manteca California USA	72	C3	37 50N	121 16W
Mantes-la-Jolie Fr.	86	F8	48 59N	1 43E
Manukau NZ	111	E6	37 00S	174 52E
Manuta Italy	89	C6	45 10N	10 47E
Manyoni Tanzania	108	L6	5 46S	34 50E
Manzanares Sp.	87	D3	39 00N	3 23W
Manzanillo Cuba	75	J4	20 21N	77 21W
Manzanillo Mexico	74	D3	19 00N	104 20W
Manzhouli China	101	M8	46 36N	117 28E
Maoming China	101	L3	21 50N	110 56E
Ma On Shan HK China	100	C2	22 26N	114 13E
Ma On Shan *mt.* HK China	100	C2	22 24N	114 16E
Maple Heights *tn.* Ohio USA	52	E1	41 24N	81 35W
Maputo Mozambique	109	L2	25 58S	32 35E
Marabá Brazil	80	H12	5 23S	49 10W
Maracaibo Venezuela	80	C16	10 44N	71 37W
Maracay Venezuela	80	D16	10 20N	67 28W
Maradi Niger	108	F10	13 29N	7 10E
Maranhão *admin.* Brazil	80	H12	5 20S	46 00W
Marañón *r.* Peru	80	B13	4 50S	77 30W
Marbella Sp.	87	C2	36 31N	4 53W
Marble Bar *tn.* Aust.	110	B5	21 16S	119 45E
Marble Canyon *tn.* Arizona USA	70	D4	36 50N	111 38W
Marburg Germany	88	B9	50 49N	8 36E
Marcus Island Pacific Ocean	114	F10	24 30N	157 30E
Mardan Pakistan	98	C6	34 14N	72 05E
Mar del Plata Argentina	81	F6	38 00S	57 32W
Mardin Turkey	96	D6	37 19N	40 43E
Maria Elena Chile	80	D9	22 18S	69 40W
Marianas Trench Pacific Ocean	114	E9	16 00N	147 30E
Maribor Slovenia	89	E7	46 34N	15 38E
Maricopa California USA	72	D2	34 04N	119 25W
Marie Byrd Land *geog. reg.* Antarctica	117		77 00S	130 00W
Marie Galente *i.* Lesser Antilles	74	Q8	15 56N	61 16W
Mariehamn Finland	88	G14	60 05N	19 55E
Mariental Namibia	109	H3	24 36S	17 59E
Mariestad Sweden	88	D13	58 44N	13 50E
Marigot Dominica	74	Q8	15 32N	61 18W
Marijampole Lithuania	88	J11	54 31N	23 20E
Marília Brazil	80	G9	22 13S	49 58W
Maringá Brazil	80	G9	23 26S	52 02W
Marion Ohio USA	71	K5	40 35N	83 08W
Marion, Lake South Carolina USA	71	K3	33 00N	80 00W
Mariposa California USA	72	D3	37 30N	119 59W
Mariscal Estigarribia Paraguay	80	E9	22 03S	60 35W
Marjayoûn Lebanon	96	N11	33 22N	35 34E
Marka Somalia	108	N8	1 42N	44 47E
Markha *r.* Russia	95	P9	64 00N	12 30E
Markovo Russia	95	V9	64 40N	170 24E
Marlette Michigan USA	52	C3	43 20N	83 04W
Marmara, Sea of Turkey	96	A7	15 40N	28 10E
Maroantsetra Madagascar	109	P4	15 23S	49 44E
Maroni *r.* Suriname	80	G14	4 00N	54 30W
Maroua Cameroon	108	G10	10 35N	14 20E
Marquesas Islands Pacific Ocean	115	N7	10 00S	137 00W
Marquette Michigan USA	71	J6	46 33N	87 23W
Marrakesh Morocco	108	C14	31 49N	8 00W
Marsabit Kenya	108	M8	2 20N	37 59E
Marsala Italy	89	D2	37 48N	12 27E
Marseilles Fr.	87	H5	43 18N	5 22E
MARSHALL ISLANDS	114	G9		
Marshfield Wisconsin USA	51	F3	44 40N	90 10W
Martaban, Gulf of Myanmar	103	B7	15 30N	92 30E
Martha's Vineyard *is.* Massachusetts USA	73	E2	41 18N	70 37W
Martinique *i.* Lesser Antilles	74	R12	14 30N	61 00W
Martin Lake Alabama USA	71	J3	33 00N	86 00W
Martinsburg West Virginia USA	73	B1	39 26N	77 58W
Martinsville Virginia USA	71	L4	36 43N	79 53W
Martin Vaz *i.* Atlantic Ocean	116	F4	21 00S	27 30W
Marton NZ	111	E4	40 05S	175 23E
Mary Turkmenistan	94	J4	37 42N	61 54E
Maryborough Aust.	110	J4	25 32S	152 36E
Maryland *state* USA	71	L4	39 00N	77 00W
Marysville California USA	70	B4	39 10N	121 34W
Masada *hist. site* Israel	96	N10	31 17N	35 20E
Masan South Korea	101	P6	35 10N	128 35E
Masaya Nicaragua	74	G2	11 59N	86 03W
Masbate *i.* Philippines	103	G6	12 21N	123 36E
Mascarene Basin Indian Ocean	113	E5	15 00S	55 00E
Maseru Lesotho	109	K2	29 19S	27 29E
Mashhad Iran	97	G6	36 16N	59 34E
Masindi Uganda	108	L8	1 41N	31 45E
Maşīrah *i.* Oman	97	G3	20 25N	58 40E
Mason Michigan USA	52	B2	42 34N	84 27W
Mason City Iowa USA	71	H5	43 10N	93 10W
Massachusetts *state* USA	71	M5	42 00N	72 00W
Massachusetts Bay Massachusetts USA	73	E3	42 00N	70 00W
Massawa Eritrea	108	M11	15 42N	39 25E
Massena New York USA	71	M5	44 56N	74 57W
Massif Central *mts.* Fr.	87	G6	45 00N	3 30E
Massif de L'Isola *mts.* Madagascar	109	N3/P3	23 00S	45 00E
Massif des Bongos *mts.* CAR	108	J9	9 00N	23 00E
Massif de Tsaratanana *mts.* Madagascar	109	P5	14 00S	49 00E
Masterton NZ	111	E4	40 57S	175 39E
Masuda Japan	102	B1	34 42N	131 51E
Masuku Gabon	108	G7	1 40S	13 31E
Masvingo Zimbabwe	109	L3	20 05S	30 50E
Matachel *r.* Sp.	87	B3	38 40N	6 00W
Matadi CDR	109	G6	5 50S	13 32E
Matagalpa Nicaragua	74	G2	12 52N	85 58W
Matale Sri Lanka	98	E1	7 28N	80 37E
Matamoros Mexico	74	D5	25 33N	103 51W
Matamoros Mexico	74	E5	25 50N	97 31W
Matanzas Cuba	75	H4	23 04N	81 35W
Matara Sri Lanka	98	E1	5 57N	80 32E
Mataram Indonesia	103	F2	8 36S	116 07E
Mataró Sp.	87	G4	41 32N	2 27E
Matehuala Mexico	74	D4	23 40N	100 40W
Matera Italy	89	F4	40 40N	16 37E
Mathura India	98	D5	27 30N	77 42E
Matla *r.* India	99	K8/K9	22 00N	88 35E
Mato Grosso *admin.* Brazil	80	F11	14 00S	56 00W
Mato Grosso *tn.* Brazil	80	F10	15 05S	59 57W
Mato Grosso do Sul *admin.* Brazil	80	G9	20 00S	55 00W
Matopo Hills Zimbabwe	109	K3	21 00S	28 30E
Matosinhos Port.	87	A4	41 08N	8 45W
Maţraḩ Oman	97	G3	23 31N	58 18E
Matsudo Japan	102	C2	35 46N	139 54E
Matsue Japan	102	B2	35 29N	133 04E
Matsumoto Japan	102	C2	36 18N	137 58E
Matsuyama Japan	102	B1	33 50N	132 47E
Matterhorn *mt.* Switz.	87	J6	45 59N	7 39E
Matuku *i.* Fiji	114	U15	19 11S	179 45E
Maturín Venezuela	80	E15	9 45N	63 10W
Maubeuge Fr.	86	G9	50 17N	3 58E
Maués Brazil	80	F13	3 22S	57 38W
Maui *i.* Hawaiian Islands	115	Y18	21 00N	156 30W
Maulvi Bazar Bangladesh	99	L10	24 30N	91 48E
Maumee Ohio USA	51	K1	41 34N	83 40W
Maumee River Ohio USA	51	K1	41 34N	83 40W
Maumere Indonesia	103	G2	8 35S	122 13E
Mauna Kea *mt.* Hawaiian Islands	115	Z17	19 50N	155 25W
Mauna Loa *vol.* Hawaiian Islands	115	Z17	19 28N	155 35W
Maungdaw Myanmar	99	M8	20 47N	92 26E
MAURITANIA	108	B11		
MAURITIUS	113	E4		
Ma Wan *i.* HK China	100	B2	22 21N	114 03E
Ma Wan Chung HK China	100	A1	22 17N	113 56E
Mawlaik Myanmar	100	G3	23 40N	94 26E
Mayādīn Syria	96	D6	35 01N	40 28E
Mayaguana *i.* Bahamas	75	K4	22 30N	72 40W
Mayagüez Puerto Rico	75	L3	18 13N	67 09W
Mayenne *r.* Fr.	86	E7	47 45N	0 50W
Maykop Russia	94	G5	44 37N	40 48E
Mayotte *i.* Indian Ocean	109	P5	13 00S	45 00E
May Pen Jamaica	75	U13	17 58N	77 15W
Mayumba Gabon	108	G7	3 23S	10 38E
Mayville New York USA	52	G2	42 15N	79 32W
Mazabuka Zambia	109	K4	15 50S	27 47E
Mazama Washington USA	42	H4	48 40N	120 15W
Mazār-e Sharīf Afghanistan	97	J6	36 42N	67 06E
Mazatenango Guatemala	74	F2	14 31N	91 30W
Mazatlán Mexico	74	C4	23 11N	106 25W
Mazeikiai Lithuania	88	J12	56 20N	22 22E
Mazirbe Latvia	88	J12	57 40N	22 21E
Mbabane Swaziland	109	L2	26 20S	31 08E
Mbaiki CAR	108	H8	3 53N	18 01E
Mbala Zambia	109	L6	8 50S	31 24E
Mbalmayo Cameroon	108	G8	3 30N	11 31E
Mbandaka CDR	108	H8	0 03N	18 28E
Mbengga *i.* Fiji	114	U15	18 24S	178 09E
Mbeya Tanzania	109	L6	8 54S	33 29E
Mbuji-Mayi CDR	109	J6	6 10S	23 39E
Mead, Lake USA	70	D4	36 10N	114 25W
Meadville Pennsylvania USA	71	K5	41 38N	80 10W
Meaux Fr.	86	G8	48 58N	2 54E
Mecca Saudi Arabia	96	C3	21 26N	39 49E
Mechelen Belgium	86	H9	51 02N	4 29E
Mecheria Algeria	108	D14	33 31N	0 20W
Mecklenburg Bay Europe	88	C11	54 00N	12 00E
Medan Indonesia	103	B4	3 35N	98 39E
Medellín Col.	80	B15	6 15N	75 36W
Medenine Tunisia	108	G14	33 24N	10 25E
Medford Oregon USA	70	B5	42 20N	122 52W
Medford Wisconsin USA	51	F3	45 08N	90 21W
Medina Saudi Arabia	96	C3	24 30N	39 35E
Medina New York USA	52	H3	43 13N	78 23W
Medina del Campo Sp.	87	C4	41 18N	4 55W
Medinipur India	99	F4	22 25N	87 24E
Mediterranean Sea Africa/Europe	87	D1/K3	35 00N	15 00E
Medvezh'yegorsk Russia	94	F9	62 56N	34 28E
Meekatharra Aust.	110	B4	26 30S	118 30E
Meerut India	98	D5	29 00N	77 42E
Mega Ethiopia	108	M8	4 02N	38 19E
Meghalaya *admin.* India	99	G5	25 30N	91 00E
Meizhou China	101	M3	24 19N	116 13E
Mekele Ethiopia	108	M10	13 32N	39 33E
Meknès Morocco	108	C14	33 53N	5 37W
Mekong *r.* Asia	103	C8	16 00N	105 00E
Mekong, Mouths of the *est.* Vietnam	103	D5	9 30N	106 45E
Melaka Malaysia	103	C4	2 11N	102 14E
Melanesia *geog. reg.* Pacific Ocean	114	E8	0 00	150 00E
Melbourne Aust.	110	G2	37 45S	144 58E
Melbourne Florida USA	71	K2	28 04N	80 38W
Melilla *territory* Sp.	87	D1	35 17N	2 57W
Melo Uruguay	81	G7	32 22S	54 10W
Melun Fr.	86	G8	48 32N	2 40E
Melville, Cape Aust.	110	G7	14 08S	144 31E
Melville Island Aust.	110	E7	11 30S	131 00E
Memmingen Germany	88	C7	47 59N	10 11E
Memphis Tennessee USA	71	J4	35 10N	90 00W
Mende Fr.	87	G6	44 32N	3 30E
Menderes *r.* Turkey	96	A6	37 50N	28 10E
Mendi PNG	110	G8	6 13S	143 39E
Mendocino California USA	72	B4	39 20N	123 47W
Mendocino Seascarp Pacific Ocean	115	M12	41 00N	145 00W
Mendota California USA	72	C3	36 44N	120 24W
Mendoza Argentina	81	D7	32 48S	68 52W
Mengdingjie China	101	H3	23 03N	99 03E
Menongue Angola	109	H5	14 36S	17 48E
Menorca *i.* Sp.	87	G4	39 45N	4 15E
Mentawai Islands Indonesia	113	J7	2 00N	99 00E
Mentor Ohio USA	71	K5	41 42N	81 22W
Merauke Indonesia	110	G8	8 30S	140 22E
Merced California USA	70	B4	37 17N	120 29W
Mercedes Argentina	81	D7	33 41S	65 28W
Mercedes Uruguay	81	F7	34 15S	58 02W
Mergui Myanmar	103	B6	12 26N	98 34E
Mergui Archipelago *is.* Myanmar	103	B6	11 00N	97 40E
Mérida Mexico	74	G4	20 59N	89 39W
Mérida Sp.	87	B3	38 55N	6 20W
Mérida Venezuela	80	C15	8 24N	71 08W
Meriden Connecticut USA	73	D2	41 32N	72 49W
Meridian Mississippi USA	71	J3	32 21N	88 42W
Merowe Sudan	108	L11	18 30N	31 49E
Merowe Dam Sudan	108	L11	18 40N	32 10E
Mersin Turkey	96	B6	36 47N	34 37E
Merthyr Tydfil UK	86	D9	51 46N	3 23W
Mesa Arizona USA	70	D3	33 25N	111 50W
Mesabi Range *mts.* Minnesota USA	51	E4	47 30N	92 56W
Mesolóngi Greece	89	H3	38 21N	21 26E
Mesopotamia *geog. reg.* Middle East	96	D6	35 00N	42 00E
Mesquite Lake California USA	72	F2	35 43N	115 36W
Messina Italy	89	E3	38 13N	15 33E
Messina RSA	109	K3	22 23S	30 00E
Meta *r.* Col.	80	C15	6 00N	71 00W
Methow River Washington USA	42	H4	48 40N	120 15W
Metlakatla Alaska USA	42	E4	55 09N	131 35W
Metz Fr.	86	J8	49 07N	6 11E
Meuse *r.* Belgium/Fr.	86	H9	50 03N	4 40E
Mexicali Mexico	74	A6	32 36N	115 30W
MEXICO	74	C5/E3		
Mexico New York USA	53	K3	43 28N	76 14W
Mexico City Mexico	74	E3	19 25N	99 10W
Mexico, Gulf of Mexico	74	F4/G4	25 00N	90 00W
Meymaneh Afghanistan	97	H6	35 55N	64 47E
Mezen' Russia	94	G10	65 50N	44 20E
Miami Florida USA	71	K2	25 45N	80 15W
Miami Oklahoma USA	71	H4	36 53N	94 54W
Mīāneh Iran	97	E6	37 23N	47 45E
Mianwali Pakistan	98	C6	32 32N	71 33E
Miass Russia	94	J7	55 00N	60 08E
Michelson, Mount Alaska USA	64	B4	69 19N	144 20W
Michigan *state* USA	71	J5/K5	45 00N	85 00W
Michigan, Lake Canada/USA	71	J5/J6	45 00N	87 00W
Micronesia *geog. reg.* Pacific Ocean	114	G8	10 00N	160 00E
Mid-Atlantic Ridge Atlantic Ocean	116	F11	15 00S	13 00W
Middle America Trench Pacific Ocean	115	R9/T9	16 30N	99 00W
Middle Andaman *i.* Andaman Islands	99	G2	12 30N	93 00E
Middleburg RSA	109	K2	31 28S	25 01E
Middle Loup *r.* Nebraska USA	70	F5	42 00N	101 00W
Middlesbrough UK	86	E11	54 35N	1 14W
Middletown Connecticut USA	73	D2	41 33N	72 39W
Mid-Indian Basin Indian Ocean	113	H5/H6	10 00S	80 00E
Mid-Indian Ridge Indian Ocean	113	F5/G3	27 00S	70 00E
Midland Michigan USA	71	K5	43 38N	84 14W
Midland Texas USA	70	F3	32 00N	102 09W
Midland Beach New York USA	73	H1	40 33N	74 07W
Mid-Pacific Mountains Pacific Ocean	114	F10	21 00N	160 00E
Midway Islands Pacific Ocean	114	J10	28 15N	177 25W
Mieres Sp.	87	C5	43 15N	5 46W
Mijares *r.* Sp.	87	E4	40 03N	0 30W
Milagro Ecuador	80	B13	2 11S	79 36W
Milan Italy	89	B6	45 28N	9 12E
Mildura Aust.	110	G3	34 14S	142 13E
Miles City Montana USA	70	E6	46 24N	105 48W
Milford Pennsylvania USA	73	C2	41 19N	74 48W
Milford Utah USA	70	D4	38 22N	113 00W
Milford Haven UK	86	C9	51 44N	5 02W
Mitford Sound *tn.* NZ	111	A2	44 41S	167 56E
Milk *r.* Canada/USA	70	D6	49 00N	112 00W
Millau Fr.	87	G6	44 06N	3 05E
Mill Creek *r.* Michigan USA	52	C3	43 10N	83 00W
Millerton New York USA	73	D2	41 57N	73 31W
Millinocket Maine USA	57	F1	45 42N	68 43W
Millville New Jersey USA	73	C1	39 24N	75 02W
Milos *i.* Greece	89	K2	36 00N	24 00E
Milton NZ	111	B1	46 07S	169 58E
Milton Keynes UK	86	E10	52 02N	0 42W
Milwaukee Wisconsin USA	71	J5	43 03N	87 56W
Mimizan Fr.	87	E6	44 12N	1 14W
Minahassa Peninsula Indonesia	103	G4	0 30N	123 00E
Minamata Japan	102	B1	32 13N	130 23E
Minas Uruguay	81	F7	34 20S	55 15W
Minas Gerais *admin.* Brazil	80	H10	17 30S	45 00W
Minatitlán Mexico	74	F3	17 59N	94 32W
Mindanao *i.* Philippines	103	G5	8 00N	125 00E
Minden Germany	88	B10	52 18N	8 54E
Minden Louisiana USA	71	H3	32 26N	93 17W
Mindoro *i.* Philippines	103	G6	13 00N	121 00E
Minicoy Island India	98	C1	8 29N	73 01E
Minneapolis Minnesota USA	71	H5	45 00N	93 15W
Minnesota *r.* Minnesota USA	71	G5	44 00N	95 00W
Minnesota *state* USA	71	H6	47 00N	95 00W
Miño *r.* Sp./Port.	87	A5	42 00N	8 40W
Minot North Dakota USA	70	F6	48 16N	101 19W
Mio Michigan USA	51	J3	44 39N	84 08W
Miram Shah Pakistan	98	B6	32 59N	70 07E
Miranda de Ebro Sp.	87	D5	42 41N	2 57W
Miri Malaysia	103	E4	4 23N	114 00E
Mirnyy Russia	95	P9	62 30N	113 58E
Mirpur Khas Pakistan	98	B5	25 33N	69 05E
Mirs Bay HK China	100	D3	22 31N	114 25E
Mirtoan Sea Greece	89	J2	37 00N	23 00E
Mirzapur India	98	E5	25 09N	82 34E
Misawa Japan	102	D3	40 42N	141 26E
Miskolc Hungary	88	H8	48 07N	20 47E
Misoöl *i.* Indonesia	103	J3	1 50S	129 55E
Misratah Libya	108	G14	32 23N	15 00E
Mississippi *r.* USA	71	H3	35 00N	90 00W
Mississippi *state* USA	71	H3/J3	32 00N	90 00W
Mississippi Delta Louisiana USA	71	J2	30 00N	90 00W
Missoula Montana USA	70	D6	46 52N	114 00W
Missouri *r.* USA	70	H4	39 00N	93 00W
Missouri *state* USA	71	H4	38 00N	93 00W

Mitchell South Dakota USA 71 G5 43 40N 98 01W
Mitchell *r.* Aust. 110 G6 16 00S 142 30E
Mitkof Island Alaska USA 42 D5 56 40N 132 45W
Mito Japan 102 D2 36 22N 140 29E
Mitú Col. 80 C14 1 07N 70 05W
Miyako Japan 102 D2 39 38N 141 59E
Miyakonojō Japan 102 B1 31 43N 131 02E
Miyazaki Japan 102 B1 31 56N 131 27E
Mizen Head *c.* RoI 86 A9 51 30N 9 50W
Mizoram *admin.* India 99 G4 23 40N 93 30E
Mjölby Sweden 88 E13 58 19N 15 10E
Mladá Boleslav Czech Rep. 88 E9 50 26N 14 55E
Mława Poland 88 H10 53 08N 20 20E
Moala *i.* Fiji 114 U15 18 34S 179 56E
Mobaye CAR 108 J8 4 19N 21 11E
Mobile Alabama USA 71 J3 30 40N 88 05W
Moçambique Mozambique 109 N4 15 03S 40 45E
Mocuba Mozambique 109 M4 16 52S 36 57E
Módena Italy 89 C6 44 39N 10 55E
Modesto California USA 70 B4 37 37N 121 00W
Moe Aust. 110 H2 38 09S 146 22E
Mogadishu Somalia 108 P8 2 02N 45 21E
Mogocha Russia 95 P7 53 44N 119 45E
Mogollon Rim *plat.* Arizona USA 70 D3 34 00N 111 00W
Mohall North Dakota USA 47 G1 48 50N 101 34W
Mohe China 101 N9 52 55N 122 20E
Mohyliv-Podil's'kyy Ukraine 88 L8 48 29N 27 49E
Mojave California USA 70 C4 35 02N 118 11W
Mojave *r.* California USA 72 E2 34 47N 117 15W
Mojave Desert California USA 72 E2 35 08N 117 21W
Mokau NZ 111 E5 38 42S 174 37E
Mokelumne *r.* California USA 72 C4 38 13N 121 05W
Mokolo Cameroon 108 G10 10 49N 13 54E
Mokp'o South Korea 101 P5 34 50N 126 25E
Molango Mexico 74 E4 20 48N 98 44W
MOLDOVA 88/89 M7
Moldova *r.* Romania 89 L7 47 00N 26 00E
Molepolole Botswana 109 K3 24 25S 25 30E
Mollendo Peru 80 C10 17 00S 72 00W
Molokai *i.* Hawaiian Islands 115 Y18 21 40N 155 55W
Molopo *r.* Southern Africa 109 J2 26 30S 22 30E
Molucca Sea Indonesia 103 G3 0 30S 125 30E
Mombasa Kenya 108 M7 4 04S 39 40E
MONACO 87 J5
Monahans Texas USA 70 F3 31 35N 102 54W
Monbetsu Japan 102 D3 42 28N 142 10E
Monbetsu Japan 102 D3 44 23N 143 22E
Monçaõ Brazil 80 H13 3 30S 45 15W
Mönchengladbach Germany 88 A9 51 12N 6 25E
Monclova Mexico 74 D5 26 55N 101 25W
Mondego *r.* Port. 87 A4 40 30N 8 15W
Mondovi Italy 89 A6 44 23N 7 49E
Monemvasia Greece 89 J2 36 41N 23 03E
Mong Kok HK China 100 B1 22 19N 114 09E
MONGOLIA 100/101 F8
Mongu Zambia 109 J4 15 13S 23 09E
Mono Lake California USA 72 D4 38 00N 119 00W
Monopoli Italy 89 F4 40 57N 17 18E
Monroe Louisiana USA 71 H3 32 31N 92 06W
Monroe Michigan USA 51 K1 41 54N 83 24W
Monrovia Liberia 108 B9 6 20N 10 46W
Montana Bulgaria 89 J5 43 25N 23 11E
Montana *state* USA 70 E6 47 00N 111 00W
Montañas de León *mts.* Sp. 87 B5 42 30N 6 15E
Montargis Fr. 86 G7 48 00N 2 44E
Montauban Fr. 87 F6 44 01N 1 20E
Montauk Point New York USA 73 E2 41 05N 71 55W
Montbéliard Fr. 87 J7 47 31N 6 48E
Mont Blanc *mt.* Fr./Italy 87 J6 45 50N 6 52E
Mont Cameroun *mt.* Cameroon 108 F8 4 13N 9 10E
Montclair New Jersey USA 73 H2 40 48N 74 12W
Mont-de-Marsan Fr. 87 E5 43 54N 0 30W
Monte Cinto *mt.* Fr. 87 K5 42 23N 8 57E
Montego Bay *tn.* Jamaica 75 U14 18 27N 77 56W
Montélimar Fr. 87 H6 44 33N 4 45E
MONTENEGRO 89 G5
Monterey California USA 70 B4 36 35N 121 55W
Monterey Bay California USA 72 C3 36 46N 121 51W
Montería Col. 80 B15 8 45N 75 54W
Montero Bolivia 80 E10 17 20S 63 15W
Monte Roraima *mt.* Guyana 80 E15 5 14N 60 44W
Monterrey Mexico 74 D5 25 40N 100 20W
Montes Claros *tn.* Brazil 80 J10 16 45S 43 52W
Montes de Toledo *mts.* Sp. 87 C3 39 35N 4 30W
Montevideo Uruguay 81 F7 34 55S 56 10W
Montgomery Alabama USA 71 J3 32 22N 86 20W
Monti del Gennargentu *mts.* Italy 89 B3/B4 40 00N 9 30E
Monti Nebrodi *mts.* Italy 89 E2 37 00N 14 00E
Montluçon Fr. 87 G7 46 20N 2 36E
Montmorillon Fr. 87 F7 46 26N 0 52E
Monto Aust. 110 J5 24 53S 151 06E
Montpelier Ohio USA 52 B1 41 35N 84 35W
Montpellier Fr. 87 G5 43 36N 3 53E
Montreux Switz. 87 J7 46 27N 6 55E
Montrose UK 86 D12 56 43N 2 29W
Montrose Colorado USA 70 E4 38 29N 107 53W
Monts d'Auvergne *mts.* Fr. 87 G6 45 30N 2 50E
Montserrat *i.* Lesser Antilles 74 P9 16 45N 62 14W
Monts Nimba *mts.* Guinea/Liberia 108 C9 7 39N 8 30W
Monywa Myanmar 100 H3 22 05N 95 12E
Monza Italy 89 B6 45 35N 9 16E
Moora Aust. 110 B3 30 40S 116 01E
Moore, Lake Aust. 110 B4 30 00S 117 30E
Moorhead Minnesota USA 71 G6 46 51N 96 44W
Moosehead Lake Maine USA 53 S5 45 40N 69 40W
Mooselookmeguntic Lake Maine USA 57 E1 44 56N 71 00W
Mopti Mali 108 D10 14 29N 4 10W
Moradabad India 98 D5 28 50N 78 45E
Morant Point Jamaica 75 U13 17 55N 76 12W
Moratuwa Sri Lanka 98 D1 6 47N 79 53E
Morava *r.* Europe 88 F8 48 00N 17 00E
Moray Firth *est.* UK 86 D12 57 45N 3 45W
Moreau *r.* South Dakota USA 70 F6 45 00N 102 00W
Moree Aust. 110 H4 29 29S 149 53E
Morelia Mexico 74 D3 19 40N 101 11W
Morenci Arizona USA 70 E3 33 05N 109 22W
Morgan Hill California USA 72 C3 37 05N 121 48W
Morgantown West Virginia USA 71 L4 39 38N 79 57W
Mori Japan 102 D3 42 07N 140 33E
Morioka Japan 102 D2 39 43N 141 08E
Morlaix Fr. 86 D8 48 35N 3 50W
Morne Diablotins *mt.* Dominica 74 Q8 15 30N 61 24W
MOROCCO 108 C14
Morogoro Tanzania 109 M6 6 49S 37 40E
Moro Gulf Philippines 103 G5 7 00N 123 00E
Morón Cuba 75 J4 22 08N 78 39W
Morondava Madagascar 109 N3 20 19S 44 17E
Moroni Comoros 109 N5 11 40S 43 16E
Morotai *i.* Indonesia 103 H4 2 30N 128 30E
Moroto Uganda 108 L8 2 32N 34 41E
Morrinsville NZ 111 E6 37 39S 175 32E
Morristown New Jersey USA 73 C2 40 49N 74 29W
Morro Bay *tn.* California USA 72 C2 35 22N 120 50W
Moscow Russia 94 F8 55 45N 37 42E
Moscow Idaho USA 70 C6 46 44N 117 00W
Mosel *r.* Germany/Fr. 88 A8 50 00N 7 00E
Moses Lake *tn.* Washington USA 70 C6 47 09N 119 20W
Mosgiel NZ 111 C2 45 53S 170 21E
Moshi Tanzania 108 M7 3 21S 37 19E
Mosquito Creek Lake *res.* Ohio USA 52 F1 41 20N 80 45W
Moss Norway 86 L13 59 26N 10 41E
Mossoró Brazil 80 K12 5 10S 37 18W
Most Czech Rep. 88 D9 50 31N 13 39E
Mostar Bosnia-Herzegovina 89 F5 43 20N 17 50E
Móstoles Sp. 87 D4 40 19N 3 53W
Mosul Iraq 96 D6 36 21N 43 08E
Motala Sweden 88 E13 58 34N 15 05E
Mothe *i.* Fiji 114 V15 18 39S 178 32W
Motherwell UK 86 D11 55 48N 3 59W
Motril Sp. 87 D2 36 45N 3 31W
Motueka NZ 111 D4 41 07S 173 01E
Mouila Gabon 108 B7 1 50S 11 02E
Moulins Fr. 87 G7 47 00N 3 48E
Moulmein Myanmar 103 B7 16 30N 97 39E
Moundou Chad 108 H9 8 35N 16 01E
Mount Darwin *tn.* Zimbabwe 109 L4 16 45S 31 39E
Mount Desert Island Maine USA 57 F1 44 22N 68 15W
Mount Gambier *tn.* Aust. 110 G2 37 51S 140 50E
Mount Hagen *tn.* PNG 110 G8 5 54S 144 13E
Mount Isa *tn.* Aust. 110 F5 20 50S 139 29E
Mount Magnet *tn.* Aust. 110 B4 28 06S 117 50E
Mount Morgan *tn.* Aust. 110 J5 23 40S 150 25E
Mount Pleasant *tn.* Michigan USA 51 J2 43 36N 84 46W
Mount Union *tn.* Pennsylvania USA 73 B2 40 22N 77 52W
Mount Vernon *tn.* Illinois USA 71 J4 38 19N 88 52W
Mount Vernon *tn.* Washington USA 42 H4 48 25N 122 20W
Moyale Kenya 108 M8 3 31N 39 04E
Moyobamba Peru 80 B12 6 04S 76 56W
MOZAMBIQUE 109 L3/M5
Mozambique Basin Indian Ocean 113 C3 35 00S 40 00E
Mozambique Channel Mozambique/Madagascar 109 N4 18 00S 42 00E
Mpanda Tanzania 109 L6 6 21S 31 01E
Mtwara Tanzania 109 N5 10 17S 40 11E
Muang Chiang Rai Thailand 103 B7 19 56N 99 51E
Muang Khon Kaen Thailand 103 C7 16 25N 102 50E
Muang Lampang Thailand 103 B7 18 16N 99 30E
Muang Nakhon Sawan Thailand 103 B7 15 42N 100 10E
Muang Phitsanulok Thailand 103 C7 16 49N 100 18E
Muchinga Mountains Zambia 109 L5 12 30S 32 30E
Mudanjiang China 101 P7 44 36N 129 42E
Mufulira Zambia 109 K5 12 30S 28 12E
Muğla Turkey 96 A6 37 13N 28 22E
Muir Woods National Monument California USA 72 B3 37 54N 122 32W
Mui Wo HK China 100 A1 22 16N 113 59E
Mukachevo Ukraine 88 J8 48 26N 22 45E
Mukalla Yemen 97 E1 14 34N 49 09E
Mulegé Mexico 74 B5 26 54N 112 00W
Mulhacén *mt.* Sp. 87 D2 37 04N 3 19W
Mulhouse Fr. 86 J7 47 45N 7 21E
Mull *i.* UK 86 B12 56 25N 6 00W
Mullett Lake Michigan USA 52 B5 45 30N 84 30W
Mullingar RoI 86 B10 53 32N 7 20W
Multan Pakistan 98 C6 30 10N 71 36E
Mumbai India 98 C3 18 56N 72 51E
Muna *i.* Indonesia 103 G2/G3 5 00S 122 20E
Muncie Indiana USA 71 J5 40 11N 85 22W
Muncy Pennsylvania USA 73 B2 41 12N 76 48W
Mundo *r.* Sp. 87 D3/E3 38 30N 2 00W
Mungbere CDR 108 K8 2 40N 28 25E
Mungla Bangladesh 99 K9 22 18N 89 34E
Munich Germany 88 C8 48 08N 11 35E
Munising Michigan USA 51 H4 46 24N 86 39W
Münster Germany 88 A9 51 58N 7 37E
Mur *r.* Europe 89 E7 48 00N 14 40E
Murat *r.* Turkey 96 D6 38 50N 40 20E
Murchison NZ 111 D4 41 50S 172 20E
Murchison *r.* Aust. 110 B4 26 00S 117 00E
Murcia Sp. 87 E2 37 59N 1 08W
Mureş *r.* Romania 89 J6 46 00N 22 00E
Murfreesboro Tennessee USA 71 J4 35 50N 86 25W
Müritz *l.* Germany 88 D10 53 00N 12 00E
Murmansk Russia 94 F10 68 59N 33 08E
Murom Russia 94 G8 55 34N 42 04E
Muroran Japan 102 D3 42 21N 140 59E
Muroto Japan 102 B1 33 13N 134 11E
Muroto-zaki *c.* Japan 102 B1 33 13N 134 11E
Murray *r.* Aust. 110 G2 35 30S 144 00E
Murray Bridge *tn.* Aust. 110 F2 35 10S 139 17E
Murray Seascarp Pacific Ocean 115 N11 32 00N 138 00W
Murrumbidgee *r.* Aust. 110 H3 34 30S 146 30E
Murupara NZ 111 F5 38 27S 176 42E
Murwara India 98 E4 23 49N 80 28E
Murzuq Libya 108 G13 25 55N 13 55E
Muş Turkey 96 D6 38 45N 41 30E
Muscat Oman 97 G3 23 37N 58 38E
Musgrave Ranges Aust. 110 E4 26 00S 132 00E
Mushin Nigeria 108 E9 6 30N 3 15E
Muskegon Michigan USA 71 J5 43 13N 86 15W
Muskegon River Michigan USA 52 A3 44 00N 85 05W
Muskogee Oklahoma USA 71 G4 35 35N 95 21W
Musselshell *r.* Montana USA 70 E6 47 00N 108 00W
Mustique *i.* Lesser Antilles 74 R11 12 39N 61 15W
Mutarara Mozambique 109 M4 17 30S 35 06E
Mutare Zimbabwe 109 L4 18 58N 32 40E
Mutsu Japan 102 D3 41 18N 141 15E
Mutsu-wan *b.* Japan 102 D3 41 05N 140 40E
Muyun Kum *d.* Kazakhstan 94 J5/K5 44 00N 70 00E
Muzaffarnagar India 98 D5 29 28N 77 42E
Muzaffarpur India 99 F5 26 07N 85 23E
Muzon, Cape Alaska USA 42 D4 54 41N 132 40W
Mwanza Tanzania 108 L7 2 31S 32 56E
Mweru, Lake CDR/Zambia 109 K6 8 30S 28 30E
MYANMAR 103 B7
Myitkyina Myanmar 101 H4 25 24N 97 25E
Mymensingh Bangladesh 99 L10 33 43N 78 54W
Myrtle Beach *tn.* USA 71 L3 22 50N 109 52W
Mys Chelyuskin *c.* Russia 95 N12 77 44N 103 55E
Mys Kanin Nos *c.* Russia 94 G10 68 38N 43 20E
Mys Navarin *c.* Russia 95 V9 62 17N 179 13E
Mys Olyutorskiy *c.* Russia 95 V9 59 58N 170 25E
Mysore India 98 D2 12 18N 76 37E
Mys Tolstoy *c.* Russia 95 T8 59 00N 155 00E
My Tho Vietnam 103 D6 10 21N 106 21E
Mytilíni Greece 89 L3 39 06N 26 34E
Mzuzu Malawi 109 L5 11 31S 34 00E

N

Naas RoI 86 B10 53 13N 6 39W
Naberezhnyye Chelny Russia 94 H8 55 42N 52 19E
Nablus Jordan 96 N11 32 13N 35 16E
Nacimiento Reservoir California USA 72 C2 34 45N 121 00W
Nacogdoches Texas USA 71 H3 31 36N 94 40W
Nadiad India 98 C4 22 42N 72 55E
Nador Morocco 108 D15 35 10N 3 00W
Nadym Russia 94 K10 65 25N 72 40E
Naestved Denmark 88 C11 55 14N 11 47E
Náfplio Greece 89 J2 37 34N 22 48E
Naga Philippines 103 G6 13 36N 123 12E
Nagaland *admin.* India 99 G5 26 00N 94 30E
Nagano Japan 102 C2 36 39N 138 10E
Nagaoka Japan 102 C2 37 27N 138 50E
Nagaon India 99 G5 26 20N 92 41E
Nagasaki Japan 102 A1 32 45N 129 52E
Nagato Japan 102 B1 34 22N 131 11E
Nagercoil India 98 D1 8 11N 77 30E
Nagornyy Russia 95 Q8 55 57N 124 54E
Nagoya Japan 102 C2 35 08N 136 53E
Nagpur India 98 D4 21 10N 79 12E
Nagykanizsa Hungary 89 F7 46 27N 17 00E
Nahariyya Israel 96 N11 33 01N 35 05E
Nairobi Kenya 108 M7 1 17S 36 50E
Najd *geog. reg.* Saudi Arabia 96 D4 25 40N 42 30E
Najrān Saudi Arabia 96 D2 17 37N 44 40E
Nakamura Japan 102 B1 33 02N 132 58E
Nakatsu Japan 102 B1 33 37N 131 11E
Nakhodka Russia 95 R5 42 53N 132 54E
Nakhon Ratchasima Thailand 103 C6 14 59N 102 06E
Nakhon Si Thammarat Thailand 103 B5 8 24N 99 58E
Nakuru Kenya 108 M7 0 16S 36 05E
Nal *r.* Pakistan 98 B5 26 10N 65 30E
Nal'chik Russia 94 G5 43 31N 43 38E
Namangan Uzbekistan 94 K5 40 59N 71 41E
Nam Dinh Vietnam 101 K3 20 25N 106 12E
Namib Desert Namibia 109 G3/H2 22 00S 14 00E
Namibe Angola 109 G4 15 10S 12 09E
NAMIBIA 109 H3
Nampa Idaho USA 70 C5 43 35N 116 34W
Nampo North Korea 101 P6 38 51N 125 10E
Nampula Mozambique 109 M4 15 09S 39 14E
Namtu Myanmar 101 H3 23 04N 97 26E
Namur Belgium 86 H9 50 28N 4 52E
Nam Wan HK China 100 B2 22 20N 114 05E
Nanao Japan 102 C2 37 03N 136 58E
Nanchang China 101 M4 28 33N 115 58E
Nanchong China 101 K5 30 54N 106 06E
Nancowry Island India 99 G1 7 59N 93 32E
Nancy Fr. 86 J8 48 42N 6 12E
Nanda Devi *mt.* India 98 D6 30 21N 79 58E
Nānded India 98 D3 19 11N 77 21E
Nanduri Fiji 114 U16 16 26S 179 08E
Nanjing China 101 M5 32 03N 118 47E
Nan Ling *mts.* China 101 L3 25 00N 112 00E
Nanning China 101 K3 22 50N 108 19E
Nanpan Jiang *r.* China 101 K3 25 00N 106 00E
Nanping China 101 M4 26 40N 118 07E
Nantes Fr. 87 E7 47 14N 1 35W
Nantong China 101 N5 32 06N 121 04E
Nantucket Island Massachusetts USA 71 M5 41 15N 70 05W
Nantucket Sound Massachusetts USA 73 E2 41 20N 70 08W
Nanuku Passage *sd.* Fiji 114 V15 16 40S 179 25W
Nanumea *is.* Tuvalu 114 H7 5 43S 176 00E
Nanyang China 101 L5 33 06N 112 31E
Nanyuki Kenya 108 M8 0 01N 37 05E
Naogaon Bangladesh 99 K10 24 49N 88 59E
Napa California USA 72 B4 38 18N 122 17W
Napier NZ 111 F5 39 30S 176 54E
Naples Italy 89 E4 40 50N 14 15E
Naples Florida USA 71 K2 26 09N 81 48W
Napo *r.* Peru 80 C13 2 30S 73 30W
Napoleon Ohio USA 52 B1 41 24N 84 09W
Napoopoo Hawaiian Islands 115 Z17 19 29N 155 55W
Nara Japan 102 C1 34 41N 135 49E
Narail Bangladesh 99 K9 23 18N 89 45E
Narayanganj Bangladesh 99 L9 23 36N 90 28E
Narbonne Fr. 87 G5 43 11N 3 00E
Narcondam Island India 99 G2 13 15N 94 30E
Nares Deep Atlantic Ocean 116 B9 26 00N 61 10W
Narew *r.* Europe 88 H10 53 00N 21 00E
Narmada *r.* India 98 C4 22 00N 75 00E
Narrogin Aust. 110 B3 32 57S 117 07E
Nar'yan Mar Russia 94 H10 67 37N 53 02E
Nasca Ridge Pacific Ocean 115 T5 20 00S 81 00W
Naseby NZ 111 C2 45 02S 171 26E
Nashik India 98 C3 20 00N 73 52E
Nashua New Hampshire USA 71 M5 42 44N 71 28W
Nashville Tennessee USA 71 J4 36 10N 86 50W
Nassau Bahamas 75 J5 25 05N 77 20W
Nasser, Lake Egypt 108 L12 22 35N 31 40E
Nässjö Sweden 88 E12 57 40N 14 40E
Natal Brazil 80 K12 5 46S 35 15W
Natchez Mississippi USA 71 H3 31 32N 91 24W
Natewa Peninsula Fiji 114 U15 16 40S 180 00
National City California USA 72 E1 32 39N 117 05W
Natron, Lake Tanzania 108 M7 2 00S 36 00E
Natuna Besar *i.* Indonesia 103 D4 3 40N 108 00E
Naturaliste, Cape Aust. 110 B3 33 32S 115 01E
NAURU 114 G7
Nausori Fiji 114 U15 18 01S 178 31E
Navadwip India 99 K9 23 25N 88 22E
Navia *r.* Sp. 87 B5 43 10N 7 05W
Naviti *i.* Fiji 114 T16 17 08S 177 15E
Navoi Uzbekistan 94 J5 40 04N 65 20E
Navojoa Mexico 74 C5 27 04N 109 28W
Navsari India 98 C4 20 58N 73 01E
Nawabganj Bangladesh 99 K10 24 35N 88 21E
Náxos *i.* Greece 89 K2 37 00N 25 00E
Nayoro Japan 102 D3 44 21N 142 30E
Nazareth Israel 96 N11 32 41N 35 16E
Nazca Peru 80 C11 14 53S 74 54W
Nazwá Oman 97 G3 22 56N 57 33E
Ndélé CAR 108 J9 8 25N 20 38E
Ndjamena Chad 108 H10 12 10N 14 59E
Ndola Zambia 109 K5 13 00S 28 39E
Neah Bay *tn.* Washington USA 42 H4 48 20N 124 38W
Néapoli Greece 89 J2 36 31N 23 03E
Nebitdag Turkmenistan 94 H4 39 31N 54 24E
Nebraska *state* USA 70 F5 42 00N 102 00W
Neche North Dakota USA 49 D1 48 59N 97 33W
Neckei *i.* Hawaiian Islands 115 K10 23 25N 164 42W
Necochea Argentina 81 F6 38 31S 58 46W
Needles California USA 70 D3 34 51N 114 36W
Negele Ethiopia 108 M9 5 20N 39 35E
Negev *d.* Israel 96 N10 30 50N 30 45E
Negombo Sri Lanka 98 D1 7 13N 79 51E
Negritos Peru 80 A13 4 42S 81 18W
Negro *r.* Argentina 81 E6 40 00S 65 00W
Negro *r.* Brazil 80 D13 0 05S 67 00W
Negro *r.* Uruguay 81 F7 33 00S 57 30W
Negros *i.* Philippines 103 G5 10 00N 123 00E
Neijiang China 101 K4 29 32N 105 03E
Nei Mongol Zizhiqu *admin.* China 101 K7 42 30N 112 30E
Neiva Col. 80 B14 2 58N 75 15W
Nek'emte Ethiopia 108 M9 9 04N 36 30E
Nellore India 98 D2 14 29N 80 00E
Nelson NZ 111 D4 41 30S 173 20E
Neman *r.* Lithuania/Russia 88 J11 55 00N 22 00E
Nemuro Japan 102 E3 43 22N 145 36E
Nemuro-kaikyō *sd.* Japan 102 E3 44 00N 146 00E

Name	Page	Grid	Lat	Long
Nenjiang China	101	P8	49 10N	125 15E
Nen Jiang *r.* China	101	P9	50 00N	125 00E
NEPAL	98/99	E5/F5		
Nerchinsk Russia	95	P7	52 02N	116 38E
Neretva *r.* Bosnia-Herzegovina	89	G5	43 30N	15 18E
Nerva Sp.	87	B2	37 41N	6 33W
Neryungri Russia	95	Q8	56 39N	124 38E
Netanya Israel	96	N11	32 20N	34 51E
Netcong New Jersey USA	73	C2	40 54N	74 42W
NETHERLANDS	86	H10		
Netzahualcóyotl Mexico	74	E3	19 24N	99 02W
Neubrandenburg Germany	88	D10	53 33N	13 16E
Neuchâtel Switz.	87	J7	46 55N	6 56E
Neufchâtel-en-Bray Fr.	86	F8	49 44N	1 26E
Neumünster Germany	88	B11	54 05N	9 59E
Neuquén Argentina	81	D6	38 55S	68 05W
Neuruppin Germany	88	D10	52 56N	12 49E
Neusiedler See *l.* Austria	88	F7	48 00N	16 00E
Neustrelitz Germany	88	D10	53 22N	13 05E
Nevada *state* USA	70	C4	39 00N	118 00W
Nevers Fr.	87	G7	47 00N	3 09E
Nevis *i.* St. Kitts and Nevis	74	P9	17 10N	62 34W
New *r.* USA	71	K4	37 00N	81 00W
New Albany Indiana USA	71	J4	38 17N	85 50W
New Amsterdam Guyana	80	F15	6 18N	57 30W
Newark New Jersey USA	71	M5	40 44N	74 24W
Newark New York USA	53	J3	43 02N	77 06W
Newark Ohio USA	71	K5	40 03N	82 25W
Newark Bay New Jersey USA	73	H1	40 40N	74 08W
New Bedford Massachusetts USA	71	M5	41 38N	70 55W
New Bern North Carolina USA	71	L4	35 05N	77 04W
Newberry Michigan USA	51	J4	46 21N	85 31W
New Braunfels Texas USA	71	G2	29 43N	98 09W
New Brighton New Jersey USA	73	H1	40 37N	74 06W
New Britain Connecticut USA	73	D2	41 40N	72 48W
New Britain *i.* PNG	110	H8/J8	4 45S	150 30E
New Brunswick New Jersey USA	73	C2	40 29N	74 26W
Newburgh New York USA	71	M5	41 30N	74 00W
New Caledonia *i.* Pacific Ocean	114	G5	22 00S	165 00E
Newcastle Aust.	110	J3	32 55S	151 46E
Newcastle Wyoming USA	70	F5	43 52N	104 14W
Newcastle upon Tyne UK	86	E11	54 59N	1 35W
New Delhi India	98	D5	28 37N	77 14E
New Dorp New York USA	73	H1	40 34N	74 06W
Newfane New York USA	52	H3	43 17N	78 42W
Newfoundland Basin Atlantic Ocean	116	D11	44 00N	40 00W
New Guinea *i.* Pacific Ocean	110	E9/H8	5 00S	141 00E
Newhalem Washington USA	42	H4	48 35N	121 20W
New Hampshire *state* USA	71	M5	43 00N	72 00W
New Hartford Connecticut USA	73	D2	41 52N	72 57W
New Haven Connecticut USA	71	M5	41 18N	72 55W
New Hebrides Trench Pacific Ocean	114	G6	15 00S	169 00E
New Iberia Louisiana USA	71	H2	30 00N	91 51W
New Ireland *i.* PNG	110	J9	3 15S	152 30E
New Jersey *state* USA	71	M4	40 00N	75 00W
New London Connecticut USA	71	M5	41 21N	72 06W
Newman Aust.	110	B5	23 20S	119 34E
New Mexico *state* USA	70	E3	35 00N	107 00W
New Milford Pennsylvania USA	53	L1	41 52N	75 44W
New Orleans Louisiana USA	71	H2	30 00N	90 03W
New Plymouth NZ	111	E5	39 04S	174 04E
Newport UK	86	D9	51 35N	3 00W
Newport Rhode Island USA	73	E2	41 29N	71 20W
Newport Vermont USA	53	P4	44 56N	72 13W
Newport Beach *tn.* California USA	72	E1	33 38N	117 55W
Newport News Virginia USA	71	L4	36 59N	76 26W
Newry UK	86	B11	54 11N	6 20W
New Siberian Islands Russia	95	R12/S12	75 00N	145 00E
New South Wales *state* Aust.	110	G3/H3	32 00S	145 00E
New Springville New York USA	73	H1	40 35N	74 10W
Newton Falls *tn.* New York USA	53	L4	44 13N	74 58W
New Ulm Minnesota USA	71	H5	44 19N	94 28W
New York New York USA	71	M5	40 40N	73 50W
New York *state* USA	71	L5	43 00N	76 00W
NEW ZEALAND	111			
Neyrīz Iran	97	F4	29 14N	54 18E
Neyshābūr Iran	97	G6	36 13N	58 49E
Ngami, Lake Botswana	109	J3	21 00S	23 00E
Ngau *i.* Fiji	114	U15	18 00S	179 16E
Ngong Ping HK China	100	A1	22 15N	113 54E
Nguigmi Niger	108	G10	14 19N	13 06E
Nguru Nigeria	108	G10	12 53N	10 30E
Nha Trang Vietnam	103	D6	12 15N	109 10E
Nhulunbuy Aust.	110	F7	12 30S	136 56E
Niagara Escarpment New York USA	54	D2	43 08N	78 50W
Niagara Falls *tn.* New York USA	71	L5	43 06N	79 04W
Niamey Niger	108	E10	13 32N	2 05E
Niangara CDR	108	K8	3 45N	27 54E
NICARAGUA	75	G2		
Nice Fr.	87	J5	43 42N	7 16E
Nicobar Islands India	99	G1	8 30N	94 00E
Nicosia Cyprus	96	B6	35 11N	33 23E
Niedere Tauern *mts.* Austria	89	D7	47 00N	14 00E
Nienburg Germany	88	B10	52 38N	9 13E
Nieuw Nickerie Suriname	80	F15	5 52N	57 00W
NIGER	108	E10		
Niger *r.* West Africa	108	F9	5 30N	6 15E
NIGERIA	108	F10		
Nihoa *i.* Hawaiian Islands	115	K10	23 03N	161 55W
Niigata Japan	102	C2	37 58N	139 02E
Niihama Japan	102	B1	33 57N	133 15E
Niihau *i.* Hawaiian Islands	115	W18	21 50N	160 11W
Nii-jima *i.* Japan	102	C1	34 20N	139 15E
Nijmegen Neths.	86	H9	51 50N	5 52E
Nikkō Japan	102	C2	36 45N	139 37E
Nikolayevsk-na-Amure Russia	95	S7	53 10N	140 44E
Nikšić Montenegro	89	G5	42 48N	18 56E
Niland California USA	72	F1	33 14N	115 30W
Nile *r.* Sudan/Egypt	108	L13	27 30N	31 40E
Nilgiri Hills India	98	D2	11 00N	76 30E
Nîmes Fr.	87	H5	43 50N	4 21E
Nimule Sudan	108	L8	3 35N	32 03E
Nim Wan HK China	100	A2	22 26N	113 56E
Nine Degree Channel *sd.* Maldives	98	C1	9 00N	73 00E
9 de Julio *tn.* Argentina	81	E6	35 28S	60 58W
Ninepin Group *is.* HK China	100	D1	22 15N	114 22E
Ninety East Ridge Indian Ocean	113	H4	20 00S	88 00E
Ninety Mile Beach NZ	111	D7	34 45S	172 58E
Nineveh *hist. site* Iraq	96	D6	36 24N	43 08E
Ningbo China	101	N4	29 54N	121 33E
Ninh Binh Vietnam	101	K3	20 14N	106 00E
Niobrara *r.* USA	70	F5	42 00N	102 00W
Nioro du Sahel Mali	108	C11	15 12N	9 35W
Niort Fr.	87	E7	46 19N	0 27W
Niš Serbia	89	H5	43 20N	21 54E
Niterói Brazil	80	J9	22 54S	43 06W
Nitra Slovakia	88	G8	48 19N	18 04E
Niue *i.* Pacific Ocean	115	K6	19 02S	169 55W
Nizamabad India	98	D3	18 40N	78 05E
Nizhneangarsk Russia	95	N8	55 48N	109 35E
Nizhnekamsk Russia	94	H8	55 38N	51 49E
Nizhnekolymsk Russia	95	U10	68 34N	160 58E
Nizhnevartovsk Russia	94	K9	60 57N	76 40E
Nizhniy Novgorod Russia	94	G8	56 20N	44 00E
Nizhniy Tagil Russia	94	J8	58 00N	59 58E
Nizhnyaya (Lower) Tunguska *r.* Russia	95	M9	64 00N	95 00E
Nízké Tatry *mts.* Slovakia	88	G8	49 00N	19 00E
Nkongsamba Cameroon	108	F8	4 59N	9 53E
Noakhali Bangladesh	99	L9	22 52N	91 03E
Nobeoka Japan	102	B1	32 36N	131 40E
Nogales Mexico	74	B6	31 20N	111 00W
Nogales Arizona USA	70	D3	31 20N	110 56W
Nojima-zaki *c.* Japan	102	C1	34 54N	139 54E
Nokrek Peak *mt.* India	99	L10	25 27N	90 21E
Nola CAR	108	H8	3 28N	16 08E
Nome Alaska USA	40	B6	64 32N	165 28W
Nordfriesische Inseln *is.* Germany	88	A11	54 00N	8 00E
Nordhausen Germany	88	C9	51 31N	10 48E
Nordvik Russia	95	P11	74 01N	111 30E
Nore *r.* RoI	86	B10	52 45N	7 21W
Norfolk Nebraska USA	71	G5	42 01N	97 25W
Norfolk Virginia USA	71	L4	36 54N	76 18W
Norfolk Island Pacific Ocean	108	G5	29 05S	167 59E
Norfolk Island Trough Pacific Ocean	114	F5	27 30S	166 00E
Norfolk Lake Arkansas USA	71	H4	36 00N	92 00W
Noril'sk Russia	95	L10	69 21N	88 02E
Normanton Aust.	110	G6	17 40S	141 05E
Norridgewock Maine USA	53	S4	44 43N	69 48W
Norris Lake Tennessee USA	71	K4	36 00N	84 00W
Norristown Pennsylvania USA	73	C2	40 07N	75 21W
Norrköping Sweden	88	F13	58 35N	16 10E
Norrtälje Sweden	88	G13	59 46N	18 43E
Norseman Aust.	110	C3	32 15S	121 47E
North Adams Massachusetts USA	73	D3	42 43N	73 12W
Northam Aust.	110	B3	31 40S	116 40E
North American Basin Atlantic Ocean	116	C10	34 00N	55 00W
Northampton Aust.	110	A4	28 27S	114 37E
Northampton UK	86	E10	52 14N	0 54W
Northampton Massachusetts USA	73	D3	42 20N	72 38W
North Andaman *i.* Andaman Islands	99	G2	13 00N	93 00E
North Australian Basin Indian Ocean	113	L5	14 00S	115 00E
North Bergen New Jersey USA	73	H2	40 46N	74 02W
North Canadian *r.* USA	70	F4	36 00N	100 00W
North Cape NZ	111	D7	34 25S	173 03E
North Carolina *state* USA	71	L4	36 00N	80 00W
North Cascades National Park Washington USA	42	H4	48 45N	121 20W
North Channel British Isles	86	C11	55 20N	5 50W
North Collins New York USA	54	D1	42 36N	78 57W
North Dakota *state* USA	70/71	F6	47 00N	102 00W
North East Pennsylvania USA	52	G2	42 13N	79 51W
Northern Ireland *admin.* UK	86	B11	54 40N	7 00W
NORTHERN MARIANAS	114	E9/F9		
Northern Territory *territory* Aust.	110	E5/E6	19 00S	132 00E
North Fiji Basin Pacific Ocean	114	H6	18 00S	173 00E
North Island NZ	111	D7/E4	39 00S	176 00E
NORTH KOREA	101	P6/P7		
North Little Rock Arkansas USA	71	H3	34 46N	92 16W
North Loup *r.* Nebraska USA	70	F5	42 00N	100 00W
North Platte Nebraska USA	70	F5	41 09N	100 45W
North Platte *r.* North America	70	F5	42 00N	103 00W
North Pole Arctic Ocean	117		90 00N	
North Stratford New Hampshire USA	53	Q4	44 46N	71 36W
North Uist *i.* UK	86	B12	57 04N	7 15W
North West Cape Aust.	110	A5	21 48S	114 10E
North West Christmas Island Ridge Pacific Ocean	115	K9	9 30N	170 00W
Northwestern Atlantic Basin Atlantic Ocean	116	A10	33 00N	70 00W
Northwest Highlands UK	86	C12	58 00N	5 00W
Northwest Pacific Basin Pacific Ocean	114	E11	35 00N	150 00E
North York Moors UK	86	E11	55 22N	0 45W
Norton Kansas USA	70	G4	39 51N	99 53W
Norwalk Connecticut USA	73	D2	41 08N	73 25W
Norwalk Ohio USA	51	K1	41 15N	82 36W
NORWAY	86	H13		
Norwegian Basin Atlantic Ocean	116	H13	67 00N	0 00
Norwegian Sea Arctic Ocean	117		70 00N	5 00E
Norwich UK	86	F10	52 38N	1 18E
Norwich Connecticut USA	73	D2	41 32N	72 05W
Norwich New York USA	53	L2	42 32N	75 32W
Noshiro Japan	102	D3	40 13N	140 00E
Nosop *r.* Southern Africa	109	J2	25 00S	20 30E
Nosy Bé *i.* Madagascar	109	P5	13 00S	47 00E
Notéc *r.* Poland	88	F10	53 00N	17 00E
Nottingham UK	86	E10	52 58N	1 10W
Nouadhibou Mauritania	108	A12	20 54N	17 01W
Nouakchott Mauritania	108	A11	18 09N	15 58W
Nova Friburgo Brazil	80	J9	22 16S	42 34W
Nova Iguaçu Brazil	80	J9	22 46S	43 23W
Novara Italy	89	B6	45 27N	8 37E
Nova Scotia Basin Atlantic Ocean	116	C10	39 00N	55 00W
Novato California USA	72	B4	38 05N	122 34W
Novaya Zemlya *is.* Russia	94	H11	74 00N	55 00E
Novgorod Russia	94	F8	58 30N	31 20E
Novi Pazar Serbia	89	H5	43 09N	20 29E
Novi Sad Serbia	89	G6	45 15N	19 51E
Novograd Volynskiy Ukraine	88	L9	50 34N	27 32E
Novo Hamburgo Brazil	81	G8	29 37S	51 07W
Novokazalinsk Kazakhstan	94	J6	45 48N	62 06E
Novokuznetsk Russia	95	L7	53 45N	87 12E
Novorossiysk Russia	94	F5	44 44N	37 46E
Novosibirsk Russia	95	L8	55 04N	83 05E
Novvy Port Russia	94	K10	67 38N	72 33E
Novvy Urengoy Russia	94	K10	66 00N	77 20E
Nowa Sól Poland	88	E9	51 49N	15 41E
Nowy Dwor Mazowiecki Poland	88	H10	52 27N	20 41E
Nowy Sącz Poland	88	H8	49 39N	20 40E
Noyes Island Alaska USA	42	D4	56 30N	133 45W
Nubian Desert Sudan	108	L12	21 00N	33 00E
Nueces *r.* Texas USA	70	G2	28 00N	99 00W
Nueva Rosita Mexico	74	D5	27 58N	101 11W
Nueva San Salvador El Salvador	74	G2	13 40N	89 18W
Nuevitas Cuba	75	J4	21 34N	77 18W
Nuevo Casas Grandes Mexico	74	C6	30 22N	107 53W
Nuevo Laredo Mexico	74	E5	27 39N	99 30W
Nu Jiang *r.* China/Myanmar	101	H3/H4	25 00N	99 00E
Nukus Uzbekistan	94	H5	42 28N	59 07E
Nullarbor Plain Aust.	110	D3	32 00S	128 00E
Numazu Japan	102	C2	35 08N	138 50E
Numedal *geog. reg.* Norway	86	K13	60 40N	9 00E
Nunivak Island Alaska USA	115	K13	60 00N	166 00W
Nuoro Italy	89	B4	40 20N	9 21E
Nuremberg Germany	88	C8	49 27N	11 05E
Nusaybin Turkey	96	D6	37 05N	41 11E
Nushki Pakistan	98	B5	29 33N	66 01E
Nyainqêntanglha Shan *mts.* China	100	F4/G5	30 00N	90 00E
Nyala Sudan	108	J10	12 01N	24 50E
Nyasa, Lake Southern Africa	109	L5	12 00S	35 00E
Nyíregyháza Hungary	88	H7	47 57N	21 43E
Nykøbing Denmark	88	C11	54 47N	11 53E
Nyköping Sweden	88	F13	58 45N	17 03E
Nyngan Aust.	110	H3	31 34S	147 14E
Nyons Fr.	87	H6	44 22N	5 08E
Nysa Poland	88	F9	50 30N	17 20E
Nysa *r.* Poland	88	E9	52 00N	14 00E
Nyūdō-zaki *c.* Japan	102	C2	40 00N	139 42E
O				
Oahe, Lake USA	70	F6	45 00N	100 00W
Oahu *i.* Hawaiian Islands	115	X18	21 30N	158 10W
Oakdale California USA	72	C3	37 40N	120 53W
Oak Harbor *tn.* Ohio USA	52	C1	41 31N	83 10W
Oak Harbor *tn.* Washington USA	42	H4	48 20N	122 38W
Oakhurst California USA	72	D3	37 20N	119 39W
Oakland California USA	70	B4	37 50N	122 15W
Oak Ridge *tn.* Tennessee USA	71	K4	36 02N	84 12W
Oamaru NZ	111	C2	45 06S	170 58E
Oaxaca Mexico	74	E3	17 05N	96 41W
Ob' *r.* Russia	94	J10	65 30N	66 00E
Oban UK	86	C12	56 25N	5 29W
Ob', Gulf of Russia	94	K10	68 00N	74 00E
Obidos Brazil	80	F13	1 52S	55 30W
Obihiro Japan	102	D3	42 56N	143 10E
Ocala Florida USA	71	K2	29 11N	82 09W
Ocana Col.	80	C15	8 16N	73 21W
Ocatlán Mexico	74	D4	20 21N	102 42W
Oceanside California USA	72	E1	33 12N	117 23W
Ōda Japan	102	B2	35 10N	132 29E
Ōdate Japan	102	D3	40 18N	140 32E
Odawara Japan	102	C2	35 15N	139 08E
Odense Denmark	88	C11	55 24N	10 25E
Oder *r.* Europe	88	E10	52 00N	15 30E
Odessa Delaware USA	73	C1	39 27N	75 40W
Odessa Texas USA	70	F3	31 50N	102 23W
Odiel *r.* Sp.	87	B2	37 32N	7 00W
Odra *r.* Europe	88	E10	52 00N	15 00E
Oeno *i.* Pacific Ocean	115	N5	23 10S	132 00W
Ofanto *r.* Italy	89	E4/F4	41 00N	15 00E
Offenburg Germany	88	A8	48 29N	7 57E
Ōfunato Japan	102	D2	39 04N	141 43E
Ogaden *geog. reg.* Africa	108	P9	7 00N	51 00E
Ōgaki Japan	102	C2	35 22N	136 36E
Ogasawara Gunto *i.* Pacific Ocean	114	E10	27 30N	143 00E
Ogbomoso Nigeria	108	E9	8 05N	4 11E
Ogden Utah USA	70	D5	41 14N	111 59W
Ogdensburg New York USA	51	P3	44 05N	74 36W
Ogooué *r.* Gabon	108	F7	0 50S	9 50E
Ohai NZ	111	A2	45 56S	167 57E
Ōhata Japan	102	D3	41 22N	141 11E
Ohio *r.* USA	71	J4	38 00N	86 00W
Ohio *state* USA	71	K5	40 00N	83 00W
Ohridsko ezero *l.* Europe	89	H4	41 00N	21 00E
Oil City Pennsylvania USA	52	G1	41 26N	79 44W
Oildale California USA	72	D2	35 25N	119 00W
Oise *r.* Fr.	86	G8	49 10N	2 10E
Ōita Japan	102	B1	33 15N	131 36E
Ojinaga Mexico	74	D5	29 35N	104 26W
Okanagan *r.* North America	70	C6	49 00N	119 00W
Okanogan Washington USA	43	L1	48 22N	119 35W
Okanogan River North America	43	L1	49 00N	119 00W
Okara Pakistan	98	C6	30 49N	73 31E
Okavango *r.* Southern Africa	109	H4	17 50S	20 00E
Okavango Basin Botswana	109	J4	19 00S	23 00E
Okaya Japan	102	C2	36 03N	138 00E
Okayama Japan	102	B1	34 40N	133 54E
Okazaki Japan	102	C1	34 58N	137 10E
Okeechobee, Lake Florida USA	71	K2	27 00N	81 00W
Okha Russia	95	S7	53 35N	143 01E
Okhotsk Russia	95	S8	59 20N	143 15E
Okhotsk, Sea of Russia	95	S7/S8	55 00N	148 00E
Oki *is.* Japan	102	B2	36 05N	133 00E
Okinawa *i.* Japan	101	P4	26 30N	128 00E
Oklahoma *state* USA	71	G4	36 00N	98 00W
Oklahoma City Oklahoma USA	71	G4	35 28N	97 33W
Oktyabr'skiy Russia	95	T7	52 43N	156 14E
Okushiri-tō *i.* Japan	102	C3	42 15N	139 30E
Olancha California USA	72	D3	36 18N	118 00W
Öland *i.* Sweden	88	F12	56 45N	51 50E
Olbia Italy	89	B4	40 56N	9 30E
Olcott New York USA	54	D2	43 20N	78 40W
Oldenburg Germany	88	B10	53 08N	8 13E
Old Saybrook Connecticut USA	73	D2	41 18N	72 23W
Old Town Maine USA	57	F1	44 55N	68 41W
Olean New York USA	51	M2	42 05N	78 26W
Olekma *r.* Russia	95	Q8	59 00N	121 00E
Olekminsk Russia	95	Q9	60 25N	120 25E
Olenek Russia	95	P10	68 28N	112 18E
Olenek *r.* Russia	95	Q11	72 00N	122 00E
Olga Washington USA	42	H4	48 40N	123 05W
Olhão Port.	87	B2	37 01N	7 50W
Olinda Brazil	80	K12	8 00S	34 51W
Olomouc Czech Rep.	88	F8	49 38N	17 15E
Olongapo Philippines	103	G6	14 49N	120 17E
Olsztyn Poland	88	H10	53 48N	20 29E
Olt *r.* Romania	89	K6	44 00N	24 00E
Olympia Washington USA	70	B6	47 03N	122 53W
Ólympos *mt.* Greece	89	J4	40 05N	22 21E
Olympus *mt.* Cyprus	96	B5	34 55N	32 52E
Olympus, Mount Washington USA	70	B6	47 49N	123 42W
Om' *r.* Russia	94	K8	55 30N	79 00E
Omagh UK	86	B11	54 36N	7 18W
Omaha Nebraska USA	71	G5	41 15N	96 00W
Omak Washington USA	43	L1	48 25N	119 30W
OMAN	97	F2/G3		
Oman, Gulf of Iran/Oman	97	G3	24 30N	58 30E
Omboué Gabon	108	F7	1 38S	9 20E
Omdurman Sudan	108	L11	15 37N	32 29E
Ommaney, Cape Alaska USA	42	C5	56 10N	134 40W
Omo *r.* Ethiopia	108	M9	7 00N	37 00E
Omolon *r.* Russia	95	U10	65 00N	160 00E
Omoloy *r.* Russia	95	R10	70 00N	132 00E
Omsk Russia	94	K8	55 00N	73 22E
Ōmuta Japan	102	B1	33 02N	130 26E
Onaway Michigan USA	52	B5	45 23N	84 14W

Oneida New York USA **51** P2 43 05N 75 39W
Oneida Lake New York USA **51** P2 43 14N 76 00W
Oneonta New York USA **53** L2 42 30N 75 04W
Onești Romania **89** L7 46 15N 26 45E
Onezhskoye Ozero *l.* Russia **94** F9 62 00N 40 00E
Ongea Levu *i.* Fiji **114** V15 19 11S 178 28W
Onitsha Nigeria **108** F9 6 10N 6 47E
Onomichi Japan **102** B1 34 25N 33 11E
Onon *r.* Russia/Mongolia **101** L9 51 00N 114 00E
Onslow Aust. **110** B5 21 41S 115 12E
Ontario California USA **70** C3 34 04N 117 38W
Ontonagon Michigan USA **71** J6 46 52N 89 18W
Oostende Belgium **86** G9 51 13N 2 55E
Opala CDR **108** J7 0 40S 24 20E
Opava Czech Rep. **88** F8 49 58N 17 55E
Opheim Montana USA **47** D1 48 56N 106 25W
Opole Poland **88** F9 50 40N 17 56E
Oporto Port. **87** A4 41 09N 8 37W
Opotiki NZ **111** F5 38 01S 177 17E
Oradea Romania **89** H7 47 03N 21 55E
Orai India **98** D5 26 00N 79 26E
Oran Algeria **108** D15 35 45N 0 38W
Orán Argentina **80** E9 23 07S 64 16W
Orange Aust. **110** H3 33 19S 149 10E
Orange Fr. **87** H6 44 08N 4 48E
Orange New Jersey USA **73** H2 40 45N 74 14W
Orange Texas USA **71** H3 30 05N 93 43W
Orange *r.* Southern Africa **109** H2 28 30S 17 30E
Orangeburg South Carolina USA **71** K3 33 28N 80 53W
Oravița Romania **89** H6 45 02N 21 43E
Orbigo *r.* Sp. **87** C5 42 15N 5 45W
Orcas Island Washington USA **42** H4 48 40N 123 05W
Orchard Park *tn.* New York USA **52** H2 42 46N 78 45W
Orcia *r.* Italy **89** C5 42 00N 11 00E
Ord Mountain California USA **72** E2 34 42N 116 50W
Ordu Turkey **96** C7 41 00N 37 52E
Örebro Sweden **88** E13 59 17N 15 13E
Oregon *state* USA **70** B5/C5 44 00N 120 00W
Oregon City Oregon USA **70** B6 45 21N 122 36W
Orël Russia **94** F7 52 58N 36 04E
Orem Utah USA **70** D5 40 20N 111 45W
Orenburg Russia **94** H7 51 50N 55 00E
Orense Sp. **87** B5 42 20N 7 52W
Orient New York USA **73** D2 41 09N 72 18W
Orihuela Sp. **87** E3 38 05N 0 56W
Orinoco *r.* Venezuela **80** E15 8 00N 64 00W
Orissa *admin.* India **99** E4 20 20N 83 00E
Oristano Italy **89** B3 39 54N 8 36E
Orizaba Mexico **74** E3 18 51N 97 08W
Orkney Islands UK **86** D13 59 00N 3 00W
Orlando Florida USA **71** K2 28 33N 81 21W
Orléans Fr. **86** F7 47 54N 1 54E
Oroville California USA **72** C4 39 32N 121 34W
Oroville Washington USA **43** L1 48 57N 119 27W
Orsk Russia **94** H7 51 13N 58 35E
Ortigueira Sp. **87** B5 43 43N 8 13W
Ortona Italy **89** E5 42 21N 14 24E
Orūmīyeh Iran **96** D6 37 40N 45 00E
Oruro Bolivia **80** D10 17 59S 67 08W
Ōsaka Japan **102** C1 34 40N 135 30E
Ō-shima *i.* Japan **102** C1 34 45N 139 25E
Oshkosh Wisconsin USA **71** J5 44 01N 88 32W
Oshogbo Nigeria **108** E9 7 50N 4 35E
Osijek Croatia **89** G6 45 33N 18 41E
Oskarshamn Sweden **88** F12 57 16N 16 25E
Oslo Norway **86** L13 59 56N 10 45E
Oslofjorden *fj.* Norway **86** L13 59 20N 10 37E
Osmaniye Turkey **96** C6 37 04N 36 15E
Osnabrück Germany **88** B10 52 17N 8 03E
Osorno Chile **81** C5 40 35S 73 14W
Ossa, Mount Aust. **110** H1 41 52S 146 04E
Osseo Wisconsin USA **51** F3 44 35N 91 13W
Ostfriesische Inseln *is.* Germany **88** A10 53 00N 7 00E
Ostrava Czech Rep. **88** G8 49 50N 18 15E
Ostróda Poland **88** G10 53 42N 19 59E
Ostrołęka Poland **88** H10 53 05N 21 32E
Ostrowiec Swietokrzyski Poland **88** H9 50 58N 21 22E
Ostrów Mazowiecka Poland **88** H10 52 50N 21 51E
Ostrów Wielkopolski Poland **88** F9 51 39N 17 50E
Osumi-kaikyo *sd.* Japan **102** B1 30 50N 131 00E
Oswego New York USA **71** L5 43 27N 76 31W
Otaki NZ **111** E4 40 46S 175 09E
Otaru Japan **102** D3 43 14N 140 59E
Otavalo Ecuador **80** B14 0 13N 78 15W
Otira NZ **111** C3 42 50S 171 34E
Otra *r.* Norway **86** J13 56 17N 7 30E
Otranto Italy **89** G4 40 08N 18 30E
Otranto, Strait of Adriatic Sea **89** G3/G4 40 00N 19 00E
Ōtsu Japan **102** C2 35 00N 135 50E
Ottawa Kansas USA **71** G4 38 35N 95 16W
Ottumwa Iowa USA **71** H5 41 02N 92 26W
Ouachita *r.* USA **71** H3 34 00N 93 00W
Ouachita Mountains USA **71** G3/H3 34 00N 95 00W
Ouadda CAR **108** J9 8 09N 22 20E
Ouagadougou Burkina **108** D10 12 20N 1 40W
Ouahigouya Burkina **108** D10 13 31N 2 20W
Ouargla Algeria **108** F14 32 00N 5 16E
Oubangui *r.* Central Africa **108** H8 0 00 17 30E
Oudtshoorn RSA **109** J1 33 35S 22 12E
Oued Dra *r.* Morocco **108** B13 28 10N 11 00W
Ouesso Congo **108** H8 1 38N 16 03E
Ouham *r.* CAR **108** H9 7 00N 17 30E
Oujda Morocco **108** D14 34 41N 1 45W
Ōu-sanmyaku *mts.* Japan **102** D2 39 20N 141 00E
Oust *r.* Fr. **86** D7 47 50N 2 30W
Outer Hebrides *is.* UK **86** B12 58 00N 7 00W
Ovalau *i.* Fiji **114** U16 17 40S 178 47E
Ovalle Chile **81** C7 30 33S 71 16W
Oviedo Sp. **87** C5 43 21N 7 18W
Owando Congo **108** H7 0 27S 15 44E
Owego New York USA **53** K2 42 07N 76 16W
Owen Falls Dam Uganda **108** L8 0 29N 33 11E
Owen Fracture Zone Indian Ocean **113** E7 10 00N 55 00E
Owensboro Kentucky USA **71** J4 37 45N 87 05W
Owens Lake California USA **70** C4 36 25N 117 56W
Owen Stanley Range *mts.* PNG **110** H8 9 15S 148 30E
Owosso Michigan USA **51** J2 42 59N 84 10W
Owyhee *r.* USA **70** C5 43 00N 117 00W
Oxford UK **86** E9 51 46N 1 15W
Oxnard California USA **70** C3 34 11N 119 10W
Oyama Japan **102** C2 36 18N 139 48E
Oyapock *r.* Brazil **80** G14 3 00N 52 30W
Oyem Gabon **108** G8 1 34N 11 31E
Ozark Plateau Missouri USA **71** H4 37 00N 93 00W
Ozarks, Lake of the Missouri USA **71** H4 38 00N 93 00W
Ozero Alakol' *salt l.* Kazakhstan **94** L6 46 00N 82 00E
Ozero Balkhash *l.* Kazakhstan **94** K6 46 00N 75 00E
Ozero Baykal *l.* Russia **95** N7 54 00N 109 00E
Ozero Chany *salt l.* Russia **94** K7 55 00N 77 30E
Ozero Il'men' *l.* Russia **94** F8 58 00N 31 30E
Ozero Issyk-Kul' *salt l.* Kyrgyzstan **94** K5 42 30N 77 30E
Ozero Khanka *l.* Asia **95** R6 45 00N 132 30E
Ozero Taymyr *l.* Russia **95** N11 74 00N 102 30E
Ozero Tengiz *salt l.* Kazakhstan **94** J7 51 00N 69 00E
Ozero Zaysan *l.* Kazakhstan **95** L6 48 00N 84 00E
Ozieri Italy **89** B4 40 35N 9 01E

P

Pabianice Poland **88** G9 51 40N 19 20E
Pabna Bangladesh **99** K10 24 00N 89 15E
Pacasmayo Peru **80** B12 7 27S 79 33W
Pachuca Mexico **74** E4 20 10N 98 44W
Pacific-Antarctic Ridge Pacific Ocean **115** M1 55 00S 135 00W
Pacific Grove California USA **70** B4 36 36N 121 56W
Pacific Ocean **114/115**
Padang Indonesia **103** C3 1 00S 100 21E
Paderborn Germany **88** B9 51 43N 8 44E
Padilla Bolivia **80** E10 19 18S 64 20W
Padma *r.* Bangladesh **99** L9 23 25N 90 10E
Padua Italy **89** C6 45 24N 11 53E
Paducah Kentucky USA **71** J4 37 03N 88 36W
Paeroa NZ **111** E6 37 23S 175 40E
Pag *i.* Croatia **89** E6 44 00N 15 00E
Pagadian Philippines **103** G5 7 50N 123 30E
Pahala Hawaiian Islands **115** Z17 19 12N 155 28W
Pahute Mesa *mts.* Nevada USA **72** E3 37 15N 116 20W
Painesville Ohio USA **51** L1 41 43N 81 15W
Paisley UK **86** C11 55 50N 4 26W
Paita Peru **80** A12 5 11S 81 09W
Pakanbaru Indonesia **103** C4 0 33N 101 30E
PAKISTAN **98** B5/C5
Pak Mong HK China **100** A1 22 18N 113 57E
Pakokku Myanmar **100** H3 21 20N 95 05E
Pak Tam Chung HK China **100** C2 22 24N 114 19E
Pakxé Laos **103** D6 15 00N 105 55E
Palana Russia **95** T8 59 05N 159 59E
Palangkaraya Indonesia **103** E3 2 16S 113 55E
PALAU **114** D8
Palawan *i.* Philippines **103** F5/F6 10 00N 119 00E
Palembang Indonesia **103** C3 2 59S 104 45E
Palencia Sp. **87** C5 41 01N 4 32W
Palermo Italy **89** D3 38 08N 13 23E
Palestine Texas USA **71** G3 31 45N 95 39W
Palestine *geog. reg.* Middle East **96** N10/N11 32 00N 35 00E
Palghat India **98** D2 10 46N 76 42E
Palk Strait India **98** D1 10 00N 80 00E
Palma de Mallorca Sp. **87** G3 39 35N 2 39E
Palmar Sur Costa Rica **75** H1 8 57N 83 28W
Palmas, Cape Liberia **108** C8 4 25N 7 50W
Palmdale California USA **72** D2 34 35N 118 07W
Palmer Land *geog. reg.* Antarctica **117** 72 00S 62 00W
Palmerston NZ **111** C2 45 29S 170 43E
Palmerston Atoll *i.* Pacific Ocean **115** K6 18 04S 163 10W
Palmerston North NZ **111** E4 40 22S 175 37E
Palmira Col. **80** B14 3 33N 76 17W
Palm Springs *tn.* California USA **72** E1 33 49N 116 33W
Palmyra Syria **96** C5 34 40N 38 10E
Palmyra New York USA **53** J3 43 04N 77 14W
Palmyra Pennsylvania USA **73** C2 40 19N 76 36W
Palmyra Atoll *i.* Pacific Ocean **115** L8 5 52N 162 05W
Palo Alto California USA **72** B3 37 26N 122 10W
Palomares Mexico **74** E3 17 10N 95 04W
Palopo Indonesia **103** G3 3 01S 120 12E
Palu Indonesia **103** F3 0 54S 119 52E
Pamiers Fr. **87** F5 43 07N 1 36E
Pampas *geog. reg.* Argentina **81** E6 36 00S 63 00W
Pamplona Col. **80** C15 7 24N 72 38W
Pamplona Sp. **87** E5 42 49N 1 39W
PANAMA **75** H1/J1
Panama Canal Panama **75** J1 9 00N 80 00W
Panama City Panama **75** J1 8 57N 19 30W
Panama City Florida USA **71** J3 30 10N 85 41W
Panay *i.* Philippines **103** G6 11 00N 122 00E
Pancake Range *mts.* Nevada USA **72** F4 38 45N 115 55W
Pančevo Serbia **89** H6 44 52N 20 40E
Panevezys Lithuania **88** K11 55 44N 24 24E
Pangkalpinang Indonesia **103** D3 2 05S 106 09E
Panipat India **98** D5 29 24N 76 58E
Pantar *i.* Indonesia **103** G2 8 30S 124 00E
Pantelleria *i.* Italy **89** D2 36 00N 12 00E
Papa Hawaiian Islands **115** Z17 19 12N 155 53W
Pápa Hungary **89** F7 47 20N 17 29E
Papantla Mexico **74** E4 20 30N 97 21W
Papoose Lake Nevada USA **72** F3 37 08N 115 52W
Papua, Gulf of PNG **110** G8/H8 8 15S 144 45E
PAPUA NEW GUINEA **110** G8/H8
Pará *admin.* Brazil **80** G13 4 30S 52 30W
Paraburdoo Aust. **110** B5 23 15S 117 45E
Paracel Islands South China Sea **103** E7 16 00N 113 30E
Paragua *r.* Bolivia **80** E11 14 00S 61 30W
Paragua *r.* Venezuela **80** E15 6 00N 63 30W
PARAGUAY **80** F9
Paraguay *r.* Paraguay/Argentina **80** F8/F9 26 30S 58 00W
Paraiba *admin.* Brazil **80** K12 7 20S 37 10W
Parakou Benin **108** E9 9 23N 2 40E
Paramaribo Suriname **80** F15 5 52N 55 14W
Paramonga Peru **80** B11 10 42S 77 50W
Paraná Argentina **81** E7 31 45S 60 30W
Paraná *admin.* Brazil **80** G9 24 30S 53 00W
Paraná *r.* Paraguay/Argentina **80** F8 27 00S 56 00W
Paranaíba *r.* Brazil **80** H10 18 00S 49 00W
Parana Panema *r.* Brazil **80** G9 22 30S 52 00W
Paranguá Brazil **80** H8 25 32S 48 36W
Paraparaumu NZ **111** E4 40 55S 175 00E
Pardo *r.* Brazil **80** K10 15 10S 40 00W
Pardubice Czech Rep. **88** E9 50 03N 15 45E
Parepare Indonesia **103** F3 4 00S 119 40E
Parintins Brazil **80** F13 2 38S 56 45W
Paris Fr. **86** G8 48 52N 2 20E
Paris Texas USA **71** G3 33 41N 95 33W
Parish New York USA **51** N2 43 24N 76 08W
Parkersburg West Virginia USA **71** K4 39 17N 81 33W
Parma Italy **89** C6 44 48N 10 19E
Parma Ohio USA **51** L1 41 22N 81 44W
Parnaíba Brazil **80** J13 2 58S 41 46W
Parnaíba *r.* Brazil **80** J12 7 30S 45 00W
Parnassós *mt.* Greece **89** J3 38 30N 22 37E
Pärnu *r.* Estonia **88** K13 58 30N 24 30E
Paroo *r.* Aust. **110** G4 29 00S 144 30E
Páros Greece **89** K2 37 04N 25 06E
Parras Mexico **74** D5 25 30N 102 11W
Pasadena California USA **72** D2 34 10N 118 08W
Pasadena Texas USA **71** G2 29 42N 95 14W
Pascagoula Mississippi USA **71** J3 30 21N 88 32W
Pasco Washington USA **70** C6 46 15N 119 07W
Paso Robles California USA **72** C2 35 38N 120 42W
Passaic New Jersey USA **73** H2 40 50N 74 08W
Passaic River New Jersey USA **73** H2 40 46N 74 09W
Passau Germany **88** D8 48 35N 13 28E
Passo Fundo Brazil **81** G8 28 16S 52 20W
Pastaza *r.* Peru **80** B13 2 30S 77 00W
Pasto Col. **80** B14 1 12N 77 17W
Patagonia *geog. reg.* Argentina **81** C3 48 00S 70 00W
Patan India **98** C4 23 51N 72 11E
Patan Nepal **99** F5 27 40N 85 20E
Patchogue New York USA **73** D2 40 46N 73 01W
Patea NZ **111** E5 39 45S 174 28E
Pate Island Kenya **108** N7 2 05S 41 05E
Paterson New Jersey USA **71** M5 40 55N 74 08W
Pathankot India **98** D6 32 16N 75 43E
Patiala India **98** D6 30 21N 76 27E
Patna India **99** F5 25 37N 85 12E
Patos Brazil **80** K12 6 55S 37 15W
Patras Greece **89** H3 38 14N 21 44E
Patterson California USA **72** C3 37 29N 121 09W
Pau Fr. **87** E5 43 18N 0 22W
Pavia Italy **89** B6 45 12N 9 09E
Pavlodar Kazakhstan **94** K7 52 21N 76 59E
Pawtucket Rhode Island USA **73** E2 41 53N 71 23W
Paysandu Uruguay **81** F7 32 21S 58 05W
Pazardzhik Bulgaria **89** K5 42 10N 24 20E
Peake Deep Atlantic Ocean **116** G11 43 00N 20 05W
Pearl *r.* Mississippi USA **71** H3 32 00N 90 00W
Pearl Harbor Hawaiian Islands **115** X18 21 22N 158 00W
Peč Kosovo **89** H5 42 40N 20 19E
Pechora Russia **94** H10 65 14N 57 18E
Pechora *r.* Russia **94** H10 66 00N 52 00E
Pecos Texas USA **70** F3 30 00N 102 00W
Pecos *r.* USA **70** F3 30 00N 102 00W
Pécs Hungary **89** G7 46 04N 18 15E
Pedreiras Brazil **80** J13 4 32S 44 40W
Pedro Juan Caballero Paraguay **80** F9 22 30S 55 44W
Peekskill New York USA **73** D2 41 18N 73 50W
Pegu Myanmar **103** B7 17 18N 96 31E
Pegunungan Barisan *mts.* Indonesia **103** C3 2 30S 102 30E
Pegunungan Maoke *mts.* Indonesia **110** F9 4 00S 137 00E
Pegunungan Muller *mts.* Indonesia **103** E4 0 00 113 00E
Pegunungan Schwaner *mts.* Indonesia **103** E3 1 00S 111 00E
Pegunungan Van Rees *mts.* Indonesia **110** F9 2 45S 138 30E
Pekalongan Indonesia **103** D2 6 54S 109 37E
Pelée, Mount Martinique **74** R12 14 47N 61 04W
Pelican Point Namibia **109** G3 22 54S 14 25E
Pelješac *i.* Croatia **89** F5 43 00N 17 00E
Pelopónnisos *geog. reg.* Greece **89** H2/J2 37 00N 22 00E
Pelotas Brazil **81** G7 31 45S 52 20W
Pematangsiantar Indonesia **103** B4 2 59N 99 01E
Pemba Mozambique **109** N5 13 00S 40 30E
Pembina Minnesota USA **49** D1 48 59N 97 20W
Peñarroya-Pueblonuevo Sp. **87** C3 38 19N 5 16W
Pendleton Oregon USA **70** C6 45 40N 118 46W
Pend Oreille Lake Idaho USA **43** M1 48 10N 116 20W
Pend Oreille River Washington USA **43** M1 48 50N 117 25W
Penedo Brazil **80** K11 10 16S 36 33W
Peng Chau *i.* HK China **100** B1 22 17N 114 02E
Peninsula de Taitao Chile **81** B4 46 30S 75 00W
Peninsular Malaysia *admin.* Malaysia **103** C4 5 00N 102 00E
Penner *r.* India **98** D2 14 30N 79 30E
Pennines *hills* UK **86** C11 54 30N 2 10W
Pennsylvania *state* USA **71** L5 41 00N 78 00W
Penn Yan New York USA **53** J2 42 40N 77 03W
Penobscot River Maine USA **57** F1 44 15N 68 30W
Penonomé Panama **75** H1 8 30N 80 20W
Penrith UK **86** D11 54 40N 2 44W
Pensacola Florida USA **71** J3 30 26N 87 12W
Pentland Firth *sd.* UK **86** D13 58 45N 3 10W
Penza Russia **94** G7 53 11N 45 00E
Penzance UK **86** C9 50 07N 5 33W
Peoria Illinois USA **71** J5 40 43N 89 38W
Pereira Col. **80** B14 4 47N 75 46W
Périgeuex Fr. **87** F6 45 12N 0 44E
Perm' Russia **94** H8 58 01N 56 10E
Pernambuco *admin.* Brazil **80** K12 8 00S 37 30W
Pernik Bulgaria **89** J5 42 36N 23 03E
Perpignan Fr. **87** G5 42 42N 2 54E
Perris California USA **72** E1 33 47N 117 14W
Perrysburg Ohio USA **52** C1 41 33N 83 39W
Persian Gulf Middle East **97** F4 27 20N 51 00E
Perth Aust. **110** B3 31 58S 115 49E
Perth UK **86** D12 56 42N 3 28W
Perth Amboy New Jersey USA **73** C2 40 31N 74 16W
PERU **80** B11
Peru Basin Pacific Ocean **115** S6 18 00S 95 00W
Peru-Chile Trench Pacific Ocean **115** T7 13 00S 77 00W
Perugia Italy **89** D5 43 07N 12 23E
Pesaro Italy **89** D5 43 54N 12 54E
Pescadero California USA **72** B3 37 15N 122 24W
Pescara Italy **89** E5 42 27N 14 13E
Peshawar Pakistan **98** C6 34 01N 71 40E
Petah Tiqwa Israel **96** N11 32 05N 34 53E
Petaluma California USA **70** B4 38 13N 12 39W
Petare Venezuela **80** D16 10 31N 66 50W
Petauke Zambia **109** L5 14 15S 31 20E
Peterborough Aust. **110** F3 33 00S 138 51E
Peterborough UK **86** E10 52 35N 0 15W
Peterhead UK **86** E12 57 30N 1 46W
Petersburg Alaska USA **42** D5 56 49N 132 58W
Petersburg Virginia USA **71** L4 37 14N 77 24W
Petoskey Michigan USA **51** J3 45 22N 84 58W
Petra *hist. site* Jordan **96** N10 30 19N 35 26E
Petrolina Brazil **80** J12 9 22S 40 30W
Petropavlovsk Kazakhstan **94** J7 54 53N 69 13E
Petropavlovsk-Kamchatskiy Russia **95** T7 53 03N 158 43E
Petroșani Romania **89** J6 45 25N 23 22E
Petrozavodsk Russia **94** F9 61 46N 34 19E
Pevek Russia **95** V10 64 41N 170 19E
Phenix City Alabama USA **71** J3 32 28N 85 01W
Philadelphia Pennsylvania USA **71** L4 40 00N 75 10W
Philippine Sea Pacific Ocean **114** C10 21 00N 130 00E
PHILIPPINES, THE **103** G7
Philippine Trench Pacific Ocean **114** C8/C9 12 00N 127 00E
Phillipsburg New Jersey USA **73** C2 40 42N 75 11W
Phnom Penh Cambodia **103** C6 11 35N 104 55E
Phoenix Arizona USA **70** D3 33 30N 112 03W
Phoenix Island Kiribati **114** J7 3 30S 174 30W
Phoenix Islands Kiribati **114** J7 4 40S 177 30W
Phôngsali Laos **101** J3 21 40N 102 06E
Phuket Thailand **103** B5 7 52N 98 22E
Piacenza Italy **89** B6 45 03N 9 41E
Piatra Neamț Romania **89** L7 46 53N 26 23E
Piauí *admin.* Brazil **80** J12 7 30S 43 00W
Pico Bolivar *mt.* Venezuela **80** C15 8 33N 71 03W
Pico Cristóbal *mt.* Col. **80** C16 10 53N 73 48W
Pico de Itambé *mt.* Brazil **80** J10 18 23S 43 21W
Picos Brazil **80** J12 7 05S 41 24W
Picton NZ **111** E4 41 18S 174 00E
Pidurutalagala *mt.* Sri Lanka **98** E1 7 01N 80 45E
Piedras Negras Mexico **74** D5 28 40N 100 32W
Pierre South Dakota USA **70** F5 44 23N 100 20W
Pierreville Trinidad and Tobago **75** V15 10 17N 61 01W
Pietermaritzburg RSA **109** L2 29 36S 30 24E
Pietersburg RSA **109** K3 23 54N 29 23E
Pigeon Michigan USA **52** C3 43 50N 83 15W
Pijijiapan Mexico **74** F3 15 42N 93 12W
Pikes Peak Colorado USA **70** E4 38 50N 105 03W
Pik Pobedy *mt.* Kyrgyzstan **94** L5 42 25N 80 15E

Name	Page	Grid	Lat	Long
Piła Poland	88	F10	53 09N	16 44E
Pilar Paraguay	80	F8	26 51S	58 20W
Pilcomayo *r.* Paraguay/Argentina	80	F9	24 00S	60 00W
Pilica *r.* Poland	88	H9	52 00N	21 00E
Pimenta Bueno Brazil	80	E11	11 40S	61 14W
Pimlico Sound North Carolina USA	71	L4	35 00N	76 00W
Pinang *i.* Malaysia	103	C5	5 25N	100 20E
Pinar del Río Cuba	75	H4	22 24N	83 42W
Píndhos *mts.* Greece	89	H3	40 00N	21 00E
Pine Bluff Arkansas USA	71	H3	34 13B	92 00W
Pine Creek *r.* Pennsylvania USA	53	J1	41 40N	77 25W
Pinecrest California USA	72	D4	38 13N	120 00W
Pine Flat Reservoir California USA	72	D3	36 52N	119 17W
Pine River Michigan USA	52	B3	43 23N	84 40W
Ping Chau *i.* HK China	100	D3	22 33N	114 26E
Ping Che HK China	100	C3	22 32N	114 10E
Pingdingshan China	101	L5	33 50N	113 20E
Ping Shan HK China	100	B2	22 27N	114 00E
Pingtung Taiwan	101	N3	22 40N	120 30E
Pingxiang China	101	K3	22 06N	106 44E
Pingxiang China	101	L4	27 35N	113 46E
Pinnacles National Monument California USA	72	C3	36 27N	121 12W
Piombino Italy	89	C5	42 56N	10 32E
Pioneer Ohio USA	52	B1	41 42N	84 33W
Piotrków Trybunalski Poland	88	G9	51 27N	19 40E
Pirapora Brazil	80	J10	17 20S	44 54W
Pireneos *mts* Sp./Fr.	87	E5/F5	42 50N	0 30E
Pirin Planina *mts.* Bulgaria	89	J4	41 00N	23 00E
Pisa Italy	89	C5	43 43N	10 24E
Pisco Peru	80	B11	13 46S	76 12W
Písek Czech Rep.	88	D8	49 18N	14 10E
Pisté Mexico	74	D3	20 44N	88 35W
Pistoia Italy	89	C5	43 56N	10 55E
Pitanga Brazil	80	G9	24 45S	51 43W
Pitcairn Islands Pacific Ocean	115	N5	25 04S	130 06W
Piteşti Romania	89	K6	44 51N	24 51E
Pittsburgh Pennsylvania USA	71	L5	40 26N	80 00W
Pittsfield Massachusetts USA	71	M5	42 27N	73 15W
Piura Peru	80	A12	5 15S	80 38W
Placerville California USA	72	C4	38 43N	120 50W
Plainfield New Jersey USA	73	C2	40 38N	74 24W
Plainview Texas USA	70	F3	34 12N	101 43W
Planada California USA	72	C3	37 18N	120 19W
Planalto de Mato Grosso *geog. reg.* Brazil	80	F11	13 00S	56 00W
Plasencia Sp.	87	B4	40 02N	6 05W
Plateau de Langres *hills* Fr.	87	H7	47 40N	4 55E
Plateau de Tchigaï Chad/Niger	108	G12	21 30N	15 00E
Plateau du Tademaït Algeria	108	E13	8 45N	2 00E
Plateaux du Limousin *hills* Fr.	87	F6	45 45N	1 15E
Platte *r.* USA	70	F5	41 00N	100 00W
Plattsburgh New York USA	71	M5	44 42N	73 29W
Plauen Germany	88	D9	50 29N	12 08E
Playa Azul Mexico	74	D3	18 00N	102 24W
Plenty, Bay of NZ	111	F6	37 48S	177 12E
Plentywood Montana USA	47	E1	48 51N	104 34W
Pleven Bulgaria	89	K5	43 25N	24 04E
Płock Poland	88	G10	52 32N	19 40E
Ploieşti Romania	89	K6	44 57N	26 01E
Plovdiv Bulgaria	89	K5	42 08N	24 45E
Plover Cove Reservoir HK China	100	C2	22 28N	114 15E
Plunge Lithuania	88	H11	55 52N	21 49E
Plymouth Montserrat	74	P9	16 42N	62 13W
Plymouth UK	86	C9	50 23N	4 10W
Plymouth Massachusetts USA	73	E2	41 58N	70 41W
Plzeň Czech Rep.	88	D8	49 45N	13 25E
Po *r.* Italy	89	C6	45 00N	10 00E
Pocatello Idaho USA	70	D5	42 35N	112 26W
Pochutla Mexico	74	E3	15 45N	96 30W
Podgorica Montenegro	89	G5	42 28N	19 17E
Podkamennaya (Stony) Tunguska *r.* Russia	95	M9	62 00N	97 30E
Podol'sk Russia	94	F8	55 23N	37 32E
Pohang South Korea	101	P6	36 00N	129 26E
Point Arena *c.* California USA	72	B4	39 57N	123 45W
Point Arguello *c.* California USA	72	C2	34 34N	120 39W
Point Buchon *c.* California USA	72	C2	35 15N	120 55W
Point Conception *c.* California USA	72	C2	34 27N	120 28W
Pointe-à-Pitre Guadeloupe	74	Q9	16 14N	61 32W
Point-Noire *tn.* Congo	108	G7	4 46S	11 53E
Point Reyes *c.* California USA	72	B4	38 00N	123 01W
Point Roberts *c.* Washington USA	42	H4	49 00N	123 06W
Point Sur *c.* California USA	72	C3	36 19N	121 53W
Poitiers Fr.	87	F7	46 35N	0 20E
Pokhara Nepal	98	E5	28 14N	83 58E
Pok Wai HK China	100	B2	22 28N	114 03E
POLAND	88	E10		
Pollensa Spain	87	G3	39 52N	3 01E
Polýgyros Greece	89	J4	40 23N	23 25E
Polynesia *geog. reg.* Pacific Ocean	115	K4	30 00S	166 00W
Pomeranian Bay Baltic Sea	88	E11	54 00N	14 00E
Pomona California USA	72	E2	34 04N	117 45W
Ponca City Oklahoma USA	71	G4	36 41N	97 04W
Ponce Puerto Rico	75	L3	18 01N	66 36W
Pondicherry India	98	D2	11 59N	79 50E
Pondicherry *admin.* India	98	D2	11 00N	79 45E
Ponferrada Sp.	87	B5	42 33N	6 35W
Ponta da Marca *c.* Angola	109	G4	16 33S	11 43E
Ponta das Salinas *c.* Angola	109	G5	12 50S	12 54E
Ponta Grossa Brazil	80	G8	25 07S	50 09W
Ponta Porã Brazil	80	F9	22 27S	55 39W
Pontchartrain, Lake Louisiana USA	71	H3	30 00N	90 00W
Ponte Leccia Fr.	87	K5	42 28N	9 12E
Pontevedra Sp.	87	A5	42 25N	8 39W
Pontiac Michigan USA	51	K2	42 38N	83 18W
Pontianak Indonesia	103	D3	0 05S	109 16E
Pontivy Fr.	86	D8	48 04N	2 58W
Poole UK	86	E9	50 43N	1 59W
Pool Malebo *l.* CDR	108	H7	5 00S	17 00E
Popacatepetl *mt.* Mexico	74	E3	19 02N	98 38W
Popayán Col.	80	B14	2 27N	76 32W
Poplar Bluff *tn.* Missouri USA	71	H4	36 16N	90 25W
Popondetta PNG	110	H8	8 45S	148 15E
Porbandar India	98	B4	21 04N	69 40E
Porcupine River Alaska USA	64	B4	67 15N	144 00W
Pordenone Italy	89	D6	45 58N	12 39E
Porirua NZ	111	E4	41 08S	174 50E
Poronaysk Russia	95	S6	49 13N	143 05E
Porsgrunn Norway	86	K13	59 10N	9 40E
Portadown UK	86	B11	54 26N	6 27W
Portal North Dakota USA	47	F1	49 01N	102 34W
Portalegre Port.	87	B3	39 17N	7 25W
Portales New Mexico USA	70	F3	34 12N	103 20W
Port Alexander Alaska USA	42	C5	56 13N	134 40W
Port Allegany *tn.* Pennsylvania USA	52	H1	41 49N	78 17W
Port Angeles Washington USA	70	B6	48 06N	123 26W
Port Antonio Jamaica	75	U14	18 10N	76 27W
Port Arthur Texas USA	71	H2	29 55N	93 56W
Port Augusta Aust.	110	F3	32 30S	137 27E
Port-au-Prince Haiti	75	K3	18 33N	72 20W
Port Austin Michigan USA	51	K3	44 02N	82 59W
Port Blair Andaman Islands	99	G2	11 40N	92 44E
Port Canning *tn.* India	99	K9	22 19N	88 40E
Port Chalmers NZ	111	C2	45 49S	170 37E
Port Clinton Ohio USA	51	K1	41 30N	82 56W
Port-de-Paix Haiti	75	K3	19 56N	72 52W
Port Elizabeth RSA	109	K1	33 58S	25 36E
Porterville California USA	72	D3	36 03N	119 08W
Port Gentil Gabon	108	F7	0 40S	8 50E
Port Harcourt Nigeria	108	F8	4 43N	7 05E
Port Hedland Aust.	110	B5	20 24S	118 36E
Port Huron Michigan USA	71	K5	42 59N	82 28W
Portimaõ Port.	87	A2	37 08N	8 32W
Port Island HK China	100	D2	22 30N	114 21E
Port Jervis New York USA	73	C2	41 23N	74 41W
Port Kaituma Guyana	80	F15	7 44N	59 53W
Portland Aust.	110	G2	38 21S	141 38E
Portland Maine USA	71	M5	43 41N	70 18W
Portland Michigan USA	52	B2	42 52N	84 53W
Portland Oregon USA	70	B6	45 32N	122 40W
Portland Canal *sd.* Alaska USA	42	E4	55 00N	130 10W
Portland Point Jamaica	75	U13	17 42N	77 11W
Portlaoise RoI	86	B10	53 02N	7 17W
Port Lincoln Aust.	110	F3	34 43S	135 49E
Port Macquarie Aust.	110	J3	31 28S	152 25E
Port Maria Jamaica	75	U14	18 22N	76 54W
Port Morant Jamaica	75	U13	17 53N	76 20W
Port Moresby PNG	110	H8	9 30S	147 07E
Port Nolloth RSA	109	H2	29 17S	16 51E
Porto Alegre Brazil	81	G7	30 03S	51 10W
Porto Amboim Angola	109	G5	10 47S	13 43E
Portobelo Panama	75	Y3	9 33N	79 37W
Port-of-Spain Trinidad and Tobago	75	V15	10 38N	61 31W
Pôrto Grande Brazil	80	G14	0 43N	51 23W
Porto Novo Benin	108	E9	6 30N	2 47E
Porto Tòrres Italy	89	B4	40 51N	8 24E
Porto-Vecchio France	87	K4	41 35N	9 16E
Pôrto Velho Brazil	80	E12	8 45S	63 54W
Portoviejo Ecuador	80	A13	1 07S	80 28W
Port Pirie Aust.	110	F3	33 11S	138 01E
Portree UK	86	B12	57 24N	6 12W
Port Said Egypt	109	S4	31 17N	32 18E
Port Shelter *b.* HK China	100	C2	22 21N	114 18E
Portsmouth Dominica	74	Q8	15 35N	61 28W
Portsmouth UK	86	E9	50 48N	1 05W
Portsmouth New Hampshire USA	71	M5	43 03N	70 47W
Portsmouth Virginia USA	71	L4	36 50N	76 20W
Port Sudan Sudan	108	M11	19 38N	37 07E
PORTUGAL	87	A3		
Posadas Argentina	80	F8	27 27S	55 50W
Potenza Italy	89	E4	40 38N	15 48E
Potiskum Nigeria	108	G10	11 40N	11 03E
Po Toi *i.* HK China	100	C1	22 10N	114 16E
Potomac *r.* Maryland USA	71	L4	39 10N	77 30W
Potosí Bolivia	80	D10	19 34S	65 45W
Potsdam Germany	88	D10	52 24N	13 04E
Potsdam New York USA	51	P3	44 40N	74 59W
Poughkeepsie New York USA	71	M5	41 43N	73 56W
Pouthisat Cambodia	103	C6	12 27N	103 40E
Poway California USA	72	E1	32 57N	117 01W
Powell, Lake USA	70	D4	37 00N	110 00W
Powers Lake *tn.* North Dakota USA	47	F1	48 34N	102 39W
Poyang Hu *l.* China	101	M4	29 00N	116 30E
Poza Rica Mexico	74	E4	20 34N	97 26W
Poznań Poland	88	F10	52 25N	16 53E
Prague Czech Rep.	88	E9	50 06N	14 26E
Prairie Dog Town Fork *r.* USA	70	F3	34 00N	101 00W
Prato Italy	89	C5	43 53N	11 06E
Pratt Kansas USA	71	G4	37 40N	98 45W
Přerov Czech Rep.	88	F8	49 28N	17 30E
Prescott Arizona USA	70	D3	34 34N	112 28W
Presidencia Roque Sáenz Peña Argentina	80	E8	6 45S	60 30W
Presidente Prudente Brazil	80	G9	22 09S	51 24W
Prešov Slovakia	88	H8	49 00N	21 10E
Prespansko ezero *l.* Europe	89	H4	41 00N	21 00E
Presque Isle *tn.* Maine USA	71	N6	46 42N	68 01W
Preston UK	86	D10	53 46N	2 42W
Pretoria RSA	109	K2	25 45S	28 12E
Préveza Greece	89	H3	38 59N	20 45E
Příbram Czech Rep.	88	E8	49 42N	14 01E
Price Utah USA	70	D4	39 35N	110 49W
Price *r.* Utah USA	70	D4	39 00N	110 00W
Prieska RSA	109	J2	29 40S	22 45E
Priest Lake Idaho USA	43	M1	49 45N	116 50W
Priestly Mountain Maine USA	53	S6	46 34N	69 23W
Priest River *tn.* Idaho USA	43	M1	48 11N	116 55W
Prijedor Bosnia-Herzegovina	89	F6	45 00N	16 41E
Prilep FYROM	89	H4	41 20N	21 32E
Prince Edward Island Indian Ocean	113	C2	46 30S	37 20E
Prince of Wales Island Alaska USA	42	D4	56 00N	132 00W
Princess Elizabeth Land *geog. reg.* Antarctica	117		72 00S	80 00E
Príncipe *i.* Gulf of Guinea	108	F8	1 37N	7 27E
Prinzapolca Nicaragua	75	H2	13 19N	83 35W
Priština Kosovo	89	H5	42 39N	21 20E
Prizren Kosovo	89	H5	42 12N	20 43E
Probolinggo Indonesia	103	E2	7 45S	113 12E
Progreso Mexico	74	G4	21 20N	89 40W
Prokop'yevsk Russia	95	L7	53 55N	86 45E
Propriá Brazil	80	K11	10 15S	36 51W
Providence Rhode Island USA	71	M5	41 50N	71 28W
Providence, Cape NZ	111	A2	46 01S	166 28E
Provideniya Russia	95	W9	64 30N	73 11E
Provincetown Massachusetts USA	73	E3	42 03N	70 12W
Provo Utah USA	70	D5	40 15N	111 40W
Prudhoe Bay *tn.* Alaska USA	64	A5	70 05N	148 20W
Pruszków Poland	88	H10	52 10N	20 47E
Prut *r.* Romania	88	K8	47 00N	28 00E
Przemyśl Poland	88	J8	49 48N	22 48E
Przeworsk Poland	88	J9	50 04N	22 30
Przheval'sk Kyrgyzstan	94	K5	42 31N	78 22E
Pskov Russia	94	E8	57 48N	28 26E
Pucallpa Peru	80	C12	8 21S	74 33W
Puebla Mexico	74	E3	19 03N	98 10W
Pueblo Colorado USA	70	F4	38 17N	104 38W
Puerto Aisén Chile	81	C4	45 27S	72 58W
Puerto Armuelles Panama	75	H1	8 19N	82 51W
Puerto Ayacucho Venezuela	80	D15	5 39N	67 32W
Puerto Barrios Guatemala	74	G3	15 41N	88 32W
Puerto Berrio Col.	80	C15	6 28N	74 28W
Puerto Cabello Venezuela	80	D16	10 29N	68 02W
Puerto Cabezas Nicaragua	75	H2	14 02N	83 24W
Puerto Carreño Col.	80	D15	6 08N	69 27W
Puerto Cortés Honduras	74	G3	15 50N	87 55W
Puerto de Morelos Mexico	74	G4	20 49N	86 52W
Puerto Escondido Mexico	74	E3	15 52N	97 02W
Puerto La Cruz Venezuela	80	E16	10 14N	64 40W
Puertollano Sp.	87	C3	38 41N	4 07W
Puerto Maldonado Peru	80	D11	12 37S	69 11W
Puerto Montt Chile	81	C5	41 28S	73 00W
Puerto Natales Chile	81	C3	51 41S	72 15W
Puerto Penasco Mexico	74	B6	31 20N	113 35W
Puerto Pilón Panama	75	Y2	9 21N	79 48W
Puerto Plata Dom. Rep.	75	K3	19 47N	70 42W
Puerto Princesa Philippines	103	F5	9 46N	118 45E
PUERTO RICO	75	L3		
Puerto Rico Trench Atlantic Ocean	116	B9	21 00N	65 00W
Puerto Santa Cruz Argentina	81	D3	50 03S	68 35W
Puerto Vallarta Mexico	74	C4	20 36N	105 15W
Pukekohe NZ	111	E6	37 12S	174 54E
Pula Croatia	89	D6	44 52N	13 52E
Pulacayo Bolivia	80	D9	20 25S	66 41W
Pulau Bangka *i.* Indonesia	103	D3	2 30S	107 00E
Pulau Belitung *i.* Indonesia	103	D3	2 30S	107 30E
Pulau Dolak *i.* Indonesia	110	F8	7 45S	138 15E
Pulau Enggano *i.* Indonesia	103	C2	5 20S	102 20E
Pulau Nias *i.* Indonesia	103	B4	1 00N	97 30E
Pulau Simeulue *i.* Indonesia	103	B4	2 30N	96 00E
Pullman Washington USA	70	C6	46 46N	117 09W
Pune India	98	C3	18 34N	73 58E
Punjab *admin.* India	98	D6	30 40N	75 30E
Puno Peru	80	C10	15 53S	70 03W
Punta Alta Argentina	81	E6	38 50S	62 00W
Punta Arenas Chile	81	C3	53 10S	70 56W
Punta del Mona *c.* Nicaragua	75	H2	11 36N	83 37W
Punta Eugenia *c.* Mexico	74	A5	27 50N	115 05W
Punta Galera *c.* Ecuador	80	A14	0 49N	80 03W
Punta Gallinas *c.* Col.	80	C16	12 27N	71 44W
Punta Gorda Belize	74	G3	16 10N	88 45W
Punta Manzanillo *c.* Panama	75	Y3	9 37N	79 36W
Punta Negra *c.* Peru	80	A12	6 06S	81 09W
Puntarenas Costa Rica	75	H2	10 00N	85 00W
Puntcak Jaya *mt.* Indonesia	110	F9	4 05S	137 09E
Punto Fijo Venezuela	80	C16	11 50N	70 16W
Puquio Peru	80	C11	14 44S	74 07W
Pur *r.* Russia	95	K10	67 00N	77 30E
Puri India	99	F3	19 49N	85 54E
Purnia India	99	F5	25 47N	87 28E
Purus *r.* Brazil	80	D12	7 00S	65 00W
Pusan South Korea	101	P6	35 05N	129 02E
Putoran Mountains Russia	95	M10	68 00N	95 00E
Puttalam Sri Lanka	98	D1	8 02N	79 50E
Putumayo *r.* Col./Peru	80	C13	2 30S	72 30W
Puy de Sancy *mt.* Fr.	87	G6	45 32N	2 48E
Pyasina *r.* Russia	95	L11	71 00N	90 00E
Pyatigorsk Russia	94	G5	44 04N	43 06E
Pyè Myanmar	103	B7	18 50N	95 14E
Pyinmana Myanmar	103	B7	19 45N	96 12E
Pymatuning Lake *res.* Ohio/Pennsylvania USA	52	F1	41 35N	80 30W
Pyongyang North Korea	101	P6	39 00N	125 47E
Pyramid Lake Nevada USA	70	C5	40 00N	119 00W
Pyrénées *mts.* Fr./Sp.	87	F5	42 50N	0 30E
Pýrgos Greece	89	H2	37 40N	21 27E
Pýrgos Greece	89	K1	35 00N	25 10E
Pysht Washington USA	42	H4	48 08N	124 25W

Q

Name	Page	Grid	Lat	Long
Qaidam Pendi China	100	G6	37 30N	94 00E
Qanâ el Manzala *can.* Egypt	109	R4	31 21N	31 56E
Qasr-e-Shīrīn Iraq	96	E5	34 32N	45 35E
Qasr Farâfra Egypt	108	K13	27 03N	28 00E
QATAR	97	F4		
Qatrāna Jordan	96	P10	31 14N	36 03E
Qattara Depression Egypt	108	K13	24 00N	27 30E
Qazvīn Iran	97	E6	36 16N	50 00E
Qezi'ot Israel	96	N10	30 53N	34 28E
Qiemo China	100	F6	38 08N	85 33E
Qila Saifullah Pakistan	98	B6	30 42N	68 30E
Qilian Shan *mts.* China	101	H6	39 00N	98 00E
Qingdao China	101	N6	36 04N	120 22E
Qinghai Hu *l.* China	101	J6	37 00N	100 00E
Qingjiang China	101	M5	33 35N	119 02E
Qinhuangdao China	101	M6	39 55N	119 37E
Qin Ling *mt.* China	101	K5	34 00N	107 30E
Qionghai China	101	L2	19 17N	110 30E
Qiqihar China	101	N8	47 23N	124 00E
Qom Iran	97	F5	34 39N	50 57E
Qomisheh Iran	97	F5	32 01N	51 55E
Quang Ngai Vietnam	103	D7	15 00N	108 50E
Quang Tri Vietnam	103	D7	16 46N	107 11E
Quanzhou China	101	M3	24 53N	118 36E
Quarry Bay *tn.* HK China	100	C1	22 17N	114 13E
Queanbeyan Aust.	110	H2	35 24S	149 17E
Queen Mary Land *geog. reg.* Antarctica	117		70 00S	90 00E
Queens *admin.* New York USA	73	D2	40 47N	73 50W
Queensland *state* Aust.	110	G5	23 00S	143 00E
Queenstown Aust.	110	H1	42 07S	145 33E
Queenstown NZ	111	B2	45 02S	168 40E
Quelimane Mozambique	109	M4	17 53S	36 51E
Querétaro Mexico	74	D4	20 38N	100 23W
Quetta Pakistan	98	B6	30 15N	67 00E
Quezaltenango Guatemala	74	F2	14 50N	91 30W
Quezon City Philippines	103	G6	14 39N	121 02E
Quibala Angola	109	G5	10 48S	14 59E
Quibdó Col.	80	B15	5 40N	76 38W
Quiberon Fr.	87	D7	47 29N	3 07W
Quilá Mexico	74	C4	24 26N	107 11W
Quillacollo Bolivia	80	D10	17 26S	66 16W
Quilon India	98	D1	8 53N	76 38E
Quilpie Aust.	110	G4	26 35S	144 14E
Quimper Fr.	86	C7	48 00N	4 06W
Quincy Illinois USA	71	H4	39 55N	91 22W
Quincy Massachusetts USA	73	E3	42 15N	71 01W
Qui Nhon Vietnam	103	D6	13 47N	109 11E
Quito Ecuador	80	B13	0 14S	78 30W
Quixadá Brazil	80	K13	4 57S	39 04W
Qullai Garmo *mt.* Tajikistan	94	K4	38 59N	72 01E
Quseir Egypt	108	L13	26 04N	34 15E

R

Name	Page	Grid	Lat	Long
Raas Caseyr *c.* Somalia	108	Q10	11 50N	51 16E
Raba Indonesia	103	F2	8 27S	118 45E
Rabat-Salé Morocco	108	C14	34 02N	6 51W
Rabaul PNG	110	J9	4 13S	152 11E
Rabnabad Islands Bangladesh	99	L8	21 58N	90 24E
Rach Gia Vietnam	103	D5	10 00N	105 05E
Racibórz Poland	88	G9	50 05N	18 10E
Radford Virginia USA	71	K4	37 07N	80 34W
Radom Poland	88	H9	51 26N	21 10E
Radom Sudan	108	J9	9 58N	24 53E
Radomsko Poland	88	G9	51 04N	19 25E
Radstadt Austria	89	D7	47 23N	13 28E
Raeside, Lake Aust.	110	C4	29 00S	122 00E
Raetihi NZ	111	E5	39 26S	175 17E
Rafaḥ Egypt	96	N10	31 18N	34 15E
Rafsanjān Iran	97	G5	30 25N	56 00E
Ragusa Italy	89	E2	36 56N	14 44E
Rahimyar Khan Pakistan	98	C5	28 22N	70 20E
Raichur India	98	D3	16 15N	77 20E
Raiganj India	99	K10	25 37N	88 12E
Raigarh India	98	E4	21 53N	83 28E
Railroad Valley Nevada USA	72	F4	38 18N	115 38W
Rainier, Mount Washington USA	70	B6	46 25N	121 45W

Raipur India 98 E4 21 16N 81 42E
Raisin, River Michigan USA 52 C1 41 55N 83 40W
Rajahmundry India 98 E3 17 01N 81 52E
Rajapalaiyam India 98 D1 9 26N 77 36E
Rajasthan *admin.* India 98 C5 26 30N 73 00E
Rajkot India 98 C4 21 18N 70 53E
Rajshahi Bangladesh 99 K10 24 24N 88 40E
Raleigh North Carolina USA 71 L4 35 46N 78 39W
Ralik Chain *is.* Pacific Ocean 114 G8 7 30N 167 30E
Ramat Gan Israel 96 N10 32 04N 34 48E
Ramgarh Bangladesh 99 L9 22 59N 91 43E
Râmnicu Vâlcea Romania 89 K6 45 06N 24 21E
Rampur Himachal Pradesh India 98 D6 31 26N 77 37E
Rampur Uttar Pradesh India 98 D5 28 50N 79 05E
Ramtha Jordan 96 N11 32 34N 36 00E
Rancagua Chile 81 C7 34 10S 70 45W
Ranchi India 99 F4 23 22N 85 20E
Randers Denmark 88 C12 56 28N 10 03E
Rangeley Maine USA 53 R4 44 58N 70 40W
Rangiora NZ 111 D3 43 19S 172 36E
Rangpur Bangladesh 99 K10 25 45N 89 21E
Rann of Kachchh *geog. reg.* India/Pakistan 98 B4/C4 24 00N 69 00E
Rapid City South Dakota USA 70 F5 44 06N 103 14W
Rapid River *tn.* Michigan USA 51 H3 45 56N 86 58W
Ra's al Hadd *c.* Oman 97 G3 22 31N 59 45E
Ra's al Khaymah UAE 97 G4 25 48N 55 56E
Râs Banâs *c.* Egypt 108 M12 23 58N 35 50E
Ras Dashen Terara *mt.* Ethiopia 108 M10 13 15N 38 27E
Râs el Barr Egypt 109 R5 31 32N 31 42E
Râs el 'Ish Egypt 109 S4 31 07N 32 18E
Ra's Fartak *c.* Yemen 97 F2 15 20N 52 12E
Rasht Iran 97 E6 37 18N 49 38E
Ras Lanuf Libya 108 H14 30 31N 18 34E
Ra's Madrakah *c.* Oman 97 G2 18 58N 57 50E
Ras Nouadhibou *c.* Mauritania 108 A12 20 53N 17 01W
Ratak Chain *is.* Pacific Ocean 114 H9 10 00N 172 30E
Rat Buri Thailand 103 B6 13 30N 99 50E
Ratlam India 98 D4 23 18N 75 06E
Ratno Ukraine 88 K9 51 40N 24 32E
Raton New Mexico USA 70 F4 36 45N 104 27W
Raurkela India 99 E4 22 16N 85 01E
Ravenna Italy 89 D6 44 25N 12 12E
Ravensburg Germany 88 B7 47 47N 9 37E
Ravensthorpe Aust. 110 C3 33 34S 120 01E
Ravi *r.* Pakistan 98 C6 31 00N 73 00E
Rawalpindi Pakistan 98 C6 33 40N 73 08E
Rawlins Wyoming USA 70 E5 41 46N 107 16W
Rawson Argentina 81 E5 43 15S 65 06W
Raymondville Texas USA 71 G2 26 30N 97 48W
Raystown Lake Pennsylvania USA 73 A2 40 10N 78 10W
Razgrad Bulgaria 89 L5 43 31N 26 33E
Reading UK 86 E9 51 28N 0 59W
Reading Pennsylvania USA 71 L5 40 20N 75 55W
Rebun-tō *i.* Japan 102 D4 45 25N 141 04E
Recherche, Archipelago of the *is.* Aust. 110 C3 35 00S 122 50E
Recife Brazil 80 L12 8 06S 34 53W
Reconquista Argentina 81 F8 29 08S 59 38W
Red *r.* USA 71 G3 34 00N 95 00W
Red *r.* USA 71 G6 46 00N 97 00W
Red Bluff California USA 70 B5 40 11N 122 16W
Redding California USA 70 B5 40 35N 122 24W
Redlands California USA 72 E2 34 03N 117 10W
Redon Fr. 86 D7 47 39N 2 05W
Redondo Beach *tn.* California USA 72 D1 33 51N 118 24W
Red Sea Middle East 96 C4/C2 27 00N 35 00E
Red Wing Minnesota USA 71 H5 44 33N 92 31W
Redwood City California USA 72 B3 37 28N 122 15W
Reed City Michigan USA 51 J2 43 53N 85 30W
Reedley California USA 72 D3 36 35N 119 27W
Reedsport Oregon USA 70 B5 43 42N 124 05W
Reefton NZ 111 C3 42 07S 171 52E
Regensburg Germany 88 D8 49 01N 12 07E
Reggio di Calabria Italy 89 E3 38 06N 15 39E
Reggio nell'Emilia Italy 89 C6 44 42N 10 37E
Rehovot Israel 96 N10 31 54N 34 46E
Reims Fr. 86 H8 49 15N 4 02E
Reinosa Sp. 87 C5 43 01N 4 09W
Rembang Indonesia 103 E2 6 45S 111 22E
Rendsburg Germany 88 B11 54 19N 9 39E
Rennes Fr. 86 E8 48 06N 1 40W
Reno Nevada USA 70 C4 39 32N 119 49W
Republic Washington USA 43 L1 48 39N 118 45W
REPUBLIC OF IRELAND 86 B10
REPUBLIC OF SOUTH AFRICA 109 J1/J2
Repulse Bay HK China 100 C1 22 14N 114 13E
Resistencia Argentina 80 F8 27 28S 59 00W
Reşiţa Romania 89 H6 45 16N 21 55E
Réthymno Greece 89 K1 35 23N 24 28E
Réunion *i.* Indian Ocean 113 E4 21 00S 55 30E
Reus Sp. 87 F4 41 10N 1 06E
Revillagigedo Island Alaska USA 42 E4 55 30N 131 30W
Rewa India 98 E4 24 32N 81 18E
Reykjanes Ridge Atlantic Ocean 116 E12 57 00N 33 00W
Reynosa Mexico 74 E5 26 05N 98 18W
Rhein *r.* Germany 88 A8 50 30N 8 00E
Rheine Germany 88 A10 52 17N 7 26E
Rhinelander Wisconsin USA 51 G3 45 38N 89 24W
Rhode Island *state* USA 71 M5 41 00N 71 00W
Rhône *r.* Switz./Fr. 87 H6 45 00N 4 50E
Ribe Denmark 88 B11 55 20N 8 47E
Ribeirão Prêto Brazil 80 H9 21 09S 47 48W
Riberalta Bolivia 80 D11 10 59S 66 06W
Richgrove California USA 72 D2 35 46N 119 04W
Richland Washington USA 70 C6 46 17N 119 17W
Richmond Aust. 110 G5 20 45S 143 05E
Richmond NZ 111 D4 41 31S 173 39E
Richmond California USA 70 B4 37 46N 122 20W
Richmond Indiana USA 71 K4 39 50N 84 51W
Richmond New York USA 73 H1 40 36N 74 10W
Richmond Virginia USA 71 L4 37 34N 77 27W
Richmondville New York USA 73 C3 42 38N 74 34W
Ridgecrest California USA 72 E2 35 37N 117 43W
Ridgeway Pennsylvania USA 52 H1 41 25N 78 40W
Riesa Germany 88 D9 51 18N 13 18E
Rieti Italy 89 D5 42 24N 12 51E
Riga Latvia 88 K12 56 53N 24 08E
Riga, Gulf of Estonia/Latvia 88 J12 57 30N 23 30E
Rijeka Croatia 89 E6 45 20N 14 27E
Rimini Italy 89 D6 44 03N 12 34E
Ringgold Isles *is.* Fiji 114 V16 16 10S 179 50W
Ringkøbing Denmark 88 B12 56 06N 8 15E
Ringkøbing Fjord Denmark 88 B11 56 00N 8 00E
Riobamba Ecuador 80 B13 1 44S 78 40W
Rio Branco *tn.* Brazil 80 D12 9 59S 67 49W
Río Cuarto *tn.* Argentina 81 E7 33 08S 64 20W
Rio de Janeiro *tn.* Brazil 80 I8 22 53S 43 17W
Rio de Janeiro *admin.* Brazil 80 J9 22 00S 42 30W
Río de la Plata *est.* Uruquay/Argentina 81 F6/F7 35 00S 57 00W
Rio de Para *r.* Brazil 80 H13 1 00S 48 00W
Río Gallegos *tn.* Argentina 81 D3 51 35S 68 10W
Río Grande *r.* Mexico/USA 70 E3/F3 30 00N 105 00W
Río Grande *tn.* Argentina 81 D3 53 45S 67 46W
Rio Grande *tn.* Brazil 81 G7 32 03S 52 08W
Río Grande *tn.* Mexico 74 D4 23 50N 103 02W
Rio Grande do Norte *admin.* Brazil 80 K12 6 00S 37 00W
Rio Grande do Sul *admin.* Brazil 81 G8 28 00S 52 30W
Rio Grande Rise Atlantic Ocean 116 E3 32 00S 36 00W
Riohacha Col. 80 C16 11 34N 72 58W
Rio Verde *tn.* Brazil 80 G10 17 50S 50 55W
Río Verde *tn.* Mexico 74 D4 21 58N 100 00W
Rishiri-tō *i.* Japan 102 D4 45 10N 141 20E
Ritter, Mount California USA 70 C4 37 40N 119 15W
Rivera Uruguay 81 F7 30 52S 55 30W
River Cess *tn.* Liberia 108 C9 5 28N 9 32W
Riverside California USA 70 C3 33 59N 117 22W
Riverton NZ 111 B1 46 22S 168 01E
Rivière-Pilote *tn.* Martinique 74 R12 14 29N 60 54W
Rivne Ukraine 88 L9 50 39N 26 10E
Riyadh Saudi Arabia 97 E3 24 39N 46 46E
Roanne Fr. 87 H7 46 02N 4 05E
Roanoke Virginia USA 71 L4 37 15N 79 58W
Robertsport Liberia 108 B9 6 45N 11 22W
Robin's Nest *mt.* HK China 100 C3 22 33N 114 11E
Roca Alijos *is.* Mexico 115 Q10 24 59N 115 49W
Rochefort Fr. 87 E6 45 57N 0 58W
Roche Harbor *tn.* Washington USA 42 H4 48 38N 123 06W
Rochester Minnesota USA 71 H5 84 01N 92 27W
Rochester New Hampshire USA 73 E3 43 18N 70 59W
Rochester New York USA 71 L5 43 12N 77 37W
Rockall Bank Atlantic Ocean 116 G12 58 00N 15 00W
Rockaway Beach New York USA 73 J1 40 33N 73 55W
Rockaway Inlet New York USA 73 J1 40 34N 73 56W
Rockford Illinois USA 71 J5 42 16N 89 06W
Rockhampton Aust. 110 J5 23 22S 150 32E
Rock Hill *tn.* South Carolina USA 71 K3 34 55N 81 01W
Rockin California USA 72 C4 38 47N 121 18W
Rock Island *tn.* Illinois USA 71 H5 41 30N 90 34W
Rock Lake *tn.* North Dakota USA 49 C1 48 49N 99 13W
Rockport Washington USA 42 H4 48 27N 121 37W
Rock Springs *tn.* Wyoming USA 70 E5 41 35N 109 13W
Rockville Maryland USA 73 B1 39 04N 77 08W
Rocky Mount *tn.* North Carolina USA 71 L4 35 46N 77 48W
Rodez Fr. 87 G6 44 21N 2 34E
Rodopi Planina *mts.* Bulgaria 89 K4 41 00N 25 00E
Rodrigues *i.* Indian Ocean 113 F5 19 43S 63 26E
Rogers City Michigan USA 51 K3 45 25N 83 49W
Rogers Lake California USA 72 E2 34 55N 117 48W
Rolette North Dakota USA 49 C1 48 40N 99 51W
Rolla Missouri USA 71 H4 37 56N 91 55W
Rolla North Dakota USA 49 C1 48 52N 99 37W
Roman Romania 89 L7 46 56N 26 56E
ROMANIA 88 H6
Rome Italy 89 D4 41 53N 12 30E
Rome Georgia USA 71 J3 34 01N 85 02W
Rome New York USA 71 L5 43 13N 75 28W
Ronda Sp. 87 C2 36 45N 5 10W
Rondônia *admin.* Brazil 80 E11 11 30S 63 00W
Rondonópolis Brazil 80 G10 16 29S 54 37W
Ronne Ice Shelf Antarctica 117 77 00S 60 00W
Roosevelt Minnesota USA 49 E1 48 48N 95 06W
Roraima *admin.* Brazil 80 E14 2 30N 62 30W
Rosamond Lake California USA 72 D2 34 50N 118 05W
Rosario Argentina 81 E7 33 00S 60 40W
Rosário Brazil 80 J13 3 0SS 44 15W
Rosario Mexico 74 A6 30 02N 115 46W
Rosario Mexico 74 C4 23 00N 105 51W
Rosario Strait *sd.* Washington USA 42 H4 48 25N 123 00W
Rosarito Mexico 74 B5 28 38N 114 02W
Roscoff Fr. 86 D8 48 43N 3 59W
Roscommon Michigan USA 51 J3 44 30N 84 35W
Roseau Dominica 74 Q8 15 18N 61 23W
Roseau Minnesota USA 49 E1 48 54N 95 43W
Roseburg Oregon USA 70 B5 43 13N 123 21W
Roselle New Jersey USA 73 H1 40 40N 74 16W
Rosenheim Germany 88 D7 47 51N 12 09E
Roseville California USA 72 C4 38 43N 121 20W
Roseville Michigan USA 52 D2 42 29N 82 52W
Rossano Italy 89 F3 39 35N 16 38E
Ross Ice Shelf Antarctica 117 80 00S 180 00
Ross Lake Washington USA 42 H4 48 50N 121 05W
Ross Lake National Recreation Area Washington USA 42 H4 48 50N 121 00W
Rosslare RoI 86 B10 52 15N 6 22W
Rosso Mauritania 108 A11 16 29N 15 53W
Ross Sea Antarctica 117 75 00S 180 00
Rostock Germany 88 D11 54 06N 12 09E
Rostov-na-Donu Russia 94 F6 47 15N 39 45E
Roswell New Mexico USA 70 F3 33 24N 104 33W
Rotorua NZ 111 F5 38 08S 176 14E
Rotterdam Neths. 86 H9 51 54N 4 28E
Roubaix Fr. 86 G9 50 42N 3 10E
Rouen Fr. 86 F8 49 26N 1 05E
Round Mountain *tn.* Nevada USA 72 E4 38 43N 117 03W
Rovigo Italy 89 C6 45 04N 11 47E
Rowta India 99 M11 26 50N 92 20E
Roxas Philippines 103 G6 11 36N 122 45E
Roxburgh NZ 111 B2 45 33S 169 19E
Royal Oak Michigan USA 52 C2 42 29N 83 09W
Royan Fr. 87 E6 45 38N 1 02W
Rub Al Khālī *d.* Saudi Arabia 97 E2 19 30N 48 00E
Rubtsovsk Russia 94 L7 51 43N 81 11E
Rudnyy Kazakhstan 94 J7 53 00N 63 05E
Rudyard Montana USA 46 G1 48 34N 110 33W
Rufiji *r.* Tanzania 109 M6 7 30S 38 40E
Rugao China 101 N5 32 27N 120 35E
Rugby UK 86 E10 52 23N 1 15W
Rügen *i.* Germany 88 D11 54 00N 14 00E
Rukwa, Lake Tanzania 109 L6 8 00S 33 00E
Rumford Maine USA 57 E1 44 33N 70 34W
Rumoi Japan 102 D3 43 57N 141 40E
Runanga NZ 111 C3 42 24S 171 15E
Ruse Bulgaria 89 L5 43 50N 25 59E
Rusk Texas USA 71 G3 31 49N 95 11W
Russas Brazil 80 K13 4 56S 38 02W
Russell NZ 111 E7 35 16S 174 07E
Russell Kansas USA 71 G4 38 54N 98 51W
Russian *r.* California USA 72 B4 38 52N 123 03W
RUSSIAN FEDERATION 94/95
Ruston Louisiana USA 71 H3 32 32N 92 39W
Ruth Nevada USA 70 D4 39 16N 114 59W
Rutland Vermont USA 71 M5 43 37N 72 59W
Rutog China 100 D5 33 27N 79 43E
Ruvuma *r.* Tanzania/Mozambique 109 M5 11 30S 38 00E
Ružomberok Slovakia 88 G8 49 04N 19 15E
RWANDA 108 K7
Ryazan' Russia 94 F7 54 37N 39 43E
Rybinsk Russia 94 F8 58 03N 38 50E
Rybinskoye Vodokhranilische *res.* Russia 94 F8 59 00N 38 00E
Rybnik Poland 88 G9 50 07N 18 30E
Ryukyu Islands Japan 101 N4 27 30N 127 30E
Ryukyu Ridge Pacific Ocean 114 C10 25 50N 128 00E
Rzeszów Poland 88 J9 50 04N 22 00E

S

Saalfeld Germany 88 C9 50 39N 11 22E
Saarbrücken Germany 88 A8 49 15N 6 58E
Saaremaa *i.* Estonia 88 J13 58 20N 22 00E
Šabac Serbia 89 G6 44 45N 19 41E
Sabadell Sp. 87 G4 41 33N 2 07E
Sabah *admin.* Malaysia 103 F4/F5 5 00N 115 00E
Sabaloka Cataract Sudan 108 L11 16 19N 32 40E
Sabhā Libya 108 G13 27 02N 14 26E
Sabi *r.* Zimbabwe/Mozambique 109 L3 20 30S 33 00E
Sabinas Mexico 74 D5 27 50N 101 09W
Sabinas Hidalgo Mexico 74 D5 26 33N 100 10W
Sabine *r.* USA 71 H3 30 00N 94 00W
Sable, Cape Florida USA 71 K2 25 08N 80 07W
Sabor *r.* Port. 87 B4 41 22N 6 50W
Sabyā Saudi Arabia 96 D2 17 07N 42 39E
Sabzevār Iran 97 G6 36 15N 57 38E
Sacramento California USA 70 B4 38 32N 121 30W
Sacramento *r.* California USA 72 C4 38 05N 121 35W
Sacramento Mountains USA 70 E3 33 00N 105 00W
Sadiya India 99 H5 27 49N 95 38E
Sado *r.* Port. 87 A3 38 15N 8 30W
Sadoga-shima *i.* Japan 102 C2 38 20N 138 30E
Säffle Sweden 88 D13 59 08N 12 55E
Safi Morocco 108 C14 32 20N 9 17W
Saga Japan 102 B1 33 16N 130 18E
Sagamihara Japan 102 C2 35 34N 139 22E
Sagamore Massachusetts USA 73 E2 41 46N 70 31W
Sagar India 98 D4 23 50N 78 44E
Sage Creek *r.* Montana USA 46 G1 48 45N 110 40W
Saginaw Michigan USA 71 K5 43 25N 83 54W
Saginaw Bay Michigan USA 71 K5 44 00N 84 00W
Sagua la Grande Cuba 75 H4 22 48N 80 06W
Sagunto Sp. 87 E3 39 40N 0 17W
Sahara Desert North Africa 108/109 C12
Saharanpur India 98 D5 29 58N 77 33E
Sahiwal Pakistan 98 C6 30 41N 73 11E
Sahuaripa Mexico 74 C5 29 00N 109 13W
Sahuayo Mexico 74 D4 20 05N 102 42W
Saidpur Bangladesh 99 K10 25 48N 89 00E
Saikhoa Ghat India 99 H5 27 40N 95 35E
Sai Kung HK China 100 C2 22 23N 114 16E
St. Albans UK 86 E9 51 46N 0 21W
St. Albans New York USA 73 J1 40 42N 73 45W
St. Albans Vermont USA 57 D1 44 49N 73 07W
St. Andrews UK 86 D12 56 20N 2 48W
St. Ann's Bay *tn.* Jamaica 75 U14 18 26N 77 12W
St. Augustine Florida USA 71 K2 29 54N 81 19W
St. Barthélémy *i.* Lesser Antilles 74 P9 17 55N 62 50W
St-Brieuc Fr. 86 D8 48 31N 2 45W
St. Cloud Minnesota USA 71 H6 45 34N 94 10W
St. Croix *i.* W. Indies 75 M3 22 45N 65 00W
St. Croix *r.* USA 71 H6 46 00N 93 00W
St-Dié Fr. 86 J8 48 17N 6 57E
St-Dizier Fr. 86 H8 48 38N 4 58E
St. Elias, Mount Alaska USA 64 B3 60 12N 140 57W
Ste. Marie Martinique 74 R12 14 47N 61 00W
Saintes Fr. 87 E6 45 44N 0 38W
St-Étienne Fr. 87 H6 45 26N 4 23E
St. Eustatius *i.* Lesser Antilles 74 P9 17 30N 62 55W
St. Francis *r.* USA 71 H4 35 00N 90 00W
St. Gallen Switz. 87 K7 47 25N 9 23E
St-Gaudens Fr. 87 F5 43 07N 0 44E
St. George's Grenada 74 R11 12 04N 61 44W
St. George's Channel British Isles 86 B9 52 00N 6 00W
St. Helena *i.* Atlantic Ocean 116 H5 15 58S 5 43W
St. Helena Bay RSA 109 H1 32 00S 17 30E
St. Ignace Michigan USA 71 K6 45 53N 84 44W
St. John North Dakota USA 49 C1 48 57N 99 43W
St. John *r.* Liberia 108 C9 6 30N 9 40W
Saint John *r.* USA 71 N6 46 00N 69 00W
St. John's Antigua and Barbuda 74 Q9 17 08N 61 50W
St. Johns Michigan USA 52 B3 43 01N 84 31W
St. Joseph Missouri USA 71 H4 39 45N 94 51W
St. Joseph River Indiana/Ohio USA 52 B1 41 12N 84 55W
St. Kitts *i.* St. Kitts and Nevis 74 P9 17 21N 62 48W
ST. KITTS AND NEVIS 74 P9
St. Laurent French Guiana 80 G15 5 29N 54 03W
St. Lawrence Island Alaska USA 115 J14 63 15N 169 50W
St-Lô Fr. 86 E8 49 07N 1 05W
St. Louis Senegal 108 A11 16 01N 16 30W
St. Louis Missouri USA 71 H4 38 40N 90 15W
St. Louis River Minnesota USA 51 E4 47 20N 92 40W
ST. LUCIA 74 R11
St. Lucia Channel *sd.* Caribbean Sea 74 R12 14 09N 60 57W
St. Maarten Lesser Antilles 74 P10 18 04N 63 04W
St-Malo Fr. 86 D8 48 39N 2 00W
St. Martin Lesser Antilles 74 P10 18 04N 63 04W
St. Mary Montana USA 46 F1 48 44N 113 26W
St. Marys Pennsylvania USA 52 H1 41 25N 78 33W
St. Moritz Switz. 87 K7 46 30N 9 51E
St-Nazaire Fr. 87 D7 47 17N 2 12W
St-Omer Fr. 86 G9 50 45N 2 15E
St. Paul Minnesota USA 71 H5 45 00N 93 10W
St. Paul *r.* Liberia 108 B9/C9 7 10N 10 05W
St. Paul Rocks Atlantic Ocean 116 F7 0 23N 29 23W
St. Petersburg Russia 94 F8 59 55N 30 25E
St. Petersburg Florida USA 71 K2 27 45N 82 40W
St. Pölten Austria 88 E8 48 13N 15 37E
St-Quentin Fr. 86 G8 49 51N 3 17E
St. Thomas *i.* W. Indies 75 L3 18 00N 65 30W
St-Tropez Fr. 87 J5 43 16N 6 39E
St. Vincent *i.* St. Vincent and The Grenadines 74 R11 13 15N 61 12W
ST. VINCENT AND THE GRENADINES 74 R11
St. Vincent Passage *sd.* St. Lucia 74 R11 13 30N 61 00W
Sakai Japan 102 C1 34 35N 135 28E
Sakākah Saudi Arabia 96 D4 29 59N 40 12E
Sakakawea, Lake North Dakota USA 70 F6 48 00N 103 00W
Sakarya Turkey 96 B7 40 47N 30 23E
Sakarya *r.* Turkey 96 B7 40 05N 30 15E
Sakata Japan 102 C2 38 55N 139 51E
Sakhalin *i.* Russia 95 S7 50 00N 143 00E
Sakhalin Bay Russia 95 S7 54 00N 141 00E
Saki Nigeria 108 E9 8 39N 3 25E
Sala Sweden 88 F13 59 55N 16 38E
Salado *r.* Argentina 81 D6 35 00S 66 30W
Salado *r.* Argentina 81 E8 28 30S 62 30W
Şalalah Oman 97 F2 17 00N 54 04E
Salamanca Mexico 74 D4 20 34N 101 12W
Salamanca Sp. 87 C4 40 58N 5 40W
Salamanca New York USA 52 H2 42 10N 78 43W
Salay Goméz *i.* Pacific Ocean 115 R5 26 28S 105 28W
Saldus Latvia 88 J12 56 38N 22 30E

Salekhard Russia 94 J10 66 33N 66 35E
Salem India 98 D2 11 38N 78 08E
Salem Massachusetts USA 71 M5 42 32N 70 53W
Salem Oregon USA 70 B5 44 57N 123 01W
Salerno Italy 89 E4 40 40N 14 46E
Salgótarján Hungary 88 G8 49 05N 19 47E
Salgueiro Brazil 80 K12 8 04S 39 05W
Salima Malawi 109 L5 13 45S 34 29E
Salina Kansas USA 71 G4 38 53N 97 36W
Salinas Ecuador 80 A13 2 15S 80 58W
Salinas California USA 70 B4 36 39N 121 40W
Salinas *r.* California USA 72 C3 36 30N 121 40W
Salinas Grandes *l.* Argentina 81 D7/E8 30 00S 65 00W
Saline Michigan USA 52 C2 42 12N 83 46W
Salisbury UK 86 E9 51 05N 1 48W
Salisbury Maryland USA 71 L4 38 22N 75 37W
Salisbury North Carolina USA 71 K4 35 20N 80 30W
Salmon Idaho USA 70 D6 45 11N 113 55W
Salmon *r.* Idaho USA 70 C6 45 00N 116 00W
Salmon Reservoir New York USA 53 L3 43 32N 75 50W
Salmon River Mountains Idaho USA 70 C5 45 00N 115 00W
Salonta Romania 89 H7 46 49N 21 40E
Salt Jordan 96 N11 32 03N 35 44E
Salt *r.* Arizona USA 70 D3 34 00N 110 00W
Salta Argentina 80 D9 24 46S 65 28W
Salt Fork *r.* Texas/Oklahoma USA 70 F3 35 00N 100 00W
Saltillo Mexico 74 D5 25 30N 101 00W
Salt Lake City Utah USA 70 D5 40 45N 111 55W
Salto Uruguay 81 F7 31 27S 57 50W
Salton Sea *l.* California USA 70 C3 33 00N 116 00W
Salvador Brazil 80 K11 12 58S 38 29W
Salween *r.* China/Myanmar 103 B8 20 00N 103 00E
Salzburg Austria 88 D7 47 48N 13 03E
Salzgitter Germany 88 C10 52 13N 10 20E
Samani Japan 102 D3 42 07N 142 57E
Samar *i.* Philippines 103 G6 12 00N 125 00E
Samara Russia 94 H7 53 10N 50 10E
Samarinda Indonesia 103 F3 0 30S 117 09E
Samarkand Uzbekistan 94 J4 39 40N 66 57E
Sāmarrā' Iraq 96 D5 34 13N 43 52E
Sambalpur India 99 E4 21 28N 84 04E
Sambas Indonesia 103 D4 1 22N 109 15E
Sambor Ukraine 88 J8 49 31N 23 10E
SAMOA 114 J6
Sámos *i.* Greece 89 L2 37 45N 26 45E
Samothráki *i.* Greece 89 K4 40 00N 25 00E
Samsun Turkey 96 C7 41 17N 36 22E
San Mali 108 C10 13 21N 4 57W
Sana Yemen 96 D2 15 23N 44 14E
Sanaga *r.* Cameroon 108 G8 4 30N 12 20E
Sanandaj Iran 97 E6 35 18N 47 01E
San Andrés Tuxtla Mexico 74 E3 18 28N 95 15W
San Angelo Texas USA 70 F3 31 28N 100 28W
San Antonio Chile 81 C7 33 35S 71 39W
San Antonio Texas USA 71 G2 29 25N 98 30W
San Antonio *r.* Texas USA 71 G2 29 00N 97 00W
San Antonio Oeste Argentina 81 E5 40 45S 64 58W
San Benito *r.* California USA 72 C3 36 45N 121 18W
San Bernardino California USA 70 C3 34 07N 117 18W
San Bernardo Chile 81 C7 33 37S 70 45W
San Carlos Venezuela 80 D15 9 39N 68 35W
San Carlos Luzon Philippines 103 G7 15 59N 120 22E
San Carlos Negros Philippines 103 G6 10 30N 123 29E
San Carlos de Bariloche Argentina 81 C5 41 11S 71 23W
San Carlos del Zulia Venezuela 80 C15 9 01N 71 58W
San Clemente California USA 72 E1 33 26N 117 36W
San Clemente Island California USA 70 C3 33 26N 117 36W
San Cristóbal Argentina 81 E7 30 20S 61 14W
San Cristóbal Mexico 74 F3 16 45N 92 40W
San Cristóbal Venezuela 80 C15 7 46N 72 15W
Sancti Spíritus Cuba 75 J4 21 55N 79 28W
Sandakan Malaysia 103 F5 5 52N 118 04E
Sanday *i.* UK 86 D13 59 15N 2 30W
Sandefjord Norway 86 L13 59 00N 10 15E
San Diego California USA 70 C3 32 45N 117 10W
Sandpoint *tn.* Idaho USA 70 C6 48 17N 116 34W
Sandusky Ohio USA 51 K1 41 27N 82 43W
Sandusky Bay Ohio USA 52 D1 41 30N 82 50W
Sandwip Island Bangladesh 99 L9 22 30N 91 25E
Sandy River Maine USA 53 R4 44 45N 70 12W
San Felipe Mexico 74 B6 31 03N 114 52W
San Felipe Venezuela 80 D16 10 25N 68 40W
San Feliú de Guixols Sp. 87 G4 41 47N 3 02E
San Fernando Mexico 74 A5 29 59N 115 10W
San Fernando Sp. 87 B2 36 28N 6 12W
San Fernando Trinidad and Tobago 75 V15 10 16N 61 28W
San Fernando California USA 72 D2 34 17N 118 27W
San Fernando de Apure Venezuela 80 D15 7 53N 67 15W
Sanford Florida USA 71 K2 28 49N 81 17W
San Francisco Argentina 81 E7 31 29S 62 06W
San Francisco Dom. Rep. 75 K3 19 19N 70 15W
San Francisco California USA 70 B4 37 45N 122 27W
San Francisco Bay California USA 72 B3 37 37N 122 15W
San Francisco del Oro Mexico 74 C5 26 52N 105 50W
Sangar Russia 95 Q9 64 02N 127 30E
Sanger California USA 72 D3 36 42N 119 33W
Sangha *r.* Africa 108 H8 2 00N 17 00E
Sangli India 98 C3 16 55N 74 37E
Sangre de Cristo Mountains New Mexico USA 70 E4 37 00N 105 00W
Sangre Grande Trinidad and Tobago 75 V15 10 35N 61 08W
Sangu *r.* Bangladesh 99 M9 22 10N 92 15E
San Jacinto Peak *mt.* California USA 72 E1 33 48N 116 40W
San Javier Bolivia 80 E10 16 22S 62 38W
San Joaquin *r.* California USA 70 B4 37 00N 120 00W
San José Costa Rica 75 H1 9 59N 84 04W
San José Uruguay 81 F7 34 27S 56 40W
San José California USA 70 B4 37 20N 121 55W
San José del Cabo Mexico 74 C4 23 01N 109 40W
San Juan Argentina 81 D7 31 33S 68 31W
San Juan Peru 80 B10 15 22S 75 07W
San Juan Puerto Rico 75 L3 18 29N 66 08W
San Juan *r.* USA 70 D4 37 00N 110 00W
San Juan Islands Washington USA 42 H4 48 30N 123 05W
San Juan Mountains Colorado USA 70 E4 37 50N 107 50W
San Julián Argentina 81 D4 49 17S 67 45W
Sankosh *r.* India/Bhutan 99 K11 26 55N 90 00E
Sankuru *r.* CDR 108 J7 4 00S 23 30E
Sanliurfa Turkey 96 C6 37 08N 38 45E
Sanlúcar de Barrameda Sp. 87 B2 36 46N 6 21W
San Luis Argentina 81 D7 33 20S 66 23W
San Luis Obispo California USA 70 B4 35 16N 120 40W
San Luis Obispo Bay California USA 72 C2 35 03N 120 39W
San Luis Potosí Mexico 74 D4 22 10N 101 00W
San Marcos Texas USA 71 G2 29 54N 97 57W
SAN MARINO 89 D5 44 00N 12 00E
San Mateo California USA 72 B3 37 33N 122 22W
Sanmenxia China 101 L5 34 46N 111 17E
San Miguel El Salvador 74 G2 13 28N 88 10W
San Miguel *r.* Bolivia 80 E10 15 00S 63 30W
San Miguel de Tucumán Argentina 80 D8 26 47S 65 15W
San Miguel Island California USA 72 C2 34 03N 120 22W
Sanming China 101 M4 26 16N 117 35E
San Nicolas de los Arroyos Argentina 81 E7 33 25S 60 15W
San Nicolas Island California USA 72 D1 33 15N 119 30W
San Pablo Philippines 103 G6 14 03N 121 19E
San Pablo Bay California USA 72 B4 38 00N 122 15W
San Pedro Argentina 80 E9 24 12S 64 55W
San Pedro Côte d'Ivoire 108 C8 4 45N 6 37W
San Pedro Dom. Rep. 75 L3 18 30N 69 18W
San Pedro Channel California USA 72 D1 33 37N 118 30W
San Pedro de las Colonias Mexico 74 D5 25 50N 102 59W
San Pedro Sula Honduras 74 G3 15 26N 88 01W
San Rafael Argentina 81 D7 34 35S 68 24W
San Rafael California USA 70 B4 37 58N 122 30W
San Rafael Mountains California USA 72 D2 34 50N 119 40W
San Remo Italy 89 A5 43 48N 7 46E
San Salvador El Salvador 74 G2 13 40N 89 10W
San Salvador *i.* Bahamas 75 K4 24 00N 74 32W
San Salvador de Jujuy Argentina 80 D9 24 10S 65 48W
San Sebastián Sp. 87 E5 43 19N 1 59W
San Severo Italy 89 E4 41 41N 15 23E
Santa Ana Bolivia 80 D11 13 46S 65 37W
Santa Ana El Salvador 74 G2 14 00N 89 31W
Santa Ana California USA 70 C3 33 44N 117 54W
Santa Barbara Mexico 74 C5 26 48N 105 50W
Santa Barbara California USA 70 C3 33 29N 119 01W
Santa Barbara Channel California USA 72 C2 34 15N 120 00W
Santa Barbara Island California USA 72 D1 33 29N 119 02W
Santa Catalina, Gulf of California USA 72 D1 33 07N 118 00W
Santa Catalina Island California USA 70 C3 33 25N 118 25W
Santa Catarina *admin.* Brazil 80 G8 27 00S 51 00W
Santa Clara Cuba 75 J4 22 25N 79 58W
Santa Clara California USA 72 C3 37 21N 121 57W
Santa Clarita California USA 72 D2 34 23N 118 33W
Santa Cruz Bolivia 80 E10 17 50S 63 10W
Santa Cruz Canary Islands 108 A13 28 28N 16 15W
Santa Cruz California USA 70 B4 36 58N 122 03W
Santa Cruz *r.* Argentina 81 C3 50 00S 70 00W
Santa Cruz Island California USA 70 C3 34 00N 119 40W
Santa Cruz Islands Solomon Islands 114 G6 11 00S 167 00E
Santa Fé Argentina 81 E7 31 35S 60 50W
Santa Fe New Mexico USA 70 E4 35 41N 105 57W
Santa Isabel *i.* Solomon Islands 114 F7 7 30S 158 30E
Santa Maria Brazil 81 G8 29 45S 53 40W
Santa Maria California USA 70 B3 34 56N 120 25W
Santa Marta Col. 80 C16 11 18N 74 10W
Santa Monica California USA 72 D2 34 00N 118 28W
Santana do Livramento Brazil 81 F7 30 52S 55 30W
Santander Col. 80 B14 3 00N 76 25W
Santander Sp. 87 D5 43 28N 3 48W
Sant' Antioco Italy 89 B3 39 04N 8 27E
Santa Paula California USA 72 D2 34 20N 119 04W
Santarém Brazil 80 G13 2 26S 54 41W
Santarém Port. 87 A3 39 14N 8 40W
Santa Rosa Argentina 81 E6 36 37S 64 17W
Santa Rosa Honduras 74 G2 14 48N 88 43W
Santa Rosa California USA 70 B4 38 26N 122 43W
Santa Rosa New Mexico USA 70 F3 34 56N 104 42W
Santa Rosa Island California USA 70 B3 34 00N 120 05W
Santa Rosalia Mexico 74 B5 27 20N 112 20W
Santa Ynez Mountains California USA 72 C2 34 31N 120 00W
Santee California USA 72 E1 32 51N 116 59W
Santiago Chile 81 C7 33 30S 70 40W
Santiago Panama 75 H1 8 08N 80 59W
Santiago de Compostela Sp. 87 A5 42 52N 8 33W
Santiago de Cuba Cuba 75 J4 20 00N 75 49W
Santiago del Estero Argentina 81 E8 27 47S 64 15W
Santiago Ixcuintla Mexico 74 C4 21 50N 105 11W
San Tin HK China 100 B3 22 30N 114 04E
Santipur India 99 K9 23 16N 88 27E
Santo Andre Brazil 80 H9 23 39S 46 29W
Santo Domingo Dom. Rep. 75 L3 18 30N 69 57W
Santo Domingo de los Colorados Ecuador 80 B13 0 13S 79 09W
Santos Brazil 80 H9 23 56S 46 22W
San Vicente El Salvador 74 G2 13 38N 88 42W
San Wai Tsuen HK China 100 B2 22 28N 114 03E
Sanxia Shuiku *res.* China 101 K4/L5 31 27N 108 00S
Sanya China 101 K2 18 25N 109 27E
São Bernardo do Campo Brazil 80 H9 23 45S 46 34W
São Borja Brazil 81 F8 28 35S 56 01W
São Francisco *r.* Brazil 80 K12 8 30S 39 00W
São José Brazil 81 H8 27 35S 48 40W
São José do Rio Prêto Brazil 80 H9 20 50S 49 20W
São José dos Campos Brazil 80 H9 23 07S 45 52W
São Luís Brazil 80 J13 2 34S 44 16W
Saône *r.* Fr. 87 H7 46 28N 4 55E
São Paulo Brazil 80 H9 23 33S 46 39W
São Paulo *admin.* Brazil 80 G9 21 30S 50 00W
São Paulo de Olivença Brazil 80 D13 3 34S 68 55W
São Tomé *i.* Gulf of Guinea 108 F8 0 25N 6 35E
SÃO TOMÉ AND PRINCIPE 108 F8
São Vicente Brazil 80 H9 23 57S 46 23W
Sapporo Japan 102 D3 43 05N 141 21E
Saqqez Iran 96 E6 36 14N 46 15E
Sarajevo Bosnia-Herzegovina 89 G5 43 52N 18 26E
Sarakhs Iran 97 H6 36 32N 61 07E
Saransk Russia 94 G7 54 12N 45 10E
Sarasota Florida USA 71 K2 27 20N 82 32W
Sarata Ukraine 89 M7 46 00N 29 40E
Saratoga Springs *tn.* New York USA 73 D3 43 05N 73 47W
Saratov Russia 94 G7 51 30N 45 55E
Saravan Iran 97 H4 27 25N 62 17E
Sarawak *admin.* Malaysia 103 E4 1 00N 111 00E
Sardindida Plain Kenya 108 M8 2 00N 40 00E
Sardinia *i.* Italy 89 B3/B4 40 00N 9 00E
Sar-e Pol Afghanistan 97 J6 36 15N 65 57E
Sargasso Sea Atlantic Ocean 116 B9 27 00N 66 00W
Sargodha Pakistan 98 C6 32 01N 72 40E
Sarh Chad 108 H9 9 08N 18 22E
Sarīr Calanscio *d.* Libya 108 J13 26 00N 22 00E
Sark *i.* British Isles 86 D8 49 26N 2 22W
Sarles North Dakota USA 49 C1 48 57N 98 59W
Sarmiento Argentina 81 D4 45 38S 69 08W
Sarny Ukraine 88 L9 51 21N 26 31E
Sarpsborg Norway 86 L13 59 17N 11 06E
Sarrebourg Fr. 86 J8 48 43N 7 03E
Sarreguemines Fr. 86 J8 49 06N 6 55E
Sartène France 87 K4 41 37N 8 58E
Sasebo Japan 102 A1 33 10N 129 42E
Sassandra Côte d'Ivoire 108 C8 4 58N 6 08W
Sassandra *r.* Côte d'Ivoire 108 C9 5 50N 6 55W
Sassari Italy 89 B4 40 43N 8 34E
Sassnitz Germany 88 D11 54 32N 13 40E
Satna India 98 E4 24 33N 80 50E
Satpura Range *mts.* India 98 C4/D4 21 40N 75 00E
Sattahip Thailand 103 C6 12 36N 100 56E
Satu Mare Romania 88 J7 47 48N 22 52E
SAUDI ARABIA 96/97 D3/F3
Sault Ste. Marie Michigan USA 51 J4 46 29N 84 22W
Saumur Fr. 87 E7 47 16N 0 05W
Saurimo Angola 109 J6 9 39S 20 24E
Sava *r.* Europe 89 G6 45 00N 16 00E
Savannah Georgia USA 71 K3 32 04N 81 07W
Savannah *r.* USA 71 K3 33 00N 82 00W
Savannakhet Laos 103 C7 16 34N 104 45E
Savanna la Mar Jamaica 75 T14 18 13N 78 08W
Savona Italy 89 B6 44 18N 8 28E
Sawahlunto Indonesia 103 C3 0 41S 100 52E
Sawu Sea Indonesia 103 G2 9 00S 122 00E
Sayanogorsk Russia 95 M7 53 00N 91 26E
Saylac Somalia 108 N10 11 21N 43 30E
Saynshand Mongolia 101 L8 45 00N 111 10E
Sayre Pennsylvania USA 53 K1 41 58N 76 03W
Say'ūn Yemen 97 E2 15 59N 48 44E
Scarborough Trinidad and Tobago 75 V15 11 11N 60 44W
Scarborough UK 86 E11 54 17N 0 24W
Schenectady New York USA 71 M5 42 48N 73 57W
Schleswig Germany 88 B11 54 32N 9 34E
Schurz Nevada USA 72 D4 38 57N 118 48W
Schwäbisch Alb *mts.* Germany 88 B8 48 00N 9 00E
Schwarzwald *mts.* Germany 88 B8 47 00N 8 00E
Schweinfurt Germany 88 C9 50 03N 10 16E
Schwerin Germany 88 C10 53 38N 11 25E
Scilly, Isles of UK 86 B8 49 56N 6 20W
Scobey Montana USA 47 E1 48 50N 105 29W
Scotia Ridge Atlantic Ocean 116 C1 53 00S 50 00W
Scotia Sea Antarctica 117 55 00S 45 00W
Scotland *admin.* UK 86 C12 56 00N 4 00W
Scott Island Southern Ocean 114 G1 66 35S 180 00
Scottsbluff Nebraska USA 70 F5 41 52N 103 40W
Scranton Pennsylvania USA 71 L5 41 25N 75 40W
Searles Lake California USA 72 E2 35 42N 117 17W
Seaside California USA 72 C3 36 36N 121 51W
Seattle Washington USA 70 B6 47 35N 122 20W
Sebewaing Michigan USA 52 C3 43 44N 83 26W
Seboomook Lake Maine USA 53 S5 45 55N 69 50W
Sedalia Missouri USA 71 H4 38 42N 93 15W
Sedan Fr. 86 H8 49 42N 4 57E
Sedro Woolley Washington USA 42 H4 48 27N 122 18W
Ségou Mali 108 C10 13 28N 6 18W
Segovia Sp. 87 C4 40 57N 4 07W
Segre *r.* Sp. 87 F4 42 00N 1 10E
Segura *r.* Sp. 87 D3 38 00N 1 00W
Seine *r.* Fr. 86 F8 49 15N 1 15E
Sekiu Washington USA 42 H4 48 10N 124 30W
Sekondi Takoradi Ghana 108 D8 4 59N 1 43W
Selat Sunda *sd.* Indonesia 103 D2 5 50S 105 30E
Selemdzha *r.* Russia 95 R7 53 00N 132 00E
Selenge *r.* Mongolia 101 J8 49 00N 102 00E
Selima Oasis Sudan 108 K12 21 22N 29 19E
Selma Alabama USA 71 J3 32 24N 87 01W
Selma California USA 72 D3 36 34N 119 36W
Semarang Indonesia 103 E2 6 58S 110 29E
Seminoe Reservoir Wyoming USA 70 E5 42 00N 106 00W
Seminole Oklahoma USA 71 G4 35 15N 96 40W
Semipalatinsk Kazakhstan 94 L7 50 26N 80 16E
Semnān Iran 97 F6 35 30N 53 25E
Sendai Honshu Japan 102 D2 38 16N 140 52E
Sendai Kyushu Japan 102 B1 31 50N 130 17E
Seneca Falls *tn.* New York USA 53 K2 42 55N 76 48W
Seneca Lake New York USA 51 N2 42 40N 77 01W
SENEGAL 108 A10
Sénégal *r.* Senegal/Mauritania 108 A11 16 45N 14 45W
Senhor do Bonfim Brazil 80 J11 10 28S 40 11W
Senj Croatia 89 E6 45 00N 14 55E
Sennar Sudan 108 L10 13 31N 33 38E
Sens Fr. 86 G8 48 12N 3 18E
Senyavin Islands Pacific Ocean 114 G8 7 00N 161 30E
Seoul South Korea 101 P6 37 32N 127 00E
Sepik *r.* PNG 110 G9 4 15S 143 00E
Sequoia National Park California USA 72 D3 36 23N 118 38W
Seram *i.* Indonesia 103 H3/J3 3 30S 129 30E
Seram Sea Indonesia 103 H3/J3 2 30S 130 00E
Serang Indonesia 103 D2 6 07S 106 09E
SERBIA 89 H5/H6
Seremban Malaysia 103 C4 2 43N 102 57E
Serenje Zambia 109 L5 13 12S 30 15E
Sergino Russia 94 J9 62 30N 65 40E
Sergipe *admin.* Brazil 80 K11 11 00S 38 00W
Sergiyev Posad Russia 94 F8 56 20N 38 10E
Seria Brunei 103 E4 4 39N 114 23E
Serian Malaysia 103 E4 1 10N 110 35E
Sérifos *i.* Greece 89 K2 37 10N 24 25E
Serov Russia 94 J8 59 42N 60 32E
Serpent's Mouth *sd.* Trinidad and Tobago 75 V15 10 10N 61 58W
Serra Brazil 80 J10 20 06S 40 16W
Serra do Mar *mts.* Brazil 80/81 H8 27 30S 49 00W
Serra do Navio Brazil 80 G14 1 00N 52 05W
Serrania de Cuenca *mts.* Sp. 87 D4/E4 40 30N 2 15W
Serra Tumucumaque *mts.* Brazil 80 F14 2 00N 55 00W
Sérres Greece 89 J4 41 03N 23 33E
Sete Lagoas Brazil 80 J10 19 29S 44 15W
Setesdal *geog. reg.* Norway 86 J13 59 30N 7 10E
Sétif Algeria 108 F15 36 11N 5 24E
Setit *r.* Sudan 108 M10 14 20N 36 15E
Seto-naikai *sd.* Japan 102 B1 34 00N 132 30E
Settat Morocco 108 C14 33 04N 7 37W
Setúbal Port. 87 A3 38 31N 8 54W
Severn *r.* UK 86 D10 52 30N 3 15W
Severnaya (North) Dvina *r.* Russia 94 G9 63 00N 43 00E
Severnaya Sos'va *r.* Russia 94 J9 62 30N 62 00E
Severnaya Zemlya *is.* Russia 95 M13 80 00N 95 00E
Severodvinsk Russia 94 F9 64 35N 39 50E
Sevier *r.* Utah USA 70 D4 39 00N 113 00W
Seville Sp. 87 C2 37 24N 5 59W
SEYCHELLES 113 E6

Name	Page	Grid	Lat	Long
Seychelles Ridge Indian Ocean	113	E6	10 00S	60 00E
Seymchan Russia	95	T9	62 54N	152 26E
Sfântu Gheorghe Romania	89	K6	45 51N	25 48E
Sfax Tunisia	108	G14	34 45N	10 43E
Sha Chau *i.* HK China	100	A2	22 21N	113 53E
Shache China	100	D6	38 27N	77 16E
Shah Alam Malaysia	103	C4	3 02N	101 31E
Shahdol India	98	E4	23 19N	81 26E
Shahjahanpur India	98	D5	27 53N	79 55E
Sha Lo Wan HK China	100	A1	22 17N	113 54E
Sham Chung HK China	100	C2	22 26N	114 17E
Sham Chun River HK China	100	B3	22 30N	114 00E
Shamokin Pennsylvania USA	73	B2	40 47N	76 34W
Sham Shek Tsuen HK China	100	A1	22 17N	113 53E
Sham Shui Po HK China	100	C1	22 20N	114 10E
Shangani *r.* Zimbabwe	109	K4	19 00S	29 00E
Shanghai China	101	N5	31 06N	121 22E
Shangqui China	101	M5	34 27N	115 07E
Shangrao China	101	M4	28 28N	117 54E
Shannon Rol	86	A10	52 41N	8 55W
Shannon *r.* Rol	86	A10	52 45N	8 57W
Shannon, Lake Washington USA	42	H4	48 35N	121 45W
Shantou China	101	M3	23 23N	116 39E
Shaoguan China	101	L3	24 54N	113 33E
Shaoxing China	101	N5	30 02N	120 35E
Shaoyang China	101	L4	27 10N	111 25E
Shaqrā' Saudia Arabia	96	E4	25 18N	45 15E
Sharjah UAE	97	G4	25 20N	55 20E
Sharm el Sheikh Egypt	96	B4	27 52N	34 16E
Sharon Pennsylvania USA	71	K5	41 46N	80 30W
Sharp Island HK China	100	C2	22 22N	114 18E
Sharp Peak HK China	100	D2	22 26N	114 22E
Shashi China	101	L5	30 16N	112 20E
Shasta Lake California USA	70	B5	40 45N	122 20W
Shasta, Mount California USA	70	B5	41 25N	122 12W
Sha Tau Kok HK China	100	C3	22 33N	114 13E
Sha Tin HK China	100	C2	22 23N	114 11E
Shatsky Rise Pacific Ocean	114	G11	34 00N	160 00E
Shebele *r.* Ethiopia/Somalia	108	N9	6 00N	44 00E
Sheberghān Afghanistan	97	J6	36 41N	65 45E
Sheboygan Wisconsin USA	71	J5	43 46N	87 44W
Sheffield UK	86	E10	53 23N	1 30W
Sheffield Pennsylvania USA	52	G1	41 43N	79 02W
Shek Kong HK China	100	B2	22 26N	114 06E
Shek Kwu Chau *i.* HK China	100	A1	22 12N	113 59E
Shek O HK China	100	C1	22 14N	114 15E
Shek Pik HK China	100	A1	22 13N	113 53E
Shek Pik Reservoir HK China	100	A1	22 14N	113 54E
Shek Uk Shan *mt.* HK China	100	C2	22 26N	114 18E
Shek Wu Hui HK China	100	B3	22 30N	114 07E
Shelby Montana USA	70	D6	48 30N	111 52W
Shelekhov Bay Russia	95	T8/T9	60 00N	157 00E
Shell Lake Wisconsin USA	51	F3	45 45N	91 56W
Shelter Island HK China	100	C1	22 19N	114 19E
Shenandoah Iowa USA	71	G5	40 48N	95 22W
Shenandoah Mountains West Virginia USA	73	B1	39 20N	78 45W
Shenandoah National Park West Virginia/Virginia USA	73	B1	39 00N	78 00W
Shenyang China	101	N7	41 50N	123 26E
Shenzhen China	101	L3	22 31N	114 08E
Shepetovka Ukraine	88	L9	50 12N	27 01E
Sherburne New York USA	53	L2	42 41N	75 30W
Sheridan Wyoming USA	70	E5	44 48N	106 57W
's-Hertogenbosch Neths.	86	H9	51 41N	5 19E
Sherwood North Dakota USA	47	G1	48 57N	101 38W
Shetland Islands UK	86	E13/E14	60 00N	1 15W
Sheung Fa Shan HK China	100	B2	22 23N	114 06E
Sham Tseng HK China	100	B2	22 22N	114 03E
Sheung Shui HK China	100	B3	22 31N	114 08E
Shiawassee River Michigan USA	52	B3	43 05N	84 12W
Shihezi China	100	F7	44 19N	86 10E
Shijiazhuang China	101	L6	38 04N	114 28E
Shikarpur Pakistan	98	B5	27 58N	68 42E
Shikoku *i.* Japan	102	B1	33 40N	134 00E
Shikotan *i.* Japan	102	E3	43 47N	148 45E
Shiliguri India	99	F5	26 42N	88 30E
Shilka *r.* Russia	95	P7	52 30N	117 30E
Shillong India	99	G5	25 34N	91 53E
Shimizu Japan	102	C2	35 01N	138 29E
Shimla India	98	D6	31 07N	77 09E
Shimoga India	98	D2	13 56N	75 31E
Shimonoseki Japan	102	B1	33 59N	130 58E
Shinano *r.* Japan	102	C2	37 40N	139 00E
Shindand Afghanistan	97	H5	33 16N	62 05E
Shingū Japan	102	C1	33 42N	136 00E
Shinjō Japan	102	D2	38 45N	140 18E
Shinyanga Tanzania	108	L7	3 40S	33 25E
Shiono-misaki *c.* Japan	102	C1	33 28N	135 47E
Shirakawa Japan	102	D2	37 07N	140 11E
Shiraoi Japan	102	D3	42 34N	141 19E
Shīrāz Iran	97	F4	29 38N	52 34E
Shiretoko-misaki *c.* Japan	102	E3	44 24N	145 20E
Shizuishan China	101	K6	39 04N	106 22E
Shizuoka Japan	102	C1	34 59N	138 24E
Shkodër Albania	89	G5	42 03N	19 01E
Shoshone California USA	72	E2	35 58N	116 17W
Shreveport Louisiana USA	71	H3	32 30N	93 46W
Shrewsbury UK	86	D10	52 43N	2 45W
Shuangliao China	101	N7	43 30N	123 29E
Shuangyashan China	101	Q8	46 42N	131 20E
Shuen Wan HK China	100	C2	22 28N	114 12E
Shui Tau HK China	100	B2	22 27N	114 04E
Shui Tsiu San Tsuen HK China	100	B2	22 26N	114 02E
Shuksan, Mount Washington USA	42	H4	48 52N	121 30W
Shumen Bulgaria	89	L5	43 17N	26 55E
Shunde China	101	L3	22 50N	113 16E
Shuqrā Yemen	97	E1	13 23N	45 44E
Shymkent Kazakhstan	94	J5	42 16N	69 05E
Sialkot Pakistan	98	C6	32 29N	74 35E
Siauliai Lithuania	88	J11	55 51N	23 20E
Šibenik Croatia	89	E5	43 45N	15 55E
Sibi Pakistan	98	B5	29 31N	67 54E
Sibiti Congo	108	G7	3 40S	13 24E
Sibiu Romania	89	K6	45 46N	24 09E
Sibolga Indonesia	103	B4	1 42N	98 48E
Sibu Malaysia	103	E4	2 19N	111 50E
Sibut CAR	108	H9	5 46N	19 06E
Sichuan Pendi China	101	J5/K5	32 00N	107 00E
Sicilian Channel Mediterranean Sea	89	D2	37 00N	12 00E
Sicily *i.* Italy	89	D2/E2	37 00N	14 00E
Sicuani Peru	80	C11	14 21S	71 13W
Sidi Barrani Egypt	108	K14	31 38N	25 58E
Sidi Bel Abbès Algeria	108	D15	35 15N	0 39W
Sidi Ifni Morocco	108	B13	29 24N	10 12W
Sidney Lanier, Lake Georgia USA	71	K3	34 00N	84 00W
Sidon Lebanon	96	N11	33 32N	35 22E
Siedlce Poland	88	J10	52 10N	22 18E
Siegen Germany	88	B9	50 52N	8 02E
Siena Italy	89	C5	43 19N	11 19E
Sierra Blanca *tn.* Texas USA	70	E3	31 10N	105 22W
Sierra de Maracaju *mts.* Brazil	80	F9	20 00S	55 00W
SIERRA LEONE	108	B9		
Sierra Madre del Sur *mts.* Mexico	74	D3/E3	17 30N	100 00W
Sierra Madre Occidental *mts.* Mexico	74	C5/D4	26 00N	107 00W
Sierra Madre Oriental *mts.* Mexico	74	D5/E4	23 30N	100 00W
Sierra Morena *mts.* Sp.	87	B3/C3	38 05N	5 50W
Sierra Nevada *mts.* Sp.	87	D2	37 00N	3 20W
Sierra Nevada *mts.* California USA	70	C4	37 00N	119 00W
Sierras de Córdoba *mts.* Argentina	81	D7/E7	32 30S	65 00W
Sífnos *i.* Greece	89	K2	37 00N	24 40E
Sighetu Marmaţiei Romania	88	J7	47 56N	23 53E
Sighişoara Romania	89	K7	46 12N	24 48E
Sigüenza Sp.	87	D4	41 04N	2 38W
Siguiri Guinea	108	C10	11 28N	9 07W
Sikar India	98	D5	27 33N	75 12E
Sikasso Mali	108	C10	11 18N	5 38W
Sikhote-Alin' *mts.* Russia	95	R6	45 00N	137 00E
Sikkim *admin.* India	99	F5	27 30N	88 30E
Sil *r.* Sp.	87	B5	42 25N	7 05W
Silchar India	99	G4	24 49N	92 47E
Silifke Turkey	96	B6	36 22N	33 57E
Silistra Bulgaria	89	L6	44 06N	27 17E
Silkeborg Denmark	88	B12	56 10N	9 39E
Silute Lithuania	88	H11	55 21N	21 30E
Silver Bay *tn.* Minnesota USA	51	F4	47 18N	91 15W
Silver City New Mexico USA	70	E3	32 47N	108 16W
Silver Creek *tn.* New York USA	52	G2	42 32N	79 10W
Silver Peak Range *mts.* Nevada USA	72	E3	37 30N	117 45W
Silver Springs *tn.* Nevada USA	72	D4	39 25N	119 14W
Silves Port.	87	A2	37 11N	8 26W
Simi Valley *tn.* California USA	72	D2	34 16N	118 47W
Simpson Desert Aust.	110	F5	24 30S	137 30E
Sincelejo Col.	80	B15	9 17N	75 23W
Sind *geog. reg.* Pakistan	98	B5	26 20N	68 40E
Sines Port.	87	A2	37 58N	8 52W
SINGAPORE	103	C4		
Singaraja Indonesia	103	F2	8 06S	115 04E
Singatoko Fiji	114	T15	18 10S	177 30E
Sinop Turkey	96	C7	42 02N	35 09E
Sintra Port.	87	A3	38 48N	9 22W
Sinuiju North Korea	101	N7	40 04N	124 25E
Sioux City Iowa USA	71	G5	42 30N	96 28W
Sioux Falls *tn.* South Dakota USA	71	G5	43 34N	96 42W
Siping China	101	N7	43 15N	124 25E
Sira *r.* Norway	86	J13	58 50N	6 40E
Siracusa Italy	89	E2	37 04N	15 19E
Sirajganj Bangladesh	99	K10	24 27N	89 42E
Siret *r.* Romania	88	L7	47 00N	26 00E
Sirte Libya	108	H14	31 13N	16 35E
Sirte Desert Libya	108	H14	30 00N	16 00E
Sirte, Gulf of Libya	108	H14	31 00N	17 00E
Sisak Croatia	89	F6	45 30N	16 22E
Sisophon Cambodia	103	C6	13 37N	102 58E
Sisteron Fr.	87	H6	44 16N	5 56E
Sitka Alaska USA	42	C5	57 05N	135 20W
Sitka Sound Alaska USA	42	C5	57 00N	135 50W
Sittwe Myanmar	100	G3	20 09N	92 55E
Sivas Turkey	96	C6	39 44N	37 01E
Siwa Egypt	108	K13	29 11N	25 31E
Sjaelland *i.* Denmark	88	C11	55 15N	11 30E
Skadarsko ezero *l.* Europe	89	G5	42 00N	19 00E
Skagen Denmark	88	C12	57 44N	10 37E
Skagerrak *sd.* Denmark/Norway	86	K12	57 30N	8 00E
Skagit River Washington USA	42	H4	48 30N	121 20W
Skagway Alaska USA	42	C6	59 23N	135 20W
Skien Norway	86	K13	59 14N	9 37E
Skierniewice Poland	88	H9	51 58N	20 10E
Skikda Algeria	108	F15	36 53N	6 54E
Skive Denmark	88	B12	56 34N	9 02E
Skopje FYROM	89	H4	42 00N	21 28E
Skövde Sweden	88	D13	58 24N	13 52E
Skovorodino Russia	95	Q7	54 00N	123 53E
Skowhegan Maine USA	53	S4	44 46N	69 44W
Skye *i.* UK	86	B12	57 20N	6 15W
Skýros *i.* Greece	89	K3	38 50N	24 35E
Slaney *r.* Rol	86	B10	52 24W	6 33W
Slatina Romania	89	K6	44 26N	24 22E
Slavonski Brod Croatia	89	F6	45 09N	18 02E
Sligo Rol	86	A11	54 17N	8 28W
Sliven Bulgaria	89	L5	42 40N	26 19E
SLOVAKIA	88	F8/H8		
SLOVENIA	89	E6		
Sluch' *r.* Ukraine	88	L9	50 00N	27 00E
Słupsk Poland	88	F11	54 28N	17 00E
Smederevo Serbia	89	H6	44 40N	20 56E
Smethport Pennsylvania USA	52	H1	41 48N	78 26W
Smoky Hills Kansas USA	70	G4	39 00N	100 00W
Smolensk Russia	94	F7	54 49N	32 04E
Smolyan Bulgaria	89	K4	41 34N	24 42E
Snake *r.* USA	70	C5	44 00N	118 00W
Snake River Plain USA	70	D5	43 00N	114 00W
Snowdon *mt.* UK	86	C10	53 04N	4 05W
Snowy Mountains Aust.	110	H2	36 50S	147 00E
Snyder Texas USA	70	F3	32 43N	100 54W
Soa-Siu Indonesia	103	H4	0 40N	127 30E
Sobat *r.* Sudan	108	L9	8 00N	33 00E
Sobral Brazil	80	J13	3 45S	40 20W
Sochi Russia	94	F5	43 35N	39 46E
Society Islands Pacific Ocean	115	L6	16 30S	153 00W
Socotra *i.* Yemen	97	F1	12 05N	54 10E
Soda Lake California USA	72	E2	35 09N	116 04W
Soda Springs *tn.* California USA	72	C4	39 19N	120 23W
Sodertälje Sweden	88	F13	59 11N	17 39E
Sodo Ethiopia	108	M9	6 49N	37 41E
Sodus New York USA	53	J3	43 14N	77 04W
Sofia Bulgaria	89	J5	42 40N	23 18E
Sogamoso Col.	80	C15	5 43N	72 56W
Sohâg Egypt	108	L13	26 33N	31 42E
Soissons Fr.	86	G8	49 23N	3 20E
Sok Kwu Wan HK China	100	B1	22 13N	114 08E
Sokodé Togo	108	E9	8 59N	1 11E
Soko Islands HK China	100	A1	22 10N	113 54E
Sokoto Nigeria	108	F10	13 02N	5 15E
Sokoto *r.* Nigeria	108	E10	13 02N	4 55E
So Kwun Wat HK China	100	B2	22 23N	114 00E
Solāpur India	98	D3	17 43N	75 56E
Soledad California USA	72	C3	36 25N	121 20W
Solikamsk Russia	94	H8	59 40N	56 45E
Solimões *r.* Brazil	80	D13	3 30S	69 00W
Sóller Spain	87	G3	39 46N	2 42E
Sologne *geog. reg.* Fr.	87	F7	47 35N	1 47E
SOLOMON ISLANDS	114	G7		
Solomon Sea PNG	110	J8	7 00S	150 00E
Solothurn Switz.	87	J7	47 13N	7 32E
Soltau Germany	88	B10	52 59N	9 50E
Solway Firth *est.* UK	86	D11	54 45N	3 40W
SOMALIA	108	N8		
Somali Basin Indian Ocean	113	E7	5 00N	55 00E
Sombor Serbia	89	G6	45 46N	19 09E
Sombrerete Mexico	74	D4	23 38N	103 40W
Sombrero Channel *sd.* India	99	G1	7 41N	93 35E
Somerset Michigan USA	51	J2	42 03N	84 22W
Somme *r.* Fr.	86	F8	50 00N	1 45E
Sommen *l.* Sweden	88	E12	58 05N	15 15E
Somoto Nicaragua	74	G2	13 29N	86 36W
Son *r.* India	98	E4	24 00N	84 00E
Sønderborg Denmark	88	B11	54 55N	9 48E
Songea Tanzania	109	M5	10 42S	35 39E
Songhua Jiang *r.* China	101	P8	46 00N	128 00E
Songkhla Thailand	103	C5	7 12N	100 35E
Song-koi *r.* China/Vietnam	101	J3	22 30N	103 00E
Sonoita Mexico	74	B6	31 53N	112 52W
Sonora California USA	72	C3	37 59N	120 21W
Sonsonate El Salvador	74	G2	13 43N	89 44W
Sopot Poland	88	G11	54 27N	18 31E
Soria Sp.	87	D4	41 46N	2 28W
Soroca Moldova	88	M8	48 08N	28 12E
Sorong Indonesia	103	J3	0 50S	131 17E
Soroti Uganda	108	L8	1 42N	33 37E
Sorraia *r.* Port.	87	A3	38 55N	9 30W
Sosnowiec Poland	88	G9	50 16N	19 07E
Soufrière *mt.* Guadeloupe	74	Q9	16 03N	61 40W
Souillac Fr.	87	F6	44 53N	1 29E
Sousse Tunisia	108	G14	35 50N	10 38E
Southampton UK	86	E9	50 55N	1 25W
Southampton New York USA	73	D2	40 53N	72 24W
South Andaman *i.* Andaman Islands	99	G2	11 30N	93 00E
South Australia *state* Aust.	110	E3/F4	27 00S	135 00E
South Australian Basin Indian Ocean	113	M3	38 00S	125 00E
South Bend Indiana USA	71	J5	41 40N	86 15W
South Carolina *state* USA	71	K3	34 00N	81 00W
South China Sea Pacific Ocean	103	E6/F7	15 00N	110 00E
South Dakota *state* USA	70	F5	45 00N	102 00W
South East Cape Aust.	110	H1	43 38S	146 48E
Southeast Indian Basin Indian Ocean	113	K3	32 00S	108 00E
Southeast Indian Ridge Indian Ocean	113	H2	45 00S	90 00E
South East Pacific Basin Pacific Ocean	115	S3	53 00S	95 00W
Southend-on-Sea UK	86	F9	51 33N	0 43E
Southern Alps *mts.* NZ	111	B2/C3	43 07S	171 13E
Southern Honshu Ridge Pacific Ocean	114	E10	25 50N	142 30E
Southern Ocean	117			
South Fiji Basin Pacific Ocean	114	H5	25 00S	176 50E
South Georgia *i.* Atlantic Ocean	116	E1	54 00S	36 30W
South Hatia Island Bangladesh	99	L9	22 19N	91 07E
South Indian Basin Indian Ocean	113	L1	55 00S	130 00E
South Island NZ	111	A1/D4	42 30S	172 00E
SOUTH KOREA	101	P6		
South Lake Tahoe *tn.* California USA	72	D4	38 55N	119 58W
South Loup *r.* Nebraska USA	70	G5	42 00N	99 00W
South Negril Point *c.* Jamaica	75	T14	18 16N	78 22W
South Orkney Islands Southern Ocean	117		60 00S	45 00W
South Platte *r.* USA	70	F5	41 00N	103 00W
South Pole Antarctica	117		90 00S	
South Sandwich Trench Atlantic Ocean	116	E2/F1	55 00S	30 00W
South San Francisco California USA	72	B3	37 39N	122 24W
South Shetland Islands Southern Ocean	117		62 00S	60 00W
South Sioux City Nebraska USA	71	G5	42 28N	96 24W
South Uist *i.* UK	86	B12	57 20N	7 15W
Southwest Cape NZ	111	A1	48 00S	168 00E
Southwest Indian Ridge Indian Ocean	113	C2	40 00S	50 00E
South West Pacific Basin Pacific Ocean	115	L4	35 00S	155 00W
Sovetsk Russia	88	H11	55 02N	21 50E
Sovetskaya Gavan' Russia	95	S6	48 57N	140 16E
SPAIN	87	C3/E3		
Spanish Town Jamaica	75	U13	17 59N	76 58W
Sparks Nevada USA	70	B4/C4	39 34N	119 46W
Spartanburg South Carolina USA	71	K3	34 56N	81 57W
Spárti Greece	89	J2	37 05N	22 25E
Spassk-Dal'niy Russia	95	R5	44 37N	132 37E
Speightstown Barbados	74	S11	13 15N	59 39W
Spencer Iowa USA	71	G5	43 08N	95 08W
Spencer Gulf Aust.	110	F2	34 00S	137 00E
Spey *r.* UK	86	D12	57 35N	3 10W
Spitsbergen *i.* Arctic Ocean	94	D12	79 00N	15 00E
Spittal an der Drau Austria	89	D7	46 48N	13 30E
Split Croatia	89	F5	43 31N	16 28E
Spokane Washington USA	70	C6	47 40N	117 25W
Spoleto Italy	89	D5	42 44N	12 44E
Spratly Islands South China Sea	103	E5/F5	8 45N	111 54E
Springbok RSA	109	H2	29 44S	17 56E
Springdale Nevada USA	72	E3	37 02N	116 46W
Springfield NZ	111	C3	43 20S	171 56E
Springfield Illinois USA	71	J4	39 49N	89 39W
Springfield Massachusetts USA	71	M5	42 07N	72 35W
Springfield Missouri USA	71	H4	37 11N	93 19W
Springfield Ohio USA	71	K4	39 55N	83 48W
Springfield Oregon USA	70	B5	44 03N	123 01W
Springfield Vermont USA	73	D3	43 18N	72 29W
Spring Mountains Nevada USA	72	F3	36 22N	115 52W
Springsure Aust.	110	H5	24 09S	148 04E
Springville New York USA	73	A3	42 30N	78 40W
Spurn Head *c.* UK	86	F10	53 36N	0 07E
Sredinnyy Range *mts.* Russia	95	T7/T8	57 00N	158 00E
Srednekolymsk Russia	95	T10	67 27N	153 35E
Sretensk Russia	95	P7	52 15N	117 52E
Srikakulum India	99	E3	18 19N	84 00E
SRI LANKA	98	E1		
Srinagar Kashmir	98	C6	34 08N	74 50E
Stafford UK	86	D10	52 48N	2 07W
Stamford Connecticut USA	73	D2	41 04N	73 33W
Standish Michigan USA	51	K2	43 59N	83 57W
Stanley Falkland Islands	81	F3	51 45S	57 56W
Stanley HK China	100	C1	22 12N	114 12E
Stanovoy Range *mts.* Russia	95	Q8	56 00N	122 30E
Stara Planina *mts.* Europe	89	J5/K5	43 00N	23 00E
Stara Zagora Bulgaria	89	K5	42 25N	25 37E
Stargard Szczeciński Poland	88	E10	53 21N	15 01E
Starogard Gdański Poland	88	G10	53 58N	18 30E
Start Point *c.* UK	86	D9	50 13N	3 38W
Staryy Oskol Russia	94	F7	51 20N	37 50E
State College Pennsylvania USA	71	L5	40 48N	77 52W
Staten Island New York USA	73	H1	40 35N	74 10W
Staunton Virginia USA	71	L4	38 10N	79 05W
Stavanger Norway	86	H13	58 58N	5 45E
Staveley NZ	111	C3	43 39S	171 26E
Stavropol' Russia	94	G6	45 03N	41 59E
Stehekin Washington USA	42	H4	48 25N	120 30W
Stendal Germany	88	C10	52 36N	11 52E
Stephens Passage *sd.* Alaska USA	42	D5	58 00N	134 00W
Sterling Colorado USA	70	F5	40 37N	103 13W

Sterlitamak Russia 94 H7 53 40N 55 59E
Steubenville Ohio USA 71 K5 40 22N 80 39W
Stewart Island NZ 111 A1 46 55S 167 55E
Steyr Austria 88 E7 48 04N 14 25E
Stillaguamish River Washington USA 42 H4 48 16N 122 00W
Stillwater Nevada USA 72 D4 39 31N 118 33W
Stillwater Reservoir New York USA 53 L3 43 55N 75 00W
Štip FYROM 89 J4 41 44N 22 12E
Stirling UK 86 D12 56 07N 3 57W
Stockbridge Massachusetts USA 73 D3 42 17N 73 19W
Stockholm Sweden 88 G13 59 20N 18 05E
Stockton California USA 70 B4 37 59N 121 20W
Stockton-on-Tees UK 86 E11 54 34N 1 19W
Stœng Trêng Cambodia 103 D6 13 31N 105 59E
Stoke-on-Trent UK 86 D10 53 00N 2 10W
Stonecutters Island HK China 100 B1 22 18N 114 08E
Stonyford California USA 72 B4 39 23N 122 34W
Stornoway UK 86 B13 58 12N 6 23W
Straits of Florida *sd.* Florida USA 71 K1 25 00N 80 00W
Stralsund Germany 88 D11 54 18N 13 06E
Stranraer UK 86 C11 54 55N 5 02W
Strasbourg Fr. 86 J8 48 35N 7 45E
Straubing Germany 88 D8 48 53N 12 35E
Stretto di Messina *sd.* Italy 89 E2 38 00N 15 00E
Strimonas *r.* Greece 89 J4 41 00N 23 00E
Stromboli *mt.* Italy 89 E3 38 48N 15 15E
Stroudsburg Pennsylvania USA 73 C2 40 59N 75 12W
Struma *r.* Bulgaria 89 J4 42 00N 23 00E
Stryy Ukraine 88 J8 49 16N 23 51E
Sturt Creek *r.* Aust. 110 D6 19 00S 127 30E
Stuttgart Germany 88 B8 48 47N 9 12E
Styr' *r.* Ukraine/Belarus 88 K9 51 30N 25 30E
Suakin Sudan 108 M11 19 08N 37 17E
Subotica Serbia 89 G7 46 04N 19 41E
Suceava Romania 88 L7 47 37N 26 18E
Sucre Bolivia 80 D10 19 05S 65 15W
SUDAN 108 K10
Sudety Reseniky *mts.* Europe 88 E9/F9 50 40N 16 00E
Sue *r.* Sudan 108 K9 7 00N 28 00E
Suez Egypt 109 T1 29 59N 32 33E
Suez Canal Egypt 109 S4 31 30N 32 20E
Suez, Gulf of Egypt 109 T1 29 56N 32 32E
Sugarloaf Mountain Maine USA 53 R5 45 02N 70 18W
Sühbaatar Mongolia 101 K9 50 10N 106 14E
Suiattle River Washington USA 42 H4 48 16N 121 20W
Sukabumi Indonesia 103 D2 6 55S 106 50E
Sukhona *r.* Russia 94 G9 60 00N 45 00E
Sukkur Pakistan 98 B5 27 42N 68 54E
Sulaiman Range *mts.* Pakistan 98 B5/C6 30 00N 70 00E
Sulawesi *i.* Indonesia 103 F3/G3 2 00S 120 00E
Sullana Peru 80 A13 4 52S 80 39W
Sulu Archipelago Philippines 103 G5 6 00N 121 00E
Sulu Sea Philippines/Malaysia 103 F5/G5 8 00N 120 00E
Sumas Washington USA 42 H4 49 00N 122 18W
Sumatra *i.* Indonesia 103 B4/C3 0 00 100 00E
Sumba *i.* Indonesia 103 F2/G1 10 00S 120 00E
Sumbawa *i.* Indonesia 103 F2 8 00S 118 00E
Sumburgh Head *c.* UK 86 E13 59 51N 1 16W
Summer Strait *sd.* Alaska USA 42 D5 56 30N 133 30W
Sunburst Montana USA 46 G1 48 56N 111 58W
Sunbury Pennsylvania USA 73 B2 40 52N 76 47W
Sunchon South Korea 101 P5 34 56N 127 28E
Sundarbans *geog. reg.* India/Bangladesh 99 K8 21 50N 88 50E
Sunderland UK 86 E11 54 55N 1 23W
Sung Kong *i.* HK China 100 C1 22 11N 114 17E
Sunnyvale California USA 72 C3 37 23N 122 00W
Sunset Peak HK China 100 A1 22 15N 113 57E
Sunshine Island HK China 100 B1 22 16N 114 03E
Suntar Russia 95 P9 62 10N 117 35E
Sunyani Ghana 108 D9 7 22N 2 18W
Suō-nada *b.* Japan 102 B1 33 50N 131 30E
Superior Wisconsin USA 71 H6 46 42N 92 05W
Sūr Oman 97 G3 22 34N 59 32E
Surabaya Indonesia 103 E2 7 14S 112 45E
Surakarta Indonesia 103 E2 7 32S 110 50E
Surat India 98 C4 21 10N 72 54E
Surat Thani Thailand 103 B5 9 09N 99 20E
Surgut Russia 94 K9 61 13N 73 20E
SURINAME 80 F14
Susquehanna River Pennsylvania USA 53 K1 41 45N 76 25W
Susuman Russia 95 S9 62 46N 148 08E
Sutlej *r.* Pakistan 98 C6 30 30N 73 00E
Suva Fiji 114 U15 18 08S 178 25E
Suwałki Poland 88 J11 54 06N 22 56E
Suzhou China 101 M5 33 38N 117 02E
Suzhou China 101 N5 31 21N 120 40E
Suzuka Japan 102 C1 34 52N 136 37E
Suzu-misaki *c.* Japan 102 C2 37 30N 137 21E
Svobodnyy Russia 95 Q7 51 24N 128 05E
Swale *r.* UK 86 E11 54 20N 2 00W
Swansea UK 86 D9 51 38N 3 57W
Swanton Ohio USA 52 C1 41 36N 83 54W
Swanton Vermont USA 53 N4 44 56N 73 08W
SWAZILAND 109 L2
SWEDEN 88 D13
Sweetwater *tn.* Texas USA 70 F3 32 27N 100 25W
Swellendam RSA 109 J1 34 01S 20 26E
Swiebodzin Poland 88 E10 52 15N 15 31E
Swindon UK 86 E9 51 34N 1 47W
Swinoujście Poland 88 E10 53 55N 14 18E
SWITZERLAND 87 J7/K7
Sydney Aust. 110 J3 33 55S 151 10E
Syktyvkar Russia 94 H9 61 42N 50 45E
Sylhet Bangladesh 99 L10 24 53N 91 51E
Sylt Germany 88 B11 54 00N 8 00E
Sylvania Ohio USA 51 K1 41 41N 83 37W
Syracuse New York USA 71 L5 43 03N 76 10W
Syr-Dar'ya *r.* Asia 94 J5 43 30N 66 30E
SYRIA 96 C6
Syrian Desert Middle East 96 C5 32 30N 39 20E
Syzran' Russia 94 G7 53 10N 48 29E
Szczecin Poland 88 E10 53 25N 14 32E
Szczecinek Poland 88 F10 53 42N 16 41E
Szeged Hungary 89 H7 46 15N 20 09E
Székesfehérvár Hungary 89 G7 47 11N 18 22E
Szolnok Hungary 89 H7 47 10N 20 10E
Szombathely Hungary 89 F7 47 14N 16 38E

T

Ţabas Iran 97 G5 33 37N 56 54E
Table Rock Lake Missouri USA 71 H4 36 38N 93 17W
Tábor Czech Rep. 88 E8 49 25N 14 39E
Tabora Tanzania 108 L7 5 01S 32 48E
Tabrīz Iran 96 E6 38 04N 46 17E
Tabuaaran Island Kiribati 115 L8 4 00N 158 10W
Tabūk Saudi Arabia 96 C4 28 33N 36 36E
Tacloban Philippines 103 G6 11 15N 125 01E
Tacna Peru 80 C10 18 00S 70 15W
Tacoma Washington USA 70 B6 47 16N 122 30W
Taegu South Korea 101 P6 35 52N 128 36E
Taejon South Korea 101 P6 36 20N 127 26E
Tafila Jordan 96 N10 30 52N 35 36E
Taganrog Russia 94 F6 47 14N 38 55E
Tagus *r.* Sp./Port. 87 B3 39 30N 7 00W
Tahat, Mount Algeria 108 F12 23 18N 5 33E
Tahiti *i.* Pacific Ocean 115 M6 17 30S 148 30W
Tahoe, Lake California USA 70 C4 39 00N 120 00W
Tahoua Niger 108 F10 14 57N 5 19E
Tai'an China 101 M6 36 15N 117 10E
Taibei Taiwan 101 N4 25 05N 121 32E
Taichung Taiwan 101 N3 24 09N 124 40E
Taihape NZ 111 E5 39 41S 175 48E
Tai Lam Chung HK China 100 B2 22 22N 114 01E
Tai Lam Chung Reservoir HK China 100 B2 22 23N 114 01E
Tai Long HK China 100 D2 22 25N 114 22E
Tai Long Wan *b.* HK China 100 D2 22 24N 114 23E
Tai Mei Tuk HK China 100 C2 22 28N 114 14E
Tai Mong Tsai HK China 100 C2 22 23N 114 18E
Tai Mo Shan *mt.* HK China 100 B2 22 25N 114 07E
Tainan Taiwan 101 N3 23 01N 120 14E
Tai O HK China 100 A1 22 15N 113 52E
Tai Po HK China 100 C2 22 27N 114 10E
Tai Shui Hang HK China 100 B1 22 17N 114 01E
Tai Tam Resevoirs HK China 100 C1 22 15N 114 13E
Tai Tam Wan *b.* HK China 100 C1 22 13N 114 13E
Tai Wai HK China 100 C2 22 23N 114 10E
TAIWAN 101 N3
Taiwan Strait China/Taiwan 101 M3 24 00N 119 30E
Tai Wan Tau HK China 100 C1 22 17N 114 17E
Taiyuan China 101 L6 37 50N 112 30E
Ta'izz Yemen 96 D1 13 35N 44 02E
TAJIKISTAN 94 J4/K4
Tajo *r.* Sp./Port. 87 B3 39 00N 7 00W
Tak Thailand 103 B7 16 51N 99 08E
Takamatsu Japan 102 B1 34 20N 134 01E
Takaoka Japan 102 C2 36 47N 137 00E
Takapuna NZ 111 E6 36 48S 174 46E
Takasaki Japan 102 C2 36 20N 139 00E
Takayama Japan 102 C2 36 09N 137 16E
Takefu Japan 102 C2 35 54N 136 10E
Takêv Cambodia 103 C6 11 00N 104 46E
Taki India 99 K9 22 35N 88 56E
Taku Inlet Alaska USA 42 C6 58 30N 134 00W
Talara Peru 80 A13 4 38S 81 18W
Talavera de la Reina Sp. 87 C3 39 58N 4 50W
Talbot, Cape Aust. 110 D7 13 49S 126 42E
Talca Chile 81 C6 35 28S 71 40W
Talcahuano Chile 81 C6 36 40S 73 10W
Taldykorgan Kazakhstan 94 K6 45 02N 78 23E
Tallahassee Florida USA 71 K3 30 26N 84 16W
Tallinn Estonia 88 K13 59 22N 24 48E
Tall Kalakh Syria 96 P12 34 45N 36 17E
Talodi Sudan 108 L10 10 40N 30 25E
Talsi Latvia 88 J12 57 17N 22 37E
Taltal Chile 80 C8 25 26S 70 33W
Tamabo Range Malaysia 103 F4 4 00N 115 30E
Tamale Ghana 108 D9 9 26N 0 49W
Tamanrasset Algeria 108 F12 22 50N 5 28E
Tamazunchale Mexico 74 E4 21 18N 98 46W
Tambov Russia 94 G7 52 44N 41 28E
Tambre *r.* Sp. 87 A5 42 55N 8 50W
Tâmega *r.* Port. 87 B4 41 40N 7 45W
Tamil Nadu *admin.* India 98 D2 12 00N 78 30E
Tampa Florida USA 71 K2 27 58N 82 38W
Tampico Mexico 74 E4 22 18N 97 52W
Tamworth Aust. 110 J3 31 07S 150 57E
Tana *r.* Kenya 108 M7 0 30S 39 00E
Tanabe Japan 102 C1 33 43N 135 22E
Tanahmerah Indonesia 110 G8 6 08S 140 18E
Tana, Lake Ethiopia 108 M10 12 20N 37 20E
Tandil Argentina 81 F6 37 18S 59 10W
Tanega-shima *i.* Japan 102 B1 31 00N 131 00E
Tanezrouft *geog. reg.* Algeria 108 D12 24 00N 0 30W
Tanga Tanzania 108 M6 5 07S 39 05E
Tangail Bangladesh 99 K10 24 15N 89 55E
Tangan *r.* India 99 K10 25 30N 88 20E
Tanganyika, Lake East Africa 109 K6/L6 7 00S 30 00E
Tanggula Shan *mts.* China 100 G5 32 30N 92 30E
Tangier Morocco 108 C15 35 48N 5 45W
Tangshan China 101 M6 39 37N 118 05E
Tanjungkarang-Telukbetung Indonesia 103 D2 5 28S 105 16E
Tannu Ola *mts.* Russia 95 M7 51 00N 92 30E
Tanout Niger 108 F11 15 05N 8 50E
TANZANIA 108/109 L6
Tapachula Mexico 74 F2 14 54N 92 15W
Tapajós *r.* Brazil 80 F12 6 30S 57 00W
Tāpi *r.* India 98 D4 21 30N 76 30E
Tappi-zaki *c.* Japan 102 D3 41 14N 140 21E
Taquari *r.* Brazil 80 F10 18 00S 57 00W
Tarakan Indonesia 103 F4 3 20N 117 38E
Tāranto Italy 89 F4 40 28N 17 15E
Tarapoto Peru 80 B12 6 31S 76 23W
Tarauacá Brazil 80 C12 8 06S 70 45W
Tarawera NZ 111 F5 38 15S 175 56E
Tarazona Sp. 87 E4 41 54N 1 44W
Tarbes Fr. 87 F5 43 14N 0 05E
Taree Aust. 110 J3 31 54S 152 26E
Tarfaya Morocco 108 B13 27 58N 12 55W
Târgovişte Romania 89 K6 44 56N 25 27E
Târgu-Jiu Romania 89 J6 45 03N 23 18E
Târgu Mureş Romania 89 K7 46 33N 24 34E
Tarija Bolivia 80 D9 21 33S 65 02W
Tarim He *r.* China 100 E7 41 00N 82 00E
Tarim Pendi China 100 E6/F6 39 00N 84 00E
Tarko-Sale Russia 94 K9 64 55N 77 50E
Tarkwa Ghana 108 D9 5 16N 1 59W
Tarn *r.* Fr. 87 G5 44 05N 1 40E
Tarnobrzeg Poland 88 H9 50 35N 21 40E
Tarnów Poland 88 H9 50 01N 20 59E
Tarragona Sp. 87 F4 41 07N 1 15E
Tarrasa Sp. 87 G4 41 34N 2 00E
Tarsus Turkey 96 B6 26 25N 34 52E
Tartary, Gulf of Russia 95 S6/S7 50 00N 141 00E
Tartūs Syria 96 C5 34 55N 35 52E
Tashkent Uzbekistan 94 J5 41 16N 69 13E
Tasman Basin Southern Ocean 114 F3 48 00S 154 00E
Tasman Bay NZ 111 D4 41 00S 173 14E
Tasmania *state* Aust. 110 H1 43 00S 147 00E
Tasman Plateau Southern Ocean 114 E3 48 00S 147 00E
Tasman Sea Pacific Ocean 111 D6 40 00S 155 00E
Tassili N'Ajjer *mts.* Algeria 108 F13 26 00N 6 20W
Tatabánya Hungary 89 G7 47 31N 18 25E
Tateyama Japan 102 C1 34 59N 139 50E
Taumarunui NZ 111 E5 38 53S 175 16E
Taunggyi Myanmar 101 H3 20 55N 97 02E
Taunton UK 86 D9 51 01N 3 06W
Taunton Massachusetts USA 73 E2 41 54N 71 06W
Taupo NZ 111 F5 38 42S 176 05E
Taupo, Lake NZ 111 F5 38 55S 175 49
Tauranga NZ 111 F6 37 41S 176 10E
Tauva Fiji 114 T16 17 31S 177 53E
Tavda *r.* Russia 94 J8 58 00N 64 00E
Taveuni *i.* Fiji 114 U15 16 40S 180 00
Tavira Port. 87 B2 37 07N 7 39W
Tavoy Myanmar 103 B6 14 02N 98 12E
Tawas City Michigan USA 51 K3 44 16N 83 31W
Tawau Malaysia 103 F4 4 16N 117 54E
Taymā' Saudi Arabia 96 C4 27 37N 38 30E
Taymyr Peninsula Russia 95 M12 75 00N 100 00E
Tayshet Russia 95 M8 55 56N 98 01E
Taz *r.* Russia 95 L10 67 00N 82 00E
Taza Morocco 108 D14 34 16N 4 01W
Tchibanga Gabon 108 G7 2 49S 11 00E
Tczew Poland 88 G11 54 05N 18 46E
Te Anau, Lake NZ 111 A2 45 13S 167 45E
Te Aroha NZ 111 E6 37 32S 175 42E
Te Awamutu NZ 111 E5 38 01S 175 20E
Tébessa Algeria 108 F15 35 21N 8 06E
Tecopa California USA 72 E2 35 51N 116 13W
Tecuci Romania 89 L6 45 50N 27 27E
Tecumseh Michigan USA 52 C2 42 01N 83 56W
Tees *r.* UK 86 D11 54 40N 1 20W
Tefé Brazil 80 E13 3 24S 64 45W
Tefé *r.* Brazil 80 D12 4 30S 65 30W
Tegal Indonesia 103 D2 6 52S 109 07E
Tegucigalpa Honduras 74 G2 14 05N 87 14W
Tehachapi California USA 72 D2 35 08N 118 27W
Tehachapi Mountains California USA 72 D2 34 52N 118 45W
Tehran Iran 97 F6 35 40N 51 26E
Tehuacán Mexico 74 E3 18 30N 97 26W
Tehuantepec Mexico 74 E3 16 21N 95 13W
Teifi *r.* UK 86 C10 52 03N 4 30W
Tejo *r.* Port. 87 B3 39 30N 8 15W
Tekapo, Lake NZ 111 C3 43 53S 170 32E
Te Kuiti NZ 111 E5 38 20S 175 10E
Tel *r.* India 98 E4 20 30N 84 00E
Tela Honduras 74 G3 15 46N 87 25W
Tel Aviv-Yafo Israel 96 N11 32 05N 34 46E
Telemark *geog. reg.* Norway 86 K13 59 42N 8 00E
Telescope Peak *mt.* California USA 72 E3 36 11N 117 05W
Teles Pires *r.* Brazil 80 F12 8 00S 57 00W
Telford UK 86 D10 52 42N 2 28W
Telsiai Lithuania 88 J12 55 59N 22 17E
Teluk Bone *b.* Indonesia 103 G3 4 00S 121 00E
Teluk Cenderawasih *b.* Indonesia 110 E9 2 15S 135 30E
Teluk Intan Malaysia 103 C4 4 02N 101 01E
Teluk Tomini *b.* Indonesia 103 G3 0 20S 121 00E
Tema Ghana 108 E9 5 41N 0 00
Temecula California USA 72 E1 33 30N 117 08W
Temirtau Kazakhstan 94 K7 50 05N 72 55E
Tempio Pausania Italy 89 B4 40 54N 9 07E
Temple Texas USA 71 G3 31 06N 97 22W
Temuco Chile 81 C6 38 45S 72 40W
Temuka NZ 111 C2 44 15S 171 17E
Tenali India 98 E3 16 13N 80 36E
Ten Degree Channel Andaman Islands/Nicobar Islands 99 G1 10 00N 93 00E
Tenerife *i.* Canary Islands 108 A13 28 15N 16 35W
Tennant Creek *tn.* Aust. 110 E6 19 31S 134 15E
Tennessee *r.* USA 71 J4 35 00N 88 00W
Tennessee *state* USA 71 J4 35 00N 87 00W
Teófilo Otôni Brazil 80 J10 17 52S 41 31W
Tepatitlán Mexico 74 D4 20 50N 102 46W
Tepic Mexico 74 D4 21 30N 104 51W
Ter *r.* Sp. 87 G4 41 55N 2 30E
Teresina Brazil 80 J12 5 09S 42 46W
Teressa Island India 99 G1 8 15N 93 10E
Termez Uzbekistan 94 J4 37 15N 67 15E
Termini Imerese Italy 89 D2 27 59N 13 42E
Ternate Indonesia 103 H4 0 48N 127 23E
Terni Italy 89 D5 42 34N 12 39E
Ternopil' Ukraine 88 K8 49 35N 25 39E
Terpeniya Bay Russia 95 S6 48 00N 144 0E
Terracina Italy 89 D4 41 17N 13 15E
Terrasini Italy 89 D3 38 09N 13 05E
Terre Haute Indiana USA 71 J4 39 27N 87 24W
Teruel Sp. 87 E4 40 21N 1 06W
Teseney Eritrea 108 M11 15 10N 36 48E
Teshio Japan 102 D3 44 53N 141 46E
Testa del Gargano *c.* Italy 89 F4 41 50N 16 10E
Teteiev *r.* Ukraine 88 M9 50 00N 29 00E
Tétouan Morocco 108 C15 35 34N 5 22W
Tetovo FYROM 89 H5 42 00N 20 59E
Texarkana Arkansas USA 71 H3 33 28N 94 02W
Texas *state* USA 70 G3 31 00N 100 00W
Texel *i.* Neths. 86 H10 53 05N 4 45E
Texoma, Lake Oklahoma/Texas USA 71 G3 34 00N 97 00W
THAILAND 103 B7/C7
Thailand, Gulf of Southern Asia 103 C6 10 50N 101 00E
Thakhek Laos 103 C7 17 22N 104 50E
Thames NZ 111 E6 37 09S 175 33E
Thames *r.* UK 86 E9 51 32N 0 50W
Thane India 98 C3 19 14N 73 02E
Thanh Hoa Vietnam 103 D7 19 49N 105 48E
Thanjavur India 98 D2 10 46N 79 09E
Thar Desert India 98 C5 27 30N 72 00E
Thásos *i.* Greece 89 K4 40 00N 24 00E
Thayetmyo Myanmar 103 B7 19 20N 95 10E
The Brothers *is.* HK China 100 A2 22 20N 113 58E
The Dalles *tn.* Oregon USA 70 B6 45 36N 121 10W
The Everglades *swamp* Florida USA 71 K2 26 00N 81 00W
The Hague Neths. 86 H10 52 05N 4 16E
Thermaïkós Kólpos *g.* Greece 89 J3/J4 40 00N 22 50E
Thermopolis Wyoming USA 70 E5 43 39N 108 12W
Thessaloníki Greece 89 J4 40 38N 22 58E
The Valley Anguilla 74 P10 18 03N 63 04W
Thief River Falls *tn.* Minnesota USA 71 G6 48 12N 96 48W
Thiers Fr. 87 G6 45 51N 3 33E
Thiès Senegal 108 A10 14 49N 16 52W
Thimphu Bhutan 99 F5 27 32N 89 43E
Thionville Fr. 86 J8 49 22N 6 11E
Thira *i.* Greece 89 K2 36 00N 25 00E
Thisted Denmark 88 B12 56 58N 8 42E
Thithia *i.* Fiji 114 V16 17 45S 179 20W
Thiva Greece 89 J3 38 19N 23 19E
Thomasville Georgia USA 71 K3 30 50N 83 59W
Thomson *r.* Aust. 110 G5 24 00S 141 00E
Thornapple River Michigan USA 52 A2/B2 42 38N 85 00W
Thousand Oaks California USA 72 D2 34 10N 118 50W
Three Kings Islands NZ 111 D7 34 10S 172 07E
Three Mile Bay *tn.* New York USA 51 N3 44 05N 76 10W
Three Points, Cape Ghana 108 D8 4 43N 2 06W
Thun Switz. 87 J7 46 46N 7 38E
Thunder Bay Michigan USA 52 C4 45 00N 83 25W
Thüringer Wald *hills* Germany 88 C9 50 00N 10 00E
Thurso UK 86 D13 58 35N 3 32W
Tianjin China 101 M6 39 08N 117 12E
Tianshui China 101 K5 34 25N 105 58E
Tiber *r.* Italy 89 D4 42 00N 12 00E
Tiberias Israel 96 N11 32 48N 35 32E
Tiberias, Lake Israel 96 N11 32 45N 35 30E
Tibesti *mts.* Chad 108 H12 21 00N 17 00E
Tiburón *i.* Mexico 74 B5 28 30N 112 30W
Ticul Mexico 74 G4 20 22N 89 31W
Tierra Blanca Mexico 74 E3 18 28N 96 21W
Tiffin Ohio USA 51 K1 41 07N 83 10W
Tighina Moldova 89 M7 46 50N 29 29E
Tikrīt Iraq 96 D5 34 36N 43 42E
Tijuana Mexico 74 A6 32 29N 117 10W
Tiksi Russia 95 Q11 71 40N 128 45E
Tilburg Neths. 86 H9 51 34N 5 05E
Timaru NZ 111 C2 44 24S 171 15E
Timimoun Algeria 108 E13 29 15N 0 14E
Timişoara Romania 89 H6 45 45N 21 15E
Timişul *r.* Romania/Serbia 89 H6 45 00N 21 00E
Timon Brazil 80 J12 5 08S 42 52W
Timor *i.* Indonesia 103 G1 9 00S 125 00E
Timor Sea Indonesia 103 H1 10 45S 126 00E
Tindouf Algeria 108 C13 27 42N 8 10W
Tinos *i.* Greece 89 K2 37 00N 25 00E
Tin Sam HK China 100 A2 22 26N 113 59E
Tinsukia India 99 H5 27 30N 95 22E
Tionesta Pennsylvania USA 52 G1 41 31N 79 30W

Tionesta Lake Pennsylvania USA 52 G1 41 30N 79 29W
Tiranë Albania 89 G4 41 20N 19 49E
Tir'at el Ismâ'ilîya can. Egypt 109 R3 30 32N 31 48E
Tir'at el Mansûriya r. Egypt 109 R4 31 12N 31 38E
Tiraz Mountains Namibia 109 H2 25 30S 16 30E
Tirso r. Italy 89 B3 40 00N 9 00E
Tiruchchirappalli India 98 D2 10 50N 78 41E
Tirunelveli India 98 D1 8 45N 77 43E
Tirupati India 98 D2 13 39N 79 25E
Tiruppur India 98 D2 11 05N 77 20E
Tisza r. Hungary/Serbia 89 H7 46 00N 20 00E
Titovo Užice Serbia 89 G5 43 52N 19 50E
Titov Veles FYROM 89 H4 41 43N 21 49E
Tittabawassee River Michigan USA 52 B3 43 50N 84 25W
Titusville Pennsylvania USA 52 G1 41 37N 79 42W
Tiu Chung Chau i. HK China 100 C2 22 20N 114 19E
Tiverton Rhode Island USA 73 E2 41 38N 71 12W
Tivoli Italy 89 D4 41 58N 12 48E
Tizimín Mexico 74 G4 21 10N 88 09W
Tizi Ouzou Algeria 108 E15 36 44N 4 05E
Tiznit Morocco 108 C13 29 43N 9 44W
Tlemcen Algeria 108 D14 34 53N 1 21W
Toamasina Madagascar 109 P4 18 10S 49 23E
Tobago i. Trinidad and Tobago 75 V15 11 15N 60 40W
Tobi-shima i. Japan 102 C2 39 12N 139 32E
Tobol r. Russia 94 J8 57 00N 67 30E
Tobol'sk Russia 94 J8 58 15N 68 12E
Tocantins admin. Brazil 80 H11 12 00S 47 00W
Tocantins r. Brazil 80 H12 10 00S 49 00W
Toco Trinidad and Tobago 75 V15 10 49N 60 57W
Tocopilla Chile 80 C9 22 05S 70 10W
TOGO 108 E9
Toi Tan HK China 100 C2 22 26N 114 19E
Toiyabe Range mts. Nevada USA 72 E4 39 20N 117 15W
Tok Alaska USA 64 B3 63 20N 142 59W
Tokelau Islands Pacific Ocean 114 J7 9 00S 168 00W
Tokushima Japan 102 B1 34 03N 134 34E
Tokuyama Japan 102 B1 34 03N 131 48E
Tokyo Japan 102 C2 35 40N 139 45E
Tolaga Bay tn. NZ 111 G5 38 22S 178 18E
Tôlanaro Madagascar 109 P2 25 01S 47 00E
Toledo Sp. 87 C3 39 52N 4 02W
Toledo Ohio USA 71 K5 41 40N 83 35W
Toliara Madagascar 109 N3 23 20S 43 41E
Tollhouse California USA 72 D3 37 01N 119 25W
Tolo Channel HK China 100 C2 22 28N 114 17E
Tolo Harbour b. HK China 100 C2 22 26N 114 13E
Tolosa Sp. 87 D5 43 09N 2 04W
Toluca Mexico 74 E3 19 20N 99 40W
Tol'yatti Russia 94 G7 53 32N 49 24E
Tomakomai Japan 102 D3 42 39N 141 33E
Tomaniivi mt. Fiji 114 U16 17 37S 178 01E
Tomar Port. 87 A3 39 36N 8 25W
Tomatlán Mexico 74 C3 19 54N 105 18W
Tombigbee r. USA 71 J3 32 00N 88 00W
Tombouctou Mali 108 D11 16 49N 2 59W
Tombua Angola 109 G4 15 49S 11 53E
Tom Price, Mount Aust. 110 B5 22 49S 117 51E
Tomsk Russia 95 L8 56 30N 85 05E
Tonalá Mexico 74 F3 16 08N 93 41W
Tonasket Washington USA 43 L1 48 42N 119 28W
Tonawanda New York USA 51 M2 43 01N 78 53W
Tonawanda Channel New York USA 54 D2 43 03N 78 55W
Tonawanda Creek r. New York USA 52 H3 43 08N 78 35W
TONGA 114 J5
Tonga Trench Pacific Ocean 114 J5 20 00S 173 00E
Tongchuan China 101 K6 35 05N 109 02E
Tong Fuk HK China 100 A1 22 14N 113 56E
Tonghai China 101 J3 24 07N 104 45E
Tonghua China 101 P7 41 42N 125 45E
Tongking, Gulf of China/Vietnam 101 K2 19 00N 107 00E
Tongling China 101 M5 30 58N 117 48E
Tônlé Sab l. Cambodia 103 C6 12 00N 103 50E
Tonopah Nevada USA 70 C4 38 05N 117 15W
Tønsberg Norway 86 L13 59 16N 10 25E
Tooele Utah USA 70 D5 40 32N 112 18W
Toowoomba Aust. 110 J4 27 35S 151 54E
Topeka Kansas USA 71 G4 39 02N 95 41W
Torbay UK 86 D9 50 27N 3 30W
Tordesillas Sp. 87 C4 41 30N 5 00W
Tormes r. Sp. 87 C4 41 03N 5 58W
Tororo Uganda 108 L8 0 42N 34 12E
Toros Dağlari mts. Turkey 96 B6 37 10N 33 10E
Torre del Greco Italy 89 E4 40 46N 14 22E
Torrelavega Sp. 87 C5 43 21N 4 03W
Torrens, Lake Aust. 110 F3 31 00S 137 50E
Torreón Mexico 74 D5 25 34N 103 25W
Torres Strait Aust. 110 G7/G8 10 00S 142 30E
Torrington Connecticut USA 73 D2 41 48N 73 07W
Tortosa Sp. 87 F4 40 49N 0 31E
Torun Poland 88 G10 53 01N 18 35E
Tosa-wan b. Japan 102 B1 33 20N 133 40E
Totoya i. Fiji 114 V15 18 56S 179 50W
Tottori Japan 102 B2 35 32N 134 12E
Touggourt Algeria 108 F14 33 08N 6 04E
Toulon Fr. 87 H5 43 07N 5 55E
Toulouse Fr. 87 F5 43 33N 1 24E
Toungoo Myanmar 103 B7 18 57N 96 26E
Tournai Belgium 86 G9 50 36N 3 24E
Tours Fr. 87 F7 47 23N 0 42E
Towanda Pennsylvania USA 53 K1 41 46N 76 27W
Townsville Aust. 110 H6 19 13S 146 48E
Towson Maryland USA 73 B1 39 25N 76 36W
Toyama Japan 102 C2 36 42N 137 14E
Toyohashi Japan 102 C1 34 46N 137 22E
Toyota Japan 102 C2 35 05N 137 09E
Tozeur Tunisia 108 F14 33 55N 8 07E
Trabzon Turkey 96 C7 41 00N 39 43E
Tracy California USA 72 C3 37 39N 121 26W
Tralee RoI 86 A10 52 16N 9 42W
Tranås Sweden 88 E13 58 03N 15 00E
Transantarctic Mountains Antarctica 117 80 00S 155 00E
Trápani Italy 89 D3 38 02N 12 32E
Traverse City Michigan USA 71 J5 44 46N 85 38W
Treinta-y-Tres Uruguay 81 G7 33 16S 54 17W
Trelew Chile 81 D5 43 13S 65 15W
Trelleborg Sweden 88 D11 55 22N 13 10E
Trenčín Slovakia 88 G8 48 53N 18 00E
Trenque Lauquen Argentina 81 E6 35 56S 62 43W
Trent r. UK 86 E10 53 30N 0 50W
Trento Italy 89 C7 46 04N 11 08E
Trenton New Jersey USA 71 M5 40 15N 74 43W
Tres Arroyos Argentina 81 E6 38 26S 60 17W
Três Lagoas Brazil 80 G9 20 46S 51 43W
Treviso Italy 89 D6 45 40N 12 15E
Trichur India 98 D2 10 32N 76 14E
Trieste Italy 89 D6 45 39N 13 47E
Tríkala Greece 89 H3 39 33N 21 46E
Trincomalee Sri Lanka 98 E1 8 34N 81 13E
Trindade i. Atlantic Ocean 116 F4 20 30S 29 20W
Trinidad Bolivia 80 E11 14 46S 64 50W
Trinidad Cuba 75 H4 21 48N 80 00W
Trinidad Colorado USA 70 F4 37 11N 104 31W
Trinidad i. Trinidad and Tobago 75 V15 11 00N 61 30W
TRINIDAD AND TOBAGO 75 M2
Trinity r. USA 71 G3 32 00N 96 00W
Tripoli Greece 89 J2 37 31N 22 22E
Tripoli Lebanon 96 N12 34 27N 35 50E
Tripoli Libya 108 G14 32 54N 13 11E
Tripura admin. India 99 G4 23 40N 92 00E
Tristan da Cunha i. Atlantic Ocean 116 G3 37 15S 12 30W
Trivandrum India 98 D1 8 30N 76 57E
Trnava Slovakia 88 F8 48 23N 17 35E
Trollhätten Sweden 88 D13 58 17N 12 20E
Trombetas r. Brazil 80 F14 1 30N 57 00W
Trona California USA 72 E2 35 46N 117 24W
Trouville Fr. 86 F8 49 22N 0 05E
Troy Alabama USA 71 J3 31 49N 86 00W
Troy Montana USA 43 N1 48 28N 115 55W
Troy New York USA 71 M5 42 43N 73 43W
Troy hist. site Turkey 96 A6 39 55N 26 17E
Troyes Fr. 86 H8 48 18N 4 05E
Trujillo Peru 80 B12 8 06S 79 00W
Trujillo Sp. 87 C3 39 28N 5 53W
Trujillo Venezuela 80 C15 9 20N 70 38W
Truk Islands Pacific Ocean 114 E8 7 30N 152 30E
Truro UK 86 C9 50 16N 5 03W
Tseung Kwan O HK China 100 C1 22 19N 114 14E
Tshane Botswana 109 J3 24 05S 21 54E
Tshuapa r. CDR 108 J7 1 00S 23 00E
Tsing Chau Tsai HK China 100 B2 22 20N 114 02E
Tsing Yi HK China 100 B2 22 21N 114 06E
Tsu Japan 102 C1 34 41N 136 30E
Tsuchiura Japan 102 D2 36 05N 140 11E
Tsuen Wan HK China 100 B2 22 22N 114 06E
Tsugaru-kaikyō sd. Japan 102 D3 41 30N 140 30E
Tsumeb Namibia 109 H4 19 13S 17 42E
Tsuruga Japan 102 C2 35 40N 136 05E
Tsuruoka Japan 102 C2 38 42N 139 50E
Tsushima i. Japan 102 A1 34 30N 129 20E
Tsuyama Japan 102 B2 35 04N 134 01E
Tua r. Port. 87 B4 41 20N 7 30W
Tuamotu Archipelago is. Pacific Ocean 115 N6 15 00S 145 00W
Tuamotu Ridge Pacific Ocean 115 M6 19 00S 144 00W
Tübingen Germany 88 B8 48 32N 9 04E
Tubruq Libya 108 J14 32 05N 23 59E
Tubuai Islands Pacific Ocean 115 M5 23 23S 149 27W
Tucson Arizona USA 70 D3 32 15N 110 57W
Tucumcari New Mexico USA 70 F4 35 11N 103 44W
Tucupita Venezuela 80 E15 9 02N 62 04W
Tucuruí Brazil 80 H13 3 42S 49 44W
Tudela Sp. 87 E5 42 04N 1 37W
Tuen Mun HK China 100 A2 22 24N 113 58E
Tukums Latvia 88 J12 56 58N 23 10E
Tula Russia 94 F7 54 11N 37 38E
Tula Mexico 74 E4 20 01N 99 21W
Tula Mexico 74 E4 23 00N 99 41W
Tulare California USA 72 D3 36 12N 119 21W
Tulare Lake California USA 72 D3 36 04N 119 45W
Tulcán Ecuador 80 B14 0 50N 77 48W
Tulcea Romania 89 M6 45 10N 28 50E
Tulkarm Jordan 96 N11 32 19N 35 02E
Tulle Fr. 87 F6 45 16N 1 46E
Tulsa Oklahoma USA 71 G4 36 07N 95 58W
Tuluá Col. 80 B14 4 05N 76 12W
Tulun Russia 95 N7 54 32N 100 35E
Tumaco Col. 80 B14 1 51N 78 46W
Tumbes Peru 80 A13 3 37S 80 27W
Tumkur India 98 D2 13 20N 77 06E
Tunduru Tanzania 109 M5 11 08S 37 21E
Tundzha r. Bulgaria 89 K5 42 00N 25 00E
Tungabhadra r. India 98 D3 15 00N 75 30E
Tung Lung Chau i. HK China 100 C1 22 15N 114 17E
Tunis Tunisia 108 G14 36 50N 10 13E
TUNISIA 108 F14
Tunja Col. 80 C15 5 33N 73 23W
Tunkhannock Pennsylvania USA 53 L1 41 32N 75 46W
Tuolumne r. California USA 72 C3 37 53N 120 09W
Tupelo Mississippi USA 71 J3 34 15N 88 43W
Tupiza Bolivia 80 D9 21 27S 65 45W
Túquerres Col. 80 B14 1 06N 77 37W
Tura Russia 95 N9 64 20N 100 17E
Turda Romania 89 J7 46 35N 23 50E
Turgay r. Kazakhstan 94 J7 50 00N 64 00E
Turia r. Sp. 87 E3 39 45N 0 55W
Turin Italy 89 A6 45 04N 7 40E
Turkana, Lake Ethiopia/Kenya 108 M8 4 00N 36 00E
TURKEY 96 B6
TURKMENISTAN 94 H4/J4
Turks and Caicos Islands W. Indies 75 K4 21 30N 72 00W
Turks Island Passage sd. W. Indies 75 K4 21 30N 71 30W
Turlock California USA 72 C3 37 30N 120 53W
Turner Montana USA 47 C1 48 51N 108 25W
Turnu Măgurele Romania 89 K5 43 44N 24 53E
Turpan China 100 F7 42 55N 89 06E
Turpan Depression China 100 F7 42 40N 89 30E
Turukhansk Russia 95 L10 65 49N 88 00E
Tuscaloosa Alabama USA 71 J3 33 12N 87 33W
Tuticorin India 98 D1 8 48N 78 10E
Tuttlingen Germany 88 B7 47 59N 8 49E
TUVALU 108 H7
Tuxpan Mexico 74 C4 21 58N 105 20W
Tuxpan Mexico 74 E4 20 58N 97 23W
Tuxtla Gutierrez Mexico 74 F3 16 45N 93 09W
Túy Sp. 87 A5 42 03N 8 39W
Tuz Gölü l. Turkey 96 B6 38 40N 33 35E
Tuzla Bosnia-Herzegovina 89 G6 44 33N 18 41E
Tver' Russia 94 F8 56 49N 35 57E
Tweed r. UK 86 D11 55 45N 2 10W
Twentynine Palms California USA 72 E2 34 09N 116 03W
Twin Falls tn. Idaho USA 70 D5 42 34N 114 30W
Twisp Washington USA 43 K1 48 22N 120 08W
Twisp River Washington USA 42 H4 48 30N 120 20W
Two Harbors tn. Minnesota USA 51 F4 47 02N 91 40W
Two Medicine River Montana USA 46 F1 48 27N 112 50W
Tyan-Shan' Kyrgyzstan 94/95 K5 41 00N 76 00E
Tyler Texas USA 71 G3 32 22N 95 18W
Tym r. Russia 95 L8 59 00N 82 30E
Tynda Russia 95 Q8 55 10N 124 35E
Tyne r. UK 86 E11 55 58N 2 43W
Tyre Lebanon 96 N11 33 16N 35 12E
Tyrone Pennsylvania USA 73 A2 40 41N 78 14W
Tyrrhenian Sea Europe 89 C4/D4 40 00N 12 00E
Tyumen' Russia 94 J8 57 11N 65 29E
Tyung r. Russia 95 P9 65 00N 119 00E
Tywi r. UK 86 D9 51 50N 4 25W

U

Uaupés Brazil 80 D13 0 07S 67 05W
Ubangi r. CAR 108 H8 4 00N 18 00E
Ube Japan 102 B1 33 57N 131 16E
Uberaba Brazil 80 H10 19 47S 47 57W
Uberlândia Brazil 80 H10 18 57S 48 17W
Ubly Michigan USA 52 D3 43 44N 82 58W
Ubon Ratchathani Thailand 103 C7 15 15N 104 50E
Ubort' r. Europe 88 L9 51 00N 27 00E
Ubundu CDR 108 K7 0 24S 25 30E
Ucayali r. Peru 80 C12 6 00S 74 00W
Uchiura-wan b. Japan 102 D3 42 30N 140 40E
Uda r. Russia 95 R7 54 00N 134 00E
Udaipur India 98 C4 24 36N 73 47E
Udaipur India 99 L9 23 32N 91 29E
Uddevalla Sweden 88 C13 58 20N 11 56E
Udine Italy 89 D7 46 04N 13 14E
Udon Thani Thailand 103 C7 17 25N 102 45E
Ueda Japan 102 C2 36 27N 138 13E
Uele r. CDR 108 K8 4 00N 27 00E
Uelen Russia 95 W10 66 13N 169 48W
Uelzen Germany 88 C10 52 58N 10 34E
Ufa Russia 94 H7 54 45N 55 58E
Ugab r. Namibia 109 H3 21 00S 15 00E
UGANDA 108 L7/L8
Uinta Mountains Utah USA 70 D5 40 00N 111 00W
Uitenhage RSA 109 K1 33 46S 25 25E
Ujjain India 98 D4 23 11N 75 50E
Ujung Pandang Indonesia 103 F2 5 09S 119 28E
Ukhta Russia 94 H9 63 33N 53 44E
Ukiah California USA 70 B4 39 09N 123 12W
Ukiah California USA 72 B4 39 09N 123 12W
Ukmerge Lithuania 88 K11 55 14N 24 49E
UKRAINE 88 J8/N8
Ulaangom Mongolia 100 G8 49 59N 92 00E
Ulan Bator Mongolia 101 K8 47 54N 106 52E
Ulan-Ude Russia 95 N7 51 55N 107 40E
Ulhasnagar India 98 C3 19 15N 73 08E
Uliastay Mongolia 101 H8 47 42N 96 52E
Ullapool UK 86 C12 57 54N 5 10W
Ulm Germany 88 C8 48 24N 10 00E
Ulsan South Korea 101 P6 35 32N 129 21E
Ulungur Hu l. China 100 F8 47 10N 87 10E
Ul'yanovsk Russia 94 G7 54 19N 48 22E
Uman' Ukraine 88 N8 48 45N 30 10E
Umbagog Lake New Hampshire/Maine USA 53 R4 44 45N 71 00W
Umm as Samim geog. reg. Oman 97 G3 22 10N 56 00E
Umm Ruwaba Sudan 108 L10 12 50N 31 20E
Umtata RSA 109 K1 31 35S 28 47E
Umuarama Brazil 80 G9 23 43S 52 57W
Una r. Bosnia-Herzegovina/Croatia 89 F6 45 15N 16 15E
'Unayzah Saudi Arabia 96 D4 26 06N 43 58E
Union New Jersey USA 73 H1 40 42N 74 14W
Union i. Lesser Antilles 74 R11 12 36N 61 26W
Union City New Jersey USA 73 H2 40 45N 74 01W
Union City Pennsylvania USA 52 G1 41 56N 79 51W
Union City Reservoir Pennsylvania USA 52 G1 41 58N 79 54W
Uniontown Pennsylvania USA 71 L4 39 54N 79 44W
Unionville Michigan USA 52 C3 43 41N 83 29W
UNITED ARAB EMIRATES 97 F3
UNITED KINGDOM 86
UNITED STATES OF AMERICA 70/71
Unst i. UK 86 E14 60 45N 0 55W
Upata Venezuela 80 E15 8 02N 62 25W
Upham North Dakota USA 49 B1 48 35N 100 44W
Upington RSA 109 J2 28 28S 21 14E
Upolu Point c. Hawaiian Islands 115 Z18 20 16N 155 52W
Upper Bay New Jersey USA 73 H1 40 40N 74 03W
Upper Hutt NZ 111 E4 41 07S 175 04E
Upper Lake tn. California USA 72 B4 39 10N 122 56W
Upper Lough Erne l. UK 86 B11 54 15N 7 30W
Upper Red Lake Minnesota USA 71 H6 48 04N 94 48W
Upper Sandusky Ohio USA 51 K1 40 50N 83 17W
Upplands Vasby Sweden 88 F13 59 30N 18 15E
Uppsala Sweden 88 F13 59 55N 17 38E
Ur hist. site Iraq 96 E5 30 56N 46 08E
Urakawa Japan 102 D3 42 10N 142 46E
Ural r. Asia 94 H6 48 00N 52 00E
Ural Mountains Russia 94 H7 57 00N 60 00E
Ural'sk Kazakhstan 94 H7 51 19N 51 20E
Uraricuera r. Brazil 80 E14 3 00N 62 30W
Urawa Japan 102 C2 35 52N 139 40E
Ure r. UK 86 E11 54 20N 1 55W
Urengoy Russia 95 K10 65 59N 78 30E
Urgench Uzbekistan 94 J5 41 35N 60 41E
Urmston Road sd. HK China 100 A2 22 23N 113 53E
Uroševac Kosovo 89 H5 42 21N 21 09E
Uruapan Mexico 74 D3 19 26N 102 04W
Urubamba Peru 80 C11 13 20S 72 07W
Uruguaiana Brazil 81 F8 29 45S 57 05W
URUGUAY 81 F7
Uruguay r. Uruguay/Argentina 81 F7 32 00S 57 40W
Ürümqi China 100 F7 43 43N 87 38E
Urziceni Romania 89 L6 44 43N 26 39E
Usa r. Russia 94 H10 66 00N 60 00E
Ushuaia Argentina 81 D3 54 48S 68 19W
Usinsk Russia 94 H10 65 57N 57 27E
Üsküdar Turkey 96 A7 41 02N 29 02E
Usol'ye-Sibirskoye Russia 95 N7 52 48N 103 40E
Ussuri r. Russia 95 R6 47 00N 134 00E
Ussuriysk Russia 95 R5 43 48N 131 59E
Ustica i. Italy 89 D3 38 00N 13 00E
Ust'-Ilimsk Russia 95 N8 58 03N 102 39E
Ustí nad Labem Czech Rep. 88 E9 50 40N 14 02E
Ust'-Kamchatsk Russia 95 U8 56 14N 162 28E
Ust'-Kamenogorsk Kazakhstan 95 L6 49 58N 82 36E
Ust'-Kut Russia 95 N8 56 48N 105 42E
Ust'Maya Russia 95 R9 60 25N 134 28E
Ust'-Nera Russia 95 S9 64 35N 143 14E
Ust'Olenek Russia 95 P11 72 59N 119 57E
Ust Urt Plateau Asia 94 H5 43 30N 55 00E
Usulután Mexico 74 G2 13 20N 88 25W
Utah state USA 70 D4 39 00N 112 00W
Utah Lake Utah USA 70 D5 40 10N 111 50W
Utica New York USA 71 L5 43 06N 75 15W
Utrecht Neths. 86 H10 52 05N 5 07E
Utrera Sp. 87 C2 37 10N 5 47W
Utsunomiya Japan 102 C2 36 33N 139 52E
Uttaradit Thailand 103 C7 17 38N 100 05E
Uttaranchal admin. India 98 D5/D6 30 00N 78 00E
Uttar Pradesh admin. India 98 E5 27 00N 80 00E
Uvalde Texas USA 70 G2 29 14N 99 49W
Uvinza Tanzania 108 L6 5 08S 30 23E
Uvs Nuur l. Mongolia 100 G9 50 10N 92 30E
Uwajima Japan 102 B1 33 13N 132 32E
Uyuni Bolivia 80 D9 20 28S 66 47W
Uz r. Slovakia 88 H8 48 30N 22 00E
UZBEKISTAN 94 H5/J5
Uzhgorod Ukraine 88 J8 48 37N 22 22E

V

Vaal r. RSA 109 K2 27 30S 25 30E
Vác Hungary 88 G7 47 46N 19 08E
Vacaville California USA 72 C4 38 21N 121 59W
Vadodara India 98 C4 22 19N 73 14E
Vaga r. Russia 94 G9 62 00N 43 00E
Váh r. Slovakia 88 F8 48 00N 18 00E
Vakh r. Russia 95 L9 61 30N 80 30E
Vakhsh r. Asia 94 J4 37 00N 68 00E
Valdepeñas Sp. 87 D3 38 46N 3 24W
Valdés, Peninsula Argentina 81 E5 42 30S 63 00W
Valdez Alaska USA 40 F6 61 07N 146 16W
Valdivia Chile 81 C6 39 46S 73 15W
Valdosta Georgia USA 71 K3 30 51N 83 51W
Valença Brazil 80 K11 13 22S 39 06W
Valence Fr. 87 H6 44 56N 4 54E

Name	Page	Grid	Lat	Long
Valencia Sp.	87	E3	39 29N	0 24W
Valencia Venezuela	80	D16	10 14N	67 59W
Valencia, Gulf of Sp.	87	F3	39 30N	0 20E
Valenciennes Fr.	86	G9	50 22N	3 32E
Valera Venezuela	80	C15	9 21N	70 38W
Valjevo Serbia	89	G6	44 16N	19 56E
Valladolid Mexico	74	G4	20 40N	88 11W
Valladolid Sp.	87	C4	41 39N	4 45W
Valle de la Pascua Venezuela	80	D15	9 15N	66 00W
Valledupar Col.	80	C16	10 31N	73 16W
Valle Grande Bolivia	80	E10	18 30S	64 04W
Vallejo California USA	70	B4	38 05N	122 14W
Vallenar Chile	81	C8	28 36S	70 45W
Valletta Malta	89	E1	35 54N	14 32E
Valley Stream *tn.* New York USA	73	K1	40 39N	73 42W
Valmiera Latvia	88	K12	57 32N	25 29E
Valparaíso Chile	81	C7	33 05S	71 40W
Van Turkey	96	D6	38 28N	43 20E
Van Buren Maine USA	57	G2	47 10N	67 59W
Vancouver Washington USA	70	B6	45 38N	122 40W
Vänern *l.* Sweden	88	D13	59 00N	13 30E
Vänersborg Sweden	88	D13	58 23N	12 19E
Van Gölü *l.* Turkey	96	D6	38 33N	42 46E
Vannes Fr.	86	D7	47 40N	2 44W
Vanua Levu *i.* Fiji	114	U16	16 20S	179 00E
Vanua Levu Barrier Reef Fiji	114	U16	17 10S	179 00E
Vanua Mbalavu *i.* Fiji	114	V16	17 15S	178 55W
VANUATU	103	N7		
Van Wert Ohio USA	51	J1	40 52N	84 35W
Varadero Cuba	75	H4	23 09N	81 16W
Varanasi India	98	E5	25 20N	83 00E
Varaždin Croatia	89	F7	46 18N	16 21E
Varberg Sweden	88	D12	57 07N	12 16E
Varna Bulgaria	89	L5	43 12N	27 57E
Värnamo Sweden	88	E12	57 11N	14 03E
Várzea Grande Brazil	80	J12	6 32S	42 05W
Vaslui Romania	89	L7	46 37N	27 46E
Vassar Michigan USA	52	C3	43 23N	83 33W
Västerås Sweden	88	F13	59 36N	16 32E
Västervik Sweden	88	F12	57 45N	16 40E
Vasyugan *r.* Russia	94	K8	59 00N	77 30E
Vättern *l.* Sweden	88	E13	58 20N	14 20E
Vatulele *i.* Fiji	114	T15	18 30S	177 38E
Vaupés *r.* Col.	80	C14	1 30N	72 00W
Växjö Sweden	88	E12	56 52N	14 50E
Vaygach *i.* Russia	94	H11	70 00N	59 00E
Vejle Denmark	88	B11	55 43N	9 33E
Velebit *mts.* Croatia	89	E6	44 00N	15 00E
Velikiye Luki Russia	94	F8	56 19N	30 31E
Veliko Tŭrnovo Bulgaria	89	K5	43 04N	25 39E
Vellore India	98	D2	12 56N	79 09E
VENEZUELA	80	D15		
Venezuelan Basin Caribbean Sea	116	B8	14 00N	67 00W
Venice Italy	89	D6	45 26N	12 20E
Venta *r.* Latvia/Lithuania	88	J12	56 05N	21 50E
Ventspils Latvia	88	H12	57 22N	21 31E
Ventura California USA	70	C3	34 16N	119 18W
Veracruz Mexico	74	E3	19 11N	96 10W
Veraval India	98	C4	20 53N	70 28E
Vercelli Italy	89	B6	45 19N	8 26E
Verde *r.* Paraguay	80	F9	23 20S	60 00W
Verde *r.* Arizona USA	70	D3	34 00N	112 00W
Verdun-sur-Meuse Fr.	86	H8	49 10N	5 24E
Vereeniging RSA	109	K2	26 41S	27 56E
Verin Sp.	87	B4	41 55N	7 26W
Verkhoyansk Russia	95	R10	67 35N	133 25E
Verkhoyansk Range *mts.* Russia	95	Q10	65 00N	130 00E
Vermilion Ohio USA	52	D1	41 24N	82 21W
Vermillion Lake Minnesota USA	51	E4	47 35N	92 28W
Vermillion Range *mts.* Minnesota USA	51	F4	48 00N	91 00W
Vermont *state* USA	71	M5	44 00N	73 00W
Vernon Texas USA	70	G3	34 10N	99 19W
Véroia Greece	89	J4	40 32N	22 11E
Verona Italy	89	C6	45 26N	11 00E
Versailles Fr.	86	G8	48 48N	2 07E
Verviers Belgium	86	H9	50 36N	5 52E
Vesuvio *vol.* Italy	89	E4	40 49N	14 26E
Vetlanda Sweden	88	E12	57 26N	15 05E
Viano do Castelo Port.	87	A4	41 41N	8 50W
Viar *r.* Sp.	87	C2	37 45N	5 50W
Viborg Denmark	88	B12	56 28N	9 25E
Vicente Guerrero Mexico	74	A6	30 48N	116 00W
Vicenza Italy	89	C6	45 33N	11 32E
Vichy Fr.	87	G7	46 07N	3 25E
Vicksburg Mississippi USA	71	H3	32 21N	90 51W
Victoria Chile	81	C6	38 20S	72 30W
Victoria Texas USA	71	G2	28 49N	97 01W
Victoria *r.* Aust.	110	E6	16 00S	131 30E
Victoria *state* Aust.	110	G2/H2	37 00S	145 00E
Victoria de las Tunas Cuba	75	J4	20 58N	76 59W
Victoria Falls Zambia/Zimbabwe	109	K4	17 55S	25 51E
Victoria Harbour HK China	100	C1	22 18N	114 10E
Victoria, Lake East Africa	108	L7	2 00S	33 00E
Victoria Land *geog. reg.* Antarctica	117		75 00S	157 00E
Victoria Peak HK China	100	B1	22 17N	114 09E
Victoria West RSA	109	J1	31 25S	23 08E
Victorville California USA	72	E2	34 31N	117 18W
Vidin Bulgaria	89	J5	44 00N	22 50E
Viedma Argentina	81	E5	40 45S	63 00W
Vienna Austria	88	F8	48 13N	16 22E
Vienne Fr.	87	H6	45 32N	4 54E
Vientiane Laos	103	C7	17 59N	102 38E
Vierzon Fr.	87	G7	47 14N	2 03E
VIETNAM	103	D7		
Vieux Fort St. Lucia	74	R11	13 44N	60 57W
Vigia Brazil	80	H13	0 50S	48 07W
Vigo Sp.	87	A5	42 15N	8 44W
Vijayawada India	98	E3	16 34N	80 40E
Vijosë *r.* Albania	89	H4	40 30N	20 00E
Vila Nova de Gaia Port.	87	A4	41 08N	8 37W
Vila Real Port.	87	B4	41 17N	7 45W
Vila Velha Brazil	80	J9	20 23S	40 18W
Vilhena Brazil	80	E11	12 40S	60 08W
Villach Austria	89	D7	46 37N	13 51E
Villa Constitución Mexico	74	B5	25 05N	111 45W
Villahermosa Mexico	74	F3	18 00N	92 53W
Villalba Sp.	87	B5	43 17N	7 41W
Villa María Argentina	81	E7	32 25S	63 15W
Villa Montes Bolivia	80	E9	21 15S	63 30W
Villanueva Mexico	74	D4	22 24N	102 53W
Villarrica Chile	81	C6	39 15S	72 15W
Villarrobledo Sp.	87	D3	39 16N	2 36W
Villa Unión Argentina	81	D8	29 27S	62 46W
Villa Unión Mexico	74	C4	23 10N	106 12W
Villavicencio Col.	80	C14	4 09N	73 38W
Villefranche-sur-Saône Fr.	87	H6	46 00N	4 43E
Villeneuve-sur-Lot Fr.	87	F6	44 25N	0 43E
Villeurbanne Fr.	87	H6	45 46N	4 54E
Vilyuy *r.* Russia	95	Q9	64 00N	123 00E
Vilyuysk Russia	95	Q9	63 46N	121 35E
Viña del Mar Chile	81	C7	33 02S	71 35W
Vinaroz Sp.	87	F4	40 29N	0 28E
Vincennes Indiana USA	71	J4	38 42N	87 30W
Vindhya Range *mts.* India	98	D4	23 00N	75 00E
Vineland New Jersey USA	71	L4	39 29N	75 02W
Vinh Vietnam	103	D7	18 42N	105 41E
Vinkovci Croatia	89	G6	45 16N	18 49E
Vinnytsya Ukraine	88	M8	49 11N	28 30E
Vinson Massif *mts.* Antarctica	117		78 02S	22 00W
Vipiteno Italy	89	C7	46 54N	11 27E
Virgin *r.* USA	70	D4	37 00N	114 00W
Virginia Minnesota USA	71	H6	47 30N	92 28W
Virginia *state* USA	71	L4	38 00N	77 00W
Virginia Beach *tn.* Virginia USA	71	L4	36 51N	75 59W
Virgin Islands W. Indies	75	M3	18 00N	64 30W
Virovitica Croatia	89	F6	45 50N	17 25E
Vis *i.* Croatia	89	F5	43 00N	16 00E
Visalia California USA	70	C4	36 20N	119 18W
Visby Sweden	88	G12	57 32N	18 15E
Vise *i.* Russia	95	K12	79 30N	77 00E
Viseu Port.	87	B4	40 40N	7 55W
Vishakhapatnam India	98	E3	17 42N	83 24E
Vista California USA	72	E1	33 12N	117 15W
Viterbo Italy	89	D5	42 24N	12 06E
Vitichi Bolivia	80	D9	20 14S	65 22W
Viti Levu *i.* Fiji	114	T15	18 10S	177 55E
Vitim Russia	95	P8	59 28N	112 35E
Vitim *r.* Russia	95	P8	58 00N	113 00E
Vitória Brazil	80	J9	20 20S	40 18W
Vitória da Conquista Brazil	80	J11	14 53S	40 52W
Vitoria Gasteiz Sp.	87	D5	42 51N	2 40W
Vitry-le-François Fr.	86	H8	48 44N	4 36E
Vityaz Trench Pacific Ocean	114	G7	9 30S	170 00E
Vivi *r.* Russia	95	M10	61 00N	96 00E
Vizianagaram India	98	E3	18 07N	83 30E
Vladikavkaz Russia	94	G5	43 02N	44 43E
Vladimir Russia	94	G8	56 08N	40 25E
Vladimir Volynskiy Ukraine	88	K9	50 51N	24 19E
Vladivostok Russia	95	R5	43 09N	131 53E
Vlissingen Neths.	86	G9	51 27N	3 35E
Vlorë Albania	89	G4	40 29N	19 29E
Vltava *r.* Czech Rep.	88	E8	49 00N	14 00E
Voi Kenya	108	M7	3 23S	38 35E
Volga *r.* Russia	94	G6	50 00N	45 00E
Volgodonsk Russia	94	G6	47 35N	42 08E
Volgograd Russia	94	G6	48 45N	44 30E
Vologda Russia	94	F8	59 10N	39 55E
Vólos Greece	89	J3	39 22N	22 57E
Volta, Lake Ghana	108	D9	7 30N	0 30W
Volturno *r.* Italy	89	E4	41 00N	14 00E
Volzhskiy Russia	94	G6	48 48N	44 45E
Vóreioi Sporádes *is.* Greece	89	J3/K3	39 00N	24 00E
Vorkuta Russia	94	J10	67 27N	64 00E
Voronezh Russia	94	F7	51 40N	39 13E
Vørterkaka Nunatak *mt.* Antarctica	117		71 45S	32 00E
Vosges *mts.* Fr.	86	J8	48 10N	6 50E
Vostochnyy Russia	95	R5	42 52N	132 56E
Vouga *r.* Port.	87	A4	40 45N	8 15W
Vranje Serbia	89	H5	42 33N	21 54E
Vratsa Bulgaria	89	J5	43 12N	23 32E
Vrbas *r.* Bosnia-Herzegovina	89	F6	44 00N	17 00E
Vršac Serbia	89	H6	45 07N	21 19E
Vryburg RSA	109	J2	26 57S	24 44E
Vukovar Croatia	89	G6	45 19N	19 01E
Vung Tau Vietnam	103	D6	10 21N	107 04E
Vunisea Fiji	114	U15	19 04S	178 09E
Vyatka *r.* Russia	94	G8	58 00N	50 00E
Vyborg Russia	94	E9	60 45N	28 41E
Vychegda *r.* Russia	94	H9	62 00N	52 00E

W

Name	Page	Grid	Lat	Long
Wa Ghana	108	D10	10 07N	2 28W
Wabash *r.* USA	71	J4	38 00N	87 30W
Wabuska Nevada USA	72	D4	39 09N	119 13W
Waco Texas USA	71	G3	31 33N	97 10W
Waddeneilanden Neths.	86	H10	53 25N	5 15E
Waddenzee *sea* Neths.	86	H10	53 15N	5 15E
Wādī al 'Arabah *r.* Israel	96	N10	30 30N	35 10E
Wādī al Masīlah *r.* Yemen	97	F2	16 00N	50 00E
Wādī el Gafra Egypt	109	R2	30 16N	31 46E
Wadi Halfa Sudan	108	L12	21 55N	31 20E
Wad Medani Sudan	108	L10	14 24N	33 30E
Wagga Wagga Aust.	110	H2	35 07S	147 24E
Wagin Aust.	110	B3	33 20S	117 15E
Waglan Island HK China	100	C1	22 11N	114 18E
Wah Pakistan	98	C6	33 50N	72 44E
Waha Libya	108	H13	28 10N	19 57E
Wahpeton North Dakota USA	71	G6	46 16N	96 36W
Waialua Hawaiian Islands	115	X18	21 35N	158 08W
Waigeo *i.* Indonesia	103	J3	0 15S	130 45E
Waihi NZ	111	E6	37 57S	175 44E
Wailuku Hawaiian Islands	115	Y18	20 54N	156 30W
Waimate NZ	111	C2	44 44S	171 03E
Waipara NZ	111	D3	43 04S	172 45E
Waipawa NZ	111	F5	39 57S	176 35E
Waipu NZ	111	F7	35 59S	174 27E
Wairoa NZ	111	F5	39 03S	177 25E
Waitara NZ	111	E5	39 00S	174 14E
Wajima Japan	102	C2	37 23N	136 53E
Wajir Kenya	108	M8	1 46N	40 05E
Wakasa-wan *b.* Japan	102	C2	35 40N	135 30E
Wakayama Japan	102	C1	34 12N	135 10E
Wakefield Rhode Island USA	73	E2	41 26N	71 30W
Wake Islands Pacific Ocean	114	G9	19 18N	166 36E
Wakkanai Japan	102	D4	45 26N	141 43E
Wałbrzych Poland	88	F9	50 48N	16 19E
Wales *admin.* UK	86	C10	52 40N	3 30W
Walhalla North Dakota USA	49	D1	48 55N	97 55W
Walker *r.* Nevada USA	72	D4	39 08N	119 00W
Walker Lake Nevada USA	70	C4	38 40N	118 43W
Wallaroo Aust.	110	F3	33 57S	137 36E
Walla Walla Washington USA	70	C6	46 05N	118 18W
Wallis and Futuna *is.* Pacific Ocean	114	J6	13 16S	176 15W
Walsenburg Colorado USA	70	F4	37 36N	104 48W
Waltham Massachusetts USA	73	E3	42 23N	71 14W
Walvis Bay *tn.* Namibia	109	G3	22 59S	14 31E
Walvis Ridge Atlantic Ocean	116	J3	30 00S	3 00E
Walyevo Fiji	114	V16	17 35S	179 58W
Wamba *r.* CDR	109	H6	6 30S	17 30E
Wanganui NZ	111	E5	39 56S	175 03E
Wang Chau *i.* HK China	100	D1	22 19N	114 22E
Wanxian China	101	K5	30 54N	108 20E
Warangal India	98	D3	18 00N	79 35E
Wardha *r.* India	98	D4	20 30N	79 00E
Warner Springs *tn.* California USA	72	E1	33 19N	116 38W
Warren Michigan USA	51	K2	42 30N	83 02W
Warren Ohio USA	71	K5	41 15N	80 49W
Warren Pennsylvania USA	52	G1	41 52N	79 09W
Warrnambool Aust.	110	G2	38 23S	142 03E
Warroad Minnesota USA	49	E1	48 59N	95 20W
Warsaw Poland	88	H10	52 15N	21 00E
Warta *r.* Poland	88	F10	52 00N	17 00E
Warwick Aust.	110	J4	28 12S	152 00E
Warwick Rhode Island USA	71	M5	41 42N	71 23W
Wasco California USA	72	D2	35 36N	119 20W
Washburn Wisconsin USA	51	F4	46 41N	90 53W
Washington *state* USA	70	B6/C6	47 00N	120 00W
Washington Crossing *tn.* New Jersey USA	73	C2	40 18N	74 52W
Washington D.C. District of Columbia USA	71	L4	38 55N	77 00W
Wash, The *b.* UK	86	F10	52 55N	0 10E
Watampone Indonesia	103	G3	4 33S	120 20E
Waterbury Connecticut USA	73	D2	41 34N	73 02W
Waterford RoI	86	B10	52 15N	7 06W
Waterloo Iowa USA	71	H5	42 30N	92 20W
Waterloo New York USA	53	K2	42 54N	76 53W
Watersmeet Michigan USA	51	G4	46 16N	89 10W
Watertown New York USA	71	L5	43 57N	75 56W
Watertown South Dakota USA	71	G5	44 54N	97 08W
Waterville Maine USA	71	N5	44 34N	69 41W
Waterville New York USA	53	L2	42 55N	75 24W
Waterville Ohio USA	52	C1	41 29N	83 44W
Watkins Glen *tn.* New York USA	53	K2	42 23N	76 53W
Watsonville California USA	72	C3	36 59N	121 47W
Wau PNG	110	H8	7 22S	146 40E
Wau Sudan	108	K9	7 40N	28 04E
Waukegan Illinois USA	71	J5	42 21N	87 52W
Waukesha Wisconsin USA	71	J5	43 01N	88 14W
Wausau Wisconsin USA	71	J5	44 58N	89 40W
Wawona California USA	72	D3	37 32N	119 39W
Waycross Georgia USA	71	K3	31 12N	82 22W
Webster New York USA	53	J3	43 13N	77 26W
Weddell Sea Southern Ocean	117		71 00S	40 00W
Weiden Germany	88	D8	49 40N	12 10E
Weifang China	101	M6	36 44N	119 10E
Wei He *r.* China	101	K5	34 00N	106 00E
Weipa Aust.	110	G7	12 35S	141 56E
Weirton West Virginia USA	71	K5	40 24N	80 37W
Wejherowo Poland	88	G11	54 36N	18 12E
Wellesley Islands Aust.	110	F6	16 30S	139 00E
Wellington NZ	111	E4	41 17S	174 46E
Wellington Kansas USA	71	G4	37 17N	97 25W
Wellington Nevada USA	72	D4	38 45N	119 23W
Wellsboro Pennsylvania USA	53	J1	41 45N	77 18W
Wellsford NZ	111	E6	36 18S	174 31E
Wellsville New York USA	52	J2	42 07N	77 56W
Wels Austria	88	D8	48 10N	14 02E
Wenzhou China	101	N4	28 02N	120 40E
Weser *r.* Germany	88	B10	53 00N	8 00E
West Australian Basin Indian Ocean	113	J4/J5	20 00S	100 00E
West Bank *territory* Israel	96	N10	32 00N	35 00E
West Bengal *admin.* India	99	F4	22 00N	88 00E
West Branch Michigan USA	51	J3	44 17N	84 16W
Westby Montana USA	47	E1	48 52N	104 04W
West Caroline Basin Pacific Ocean	114	D8	3 00N	136 00E
West Chester Pennsylvania USA	73	C1	39 57N	75 36W
Western Australia *state* Aust.	110	B2/D7	25 00S	117 00E
Western Ghats *mts.* India	98	C3/D2	15 30N	74 00E
WESTERN SAHARA	108	A12		
Western Sayan *mts.* Russia	95	L7/M7	52 30N	92 30E
Westerwald *geog. reg.* Germany	88	A9/B9	50 00N	8 00E
West European Basin Atlantic Ocean	116	G11	47 00N	18 00W
West Falkland *i.* Falkland Islands	81	E3/F3	51 00S	60 40W
Westfield Massachusetts USA	73	D3	42 08N	72 45W
Westfield New York USA	52	G2	42 20N	79 34W
West Grand Lake Maine USA	57	F1	44 15N	68 00W
Westhope North Dakota USA	47	G1	48 57N	101 02W
West Indies *is.* Caribbean Sea	75	K4/L4	22 00N	69 00W
Westlake Ohio USA	52	E1	41 25N	81 54W
West Lamma Channel HK China	100	B1	22 14N	114 05E
West Marianas Basin Pacific Ocean	114	D9	16 00N	137 30E
West Memphis Arkansas USA	71	H4	35 09N	90 11W
West Palm Beach *tn.* Florida USA	71	K2	26 42N	80 05W
West Plains *tn.* Missouri USA	71	H4	36 44N	91 51W
Westport NZ	111	C4	41 45S	171 36E
Westport RoI	86	A10	53 48N	9 32W
Westport California USA	72	B4	39 39N	123 47
Westport Connecticut USA	73	D2	41 08N	73 21W
West Siberian Lowland Russia	94	K8/K9	60 00N	75 00E
West Virginia *state* USA	71	K4	39 00N	81 00W
Wetar *i.* Indonesia	103	H2	7 15S	126 45E
Wewak PNG	110	G9	3 35S	143 35E
Wexford RoI	86	B10	52 20N	6 27W
Weymouth UK	86	D9	50 37N	2 25W
Weymouth Massachusetts USA	73	E3	42 13N	70 59W
Whakatane NZ	111	F6	37 58S	176 59E
Whangarei NZ	111	E7	35 43S	174 19E
Wharfe *r.* UK	86	E11	54 10N	2 05W
Wharton Pennsylvania USA	52	H1	41 31N	78 00W
Wharton Basin Indian Ocean	113	J5	15 00S	100 00E
Whatconi, Lake Washington USA	42	H4	48 40N	122 26W
Wheeler Lake Alabama USA	71	J3	34 00N	87 00W
Wheeling West Viriginia USA	71	K5	40 05N	80 43W
Whidbey Island Washington USA	42	H4	48 20N	122 38W
White *r.* Arkansas USA	71	H4	35 00N	92 00W
White *r.* Nevada USA	72	F4	38 40N	115 10W
White *r.* South Dakota USA	70	F5	43 00N	103 00W
White Nile Dam Sudan	108	L11	14 18N	32 20E
White Sea Russia	94	F10	66 00N	37 30E
White Volta *r.* Ghana	108	D9	9 30N	1 30W
Whitewater Montana USA	47	D1	48 46N	107 37W
Whitewater Creek *r.* Montana USA	47	D1	48 46N	107 36W
Whitianga NZ	111	E6	36 49S	175 42E
Whitney, Mount California USA	70	C4	36 35N	118 17W
Whitney Point *tn.* New York USA	73	C3	42 20N	75 58W
Whyalla Aust.	110	F3	33 04S	137 34E
Wichita Kansas USA	71	G4	37 43N	97 20W
Wichita *r.* Texas USA	70	F3	33 00N	100 00W
Wichita Falls *tn.* Texas USA	71	G3	33 55N	98 30W
Wick UK	86	D13	58 26N	3 06W
Wickliffe Ohio USA	52	E1	41 38N	81 25W
Wicklow RoI	86	B10	52 59N	6 03W
Wicklow Mountains RoI	86	B10	53 00N	6 20W
Wiener Neustadt Austria	88	F7	47 49N	16 15E
Wieprz *r.* Poland	88	J9	51 00N	23 00E
Wiesbaden Germany	88	B9	50 05N	8 15E
Wildrose North Dakota USA	47	F1	48 38N	103 11W
Wilhelm II Land *geog. reg.* Antarctica	117		70 00S	90 00E
Wilhelmshaven Germany	88	B10	53 32N	8 07E
Wilkes-Barre Pennsylvania USA	71	L5	41 15N	75 50W
Wilkes Land *geog. reg.* Antarctica	117		68 00S	105 00E
Willemstad Curaçao	75	L2	12 12N	68 56W
Williams California USA	72	B4	39 09N	122 09W
Williams Minnesota USA	49	E1	48 45N	94 55W
Williamsport Pennsylvania USA	71	L5	41 16N	77 03W
Williston North Dakota USA	70	F6	48 09N	103 39W
Willits California USA	72	B4	39 23N	123 22W
Willmar Minnesota USA	71	G6	45 06N	95 03W
Willoughby Hills *tn.* Ohio USA	52	E1	41 35N	81 29W
Willow Creek *r.* Montana USA	46	G1	48 40N	111 20W

Name	Page	Grid	Lat	Long
Willow River Michigan USA	52	D3	43 50N	82 58W
Willows California USA	72	B4	39 32N	122 10W
Willow Springs *tn.* Missouri USA	71	H4	36 59N	91 59W
Wilmington Delaware USA	71	L4	39 46N	75 31W
Wilmington North Carolina USA	71	L3	34 14N	77 55W
Wilson New York USA	54	D2	43 15N	78 50W
Wilson North Carolina USA	71	L4	35 43N	77 56W
Wiluna Aust.	110	C4	26 37S	120 12E
Winchendon Massachusetts USA	73	D3	42 41N	72 03W
Winchester UK	86	E9	51 04N	1 19W
Winchester Virginia USA	71	L4	39 11N	78 12W
Windhoek Namibia	109	H3	22 34S	17 06E
Wind River Range *mts.* Wyoming USA	70	E5	43 00N	109 00W
Windsor Locks *tn.* Connecticut USA	73	D2	41 55N	72 37W
Windward Islands Lesser Antilles	75	M2	12 30N	62 00W
Windward Passage *sd.* Cuba/Haiti	75	K3/K4	20 00N	73 00W
Winnemucca Nevada USA	70	C5	40 58N	117 45W
Winona Minnesota USA	71	H5	44 02N	91 37W
Winslow Arizona USA	70	D4	35 01N	110 43W
Winston-Salem North Carolina USA	71	K4	36 05N	80 18W
Winterthur Switz.	87	K7	47 30N	8 45E
Winthrop Washington USA	42	H4	48 35N	120 10W
Winton Aust.	110	G5	22 22S	143 00E
Wisconsin *r.* Wisconsin USA	71	H5	45 00N	90 00W
Wisconsin *state* USA	71	H6/J6	45 00N	90 00W
Wisconsin Rapids *tn.* Wisconsin USA	51	G3	44 23N	89 51W
Wisła *r.* Poland	88	G10	53 00N	19 00E
Wisłok *r.* Poland	88	J9	50 00N	22 00E
Wismar Germany	88	C10	53 54N	11 28E
Wittenberg Germany	88	D9	51 53N	12 39E
Wittenberge Germany	88	C10	52 59N	11 45E
Włocławek Poland	88	G10	52 39N	19 01E
Wolcott New York USA	53	K3	43 13N	76 49W
Wolfsberg Austria	89	E7	46 50N	14 50E
Wolfsburg Germany	88	C10	52 27N	10 49E
Wollongong Aust.	110	J3	34 25S	150 52E
Wolverhampton UK	86	D10	52 36N	2 08W
Wompah Aust.	110	G4	29 04S	142 05E
Wong Chuk Hang HK China	100	C1	22 15N	114 10E
Wonju South Korea	101	P6	37 24N	127 52E
Wonsan North Korea	101	P6	39 07N	127 26E
Woodfords California USA	72	D4	38 47N	119 50W
Woodland California USA	72	C4	38 42N	121 47W
Woodlark Island PNG	110	J8	9 10S	152 50E
Woodville NZ	111	E4	40 21S	175 52SE
Woodward Oklahoma USA	70	G4	36 26N	99 25W
Woonsocket Rhode Island USA	73	E2	42 01N	71 30W
Worcester RSA	109	H1	33 39S	19 26E
Worcester UK	86	D10	52 11N	2 13W
Worcester Massachusetts USA	71	M5	42 17N	71 48W
Workington UK	86	D11	54 39N	3 33W
Worland Wyoming USA	70	E5	44 01N	107 58W
Worthing UK	86	E9	50 48N	0 23W
Worthington Minnesota USA	71	G5	43 37N	95 36W
Wrangel Island Russia	95	V11	61 30N	180 00
Wrangell Alaska USA	42	D5	56 28N	132 23W
Wrangell Island Alaska USA	42	D5	56 25N	132 05W
Wrangell Mountains Alaska USA	64	B3	62 00N	143 00W
Wrangell-St. Elias National Park Alaska USA	64	B3	62 00N	142 30W
Wrexham UK	86	D10	53 03N	3 00W
Wrights Corner New York USA	54	D2	43 10N	78 45W
Wrightsville Pennsylvania USA	73	B2	40 02N	76 32W
Wrocław Poland	88	F9	51 05N	17 00E
Wu Chau Tong HK China	100	C2	22 30N	114 18E
Wuhai China	101	K6	39 40N	106 40E
Wuhan China	101	L5	30 35N	114 19E
Wuhu China	101	M5	31 23N	118 25E
Wukari Nigeria	108	F9	7 49N	9 49E
Wu Kau Tang HK China	100	C3	22 30N	114 15E
Wuppertal Germany	88	A9	51 15N	7 10E
Wurno Nigeria	108	F10	13 18N	5 29E
Wurtsboro New York USA	73	C2	41 35N	74 29W
Würzburg Germany	88	B8	49 48N	9 57E
Wusul Jiang *r.* China	101	Q8	47 00N	134 00E
Wutongqiao China	101	J4	29 21N	103 48E
Wuxi China	101	N5	31 35N	120 19E
Wuyi Shan *mts.* China	101	M4	26 00N	116 30E
Wuzhou China	101	L3	23 30N	111 21E
Wyandotte Michigan USA	51	K2	42 11N	83 10W
Wye *r.* UK	86	D10	51 50N	2 40W
Wyndham Aust.	110	D6	15 30S	128 09E
Wyoming Michigan USA	51	J2	42 54N	85 44W
Wyoming *state* USA	70	E5	43 00N	108 00W

X

Name	Page	Grid	Lat	Long
Xaafuun Somalia	108	Q10	10 27N	51 15E
Xam Hua Laos	101	J3	20 28N	104 05E
Xánthi Greece	89	K4	41 07N	24 56E
Xiamen China	101	M3	24 28N	118 05E
Xi'an China	101	K5	34 16N	108 54E
Xiangfan China	101	L5	32 05N	112 03E
Xiangkhoang Laos	103	C7	19 21N	102 23E
Xiangtan China	101	L4	27 48N	112 55E
Xianyang China	101	K5	34 22N	108 42E
Xigaze China	100	F4	29 18N	88 50E
Xi Jiang *r.* China	101	L3	23 30N	111 00E
Xingtai China	101	L6	37 08N	114 29E
Xingu *r.* Brazil	80	G12	5 00S	54 00W
Xining China	101	J6	36 35N	101 55E
Xinjiang Uygur Zizhiqu *admin.* China	100	E7/F7	41 00N	85 00E
Xinjin China	101	N6	39 25N	121 58E
Xiqing Shan *mts.* China	101	J5	34 00N	102 30E
Xizang Zizhiqu *admin.* China	100	E5/G5	33 30N	85 00E
Xochimilco Mexico	74	E3	19 08N	99 09W
Xuanhua China	101	M7	40 36N	115 01E
Xuchang China	101	L5	34 03N	113 48E
Xuwen China	101	L3	20 25N	110 08E
Xuzhou China	101	M5	34 17N	117 18E

Y

Name	Page	Grid	Lat	Long
Yablonovy Range *mts.* Russia	95	N7/P7	51 30N	110 00E
Yabrūd Syria	96	P11	33 58N	36 39E
Yaizu Japan	102	C1	34 54N	138 20E
Yakima Washington USA	70	B6	46 37N	120 30W
Yakima *r.* Washington USA	70	B6	47 00N	120 00W
Yaku-shima *i.* Japan	102	B1	30 00N	130 30E
Yakutat Alaska USA	42	A6	59 50N	139 49W
Yakutat Bay Alaska USA	42	A6	59 50N	140 00W
Yakutsk Russia	95	Q9	62 10N	129 50E
Yalu *r.* China/North Korea	101	P7	41 00N	126 00E
Yamagata Japan	102	D2	38 16N	140 16E
Yamaguchi Japan	102	B1	34 10N	131 28E
Yamal Peninsula Russia	94	J11	72 00N	70 00E
Yambio Sudan	108	K8	4 34N	28 21E
Yambol Bulgaria	89	L5	42 28N	26 30E
Yamburg Russia	95	K10	68 19N	77 09E
Yamoussoukro Côte d'Ivoire	108	C9	6 50N	5 20W
Yamuna *r.* India	98	E5	26 00N	80 30E
Yamunanagar India	98	D6	30 07N	77 17E
Yana *r.* Russia	95	R10	69 00N	135 00E
Yanbu'al Baḥr Saudi Arabia	96	C3	24 07N	38 04E
Yangcheng China	101	N5	33 23N	120 10E
Yangon Myanmar	103	B7	16 47N	96 10E
Yangquan China	101	L6	37 52N	113 29E
Yanji China	101	P7	42 52N	129 32E
Yanjing China	101	H4	29 01N	98 38E
Yankton South Dakota USA	71	G5	42 53N	97 24W
Yantai China	101	N6	37 30N	121 22E
Yaoundé Cameroon	108	G8	3 51N	11 31E
Yap Islands Pacific Ocean	114	D8	9 30N	138 09E
Yap Trench Pacific Ocean	114	D8	10 00N	139 00E
Yaqui *r.* Mexico	74	C5	28 00N	109 50W
Yarlung Zangbo *r.* China	100	G4	29 00N	92 30E
Yaroslavl' Russia	94	F8	57 34N	39 52E
Yarumal Col.	80	B15	6 59N	75 25W
Yasawa *i.* Fiji	114	T16	16 50S	177 30E
Yasawa Group *is.* Fiji	114	T16	17 00S	177 40E
Yatsushiro Japan	102	B1	32 32N	130 35E
Yau Tong HK China	100	C1	22 18N	114 14E
Yavari *r.* Peru/Brazil	80	C13	5 00S	72 30W
Yawatahama Japan	102	B1	33 27N	132 24E
Yazd Iran	97	F5	31 54N	54 22E
Yazoo *r.* Mississippi USA	71	H3	33 00N	90 00W
Ye Myanmar	103	B7	15 15N	97 50E
Yekaterinburg Russia	94	J8	56 52N	60 35E
Yell *i.* UK	86	E14	60 35N	1 10W
Yellow Sea China	101	N6	35 30N	122 30E
Yellowstone *r.* USA	70	E6	46 00N	108 00W
Yellowstone Lake Wyoming USA	70	D5	44 30N	110 20W
YEMEN REPUBLIC	96/97	D2/E2		
Yenisey *r.* Russia	95	L9	64 00N	87 30E
Yenisey, Gulf of Russia	95	K11	72 30N	80 00E
Yeniseysk Russia	95	M8	58 27N	92 13E
Yeppoon Aust.	110	J5	23 05S	150 42E
Yerington Nevada USA	72	D4	39 00N	119 11W
Yesilirmak *r.* Turkey	96	C7	41 00N	36 25E
Ye Xian China	101	M6	37 10N	119 55E
Yiannitsá Greece	89	J4	40 46N	22 24E
Yibin China	101	J4	28 42N	104 30E
Yichang China	101	L5	30 46N	111 20E
Yinchuan China	101	K6	38 30N	106 19E
Yingkou China	101	N7	40 40N	122 17E
Yining China	100	E7	43 50N	81 28E
Yi Pak HK China	100	B1	22 18N	114 01E
Yirga Alem Ethiopia	108	M9	6 48N	38 22E
Yiyang China	101	L4	28 39N	112 10E
Yoakum Texas USA	71	G2	29 18N	97 20W
Yogyakarta Indonesia	103	E2	7 48S	110 24E
Yoichi Japan	102	D3	43 14N	140 47E
Yokadouma Cameroon	108	H8	3 26N	15 06E
Yokkaichi Japan	102	C1	34 58N	136 38E
Yokohama Japan	102	C2	35 27N	139 38E
Yokosuka Japan	102	C2	35 18N	139 38E
Yokote Japan	102	D2	39 20N	140 31E
Yola Nigeria	108	G9	9 14N	12 32E
Yonago Japan	102	B2	35 27N	133 20E
Yonezawa Japan	102	D2	37 56N	140 06E
Yonkers New York USA	73	D2	40 58N	73 53W
Yonne *r.* Fr.	86	G8	48 00N	3 15E
York UK	86	E10	53 58N	1 05W
York Pennsylvania USA	71	L4	39 57N	76 44W
York, Cape Aust.	110	G7	10 42S	142 32E
Yosemite National Park California USA	72	D3	37 30N	119 00W
Yosu South Korea	101	P5	34 50N	127 30E
Youghal RoI	86	B9	51 51N	7 50W
You Jiang *r.* China	101	K3	23 30N	107 00E
Youngstown New York USA	52	G3	43 14N	79 01W
Youngstown Ohio USA	71	K5	41 05N	80 40W
Youngsville Pennsylvania USA	52	G1	41 52N	79 22W
Ypsilanti Michigan USA	52	C2	42 15N	83 36W
Ystad Sweden	88	D11	55 25N	13 50E
Yuba City California USA	70	B4	39 09N	121 36W
Yūbari Japan	102	D3	43 04N	141 59E
Yucatan *p.* Mexico	74	G3	19 00N	89 00W
Yucatan Basin Caribbean Sea	115	T9	20 00N	85 00W
Yucca Lake Nevada USA	72	F3	37 00N	116 02W
Yuci China	101	L6	37 40N	112 44E
Yuen Long HK China	100	B2	22 26N	114 02E
Yugakir Plateau Russia	95	T10	66 30N	156 00E
Yu Jiang *r.* China	101	K3	23 00N	109 00E
Yukon Flats National Wildlife Refuge Alaska USA	64	A4	66 30N	147 30W
Yuma Arizona USA	70	D3	32 40N	114 39W
Yumen China	101	H6	39 54N	97 43E
Yung Shue Wan *tn.* HK China	100	B1	22 13N	114 06E
Yurimaguas Peru	80	B12	5 54S	76 07W
Yuzhno-Sakhalinsk Russia	95	S6	46 58N	142 45E
Yverdon Switz.	87	J7	46 47N	6 38E
Yvetot Fr.	86	F8	49 37N	0 45E

Z

Name	Page	Grid	Lat	Long
Zaanstad Neths.	86	H10	52 27N	4 49E
Zābol Iran	97	H5	31 00N	61 32E
Zabrze Poland	88	G9	50 18N	18 47E
Zacapa Guatemala	74	G3	15 00N	89 30E
Zacatecas Mexico	74	D4	22 48N	102 33W
Zacatecoluca El Salvador	74	G2	13 29N	88 51W
Zadar Croatia	89	E6	44 07N	15 14E
Zafra Sp.	87	B3	38 25N	6 25W
Żagań Poland	88	E9	51 37N	15 20E
Zagreb Croatia	89	E6	45 48N	15 58E
Zagros Mountains Iran	97	E5/F5	32 45N	48 50E
Zāhedān Iran	97	H4	29 32N	60 54E
Zahlé Lebanon	96	N11	33 50N	35 55E
Zakopane Poland	88	G8	49 17N	19 54E
Zákynthos *i.* Greece	89	H2	37 45N	20 50E
Zalaegerszeg Hungary	89	F7	46 53N	16 51E
Zalău Romania	89	J7	47 10N	23 04E
Zaltan Libya	108	H13	28 15N	19 52E
Zambeze *r.* Mozambique	109	L4	16 00S	34 00E
Zambezi Zambia	109	J5	13 33S	23 08E
Zambezi *r.* Zambia/Zimbabwe	109	J4	16 00S	23 00E
ZAMBIA	109	J5/L5		
Zamboanga Philippines	103	G5	6 55N	122 05E
Zamora Sp.	87	C4	41 30N	5 45W
Zamość Poland	88	J9	50 43N	23 15E
Zanderij Suriname	80	F15	5 26N	55 14W
Zanesville Ohio USA	71	K4	39 55N	82 02W
Zanjān Iran	97	E6	36 40N	48 30E
Zanthus Aust.	110	C3	31 01S	123 32E
Zanzibar Tanzania	109	M6	6 10S	39 12E
Zanzibar *i.* Tanzania	108/109	M6	6 10S	39 13E
Zaozhuang China	101	M5	34 53N	117 38E
Zaragoza Sp.	87	E4	41 39N	0 54W
Zarand Iran	97	G5	30 50N	56 35E
Zaraza Venezuela	80	D15	9 23N	65 20W
Zarembo Island Alaska USA	42	D5	56 30N	132 50W
Zaria Nigeria	108	F10	11 01N	7 44E
Zarqa Jordan	96	C5	32 04N	36 05E
Zefat Israel	96	N11	32 57N	35 27E
Zell-am-See *tn.* Austria	89	D7	47 19N	12 47E
Zenica Bosnia-Herzegovina	89	F6	44 11N	17 53E
Zephyr Cove *tn.* Nevada USA	72	D4	39 07N	119 57W
Zeya Russia	95	Q7	53 48N	127 14E
Zeya *r.* Russia	95	Q7	53 00N	127 30E
Zêzere *r.* Port.	87	B3	39 50N	8 05W
Zgierz Poland	88	G9	51 52N	19 25E
Zgorzelec Poland	88	E9	51 10N	15 00E
Zhambyl Kazakhstan	94	K5	42 50N	71 25E
Zhangjiakou China	101	L7	40 51N	114 59E
Zhangzhou China	101	M3	24 31N	117 40E
Zhanjiang China	101	L3	21 10N	110 20E
Zhengzhou China	101	L5	34 45N	113 38E
Zhezkazgan Kazakhstan	94	J6	47 44N	67 42E
Zhigansk Russia	95	Q10	66 48N	123 27E
Zhmerynka Ukraine	88	M8	49 00N	28 02E
Zhob Pakistan	98	B6	31 30N	69 30E
Zhob *r.* Pakistan	98	B6	30 55N	68 01E
Zhoukou China	101	L5	33 35N	114 41E
Zhuzhou China	101	L4	27 53N	113 07E
Zhytomyr Ukraine	88	M9	50 18N	28 40E
Zibo China	101	M6	36 51N	118 01E
Zielona Góra Poland	88	E9	51 57N	15 30E
Zigong China	101	J4	29 25N	104 47E
Ziguinchor Senegal	108	A10	12 35N	16 20W
ZIMBABWE	109	K4/L4		
Zinder Niger	108	F10	13 46N	8 58E
Ziqudukou China	100	H5	33 03N	95 51E
Zlatoust Russia	94	H8	55 10N	59 38E
Zlín Czech Rep.	88	F8	49 14N	17 40E
Znojmo Czech Rep.	88	F8	48 52N	16 04E
Zolochev Ukraine	88	K8	49 49N	24 53E
Zomba Malawi	109	M4	15 22S	35 22E
Zonguldak Turkey	96	B7	41 26N	31 47E
Zouar Chad	108	H12	20 30N	16 30E
Zouérate Mauritania	108	B12	22 44N	12 21W
Zrenjanin Serbia	89	H6	45 22N	20 23E
Zújar *r.* Sp.	87	C3	38 35N	5 30W
Zunyi China	101	K4	27 35N	106 48E
Zürich Switz.	87	K7	47 23N	8 33E
Zvishavane Zimbabwe	109	L3	20 20S	30 02E
Zwickau Germany	88	D9	50 43N	12 30E
Zyrardów Poland	88	H10	52 02N	20 28E
Zyryanka Russia	87	T10	65 42N	150 49E

Glossary

Ákra	cape (Greek)
Älv	river (Swedish)
Bahia	bay (Spanish)
Bahr	stream (Arabic)
Baie	bay (French)
Bugt	bay (Danish)
Cabo	cape (Portugese; Spanish)
Cap	cape (French)
Capo	cape (Italian)
Cerro	hill (Spanish)
Chaîne	mountain range (French)
Chapada	hills (Portugese)
Chott	salt lake (Arabic)
Co	lake (Chinese)
Collines	hills (French)
Cordillera	mountain range (Spanish)
Costa	coast (Spanish)
Côte	coast (French)
-dake	peak (Japanese)
Danau	lake (Indonesian)
Dao	island (Chinese)
Dasht	desert (Persian; Urdu)
Djebel	mountain (Arabic)
Do	island (Korean; Vietnamese)
Embalse	reservoir (Spanish)
Erg	dunes (Arabic)
Estrecho	strait (Spanish)
Estreito	strait (Portugese)
Gebel	mountain (Arabic)
Golfe	gulf; bay (French)
Golfo	gulf; bay (Italian; Spanish)
Gölü	lake (Turkish)
Gora	mountain (Russian)
Gunto	islands (Japanese)
Gunung	mountain (Indonesian; Malay)
Hafen	harbour (German)
Hai	sea (Chinese)
Ho	river (Chinese)
Hu	lake (Chinese)
Île; Isle	island (French)
Ilha	island (Portugese)
Inseln	islands (German)
Isla	island (Spanish)
Istmo	isthmus (Spanish)
Jabal; Jebel	mountain (Arabic)
Jezero	lake (Serb-Croat)
Jezioro	lake (Polish)
Jiang	river (Chinese)
-jima	island (Japanese)
-kaikyō	strait (Japanese)
Kamen'	rock (Russian)
Kap	cape (Danish)
Kepulauan	islands (Indonesian)
-ko	lake (Japanese)
Lac	lake (French)
Lago	lake (Italian; Portugese; Spanish)
Laguna	lagoon (Spanish)
Ling	mountain range (Chinese)
Llyn	lake (Welsh)
-misaki	cape (Japanese)
Mont	mountain (French)
Montagne	mountain (French)
Monts	mountains (French)
Monti	mountains (Italian)
More	sea (Russian)
Muang	city (Thai)
Mys	cape (Russian)
-nada	gulf; sea (Japanese)
-nama	cape (Japanese)
Ostrova	islands (Russian)
Ozero	lake (Russian)
Pergunungan	mountain range (Indonesian)
Pendi	basin (Chinese)
Pic	summit (French; Spanish)
Pico	summit (Spanish)
Pik	summit (Russian)
Planalto	plateau (Portugese)
Planina	mountain range (Bulgarian; Serb-Croat)
Poluostrov	peninsula (Russian)
Puerto	port (Spanish)
Pulau-pulau	islands (Indonesian)
Puncak	mountain (Indonesian)
Punta	cape (Italian; Spanish)
Ras; Râs	cape (Arabic)
Ra's	cape (Persian)
Rio	river (Portugese; Spanish)
Rivière	river (French)
Rubha	cape (Gaelic)
-saki	cape (Japanese)
Salina	salt pan (Spanish)
-san	mountain (Japanese)
-sanchi	mountains (Japanese)
-sanmyaku	mountain range (Japanese)
Sebkra	salt pan (Arabic)
See	lake (German)
Selat	strait (Indonesian)
Seto	strait (Japanese)
Shan	mountains (Chinese)
-shima	island (Japanese)
-shotō	islands (Japanese)
Sierra	mountain range (Spanish)
Song	river (Vietnamese)
-suidō	strait (Japanese)
Tassili	plateau (Berber)
Tau	island (Chinese)
Teluk	bay (Indonesian)
-tō	island (Japanese)
Tonle	lake (Cambodian)
-wan	bay (Japanese)
-zaki	cape (Japanese)
Zaliv	bay (Russian)

70 Wynford Drive, Don Mills, Ontario M3C 1J9
www.oupcanada.com

Oxford University Press is a department of the University of Oxford. It furthers the University's objective of excellence in research, scholarship, and education by publishing worldwide in

Oxford New York
Auckland Cape Town Dar es Salaam Hong Kong Karachi
Kuala Lumpur Madrid Melbourne Mexico City Nairobi
New Delhi Shanghai Taipei Toronto

With offices in
Argentina Austria Brazil Chile Czech Republic France Greece
Guatemala Hungary Italy Japan Poland Portugal Singapore
South Korea Switzerland Thailand Turkey Ukraine Vietnam

Published in Canada by Oxford University Press

First Published 2009

ISBN 978-0-19-542924-4

Oxford University Press is committed to our environment. This book is printed on Forest Stewardship Council certified paper, harvested from a responsibly managed forest, and contains a minimum of 10% post-consumer waste.

Printed and bound in Canada.

1 2 3 4 — 11 10 09 08

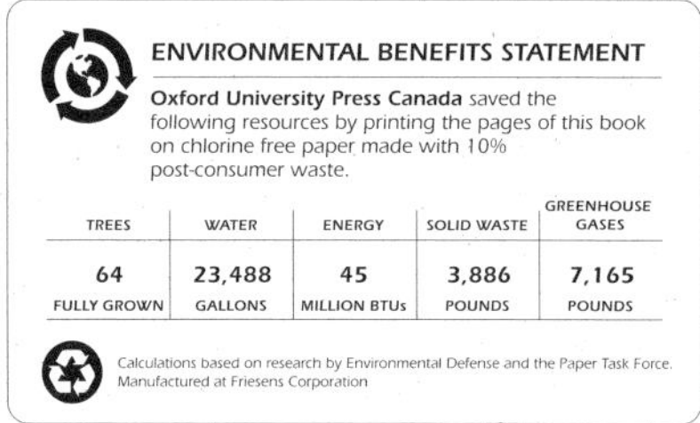

ENVIRONMENTAL BENEFITS STATEMENT

Oxford University Press Canada saved the following resources by printing the pages of this book on chlorine free paper made with 10% post-consumer waste.

TREES	WATER	ENERGY	SOLID WASTE	GREENHOUSE GASES
64 FULLY GROWN	23,488 GALLONS	45 MILLION BTUs	3,886 POUNDS	7,165 POUNDS

Calculations based on research by Environmental Defense and the Paper Task Force. Manufactured at Friesens Corporation

Credits
Contributor: Kingsley Hurlington

Cartographic Project Manager/Editor: Caleb Gould
Cartographic Editor: Karen Brittin
Cartographic Technician: Tracey Learoyd

Photo research: Suzanne Williams of pictureresearch (UK); Lynn McIntyre (Canada

Every possible effort has been made to trace the original source of the material contained in this book. Where the effort has been unsuccessful, the publisher wou be pleased to hear from the copyright holders to rectify any omission.

Photos
cover photo: Satellite image courtesy of WorldSat Int. Inc. 2008

Corbis **132** (desert/Dave G. Houser), **133** (tundra/Staffan Widstrand), **133** (semi-desert/Charles & Josette Lenars); Courtesy Hubble data: NASA , ESA, and A. Zezas (Harvard-Smithsonian Center for Astrophysics); GALEX data: NASA, JPL-Caltech, GALEX Team, J. Huchra et al. (Harvard-Smithsonian Center for Astrophysics), Spitzer data: NASA/JPL/Caltech/Harvard-Smithsonian Center for Astrophysics **10** Earth in Space; Jean du Boisberranger / Getty Images **132** Mixed Forest Trois-Rivieres, QC; NASA **154**; NASA Images courtesy of the MODIS Rapid Response Team at Goddard Space Flight Center **81** (1986), **81** (2001); NASA / Science Source / First Light 7 Earth; NASA Visible Earth **152**; Courtesy National Snow and Ice Data Center, NSIDC Arctic Snow and Ice News Fall 2007 / WorldSat International Inc. **64** Polar ice; Photolibrary.com **132** (temperate grasslands/Sean Morris), **132** (tropical rainforest/Michael Fogden), **132** (evergreen trees and shrubs/David Fox), **133** (Coniferous Forest/David Tipling), **133** (mountains/Martyn Colbeck), **133** (tropical grasslands/Stan Osolinski), **133** (thorn forest/Gerald Thompson); Science Photo Library **99** (Cnes, 1990 Distribution Spot Image), **109** (M-Sat Ltd), **129** (NOAA), **131** (NASA/Goddard Space Flight Center), **132** (ice/Simon Fraser); Courtesy of UNEP **130** (1989), **130** (2003); WorldSat International Inc. **9** Vancouver, looking North, Edmonton, **44** Calgary, **45** Vancouver, Rocky Mountains-Kicking Horse Pass, Victoria **48** Indian Head, SK, Winnipeg. **53** Golden Horse Shoe, **55** Toronto, **58** Montreal, **59** Ottawa, Halifax, **61** Beloeil, Québec, Québec City, Bobcaygeon, ON, Manicouaga Reservoir, QC, **62** Dawson City, Yukon, Mackenzie Delta, L'Anse aux Meadows, NL, St. John's, NL; **67** North America, **77** South America, **83** Europe, **91** Asia, **105** Africa

12–13 Provincial and territorial flags courtesy of: Legislative Services, Tourism, Parks, Recreation and Culture, Government of Alberta; Copyright © Province of British Columbia. All rights reserved. Reprinted with permission of the Province of British Columbia. www.ipp.gov.bc.ca; Communications Services Manitoba, Manitoba Government; Government of Newfoundland and Labrador; Communications New Brunswick; Legislative Assembly of the NWT; Crown Copyright Province of Nova Scotia. Used with permission; Legislative Assembly of Nunavut; Government of Ontario; Government of PEI, Provincial Treasury; Direction des communications, Ministère du Conseil exécutif du Québec - Justice; Office of Protocol and Honours, Saskatchewan Government Relations; Office of Protocol, Government of Yukon.

Maps
All maps in this atlas have been adapted from various sources. Following are credi for major contributions:

Natural Resources Canada, *The Atlas of Canada*: **14** main map "Age of Rocks"; **22** righ "Soil Capability for Agriculture";

Natural Resources Canada, *The Atlas of Canada, 1st ed.*: **36** "Density of Population, 1901 [Eastern Canada]", "Density of Population, 1901 [Western Canada].

Natural Resources Canada, *The Atlas of Canada, 5th ed.*: **14** inset "Glaciers"; **15** main map "Terrestrial Ecoregions, 1993", inset "Wetland Regions, 1986"; **16** top and middle "Temperature—January and July; **17** top left "Precipitation", middle left: "Snowfall"; **18** top "Heating Degree-days"; **19** "Climatic Regions: Thornthwaite Classification Moisture Regions"; **28** "Energy and Minerals, 1985"; **38** "Indian and Inuit Communities and Languages, 1980"

Natural Resources Canada, *The Atlas of Canada*, Agriculture: **23** top "Grape Area in Production, 2001"; "Area Irrigated in Western Canada, 2001"; "Change in Greenhouse Area, 1991-2001"; "Very Large Livestock Farms, 2001"; "Very Large Livestock Farms, 2001 (Western Canada)"

39 Natural Resources Canada, *The Atlas of Canada, History, 1639 to 1949:* "Territorial Evolution of Canada (1667 to 1949)"

24 Natural Resources Canada: various Natural Hazards maps at http://atlas.nrcan.gc.ca/site/english/maps/environment/naturalhazards

17 bottom left: David Phillips, "Thunderstorms" in *The Climates of Canada*. (Ottaw Minister of Supply and Service Canada), © Her Majesty The Queen in Right of Canada Environment Canada, 1990. Reproduced with the permission of the Minister of Public Works and Government Services Canada.

tistics

tistics Canada information is used with the permission of Statistics Canada. Users : forbidden to copy this material and/or redisseminate the data, in an original modified form, for commercial purposes, without the expressed permission of .atistics Canada. Information on the availability of the wide range of data from tatistics Canada can be obtained from Statistics Canada's Regional Offices, its World Vide Web site at http://www.statcan.ca, and its toll-free access number 1-800-263-1136.

12–13 Statistics Canada, "Population and dwelling counts, for Canada, provinces and territories, 2006 and 2001 censuses - 100% data (table)", "Population and Dwelling Count Highlight Tables", 2006 Census, Catalogue no. 97-550-XWE2006002, Ottawa, 13 March 2007, http://www12.statcan.ca/english/census06/data/popdwell/Table.cfm?T=101&SR=1&S=0&O=A&RPP=25&PR=0&CMA=0, accessed 21 April 2008.

21 Fish catches by quantity and value Fisheries and Oceans Canada, "1990 Atlantic & Pacific Coasts Commercial Landings, by Province (metric tonnes, live weight)"; "2006 Atlantic & Pacific Coasts Commercial Landings, by Province (metric tonnes, live weight)"; "1990 Value of Atlantic & Pacific Coasts Commercial Landings, by Province (thousand dollars) 2006"; "Value of Atlantic & Pacific Coasts Commercial Landings, by Province (thousand dollars)"; Major world fishing countries, 2004 Food and Agriculture Organization of the United Nations, FishStat, 2001-2004; Aquaculture value by species, 2005 Adapted from Statistics Canada. "Aquaculture Statistics 2006", Table 1-15, 2005, Catalogue 23-222-X, http://www.statcan.ca/english/freepub/23-222-XIE/2006000/tablesectionlist.htm.

23 Farm types, 2006, Pasture land by province, Cropland by province, Canada farm land, 2006 Adapted from Statistics Canada, "2006 Census of Agriculture, Farm Data and Farm Operator Data", Catalogue 95-629-XWE, Table 4.3-2. http://www.statcan.ca/english/freepub/95-629-XIE/4/4.3-2_A.htm.

25 Greenhouse gas emissions by province, 2004 Environment Canada, *National Inventory Report, 1990–2004*, Greenhouse Gas Sources and Sinks in Canada, Annex 12: Provincial/Territorial Greenhouse gas emission tables, 1990-2004; **Greenhouse gas emissions by sector, 2004** Environment Canada, *National Inventory Report, 1990–2004*, Greenhouse Gas Sources and Sinks in Canada, Annex 8: Canada's Greenhouse Gas Emission Tables, 1990–2004, Table A8-2: Canada's 1990-2004 Greenhouse Gas Emissions by Sector http://www.ec.gc.ca/pdb/ghg/inventory_report/2004_report/ta8_2_e.cfm; **Contribution of Canadian greenhouse gas emissions to future global warming** Environment Canada, *National Inventory Report, 1990–2004*, Greenhouse Gas Sources and Sinks in Canada, Table S-2: Canada's GHG Emissions by Gas and Sector, 2004, http://www.ec.gc.ca/pdb/ghg/inventory_report/2004_report/ts_2_e.cfm; **Observed trends in temperature** Henry Hengeveld, Bob Whitewood, and Angus Fergusson, "Observed trends in temperatures across southern Canada since 1900 and all of Canada since 1948", Figure 1.9, in *An Introduction to Climate Change: A Canadian perspective.* (Downsview: Environment Canada, 2005), p. 10, www.msc.ec.gc.ca/education/scienceofclimatechange

26 Population by ecozone, 2001 Adapted from Statistics Canada, *Human Activity and the Environment: Annual Statistics, 2006*, Catalogue 16-201-XWE, Table 3.3 and Map 2.2. http://www.statcan.ca/english/freepub/16-201-XIE/2006000/t071_en.htm?.

28 Metallic mineral production of Canada, 2006; Nonmetallic mineral production of Canada, 2006 Adapted from Statistics Canada, *Canada's Mineral Production, Preliminary Estimates, 2006*, Catalogue 26-202-XIB, Table 1, http://www.statcan.ca/english/freepub/26-202-XIB/26-202-XIB2007000.pdf, accessed June 2007.

29 Coal imports and exports, Coal consumption by province Adapted from Natural Resources Canada, *Canadian Minerals Yearbook 2005*, pp. 20.1, 20.3-20.4, © Her Majesty the Queen in Right of Canada, 2007; **Crude oil transfers, Natural gas transfers** National Energy Board, *Annual Report 2005 to Parliament*, pp. 23, 27. Reproduced with the permission of the Minister of Public Works and Government Services Canada, 2008.

30 Electricity trade National Energy Board, *Annual Report 2005 to Parliament*, p.30. Reproduced with the permission of the Minister of Public Works and Government Services Canada, 2008.

31 provincial data Adapted from Statistics Canada, 2006, National and Provincial Principal Statistics from the Annual Survey of Manufactures and Logging (ASML), CANSIM Database http://cansim2.statcan.ca/, Tables 301-0006 and 301-0007; **CMA data** Adapted from Statistics Canada, Summary Statistics of Manufacturing Industries, by Census Metropolitan Areas (CMA), Annual Survey of Manufactures and Logging (ASML), 2003.

32–33 Trade (exports) and Trade (imports) Adapted from Statistics Canada, *Imports by Country*, Catalogue 65-006, vol. 63 no. 04, January to December 2006, 19 February 2007; *Exports by Country*, Catalogue 65-003, vol. 63 no. 04, January to December 2006, 5 March 2007.

36 Census Metropolitan Areas Adapted from Statistics Canada, "2006 Census of the Population, Population and Dwelling Count Highlight Tables, Population and dwelling counts for census metropolitan areas, 2006 and 2001 censuses—100% data", Catalogue 97-550-XWE2006002, http://www12.statcan.ca/english/census06/data/popdwell/Table.cfm?T=205&RPP=50.

37 Population, 2006 Adapted from Statistics Canada, "Age and Sex, 2006 counts for both sexes, for Canada, provinces and territories - 100% data (table)". Age and Sex Highlight Tables. 2006 Census, Catalogue 97-551-XWE2006002, Ottawa, 17 July 2007. http://www12.statcan.ca/english/census06/data/highlights/agesex/index.cfm?Lang=E, accessed 18 April 2008; **Population by mother tongue, 2006** Adapted from Statistics Canada, "Population by mother tongue and age groups, 2006 counts, for Canada, provinces and territories – 20% sample data (table)". Language Highlight Tables. 2006 Census, Catalogue 97-555-XWE2006002, Ottawa, 4 December 2007, http://www12.statcan.ca/english/census06/data/highlights/Language/Table401.cfm?Lang=E&T=401&GH=4&SC=1&S=99&O=A, accessed 18 April 2008; **Immigrant population for selected CMAs, 2006** Adapted from Statistics Canada, "Population by immigrant status and period of immigration, 2006 counts, for Canada and census metropolitan areas and census agglomerations – 20% sample data (table)". Immigration and Citizenship Highlight Tables. 2006 Census. Catalogue 97-557-XWE2006002, Ottawa, 4 December 2007, http://www12.statcan.ca/english/census06/data/highlights/Immigration/Table403.cfm?Lang=E&T=403&GH=8&SC=1&S=0&O=A, accessed 18 April 2008; **Immigrant population by province or territory, 2006** Adapted from Statistics Canada, "Population by immigrant status and period of immigration, 2006 counts, for Canada, provinces and territories – 20% sample data (table)". Immigration and Citizenship Highlight Tables. 2006 Census. Catalogue 97-557-XWE2006002, Ottawa, 4 December 2007, http://www12.statcan.ca/english/census06/data/highlights/Immigration/Table403.cfm?Lang=E&T=403&GH=4&SC=1&S=99&O=A, accessed 18 April 2008; **provincial pie charts** Adapted from Statistics Canada, "2001 Census of the Population, Ethnocultural Portrait of Canada: Highlight Tables, Ethnic Origins", Catalogue 97F0024XIE2001006; **map lower left Natural increase values** Adapted from Statistics Canada, "Population Change 2001-2006" Natural Increase - Annual Demographic Estimates: Canada, Provinces and Territories - 2005-2006, Table 4-11: Annual estimates of demographic components, national perspective-Natural increase, Catalogue 91-215; **map lower left Interprovincial migration values** Adapted from Statistics Canada "2001 Census: analysis series, Profile of the Canadian population by mobility status: Canada, a nation on the move", Table: "Net migrants and net migration rates, provinces and territories, 1976 to 2001" p. 20, Catalogue 96F0030XIE2001006, http://www12.statcan.ca/english/census01/products/analytic/companion/mob/pdf/96F0030XIE2001006.pdf; map lower left International migration values Adapted from Statistics Canada, "Population Change 2001-2006" Net international migration - Annual Demographic Estimates: Canada, Provinces and Territories - 2005-2006, Table 4-13: Annual estimates of demographic components, national perspective-Net international migration, Catalogue 91-215; **map lower left percentages for Immigrants arriving in Canada by place of birth, 2001-2006** Adapted from Statistics Canada, "Place of birth for the immigrant population by period of immigration, 2006 counts and percentage distribution, for Canada, provinces and territories – 20% sample data (table)". Immigration and Citizenship Highlight Tables. 2006 Census, Catalogue 97-557-XWE2006002, Ottawa, 4 December 2007, http://www12.statcan.ca/english/census06/data/highlights/Immigration/Table404.cfm?Lang=E&T=404&GH=4&SC=1&S=1&O=D, accessed 21 April 2008.

38 Aboriginal population, 2006; Aboriginal peoples, 2006, Where the aboriginal population live, 2006 Adapted from Statistics Canada, "Aboriginal Peoples Highlight Tables, 2006 Census", Catalogue 97-558-XWE2006002, Table 1: "Aboriginal identity population by age groups, median age and sex", http://www12.statcan.ca/english/census06/data/highlights/aboriginal/index.cfm?Lang=E

40–65 land area statistics "Facts about Canada—Land and Freshwater Areas", 2001 data courtesy of Natural Resources Canada, Canada Centre for Remote Sensing; **Census population** Adapted from Statistics Canada: "Population and Dwelling Counts", 2006 Census, Catalogue 97-550-XWE2006002, July 2007, http://www.statcan.ca/bsolc/english/bsolc?catno=97-550-X2006002; "Population urban and rural, by province and territory", http://www40.statcan.ca/l01/cst01/demo62a.htm; **Census Metropolitan Areas, 2006, Other important urban centres, 2006** Adapted from Statistics Canada, "Population and dwelling counts, for Canada, provinces and territories, 2006 and 2001 censuses - 100% data (table)". Population and Dwelling Count Highlight Tables, 2006 Census, Catalogue 97-550-XWE2006002, Ottawa, 13 March 2007. http://www12.statcan.ca/english/census06/data/popdwell/Table.cfm?T=101&SR=1&S=0&O=A&R PP=25&PR=0&CMA=0, accessed 18 April 2008; Gross Domestic Product Adapted from Statistics Canada, "Gross Domestic Product (GDP) at basic prices, by North American Industry Classification System (NAICS) and province, annual (dollars)", CANSIM 379-0025, http://cansim2.statcan.ca/cgi-win/CNSMCGI.PGM, accessed June 2007.

World Flags

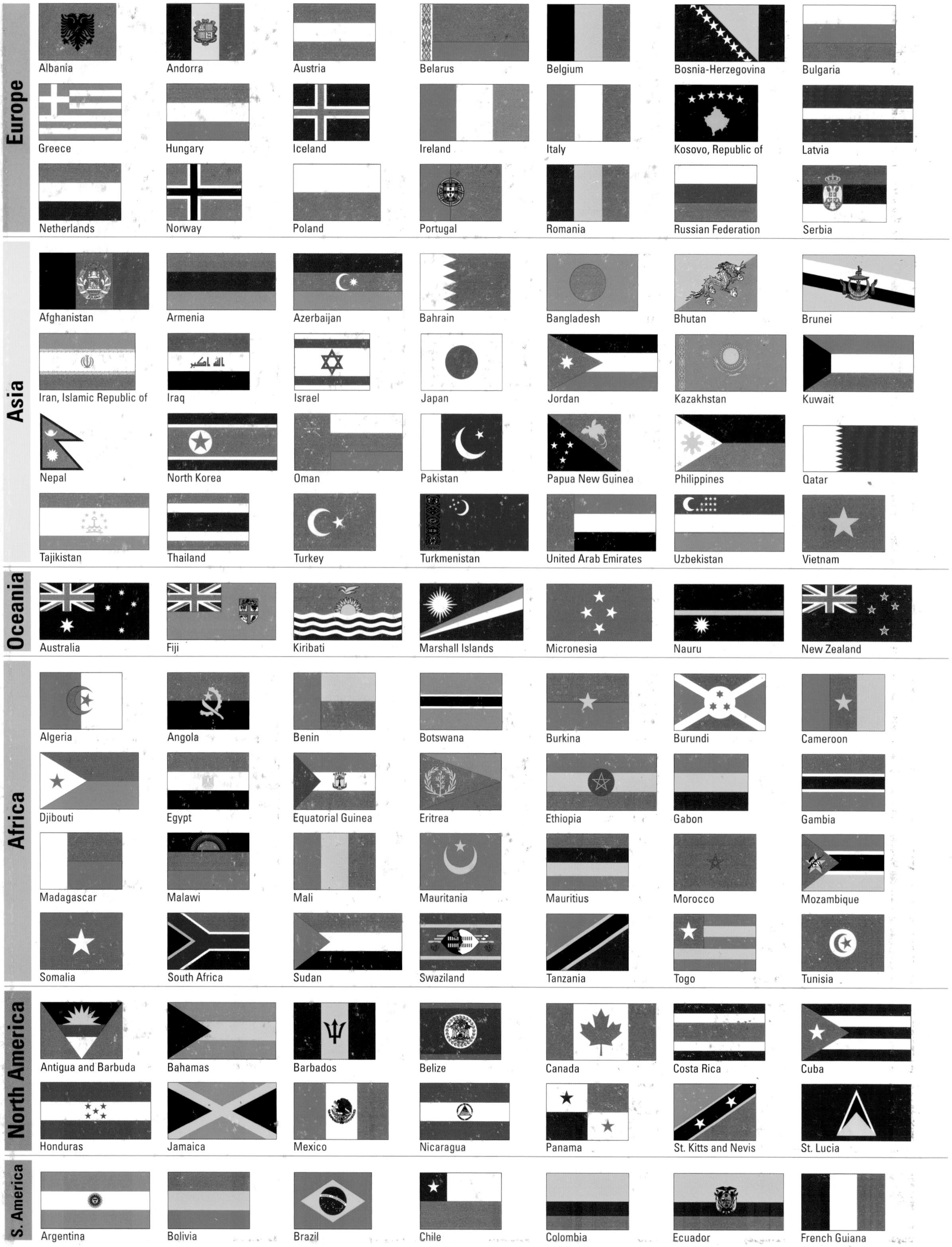

Europe

Albania
Andorra
Austria
Belarus
Belgium
Bosnia-Herzegovina
Bulgaria
Greece
Hungary
Iceland
Ireland
Italy
Kosovo, Republic of
Latvia
Netherlands
Norway
Poland
Portugal
Romania
Russian Federation
Serbia

Asia

Afghanistan
Armenia
Azerbaijan
Bahrain
Bangladesh
Bhutan
Brunei
Iran, Islamic Republic of
Iraq
Israel
Japan
Jordan
Kazakhstan
Kuwait
Nepal
North Korea
Oman
Pakistan
Papua New Guinea
Philippines
Qatar
Tajikistan
Thailand
Turkey
Turkmenistan
United Arab Emirates
Uzbekistan
Vietnam

Oceania

Australia
Fiji
Kiribati
Marshall Islands
Micronesia
Nauru
New Zealand

Africa

Algeria
Angola
Benin
Botswana
Burkina
Burundi
Cameroon
Djibouti
Egypt
Equatorial Guinea
Eritrea
Ethiopia
Gabon
Gambia
Madagascar
Malawi
Mali
Mauritania
Mauritius
Morocco
Mozambique
Somalia
South Africa
Sudan
Swaziland
Tanzania
Togo
Tunisia

North America

Antigua and Barbuda
Bahamas
Barbados
Belize
Canada
Costa Rica
Cuba
Honduras
Jamaica
Mexico
Nicaragua
Panama
St. Kitts and Nevis
St. Lucia

S. America

Argentina

Bolivia

Brazil

Chile

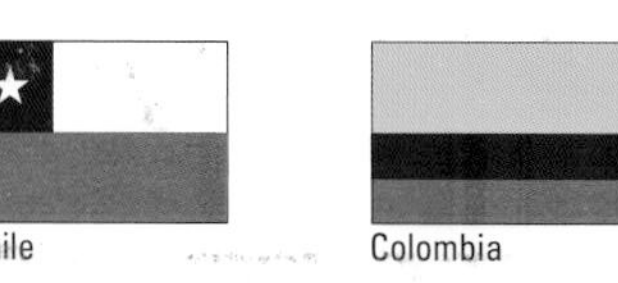
Colombia

Ecuador

French Guiana